Judicial combat illustrating a plea roll of 1249:KB 26/233 (see pages 32–34)

General Editors

R. F. HUNNISETT

J. B. POST

MEDIEVAL LEGAL RECORDS

edited in memory of

C. A. F. MEEKINGS

LONDON

HER MAJESTY'S STATIONERY OFFICE

First published 1978

ISBN 0 11 440085 7*

CONTENTS

PREFACE

This volume owes both its existence and its nature to the widespread feeling, produced by the news of his retirement on 30 September 1974, that the career of Mr C. A. F. Meekings at the Public Record Office should be honoured in a suitable manner. His career, which is briefly sketched in the accompanying Memoir, had many facets; but preëminently it was notable for his work on the medieval records of the English courts of common law, on which he is universally recognised as the foremost authority of his generation. His scholarship was only equalled by the generosity with which he always shared his knowledge and insights with others, so that there can be few working in this field who are not considerably in his debt. It was therefore natural that a number of his 'pupils' should decide to collaborate in producing this volume which they dedicate to him as a token of their gratitude and respect. It is a collection of short legal records, or extracts from records, each edited by one of his former colleagues or other friends. Both their chronological range – from the early thirteenth to the late fifteenth century – and their variety of content aptly reflect the extent of Meekings' own interests and expertise. Meekings died on 20 January 1977, so that this volume, which was intended to celebrate an active historian, is published as a memorial.

The general editors would like to thank their fellow contributors for their ready coöperation at all stages, and particularly for their forbearance and understanding during the inevitably lengthy periods necessary for general editorial work and for indexing. They much appreciate the interest taken in the volume by Dr Susan Hall since the death of her husband, G. D. G. Hall, who had, however, himself completed the work on his contribution. They also wish to acknowledge the valuable editorial assistance rendered by Public Record Office colleagues, notably by Mr D. G. Clark and Miss H. R. Shelton. The size of the volume, the consequent need to keep costs to a minimum and the varying nature of the contributions combined to create unusually complex problems of presentation and layout. Here the assistance of Mr David Napthine, formerly of Her Majesty's Stationery Office, has been invaluable. His consistency of approach, attention to detail, ready appreciation of difficulties, and sensible ideas for their solution have contributed more than could reasonably have been asked of him.

The documents calendared and transcribed are nearly all in the Public Record Office, but in a few contributions the public records are supplemented by manuscripts preserved elsewhere. They are specified in the Table of Other Manuscripts Cited and also in the particular contributions. The general editors and the Public Record Office gratefully acknowledge the permission to print them granted by the Trustees of the British Library, the Honourable Society of Lincoln's Inn, Lieutenant Colonel P. T. Clifton and Nottingham University, the Trustees of the Shakespeare Birthplace Trust and the trustees of the Palmer-Morewood estate; the permission granted by the Trustees of the Ames Foundation to Mr Hector to use material from one of their forthcoming volumes; and the permission of the Selden Society to reproduce the frontispiece of volume I of that society's publications as the frontispiece of this book.

PUBLIC RECORD OFFICE

EDITORIAL NOTE

The editorial conventions applied throughout this volume are those which have recently been described in R. F. Hunnisett, *Editing Records for Publication* (British Records Association, Archives and the User No. 4, 1977). Three may usefully be mentioned here. Unfootnoted textual words and passages printed within square brackets have been supplied by the editor at points where the manuscript is defective; unfootnoted angle brackets contain process interlineation; and the choice between the letters 'u' and 'v', 'c' and 't', and 'i' and 'j' has been determined by the spelling of the modern English word or derived word. A few editors have felt that not every convention recommended was appropriate for their contributions. Throughout the volume, numbers printed within square brackets refer to textual entries within the same contribution.

TABLE OF ABBREVIATIONS

For full details of printed works published by HMSO see *British National Archives* (London, HMSO, Government Publications Sectional List No. 24, revised annually). Call numbers of record classes in the Public Record Office are defined in the next table.

Add.
Additional

Am. Jnl Leg. Hist.
The American Journal of Legal History

Arch.
Archaeologia/Archaeological

BIHR
Bulletin of the Institute of Historical Research

BL
British Library

BNB
Bracton's Note Book . . ., ed. F. W. Maitland, 3 vols (London, 1887)

Bracton (I–II)
Bracton, De Legibus et Consuetudinibus Angliae, ed. G. E. Woodbine, trans. & rev. S. E. Thorne, 2 vols (Cambridge, Mass, 1968)

Bracton (III–IV)
Bracton, De Legibus et Consuetudinibus Angliae, ed. G. E. Woodbine, 2 vols (New Haven, Conn, 1940–2)

Bull. Jn Rylands Lib.
Bulletin of the John Rylands University Library of Manchester

CAD
A Descriptive Catalogue of Ancient Deeds in the Public Record Office (HMSO)

CCR
Calendar of the Close Rolls preserved in the Public Record Office (HMSO)

CCW
Calendar of Chancery Warrants preserved in the Public Record Office, AD 1244–1326 (HMSO)

CChR
Calendar of the Charter Rolls preserved in the Public Record Office (HMSO)

CFR
Calendar of the Fine Rolls preserved in the Public Record Office (HMSO)

CIM
Calendar of Inquisitions Miscellaneous (Chancery) preserved in the Public Record Office (HMSO)

CIPM
Calendar of Inquisitions Post Mortem and other Analogous Documents preserved in the Public Record Office (HMSO)

CJCP
chief justice of common pleas

CJKB
chief justice of king's bench

CLR
Calendar of the Liberate Rolls preserved in the Public Record Office (HMSO)

CMR
Calendar of Memoranda Rolls (Exchequer) preserved in the Public Record Office, Michaelmas 1326–Michaelmas 1327 (HMSO)

CPL
Calendar of Entries in the Papal Registers relating to Great Britain and Ireland: Papal Letters (HMSO)

CPR
Calendar of the Patent Rolls preserved in the Public Record Office (HMSO)

CRR
Curia Regis Rolls . . . preserved in the Public Record Office (HMSO)

Ch.
Charter

Cl D
Clifton of Clifton Deeds

Close R.
Close Rolls of the reign of Henry III preserved in the Public Record Office (HMSO)

DNB
Dictionary of National Biography, 63 vols (London, 1885–1900)

DR 37
Archer Collection

EHR
The English Historical Review

EPNS
English Place-Name Society

Eng. Govt at Work
The English Government at Work, 1327–1336, ed. J. F. Willard, W. A. Morris, J. R. Strayer and W. H. Dunham Jr, 3 vols (Cambridge, Mass, 1940–50)

Ex. Rot. Fin.
Excerpta e Rotulis Finium in Turri Londinensi asservatis, Henrico Tertio Rege, ed. C. Roberts (RC, 1835–6)

Fdn
Foundation

Fedn Old Corn Socs
Federation of Old Cornwall Societies

Foedera
Foedera, Conventiones, Litterae, . . ., ed. T. Rymer, [3rd edn], 4 vols (RC, 1816–69)

Foss, *Biog. Judges*
E. Foss, *A Biographical Dictionary of the Judges of England, 1066–1870* (London, 1870)

Foss, *Judges of England*
E. Foss, *The Judges of England* . . ., 4 vols (London, 1848–51)

G. E. C.
G. E. C[ockayne], *The Complete Peerage* . . ., 2nd edn, 12 vols (London, 1910–59)

HMC
Historical Manuscripts Commission

HWRO 009
County of Hereford and Worcester Record Office, Documents relating to the Estates of the Bishop of Worcester

HWRO 705
County of Hereford and Worcester Record Office, A Collection

HWRO 716
County of Hereford and Worcester Record Office, Bishops' Registers

Harl.
Harleian

Hdbk Brit. Chron.
Handbook of British Chronology, 2nd edn, ed. F. M. Powicke and E. B. Fryde (R. Hist. Soc. Guides & Handbooks No. 2, London, 1961)

Hdbk of Dates
Handbook of Dates for Students of English History, ed. C. R. Cheney (R.Hist.Soc. Guides & Handbooks No. 4, London, 1945)

Hist. Jnl
The Historical Journal

Holdsworth
W. S. Holdsworth, *A History of English Law,* 17 vols (London, 1922–72): vol. I is 7th edn (1956) and vols II–III are 3rd edn (1923)

J
justice

JCP
justice of common pleas

JKB
justice of king's bench

JP
justice of the peace

Jnl R. Instn Corn
Journal of the Royal Institution of Cornwall

KS
king's serjeant

King's Bench
Select Cases in the Court of King's Bench . . ., ed. G. O. Sayles, 7 vols (SS LV, LVII, LVIII, LXXIV, LXXVI, LXXXII, LXXXVIII, 1936–71)

L & I Soc.
List & Index Society

Law Qtly Rev.
The Law Quarterly Review

Occ. Papers
Occasional Papers

PR
Pipe Roll

PRO L & I
Public Record Office Lists and Indexes

PRS
Pipe Roll Society

Parl. Writs
The Parliamentary Writs and Writs of Military Summons . . ., ed. F. Palgrave, 3 vols (RC, 1827–34)

Pat. R.
Patent Rolls of the reign of Henry III preserved in the Public Record Office (HMSO)

Pollock & Maitland
F. Pollock and F. W. Maitland, *The History of English Law before the time of Edward I,* 2 vols, 2nd edn (Cambridge, 1898)

Procs before JPs
Proceedings before the Justices of the Peace in the Fourteenth and Fifteenth Centuries, ed. B. H. Putnam (Ames Fdn, 1938)

Procs Brit. Acad.
Proceedings of the British Academy

RC
Record Commission

RP
Rotuli Parliamentorum . . ., 6 vols [London, 1783]

RS
Rerum Britannicarum Medii Aevi Scriptores [Rolls Series]

Reg. Brev.: Orig./Jud.
Registrum Brevium tam Originalium quam Judicialium, 4th edn (London, 1687)

Rot. Litt. Claus.
Rotuli Litterarum Clausarum in Turri Londinensi asservati, 2 vols, ed. T. D. Hardy (RC, 1833–44)

SR
The Statutes of the Realm, 11 vols (RC, 1810–28)

SS
Selden Society

Sa AC
Sandwich Chamberlains' Accounts

Soc.
Social/Society

Supp. ser.
Supplementary series

TRHS
Transactions of the Royal Historical Society

VCH
The Victoria History of the Counties of England

Vesp.
Vespasian

Wm Salt Arch. Soc., *Hist. Colls*
The William Salt Archaeological Society, *Collections for a History of Staffordshire*

YB
Year Book(s)

TABLE OF PUBLIC RECORD OFFICE CLASSES CITED

Classes marked with an asterisk contain documents printed either completely or partially in this volume.

C 1
Early Chancery Proceedings

C 4
Chancery Proceedings, Answers, etc.

C 44
Placita in Cancellaria (Tower Series)

C 47
Chancery Miscellanea

C 49
Chancery, Parliamentary and Council Proceedings

C 66
Chancery, Patent Rolls

C 67
Chancery, Patent Rolls (Supplementary) [Pardon Rolls cited]

C 69
Chancery, Redisseisin Rolls

C 81
Chancery, Warrants for the Great Seal, Series I

C 85
Chancery, Significations of Excommunication

C 88
Chancery Files (Tower and Rolls Chapel Series), Records upon Outlawries

C 131
Chancery, Extents for Debts, Series I

C 132
Chancery, Inquisitions Post Mortem, Series I, Henry III

C 136
Chancery, Inquisitions Post Mortem, Series I, Richard II

C 139
Chancery, Inquisitions Post Mortem, Series I, Henry VI

C 140
Chancery, Inquisitions Post Mortem, Series I, Edward IV

C 143
Chancery, Inquisitions Ad Quod Damnum

C 145
Chancery, Miscellaneous Inquisitions

C 146
Chancery, Ancient Deeds, Series C

C 239
Chancery, Extents for Debts, Series II

C 241
Chancery, Certificates of Statute Merchant and Statute Staple (Tower and Rolls Chapel Series)

*C 244
Chancery Files (Tower and Rolls Chapel Series), Corpus Cum Causa

C 250
Chancery Files (Tower Series), Habeas Corpus Cum Causa

C 251
Chancery Files (Tower and Rolls Chapel Series), Non Sunt Inventi

C 253
Chancery Files (Tower and Rolls Chapel Series), Sub Pena

C 254
Chancery Files (Tower and Rolls Chapel Series), Dedimus Potestatem

C 256
Chancery Files (Tower and Rolls Chapel Series), Various Summonses

C 260
Chancery Files (Tower and Rolls Chapel Series), Recorda

CP 25
Common Pleas, Feet of Fines

*CP 40
Common Pleas, De Banco Rolls

*CP 52
Common Pleas, Writs

DL 29
Duchy of Lancaster, Ministers' Accounts

DL 42
Duchy of Lancaster, Miscellaneous Books

DURH 3
Palatinate of Durham, Cursitor's Records

E 13
Exchequer of Pleas, Plea Rolls

*E 28
Exchequer, Treasury of the Receipt, Council and Privy Seal Records

E 36
Exchequer, Treasury of the Receipt, Books

*E 40
Exchequer, Treasury of the Receipt, Ancient Deeds, Series A

*E 41
Exchequer, Treasury of the Receipt, Ancient Deeds, Series AA

E 101
Exchequer, King's Remembrancer, Accounts, Various

E 136
Exchequer, King's Remembrancer, Escheators' Accounts

E 143
Exchequer, King's Remembrancer, Extents and Inquisitions

E 159
Exchequer, King's Remembrancer, Memoranda Rolls

*E 163
Exchequer, King's Remembrancer, Miscellanea

E 164
Exchequer, King's Remembrancer, Miscellaneous Books, Series I

E 179
Exchequer, King's Remembrancer, Subsidy Rolls, etc.

E 199
Exchequer, King's Remembrancer, Sheriffs' Accounts, etc.

E 202
Exchequer, King's Remembrancer, Writs

E 207
Exchequer, King's Remembrancer, Bille

E 357
Exchequer, Pipe Office, Escheators' Accounts

E 358
Exchequer, Pipe Office, Miscellaneous Accounts

E 364
Exchequer, Pipe Office, Rolls of Foreign Accounts

*E 368
Exchequer, Lord Treasurer's Remembrancer, Memoranda Rolls

E 371
Exchequer, Lord Treasurer's Remembrancer, Originalia Rolls

E 372
Exchequer, Pipe Office, Pipe Rolls

E 401
Exchequer, Exchequer of Receipt, Enrolments and Registers of Receipts

E 404
Exchequer, Exchequer of Receipt, Writs and Warrants for Issues

IND
Index

*JUST 1
Justices Itinerant, Assize and Gaol Delivery Justices, etc., Eyre Rolls, Assize Rolls, etc.

*JUST 2
Justices Itinerant, Assize and Gaol Delivery Justices, etc., Coroners' Rolls

JUST 3
Justices Itinerant, Assize and Gaol Delivery Justices, etc., Gaol Delivery Rolls

*KB 9
King's Bench, Ancient Indictments

*KB 26
King's Bench, Curia Regis Rolls

*KB 27
King's Bench, Coram Rege Rolls

KB 29
King's Bench, Controlment Rolls

KB 37
King's Bench Files, Brevia Regis

KB 145
King's Bench Files, Recorda

PRO 12
Public Record Office, Registers, Repairs

*SC 1
Special Collections, Ancient Correspondence

*SC 2
Special Collections, Court Rolls

SC 6
Special Collections, Ministers' and Receivers' Accounts

SC 11
Special Collections, Rentals and Surveys

*SP 46
State Papers, Domestic, Supplementary

TABLE OF OTHER MANUSCRIPTS CITED

Collections marked with an asterisk contain manuscripts printed either completely or partially in this volume.

Bodleian Library
  Dodsworth MSS

British Library
  Additional Charters
  *Additional MSS
  Cotton MSS
  Egerton Rolls
  Harleian Charters
  Harleian MSS
  Lansdowne MSS

Cambridge University Library MSS

County of Hereford and Worcester Record Office (St Helen's, Worcester)
  Bishops' Registers
  Collection 705: 7 (B.A. 57)
  Documents relating to the Estates of the Bishop of Worcester

Derby Central Library
  *Palmer-Morewood Collection

Guildhall Library
  Commissary Court of London Registers

Hampshire Record Office
  Winchester Pipe Rolls

Henry E. Huntington Library
  Battle Abbey MSS

Kent Archives Office
  Sandwich Chamberlains' Accounts

Lambeth Palace Library
  Register of Archbishop Arundel

Lincoln's Inn
  *Hale MSS

Lincolnshire Record Office
  Bishops' Registers

Nottingham University Library
  *Clifton of Clifton Deeds

Shakespeare Birthplace Trust
  *Archer Collection

C. A. F. MEEKINGS

A MEMOIR

Omnibus ad quos presentes
Venerint versus patentes,
Re dignam non competentes
Assequi virtutem,
Nos, cohors historicorum
Custodumque recordorum
Temporum preteritorum,
Plurimam salutem.

Notum universitati
Vestre sit quod, pietati
Pariter et veritati
Aurem inclinantes
Et memoriam sodalis,
Cui non remanet equalis
Interpres fori regalis,
Juste honorantes

(Qui quidem tot nobis plana
Fecit, et Bractoniana
Et de curiis arcana
Exhibendo puncta;
Quique tot pulverulenta
Agnovit videns fragmenta,
Que nunc sunt additamenta
Rotulis rejuncta)

Pro serviciis immensis
Studio nostro impensis
Et pro lucernis accensis,
Qua defecit lumen,
Socii nostri prefati
Nos laboribus ditati
Animi hoc pignus grati
Edimus volumen.

Acanthostaphyle

A young man joining the staff of the Public Record Office between the wars could not long remain unaware of the existence or the influence of a group of Olympians to whom his immediate seniors were apt to refer with affectionate irreverence as 'the pundits'. From the better informed he might learn that 'the pundits' were the survivors or the successors of a Publications Committee set up in deference to a recommendation of the 1910 Royal Commission on the Public Records. He was presumed not to need telling how their status had been achieved. Such Assistant Keepers still in post as the great S. C. Ratcliff had manifestly grown old and wise in daily contact with the records; and in similar daily contact such acknowledged pundits as Hubert Hall and Charles Johnson had grown even older and even wiser.

We were thus scarcely prepared to find in 1947 that in Cecil Meekings we were acquiring a colleague in his early thirties who, before coming to join us, had already won the sort of respect that we associated with considerable seniority. In the two or three years between the end of a distinguished undergraduate career at Jesus College, Cambridge (a First Class in the History Tripos, 1935–6; George Williams Prize, 1935; Lightfoot Scholarship, 1936) and the outbreak of war in 1939 he had worked with such industry and insight on an edition of the Surrey Fines for 1509 to 1558 that its Introduction was at once hailed as a text-book treatment of post-medieval fines in general. The same industry and insight had been enlisted in the period immediately following the war when, after service in East Africa and before demobilisation, he was seconded from regimental duties to become Archives Officer to the British Control Commission for Germany.

The editorship of the Surrey Fines and the appointment to the Control Commission may have owed something to the benevolent interest of the then unknighted Hilary Jenkinson (whose remarkable eye for a rising talent was never better demonstrated), but Meekings' achievements during the next thirty years or so were all his own. The contents of the present volume are in themselves inadequate evidence of the number and diversity of the academic interests which have benefited from his work, published and unpublished, or from his help and advice. Like the appended bibliography of his own writings on legal history, they do not even completely reflect his work on legal records: the many years of sorting, listing and analysing both those already available to the public and the dauntingly large number formerly residing in chaos and grime in unwelcoming sacks. New lists, often detailed and rather complex, and innumerable amendments and corrections to existing lists bear witness from the search room shelves to his labours. Although his work on the legal records of the medieval and early modern periods was the supreme achievement of his career, this interest was of relatively late development. Earlier it had seemed more probable that he would specialise in financial records, and he had both worked and written on the medieval exchequer and the seventeenth-century hearth tax. Indeed, his interests remained remarkably catholic, as is attested by his magisterial reviews of books about modern German archives. Nor are his services to orthodox scholarship the only manifestation of qualities which have been displayed to advantage in fields as remote from medieval legal institutions as philately and the history of the Fulham Football Club.

He himself derived great personal satisfaction from his service as Librarian of the Public Record Office. When he was appointed to the post in 1953 the somewhat empirical principles upon which the Library was arranged and administered remained what they had been at the time of Charles Johnson's retirement in 1930. Meekings at once set himself to introduce the changes which the accessions of a quarter of a century had made necessary. He needed all his patience to win for those changes the approval of some of his most senior colleagues, who perhaps did not always realise that what they regarded as the logical place for a book was in fact only the one they were used to. After concessions on both sides the encounter may be said to have ended in an honourable compromise, to which Meekings' subject catalogue on cards stands as an enduring monument. To the ordering and purchase of books he brought an informed and active interest which has turned what was previously a very good library for its purpose into a truly excellent one.

His versatility seemed to many of his associates to arise from a rare empathy, having about it no trace of either the sentimental or the patronising, which, in his dealings with records, enabled him to see the procedures and the problems of the past in their contemporary setting and clarified for him what Plucknett, in an admirable phrase, called 'the relation between documents and facts'. Sir Cyril Flower and Lady Stenton, both highly conscientious editors, took diametrically opposed views of the 'value' of essoins, which they both considered purely as evidence of litigation or of the survival of litigants. Meekings, for his part, studied essoins as a naturally evolved element in the administration of a legal system. When he was shown a Year Book case in which a chief justice used language implying that a plaintiff's essoin was almost a kind of default, Meekings' mildly shocked disapproval was precisely such as might have been occasioned by a frivolous irregularity on the part of a colleague.

The award of the OBE to Meekings in the New Year Honours of 1973 gave great pleasure to all the generations of his colleagues in the Public Record Office and to his many friends and admirers outside it. It was with corresponding pleasure that some of them united to prepare and to offer to him this volume as a token of their regard and gratitude.

As will be clear from the preface, the contributors confidently expected that Meekings himself would be among their most discerning readers. Their contributions therefore reflect their views not only of the breadth and maturity of his scholarship but also of his character and attitudes, including his sense of humour and his taste for pastiche.

L. C. H.

LEGAL WRITINGS OF C. A. F. MEEKINGS

Abstracts of Surrey Feet of Fines, 1509–1558 (Surrey Rec. Soc., XIX, 1946)

'Six Letters concerning the Eyres of 1226–8', *EHR*, LXV (1950), 492–504

'Henry de Bracton, Canon of Wells', *Notes & Queries for Somerset and Dorset*, XXVI (1951–4), 141–3

'Alan de Wassand (†1257)', *Yorks Arch. Jnl*, XXXVIII (1952–5), 465–73

'Martin Pateshull and William Raleigh', *BIHR*, XXVI (1953), 157–80

Curia Regis Rolls, XI–XV (1955–72), Introductions

'Justices of the Jews, 1218–68: A Provisional List', *BIHR*, XXVIII (1955), 173–88

'The Rutland Eyre of 1253: A Correction', *EHR*, LXXI (1956), 615–18

'Sir William Bonquer', *Notes & Queries*, CCI (1956), 54–6

'The Pipe Roll Order of 12 February 1270', in *Studies presented to Sir Hilary Jenkinson*, ed. J. Conway Davies (Oxford, 1957), 222–53

'More about Robert Carpenter of Hareslade', *EHR*, LXXII (1957), 260–9

'Roger of Whitchester (†1258)', *Arch. Aeliana*, 4th ser., XXXV (1957), 100–28

Chertsey Abbey Cartularies, II, pt 1 (Surrey Rec. Soc., XII, 1958), Introduction and Notes to the Text

'A Roll of Judicial Writs', *BIHR*, XXXII (1959), 209–21

Crown Pleas of the Wiltshire Eyre, 1249 (Wilts Arch. & Nat. Hist. Soc., Recs Branch, XVI, 1960)

'Adam fitz William (d. 1238)', *BIHR*, XXXIV (1961), 1–15

'Robert of Nottingham, Justice of the Bench, 1244–6', *BIHR*, XLI (1968), 132–8

List of Various Common-Law Records (PRO L & I, Supp. ser., I, 1970)

'Martin de Pateshull of Good Memory my Sometime Lord', *BIHR*, XLVIII (1974), 224–9

'Early King's Bench Stamps, 1584–96', *Jnl Soc. Archivists*, V (1974–7), 90–3

'Thomas Kerver's Case, 1444', *EHR*, XC (1975), 331–46

(with R. E. Latham) 'The Veredictum of Chippenham Hundred, 1281', in *Collectanea*, ed. N. J. Williams (Wilts Arch. & Nat. Hist. Soc., Recs Branch, XII, 1956), 50–128

(with P. Shearman) *Fitznells Cartulary: A Calendar of Bodleian Library MS. Rawlinson B 430* (Surrey Rec. Soc., XXVI, 1968)

Changes in the assize utrum between the constitutions of Clarendon and Bracton

edited by

ALEXANDRA NICOL

The assize utrum is first found in statute law in 1164 when it appears as clause 9 of the constitutions of Clarendon.[1] There it is a preliminary form of action, deciding to which court the plea should go, and the demandant could be either a cleric or a layman. Less than a century later Bracton describes it as an assize which settles both possession and right and which Martin Pattishall had at one time forbidden to laymen;[2] it had become 'the parson's writ of right'.[3] This article examines these two changes, looking first at the function of the assize and then at the personnel.

In the constitutions of Clarendon it is said that a jury should decide whether a disputed tenement were alms or lay fee. If it belonged to alms the plea went to the church courts; if it belonged to lay fee the plea went to the king's court, unless both parties claimed to hold of the same lord in which case it went to the lord's court. There is no evidence of utrum working in this way. In 1206 there is a jurata utrum in which the tenant who is described as holding lay fee has a charter which says he holds in alms; as both parties, therefore, claim to hold in alms the case is sent to the church courts.[4] This case has been described as an example of utrum being used as 'an administrative device deciding in cases of conflict of competence',[5] but as the recognition was held in the lay court and it was decided that the land was alms without the jury giving a verdict this cannot be accepted. There is another case in 1219 in which the same thing happens.[6] These two cases tell us that the church courts were competent at this time to hear cases concerning land held in free alms, but they tell us nothing about the function of the assize utrum.

We would not expect to find utrum acting as a preliminary assize as late as 1206 because in the assize as described by Glanvill[7] it seems that seisin was delivered to the successful party after the assize. Glanvill does not specifically say this, but he does say that the recognition proceeds in the manner stated for other recognitions. This must refer to his section on mort d'ancestor which includes a writ for delivering seisin after the recognition.[8] The vocabulary used by Glanvill suggests the same thing, for he says that if a tenement be proved to be ecclesiastical fee, 'licet peti possit' by the losing party to hold it from the church. If seisin had not followed the recognition the word 'peti' would be misleading.

The delivery of seisin after the assize marks an important development since 1164, and in particular the loss of jurisdiction by the ecclesiastical and lords' courts should be noted. It is of interest that there is no evidence of opposition to this loss. The acceptance could be connected with the invention of other assizes as a result of which seisin could change hands, for there was less reason for resisting in utrum once the principle was established.

The utrum writ in Glanvill is included in his book on recognitions. In his introductory paragraph to this book he says that he has so far discussed pleas about right and there remain those concerned with seisin only. These are most often settled by recognition and therefore he will now consider the various kinds of recognition.[9] He does not say specifically that the recognitions which follow are concerned with seisin only, but he does suggest that those assizes which are settled by recognition and which are discussed in this book are considered to settle seisin as opposed to right. Certainly after the other assizes in this book the losing party can take out another writ, for example, of right or advowson, to pursue his claim to the land or church. With utrum, however, the case is somewhat different. In the utrum writ in Glanvill the parson claimed the land as free alms of the church of which he was parson and the jurors decided whether the land were lay fee of a named person or ecclesiastical fee. The question that arises here is at what level had the successful party gained seisin.

Let us consider first a verdict that the land was lay

1 *Select Charters . . .*, ed. W. Stubbs, 9th edn, revised by H. W. C. Davis (Oxford, 1913), 165–6.

2 Bracton, f.285b (III, 329).

3 Britton, IV, 7.2 (ed. F. M. Nichols, Oxford, 1865, II, 207).

4 *CRR*, IV, 291 (Oxon). The question is whether the land is free alms or lay fee of the barony of the abbot of Westminster. The abbot's charter describes the land as alms, but we would not expect this to be justiciable in the church courts: see the constitutions of Clarendon, c.11 (Stubbs, *Select Charters*, 166); *Tractatus de Legibus et Consuetudinibus regni Anglie qui Glanvilla vocatur*, VII, 1 (ed. G. D. G. Hall, London, 1965, 74).

5 *Royal Writs in England from the Conquest to Glanvill*, ed. R. C. Van Caenegem (SS, LXXVII, 1959), 328 n.3.

6 *Rolls of the Justices in Eyre for Lincolnshire, 1218–1219, and Worcestershire, 1221*, ed. D. M. Stenton (SS, LIII, 1934), no. 333.

7 Glanvill, XIII, 23–25 (ed. Hall, 163–4).

8 ibid., XIII, 8 (ed. Hall, 153).

9 ibid., XII, 1 (ed. Hall, 148–9).

fee of a named person. What further action could the parson bring? He could, of course, claim the land in his own right and not by right of the church, but if he did so he would be claiming as a third party; his claim would not be connected with the utrum assize. He could also bring a jury of attaint[10] but such a jury could not settle the matter at a higher level than utrum, it could merely reverse the jurors' decision.

The one form of action which could possibly overrule the utrum decision and after the assize settle the dispute at a higher level is the writ of right. In Glanvill this writ is available to a claimant to hold in free alms.[11] This must mean that parsons could bring it, but by the time Bracton was writing this had changed, and the writ was not available to them.[12] There is evidence of parsons bringing writs of right claiming land 'ut jus ecclesie' quite regularly until 1212[13] and there are two cases in the 1220s.[14] None of these cases, however, follows an utrum case.[15] Indeed Glanvill, by specifying how the losing party could pursue his claim to the land following a verdict of ecclesiastical fee, implies that nothing could follow a verdict of lay fee. Therefore the assize was settling more than possessory title when the verdict was lay fee. This conclusion is to some extent anticipated by the verdict being that the land is lay fee of a named person, and not just lay fee.

There follows the question whether the church could hold lay fee. It is a question that we shall hold over while we discuss the other possibility in Glanvill's assize utrum, a verdict of ecclesiastical fee. Glanvill tells us what further case could follow, for although a verdict of ecclesiastical fee meant that the land could never again be lay fee, nonetheless the losing party could claim to hold it from the church for certain services. To do this he had to go to the church courts.[16] A verdict of ecclesiastical fee at this date, therefore, meant that the church had established a claim either to hold the land in demesne or to hold the services from it.

By Bracton's day a verdict in favour of the parson did not include the phrase 'ecclesiastical fee'; instead the land was said to be free alms. Free alms did not, however, include land held from the church for services, which was regarded as lay fee.[17] This was firmly established by 1228, but not before then. Thus in a case in 1224 the jurors said that the land was the fee of the church because the tenant and his ancestors had always held it from the church and they had never heard that the church had held it in demesne. The case ends in a final concord.[18] After 1228 the verdict would have been that the land was lay fee and only the services were free alms. It is more on the Glanvill pattern than any other case and the vocabulary partly accounts for this, for Glanvill talks of ecclesiastical fee and here we have fee of the church. In no other cases do the jurors use such expressions. What they both seem to mean is that if the church held the land in demesne then the land was free alms; if the land were held from the church for services then it was ecclesiastical fee.

There are two pieces of evidence against this argument: final concords in which the land is acknowledged to be free alms of the church and the lay party is then granted that land to hold from the parson and his successors for services.[19] The latter of the con-

[10] There are very few juries of attaint following utrum; the earliest is in 1221, following an utrum case of 1205 (*CRR*, III, 279 (Glos); IV, 3, 8; *Pleas before the King or his Justices, 1198–1212,* ed. D. M. Stenton, III (SS, LXXXIII, 1966), no. 1644). The jury of attaint is in *Rolls of the Justices in Eyre for Gloucestershire, Warwickshire and Shropshire, 1221–1222,* ed. D. M. Stenton (SS, LIX, 1940), no. 77.

[11] Glanvill, XII, 3 (ed. Hall, 137).

[12] Bracton, f.287 (III, 333).

[13] e.g. *CRR*, I, 247–8 (Yorks); IV, 102, 206–7, 265 (Norf); VI, 259, 263 (Derb). Bracton says that a parson could bring an action claiming escheat for which he could rely on a predecessor's seisin of services (Bracton, f.287b: III, 333–4). We sometimes find a parson claiming land as right of his church which later turns out to be escheat, e.g. KB 26/125, mm.16, 22d; other stages of this case are in ibid., mm.12Bd, 6d, 24d; 131, m.2d. These are to be published as *CRR*, XVII, nos. 140, 186, 293, 2463, 2499; XVIII, no. 664.

[14] *CRR*, XII, no. 2188; XIII, no. 1790.

[15] The only possible example is the plea of right in 1229 (*CRR*, XIII, no. 1790), for in 1226 the itinerant justices were instructed to take an utrum case with the same demandant and tenant, and the same amount of land in the same place: *Pat.R. 1225–32,* 80. There is nothing to indicate that it is the same piece of land.

[16] Glanvill, XII, 25 (ed. Hall, 148). The assize retains here something of its preliminary nature.

[17] Bracton, f.286–286b (III, 331). e.g. JUST 1/819, m.12d; 174, m.12d.

[18] *CRR*, XI, no. 1755; also in *BNB,* III, no. 1075. Other stages of the case are in *Pat.R. 1216–25,* 485; *CRR*, XI, no. 2889; *Feet of Fines for Essex,* I, ed. R. E. G. Kirk (Essex Arch. Soc., 1899–1910), no. 125.

[19] *Abstracts of Final Concords, temp. Richard I, John and Henry III,* I, ed. W. O. Massingberd and W. Boyd (London, 1896), 139–40 (no. 84). The assize leading to this is in *Eyre for Lincs & Worcs,* nos. 369, 459. Other stages are in ibid., nos. 225, 432, 807, 834; *CRR,* XIII, no. 1010.

cords is in 1228 by which date land not held by the church in demesne would be said by jurors to be lay fee.[20]

It is significant that in 1224 the jurors do not give a verdict of church fee and that they take services into account. This approach to services marks the main development in the assize. In Glanvill a verdict of ecclesiastical fee meant that the losing party could pursue his claim to hold the land in the church courts. Later this would be included in the assize. At first, however, this had to be by consent, as we find in 1206 when there is a jurata to decide whether land is free alms of the parson holding in demesne or lay fee of the other party holding from the church.[21] Although later the words *jurata utrum* were used instead of *assisa utrum* this was not so before the 1220s when a jurata means that the parties have consented to it.

So far we have discussed services only when they were owed by a tenant of the church. What was the position if the church owed services? A case of 1219 shows clearly, when the jurors in Lincolnshire were in a quandary, not knowing if the land were free alms or lay fee. The church had been seised of the land for a very long time, but the jurors did not know whether it were free alms because the church owed services. The case went to Westminster where it was said that since many lands were given to churches in alms, some in free, pure and perpetual alms giving no services and others in free alms only, for which services that were owed were given, therefore the prioress claiming free alms was given seisin.[22]

Here, therefore, we have a statement that land held by parish churches in demesne is regarded as free alms, regardless of whether it owes services. Later this had to be so, as utrum was the only form of action available to parsons except when they could rely on their own seisin, so if they claimed land as demesne land of their church they had to claim that it was free alms. There are no cases after 1219 in which a claim to free alms is questioned because services are owed for the land.

Here we pick up the point about lay fee and the question whether the church could hold it. Was land held by the church and owing services always regarded as free alms? The 1219 case seems to be establishing a principle, as it had to be sent to Westminster for solution, which suggests that it was not always so regarded. Moreover, the 1219 case fits quite well with the evidence of parsons bringing writs of right for land claimed as the right of their churches. Until 1212 they come up quite regularly but after that I have only found two cases.[23] It could be, therefore, that before 1219 land held by the churches for services was regarded as lay fee, and to claim it a parson had to bring a writ of right. There is some evidence for this view in that in none of the utrum cases before 1219 are services owed for land that is said to be free alms. In some of the writs of right before 1219 we find that the parson is claiming that the land is free alms,[24] as Glanvill said he could,[25] and this helps explain the cases after 1219. In these the land is not said to be alms, but the reports of the cases are not long.

There can be no real proof of the suggestion that before 1219 land for which the church owed services was regarded as lay fee. The evidence for free alms tenure is about large landholders, that is, the religious houses and cathedral churches.[26] This suggestion would explain one puzzling early case in which the demandant claimed lay fee and later stated that he was claiming only the services.[27] The only explanation for the demandant bringing utrum for such a claim is that the church could hold lay fee and give services. It is still a strange action to bring, for, as we have seen, the jurors in Glanvill are asked to decide whether the land is lay fee of a named person and seisin was delivered as a result. A verdict of lay fee in this case, therefore, would have given the demandant seisin of the land, not just the services. As it happened, in this case the tenant had a charter from the demandant's father, and although this was challenged by the demandant judgment was that the tenant should hold in peace.

This establishment of the fact that the land held by the church in demesne was free alms was paralleled by the change whereby land held from the church for

[20] e.g. JUST 1/819, m.12d.

[21] *CRR*, IV, 193 (Lincs). This is part of a long case. Other stages are found in *Pleas before the King or his Justices*, III, nos. 1071, 1941; *CRR*, III, 172, 229; IV, 195, 233; *Feet of Fines, Lincolnshire, 1199–1215*, ed. H. S. Walker (PRS, New ser., XXIX, 1953), no. 209; *The Earliest Lincolnshire Assize Rolls, A.D. 1202–1209*, ed. D. M. Stenton (Linc. Rec. Soc., XXII, 1924), no. 1431.

[22] *BNB*, II, no. 21.

[23] *CRR*, XII, no. 2188; XIII, no. 1790.

[24] e.g. *CRR*, III, 43 (Yorks); preceded by ibid., II, 247, 307.

[25] Glanvill, XII, 3 (ed. Hall, 137).

[26] Discussions on free-alms tenure inevitably concentrate on these: e.g. E. G. Kimball, 'Tenure in Frank Almoign and Secular Services', *EHR*, XLIII (1928), 341–53.

[27] *Rotuli Curiae Regis*, ed. F. Palgrave (RC, 1835), I, 190–1 (Essex).

services was regarded as lay fee. This had an obvious effect upon the assize for it now decided what services were owed for the land and did not leave this unsettled. No further case could be brought about the land, and the assize did indeed settle both possession and right.

In addition to this change in the function of the assize a limitation was imposed upon who could bring it. In the constitutions of Clarendon it can be brought by either party, and although in Glanvill's writ the demandant is a parson there is no indication that the assize was not also available to laymen. In the cases up to the early 1230s parsons are most frequently the demandants but laymen also bring the assize. This, however, changed and Bracton tells us that Pattishall had once forbidden the assize to laymen, although when Bracton was writing they were once more allowed to bring it.[28]

Bracton gives as an example of Pattishall forbidding the assize to laymen a case of 1227.[29] In this case, however, the layman acknowledged that he had never had seisin of the land and it is for this reason that the writ did not lie; there is no suggestion that the writ would have fallen if he could have claimed his own seisin. This idea that the lay demandant had to be able to base his claim on his own seisin is not found until the mid 1220s. Thus in one case of 1221, quoted by Bracton as an example of laymen being allowed the assize, the jurors take the seisin of the demandant's mother and grandmother into account, although the demandant claimed that his mother had died seised which made the seisin fairly near his own.[30] In another case the church is acknowledged as having had seisin for a long time, but this is a jurata utrum following a prohibition plea, after which the church had been given seisin until the status of the land could be sorted out by a jurata.[31] It is, therefore, a special case. When we move on to 1224 we find that a layman who bases his claim on his grandfather's seisin is told to get a writ of right;[32] and in 1227 the tenant successfully claims that as the demandant is not founding his claim on seisin, which only the parson can do, the writ should not lie [1].

The evidence that the layman had by the mid 1220s to rely on his own seisin to bring the assize is contradicted by only one source: the Irish Register where an utrum writ is followed by the comment that the writ could be sought by a cleric or a layman.[33] The prefatory writ to the register is dated 1227,[34] but the case evidence makes it clear that the writ was not available to laymen without qualification.

There are only three later cases brought by laymen. The first, in 1229, fits the pattern, for the tenants claim that the assize should not continue as the demandant had no right in the land nor did he through whom he claimed; neither of them had had seisin. The demandant withdrew.[35] In a case in 1235 the parson claims long seisin for the church and the court adjourns while it is considered whether the writ should lie.[36]

The only other utrum case after 1227 with a lay demandant is a jurata following another plea;[37] it is interesting because Bracton tells us of one situation in which there could be an utrum case when the tenant was a parson. This is if a layman brings a writ of right the cleric could place himself on a jurata utrum. Bracton qualifies this by saying that he could only do so if whoever testified was able to do so from his own memory. He also says that on account of this a case of ownership is not turned into one merely of possession. If the time lapse was too long the parson would, with permission, place himself on the grand assize.[38]

What Bracton says ties in with the limitations imposed on laymen bringing utrum by an original writ, and here we have the explanation for their being able to bring utrum only when they could rely on their own seisin. For utrum was for the layman a possessory action; only when it was used in a plea of right as a jurata was this not so. It is, therefore, not surprising that we do not find them bringing it, for the assize of novel disseisin was the more obvious one to use.

If the assize was not absolutely forbidden to lay-

[28] Bracton, f.285b (III, 329). [29] *BNB*, III, no. 1923.

[30] *Eyre for Lincs & Worcs*, no. 976.

[31] *CRR*, XI, nos. 62, 902.

[32] *BNB*, III, no. 1020; also in *CRR*, XI, no. 1842. Preceded by *Pat.R. 1216–25*, 408 and *Rot. Litt. Claus.*, I, 631b. The demandant brought a writ of right in *CRR*, XI, no. 2751.

[33] *Early Registers of Writs*, ed. E. de Haas and G. D. G. Hall (SS, LXXXVII, 1970), 8 (no. 21).

[34] ibid., 1.

[35] *BNB*, II, no. 368. [36] ibid., III, no. 1156.

[37] *CRR*, XIV, no. 998; following ibid., XIII, no. 2580.

[38] Bracton, f.287–287b (III, 333).

men their use of it was greatly limited, in contrast to the parson, who could claim at least within the limits for the writ of right.[39] The reason for this, according to Bracton, was that other forms of action were available to laymen. This is not, however, a very convincing reason, especially as Bracton tells us that laymen can now once more bring it. The explanation may lie in the form that the developed assize took, when the parson very frequently in his count would claim that a predecessor, maybe in a previous reign, had held the land in demesne, taking profits from it, and that he had unjustly alienated it. This unjust alienation is important, for once the church had land as free alms it remained as free alms, unless it was granted away with the permission of the bishop and patron.[40] The tenant holding lay fee could claim either that the previous parson had not held the land in demesne by right of his church, or that the alienation was just. The layman as demandant was in a different position for if one of his ancestors had granted away the land to the church the restrictions on alienations by churches and parsons were absent, and it would be difficult to prove that the alienation was unjust. Unless the jurors could go back to the point at which the church had gained seisin the fact that the church was holding the land in demesne would indicate that the land was free alms. This explains why there is the emphasis on the lay demandant having had seisin, or the 'tempus probationis' being within living memory. When the parson was demandant the issue could in no way be prejudged by the church's seisin.

The question that follows, of course, is whether a grand assize were fairer. In the grand assize there may have been more stress on title and less on seisin, and therefore instead of the church's seisin influencing the verdict the title would have to be proved. There is no real reason, however, why this could not have been included in the assize, which could be why Bracton saw no reason for not allowing them the use of it. It was limited for them at a time when it was gaining its established form as an action that settled both possession and right and when there was a stress on the church having held the land in demesne, and this may account for the limitation.

There remains one final question, which is why clerics could not bring the writ of right after a certain time. Bracton tells us that they could not because gifts were made to the church and not to the parson and his successors; he could not therefore plead his predecessors' seisin and so the writ was not allowed to him.[41] This had not, however, prevented parsons from bringing writs of right as late as 1229, and as they are allowed a writ of entry it is, as Maitland remarks, somewhat anomalous.[42] If the church could hold lay fee until 1219, for which the parson had to bring a writ of right, the establishment of all demesne land of the church as free alms would curtail its use. This does not suggest, however, that they could not still bring it for free alms. One possible explanation is that a writ of right had in the first instance to be addressed to the lord, and in the case of free alms for which no services were owed, the parson may not have known who was the lord.

Various aspects of the assize have not been examined, for example its use by cathedral churches and religious houses, and changes in the vocabulary which were contemporaneous with the developments that we have discussed. The most important changes in the assize, however, are those we have discussed, that is, the change in its function and in the rôle of the laymen.

[39] [2] is the only utrum case to mention a date of limitation. Bracton does not mention a date of limitation for utrum, but Britton says it is the same as for the writ of right: Britton, IV, 7.2 (ed. Nichols, II, 207). His statement is contradicted by statements in Fleta, V, 21 (*Fleta, Seu Commentarius Juris Anglicani*, ed. J. Selden (London, 1647), 333) and one of the Year Books: *YB 21–22 Edw. I*, ed. A. J. Horwood (RS, 1873), 456.

[40] Fleta, V, 21 (ed. Selden, 333); Britton, IV, 8.1 (ed. Nichols, II, 208). If a parson granted away land in a final concord the assent of the bishop had to be sought: e.g. *CRR*, XIII, nos. 1010, 2149, following nos. 1058, 1818. There is less record of the presence of the patron, but see, for example, KB 26/121, m.23 (Norf), to be printed as *CRR*, XVI, no. 1659.

[41] Bracton, ff.286b–287 (III, 331–2).

[42] Pollock & Maitland, 249 n.2, quoting Bracton, f.287b (III, 334). I have found no cases of parsons bringing writs of entry for their churches, but there is one in BL, MS Lansdowne 564.

TEXT

[1]
JUST 1/229, m.6

[Placita et assise apud Chelmesford die dominica proxima post festum Sancti Luce Ewangeliste [24 Oct. 1227]]

Assisa venit recognitura si[43] una virgata terre cum pertinenciis in Messing' sit libera elemosina[44] prioris de Colum ut pertinens ad[45] ecclesiam suam de Mestinges an laicum feodum Thome Baynard et Ismania[46] uxoris eius, quam terram prior de Colun tenet. Qui venit et dicit quod assisa non debet inde fieri quia istud breve non competit laico qui[47] extra saisinam set solum persone qui est extra saisinam.[48] Alius hoc cognoscit. Ideo consideratum est quod assisa non jacet et perquirat[49]

[2]
JUST 1/62, m.22

[Placita et assise apud Wycumb' [16 Henry III]]

Assisa venit recognitura utrum quatuor viginti et octo acre terre cum pertinenciis in Aylesbyres sint libera elemosina pertinens ad ecclesiam Willelmi persone ecclesie de Aylesbyres an laicum feodum Nigelli de Caldekot' Johannis filii Nigelli Willelmi filii Nigelli et Agnetis filie Nigelli unde Nigellus de Caldekot' xxix acras Johannes filius Nigelli xxix acras Willelmus filius Nigelli xv acras et Agnes filia Nigelli xv acras terre inde tenent. Qui omnes veniunt. Et Johannes et alii vocant ad warantum predictum Nigellum qui presens est et eis warantizat et respondet de toto. Et dicit quod assisa non debet inde fieri quia pater suus ante ipsum tenuit terram illam iiij^{xx} annis et ipse post eum iam tenuit illam iiij^{xx} annis. Et desicut terminum viij^{xx} annorum excedit terminum brevis de recto petit judicium si debeat ad hoc breve respondere. Dicit etiam quod Walensis pater suus feofatus fuit de terra illa et profert cartam cuiusdam[50] Roberti Linc' episcopi et capituli Sancte Marie Linc' que testatur quod idem episcopus et capitulum concesserunt predicto Walensi homini Willelmi archidiaconi Norht' totam terram de Caldekotes que pertinet ad ecclesiam de Eylesbir' heriditario jure tenendam ipsi et heredibus suis per annuam pensionem decem solidorum sicut dominus suus Willelmus archidiaconus Norht' de cuius prebenda est dedit ei. Idem autem episcopus et capitulum hanc donationem concedunt et presentis scripti testimonio confirmant. Teste etc.

Et Willelmus venit et dicit quod carta ista non debet ei nocere. Quia continetur in carta illa quod episcopus et capitulum confirmant ei totam predictam terram de Caldekot' sicut dominus suus Willelmus archidiaconus Norht' illam ei dedit et ipse nichil ostendit de feofamento ipsius archidiaconi. Preterea dicit quod semper consuetum fuit et esse debet quod in omnibus cartis per capitulum confectis debet apponi nomen et sigillum decani quicumque fuerit et ipse Nigellus nichil[50] ostendit de concessione decani. Preterea dicit quod dominus rex est advocatus predicte ecclesie qui dedit predictam ecclesiam et[50] prebendavit Linc' ecclesie et nichil ostendit de domino rege nec de aliquibus antecessoribus suis. Preterea dicit quod in carta sua continetur quod ipse et heredes sui[51] debent tenere predictam terram per pensionem x solidorum per annum ipse recessit de carta illa et reddit per annum xl solidos. Et petit judicium desicut ipse cognoscit quod pater suus inde feofatus fuit et ipse nichil ostendit de feofamento.

Et Nigellus venit et dicit quod cum decanus sit de capitulo Linc' et carta sua loquitur de episcopo et capitulo et nulla sit mentio de aliqua persona eiusdem capituli nulla debet fieri mentio de decano cum ipse decanus sit de capitulo. Ad hoc quod dicit quod nichil ostendit de feofamento Willelmi archidiaconi dicit quod domus sua combusta fuit in qua carta illa simul cum pluribus aliis cartis combusta fuit et quod habuit cartam et quod ita combusta fuit ponit se super patriam si opus fuerit. De hoc quod dicit quod ipse recessit de carta sua quam ostendit sub nomine episcopi dicit quod revera ipse non debet de jure de predicta terra non tantum x solidos nomine pensionis sed tempore quo Herbertus archidiaconus tenuit ecclesiam de[52] Eylesbyr' venit ipse Herbertus et cepit eum et duxit apud Wynt' et ibi eum inprisonavit

[43] *si* is used instead of *utrum* quite frequently until 1228.

[44] Followed by *pertinens ad ecclesiam ad ecclesiam,* struck through.

[45] Followed by *pertinens,* struck through.

[46] Recte *Ismanie.*

[47] *est* possibly omitted.

[48] Followed by *et iam*?, deleted.

[49] The report of the case ends abruptly here.

[50] Interlined.

[51] *et heredes sui* interlined.

[52] *ecclesiam de* repeated.

et tenuit eum in prisona quousque concederet ei xl solidos per annuum redditum pro predicta terra. [*Marginated*] Westm'. Ad judicium.
[*There then follows a long space.*]

Dies datus est eis de audiendo judicio suo apud Westm' a die Sancti Martini in xv dies. Et decanus ponit loco suo Robertum de Herpeford vel Willelmum de Dinigton'.

Highway robbery and trial by battle in the Hampshire eyre of 1249

edited by

M. T. CLANCHY

INTRODUCTION*

The documents edited here concern a robbery in the pass of Alton and related crimes tried at Winchester in the eyre of January–February 1249. They comprise a detached membrane from a Hampshire eyre roll, now classified as a Curia Regis Roll, and select crown pleas from the parent roll. The detached membrane, KB 26/223 (formerly 216), has been well known in part for centuries because it has at its head a drawing of a judicial combat (Frontispiece). Nor have the pleas concerning the Alton robbery in the parent roll, JUST 1/776, been neglected, since Matthew Paris gave a detailed account of the trial in his *Chronica Majora.*[1] A synopsis of Matthew's narrative, divided into sections using an alphabetical notation [a–t], has been appended to the Introduction for convenience of reference. The two rolls, KB 26/223 and JUST 1/776, were not associated with each other until Mr Meekings showed that KB 26/223 had originally been part of JUST 1/776 and that both documents consequently concerned the Hampshire eyre of 1249.[2] This edition aims to restore KB 26/223 to its original context and to provide a text of documents which are today in poor condition and difficult to read. These crown pleas are unusual in containing details of such rarely recorded events as trial by combat, the corruption of jurors and the involvement of men of the knightly class in organised crime.

Description and history of the documents

The whole of what remains legible of KB 26/223 has been transcribed below [1–12], even though most enrolments do not specifically concern the Alton robbery. The membrane is entitled on its face 'Apella probatorum' and was evidently intended to be a special section for approvers' accusations from a wide area; a membrane of similar type is extant from the Warwickshire eyre of 1247.[3] Despite its title, KB 26/223 is not devoted exclusively to approvers' business, as [6] and [7] on the face and [8] on the dorse are indictments concerning the Alton robbery. Consequently on the dorse of the membrane 'et malefactoribus in passu de Aulton' has been added to the heading 'Adhuc de probatoribus'. Though brief, [6] is the most important single enrolment about the Alton robbery because it names the principal thieves and mentions William Pope, the only offender actually named by Matthew Paris [q].

From the parent roll, JUST 1/776, all pleas have been extracted which mention crimes in the pass of Alton. All such pleas probably concern the great robbery described by Matthew Paris, except [25] which looks like an unconnected case of homicide. Other pleas have been included which reasonable supposition associates with the robbery, even though they do not specifically refer to Alton. For example, [18] indicts John de Bendinges of robbery without specifying a place, whereas he is explicitly said to be one of the Alton robbers at [6] and [7]. In addition, enrolments naming the jurors of Alton, Odiham and Selborne hundreds have been included because some of them were alleged to be implicated in the robbery. The foreman for each hundred has been named [13, 24, 29] together with the appropriate lists of jurors from the end of the plea roll [46–8]. One other plea [28] has been extracted because it concerns an accusation by Walter Bloweberme [4, 5, 11], the chief approver in KB 26/223. The enrolments selected from JUST 1/776 have been numbered consecutively, following on from KB 26/223. This sequence is arbitrary, as it cannot be established where KB 26/223

* I am grateful to Mr H. R. T. Summerson for commenting on my introduction. He is making a study of law enforcement in Henry III's reign, and I owe him the references indicated by (HRTS).

[1] *Matthaei Parisiensis . . . Chronica Majora,* ed. H. R. Luard (RS, 1872–84), V, 56–60. A shortened version appears in *Matthaei Parisiensis . . . Historia Anglorum sive . . . Historia Minor,* ed. F. Madden (RS, 1866–9), III, 46–7. J. G. Bellamy has discussed the robbery in his *Crime and Public Order in England in the Later Middle Ages* (London, 1973), 42–5; but he has not taken account of Mr Meekings' identification of the manuscripts and he misunderstands some of the other sources. In what follows I have corrected errors and omissions in Bellamy's narrative without comment. His most misleading statements (at p.43) arise from misinterpreting Matthew Paris: the merchants came to the king in 1249, not 1248; the bishop of Taunton was not involved, as Taunton has never had a bishop; about 30 malefactors were hanged (below, 37, 47), not 300.

[2] *Crown Pleas of the Wiltshire Eyre, 1249,* ed. C. A. F. Meekings (Wilts Arch. & Nat. Hist. Soc., Recs Branch, XVI, 1960), 6 n.3, 25 n.9, 91 n.7.

[3] JUST 1/952, m.45; Meekings in *Wilts Crown Pleas 1249,* 91 n.6. KB 26/223 does not include all appeals by approvers from the Hants eyre, as another appears in the gaol delivery section of JUST 1/776 (m.37, Winchester city, not transcribed here). The separate gaol delivery section is exceptional: Meekings in *Wilts Crown Pleas 1249,* 18.

was originally placed among the membranes of JUST 1/776. In the translations of the enrolments repetitious use of 'and' and 'aforesaid' or 'said' has been omitted.

The parent roll, JUST 1/776, is typical in its dimensions and format of eyre rolls of the period. The membranes vary in width between 16 and 17 centimetres and in length between 60 and 68 centimetres. The crown pleas are written mainly in one hand which is small and rather compressed.[4] There is possibly a different hand at work in the list of presenting juries [46–8] and certainly another larger hand in the first membrane (m. 23) of crown pleas. The roll is a subsidiary roll and not the main roll of the principal justice of the circuit, Henry Bath. Mr Meekings suggests that it was made for William Breton, one of the justices accompanying Henry Bath.[5] The detached membrane KB 26/223 varies in width between 16 and 16·4 centimetres and is 38 centimetres long, distinctly shorter than the membranes of JUST 1/776. Most of the enrolments are written in the same small hand as the crown pleas of JUST 1/776. The membrane can be shown to have once been a part of JUST 1/776 because it has two pairs of holes at the head (see Frontispiece) which match the similar pairs of holes on JUST 1/776 (e.g. on m.28).

The condition of the documents is at some points very poor. KB 26/223 has suffered from too much handling and exposure to light since the seventeenth century and is today scarcely legible. Some parts respond well to ultra-violet light [e.g. 8], but on others it has no effect. I have benefited considerably from a transcript made in 1949 by Mr Meekings and Mr L. C. Hector and also from a text of [4] and [5] by Edward Bisshe printed in 1654. The condition of JUST 1/776 is more varied. Some membranes (e.g. m.30) are in excellent condition, whereas particular enrolments on others are difficult to read. On membrane 27 items [14–17] respond well to ultra-violet light, but it has no effect on the latter enrolments on the tail of membrane 29d, where the parchment has been rubbed. Another enrolment which may concern the Alton robbery follows [31] at the damaged tail of the membrane, but it has been omitted from this edition as no names or significant details can be extracted.

The history of the documents is closely related to their poor state of preservation. JUST 1/776, including membrane KB 26/223, was one of those plea rolls which was not brought back from the Tower of London to Westminster after Bishop Stapleton's array of records in 1320–6.[6] The Tower records were on the whole not so carefully kept as those at Westminster. Our roll attracted particular attention from antiquaries in the seventeenth century because of the drawing of the combat on KB 26/223. In 1654 a fanciful engraving of the drawing by Robert Vaughan and a transcript of [4] and the first paragraph of [5] were published among Edward Bisshe or Bisse's notes accompanying an edition of Upton's *De Studio Militari.*[7] Bisshe describes the document as being in the Tower in a roll of the year 33 Henry III, that is, at that time KB 26/223 was still an integral part of JUST 1/776. So it must likewise have been when William Prynne, keeper of the Tower records from 1660 to 1669, wrote 'duellum' on the dorse of the last membrane (m.44d) of JUST 1/776, referring presumably to the drawing on KB 26/223.[8] The two documents were still together when the pairs of holes were made through the membranes, as they affect both JUST 1/776 and KB 26/223. These holes were probably made after Bisshe's time, as they are not discussed in his description of the drawing, even though one of them affects the face of the combatant, Walter Bloweberme (Frontispiece). These holes may have been made by Prynne, who is known to have maltreated other records in his keeping. They were perhaps intended to facilitate hanging the roll up with string.

Mr Meekings suggests that Prynne may likewise have been responsible for removing KB 26/223 from its parent roll JUST 1/776.[9] If so, that was presumably done after he had written 'duellum' on the parent roll. KB 26/223 had certainly been removed by 1711, when Thomas Madox published a more accurate engraving of the combat drawing in his *History and Antiquities of the Exchequer.*[10] He evidently did not know the provenance of the membrane, as he described it as being 'written in a little hand, of the reign (as I guess upon view) of

[4] The same hand is evident in JUST 1/996: Meekings in *Wilts Crown Pleas 1249*, 25.

[5] For a biography of William see ibid., 129–30. He was a friend of the bishop of Winchester: ibid., 13; below, 40.

[6] Meekings in *Wilts Crown Pleas 1249*, 24, 25 n.9.

[7] *Nicholai Uptoni De Studio Militari* (London, 1654), Appendix 'In Nicholaum Uptonum Notae', 36–7.

[8] Meekings in *Wilts Crown Pleas 1249*, 25 n.9.

[9] ibid.

[10] [Folio edn] (London, 1711), 383. The drawing was republished in the quarto edn (1769), I, 551. Another

K. Henry III'. Madox added that the membrane 'hath suffered by time or weather so that some parts of it are scarce legible' and he drew attention to the pairs of holes, one of which 'passeth through the face of Walter Bloweberme'. In a footnote he appended a transcript of the first paragraph of [5], omitting the words 'ad domum Edeline' which had been legible in Bisshe's time. It is reasonable to conclude therefore that KB 26/223 was removed from JUST 1/776 and damaged in the process between 1660 and 1710.

During the overhaul of records which followed the reforming legislation of the nineteenth century Hubert Hall, who had been appointed a junior clerk in the Public Record Office in 1879, rediscovered KB 26/223 'amongst a heap of refuse where it had probably lain from the time of Madox'.[11] Hall says that he had it 'repaired and restored to a place of safety'. This is doubtless the repair done in October 1887, of which a note survives at the Public Record Office.[12] Hall adds that he had a new copy made of the combat drawing and this was published in 1890 in his *Court Life under the Plantagenets.*[13] The engraving made for Hall is, however, inferior both in artistic quality and in accuracy to that done for Madox in 1711. Fortunately Hall had told F. W. Maitland of his discovery, probably early in 1887 before the document was repaired. Maitland commissioned the Woodburytype Company to make a photographic reproduction of the drawing from the original manuscript, a relatively novel process at the time. The Woodburytype reproduction was then published by him in 1888 as the frontispiece to his *Select Pleas of the Crown,* launching the Selden Society. That frontispiece (republished as a frontispiece to this book) is the most accurate record of the combat drawing. Maitland insisted on its accuracy when he wrote in 1889 to George Neilson, who was about to publish *Trial by Combat:* 'I think that there can be no reasonable doubt that the Woodburytype has reproduced our friend Mr. Blowberme to a hair; but if I get a chance I will glance at the original picture'.[14] These words incidentally suggest that Maitland had difficulty in getting convenient access to the manuscript. That would also explain why he was no better informed than Madox had been about the date or provenance of KB 26/223. Nor evidently did Maitland make his transcript of [5] from the original document, but from Madox, as he (like Madox) omits the second paragraph of the text.[15]

As Maitland's reputation and that of the Selden Society grew in the 1890s, scholarly prominence was assured to the combat drawing. In 1901 it became known to the wider reading public when the publishers Cassell and Co. used a touched-up version of the Selden Society's frontispiece, omitting the names on the original, as an illustration to accompany Maitland's article on English law in their *Social England: a Record of the Progress of the People.*[16] This version of the drawing has subsequently appeared elsewhere, for example, in L. F. Salzman's *English Life in the Middle Ages* where it is ascribed to the year 1270.[17] The original drawing was exhibited in the museum of the Public Record Office from its opening in 1902 until the mid-1960s, when it was removed to prevent further deterioration.[18]

The present condition of KB 26/223 is worse than it was when Maitland had it photographed in c 1887. To the naked eye the figures of the two combatants are mere shadows of those portrayed in the Selden

engraving, based on that made for Madox, was published in E. A. Kendall, *Argument . . . on Wager of Battle,* 3rd edn (London, 1818), at p.305 in the British Library copy.

[11] H. Hall, *Court Life under the Plantagenets* (London, 1890), 207. Hall's career is outlined by C. Johnson, 'Hubert Hall, 1857–1944', *TRHS,* 4th ser., XXVIII (1946), 2.

[12] PRO 12/1: 'Chancery (Tower) "Ordeal by Battle" Assize Roll. 1 membrane repaired by G. Merton for Mr Selby.' I owe this reference to Dr P. A. Brand.

[13] fig. 21 at p.93.

[14] Letter of 19 June 1889. I owe this reference to Professor Stones: *F. W. Maitland: Letters to George Neilson,* ed. E. L. G. Stones (Glasgow, 1976), 5. It is probable that Neilson had questioned whether the combatants had pudding-basin haircuts: below, 34.

[15] *Select Pleas of the Crown, A.D. 1200–1225,* ed. F. W. Maitland (SS, I, 1887), xxix–xxx.

[16] ed. H. D. Traill and J. S. Mann, [illust. edn] (London, 1901), I, 414.

[17] (Oxford, 1926), 223.

[18] H. C. Maxwell Lyte, *Catalogue of . . . the Museum of the Public Record Office,* [1st edn] (London, 1902), Case H, no. 93. Our roll was described vaguely as 'Fragment of an assize roll – 13th century' until the 9th edn of the *Catalogue* in 1922, when it appeared more accurately as 'Fragment of plea roll – 33 Henry III'. When the Museum was reopened after 1945, our roll was transferred from Case H, which had been for 'Curiosities', to 'Legal Records': *Catalogue* (1948 edn), Case C, no. 1. In the abbreviated edition of the *Catalogue* (1956) our roll is correctly described as: 'Membrane of Hampshire eyre roll with drawings illustrating a case decided by judicial combat (Trial by Battle) – 1249', Wall Case IX, no. 3.

Society frontispiece, the hill on which the gallows stands has disappeared, and the names of the persons are illegible. Even on an enlarged photograph, taken under ultra-violet light, there is less detail than in the Selden Society version. That is why the latter has been reproduced here instead of a new photograph of the original. This deterioration seems to have been caused by repeated exposure to light and wear in the Office's museum, compounded by ill-judged repair work, whereby fine gauze has been stuck over the drawing obscuring its remaining details. All in all, these documents have suffered neither from neglect nor from natural deterioration over time, but from too much indiscriminate attention in the last three centuries.

Trial by battle and approvers

The aim of trial by battle was to establish the truth by divine intervention: God would ensure that the innocent party triumphed. Battle was essentially therefore an ordeal, similar in function to other trials by ordeal such as those of hot iron or water.[19] Battle was not seen as a simple matter of the physically superior or more expert fighter winning. Right would triumph over might, and the court sometimes gave the stronger party a handicap, such as requiring him to fight with a hand tied or standing in water. Nevertheless, by the mid-thirteenth century trial by battle, like the other ordeals, was going out of favour both with the church and with English royal lawyers. Civil and criminal cases which had earlier required it were usually tried by a jury instead.

In criminal cases battle had formerly been the routine procedure in an appeal of felony. By that procedure the aggrieved party, A, appealed (i.e. accused) B of committing a felony affecting A or one of his kinsmen. A might allege, for example, that B had killed his brother or broken into his house. A undertook to prove his allegation 'by his body', that is, by combat with B. By 1249 such an allegation was no longer considered a private matter between A and B: it was a plea concerning the king's peace and was to be tried, not by combat, but by a jury of the neighbourhood giving their verdict. Bracton states this as a principle in his *De Legibus* (contemporary with our pleas): 'when the appellee offers to defend himself by his body he will not be heard, because the king does not fight, nor has he any champion other than the country' (i.e. the jury of the neighbourhood).[20] Mr Meekings has examined more than a thousand such appeals recorded in plea rolls between 1234 and 1249 and in none was a duel actually fought.[21]

Nevertheless, battle had not been entirely eliminated from criminal trials, as it still continued in accusations brought by approvers.[22] Although accusations by approvers were classified as appeals of felony, they were essentially different from the type of appeal described above. In an ordinary appeal of felony the aggrieved party accused another person of seriously hurting him or his kindred, whereas an approver was an accused criminal who had admitted his guilt and appealed another person of being his accomplice in exchange for a reduction of punishment. The approver was not an allegedly innocent and aggrieved party like the accuser in an ordinary appeal of felony. Nor was a combat between an approver and his adversary an ordinary ordeal in which both parties protested their innocence and asked God to decide between them. The approver had already admitted his guilt and was fighting, not for his own right, but to save himself from being hanged. Yet a vestige of the idea of testing righteousness remained, as the king was considered to be the aggrieved and innocent party upon whose behalf the approver fought those who had broken the king's peace. Hence an approver was the king's 'prover' and was known as his 'child' or even as his 'son'.[23] Thus although it was a rule that 'the king does not fight, nor has he any champion', he still did have a champion in the exceptional person of his approver.

At a less theoretical level, the royal government used the approver as a prosecutor and intimidator when no better proof could be obtained. The practical

[19] In general see G. Neilson, *Trial by Combat* (Glasgow, 1890); H. C. Lea, *Superstition and Force*, 4th edn (Philadelphia, Pa, 1892).

[20] Bracton, f.142b (II, 402).

[21] Meekings in *Wilts Crown Pleas 1249*, 70. But three such duels were fought between 1250 and 1260: at Eye (Suff) gaol delivery in 1250 (JUST 1/1177A, m.4d); at the Herts eyre of 1255 (JUST 1/320, m.29); at the Cambs eyre of 1260: *Assizes held at Cambridge, 1260*, ed. W. M. Palmer (Linton, 1930), 42 (HRTS).

[22] In general see F. C. Hamil, 'The King's Approvers', *Speculum*, XI (1936), 238–58.

[23] *Placita Corone*, ed. J. M. Kaye (SS, Supp. ser., IV, 1966), 24 (lenfant le Roy), 20 (fiz le Roy). Cf. Meekings in *Wilts Crown Pleas 1249*, 91.

aspect of the procedure is emphasised by the author of the 'Dialogue of the Exchequer' (c 1179): 'when some notorious criminal is apprehended by the king's officers of the peace, crime being so rife, the justices sometimes consent, as an extreme measure to purge the country of criminals, that if such a man confesses and turns king's evidence against his associates, and succeeds in proving by battle a charge against one or more of them, he may escape the death he has deserved, and save his skin by losing his civil rights and abjuring the realm.'[24] The procedure of accusation by approver must have been repugnant to those English jurists trained in Roman law and natural justice at Bologna or to theologians and canon lawyers from Paris,[25] yet it persisted when the other ordeals disappeared because of its usefulness, even though it was frequently abused.[26]

Accusation by approver had two advantages for the royal government. Firstly, it provided information about other suspects which could not readily be obtained by local officials and jurors. Medieval English law was far from unique in encouraging accused persons to give evidence against each other in return for mitigation of punishment. The second advantage of accusation by approver was peculiarly medieval. In the twelfth century an accused person could be compelled to stand trial by ordeal, whether ordeal by combat or by iron or whatever, because he must submit to the judgment of God. But when jury trial replaced ordeals as the normal mode of proof, the accused could not be compelled to submit to that, because a jury's verdict was not a judgment of God but the testimony of fallible men.[27] In theory jury trial had to be chosen by the accused. As the jury's verdict consisted essentially of a collective statement about the accused's reputation by local men of property speaking from their own knowledge, no stranger, particularly if he were a poor vagrant, would willingly submit to it. In *Placita Corone* (written in c 1274 but based on cases of the mid-thirteenth century) an accused cattle thief says to the judge: 'Sir, I am a stranger in these parts and less known to these good people than I would need be. Hence I dare not trust myself to their verdict.'[28]

Gangs of highwaymen moving from place to place, who were common throughout England according to Matthew Paris [d], were the least likely of accused to submit to trial by jury. By 1300 the peine forte et dure had been developed to compel the accused to plead by progressively crushing him to death with iron weights. In the mid-thirteenth century various pressures, both mental and physical, were no doubt used to compel suspects to submit to trial by jury.[29] If these failed, however, an accusation by an approver was uniquely useful, since the accused could not stand mute: he must submit to the combat because it was a judgment of God.[30] The threat of trial by battle might thus be used by the court to coerce an accused person, if he were not prepared to fight, into making a confession or 'choosing' the more modern form of trial by jury.

The procedure of trial by battle by approver consequently played an important supportive rôle in the administration of the criminal law in the thirteenth century, by discovering suspects and paradoxically by reinforcing trial by jury. Approvers were common, but actual combats were rare. Professor Pugh estimates that there was about one combat a year in the reign of Edward I.[31] For the mid-thirteenth century no such statistics are available, as most approvers were sent to Newgate, whose gaol delivery rolls only begin as a continuous series in 1273.[32] Mr Meekings cites an example of a combat in the Suffolk eyre of 1240 and others have been noted in the eyres of Wiltshire and Kent, both in 1241, and of Sussex in 1262.[33] The chancery rolls occasionally record permission for a successful approver to abjure the realm after convicting the required number of appellees,[34] but such records do not necessarily mean that any combats actually

24 *Dialogus de Scaccario,* ed. C. Johnson (London, 1950), 87–8.

25 e.g. Thomas Chobham objected to approvers: J. W. Baldwin, *Masters, Princes and Merchants* (Princeton, N.J., 1970), I, 329–30.

26 Abuses are discussed by Hamil, *Speculum,* XI, 248–50.

27 Pollock & Maitland, II, 650.

28 *Placita Corone,* 18.

29 The subject is obscure. Bracton (f.142b: II, 402) says that an accused person who refuses trial by jury is 'per hoc quasi convictus' and that he can be coerced to stand trial; but *Placita Corone* (23–4) shows how a suspect has to be tricked by the judge into accepting jury trial.

30 I differ here from Professor R. B. Pugh, who says that an appellee might stand mute: 'Some Reflections of a Medieval Criminologist', *Procs Brit. Acad.,* LIX (1973), 91.

31 ibid.

32 ibid., 104; Meekings in *Wilts Crown Pleas 1249,* 91.

33 ibid., 91–2; JUST 1/818, m.48d (Suff); JUST 1/37, m.31d (Berks roll referring to a case in Wilts); JUST 1/359, m.29d (Kent); JUST 1/912A, m.44d (Sussex) (HRTS). This list is not exhaustive.

34 Hamil, *Speculum,* XI, 247 n.3; *Close R. 1237–42,* 5; *1247–51,* 62.

took place. The approver might win his convictions by the flight of his opponents [5] or by their being convicted by a jury. The crown was satisfied provided that the appellees had been eliminated, since the intention of the procedure was to purge the country of criminals, not to encourage duels between the king's subjects.

The Hampshire eyre roll is therefore remarkable, as it records two combats [3, 5] in which the approver actually fought a duel and defeated the appellee, another combat [12] in which the outcome is unknown because the text is illegible, and a fourth case [9] in which the approver withdrew after the appellee had offered battle. One of the successful approvers, Reynold Sutor of Scotland [3], accused three other men who were acquitted by juries [2, 10], a woman [1] upon whom the jury's verdict is not recorded, and another appellee who accepted the challenge [12]. Reynold's ultimate fate is unknown, as he does not appear in other records and the Hampshire roll is incomplete. The other successful approver, Walter Bloweberme [5], is recorded to have convicted ten appellees: six at Guildford, presumably in the Surrey eyre of May–June 1248 (no plea roll extant), and four in the Hampshire eyre (one by combat and three by flight). Of the latter four, the appellee defeated by combat is Hamo Stare [5], but only one of the three fugitives has been identified: Henry Clop [28] who escaped and abjured the realm. In addition Walter accused two men who were acquitted by a jury [11] and another man [4] who was presumably acquitted, as no person found guilty by a jury is mentioned among Walter's four successful convictions in the Hampshire eyre [5].

Despite these failures, Walter is that rare phenomenon, a successful approver who was permitted to abjure the realm after completing his quota of convictions [5]. Nevertheless the story did not end happily for him. In October 1250 he was tried before the justices of the bench at Westminster, because he had again been arrested and turned approver.[35] This time he accused twenty persons in all: twelve who had been arrested in the archbishop of Canterbury's liberty in Kent, and another eight whom he alleged had committed a robbery with him at St Albans. But the court referred to the rolls of the Hampshire eyre of 1249 and found that he had previously turned approver, triumphed in combat and abjured the realm. He was therefore handed over to the bailiffs of the archbishop's liberty for execution and was presumably hanged. Even if Walter had actually abjured the realm after the Hampshire eyre, perpetual exile would have been hazardous for such a man. The successful approver forswore the protection of the king's peace, yet he could expect no quarter from his exiled accomplices, like Henry Clop [28], whom he had either betrayed or falsely accused.

These records of approvers conflict in some respects with what is said about the procedure in contemporary law books. Bracton and *Placita Corone* both insist that an approver invariably fails if he accuses a man who is subsequently acquitted by a jury.[36] Yet Reynold [2, 10] and Walter [4, 11] both made such unsuccessful accusations without being summarily hanged. There was logic in Bracton's doctrine because acquittal by a jury demonstrated that the approver was untruthful. Thereafter he could not appeal to God to uphold his righteousness in ordeal by combat and furthermore he had dishonoured the king whose 'son' he was. In *Placita Corone* the judge forbids the approver 'in the name of God and in the king's name' to accuse any man wrongfully and the approver replies in peril of his soul.[37] One exception is, however, allowed to the rule that the approver may make no wrong accusation: he must not make such an accusation 'without good reason'.[38] Perhaps Reynold and Walter were considered to have had good reasons for their accusations, even though the appellees were acquitted. Alternatively, in the exceptional circumstances of the Hampshire eyre of 1249, the need to obtain accusations and eliminate criminals from an area which Matthew Paris describes as 'infected by larceny' [c] may have led the judges to override those principles of divine and natural justice upon which the law was supposed to be based.[39]

A minor discrepancy between the law books and our record concerns the number of persons, ten appellees, whom Bloweberme had undertaken to convict. *Placita Corone* says that an approver may expect a pardon if he can make nine combats, presumably meaning if he can obtain nine convictions.[40] Bracton says the number is agreed upon

[35] KB 26/143, m.16d. This record says that Walter convicted 9 persons in the Hants eyre, whereas our roll [5] has 10 persons. Cf. below, 34–6.

[36] Bracton, f.152 (II, 429); *Placita Corone*, 24.

[37] ibid., 20. [38] 'sanz acheson': ibid., 20.

[39] The theoretical basis of the law is expounded by Bracton, ff.1–4b (II, 21–8).

[40] *Placita Corone*, 24. Cf. above, n.35.

between the approver and the king; the writ he cites mentions *quinque vel tot* (five or some other number).[41] In 1237 one approver was allowed to abjure the realm after obtaining five convictions.[42] Thus a hard bargain had been driven with Bloweberme, who had to convict ten. Matthew Paris mentions approvers in his account of the Hampshire eyre and says that William Pope obtained about fifteen convictions [q], a remarkably high number. But there is an ambiguity in Matthew's text depending on how it is punctuated. Luard's edition reads . . . *circiter quindecim; appelavit; qui convicti* . . . , thus making *quindecim* refer to the number of wine casks in William Pope's cellar [q] and leaving the number of convictions unspecified. The manuscripts read . . . *circiter xv. appelavit. qui convicti* . . . The full point after *xv* is probably not a stop, as it was the usual practice to terminate numerals in this way. With modern punctuation and extensions the text best reads . . . *circiter quindecim appelavit, qui convicti* . . . , meaning that William did indeed obtain about fifteen convictions. Ambiguity is compounded by Matthew's next sentence [r], which says that one man (*unus*) delivered the neighbourhood of six thieves by combat. Maitland interpreted *unus* as referring to William Pope and says that he fought six combats.[43] More plausibly, *unus* refers to another unnamed approver, probably Walter Bloweberme [5] whose success may have been reported to Matthew. A final difficulty with Matthew's version is that William Pope may not have been an approver at all, as is explained below in the discussion of accusations in the Hampshire eyre.

The drawing of the combat

Walter Bloweberme's unusual success, which seems echoed in Matthew Paris's narrative [r], may be the reason why his combat with Hamo Stare [5] is depicted at the head of KB 26/223. That picture (see Frontispiece) merits analysis, even though it has been frequently noticed and is now spoiled. Its history and present physical condition have already been described in the discussion of the documents.[44] The composition occupies the head of KB 26/223 and is approximately the same width as the membrane, 16.4 centimetres. The height of the picture, from the top of the membrane to the line where the text [1] begins, is 4·8 centimetres. The figures and ornament are drawn with a pen, using the same type of black ink as in the text of the plea roll. The condition of the parchment is too poor to establish whether there was any preliminary under-drawing. The drawing is contemporary with the text of the plea roll. On paleographic grounds the handwriting of the names above the heads of the combatants and the ornamented capital letters on the left are typical of the period. The drapery, particularly at the hems of the tunics of the combatants, is likewise characteristic of English drawings of the mid-thirteenth century.[45] The gallows and the hanging figure are similar in style, though not in detail, to Matthew Paris's drawing of hanged men.[46] The ensemble of ornamented heading, closely written text, and caricatured persons in movement with names attached to them is typical of contemporary pictorial narrative technique which is seen at its best in the *Chronica Majora* of Matthew Paris.[47] Other thirteenth-century drawings of men fighting with war hammers and shields have been noted, but they are not of English provenance and date from late in the century.[48]

The identity of the artist cannot be established. The handwriting of the names above the combatants is similar to, though not necessarily the same as, the text of the plea roll. It is therefore possible that the drawing was done by the clerk who wrote much of the roll. Scribes of plea rolls quite frequently made marginal doodles; there are, for example, three grotesque little human heads in left profile introducing enrolments in the civil pleas

41 Bracton, f.152 (II, 429, 430).

42 *Close R. 1237–42*, 5.

43 Pollock & Maitland, II, 655. Re William Pope see below, 35, 42, 43.

44 Above, 27–9. In commenting on the drawing I have received very helpful advice from Dr G. D. S. Henderson (Cambridge Univ. Dept of History of Art) and Miss Claire Pace (Glasgow Univ. Dept of History of Fine Art). Unless otherwise stated, however, the opinions expressed are my own.

45 M. Rickert, *Painting: Britain in the Middle Ages,* [1st edn] (London, 1954), plates 102–4, 106, 112.

46 M. R. James, 'The Drawings of Matthew Paris', *Walpole Soc.*, XIV (1926), plate X, f.60. In our drawing the head of Hamo Stare is blindfolded (as in Matthew's drawing of hanged men), not surmounted by a circlet or crown as in the engraving done for Madox's *History of the Exchequer:* above, n.10.

47 Matthew's technique is analysed by P. Brieger, *English Art 1216–1307* (Oxford History of English Art, IV, 1957), 138–40, and R. Vaughan, *Matthew Paris* (Cambridge, 1958), 211–12.

48 L. M. C. Randall, *Images in the Margins of Gothic Manuscripts* (Berkeley, Calif, 1966), 185.

section of JUST 1/776 (mm.1, 16, 18). Scribes occasionally also wrote facetious comments on the rolls.[49] Nevertheless our drawing is more elaborate and larger than the scribes' usual facetious marginalia and it occupies a prominent position at the head of a membrane. It is best compared, not with the occasional doodles of the justices' clerks, but with the elaborate drawing heading a membrane on an exchequer receipt roll of 1233 caricaturing prominent jews of Norwich.[50] In my view such elaborate compositions were not done on the clerk's own initiative, even if they were executed by one of the scribes, but were ordered by higher authority. Perhaps our drawing was commissioned by William Breton, the judge for whom the roll was probably made, or even by Henry III himself, although it is not up to the standard that such a connoisseur might have required. There would have been no shortage of draughtsmen competent to make our drawing either in the circle of the king or of the bishop at Winchester. In Dr Henderson's opinion the artist has 'a sort of first-hand vigour', which catches the effort and tension of the combat, although the sketch of the hanging is of poorer quality.

The subject matter of the drawing requires explanation. On the right Walter Bloweberme (in profile) and Hamo Stare (three-quarter face) are fighting their combat. In the centre of the picture Hamo is hanged on a gibbet, standing on a stylised hill, after losing the combat. Although the faces of the combatants seem caricatured (only Hamo's face can now be distinguished owing to the poor state of the picture) and the hanging scene is stylised, the artist appears to have aimed at verisimilitude in his treatment of the weapons and costume of the combatants. Perhaps that was because they seemed remarkable to him. (Matthew Paris likewise aimed at drawing unfamiliar things accurately, such as the elephant sent to Henry III by St Louis in 1255.[51]) The combatants are not using the ordinary weapons of the time. Approvers were provided with special outfits, usually at the crown's expense.[52] Fortunately the bill survives for equipping one of the combats in the Hampshire eyre, as it was charged to the bishop of Winchester's Waltham account and recorded on his pipe roll.[53] It specifies the following items:

purchase of 2 shields	13s. 4d.
emending the same	8d.
purchase of 2 staves	3s.
purchase of white leather felt linen cloth for armour and tunics	8s. 3d.
wages of an armourer to make arms and equip the combatants	2s.

Taking these items in the order in which they come on the bishop's account starting with the shields, it is worth noting that these were 'emended' after purchase, meaning either that they were adapted for this special use or that they had to be repaired. The large rectangular shields in the drawing are different from the smaller kite-shaped or heart-shaped shields of Matthew Paris's combat drawings and similar illustrations.[54] They are like later archers' shields, but seem in fact to be the type of shield distinctive of a champion. On the seal (date c 1190) of Bernard Champion (*Bernardus Pugil*) is depicted a similar rectangular shield intersected by a war hammer.[55] Likewise the seal of Henry Marshal, champion of the abbot of Glastonbury in 1258, depicts a large rectangular shield.[56]

The two staves listed in the account have become in the drawing what look like double iron-headed war hammers, with cord wound tightly round their hafts.

[49] Meekings in *Wilts Crown Pleas 1249*, 25.

[50] E 401/1565, m.1. Illustrated by L. O. Pike, *History of Crime in England* (London, 1873), I, frontispiece; V. D. Lipman, *The Jews of Medieval Norwich* (Jewish Hist. Soc., 1967), 33; J. Gillingham, *Life and Times of Richard I* (London, 1973), 54–5.

[51] James, *Walpole Soc.*, XIV, plate VI; Vaughan, *Matthew Paris*, 256–7, plate XXI.

[52] Hamil, *Speculum*, XI, 245 n.6.

[53] 'In ij scutis emptis ad latrones debellandos xiij s. iiij d. In eisdem emendandis viij d. In baculis emptis iij s. In albo coreo et feutre emptis et lineo panno, et ad armas et ad tunicas armaturas viij s. iij d. In stipendis cuiusdam hominis ad armas facere et ad eosdem armandos ij s.' (Hants Rec. Off., Winchester Pipe Roll 159290, m.28: Meekings in *Wilts Crown Pleas 1249*, 91). I am grateful to Mr C. R. Davey, Deputy County Archivist, for assistance.

[54] James, *Walpole Soc.*, XIV, plates II, VIII, XVII, XVIII. Actual shields are illustrated by G. F. Laking, *European Armour and Arms* (London, 1920), I, 76–82.

[55] W. Brown, 'Trial by Combat', *Yorks Arch. Jnl*, XXIII (1915), 302. Brown describes the hammer as having a square buckler on each side, whereas more probably it intersects a rectangular shield. C. H. Hunter Blair had mistakenly interpreted the seal as belonging to a miller: 'Durham Seals', *Arch. Aeliana*, 3rd ser., VII (1911), 294 (no. 220).

[56] Illustrated in Robert Vaughan's engraving of our combat: above, 27. Cf. Neilson, *Trial by Combat*, 53–4.

Like the shields, these hammers are unusual. The champion, Henry Marshal, carries a small battle axe, which was evidently a contemporary weapon as a similar one is illustrated by Matthew Paris.[57] Our weapons, on the other hand, are not axes but picks, or more accurately (as they seem to have blunt tips) double-headed hammers. The hammer on the seal of Bernard Champion is very similar to ours. Judging from other descriptions, the weapons used in judicial combats were normally small hammers or axes of archaic design. In a description of another fight by an approver (also at Winchester) in 1456 it is said that the weapon is to have at one end a horn of iron, made like a ram's horn and as sharp as possible.[58] Brunner suggested that the weapons used in combats aimed to simulate the ancient Frankish war axe.[59] Neilson surmised that the mention of animal horn might take the origins of the weapon back into pre-history before man's use of metal.[60] In the combat at Winchester in 1456 the appellor's archaic weapon broke almost at the first blow and the combatants had to fight with their hands and feet.[61] The weapons used in our combat look more practical, even if they have archaic features.

According to the drawing, the combatants have no metal body armour. The bishop of Winchester's pipe roll refers to *tunicas armaturas,* which must mean protective tunics of leather and felt if the drawing is correct. The reference in the pipe roll to 'white' leather is significant, as white sheep's leather was also prescribed in the combat of 1456.[62] Whether the colour had archaic or symbolic significance, or whether it was just to make a good show, has not been established. Dr Henderson considers the cross-gartering on the combatants' legs to be unusual in the thirteenth century. That may also be an archaism. The gartering is similar to that worn by some of the Norman horsemen in the Bayeux Tapestry.[63]

Finally the pudding-basin haircuts of the combatants are noticeable. There is good evidence that champions had a distinctive tonsure. Difficulty arises because Neilson argued that a champion's head should be completely shaved and observed that our combatants' heads are not shaven.[64] In fact our combatants are distinctly shaven below the crown and there is no firm evidence for complete shaving. The pudding-basin haircut was perhaps the type of tonsure distinctive of a champion.

Accusations in the Hampshire eyre

The combat between Walter Bloweberme and Hamo Stare and the other appeals by approvers recorded on KB 26/223 do not directly concern the Alton robbery, as they specify thefts of clothing committed over a wide area in the south (the Isle of Wight, Southampton, Winchester and Salisbury), whereas the Alton robbery concerned the more ambitious theft of a sum of money from foreign merchants. Nevertheless, both the plea roll and Matthew Paris link the two. KB 26/223 records important indictments about the Alton robbery in the middle of its appeals by approvers [6–8]. Matthew mentions accusations by approvers [q–r] in his garbled description of William Pope, as already noted.[65] He may also have used general reports about the approvers' trials to create his picture of an infamous region [d] infected by larceny [c], which made the king himself ashamed of his birthplace at Winchester [i].

The king's government may likewise have hoped to find some link between its approvers and the Alton robbery, as it took the unusual step of assembling approvers at Winchester instead of trying them at Newgate. On 5 February 1249, in the middle of the Hampshire eyre and shortly after Henry III had visited Winchester on 24–25 January, the sheriffs of London were instructed to send all the malefactors who were to be named by Anketin Mallory, a royal officer, down to Winchester to appear before the justices in eyre.[66] These malefactors probably included Walter Bloweberme, as the sheriff of Surrey had been ordered two days earlier to send five approvers from Guildford gaol to Newgate.[67] Bloweberme, it will be remembered,

57 James, *Walpole Soc.*, XIV, plate XVI, f.159v.

58 'William Gregory's Chronicle of London' in *The Historical Collections of a Citizen of London in the Fifteenth Century,* ed. J. Gairdner (Camden Soc., New ser., XVII, 1876), 200.

59 Pollock & Maitland, II, 634.

60 Neilson, *Trial by Combat,* 54 n.2.

61 'Gregory's Chronicle of London', 202.

62 ibid., 200.

63 C. H. Gibbs-Smith, *The Bayeux Tapestry* (London, 1973), plates 46, 51. Cf. the legs of King David in an English psalter of the later 11th century: F. Wormald, 'An English 11th Century Psalter', *Walpole Soc.*, XXXVIII (1962), plate 27.

64 Neilson, *Trial by Combat,* 55–6, 148; Hamil, *Speculum,* XI, 245 n.7.

65 Above, 32.

66 *CLR 1245–51,* 219.

67 ibid., 218–19.

had obtained six convictions at Guildford as part of his contract [5] before fighting at Winchester. Another pair of approvers, William Scot and Robert alias Nicholas Winchelsea, who were still lodged in Winchester castle gaol on 17 May 1249,[68] were later suspected of being involved in a robbery in the pass of Alton.[69] But their complicity was never proved and they were released and permitted to go to the Holy Land in February 1253.[70] An additional problem with them is that William Scot was already in prison at Aylesbury (Bucks) in July 1248, two months before the great Alton robbery took place.[71] There is no firm evidence that accusations by approvers and trial by battle played any direct part in identifying or convicting those involved in the Alton robbery. No extant accusations were brought by Scot and Winchelsea and the case against themselves was never proved. Hence they cannot have confessed to the robbery, which is the first step an approver must take before accusing anyone else. One man, John Harvest, who was indicted of aiding the robbers and acquitted [34], turned approver some time after the eyre and was hanged;[72] but he does not seem to have affected the outcome in 1249.

Matthew Paris again brings combat into his narrative where he says that the robbed Brabantine merchants offered trial by battle against those they accused [b]. Such a challenge as that, by an innocent and aggrieved party against a suspect, is quite distinct from an approver's accusation, as has already been explained. Battle would no longer have been admissible in practice under English law. Either the merchants were resorting to their own legal custom, or more probably they had been advised to proceed by appeal of felony in order to bring the case automatically into the king's court and to claim compensation. In an appeal of felony the original appellor, although he was no longer permitted to fight, could compel a suspect to 'stand to right' even after he had been acquitted in the king's court.[73] Thus William Arundel, who was acquitted by a jury, was ordered to 'find sureties to stand to right if the aforesaid merchants wish to proceed against him' [20].

There remains in the context of appeals of felony the problem of whether William Pope, who was involved in the Alton robbery, was an approver as alleged by Matthew Paris [q]. The plea roll [6] records that William was indicted of harbouring outlaws from the pass of Alton and that he was found guilty by a jury of being a party to the robbery. But no sentence is recorded against him and there is a blank space (not an illegible gap) on the membrane. Evidently he was not hanged, as he is said to have abjured the realm in a royal writ dated 21 September 1249.[74] Whether he abjured after escaping from custody or was permitted to abjure because he became an approver cannot be definitely established. No accusations brought by him as an approver are extant on the plea roll, nor is he referred to as an approver in subsequent records. William Pope may feature prominently in Matthew's narrative only because his surname appealed to Matthew's anti-papal prejudices, as he relished the pun of a pope being a thief.

Approvers are unlikely to have played a significant part in obtaining convictions in the Alton robbery anyway. According to Matthew the difficulty in obtaining convictions was caused by the jurors refusing to indict persons in the first place [e] or to bring in verdicts of guilty [c], because they were themselves confederates of the thieves [i]. Such a conspiracy of influential local men was not going to be broken by accusations coming from approvers, because a man of standing when accused by an approver could immediately demand trial by jury, since 'a self-confessed thief has no right to speak against a man of good faith (*fidelem vocem*) who is able and willing to put himself on the country'.[75] If the jurors were corrupt, such a 'faithful' man would then be acquitted, provided he were one of their group. Approvers were useful for obtaining convictions against poor vagrants, about whom nothing was known in the locality, but

[68] ibid., 235. In the Wilts eyre of April–June 1249 a William Scot of Warminster was appealed of rape in his absence and then outlawed as a thief: *Wilts Crown Pleas 1249*, no. 310. This looks like the same William who had been transferred from Winchester gaol to Wilton on 17 May, but in that case it is difficult to see why he was outlawed as absent.

[69] *Close R. 1247–51*, 403, 411.

[70] ibid. *1251–3*, 315–16.

[71] ibid. *1247–51*, 66, 69. The great robbery occurred in September: below, 38.

[72] JUST 1/778, m.44.

[73] *Placita Corone*, 6. Procedure in appeals of felony is explained above (29–32) and the merchants' claim to compensation below (39).

[74] *Close R. 1247–51*, 202. Cf. *Ex. Rot. Fin.*, II, 137; above, 32; below, 37, 42–3.

[75] Bracton, f.152 (II, 429).

not for breaking up conspiracies of jurors concealing crimes committed by their own class. Against the latter there was no sure remedy because the king, as Matthew has Henry III say [i], was but one man; his government depended on the local gentry to identify criminals in indictments and then to bring in honest verdicts.

Matthew's allegation that some Hampshire jurors were corrupt is corroborated by the plea roll, where three jurors are accused of perturbing [21] and impeding [30] their fellows so that they could not speak the truth. John Boarhunt, one of those accused [30], was in fact the foreman of the Selborne panel of jurors [29]. Richard Kitcombe, one of the electors of the Selborne jury [48], was hanged for his part in the Alton robbery [30]. Furthermore, the jury lists of Odiham and Selborne hundreds [47–8] are short of persons, which likewise may suggest the removal of corrupt jurors. The name of William Bullock, one of the Odiham jurors charged with corruption [21], does not appear in the list of jurors [47]. It may also be significant that the amount of Selborne hundred's fine before judgment was left blank on the plea roll [29], implying perhaps that it would be abnormally large.[76] There is no evidence from the plea roll, however, to support Matthew's larger allegation [k–l] that two new sets of jurors from the whole of Hampshire were selected by the king's personal command because of corruption. Yet the plea roll does suggest that the court was dissatisfied with some of the acquittals, as it ordered a verdict on William Sinclair [19] from another three panels of jurors, although he had already been acquitted by the exceptionally high number of four panels. The normal criminal jury of the time comprised the jury of the hundred concerned and representatives of four neighbouring townships. In the Alton indictments, on the other hand, the accused was sometimes tried by a jury of two [41], three [6, 8], four [19, 33], or even most exceptionally seven [19] hundreds.

Matthew Paris probably simplified and overdramatised the process by which the juries made their indictments. He says that the first new set of jurors refused to name anyone [k], whereas the second panel made a sudden flood of accusations when they heard that their predecessors were in a dungeon awaiting hanging [1]. It is unlikely that the jurors would really have feared the death penalty if they remained silent, even though aiding felons (supposing that could be proved) was a capital offence. Yet the plea roll does record that the three corrupt jurors were remanded in custody; so they may have been temporarily lodged in a dungeon in Winchester castle where the eyre was being held. They were released on making fines: quite a small fine of 40 shillings on his own surety in the case of John Boarhunt [30]; a larger fine of 100 shillings for William Bullock [21]; and the considerable sum of £40 (60 marks) in the case of Thomas Aston [21].[77] The reluctance of jury panels to make accusations was probably broken down by the judges cross-examining individual jurors, as Bracton recommends,[78] rather than by the rhetoric of the king [i] or the bishop of Winchester [j], although the effects of royal and divine sanctions should not be entirely ruled out.

Nor does the plea roll entirely support Matthew Paris's suggestion that numerous thefts and crimes were revealed by the new jurors [1]. Sixty-four persons were charged with offences concerning the Alton robbery, but the great majority of these were indicted of consorting with, harbouring or otherwise assisting the robbers. Only twelve of the sixty-four were charged with actual robbery or larceny and five of these were acquitted [16, 19, 44–5]. The remaining seven were found guilty, but all of them had escaped [7, 15, 17–18] except the Selborne juror, Richard Kitcombe [30]. He had been indicted of larceny and found guilty of supplying a pig and two sheep to the outlaws in Alton wood. Whether he had acted entirely of his own free will is doubtful, as the unidentified outlaws of Alton wood (who make repeated appearances in the plea roll) obtained food by force [33–4] and intimidated local people [32].

Of the sixty-four persons charged either with being principals or accessories to the robbery, twenty-five were found guilty, twenty-five were acquitted, twelve were remanded in custody for lesser offences [27, 32–5], and on two [26, 31] no verdict was recorded. Of those found guilty, thirteen were outlawed in their absence [7, 15, 17, 22, 26, 36], two escaped and abjured the realm [42–3], one was committed to the bishop as a clerk convict [38], and nine are

[76] Fines before judgment are explained by Mr Meekings in *Wilts Crown Pleas 1249*, 113. The amount of Selborne's fine is not known, as the portion of the amercement roll (JUST 1/776, m.41d) recording it is damaged. The fines of Alton and Odiham hundreds [24, 13] were not abnormally large.

[77] Below, 45.

[78] Bracton, f.143b (II, 405–6).

presumed to have been hanged [6, 8, 27, 30–1, 38–9, 41]. Of those presumed hanged, it can be established that at least one, William Pope [6], was reprieved. These statistics are of limited value because the plea roll is badly damaged and evidently incomplete, as there are no presentments from the city of Winchester,[79] which was deeply involved in the robbery according to Matthew Paris [i]. Despite the lesser number on the plea roll, Matthew's statistic of about thirty hanged and a similar number imprisoned [o] may not be inaccurate.[80]

Matthew also notes that some of the accused found sanctuary in churches [n], which is corroborated by [42] and [43]. Likewise his statement that people took advantage of the crowd to escape [n] seems to be confirmed by the plea roll's record that Richard Lacfeud escaped between being taken out of Winchester gaol by the sheriff and reaching the place of trial [42]. The important fact which Matthew does not report is that many people were acquitted, although in a different context he states that at the beginning of his narrative [c]. There is no way of knowing whether the acquittals were in fact ill-founded. Nor does either Matthew or the plea roll explain the rôle in the robbery or the identity of those vaguely and repeatedly described as 'outlaws'. No person described as an outlaw of Alton wood was arrested and tried. Some of the robbers were found guilty and outlawed, for example John de Bendinges [7, 18], but such men would not have been described as outlaws at the time of the trial.

The robbery in the pass of Alton

From Matthew Paris's narrative and the public records, including the plea roll, it is possible to establish the main details of the robbery near Alton which the trial principally concerned. The place of the robbery, the 'pass of Alton', can be approximately identified. Enrolment [25], recording a homicide there, states that the neighbouring vills of Alton, Medstead and Chawton failed to come to the inquest. That suggests that the pass of Alton lay in a triangle south-west of Alton with the churches of Alton, Medstead and Chawton at its corners. The approximate centre of this triangle is Chawton Park Farm (National Grid reference SU 697376), 1½ miles south-west of Alton. In 1269 a charter confirmed a grant of woodland to Ellis Rochester, a royal marshal, 'in that part of the high road, which extends from the king's manor of Alton to Alresford . . . in the pass called the pass of Alton'; a further confirmation in 1271 defined the area more closely as 'the pass by which the road runs from Alton to Medstead'.[81] There were various ancient roads from Southampton to Alton and thence to London.[82] The road which ran from Alresford (about half way between Winchester and Alton) to Alton via Medstead, on which the pass of Alton lay (according to these charters), was a ridgeway running through woods following the comb of the hills. William Cobbett describes riding in 1825 from Alton to Alresford via Medstead 'in order to have fine turf to ride on, and to see, on this lofty land that which is, perhaps, the finest *beech-wood* in all England'.[83] A broad bridle-path, comprising a series of parallel cart-tracks, can still today be picked up east (Grid reference 703378) of Chawton Park Farm and followed west south-westwards. The path ascends at a gentle but steady gradient through the beech woods today called Alton Forest. The pass of Alton doubtless lay somewhere here. The word 'pass' in this context does not describe a defile between the hills but a clear passage through the trees. This meaning is suggested by the topography, as the road runs on top of the hills, and also by a writ to the sheriff of Hampshire dated 3 June 1249, ordering him to have the trees felled in Alton wood on both sides 'next to the pass of the same wood'.[84]

By the fourteenth century, when William Langland wrote *Piers Plowman,* the pass of Alton had become a place of proverbial notoriety for thieves. Only Langland's allegorical figure of absolute Poverty could pass through it with safety because he possessed nothing.[85] That notoriety may have originated from

[79] One Winchester city plea appears in the gaol delivery section of the roll: above, n.3. Mr Meekings has suggested to me that Winchester city's crown pleas may have been recorded in a coram rege roll which is no longer extant. Amercements from Winchester soke, recorded in the bishop's Pipe Roll (Hants Rec. Off., 159290, m.34), are unremarkable. *VCH Hants,* V, 47, is mistaken to associate them with the Alton robbery.

[80] In *Historia Anglorum* Matthew arbitrarily increased the number of hanged from 30 to 100: below, 47.

[81] *CChR,* II, 122–3, 172; below, 42.

[82] C. F. C. Hawkes, 'Old Roads in Central Hants', *Papers & Procs Hants Field Club,* IX (1920–4), map at p.332.

[83] W. Cobbett, *Rural Rides* (London, 1830), 281 (30 Oct. 1825).

[84] *Close R. 1247–51,* 167.

[85] '. . . thorw the pas of Altoun
Pouerte myghte passe withoute peril of robbynge'
The Vision of William concerning Piers the Plowman . . . , ed. W. W. Skeat (Oxford, 1886), I, 432–3 (C Text, Passus XVII, lines 139–40).

the robbery of 1248, as there are no references specifically to the pass of Alton earlier than that year. In the previous extant eyre roll of 1236, neither the pass of Alton nor large robberies in Alton, Odiham and Selborne hundreds are mentioned.[86] Nevertheless in 1237 or 1238 a servant of a foreign merchant, Hector Araz (? Arras), had been robbed when going through the Alton neighbourhood (*transeunte per partes Aulton'*). The king ordered the bishop of Winchester to return Hector's chattels, which had been found at Southampton and were presumably confiscated from the thief, if Hector could prove that they were his.[87] This case provides precedents both for robbery of a merchant in the Alton area and for compensating him by returning his goods.

Further trouble had evidently occurred in 1248, before our robbery, as royal serjeants were appointed to guard the pass of Alton that spring or summer. Payment for their liveries was authorised on 28 June 1248 and arrears of their wages on 2 July.[88] The main robbery seems to have happened early that autumn (while the beech leaves still provided cover for an ambush), since Ralph Wauncy was ordered on 23 September 1248 to conduct an inquiry in Hampshire, Sussex and Surrey concerning a robbery 'lately committed at Alton'.[89] The wide area covered by his commission suggests that it concerned the great robbery. There is no evidence, however, that Ralph, who was connected with the king's household,[90] ever did hold this inquiry.

Matthew Paris says that Henry de Mara (or de la Mare) unsuccessfully conducted an inquiry [e]. Henry's visit is confirmed by [26] which mentions that Alton had already been amerced by him. The plea roll also refers to Henry as a justice of gaol delivery, where it lists fugitives outlawed by him and his fellows.[91] These references show, incidentally, that Henry was not entirely unsuccessful in his visit. He was a justice of the court coram rege at the time and may have been commissioned for the Alton inquiry in place of Ralph Wauncy, although there is no record of that in the extant documents. Henry ceased to be a coram rege justice in or after February 1249,[92] the time of the Hampshire eyre; perhaps his dismissal or resignation was connected with his failure there.

By the end of October 1248 the two principal robbers, John de Bendinges and John Barkham, had been arrested and imprisoned in London. That is known because a writ dated 30 October 1248 ordered the sheriffs of London to send them to Reading to appear before the king's justices on 5 November.[93] This trial was probably held before the coram rege judges, of whom Bracton was one,[94] as the king was nearby at Windsor from 2 to 5 November. It is possible that Henry de la Mare was sent down to Hampshire after the trial at Reading had revealed how the local gentry were implicated in the robbery. Some inquiries had certainly been completed before the end of the year, as Master Geoffrey, described as 'formerly the king's cook', was deprived of his royal lands in Mapledurham (near Petersfield) on 19 December 1248.[95] The plea roll records that a man of his, Ellis Blunt, had supplied food to the outlaws in Alton wood [15].

These events, preceding the Hampshire eyre which opened at Winchester on 14 January 1249, are at variance at some points with the record both of the plea roll and of Matthew Paris. John de Bendinges, John Barkham and Richard Bennet were the principal robbers according to the plea roll [6–7]. Nothing is known of Richard Bennet, but the other two had been imprisoned by October 1248, as already discussed. Yet the plea roll records that John de Bendinges, 'fearing for himself', had fled [22]. Certainly John escaped and survived, as both he and John Barkham were later pardoned.[96] But the plea roll makes no

[86] JUST 1/775, mm.15, 15d, 21, 24d.

[87] *Close R. 1237–42,* 25 (HRTS).

[88] *CLR 1245–51,* 190, 191.

[89] *CPR 1247–58,* 28.

[90] He is named among royal officers witnessing a deed in May 1249: *Close R. 1247–51,* 227. He had received gifts from the king in 1247: *CLR 1245–51,* 115, 148. He was not a local man, as his lands lay in Norfolk, Suffolk and Wilts: *Book of Fees,* II, 905, 919, 712, 724. But he may have been a kinsman of Nicholas Wauncy, sheriff of Surrey and Sussex 1249–52.

[91] JUST 1/776, m.33d (Bountisborough hundred), not transcribed here. As Henry was an assize commissioner in Hants in 1248 (C 66/59, mm.5d, 6d: uncalendared commissions on the dorse of the patent roll) (HRTS), he may have held a gaol delivery commission at the same time. He held land in Broughton, Hants: *Books of Fees,* II, 702. Other persons surnamed 'de la Mare' (though not forenamed 'Henry') witnessed Selborne charters in this period and made grants to the priory: *Calendar of Charters and Documents . . . of Selborne and its Priory,* ed. W. D. Macray (Hants Rec. Soc., 1891, 1894). Henry may therefore have had personal connections with the Alton-Selborne region.

[92] C. A. F. Meekings in *List of Various Common-Law Records* (PRO L & I, Supp. ser., I), 40.

[93] *CLR 1245–51,* 207.

[94] Meekings in *List of Various C–L Recs,* 40.

[95] *Close R. 1247–51,* 132.

[96] Below, 41.

mention of his having escaped from captivity and gives the impression that he had simply fled from the locality. If he and John Barkham had escaped during their trial at Reading in Berkshire, their escape would not have concerned a Hampshire jury; that may be why our plea roll makes no reference to it.[97]

In his narrative Matthew Paris gives the impression that the king knew nothing about the Alton robbery until he was told of it by the Brabantine merchants when he arrived at Winchester shortly before Lent in 1249 [a–b]. In fact the king must have been informed of the trial coram rege on 5 November 1248, even if he had not personally authorised the inquiry by Ralph Wauncy on 23 September. He had also dismissed Master Geoffrey, his cook, before the merchants made their complaint. Matthew may therefore have been romancing when he says that the merchants recognised the faces of the thieves among the king's court [b], as no other members of the royal household are known to have been involved. It is possible, however, that the merchants recognised some of the thieves' associates among the assembled knights and jurors of Hampshire and mistook them for members of the king's court. They might have seen, for example, Richard Kitcombe, the Selborne juror [48] who was subsequently hanged [30].

Another problem with Matthew's account is that Henry III was not at Winchester, but at Clarendon, shortly before Lent in 1249.[98] That year he resided at Clarendon from 28 January to 25 February, and Lent began on 17 February (Ash Wednesday). He visited Winchester both before and after his stay at Clarendon, as it lay on the route to London. The king was at Winchester on 24–25 January and 27 February–2 March. The former date (24–25 January) was ten days after the eyre had opened, but more than three weeks before Lent. Nevertheless this is probably the time which Matthew means, as the eyre had effectively finished by mid-February. The principal robbers, John de Bendinges and John Barkham, had certainly been judged by 10 February 1249, as their forfeited lands were ordered to be set to waste on that day.[99] Exactly when and how the king's intervention took place remains an unresolved problem, as there is no reference to it in any form in the plea roll.

It is possible that the king concerned himself with the Alton robbery on both his visits to Winchester. The two merchants of Brabant, whom Matthew Paris does not name [a], seem to tally with Thomas Wales (? Walloon) and Reyner Lewe,[100] who were paid £122 from the issues of the Hampshire eyre in compensation for their loss in a robbery in the pass of Alton. These are also presumably the overseas merchants, who are mentioned, but not named, in the plea roll [6–7, 19–20]. Matthew gives the impression that negotiations between the king and the merchants were protracted [d]. Perhaps the compensation was settled during the king's second visit to Winchester. Thomas Wales was authorised to have £16 on 4 March 1249 (two days after Henry III had left Winchester for London) and Reyner Lewe £106 on 16 March. The sums had probably been paid out by the end of May.[101] The total of £122 compensation tallies quite well with Matthew's statement [b] that the merchants claimed 200 marks (£133 6s. 8d.). It also tallies with the extraordinarily large sum of £136 12s. 6½d. at which John de Bendinges' chattels were assessed in the plea roll [22]. It looks as if the whole sum of money, which had probably been stolen in cash, was recovered when John was arrested. If the merchants knew that, they would have been even more determined to claim compensation. It was not usual practice to compensate for thefts, as felons' chattels were an emolument of justice forfeit to the king, but in this case Matthew says that the king's counsellors warned him of international reprisals if the merchants were not satisfied [f].

There is less substance to Matthew's allegation that the robbers had stolen the king's wines and drunk them [h], as such a theft is not recorded in the Hampshire plea roll nor in the printed public records at this time. In *Historia Anglorum* Matthew gave an embroidered account of the same incident, which had evidently caught his fancy.[102] There are numerous references in the chancery rolls of the time to the purchase and transport of wines, but none to a theft. Certainly Henry III enjoyed a drink; for example, in November 1249 the keepers of his wines at Winchester

[97] Above, n.93. Neither the coram rege roll nor the appropriate Berks eyre roll is extant.

[98] Itinerary of Henry III (PRO, typescript), 206–7.

[99] *Ex. Rot. Fin.*, II, 48–9.

[100] Reyner is named among Brabantine merchants who received royal safe-conducts in Aug.–Sept. 1242: *CPR 1232–47*, 302 (HRTS). His place of origin is there spelt *Lewes*, which may refer to Looz, although that town was subject to Liège and not directly to Brabant. *Lewe* (the form of the name in n.101 below) should probably not be identified with Louvain, the capital of Brabant, as that is rendered *Luveyn* in the safe-conducts above.

[101] *CLR 1245–51*, 221, 222, 236. Cf. E 372/93, r.8d.

[102] Above, n.1.

were ordered to provide wines 'to make precious and delicate drinks for the king'.[103] Matthew's story of a theft should not be entirely ruled out, however, since the king's baggage train was indeed later attacked in the pass of Alton in the period of the baronial rebellion.[104]

Another statement of Matthew's which has caused difficulty is that the thieves came from the neighbourhood of Alton and from the bishop's liberty of Taunton [1], 'de libertate episcopi de Tantona'. The bishop of Winchester's liberty at Taunton in Somerset must be meant, as there is no place in Hampshire which can be identified with *Tantona.* The Alton conspiracy certainly extended into neighbouring counties (Berkshire, Surrey and Sussex, for example), but Somerset is more surprising as Taunton is about 90 miles west of Alton. Matthew's statement cannot be verified from other sources. No plea roll is extant from the Somerset eyre of July 1249, at which crown pleas from the bishop of Winchester's liberty at Taunton would have been heard. Nor do the Taunton sections of the bishop's pipe rolls refer to the chattels or fines of anybody involved in the Alton robbery. Nevertheless the reference to Taunton is not the sort of detail which Matthew would have invented or misrepresented, as it is inessential to his interpretation of events.

Even if doubt about Taunton in Somerset remains, the bishop of Winchester's liberties in Hampshire were indeed involved: in Bishops Sutton hundred [43] and possibly also in Bishops Waltham [28]. The liability of the bishop helps explain his intervention in the trial, as recounted by Matthew [j]. The bishop at the time was William Raleigh, who had been a royal justice himself, although he had quarrelled with the king on becoming bishop. Nevertheless the two had been reconciled at Christmas 1246.[105] He may have discussed the robbery with the king well before the eyre of January 1249, as the two were together at Westminster on 13 October 1248,[106] the approximate time of the arrest of John de Bendinges and John Barkham. Bishop Raleigh was also a friend of William Breton, the justice for whom our roll was probably made.[107]

The aftermath of the robbery

Matthew Paris's conclusion that the malefactors were disposed of by divine vengeance [s] and that his story illustrates how effectively their conspiracy was broken up [t] is too simple. The government was still instructing the sheriff of Hampshire at Christmas 1251 to have a 'diligent and cautious investigation made' concerning certain men of Winchester and Alton.[108] Many of the robbers and their accomplices had escaped, although penalties were exacted against those fugitives who possessed property. The lands of William Pope [6] were granted to Ellis Rochester, a royal marshal, in August 1252.[109] The seized chattels of Adam Limesy [43] are listed in detail in the bishop of Winchester's pipe roll,[110] because they were due to the bishop and not to the sheriff as stated in the plea roll. They comprised 1 horse, 3 colts, 5 oxen, 1 cow, 3 calves, 5 pigs, 4 piglets, 83 sheep (*multones*) and 33 ewes (*matrones*). Under both 'sheep' and 'ewes' there is also noted: *In dono domini episcopi uxor Ade de Lymes* (Adam's wife is in the bishop's gift). The bishop's clerk had a cruel sense of humour.

The seizure of the lands of the principal robbers, John de Bendinges and John Barkham, gave rise to numerous memoranda in the royal records. Sheriffs were ordered to prepare to make waste their lands, fields, pastures, woods, gardens and houses on 10 February 1249;[111] these were then committed to Godfrey Liston, the keeper of Windsor.[112] In October 1249 Godfrey was authorised to spend £40 from their lands on the king's works at Windsor.[113] Similarly in December 1249, 20,000 shingles (wooden tiles) were ordered from John de Bendinges' lands to roof royal buildings in Winchester.[114] In the same month the king made a presentation to the church of Barkham, of which John Barkham had been the patron.[115] In June–July 1250, the king's year and

103 *Close R. 1247–51,* 242.

104 Below, n.139.

105 Matthew Paris, *Chronica Majora,* IV, 590.

106 ibid., V, 28–9.

107 Meekings in *Wilts Crown Pleas 1249,* 13. Concerning Raleigh's Hants connections see also C. A. F. Meekings, '"Martin Pateshull of Good Memory my Sometime Lord"', *BIHR,* XLVII (1974), 224–9.

108 *Close R. 1251–3,* 183.

109 Below, n.135.

110 Hants Rec. Off., 159290, m.30d; below, 44, 47.

111 Above, n.99. The procedure is explained by Bracton, f.129 (II, 364).

112 *Rotulorum Originalium in Curia Scaccarii Abbreviatio,* ed. H. Playford (RC, 1805–10), I, 11.

113 *CLR 1245–51,* 256.

114 *Close R. 1247–51,* 251.

115 *CPR 1247–58,* 55.

day of waste being completed, the lands were surveyed and returned to their lords.[116]

For owners of property justice was tempered by mercy. Small gifts were made to the wives of the fugitives to enable them to survive. William Pope's wife, Joan, was granted a quarter of corn from his chattels in September 1249.[117] At the same time John Barkham's wife, Alice, was given 5 quarters of rye and 2 marks.[118] The next autumn Alice was allowed £10 to maintain herself and her children.[119] At Christmas 1251 John himself was pardoned at York at the instance of Alexander III, king of Scots, on the occasion of Alexander's marriage to Margaret, Henry III's daughter.[120] Alexander's intercession perhaps indicates that John had escaped to Scotland and won favour there, though it is as likely that John was simply taking advantage of a great occasion to sue for mercy. Alexander may not have been personally involved, since he was only eleven years old at the time.

Certainly an outlaw needed an influential patron to be pardoned such a flagrant offence as highway robbery in the middle of the thirteenth century. Bracton says that the committer of a felony ought never to be admitted back to grace, 'or only with great hesitation', because such ease of pardon would encourage others to offend.[121] Nevertheless, such outlawries were reversed in Bracton's time, usually through the king's young kinsmen acting as intercessors. As well as John Barkham, his partner in crime, John de Bendinges, was pardoned in March 1254 at Meilhan-sur-Garonne in Gascony at the instance of Guy de Lusignan, the king's half-brother.[122] In September 1254 Adam Limesy [43] was pardoned at Bordeaux at the instance of Edward, Henry III's eldest son.[123] Finally in December 1254 John Barkham was pardoned again, this time at Boulogne at the instance of Henry of Almain, the king's nephew.[124]

These pardons do not necessarily imply that punishments were too light, although they do emphasise how offenders were not all treated uniformly. Nor do we know exactly what mitigating circumstances, or their opposite, may have influenced the court in reaching its decisions. From the records available it is pointless to speculate about the real degree of guilt or innocence of the accused, and still less to decide whether the punishments were absolutely just. Bracton insists that men who had been justly outlawed by due process (like the Alton robbers) were restored to nothing by a pardon except the king's peace. They were not restored to homages, tenements or inheritances and no one was bound to them by virtue of previous obligations: 'the inlawed may in truth be said to be, so to speak, new-born infants and new men, as though newly created'.[125] How successfully the pardoned Alton robbers started anew in 1254 and whether they were accepted back into county society can be established only in the case of Adam Limesy. In the Hampshire eyre of 1256 he had disappeared and was suspected of homicide. So he was outlawed once more; this time he was found to have no chattels.[126]

In the pass of Alton itself the king's government took consistent and sensible steps to stop robberies, but without much success. Royal serjeants, led by Richard Brown, who had probably served on the Welsh border, had been appointed to keep guard there by June 1248.[127] There is no evidence that any of these serjeants was implicated in the robbery, as Matthew Paris seems to suggest [m], unless John de Bendinges was one of them.[128] It is true, however, that their stipends were sometimes in arrears,[129] as Matthew likewise implies [p]. In the summer after the robbery the pass of Alton was ordered to be widened by felling the trees on each side of the road.[130] Two summers later, in May 1251 (when the leaves would have begun to provide cover), a writ was sent to all sheriffs warning them of highwaymen in 'passes' and ordering watch to be kept by several men in each village.[131] That provision may have originated from the counsellors' advice to the king in the Hampshire eyre of 1249, as recounted by Matthew Paris [d]. Early in 1253 the men of Alton, guarding the pass under such conditions, petitioned the king to

116 *Ex. Rot. Fin.*, II, 80–3; *CPR 1247–58*, 69; *CIPM*, I, no. 176; *Close R. 1247–51*, 306.

117 ibid., 202.

118 *CLR 1245–51*, 252.

119 ibid., 304.

120 *CPR 1247–58*, 121.

121 Bracton, f.132b (II, 372); cf. ff.131b, 133 (II, 369, 375).

122 *CPR 1247–58*, 282.

123 ibid., 336; below, 44.

124 *CPR 1247–58*, 388.

125 Bracton, f.133 (II, 374).

126 JUST 1/778, m.52d (HRTS); above, n.123; below, nn.167–70.

127 *Close R. 1247–51*, 76, 145; above, n.88.

128 Below, 43.

129 *CLR 1245–51*, 191; *Close R. 1251–3*, 114.

130 Above, n.84.

131 *Close R. 1247–51*, 540.

compel more of their neighbours (particularly Robert St John) to assist with this duty.[132] Whether salaried royal serjeants were still being employed there is unclear; they certainly had been in the preceding June, when they were headed by Nicholas Dismars.[133] In the next Hampshire eyre of January 1256, two enrolments specifically concerned the pass of Alton: Clement son of Sephare Driver, suspected of robbery there, was handed over to the bishop's official as a clerk convict; Samson Bulstede, indicted of harbouring malefactors there, was acquitted. Both these cases may refer to the robbery of 1248, like that of John Harvest [34], who had been acquitted in 1249 but subsequently turned approver.[134]

The best hope of protecting the pass had arisen in August 1252, when Ellis Rochester (alias Hertford) was granted all the land which William Pope had formerly held there.[135] Ellis, who is described as the king's serjeant or marshal and once as the 'marshal of the king's horses',[136] was evidently a professional soldier. Further grants and confirmations were made to him in the pass in 1255, 1257 and 1259.[137] Ellis remained loyal to the king in the civil war and was rewarded by similar grants in 1269 ('for laudable service') and in 1271.[138] For two decades therefore the pass of Alton was under the guardianship of a dependable professional soldier. Nevertheless the king complained to the baronial council in 1261 that his baggage train had been robbed in the pass.[139] Probably as a result of that complaint, the woodland in the pass was surveyed and valued in 1262 preparatory to felling the trees.[140] In that survey, and also in an inquiry held by the Hampshire eyre justices in 1263,[141] robberies and homicides were said to be committed often, and even daily, in the pass. The war had evidently delayed clearing the trees, as William Wintershill (who had conducted the survey in 1262) was ordered in May 1269 to go to the pass of Alton to dispatch the king's business there.[142] At the same time Ellis Rochester was granted the surveyed woodland, on condition that he felled the trees and brought the land under cultivation.[143]

Matthew Paris concludes his story with the remark that Winchester and Hampshire incurred an indelible stain of infamy from the great robbery [s]. It may indeed have entered into popular consciousness, as *Piers Plowman* suggests,[144] but its memory had evidently been erased in some local areas as early as 1280. The Winchester-Hyde annalist at that time records nothing about the eyre of January 1249 except the names of the justices, some of which he gets wrong.[145]

The gentry and the robbery

Matthew Paris alleges that among those arrested and hanged were royal officers of the region, rich men with lands valued at £50 or more, and even members of the king's own household [m]. The last allegation seems exaggerated, as the plea roll records only that a man of Master Geoffrey the king's cook had supplied food to the robbers [15]. Master Geoffrey himself was speedily dismissed.[146] It is also doubtful whether any royal officers of the region (sheriffs, bailiffs, serjeants guarding the pass, for example) were implicated.[147] Nevertheless Matthew is certainly correct in saying that the robbery involved men of good standing. Two of the principal robbers, John de Bendinges and John Barkham, were certainly of knightly status, although nothing has been discovered about the third principal, Richard Bennet [6–7]. The biographical details of the accused which follow do not claim to be exhaustive and derive mainly from records which have been printed and indexed.

John de Bendinges was probably the leader of the robbers, as he was in possession of a sum of money which tallied with the amount stolen.[148] He was a junior member of the Bendinges family, whose main lands lay 6 or 7 miles north of Alton in Odiham hundred.[149] His exact relationship to the other

132 ibid. *1251–3,* 441.

133 ibid., 114.

134 JUST 1/778, mm.43d (HRTS), 46; above, n.72.

135 *Ex. Rot. Fin.*, II, 137; *Close R. 1251–3,* 137; *CChR*, I, 401.

136 *Close R. 1254–6,* 197.

137 ibid., 32, 197; *CChR*, II, 1, 19.

138 Above, 37; below, n.141.

139 *Documents of the Baronial Movement of Reform and Rebellion, 1258–1267,* ed. R. F. Treharne and I. J. Sanders (Oxford, 1973), 214, 230.

140 *CPR 1258–66,* 234; *CIM*, I, no. 269.

141 *CChR*, II, 122. Copy in A. W. Goodman, *Chartulary of Winchester Cathedral* (Winchester, 1927), 35–6.

142 *CLR 1267–72,* 81.

143 Above, nn.138, 141.

144 Above, n.85.

145 'Annales Monasterii de Wintonia' in *Annales Monastici,* II, ed. H. R. Luard (RS, 1865), 91. Cf. N. Denholm-Young, 'The Winchester-Hyde Chronicle', *EHR*, XLIX (1934), 85.

146 Above, 39.

147 Above, 41; below, 43.

148 Above, 39.

149 *VCH Hants,* IV, 75, 84, 93, 110.

Bendinges is unclear.[150] When his lands were seized after his outlawry, he was found to have 3 virgates in Odiham held from Thomas son of Peter de Bendinges, a minor, who was a tenant of Chertsey abbey.[151] In addition John had woodland in Winchfield (north of Odiham), a manor which the Bendinges held from Chertsey abbey;[152] 20,000 shingles were ordered from his woods there after they were confiscated[153] and the plea roll records that he was harboured in Winchfield [18]. Neither a wife nor children of John are mentioned in the records. He was an experienced horseman and soldier at the time of the robbery, who had fought as one of the king's serjeants at arms in Wales in 1245 and 1246.[154] He may possibly therefore have been one of the royal serjeants appointed to guard the pass of Alton in 1248, as well as being a landlord there. He was sufficiently prosperous to have a reeve [23] and had litigated with the prioress of Wintney (Hants) in the Berkshire eyre of 1248; he settled with her for 20 marks.[155] None of these facts explains why he committed highway robbery that autumn, but they do suggest his suitability for the crime: he had military experience, he knew the ground and he had personal connections in the neighbourhood.

John Barkham (sc. Barkham near Wokingham in south Berkshire) was a younger man, who had been presented as a squire holding a whole knight fee in the Berkshire eyre of June–July 1248.[156] He was chief lord of his fee and held it from Henry Earley, a tenant in chief of the honor of Windsor.[157] John was potentially therefore a royal knight of Windsor, whose family would have been personally known to the king. He had adequate, if not generous, resources to sustain his status, as his chattels (forfeit to the king for his crime) were valued at 28 marks and the 'year, day and waste' of his lands at £58 10s. 4d.[158] Although he had scarcely attained his majority – he is described as being under age in the Berkshire eyre of 1248 – he had a wife and children.[159] How he first met John de Bendinges is not known. The latter had connections in Berkshire, as he obtained quittance from attending the eyre there in 1248[160] and may have been a kinsman of Gunnora de Bendinges, who had property in Tidmarsh and Pangbourne on the Thames.[161] A closer connection may be that Winchfield, where John de Bendinges resided, and Barkham are only 8 miles apart although in different counties. As with John de Bendinges, there is no clue as to why John Barkham committed robbery. Unlike John de Bendinges, he was head of his family and at the start of a knightly career at the time of the robbery.

A number of accessories to the robbery can likewise be shown to have been gentlemen; in one or two cases there are facts suggesting possible motives. William Pope [6], a tenant in chief of the king,[162] who is described by Matthew Paris as a man abounding in worldly goods [q], held the land where the pass of Alton lay (which was subsequently granted to Ellis Rochester).[163] Although William is named four times as a witness in the charters of Selborne priory,[164] his family is difficult to trace. In the Hampshire eyre of 1236 a Walter Pope was reported to have taken sanctuary in Alton church after killing a man and had abjured the realm. His chattels had been valued at £25 8s. 8d., a relatively large sum which indicates that Walter was a man of substance.[165] The coincidence of surname, place and status suggests that Walter and William were kinsmen, in which case Walter's outlawry may have caused William to become disaffected from the king's peace. The plea roll of 1249 says that William consented to the thieves going out from his house to commit the robbery in the pass [6]; but perhaps they intimidated him as they needed to use his land. An alternative or additional motive for William's involvement may be that he was in debt to Elias son of Chera, a jew of Winchester.[166]

[150] An assize of mort d'ancestor in the eyre of 1236 (JUST 1/775, m.10) shows that another John de Bendinges, the uncle of Peter, had held land in Hartley Mauditt.

[151] *CIPM,* I, no. 176; *Close R. 1247–51,* 306; *Ex. Rot. Fin.,* II, 80, 81; *CPR 1247–58,* 69.

[152] *Chertsey Abbey Cartularies,* II, pt 1 (Surrey Rec. Soc., XII, 1958), no. 905.

[153] Above, n.114.

[154] *Close R. 1242–7,* 335, 458–9 (loss of horses in the king's service); *CLR 1245–51,* 98.

[155] *The Roll and Writ File of the Berkshire Eyre of 1248,* ed. M. T. Clanchy (SS, XC, 1972–3), no. 576; CP 25(1)/203/8, no. 14.

[156] *Berks Eyre 1248,* no. 964.

[157] ibid., no. 186 (our John is distinct from 'John son of Robert Barkham'); *Book of Fees,* II, 845, 848, 857; *Ex. Rot. Fin.,* II, 82–3.

[158] E 372/96, r.3d (HRTS).

[159] *Berks Eyre 1248,* no. 127; above, 41.

[160] *Close R. 1247–51,* 115.

[161] *BNB,* III, no. 1176.

[162] *Close R. 1254–6,* 32.

[163] Above, 37, 40.

[164] *Selborne Priory Charters* (1891), 27; (1894), 26, 29, 30.

[165] JUST 1/775, m.15 (HRTS).

[166] *Close R. 1254–6,* 32, 197. Re Elias son of Chera see *Calendar of the Plea Rolls of the Exchequer of the Jews,* I, ed. J. M. Rigg (Jewish Hist. Soc., 1905), indexed refs.

Adam Limesy, a horse thief who was indicted of complicity in the Alton robbery [43], is the clearest example of a gentleman in adverse circumstances who may have turned to crime as a solution to his problems. His father, Roger, was murdered in 1234 owing more than £276 to the crown and the family had been in debt since before 1200.[167] Adam had alienated some of his indebted inheritance at West Tisted (7 miles south-west of Alton) in the early 1240s to Selborne priory and Newark priory (near Guildford) in exchange for an income for life.[168] But he had evidently retained some property, as his lands and chattels were valued at more than £31 at the time of his flight [43], including 138 domestic animals in Bishops Sutton hundred which went to the bishop of Winchester. As already mentioned, Adam was pardoned in 1254 but he was outlawed again in 1256, this time owning nothing.[169] Some of his lands evidently remained with Selborne and Newark priories, since his father's debts were still being demanded from them in 1266.[170]

Other accessories to the robbery were evidently men of standing, although less information is available about them. Richard Kitcombe, who was hanged [30], had lands worth more than £30, presumably situated at Kitcombe (2½ miles south of the pass of Alton). He was also an elector of the Selborne jury [48] in 1249 and had been one of the two foremen of the same jury in the eyre of 1236.[171] Like William Pope and Adam Limesy, he witnessed charters for Selborne priory in the 1240s.[172] Miles Merchant of Alton, who was outlawed with his son [26], was poor compared with these landowners, yet he had 25 shillings in chattels and a house in Alton belonging to his wife.[173] Richard Lacfeud, who abjured the realm, was a free man [42], though nothing more has been discovered about his wealth and status. Similarly Henry King of Priors Dean, who was hanged [41], had property worth more than £6.

Clerics and monks were involved in the robbery. Thomas Clerk of Priors Dean, who wrote letters for the outlaws [38], successfully claimed his clergy, although he was married and had a lay fee. Enrolment [39] suggests that canons of Durford abbey (in Rogate, Sussex, 12 miles south-east of Alton) were implicated, as a message was delivered from the Alton outlaws to their cellarer. This is credible, since William, former abbot of Durford, and other canons were accused of homicide in the Sussex eyre of November 1249 and it was also attested that outlaws had been harboured in the abbey.[174]

Some other persons of status were accused of being accessories to the robbery, but were either acquitted or fined for lesser offences. As trial juries were alleged to be corrupt, it is possible that some of these accused were more deeply implicated than the plea roll records. Cecily Colemore, who offered the very large sum of 100 marks to have a special jury [33], must have had influence to find sureties capable and willing to back it. William Arundel, who was acquitted but obliged to find sureties [20], appears to be an important man. According to the Selborne priory charters there were two persons of that name in the region at the time. One was William son of Hugh, lord of Upton Grey (6 miles north of Alton) and of half a knight fee in Ludshott (in Bramshott in Alton hundred), who made gifts to Selborne priory in 1236–7.[175] The other was William son of John, usually called 'Willelmus de Arundel de la Wyke' in the Selborne priory witness lists;[176] Wyke can probably be identified with Upper Wick (1 mile north of Selborne). The William accused at [20] is most likely the former, while the Selborne juror of the same name [48] is probably the latter.

Lawrence Talbot [19], who was tried by the same enlarged jury as William Arundel [20], held 2 knight fees in Crofton (in Titchfield near Fareham).[177] William Sinclair, who was tried with him [19], may not be the knight of that name who held lands in Buckinghamshire.[178] Yet our William Sinclair was

167 *Ex. Rot. Fin.*, I, 257; *VCH Hants*, III, 59; *Selborne Priory Charters* (1891), 59. Roger's debts were still being entered on the pipe rolls at the time of Adam's exile: e.g. E 372/94, r.2.

168 *VCH Hants*, III, 59; CP 25(1)/203/7, no. 276.

169 Above, 40–1.

170 *Selborne Priory Charters* (1891), 59.

171 JUST 1/775, m.24d.

172 *Selborne Priory Charters* (1891), 29, 34.

173 *CIM*, I, no. 532; below, n.182. In 1237 Miles had been imprisoned for homicide, but he was released on a writ de odio et atia: *Close R. 1234–7*, 421.

174 JUST 1/909A, m.21 (Dumpford hundred). William had certainly been abbot in 1237–44, but he was replaced by Valentine in or before November 1249: Durford cartulary, BL, MS Cotton Vesp. E. XXIII, ff.33, 74, 73v. Valentine had acted as attorney for Abbot William in 1241: CP 25(1)/203/7, no. 266.

175 *Selborne Priory Charters* (1891), 21, 22, 25; *Book of Fees*, II, 693; *VCH Hants*, III, 383; CP 25(1)/203/7, no. 272.

176 *Selborne Priory Charters* (1891, 1894), indexed refs.

177 *Book of Fees*, II, 704. Cf. JUST 1/776, m.12; CP 25(1)/203/8, no. 41.

178 *Book of Fees*, I, 462, 463, 468, 471; II, 875, 1172, 1214, 1256.

certainly of knightly status, as he had been elected to three grand assize inquests in the Hampshire eyre of 1236.[179] John Otter, accused of confederacy [27], had witnessed a number of charters for Selborne priory, mainly concerning Thedden near Alton.[180] He was of sufficient status to answer at the exchequer for arrears from the farm of Alton[181] and to serve on the inquest into the property of Miles Merchant of Alton, who had been outlawed [26].[182] Like John Otter, Walter Bulstede (of Bulstede in Thedden) had witnessed charters for Selborne priory[183] and was considered sufficiently trustworthy to serve on an inquest in July 1250 into the tenements of John de Bendinges,[184] even though Walter had been indicted of harbouring outlaws from Alton [14]. Similarly Gilbert Hattingley (sc. Hattingley in Medstead), charged with harbouring [37], held other lands in Hampshire and witnessed charters for Selborne priory, as did his son and fellow accused, William.[185] Also from near Medstead, William Soldridge [35] appears as a witness on a Selborne priory charter.[186]

Three of the presenting jurors were found guilty of obstructing the course of justice.[187] They would have been persons of status by virtue of their office, as theoretically only free and lawful men were selected for it. The two jurors from Odiham hundred [21], Thomas Aston and William Bullock, are obscure, but a few suggestive facts can be discovered about them. Thomas had served on an assize of mort d'ancestor inquest in the eyre of 1236 concerning the Bendinges family.[188] He was also sufficiently prosperous to pay half his fine of 60 marks by 1251.[189] William was probably of the family who gave their name to Bullocks Farm (1½ miles east of Odiham). A William Bullock had held a virgate of land at Murrell in Odiham in 1219.[190] More significantly, William may have been involved with one of the principal robbers, John Barkham. In the Berkshire eyre of 1248, three months before the robbery, John and a William Bullock were co-defendants in an action for common of pasture in Barkham.[191] As Barkham and Odiham are only ten miles apart, the same William Bullock may be involved in both instances. The third corrupt juror, John Boarhunt [30], is more firmly documented. His family gave their name to Burhunt Farm (1 mile south-east of Selborne) and he was the foreman of the Selborne jury [29]. The exact nature of his offence in 1249 is unclear. His fine was relatively small [30] and, unlike the other two convicted jurors [21], he was not required to find sureties. He was a presenting juror for Selborne again in the eyre of 1256 and heads the list of names, but he was also found in that eyre to have wrongfully indicted Osbert Breach of harbouring malefactors.[192] He made grants to Selborne priory and witnessed documents concerning it throughout the period 1235–66.[193]

Taken together, these biographical fragments suggest that the Alton robbery comprised a conspiracy of local gentlemen, as Matthew Paris alleged [e]. Two of the three principals and about twenty of the sixty or so persons indicted as accessories can be shown to have been freemen of the Alton region at the least. Considering how sparse information usually is in this period about persons named in criminal indictments, this result is remarkable. The robbery was an exceptional venture. The sum stolen (200 marks, probably in cash) was unusually large. The thieves were sophisticated: they communicated by letters written by clerks [38–9] and acted with daring effrontery in obtaining food from the royal kitchen [15] and perhaps also in drinking the king's wine [h].[194] Exceptionally too, there is no firm evidence that the thieves killed anyone in the course of the robbery, although Matthew Paris says in general terms that homicides were committed [o] and a homicide in the pass of Alton is recorded at [25].

A number of studies have been made of gentry involved in crime, the most notable being Professor

[179] JUST 1/775, mm.2(bis), 3d.

[180] *Selborne Priory Charters* (1894), indexed refs. Cf. ibid. (1891), 25, 27, 36.

[181] E 372/94, r.2. John answered together with John Swell and Adam Gurdon.

[182] C 145/22, no. 11; above, n.173.

[183] *Selborne Priory Charters* (1894), 23, 25, 28.

[184] C 132/9/12; above, n.151.

[185] *Book of Fees*, II, 694; *VCH Hants*, III, 246; *Selborne Priory Charters* (1894), indexed refs; CP 25(1)/203/7, no. 232.

[186] *Selborne Priory Charters* (1894), 46.

[187] Above, 36.

[188] JUST 1/775, m.10; above, n.150.

[189] E 372/95, r.35.

[190] *VCH Hants*, IV, 93.

[191] *Berks Eyre 1248*, nos. 186, a190.

[192] JUST 1/778, mm.63, 44.

[193] *Selborne Priory Charters* (1891), 28, 32, 43, 50–1, 57–8 (grants); ibid. (1891, 1894), indexed refs (witness).

[194] Above, 39–40.

Stones' account of the Folvilles of Ashby Folville in Leicestershire in the period 1326–47.[195] If one compares the Alton robbers with the Folville gang, the government seems more efficient in 1249 than it was a century later. In the Alton robbery two of the principals were promptly arrested and the stolen money recovered. The fact that John de Bendinges and John Barkham subsequently escaped and were ultimately pardoned[196] does not necessarily indicate, despite Matthew Paris [d], that the government was grossly inefficient. It may show rather that the harshness of the criminal law was mitigated where gentlemen were concerned. Our records demonstrate how poor men were humiliated by trial by battle and hanged for stealing clothes [9], coats [3, 5, 12] and shoes [4], whereas gentlemen were pardoned for taking 200 marks. Destitute aiders of the robbers were sentenced to death while the principals escaped: Alice Gosepaun who had no chattels was hanged [27], as was William Godshill who pleaded that he had been compelled to act as a messenger for the thieves [39]. This is not to suggest that such people were necessarily innocent, but to contrast their cases with that of Cecily Colemore [33], who paid 100 marks to have a special jury which acquitted her.[197] Clergy also, of course, were exempt from the death penalty [38].

Such lack of uniformity in treating offenders does not in itself imply that the king's justices were persistently corrupt. Their attitude seems to have been that wrongdoers should indeed be punished with equal severity, but that did not mean that all punishments would be the same. Each malefactor must offer an equivalent recompense to the king for his offence. Gentlemen like John de Bendinges and John Barkham had lands which the king could confiscate and despoil, whereas a poor man had nothing to offer the king except his own person. The only alternative to hanging for a propertyless man was to turn approver and use his body in the king's service. The pardoning of John de Bendinges and John Barkham may not therefore have been because the king was weak, although later in the century pardons became more numerous and cynical. Henry III may have thought that they, as gentlemen, had suffered their due. To be generous and merciful was a royal virtue; the king's mercy was arbitrary, but so was the whole tenor of government in thirteenth-century England. His capricious mercy mitigated the hideous penalties of hanging, combat and mutilation which tradition demanded. On the whole, of course, it was men of influence and not the poor who benefited from the prerogative of mercy.

Like the king, local communities seem to have softened the rigours of the law for those with whom they sympathised. A striking feature of all plea roll records is that many of the accused fled or escaped. In our roll, for example, Richard Lacfeud escaped from the custody of the sheriff himself [42], and Henry Clop [28] and Adam Limesy [43] likewise got away; all three fled to sanctuary. Such escapes may have been collusive when leaders of local communities felt that one of their neighbours should not be judicially killed. The community had, however, to be prepared to pay a heavy fine for permitting an escape; for example Bishops Waltham hundred was fined 66s. 8d. for Henry Clop's escape.[198] Localised mercy may likewise be at work in the jurors' refusal to indict and in the large number of acquittals; we need not assume with Matthew Paris [c] that all such conduct was caused by corruption. In the Alton case local communities would have been understandably reluctant to pursue in the first place and subsequently accuse landlords like John de Bendinges and John Barkham who had the power to retaliate. Nevertheless, in our case the principals were arrested even though they subsequently escaped. The complex and fragmented story of the Alton robbery does not support the simplistic proposition that royal justice was corrupt and venal, but it does emphasise the importance of social status in determining the heinousness of crimes. As in the Anglo-Saxon law codes, punishments were scaled to a hierarchy of persons as much as to the gravity of offences.

Matthew Paris and the plea roll

As comparisons have been made throughout this introduction between Matthew Paris's version of events and the plea roll's, it is appropriate to conclude with an assessment of their relative value. Criticism of Matthew's narrative does not imply that he is less valuable as a historical source than the legal records. The plea roll likewise contains contradictions and

[195] E. L. G. Stones, 'The Folvilles of Ashby-Folville, Leicestershire, and their Associates in Crime, 1326–1347', *TRHS*, 5th ser., VII (1957), 117–36. Cf. bibliography in Bellamy, *Crime and Public Order*, 208–9.

[196] Above, 38.

[197] By 1251 she had paid the sheriff £20 (= 30 marks) and still owed 70 marks: E 372/95, r.35.

[198] Hants Rec. Off., Winchester PR 159290, m.34.

makes mistakes. It says, for example, that John de Bendinges had no chattels at [18] and £136 at [22], or that Adam Limesy's chattels were answered for by the sheriff [43] whereas they went to the bishop of Winchester.[199] More importantly the plea roll makes omissions which can mislead. It fails to state that William Pope [6] abjured the realm,[200] or that John de Bendinges [22] had escaped from custody.[201] Similarly we would never know from the plea roll that Henry III had personally intervened in the trial at Winchester. Some such omissions are not really mistakes at all, as they derive from the nature of the record. It was not the eyre roll's business to record the king's speech to the men of Hampshire and there may also have been a separate coram rege plea roll which is now lost.[202] The principal limitation of crown plea rolls as historical records is that their main function was to record decisions of the court, usually concerning payments due to the crown, in proper form. The routines of legal process, however carefully recorded, were neither the substance of the law nor its political and social reality.

Matthew Paris by contrast puts formal legal processes into a dynamic political context, which is credible though obviously over-dramatised. The Alton robbery doubtless was discussed by the king's council [d] and its implications assessed [f]. Henry III probably did speak to the men of Hampshire [g], as he delivered comparable addresses on other occasions.[203] The bishop of Winchester may well have used ecclesiastical censures [j], since these would have impressed some of the jurors speaking on oath. We also owe to Matthew Paris some circumstantial details which would not be known otherwise, such as that the overseas merchants described in the plea roll [19] came from Brabant [a]. Many of the details of his narrative which can be tested by comparison with other records turn out to be true, or at least based on fact. Matthew was accurate, for example, about the sum of money stolen [b], the commission to Henry de la Mare [e], the involvement of men from Alton in the robbery [1], and perhaps even about the rôle of William Pope [q].[204]

Like the plea roll, Matthew Paris's chronicle has to be interpreted within its own terms of reference. Although his narrative seems naïve and unsophisticated, its structure is complex. He had an eye for detail and a regard for documentary records, but he also intended his chronicle to read well and contain didactic material. His eye for detail is shown by the particular examples just mentioned. His regard for records is exemplified in the collection of documents (*Liber Additamentorum*) which he appended to the *Chronica Majora.* He may have possessed documentary material concerning the Alton robbery, as he referred the reader to the *Liber Additamentorum* for further information about it.[205] In fact, however, there are no documents concerning the robbery in the *Liber* and Matthew's reference to it was emended by a superimposed slip of vellum directing the reader to the 'rolls of the king's clerks' instead.[206] As Matthew is known to have had access to official royal records on other occasions,[207] it is possible that he had seen one of the plea rolls or related documents, even if he did not possess copies of them.

However good the sources of his information may have been, Matthew aimed to be more than a collector of documents and facts for their own sake. He wanted to give his facts life and significance. Thus at the end of his narrative of the Alton robbery, he half apologises to the reader for discussing it so fully and diffusely and explains that he has done so for the moral purpose of demonstrating how conspiracies are weak [t]. From the point of view of the historian today, Matthew has not discussed the robbery nearly fully enough and his didactic purpose has made him lose interest in what really happened to the robbers after the trial. Furthermore his determination to tell a good story makes him casual even about those facts which he had originally grasped. For example, his statistic of about thirty persons hanged [o] in *Chronica Majora* becomes a hundred persons in *Historia Anglorum* written subsequently.[208]

Matthew's inconsistencies and vagaries have led Professor Vaughan to conclude that he is 'basically unreliable as a historical source'.[209] Judging by

[199] Above, 44. [200] Above, 35. [201] Above, 38.

[202] Above, n.79.

[203] M. T. Clanchy, 'Did Henry III have a policy?', *History,* New ser., LIII (1968), 205–10.

[204] Above, 39; 38; 40; 45; 32.

[205] The reference is in the shortened version of the story in *Historia Anglorum,* III, 47 n.5 (above, n.1), not in the *Chronica Majora.* The relationship of the *Historia Anglorum,* the *Chronica Majora* and the *Liber Additamentorum* is discussed by Vaughan, *Matthew Paris,* summary at pp.76–7.

[206] Matthew's use of vellum slips for emendations is discussed by Vaughan: ibid., 122–3.

[207] ibid., 17–18.

[208] Matthew Paris, *Historia Anglorum,* III, 47; above, 37.

[209] Vaughan, *Matthew Paris,* 134.

Matthew's account of the Alton robbery, the only part of his chronicle which has been subjected to detailed criticism from external sources, Vaughan's verdict is too severe. Matthew is not basically, but superficially, unreliable as a historical source. His love of drama and his strong prejudices (against papal and royal officials, for example) are self evident. But beneath the surface his narrative is based on numerous truthful details about events in his time, which can be extracted from the artistic setting he gave them and used by the historian. Unfortunately his superficial prejudices have had more influence on modern historical writing than the circumstantial details.[210] Matthew Paris and the compiler of the plea roll constructed their narratives in different ways. The justices' clerks were expected to be exact, decisive and formal in their memoranda, whereas Matthew aimed to retain his readers' and hearers' interest by being discursive, suggestive and personal. Each type of narrative has advantages and shortcomings for the historian and neither can claim a monopoly of truth.

[210] Clanchy, *History*, New ser., LIII, 204.

Appendix to Introduction

SYNOPSIS OF MATTHEW PARIS'S NARRATIVE

(Text in *Chronica Majora,* V, 56–60)

[a] Shortly before Lent in 1249, when the king arrived at Winchester, two unnamed merchants from Brabant came to him.

[b] They complained that they had been attacked and robbed of two hundred marks and alleged that they recognised the faces of the thieves among the king's court. They challenged those they accused to trial by battle.

[c] The suspected persons were arrested, but were liberated by the verdict of a jury of the neighbourhood. This was not surprising because the whole neighbourhood was infected by larceny.

[d] Nevertheless, the merchants still demanded their money from the king, who sought the advice of his counsellors. They told him that highway robbery was a frequent occurrence throughout England and that the justices in eyre should have cleaned up this infamous neighbourhood.

[e] The counsellors believed that there was a conspiracy in the neighbourhood whereby no one would accuse anyone else. The royal justice, Henry de Mara, had been there with his fellows, but he proved ineffective because the men whom he had chosen for inquests were confederates of the thieves.

[f] The counsellors also pointed out to the king the political and economic implications of the case, since Winchester was an important city for trade and the duke of Brabant might retaliate by seizing English merchants' goods.

[g] So the king had the bailiffs and freemen of Hampshire assembled in the hall of Winchester castle and upbraided them.

[h] He alleged that even his own wines had been stolen and drunk by the thieves.

[i] The king said that he was but one man and depended on support and coöperation to rule the kingdom. He was ashamed of Winchester, which was his birthplace. He believed that the citizens were accomplices and confederates of the thieves and threatened to have them tried as traitors at a convocation of all the counties of England.

[j] The bishop of Winchester calmed the king's anger, but supported him by excommunicating everybody who failed to reveal the truth about the matter.

[k] Twelve jurors were therefore chosen from the men of Winchester and Hampshire to give the names of the thieves, but after long deliberation they refused to name anyone. So the king ordered them to be thrown into a dungeon and another twelve were chosen.

[l] The second set of jurors, when they heard that the first set were in prison awaiting hanging, loosed their tongues. They disclosed numerous thefts and crimes, committed especially by men from the neighbourhood of Alton and from the bishop's liberty of Taunton.

[m] Among those arrested and hanged were rich men of good standing, royal keepers of the peace and bailiffs of that region, men with horses, households and fifty or eighty poundsworth of land, and even some retainers and archers of the king's own household.

[n] Some of the accused found sanctuary in churches and others promptly fled. Some people from Winchester took advantage of the confusion and escaped through the crowd.

[o] Those under arrest confessed to appalling thefts and killings. About thirty persons were convicted and hanged and a similar or greater number were imprisoned awaiting judgment.

[p] The members of the royal household who were hanged blamed their conduct on the king, because their stipends were in arrears.

[q] Among the thieves was one, called William Pope, who became an appellor. He was a rich man with casks full of wine in his cellar. He appealed about fifteen persons, who were convicted and hanged forthwith.

[r] One man did the king good service by fighting and he delivered the neighbourhood of six thieves.

[s] Thus the malefactors were disposed of by the vengeance of God, but Winchester, Southampton and the whole of Hampshire incurred an indelible stain of infamy.

[t] These events have been fully and diffusely described so that it may be clear to all that conspiracies of malefactors are weak, because they create confusion among themselves.

TEXT

KB 26/223, m.1

APELLA PROBATORUM

APPEALS OF APPROVERS

[1] Reginaldus Sutor de Scotia captus pro latrocinio devenit . . . probator domini regis. Et idem Reginaldus venit et appellat Cristianam Gray de Suthampton' . . . dicens quod predicta Cristiana quampl[uries] receptavit eum in domo sua et alios latrones et cum latrocinio . . . et latrocinia eorum ex corde . . . et quod hoc sit verum offert probare per corpus suum sicut curia . . Et Cristiana venit et . . . totum et de bono et malo ponit se super patriam.

Reynold Sutor of Scotland, arrested for larceny, has become an approver of the lord king. The same Reynold comes and appeals Christian Grey of Southampton, saying that Christian frequently harboured him and other thieves in her house and larcenously [? did this] and heartily [? abetted] their thefts, and he offers to prove that this is true by his body as the court [shall adjudge]. Christian comes and [denies] everything and for good or ill puts herself on [the verdict of] the country. [*Verdict not recorded*].

[2] Idem Reginaldus appellat Robertum Hrdman et Philippum filium suum de cons[ortio] latrocinii simul fuerunt in burgando duas domos in Insula, in villa de Kingeston' unam domum et unam domum ad quandam grangiam de Quarrere, et offert etc. Et predicti Robertus et Willelmus veniunt et defendunt totum et de bono et malo . . . se super patriam quod non sunt culpabiles. Et quia dictus appellator sic aperte loquitur versus eos, ideo custodiantur.

Postea venerunt predicti . . . et ponunt se super totam Insulam. Juratores dicunt quod non sunt culpabiles. Ideo inde quieti etc.

The same Reynold appeals Robert Herdman and Philip his son of confederacy in larceny [in that] together they burgled 2 houses in the Isle of Wight, 1 house in the vill of Kingston and 1 house at a certain grange of Quarr [abbey], and he offers [to prove this as above]. Robert and William [? *recte* Philip] come and deny everything and for good or ill [put] themselves on [the verdict of] the country that they are not guilty. Because the said appellor speaks thus openly against them, they are to be taken into custody.

Later the aforesaid [? Robert and Philip] come and put themselves on [the verdict of] the whole Isle. The jurors say that they are not guilty. So they [are] acquitted thereof.

[3] [*Marginated*] Suspendatur
Idem Reginaldus venit et appellat Walterum le Coc de Suthampton' . . . dicens quod . . . cum eo in villa de Knecton' in Insula de Wyth' et i[ntrav]erunt quandam domum et bona in eadem domo inventa asportaverunt, unde habuit ad partem suam unam supertunicam et unam tunicam . . . alia etc. et quod hoc sit verum offert probare per corpus suum etc. Et dictus Walterus venit et defendit totum etc. et dicit quod vult se defendere per corpus suum etc. Et ideo consideratum est quod sit duellum inter eos. Et est duellum inter eos percussum, et dictus Walterus succubuit. Ideo ad judicium de eo tanquam de convi[cto].

[*Marginated*] He is to be hanged
The same Reynold comes and appeals Walter Cook of Southampton, saying that [? Walter was] with him in the vill of Knighton in the Isle of Wight and they entered a certain house and carried off the goods in the house, whereof [Walter] had as his share 1 overcoat and 1 coat [? and many] other things, and he offers to prove that this is true by his body [as above]. Walter comes and denies everything and says that he is willing to defend himself by his body. So it is adjudged that there be battle between them. The battle between them is struck and Walter has given in. So to judgment on him as a convict.

[4] Walterus Bloweberme probator venit et appellat Walterum[211] Smallys de Wynton' de latrocinio, dicens quod dictus Walterus fuit cum eo apud Sar' ad Pentecosten et ibi simul furabantur pannos, sotulares et multa alia, et quod hoc sit verum offert ut prius etc. Et dictus Walterus venit et defendit totum et de bono et malo [ponit se super][212] patriam . . .

Walter Bloweberme, an approver, comes and appeals Walter Small of Winchester of larceny, saying that Walter was with him at Salisbury at Whitsun and there together they stole clothes, shoes and many other things, and he offers to prove that this is true as above. Walter comes and denies everything and for good or ill

[211] Interlined.

[212] No longer legible; supplied from transcript made by Edward Bisshe before 1654.

puts himself on [the verdict of] the country . . . [*Verdict illegible*].

[5] Idem Walterus venit et appellat Hamonem le Stare de Wynton' per eadem verba, scilicet [quod fuerunt ad domum Edeline][213] de Cruce apud Wynton' et ibi [furati erant][214] pannos et alia bona, unde [dictus][214] Hamo habuit ad partem suam duas tunicas, unam scilicet de panno de Hybernia et unam tunicam partitam de panno de Abendon' et de burello de London', et quod simul fuit cum eo ad faciendum dictum latrocinium offert disrationare per corpus suum sicut curia consideraverit etc. Et Hamo venit et defendit totum . . . quod vult se defendere per corpus suum etc. Ideo consideratum est quod duellum sit inter eos etc. Et . . . [duel]lum inter eos percussum, et predictus Hamo succubuit. Ideo ad judicium de eo etc. Nulla habuit catalla.

. . . quia dictus Walterus fecit disrationationem suam de x, sicut convenit, scilicet apud Gudeford' de vj . . . devenit probator, qui devenerunt probatores. Et appellavit alios quatuor, et unus defendit se per [corpus s]uum et convictus fuit, et tres fugerunt. Ideo consideratum est quod dictus Walterus abjuret regnum.

The same Walter comes and appeals Hamo Stare of Winchester by the same words, namely that they were at the house of Edeline Cross at Winchester and there stole clothes and other goods, whereof Hamo had as his share 2 coats, namely 1 of Irish cloth and 1 partly of Abingdon cloth and [partly] of London burel, and that [Hamo] was a party with him in committing the said larceny he offers to prove by his body as the court shall adjudge. Hamo comes and denies everything [and says] that he is willing to defend himself by his body. So it is adjudged that there be battle between them. The battle between them [is] struck and Hamo has given in. So to judgment on him. He had no chattels.

Because Walter has made his proof against 10 [appellees], as he agreed, namely on 6 at Guildford . . . who became approvers, and he has appealed another 4 – and 1 defended himself by his body and was convicted, and 3 have fled – it is therefore adjudged that Walter may abjure the realm.

[6] Willelmus la Pape de Aulton' rettatus de receptamento utlagatorum de passu de Aulton' venit et defendit totum et de bono et de malo[215] ponit se super tria hundreda, scilicet Aulton', Seleburn' et Odyham. Juratores dicunt quod culpabilis est, quia dicunt quod Johannes de Bendinges, Johannes de Bercham et Ricardus Benet robav[erunt] quosdam mercatores in passu de Aulton', et predicti exierunt de domo predicti Willelmi ad depredandum predictos mercatores in predicto passu, et quod eis consentiens fuit.

William Pope of Alton, accused of the harbouring of outlaws from the pass of Alton, comes and denies everything and for good or ill puts himself on [the verdict of] 3 hundreds, namely Alton, Selborne and Odiham. The jurors say that he is guilty, because they say that John de Bendinges, John Barkham and Richard Bennet robbed certain merchants in the pass of Alton and the aforesaid [persons] went out from William's house to intercept those merchants in that pass, and he was a party with them.

[7] Johannes de Bendinges, Johannes de Bercham et Ricardus Benet, rettati de roberia et maxime de passu . . . quod fuerunt in consortio utlagatorum in passu de Aulton' et quod similiter robaverunt in eodem passu, non . . . dicunt quod predicti Johannes et Johannes et Ricardus Benet predaverunt predictos mercatores et sunt consortes utlagatorum. Ideo ex[igantur et] utlagentur. Catalla . . .

John de Bendinges, John Barkham and Richard Bennet, accused of robbery and most especially concerning the pass [? of Alton and certain merchants, and] that they were in confederacy with outlaws in the pass of Alton, and that likewise they committed robbery in the same pass, [have] not [come. The jurors] say that the aforesaid John and John and Richard Bennet did plunder the aforesaid merchants and they are consorters with outlaws. So they are to be exacted and outlawed. Chattels . . . [*value illegible*].

Membrane 1d

ADHUC DE PROBATORIBUS ET MALEFACTORIBUS IN PASSU DE AULTON' ET EORUM RECEPTAMENTO

STILL CONCERNING APPROVERS AND MALEFACTORS IN THE PASS OF ALTON AND THE HARBOURING OF THEM

[8] Ricardus Forestarius rettatus . . . de consortio utlagatorum venit et defendit totum et de bono et malo ponit se super patriam, tria hundreda scilicet

213 Supplied from transcript by Edward Bisshe; *Edeline* corrected from Bisshe's *Edelme*.

214 Supplied from Bisshe's transcript.

215 Followed by *et*.

Aulton', Seleburn' et Odyham. Juratores dicunt quod culpabilis est de predicto . . . consortio. Ideo ad judicium de eo. Suspendatur.

Richard Forester, accused of confederacy with outlaws, comes and denies everything and for good or ill puts himself on [the verdict of] the country, namely the 3 hundreds of Alton, Selborne and Odiham. The jurors say that he is guilty of confederacy. So to judgment on him. He is to be hanged.

[9] Johannes Throstel[216] appellator venit et appellat Ricardum Thynnok' de Berton' et Walterum Fydelek' de consortio et latrocinio pannorum et aliorum latrociniorum etc. et hoc offert probare per corpus suum etc. Et predicti Walterus et Ricardus veniunt et defendunt totum et . . . latrocinium et consortium dicti Johannis, et de bono et malo ponunt se super patriam.

Idem Johannes venit et appellat Matheum Bere de Berton' per eadem verba, et offert etc. Et dictus Matheus venit et defendit totum et omne latrocinium et consortium etc. et offert defendere se per corpus suum etc.

Postea venit dictus Johannes appellator et retrahit se. Ideo ad judicium de eo tanquam de convicto. Nulla habuit catalla. Et super hoc venit dictus Matheus simul cum predictis Ricardo et Waltero et de bono et malo ponunt se super patriam. Juratores dicunt quod non sunt culpabiles. Ideo inde quieti. Et invenerunt plegios de fidelitate etc.

John Throstle, an approver, comes and appeals Richard Thynnok of Barton and Walter Fydelek of confederacy and the larceny of clothes and of other larcenies, and he offers to prove this by his body. Walter and Richard come and deny everything and [every] larceny and confederacy with John, and for good or ill put themselves on [the verdict of] the country.

The same John comes and appeals Matthew Bere of Barton by the same words, and offers [to prove this by his body]. Matthew comes and denies everything and every larceny and confederacy [with John], and he offers to defend himself by his body.

Later John, the appellor, comes and retracts. So to judgment on him as a convict. He had no chattels. Thereupon Matthew comes, together with Richard and Walter, and for good or ill they put themselves on [the verdict of] the country. The jurors say that they are not guilty. So they [are] acquitted thereof. They have found sureties of [good] faith.

[216] Reading uncertain.

[10] I[dem] Reginaldus Sutor venit et appellat Matheum Herbert le peleter de consortio latrocinii pannorum et de receptamento suo, et hoc offert probare per corpus suum. Et dictus Matheus venit et defendit totum et de bono et malo ponit se super patriam. Juratores dicunt quod non est culpabilis. Ideo inde quietus.

The same Reynold Sutor comes and appeals Matthew Herbert, pelter, of confederacy in the larceny of clothes and of harbouring him, and he offers to prove this by his body. Matthew comes and denies everything and for good or ill puts himself on [the verdict of] the country. The jurors say that he is not guilty. So he [is] acquitted thereof.

[11] Ricardus Leyere, Walterus le Flesmangere, rettati de latrocinio per Walterum Bloueberm', veniunt et defendunt totum et de bono et malo ponunt se super patriam. Juratores dicunt quod non sunt culpabiles. Ideo inde quieti.

Richard Leyere [and] Walter Fleshmonger, accused of larceny by Walter Bloweberme, come and deny everything and for good or ill put themselves on [the verdict of] the country. The jurors say that they are not guilty. So they [are] acquitted thereof.

[12] Idem Reginaldus Sutor venit et appellat Herbertum le Filur de Petresfeud' de consortio et receptamento suo et aliorum latronum et quod emit de eo tres supertunicas furatas, et offert etc. Et Herbertus venit et defendit . . . offert . . . corpus suum etc. . . . duellum inter eos . . .

The same Reynold Sutor comes and appeals Herbert Filer of Petersfield of confederacy and of harbouring him and other thieves, and that he bought from him 3 stolen overcoats, and he offers [to prove this by his body]. Herbert comes and denies [? everything and] he offers [to defend himself by] his body. [? So it is adjudged that there be] battle between them . . . [*Outcome illegible*].

JUST 1/776, m.23

PLACITA CORONE DE COMITATU SUHAMPT' DE ITINERE H. DE BATHON' ET SOCIORUM SUORUM JUSTICIARIORUM ITINERANTIUM APUD WYNTON' IN CRASTINO SANCTI YLLARII ANNO REGNI REGIS H. XXXIIJ

PLEAS OF THE CROWN OF THE COUNTY OF SOUTHAMPTON OF THE EYRE OF HENRY BATH AND HIS FELLOW JUSTICES IN EYRE AT

WINCHESTER ON THE MORROW OF ST HILARY IN THE 33RD YEAR OF THE REIGN OF KING HENRY

Membrane 27

HUNDREDUM DE ODYHAM VENIT PER XIJ

THE HUNDRED OF ODIHAM COMES BY 12

[13] De Willelmo de Cufaude et sociis suis xij juratoribus de fine ante judicium – ij marce.

From William Cufaude and his fellows, 12 jurors, for a fine before judgment: 2 marks.

[14] Walterus de Bolestede rettatus de receptamento utlagatorum de passu de Aulton' venit et defendit totum et de bono et malo ponit se super patriam. Juratores dicunt quod non est culpabilis. Ideo inde quietus.

Walter Bulstede, accused of the harbouring of outlaws from the pass of Alton, comes and denies everything and for good or ill puts himself on [the verdict of] the country. The jurors say that he is not guilty. So he [is] acquitted thereof.

[15] [*Marginated*] Exigatur, utlagetur
Elias le Blund, homo Magistri Galfridi coci domini regis, rettatus de latrocinio, consortio et cibaria utlagatorum in bosco de Aulton', non venit. Juratores dicunt quod culpabilis est. Ideo exigatur et utlagetur. Et fuit receptatus in curia domini regis. Nescitur de catallis.

[*Marginated*] He is to be exacted [and] outlawed
Ellis Blunt, a man of Master Geoffrey the lord king's cook, accused of larceny, confederacy and [? supplying] victuals for outlaws in Alton wood, has not come. The jurors say that he is guilty. So he is to be exacted and outlawed. He was harboured in the court of the lord king. [The value] of his chattels is not known.

[16] Henricus le Bret et Willelmus le Beche rettati de roberia et consortio utlagatorum in bosco de Aulton' veniunt et defendunt totum et de bono et malo ponunt se super patriam. Juratores dicunt quod non sunt culpabiles. Ideo inde quieti.

Henry Bret and William Beech, accused of robbery and confederacy with outlaws in Alton wood, come and deny everything and for good or ill put themselves on [the verdict of] the country. The jurors say that they are not guilty. So they [are] acquitted thereof.

[17] [*Marginated*] Misericordia
Rogerus le Messer de Standeford rettatus de latrocinio et consortio utlagatorum passus de Aulton' non venit. Juratores dicunt quod culpabilis est. Ideo exigatur et utlagetur. Non fuit in decenna set fuit de manupastu Willelmi Mauduit, ideo in misericordia. Nulla habuit catalla.

[*Marginated*] Amercement
Roger Messor of Standford, accused of larceny and confederacy with outlaws of the pass of Alton, has not come. The jurors say that he is guilty. So he is to be exacted and outlawed. He was not in a tithing, but was from William Mauduit's household. So [it is] in mercy. He had no chattels.

[18] [*Marginated*] Exigantur, utlagentur, misericordia
Willelmus le Messer et Johannes de Bendinges rettati de roberia non venerunt. Juratores dicunt quod culpabiles sunt. Ideo exigantur et utlagentur. Et fuerunt receptati in villa de Wynchefeud extra decenna, ideo in misericordia. Nulla habuerunt catalla.

[*Marginated*] They are to be exacted [and] outlawed, amercement
William Messor and John de Bendinges, accused of robbery, have not come. The jurors say that they are guilty. So they are to be exacted and outlawed. They were harboured in the vill of Winchfield outside the tithing. So [it is] in mercy. They had no chattels.

[19] Willelmus de Sancto Claro rettatus de receptamento et consortio utlagatorum passus de Aulton' et de roberia facta in [pas]su de Aulton', et Laurencius Thalebot rettatus de consortio Johannis de Beddinges et maxime quod debuit ac[como]dasse equum suum ad depredandum mercatores transmarinos in eodem passu de Aulton' et fuit[217] consentiens dicte roberie, veniunt et defendunt totum et de bono et malo ponunt se super patriam, scilicet hundreda de Sutton', Thychefeud', Aulton' et Odyham. Juratores dicunt quod dictus Laurencius non est culpabilis de consortio et est ideo inde quietus. Adduntur hundreda de Menes, Farham et Waltham. Juratores dicunt per eorum sacramentum quod predictus Willelmus non est culpabilis de receptamento nec de consortio et est inde quietus.

William Sinclair, accused of the harbouring of and confederacy with outlaws of the pass of Alton and of robbery done in the [same] pass of Alton, and Lawrence Talbot, accused of confederacy with John

[217] *et fuit* interlined.

de Bendinges and most especially that he was obliged to lend his horse to intercept the overseas merchants in the same pass of Alton and was a party to the robbery, come and deny everything and for good or ill put themselves on [the verdict of] the country, namely the hundreds of Bishops Sutton, Titchfield, Alton and Odiham. The jurors say that Lawrence is not guilty of confederacy and so he is acquitted thereof. The hundreds of Meon, Fareham and Bishops Waltham are added: the jurors say on their oath that the said William is not guilty of harbouring nor of confederacy and so he is acquitted thereof.

[20] Willelmus de Arundel rettatus de predicto receptamento venit et defendit totum et de bono et malo ponit se super predicta hundreda. Juratores dicunt quod predictus Willelmus non est culpabilis de predicto receptamento nec de aliquo et est ideo inde quietus. Ita quod inveniat plegios standi recto si predicti mercatores robati velint sequi versus eum et invenit hos plegios, scilicet Willelmum de Ramuse, Nicholaum de Langerisse, Nicholaum de Valung', Ricardum de Prevet, Ricardum de Aldewyk', Johannem Taylard.

William Arundel, accused of the aforesaid harbouring, comes and denies everything and for good or ill puts himself on [the verdict of] the aforesaid hundreds. The jurors say that William is not guilty of the harbouring nor of anything and so he is acquitted thereof. In order that he may find sureties to stand to right if the aforesaid merchants wish to proceed against him, he has found these sureties: namely William Romsey, Nicholas Langrish, Nicholas Valognes, Richard Privett, Richard Aldwick [and] John Taillard.

[21] [*Marginated*] Custodiantur, C solidi
Thomas de Eston' et Willelmus Bullok' duo ex xij juratoribus turbabunt socios suos juratores ita quod non poterant dicere veritatem in veredicto suo et maxime de passu de Aulton'. Ideo custodiantur. Postea venit dictus Willelmus et finem fecit pro C solidis [si] placet domino regi per plegium Hugonis de Wingham, Roberti de Fraxino, Ricardi de Iabinton', Henrici de Berkham', Willelmi Greg', Walteri de Belstede, Radulfi le Jovene de Bynteworth', Alani de Molendino de Graywell', Johannis le Clop', Johannis Wastehose, Willelmi de la Legh', Johannis de Bovill'.

[*Marginated*] lx marce
Postea venit dictus Thomas et finem fecit pro lx marcis per plegium Hugonis de Wyngham, Johannis le Clop', Radulfi le Jovene de Bynteworth', Henrici de Berkham', Walteri de Welstede, Alani de Molendino, Johannis de Bvill', Willelmi Greg', Willelmi de la Leg', Johannis Wastehose, Galfridi Fabri de Bynteworth', Johannis de la Holte de eadem, Thome filii Jordani de eadem.

[*Marginated*] They are to be taken into custody, 100 shillings
Thomas Aston and William Bullock, 2 of the 12 jurors, perturbed their fellow jurors so that they could not speak the truth in their verdict and most especially concerning the pass of Alton. So they are to be taken into custody. Later William came and made a fine for 100 shillings if it pleases the lord king by surety of Hugh Wingham, Robert Ash, Richard Avington, Henry Burkham, William Greg, Walter Bulstede, Ralph Young of Bentworth, Alan Mill of Greywell, John Clop, John Wastehose, William Leigh [and] John Bovill.

[*Marginated*] 60 marks
Later Thomas came and made a fine for 60 marks by surety of Hugh Wingham, John Clop, Ralph Young of Bentworth, Henry Burkham, Walter Bulstede, Alan Mill, John Bovill, William Greg, William Leigh, John Wastehose, Geoffrey Smith of Bentworth, John Holt[218] of the same [and] Thomas son of Jordan of the same.

[22] [*Marginated*] Exigatur, utlagetur; vj^{xx}xvj libri et xij solidi vj denarii obolus
Johannes de Bendingkes rettatus de receptamento ultagatorum passus de Aulton' et de consortio eorum, timens sibi, fugit. Ideo exigatur et utlagetur. Catalla sua cum anno die et vasto vj^{xx}xvj libri xij solidi vj denarii obolus.

[*Marginated*] He is to be exacted [and] outlawed; 136 pounds, 12 shillings, 6½ pence
John de Bendinges, accused of the harbouring of outlaws of the pass of Alton and of confederacy with them, fearing for himself, has fled. So he is to be exacted and outlawed. His chattels with year, day and waste: 136 pounds, 12 shillings, 6½ pence.

[23] Rogerus de Thyilherst prepositus Johannis de Bendinges rettatus de consortio utlagatorum passus de Aulton' venit et defendit totum et de bono et malo ponit se super patriam. Juratores dicunt quod non est culpabilis. Ideo inde quietus.

Roger Tilehurst, reeve of John de Bendinges, accused of the harbouring of outlaws of the pass of Alton, comes and denies everything and for good or ill puts himself on [the verdict of] the country. The jurors say that he is not guilty. So he [is] acquitted thereof.

[218] sc. Holt End in Bentworth.

Membrane 27d

HUNDREDUM DE AULTON' VENIT PER XIJ

THE HUNDRED OF ALTON COMES BY 12

[24] De Jacobo de Molendinis et sociis suis xij juratoribus de fine ante judicium – C solidi.

From James Mill and his fellows, 12 jurors, for a fine before judgment: 100 shillings.

[25] [*Marginated*] Murdrum, misericordie
Quidam extraneus inventus fuit occisus in passu de Aulton'. Ricardus Squirel primus inventor venit et non malecreditur. Nescitur quis eum occidit. Nulla Englescheria, ideo murdrum. Et villate de Aulton', Myddeste et Chauton' non venerunt plenarie ad inquisitionem etc. Ideo in misericordia.

[*Marginated*] Murder, amercements
A certain stranger was found killed in the pass of Alton. Richard Squirrel, the first finder, comes and is not suspected. Who killed him is not known. No Englishry, so a murder [fine]. The vills of Alton, Medstead and Chawton did not come in full to the inquest. So [they are] in mercy.

[26] [*Marginated*] Exigantur, utlagentur, xxv solidi, misericordie, xx solidi
Mylo le Marchant de Aulton' et Nicholaus filius suus[219] rettati de receptamento utlagatorum dc passu de Aulton', Herebertus de Yuesete et Stephanus de Wydehale rettati de eadem, non venerunt. Juratores dicunt quod predicti Mylo et Stephanus sunt culpabiles de consortio utlagatorum, et Herebertus culpabilis est. Ideo exigantur et utlagentur. Et Mylo[220] fuit receptatus in villa de Aulton' et dicta villa fuit amerciata coram domino Henrico de Mara. Catalla sua xxv solidi unde vicecomes respondeat. Et Herbertus et Stephanus fuerunt in decenna de Wyuehal', ideo in misericordia. Catalla dicti Herberti xx solidi unde idem vicecomes respondeat. Et Stephanus nulla habuit catalla.

[*Marginated*] They are to be exacted [and] outlawed, 25 shillings, amercements, 20 shillings
Miles Merchant of Alton and Nicholas his son, accused of the harbouring of outlaws of the pass of Alton, [and] Herbert Ewshott and Stephen Willhall,[221] accused of the same, have not come. The jurors say that Miles and Stephen are guilty of confederacy with outlaws, and Herbert is guilty. So they are to be exacted and outlawed. Miles was harboured in the vill of Alton and the said vill was amerced before the lord Henry de la Mare. His chattels: 25 shillings for which the sheriff is answerable. Herbert and Stephen were in the tithing of Will Hall. So [it is] in mercy. Herbert's chattels: 20 shillings for which the same sheriff is answerable. Stephen had no chattels. [*No verdict recorded on Nicholas*].

[27] Matheus de Hertl', Henricus le Macun, Johannes le Oter, Nicholaus le Synker,[222] Alicia Gosepaun', Adam Wodekok', Stephanus le Blake, Stephanus le Forester, Johannes le Wodeward, Stephanus Wyard, Johannes le Nuk rettati de consortio et receptamento utlagatorum de passu de Aulton' veniunt et defendunt totum et de bono et malo ponunt se super patriam. Juratores dicunt quod predicta Alicia culpabilis est. Ideo ad judicium de ea. Nulla habuit catalla. Dicunt etiam quod predicti Adam Wodecok', Stephanus Forestarius, Johannes Wodeward viderunt predictos utlagatos et non levaverunt hutesium. Ideo custodiantur. Set Stephanus Wyard et Johannes le Nug in nullo sunt culpabiles. Ideo inde quieti. Postea venit Stephanus le Forester et finem fecit per j marcam per plegium Petri de Turvill'. Postea venerunt predicti Matheus de Hertl', Johannes le Oter et alii. Non sunt culpabiles. Ideo inde quieti.

Matthew Hartley,[223] Henry Mason, John Otter, Nicholas Sinker, Alice Gosepaun, Adam Woodcock, Stephen Black, Stephen Forester, John Woodward, Stephen Wyard [and] John Nug, accused of confederacy and of the harbouring of outlaws from the pass of Alton, come and deny everything and for good or ill put themselves on [the verdict of] the country. The jurors say that Alice is guilty. So to judgment on her. She had no chattels. [The jurors] also say that Adam Woodcock, Stephen Forester [and] John Woodward saw the outlaws and did not raise the hue. So they are to be taken into custody. But Stephen Wyard and John Nug are guilty of nothing. So they [are] acquitted thereof. Later Stephen Forester came and made a fine of 1 mark by surety of Peter Turville. Later Matthew Hartley, John Otter and the others came. They are not guilty. So they [are] acquitted thereof.

219 *et Nicholaus filius suus* interlined.

220 Interlined.

221 sc. Will Hall in Alton.

222 *Johannes le Oter, Nicholaus le Synker* interlined.

223 sc. Hartley Mauditt.

Membrane 28

HUNDREDUM DE WLPITTE VENIT PER XIJ

THE HUNDRED OF WOOLPIT[224] COMES BY 12

[28] [*Marginated*] Evasio, [vi]ij solidi, v denarii
Henricus le Clop appellatus per Walterum Bloueberme captus fuit et evasit de custodia ville de Waltham et fugit ad ecclesiam Sancti Suthini et cognovit se esse latronem et abjuravit regnum. Ideo villata de Waltham respondeat de evasione. Catalla sua viij solidi v denarii unde episcopus Wynton' respondeat.

[*Marginated*] Escape, 8 shillings, 5 pence
Henry Clop, appealed by Walter Bloweberme, was arrested and escaped from the custody of the vill of Bishops Waltham and fled to St Swithun's church and acknowledged himself to be a thief and abjured the realm. So the vill of Bishops Waltham is answerable for the escape. His chattels: 8 shillings, 5 pence for which the bishop of Winchester is answerable.

Membrane 29d

HUNDREDUM DE SELEBURNE VENIT PER XIJ

THE HUNDRED OF SELBORNE COMES BY 12

[29] De Johanne de Burhunte et sociis suis xij juratoribus de fine ante judicium –.

From John Boarhunt and his fellows, 12 jurors, for a fine before judgment: [*blank*].

[30] [*Marginated*] Suspendatur
Ricardus de Ketecumbe et Cristiana uxor eius[225] rettati de latrocinio et receptamento utlagatorum passus de Aulton' veniunt et defendunt totum et de bono et malo ponunt se super patriam. Juratores dicunt quod predictus Ricardus[226] culpabilis est de consortio et receptamento predictorum utlagatorum, quia dicunt quod cibaria predictorum utlagatorum decoquabantur in domo predicti Ricardi, scilicet unus porcus et duo multones et de dicta domo destinebantur predicta cibaria predictis utlagaṭis ad boscum de Aulton'. Ideo ad judicium de eo etc.

[*Marginated*] xl solidi
Et testatum est quod predicta Cristiana non fuit consentiens receptamento predictorum utlagatorum nisi per compellationem dicti Ricardi viri sui. Ideo inde quieta. Et Johannes de Burhunte unus xij juratorum convictus est quod impedivit predictos juratores quod non poterant dicere veritatem. Ideo ipse custodiatur. Postea venit dictus Johannes et finem fecit pro xl solidis per plegium suum. Catalla dicti Ricardi de Kytecumbe cum anno die et vasto super feodum episcopi Exon' xij libri xviij solidi v denarii. Item super feodum Constancie de Pontelarch' et anno etc. xvij libri iij solidi viij denarii unde vicecomes respondeat de toto.

[*Marginated*] He is to be hanged
Richard Kitcombe and Christian his wife, accused of larceny and the harbouring of outlaws of the pass of Alton, come and deny everything and for good or ill put themselves on [the verdict of] the country. The jurors say that Richard is guilty of confederacy and of the harbouring of the outlaws, because they say that the outlaws' victuals were cooked in Richard's house, namely 1 pig and 2 sheep, and those victuals were dispatched from that house to the outlaws at Alton wood. So to judgment on him.

[*Marginated*] 40 shillings
It is attested that Christian was not a party to the harbouring of the outlaws except by compulsion of Richard her husband. So she [is] acquitted thereof. John Boarhunt, 1 of the 12 jurors, is convicted of having impeded the jurors so that they could not speak the truth. So he is to be taken into custody. Later John came and made a fine of 40 shillings on his own surety. Richard Kitcombe's chattels with year, day and waste on the fee of the bishop of Exeter: 12 pounds, 18 shillings, 5 pence. Also on the fee of Constance Pont de l'Arche and year, [day and waste] : 17 pounds, 3 shillings, 8 pence for the whole of which the sheriff is answerable.

[31] [? Ricardus] de Westedenn' de Thy. . . e rettatus de consortio et receptamento utlagatorum passus de Aulton', [? Alanus] de Neuton' rettatus de eadem, et Radulfus de Ores rettatus de diversis latrociniis, veniunt et de[fendunt] . . . bono et malo ponunt se super patriam. Juratores dicunt quod predictus Ricardus de Westeden' culpabilis est . . . Radulfus de Ores culpabilis est . . .

[? Richard] Westdean of [*illegible*], accused of confederacy and the harbouring of outlaws of the pass of Alton, [? Alan] Newton[227] accused of the same, and Ralph Noar[228] accused of several larcenies, come

[224] Woolpit hundred must here be Bishops Waltham, not Finchdean. This is proved by the following entry and by the fact that the crown pleas of Finchdean hundred are enrolled separately, at m. 23.

[225] *et Cristiana uxor eius* interlined.

[226] *predictus Ricardus* interlined.

[227] Newton Valence?

[228] sc. Noar Hill in Newton Valence.

and deny [everything and for] good or ill put themselves on [the verdict of] the country. The jurors say that Richard Westdean is guilty . . . Ralph Noar is guilty . . .

Membrane 30

ADHUC DE HUNDREDO DE SELEBURN'

STILL CONCERNING THE HUNDRED OF SELBORNE

[32] [*Marginated*] Custodiatur, xl solidi
Petrus Pistor de Seleburn' et Johannes Clericus de Wynteneye rettati de consortio utlagatorum passus de Aulton' veniunt. Et Johannes clericus est, et dicit quod non vult hic respondere. Et super hoc venit officiarius episcopi Wynton' et petit ipsum tamquam clericum et liberatur ei. Et Petrus le Pestur defendit totum et de bono et malo ponit se super patriam. Juratores dicunt quod predicti Johannes Clericus et Petrus non sunt culpabiles de consortio predictorum utlagatorum, set dicunt quod predictus Petrus incidit inter predictos utlagatos et ipsi vi abstulerunt ei unum cornu. Et quia ipse non levavit uthesium, ideo ipse custodiatur. Postea venit predictus Petrus[229] et finem fecit pro xl solidis per plegium Henrici Ward de Aulton'. Postea venerunt predicti Walterus, Stephanus et Willelmus et finem fecerunt pro ij marcis per plegium prioris de Suthwyk'.[230]

[*Marginated*] He is to be taken into custody, 40 shillings
Peter Baker of Selborne and John Clerk of Hartley Wintney, accused of confederacy with outlaws of the pass of Alton, come. John is a clerk and says that he does not want to answer here. Thereupon the bishop of Winchester's official comes and claims him as a clerk and he is to be delivered to him. Peter Baker denies everything and for good or ill puts himself on [the verdict of] the country. The jurors say that John Clerk and Peter are not guilty of confederacy with the outlaws, but they say that Peter fell in with the outlaws and they took away from him by force 1 horn. Because he did not raise the hue, he is to be taken into custody. Later Peter came and made a fine for 40 shillings by surety of Henry Ward of Alton. Later the aforesaid Walter, Stephen and William came and made a fine for 2 marks by surety of the prior of Southwick.

[33] [*Marginated*] C marce, custodiatur
Cecilia de Colemere rettata de receptamento utlagatorum et cibariis eis missis ad boscum venit et defendit totum et de bono et malo ponit se super patriam. Et pro habenda inquisitione quatuor hundredorum, scilicet Seleburn', Hodyham, Aulton' et Sutton' offert domino regi C marcas et recipiuntur si placet domino regi per plegium Roberti de Horpenham de Berk', Nicholai de Ingepenn' de eadem, Roberti de la Sale de Lamborn', Henrici de Sewell' de Berk' et Johannis Kokyn de eadem. Postea veniunt juratores predictorum hundredorum et dicunt quod non est culpabilis de receptamento nec de dicto consortio, nisi simul per nuncios suos transmisit eis cibaria ad boscum et hoc pro timore eo quod minabuntur ei. Ideo custodiatur etc.

[*Marginated*] 100 marks, she is to be taken into custody
Cecily Colemore, accused of the harbouring of outlaws and of sending victuals to them at the wood, comes and denies everything and for good or ill puts herself on [the verdict of] the country. She offers the lord king 100 marks to have an inquest of 4 hundreds, namely Selborne, Odiham, Alton and Bishops Sutton, and they are received if it pleases the lord king by surety of Robert Orpenham of Berkshire, Nicholas Inkpen of the same, Robert de la Sale of Lambourn, Henry Sewell of Berkshire and John Cocking of the same. Later the jurors of the aforesaid hundreds come and say that she is not guilty of harbouring nor of the said confederacy, except that she once sent victuals over to the [outlaws] at the wood by her messengers and [she did] this from fear because they were threatening her. So she is to be taken into custody.

[34] [*Marginated*] Custodiantur, custodiatur, j marca
Walterus prepositus prioris de Shuwik',[231] Adam de Myreifeud, Stephanus le Jovene, Johannes Hervest et Willelmus de la Lode et Mylesenta de Colle rettati de receptatione utlagatorum et de cibariis eis missis ad boscum de Aulton', veniunt et defendunt totum et de bono et malo ponunt se super patriam. Juratores dicunt quod non sunt culpabiles. Ideo inde quieti. Quia dicunt quod non receptaverunt utlagatos set dicunt quod utlagati venerunt ad domos predictorum Walteri, Stephani, Johannis et Mylesente et cibaria in predictis domibus inventa vi asportaverunt. Et ipsi non levaverunt uthesium. Ideo ipsi custodiantur. Et

229 Interlined.

230 This sentence refers to [34].

231 The *Sh* is uncertain; possibly changed from *Sci,* for *Sancti.*

predictus Willelmus de la Lode vidit eos et loquebatur cum eis et non levavit uthesium. Ideo ipse custodiatur. Postea venit predicta Mylesenta et finem fecit per j marcam per plegium Symonis de Anvers.[232]

[*Marginated*] They are to be taken into custody, he is to be taken into custody, 1 mark
Walter the reeve of the prior of Southwick, Adam Merryfield, Stephen Young, John Harvest, William de la Lode and Millicent Goleigh, accused of the harbouring of outlaws and of sending victuals to them at Alton wood, come and deny everything and for good or ill put themselves on [the verdict of] the country. The jurors say they are not guilty. So [they are] acquitted thereof. Because [the jurors] say that they did not harbour the outlaws, but they say that the outlaws came to the houses of Walter, Stephen, John and Millicent and carried off by force the victuals found in those houses. [Walter and the others] did not raise the hue. So they are to be taken into custody. William de la Lode saw the [outlaws] and spoke with them and he did not raise the hue. So he is to be taken into custody. Later Millicent came and made a fine of 1 mark by surety of Simon Danvers.

[35] [*Marginated*] Custodiantur
David de la Dune et Willelmus de Solrige rettati de latrocinio et de receptamento utlagatorum veniunt et defendunt totum et ponunt se super patriam. Juratores dicunt quod predicti utlagati venerunt ad domum predictorum Davidis et Willelmi, set dicunt quod non fuerunt consentientes predictis utlagatis. Et quia non levaverunt uthesium post predictos utlagatos, ideo custodiantur.

[*Marginated*] They are to be taken into custody
David Down and William Soldridge, accused of larceny and of the harbouring of outlaws, come and deny everything and put themselves on [the verdict of] the country. The jurors say that the outlaws came to the house of David and William, but they say that [David and William] were not parties with the outlaws. Because they did not raise the hue after the outlaws, they are to be taken into custody.

[36] [*Marginated*] Exigantur, utlagentur, misericordia, misericordia, misericordia, capiatur
Osbertus le Messer de Neweton', Willelmus Page de Tysted, Galfridus serviens Cecilie de Kernet, Juliana vidua de Dene rettati de receptamento utlagatorum passus de Aulton' non venerunt. Juratores dicunt quod culpabiles sunt. Ideo exigantur et utlagentur. Et Osbertus non fuit in decenna et fuit receptatus in villa de Neuton', ideo in misericordia. Et Willelmus Page fuit in decenna de Tystede, [ideo] in misericordia. Nulla habuit catalla. Et Galfridus fuit receptatus in villa de Colemere extra decenna, ideo in misericordia. Nulla habuit catalla. Et Juliana nulla habuit catalla. Postea testatum est quod predictus Osbertus non fuit consentiens utlagatis set quod loquebatur utlagatis et non levavit uthesium. Ideo capiatur pro uthesio non levato.

[*Marginated*] They are to be exacted [and] outlawed, amercement, amercement, amercement, he is to be arrested
Osbert Messor of Newton Valence, William Page of East Tisted, Geoffrey the servant of Cecily Kernet [and] Gillian the widow of [Priors] Dean, accused of the harbouring of outlaws of the pass of Alton, have not come. The jurors say that they are guilty. So they are to be exacted and outlawed. Osbert was not in a tithing and he was harboured in the vill of Newton Valence, so [it is] in mercy. William Page was in the tithing of East Tisted, so [it is] in mercy. He had no chattels. Geoffrey was harboured in the vill of Colemore outside the tithing. So [it is] in mercy. He had no chattels. Gillian had no chattels. Later it is attested that Osbert was not a party with the outlaws, but that he spoke with the outlaws and did not raise the hue. So he is to be arrested for not having raised the hue.

[37] Gilbertus de Hattingelg' et Willelmus filius eius rettati de receptamento utlagatorum passus de Aulton' veniunt et de bono et malo ponunt se super patriam. Juratores dicunt quod non sunt culpabiles. Ideo inde quieti.

Gilbert Hattingley and William his son, accused of the harbouring of outlaws of the pass of Alton, come and for good or ill put themselves on [the verdict of] the country. The jurors say that they are not guilty. So they [are] acquitted thereof.

[38] [*Marginated*] Capiatur
Johannes Bissup et Galfridus de Westden' et Thomas Clericus de Dene rettati de receptamento utlagatorum veniunt et defendunt totum. Et Thomas dicit quod non vult hic respondere quia clericus est. Super hoc venit officiarius episcopi Wynton' et petit ipsum tanquam clericum et liberatur ei etc. Et quia uxoratus est et habet laicum feodum, preceptum est vicecomiti quod capiat terram suam in manum domini regis.

232 cf. the last sentence of [32].

Et predicti Johannes et Galfridus de bono et malo ponunt se super patriam. Juratores dicunt quod predictus Thomas Clericus culpabilis est de consortio utlagatorum in passu de Aulton' et quod fecit brevia utlagatis. Ideo committatur gayole officiarii episcopi tanquam convictus. Dicunt etiam quod predictus Galfridus de Westdenn' culpabilis est de predicto consortio predictorum utlagatorum. Ideo ad judicium de eo. Set dicunt quod Johannes Bissup non est culpabilis de consortio nec de receptamento. Ideo inde quietus.

[*Marginated*] [Land] is to be taken [into the king's hand]
John Bishop and Geoffrey Westdean and Thomas Clerk of Priors Dean, accused of the harbouring of outlaws, come and deny everything. Thomas says that he does not want to answer here because he is a clerk. Thereupon the bishop of Winchester's official comes and claims him as a clerk and he is to be delivered to him. Because he is married and has a lay fee, the sheriff is ordered to take his land into the hand of the lord king. John and Geoffrey put themselves for good or ill on [the verdict of] the country. The jurors say that Thomas Clerk is guilty of confederacy with outlaws in the pass of Alton and that he made writs for the outlaws. So he is to be committed to the gaol of the bishop of Winchester's official as a convict. They also say that Geoffrey Westdean is guilty of confederacy with the aforesaid outlaws. So to judgment on him. But they say that John Bishop is not guilty of confederacy nor of the harbouring. So he [is] acquitted thereof.

[39] [*Marginated*] Menes, suspendatur
Willelmus de Godeshull' et Gilbertus de Collegh' rettati de consortio et receptamento utlagatorum veniunt. Et dictus Gilbertus defendit expresse consortium et receptamentum dictorum utlagatorum et ponit se super patriam etc. Et Willelmus bene cognovit quod vi et timore compulsus tulit quoddam breve apud Dureford', quod quidem breve tradidit celarario de Dureford' ex parte dictorum utlagatorum set nescivit quid continebatur in predicto brevi, et nunquam aliud consortium habuit cum eis nec eos receptavit, et de hoc ponit se super patriam. Juratores dicunt quod predictus Gilbertus non est culpabilis de consortio nec de receptamento. Ideo inde quietus. Set dicunt quod predictus Willelmus culpabilis est de consortio et receptamento. Ideo ad judicium de eo. Catalla sua . . .

[*Marginated*] Meon, he is to be hanged
William Godshill and Gilbert Goleigh, accused of confederacy and the harbouring of outlaws, come. Gilbert expressly denies confederacy and the harbouring of the outlaws and puts himself on [the verdict of] the country. William has readily acknowledged that, compelled by force and fear, he brought a certain writ to Durford [abbey], which writ he handed over to the cellarer of Durford on behalf of the outlaws, but he did not know what was contained in the writ and never had any other confederacy with them, nor did he harbour them, and thereon he puts himself on [the verdict of] the country. The jurors say that Gilbert is not guilty of confederacy nor of harbouring. So he [is] acquitted thereof. But they say that William is guilty of confederacy and harbouring. So to judgment on him. His chattels: [*blank*].

[40] [*Marginated*] Fallegh'
Juliana Quakepel et Margeria filia sua rettate de consortio et receptamento utlagatorum predictorum veniunt et defendunt totum et de bono et malo ponunt se super patriam. Juratores dicunt quod non sunt culpabiles. Ideo inde quieti.

[*Marginated*] Fawley
Gillian Quakepel and Margery her daughter, accused of confederacy and the harbouring of the aforesaid outlaws, come and deny everything and for good or ill put themselves on [the verdict of] the country. The jurors say that they are not guilty. So they [are] acquitted thereof.

Membrane 30d

ADHUC DE HUNDREDO DE SELEBURN'

STILL CONCERNING THE HUNDRED OF SELBORNE

[41] [*Marginated*] Suspendatur, x marce
Henricus King de Dene rettatus de receptatione latronum et maxime de receptatione utlagatorum de passu de Aulton' venit et defendit totum et de bono et malo ponit se super patriam, scilicet hundreda de Berton' and Seleburn'. Juratores dicunt quod culpabilis est de receptatione dictorum utlagatorum et quod pluries eos receptavit et eis misit ciseram ad potandam ad boscum. Ideo ad judicium de eo. Postea venit prior de Suthwyk' et finem fecit pro catallis sui[233] cum anno die et vasto per x marcas per plegium suum.

[233] Recte *suis.*

[*Marginated*] He is to be hanged, 10 marks
Henry King of Priors Dean, accused of the harbouring of thieves and most especially of the harbouring of outlaws from the pass of Alton, comes and denies everything and for good or ill puts himself on [the verdict of] the country, namely the hundreds of Barton Stacey and Selborne. The jurors say that he is guilty of the harbouring of the said outlaws and that he harboured them many times and sent them cider to drink at the wood. So to judgment on him. Later the prior of Southwick came and made a fine for his chattels with year, day and waste for 10 marks on his own surety.

[42] [*Marginated*] Abjuravit
Ricardus Lacfeud [rettatus] de consortio et receptamento utlagatorum passus de Aulton' captus fuit et imprisonatus in gayola Wynton' et de illa prisona liberatus fuit Nigello Clerico tunc vicecomiti ad ducendum ipsum coram justiciariis. Et dictus Ricardus evasit et fugit ad ecclesiam Sancti Suthwini Wynton' et abjuravit regnum. Non fuit in decenna quia liber. Catalla sua . . .

[*Marginated*] He has abjured
Richard Lacfeud, accused of confederacy and the harbouring of outlaws of the pass of Alton, was arrested and imprisoned in Winchester gaol and was delivered from that prison to Neil Clerk, the then sheriff, to conduct him before the justices. Richard escaped and fled to St Swithun's church at Winchester and abjured the realm. He was not in a tithing because he [was] a freeman. His chattels: [*blank*].

Membrane 32d

HUNDREDUM DE SUTTON VENIT PER XIJ

THE HUNDRED OF BISHOPS SUTTON COMES BY 12

[43] [*Marginated*] Abjuravit, xxxj libri, xij solidi
Adam de Lymesi rettatus de receptamento et consortio utlagatorum in passu de Aulton' timens sibi posuit se in ecclesia de fratrum predicatorum de Wynton' et cognovit se esse latronem de uno equo quem furabatur apud Lundun' et abjuravit regnum. Et fuit liber. Catalla sua cum anno die et vasto xxxj libri xij solidi unde vicecomes respondeat.

[*Marginated*] He has abjured, 31 pounds, 12 shillings
Adam Limesy, accused of the harbouring of and confederacy with outlaws in the pass of Alton, fearing for himself, put himself in the church of the friars preacher of Winchester and acknowledged himself to be the thief of 1 horse which he stole at London and he has abjured the realm. He was a freeman. His chattels with year, day and waste: 31 pounds, 12 shillings for which the sheriff is answerable.

Membrane 37

DELIBERATIO GAYOLE

GAOL DELIVERY

[44] [*Marginated*] Hundredum de Basingestok'
Walterus le Buteler rettatus de latrocinio et consortio utlagatorum passus de Aulton' venit et defendit totum et de bono et malo ponit se super patriam. Juratores dicunt quod non est culpabilis. Ideo inde quietus.

[*Marginated*] Basingstoke hundred
Walter Butler, accused of larceny and confederacy with outlaws of the pass of Alton, comes and denies everything and for good or ill puts himself on [the verdict of] the country. The jurors say that he is not guilty. So he [is] acquitted thereof.

[45] [*Marginated*] Seleburn'
Gilbertus de Norton' rettatus de latrocinio et consortio utlagatorum passus de Aulton' venit et defendit totum et de bono et malo ponit se super patriam. Juratores dicunt quod non est culpabilis. Ideo inde quietus.

[*Marginated*] Selborne
Gilbert Norton, accused of larceny and confederacy with outlaws of the pass of Alton, comes and denies everything and for good or ill puts himself on [the verdict of] the country. The jurors say that he is not guilty. So he [is] acquitted thereof.

Membrane 38

[KALENDAR OF JURIES OF PRESENTMENT]
[jur' = juratus]

[46] [H]undredum de [A]ulton'

Idem N. [Nicholaus Longus] ballivus	jur'
Electores: Galfridus Serviens	jur'
Jacobus de Molend'	jur'
Johannes de Chauton'	jur'
Henricus Wyard	jur'
Andreas de Hogges	jur'
Matheus de Merham	jur'
Radulfus de Bello	jur'
Johannes de Brembessete	jur'
Willelmus Huse	jur'

Johannes de Aulton'	jur'
Ricardus Sygar	jur'
Nicholaus Snelle	jur'

[47] Hundredum de Odiham

Robertus Wastehose ballivus		jur'
Electores: Henricus de Berkeham		jur'
Willelmus de Cofaude		jur'
Robertus de Cofaude	jur'	
Willelmus de la Byry	jur'	
Thomas de Eston'	jur	
Ricardus de la Rigge	jur'	
Willelmus de la Lye	jur'	
Johannes Wastehose	jur'	
Willelmus Lancelenehe	jur'	
Johannes de Bovile	jur'	

[*10 jurors only*]

[48] Hundredum de Seleburn'

Henricus de Brondn' ballivus		jur'
Electores: Ricardus de Ketecombe		jur'
Hugo de Westwode		jur'
Radulfus Cherculf	jur'	
Ricardus de la Rude	jur'	
Robertus Oiselur	jur'	
Johannes Burhunte	jur'	
Galfridus Lamkashard	jur'	
Robertus Mutun	jur'	
Willelmus de Arundell'	jur	

[*9 jurors only*]

Oldcotes v. d'Arcy

edited by

P. A. BRAND

INTRODUCTION

Either on, or a few days before, 1 November 1272,[1] Ingram of Oldcotes entered into an agreement with Roger d'Arcy. Roger was to make Ingram a knight by 24 June 1273;[2] and, once he had become a knight, to provide food and clothing both for him and for an esquire and two grooms, and to maintain three horses for his use, for the rest of Ingram's lifetime. In return, Ingram granted Roger for life all his lands in Styrrup, Oldcotes and Bugthorpe,[3] to be held for the nominal annual rent of one penny and the forinsec service owed to the lord of the fee. Roger, who took an oath to observe the agreement, also agreed that if at any time he failed to carry out any of the conditions, Ingram might reënter the lands, and that he would not bring an assize of novel disseisin or any other legal action for their recovery if he did so.

The agreement was recorded in two separate legal instruments. One was a charter in Ingram's name granting Roger his lands for life in return for the payment of the annual rent of one penny and the performance of the forinsec service to the lords of the fee but saying nothing of the other conditions under which the grant had been made. This was deposited for safe-keeping with the mayor of Lincoln, William of Holgate.[4] The other was a bipartite chirograph sealed by both Ingram and Roger recording the other conditions of the grant of which both parties kept a part.[5]

It was this agreement that subsequently gave rise to litigation between the Oldcotes and d'Arcy families which lasted, with intermissions, for almost forty years. The principal stages in this litigation are recorded in the documents here printed.[6]

I

Ingram of Oldcotes was a great-nephew of the Philip of Oldcotes who, after suffering for his loyalty to John during Richard's reign,[7] had been in joint charge with Hubert de Burgh of the castle of Chinon when it was captured in 1206, and had subsequently risen to a position of some importance as one of John's trusted agents in the north of England, being joint custodian of the vacant see of Durham from 1209 to 1217 and sheriff, either alone or with others, of the county of Northumberland from 1212 to 1220.[8] By the time of his death late in 1220, when about to take up the position of seneschal of Poitou,[9] Philip had made considerable additions to his original landed possessions, which consisted of no more than a single knight fee in Styrrup and Oldcotes[10] held of the honor of Tickhill[11] which he

[1] Neither of the documents which recorded the agreement was dated, to judge from what seem to be full transcripts of them given in plea roll enrolments of 1274 and 1280 [1, 2]. It is, however, clear from [1] that Roger d'Arcy entered into seisin of the lands at All Saints' day (1 Nov.) 1272; and probable, therefore, that the agreement was drawn up either on that day or a few days previously.

[2] In the original agreement, the date set was the nativity of St John the Baptist 57 Henry III. Henry III, however, died at the very beginning of his fifty-seventh regnal year, on 16 November 1272, some eight months before the feast day. It seems reasonable to assume that there was a general legal rule for the transposition of such dates in legally binding contracts into dates in the reign of the late king's successor.

[3] These places are identified in note A, below, 93.

[4] It is given in full in [1].

[5] It is given in full, with only minor verbal differences, in both [1] and [2].

[6] A chronology of some of the more important dates in this litigation will be found below at Appendix I. Previous accounts of, or references to, various parts of the litigation and to its background will be found in R. Thoroton, *The Antiquities of Nottinghamshire,* 2nd edn, with additions by J. Throsby (London, 1790–7), III, 422–3; *Placitorum . . . Abbreviatio* (RC, 1811), 229; J. Raine, *The History and Antiquities of the Parish of Blyth in the Counties of Nottingham and York* (Westminster, 1860), 164; G.E.C., IV, 51 note h, 55 notes c, d; D. W. Sutherland, *The Assize of Novel Disseisin* (Oxford, 1973), 143 n.2.

[7] *PR 6 Ric. I,* ed. D. M. Stenton (PRS, New ser., V, 1928), 85.

[8] J. C. Holt, *The Northerners* (Oxford, 1961), 222–4: M. H. Dodds, *A History of Northumberland,* XII (London, 1926), 259–61.

[9] *Pat. R. 1216–25,* 250; *Rot. Litt. Claus.,* I, 446.

[10] There is no direct evidence from Philip's own lifetime that the knight fee was in these two places: but in 1242/3, three of his descendants are to be found holding a knight fee of the honor of Tickhill in Styrrup (*Book of Fees,* 979), and an apparently trustworthy late thirteenth-century genealogy of the Oldcotes family in the Welbeck cartulary (BL, MS Harl. 3640, f.167) states that Philip held a knight fee in Oldcotes and Styrrup. There is also the evidence of his own surname.

[11] He was holding this knight fee from at least the beginning of John's reign: *PR 2 John,* ed. D. M. Stenton (PRS, New ser., XII, 1934), 14; *PR 3 John,* ed. D. M. Stenton (PRS, New ser., XIV, 1936), 100; *Book of Fees,* 33.

probably inherited from his father, Gerard of Styrrup.[12] The most valuable of these acquisitions seem to have been the extensive lands in Nafferton, West Matfen and Lorbottle and houses in Newcastle upon Tyne that were held by the serjeanty of acting as coroner for the county of Northumberland south of the river Coquet and as forester in fee for the whole county, which were granted to him during pleasure in 1210 and in fee in 1213.[13] The lands at Nafferton and West Matfen alone were valued in 1219 at £20 a year;[14] the land at Lorbottle, then held by John de Neville, presumably in right of the dower of his wife Isabel, widow of the previous tenant of the serjeanty, Sewal fitz Henry, were then said to be worth another £5 a year.[15] By 1250, when the lands of the serjeanty were arrented by Robert Passelewe, they were valued at over £60 a year;[16] and in 1279, when they were again appraised, their gross value was said to be between £70 and £80 a year, though from this £32 had to be deducted for rent paid to the king in lieu of the services formerly performed for the land.[17] Philip had also acquired, probably in fee, the salmon fishery of Pool in Ord near Tweedmouth, later in Northumberland, but then in the northern part of the liberty of Durham,[18] which was probably worth a sum closer to the fifty marks a year at which it was valued in June 1278[19] than the eight marks a year at which the prior of Durham claimed he leased it in 1279.[20] Philip's probable acquisitions also include a moiety of the vill of Kibblesworth in county Durham,[21] and the whole of the vill of Seaham in the same county;[22] by 1219 he had also acquired the lands previously held by Master Alan of Bolsover, physician to King John, in Canwick and Lincoln in Lincolnshire, and in Retford, Gringley, Sturton le Steeple, Wiseton, Fenton and Leverton in Nottinghamshire.[23] The value of these acquisitions is not known.

Philip had no surviving issue at the time of his death, and so was succeeded by his five sisters: Alice, who at the time of Philip's death seems to have been unmarried; Margaret or Margery, who was married to Hamlin of Bugthorpe; Juliana, who was married to Alfred of Barnby; Isabel, who was married to Thomas of 'Stretton'; and Constance, who was married to Daniel son of Nicholas otherwise Daniel of Newcastle.[24]

[12] The Welbeck genealogy (above, n.10) is the authority for Philip's parentage; but it does not specifically state that either this Gerard or another Gerard of Styrrup, who was Philip's grandfather, ever held the knight fee. There is no detailed 1166 *carta* for the honor of Tickhill, as it was in the king's hands at the time.

[13] For the 1210 grant see *PR 12 John*, ed. C. F. Slade (PRS, New ser., XXVI, 1951), 107; *PR 13 John*, ed. D. M. Stenton (PRS, New ser., XXVIII, 1953), 206; *Book of Fees*, 204. For the 1213 grant see *Rotuli Chartarum . . .*, ed. T. D. Hardy (RC, 1837), 190. The previous tenant of the serjeanty, Sewal fitz Henry, had been granted it only in 1191 (*PR 2 Ric. I*, ed. D. M. Stenton (PRS, New ser., I, 1925), 19), a grant confirmed by John in 1200 (*Rot. Chart.*, 76), but died, apparently without heirs, towards the end of 1210. The 1213 grant to Philip included a clause saving the rights of any possible heirs of Sewal fitz Henry.

That the duties of the serjeanty included not only acting as coroner south of the Coquet, but also acting as forester in fee is not mentioned in the accounts of the duties of the tenant of the serjeanty given in 1198 and 1212 (*Book of Fees*, 5, 204), but is mentioned in the writ of July 1221 which gave Philip's heirs seisin of the lands held with the serjeanty: *Ex. Rot. Fin.*, I, 67–8.

[14] *Book of Fees*, 249.

[15] ibid. For John de Neville's marriage to Sewal's widow see *PR 12 John*, 134; *CRR*, V, 311; VII, 311.

[16] *Book of Fees*, 1192–3.

[17] E 143/1/7, no. 19. On the serjeanty, its lands and tenants see generally Dodds, *History of Northumberland*, XII, 257–78.

[18] In 1279 the prior of Durham, then tenant of the fishery, denied that Philip had ever held the fishery in fee (E 143/1/7, no. 19d), a claim subsequently supported by the verdict of a jury taken before Geoffrey of Newbold, chancellor of the exchequer: J. Raine, *The History and Antiquities of North Durham* (London, 1852), 249 note k. However, the treasury at Durham contains a charter of Henry of Ord, the previous tenant of the fishery, granting it to Philip in fee (Raine, *North Durham*, appendix, 132, no. DCCXLVII); and the evidence of the charter is supported by the testimony of witnesses produced on behalf of the bishop of Durham against the prior and chapter in 1228: *Feodarium Prioratus Dunelmensis*, ed. W. Greenwell (Surtees Soc., LVIII, 1872), 224–30. For the tangled later history of the fishery, involving the claims of Philip's heirs, Master William of Greenlaw, and Durham priory, see Raine, *North Durham*, 249 note k, and *Feodarium . . . Dunelmensis*, 224–30.

[19] E 143/1/7, no. 3, m.1.

[20] E 143/1/7, no. 19d.

[21] Note B, below, 93.

[22] Note C, below, 93–4.

[23] Note D, below, 94.

[24] The original mandate to give Philip's sisters seisin of his lands, issued on 22 Jan. 1221 (*Rot. Litt. Claus.*, I, 446), does not mention any of the husbands: but they are all mentioned in further mandates of 6 July 1221 relating to the Northumberland serjeanty lands: *Ex. Rot. Fin.*, I, 67–8; *Pat. R. 1216–25*, 296. In the Northumberland eyre of 1227 it was said that all the sisters had been married before Philip's death: *Book of Fees*, 371. The fact that three out of the four sisters who had husbands, had husbands whose names probably indicate origins in fairly close proximity to Styrrup and Oldcotes – Hamlin of Bugthorpe probably came from the Bugthorpe near Maltby, Yorks (note A, below, 93); Alfred of Barnby probably came from Barnby Moor about three miles SE of Blyth; and Thomas of 'Stretton' may have come from

Ingram was the grandson and heir of the second of the sisters, Margaret/Margery.[25] She and her husband Hamlin were still alive at Michaelmas 1238, when they were parties, together with others of Philip's heirs, to a final concord relating to land in Matfen;[26] but both they and their son, Geoffrey, were dead by 1242/3 when Ingram of Oldcotes appears (under the name of Ingram son of Geoffrey) as one of the tenants of the knight fee in Styrrup held of the honor of Tickhill together with Thomas of 'Stretton' and his wife Isabel and Norman son of Alfred (of Barnby).[27] Ingram's share of Philip's lands seems to have consisted only of the Nottinghamshire portion of the lands inherited by Margaret/Margery, less the lands donated by her and Hamlin to the religious houses of Welbeck, Roche and Blyth,[28] but plus certain other lands which he acquired in the early 1250s from his great-aunt Isabel, who was by then the widow of Thomas of 'Stretton'.[29] The total value of these lands in Oldcotes, Styrrup and Nornay,[30] less any lands which he had himself alienated prior to 1272 or which Roger d'Arcy alienated between 1272 and 1279, amounted, according to an inquisition held in 1279 into the value of these and other lands in Nottinghamshire once held by Philip of Oldcotes, to some £7 13s. 7d. a year,[31] and what seem to have been roughly the same lands were valued in 1313 at £10 a year.[32] What happened to Margaret/Margery's share of Philip's lands in Northumberland is unclear. Ingram's name is never found in connection with these lands;[33] and while it is possible that Hamlin and Margaret/Margery exchanged or sold their share to others of Philip's heirs, it seems equally possible that it went to one or both of the two tenants, John of Brafferton[34] and Robert of Oldcotes,[35] who, in the mid-thirteenth century held substantial portions of the Northumberland serjeanty lands but cannot be accounted for either as heirs or alienees of Philip's other sisters or as heirs of known subtenants of the serjeanty.

Ingram probably also inherited land from his paternal grandfather. As has been seen, Ingram's charter to Roger d'Arcy spoke of lands in Bugthorpe, as well as in Oldcotes and Styrrup;[36] it is reasonable

the Sturton le Steeple about ten miles east of Blyth – also suggests that they may have married before their brother achieved prominence.

25 That Ingram was grandson of Hamlin and Margaret/Margery is shown by the Oldcotes family genealogy in the Welbeck cartulary (above, n.10), which also shows that his father's name was Geoffrey. This is confirmed by deeds in the Blyth cartulary (*The Cartulary of Blyth Priory,* ed. R. F. Timson, Thoroton Soc., XXVII, XXVIII, 1973, nos. 115–6) which show Ingram of Oldcotes, son of Geoffrey of Bugthorpe, confirming grants made to Blyth by Hamlin [of Bugthorpe] and Margaret; and confirming all the grants made to Blyth by Gerard of Styrrup, Philip of Oldcotes and his other ancestors. Among the Harleian Charters (BL, Harl. Ch. 112.G.43) there is a grant apparently by Ingram relating to land in Styrrup in which he simply calls himself Ingram son of Geoffrey of 'Bythetorp' (Bugthorpe).

26 CP 25(1)/181/17, no. 189.

27 *Book of Fees,* 979. The suggestion made by Timson (*Blyth Cartulary,* xl), that Ingram's father, Geoffrey, was still alive in 1242/3, is the result of a mistaken identification of Ingram's father with a Geoffrey of Bugthorpe who is associated with, and takes his surname from, the East Riding Bugthorpe.

28 For these gifts see CP 25(1)/182/6, no. 189; *Rot. Hund.,* II, 304; Welbeck cartulary (BL, MS Harl. 3640), f.73; *Blyth Cartulary,* nos. 113, 114.

29 The extent of Ingram's acquisitions from Isabel is unclear, as our knowledge of these acquisitions is derived solely from the Oldcotes family genealogy in the Welbeck cartulary (above, n.10), which merely states that Isabel during her widowhood granted all her Nottinghamshire lands to Ingram, Norman son of Alfred (of Barnby) and the abbey of Welbeck. Isabel's husband was still alive in Nov. 1251 (*Northumberland Pleas . . . 1198–1272,* Newcastle upon Tyne Rec. Ser., II, 1922, no. 516) but was dead by Feb. 1253: *Ex. Rot. Fin.,* II, 153. Isabel herself was dead by June 1256: ibid., 233.

30 Nornay is a hamlet just outside Blyth, about a quarter of a mile to the north on the road towards Styrrup. It is probable that the lands here are to be identified with those elsewhere said to be in Blyth and may for the purposes of the original agreement have been regarded as being in Styrrup.

31 E 143/1/7, no. 15, m.2. This is the valuation of the lands held by Roger d'Arcy by virtue of Ingram's grant. See note E, below, 94–5.

32 C 143/91, no. 7. See below, 91, for the circumstances of this valuation.

33 His name does not appear in connection with the 1250 arrentation of the serjeanty lands (*Book of Fees,* 1192–3) nor is it found in the lists of the Northumberland tenants of Philip of Oldcotes' lands provided by inquisitions in 1278 and 1279: note E, below, 94–5.

34 For his holding in 1250 see *Book of Fees,* 1192; and for the subsequent history and descent of this holding see *CIPM,* I, no. 771; *Ex. Rot. Fin.,* II, 531; *Rot. Hund.,* II, 21. In 1278 his descendant, Richard of Brafferton, was said to hold 79 acres of the serjeanty once held by Philip of Oldcotes (E 143/1/6, no. 7); and in 1279 this was said to be worth, after the payment of services, 25s. 10d. a year: E 143/1/7, no. 19.

35 For his holding in 1250 see *Book of Fees,* 1192. He was succeeded in 1266 by a son named Simon (*CIPM,* I, no. 630), whose land by 1279 was reduced in value from the 38s. a year it had been worth in 1250 to only 8d. a year after services had been paid: E 143/1/7, no. 19.

36 Above, 64.

to assume that these lands came to him from Hamlin of Bugthorpe. How extensive such lands were is not known. All that is known about them is that they included some reasonably valuable woodland, as Ingram's son, Robert of Oldcotes, recovered forty-two shillings, three times the amount of damage done, for the 'wasting' of woods there by Ingram's widow, Elena, and her husband, John le Keu, in the early fourteenth century.[37]

Since Ingram was named as one of the tenants of the Styrrup fee in 1242/3,[38] he may already then have been of age.[39] In 1256–7 he was amerced one mark for a false claim, probably in the honor court of Tickhill,[40] and in 1257, when, although not yet a knight, he was named as one of the jurors on an attaint jury taken before Gilbert of Preston at Granby in Nottinghamshire.[41] In 1258 he was an unattached co-defendant with several others (including the constable of Tickhill) in an assize of novel disseisin concerning land at Ordsall in Nottinghamshire, heard before the justiciar, Hugh Bigod.[42] During the disorders of the 'baronial reform' period, he seems to have participated, with a large number of other men from northern Nottinghamshire and southern Yorkshire, principally from Retford, Tickhill and Rotherham, in an attack on the manor and castle of Sheffield, which belonged to a prominent royalist, Thomas de Furnivall. According to Furnivall, this attack involved not only the burning of his manor and castle, but also the looting of goods and chattels to the value of £3,000: it probably took place in August or September 1265.[43] Among his fellow defendants in a case brought by Furnivall in the court coram rege in 1265 and 1266 against the alleged participants in this attack was one John of Bugthorpe, who may have been his brother:[44] both men were attested at Easter 1266 to be in prison at Knaresborough.[45] However, despite his alleged participation in the attack, Ingram does not seem to have purchased a pardon or to have been caught by the proceedings under the dictum of Kenilworth against baronial partisans. By Easter 1267 at latest, he was out of prison and able to plead as defendant in an assize of mort d'ancestor brought against him by Simon son of Robert of Laughton concerning a messuage and one bovate in Letwell, a village in Yorkshire about two miles SW of Oldcotes.[46] Other evidence which sheds a somewhat uncertain light on Ingram's activities during this period includes an appeal for imprisonment and breach of the peace brought against him and some nine others by Stephen son of Stephen of 'Frismareis', in which Stephen was nonsuited at the Yorkshire eyre of 1268;[47] and the accusations of petty extortions made against him as one of the bailiffs of the honor of Tickhill during

[37] CP 40/142, m.28. The waste found involved the cutting down of 55 small oaks worth 3d. each and one small oak worth 4d.

[38] Above, 66.

[39] There is no suggestion that the land was being held by a guardian on his behalf.

[40] SC 6/1094/11, m.2: accounts of the lands of the Lord Edward for 41 Henry III, section relating to Tickhill, subsection relating to the profits of Tickhill court(s).

[41] JUST 1/1185, m.3d. The jurors of an attaint jury should all have been knights: *Early Registers of Writs*, ed. E. de Haas and G. D. G. Hall (SS, LXXXVII, 1970), CA 50, CC 175, CC 182 (pp.31, 86, 90).

[42] JUST 1/1187, m.16.

[43] Furnivall had commenced proceedings in the court coram rege against Ingram and some thirty other men in connection with this attack by the quindene of Michaelmas 1265 (mid-Oct.): KB 26/174, m.4d; proceedings which he continued to prosecute in Hilary and Easter terms in 1266: KB 26/175, mm.8, 25d; C 47/14/3, nos. 16–17. The verdict of a jury in a separate case also heard coram rege (*Thornhill of Wath* v. *le Tyeys:* KB 26/175, m.9) suggests, though the wording of the verdict is not entirely clear, that the burning of Sheffield castle took place between the battle of Evesham (4 Aug. 1265) and the public proclamation of the king's peace on 16 September 1265: *CIM,* 1, no. 321.

[44] Ingram of Oldcotes and a brother named John were convicted, together with one Amice of Bugthorpe, of the disseisin of Richard of Clifton and his wife Isabel at Braithwell, Yorks, a village about two miles north of Maltby, in an assize heard at Easter 1272: JUST 1/1052, m.15. One John of Bugthorpe and his wife Hawise were convicted of the disseisin of Hugh son of Elias of Styrrup at Styrrup in the Nottinghamshire eyre of 1280–1 (JUST 1/668, m.6d); John of Bugthorpe also appears as a co-defendant with Constance de Béarn in a novel disseisin case relating to a windmill in Gringley in 1276: KB 27/14, m.11.

[45] The reason for their imprisonment is not stated. This may have been during the period when Luke de Tany was acting as constable both of Tickhill and of Knaresborough (*CPR 1258–66,* 442); it is possible that they were transferred for safe-keeping from Tickhill to Knaresborough.

[46] JUST 1/1194, m.15. The pleadings and verdict, which went against Ingram, indicate that he had either a rent charge of 2s. or a paramount lordship over the land in question.

[47] JUST 1/1051, m.15d. Of the other defendants, at least four came from Bawtry, Yorks, just three miles due east of Tickhill. A jury taken at the king's suit subsequently acquitted Ingram and the other defendants.

the period when John Basset was constable of Tickhill castle in the hundred rolls inquiry of 1274.[48]

In 1273 Ingram was attacked by Thomas de Furnivall and his men, possibly in revenge for his participation in the 1265 attack on Furnivall's manor and castle of Sheffield,[49] and subsequently Ingram brought an appeal, alleging maiming and breach of the peace, against Furnivall himself, Saer of Huntingfield and nine others, in the court coram rege. This appeal can be traced on the plea rolls in Hilary and Easter terms 1274, but does not appear on the roll for Michaelmas term 1274 or subsequently.[50] The attack and subsequent appeal are also mentioned in cases in 1286 [4][51] and 1309 [9]: and if this part of the 1286 jury verdict is to be believed, the date at which the attack took place can be confined within narrower limits, as having taken place between 24 June 1273 and the end of the same year.[52]

As for the other party to the 1272 agreement, Roger d'Arcy, he seems to have been a younger son of the Philip d'Arcy who held the barony of Nocton in Lincolnshire, and who was succeeded in 1264 by his eldest son, Norman.[53] Since Norman was said in 1264 to be twenty-eight years of age, Roger can then have been no more than twenty-seven and may conceivably have been several years younger than that.[54] Either in 1263 or 1264 he took part with his brother Norman, his uncle Thomas, the noted baronial partisans John d'Eyvill and Adam de Neufmarché, and many others, in looting the goods of the Cahorsin money-lender, Peter Beraud, at various places in Lincolnshire.[55] These attacks seem to have been connected with the financial hold which Beraud had gained over both the d'Arcy family[56] and its monastery of Nocton Park.[57] In June 1264 Roger and his brother Norman, who were said to have been captured at Hull, were in prison at Scarborough, in the custody of its royalist constable, John of Octon. Their release was ordered at the same time as similar mandates were sent to other royalists for the release of their baronial prisoners.[58] This mandate may have been observed, although Octon did not surrender the castle until December, for Norman d'Arcy at least was out of captivity by 1 July 1264, when the king took his homage.[59] Both Norman and Roger and their uncle Thomas seem subsequently to have been among the 'disinherited', those who refused to accept the terms of the dictum of Kenilworth and continued to hold out against the king; for it was only in June 1267, after the earl of Gloucester's march on London and settlement with the king, that they received a safe-conduct to return home, and then a pardon for their part in the recent disturbances.[60] Roger was also responsible, at some date prior to March 1268, when he received a pardon for this at the instance of John de la Lynde, for the killing, in circumstances which are not explained, of one Master Robert of London.[61]

Subsequently, Roger occurs with his mother Isabel as a defendant in an assize of novel disseisin heard in the Lincolnshire eyre of 1271/2,[62] and

[48] *Rot. Hund.*, II, 307; JUST 1/1060, mm.19–20.

[49] Uncertain light on Ingram's relations with Furnivall immediately prior to the attack is shed by Roger's allegation, in a case in the Nottinghamshire eyre of 1280–1 in which he attempted to vouch Ingram to warranty for one acre sought against him by Simon of Styrrup, that Ingram had taken his homage on the day of the Assumption 1 Edward I (?18 May [*Assumptio Domini*] or 15 Aug. 1273) at Tickhill castle in the presence of Thomas de Furnivall and others. Ingram denied this, but before the issue was decided by a jury Simon was nonsuited: JUST 1/668, m.11. Cf. ibid., m.20d; JUST 1/148, m.18.

[50] KB 27/7, m.15 (morrow of the Purification); 9, m.8d (3 weeks or month after Easter). The roll for the intervening Trinity term does not survive.

[51] Note that here the identity of the attackers is not revealed.

[52] The attack is said to have taken place after the latest date set for Ingram to receive his knighthood: it must have taken place not later than the end of 1273 for Ingram to have been suing his appeal by Hilary term 1274.

[53] G.E.C., IV, 54.

[54] *CIPM*, I, no. 577.

[55] Roger appears in a long list of Lincolnshire defendants being sued by Beraud in the court coram rege in Michaelmas 1268 (KB 26/186, m.21d): he does not appear in similar lists in Michaelmas 1269 (KB 26/193, m.24d), Hilary 1270 (KB 26/197, mm.2, 10) or Trinity 1271 (KB 26/204, m.19). For other defendants against whom process was sued in Yorkshire, Nottinghamshire and Norfolk see KB 26/186, m.21d; 193, mm.20, 21, 25d, 29; 197, mm.9d, 10d; 204, m.19. The uncertainty about the date comes from the fact that of three cases brought by similar writs which came to trial, two were said to be concerned with seizures made in June 1263 (KB 26/197, m.10; 193, m.20), the third with seizures made in June 1264 (KB 26/186, m.18d). The latter seems the more probable date, as far as the political circumstances are concerned.

[56] cf. KB 26/186, mm.25, 25d; E 159/36, m.ld.

[57] cf. KB 26/189, mm.6, 25; 185, m.21d; 193, m.20d; 196, m.18; E 368/42, m.5. For some other aspects of Beraud's career in England see *CPR 1258–66,* 70, 172, 283, 448, 482; *1266–72,* 172, 463, 538, 556.

[58] ibid., *1258–66,* 360, 390–1.

[59] *Ex. Rot. Fin.*, II, 409.

[60] *CPR 1266–72,* 78–80: by this date Roger had been knighted, since the pardon is to him as Roger d'Arcy, knight.

[61] ibid., 209.

[62] JUST 1/483, m.35d.

was in trouble in the court coram rege late in 1273 and early in 1274 for having, some time late in Henry III's reign, attacked the servants of the sheriff of Lincolnshire who had been sent to replevy the cattle of one Robert de Lisle.[63]

According to the appeal made in September 1274 before the Newgate gaol delivery justices by one Peter of 'Scabbehawe', an approver who subsequently withdrew his appeal, men of Roger's household, though not Roger himself, had participated with Ingram's sons, William and Gilbert, and others in a robbery in a wood at Maltby in Yorkshire shortly before Christmas 1273;[64] and Roger himself, either shortly before or shortly after his agreement with Ingram, seems to have been involved in disturbances at Rothwell and Cuxwold in north-east Lincolnshire connected with disputes over title to land there,[65] and to have participated in disseisins at Keelby near Stallingborough in Lincolnshire[66] and at Great Coates also in Lincolnshire.[67] It was probably also at about this time that Roger acquired an interest in land at Sproatley in Holderness in Yorkshire from Simon de Vere, an interest which he later quit-claimed to the king.[68] By 1280/1, Roger seems to have been in minor orders;[69] when he acquired them is uncertain.

The nature and terms of the agreement also call for comment. Arrangements involving the surrender of the whole of the grantor's land in return for support for the remainder of his lifetime, seem to have been comparatively common at the level of the peasant cultivator. Here the grantee was usually a close relation, often the heir apparent, of the grantor, who was now too old or infirm to cultivate the land himself.[70] It is, however, less clear how common such arrangements were at a higher level, where the grantor was not himself the cultivator of the soil: though the fact that Bracton mentions such agreements in his treatise suggests that they were by no means unknown.[71] The most curious feature of the agreement, clearly, however, was that it required Roger to make Ingram a knight, the costs of the knighting being borne by Roger.[72] It is generally held that knighthood was a status which men were increasingly unwilling to adopt in the thirteenth century, both because of the high costs involved in the purchase of appropriate horses and armour[73] and because of the heavy administrative and judicial burdens laid upon the knightly class: and that it was the growing unwillingness of those who would once have automatically taken up knighthood to do so that led to the frequent distraints of knighthood under Henry III, Edward I and their successors.[74] This agreement, however, is a useful reminder that knightly status clearly also possessed attractions ranging from the financial – a higher rate of pay on

63 KB 27/1, m.8d; 7, m.10d. It was probably the same incident that was the subject of a presentment by the wapentake of Manley in the Lincolnshire eyre of 1281–4: JUST 1/486, m.25d.

64 JUST 3/35A, m.1. Ingram's son William is described as such, Gilbert merely as Gilbert of Oldcotes, but it seems reasonable to identify him with the son of Ingram who put Roger d'Arcy in seisin of Ingram's lands in 1272. Other robberies mentioned in the retracted appeal involved members of the household of Thomas de Furnivall, including the tutor of his children, and the steward of Adam de Neufmarché.

65 KB 27/14, m.13d; 26, m.43d. When the king was at Lincoln in Easter 1276 he was also arraigned at the king's suit for being, as it was alleged, a public disturber of the king's peace, plundering cattle, corn and other goods and extorting money by threats: KB 27/14, m.12d.

66 JUST 1/484, m.4. 67 KB 27/12, m.32d.

68 *Calendar of the Plea Rolls of the Exchequer of the Jews* (Jewish Hist. Soc.), II, ed. J. M. Rigg (1910), 306; III, ed. H. Jenkinson (1929), 135, 253; IV, ed. H. G. Richardson (1972), 77; *CCR 1272–9*, 166, 169; JUST 1/1235, m.25d; 1238, mm.3d, 8.

69 Note F, below, 95.

70 G. C. Homans, *English Villagers of the Thirteenth Century* (Cambridge, Mass, 1941), 141–59.

71 Bracton, ff.18–18b, 47 (II, 69–70, 145). For litigation about other similar agreements see, e.g., the following cases: *Wombe* v. *Wombe* (CP 40/13, m.48d); *Makejoy* v. *Comyn* (CP 40/17, m.117); *Dunmow* v. *Draper* (CP 40/31, m.5); *Park* v. *le Brun* (CP 40/19, m.39; 27, m.129; 29, m.23d).

72 There is some ambiguity in the wording of the agreement as to whether Roger is to dub Ingram himself or to ensure the performance of the ceremony by another. In the subsequent litigation, however, it seems to be assumed that it was Roger himself who would have conferred knighthood. This is important evidence for the view that at this date in England, as much later was still the case in France, knighthood could still be conferred by anyone who was himself a knight rather than just by the king, his deputies, and captains of armies in the field: cf. F. M. Nichols, 'On Feudal and Obligatory Knighthood', *Archaeologia,* XXXIX (1863), 208–12. Michael Powicke's belief (*Military Obligation in Medieval England,* Oxford, 1962, 104) that by 1274 there existed a royal monopoly on the conferring of knighthood is mistaken: the evidence he cites shows only that by 1274 the crown claimed a monopoly of distraining men to take up knighthood.

73 H. M. Chew, *The English Ecclesiastical Tenants-in-Chief and Knight Service* (London, 1932), 89–90.

74 Powicke, *Military Obligation,* 69–80; N. Denholm-Young, 'Feudal Society in the Thirteenth Century: the Knights', in *Collected Papers on Mediaeval Subjects* (Oxford, 1946), 56–67.

campaigns[75] – to the social – the prestige of belonging to a class which was increasingly separating itself off from the main body of mere freeholders[76] and the glamour associated with knighthood by the cult of chivalry.[77] Which of these factors weighed most with Ingram is uncertain. It is, however, legitimate to speculate that the social status associated with knighthood may have been particularly attractive to one who must have been aware of his relationship to Philip of Oldcotes, who had in his day been a man of influence and importance; and that Ingram's tenure of lands in Oldcotes and Styrrup may have made him particularly susceptible to the attractions of knightly status as an entrée to the world of chivalry, since those lands were close to one of the most important English tournament grounds, that which lay between Tickhill and Blyth.[78] Tournaments were, of course, closely associated with the cult of chivalry and knighthood.[79] Certainly, if the 1279 valuation of his lands was anything near accurate,[80] and provided this valuation covered most of his lands, as it probably does, then Ingram's lands were worth only a little over a third of the annual value at which tenants were normally expected or distrained to assume knighthood:[81] there was therefore never any question of Ingram otherwise being forced to take up knighthood.

As for the attractions of the agreement to Roger, these are even more speculative. If, and this is by no means certain, Roger entered into the agreement with Ingram in good faith, then it may have been because the prospect of possessing land of his own, even on fairly harsh terms, was an attractive one to the landless younger son of a minor baronial family; and since Roger was probably at that time on good terms with Ingram, he may even have hoped that he might subsequently be able to induce Ingram to make over the lands to him entirely. Moreover, Roger was probably somewhat younger than Ingram and may have hoped to recoup his initially high capital expenditure not only from the difference between the value of Ingram's lands and the costs of fulfilling the regular obligations to Ingram during Ingram's lifetime but also from the profit which he would derive from it during the period between Ingram's death and his own. During this period he would, of course, have no further obligations under the agreement but would be entitled to continue holding the lands. It is, however, possible that from the first Roger intended to renege on the agreement once he had entered into the lands: and then his motives in doing so are even more obvious.

The 1272 agreement between Ingram and Roger was, as has been seen already,[82] embodied in two quite separate instruments: a charter by which Ingram granted his lands to Roger for life, apparently without condition, and a chirograph setting out in detail the conditions under which the grant had been made. There seem to have been no technical legal reasons why grant and conditions should not both have been contained in a single instrument, one which would have made it clear that the grant was being made only in return for the fulfilment of the conditions; and Ingram may well have subsequently regretted that this was not done. It was, however, probably at his own prompting that things were done in this way: his motive being to hide the fact that he had in effect purchased his knighthood. For this it was necessary that the charter of feoffment, which would in the normal course of events become publicly known when Roger was put in seisin of his lands, should make no mention of this or the other conditions on which that feoffment had been made. These were instead recorded in a separate agreement, which, provided it was kept, need never become general knowledge.[83]

75 Powicke, *Military Obligation,* 68.

76 The best evidence for this growing sense of social exclusiveness lies, I think, in the change to be found in charters from the early or mid-thirteenth century which led to knightly witnesses being described as such and being given precedence over other witnesses. The exact chronology of this change awaits a detailed study of English charter practice.

77 Powicke, *Military Obligation,* 68.

78 The local historian Raine (*History of Blyth,* 168) conjectured more specifically on topographical grounds that it lay between Blyth and Styrrup. Ingram's lands would, therefore, have been very close to it indeed.

79 N. Denholm-Young, 'The Tournament in the Thirteenth Century', in *Studies in Medieval History presented to F. M. Powicke,* ed. R. W. Hunt, W. A. Pantin and R. W. Southern (Oxford, 1948), 240–68. Tournaments were forbidden at Blyth in April 1273, and again in January 1274: *CPR 1272–81,* 8, 41.

80 Above, 66.

81 This was £20 a year: Powicke, *Military Obligation,* 72–80. The lowest level to which it fell was £15 a year, in 1256; under Edward I, it never fell below £20 a year, and eventually became fixed at £40 a year: ibid., 105–9.

82 Above, 64.

83 This would explain why Ingram's letters patent for his son Gilbert to put Roger in seisin of his lands also only mentions the charter of feoffment and not the chirograph.

II

Shortly after the agreement Ingram and Roger fell out with each other. Ingram may have had second thoughts about the wisdom of the agreement and attempted to terminate it by refusing to accept knighthood from Roger.[84] More probably, Roger saw and seized an opportunity of retaining Ingram's lands without carrying out the expensive obligations which this was intended to entail. At all events, Ingram soon ejected Roger from his lands, for early in July 1273 Roger purchased a writ of novel disseisin against Ingram, claiming that he had been disseised of lands in Oldcotes, Bugthorpe and Styrrup.[85] From the sequel it is clear that Roger must have been successful in the assize and recovered the lands.[86]

It was probably after the hearing of this assize – though the exact chronology is uncertain – that Ingram was assaulted by Thomas de Furnivall and his men,[87] and it is possible that it was the hundred marks which he was later said to have received for abandoning his appeal against them [5] that enabled Ingram to embark on his first counteraction against Roger for the recovery of his lands. This was an action brought by a writ of entry ad terminum qui preteriit and both parties appeared and pleaded it in Michaelmas term 1274 [1].[88] The choice of action seems to have been made with care. Ingram was barred by the verdict in Roger's favour in the 1273 assize from bringing an assize of novel disseisin himself against Roger.[89] He could have brought an action of covenant for the enforcement of the chirographed agreement of 1272, but in such an action he would have been able to recover damages, but not his land. Alternatively he could have brought an action by writ of right, though such actions tended, for procedural reasons, to be both hazardous and slow.[90] An action by writ of entry had the advantage both of being swifter and easier than action by writ of right, and of being sufficiently 'high in the right' that the demandant was not barred by the adverse assize verdict. Writs of entry ad terminum qui preteriit were, it was true, generally used only for the recovery of land which a lessee had gone on holding at the end of his lease or a tenant at will gone on holding when the lessor wished to terminate his lease, or a mortgagor gone on holding when the debt was paid; or from the alienees of such tenants or lessees, when such tenants or lessees had purported to alienate the land they thus held. Prima facie, at least, therefore, Ingram's case was not one covered by the action. When the case came to court, however, Ingram ingeniously claimed that, through the combined operation of the charter and the chirographed agreement, Roger had in effect been a lessee who had held for a term which commenced on 1 November 1272 (the day he had been put in seisin of Ingram's lands) and terminated on 24 June 1273 (the day by which he was to have made Ingram a knight, but had failed to do so): Roger was, therefore, now in exactly the same position as any other termor or lessee who held on to land after his term or lease had expired. As evidence for this contention, Ingram produced his part of the chirographed agreement.

Roger in reply admitted that he was a lessee but claimed that his term had not expired, since his lease was for life. The terms on which he had received the

[84] This is the suggestion of the pro-d'Arcy jury verdict in [4], which stated that it had been Ingram who, when the day had come for him to be knighted, had made difficulties ('quesivit occasiones'), as a result of which the two men had separated without Ingram receiving his knighthood.

[85] C 66/92, m.10: enrolment of the commission to the two justices assigned to hear the assize. It was probably issued on 8 July 1273 since it occurs, without date, between two entries of that date: the other entries on the membrane, where dated, are all of early July. Roger paid 20s. for this assize: E 371/37, m.4.

[86] Why Roger was successful in the assize is not at all clear. One would have expected that Ingram could have justified his entry by means of the chirographed agreement which specifically safeguarded his right of reëntry. If, however, by 1273 Roger had already acquired the charter of feoffment which he pleaded in 1274 (below, 72), it may be that it was by pleading this that he won his case. Curiously, the John of Octon commissioned with Elias of Beckingham to hear the assize seems to be the same man as the man of that name who had been constable of Scarborough in 1264, and therefore for a while Roger d'Arcy's gaoler: above, 68.

[87] Above, 68.

[88] Unfortunately no common pleas plea rolls survive for terms between Trinity 1273 and Michaelmas 1274, so that it is impossible to know when the action started. Nor is it certain when Ingram abandoned his appeal against Furnivall and his men, though this must have been between Easter and Michaelmas 1274: above, 68. Any causal link between the two is, therefore, highly speculative.

[89] For the rule that two assizes could not both consider the same facts see Sutherland, *Assize of Novel Disseisin,* 142–3.

[90] It was, in particular, up to the tenant to choose whether he would opt for trial by battle or the grand assize. Roger might well have been more confident than Ingram as to the outcome of a trial by battle.

land were, he claimed, those laid down in Ingram's charter of feoffment, which he now produced and which made him a tenant for life;[91] and in additional support of his argument he produced the letters of attorney made by Ingram for his son Gilbert to put Roger in seisin of the lands, which spoke only of Roger receiving seisin in accordance with Ingram's charter and said nothing of the chirographed agreement or of Roger receiving seisin subject to the agreement as well as to the charter. He was not, it will be noted, denying the genuineness of the chirographed agreement: all that he was denying was that it had any relevance to the present case.[92] The justices adjudged that a jury should decide the crucial issue of whether Roger had entered the land 'by' the charter of feoffment, as he claimed, or 'by' the chirographed agreement, as Ingram claimed.[93]

In the following Easter term, at the return day appointed for the appearance of the jury, a jury duly appeared, but was rejected by the justices on the grounds that all the jurors were poor and none of them was a knight. The case was therefore adjourned to Michaelmas term and the sheriff ordered to produce a new jury of whom at least six were to be knights.[94] No adjournment is recorded on the Michaelmas plea roll,[95] but in that for Hilary term 1276 a further adjournment to Trinity term is recorded.[96] Then, like so many others, this case disappears from the rolls, without any note either that the demandant has failed to prosecute or that a verdict has been given.[97] All that we do know is that Roger remained in seisin of the land.[98]

III

The first recorded adjournment in Ingram's second action against Roger for the recovery of his lands[99] was in Hilary term 1279, when the sheriff returned that since Ingram had not found pledges to prosecute his action, he had not summoned Roger. Ingram now found pledges,[100] and it was ordered that Roger be summoned for Easter term.[101] In Trinity term 1279 Roger sought a view of the land, the case being adjourned to Michaelmas term to allow the view to be made.[102] No enrolment relating to the case is to be found on the plea roll for Michaelmas term 1279, probably because Roger had been essoined; but in the following term, Hilary 1280, both parties appeared and pleaded [2]. The form of action

[91] It will be remembered that this had been left in the safe-keeping of the mayor of Lincoln. How and when Roger obtained possession of it is not clear.

[92] The implication of this seems to be that if Ingram wishes to attempt to enforce the chirographed agreement, he must bring an action of covenant, though in this he will only recover damages, not his land.

[93] Ingram was not, of course, claiming that the charter was invalid; only that its provisions were overriden by or subject to those of the chirograph.

[94] CP 40/9, m.41d. The return day first appointed for the jury's appearance was five weeks after Easter. The adjournment then made was to a month after Michaelmas, though if the chief justice, Seyton, should in the meanwhile go to Nottinghamshire the jury was to be taken before him then. In the rejection of the jury for containing no knights may be seen a reasonable insistence on the normal requirement stipulated in writs for juries that they contain both knights and free men; the requirement that the jury should contain at least six knights is more extraordinary and was probably the result of the acceptance by the justices of a proffer to the king for such a jury from one of the parties.

[95] Possibly because Roger was essoined.

[96] CP 40/13, m.66d. The adjournment was from the octave or quindene of Hilary to the octave of St John the Baptist: again there was a provision that the jury be taken by a justice, this time the puisne justice, John de Lovetot, if he went to Nottinghamshire in the meanwhile.

[97] In Trinity term 1276, Roger is noted on the roll (CP 40/15, m.29) as bringing an action of debt for 58 marks against Ingram. Roger had been essoined and it is his essoiner, the anonymous John Pye, who sues the default. Ingram is to be attached for a return day in Michaelmas term. No further stages of the case nor any pleadings in it have, however, been found, and it is impossible to know what significance should be attached to it.

[98] This is clear from the sequel, the reopening of litigation in 1279 with Ingram again demandant and Roger again tenant. Moreover, an assize of novel disseisin brought by one William son of Robert of Blyth for land in Oldcotes in October 1276 named both Ingram and Roger as disseisors, which would probably only have been appropriate if Roger had still been in seisin of some, if not all, of Ingram's land (C 66/95, m.7d); and in July 1277, when vouched by the king to warranty in a case involving land at Sproatley, Yorks, Roger, who was said to be in Wales, presumably with the king's army, was mainperned by men from Oldcotes: JUST 1/1235, m.25d. Roger was also named as tenant of the land in February 1279 by the inquisition into the Nottinghamshire lands once held by Philip of Oldcotes: above, 66.

[99] The detailed specification of the tenements being sought is identical with that given in [1], other than in the omission of the garden there mentioned. Possibly this was now considered as being part of the appurtenances of the land.

[100] They were John of Stoke of Nottinghamshire and Richard le Brid of Norfolk.

[101] CP 40/28, m.7d.

[102] CP 40/30, m.5. The adjournment was made at the octave of Trinity, and was to the octave of Michaelmas.

Ingram was now using was cessavit per biennium, created just a year and a half earlier by chapter 4 of the statute of Gloucester.[103] At first sight, at least, the new action was well suited to the facts of Ingram's case. It allowed a demandant to recover and hold in demesne any land which had been demised in return for annual renders of money or food and clothing, where the payment of the rent or render had ceased for two years or more, provided that the sum of money or the value of the food and clothing amounted to at least one quarter of the true annual value of the land; and clearly Ingram wanted to recover his land, could show that Roger had not made the renders of food and clothing due under their agreement for at least two years, and could also probably show that the renders would have amounted to at least a quarter of the annual value of the land. There were, however, also other conditions which had to be met before an action of cessavit per biennium could succeed. It seems almost certain[104] that the statute applied only to lands granted away in perpetuity, at fee farm, and could not be used where lands had been granted only for a term of years or for a single lifetime.[105] Ingram had granted his lands to Roger only for Roger's lifetime;[106] but now, in order to bring his case within the purview of the statutory action, he seems, to judge from his count as recorded on the rolls, to have claimed that the original grant had been one to both Roger and his heirs.[107] The demandant had also, under the provisions of the statute, to be able, if necessary, to show that the land concerned had lain 'fresh', that is, bare of distrainable chattels,[108] for the two years during which the services had ceased; and although it is known that the land in Oldcotes had lain 'fresh' for part at least of the two years immediately preceding the bringing of the action,[109] it seems doubtful, considering the value of the land, whether it had really lain 'fresh' for the whole of the necessary period. A further potential weakness in Ingram's case was that, although the statute did apply to demisals made before its enactment as well as to those made after it, only time which had elapsed since the enactment of the statute counted in calculating the two years during which services had ceased which had to elapse before the action could be brought;[110] and by Trinity term 1279 less than a year had elapsed since the enactment of the statute. A final, and possibly fatal, weakness in Ingram's case resulted from the way in which the original agreement had been recorded. Roger could probably have argued on the basis of the original charter that the only service, as such, which he owed Ingram for the land, was a penny rent: and that it was only for arrears of this rent, and not for arrears of the food and clothing promised in the chirographed agreement, that Ingram would have been entitled to distrain, the more so as in the original agreement Ingram was given only the right to reënter on a default, and not a right to distrain for arrears. If this was so, then Ingram was not entitled to bring the action of cessavit per biennium, since a penny was nowhere near a quarter of the value of the land.

Surprisingly, when Ingram had made his count, in which he claimed that Roger was now six years in arrears with the food and clothing promised in the chirographed agreement, Roger took none of these possible lines of defence, although any of them would have sufficed to quash Ingram's action. That which he did use was, however, potentially even more serious for Ingram. After an express

103 6 Edw. I, c.4. For the form of the writ see *Reg. Brev.: Orig.*, f.237v; and on the action generally see T. F. T. Plucknett, *The Legislation of Edward I*, 2nd edn (Oxford, 1962), 90–1, and Milsom in *Novae Narrationes*, ed. S. F. C. Milsom and E. Shanks (SS, LXXX, 1963), liv–lix.

104 Some texts of the statute do, it is true, speak of land granted at 'farm' rather than at 'fee farm'. However, the writ based on the statute (see previous note) covered only tenements demised at fee farm.

105 The later doctrine was that cessavit per biennium, as given by the statute of Gloucester, could only be brought against a life tenant where the reversion was to somebody other than the demandant or his heir: E. Coke, *The Second Part of the Institutes of the Laws of England* (1797 edn, citations by original enumeration), 296.

106 See [1], in which both parties agree on this point, though Ingram wishes to make the grant a qualified one.

107 Ingram and his heirs later reverted to the claim that the grant had been only for life.

108 The primary, common law remedy of the grantor and his heirs when the grantee, his heirs or alienees failed to perform services owed them was to distrain them by the chattels found on the land. Only if the land was 'fresh', could they be said to lack this remedy and need the alternative remedy provided by statute. Such seems to be the rationale for this proviso of the statute.

109 It was attested in January 1278 that Roger was leaving his Nottinghamshire lands fallow, and that there were no chattels to be found on them: JUST 1/1238, m.8.

110 This is the rule laid down in the 'Explanations' of the statute of Gloucester, issued shortly after its enactment: *SR*, I, 50. It is referred to, but waived with the tenant's consent, in the earliest cessavit per biennium action found on the rolls: *Park* v. *le Brun*, heard in Easter term 1279: CP 40/29, m.23d.

acknowledgment of the chirographed agreement and of the fact that it had once been valid, he claimed that, at an unspecified date after the making of the agreement, he had surrendered the tenements in question to Ingram, subsequently receiving them back by a new enfeoffment. This second enfeoffment had, he claimed, given the land to him and his heirs unconditionally. He therefore was no longer obliged to perform the services which Ingram claimed; nor could they be in arrears.

It seems clear that either Ingram or Ingram's legal representative at once saw and appreciated the strongest point in this claim, the fact most likely to convince a jury that Roger's account was substantially correct: that Roger's seisin of the land had indeed been interrupted by a period during which Ingram had been in seisin of the land. He therefore took pains to explain just how this had occurred: that he had in fact ejected Roger from the tenements when Roger had refused to find the food and clothing due under the agreement, and that Roger had then recovered seisin of the tenements by an assize of novel disseisin heard before Octon and Beckingham.[111] There had never been any surrender of the tenements and subsequent refeoffment, as Roger was now claiming. The two parties therefore now put themselves on a jury as to whether there had ever been a second enfeoffment or not.

The pleadings in this second counteraction by Ingram against Roger clearly mark an important stage in the development of the dispute between them. In the first action, neither party seems to have been lying. Roger had been able to defend himself by using the technical weaknesses of Ingram's case, more particularly the defects of the written instruments in which the original agreement had been recorded, and a jury might well have found for him quite justly on the facts of the case. Now, however, the stories told by the two parties were in direct contradiction to each other: and it seems plain that one of them must have been lying.[112] Since Ingram's account is that which is testable by other evidence – we know that Roger did recover the tenements by an assize of novel disseisin taken by Octon and Beckingham[113] – it is difficult not to conclude that it was Ingram who was now telling the truth, and Roger who was lying.[114] That Roger was now claiming to hold by an unconditional feoffment in fee to himself and heirs also marks a significant development, a significant upping of the stakes in the dispute.[115] Now Roger was claiming the fee of the land, to hold it in perpetuity: hitherto both sides had been agreed that all that was at stake was a life interest in the land.

After the pleadings in Hilary term 1280, the case was adjourned to the following Trinity term for the production of a jury. Roger now appears to have attempted to secure the dismissal of the case by means of a piece of trickery. At the appointed return day, the octave of Trinity, Ingram, and possibly also Roger, was essoined,[116] and the case adjourned to Michaelmas term, to the morrow of All Souls. Roger, however, notwithstanding Ingram's essoin, proceeded to sue a default against Ingram: that is, waited till Ingram's essoiner had departed, and then claimed that Ingram, the demandant, had neither appeared nor been essoined at the return day to which the parties had

[111] This largely tallies with the other evidence which we have about what had happened in 1273 (above, 71): though the pleading in the litigation of 1274 [1] and the details of the agreement suggest that Ingram's reëntry into the tenements was because Roger had failed to knight him rather than for failure to provide food and clothing under the agreement, the latter obligation only arising once the former had been fulfilled. Ingram may have needed to keep his pleading consistent with the claim he was making in this action that it had been the food and clothing which had not been supplied for over two years.

[112] It would, I suppose, be possible to argue that the stories told by Ingram and Roger were, in reality, not alternative explanations of the same observable sequence of events: Roger seised, Ingram seised, Roger seised; but explanations of two non-simultaneous though identical sequences of events, Ingram having become seised of the land twice rather than once between the date of the original agreement and 1279. This seems extremely unlikely, however, since, if this was so, one would have expected one of the parties to make the point.

[113] Above, 71.

[114] It must, however, be conceded that even Ingram was not entirely truthful in 1279: see above 73 and n.111. It may be significant that Roger produced no charter of feoffment to bear out the story of the alleged second feoffment: no such charter was produced in pleading until 1305 when one was produced by Roger's son John [8].

[115] Ingram, of course, for technical reasons, as we have seen, was also in 1280 saying that the original feoffment under which Roger was holding the land had been of Roger and his heirs. It is, however, unlikely that Roger's defence was influenced by this, and probable that he would in any case have unilaterally upped the stakes.

[116] Ingram's essoin was made before one of the puisne justices, Roger of Leicester, who later 'recorded' the fact [2]. Ingram, according to the same record, claimed that Roger had been essoined at the same return day, but Roger's pleading makes no mention of the fact and the default was sued by him, not his essoiner. It is probable, therefore, that the clerk who wrote the plea roll misunderstood what Ingram was saying on this point, and that what he really said in court was that he, rather than Roger, had been essoined.

been adjourned, so that he had failed to prosecute his action. Ingram's nonsuit, and consequent amercement for failure to prosecute, were therefore duly entered on the roll.[117] A general eyre was then summoned for the county of Nottingham for the morrow of All Souls 1280. To this were automatically adjourned all the Nottinghamshire pleas then pending in the common bench and, as was customary, the bench justices sent to the justices in eyre all the relevant writs and records of such adjournments and pleadings as had been recorded up to that date. The writs and record of *Oldcotes* v. *d'Arcy* were duly sent with the rest to the justices in eyre, John des Vaux and his companions, and Ingram appeared before them and asked that the jury deliver its verdict. Roger also appeared, but objected to the case proceeding and the jury giving its verdict on the grounds that Ingram had been nonsuited in the previous Trinity term. As was usual in such a case, he put himself on the record of the rolls and Ingram did likewise,[118] that is, they both agreed that the case should be decided, on the basis of what the rolls recorded, which of them the rolls supported. The case was now once more adjourned to allow time for the rolls to be searched.[119] During the intervening period, however, one of the parties, probably Ingram, went to chancery and obtained a writ to adjourn the case back into the bench for Hilary term 1281;[120] where, probably after some investigation and discussion between the justices, the default entered on the chief justice's roll was quashed, on the basis of Leicester J's record of the essoin made by Ingram before him, and all proceedings since the parties had put themselves upon the verdict of a jury were in effect declared void.[121] The sheriff of Nottinghamshire was therefore ordered afresh to produce a jury in the bench for Easter term 1281.

When the jurors failed to appear at the appropriate return day, the case was again adjourned, this time to Trinity term, and the sheriff ordered to take appropriate measures to secure their attendance.[122] No entry relating to the case is to be found on the plea roll for Trinity term, possibly because one of the parties had been essoined: but the following Michaelmas a brief entry records that the case has been adjourned sine die because Roger was in prison at Nottingham.[123]

Roger was probably subsequently acquitted of the offences with which he had been charged and for which he had been imprisoned;[124] but before Ingram could restart proceedings for the recovery of his lands, Roger had died. The exact date of his death is not known: it must, however, have occurred between November 1281 and August 1282.[125]

[117] CP 40/34, m.47d: the entry was subsequently cancelled with a note explaining that it had been entered in error since Ingram had been essoined. It is possible that a different justice (or justices) was responsible for adjudging the default than had been responsible for adjudging the essoin, and that this made the deceit easier to practice. Certainly, as far as the essoin was concerned, it was the record of Leicester, a puisne justice (see previous note) and not the record of the chief justice that was followed: while the default was duly entered on the roll of the chief justice. This seems to be a case where the record of a puisne justice was preferred to that of the chief justice.

[118] The proceedings before the justices in eyre at Nottingham are recorded both in a postea to the enrolment of the original pleadings in the bench [2] and in the plea rolls of the justices in eyre themselves, e.g. JUST 1/668, m.8d (des Vaux's roll). The only difference of any possible significance between them is that in the eyre justices' rolls Roger is said to have 'put himself' on the record of the rolls of the chief justice, Thomas of Wayland, while in the common pleas roll, he is said to have put himself on the record of the rolls of the justices of the common bench.

[119] The adjournment was to the Sunday after the feast of St Andrew the apostle (1 Dec. 1280). Since the eyre had only opened on the morrow of All Souls (3 Nov.), the first hearing must have been very soon after it opened.

[120] The adjournment was to the octave of Hilary 1281. Adjourning the case back to the bench was clearly, in this case anyway, a sensible and reasonable idea. The actual judgment in the case was given a fortnight later, at the octave of the Purification.

[121] Curiously, although the default was said to have been sued 'in decepcionem curie', there is no indication of any attempt to institute proceedings against Roger or his essoiner or attorney for this deception.

[122] CP 40/39, m.45d: the adjournment was from 3 weeks after Easter to the quindene of St John the Baptist.

[123] CP 40/42, m.130: the membrane is assigned by its heading to the octave or quindene of St Martin. The Nottingham of the entry is almost certainly an error for York: note F, below, 95.

[124] That he was never convicted of the offences is clear from the fact that his lands did not escheat, and that his son was able in 1284 to claim to be holding by hereditary descent from his father [4]. The fact that in 1286 the jury said in their verdict that Ingram had entered the lands on the day that Roger died and that Ingram was present in the vill 'tempore mortis ipsius Rogeri' [5] suggests strongly that Roger died in Oldcotes rather than in York or Nottingham. If this be so, then he must have been acquitted of the charges against him.

[125] These limiting dates are provided by the date of the commission for his delivery and of the attestation in the bench that he was in prison (note F, below, 95) and by the date when an assize of novel disseisin was being brought against his widow [3].

IV

Roger's death was a severe blow to Ingram's chances of a speedy recovery of his lands, a blow that was potentially more serious even than Roger's imprisonment. True, Roger's imprisonment had led to a complete suspension of proceedings. This was necessary because the law regarded the prisoner as being in a position analagous to that of the madman or minor, incapable of managing his own affairs, and also because the justices regarded themselves as bound to protect the interests both of the king and of the lords of whom the prisoner held, which might have been damaged by collusive litigation to defraud them of their rights against the prisoner's land and chattels on any possible conviction. Once Roger had been acquitted, however, Ingram could take up his action against him at the point at which proceedings had been suspended; and even had Roger been convicted, Ingram would have been able to recover the lands from the lady to whom they had escheated, though this would have meant bringing an entirely new action. The opponent Ingram now faced, as a result of Roger's death, however, was a child aged only one or two, John d'Arcy, Roger's son and heir;[126] and the law was in general extremely generous to those minors who were able to claim that their fathers had died seised in fee.

In most circumstances they could secure the postponement of any litigation brought against them for such tenements until they came of age at twenty-one.[127] Ingram was, therefore, faced with the possibility of something like a twenty-year wait before he could even start bringing an action for the recovery of his lands.

Ingram acted at once. According to the most circumstantial, and possibly at this point the most trustworthy, account,[128] Ingram was present in 'the vill'[129] at the time of Roger's death, and at once took seisin of the tenement by entering the chief messuage belonging to it. Such an entry had much to recommend it. Although minor tenants had considerable procedural advantages, minors claiming land were in a much less advantageous position: their incapacity working here against them rather than for them. Certainly, John would have been able in the circumstances to bring the assize of mort d'ancestor against Ingram for the tenements: but Ingram would in his defence have been allowed to plead that John's father had not died seised in fee, an allegation which he would not have been allowed to use in bringing an action himself against John.

What went wrong with Ingram's plans was not, as might have been expected, that he was in turn ejected by the d'Arcys; but rather that on the Wednesday immediately following the Monday on which Roger's death had occurred and Ingram had entered the tenements[130] he was ejected by the bailiff of Constance de Béarn, lady of Tickhill, of whom the lands were held.[131] What made things worse was that the bailiff, instead of keeping the lands in the hands of his mistress until it was settled who was entitled to hold them, handed them straight over to the friends and/or relations[132] of John d'Arcy for them to hold them in his name.

Just why the bailiff acted in this way and whether he was acting on his own initiative or on instructions in so doing is not clear.[133] What is clear is that quite soon afterwards, in an attempt to recover the lands from which he had just been ejected, Ingram pur-

[126] For John's age see below, n.142.

[127] The only general exception to this rule was that introduced by statute in 1275 allowing writs of entry sur disseisin in certain cases to be brought against minors: 3 Edw. I (Westminster I), c. 47.

[128] This is the verdict of an assize of novel disseisin in 1286 [5]. The main reason for trusting it here is that elsewhere its account seems overwhelmingly to favour the d'Arcy family; but here alone it directly contradicts the account of events given by John d'Arcy's guardian [4]. This suggests that the events were too well known and too fresh in the memory for the jurors to accept or give a palpably false version of them.

[129] Presumably Oldcotes is meant.

[130] The 1286 verdict is here at direct variance with that of the 1282 assize [3] which says that Ingram was seised only from daybreak to the third hour of a single day, not for three days. Possibly the jurors in 1282 intended, by minimising the period Ingram was seised, to make more comprehensible and excusable Constance's action, as chief lady of the fee, in seising the land into her hands, to give rise to fewer awkward questions about the reason for the delay.

[131] Note G, below, 95.

[132] The word *amici* is ambiguous and can mean either; possibly both are meant.

[133] One possibility is that he was acting on instructions from the honor court of Tickhill or on a complaint made there by Isabel d'Arcy. Certainly later on in the century, the honor court is known to have met every third Wednesday: CP 52/writ file for quindene of Hilary 24 Edw. I, Yorks section (session of court on 21 Dec. 1295); CP 52/writ file for octave of Trinity 28 Edw. I, Yorks section (sessions of court on 4 and 25 May 1300); SC 11/543 (list of tenants of honor and obligations, including three-weekly suit to Tickhill).

chased an assize of novel disseisin in which he named as his disseisors Isabel, the widow of Roger d'Arcy, John, his son and heir, John de Launde, Constance de Béarn and William son of Jordan of Tickhill. The assize was heard at Nottingham before Nicholas of Stapleton and Elias of Beckingham, probably on 8 August 1282 [3].[134] There are some curious points about this assize. Although the assize's verdict indicates that the d'Arcys were, at the time the assize was taken, the tenants of the lands which were at stake in the assize,[135] neither Isabel d'Arcy nor John d'Arcy nor John de Launde, who is known from other evidence to have been an associate of the d'Arcy family,[136] appeared in court to defend the d'Arcy interest in the lands; and it was even attested in court that they had not been attached to appear because they had not been found. It is difficult to resist the conclusion that Ingram must have found some way of ensuring that they did not hear about the assize until it was finished and he was being put back in seisin of the tenements.

The otherwise unexplained debt recognisance to Constance de Béarn entered into by Ingram at the time of the 1282 assize also suggests that there may have been an element of collusion about the assize: that this may have been Constance's price for agreeing when the assize was heard not to justify her own action and that of her bailiff in terms of the rights of the d'Arcy family, but merely to claim that she had entered as chief lady of the fee on d'Arcy's death,[137] leaving William son of Jordan of Tickhill[138] to take the sole blame for handing over seisin of the tenements to the d'Arcys even though in doing so he had probably been acting as her bailiff and may even have been acting on her instructions.[139]

Ingram was clearly successful in 1282 not only in making sure that the d'Arcy family did not appear and that Constance de Béarn did not make their case for them even in their absence, but also in persuading the assize jury that his entry had been the justified entry of a reversioner, for they found that he had entered into the tenements 'ut de libero tenemento', a verdict which implies a complete acceptance of Ingram's case.[140] So he was back in seisin of his lands as a result of the assize with the added bonus of a jury verdict in his favour to strengthen his title to the tenements.

Almost immediately, however, Ingram granted the lands to John of Stonegrave[141] for John's life: though whether the grant was made for financial or for other reasons is not clear. It was John of

[134] There are three feast days of St Lawrence: 3 Feb., 10 Aug. and 17 Oct.; but the debt acknowledged by Ingram to Constance on the same membrane, payable at the feast of the Assumption of the Virgin Mary (15 Aug.) in the same year excludes the last. This means, however, that the Saturday before St Lawrence could be either 31 January or 8 August 1282. The latter date seems more probable. In this assize all the lands are said to be in Oldcotes; but the description of these lands tallies with those given in 1280 [2] for all the lands in Oldcotes, Styrrup and Blyth. Clearly the same lands were in question.

[135] It is in keeping with the position of the d'Arcys as beneficiaries of the disseisin but not participants in it that Ingram was amerced for a false claim against them, but the amercement was immediately pardoned. It was by this date necessary to name the actual tenants of the land in novel disseisin, even when they had played no part in the disseisin, if one wished to recover the land which they were holding: Sutherland, *Assize of Novel Disseisin,* 57.

[136] He had received a safe-conduct to go wherever he wished on 24 June 1267, at the same time as Norman and Roger d'Arcy (*CPR 1266–72,* 78); and on 30 June 1267 he had been pardoned together with Norman and Roger and their uncle Thomas for his part in the recent disturbances: ibid., 79–80. In 1277 he served with Norman d'Arcy in Wales: *Parl. Writs,* I, 206.

[137] It is unfortunate that the sole surviving record of the pleadings in this assize is heavily damaged; and that it is therefore impossible to be certain just what exactly was pleaded on this occasion by Constance. Such a pleading would, however, fit the verdict as well as what can be read of the pleadings.

[138] William son of Jordan of Tickhill is almost certainly to be identified with the unnamed bailiff of Constance mentioned in the 1286 assize verdict [4] as having disseised Ingram, particularly as he stated in 1282 that he himself made no claim to the tenements and was in the end the only defendant convicted of disseisin. That he was later one of Constance's agents is certain: in June 1284 he was appointed as her general attorney for two years (*CPR 1281–92,* 127), at Michaelmas 1287 he was acting as her general attorney (KB 27/107, m.51) and in 1290 and 1292 he was again appointed as her general attorney for periods of two years: *CPR 1281–92,* 337, 492. He is also mentioned as a bailiff of Tickhill in the Yorkshire eyre of 1293: JUST 1/1101, m.33; cf. m.33d.

[139] Note H, below, 95–6.

[140] There was, of course, always a danger that, even in the absence of the d'Arcys, a jury might find in their favour. In theory, an assize gave its verdict from its own knowledge rather than from evidence supplied by the parties.

[141] Note I, below, 96.

Stonegrave, therefore, who was the tenant of the lands when, in May 1284, Roger d'Arcy's son, John, or rather his guardian acting on his behalf,[142] brought an assize of novel disseisin against Constance de Béarn, William son of Jordan of Tickhill, Ingram, and John of Stonegrave, alleging that they had disseised him of the land which Ingram had recovered by the 1282 assize verdict,[143] in what was clearly an attempt to undo the effects of that verdict [4]. This second assize was taken before John of Mettingham and Thomas of Sodington at Bultham in Nottinghamshire on 12 May 1284. Of the several defendants, neither Constance de Béarn nor William son of Jordan of Tickhill put in an appearance,[144] and John of Stonegrave appeared only to plead that, if there had been a disseisin, this had been Ingram's doing, as he had entered under a subsequent grant by Ingram. The whole burden of the defence rested, therefore, on Ingram. He at once objected to the assize being heard on the grounds that the 1282 assize had been concerned with the same land and had given its verdict for him against the present plaintiff. To allow the present assize to pass, therefore, would be to allow an assize to be taken 'on' an assize, that is, would be to allow two assizes to give verdicts on the same set of facts, with the attendant possibility that one verdict would contradict the other.[145]

John's guardian was, however, ready with an answer to this argument. The 1282 assize had, he alleged, been collusive; but, in any case, that assize had been concerned only with an alleged disseisin of Ingram and not with an earlier disseisin by Ingram of John. John had been in the tenement at his father's death and been seised for three days until Ingram had disseised him. This disseisin had never been remedied, nor had it even been considered by the previous assize, which had been concerned only with subsequent events. To allow the present assize to pass was, he implied, therefore, not to allow an assize to be taken 'on' an assize. The justices seem to have accepted this argument, for it was adjudged that the assize be taken.

Pleading seems to have taken place in the absence of a jury, or, at least, in the presence only of an inadequate number of jurors, for the assize was now adjourned for lack of jurors to another day about two months later.[146] For some unexplained reason, however, the justices themselves failed to appear at the day to which the parties had been adjourned: and the case stood over sine die for over two years[147] until it was resummoned for 20 September 1286 at Nottingham before the same John of Mettingham and others.[148] A sufficient number of jurors now appeared and a verdict was given [5].

This verdict covered not only the sequence of events since Roger d'Arcy's death, but also the events which preceded it, as far back as the initial 1272 agreement between Ingram and Roger. As to the events since Roger's death, the jury explicitly rejected the account of them advanced by John's guardian in the 1284 pleadings: it had been Ingram and not John who had been the first to enter the lands after Roger's death. The legal status of this entry was, however, called into question by the first part of the verdict which suggested that by the time of his death Roger had acquired the fee of the lands. Possibly because of their uncertainty as to the exact legal position, the assize did not state whether or not Ingram and his fellow defendants had in fact disseised John d'Arcy;[149]

142 John was still a minor in Easter 1301 (CP 40/138, m.25), but was of age by Trinity 1302: CP 40/143, m.70. He must therefore have been born in 1280 or 1281 and can only have been aged 3 or 4 in 1284. See further note J, below, 96.

143 The land was more correctly described this time as being in Styrrup and Blyth as well as in Oldcotes: above, n.134. It is, however, also described slightly differently from the way in which it had been described in 1274, 1280 and 1282 [1, 2, 3]: the single message becoming 2 messuages, the hundred acres of arable becoming 120 acres, the 25 acres of meadow becoming 30 acres, the 4 marks of rent becoming 5, and the two-fifths of a mill decreasing to one quarter. The reason for these changes is not known, though it may be relevant to note that this is the first occasion that the tenements had been specified in a demand by a representative of the d'Arcy interest: and that their figures may have been slightly different from Ingram's. It seems clear beyond doubt, however, that it was still basically the same lands which were in question.

144 Constance may still have been out of seisin of Tickhill: note G, below, 95.

145 The implication was that, if John wished to reverse the earlier verdict, he had to do this either directly by attainting the jurors or indirectly by bringing an action which was 'higher in the right'.

146 The adjournment was to the morrow of St Mary Magdalen (23 July).

147 It is possible that the delay was the result of influence exercised on Ingram's behalf by Elias de Hauvill: below, 82.

148 The others were probably Elias of Beckingham, Walter of Stirchley and Walter of Amersham who had been commissioned in August 1285 to hear Nottinghamshire assizes with Mettingham: *CCR 1279–88*, 365.

149 Jurors in assizes of novel disseisin were allowed to do this by 13 Edw. I (Westminster II), c.30.

and their verdict was followed by further legal argument between the two sides. Ingram, clearly sensing the danger to his position in that part of the verdict which suggested that Roger had died seised of the fee of the tenements, attempted to estop any claim by John as Roger's heir to hold in fee by vouching the record of the common bench rolls to prove that Roger had admitted in court that he held only for life under Ingram's charter.[150] John's guardian, clearly thinking not of the 1274 litigation but of the litigation of 1280, showed himself equally willing to vouch the bench rolls to show that Roger had always claimed to hold in fee by Ingram's charter of feoffment.

These appeals to the record of the bench rolls led to a further adjournment of the case, to 7 January 1287,[151] for those rolls to be searched. Ingram now had the case removed into the court coram rege,[152] but when judgment in the assize was finally given late in October 1287,[153] after the common bench plea rolls had been examined, it was in John's favour [6]. The justices held that Ingram's entry after Roger's death had been an intrusion,[154] since the verdict of the assize which suggested that Roger had died seised of the fee of the tenements was supported by the record of the common bench which showed that Roger, when impleaded by Ingram, had always claimed the fee of the tenements.[155]

V

The crucial factor in Ingram's loss of his lands in 1287, therefore, was that part of the assize jury's verdict which suggested that Roger had died seised of the lands in fee. In view of its critical importance and because the story recounted by the assize is at variance at several points with the account of events between 1272 and 1280 given hitherto, this part of the verdict will be examined more closely.[156]

The story told in the verdict was a long and complex one. It started with the agreement between Ingram and Roger, by which, in return for Ingram granting Roger his lands for Roger's life, Roger agreed to make Ingram a knight and find all the necessary expenses attendant on the ceremony. It was Ingram who was, according to the verdict, to blame for the breach between himself and Roger which had led to him not taking knighthood at the day fixed for him to do so. After the breach, Ingram had been attacked by unnamed assailants; as soon as he had recovered, he had gone to Roger to seek his assistance in getting justice against his attackers. Roger, however, had refused to comply, unless Ingram would provide some form of assurance that he would abide by his counsel in prosecuting them. This Ingram had provided in the form of a charter of feoffment, granting the land to Roger and his heirs, which was deposited with a neutral third party, Roger son of Benedict of Lincoln, who was to surrender the charter to Roger d'Arcy only if Ingram failed to abide by d'Arcy's counsel. Roger d'Arcy had then begun to sue on Ingram's behalf against his attackers until Ingram, without Roger's prior knowledge and without asking his advice, had settled with his attackers for one hundred marks, thereby forfeiting the charter and the fee of his lands. Roger d'Arcy had then gone to Roger son of Benedict, with whom the charter was deposited, and requested its surrender; the latter had, quite properly, refused to comply in the absence of Ingram, but had eventually done so by royal order[157] after having been impleaded by Roger for this purpose. Ingram had subsequently gone to the king's court,[158] and, acting on the advice of one Elias de Hauvill (whom he had met there), he had proceeded to eject Roger from the tenements. Roger had then, however, recovered the lands in an assize of novel disseisin heard before John de Lovetot at Newark, at which he had, for the first time, produced the charter granting him the lands in fee. Subsequently, acting again on the advice of Elias de Hauvill, Ingram had impleaded Roger in the common bench: but, although the plea had been pending for a considerable period of time and the jurors

[150] Clearly a reference to the 1274 pleadings [1].

[151] The morrow of the Epiphany.

[152] This, too, may have been done at the instance of Elias de Hauvill: below, 82.

[153] At Michaelmas 3 weeks, that is between 20 and 26 October.

[154] And therefore, or so the judgment implies, tantamount to a disseisin.

[155] This is clearly a reference to the position taken by Roger in the 1280 pleadings [2]. Even if the court was aware of the earlier pleadings in 1274 [1], to which Ingram had appealed, it is likely that they would have disregarded them in favour of the later ones, since Roger could, on the facts revealed, well have acquired the interest in fee at some date after 1274 and prior to 1280. Ingram must have been hoping that John's guardian would not know of the 1280 pleadings.

[156] See [5] and Appendix II.

[157] The reference is presumably to a writ of judgment after a verdict in an action of detinue of charter.

[158] The reference is clearly to the curia regis in a social rather than a judicial sense.

were uncertain about the details, they were certain that Roger had continued in seisin of the lands and had died seised of them.

The first point which must be made in commenting on the verdict is the complete lack of corroborative evidence for two of the most important parts of the account: the action allegedly brought by Roger d'Arcy against Roger son of Benedict of Lincoln for the surrender of the charter unconditionally enfeoffing him in fee,[159] and the assize heard before John de Lovetot at Newark, in which Roger recovered seisin by pleading the enfeoffment in fee.[160] The second point to be made is that the account has a number of significant omissions, omissions of facts which are well attested by other surviving evidence, but which would have proved difficult to reconcile with this account of the Oldcotes–d'Arcy relationship. The verdict does not, for example, mention the first action brought by Ingram against Roger which was pending in the common bench between 1274 and 1276, and in which Roger admitted that he had only a life interest in the land – an admission which would have been difficult to reconcile with the chronology of Ingram's alleged forfeiture of his reversion to the tenements, which should have already taken place at the time that Ingram brought his action and Roger made his admission, even if Roger was not yet in possession of the charter of feoffment.[161] Nor does the verdict mention the fact that the original agreement stipulated not only that Roger should make Ingram a knight, but also that he should keep him and his servants in food and clothing for the rest of his life, and that Ingram therefore had a substantial and continuing interest in the land – which would make it even less plausible that, in return for just a hundred marks, he should forfeit not only the reversion to the lands but also his own right to maintenance. Nor, finally, does the verdict mention the fact that Ingram's right of reëntry was safeguarded under the original agreement and that he had exercised that right, only to be subsequently ejected himself as a result of an assize of novel disseisin brought by Roger – ejectment and assize being difficult to reconcile with the situation portrayed by the assize verdict of Ingram turning to Roger after the attack and trusting him sufficiently to reach the agreement about the enfeoffment in fee with him.

The balance of probabilities therefore suggests that this account, where it differs from that already given, must be rejected as false; and it is difficult to resist the conclusion that what we have in the verdict is the d'Arcy family's version of the events of 1272–80, adopted entirely as its own by the jury.[162] This version was one woven around certain true and probably generally known elements: the original Oldcotes–d'Arcy agreement, the attack on Ingram and his settlement with his assailants, the second action in the common bench in which Roger had claimed to hold the tenements in fee and in which Ingram probably had received assistance from Elias de Hauvill.[163] The most important part of the story, however, that which purported to show how Roger had acquired the fee of the tenements, was untrue.

159 The action of detinue of charter could, it is true, be brought in the county as well as in the common bench: *Early Registers of Writs,* CC 147, R 515 (pp. 77, 229). However, the verdict mentions Roger going many times (*pluries*) to the king's court to get writs (*brevia*) for the release of the charter, which suggests an action in the bench. No such action is to be found on the bench plea rolls between Michaelmas 1274 and 1279. The settlement cannot have been made before Easter 1274 (above, 68); it is unlikely that the litigation could have been brought and concluded in Trinity 1274, the only intervening term for which rolls do not survive.

160 The assize would have had to have been brought between 1274, when Ingram settled with his assailants, and 1279, when Ingram started impleading Roger in the common bench. There is no trace on the patent rolls of any commission for such an assize; nor did Lovetot act in Nottinghamshire assize commissions during this period.

161 The pleadings in that first action would also have revealed that the arrangements for the custody of the charter granting the lands for life to Roger, that it should be left in the hands of a neutral third party, the mayor of Lincoln, William of Holgate, were suspiciously similar to those mentioned in the assize's verdict as having been made for the custody of the charter granting Roger the lands in fee, the custodian on this occasion being Holgate's immediate successor as mayor of Lincoln, Roger son of Benedict: J. W. F. Hill, *Medieval Lincoln* (Cambridge, 1948), 382. It might, of course, be argued that such arrangements for the safe custody of charters in the hands of a neutral party were common, and were quite likely to have occurred in the case of two different charters; but it seems unlikely that Ingram would have again consented to such an arrangement, after the first arrangement had so signally failed to protect his rights.

162 It is at first sight difficult to reconcile this with the fact that, in its account of events since Roger d'Arcy's death, the assize explicitly rejected the d'Arcy family view. It may be that these later events were too well known for the d'Arcy account to be believed: in any case, the exact sequence of events since Roger's death became a matter of no importance once the jury had by their verdict shown that Roger had died seised in fee, thereby substituting a better reason for Ingram to be convicted of disseisin than that which the d'Arcys had previously suggested in pleading.

163 Above, 64, 71–5.

VI

John d'Arcy, through his guardian, recovered seisin of the lands in Oldcotes, Styrrup and Blyth late in October 1287. He did not remain in undisputed possession of them for long. No later than 18 July 1288 he was bringing an action of redisseisin against two of the defendants named in the previous assize, Constance de Béarn and her bailiff, William son of Jordan of Tickhill, alleging that he had again been disseised of the lands he had recovered in that assize.[164] Since this action, like all other actions brought by writs of redisseisin, was heard in the county court, no record of it survives; it is therefore not known why, or on what pretext, Constance and her bailiff had disseised John.[165] However, either by a judgment in this action or by a settlement reached out of court, John again recovered the lands.

A further challenge to John's possession of the lands was launched by Ingram and John of Stonegrave on 10 June 1291, when they purchased a writ of error, alleging error in the record and process of the 1284–7 assize, and ordering the justices of the court coram rege to correct any errors found in the record of that assize.[166] In Easter term 1292 it was adjudged that the court proceed to examine the record notwithstanding the absence of John d'Arcy, who had been duly warned to appear by a writ of scire facias, but that the examination be put off till the following Trinity term. At the day appointed, not only Ingram and John but also John d'Arcy's guardian appeared; and the writ of error and the whole of the earlier proceedings were enrolled. There was, however, as yet no detailed examination of the record and of its alleged errors, and the parties were again adjourned to the following Michaelmas term. Further adjournments were then made to Hilary term 1293 and thence to Easter term when, finally, the court found time for Ingram and John to show the errors in the record.[167] Since there was a separate procedure of attaint for reversing the verdict of an assize or jury, the legal rules allowed error to be assigned only in the procedure followed in the case under review or in the judgment rendered in it by the justices. Ingram and John therefore confined themselves to alleging two errors in the procedure and three in the substantive law of the judgments in the earlier assize. The errors in process were, they alleged, that the 1286 assize justices had taken the jury's verdict without reättaching the parties or giving them any prior warning of the hearing of the case;[168] and that the justices of the court coram rege had, after an initial adjournment from the quindene of Hilary to the octave of the Purification, failed to make any further adjournment of the case, thereby putting it sine die, but had nonetheless given judgment in the case at Michaelmas 1287 when the parties had no day for appearance then.[169] As for the errors in law, the first had been made by the original assize justices in allowing the assize to be taken despite Ingram's, as it turned out, justified objection that the assize would be rehearing and retrying matters already tried and decided by another assize.[170] The second error had been made by the justices of the court coram rege who had decided on the basis of the charter granting him the lands in fee that Roger had died seised of the lands in fee. That charter was, however, they alleged, of no effect in law both because it had been handed over to Roger in violation of the conditions of its deposit and because it had never been read out publicly nor known about before it was produced at the assize heard before Lovetot. The third error, also made by the justices of the court coram rege, was a corollary of the first two. They had been wrong in supposing in their judgment that Ingram had intruded into the land on Roger's death and had no estate other than that acquired by

[164] C 69/1, m.13; cf. E 371/51, m.25. It will be remembered that neither Constance nor William had in fact put in an appearance for that assize.

[165] See note K, below, 96, for one possible conjecture.

[166] A resumé of the contents of the writ together with the subsequent proceedings are given in [7]. Unlike most writs of error, which alleged error in the proceedings of a lower court and authorised a higher court to examine them, in this writ the court coram rege was being authorised, in effect, to correct its own errors. The availability of such a writ may have been connected with the dismissal of Hengham, chief justice of the court at the time the earlier assize was heard, or with assistance rendered to Ingram by Elias de Hauvill: below, 82.

[167] The adjournments are all recorded in a postea to the enrolment of the record of the earlier case and of the writ of error made in Trinity term 1292: see [7]. Here too is recorded Ingram and John's assignment of errors in the record.

[168] No such reattachment or warning is mentioned in the record [5] though it is said that the assize was 'resummoned'. If indeed it is true that neither Ingram nor John of Stonegrave received prior warning of the hearing, this might go some way to explaining why the jury's verdict so favoured the d'Arcys.

[169] This is, prima facie, an error supported by the record [6]: but it seems to have been a common practice not necessarily to enter all the adjournments in the case, even when these were made.

[170] On this point and the legal issues it raised see Sutherland, *Assize of Novel Disseisin*, 143.

intrusion, for his initial entry had been rightful, not an intrusion; and, at the time the 1284 assize was brought, he had possessed an estate in the land that had been recognised, and indeed in some senses acquired, by and through the assize verdict of 1282.

Before John d'Arcy and his guardian had a chance to reply to these points, the case was again adjourned, to the following Trinity term, and further adjournments continued to be made in the case down to Easter term 1294 when it disappears from the rolls.[171] Curiously, indeed inexplicably,[172] in the following term, Trinity term 1294, however, there is an entry on the coram rege roll recording process on a writ of error being brought by Ingram, but one alleging error in the record and process of the 1282 assize heard by Stapleton [3] in which he had recovered his tenements against Roger's widow, Isabel, his son, John, Constance de Béarn and others.[173] The sheriff of Nottinghamshire had, according to his return, warned Isabel and the others to appear before the common bench at Westminster rather than coram rege: he was therefore ordered to repeat the procedure for the following term, Michaelmas 1294. Further stages of process on this writ are to be found on the plea rolls for that term[174] and for Hilary 1295;[175] after which this action too disappears from the rolls.

There also appears on the patent roll at the end of December 1292 or beginning of January 1293 a commission to John of Mettingham and Elias of Beckingham to take an assize of novel disseisin brought by Elias de Hauvill against John d'Arcy and others for lands in Oldcotes, Styrrup and Blyth.[176] This is the first definite indication that Elias, the man named by the jury in the 1286 verdict as having advised Ingram to eject Roger and subsequently to implead him in the common bench [5], had acquired an interest in the disputed lands. The commission does not reveal the extent of this interest nor how he had acquired it, but it seems certain that he had acquired it from Ingram, presumably as the price of his assistance,[177] and probably at some date between 1282 and 1287.[178] Its extent can probably be gauged by adding together the messuage, bovate and ten shillings' worth of rent sought by Ingram's son and heir Robert from his stepmother in 1303/4, which she claimed was her dower, but he claimed was land demised by Ingram to Elias for Elias's life before Ingram had married her,[179] with the two-thirds of two bovates, half a mill and ten shillings' worth of rent in Styrrup and Oldcotes of which Roger d'Arcy's widow, Isabel, sought a third in dower against Ingram's heir, Robert, in 1299.[180] Elias de Hauvill was clearly a man of considerable importance in the king's entourage,[181] but had probably become known to Ingram through his local connections.[182] Since he is known to have brought his influence to bear in other cases in return for reward,[183] it is not perhaps entirely fanciful to suggest that it may have been his influence which had secured a two-year postponement of the assize in 1284, the subsequent removal of that case into the court coram rege, and the writ of error of 1291.

No record survives of the assize brought by Elias against John. The sequel, however, indicates that Elias must have been successful in recovering the lands, for, probably in June 1294, a further commission was enrolled on the patent roll empowering the justices Battisford and Howard to take a 'certification' concerning a tenement in Oldcotes in which Elias was the defendant and John d'Arcy, Robert of Plumpton and his wife Isabel, Robert of Annesley, Adam of 'Osgoteby' and Robert of 'Osgoteby' were the plain-

171 No further adjournments were recorded on the membrane on which earlier adjournments are recorded; and the later plea rolls have also been checked for the case but without success.

172 It is impossible to see what motive Ingram could have had for wishing to impugn the judgment given in that assize. A clerical error of some sort must be suspected.

173 KB 27/141, m.27 (quindene of St John the Baptist).

174 KB 27/142, m.48 (Michaelmas 3 weeks).

175 KB 27/143, m.15d (quindene of Hilary).

176 C 66/112, m.23d.

177 It is, however, just possible that Ingram parted with the land to Elias in return for a settlement of the debt case Elias was bringing against him between 1283 and 1285 or the trespass case he was bringing against him in 1285: below, n.182.

178 These limiting dates are those of the period during which Ingram had control of his lands. Since Elias was not named among the defendants in the 1284 assize, he probably did not acquire his interest till after 1284.

179 CP 40/151, m.5d. This is presumably a third of Elias's entire holding.

180 CP 40/130, m.255d. She presumably demanded only a third of two-thirds of the tenement because one third of it was held in dower by Ingram's widow. The only satisfactory explanation of Ingram's heir's possession of this two-thirds is that he had successfully claimed the reversion of the land on Elias's death. He had not as yet recovered any of the land held by the d'Arcy family.

181 Note L, below, 96–7.

182 Note M, below, 97.

183 In 1292 he was accused of, and did not attempt to deny, champerty in two other pleas, that is, support of litigants in return for a share of whatever was at stake in the litigation: *RP*, I, 92–3.

tiffs.[184] The certification was, however, probably never taken, for the justices commissioned in June 1294 were on 7 July 1294 ordered to adjourn the case sine die,[185] Elias having gone with the king to Gascony; and the case probably remained so adjourned until Elias's death, which took place on, or shortly before, 6 January 1297 [186]

VII

Ingram of Oldcotes was now also dead,[187] though he had still been alive as late as January 1295;[188] and by June 1300 his widow, Elena, had married again, this time to one John le Keu[189] who held lands in Cornwall.[190] Ingram's heir, who inherited not only a right of reversion to the lands held by Elias de Hauvill but also Ingram's claims to the lands held by the d'Arcys, was his eldest[191] surviving son, Robert.[192]

Robert seems to have acted swiftly at Elias's death. At once, or almost at once, he entered the lands Elias had held by his father's grant, thereby enforcing his claim to the reversion: and he was in seisin of them, or rather of two-thirds of them,[193] by Michaelmas 1299, when he was impleaded by Roger d'Arcy's widow, Isabel, and her third husband, Simon Warde senior, for a dower third of his two-thirds of them.[194] Robert[195] denied that Roger d'Arcy had ever been seised in fee. He said that he had never had more than a life interest in the land and that Isabel was therefore not entitled to dower in it. After some delays due to difficulties in securing the attendance of a jury, a verdict was eventually given, in Robert's favour, in Hilary term 1301.[196]

Even before the verdict in his favour,[197] Robert had gone over on to the offensive in attempting to

184 C 66/113, m.17. The plaintiffs in this case are probably the unspecified other defendants of the previous assize. Isabel was Roger d'Arcy's widow (below, n.194) and Robert of 'Osgoteby' was John d'Arcy's guardian. 'Certification' was a third way of reversing the verdict of an assize of novel disseisin: but one that did not require either the assignment of error in process or judgment (as did error) or the conviction of the jurors of the original assize for making a false oath (as did attaint). All that was required was that the losing party should be able to show new matter in his favour which he had for some reason been unable to raise or show at the time the original assize was taken. The process of 'certification' could also on occasion be employed where more information was needed before final judgment was given in an assize, that is, where there was no judgment to reverse: cf. Sutherland, *Assize of Novel Disseisin*, 74–6. What had happened here, clearly, was that Elias had been successful in the 1292/3 assize and the defendants in that case were now attempting to reverse that verdict.

185 *Rôles Gascons*, III, no.3363. Cf. JUST 1/1299, m.9: an essoin in the case by Elias cancelled with the note: 'Quia sine die per breve regis'.

186 *CFR*, I, 381.

187 That Ingram had died before Elias de Hauvill was asserted in pleading, and not denied, in a case in Easter term 1304: CP 40/151, m.5d.

188 He was still suing at the quindene of Hilary 1295: KB 27/143, m.15d.

189 In Trinity term 1300 Ingram's heir, Robert, was suing them together for the wasting of woods in Bugthorpe: CP 40/139, m.30d.

190 This was attested in court at Michaelmas 1303: CP 40/145, m.345d. The lands were in a place called 'Pelrith', which I have not been able to identify.

191 Ingram had at least four other sons and one daughter: note N, below, 97–8.

192 That Robert cannot have been Elena's son but must have been Ingram's son by a previous marriage is clear from two cases brought by Robert with Ralph of Cotes and his wife Sibyl and Sibyl's sister, Agnes, for land in Norwell, Notts, in Easter 1302 (CP 40/142, m.36; for earlier stages in the litigation see CP 40/135, m.186d; 139, m.30d), in which the demandants' title was based on the seisin of the grandfather of Agnes, Sibyl and Robert, one Robert de Tany. Since Robert's paternal grandfather was Geoffrey of Bugthorpe (above, 66), Robert de Tany must have been Robert's maternal grandfather, but at this date Elena was still alive, and Robert would not have been able to claim on the seisin of his maternal grandfather if his mother had still been alive. There is no evidence, however, that this previous wife of Ingram was named Denise (Timson in *Blyth Cartulary*, xlii), a belief apparently the result of the confusion between Ingram of Oldcotes and the Ingram of Styrrup who was one of the bastard sons of Alice of Styrrup (Welbeck Cartulary: BL, MS Harl. 3640, ff.77, 167), and who did have a wife named Denise: *Blyth Cartulary*, no.131.

193 The other third was presumably held by Ingram's widow in dower; and was the land which Robert sought against her in 1303/4: above, 82. There is no trace on the rolls of an action brought by Isabel for a third of this third.

194 CP 40/130, m.255d. See further note O, below, 98.

195 He was also defending a toft which Henry del Grene held under a short lease, for which he had been vouched to warranty.

196 The adjournments and verdict are entered as a postea to the enrolment of the pleadings. The verdict does not state on what grounds the jury reached their verdict.

197 Robert must have purchased his writ against Isabel and her husband on 6 March 1300, since the scire facias sued out by Robert in Michaelmas 1308 to complete the recovery of the lands he had sought against her in this action, ordered the sheriff to give her warning of the recovery of the lands she had held at this date: CP 40/173, m.105. The writ against John was probably purchased the same day.

recover the lands his father had once held which were now in the hands of Roger's widow, Isabel, and her husband, and of Roger's son and heir John.[198] The process of recovering Isabel's share was slow and not entirely uneventful. At Easter term 1301[199] both Isabel and Simon defaulted, and a grand capë was awarded for the following Michaelmas term.[200] They seem then to have failed to replevy the land in time, for at the next return day Robert sought judgment on their default, and they were driven to deny that they had ever been summoned and to wage their law that this was so. The wager was adjourned to the following Easter term,[201] when Isabel was essoined, and the case further adjourned to Trinity term 1302. In that term, Simon was essoined of the king's service but Isabel defaulted, and a petty capë was therefore awarded for the following Michaelmas term.[202] The case then disappears from the rolls for two years until Michaelmas 1304, when it was resummoned upon the expiry of a protection granted to John d'Arcy while on the king's service in Scotland:[203] from the resummons it appears that process in the case had in fact continued to Michaelmas 1303, and that between Michaelmas 1302 and Michaelmas 1303 Isabel had vouched John, presumably as the warrantor of her dower. At Michaelmas 1304 she renewed her voucher, and the case was again adjourned, this time to a return day in Easter term 1305. John defaulted at this return day, and a capë ad valenciam was therefore awarded against him for Michaelmas term 1305.[204] Successive failures to execute the writ on time or at all led to further adjournments of the case; and it was only in Trinity term 1306 that it was finally adjudged that Robert recover his father's lands from Isabel, and Isabel receive lands to the same value in exchange from her warrantor John d'Arcy.[205] Robert did not, however, at once sue out execution of this judgment, possibly because his suit against John was still pending,[206] and, since he had allowed more than a year to pass since the original judgment, Robert had[207] to sue out a scire facias to warn Isabel that he was now seeking execution of the 1306 judgment before this could be done. This was duly returned at Michaelmas term 1308.[208]

The recovery of Isabel's share of Ingram's lands was accomplished without Robert's title to them ever being submitted to the verdict of a jury, Isabel and her warrantor John allowing them to pass by default to Robert. Things were different, however, when it came to the lands which John held in his own right. The action which Robert brought against John was a writ of entry which alleged that Robert had 'entered' the land, that is, that he derived his title to it, through Roger d'Arcy,[209] to whom Ingram of Oldcotes, Robert's father, whose heir he was, had granted the lands only for life; and that since Roger was now dead, the lands ought to revert to Robert (as Ingram's heir). Robert described the lands as being two-thirds of one messuage, one hundred acres of arable, twenty acres of meadow and thirty-five shillings of rent in Blyth, Styrrup and Oldcotes.[210]

Both parties appeared in court at Easter term 1301. John claimed that he was still a minor and that since his father had died seised of the lands in fee he was

198 He was also at the same time engaged in litigation against his stepmother and her second husband, John le Keu: note P, below, 98.

199 The form of action Robert was using against Isabel is nowhere stated. It is, however, probable that it was an action of entry ad terminum qui preteriit in the post, similar to that brought against John: note Q, below, 98–9, and [8].

200 CP 40/138, m.25: the adjournment was to the octave of Michaelmas.

201 CP 40/135, m.6: the adjournment was to the quindene of Easter.

202 CP 40/143, m.61d.

203 CP 40/149, m.197d. Presumably John was fighting in the king's army in Scotland.

204 CP 40/155, m.22.

205 CP 40/160, m.67d.

206 There may have been a danger that if he sued out execution of the judgment against Isabel while his action was still pending against John, she would recover by judgment lands to the value of those she had lost from the lands John held that were being sought against him by Robert: and that Robert would, by the final judgment against John, only recover the lands John was still holding and not those that Isabel now held. It is possible that it would have required a further action against Isabel before those lands acquired in exchange could be recovered. When Robert finally sued out judgment against Isabel, John's successor in title, Constance de Béarn, was still being impleaded by him; but he obtained judgment against her within the year allowed for the execution of the second judgment.

207 Under the provisions of 13 Edw. I (Westminster II), c.45.

208 CP 40/173, m.105. There is a contemporary copy of this enrolment among the Clifton of Clifton Deeds: Nottingham Univ. Lib., Cl D 56. There is no indication in this entry that the court was aware that John d'Arcy's own lands had in the interim escheated.

209 That is, in this case, by inheritance from: the formulae of the writ could also be used to cover title derived from an alienation.

210 The discrepancy between these totals and those of the 1299 dower case brought by Isabel (above, 82) is unexplained; but the same lands must have been in question.

not as yet required to answer Robert's writ.[211] The case was therefore adjourned sine die until John came of age; this was not long afterwards, for in Trinity term 1302 Robert sued out a resummons against him, and on his default a grand capë was awarded against him, returnable in Michaelmas term.[212] The case then again disappears from the rolls until Easter term 1305,[213] when a further capë was awarded for the following Michaelmas term on a default by John.[214] Both parties then appeared in court to plead: and on this occasion, John made a substantive defence to Robert's action [8]. As might, perhaps, have been expected, John claimed that he was in the land under a grant in fee by Ingram to Roger and he proferred an alleged charter of Ingram to this effect.[215] Robert denied that the charter was genuine, and both parties therefore put themselves on the verdict of a jury[216] as to whether or not it was genuine.

The jury was to have appeared to give its verdict in Hilary term 1306, but the sheriff's failure to secure the appearance of an adequate number of jurors led to repeated postponements of the verdict down to Michaelmas term 1306 [8].[217] Robert of Saltfleetby, John's attorney, now appeared to inform the court that John had been outlawed at the session of the Lincoln county court held immediately after St John the Baptist's day (24 June) 1306, for failure to appear to answer various charges of trespass and felony made against him at a session of Peter de Mauley and his fellows, justices of oyer and terminer, held at Lincoln. Robert of Oldcotes, who may have suspected a trick, denied that John had been outlawed and agreed that the truth be discovered by reference to the justices' rolls.[218]

John's attorney was, however, telling the truth. The records show that John's exaction to outlawry had been ordered by the oyer and terminer justices at their session held at Lincoln on 5 July 1305,[219] for failure to appear before them to answer indictments alleging that he, with others, had taken part in a robbery at the house of the rector of Lea in the wapentake of Corringham, at which horses and other goods to the value of a hundred shillings had been taken,[220] and also that he had been one of the principal participants in the murder of one Ralph le Messer of Nettleton at Stow in the wapentake of Manley at Michaelmas 1303.[221] They also show that he had indeed subsequently been outlawed.[222] His exaction had also, it seems, been ordered at the oyer and terminer session held by the same justices at Nottingham on 19 August 1305[223] for failure to appear before them to answer an indictment alleging that he had with others been poaching in the park of Philip of Willoughby at Oldcotes.[224] John's lands at

211 CP 40/138, m.25.

212 CP 40/143, m.70. The adjournment was to the return day of the morrow of All Souls.

213 During at least part of this period John had a protection while on service in Scotland: above, 84.

214 CP 40/155, m.22. This entry shows that John had essoined himself of the king's service at Trinity term 1304.

215 It should be noted that this is the first occasion on which this alleged charter of feoffment had been produced in pleading, although Roger had been claiming to hold by a feoffment in fee as long ago as 1280 [2].

216 This was to include the one surviving witness of the alleged grant, William de Cressy, who is probably to be identified with the William de Cressy of Hodsock, Notts, close to Oldcotes and Styrrup, who was born about 1245 and died in April 1311: G.E.C., III, 528–9.

217 CP 40/160, m.67.

218 He may conceivably have suspected delaying tactics on John's part or, if he knew of the outlawry, hoped that John would secure its annulment before the justices reported back, so that the case could continue. He would, in any case, have gained nothing from acknowledging that John had been outlawed since this would have led to an immediate dismissal of his case.

219 The Monday after the octave of St John the Baptist.

220 JUST 1/508, m.7.

221 ibid., m.4. According to a jury verdict on one Roger Takel' or Tackel', who appeared to answer a similar charge and who pleaded his clergy, John and Philip of Eleigh had done the actual killing, while Roger and Simon son of Modde of Knaith had been accessories to it. At the same session, one John son of Roger d'Arcy of Nocton was presented by the wapentake of Aveland for having stolen goods to the value of 10s. at Nocton; but since he appeared, pleaded his clergy and found pledges for future good behaviour, this is almost certainly a different man: JUST 1/508, m.11d.

222 JUST 1/508, m.21(1)d. One of John d'Arcy's modern descendants, R. F. D'Arcy, in his *Life of John, First Baron Darcy of Knayth* (London, 1933), 17, being unaware of this evidence, thought that although John's outlawry might 'to modern readers . . . seem a serious matter', it was 'probably nothing of the kind. Most likely he was in attendance on the Earl [of Pembroke] and on this account did not appear at an array of arms. It is very unlikely that he, as a member of an earl's retinue, would have done any punishable wrong.'

223 The Thursday after the Assumption of the Virgin Mary 33 Edward I.

224 JUST 1/676, m.1d: he is described in this entry as John d'Arcy, 'skutifer'.

Oldcotes and elsewhere were probably seized into the king's hands within days of his being outlawed in Lincolnshire, for a subsequent inquisition stated that lands lately held by him in Blyth, Oldcotes and Styrrup had been in Edward I's hands for the year and a day which the king always enjoyed on the conviction or outlawry of a felon, and Edward I died on 7 July 1307.[225] John's outlawry also meant that the land escheated, after the king had enjoyed his year and a day, to the lady of whom the land was held, Constance de Béarn, lady of the honor of Tickhill: and on 7 November 1307, the sheriff of Nottinghamshire was ordered to return the land to her.[226] Although John d'Arcy was subsequently, both on 19 May 1307 and again on 20 January 1308, pardoned his outlawry at the request of Aymer de Valence, earl of Pembroke, into whose service he had entered,[227] and later became in his own right a man of considerable importance,[228] he seems never subsequently to have attempted to regain the interest he had once possessed in the Oldcotes lands and now passes out of the story.[229]

No further stages of process in Robert's action against John seem to have been entered on the rolls after Michaelmas 1306, nor does there seem to have been any note entered on the roll showing that the case had gone sine die because the justices' rolls showed that John had indeed been outlawed. The next entry relating to Robert's attempts to recover the lands does not occur until 1308, when Robert brought, but failed to prosecute, an assize of novel disseisin against Constance de Béarn, to whom the land had escheated, before the assize justices at Nottingham.[230] This was in September 1308: and it is certain that by then he had already purchased a writ of entry against Constance for the same lands which he had probably decided to prosecute instead. Certainly an enrolment of proceedings in the writ of entry in Michaelmas term 1308[231] shows that prior to the quindene of Michaelmas, at which she defaulted, she had already been essoined once.[232] She defaulted again at the return day in Hilary term 1309 to which the case had been adjourned: but, before judgment could be given that Robert recover the lands by these two defaults, it was attested in court that the lands were appurtenant to the honor of Tickhill,[233] which Constance held only for life, and whose reversion belonged to the crown. Judgment was therefore suspended until the king was consulted, and the case adjourned to the following Easter term.[234]

Robert now proceeded to petition king and council,[235] recounting the story of his action against John d'Arcy,[236] explaining his title to d'Arcy's lands, and explaining also how he had prosecuted his action against Constance de Béarn down to the stage where judgment would have been awarded at Hilary term 1309. He requested that they give the justices instructions to 'do justice' in his case. The petition was probably dealt with in the parliament which opened at

225 C 145/68, no.10 (*CIM*, II, no.10). The land was stated in the inquisition to be 1 messuage, 120 acres of arable, 2 acres of meadow and 35s. rent: in fact John only held two-thirds of this.

226 *CCR 1307–13*, 5.

227 *CPR 1301–7*, 528; *1307–13*, 44.

228 G.E.C., IV, pt 1, 54–8.

229 Robert Russell, the man who eventually acquired the lands, did however take the trouble to secure from him a quitclaim of any right or possible right to the lands which his father had once held in Oldcotes, Styrrup and Blyth: Nottingham Univ. Lib., Cl D 329. Since the quitclaim was one to both Robert Russell and to his wife Cecilia, it was probably made after Michaelmas 1310, when Robert settled this and other lands on himself and Cecilia jointly: below, n.258.

230 JUST 1/1347, m.13.

231 CP 40/173, m.185. The lands were now, more correctly, described as being two-thirds of a messuage, 120 acres of arable, 20 acres of meadow and 25s. rent.

232 This indicates that proceedings on the writ must have started in Trinity term or before, and that the case was already pending when Robert was nonsuited in the assize.

233 Presumably in the sense that the land had come to Constance by escheat by virtue of her position as lady of the honor of Tickhill.

234 CP 40/174, m.201. See also [9].

235 [10], which is a contemporary copy of the original petition which does not itself survive. The petition had attached to it a copy of the entry relating to the case enrolled on the Hilary 1309 plea roll: CP 40/174, m.201. A copy of this entry is also to be found among the Clifton of Clifton Deeds: Nottingham Univ. Lib., Cl D 58.

236 Robert was not entirely truthful in this part of his petition, since he suggested in it that he had been seeking against Constance the same quantities of land that he had previously sought against John, which was not true: above, at n.231. He also suggested that the plea had gone sine die at the death of Edward I and that it was only when the plea was resummoned at Hilary term 1308 that it was attested that John d'Arcy had been outlawed. There is, however, no enrolment relating to the plea on the plea roll for that term (CP 40/169) and, as has been seen, John's outlawry had been previously attested but denied by Robert. Presumably the latter deception was necessary to explain how Robert had become aware of the outlawry, without mentioning Robert's earlier denial of the fact.

Westminster on 27 April 1309: and the council seem, to judge from an enrolment relating to the case at Trinity 1309 [9],[237] to have given instructions for the court to enquire into Robert's title to the land before he was to be allowed to recover it. A jury, which was to include at least six knights,[238] was therefore summoned for Trinity term 1309 to give its verdict as to whether or not Constance really had only 'entered' the land, that is, gained her title to it, after Ingram of Oldcotes had granted it for life to Roger d'Arcy, and whether or not, consequently, the land ought now to revert to Robert (as Ingram's heir) since Roger was now dead.[239]

The jury duly appeared in the common bench in Trinity term 1309 [9] and proceeded to give a verdict in Robert's favour. Before he could recover the land, however, he had to put in yet another petition to king and council to request their permission for the justices to give judgment in accordance with the jury's verdict.[240] This was duly authorised by a privy seal writ dated 12 July 1309:[241] and the lands were then finally awarded to Robert.

VIII

The 1309 jury verdict was the first detailed and reasoned verdict to have been given on the Oldcotes–d'Arcy dispute since 1286;[242] it was also the final verdict to be given in the dispute, the one which at last undid the remaining effects of the pro-d'Arcy verdict of 1286, and restored to Robert the remainder (and also the largest part) of the lands which had once belonged to his father. It is, therefore, a verdict which deserves closer examination.

The first thing to be noticed about it is that it concentrates almost entirely on the events of the 1270s, the events which had allegedly led to Roger d'Arcy acquiring from Ingram of Oldcotes a charter, appearing to grant him the fee of Ingram's land – a sequence of events from which it was possible for the justices now to conclude that Roger had never acquired the fee of the land.[243] It says nothing about how Roger had used the charter once he had acquired it or, more importantly, of how the land had descended to John d'Arcy on Roger d'Arcy's death and had subsequently passed to Constance de Béarn when John d'Arcy's lands had escheated on his outlawry for felony.[244] The only subsequent 'event', if it can be so called, in which any interest was shown was Robert's inheriting of Ingram's claim to the lands in question: a fact confirmed by the jurors under interrogation by the justices. While such a narrowing down of the issue to a single point was the normal practice in litigation between private parties in the common bench, it is much more surprising to find it in a case like this, where the crown was effectively the tenant of the land, particularly as it was clearly at a considerable practical disadvantage as against the demandant.[245] There are, I think, however, a number of possible

237 The council's answer to the petition would have been endorsed on the original petition, but this endorsement was not copied on to the dorse of the copy of the petition among the Clifton of Clifton Deeds [10]. There is no reason to doubt that it was accurately summarised by the clerk responsible for the plea roll enrolment.

238 They were to be six 'belted' knights, that is, men who had actually taken knighthood. This requirement as to the jury's composition was presumably connected with the king's interest in the case, and the wish therefore to ensure that the jurors were as solid and respectable as possible.

239 In form, the writ used by Robert was a writ of entry in the post: note Q, below, 98–9.

240 The petition does not survive, but is given in full on the plea roll [9].

241 This writ too is given in full on the plea roll [9].

242 There had of course been (in 1301) a verdict in Robert's favour in the case which Isabel d'Arcy had brought against him for dower in the lands of which her husband had died seised, where the jury had found that Roger d'Arcy had never been seised of the lands in fee (above, 83); but no reasons were given for the verdict, nor any account of the main events of the Oldcotes–d'Arcy relationship.

243 The reasoning behind the judgment seems to be that, since the jury's verdict had shown that Roger had wrongfully acquired the charter of feoffment, he had not thereby acquired any additional estate in the land, which he already held for life by Ingram's grant. Presumably the jury's verdict was intended from the first to allow this inference to be drawn.

244 The justices had been instructed by the council to inquire into Robert's right in accordance with the form of the writ he had brought against Constance. One would, therefore, have expected them to inquire not only into the alleged flaw in Constance's title (that Roger d'Arcy had only held the land for life) but also into the allegation that she had in fact entered the land only 'after' (and by implication, indirectly under) this allegedly flawed title. Nor do the justices seem to have made any attempt to check up, by inquiring from the jurors, as to whether Roger, John or Constance had ever subsequently received a release or quitclaim to the lands from either Ingram or Robert.

245 The crown was hardly in a position here to know much about the detailed earlier history of the tenement, nor even to know of the existence of quitclaims or releases, which would have been with the d'Arcy family or Constance de Béarn.

explanations for this. Despite the apparently negative evidence of the enrolment, there may in effect have been some pleading between Robert's legal representative and the legal representative of the crown which narrowed down the issue between the parties; or, again despite the negative evidence of the enrolment, the jurors' verdict as delivered may also have covered the other points; or, and this is perhaps the most likely explanation of all, the justices may have construed the instruction to enquire into Robert's right to the land in accordance with the form of the writ in the narrowest possible way, one which excluded any possible interest in the subsequent history of the land after Roger had purportedly received a charter granting him the land in fee.

A further feature of the verdict which is also worthy of notice is the closeness of its relationship to that part of the 1286 assize verdict which had dealt with the events of the same period.[246] Both verdicts take as their starting-point a life grant by Ingram to Roger of the whole of his lands: though in the 1309 verdict this is said to have been an unconditional grant, whereas in 1286 it was stated that the grant had been made in return for Roger making Ingram a knight. Both narratives then refer to an attack on Ingram,[247] and explain how it had been this attack which had led to Ingram making a second charter of feoffment to Roger, though this time one granting him the lands in fee. Ingram had, both accounts agree, gone to Roger d'Arcy to seek his assistance in the prosecution of his assailants; that Roger d'Arcy had been unwilling to help him unless he would provide some security that he would not settle with the assailants without his knowledge and consent; and that Ingram had agreed to provide such security in the shape of a charter granting Roger his lands in fee, which was deposited for safe-keeping in the hands of Roger son of Benedict, the mayor of Lincoln. According to the 1286 verdict, the sole condition of the deposit had been that Roger son of Benedict should hand the charter over to Roger d'Arcy if Ingram did break his promise and settle with his assailants without Roger's consent. In 1309, however, the jury stated that it had been agreed that Roger d'Arcy should get the charter only if he fulfilled three conditions, that is, that he should make Ingram a knight, that he should keep him in food and clothing for the remainder of his life in a manner befitting his new status, and that he should provide him with the required assistance against his assailants. Both verdicts agree in recounting how subsequently Roger d'Arcy had approached Roger son of Benedict to ask for the surrender of the charter and had been refused,[248] and in stating that Roger d'Arcy had nonetheless subsequently managed to acquire the charter. In 1286, however, this subsequent acquisition of the charter was shown to have been made in a perfectly proper manner, as a result of Roger d'Arcy successfully impleading Roger son of Benedict for the charter, whereas in 1309 d'Arcy was said to have acquired it only by ambushing Roger son of Benedict as he was on his way to Boston fair and then keeping him captive until he surrendered it.

In its main outlines, therefore, the 1309 verdict is in agreement with the 1286 verdict. Both agree that there had been not one but two feoffments, both agree that the second feoffment was made because Roger had demanded some security from Ingram that he would not settle with his assailants without his consent before he would assist him in litigation against them, and both agree that the charter had been deposited with Roger son of Benedict, mayor of Lincoln. What is curious about this is that it is just this portion of the 1286 verdict that we previously dismissed as complete invention – the whole story of the forfeited feoffment in fee being no more than an ingenious but entirely invented tale, intended to justify the d'Arcy claim to the fee of the tenements.[249]

There are, I believe, two possible explanations for this phenomenon. One is that this part of the 1286 verdict really does possess at least a kernel of truth: that where the two accounts are in agreement, they are both telling the truth. This seems unlikely. For the one transaction which they describe that can be checked against other evidence, the original life grant by Ingram to Roger, neither account is reliable: the 1309 verdict describing it as an unconditional grant, the 1286 verdict omitting to state that it was conditional on Roger providing Ingram with food and

246 See Appendix II for a comparison of the two verdicts.

247 In the 1286 verdict, this is preceded by an account of how, when the day had come for Ingram to be knighted, Ingram and Roger had quarrelled and the ceremony not taken place, the blame for this being put on Ingram's shoulders. No such episode appears, for obvious reasons, in the 1309 verdict.

248 In the 1286 verdict, however, it is made clear that it was a reasonable request since Ingram had settled with his assailants without Roger's knowledge, whereas in the context of the 1309 verdict's story the request is clearly unreasonable as the conditions had not yet been fulfilled that would have allowed Roger to claim the charter.

249 Above, 79–80.

clothing for himself and three servants for the remainder of his life as well as on making him a knight, and neither account noting that the charter had been deposited with the mayor of Lincoln, William of Holgate. There are also good grounds for scepticism about other parts of the two accounts, those which cannot be directly checked against other evidence, which are, when taken together, enough, I believe, to cast doubt on the whole story of the alleged second feoffment. To start with, there are the alleged arrangements for the custody of the second charter. Both accounts agree that it had been deposited, conditionally, with the mayor of Lincoln, Roger son of Benedict. Such an arrangement is suspiciously similar to that which is known to have been made in connection with the first charter: and it is even more suspicious that neither account mentions such an arrangement in connection with that charter.[250] Then there are the alleged reasons for Ingram making the charter: that Ingram wanted Roger's help in prosecuting his assailants, and that Roger refused to give such help without some security that Ingram would not settle with his assailants independently. While this is easily credible in the context of the story told in the 1309 verdict, which says nothing of any previous discord between Ingram and Roger,[251] and just credible in the context of the story told in the 1286 verdict, which speaks only of a disagreement between the two men when the day had come for Ingram to take knighthood which had led to the ceremony not taking place and which had been the fault of Ingram, it is really very difficult to believe in the context of the actual known events of 1273–4, Ingram's ejection of Roger from his lands and Roger's subsequent recovery of the same lands in an assize of novel disseisin.[252] Finally, there is the chronology of Roger's acquisition of the charter of feoffment in fee. Both stories seem to imply that Roger acquired it soon after it had been made: but this is quite impossible to reconcile with the fact that in 1274 Roger was still claiming only a life tenure of the land.[253]

The second and, I think, more plausible explanation of the closeness of the relationship between the story told in the pro-d'Arcy verdict of 1286 and the story told in the pro-Oldcotes verdict of 1309 would be that when Robert of Oldcotes or his lawyer came in 1309 to show Robert's right to the lands to the jury, it was for some reason impossible for him to deny the main outlines of the story told by the assize jury in 1286, only possible to alter some of the details of it: though whether this was because the 1309 jury had been told by the king's attorney of the earlier verdict or because they had become aware of it in some other way,[254] or because Robert or his lawyer themselves were unaware of any other alternative account of those events than that provided by the 1286 verdict, is unclear.[255] On balance, however, the last explanation seems the most likely, since the verdict indicates that the jurors were markedly pro-Oldcotes in their sympathies and willing because of this to accept and advance as their own an account of the events of the 1270s that showed markedly less internal consistency than had the account given by the 1286 jury.[256]

IX

It would have been nice to have been able to end the d'Arcy-Oldcotes story at the point in 1309 when Robert of Oldcotes appeared finally to have recovered the whole of his father's lands, and to have been able to point to the slow but sure triumph of medieval justice. But litigation in the thirteenth century, as now, was an expensive business and for most of the thirty-six years during which the dispute had been in and out of the courts the Oldcotes family had been out of possession of the lands. It was almost certainly, therefore, financial pressures, the debts

[250] It might be objected that there could have been two such arrangements, but this seems unlikely, particularly as the first arrangement had not in practice stopped Roger from obtaining the charter without fulfilling the necessary conditions.

[251] Though this of course makes it difficult to understand why Roger should demand such a security.

[252] Above, 71.

[253] Above, 71–2.

[254] It might conceivably have become, in the local memory, the 'true' account of these events.

[255] That the justices may have been aware of the earlier verdict is suggested by their supplementary question to the jury, asking whether or not Ingram had settled with his attackers.

[256] Thus no real motive is supplied for Roger's wish to have some security that Ingram would not settle with his assailants without his knowledge; and that security turns out to be a charter of fee deposited with a third party, and to be surrendered only after Roger had fulfilled a number of extremely onerous conditions (even less understandable when the first charter granting Roger a life interest is said to have been unconditional) rather than when Ingram had failed to fulfil certain conditions. All these defects result from changes in the story whose general effect is to put Ingram in a better light and Roger in a worse light.

incurred in the process of litigation, that led Robert of Oldcotes in Hilary term 1309, the term immediately following that in which he had sued out a writ of scire facias for execution of his judgment for the recovery of the lands held by Roger d'Arcy's widow, Isabel, to part with those same lands to one Robert Russell in return for the payment of one hundred pounds,[257] and which also led him, not later than the Michaelmas term of the following year, to part with the remainder of the lands he had so recently recovered, to the same man.[258] Thereafter, apart from one appearance in the records in Michaelmas 1314, when he was impleading the prior of Blyth in the common bench for 3½ acres of arable in Oldcotes and Styrrup,[259] Robert of Oldcotes disappears entirely from view;[260] and there is no evidence that either he, or any descendants he may have had, ever regained any kind of interest in the Oldcotes lands.

Who then was this Robert Russell who eventually acquired the whole of the Oldcotes lands? Robert Russell, often described as Robert Russell of Tickhill, was a lawyer. His first known appearance as such is in the Yorkshire eyre of 1293 where he acted as sub-attorney of the general attorney of Constance de Béarn, and as attorney for several other Tickhill litigants.[261] Between 1297 and 1300 he is to be found acting as an attorney in the common bench;[262] but in 1301 he was bailiff of the court of the honor of Tickhill.[263] In 1309 he is again to be found as an attorney in the bench, though now it is for the king that he is acting, in two quare impedit actions, one concerning the prebend of Riccall in York minster, the other the archdeaconry of Richmond.[264] From 1310 to the early 1330s he was active as a serjeant pleader in the bench;[265] and, as was normal for a man of such standing in the courts, was named on a number of oyer and terminer and other commissions in Lincolnshire, Nottinghamshire and Yorkshire.[266] Already in 1299 he was possessed of at least a seignory in Tickhill;[267] and in 1300 he recovered land at Brampton en le Morthen by an assize of novel disseisin heard in the common bench.[268] In addition to the Oldcotes lands he had, by 1310, also acquired one messuage, one carucate and eighteen shillings'

257 CP 25(1)/184/20, no.10.

258 No final concord or other deed seems to survive recording this transaction; but that it must have occurred not later than Michaelmas 1310 is plain both from the fact that in that term Robert Russell was in a position to settle on himself and his wife Cecilia and the heirs of their bodies the whole of the manor of Oldcotes, together with other lands in Great Morton by Babworth (CP 25(1)/184/20, no.31), and from the fact that in that same term Robert Russell was being sued by Ingram's widow, Elena, and her second husband, John le Keu, for a dower third both of the manor of Oldcotes and of 120 acres of arable, 30 acres of meadow and 5 marks rent in the same vill: CP 40/183, m.175.

259 CP 40/207, m.336d. Robert's action against the prior was by the writ of cessavit per biennium given by 13 Edw. I (Westminster II), c.21, and in it he claimed that the prior's predecessor, who had held the land of Ingram of Oldcotes, had failed to perform the services due to Ingram for two years. The prior denied that his predecessor had held the land of Ingram.

260 Neither his name nor that of anyone who seems to have been connected with him appears in the lay subsidy list of 1 Edward III: E 179/159, no. 4.

261 JUST 1/1096, mm.17d, 18, 20d.

262 CP 40/121, m.324d (acting for Master Robert de la Forth in a Notts plea of debt); 125, mm.287d (acting for the abbot of Roche in several Yorks pleas), 296 (acting for several men of Tickhill in a Yorks trespass plea), 296d (acting for the abbot of Roche in a Yorks land plea), 302 (acting for a Tickhill man in a Yorks plea of covenant); 130, mm.376d (acting for the abbot of Roche in three Yorks pleas, and for a minor in the same county), 378d (acting for William de Cressy in Notts and Lincs pleas); 132, mm.220 (acting for Walter Fotstande of Tickhill in a Yorks plea), 220d (acting for a minor in a Yorks plea).

263 CP 52/morrow of All Souls, 29/30 Edw. I: causa clause of a writ of accedas ad curiam to the sheriff of Yorks, alleging that Robert Russell, bailiff of the court of Tickhill, before whom a plea of replevin between Walter Fotstandard of Tickhill and John del Chaumbre of Stainton was pending, received an annual pension of 6s. 8d. from Walter Fotstandard's chamber. It may have been as a Tickhill bailiff, rather than in his own right, therefore, that Robert Russell was answerable for the king's year, day and waste of the Oldcotes lands on the outlawry of John d'Arcy: C 145/68, no.10.

264 CP 40/179, m.208d.

265 *YB 3–4 Edw. II* (SS, XXII), xliv; *YB 4 Edw. II* (SS, XLII), 1xx; *YB 5 Edw. II* (SS, LXIII), xlviii; *YB 5 Edw. II* (SS, XXXI), l; *YB 5 Edw. II* (SS, XXXIII), xliv; *YB 6 Edw. II* (SS, XXXIV), 70–1, 97, 202; *YB 6 Edw. II* (SS, XXXVIII), xxxix; *YB 6 Edw. II* (SS, XLIII), lii; *YB 6 & 7 Edw. II* (SS, XXXVI), 1x; *YB 7 Edw. II* (SS, XXXIX), lvi; *YB 8 Edw. II* (SS, XLI), xlvii, 35, 59, 84, 112, 128, 136; *YB 8 Edw. II* (SS, XXXVII), liii, 77, 84, 133; *YB 9 Edw. II* (SS, XLV), li; *YB 10 Edw. II* (SS, LII), xlvi; *YB 10 Edw. II* (SS, LIV), xlviii; *YB 11 Edw. II* (SS, LXI), xxxviii; *YB 12 Edw. II* (SS, LXV), lxiv; CP 40/244, m.166 (Mich. 1322); 261A, m.13 (Pas. 1326); 273, m.19 (Trin. 1328); 288, m.75d (Hil. 1332).

266 *CPR 1313–7*, 229, 232, 419; *1317–21*, 372, 469, 536; *CIM*, II, no. 493; *CPR 1321–4*, 370, 447; *1324–7*, 74, 289; *1327–30*, 83, 84, 86, 217, 350; *1330–4*, 133, 139, 140, 284, 287, 313; *CIM*, II, no. 1362; *CPR 1334–8*, 206, 289.

267 CP 40/127, m.116.

268 CP 40/132, m.14d.

worth of rent at Great Morton by Babworth in Nottinghamshire;[269] and by 1312, he had also acquired land at Alderthwaite in Nether Hoyland in Wath upon Dearne in south Yorkshire from the Neufmarché family.[270] In January 1313 an inquisition ad quod damnum into the proposed alienation to the priory of Monk Bretton of one pennyworth of rent and the advowson of the church of Hooton Roberts found that Robert Russell also held a half of a knight fee in Oldcotes[271] worth £10 a year (this was clearly the land acquired from Robert of Oldcotes), tenements in Tickhill worth 100s. a year, both held of the honor of Tickhill, and lands in Alderthwaite, held of Pain de Tibetot for the service of one eighth of a knight fee, and worth five marks a year:[272] curiously, nothing is said of the other lands, though whether this was because they had been sold or because the jurors did not know of their existence is not clear.

Although soon after acquiring the Oldcotes lands Robert Russell became involved in protracted litigation with the prior of Blyth arising out of a dispute about pasture rights in Oldcotes,[273] and in the Nottinghamshire eyre of 1329–30 he and Cecilia were impleaded by one John of Hadham for one messuage, twenty acres and three shillings' worth of rent in Styrrup, of which his grandfather had allegedly been disseised by Ingram of Oldcotes,[274] Robert Russell's title to the bulk of the Oldcotes lands seems never to have been challenged, and, probably in the mid or late 1330s, he was succeeded in a peaceable possession of the Oldcotes lands by his son, also named Robert.[275] This second Robert was dead by 1362 and was succeeded in turn by his son Edmund[276] who, in 1379, granted the Oldcotes lands to John de Cressy, lord of Hodsock.[277]

Ironically, then, at the end of thirty-six years of litigation between the Oldcotes and d'Arcy families, it was the successful local lawyer, Robert Russell, who was left in possession of the disputed lands, and not either of the two families. It would be difficult to find a neater illustration of the truth of the general maxim that it is only the lawyers and never litigants who benefit from litigation.

X

What can be learnt from *Oldcotes* v. *d'Arcy*? It provides a useful reminder that the status of knighthood could still in the 1270s possess powerful attractions for a man like Ingram of Oldcotes, even though he was in no sense a professional soldier. It also seems to show that as yet the crown had no monopoly over the conferring of knighthood; and that it was a status that might even, in exceptional circumstances, be

269 In which year he settled that land and the Oldcotes lands jointly on his wife and himself: above, n.258. It is possible of course, that he had inherited this land: but more likely that he had purchased it.

270 CP 40/195A, m.61.

271 There was some doubt about what services were owed for the Oldcotes lands. In a list of tenants of the honor of Tickhill, compiled probably in 1311, Robert Russell was said to hold a whole knight fee of the honor: SC 11/545. In 1315, he purchased a writ to the barons of the exchequer authorising an inquiry into other tenants of the lands late of Philip of Oldcotes in Oldcotes, Gringley and Retford, who ought, he alleged, to be contributing to the scutage of one knight fee owed by those lands for the campaigns of 28, 30 and 34 Edward I: E 159/89, m.15. By 1346 one half of a knight fee was said to be held by Robert Russell and John Styrrup, the other half by the prior of Blyth, the abbot of Roche and the prioress of Hampole: *Feudal Aids,* IV, 115.

272 C 143/91, no.7. For the licence see *CPR 1307–13,* 529.

273 CP 40/216, m.20d (Mich. 1316): the prior and his fellow defendants were said to have been joined together by a corporal oath sworn at Blyth at mid-Lent 1311 and to have depastured the land of Robert Russell and Cecilia in Oldcotes with their animals on 2 May in the same year. They were also said to have attacked Robert's servants when they attempted to impound the animals. For other litigation between Russell and the prior of Blyth see CP 40/201, m.20, and 216, m.100d (this case also reveals the existence of at least two sub-tenants of the Oldcotes fee who, among other services, owed three-weekly suit to the court of the fee).

274 JUST 1/685, mm.31d, 46d. See also note C, below, 94.

275 The exact date of Robert (I)'s death is not known: it may be significant that commissions naming him cease in 1336. In 1337 a debt was acknowledged on the close roll to Robert son of Robert Russell: *CCR 1337–9,* 278.

276 Nottingham Univ. Lib., Cl D 428: renewed quitclaim to Edmund of lands in Styrrup, Oldcotes, Farworth and Nornay which had been granted to Robert in 1357 (Cl D 426–7), and confirmed to him two years later: Cl D 549; cf. CP 25(1)/185/32, no.335.

277 JUST 1/694/2, m.10: assize of novel disseisin brought by Sir Thomas Hercy and others in 1414 against John Longespy of Dunham and his wife Sibyl, sister and heiress of Edmund Russell, who had entered the lands on the grounds that Edmund's alienation to John de Cressy had broken the 1310 settlement of the tenements by Robert Russell: above, n.258. Among the Clifton of Clifton deeds in Nottingham Univ. Lib. there is a quitclaim by one Cecilia Russell to John de Cressy of all right to the manor of Oldcotes and to lands in Styrrup, Farworth and Nornay dated 1381 (Cl D 619): her relationship to Edmund is not, however, known.

purchased from another knight, though the actual purchase had for social reasons to be kept concealed. The detailed conditions laid down in the original agreement about the clothes with which Ingram was to be provided each year, the number of horses for whose upkeep Roger was to be responsible, and the number and type of servants whom Roger was to support on Ingram's behalf suggest, moreover, at least the minimum standard of living that a knight would be expected socially to maintain in the 1270s.

Though it is impossible to say just how typical he was of others in a like position, it is at least of interest to note how Roger d'Arcy, the younger son of a somewhat impoverished baronial family, turned to extortion, disseisins, robbery, trickery and probably also murder in an effort to make his way in the world; and the career of his son, John d'Arcy, seems to show how easy it was for a talented man to rise to the highest positions in the state even after a somewhat chequered earlier career of murder, robbery and poaching. The attack by Thomas de Furnivall and his men on Ingram of Oldcotes, too, helps remind us that violence to the person was still for many people in late thirteenth-century England well within, or only just outside, the perceived range of socially acceptable behaviour, even if it was against the king's peace.

As for the litigation proper, *Oldcotes* v. *d'Arcy* provides in the first action brought by Ingram against Roger an illuminating example of an ingenious attempt to extend the scope of the writ of entry ad terminum qui preteriit to cover something that was in truth neither a lease nor a 'gage' of land; and in the second action brought by Ingram a very early example of the use of the writ of cessavit per biennium which had just been provided by the statute of Gloucester. The proceedings by writ of error brought by Ingram and John of Stonegrave, too, are of some interest as showing the court coram rege apparently correcting its own errors. More generally, *Oldcotes* v. *d'Arcy* shows just how slow English justice could be by the late thirteenth century, if both parties to litigation used to the full the various delaying tactics open to them and the various ways of reopening apparently settled cases. Indeed, had John d'Arcy not been outlawed in 1307, it is quite possible that the litigation would have gone on even longer.

The chief value of *Oldcotes* v. *d'Arcy*, however, lies, I think, in the comparative completeness of the surviving records relating to the litigation and the amount of collateral evidence which can be found and used to shed light on it. Usually, all one has to work on is the pleadings and some of the record relating to the process in a single case and little if any relevant collateral evidence. One, therefore, has little real chance of discovering why the plaintiff is using one form of action rather than another, why the defendant makes the defence which he does, which of them is telling the truth, whether the jury's verdict, when it is known, is or is not truthful. Here, because one has the record of several successive but interrelated cases and also a reasonable amount of other evidence, one can begin, with some approach to certainty, to do all these things. This allows one to understand something of the tactical manoeuvring that is going on behind the bare record set down on the plea roll, something too of how juries arrived at their verdicts, and of how unsafe it is to trust such verdicts even when what they say is supported by a mass of circumstancial detail.

Oldcotes v. *d'Arcy* is only a small piece of a very much larger jigsaw puzzle, whether that puzzle is the structure and workings of late thirteenth-century English society or how the English legal system functioned in the reign of Edward I. But it is only by fitting together small pieces like *Oldcotes* v. *d'Arcy* that we can ever really hope to understand these things, that something like a true picture can ever emerge.

Supplementary Notes to Introduction

A. Styrrup, which is in Nottinghamshire, is about two miles NNW of Blyth, Notts, and about two miles SSE of Tickhill, Yorks, and almost on a direct line between the two places. Oldcotes, which is also in Nottinghamshire, is about two miles WNW of Blyth, and about a third of the way from Blyth to Maltby, Yorks. The Bugthorpe in Yorkshire mentioned in the agreement is clearly not the East Riding Bugthorpe, but a Bugthorpe variously described as being *juxta Malteby* (in a case of 1278, in which it is alleged that there are two places called 'Buggethorp' in Yorkshire, this one, and *Buggethorp super le Wauz,* that is, on the Wolds, clearly the East Riding Bugthorpe: CP 40/27, m.83) or *juxta Tikehull* (e.g. CP 40/136, m.147d). The English Place Name Society volume for the area (A. H. Smith, *The Place-Names of the West Riding of Yorkshire,* pt I, EPNS, XXX, 1961, 139) notes 'Bughthrop' only as a field name in the parish of Maltby, but in a late eighteenth-century Yorkshire topographical work (J. Tuke, *An Alphabetical Index of all Towns, Villages, Hamlets etc. in the county of York,* York, 1792) it is still said to be a locality in the parish of Maltby; and in J. Tuke, *Map of the County of York* (York, 1816) it is shown about one mile east of Maltby, and about a quarter of a mile due south of the road from Maltby to Tickhill. Perhaps because of possible complications arising from the fact that the Bugthorpe land was in Yorkshire – the other lands were all in Nottinghamshire – Bugthorpe is not generally mentioned in the litigation about the lands between the Oldcotes and d'Arcy families. The litigation does, however, also additionally mention land in Blyth, Notts, which may have been regarded as being appurtenant to the other Nottinghamshire lands for the purposes of the original agreement.

B. That Philip had before his death acquired lands in Kibblesworth is shown by a deed (quoted in *Feodarium . . . Dunelmensis,* 105 n.2) by which he agreed to pay by the hands of his men of Kibblesworth seven marks a year to the prior and convent of Durham for the lifetime of Alice of Kibblesworth, the prior and convent paying the seven marks on Philip's behalf to the said Alice. It is possible that his interest was acquired from the same Alice of Kibblesworth. After his death, one of his sisters and coheiresses, Constance, who was married to Daniel of Newcastle, exchanged lands in Styrrup and Oldcotes for lands in Kibblesworth and Matfen with another of Philip's sisters and coheiresses, Juliana, and her husband, Alfred of Barnby (Nottingham Univ. Lib., Cl D 343, 344); and in 1228 one Reginald 'de Radho' and his wife Parnel by means of a final concord remitted to Daniel and Constance all right in 5 bovates, 25 acres and a messuage in Kibblesworth (*Feet of Fines: Northumberland and Durham*, Newcastle upon Tyne Rec. Ser., X, 1931, no. 278), at the same time as they remitted all claim to (the other) half of Kibblesworth to one John of Kibblesworth: ibid., no. 279. The subsequent history of the Oldcotes family interest in Kibblesworth is probably that on the death of Constance in 1240/1, it descended together with land in Nafferton and Matfen to the daughter of Constance who had married Richard de Scruteville (J. Hodgson, *History of Northumberland,* pt III, vol. III, Newcastle, 1835, col. 193), which Richard was the tenant, at the 1250 arrentation of the lands of the serjeanty, of lands in Nafferton and Matfen worth £10 5s. 2d. for which he was thenceforth to pay an annual rent of £4 and to perform the service of a quarter of a knight fee: *Book of Fees,* 1192. From this Richard the land in Kibblesworth probably descended, like the land in Nafferton, to the Walter de Scruteville who died in 1301, leaving a son named Richard, and who had held the Nafferton land of the king for 6 marks (£4) a year (*CIPM,* IV, no. 57); and to have subsequently descended to one Thomas de Scruteville who, according to an inquisition held in 1374, had been tenant of land in Nafferton held of the king for £4 a year and had died in 1351 leaving a son John, who was now aged 30 or more: ibid., XIV, no. 55. Certainly a Thomas de Scruteville, who is probably the same man, was said in a Durham inquisition post mortem of 1357 to have died seised of a moiety of Kibblesworth, together with lands in neighbouring Ravensworth and Lamesley, and to have a son and heir, John, aged 22 or over: DURH 3/2, f.54v.

C. The evidence for this acquisition is only indirect. What is clear is that the manor was subsequently divided between the Eland and Hadham families, descendants of the other two daughters and coheiresses of Constance of Nafferton, widow of Daniel of Newcastle (see the preceding note for the Scruteville family, descendants of the third daughter), which may indicate that the manor was purchased by Daniel and Constance or either of them, but is more likely to mean that it too was inherited from Philip of Oldcotes.

The Eland moiety of manor and advowson is first mentioned in the inquisition post mortem of William of Eland in 1281 (*CIPM,* II, no. 396), but this, in mentioning also William's lands at West Matfen, Nafferton and Lorbottle, allows him to be identified with the William of Eland who succeeded his father, Richard, in lands in these places in 1261: ibid., I, no. 494. This Richard can in turn be identified with the Richard of Eland who was married to one of the daughters of Constance of Nafferton in 1240/1 (Hodgson, *Northumberland,* pt III, vol. III, col. 193), and whose share of the serjeanty lands was arrented in 1250: *Book of Fees,* 1192. The William of Eland who died in 1281 was succeeded by his son Richard, who in turn was succeeded in 1290 by a brother named John: *CIPM,* II, no. 767. It was this John who in 1295 made an agreement with John of Hadham in Seaham church to observe the original division of their common inheritance made between Hawise of Hadham and Maud of Eland: R. Surtees, *The History and Antiquities of the County Palatine of Durham* (London, 1816–40), I, 269. The agreement of 1295 is the first evidence indicating a possible Hadham interest in Seaham: but the Hawise of Hadham mentioned in the agreement was clearly the unnamed third daughter of Constance of Nafferton who was married to Walter of Hadham at her mother's death in 1240/1 (Hodgson, *Northumberland,* pt III, vol. III, col. 193) and who was still a joint tenant with Walter of the Northumberland serjeanty lands in 1274/5 (*Rotuli Hundredorum* . . . (RC, 1812–18), II, 21). The John of Hadham of the 1295 agreement seems to have succeeded his mother (who is here called Hawise de Scouland) in her Northumberland lands, and therefore presumably also at Seaham, in 1281 (*CIPM,* II, no. 394); and in 1303 he settled his lands in Seaham on his son and heir, Thomas of Hadham: Surtees, *Durham,* I, 269. By 1329/30, this Thomas had been succeeded by another John, to judge from pleadings in the Nottinghamshire eyre on a writ of entry for land in Styrrup brought on an alleged disseisin of the John of Hadham of Edward I's reign by Ingram of Oldcotes (JUST 1/685, m.31d). That the two John of Hadhams are the same is clear from a note in the Welbeck cartulary (BL, MS Harl. 3640, f.167) which mentions John of Hadham, the descendant of Constance of Nafferton, as having been disseised of land in Styrrup because he had refused to do homage to the lord of Oldcotes; and it was probably this John who died seised of land in Seaham in 1345: *Registrum Palatinum Dunelmense,* ed. T. D. Hardy (RS, 1873–8), IV, 367–8.

D. For the mandates to the sheriffs of Lincs and Notts issued on 20 September 1219 which ordered them to restore to Philip these lands, which Master Alan had given to Philip during his lifetime, see *Rot. Litt. Claus.,* I, 400, 400b. The lands had originally been granted to Master Alan by King Richard, a grant which John confirmed in 1200: *Rot. Chart.,* 48. The 1219 mandate to the sheriff of Lincs and the 1200 confirmation speak only of lands in Lincoln city, but Philip seems also to have acquired from Master Alan an interest in Canwick, just outside Lincoln: *Book of Fees,* 177, 360, 1041. All the Nottinghamshire lands, other than mills at Retford, were part of the former royal soke of Oswaldbeck: 75s. 3d. was allowed the sheriff of Notts in the farm of his county for this land. This allowance was stated until the last quarter of 3 Henry III to be for land granted to Master Alan de Bolsover; thenceforth the allowance was for land held by Philip, and then by his heirs: *PR 16 John,* ed. P. M. Barnes (PRS, New ser., XXXV, 1959), 156; E 372/63, m.16; E 372/125, m.22; etc.

E. Philip of Oldcotes had owed jointly with Amery, archdeacon of Durham, the sum of £651 6s. 6d., being the debit balance on an account for the custody of the vacant bishopric of Durham from Martinmas 1211 to Martinmas 1212 as entered on the pipe roll for 14 John: *PR 14 John,* ed. P. M. Barnes (PRS, New ser., XXX, 1954), 46. This debt subsequently disappears from the pipe roll, only to reappear again over half a century later in John le Moyne's account for the honor of Peverel in the counties of Leicester, Buckingham, Oxford and Northampton for the period 8 December 1268 to 8 September 1270, entered on the pipe roll for 55 Henry III: E 372/115, m.4. The reasons for its reappearance at this date and in this place on the roll are not known: though it may be relevant to the latter question that Philip had at one time held half a knight fee of the honor of Peverel in Leicestershire in right of his wife: *PR 3 John,* 99; *PR 14 Hen. III,* ed. C. Robinson (PRS, New ser., IV, 1927), 86; *CRR,* V, 311; VII, 311. In the following year the debt was transferred to the Northumberland section of the roll (E 372/116, m.23d), where it continued to appear each year down to 8 Edward I.

Responsibility for the debt was then divided equally between the tenants of the lands of both debtors, Philip's share of the debt being further divided between the tenants of his lands in Northumberland and Nottinghamshire, and the individual responsibility of the Northumberland tenants recorded in full on the roll: E 372/124, m.12d. The pipe roll for the following year records in full the individual shares of the Nottinghamshire tenants in the debt: E 372/125, m.22d. These apportionments were based on the valuations of the lands once held by Philip of Oldcotes made by juries before a clerk of the exchequer, Richard of Stamford, in February 1279; separate inquisitions being held in Nottinghamshire (E 143/1/7, no. 15, mm.1–2) and Northumberland: ibid., no. 15, m.3, and no.19. It is from the former that the valuation of the lands which Ingram inherited from Philip is derived. Previous inquisitions into the tenants of Philip's lands in Northumberland had been held before the local sheriff in February and June 1278 (E 143/1/6, no. 7; 7, no. 3): and it was probably about this time that an inquest, now damaged, was held to inquire whether Philip of Oldcotes had held any land of the honor of Lancaster in Lincolnshire: E 143/1/2, no.33. For other references relating to this apportionment see E 159/47, m.11; E 159/51, m.11; E 13/6, m.20. The tenants of the Durham lands, the fishery of Pool and the lands Philip acquired from Master Alan of Bolsover all seem to have escaped inclusion in the apportionment, though the exchequer was at least aware of Philip's interest in the fishery (above, n. 18) and that he had held land in Lincolnshire.

F. Roger had been indicted in the Nottinghamshire eyre of 1280–1 for the homicide of his former servant, Gilbert of Nettleton; but he seems to have been cleared of the charge after having pleaded his clergy during the course of that eyre, that is, probably by December 1280 and, at latest, by June 1281, by the verdict of an ex officio jury: JUST 1/669, m.5. In the Yorkshire eyre of 1279–81, however, his exaction had been ordered after he had been presented by the wapentake of Birdforth for the robbery of a 'certain vicar' coming from London by way of Stamford and crossing Allerton moor: JUST 1/1070, m.23 (that this is the same Roger d'Arcy is clear from the fact that it was attested that he possessed lands and chattels at Oldcotes, Notts); and subsequently, probably in late November or early December 1281, two of the justices who had been among those holding the Yorkshire eyre, the chief justice, John des Vaux, and Roger Loveday, were commissioned to deliver York gaol of Roger d'Arcy, who had surrendered to gaol after having been put in exigent for robbery and other trespasses: C 66/101, m.22d (*CPR 1281–92,* 42).

G. Constance de Béarn, vicomtesse of Marsan, was the widow of Henry of Almain, murdered at Viterbo in 1271. In 1272 she was claiming the castle and honor of Tickhill as part of her dower (*CPR 1266–72,* 619); and in May 1274 she gained partial control of these (*CPR 1272–81,* 49; but see ibid., 58 and *Rôles Gascons,* ed. F. Michel and C. Bémont (Paris, 1885–1906), II, no. 21). In November 1276, Edward I seems to have resumed control of them (*CFR,* I, 75), a control which he maintained until March 1279 when they were again restored to her: *CPR 1272–81,* 305. In January 1283, Constance was still being styled 'lady of Tickhill' (*CPR 1281–92,* 54), and as late as July 1283 she was still on good enough terms with Edward for payments due from the Bordeaux customs under her dower arrangements to be ordered to be made: *Rôles Gascons,* II, no. 771. Later in 1283, and for most of 1284, as the result of a dispute over the county of Bigorre in Gascony (F. M. Powicke, *The Thirteenth Century 1216–1307* (Oxford, 1953), 287 n.1), Tickhill was again in the king's hands (hence the references in Kirkby's quest to land held of the king of the honor of Tickhill: e.g. *Feudal Aids,* VI, 1–7). The Bigorre dispute was finally settled in October 1284 (*Rôles Gascons,* II, nos. 815–6, and cf.779–86), and the honor and castle probably restored to her at about the same time (Wheatley, a demesne manor of the honor, was in her hands by Michaelmas 1284: E 136/3/3; the Nottinghamshire section of Kirkby's quest refers to her as lady of the honor of Tickhill). She then remained in control of the honor, probably continuously, till 1294/5, when she took the wrong side in Edward I's French war; for evidence of her interest in Tickhill during this period see e.g. *CPR 1281–92,* 353 (4 May 1290), and JUST 1/1098, m.46 (Yorks eyre, 1293). By December 1295 at latest, Edward was again in control of the honor (*CFR,* I, 368: but see SC 6/1087/16, m.2, which states that Edward I did not resume control of Tickhill till 9 January 1296), which he granted in August 1299 to Amaneus de la Bret: *CPR 1292–1301,* 433. Constance again recovered the honor in 1304 (*CPR 1301–7,* 290), holding it until June 1312: *CFR,* II, 137.

H. It is possible that there is another explanation for the way in which Constance de Béarn and William son of Jordan of Tickhill changed sides during the course of 1282. It may have been at this time that Ingram entered Constance's service: certainly in Hilary term 1283 he and his son Peter and one William le Keu of Wysall were being impleaded in the common bench by the abbot of Garendon for distraining him by plough-animals at Rempstone in Nottinghamshire and driving the distresses into Yorkshire (CP 40/48, m.11d), the abbot simultaneously impleading one William de Bowes of Costock also in the common bench in an action of fin fet to acquit him of services being demanded by the keeper of the honor of Tickhill for lands in Rempstone (ibid.), and in the same term John de Lovetot, probably to be identified with the justice of that name, was impleading Ingram, William son of Jordan of Tickhill and Bernard 'le Gascuyn', constable of Tickhill, for carrying off goods worth twenty marks from his house at Car Colston in Nottinghamshire and various other related trespasses (CP 40/48, m.1d), both pleas suggesting that, at the time of the misdeeds complained of, Ingram was an agent or some sort of bailiff for Constance de Béarn at Tickhill.

I. John was the third son but eventual heir of Simon of Stonegrave, and married one of the heiresses to the Beauchamp barony of Bedford. He served against the Welsh in 1277, 1283 and 1287, against the Scots in 1291, and in Gascony in 1294; and was frequently commissioned for enquiries in Yorkshire, including the 1279 hundred rolls inquiry: G. E. C., XII, pt 1, 276, (Stayngreve). Although at his death in 1295 he held no land of the honor of Tickhill (*CIPM,* III, nos. 277–8), in 1277 he had acquired a five-year lease and then a life lease of land in Stainton, held of the honor of Tickhill, and about three miles east of Tickhill itself: *CPR 1272–81,* 203, 242. An undated and damaged letter from Anthony Bek to the chancellor, Burnell, which must date from before July 1284 when Bek was elected bishop of Durham, suggests that Stonegrave entered the lands during the period in 1283–4 when the honor of Tickhill was in the king's hands (above, note G), since Bek asks for the manor of Oldcotes, seized into the king's hands because it had been suggested to the king that Stonegrave had entered it without the king's permission, to be returned to Stonegrave, as he had received the permission of Thomas de Normanville, custodian of the honor, to enter it: SC 1/22, no. 107.

J. John d'Arcy's guardian is not named in the 1284 pleadings [4], but after the assize was resummoned, and when there were further pleadings on it, in 1286, he is named as Robert of 'Osegoteby'. Although there are three Osgodbys or Osgoodbys in Lincolnshire and another three in Yorkshire, which makes identification of men with this toponymic problematic, it does seem quite possible that Robert was a relation of the important and well known chancery clerk, Adam of 'Osgoteby': certainly an Adam of 'Osegoteby' was named together with Robert, John d'Arcy, John's mother, Isabel, and her second husband, Robert of Plumpton, in a writ relating to subsequent proceedings concerning this land in August 1294: above, 82–3. Robert of 'Osegoteby' seems himself to have been an associate of Isabel's second husband. In 1300 he occurs with Robert's son, also named Robert, Isabel, and Isabel's third husband, Simon Warde senior, as an executor of Robert of Plumpton's will: CP 40/134, m.185.

K. One possible conjecture to explain the disseisin alleged in 1288 is that Constance may have been acting to safeguard the feudal incidents hitherto owed for the Oldcotes-Styrrup lands. Ingram of Oldcotes had held them by military tenure (above, 66) and therefore owed scutage, and his heirs, if under age, would probably have been in wardship to the lords of Tickhill. John d'Arcy seems to have claimed to be holding in socage, with Ingram as mesne receiving a nominal annual rent, possibly the penny laid down in the 1272 agreement: this would explain why John's guardian, as named in the pleadings of 1286, was an associate of Isabel d'Arcy's second husband (above, note J), Isabel being the rightful guardian of any land held in socage descending to John from his father. It would also explain why, as will be seen, Isabel brought an action against John for her dower in 1297 (below, note O). Until John came to the age of fifteen, the age at which a socage wardship ended, Isabel would have held the whole of the lands which Roger held at his death, two-thirds as socage guardian, one-third in dower, with no need to physically divide them. Once the wardship ended, however, some sort of partition was necessary. Constance may have been trying to insist that John hold directly of her and perform military service, thereby preserving the value of the feudal incidents the land owed.

L. Elias de Hauvill first appears in the records in 1276 when arrested for various trespasses after having been employed in the king's service in Gascony as custodian of the castles of Bayonne and Sault-de-Navailles (*CCR 1272–9,* 304; *CPR 1272–81,* 194); he was soon released and in December 1276 had permission to bring five horses over from Wissant for the king's use: ibid., 184. In 1277 he was on the king's service in Wales, where he acted as one of the marshals of the army in West Wales (*CPR 1272–81,* 194;

E 101/3/19); and in 1280 was one of the witnesses to a grant to John le Butler made on the king's behalf by the king's steward: *CPR 1272–81,* 426. In 1283 he was again serving in Wales (*CCW 1244–1326,* 14), and in 1284/5 served with Walter of Bath, a canon of Wells, on an embassy to the papal curia which was intended to secure the grant of a crusading tenth: *CPR 1281–92,* 135; SC 1/47, no. 125; *Foedera,* I, pt ii, 652, 659. In 1285 and 1286 he was in receipt of a fee in the royal household (C 47/4/3, m.28); and at the end of 1286 he went on another embassy with Walter of Bath, this time to the king of France: ibid., m.30d. During 1288/9 he was abroad with the king (*CCR 1288–96,* 37; *Rôles Gascons,* II, no. 1442), and in January 1290 he was once more sent abroad on the king's service: *CPR 1281–92,* 337–8. In May 1290 in a Gascon grant he was styled a knight of the king's household (*Rôles Gascons,* II, no. 1785), and in September and November 1290 he received protections while on the king's service in Scotland: *CPR 1281–92,* 384, 412. It was he that was sent with Anthony Bek to meet the Maid of Norway and her father: J. Stevenson, *Documents Illustrative of the History of Scotland* (Edinburgh, 1870), I, 144–5. In March 1291 the castle and forest of Rockingham were committed to him during pleasure (*CFR,* I, 290; *CPR 1281–92,* 424); to these were added, in June 1293, the stewardship of the king's forest between the bridges of Oxford and Stamford: *CFR,* I, 324. In 1291 and 1292 he was on the king's business in Scotland (*Foedera,* I, pt ii, 768, 772; *CPR 1281–92,* 434), and in 1294 he went with Edward I to Gascony: e.g. *Rôles Gascons,* II, nos. 2743–5, 2883, 3011. He was also employed between 1278 and 1294 on various judicial commissions: *CPR 1272–81,* 294; *1281–92,* 211, 323, 510, 521; *1292–1301,* 45, 46.

M. Elias held land at Braithwell, two miles north of Maltby (*Early Yorkshire Charters,* VIII, ed. C. T. Clay (Yorks Arch. Soc., Rec. Ser., Extra ser., VI, 1949), 170–1; *CChR,* II, 339; CP 40/89, m.51d), close to Oldcotes and Styrrup: for Ingram's connections with Braithwell, see above, n.44. They had probably become acquainted by 1280, the year in which, according to pleadings in a trespass case heard in the court coram rege in Trinity term 1285 (KB 27/92, m.33; for earlier stages see KB 27/75, m.5; 79, m.17d; 81, m.8d), Ingram took chattels of Elias to the value either of a hundred shillings (this is the sum mentioned in the pleadings) or of a hundred pounds (this is the sum mentioned in the earlier stages of the case) at the house of William of Dunton at London. No verdict has been found in this case, nor do the pleadings explain the exact circumstances of the case. Also unexplained is an action of debt Elias brought against Ingram in the common bench, of which procedural stages are to be found between Easter term 1283 and Hilary term 1285, and from which Elias had licence to recede in Trinity term 1285. CP 40/49, m.19d, 50, m.30; 51, m.62d; 53, m.66; 55, m.54; 57, m.38d; 58, m.71. The amount in question is probably the 50 marks mentioned in the initial enrolment, though subsequent enrolments saw its transmutation into 500 and then 20 marks.

N. In addition to his heir Robert, Ingram of Oldcotes had at least four other sons and one daughter: (1) *William,* who was named among the defendants in an assize of novel disseisin concerning land in Blyth in 1271 (JUST 1/1052, m.8), was among those appealed by the approver, Peter of 'Scabbehawe' in September 1274 (above, 69), and was among those put in exigent after the Yorkshire eyre of 1279–81 for a robbery at Hampole: JUST 1/1060, mm.18d, 19. (2) *Gilbert,* who was the son entrusted with the duty of putting Roger in seisin of Ingram's lands in 1272 (above, n.64), and was probably also among those appealed in 1274: above, 69. (3) *Ingram,* who was being impleaded by Roger d'Arcy's widow, Isabel, and her third husband, Simon Warde, for a dower third of 6 marks rent in Oldcotes at Michaelmas term 1298, and who claimed that Roger had never been seised of the rent in fee either at the time of their marriage or since: CP 40/125, m.38. The Oldcotes in the plea roll enrolment of this case is said to be an Oldcotes by Carlton in Lindrick; and in an original writ relating to the case, returnable at the octave of Michaelmas 1298 and issued on 11 August, the rent is said to be both in Oldcotes by Carlton and Oldcotes by Tickhill: CP 52/Edward I. It is, however, clear that Oldcotes by Carlton and Oldcotes by Tickhill are, at most, two sides of the same vill, since the Oldcotes near Blyth and Styrrup lies about 2½ miles north of Carlton in Lindrick and about 3 miles south of Tickhill. (4) *Peter,* impleaded with his father in the common bench in Hilary term 1283 for distraining the abbot of Garendon by his plough-animals at Rempstone (above, note H). (5) *Margery,* who was found in 1279 not to hold any of the lands once held by Philip of Oldcotes (E 143/1/7, no. 15), and who is probably to be identified with the Margery married to John Syriot otherwise Myniot, who claimed to hold 1 acre of land in Oldcotes jointly with her husband by Ingram's feoffment in the Nottinghamshire eyre of 1280/1, when her husband lost it by default to Simon of Styrrup: JUST 1/664, m.16d.

O. Isabel and Simon were also claiming at the same time (above, 83–4) a dower third of the lands held by John, which were described as 1 messuage, 2 bovates and 26 acres of arable, 22 acres of meadow and 22s. rent in Oldcotes and Styrrup. John, with the court's permission, conceded her claim. Isabel's second husband, Robert of Plumpton, was still alive in 1294 when he was among those bringing a certification of an assize of novel disseisin for lands in Oldcotes (above, 82–3); he was dead by 28 February 1297 when Isabel alone purchased a writ of dower against John for land Roger had held in Oldcotes, Styrrup and Blyth: CP 52/quindene of Easter, 25 Edw. I. Isabel was married to Simon Warde by Michaelmas 1298, when together they sued Ingram's son Ingram for a rent in Oldcotes: CP 40/125, m.135. After the death of Simon in 1306, she married yet again, this time to Henry of Keighley: G. E. C., XII, pt 2, 347; W. P. Baildon, 'The Keighley Family', *Yorks Arch. Jnl,* XXVII (1924), 20–1. The mistaken belief that the Isabel who was married successively to Robert of Plumpton, Simon Warde, and Henry of Keighley, was the daughter of Serlo of Westwick (G.E.C., XII, pt 2, 347; W. P. Baildon, *Baildon and the Baildons* [n.d., privately, Letchworth, 1912–27], I, 235) is due to a confusion between two different men named Robert of Plumpton, both of whom were sons of two different men named Nigel of Plumpton. The first Robert who was a son (but not the heir) of Nigel of Plumpton was indeed married to an Isabel who was the daughter of Serlo of Westwick, but the marriage took place in 1208 and Robert was dead by mid-century: *Yorkshire Deeds,* V, ed. C. T. Clay (Yorks Arch. Soc., Rec. Ser., LXIX, 1926), 102–4. The second Robert, the Robert married to this Isabel, was not only the son but also the heir of another Nigel of Plumpton and aged only 4½ in 1271: *CIPM,* I, no. 751. This Isabel was the daughter of Sir William d'Aton: G. E. C., IV, pt 1, 55.

P. At Trinity term 1300 Robert of Oldcotes was bringing an action against his stepmother and her second husband, John le Keu, for wasting woods in Bugthorpe which he had granted to Elena for life: CP 40/139, m.30d; for subsequent stages in the mesne process see CP 40/135, m.169; 136, m.147d. After continued defaults, it was finally adjudged at Easter 1302, under the provisions of the statute 13 Edw. I (Westminster II), c.14, that the sheriff of Yorks go and view the alleged waste: CP 40/142, m.28. At Hilary 1303 he returned that he and a jury had found waste to the value of 14s.: ibid.: recorded in a postea. It was therefore adjudged, under 6 Edw. I (statute of Gloucester), c.5, that Robert recover the place wasted and triple the damages: but Robert had considerable difficulty in securing these damages: CP 40/147, m.11; 148, m.42; 145, m.345d. Robert also commenced at Trinity 1303 an action against John and Elena for the recovery of one messuage, one bovate and 10s. rent in Oldcotes: CP 40/148, m.42. At Easter 1304 Elena came and prayed to be 'received' just as judgment was about to be given by default, claiming that she held in dower as of the endowment of Ingram. Robert claimed that Ingram had never been seised of the land at any time during his marriage to Elena, since he had demised the land to Elias before his marriage to her and had predeceased Elias: CP 40/151, m.5d. Robert also impleaded John and Elena in 1303/4 for the return of twelve charters: for procedural stages see CP 40/146, m.35d; 148, m.68; 145, m.385d; 151, m.91.

Q. All writs of entry alleged a single flaw in the present tenant's title, as a result of which the demandant had a better title to the land than the tenant in question. Where the present tenant was the first to hold under the flawed title, or where the subsequent devolutions of the tenement could be described in the writ by the use just once each of the Latin prepositions *per* and *cui* (the number of devolutions this would cover varied with the kind of flaw in title alleged), then the demandant had to bring a writ 'within the degrees', one which did mention the flaw in title and the subsequent devolutions of the tenement; but if there had been so many devolutions that they could not all be comprehended within a writ of this form, then from 1263/7, by statutory provision, the demandant could bring a writ of entry in the post, alleging simply that the tenant had entered the land after (and by implication indirectly under) an original 'wrongful' transaction which 'flawed' his title to the land without recounting its subsequent devolutions: 43 Hen. III, c. 27 n.11 (unnumbered additional clause of the revised provisions of Westminster of 1263); 52 Hen. III (stat. Marlborough), c.29. In the present instance, it had been possible [8] to reach John d'Arcy by a writ within the degrees, one stating that he had 'entered' the land *per* Roger d'Arcy (i.e. by inheritance from him) *cui* Ingram of Oldcotes had demised the land for life: but the further devolution of the tenement, by escheat, to Constance took the land out of reach of a writ 'within the degrees', where it could only be reached by a writ 'outside the degrees', that is, in the post in the form of the present writ.

Appendix I to Introduction

CHRONOLOGY OF SIGNIFICANT DATES
IN *OLDCOTES* v. *D'ARCY*

1 Nov. 1272
Roger d'Arcy acquires seisin of lands of Ingram of Oldcotes.

24 June 1273
Date fixed in agreement as that by which Roger was to make Ingram a knight.

July 1273
Roger purchases assize of novel disseisin against Ingram, to be heard before Octon and Beckingham.

? between June and Dec. 1273
Attack on Ingram by Furnivall and his men.

Feb. 1274
Ingram brings appeal against Furnivall in court coram rege.

Nov. 1274
Pleading in Ingram's first action against Roger in the common bench [1].

Jan. 1276
Last recorded adjournment in Ingram's first action.

July 1277
Roger in Wales [? with the king's army].

Aug. 1278
Enactment of the statute of Gloucester.

Jan. 1280
Pleading in Ingram's second action against Roger in the common bench [2].

June 1280
Roger attempts to secure dismissal of case for want of prosecution.

Nov. 1280
Nottinghamshire eyre opens: to which Ingram's second action adjourned.

Jan./Feb. 1281
Quashing of Ingram's alleged default.

Nov. 1281
Ingram's second action adjourned sine die, because Roger in prison.

between Nov. 1281 and Aug. 1282
Death of Roger d'Arcy.

? 8 Aug. 1282
Ingram recovers lands by assize of novel disseisin before Stapleton and Beckingham at Nottingham [3].

12 May 1284
John d'Arcy brings assize of novel disseisin against Ingram and others before Mettingham and Sodington at Bultham [4].

20 Sept. 1286
Verdict given in that assize before Mettingham and others at Nottingham [5].

Jan./Feb. 1287
Assize adjourned into court coram rege.

Oct. 1287
Judgment given in assize for John d'Arcy [6].

18 July 1288
John d'Arcy purchases writ of redisseisin against Constance de Béarn and others.

10 June 1291
Ingram and John of Stonegrave purchase writ of error to reverse 1287 judgment.

Dec. 1292/Jan. 1293
Elias de Hauvill purchases assize of novel disseisin against John d'Arcy and others.

April/May 1293
Ingram and John of Stonegrave assign errors in error proceedings in court coram rege [7].

Nov. 1293
Last recorded adjournment in error proceedings.

June 1294
John d'Arcy and others bring certification against Elias de Hauvill.

July 1294
Elias de Hauvill goes with king to Gascony: certification put sine die. First adjournment in second error proceedings coram rege on 1282 judgment.

Jan. 1295
Last recorded adjournment in second error proceedings.

between Jan. 1295 and Jan. 1297
Death of Ingram of Oldcotes.

Jan. 1297
Death of Elias de Hauvill.

28 Feb. 1297
Isabel d'Arcy purchases writ of dower against John d'Arcy.

Oct. 1298
Isabel and third husband, Simon Warde, plead in dower action against Ingram son of Ingram of Oldcotes.

Oct./Nov. 1299
Pleading in dower action brought by Isabel and Simon against Robert of Oldcotes; John d'Arcy agrees to give dower third.

6 March 1300
Robert of Oldcotes purchases writs of entry against Isabel d'Arcy [and John d'Arcy].

Jan. 1301
Verdict for Robert in dower action brought by Isabel and Simon.

April 1301
John d'Arcy appears and pleads nonage in Robert's action against him.

June 1303
First adjournment in Robert's action against stepmother Elena and husband John le Keu for lands in Oldcotes.

Oct./Nov. 1303
Murder of Ralph le Messer of Nettleton by John d'Arcy: John has protection while on king's service in Scotland.

July 1305
John d'Arcy's outlawry ordered at session of oyer and terminer justices in Lincs.

Oct. 1305
Pleading in Robert's action against John d'Arcy [8].

June 1306
Judgment by default in Robert's favour in case against Isabel; John d'Arcy outlawed in Lincs.

7 Nov. 1307
Mandate for livery of John d'Arcy's lands to Constance de Béarn.

Sept. 1308
Robert nonsuited in assize of novel disseisin against Constance.

Jan. 1309
Robert conveys lands recovered from Isabel to Robert Russell; judgment on Constance's default in action brought by Robert in common bench for Oldcotes lands suspended.

June 1309
Jury verdict in Robert's favour [9].

12 July 1309
Privy seal writ authorises judgment for Robert against Constance.

Oct./Nov. 1310
Robert Russell settles Oldcotes lands on self, wife and heirs of bodies.

Appendix II to Introduction

THE OLDCOTES-D'ARCY RELATIONSHIP 1272–81: THE DIFFERENT ACCOUNTS OF WHAT HAPPENED

A. *What actually happened*	B *The 1286 jury verdict's account*	C *The 1309 jury verdict's account*
1. Initial agreement made about 1 November 1272 (a) terms (i) Roger to get Ingram's lands for life. (ii) Roger to make Ingram a knight by 24 June 1273. (iii) Roger to provide food and clothing for Ingram and 3 servants for life etc. (b) Charter of feoffment deposited with William of Holgate, mayor of Lincoln.	1. Initial agreement [no date given or suggested] (a) terms (i) Roger to get Ingram's lands for life. (ii) Roger to make Ingram a knight [but no time limit mentioned]. (iii) [No mention of food and clothing requirement]. (b) [No mention of deposit of charter of feoffment].	1. Initial agreement [no date given or suggested] (a) terms (i) Roger to get Ingram's land for life. (ii-iii) [Not mentioned]. (b) [Not mentioned].
2. Knighting did not take place by 24 June 1273: responsibility uncertain.	2. When day came for Ingram to be knighted, he had made difficulties, leading to a rupture between himself and Roger.	2. [Not mentioned].
3. Ingram disseises Roger, June/July 1273.	3. [Not mentioned].	3. [Not mentioned].
4. Roger recovers land in assize of novel disseisin before Octon and Beckingham, ? in July 1273.	4. [Not mentioned].	4. [Not mentioned].
5. Attack on Ingram by Furnivall and others, ? between July and Dec. 1273.	5. Attack on Ingram by unnamed assailants.	5. Attack on Ingram by Furnivall and his men.
6. [No evidence of this].	6. Ingram goes to Roger to seek his aid in prosecuting his assailants.	6. Ingram goes to Roger to seek his aid in prosecuting his assailants.
7. [No evidence of this].	7. Roger demands assurance that Ingram will not settle with his assailants without asking his advice. Ingram provides this through a charter granting him the lands in fee. The charter is deposited with Roger son of Benedict: he is to surrender it to Roger d'Arcy only if Ingram settles with his assailants without his advice.	7. Roger demands assurance that Ingram will not settle with his assailants without asking his advice, and asks for a charter granting him the land in fee as such assurance. The charter is deposited with Roger son of Benedict, mayor of Lincoln, who is to surrender it to Roger d'Arcy only if he makes Ingram a knight, finds Ingram food and clothing for life, and assists Ingram in prosecuting his assailants. If any of these conditions are not fulfilled, the charter is to be returned to Ingram.

8. Ingram prosecutes Furnivall and others in Hilary and Easter terms, 1274.	8. Roger commences prosecution of Furnivall and others on Ingram's behalf.	8. [Not mentioned].
9. ? Ingram makes a settlement out of court with Furnivall, between Easter and Michaelmas, 1274.	9. Ingram, without Roger's knowledge or consent, settles with Furnivall for 100 marks.	9. Ingram does not settle with Furnivall.
10. Ingram pleads against Roger in the common bench: Roger claims to hold only for life, Michaelmas 1274.	10. [Not mentioned].	10. [Not mentioned].
11. Adjournments of case till Hilary 1276.	11. [Not mentioned].	11. [Not mentioned].
12. [No evidence for this].	12. Immediately after Ingram settling with Furnivall, Roger d'Arcy goes to Roger son of Benedict and asks for charter, which is now forfeit. He refuses to hand it over in the absence of Ingram.	12. At an unspecified date after the agreement, Roger d'Arcy goes to Roger son of Benedict to ask for the charter. He refuses to hand it over in the absence of Ingram.
13. [No evidence for this].	13. Roger d'Arcy impleads Roger son of Benedict for the surrender of the charter. He eventually secures it by a judgment in his favour.	13. Roger d'Arcy ambushes Roger son of Benedict and keeps him prisoner till he surrenders the charter. He then expels Ingram from his house and refuses to carry out the agreement between them (7 above).
14. [No evidence for this but cf. 3].	14. Acting on the advice of Elias de Hauvill, Ingram ejects Roger from his lands.	14. } No subsequent events are mentioned.
15. [No evidence for this but cf. 4].	15. Roger recovers the lands by an assize of novel disseisin before John de Lovetot at which the charter is produced.	15. } No subsequent events are mentioned.
16. Ingram brings a second action against Roger in the common bench, which is put sine die by Roger's imprisonment.	16. Ingram brings an action against Roger in the common bench, which pends for a long time. Roger dies seised.	16. } No subsequent events are mentioned.

TEXT

[1]
CP 40/5, m.97

[*Marginated*] Noting'
Ingeramus de Ulecotes petit versus Rogerum[278] de Arcy unum mesuagium, centum acras terre, viginti et quinque acras prati, quatuor marcatas redditus, unum gardinum et duas partes quinque parcium unius molendini cum pertinenciis in Ulecotes, Styrap et Blida, que idem Ingeramus ei dimisit ad terminum qui preteriit etc. Et unde dicit quod dimisit ei ad terminum incipientem ad festum Omnium Sanctorum anno regni Henrici regis patris regis nunc quinquagesimo septimo usque ad festum nativitatis Sancti Johannis Baptiste proximo sequens, infra quem terminum predictus Rogerus debuit fecisse predictum Ingeramum militem sumptibus ipsius Rogeri per quoddam scriptum de convencione quod profert in hec verba. Hec est convencio facta inter Rogerum de Arcy militem ex una parte et Ingeramum de Ulecotes ex altera, videlicet quod predictus Rogerus sumptibus suis propriis faciet dictum Ingeramum militem citra festum nativitatis Sancti Johannis Baptiste anno regni domini Henrici regis filii regis Johannis quinquagesimo septimo seu ad ultimum ad festum predictum sine ulteriori dilacione. Insuper, ipso Ingeramo facto milite, dictus Rogerus ex tunc inveniet eidem Ingeramo omnibus diebus vite sue omnia necessaria in victu et vestitu honorifice, scilicet in lineis et laneis, in lecto et calciamentis, scilicet singulis annis duas robas et duas capas vel duo garniamenta loco caparum et unum tabardum et eciam tres equos qui sustentabuntur ad custus ipsius domini Rogeri in feno et avena et sellas et falera ad sectam eiusdem domini Rogeri. Insimul unum armigerum et duos garciones in victu et vestitu, lineo et laneo, ac calciamentis et omnibus rebus aliis prout militis interest sustentari omnia et singula decenter inveniet dicto domino Ingeramo quoad vixerit sine murmure et bono zelo. Et vero contingat quod absit, quod dictus Rogerus in aliqua sustentacione prescriptorum in parte vel in toto aliquo modo defecerit, extunc vult et concedit dictus Rogerus quod idem dominus Ingeramus legitime possit ingredi et tenere sibi et heredibus suis inperpetuum omnes terras et tenementa et omnes possessiones de Ulecotes, Styrap et Buggethorpe cum pertinenciis que et quas prefatus dominus Ingeramus per cartam suam feoffamenti dicto domino Rogero dedit et confirmavit; et quod illa carta cassatur omnino et nullius valoris sit vel momenti, que quidem carta assensu et bona voluntate ambarum parcium relicta est in deposito domini Willelmi de Holgate tunc maioris Linc'. Omnia autem et singula fideliter tenere et in nullo contravenire per breve de nova disseisina nec per aliquod tenementum sibi calumpniandum nec aliquo alio modo dictus dominus Rogerus pro se et heredibus suis fideliter promisit sacramento prestito corporali. In cuius rei testimonium presenti scripto cirographato partes hinc inde sigilla sua apposuerunt etc.

Et Rogerus venit. Et defendit jus suum quando etc. Et dicit quod non dimisit ei predicta tenementa ad terminum qui preteriit, immo ad terminum vite ipsius Rogeri per cartam suam quam profert in hec verba. Sciant presentes etc. quod ego Ingeramus de Ulecotes dedi, concessi et hac presenti carta mea confirmavi domino Rogero de Arcy ad totam vitam suam omnes terras meas et tenementa et omnes possessiones de Ulecotes, de Styrap et de Buggethorp' cum omnibus pertinenciis suis, libertatibus et asiamentis que michi accidunt vel accidere poterunt infra predictas villas et extra, tenendas et habendas eidem domino Rogero libere etc. quam diu vixerit, faciendo inde capitalibus dominis feodorum servicia debita et consueta, reddendo inde annuatim michi et heredibus meis vel assignatis unum denarium ad Pascha pro omni servicio etc. Et ego Ingeramus et heredes mei omnia predicta tenementa cum pertinenciis prefato domino Rogero quam diu vixerit contra omnes gentes warantizabimus, acquietabimus et defendemus. Post decessum vero predicti domini Rogeri omnia predicta tenementa michi et heredibus meis vel assignatis sine diminucione revertentur et remanebunt absque alicuius contradiccione inperpetuum. Et ad majorem huius rei securitatem presenti scripto sigillum meum apposui etc.

Et Ingeramus dicit quod predictus Rogerus numquam habuit ingressum in predictis tenementis per predictam cartam; immo per predictum scriptum de convencione. Et hoc paratus est verificare per patriam.

Et Rogerus dicit quod ipse habuit ingressum in predicta tenementa per predictam cartam. Dicit enim quod idem Ingeramus constituit quemdam certum attornatum suum, scilicet Gilbertum de Ulecotes filium suum, ad ponendum predictum Rogerum in seysina de predictis tenementis secundum tenorem predicte carte per litteras ipsius Ingerami patentes

[278] Corrected from *Robertum*.

sigillo suo signatas quas profert in hec verba. Universis presentes litteras etc. Ingeramus de Ulecotes salutem. Noveritis me fecisse et constituisse certum et verum attornatum meum Gilbertum de Ulecotes filium meum ad ponendum dominum Rogerum de Arcy militem in seysinam terrarum mearum et tenementorum et possessionum cum pertinenciis in Ulecotes, Styrap et de Buggethorp' secundum tenorem carte feoffamenti quam dictus dominus Rogerus de me habet. In cuius rei testimonium predicto Gilberto has litteras meas tradidi patentes sigillo meo signatas etc. Unde dicit quod predictus attornatus per predictas litteras patentes posuit ipsum in seysina de predictis tenementis secundum tenorem predicte carte. Et hoc paratus est verificare sicut curia consideraverit etc. Ideo preceptum est vicecomiti quod venire faciat hic a die Pasche in quinque septimanas xij etc. per quos etc. Et qui nec etc. ad recognoscendum in forma predicta. Quia tam etc.

[CP 40/5 *is the plea roll of the court of common pleas for Michaelmas term 2/3 Edward I (1274). M.97 is headed*: Adhuc de quindena Sancti Martini. Seyton'.]

[2]
CP 40/32, m.17

[*Marginated*] Noting'
Ingramus de Ulcotes petit versus Rogerum Darcy unum mesuagium, centum acras terre, viginti et quinque acras prati, quatuor marcatas redditus, et duas partes quinque parcium unius molendini cum pertinenciis in Ulcotes, Styrap et Blye que idem Ingramus dimisit prefato Rogero inveniendo ei necessaria usque ad quartam partem veri valoris terre predicte ad totam vitam ipsius Ingrami, et que ad predictum Ingramum reverti debent per formam statuti de consilio domini regis nunc[279] inde provisi eo quod predictus Rogerus in dictis necessariis inveniendis per sex annos iam cessavit etc. Et unde queritur quod cum convenisset inter predictum Rogerum ex una parte et ipsum Ingrammum ex altera, videlicet quod predictus Ingramus dimisit predicto Rogero predicta tenementa tenenda sibi et heredibus suis et ipsum inde in seysinam posuit[280] sub hac forma, videlicet quod predictus Rogerus sumptibus suis propriis faceret dictum Ingramum militem ad festum nativitatis Sancti Johannis Baptiste anno regni Henrici patris regis nunc quinquagesimo septimo, et quod[281] ex tunc inveniret eidem Ingramo tota vita[282] ipsius Ingrami omnia necessaria sua usque ad quartam partem veri valoris predictorum tenementorum, predictus Rogerus iam sex annis elapsis subtraxit[283] eidem Ingrammo predicta necessaria et ea ei reddere contradixit. Et inde producit sectam. Profert eciam quoddam scriptum de convencione inde inter predictos Ingramum et Rogerum ad modum cyrographi[284] confectum in hec verba.

[*There follows a full transcript of the deed in a version that closely resembles that already given in* [1].]

Et Rogerus venit et bene cognoscit predictam convencionem.[285] Et dicit quod nichil juris clamare potest in predictis tenementis. Dicit enim quod predictus Rogerus post predictam convencionem inter eos factam reddidit predicto Ingranmo predicta tenementa; et quod[286] idem Ingramus post redicionem illam fuit inde in seysina. Et postea eundem Rogerum de eisdem tenementis pure, sine aliqua condicione, feofavit et ipsum inde in seysinam posuit[287] tenendum sibi et heredibus suis inperpetuum. Et hoc paratus est verificare sicut curia consideraverit.

Et Ingramus dicit quod predictus Rogerus post predictam convencionem inter eos factam subtraxit eidem Ingrammo predicta necessaria sua contra predictam convencionem ob quam quidem subtraccionem idem Ingramus intravit in eisdem tenementis et predictum Rogerum de eisdem ejecit; ita quod predictus Rogerus, senciens se inde gravatum, impetravit quoddam breve assise[288] nove disseisine versus predictum Ingramum de eisdem tenementis coram J. de Oketon' et Elia de Bekyngham justiciariis domini regis ad hoc assignatis per quam quidem assisam idem Rogerus recuperavit predicta tenementa versus eum. Et quod ipse Rogerus[288] nuncquam post predictam convencionem inter eos factam ei reddidit predicta tenementa nec idem Ingramus postea ipsum Rogerum de eisdem tenementis feofavit set ea tantummodo versus eum per[288] predictam assisam recuperavit ponit se super patriam, et Rogerus similiter. Ideo preceptum est vicecomiti quod venire faciat hic in octabis Sancte Trinitatis xij etc. per quos etc. et qui nec etc. ad recognoscendum in forma predicta, quia tam etc.[289]

279 *domini . . . nunc* interlined above *nostro,* cancelled.

280 MS *ponuit*? 281 Interlined.

282 Followed by *vita,* cancelled.

283 Followed by *se inveniendi,* cancelled.

284 *ad . . . cyrographi* interlined.

285 *et . . . convencionem* interlined.

286 Interlined. 287 MS *ponuit*? 288 Interlined.

289 The remainder of the entry has been added later.

Postea per communem summonicionem itineris comitatus Noting' posita fuit jurata coram J. de Vaus et sociis suis capienda in eodem comitatu coram quibus placitatum[290] fuit in hec verba. Ingeramus de Ulecotes in curia regis apud Westm' petiit versus Rogerum de Ercy unum mesuagium, centum acras terre, viginti et quinque acras prati, quatuor marcatas redditus et duas partes quinque parcium unius molendini cum pertinenciis in Ulecotes, Stirap' et Blye, que idem Ingeramus dimisit predicto Rogero pro inveniendo ei necessaria usque ad quartam partem veri valoris terre predicte ad totam vitam ipsius Ingerami et que ad predictum Ingeramum reverti debent per formam statuti domini regis nunc inde provisi, eo quod predictus Rogerus in dictis necessariis inveniendis [*schedule*] per sex annos iam cessavit etc. idem Rogerus venit in eadem curia apud Westm' et posuit se inde in juratam patrie in forma et forma cuius continetur in recordo quod prefati justiciarii de banco hic retornaverunt. Et modo venit predictus Ingeramus et similiter predictus Rogerus. Et predictus Ingeramus petit quod jurata procedat in forma qua placitaverunt. Et predictus Rogerus dicit quod nulla jurata inde procedere debet eo quod nullum habet diem hic. Dicit enim quod ipse habuit diem de eadem jurata coram justiciariis apud Westm' in octabis Sancte Trinitatis anno regis nunc octavo, ad quem diem ipse optulit se quarto die versus predictum Ingeramum et eodem die idem Ingeramus fecit defaltam ob quam consideratum fuit quod predictus Rogerus iret inde sine die et quod predictus Ingeramus et plegii sui de prosequendo essent in misericordia; et de hoc ponit se super recordum rotulorum justiciariorum de banco etc. Et concedit quod si convincatur quod ipse predicto die per judicium curie regis apud Westm' de predicto placito non rescessit quietus, quod ipse amittat seisinam suam de predictis tenementis cum pertinenciis.

Et Ingeramus bene cognoscit quod ipsi habuerunt diem apud Westm' ad predictas octabas Sancte Trinitatis, ad quem diem predictus Rogerus se essoniavit de malo veniendi et essonium illud adjudicatum fuit et adjornatum in crastino Animarum ibidem; et dicit quod interim summonitum fuit iter istud per quam summonicionem ipsi habent diem hic, et quod predictum essonium fuit adjudicatum et adjornatum sicut predictum est ponit se super recordum eorundem rotulorum. Dies datus est eis hic dominica proxima post festum Sancti Andree apostoli, et interim querentur rotuli etc. Postea ad diem illum mandavit dominus rex justiciariis suis hic breve suum in hec verba. Edwardus etc. justiciariis suis itinerantibus in comitatu Noting' salutem. Quia quibusdam certis de causis volumus quod loquela que fuit coram justiciariis de banco per breve nostrum inter Ingeramum de Houlecotes et Rogerum de Arcy de manerio de Ulecotes cum pertinenciis et que una cum quibusdam aliis loquelis predicti comitatus per prefatos justiciarios coram vobis atterminata est coram prefatis justiciariis in octabis Sancti Hillarii remittatur ibidem terminandum, vobis mandamus quod loquelam illam coram prefatis justiciariis nostris ad diem predictum atterminetis, partibus eundem diem prefigentes quod tunc sint ibi in loquela illa facture et recepture quod de jure fuerit faciendum, et mittatis ibi hoc breve. Teste me ipso apud Westm' xxvj die novembris anno regni nostri nono. Et eis mittunter. Et preceptum est vicecomiti quod habeat corpora juratorum ad eundem terminum. Postea in octabis Purificacionis Beate Marie quia Rogerus de Leyc' recordatur quod adjornavit predictum essonium predicti Ingerami versus predictum Rogerum de predicto placito sicut predictum est, et compertum est quod postea in decepcionem curie secuta fuit predicta defalta et ex inproviso minus rite adjudicata consideratum est coram justiciariis de banco quod defalta illa adnichiletur et predictum placitum sit in eodem statu in quo fuit prius quando posuerunt se in predictam inquisicionem. Et preceptum est vicecomiti quod venire faciat hic a die Pasche in tres septimanas xij etc. ad recognoscendum in forma predicta. Idem dies datus est predictis Ingeramo et Rogero in banco.

[CP 40/32 *is the plea roll of the court of common pleas for Hilary term 8 Edward I (1280). M.17 is headed*: Adhuc de octabis Sancti Hillarii. Weyl'.]

[3]
JUST 1/1257, m.10

[*Marginated*] Notingham
Ingeramus de Ullecotes cognovit quod debet Constancie de Byerne quadraginta libras quas ei reddet ad festum Assumpcionis Beate Marie hoc anno. Et nisi fecerit, concedit quod vicecomes fieri faciat de terris et catallis etc. . . .
[*Marginated*] Notingh'
Assisa venit recognitura si Isabella que fuit uxor Rogeri de Arsy et Johannes filius eius, Johannes de Launde, Constancia de Byerne et Willelmus filius Jordani de Tykehull' injuste etc. disseisiverunt Ingeramum de Ullecotes de libero tenemento suo in Oulecotes post primam etc. Et unde queritur quod disseisiverunt eum de uno mesuagio, centum acris

290 or *placitum*?

terre, xxv acris prati, quatuor marcatis redditus et duabus partibus unius molendini, ipso molendino partito in quinque partes, cum pertinenciis etc.

Et predicti Isabella et Johannes filius eius et Johannes de la Launde[291] non venerunt nec fuerunt atachiati quia non fuerunt inventi. Ideo capiatur assisa versus eos per defaltam. Et predicta Constancia venit per quendam ballivum suum Bernardum Mark'. Et similiter predictus Willelmus filius Jordani venit; et dicit quod nullam injuriam vel disseisinam ei fecit quia dicit quod nichil clamat in predicto tenemento. Et predicta Constancia dicit quod nullam injuriam nec disseisinam ei fecit quia dicit quod ipsa tanquam capitalis domina predictorum tenementorum seysivit predicta tenementa in manu sua post mortem Rogeri [de Arsy qui][292] de ea tenuit ne . . . in predictis tenementis petit quod inquiratur . . . venit quod idem Rogerus de . . . Ingerami ad . . . ipse Ingeramus . . . bona et pacifica seisina . . . disseisiverunt et de hoc ponit super assisam. Juratores dicunt super sacramentum suum [quod predictus] Ingeramus intravit in predictis tenementis ut de libero tenemento suo et seysinam suam continuavit a mane usque ad horam terciam quousque predictus Willelmus filius Jordani de Tykehull' ipsum inde injuste disseisivit. Ideo consideratum est quod predictus Ingeramus recuperet seysinam suam de predictis tenementis et predictus Willelmus in misericordia. Et requisiti si predicti Isabella, Johannes filius eius et Johannes de la Launde fuerunt ad predictam disseisinam dicunt quod non. Ideo predictus Ingeramus in misericordia pro falso clamore versus eosdem Isabellam et alios. Perdonatur per justiciarios.

Dampna xl solidi versus predictum Willelmum de Tykehull. Totum clericis.

[JUST 1/1257 *is the plea roll of Nicholas of Stapleton recording assizes etc. heard before him and Elias of Beckingham in Northamptonshire, Rutland, Nottinghamshire, Derbyshire, Leicestershire, Lincolnshire and Shropshire, 10–11 Edward I (1282–3). M.10 is headed*: Stapelton. Assise, jurate et attincte capte apud Notingham coram Nicholao de Stapelton et Elia de Bekyngham justiciariis assignatis die sabbati proxima ante festum Sancti Laurencii anno regni regis Edwardi decimo, decimo, decimo, decimo, decimo.]

[4]
JUST 1/1259, m.1d

[*Marginated*] Notingh'

Assisa venit recognitura si Constancia de Byerne, Willelmus filius Jordani de Tykehull', Ingeramus de Ulcotes et Johannes de Steyngreve injuste etc. disseisiverunt Johannem filium Rogeri de Arcy de libero tenemento suo in Oulecotes, Styrap' et Blyda post primam etc. Et unde queritur quod disseisiverunt eum de duobus mesuagiis, sexies viginti acris terre, triginta acris prati, quinque marcatis redditus et quarta parte unius molendini cum pertinenciis etc.

Et Willelmus et Constancia non veniunt. Et Constancia fuit attachiata per Rogerum filium Willelmi filii Ricardi de Grengeley et Thomam Srifrand de eadem. Ideo ipsi in misericordia.[293] Et Willelmus de Tykehull' non fuit attachiatus quia non fuit inventus. Ideo capiatur assisa versus eos per defaltam. Et Johannes et Ingeramus veniunt. Et Johannes dicit quod ipse tenet predictum tenementum de dono predicti Ingerami, unde dicit quod ipse nullam injuriam aut disseisinam predicto Johanni filio Rogeri fecit; immo si aliqua injuria aut disseisina eidem inde facta fuisset, facta fuit per ipsum Ingeramum et alios et non per ipsum. Et Ingeramus dicit quod assisa non debet inde fieri. Dicit enim quod de isto eodem tenemento arramiavit ipse alias in curia domini regis coram N. de Stapelton' et E. de Bekingham justiciariis assignatis quandam assisam nove disseisine versus istum Johannem qui modo queritur; ita quod per assisam illam recuperavit ille seisinam suam inde versus eum. Unde petit judicium si assisa debeat inde capi super assisam.

Et Johannes de Arcy visus est in curia et est infra etatem. Et per custodem suum dicit quod ipse nescit placitare nec aliquid dicere nisi tantum petere assisam. Et nichilominus ad declaracionem status ipsius Johannis de Arcy dicit custos suus quod Rogerus de Arcy pater ipsius Johannis obiit seysitus de predicto tenemento ut de feodo. Et idem Johannes hora mortis ipsius Rogeri fuit in eodem tenemento et post mortem suam remansit in eodem per tres dies continue in bona et pacifica seisina ut filius eius et heres quousque ipse Ingeramus et alii ipsum inde injuste etc. disseisiverunt. Et qualitercumque contigisset postea quod idem Ingeramus per collusionem inter

291 *et Johannes de la Launde* interlined.

292 There is a hole in the parchment at this point, caused by damp. The words supplied are conjectural.

293 *misericordia* is also marginated.

ipsum et prefatam Constanciam que est capitalis domina ipsius feodi tulisset aliquam assisam nove disseisine de isto tenemento, assisa illa non transiit neque capta fuit de tempore quo idem Johannes de Arcy habuit statum aut seisinam, immo de tempore subsequenti; ita quod injuria et disseisina eidem Johanni facta nondum correcta est. Et quod ita sit petit quod inquiratur per assisam. Ideo capiatur assisa. Set ponitur in respectum pro defectu recognitorum usque in crastino Sancte Marie Magdalene.

[JUST 1/1259 *is the plea roll of John of Mettingham recording various special assizes etc. heard before him and other justices in Nottinghamshire, Lincolnshire, Suffolk, Norfolk and Middlesex, 11–13 Edward I (1282–5). M.1d is headed*: Placita coram J. de Metingham et magistro T. de Sodington' justiciariis assignatis apud Bultham die veneris proxima ante festum Sancti Dunstani anno regni domini regis E. duodecimo.]

[5]
JUST 1/671, m.3

[*Marginated*] Notingh'
Assisa coram J. de Metingham et magistro T. de Sodington' justiciariis assignatis apud Bultham die veneris proxima ante festum Sancti Dunstani anno regni domini regis nunc duodecimo venit recognitura si

[*There then follows a transcript of* [4] *with no significant variants. It then continues*]

Ad quem diem assisa remansit per absenciam justiciariorum. Postea resummonita fuit assisa ista coram justiciariis hic. Ad quem diem partes et assisa venerunt.

Juratores dicunt super sacramentum suum quod predictus Ingeramus, cuius tenementum istud fuit, voluit dudum miles fieri et dedit terram suam cuidam Rogero de Arcy patri predicti Johannis qui nunc queritur, cuius heres ipse est, tenendum ad terminum vite ipsius Rogeri per sic quod conferret ei arma militaria et omnes custus ad hoc pertinencia inveniret. Et cum dies arma suscipiendi venisset idem Ingeramus quesivit occasiones per quod recesserunt abinvicem quasi discordes. Et cum idem Ingeramus elongasset se a predicto Rogero venerunt quidam inimici ipsius Ingerami et maletractaverunt eum et vulneraverunt, ita quod de vita eius disperabatur; et quamcito Ingeramus convalescebat rediit ad prefatum Rogerum et supplicavit quod foret ei in subsidium perquirendi sibi justiciam de tam enormi transgressione sibi illata. Et Rogerus dixit quod quia idem Ingeramus fuit mutabilis, voluit habere securitatem quod non iret extra consilium suum de facto illo. Et[294] Ingeramus fecit ei quandam cartam de feoffamento tenendum predictam terram eidem Rogero et heredibus suis in feodo, que quidem tradita fuit in equali manu cuidam Rogero filio Benedicti de Linc' custodienda, ipsaque eidem Rogero liberanda si contigisset prefatum Ingeramum extra consilium ipsius Rogeri super facto predicto aliquid operari. Et dicunt quod idem Rogerus viriliter et diligenter incepit sequi versus transgressores ipsius Ingerami, donec idem Ingeramus relinquens consilium ipsius Rogeri sine scitu et voluntate sua remisit accionem suam transgressoribus per finem centum marcarum quas ei ob inde dederunt. Et statim idem Rogerus super hoc accessit ad predictum Rogerum filium Benedicti et peciit quod predictam cartam eidem liberaret, quod quidem extra presenciam ambarum parcium facere precise recusavit, propter quod Rogerus de Arcy pluries accessit ad curiam regis et impetravit brevia pro predicta carta sibi liberanda, tandem vero quod prefatus Rogerus filius Benedicti per preceptum regis cartam illam Rogero de Arcy liberavit. Et super hoc prefatus Ingeramus accessit ad curiam et posuit se in consilio cuiusdam Elye de Hauvill, ita quod prefatus Rogerus de Arcy fuit de predicta terra postea ejectus et disseysitus: super quo idem Rogerus statim sibi perquisivit per quandam assisam nove disseisine captam coram Johanne de Lovetot justiciario assignato apud Neuwerk' et ibi ostendit predictam cartam de feodo quam predictus Ingeramus fecerat et recuperavit seisinam suam de terra predicta. Et juratores quesiti si carta illa de feodo uncquam scita, lecta vel audita fuisset in patria, dicunt quod non nisi ad horam illam quando assisa capta fuit coram prefato Johanne de Lovetot. Set dicunt quod predictus Ingeramus postea perquisivit breve domini regis per consilium prefati Elye et fecit predictum Rogerum venire coram justiciariis domini regis apud Westm' et ibi pendebat placitum diucius inter eos, set qualiter seu quomodo placitum illud fuit deductum ignorant; set bene sciunt quod predictus Rogerus semper remansit seysitus et obiit seysitus. Et dicunt quod obiit per quemdam diem lune et statim predictus Ingeramus, qui presens fuit in villa tempore mortis ipsius Rogeri, intravit in capitale mesuagium predicti tenementi et ibidem remansit usque diem mercurii proximo sequentem quod ballivus Constancie de Byerne capitalis domine venit et amovit eundem Ingeramum et tradidit seisinam predicti tenementi amicis predicti Johannis de Arcy tenendum nomine ipsius Johannis.

294 Interlined.

Et prefatus Ingeramus impetravit sibi statim per assisam nove disseisine captam coram N. de Stapelton' et E. de Bekyngham et seisinam suam inde recuperavit; et cum tenementum illud per aliquod tempus in manu sua tenuisset dimisit illud predicto Johanni de Steyngreve ad terminum vite ipsius Johannis tenendum.[295]

Et super hoc predictus Ingeramus dicit quod predictus Rogerus de Arcy cognovit in curia domini regis coram justiciariis apud Westm' quod ipse nichil habuit in predictis tenementis[296] nisi ad terminum vite sue tantum et de hoc habuit cartam ipsius Ingerami. Et hoc paratus est verificare per recordum de banco. Et Robertus de Osegoteby custos predicti Johannis dicit ex adverso quod prefatus Rogerus in prefata curia domini regis apud Westm' clamavit semper feodum et liberum tenementum in predictis tenementis per cartam ipsius Ingerami quam habuit inde de feodo. Et hoc paratus est verificare pro ipso Johanne per recordum.[297]

Dies datus est eis de audiendo judicio suo[298] apud Graham in crastino Epiphanie Domini. Et dictum est partibus quod interim faciant scrutari rotulos ad certiorand' etc. Postea ad diem illud apud Graham venit prefatus Johannes per custodem suum et similiter[299] predictus Ingeramus[300] venit et detulit breve domini regis per quod dominus rex mandavit justiciariis hic quod mitterent recordum istud coram eo, ita quod illud habeat a die Sancti Hillarii in xv dies ubicumque etc. Et ei mittitur per custodem predicti Johannis. Idem dies datus est partibus etc.

[JUST 1/671 *is the plea roll of John of Mettingham recording assizes etc. heard before him and others in Nottinghamshire, 14–17 Edward I (1286–9). M.3 is headed*: Adhuc de assisis captis apud Notingham die veneris in vigilia Sancti Matthei anno xiiij^{mo}.]

[6]
KB 27/107, m.24

[*Marginated*] Notingh'
Assisa alias coram J. de Metingham

[*There then follows a transcript of* [5] *with no significant variants. It then continues*[301]]

Postea coram rege dies datus est partibus in octabis Purificacionis Beate Marie ubicumque ut de die in diem etc. Postea coram domino rege a die Sancti Michaelis in tres septimanas [anno] regis nunc quintodecimo scrutatis rotulis de banco et recordis et processibus predicte loquele habite inter predictos Rogerum et Ingeramum que resident in ligula recordorum de termino Sancti Michaelis anno predicto auditis et intellectis; et[302] quia compertum est quod predictus Rogerus obiit seisitus et[303] quod predictus Ingeramus post mortem predicti Rogeri se intrusit [in predictis] tenementis nec aliquid habuit in eisdem nisi per intrusionem; et predictus Johannes filius Rogeri intravit [in eisdem] ut filius et heres ipsius Rogeri propinquior; et compertum sit per recordum de banco quod predictus Rogerus semper clamavit feodum et liberum tenementum in predictis tenementis per factum [ipsius Ingerami, consideratum] est quod predictus Johannes filius Rogeri recuperet seisinam suam de [predictis tenementis versus predictum Ingeramum et] alios. Et Ingeramus et alii in misericordia.

[Dampna xl] marce, unde cleric[is R. de Hengham x marce et clericis J. de Metyngham x marce].

[KB 27/107 *is the plea roll of the court coram rege for Michaelmas term 15/16 Edward I (1287). M.24 has no heading, but the heading of m.24d is*: Adhuc de tribus septimanis Sancti Michaelis et de mense anno supradicto.]

[7]
KB 27/132, m.21

Dominus rex mandavit dilecto et fideli suo Gilberto de Thornton et sociis suis[304] ad placita ipsum sequencia audienda et terminanda assignatis[305] in hec verba. Cum Johannes filius Rogeri Darcy arramiaverit quandam assisam nove disseisine versus Constanciam de Byerne, Willelmum filium Jordani de Tykehull', Ingeramum de Oulecotes et Johannem de Stayngreve de tenementis in Oulecotes, Styrap et Blye coram dilectis et fidelibus nostris Johanne de Metyngham et magistro Thoma de Suddington' justiciariis nostris ad hoc assignatis, et postea loquela coram nobis fuerit devoluta, vobis mandamus quod, scrutatis rotulis

[295] In the margin a little below this point is the note: *dampna si qua xl marce.*

[296] *in . . . tenementis* interlined.

[297] The following paragraph is separated from this one by a blank space of about five inches.

[298] *de . . . suo* interlined.

[299] *prefatus . . . similiter* interlined.

[300] Followed by *et tulit breve de,* deleted.

[301] The membrane is damaged on the right-hand side and at the bottom. Words in brackets are supplied from the transcript of [6] in [7].

[302] Interlined.

[303] *quod . . . et* interlined.

[304] Interlined.

[305] Followed by *salutem,* deleted.

nostris de tempore quo Radulfus de Hengham placita nostra tenuit, qui sunt in custodia vestra, ut dicitur, errorem si quem in eisdem recordo et processu inveneritis sine dilacione sicut alias in casu consimili vestro officio fieri consuevit corrigi faciatis. Teste me ipso apud Norham x die junii anno regni nostri decimo nono.[306] Pretextu cuius brevis preceptum fuit vicecomiti quod scire faceret predicto Johanni filio Rogeri Darcy per duos legales homines etc. ad tenementa predicta, si ipse non sit inventus etc., quod esset coram rege a die Pasche in tres septimanas ubicumque etc. auditurus recordum et processum etc., et ulterius etc. Ad quem diem[307] ipse non venit, et vicecomes mandavit quod scire fecit ei per Henricum filium Rogeri de Carleton' et Ricardum Shynhose de eadem. Ideo consideratum fuit quod procederetur ad examinacionem recordi predicti per ipsius defaltam, set ponebatur in respectum usque a die Sancte Trinitatis in xv dies ubicumque etc. Ad quem diem predictus Johannes filius Rogeri Darcy per Robertum de Osegoteby custodem suum venit, et, scrutatis rotulis predicti Radulfi de Hengham de termino Sancti Michaelis anno regni regis nunc quintodecimo incipiente sextodecimo, invenitur recordum cuius tenor talis est.

[*There then follows a transcript, continuing onto membrane 21d, identical, other than in minor points, with* [6]. *It then continues*]

Postea dies datus est Ingeramo de Ulecotes querenti et Johanni filio Rogeri Darcy per Robertum de Osegoteby custodem suum de placito terre unde recordum a die Sancti Michaelis in xv dies ubicumque prece parcium etc. Ad quem diem venit predictus Ingeramus et similiter predictus Johannes per custodem suum. Et datus est eis dies a die Sancti Hillarii in xv dies coram rege ubicumque etc. Ad quem diem venerunt partes predicte; et datus est eis dies a die Pasche in unum mensem ubicumque etc. Et Ingeramus amovet Henricum de Cavenby quem prius loco suo etc. Ad quem diem venerunt partes et similiter Johannes de Stayngreve qui habet diem nunc versus predictum Johannem Darcy etc.[308] Et quesitum est a predictis Johanne de Stayngreve et Ingeramo in quo erratum est in predictis recordo et processu. Dicunt quod erratum est in eo ubi assisa quam Johannes Darcy arramiavit versus predictum Ingeramum et alios per absenciam justiciariorum remansit capienda, justiciarii postea ad capcionem assise illius processerunt et sine premunicione vel reattachiamento parcium assisam illam ceperunt. Dicunt eciam quod erratum est in eo ubi assisa per predictum Johannem Darcy fuit arramiata versus predictum Ingeramum et alios, ibi ex parte predicti Ingerami fuit allegatum quod assisa non deberet inde fieri, eo quod idem Ingeramus alias in curia regis eadem tenementa per assisam nove disseisine recuperavit, et inde petit judicium si assisa super assisam de eisdem tenementis et de eodem tempore fieri deberet. Et justiciarii non allocata excepcione sua ad capcionem assise processerunt. Dicunt eciam quod erratum est in eo ubi predictus Johannes Darcy dixit quod habuit feodum in predictis tenementis per cartam ipsius Ingerami, invenitur[309] in recordo quod illa carta fuit tradita in equali manu cuidam Rogero filio Benedicti de Linc' custodiendum, et idem Rogerus filius Benedicti sine scitu et voluntate ipsius Ingerami cartam illam predicto Rogero Darcy liberavit et quod numquam fuit lecta vel scita; et sic per illam cartam nunquam statum habuit nec feodum clamare potuit, et per consequens justiciarii virtute illius carte vacue adjudicaverunt filium feodum, ubi pater non habuit nisi liberum tenementum.[310] Item dicunt quod erratum est in eo quod ubi loquela primo venit coram domino rege a die Sancti Hillarii in xv dies anno regni regis nunc xv et deinde datus fuit dies partibus in octabis Purificacionis Beate Marie proximo sequentibus, ad quem diem loquela remansit sine die, et postea a die Sancti Michaelis in tres septimanas proximo sequenti redditum fuit judicium super grosso assise in absencia parcium et ubi partes non habuerunt diem in curia. Preterea dicunt quod erratum est in reddicione judicii predicti, quia ubi dominus Radulfus de Hengham supponit in judicio suo quod predictus Ingeramus intrusit se in predictis tenementis post mortem predicti Rogeri Darcy nec aliquid habuit in eisdem tenementis nisi per intrusionem, illud non est verum, quia invenitur in quodam recordo coram rege hic returnato quod predictus Ingeramus presens in villa statim et primus post mortem predicti Rogeri Darcy intravit in predictis tenementis et inde fuit in pacifica seisina ut de jure suo quousque fuit inde ejectus et postea tenementa illa per assisam nove disseisine recuperavit,[311] unde manifeste patet quod predictus Ingeramus non intrusit se in predictis tenementis. Unde petunt quod, inspectis erroribus supradictis, recordum et processus predicta irritentur

[306] *Notyngh'* marginated.

[307] *Ad . . . diem* interlined above *et,* deleted.

[308] *et . . . etc.* interlined.

[309] Repeated.

[310] *non scribatur* marginated opposite this point.

[311] Interlined.

et pro nullo habeantur etc. et eis justicia fiat etc. Et super hoc dies datus est predictis Ingeramo et Johanni de Stayngreve et predicto Johanni Darcy a die Sancti Johannis Baptiste in xv dies ubicumque etc., salvo predicto Johanni Darcy quicquid pro se voluerit dicere pro statu suo salvando etc. Et deinde datus est dies predictis partibus in crastino Sancti Martini coram rege ubicumque etc., salvo predicto Johanni Darcy quicquid pro se voluerit dicere in forma predicta etc. Ad quem diem venerunt predicti Ingeramus et Johannes de Stayngreve etc. et similiter predictus Johannes Darcy per custodem suum, et datus est eis dies a die Pasche in tres septimanas coram rege ubicumque etc., salvo predicto Johanni Darcy quicquid pro se voluerit dicere etc. ut prius etc.

[KB 27/132 *is the plea roll of the court coram rege for Trinity term 20 Edward I (1292). M.21 is headed*: Adhuc de quindena Sancte Trinitatis. Rex. Thornton; *and m.21d*: Adhuc de recordo de Steyngreve et de Ulecotes.]

[8]
CP 40/153, m.37d

[*Marginated*] Not'
Robertus filius Ingelrami de Ulecotes petit versus Johannem filium Rogeri Darcy duas partes unius mesuagii, centum acrarum terre, viginti acrarum prati et triginta et quinque solidatarum redditus cum pertinenciis in Blida, Stirap et Ulecotes juxta Blidam ut jus et hereditatem suam, et in quas idem Johannes non habet ingressum nisi per Rogerum Darcy, cui Ingelramus de Ulecotes pater predicti Roberti, cuius heres ipse est, illas dimisit ad vitam ipsius Rogeri et que post mortem predicti Rogeri ad prefatum Robertum reverti debent.

Et Johannes per attornatum suum venit. Et defendit jus suum quando etc. Et bene defendit quod predictus Ingelramus non dimisit predicta tenementa predicto Rogero ad aliquem terminum, immo in feodum per cartam ipsius Ingelrami quam profert, et que testatur quod idem Ingelramus dedit, concessit et carta sua confirmavit predicto Rogero manerium de Ulecotes cum pertinenciis tenendum eidem Rogero et heredibus suis in perpetuum etc., unde petit judicium etc.

Et Robertus dicit quod carta illa ei nocere non debet etc. quia dicit quod carta illa non est factum predicti Ingelrami patris sui etc., et hoc petit quod inquiratur per patriam et per testes in predicta carta nominatos etc. Et Johannes similiter. Ideo preceptum est vicecomiti quod venire faciat hic in octabis Sancti Hillarii Willelmum de Cressy testem nominatum etc. alii testes obierunt etc. et preter illum xij etc. per quos etc. et qui nec etc., quia tam etc. ad recognoscendum etc. quia tam etc. Et sciendum quod scriptum dedictum remanet in custodia J. Bacun clerici regis.[312] Postea, continuato processu usque in crastino Animarum anno regni regis nunc xxxiiij^{to}, venit predictus Robertus per attornatum suum et predictus Johannes non venit; set quidam Robertus de Saltfleteby venit et dicit quod ipse est attornatus predicti Johannis in loquela predicta, et dicit quod idem Johannes ad proximum comitatum tentum apud Linc' post festum nativatis Sancti Johannis Baptiste anno regni regis nunc xxxiiij^{to} pro diversis transgressionibus et feloniis sibi impositis coram Petro de Malo Lacu et sociis suis justiciariis domini regis ad[313] transgressiones et felonias apud Linc' audiendas et terminandas assignatis utlagatus est etc. Et de hoc ponit se super recordum rotulorum predictorum justiciariorum etc. Et Robertus dicit quod predictus Johannes non est utlagatus etc. Ideo datus est eis dies hic a die Pasche in xv dies etc. Et interim scrutantur rotuli etc.

[CP 40/153 *is the plea roll of the court of common pleas for Michaelmas term 33/34 Edward I (1305). M.37d has no heading, but the heading of m.37 is*: Adhuc de octabis Sancti Michaelis. Hengham.]

[9]
CP 40/178, m.356

[*Marginated*] Noting'
Robertus filius Ingelrami de Ulecotes alias in curia hic, scilicet in crastino Purificacionis Beate Marie proximo preterito, optulit se quarto die versus Constanciam de Byerne de placito duarum parcium unius mesuagii, centum et viginti acrarum terre, viginti acrarum prati, et viginti et quinque solidatarum redditus cum pertinenciis in Blida, Styrap' et Ulecotes juxta Blidam quas clamavit ut jus etc. Et ipsa non venit; et alias fecit defaltam, scilicet a die Sancti Michaelis in tres septimanas proximo preteritas,[314] postquam summonita etc., ita quod tunc preceptum fuit vicecomiti quod caperet predictas duas partes in

[312] The remainder of the entry is in a smaller hand, and was clearly added later.

[313] Followed by *diversas,* deleted.

[314] *proximo preteritas* interlined.

manum domini regis etc., et diem etc., et quod summoneret eam etc. quod esset hic ad prefatum crastinum etc. Et vicecomes tunc mandavit diem capcionis etc., et quod summonuerat eam etc. Et quia testatum fuit hic quod predicta tenementa sunt de pertinenciis ad honorem de Tikehull' quem quidem honorem eadem Constancia tenet ad terminum vite sue de hereditate domini regis etc. ideo cessavit execucio etc. quousque locutum fuisset cum domino rege etc. Et datus fuit dies predicto Roberto hic a die Pasche in unum mensem proximo preteritum[315] etc. Et interim loquendum cum domino rege. Postea ad diem illum venit predictus Robertus. Et quia per peticionem coram domino rege et eius consilio exhibitam concordatum fuit[316] per consilium etc. quod inquiratur de jure ipsius Roberti secundum formam brevis quod ipse versus eam impetravit, cuius forma talis est. Et in quas eadem Constancia non habet ingressum nisi post dimissionem quam Ingelramus de Ulecotes pater predicti Roberti, cuius heres ipse est, inde fecit Rogero de Ercy ad vitam ipsius Rogeri, et que post mortem ipsius Rogeri ad prefatum Robertum reverti debent etc. Et unde idem Robertus dixit[317] quod predictus Ingelramus pater etc. fuit seisitus de predictis tenementis ut de feodo et jure tempore pacis tempore domini regis Edwardi patris domini regis nunc, capiendo inde explecia ad valenciam etc., et de ipso Ingelramo descendit jus etc. isti Roberto qui nunc petit ut filio et heredi; et in quas etc. nisi post dimissionem etc., et hoc paratus fuit verificare per patriam. Ideo preceptum fuit vicecomiti quod venire faceret hic ad hunc diem scilicet[318] in octabis Sancti Johannis Baptiste xij etc. de visneto predicto, quorum sex ad minus sint milites gladio cincti etc., per quos etc., et qui predictum Robertum nulla affinitate etc. ad recognoscendum de jure etc. Ad quem diem predictus Robertus venit; et Constancia non venit. Et juratores veniunt. Qui dicunt super sacramentum suum quod predictus Ingelramus fuit seisitus de predictis tenementis ut de jure suo, qui tenementa illa dimisit predicto Rogero Darcy militi ad terminum vite ipsius Rogeri; et quia predictus Ingelramus fuit vulneratus et mahemiatus per Thomam de Furnivall' et suos, peciit auxilium de ipso Rogero contra predictum Thomam et suos de transgressione illa, et idem Rogerus concessit ei auxilium suum; et, pro securitate habenda quod predictus Ingelramus non pacificaret cum predicto Thoma de predicta transgressione absque eius consilio, peciit cartam sibi fieri de feoffamento de predictis tenementis. Qui quidam Ingelramus fecit cartam de feoffamento de predictis tenementis, tali convencione quod idem Rogerus faceret ipsum Ingelramum militem sumptibus ipsius Rogeri, et quod inveniret eidem Ingelramo omnia necessaria sua tota vita ipsius Ingelrami honesta et tanquam militi competencia, et ei esset in auxilium contra predictum Thomam ut haberet emendam de transgressione illa; quam quidem cartam idem Ingelramus tradidit custodiendum cuidam Rogero filio Benedicti maiori Linc', ita videlicet quod si[319] idem Rogerus teneret eidem Ingelramo convencionem predictam quod carta illa traderetur predicto Rogero, et si idem Rogerus non teneret eidem Ingelramo convencionem illam, tunc carta illa retraderetur eidem Ingelramo. Et postea idem Rogerus Darcy accessit ad predictum Rogerum filium Benedicti et peciit cartam illam sibi liberari, qui quidem Rogerus filius Benedicti ei respondit quod cartam illam non liberaret sine presencia, assensu et voluntate ipsius Ingelrami; ob quod predictus Rogerus Darcy insidiabatur ipsi Rogero filio Benedicti ad capiendum ipsum, et obviando ei in via cum bonis suis versus nundinas Sancti Botulphi ipsum Rogerum filium Benedicti cum bonis suis cepit et ipsum imprisonavit et in prisona detinuit. Qui quidem Rogerus filius Benedicti per vim prisone liberavit eidem Rogero Darcy cartam illam sine assensu et voluntate ipsius Ingelrami. Et statim postquam cartam illam habuit ipsum Ingelramum a domo sua expulit et fugavit et noluit aliquid facere de convencione predicta. Et juratores quesiti si predictus Ingelramus fecit pacem cum predicto Thoma de predicta transgressione, dicunt quod non. Quesiti eciam si predictus Robertus sit heres ipsius Ingelrami propinquior dicunt revera quod idem Robertus est heres propinquior ipsius Ingelrami.

Et postea dominus rex misit hic billam ipsius Roberti justiciariis suis hic in hec verba. A nostre seignur le rey mustre Roberd le ffiz Ingram de Ulecotes qe come il porta sun bref' devaunt justices du baunk' en temps le rey qe mort est lan xxix [vers][320] Johan le ffiz Roger Darcy e play entre eaux continue qe le dit Robert fut arecoverir par juge[ment] vers le dit Johan, ne fuit la felonie le dit Johan, par quei il fut utlage, e issi sun play vers [le] dit Johan amorty, e en le terme de Saint Hillary lan de nostre seignur le roy qore est primer dit fut au dit Robert en curt qil

[315] *proximo preteritum* interlined. [316] Interlined.

[317] Altered from *dicit.* [318] *ad . . . scilicet* interlined.

[319] Interlined.

[320] The right-hand margin is worn, and the words in brackets are conjecturally supplied.

susiet vers Constance de Byerne, qe les ditz tenemenz come sa eschete par la felonie le dit Johan, e issi ad il suy vers la dite Constaunce[321] tanqe a jugement. Temoigne fut qe ele ces tenemenz tient cum sa echete par la resoune qe les ditz tenemenz furent tenuz del honur de Tikehill', le quel honur ele tient a terme de vie del heritage nostre seignur le roy, e issi demora le jugement tanqe nostre seignur le rey fut conseille. E par peticion livere a nostre seignur le rey comande fut qe dreiture fut fait au dit Robert par quoi le justices on enq . . . par bon enqueste qe Johan Darcy ne yaveit rien de dreit ne qe Rogier sun pere rien ne y aveit fors qe terme de vie du lees Ingeram de Ulecotes piere le dit Robert, qi eir il est. Par quoi le dit Robert prie a nostre seignur le roy qe luy plese comaunder a ses justices quil renddent jugement sulonc verdit de la dite enqueste, issi qe droit luy soit fait.

Insuper idem dominus rex misit breve suum hic in hec verba. Edward par la grace de dieu roy Dengleterre seignur Dirlaunde et ducs Daquitayne a noz chers et feaus monsur William de Bereford e ses compaignouns nos justices du bau[nk] [322] [*membrane* 356d] saluz. Nous vous enveoms deinz cestes lettres une peticion qe nus est baillie de part Robert le fiz Ingram de Ulcotes e vous mamdoms qe si les choses qe i sunt contenues seient veritables, a dunques ailliez avaunt au jugement solome la ley e losage de nostre reaume nouncountreesteaunt qe la chose nus tuche si com meisme la peticion fait mencion. Don' souz nostre prive seal a Waltham le xij jour de juyl lan de nostre regne tierz. Cuius peticionis tenor superius irrotulatur.

Et quia convictum est per juratam predictam quod predictus Ingelramus pater predicti Roberti, cuius jus et hereditas predicta tenementa fuerunt et qui de tenementis illis seisitus fuit in dominico suo ut de feodo et jure, dimisit eadem tenementa cum pertinenciis prefato Rogero tenenda ad terminum vite ipsius Rogeri tantum et quod idem Rogerus nullum alium statum habuit in vita sua in eisdem tenementis nisi ad terminum vite etc.,[323] et quod predictus Robertus est filius et heres ipsius Ingelrami propinquior, consideratum est quod predictus Robertus recuperet seisinam suam versus ipsam Constanciam de predictis tenementis per defaltam predictam. Et Constancia in misericordia etc.

[CP 40/178 *is the plea roll of the court of common pleas for Trinity term 2/3 Edward II (1309). M.356 is headed*: Adhuc de quindena Sancti Johannis Baptiste. Bereford'. *M.356d has no heading.*]

[10]

Nottingham Univ. Lib., Cl D 57

[*Marginated*] Notingh'

A nostre seignour le roi mustre Robert de Ulecotes qe comme il porta soen bref dentre devant justices du bank en temps le roi qe mort est lan de soen regne vint et noefime a la quinzeine de Pasche vers Johan Darcy et demanda vers lui les deux parties dun mes, cent acres de terre, vint acres de pre, vint et cink souze de rente ove les apurtenances en Blie, Stirap et Ulecotes pre de Blie comme soen droit et en les queux le dit Johan nad entre si noun par Roger Darcy a qi Ingram de Ulecotes piere le dit Robert, qi heir il est, ceo lessa a terme de la vie mesme celui Roger et les queux apres la mort' lavantdit Roger a lavantdit Robert comme filz et heir Ingram revertir devient. Et issi est ceo plai continue en bank' par proces tank' lendemein des almes lan xxxv qe la parole demora sanz jour par la mort' le roi et pendant ceo plai Johan Darcy fit felonie pur quei il fut utlage, par quei Constance de Biern' dame del honeur de Tikehill' de qi ceux tenements fuerent tenuz les seisi comme sa eschete. Et as utaves de Seint Hillar' lan nostre seigneur le roi quore est premer a la resomonse qe Robert suy vers le dit Johan Darcy fu la curt' acertee par respons du viscont' del utlagerie Johan et qe Constance fu seisi de ceu tenement comme sa eschete. Dit fu par la curt a Robert qil suyt vers la dite Constance. Et issi a Robert suy vers Constance si comme le record cosu a ceste bill purporte. Purquei le dit Robert prie a nostre seigneur le roi et a soen conseil qe le forfait Johan Darcy pendant soen plee ne lui soit desturbant de soen droit, et qe il pleise a nostre seigneur le roi et a soen conseil commander qe dreiture lui soit fait.

[321] Interlined.

[322] The right-hand margin is damaged; the letters in brackets are supplied. Followed below by: *In tergo respice de eodem.*

[323] *et quod . . . vite etc.* interlined.

Letters to John Mettingham, 1296

edited by

FRANKLIN J. PEGUES

INTRODUCTION

Sometime during the Michaelmas term of 1296 or shortly thereafter, John Mettingham, chief justice of the common bench, had one of his clerks transcribe in his copy of the plea roll for that term thirty letters which several persons had addressed to him on certain aspects of judicial business.[1] No judge to our knowledge had used the plea roll as a letter registry before Mettingham and none would use it in such a way again. In format, structure and content the plea rolls had scarcely changed across the first half of the thirteenth century;[2] in the second half they underwent several developments and these innovations increased in frequency toward the end of the century. Two well-known changes occurred about the beginning of Edward I's reign: the recorded pleas heard coram rege became permanently distinguishable as the king's bench plea roll, and the record of the pleas heard 'at Westminster' became identifiable as the 'placita de banco' or common bench plea rolls.[3] These two series were the results of a long development out of an undifferentiated curia regis roll at the beginning of the century. Another change that is not so well known was the decision about 1272 to transcribe the list of attorneys on separate membranes at the end of the plea roll rather than distribute them in irregular fashion throughout the recorded pleas.[4] Apart from these developments, the common bench plea rolls remained substantially unchanged in the 1280s and, despite several changes in the last decade of the century, the inclusion of the Mettingham letters in 1296 comes as a distinct surprise to the plea roll student.

Of the thirty enrolled letters, twenty-six were sent to Mettingham from wardens of the sea coasts, and by this group of letters we are brought up sharp against one of the most urgent defence measures taken during Edward I's reign. Among the military provisions made by the August parliament of 1295 to prepare for hostilities with France, one established a watch system for the coasts of East Anglia, Essex, Kent and the southern counties.[5] Sixteen of the twenty-six letters came from William Bovill who was appointed warden of the Suffolk coasts in December.[6] Four [7, 10, 21, 22] were from Peter Roscelyn who kept the coasts of sixteen hundreds on the north shore of Norfolk, while Robert Maltby, warden of the coast adjacent to Norwich and of sixteen other hundreds sent only one letter [26].[7] John Botetourt who seems to have been concerned with the area around Yarmouth and Lothingland hundred also sent one letter [30]. Finally, Richard Huish, warden of the Cornish coasts, dispatched four letters to Mettingham [19, 20, 23, 27].[8] A collector of the eleventh in a Suffolk hundred wrote one of the remaining four letters [3], a customs collector at Boston wrote another [24], and Roger Brabazon, Mettingham's fellow chief justice in the king's bench, sent two [28, 29].

While the concerns of the coast-guard system dominate the thirty letters, all contain essentially the same request or petition: that persons who were in the king's service be kept faultless from judicial obligations, either in general terms or for specific assignment dates and actions. The first letter which was from Bovill seemed to describe the general situation. He had established in each hundred in Suffolk two constables who must guard the coast. Peter Bedingfield and Robert Chamberlain were the two elected from their hundred, and they could not absent themselves without great peril to the neigh-

[1] CP 40/115, mm.230, 230d.

[2] The standard introduction to the early plea rolls is that by C. T. Flower, *Introduction to the Curia Regis Rolls, 1199–1230 A.D.* (SS, LXII, 1943). The first three chapters are particularly helpful for the topic under discussion here.

[3] See Sayles in *King's Bench,* I, xi–xl, for further comment on the emergence of two 'benches' and their respective records.

[4] This feature had almost become regularised by the end of the 1260s. The former system of dispersing them among the pleas may be seen in the published *Curia Regis Rolls.*

[5] The system was instituted in a series of letters dated 28 and 30 Aug. 1295: *CCR 1288–96,* 454–6.

[6] See *CPR 1292–1301,* 169, for the letter of 6 Dec. 1295 to Bovill. Bovill's letters to Mettingham are [1, 2, 4, 6, 8, 9, 11–18, 25].

[7] The appointments of Roscelyn and Maltby bear the same date as Bovill's (6 Dec.), although the three men seem also to have received a general appointment to their tasks shortly after the August parliament devised the plan: *CCR 1288–96,* 455.

[8] Neither Huish's nor Botetourt's appointments can be found in the close or patent rolls, although Botetourt was noted as a warden as early as 28 Sept. 1295: *CPR 1292–1301,* 149.

bourhood. Therefore, he asked Mettingham that 'if these two have anything to do' before him, that he 'save them without damage' [1]. This was a request in a most general way that for an unspecified period of time and in unspecified instances these two men should not suffer damage for non-appearance in the common bench. Bovill sent at least two other letters to Mettingham that were couched in the same general language: in one of these [5] he asked that three constables be saved in the bench 'lest they lose their issues' and, in another, that the chief justice help and save a certain man of the coast guard 'lest he be prosecuted before you for his defaults or lose his issues' [8]. In these letters Bovill did not seem to be thinking of specific judicial events, legal actions or assignment dates from which he wanted these men excused.

In two other types of letters, Bovill wrote in less general language and then, finally, in specific terms of the legal actions to which he referred. By far the largest group of letters from Bovill and his fellow coastal wardens, Peter Roscelyn, Robert Maltby, Richard Huish and John Botetourt, spoke in general terms of inquests, juries and assizes to which their men had been named and from which they should be excused or 'saved from damage', as the phrase was repeatedly used. Bovill usually mentioned 'en plusurs enquestes' [4, 6, 12–14, 17, 18]; Peter Roscelyn's men were involved 'en jures e en assises' [7, 21, 22]; and Richard Huish in Cornwall spoke on one occasion of persons who were 'en jurees e enquestes' [23]. In none of these cases was a date mentioned or a legal suit specified, although Roscelyn stated that his men had been continuously on duty since Hilary term.[9] In two other letters [9, 15] Bovill mentioned an assignment date, in one case the third week after Easter, and in another the Monday after the feast of St Augustine while still failing to give notice of the legal suit that was in progress. But in seven other letters the coastal wardens gave exact information on persons, legal actions and dates, as Bovill did when he informed Mettingham that five men had been in his service by the king's command on the Thursday after the quindene of Easter when they were assigned to be in an inquest connected with the grand distress between Robert son of William Blundeston and Adam, parson of Blundeston church [2].[10] In one instance, we can glimpse the progress of a suit through two letters of Richard Huish who wrote the first to Mettingham in late spring or early summer, asking that Hugh Peverel be excused from duty in an inquest on the octave and quindene of Trinity which had been summoned in a plea of land between four persons as demandants and a fifth as tenant [19; cf. 20]. The inquest was eventually reassigned to the morrow of St Martin, and Huish, asking that Peverel be excused again, probably wrote the second letter during the early part of Michaelmas term [27]. In these cases, and in most others, the wardens spoke of the assignment dates as points in the future, but in a few letters [e.g. 2, 9, 25] they refer to the court days as having already passed.

These matters are important because we must ascertain as closely as possible the class or category of petition represented by the letters so that we may better describe the authority of the judges to grant petitions, and the expectations and needs of those who sent them. Twenty-eight of the thirty letters have a common characteristic: they concern men who were in the king's service and therefore had not been or would not be able to appear when summoned in legal process. There were several provisions for persons who could not appear personally on their appointed day in court. If they were litigants, properly appointed attorneys could attend to their business. But attorneys had no necessary connection with the problem of non-appearance: in the late thirteenth century most parties who could afford it preferred to litigate through attorneys even when they were able to be personally present on every occasion. When the litigant was obliged to be personally present, he could still avoid it if he cast an essoin by virtue of being ill, or of being unable to continue his journey to the court once he had begun it, or of being in the king's service. Of these three conditions of essoin the king's service is of special interest to us here.

The casting and recording of essoins was in the jurisdiction of the bench, but apart from the essoin rolls and the plea rolls, both kept by bench clerks, there is not a large number of petitions or letters dealing with essoin, and when they occur they are directed to the chancery rather than to the bench. They seem invariably to request a warranty of essoin and are best illustrated by Robert Tibetot's letter to William Hamilton in which he noted that since John Crow, bearer of the letter, 'was in the king's service with us three weeks after Easter past, and was essoined for

[9] It must be assumed that these terms refer to Easter and Hilary 1296. See [8, 18, 21].

[10] In [5] Bovill asked that three other men be excused from the same inquest in this same suit.

that time of the king's service before the justices of the bench, we pray and request that you provide him with the king's writ of warranty to the justices of the bench against his assigned day which is the quindene of Michaelmas'.[11] The earl of Lincoln, who was often at the head of a military force in the field, had many occasions to send similar requests. In 1277 he explained to Robert Burnell that a man in his company had essoined himself of the king's service for a plea in a private court, and the earl asked the chancellor to send a writ to the man's lord or his bailiffs so that the essoin would be allowed.[12] John St John while on service in Scotland informed John Langton that one of his men was impleaded before Roger Brabazon in the king's bench and was assigned his day. However, St John had made a hurried trip to London at the king's command and while there had his man essoined of the king's service before the justices. He therefore wanted the chancellor to send a writ to the justices 'to warrant this essoin so that he not incur loss or damage on that day for service of our lord the king'.[13]

There were many instances, however, in which these same persons, and others in similar circumstances, wrote to the chancery about their men involved in legal actions without speaking in terms of essoin or warranty of essoin. By such letters we are given to understand that essoin was not the only way to deal with judicial non-appearance of men in the king's service. There was the inevitable case of the person in the king's service who had been presumably unable to cast an essoin and who had missed his day in court, thereby defaulting and incurring the usual penalties. Sometimes the word 'default' did not occur in the request; the earl of Surrey noted on one occasion that one of his men was in the king's service at Newcastle on the same day that he was impleaded in the bench in a plea of debt. He asked the chancellor to do 'in this matter what was appropriate according to reason'.[14] We are permitted to assume that the chancellor would send a writ to the bench directing the justices not to put the man in default. Reginald Grey spoke more directly when he asked the chancellor not to let his man 'be put in default on account of his absence on that day'.[15] 'Default' was also the word used on at least two occasions in 1294 when the chancery sent letters to the justices of the bench not to put certain men in default because they had missed their assigned days in court.[16] The request to chancery and the subsequent order from chancery not to put a man in default was the way to deal with a retroactive situation, with a particular instance of judicial non-appearance that had occurred in the past. These letters to the chancellor must be considered as chancery petitions in the same way that requests for warranties of essoin were chancery petitions.

The best solution for the person in the king's service was to preclude his judicial non-appearance by putting in respite a given plea or all pleas involving him, either for a term or until he had completed his service. Like petitions for warranty of essoin and petitions to save from default, letters asking for respite went to the chancery and must also be considered as petitions. A good example is the earl of Lincoln's petition to Robert Burnell in 1282 in which he asked the chancellor to order for his valet 'a writ of our lord the king to the justices of the bench to put the pleas touching him in respite for as long as he

[11] SC 1/26, nos. 13, 14. Other examples of warranty of essoin are found in SC 1/27, no. 184 (dated 31 May 1297), where the earl of Surrey asked that one of his men in Scotland have warranty of essoin 'solom les usages de la court'; SC 1/23, no. 178, to Robert Burnell from the forest justice, Roger Strange; SC 1/25, no. 99, to Hamilton as deputy chancellor about an essoin cast before eyre justices at Huntingdon (1286); and SC 1/25, no. 100, to Hamilton (1288) from Reginald Grey, justice of Chester.

[12] SC 1/23, no. 156: '. . . ke vous li voillez fere aver la lettre le rey a mon sire Regnaud le fuiz Perres ou a ses baillis ke le essoyne li seit allue'. See also *Calendar of Ancient Correspondence concerning Wales,* ed. J. G. Edwards (Cardiff, 1935), 123–4.

[13] SC 1/27, no. 136: '. . . dont nous vous prioms si vous plest qe vous le voille graunter bref as ditz joestices pur garantir cele assoigne issint qil ne encourge perde ne damage a cele journee pur le service nostre seignur le rey'.

[14] SC 1/27, no. 188: 'Jaen counte de Warenne a son trescher ami sire John de Langeton chaunceler nostre seignor le reys saluz e cheres amistez. Sire, nous vous feisons a saver e tesmoigons qe Robert de Cleseby fu ove nous en servise nostre seignor le rey au Noef Chastel sour Tyne, lendemayn de la Purificacyon nostre Dame cest an, au queu jour meime celuy Robert fu empledez devant les justices du baunc par un H. de Cleseby de ple de dette, a ceo quil dit. Dount nous vous prioms qe vous voellez de ceste chose fere ceo qe li appent solom reeson'.

[15] SC 1/28, no. 128: '. . . propter absenciam suam quo ad illum diem ponatur in defaltam'.

[16] The two letters are in *CCR 1288–96,* 369–70, and are the only two instances of such a royal order in this volume of letters close.

remains with us in Wales, for you must know that we can not permit him to leave'.[17] The king's brother wrote to the chancery in November 1295 asking for respite for the men going to Gascony, and William Leybourne, as admiral, sent similar petitions for the men serving in his fleet.[18] Contrary to what we might expect, such letters are not numerous, and if we are to assume that in all cases the chancery dispatched letters in the king's name to the bench, as the earl of Lincoln requested, ordering the justices to put such pleas in respite, we discover that such letters of respite are in scant supply, either in extant chancery correspondence or in judicial materials of the bench. Examples are two letters of 1296: in the first, written under the privy seal, the king ordered the bench justices to respite pleas for a particular man serving in Scotland, and in the second he asked that they respite until otherwise ordered his own suit against twenty-seven men who had been appealed of homicide. He wished to show favour to them because they were setting out in his service to Scotland.[19]

In sum then, we have seen that while judicial non-appearance lay clearly in the jurisdiction of the bench justices, the treatment of it, especially for men in the king's service, whether by warranty of essoin, requests not to put in default, or respite from pleas, was secured through petitions to the chancery which were presumably granted by sending letters in the king's name to the bench. Parties other than the king did not address the bench directly in such matters. This is all in contrast to the thirty letters which were sent to Mettingham in 1296. But before returning to these letters we must note two instances in which persons who were not chancery officials did in fact write directly to the bench about persons in the king's service. One of these, from Roger Strange (Lestrange), the forest justice, causes us to believe that there must have been many such letters on numerous other occasions. The letter concerned two verderers of Cannock forest who were summoned to be before Mettingham on a certain day for an assize between two litigants and they had previously been ordered to testify before Roger on certain articles concerning forest business. Observing that the king would suffer great damage if they did not complete their prior assignment first, he asked the chief justice to excuse them on this occasion so that 'they would not suffer loss in any way for prosecution of their absence'.[20] The other letter is a most unusual one and can be understood only against a background of extreme military urgency. It was probably written in 1297–8 when Edward was deeply involved in military operations in Scotland. John Lisle, a baron of the exchequer, assumed the duty of reminding the bench that knights, serjeants and other men of Yorkshire had been ordered to be continuously equipped and ready to go to Scotland for military service, and that many were impleaded. Furthermore, those who were attached and distrained to be before the bench for inquests and juries in Hilary term could not come. Lisle then informed Mettingham and his colleagues that he had enjoined the sheriff to make his return in such writs to this effect, 'that he had done nothing because of the war in Scotland. And may it please you not to challenge this return'.[21]

This survey of the ways of treating judicial non-appearance for men in the king's service indicates that the bench justices could act in such matters only when they received authority to do so from the chancery. Why did the authors of the thirty letters not address their requests to the chancery? We have already noted a characteristic that was common to twenty-eight of the thirty letters: they concerned men in the king's service. Those letters that contain

[17] SC 1/23, no. 159: '. . . ke vous luy voillez fere aver un bref nostre seignur le rey a justises du baunk de mettre les ples que luy tuchent en respit taunt cum il demort oraparmeimes avec nus en Gales, kar sachez que nus nel purrums oraparmeimes deporter'.

[18] See SC 1/28, no. 120 for Edmund's letters; he also sought permission for them to make attorney during their absence. Leybourne's letters are SC 1/27, nos. 87–9. While constable of the army in Wales, Nicholas Segrave requested respite for men serving with him: ibid., nos. 152–4.

[19] SC 1/45, no. 74; *CCR 1288–96,* 475.

[20] SC 1/30, no. 133: 'A ses chers amys sire John de Metingham e ses compaynouns justices nostre seignur le rey du baunk, Roger le Estrange, saluz e cheres amistez. Por ceo chers amis qe Richard de Barton e Rauf de Byssebury verders de la forest de Cannok sount somuns de estre devaunt vous a treys semaines de Paske pur un assise entre Elyz de Tryngeston e Richard de Mortimer, e les avauntdis Richard e Rauf sunt assingnes par bref nostre seignur le rey de enquere par certeins articles de com bien il se peut aprower ou la forest avauntdit e qe il me certefient de ceo a treis semeynes de Paske parunt e ne pount en nule manere estre devaunt vous au jour avaunt nome sy le rey ne eust graunt damage, vous pry chers amys qe vous les eet por escuse a ceste fethe e qe il ne soient de riens perdaunt par acheson de lor absence. E chers amys sy riens voillet vers mey qe jeo pusse fere me facez asaver com a cely qe est tut vostre. A Deu chers amys qe vous gard.'

[21] SC 1/30, no. 136: '. . . enjoint est par moy au vesconte ke il faite sun retour en teus brefs qe il ren nad fet pur la gwere de Escote. E de ceo retur sy le vous plest ne le voillez chalangir.'

specified information have a second common feature that probably explains the decision to send them to Mettingham: the men for whom they were written were never in any instance described as litigants but were all involved in jury duty, whether that duty was referred to as jury, assize or inquest.[22] On the other hand, in the petitions for warranty of essoin, saving from default, and respite from pleas, all of which were sent to the chancery, the men concerned were invariably one of the two litigating parties – plaintiff or defendant, claimant or tenant. Roger Strange stated clearly in his letter to Mettingham that his two men were not litigants but were to serve as jurors in the assize, and the language of his request was similar to that used in certain of the plea roll letters.[23] John Lisle noted that many of the king's men were impleaded in pleas of debt and land, but he gave special attention to 'those who are attached and distrained to be before you this term of Saint Hilary in inquests and juries . . .' In any event, he did not ask for respite from pleas, or relief from any kind of judicial liability; he simply informed Mettingham and his colleagues that he had instructed the sheriff to do nothing by way of executing the writs. His letter was, in effect, not a request or a petition but a notification under circumstances of emergency.[24]

In addition to the twenty-six letters from coastal wardens that were addressed to Mettingham and enrolled in the 1296 Michaelmas plea roll, there is at least one other letter from a warden not among those in the plea roll, and it seems at first glance to contradict our conclusion that respite from pleas could be sought only through chancery petition, and that petitory letters directed to the bench concerned only jurors and never litigants. This particular letter is found among the volumes of Ancient Correspondence and appears to be the only letter in that series from a coastal warden. Adam Gurdon had been assigned to the coast about Southampton and wrote to Mettingham, probably in 1296, informing him that Edmund Hyde had been occupied in the coast guard and was also being impleaded before Mettingham in the bench in a plea of land. Adam asked Mettingham to respite the plea during the remainder of Edmund's service.[25] Did Mettingham, knowing that he as chief justice could not grant respite from pleas without a chancery order, send it to the chancery for appropriate action, and are we to understand that because of Mettingham's action Gurdon's letter found its way into chancery materials and subsequently into Ancient Correspondence rather than remaining in some group of bench materials or being enrolled in the 1296 plea roll?

If we consider the 1296 plea roll letters to Mettingham as 'judicial petitions', analogous in their jurisdictional nature to the several categories of chancery petitions, we are confronted with the specific question whether other types of petitions came to the bench directly from petitioners, and with the general question of judicial correspondence whether of a petitory nature or not. To speak only of the reign of Edward I, it is well known that the close and patent rolls contain hundreds of chancery letters creating judicial commissions, and even of letters dealing with such secondary matters of judicial business as the custody of rolls and the solution of problems arising in connection with the conduct of eyre and assize commissions. They often reflect petitory requests as when they grant quittance of common summons of the eyre to persons in the king's service.[26] Except on the few occasions already mentioned, they do not deal with judicial non-appearance in the bench. In fact letters patent and close were rarely sent to the bench. Of some five thousand letters close in the published calendar for 1272–9, only five were directed to the bench,[27] and of another five thousand

[22] Of the 30 letters, 25 specify that the men have been put on juries. The remaining 5 were from Bovill asking that Mettingham give a general excuse and do not note the exact legal involvement.

[23] Roger's plea, 'qe il ne soient de riens perdaunt par acheson de lor absence', echoes Bovill's 'qe il ne perdunt lur issues' [5], and 'ne qe il ne perde ses issues' [8], and is similar to the Latin of William Bourne 'et quod in nullo sit perdens nec gravatus pro absencia sua' [24].

[24] An example of the kind of warrant that would have led to Lisle's action is the letter that the king sent to the chancellor in 1296 ordering him to tell the sheriff of Yorks that because of the Scottish war no one in his bailiwick was to be delayed for assizes, juries, gaol deliveries and 'other such things': *CCW*, I, 67.

[25] SC 1/30, no. 100: '. . . e meme celu Emund est en pleyde devant vos en banke par un Water du Park en play du terre, vos prie, sire, chirement ke vos voylet respiter celu play durant la garde ke il ne purreyt mie ove nus demurer e atendre a son play'. Gurdon was noted as a coastal warden in *CCR 1296–1302,* 74, where the king instructed the coast guard in Nov. 1296 to reduce the watch during the winter months.

[26] For quittance of common summons of the Wilts eyre in 1288, see ibid., *1288–96,* 29, involving some fifty persons.

[27] ibid., *1272–9,* 378, 440, 484, 526, 583.

of 1288–96, eleven were addressed to the bench.[28] Of these sixteen, two were orders to save litigants from default for non-appearance[29] and a third was an order for respite from pleas;[30] all three concerned men in the king's service, and seem to represent responses to petitions to chancery. The remaining thirteen involve appointments and other administrative business.

Among the materials assembled in Ancient Correspondence, there is a large number of letters from chancery officials to justices, from justices to chancery, a few from judges to judges, and a very few from the king to one or the other of the benches. By far the largest part of this correspondence concerns eyre justices and the business of the eyres. The judges on circuit or on assize commissions had frequent cause to write to chancery for directions and advice, and chancery officers had just as frequent cause to communicate with eyre officials.[31] On the one hand, this 'judicial correspondence' illustrates the complete management of eyre justice by the chancery and the complete absence of any jurisdiction by the common bench over the business of the circuits. On the other hand, it offers evidence again of how infrequently anyone – king, chancery or other persons – addressed the justices of the common bench. Occasionally, private persons wrote to justices on eyre and sent what may be called 'eyre petitions'. There may well have been a large number of these but few have survived, and we know little or nothing about the response to them.[32] Except for Adam Gurdon's petition to Mettingham already noted, there is nothing else in Ancient Correspondence that can be called a 'judicial petition' unless it be the earl of Lincoln's letter of 1277 asking the bench justices not to let a woman suffer damage in a suit because her husband was in the king's service.[33]

We are left with the impression that apart from the authority of the common bench judges to regulate the internal progress of cases and to render judgment, the area of their discretionary action was narrow, and this may account not only for the extremely small volume of correspondence in general that was addressed to them, but also for what seems to have been the only type of 'judicial petition' that called for their independent decisions. Judicial writs were issued by the bench at a particular point in legal proceedings and did not need an external request. The adjournment and reassignment of cases also followed established procedures, and judges' decisions to permit fines do not appear to have been the result of written petitions.[34] In effect, then, persons other than the king and chancery officers had few if any occasions to write to justices of the bench, and the latter, aside from the areas noted above and certain powers of adjudication in the casting of essoins and the recognition of attorneys, had little if any authority to grant petitions except in the matter of jury duty.

Mettingham's decision to have these 'judicial petitions' enrolled in the plea roll must be regarded as an administrative innovation rather than a response to a new type of correspondence. Even if the creation of the coast guard in 1295 made large numbers of men unable to fulfil judicial obligations, requests to excuse men from jury service as contained in the letters from Roger Brabazon, Ralph Beaumont, William Bourne and Roger Strange must have occurred from time out of mind, and there must have been many of them in every judicial term, year after year. It is unlikely that these thirty letters constitute the total for the year or for any term in 1296, and we must simply admit that, for unknown reasons, Mettingham or someone decided to register this particular group. A reasonable conjecture would suggest that Mettingham, seeing the possibility of an enormous increase in such petitions because of the coast guard, and of a very large number of men unable to

[28] ibid., *1288–96*, 64, 200, 219, 291, 294, 305, 369, 370, 411, 475, 516.

[29] ibid., 369, 370. These concerned Henry Grey and William Barrage.

[30] ibid., 475. The respite concerned the men appealed of homicide who had subsequently entered the king's service in Scotland.

[31] For only a few examples among many, see the letter from Solomon Rochester on eyre in Norfolk informing John Kirkby why he had not yet sent estreats to him (SC 1/10, no. 126), or from Robert Burnell to Rochester, telling him that he could not send a certain writ requested because such a writ must be made only by the king's special authority: SC 1/31, no. 19.

[32] For such petitions, see SC 1/30, nos. 20, 20a, 31; 11, no. 96. Those noted from SC 1/30 were apparently first sewn to the eyre rolls, perhaps by the clerks of the eyre justices, and later detached.

[33] SC 1/30, no. 117 (dated at Shrewsbury, 30 Jan. 1277). There is again the possibility that this letter is in the collection of Ancient Correspondence because at some point it became part of chancery materials.

[34] The king occasionally directed the bench justices to permit a fine to be made: e.g. *CCR 1288–96*, 305.

make judicial appearance, decided to have them recorded to keep legal procedure as orderly and clear as possible.

There is also the possibility that Mettingham intended the 1296 enrolment to become a permanent feature of the chief justice's plea roll, for this decade saw several innovations in record keeping, especially in judicial records. In 1288, chancery clerks had begun to sign their names in the lower right corner of original writs, and this practice was taken over by bench clerks writing judicial writs in 1292, although it is uncertain if Mettingham was responsible for this move.[35] Within the plea roll itself, charters seemed to be enrolled after Hilary 1290, the term in which Mettingham became chief justice, and this became a long-lived feature of the plea rolls.[36] The 1290s may well have been the period when the assignment dates for replevins were drawn up in a continuous list and inserted just before the attorney membranes. It was also in this decade that the growing formal organisation of the king's pleaders and attorneys produced the idea of grouping all pleas sued for the king on certain membranes, often with the prefixed title of 'pro rege'.[37] But while this section occurred frequently, it never became a standard part of the plea roll. Finally, there are the thirty letters of the 1296 Michaelmas roll and these too must be considered an innovation although they proved to be a very temporary one.

Whether John Mettingham was responsible for these plea roll changes or not, he was the presiding officer of the bench during this period and must be considered as the person who oversaw, and approved of, the changes.[38] For a man who governed the common bench for a dozen years he is one of the more obscure judicial figures of Edward's reign.[39] His public career is documented well enough in the close and patent rolls, certainly as well as similar careers of most of his colleagues. We know nothing of him before he was assigned to a general assize commission in 1274 with Geoffrey Lewknor,[40] and from then until he was named chief justice of the common bench in January 1290 he was continuously busy in assize and oyer and terminer commissions and on eyre circuits. He began his career as an eyre judge in the autumn of 1278 upon the commissioning of the first series of circuits by Edward I, and during the next eleven years served on eyre in ten counties.[41] He must be counted as one of the busiest judges during the 1280s, the last great decade of the eyres. Yet, there is nothing in the records that points to him as a more distinguished or more prominent judge than any of ten other colleagues engaged in the same work, men like John Vaux, William Saham, Richard Boyland and Thomas Sodington. He was probably not given the chief position in a commission until the Dorset eyre of 1288.[42]

When Edward reconstituted the common bench in

[35] The first signatures of chancery clerks occur on writs dated in Oct. 1288 and composed for the quindene of Hilary 1289. These are in the Bench Writ Files (CP 52), quindene of Hilary 17 Edw. I. In May 1292 bench clerks began putting their signatures on judicial writs for the octave of Michaelmas: ibid., octave of Michaelmas 20/21 Edw. I.

[36] The charters were enrolled on membranes immediately following the pleas, and before the attorney membranes. They concerned most often bench officers, although certain ones seem to deal with persons not connected with the bench. There is no recognisable charter section in the Hilary 1290 roll, but a charter, containing a grant of land by William Gisleham who had just become a bench justice, was inserted within the plea membranes: CP 40/81, m.99d. By 1293 the charter section of the plea roll was definitely established. See, e.g., CP 40/101, mm.178–80, for Trinity term 1293.

[37] The 'pro rege' title appears to occur for the first time in Easter 1297 (CP 40/118, mm.128–129d) where a large number of pleas are sued for the king by several persons. A 'pro rege' section occurs again in Trinity 1297: CP 40/119, mm.147–148d. In both rolls, and in later rolls, other pleas sued for the king appear in random fashion throughout the roll. In the Michaelmas plea roll of 1297 the 'pro rege' pleas are labelled at the foot, and occupy the last three membranes before the enrolled charters: CP 40/121, mm.307–309d.

[38] An officer of the bench other than Mettingham could have been responsible for changes in the plea roll. A likely person was the keeper of rolls and writs. John Lovell held this office for the first two years of Mettingham's chief justiceship, and John Bacon, who eventually became a judge himself, held it for the remainder of Mettingham's career: Sayles in *King's Bench,* I, cxlviii–cxlix. Another possibility was Mettingham's chief clerk, the person who was in charge of his plea roll. Henry Hales may have been such a person; Sayles discovered him as Mettingham's clerk in an assize commission in 1289: ibid., lxxx.

[39] Mettingham does not appear in *DNB*. Dugdale, *Origines Juridiciales . . .*, 2nd edn (London, 1671), called Mettingham a serjeant at law in 1276 on the one hand (Chronica series, 25), and a king's bench justice on the other (ibid., 26). Foss, *Judges of England,* III, 132, repeated this misreading of the liberate rolls. See Sayles in *King's Bench,* I, xli, for corrections of Dugdale.

[40] *CCR 1272–9,* 136. The commission included twelve counties.

[41] See ibid., 479, 504, for the first of these commissions to Cumberland, Westmorland and Northumberland.

[42] *CPR 1281–92,* 294, and *CCR 1279–88,* 536, have the commission for the Dorset eyre. He had been named chief justice of the Kent eyre a few weeks earlier but that commission was cancelled: ibid., 529.

January 1290, in the wake of the judicial scandals that had come to light upon his return from France a few months earlier, he chose Mettingham as the chief justice because of his large judicial experience and especially because he was one of the very few untainted by the accusations of bribery and corruption.[43] He directed the common bench during a most crucial period when it first began to assimilate the large amount of statutory legislation from the earlier part of the reign that had to be applied and interpreted in everyday litigation. His rôle in this process may never be fully understood, but there are materials for study of this question and a cursory examination of them suggests that he was an important influence in legal development and that he ruled his court with fairness and competence.[44] As to family, social background and private business, one can say more about most of his colleagues, both on eyre and in the bench, that about Mettingham. The usual land and rental transactions that enable us to estimate the material worth and social connections of persons high in the king's service are absent in his case.[45]

[43] *State Trials of the Reign of Edward the First, 1289–1293*, ed. T. F. Tout and H. Johnstone (Camden 3rd ser., IX, 1906).

[44] The material is to be found in the law reports of the 1290s, most of which are unpublished. There is sometimes extended comment by Mettingham in these reports on matters of legal substance; at other times he ruled on points of law, and on occasion there are specific 'nota' attributed to him. For examples, see BL, Add. MS 37657, ff.20, 21v, 22v.

The lack of sufficient information about Mettingham's life and conduct as a chief justice that might explain why he had these letters enrolled should not prevent us from estimating the significance of the letters themselves. They provide a rare kind of information on the management and nature of the coast guard, coming as they do from the men who served in it; in this respect they afford a unique glimpse of this unusual defence measure and of the attitudes of the men who managed it. As legal documents they lead us to conceive of a class of administrative correspondence which we may tentatively classify as judicial petitions. They also cast new light on the obscure question of the discretionary authority that judges of either bench were able to exercise. It is perhaps equally important to speculate on the body of knowledge we would possess if Mettingham had decided to continue enrolling in each term this kind of letter as well as all letters of a petitory nature. We would understand better various administrative operations and various aspects of judicial process than we now do.

[45] Pertinent cartularies and other ecclesiastical materials may yield additional information on Mettingham. He was the executor of a bench clerk, Aunger Ripon, in 1294 (CP 40/106, m.133), from whom he received in legacy two houses and several shops in Southwark and fifteen acres in Lambeth. He established these as revenue sources in 1297 for the lifetime of his sister, Beatrice: CP 40/116, m.135.

TEXT

CP 40/115, m.230

ROTULUS DE LITTERIS MISSIS JUSTICIARIIS DE BANCO PER CUSTODES SUPER COSTERAM MARIS DE TERMINIS PASCHE, SANCTE TRINITATIS ET MICHAELIS ANNO REGNI REGIS EDWARDI FILII REGIS HENRICI VICESIMO QUARTO

[1] [*Marginated*] Littera W. de Bovyle
A sun cher seignur e amy, sire Johan de Metingham, justice nostre seignur le rey, Williame de Bovile, saluz, reverences e honurs. Sachez, sire, qe jeo ay establi en chescun hundred en Suffouke[46] a la garde de la mer fere deus conestables dunt sire Peres de Bedingfeld e sire Roberd le Chaumberleyn sunt les deus elus en le hundred de Hoxne les queus ne pount estre deportez pur perils qe pount avenir en nos parties. Dunt jeo vus pri, cher sire, qe si ceus deus eeunt a fere devaunt vous qe vus les volyez sauver saunz damage. Saluz, cher sire.

[2] [*Marginated*] W. de Bovile
A sire Johan de Metingham, justice nostre seignur le rey en baunke, Williame de Bovyle, saluz e cheres amistes. Sachez, sire, qe Geffrey de Askeby, Bartolmeu Love, Thomas de Habelund, Emund de Heygham e Williame Wynny par comaundement qe nus les feseymes de par nostre seignur le rey furunt devaunt nus le joudy procheyn apres la quynseyne de la Pasche a oyr e fere ceo qe nus lur comaunderums a la garde de la mer fere, issi qe devaunt vous ne poeyunt estre a ceo jur en un enqueste en la quele il furent mys par la graunt destresse entre Roberd le fiz Williame de Blundestone e Adam persone del eglise de Blundestone. Par quey, sire, si vus plest, a ceu jur par cele defaute ne voillyez suffrir qil seyunt grevez. A Deu, sire, qe vus gard.[47]

[3] [*Marginated*] R. Bomund
Domino suo et amico si placet, domino J. de Metingham, suus R. Bomund, clericus, salutem. Quia Johannes de Honterston, Johannes Lambyn de Langham et Bartholomeus de Livermere qui coram vobis in banco in quindena Pasche in quadam jurata facienda summoniti fuerunt ad taxationem et collectionem undecime in hundredo de Blakeburne faciendas deputantur, ipsos si placet conservare velitis indemnes. Valeat dominatio vestra per tempora diutina.

[4] [*Marginated*] W. de Bovile
A sun cher seignur e amy, sire Johan de Metingham, justice nostre seignur le rey, le seon lyge Williame de Bovile, saluz e tuz honurs e reverences. Pur ceo, cher sire, qe Johan de Redesham le jeovene est mys en plusurs enquestes devaunt vus e il est fet par moy e par paiis chef conestable del hundred de Wayneford e son companyon Johan de Buresyerd[48] pur agister le genz a armes qe funt la garde a la mer, vus pri, cher sire, si pleysir vus est qe meymes ceus devaunt vus voillyez sauver saunz damage. A Deu, sire, qe vus gard, cors e alme.

[5] [*Marginated*] W. de Bovile
A sun cher seignur e amy, sire Johan de Metingham, justice nostre seignur le rey, le seon Williame de Bovyle, saluz e tus honurs. Sachez, sire, qe nus avum eleu e assigne Wauter de Ubbestone, Emun le Sauvage e Geffrey Kempe, conestables del hundred de Blythyngg,[49] de agister e ordiner le genz del hundred de la garde a la mer fere. Dunt jeo vus pry, cher sire, qe vus le volyez sauver issi qe il ne perdunt lur issues kar sachez, sire, qe il ne pount nent estre hors del pays. Saluz, sire.

[6] [*Marginated*] W. de Bovyle
A son trescher seignur e amy, sire Johan de Metingham, justice nostre seignur le rey en baunke, le seon lyge Williame de Bovyle, si luy plest, saluz ou tuz honurs e reverences. Cher sire, pur ceo qe Roberd de Sanecroft e Rauf le fiz Richard sunt mis en plusurs enquestes devaunt vus e il sunt chef conestables del hundred de Wayneford pur agister le genz a armes e funt la garde a la mer, vus pri, sire, cherement qe meymes ces devaunt vus voillyez sauver saunz damage. Saluz.[50]

46 All the letters from Bovill concerned Suffolk hundreds.

47 This letter probably concerns Lothingland hundred since Blundeston and several of the places associated with the personal names are in that hundred.

48 See [17] for a second petition for these two constables.

49 A specific request was made for Walter Ubbeston in [9] and a general request for Edmund Savage in [17].

50 In [4] two other men seemed to be chief constables of Wangford hundred. Sancroft appears again in [8].

[7] [*Marginated*] P. Roscelyn
A sun trecher amy, sire Johan de Metingham, justice nostre seignur le rey, le son Pers Roscelyn, si luy plest, saluz e cheres amites. Pur ceo qe jay assigne Roger de Perers un de conestables sur la garde de la mer en le cunte de Norf' si com comaunde me est par nostre seignur le rey a mettre ceus qe meuz seuent e purunt la garde fere, e le vescunte a respoundu de sa meynpris e des ses issues de estre devaunt vus a Lundres en jures e en assises a quei il ne put atendre, vus pri, sire, si vus plest, qe memes celi Roger taunt com il est en le service nostre seignur le rey sur cele garde saunz damage le voilliez sauver. A Deu, sire, qe vus gard tu jurs.

[8] [*Marginated*] W. de Bovyle
A sun cher seignur e amy, sire Johan de Metingham, justice noster seignur le rey, le soen Williame de Bovyle, saluz, reverences e honurs. Cher sire, pur ceo qe Roberd de Sanecroft fust assigne a la garde e la veyle fere de la mer pus la feste de Seynt Illere en ca e uncore est continuaument demoraunt, vus pry, cher sire, si pleysir vus seyt, qe memes celuy Roberd voliez eyder e sauver qe il ne seie enchesune devaunt vus pur ses defautes ne qe il ne perde ses issues kar jeo luy ay promys par la fiaunce qe jeo ay en vus qe jeo luy sauveray saunz damage. Si ren voyllyez vers moy qe fere pusse com a vostre lyge, me maundez. Saluz qe Deus vus gard.[51]

[9] [*Marginated*] W. de Bovyle
A sun trecher seygnur e amy, si luy plest, sire Johan de Metingham, chef justice du baunke nostre seignur le rey, le seon Williame de Bovyle, saluz, honurs e reverences. Pur ceo qe Wauter de Ubbestone fut a tres semeynes de Paske a la garde de la mer a chyvaus e armes par nostre comaundement, issi qe en nule manere ne pout estre devaunt vus a Lundres a jour avaunt nomee, vus pri, si le vus plest, qe par encheson de cele defaute de damage luy voillyez sauver, kar le avauntdit Wauter e Emun le Sauvage sunt chef conestables jures en le hundred de Blithingg. Saluz.[52]

[10] [*Marginated*] P. Roscelyn
A sun trecher amy, mun sire Johan de Metingham, justice nostre seignur le rey, le soen chyvaler, Pers Roscelyn, gardeyn de la costere de la mer de Norf',[53] si luy plest, saluz e tuz honurs. Sachet, cher sire, qe Wauter de Calthorpe est conestable del hundred de Galhowe qe est sur la mer par mun assignment, par quey il ne put atendre de estre en jure ne en assise hors de sa balie pur dute de nos enemies. Pur quey, cher sire, jeo vus pri qe ses issues e ses meynpernurs seyunt sauvez devaunt vus en baunke, si le vus plest. Saluz, cher sire, qe Deu vus sauve tu jurs.

[11] [*Marginated*] W. de Bovyle
A sire Johan de Metingham, justice nostre seignur le rey en baunke, Williame de Bovyle, saluz e cheres amites. Sachez, sire, qe Johan del Auneye, Nicole e Simund del Gap de Suthjernemuthe par comaundement qe nus les feseymes de par nostre seignur le rey furent devaunt nus le judi prochein apres la quinzeyne de la Pasche a oyr e fere ceo qe nus lur comaunderuns a la garde de la mer fere, issi qe devaunt vus ne poeyunt estre a ceo jur en un enqueste en la quele il furunt mys par la graunt destresse entre Roberd le fiz Williame de Blundestone e Adam persone de le eglise de Blundestone, par quey, sire, si vus plest, a cel jour par cele defaute ne voillyez suffrir qil seyent grevez. A Deu qe vus gard.[54]

[12] [*Marginated*] W. de Bovyle
A sun cher seignur e amy, sire Johan de Metingham, justice nostre seignur le rey, le soen lyge Williame de Bovile, saluz e quanke qe il pout de honurs e de reverences. Sachez, cher sire, qe Richard le fiz Roberd de Playford, Aundrew de Thunderle, Johan Bertelmew, Thomas Talenas, William de Hoo, Johan fiz Gerard de Hoo, William de Ramesholt, Austyn de Kenebrok ke sunt chef conestables en la fraunchise Seynt Andree en divers lous e sunt continuement demoraunz a chivaus e armes sur la mer, e memes celuy Rychard e ses compaynons sunt somuns devaunt vus en diverses enquestes e sunt mys a lur issues, vus pri, cher sire, si pleysir vus seyt, qe meme ceus saunz damage voilez sauver. Saluz qe Deu vus gard.[55]

[13] [*Marginated*] W. de Bovyle
A sun trecher seignur e amy, sire Johan de Metingham,

[51] See [6] for Sancroft.

[52] See [5] for Ubbeston and [5, 17] for Savage.

[53] Except for [7], Roscelyn, as warden of the Norfolk coast, identified his office in all letters to Mettingham.

[54] This case was also the subject of [2] where five other men were put on the same inquest.

[55] The franchise of St Andrew probably refers to the cathedral priory of St Andrew, Rochester, which held the Benedictine priory of Felixstowe and various lands in Suffolk: *VCH Suff*, II, 80.

justice nostre seignur le rey en baunke, le seon lige William de Bovyle, saluz, reverences e honurs. Sachez, cher sire, qe sire Johan de Ketelberge est demoraunt a chyvaus e armes a la garde de la mer fere, e il est en divers enquestes devaunt vus e est a ses issues. Vus pry, cher sire, qe le vaundit sire Johan saunz damage de vaunt vus voliez sauvez. Saluz, cher sire, qe Deu vus gard.[56]

[14] [*Marginated*] W. de Bovyle
A sun cher seygnur, sire Johan de Metingham, le seon lyge Williame de Bovyle, saluz e quant qe il put de honur e de reverences. Sachet, cher sire, qe Williame de Hoo est chef conestable del hundred de Lose en la fraunchise de Seynt Andree[57] e est continuement demoraunt pres de la mer a chivaus e a armes a la garde fere, e il est somons devaunt vus en diverses enquestes e est mys a ces issues, par quey jeo vus pri, cher sire, qe memes celuy Williame voylez, si pleysir vus seyt, sauver saunz damage. Saluz.

[15] [*Marginated*] W. de Bovyle
A sun trescher amy si luy plest, sire Johan de Metingham, justice nostre seignur le rey, le seon Williame de Bovyle, gardein de la mer de Suff',[58] saluz e tous honurs. Cher sire, jeo vus pri, si vus plest, pur men amy Williame de Cramavile, conestable del hundred de Thinghowe en la fraunchise Seyn Emun, qy est a Waltone a la mer pur la garde fere e qy somouns devaunt vus en baunke en enquestes le lundi procheyn apres la feste Seynt Austyn, qe vus, cher sire, si vus plest, luy voylez sauver, pur lamur de moy, ses issues e de tuz damages. Saluz.

[16] [*Marginated*] W. de Bovyle
A sun trecher seignur e amy, si luy plest, sire Johan de Metingham, justice nostre seignur le rey, le seon lyge Williame de Bovyle, saluz, honurs e reverences. Pur ceo, cher sire, qe Johan Ermenger e Gilberd de Clovile sunt chef conestables del hundred de Plumbesgate en la fraunchise Seynt Andre e sunt illoc continuement a la garde de la mer e sunt destrynz par la graunt destresse a estre devaunt vus ore a la quinzeyne de la Trinite en une enqueste entre Howe Pecche et dame Jone Pecche, cher sire, pur quei jeo vus pri cherement qe meme ces Johan e Gyleberd devaunt vus a ceu jour saunz damage volyez sauver. Saluz en Deu.

[17] [*Marginated*] W. de Bovyle
A sun trecher seignur e amy, sire Johan de Metingham, justice nostre seignur le rey en baunke, le seon lyge Williame de Bovyle, saluz, reverences e honurs. Sachez, cher sire, qe Johan de Buresyerd e Johan le fiz Wauter de Redisham sunt chef conestables del hundred de Wayneford e agistez devaunt mey e me companynons a chivaus e a armes a la garde de la mer fere de jur e de nuyt, e illouke sunt demoraunt continuament si com il sunt a goynt par le rey e il sunt mis a lur issues a estre devaunt vous en diverses enquestes. Vus pri, cher sire, qe les avaundiz Johan e Johan saunz damage de vaunt vus, si pleysir vus est, voilliez sauver. Et sachez, sire, qe Emun le Sauvage est un de chef conestables en le hundred de Blyinghe e est demoraunt a chevaus e a armes a la garde de la mer en la furme avaundite e est a ces issues de estre devaunt vus. Vus pri, cher sire, qe meymes celuy Edmun voylliez sauver saunz damage. Saluz.[59]

Membrane 230d

[18] [*Marginated*] W. de Bovyle
A sun cher seignur e amy, sire Johan de Metingham, justice nostre seignur le rey en baunke, le seon lyge Williame de Bovyl, saluz e quant qe il put de honurs e de reverences. Sachez, cher sire, qe Johan de Ulvestone est chef conestable en le hundred de Thrindling pus la Pasche en ca e uncore est a hore demourt a chevaus e armes sur la mer continuaument e il est en divers enquestes de vaunt vus, pur quey jeo vus pri, cher sire, qe memes celuy Johan devaunt vus voylliez saunz damage sauver si pleysir vus seyt. Saluz.

[19] [*Marginated*] R. de Hywys
A sun cher seignur e amy, sire Johan de Metingham, justice nostre seignur le rey en baunke de Weymouster e ses compaynuns, Richard de Hywys, gardeyn de la marine en Corwaylle, saluz cum a sey. Cher sire, sachez qe sire Huwe Peverel est su la mer par comaundement le rey avaundit, pur la que choses jeo vus pri qe le vaundit Huwe Peverel[60] ne soit en damage en

56 This letter may refer to Loes hundred where Kettleburgh is located.

57 In [12] William Hoo was named as one of eight chief constables in various places in the franchise of St Andrew.

58 This is the only letter in which Bovill referred to his office by a title.

59 See [4] for Bruisyard and Redisham, and [5, 9] for Savage.

60 Hugh Peverel occurs again in [20, 27]. The case in [27] was apparently a different case from the one mentioned here.

les enquestes dunt il est mys entre Gilberd de la Coudreye e Ysoude sa femme e Michel de Bray e Thomas de Polmorrenna demaundaunt e Thomas de Penros de play de terre dunt sun jur est as utaves de la Trinite e a quinzeyne. Saluz e si ren voyllez en vers moy maundez com a vostre.

[20] [*Marginated*] R. de Hywys
A sun cher seignur e amy si luy plest, sire Johan de Metingham, justice nostre seignur le rey du baunke de Weymonster, le sun Richard de Hywys, gardein de la mer en Corwaylle, saluz com a sey. Cher sire, sachez qe sire Huwe Peverel[61] qe e lenqueste entre nostre seignur le rey pleyntyf e Richard Bacyn e Annore sa femme defendaunz devaunt vus, es sus la garde de la mer en Corwayyle par mun comaundement pur la quele chose jeo vus pri e requer qe il ne seyt en damages devaunt vus a quinzeyne de la Trinite. E sachez, cher sire, qe vus me avet mis en graunt travayl e en graunt despenses qe pus qe jeo parlay a vus ne jeo ne fu en ma mesun demeyne une nuyt entere e nus avont sus la mer cynkant chyvaus covert e cynquante mil hommes a pe. Saluz.

[21] [*Marginated*] P. Roscelyn
A sun cher amy, mun sire Johan de Metingham, justice nostre seignur le rey, Pieres Roscelyn, assigne a la garde de la mer en le cunte de Norf', saluz e bon amur. Sachez, sire, qe Simon de Chesterfeld, Rauf de Bek, Richard le Keu, Williame de Refham e Rauf de Bretham sunt a la garde de la mer continueument e umt este par mun assignement pus la Paske, issi qe il ne poeient estre de vaunt vus en jures ne en assises dunt, sire, vus pri qe lur meynprise e lur issues, si vous plest, voliez sauver. Saluz.

[22] [*Marginated*] P. Roscelyn
A sun cher amy, mun sire Johan de Metingham, justice nostre seignur le rey, le sens, si luy plest, Peres Roscelyn, gardeyn de les parties de la mer en le counte de Norff', saluz en bon amur. Sachez, sire, qe Jehan del Ile, Martin de Suthmere e William de Seccheford sunt jurees de vaunt moy de estre sur la garde de la mer issi qe il ne pount estre en jurees devaunt vus par quey vus pry, sire, qe lur issues e lur meinprise, si vus plest, voylliez sauver. Saluz.

[23] [*Marginated*] R. de Hywys
A sun trecher seignur, si luy plest, honur e reverence touz jours. Trecher sire, pur ceo qe sire Johan de Lambron, Johan de Kellerion, Thomas de Trelegh et Johan le Petyt de Tresulwethen, ausi com touz les autres gentiz hommes del cunte de Corwalle par le comaundement le rey sunt de jour en jour sur la costere de la mer devaunt mei pur fere la garde come lun fet par tut Engletere, les queus sunt en jurees e enquestes devaunt vus par unt il porrunt encoure graunt damage en perte taunt com il servunt le rey, taunt en facez, si le vus plest, qe vos genz de Corwallie sentent vostre eyde com tut tens unt fet. Saluz.

[24] [*Marginated*] W. de la Bruere
Viris providis et discretis, domino J. de Metingham et sociis suis, justiciariis domini regis, Willelmus de la Burne, clericus domini regis ad custumam suam apud Sanctum Botulphum custodiendam deputatus, salutem cum omni reverencia et honore. Sciatis quod Johannes de Fenne mecum in societate est assignatus ad predictam custumam recipiendam et custodiendam per Johannem del Yle, baronem de scaccario, loco Thome Peyt, quondam socii mei, nuper defuncti. Ita quod idem Johannes de Fenne coram vobis apud Westmonasterium in octabis Sancti Michaelis interesse non potest in jurata inter magistrum de Malteby et Petrum de Gypthorp in comitatu Linc' sine maximo dispendio domini regis quo circa vestram rogo discretionem quatinus absenciam dicti Johannis de Fenne si placet habere velitis excusatam in hoc parte et quod in nullo sit perdens nec gravatus pro absencia sua. Valete.

[25] [*Marginated*] W. de Bovyle
A soen trecher seignur e amy, si luy plet, sire Johan de Metingham, justice nostre seignur le rey, le soen lyge William de Bovyle, saluz, reverences e honurs. Pur ceo qe Phelip de Bockyngg fut mis par meynprise de estre devaunt vous en un enqueste entre Roger le fiz William le Deneys e Johan le Clerke de Codenham a la quinzeyne de Sein Michel au queu jour meymes celuy Phelip fut devaunt mey e mes compaynons a Walton a la mer pur la garde fere si come nus aveymes comaundement de par nostre seignur le rey, por quey jeo vus pri, cher sire, si vus plest, qe vus luy voylliez sauver saunz damage por la defaute de cele jurnee. Saluz.

[26] [*Marginated*] R. de Mauteby
A ses cheres seignurs e amys, sire Johan de Metingham e ses compaynons, justices du baunke nostre seignur le rey, lur Roberd de Mauteby, gardeyn de la mer, saluz. Pur ceo qe Johan de Pykeryngg, William de Holvestone sunt jurez al office de connestablie en le

[61] See [19, 27] for other petitions for Hugh Peverel.

hundre de Flegg' a la garde fere de la mer, vus pri qe en enquestes en les queus il sunt sumouns devaunt vous, les voyllyez desporter taunt com la garde dure, issi qe il ne seyent amerciez. Saluz.

[27] [*Marginated*] R. de Hywys
A sun cher seignur, sire Johan de Metingham, justice nostre seignur le rey du baunke e ses compaynuns, le soen Richard de Hywys, gardeyn de la mer en Corwaylle, saluz. Sachet qe sire Huwe Peverel[62] est a la garde de la mer en Corwaylle par nostre comaundement pur la que chose jeo vus pri qe le vaunt dit Huwe ne seyt en damage devaunt vus lendemeyn de Seyn Martin en le enqueste dunt il e mis entre Michel de Bray demaundaunt e Gilberd de la Coudrey tenaunt en play de terre. E remembrez vus, cher sire, de covenaunt qe vus me feytes taunt com je fu gardeyn de la mer qe jeo ne serei devaunt vus en baunke en damage en issues ne en amerciemens taunt com je fuse en cele garde, par hunt jeo fu en graunt damage al conte de Deveneshyre. Pur la que chose jeo vus pry, cher sire, qe de damages devaunt vus me gardez. Saluz.

[28] [*Marginated*] R. Brabazun
A sages homme e sun trecher compaynoun e amy, sire Johan de Metingham, justice nostre seignur le rey, le soen en tutes choses Roger Brabazon, saluz e quant qe il seet e peot de amur e de amiste. Pur ceo, sire, qe un William Buntyng de Estaunford devroit aver este devaunt vous en une juree entre la persone de le eglise de Seyn Michel le majour de Estaunford e Gilberd de Chasterton a treis semeynes de Seyn Michel e il fut taunt en mun service al oure qe il ne pout estre. Je vus pry cherement qe vus luy voliez de ceo fere grace issint qe il ne seyt mye par cel enchesun en damage pur le amur de moy. Vostre voluntir, sire, en tutes choses si le vus plest me voylliez maunder com a celuy qe volunters la fra a seon poer. Saluz.[63]

[29] [*Marginated*] R. Brabazun
A sages homme e seon trecher compaynon e amy si luy plest, sire Johan de Metingham, justice nostre seignur le rey, le seon Roger Brabazoun, saluz e quant qe il seet e peot de amur e de amite. Pur ceo qe un chivaler, sire Beneyt de Rolliston, mon veysin, qe est mis en une juree devaunt vus me ad requys qe jeo vus tesmoigne sun estat. Sire, jeo faz a saver qe il est tel estat de cors e de chateus e de age qe il ne pout venir. Dount jeo vus pry qe vus luy vollyez de ceo aver escuse pur lamur de moy. Saluz.

[30] [*Marginated*] J. Buteturte
A sun trecher amy, sire Johan de Metingham, justice nostere seignur le rey, Johan Buteturte, saluz e amistez en tutes choses. Pur ceo qe sire Johan de Estafford porta la lettre le rey a Jernemue pur especiaument une garde fere e primerment en parties de Jernemue e de Luthynglond dunt graunt damage poreyt avenir a reaume si cele garde ne seyt estreytement fete, a la quele garde a fere en Luthinglaund sunt eluz e jurez Johan Guntone, Nicole Sywath', Johan de Enges, Henry de Enges, Thomas de Habelund, Edmon de Heyham,[64] E. de Corton e Johan dil Aunoy, vus priums, cher sire, si com nos sumes de vostre amiste e pur lamur le rey e du reaume qe vus les eyez e sensez a jours qe il sunt somuns de vaunz vus e ajournez a saver au mey de la Seyn Michel e as utaves de la Seyn Martyn. Cher sire, taunt en facez qe eus seyent saunz damage pur ceo qe eus ne venent devaunt vous. Car, certeynement, sire, nous ne les pouom desporter par la costere ou il devient la garde fere pur graunt peril qe purreit avenir par lur absence. Saluz a Deu qe vus gard.

[62] See [19, 20] for Hugh Peverel.

[63] This and [29] were from Roger Brabazon CJKB.

[64] Thomas Hapland and Edmund Higham were in Bovill's jurisdiction in [2].

A coroners' roll of the liberty of Wye, 1299–1314

edited by

R. F. HUNNISETT

INTRODUCTION

This small roll, which was discovered in 1973 among previously unsorted legal miscellanea in the Public Record Office and has been added to the class of Coroners' Rolls as no. 276, is interesting and important in several respects. It is the only coroners' roll so far known to have survived from a liberty other than a borough as a result of a general eyre, and it is therefore the earliest of its kind yet discovered; it is believed to be unique in that some of the cases entered on it were held by coroners elected for the body of the county and others by coroners appointed by the lord of the liberty; and none of the cases resulted in an entry of any kind on the eyre roll. These facts and the make-up of the coroners' roll shed some further light on the subject of record keeping by medieval coroners and their clerks, although they give rise to more problems than they solve.

Very few franchisal coroners' rolls survive from any part of the middle ages.[1] The great majority of the rolls deriving from general eyres belonged to county coroners, the only others previously known belonging to coroners of the boroughs of Bedford, Northampton, Kings Lynn and Great Yarmouth, and the city of London.[2] A further small number of borough rolls of similar date are preserved in local record offices and elsewhere,[3] but, so far as is known, the Wye roll is the only non-borough franchisal roll surviving anywhere for the period of the general eyre. Fewer liberties had the right to have their own coroners before 1330 than later,[4] and the Wye roll may therefore remain the earliest extant franchisal coroners' roll.

It survives as a result of the special eyre held for the liberty in 1314. The manor of Wye, to which the hundred belonged,[5] had been granted to the newly-founded abbey of Battle by William the Conqueror,[6] and in 1271 the abbot was granted the right to have a special eyre for all pleas concerning him and his tenants whenever there was a general eyre in any county in which he had lands and men, the pleas to be held by one of the eyre justices and the abbot's steward.[7] A tradition was established that such special eyres followed the general eyre. Thus a general eyre, held by John Berwick and his fellows for Kent, began at Canterbury on 12 April 1293, and after it had ended William Barford (de Bereford), one of the justices, and Luke de la Gare, the abbot's steward, held a special eyre at Wye for the abbot's liberty from 7 January 1294.[8] Similarly the royal justices under Harvey Stanton opened the main Kent eyre at Canterbury on 1 July 1313 and it continued, with adjournments, at Canterbury and Rochester until 8 June 1314, after which the Wye eyre was held by Henry Spigurnel, a justice, and William Northhoo, the abbot's steward, from 25 June.[9]

The abbots of Battle based their claim to appoint their own coroners for Wye and all their other lands on charters of the Conqueror and his successors which granted the abbey wide-ranging regalian rights in the most general terms.[10] The argument was that by such general words the Conqueror and his successors intended that Battle abbey and all its possessions should be outside the control of royal officials and that if coroners had been in existence in the eleventh century the abbot would have been given the right to appoint his own.

No such appointments were made for more than half a century after the introduction of the office of coroner in 1194. It is certain that Wye had no coroner of its own before the Kent eyre of 1255,[11] but the abbot probably began to appoint coroners there almost immediately after it. Ralph de Greston was coroner of the abbot's half-hundred of Battle throughout the period between the Sussex general

[1] They are listed in R. F. Hunnisett, 'The Medieval Coroners' Rolls', *Am. Jnl Leg. Hist.*, III (1959), 324–59.

[2] ibid., 324–6. See ibid., 206–8 for the preservation of coroners' rolls with the eyre rolls.

[3] ibid., 357–9.

[4] R. F. Hunnisett, *The Medieval Coroner* (Cambridge, 1961), 139–42.

[5] *Placita de Quo Warranto. . .*, (RC, 1818), 334–5.

[6] *CChR*, III, 196–7; W. Dugdale, *Monasticon Anglicanum*, ed. J. Caley, H. Ellis and B. Bandinel (London, 1846), III, 244.

[7] *CPR 1266–72*, 601–2.

[8] JUST 1/376; 378A.

[9] JUST 1/383; 384A; F. J. Pegues, 'A monastic society at law in the Kent eyre of 1313–1314', *EHR*, LXXXVII (1972), 550, 564.

[10] JUST 1/384A, m.8; *Plac. Quo Warr.*, 333–5; *Monasticon*, III, 244.

[11] JUST 1/361, m.49.

eyres of November 1255 and November 1262.[12] No earlier Battle coroner is known and it is inherently probable that the abbot began appointing coroners in his Kent and Sussex lands at the same time.[13] Certainly three successive coroners for Wye are known to have been appointed by abbots before 1284 and at least the first two of these were appointed in the reign of Henry III. The first was William Leaute, who was succeeded in turn by Thomas Shorne and Thomas Brownman.[14] Shorne was in office throughout the period between the Kent eyres of 1262–3 and 1271,[15] and quite possibly for longer. Brownman died some time between 1279 and 1284. At one point in the 1314 Wye eyre roll he is said to have died thirty years before the eyre, that is, in 1284, whereupon the then abbot of Battle through negligence omitted to appoint a successor and the county coroners intruded into the office of coroner in the hundred; and at another point he is said to have died thirty-one years earlier, that is, in 1283, during an abbatial vacancy which allowed the county coroners to intrude.[16] The round number would normally be regarded as less likely to be exact than thirty-one years, but unfortunately the apparent precision of the latter is undermined by the fact that there was no abbatial vacancy at Battle in 1283, since Henry Aylesford was abbot from 1281 until 1297.[17]

The 1294 Wye eyre roll not only throws no light on the problem, but complicates it even further. It merely names 'the coroners of the county who performed the office of coroner in that liberty after the eyre of John Reigate', namely Ralph Pivington, Robert Kingsnorth (Kingsnoad) and John Sissinghurst (Saxinghurst).[18] The natural interpretation of this statement would be that these three county coroners had successively acted as coroners of Wye throughout the period between the eyres of 1279 and 1294: in other words, the county coroners intervened in the liberty immediately after the 1279 eyre. But if this were so, the intervention did not coincide with an abbatial vacancy as there was no such vacancy between 1261 and 1281.[19] It is quite possible that the county coroners did not intervene until 1281. The fact that the abbot had ceased to appoint coroners was not questioned at the 1294 eyre, but this may well be because Brownman's heirs or assigns did not appear then to answer for the period 1279–1281 and, in the absence of his rolls, none of his cases was presented.

The situation in the abbot of Battle's lands in other counties is no clearer. In only one of them, the half-hundred of Battle, is he known with certainty to have had coroners of his own in the thirteenth century. In another, the manor of Bromham in Wiltshire, there is a possibility that he did, although the earliest named coroner of the abbot there so far discovered was in office as late as 1384.[20] At the special eyre for Bromham in 1289 it was stated that the abbot had no coroner of his own within the liberty, but that Philip Strugge, 'the king's coroner for the body of the county', answered for his time for crown pleas within the liberty.[21] Strugge seems to have been the only coroner acting in the liberty since the previous eyre of 1281, but the eyre roll is otherwise ambiguous. It could imply that the abbot had never had his own coroner at Bromham, but this is never stated in respect of the abbot's lands in other counties where it would have been true. It is therefore rather more probable that the eyre roll meant that at one time the abbot had had coroners of his own, but not since the previous eyre. On this interpretation it may well have been that the abbot abandoned his right to appoint in Kent and Wiltshire at the same time, which would mean that Brownman died no later than 1281. Unfortunately there is no surviving evidence about Bromham coroners in the years immediately before 1281.

It is even uncertain whether or not the abbot ceased to exercise his right to appoint coroners in his Sussex lands. The Sussex county coroners seem not to have acted in the half-hundred of Battle during the relevant thirty years. A Reynold Beech became coroner there in 1286 and again in 1305, but it may be significant that on each occasion he was elected in

[12] JUST 1/912A, m.37.

[13] There is no evidence on the eyre rolls that the abbot appointed his own coroners for his lands in other counties so early.

[14] JUST 1/384A, m.10.

[15] *Plac. Quo Warr.*, 334, citing from the 1271 Wye crown pleas which have not survived on the extant eyre rolls (JUST 1/364–366). The roll for the Wye eyre held after the Kent eyre of 1279 is also missing.

[16] JUST 1/384A, mm.8, 10.

[17] *VCH Sussex*, II, 55.

[18] JUST 1/378A, m.5.

[19] *VCH Sussex*, II, 55.

[20] *VCH Wilts*, V, 24 n.95.

[21] JUST 1/1013, m.26d.

the local court and not appointed by the abbot, at least not formally.[22]

The exact date of Brownman's death must therefore remain in doubt, but it was followed by something like thirty years during which the county coroner for Scray lathe, in which the hundred of Wye lay, carried out the duties of coroner within the liberty also.[23] Then, on 4 October 1312 the abbot obtained a charter confirming many of Battle's earliest charters and stating that no rights granted by them should be abrogated by reason of non-usage.[24] By virtue of this charter the abbot resumed his right to appoint his own coroners for Wye about a year and a half before the 1314 Wye eyre.[25]

Six coroners officiated in the liberty of Wye between the eyres of 1294 and 1314: the first four were elected county coroners and the other two were appointed by the abbot. The roll printed below contains inquests taken by four of the six. The earliest in date [5, 10] was held by John Sissinghurst on or around 22 February 1299. This is the only inquest on the roll taken by Sissinghurst, who had been elected county coroner for Scray lathe during the main Kent eyre of 1293 and had answered at the Wye eyre of 1294 for the brief period since his election, during which he had acted as coroner in the liberty.[26] He apparently had an unbroken period of office until he was replaced at a date unknown by John Pivington, and he was dead by the time of the 1313–14 eyre.[27] Pivington had answered at the 1294 Wye eyre for his father Ralph, a former county coroner by then dead, in respect of the liberty, although Ralph had personally attended at least the opening of the main Kent eyre in the previous year to answer for his Scray lathe jurisdiction.[28] On 15 June 1310 a writ de coronatore eligendo ordered John's replacement, alleging that he was insufficiently qualified.[29] This may never have been executed since the one case [3, 4] by which he is represented on the coroners' roll is an inquest held as late as 6 April 1311, although it must have been taken very shortly before he was replaced anyway. He was still alive during the 1313–14 eyre, which he attended, as did his two successors, John Aldglose and John Oveny.[30] These were the last two county coroners to act in Wye and there is no case of either of them on the roll, but they can have been in office for little more than eighteen months altogether, if for so long.

By contrast, the coroners' roll contains three inquests held by Hamo Pester, the first of the abbot's coroners after the resumption of his right to appoint, although he also had only a short period of office. The earliest [1, 2, 7] concerned a death which occurred on 21 February 1313, of which presentments were made on the following day; the second inquest [8] was held on 10 November 1313, the death having occurred on 7 November; and the third inquest [9] is undated but must have been taken shortly after the death on 30 November 1313. Hamo Pester died in office before the eyre, whereupon the abbot appointed Richard Coombe to succeed him and he was still coroner of the liberty during the eyre.[31] The final inquest on the roll [6] was held by him. It is also undated, but was held after the death of a man on 7 June 1314. The roll thus contains only two cases of the four county coroners who acted within the liberty from early 1294 until the end of 1312, but four inquests held by the abbot's two coroners in the remaining year and a half.

The way in which these inquests were entered on the roll is instructive. The roll as it has survived consists of a single membrane, measuring 17½ by 5½ inches, with two pieces of parchment sewn to the face, the top piece (schedule 1) being 6½ inches wide and 1½ inches long, and the other (schedule 2) nearly 7 inches wide and 2½ inches long. The cases are arranged as follows. The first two entries [1, 2] on the face of the main membrane are almost identical versions of Pester's first case, but the third [3], written right at the bottom after a space, is Pivington's inquest. The dorse begins with a different version [7] of the first Pester case, in the form of an inquest as opposed to hundred jurors' presentments, followed by Pester's other two inquests [8, 9] in chronological order and finally, at the foot of the membrane after a fairly long space, by Sissinghurst's inquest of 1299 [10]. The first schedule contains very summary versions [4, 5] of the Pivington and Sissinghurst

22 Henry E. Huntington Lib., Battle Abbey MSS, vol. 5, nos. 141, 241; R. F. Hunnisett, 'A Mediaeval Battle Coroner', *Sussex Notes & Queries*, XVI, 28–9.

23 JUST 1/384A, mm.8, 10.

24 *CChR*, III, 195–7; *Plac. Quo Warr.*, 333–5; JUST 1/384A, m.8.

25 JUST 1/384A, m.8.

26 JUST 1/376, mm.1, 61d; 378A, m.5.

27 JUST 1/383, m.4; 384A, m.8.

28 JUST 1/376, m.1; 378A, m.5.

29 *CCR 1307–13*, 215, where he is called Pynynton.

30 JUST 1/383, m.4; 384A, m.8.

31 JUST 1/384A, m.8.

inquests which are on the main membrane, while schedule 2 contains a new case [6], that held by Richard Coombe.

The arrangement of the entries suggests that what we have is basically Pester's roll. His cases are entered in strict chronological order on the main membrane, and both the face and the dorse have headings which incorporate his name. Indeed, five of the ten entries, comprising three of the six distinct cases, are his. Not only that, but the other two cases entered on the main membrane were written at the very foot of the face and the dorse, with considerable gaps separating them from Pester's cases. They are earlier in date, Sissinghurst's inquest considerably so, and could well have been added in the blank spaces of Pester's roll shortly before the eyre. Presumably the first schedule had by then already been attached; if it had not, it would have been unnecessary since it merely contains a brief note of these same two earlier cases. It may originally have contained only the note of Pivington's inquest of 1311, that of Sissinghurst's having apparently been added beneath it slightly later. Finally, the second schedule, containing Coombe's inquest, was presumably sewn on shortly before the eyre. Indeed, the inquest itself can have been held little more than a fortnight before the eyre began. It is much more typical of an item from a normal coroner's file, with the panel of jurors on its dorse, than are the brief notes on the first schedule which do not even give the verdict.[32]

An analysis of the handwriting supports the main points in the last paragraph. It is uncertain exactly how many different hands there are on the roll proper. The first two entries may or may not be in the same hand; at least they seem not to have been written at precisely the same time. The first two entries on the dorse [7, 8] were certainly written by the same clerk and the third [9] very probably was, but his handwriting is not found anywhere on the face. The bottom entries of the face and dorse [3, 10] are written in an identical hand which is different from that of all the other entries. Finally, all three cases on the schedules are written in different hands, none being represented on the roll proper.

The arrangement and appearance of the roll therefore suggest that it was essentially the roll of Hamo Pester, to which a few cases dealt with by other coroners were either added in suitable blank spaces or attached as the Wye coroners' rolls were hastily compiled on the eve of the eyre from the material in the coroners' files. The fact that two inquests are noted on a schedule and also entered on the roll proper could be confirmation of the speed with which the work was carried out: time might have been found at the last minute to enter them fully, the schedule being left attached by mistake.[33] Schedule 1 is certainly not the file membrane from which entries [3] and [10] were enrolled. The roll contains far more information, such as the names of the jurors and the verdict, although it is interesting that both versions of Pivington's inquest describe the year simply as *anno regni regis Edwardi quarto* despite the fact that the king was Edward II (who is never distinguished from Edward I anywhere on the roll[34]), and that both versions of the Sissinghurst inquest give it the same impossible date of Thursday the feast of St Peter's chair 27 Edward [I], in which year St Peter's chair was a Sunday. Indeed, roll and schedule contain no conflicting information: the deceased in Sissinghurst's inquest is called Richard son of Robert Boughton (de Boctone) on the schedule and Richard son of Robert Boughton Aluph (de Bocton Allulphi) on the roll, but that is not significant. This agreement is in marked contrast to the considerable variations between the versions of inquests entered on coroners' rolls and those found on pieces from their files in the later fourteenth century in Warwickshire.[35] Incidentally, it could be significant that it is the two inquests held by county coroners which are briefly noted on the first schedule. The notes are too brief to have been of use at the eyre and they could have been written as an aide-mémoire when the Wye cases were separated from those of the rest of Scray lathe.

The theory that what has survived is Hamo Pester's roll with a few last-minute accretions unfortunately needs considerable modification before it can explain all the difficulties which emerge from a closer examination of its contents. One of the greatest difficulties

32 For a description of items from coroners' files see R. F. Hunnisett, 'The Reliability of Inquisitions as Historical Evidence', in *The Study of Medieval Records: Essays in Honour of Kathleen Major,* ed. D. A. Bullough and R. L. Storey (Oxford, 1971), 211–22.

33 For other evidence of the speed with which coroners' rolls were compiled for general or 'superior' eyres see ibid., 211; Hunnisett, *Am. Jnl Leg. Hist.*, III, 99–100, 118–19.

34 It is interesting that the contemporary Wye hundred court rolls similarly never call Edward II 'Edward son of King Edward': SC 2/182/8–9.

35 Hunnisett in *Study of Medieval Records,* 212–27.

in the way of that interpretation is presented by the first of Pester's inquests, which is the subject of no less than three of the seven entries on the roll proper, the first two [1, 2] on the face and the other [7] on the dorse. In all three entries the information given about the fatality and about the first finder and four nearest neighbours and their sureties is exactly the same and is expressed in identical words. But whereas [7] is in the form of an inquest, as are Pester's other cases and the two earlier cases on the roll proper, beginning *Inquisitio capta,* the other versions are in the form of presentments made by the hundred of Wye.

There are good reasons for believing that these presentments were made at the coroner's inquest and not at the hundred court, although that is not stated. One reason is that they were made at Bempson, not at Wye where the hundred court normally sat.[36] It is not stated that the inquest was held at Bempson, but it should have been because the death occurred there. Secondly, there is the evidence of the dating. The second presentment was made on Thursday, 22 February 1313, the day after the death. Part of the date of the first presentment is missing, having been torn away, but it is dated by reference to the same feast day as the second and so it could not have been made later than 1 March; and there is only just enough room for the missing words of the date to have comprised the feast of St Peter's chair itself, 22 February, and not a day before or after it. The Wye hundred court frequently sat on two successive days and occasionally on two non-adjacent days in the same week,[37] but there can have been no session during the period 22 February to 1 March 1313. In normal times the Wye hundred court met every three weeks. Earlier in 1313 it had sat on Wednesday, 3 January, on Thursday, 25 January, and on Wednesday, 14 February.[38] The hundred court rolls for the rest of the year have not survived, but the court was obviously not due to meet again until a fortnight after the death had occurred and practically a week after the last possible date for the presentment enrolled first. By contrast, although the inquest itself is undated, it is unlikely to have been held earlier than 22 February, which is a highly probable date for it. The dating thus suggests that both presentments were made on the same day and at the inquest. Thirdly, no coroners' cases seem to have been presented at the Wye hundred court at this time, and those lesser matters which were presented there were presented by individual borghs and not by the whole hundred.[39] Finally, the inquest, unlike the others on the roll, is said to have been taken by twelve named jurors together with the four neighbouring townships and the commonalty of the whole hundred. [1] and [2] must therefore be the presentment made at the inquest by the hundred jurors.

But did they make a single presentment or the identical presentment twice? If the former, it must be concluded that the whole entry was written out again merely because the first time it was erroneously stated that the hundred had come and made its presentment in its entirety whereas two men had not attended. Normally the words 'preter Johannem Waryn et Johannem atte Felde' would in that event have been inserted as an interlineation, as is in fact done with two words erroneously omitted from the second presentment. Moreover, if the second presentment is a corrected version of the first, one would expect the first to have been cancelled and it is not. Yet it is inconceivable that the hundred made two identical presentments at the same inquest, especially as the twelve named jurors must have been representative free men of the hundred, as was the rule elsewhere.[40] Just possibly Warren and Field arrived late and associated themselves with a presentment already made, but that ought not to have led to two entries on the coroners' roll, each under a separate heading and in reverse order. Another hypothesis is that only one of the presentments was made by the hundred jurors, the other being that of the four townships but attributed to the hundred by a scribal error. This is highly conjectural and in no way explains the basic problem: why the verdict of a very unimportant inquest should have been enrolled three times in identical words under three separate headings, when [7] by itself is fully adequate in that it attributes the verdict to all three bodies in attendance – the twelve jurors, the four townships and the commonalty of the hundred. It is true that this inquest is unique in that Pester's others were taken by the oath of twelve (once eleven) men and four townships, but the presence of the hundred hardly warrants the entry of the case in triplicate. His other inquests are of equal importance but are entered only once.

36 J. K. Wallenberg, *The Place-Names of Kent* (Uppsala, 1934), 380.

37 Thus in 1285 it met on Tuesday and Friday, 9 and 12 Jan.; on Wednesday and Thursday, 31 Jan. and 1 Feb.; and on Wednesday and Thursday, 21 and 22 Feb.: SC 2/182/1, mm.5–7.

38 SC 2/182/8, m.10.

39 SC 2/182/1–9.

40 Hunnisett, *Medieval Coroner,* 14–15.

The answer could well be that the enrolling clerk was initially uncertain exactly how to enrol this inquest and that the first two entries were of the nature of experiments, their form being discarded in favour of that of [7] by a second clerk who continued with the enrolment of Pester's cases in the same style. [1] and [2] would no longer have been needed, but nobody bothered to cancel them. It may be significant that the third version [7] is, like the other two, entered beneath a heading, which reads 'Placita corone coram Hamone le Pestur coronatore abbatis de Bello in libertate sua de Wy anno sexto'. Neither of his other cases depends upon this heading: they derive from the next regnal year. Perhaps, then, even Pester's last two cases were enrolled hastily, and it is possible that the whole membrane was originally intended to contain only the Bempson inquest. Indeed, it may even have initially been on Pester's file with only [1] and [2] upon it.

However that may be, it is not merely the fact that the first two entries are uncancelled that is noteworthy. It is equally remarkable that the whole roll is uncancelled. The great majority of coroners' rolls which derive from general eyres are completely cancelled by a line drawn down the centre of every membrane. The few exceptions include some of the rolls from those counties in which contemporary county coroners all recorded every case, irrespective of which coroner had dealt with it: not all such rolls were used for checking the hundred jurors' presentments at the eyre and some therefore escaped cancellation.[41] But only one coroner acted in the liberty of Wye at any one time. Even if every Kent county coroner had kept a record of his own and his colleagues' cases between 1294 and 1312, as was the practice in the 1340s,[42] they would not have recorded or even known about the inquests held by the coroners appointed by the abbot of Battle in 1313–14.

It is tempting to associate the lack of cancellation of the Wye coroners' roll with the fact that none of its cases appears in any form on the Wye eyre rolls of 1314. There are many Wye coroners' cases on the eyre rolls, but they all resulted in a forfeiture or amercement of some kind or in an order for further action.[43] Cases which resulted in no financial issues or further proceedings were often not recorded, and it may be significant that the six cases on the coroners' roll comprise two natural deaths in gaol and four deaths by misadventure. But the theory which these facts suggest – that there was one Wye coroners' roll for natural deaths and fiscally unremunerative misadventures and that another or others were compiled for the rest of the misadventures, the homicides and the suicides – is untenable. It is inconceivable that these six cases were deliberately brought together before the eyre because they were the only Wye coroners' cases arising between 1294 and 1314 which were expected not to lead to forfeitures. It is true that that could have been confidently predicted of the deaths in gaol, and that no deodands were involved in three of the other cases. But the fourth misadventure [8] concerned the death of a four-year-old boy who fell into a vat full of boiling water and the coroner recorded that the vat was worth 4d. and that Robert Staple was answerable for it. It is possible that the vat would not have been forfeited at the eyre because it had not caused the death by moving, but that could not have been guaranteed in advance. Moreover, the two jurors of the hundred who did not attend the inquest in [2] could have been expected to be amerced, and there could never be any certainty that there would be no defaults by first finders and neighbours at the eyre or variations between the hundred jurors' presentments and the coroners' roll, with consequent amercements. The 1314 Wye eyre rolls contain three deaths by misadventure which involved no deodands. They are very similar to the misadventures on the coroners' roll, two being deaths of young children who had fallen into a ditch and a well and the other the death of a man who had fallen from a ladder. They were enrolled because in one case the first finder and in another two of the neighbours did not attend the eyre and therefore their sureties were amerced, and in the third case a man

41 Hunnisett, *Am. Jnl Leg. Hist.*, III, 112, 206–7.

42 In 1348 the sheriff and three county coroners held an inquest at Shinglewell which found that when several houses in Shinglewell were burnt down in 1344, one of them was the house of Michael Ifield, a Kent coroner, whose chapel, in which was a chest containing the rolls and memoranda of his office, was also destroyed. But the jurors added that 'the rolls and remembrances of the other coroners should suffice for the eyre because every coroner in that county is ingrosser and remembrancer of the other offices': *CIM*, III, no. 7; cf. *CPR 1348–50*, 197–8. The estreats of the Kent coroners' rolls of the period 1314–37 are in a roll which is arranged by lathes and whose headings suggest that each coroner enrolled only the cases arising in his own lathe, although that is not absolutely certain: JUST 2/47. There is no earlier evidence, although the fact that Kent coroners' districts were quite distinct (the five lathes and the hundred of Milton) might be expected to have made it likely that each recorded only his own cases.

43 JUST 1/384A, mm.8d, 9.

(John de By, possibly the surety of [6]) had falsely presented that he was a neighbour.[44] In at least two of these cases the amercements could not have been anticipated by the compilers of the coroners' rolls. All this aside, the theory that our six cases were deliberately segregated for administrative convenience finally breaks down on the fact that even if no issues had arisen from them they should still have been presented at the eyre and the roll should then have been cancelled.

Another theory which must be considered is that the six cases were never presented at the eyre. There is no need to assume that there was a conspiracy betwen the coroners or their clerks and the hundred jurors to prevent them from coming before the justices. The innocuous nature of the cases compared with many of those on the eyre rolls virtually precludes that, as do the survival of the roll as a result of, and doubtless with the other records of, the eyre and, indeed, its very compilation for that event. Nevertheless it is possible that the cases were not presented, perhaps because the hundred jurors depended for their information on the coroners' files or rolls and for some reason these cases were not available when they drew up their veredictum.

There is a remote possibility that the surviving roll is uncancelled because it was not the copy handed in at the eyre, but the one compiled for the abbot of Battle: that it remained among his records after the close of the eyre and ultimately took its place among the public records along with numerous other Battle abbey documents after the Dissolution. It is true that the abbot seems to have retained copies of the eyre and gaol delivery rolls relating to his liberty and a few of these are now in the Public Record Office,[45] but they were as handsomely engrossed as the justices' copies. It is just possible that the abbot's officials were content to preserve a record of coroners' cases in a contrastingly unpleasing form, but highly unlikely.

The most persuasive theory for the non-cancellation of the roll is that it was a draft: that either it was intended from the outset to be a draft or an experimental membrane from which a fair copy was made, or it became clear after the second and third thoughts about Pester's first case that it could never be submitted at the eyre and it was therefore used as a draft-cum-file.[46] The cases would have been rewritten in a far more uniform manner, each only once. The form of [7] would certainly have been adopted for Pester's first case, and so the fact that two members of the hundred had defaulted would not have been revealed at the eyre. Even the price and custody of the vat may possibly have been omitted from the fair copy of [8]. Only the fair copies of the cases would have been cancelled, and their absence from the eyre rolls may genuinely be because no forfeitures or amercements were incurred.

The fair copies were probably entered on separate rolls for each of the coroners who had acted within the liberty. According to the Wye eyre rolls, Richard Coombe came with his rolls at the opening of the eyre, while Gilbert and Richard Pester, Hamo's heirs, came with his rolls to answer for his period of office.[47] It would therefore appear that separate rolls were compiled and presented for both Pester's and Coombe's periods of office. The rolls of the Scray lathe coroners are not specifically mentioned, although their failure to present them certainly would have been. Four kinsmen and heirs came and answered for John Sissinghurst, while Pivington, Aldglose and Oveny were merely said to have answered for their time – the same expression as is used on the rolls of the main Kent eyre in respect of their county jurisdiction.[48] Each of these coroners must have had his own roll.

It would be interesting to know whether behind the rolls of these county coroners there lay two files, with the Wye cases always preserved separately, or only one. Very probably the Wye cases were not kept separately until the abbot of Battle resumed his right to appoint coroners. Indeed, it may be that the rolls which the county coroners presented at Canterbury in 1313 contained their Wye cases as well as those arising in the rest of Scray lathe, and it is even possible that their rolls for the liberty were com-

[44] ibid., m.8d. Some time between the 1314 eyre and Michaelmas 1337 a John de By was indicted for the death of John Wetham at the inquest held by the abbot of Battle's coroner and forfeited chattels worth 49s.: JUST 2/47, m.6d.

[45] The abbot's steward's copy of one membrane of the 1314 Wye eyre roll is now among the Wye hundred court rolls: SC 2/182/10. A number of Battle gaol delivery rolls are in the Huntington Library.

[46] A few examples of both kinds of draft coroners' rolls, intended and inadvertent, survive in the Public Record Office, although not from the period of the general eyre. They are virtually all cancelled either by lines drawn through the cases or by words such as *irrotulatur:* Hunnisett, *Am. Jnl Leg. Hist.*, III, 122–3.

[47] JUST 1/384A, m.8.

[48] ibid.; JUST 1/383, m.4. Six kinsmen and heirs answered for Sissinghurst at the main Kent eyre.

piled from these composite rolls after all the pleas of the crown from the body of the county had been heard. Certainly Sissinghurst's inquest [10] could not have been entered on the surviving roll until after the enrolment of Pester's last inquest [9] which was held five months after the opening of the Kent eyre; and Pivington's inquest [3] was written at the same time as Sissinghurst's. The theory advanced above, that the summary note of these two inquests (schedule 1) was sewn to the roll to serve as an aide-mémoire for their eventual enrolment, would be greatly strengthened if these enrolled cases were copied from the county coroners' rolls rather than from their files. In either event, the enrolment of two inquests taken by county coroners together with those of the abbot's coroners may represent a first attempt at bringing all the Wye cases together, later abandoned in favour of the compilation of a separate roll for each coroner.

The descriptions of the four coroners represented on the roll also suggests its experimental nature. Pivington and Sissinghurst are merely called coroners. In his sole inquest Coombe is given his full title of 'coroner of the abbot of Battle in his liberty of Wye'. Pester is similarly described once, in the heading of [7]; in the headings of [1] and [2] he is called 'coroner of Wye', in the body of [7] and in [8] 'the king's coroner of Wye', and in [9] 'the king's coroner'. It is understandable that there might have been some doubt as to how the county coroners should be described when acting in the liberty, but the varied descriptions accorded to Pester in only three different cases spanning less than a year can only be explained as experiments by clerks who were feeling their way in the new situation.

There is a similar lack of uniformity in the presentation of the cases. The exceptional nature of the first two versions of Pester's first case [1, 2] and the brief notes of the county coroners' cases made on schedule 1 [4, 5] have already been discussed. Of the other six entries, all different cases, only the inquests held by Pivington and Sissinghurst [3, 10] are in identical form, beginning 'Inquisitio capta coram A coronatore apud Wy die . . . de morte B mortui in prisona de Wy per [12 names] juratos qui dicunt per sacramentum suum quod . . .' Their verdicts are also identical and given in the same words. Both were natural deaths in gaol, which were normally phrased fairly formally, and it may well be significant that not only were both held by county coroners whose inquests had probably come to be written in a standard form but they were entered on the roll by the same clerk.

Pester's three inquests are all expressed differently. The first [7] begins 'Inquisitio capta coram A coronatore . . . per sacramentum [12 names] vina [*sic*] cum quatuor proximis villatis et comunitate totius hundredi qui dicunt quod accidit . . .'; the second [8] begins 'Inquisitio capta coram A coronatore . . . die . . . per [12 names] una cum quatuor proximis vllatis [*sic*] qui dicunt per sacramentum suum quod accidit . . .'; and the third [9] 'Inquisitio capta coram A coronatore . . . per sacramentum [11 names] una cum quatuor proximis villatis qui dicunt quod accidit . . .' Even if one either ignores the first, which is unique not only in Wye but, so far as is known, anywhere in the middle ages in apparently having three separate juries for a very unexceptional inquest[49] and is most unexpected in a small Kent hundred, or passes it off as an aberration perpetrated in what was possibly his first case by the first Wye franchisal coroner for nearly thirty years or even as the efforts of a later clerk trying to make some sense of [1] and [2], there are still differences in presentation in the other two. The accounts of the fatalities, however, proceed in a very similar way in all three entries, and they all end with the names and sureties of the first finder and four neighbours, [8] adding the information about the potential deodand.

Coombe's case [6] is in an utterly different form, although it might not have differed from the file versions of some of the others. Nevertheless it is a form which is well known elsewhere,[50] being in two paragraphs. The first is the narrative, beginning 'Accidit in . . . die . . . quod' and ending with the names and sureties of the first finder and four neighbours; while the second merely reads: 'Inquisitio capta per A coronatorem . . . et nichil aliud potuit inquireri nisi per infortunium'. The twelve jurors are listed on the dorse.

The roll presents one final mystery. The enrolled version of Pivington's case [3] names the twelve inquest jurors, three of whom have letters written above their names. The seventh is marked 'c', the eighth 'b' and the ninth 'a', quite possibly by the enrolling clerk, although the letters are too small for certainty. Indeed, they are so small that not only do they not stand out, but without a close inspection it is very possible to miss them altogether or to dismiss them as meaningless flourishes or unnecessary marks

[49] Hunnisett, *Medieval Coroner*, 13–16; cf. 21.

[50] Hunnisett, *Am. Jnl Leg. Hist.*, III, 110.

of abbreviation. This suggests that they were written for the writer's own purposes. Superior letters were used in the middle ages to correct the order of words written out of order, although the normal method of switching the positions of two words or names was to write 'b' over the first and 'a' over the second.[51] A word or name, such as the middle of the three jurors, whose position was to remain unchanged would not usually be marked at all. The letters are all written immediately above the forenames, but the correction must apply to the whole names and not to the forenames alone since they are John, Simon and John in both the existing and the corrected order. It has been suggested[52] that the clerk incorrectly marked the three names, possibly because he did not understand the instructions given to him by someone who had checked his work, perhaps a superior clerk or even the coroner himself; and that he should have written 'b' over the first and 'a' over the second, so listing the jurors in four groups of three, each group being in alphabetical order of surnames except that the first juror of the second group, the only one to be described in terms of a place, is alphabetised by the place. This theory is possibly a little too elaborate, especially as none of the other lists of jurors is arranged in such a way. But somebody obviously thought it important that the jurors should be in a different order, probably the order in which they were named in the file or roll from which the case was copied. The correction marks were presumably added when it became obvious that a better arrangement of the Wye coroners' rolls was needed before they could be presented to the justices.

[51] L. C. Hector, *The Handwriting of English Documents*, 2nd edn (London, 1966), 50.

[52] By Dr J. B. Post, to whom I am much indebted for reading this introduction and for making valuable suggestions for its improvement.

TEXT

JUST 2/276, m.1

Placita corone coram Hamone le Pestur coronatore de Wy . . .[53]

[1] Hundredum de Wy venit integre[54] apud Beaumondeston[e die jovis in festo Beati[55]] Petri in cathedra proximo preterito et presentat quod accidit in predicta [borga de Beaumondestone[56]] in nocte diei mercurii proxime ante festum Sancti Petri in cathedra circa [horam ignitegii quod] cum Wymarca uxor Laurencii ate Wyk' perrexisset de domo sua et [ivisset usque ad c]uriam Willelmi de la Haye apud Beaumondestone et dimisisset in domo predicta quendam Willelmum filium suum etate quinque annorum; cum autem ipsa Wymarca rediret versus domum suam predictam invenit eam igne accensam et conburentem;[57] et cum venisset ad domum invenit predictum Willelmum filium suum in dicta domo conbustum sine aliqua felonia alicui inponenda. Primus inventor[58] predicta Wymarca mater eiusdem Willelmi quam Willelmus Red et Godefridus atte Napeltone manuceperunt ad habendum coram justiciariis itinerantibus apud Wy quandocunque etc. Quatuor proximi visini Johannes Bercarius quem Rogerus Pistor et Thomas Galon manuceperunt; secundus Thomas Galon quem Simon Gaugi et Stephanus Gaugi manuceperunt; tertius Johannes Gaugi quem Ricardus Jordain et Johannes Welshe manuceperunt; quartus Ricardus Red quem Johannes atte Napeltone et Willelmus Ylente manuceperunt.

Placita corone coram Hamone le Pestour coronatore de Wy anno regni regis Edwardi sexto

[2] Hundredum de Wy venit integre preter Johannem Waryn et Johannem atte Felde apud Beaumondestone die jovis in festo Beati Petri in cathedra proximo preterito et presentat quod accidit in predicta borga de Beaumondestone in nocte diei mercurii proxime ante festum Sancti Petri in cathedra circa horam ignitegii quod cum Wymarca uxor Laurencii atte Wyck' perrexisset de domo sua et ivisset usque ad curiam Willelmi de la Haye apud Beaumondestone et dimisset[59] predicta in domo[60] quendam Willelmum filium suum etate quinque annorum; cum autem ipsa rediret versus domum suam predictam invenit eam igne accensam et conburentem; et cum venisset ad domum invenit predictum Willelmum filium suum in dicta domo conbustum sine aliqua felonia alicui inponenda. Primus inventor predicta Wymarca mater eiusdem Willelmi quam Willelmus Red et Godefridus atte Napeltone manuceperunt ad habendum coram justiciariis itinerantibus apud Wy quandocunque etc. Quatuor proximi visini Johannes Bercarius quem Rogerus Pistor et Thomas Galon manuceperunt; secundus Thomas Galon quem Simon Gaugi et Stephanus Gaugi manuceperunt; tertius Johannes Gaugi quem Ricardus Jordayn et Johannes Welshe manuceperunt; quartus Ricardus Red quem Johannes atte Napeltone et Willelmus Ylente manuceperunt.

[3] Inquisitio capta coram Johanne de Pyvyntone coronatore apud Wy die martis proxima post festum Sancti Ambrosii anno regni regis Edwardi quarto de morte Matillidis filie Johannis Clement de Redynges mortui[61] in prisona de Wy per Thomam de Aledon', Ricardum de Bronesforde, Thomam de Bronesforde,

[53] The top right corner of the membrane is torn away. It is possible that no words have been lost from this heading. There would have been insufficient room for *anno regni regis Edwardi sexto* as in the next heading, but enough for *anno sexto* which would agree with the heading on m.1d. Missing passages in the next four lines are supplied from [2].

[54] Both here and in [2] the MS has *integr'*, so that *integrum* is an alternative extension.

[55] There is just room for these words in the missing space, but not enough for any other day described with reference to St Peter's chair.

[56] The available space was such that *Beaumondestone* may well have been contracted or suspended.

[57] This is the only place on the roll where the first three letters of either *conburentem* or *conbustus* are written in full. Normally the conventional sign for 'con' is used, which has therefore been rendered *con,* as has *conburentem* in [7] which begins with the letters *co* written with a stroke over the *o*.

[58] Here and in [2] the MS reads *prim' invent',* but the first word ends with the normal 'us' suspension. In [7, 8, 9], where the first finders were also female, *prim' invent'* is found again, although *prim'* there has only a general mark of suspension. But it has still been extended not as *prima inventrix* but as *primus inventor* which is more likely to have been intended anyway and which also agrees with [1, 2].

[59] Recte *dimisisset.*

[60] *in domo* interlined; the insertion mark was erroneously made after the word *predicta* instead of before it.

[61] Recte *mortue.*

Willelmum Mot de Bronesforde, Gilbertum Dod, Gilbertum German, Johannem Cock',[62] Simonem Carpentarium,[63] Johannem Herebaldone,[64] Humfridum Beltyng', Ricardum Cranebrok' et Simonem Ismongere juratos qui dicunt per sacramentum suum quod predicta Matillis obiit de morte sua naturali et non per aliquam duriciam prisone nec aliquam maliciam custodis gaole predicte seu alterius cuiuscunque.

First schedule

[4] De morte Matillidis filie Johannis Clement de Redynges capte et in prisona de Wy detente que in eadem prisona obiit facta fuit inquisitio per Johannem de Pyvynton' coronatorem die martis proxima post festum Sancti Ambrosii episcopi anno regni regis Edwardi quarto.

[5] De morte Ricardi filii Roberti de Boctone qui obiit in prisona de Wy facta fuit inquisitio coram J. de Saxingherst' die jovis in festo Sancti Petri in cathedra anno regni regis Edwardi xxvij^{o}.[65]

Second schedule

[6] Accidit in borga de Socumbe die veneris ante festum Sancti Barnabe apostoli[66] anno regni regis Edwardi septimo quod cum quidam Hamund'[67] atte Hale venisset de Wy et cum venisset in quadam[68] via vocata Partiesst . . .[69] ignitegii cecidit in quandam fossatam plenam aque et statim submersit et obiit. Primus inventor Simon filius Arnoldi atte Hale quem Thomas de Socumbe et Stephanus de Socumbe manuceperunt. Quatuor proximi vicini Robertus Party quem Willelmus Jordain et Johannes Eslynge manuceperunt; Reginaldus Longe quem Stephanus Barri et Matheus Textor manuceperunt; Rogerus Stonekere quem Stephanus Faber et Stephanus Barri manuceperunt; Johannes Eslyng' quem Gilbertus Frode et Johannes By manuceperunt.

Inquisitio capta per Ricardum de Cumbe coronatorem domini abbatis de Bello in libertate [sua[70]] de Wy et nichil aliud potuit inquireri nisi per infortunium. [*Dorse*] Juratores in inquisitione: Ricardus atte Pette, Ricardus de Bronesforde, Willelmus Ferebras, Johannes Croiascre,[71] Stephanus Bronman, Ricardus Bronman, Johannes atte Hesele, Willelmus de Senche, Thomas Reynaud, Rogerus Trippe, Ricardus atte Dele, Bartholomeus atte Toune.

Membrane 1d

[Placita corone[72]] coram Hamone le Pestur coronatore abbatis de Bello [in libertate s]ua de Wy anno sexto

[7] [Inquisitio cap]ta coram Hamone le Pestur coronatore domini regis de Wy per [sacramentum Si]monis Gaugi, Johannis Welshe, Gilberti le Cupere, Johannis Amys, . . .[73] atte Napeltone, Ricardi de Chelbertone, Johannis de Benynden, . . . ente,[74] Ricardi Thunder, Willelmi Risset, Willelmi de Chelbtone[75] et Johannis le Heare vina[76] cum quatuor proximis villatis et comunitate totius hundredi qui dicunt quod accidit in borgha de Beaumondestone in nocte diei mercurii proxime ante festum Sancti Petri in cathedra circa horam ignitegii anno regni regis Edwardi sexto quod cum Wymarca uxor Laurencii atte Wyck' perrexisset de domo sua et iviset usque ad curiam Willelmi de la Haye apud Beaumondestone et dimisisset in domo predicta quendam Willelmum filium suum etate quinque annorum; cum autem ipsa Wymarca rediret versus domum suam predictam invenit eam igne accensam et conburentem; et cum venisset ad domum invenit predictum Willelmum filium suum in dicta domo conbustum per infortunium.[77] Primus inventor predicta Wimarca[78] mater

[62] *c* is written above this name.

[63] *b* is written above this name.

[64] *a* is written above this name.

[65] This date is so given in the fuller version of the case [10] as well, but the feast of St Peter's chair (22 Feb.) was a Sunday in the year 27 Edward I (1299).

[66] *ante festum Sancti Barnabe apostoli* interlined; the normally preceding *proxima* is omitted.

[67] The reading of this word is not certain as it is badly rubbed.

[68] Struck through.

[69] Several words at the end of this line are illegible.

[70] This word is illegible but can be confidently supplied.

[71] Recte *Croisacre.*

[72] These words and those in square brackets at and near the beginning of the following entry can be supplied with confidence. The top left corner of the membrane is missing.

[73] Probably either *Godefridi* or *Johannis* is missing.

[74] Possibly *Willelmi Elente.*

[75] For *Chelbertone.*

[76] Recte *una.*

[77] *per infortunium* interlined.

[78] The *m* of *Wimarca* is formed from one or more previously written letters, probably *rc.*

predicti Willelmi quam Willelmus Red et Godefridus atte Napelton' manuceperunt. Quatuor proximi visini Johannes Bercarius quem Rogerus Pistor et Thomas Galun manuceperunt; Thomas Galon quem Simon Gaugi et Stephanus Gaugi manuceperunt; Johannes Gaugi quem Ricardus Gaugi et Johannes Whelshe manuceperunt; Ricardus Red quem Johannes ate Napelton' et Willelmus Elente manuceperunt.

[8] Inquisitio capta coram Hamone le Pestur coronatore domini regis de Wy die sabbati proxima ante festum Sancti Martini anno regni regis Edwardi septimo per Johannem de Herebaldone, Johannem Cock', Willelmum Stokemed, Hamonem Cissorem, Ricardum Cranebrok', Thomam Elham, Willelmum Artur, Rogerum Herward, Simonem Ismongere, Ricardum Cocum, Ricardum Braburn' et Gwydonem de Olunteghe una cum quatuor proximis vllatis[79] qui dicunt per sacramentum suum quod accidit in borga de Beaudr' in Wy die mercurii proxima ante predictum festum Sancti Martini anno predicto circa horam vespertinam quod cum quidam Thomas filius Cecilie Chynne etate quatuor annorum venisset per quandam cuvam aque bullantis plenam et voluit tetigisse dictam aquam per infortunium cecidit in eandem et propter caliditatem aque subiit mortem. Primus inventor Juliana filia Ricardi atte Bertone quam Galfridus Molendinarius et Willelmus Cuden' manuceperunt. Quatuor proximi visini Willelmus le Webbe quem Simon Gerard et Matheus le Webbe manuceperunt; Rogerus Milde quem Ricardus Cocus et Galfridus Sebaryn manuceperunt; Gilbertus Selke quem Ricardus Malekyn et Ricardus Vitele manuceperunt; Robertus Pistor quem Willelmus de Bronesford' et Thomas Helere manuceperunt.

Precium predicte cuve unde Robertus de Stapele respondebit iiij d.

[9] Inquisitio capta coram Hamone le Pestur coronatore domini regis per sacramentum Gilberti Dod, Gilberti German, Thome Humfrey, Reginaldi atte Brok', Willelmi Michel, Godefridi Aghemond', Johannis Croisacre, Thome Reynaud, Johannis atte Wall', Simonis Isimongere et Henrici Romeys una cum quatuor proximis villatis qui dicunt quod accidit in borga de Beaudregg' apud Wytherston' die veneris in festo Beati Andree apostoli anno regni regis Edwardi septimo quod cum quedam Johanna uxor Roberti Knoutte invisset[80] mane de domo sua ad ecclesiam de Wy et dimisisset quendam Johannem filium suum etate trium annorum in eadem domo et cum dicta Johanna rediret invenit domum suam predictam suo igne proprio per infortunium accessam[81] et illuminatam et dicto Johanne filio suo in eadem extracto tamen dicto Johanne vivo iam vixit per predictam diem et noctem et obiit. Primus inventor predicta Johanna mater eius quem[82] Ricardus Knoutte et Thomas Selke manuceperunt. Quatuor proximi visini Robertus Aghemond quem Edmundus Geryn et Willelmus Flaoner manuceperunt; Stephanus Bronman quem Simon Dod et Thomas Reynaud manuceperunt; Ricardus Bronman quem Thomas de Dodeston' et Bertramus de Gotele manuceperunt; Robertus Lewe quem Godefridus Aghemond et Jordanus Frenshe manuceperunt.

[10] Inquisitio capta coram Johanne de Saxyngeherst coronatore apud Wy die jovis in festo Beati Petri in cathedra anno regni regis Edwardi xxvij^{o} de morte Ricardi filii Roberti de Bocton' Allulphi mortui in prisona de Wy per Thomam de Aledon', Ricardum Cranebrok', Willelmum Uppehelle, Robertum atte Forde, Godefridum Fullonem, Adam Frode, Willelmum Beltinge, Johannem Colebrond, Willelmum de Bronesforde, Johannem Cock', Godefridum Aghemond et Humfridum Beltynge juratos qui dicunt per sacramentum suum quod predictus [Ricardus[83]] obiit de morte sua naturali et non per aliquam duriciam prisone nec aliquam maliciam custodis gaole predicte seu alterius cuiuscunque.

[79] MS *vll'.*

[80] Recte *ivisset.*

[81] Recte *accensam.*

[82] The use of *quem* rather than *quam* confirms the reading of *primus inventor:* above, n.58.

[83] Inadvertently omitted.

Early trailbaston proceedings from the Lincoln roll of 1305

edited by

ALAN HARDING

INTRODUCTION

On 20 September 1304, Edmund Deincourt, Robert Willoughby and Thomas Burnham were ordered to hold an inquest in Lincolnshire, Nottinghamshire and Derbyshire concerning malefactors and peace-breakers who were moving about the woods and parks (*vagantur et discurrunt in boscis, parcis et aliis locis diversis*) and committing murders, depredations, burnings 'et alia dampna' to the peril of travellers and dwellers in those parts (*tam hominum per partes illas transeuntium quam ibidem commorantium*): such malefactors and their harbourers were to be arrested and delivered to the sheriffs for safe-keeping till the normal delivery of the gaols or further orders from the king.[1] This was a 'commission to arrest vagabonds' of a type which can be traced at least as far back as the earliest years of Edward I's reign.[2] Some quite new clauses were added to this old style when the commission was reissued on 23 November 1304 to Deincourt, Burnham and William Cressy.[3] The commissioners were not only to inquire 'qui sunt illi malefactores et eorum scienter receptatores et eis consentientes' (to this point, in the exact terms of the old commission), but also who had made agreements with them (*pro muneribus suis pactum fecerunt cum malefactoribus*) and hired them (*eos conduxerunt*) to assault people in public places such as fairs and markets out of hatred, envy and malice (*inimicitia, invidia, malicia*) and even for simply telling the truth on assizes, juries, recognitions and inquests concerning felonies, with the result that jurors feared to give verdicts or make indictments; who had given and received rewards for these purposes; and who encouraged, nourished and maintained such malefactors in their malice. The writ then returned to the old provisions about arrest and safe custody, but the inclusion of the new details of the criminal activity which was to be investigated had brought into being what was to be known within a few months as the commission of trailbaston.

The commission of 23 November for Lincolnshire, Nottinghamshire and Derbyshire, and others issued for Yorkshire, for Norfolk and Suffolk and for Lancashire between November and March 1305, were still only for inquiry, arrest and safe custody until the king sent further orders.[4] Such a 'great multitude' were taken in, that on 21 March 1305 the king had to empower the commissioners to replevy them by sufficient mainpernors, since he could not yet provide for their final delivery.[5] It was left for the parliament which had been convened on 28 February to turn the commission of inquiry into a commission to do justice. The *Ordinatio de trailbastons,* as the marginal caption on the parliament roll called it, laid down the procedure to be followed by the justices assigned by the king to inquire about, hear and determine felonies and trespasses committed in various counties.[6] The justices were to supersede the 'inquisitores', whose inquiries had missed some crimes 'pro temporis brevitate seu alia causa', and to 'judge and punish' all those indicted before themselves or the earlier inquest of offences committed between the feast of St John the Baptist 1297 and Easter 1305: crimes from before August 1297 were to be left for a general eyre or until the king ordained afresh concerning them. The offences within the justices' competence were divided into two classes, which were to be prosecuted in rather different ways. Those who maltreated jurors who told the truth; or attacked people in fairs, markets or other public places from hatred, envy or malice aforethought (*preconceptis*); or hired such

[1] C 66/124, m.8d (*CPR 1301–7,* 284).

[2] See for example C 66/94, m.16 (*CPR 1272–81,* 100; and cf. 103, 111, 115–17): the inhabitants of Gloucestershire to aid the sheriff in arresting malefactors moving about the county in 1275; *CPR 1272–81,* 473: Geoffrey Pitchford to hold an inquest concerning vagabonds in nine counties in 1281; *CPR 1281–92,* 46: three knights to hold an inquest concerning vagabonds in Northamptonshire in 1282 and deliver those they find to the sheriff; C 66/105, m.25 (*CPR 1281–92,* 215): Geoffrey Pitchford and William Fitz Warren to hold an inquest in 1285 in Oxfordshire, Berkshire and Hertfordshire concerning malefactors who 'vagantur et discurrunt et ibidem receptantur in maximum periculum et dampnum tam fidelium regni nostri per partes illas transeuntium quam ibidem existentium', their harbourers and 'consentientes', and deliver them into safe custody; C 66/112, m.22d (*CPR 1292–1301,* 44): Robert Mallet and Thomas Bellhouse to do the same in 1292 in Lincolnshire, Northamptonshire and Cambridgeshire, and also to do full and swift justice on those arrested.

[3] C 66/125, m.23d (*CPR 1301–7,* 343); the commission is printed from the fine roll in *Parl. Writs,* I, 407.

[4] ibid.

[5] *CPR 1301–7,* 348.

[6] *RP,* I, 178. For the origins of trailbaston, see also *Memoranda de Parliamento,* ed. F. W. Maitland (RS, 1893), liii; H. M. Cam, *Studies in the Hundred Rolls,* in Oxford Studies in Soc. & Leg. Hist., ed. P. Vinogradoff, VI (Oxford, 1921), 73–9; Sayles in *King's Bench,* IV, liv-lxvi.

malefactors or harboured them afterwards; or incited or aided such acts; or abused their power and lordship by selling their protection and advocacy (*ratione potestatis aut dominii eorum alios in protectionem et advocationem eorum pro suo dando susceperunt*): all those indicted of such 'enormous' trespasses were to be tried at the king's suit if no private accuser appeared to prosecute, and on either suit were to be exacted and outlawed in case of non-appearance, or if present and found guilty were to be committed to gaol till they redeemed themselves. But those indicted, arrested and imprisoned for 'light and personal' trespasses were to be released under sureties of good behaviour (*quod extunc bene et honeste, et pacifice, versus quoscumque de regno se gerent, nemine injuriando seu injuriari procurando*), answering only to the private complainants if these chose to prosecute (*ad respondendum querentibus cum versus eos secundum legem communem sequi voluerint*).

This first parliament of 1305, which was still in session at the beginning of April,[7] made another ordinance for the benefit of 'the justices assigned to hear and determine various felonies and trespasses'. The term 'conspirators' was the subject of an 'ordinatio et finalis diffinitio', a transcript of which was ordered to be made available to the justices.

The actual assignment of the trailbaston commissioners is contained in writs of 6 April and 28 May 1305.[8] The writ of 6 April refers to the 'ordinance delivered in our parliament' and follows its terms, except that it does not repeat the instructions about prosecution and it adds a new offence after the selling of protection (itself the main addition of the parliamentary ordinance to the list in the commission of November 1304) or perhaps merely elaborates it: the commissioners are now to concern themselves also with the extortion of money by threats (*et de illis qui pecuniam ab aliquo per graves minas ei factas maliciose extorserunt*).

Because the whole of England was now to be covered in five circuits, the personnel of the judicial commissions had to be different from that of the commissions of inquiry. The justices for the circuit comprising Yorkshire, Northumberland, Cumberland, Westmorland, Lancashire, Nottinghamshire, Derbyshire, Warwickshire, Leicestershire and Lincolnshire included, like each of the other parties, a professional judge, who was always to sit though one or two of the other justices might be absent: for this circuit he was John Lisle (*de Insula*), baron of the exchequer. But the leader of the party was Peter Mauley, holder of the barony of Mulgrave in Yorkshire, whose previous service to King Edward had been in the wars in Wales, Scotland and Gascony. The king had just paid over more than £600 from the issues of the vacant bishopric of Lincoln to certain merchants of Bayonne to release Peter from a debt for which he had been kept hostage in London.[9] Second in the list came Deincourt, lord of Thurgarton in Nottinghamshire and various lands in Lincolnshire, and leader of the inquest in Lincolnshire, Nottinghamshire and Derbyshire, who had been with the king in his army of Scotland in 1303.[10] Next came William Vavasour, who had led the inquest in his home county of Yorkshire but had made his name at the siege of Caerlaverock in 1300; he had also served on commissions of array and purveyance in Yorkshire.[11] The remaining member of the party as it began its hearings at Lincoln on Monday, 5 July 1305, was Thomas Fishburn, who had appeared on numerous judicial commissions in these counties, sometimes in harness with John Lisle. He had replaced Adam Middleton, another professional lawyer included in the original commission in April who was now busy hearing assizes with Henry Sutton on the same circuit; in May 1306 he was in turn replaced by Henry Sutton on the trailbaston commission because he was preoccupied with his duties as attorney of the earl of Lincoln.[12]

The commission of oyer and terminer was reissued to the justices on 14 October 1305, 'according to the form of the ordinance made by the king and council in this behalf delivered to them in parliament'.[13] In 1305, Mauley and his colleagues sat in Yorkshire, Lincolnshire and Nottinghamshire; and in 1306 in Warwickshire, Leicestershire, Derbyshire and Lancashire.[14] The commission was further renewed on 21 February 1307, with William Barford (de Bereford) and Adam Middleton in the place of Lisle

[7] *Hdbk Brit. Chron.*, 513. The Ordinance of Conspirators is printed in *RP*, I, 183, and *SR*, I, 145.

[8] Printed in *Parl. Writs*, I, 408; calendared in *CPR 1301–7*, 352, 354, as commissions of oyer and terminer concerning vagabonds.

[9] Foss, *Biog. Judges*, 426; *CCW*, I, 65, 93, 144, 174, 207, 224; *CPR 1301–7*, 336.

[10] Foss, *Biog. Judges*, 221; *CCR 1302–7*, 388.

[11] Foss, *Biog. Judges*, 689; *CPR 1301–7*, 2, 64, 99, 159.

[12] ibid., 380, 399, 404, 475.

[13] ibid., 404.

[14] See *List of Plea Rolls of Various Courts* (PRO, L & I, IV).

and Sutton; but on April 25 a separate party was commissioned for Northumberland, Cumberland and Westmorland, which Mauley's group had never reached.[15] In 1307, Warwickshire, Leicestershire, Lincolnshire and Yorkshire at least were visited again, for the hearing of assizes as well as 'placita corone' and 'de querelis et transgressionibus'.[16] On 8 June 1307, the king reminded Mauley's party, in a writ issued at Carlisle, that it was still his intention that they should intermeddle only with felonies and trespasses perpetrated from the twenty-fifth year of his reign until the thirty-third year, but empowered them to proceed with the cases from before the said term which they had improperly allowed to be commenced before them.[17] When the justices began their session at Lincoln on Wednesday, 12 July 1307, King Edward had been dead five days.[18]

The cases printed below have been selected[19] from the first twenty-five membranes of JUST 1/509, which record the 'placita' heard by Mauley and his colleagues in the summer of 1305. On membrane 26 begin the assizes heard in July 1307, and the remaining membranes (29–40) contain further entries 'de placitis et querelis' or 'de petitionibus et querelis', essoins and a 'rotulus de diversis preceptis'. The cases of those indicted before the justices at Lincoln in 1305 and tried or exacted and outlawed at the king's suit only are contained in a separate roll, JUST 1/508. Many counties have the two complementary rolls of proceedings under the 1305 commissions, one of 'Placita, Querele et Assise' or 'Placita de transgressionibus' or 'Placita de querelis et bilettis', the other of 'Placita corone' or 'Indictamenta' or 'Placita indictamentorum'.[20] Of the Lincoln rolls, only the 'placita' of the first part of JUST 1/509 have been selected for editing, because they are a coherent group which in substance are fully representative of the offences which the trailbaston commission was created to deal with, and also show most clearly the interdependence of jury presentment and private complaint which it will be suggested is the distinctive mark of the trailbaston proceedings.

The commissions of 1305 have often been used by historians as evidence of the disruption of English society in the last years of Edward I, under the pressures of war with France and Scotland and of the arbitrary government war required.[21] It does seem likely that the violence of the 'trailbastons' had been fostered by war service. The singer of the Trailbaston Song, who complains that his servant will present a bill against him if he only punishes him with a cuff or two, has served King Edward 'in Flanders, Scotland, in Gascony his own land' but now cannot make an honest living. He has only to have a knowledge of archery to be accused by his neighbour of being a member of a 'company' who shoot in the woods. If he can get hold of some of the cruel trailbaston justices, he will break their limbs and cut out their tongues; meantime he urges everyone to escape the uncertain common law by joining him in the green forest of Belregard.[22] Langtoft almost seems to regard the capture of William Wallace, 'mestre de larouns' (taken, tried and executed in August 1305), as an achievement of the trailbaston measures.[23] The restriction of the commission's jurisdiction to offences in the period from the late summer of 1297, the time of the Flemish expedition and the political crisis which accompanied it, emphasised that trailbaston was an emergency measure for wartime.[24] Langtoft recounts how King Edward travelled through Lindsey on his way south from Scotland in late 1304, discovering as he went who had broken his peace 'while he was in his war in Scotland'.[25] In 1318, King Robert was to make an ordinance for Scotland *De transgress-*

[15] *CPR 1301–7*, 542–3.

[16] M.26 of the Lincoln trailbaston roll is headed 'Assise capte apud Lincoln' coram Petro de Malo Lacu et sociis suis justiciariis domini regis ad assisas coram quibuscumque justiciariis arramiatis vel arramiandas capiendas assignatis die mercurii proximo post quindenam Sancti Johannis Baptiste anno regni regis Edwardi filii regis Henrici tricesimo quinto'. Cf. the rolls of the other counties as listed in *List of Plea Rolls*.

[17] *CCR 1302–7*, 503.

[18] He died at Burgh by Sands, near Carlisle, on 7 July.

[19] About one-eighth of the approximately 400 cases on the 25 membranes have been used, but these 53 entries are naturally some of the longest and most interesting.

[20] See Cornwall, Derbyshire, Nottinghamshire, Warwickshire, Yorkshire, etc. in *List of Plea Rolls*.

[21] Most recently by N. Denholm-Young, *History and Heraldry, 1254–1310* (Oxford, 1965), 125–7, and Michael Prestwich, *War, Politics and Finance under Edward I* (London, 1972), 287–90.

[22] *Anglo-Norman Political Songs*, ed. I. S. T. Aspin (Anglo-Norman Text Soc., 1953), 67–78.

[23] *The Chronicle of Pierre de Langtoft*, ed. T. Wright (RS, 1866–8), II, 359–63.

[24] *RP*, I, 178; *CCR 1302–7*, 503.

[25] Langtoft, *Chronicle*, II, 359.

oribus venientibus ad exercitum, inviting complaints (*querimonie*) of trespass.[26]

Both judges and accused were often veterans of the wars. It is perhaps significant that the old soldier of the Trailbaston Song reserves his wrath for the professional judges and respects Martyn, a Scottish veteran, as a pious man.[27] Ranulf Friskney, knight, accused of extorting 15s. from a complainant for calling off his men, and also of retaining 'ad robas suas tamquam familiares' criminals actually indicted before him at Boston as one of the justices appointed in 1300 to punish infringements of the charters and to enforce the peace according to the statute of Winchester, produced a general pardon granted him in 1299 for his 'good service' in Scotland but only after a verdict had been given against him, so that the case was adjourned to the next parliament for judgment [43, 45].[28] The references in other cases [15, 38, 39] to groups of knights and squires, horse and foot, and the virtual siege of a house, 'viriliter . . . sagittando ad hostium et fenestras', suggest a society habituated to warfare.

In two particular ways wartime conditions caused disturbance. In the absence of tenants in the king's service, disputed lands were gained by legal action, violent assault or more usually by the pressure of threats and persistent minor acts of violence. Justices of assize were sent out in 1305 to work in parallel with the justices of trailbaston, but the latter inevitably found themselves dealing with violence which arose from questions of seisin, even before they began to hear assizes formally in 1307. It was found that Sir John Deyvill of Egmanton and other knights and squires had broken up a meeting of the shire court at Lincoln, held at the same time as the Lincoln parliament of 1301, in anger at the adjournment of a case about the lands of the wife of John Deyvill of Anston [15].[29] Disruption of cultivation by distraint [25, 27, 53], the driving-off of plough-oxen [7], the removal of the wheels of carts [24] and threats to the labourers [10, 27] seem often to be directed to forcing tenants from their manors [23].

Purveyance of war supplies was the other disruptive factor. The justices of trailbaston were told [42] how William Wormley, commissioned to buy corn for the king, sealed up the door of a house barred against him by a servant of Sir Ranulf Friskney; and how, when this was reported to him, Ranulf sought William out, knocked him down and had him thrown into a lake, his seal broken and his warrant trampled underfoot. The violence in fairs and markets, which was one of the commission's major concerns [3, 5, 9, 14, etc.], was surely connected with purveyance for war. In 1298 there had been a commission, not dissimilar to trailbaston in organisation, to hear and determine complaints of the grievances done to the people in the king's name on account of the war, and William Wormley had then figured obscurely as one of the accused.[30] In a sense, trailbaston was concerned with both sides of a situation, the violence of the people as well as of officials, whereas the commission of 1298 had been concerned with only one. The lay justices of 1305 had sometimes themselves been involved as purveyors for the king. Deincourt, for instance, had been instructed in 1302 to 'use all friendly ways' to induce the regular clergy of Lincolnshire to agree to a purveyance of grain.[31]

It would be hard to prove that there was anything new in the scale of the violence uncovered in 1305, but there was a new awareness, both in the commission and in the actual cases, of calculated and organised, as opposed to casual, violence, which can perhaps be linked with real changes in society and institutions. As the commission invited them to do, juries were at pains to distinguish 'malicious' and 'preconceived' violence from spontaneous aggression 'ex inpetu animi', which is clearly regarded as less serious.[32] The element of organisation is shown by verdicts that injuries were inflicted 'ex precepto', or 'per vices', or 'per procurationem et abettum', or that the malefactors were hired.[33] Something more than the working-out of old feuds seems to be indicated by the bizarre and methodical brutality. Victims have their doors and windows broken down, their limbs

[26] *The Acts of the Parliaments of Scotland,* ed. T. Thomson and C. Innes (RC, 1814–75), I, 467.

[27] *Anglo-Norman Political Songs,* 70 (stanza 9).

[28] *Parl. Writs,* I, 398–400.

[29] In *Flores Historiarum* the first business of the inquest 'quod Anglice dicitur Traillebaston' is given as the detection of 'intrusores alienarum terrarum qui propter timorem conquerentium ipsas terras vel praedia in manus potentium alienarent': *Flores Historiarum per Matthaeum Westmonasteriensem collecti,* ed. H. R. Luard (RS, 1890), III, 122.

[30] The Lincolnshire proceedings of 1298 were meticulously edited by W. S. Thomson in *A Lincolnshire Assize Roll for 1298* (Linc. Rec. Soc., XXXVI, 1944): see no. 149 for the reference to William Wormley.

[31] *Parl. Writs,* I, 405.

[32] [1, 5, 6, 8, 12, 19, 21, 26, 33, 41, 42.]

[33] [1, 5, 7, 21, 26, 28, 32, 34, 35, 36, 38.]

fractured, the soles of their feet slashed and their wives kicked in front of their eyes; they are trampled under the feet of horses and dragged off to taverns to drink their own blood; a horse ridden by a canon has its tail cut off and a boy is made to kiss its rump.[34] This looks like terrorism calculated to back up threats and sustain 'protection rackets': it will be recalled that the parliamentary 'ordinance of trailbastons' introduced a new clause about lords who sold their protection, and that the trailbaston commissions added a further clause about extorting money by menaces.[35] Several of the stories[36] told in the Lincolnshire cases end with 'treaties' agreed to by the victims in the face of violence and 'verba contumeliosa'. In one instance [22] the negotiations 'de amore' took place in the chapel of the persecutor, Philip Darcy, knight, perhaps to lend the victim some protection. The common beaters of men 'pro lucro recipiendo' may be presumed to have acted for people of more exalted rank [1, 9, 10, 13, 14, 29]. Sir Ranulf Friskney, 'justiciarius . . . ad pacem domini regis observandam', maintained known malefactors 'ad robas suas' to beat men in fairs and markets [45].

The other main concern of the justices of trailbaston, beside organised violence and protection rackets, was conspiracy. 'Conspirators' were defined for the benefit of the justices in the same parliament from which came the 'ordinance of trailbastons'. It may have been the experience of Peter Mauley and his colleagues when they arrived at York in the spring of 1305 which convinced the king that 'trailbastons' would not be punished unless 'conspirators' were dealt with also. Mauley reported that all 'great matters' were being concealed from the commission 'par procurement e aliaunces des genz du pais' and complained that their commission ('dont nous vous enveyoms le transescrit') did not include such conspiracies. On 29 May, the king ordered his council to make the necessary amendment of the commissions, and the Lincoln roll contains its membranes 'de conspiratoribus'.[37]

The 'enormous trespass' of conspiracy, as it had begun to be defined in the last decades of the thirteenth century, was essentially the concerted abuse of legal procedure. It was first of all an offence of sheriffs and their bailiffs who 'falsely and maliciously' persuaded approvers to accuse innocent men. The linked offences of champerty and maintenance (the instigation or support of pleas by others, for spite or a share in the winnings) also seems first to have engaged the king's concern as activities of his own ministers, though the eyre of 1294 found throughout Yorkshire 'so many and so influential maintainers of false plaints and champertors and conspirators leagued together to maintain any business whatsoever etc. that justice and truth are completely choked'.[38] Already in 1293 it had been provided by a parliamentary ordinance 'De Conspiratoribus' that complainants of champerty and maintenance should take their 'querelae' to king's bench and get writs of attachment under the chief justice's seal; the actions were to be heard in king's bench or the next eyre, and the convicted punished 'graviter . . . per prisonam et redemptionem'.[39] The Articuli super Cartas of 1300 ordered that a sheriff or bailiff who included suspicious persons in a jury should pay the plaintiff 'his damages double'; and that 'in right of Conspirators, false informers, and evil procurers of dozens, inquests, assizes and juries', justices of the bench and of assize should act on mere complaint, despite the provision of the writ in 1293.[40] The definition of conspirators for the benefit of the trailbaston commissioners put first those who bound themselves by agreement 'falsely and maliciously to indict or acquit men' and then went on to 'such as retain men in the country with liveries or fees for to maintain their malicious enterprises'.[41]

The cases heard by the justices of 1305, the first collection of cases of conspiracy which we have, bear out this association of the organised violence of the 'trailbastons' with the corruption of legal processes by the 'conspirators'. One man had been beaten up for revealing a secret agreement at a meeting of a riding court [1]. When he broke up a shire court at Lincoln, John Deyvill of Anston had with him two pleaders in that court who were of his livery [15]. Sir Ranulf Friskney, a 'custos pacis' himself in 1301, was a 'communis sustentator et manutentor placitorum et

34 [5, 6, 17, 19, 21, 24, 32, 42, 43.]

35 Above, 145.

36 [14, 15, 17, 18, 20, 22, 24, 43.] Sometimes it is land which is extorted in this way [23, 25, 27].

37 *RP*, I, 183; *SR*, I, 145; Sayles in *King's Bench*, II, cxlix–cli; G. O. Sayles, 'The Dissolution of a Gild at York in 1306', *EHR*, LV (1940), 83–98. See the heading of m.18 and [46–52].

38 P. H. Winfield, *The History of Conspiracy and the Abuse of Legal Procedure* (Cambridge, 1921); Sayles in *King's Bench*, III, liv ff; *SR*, I, 139 (c.11), 216.

39 *RP*, I, 96.

40 cc. 9, 10: *SR*, I, 139.

41 *RP*, I, 183.

querelarum'; he had been threatening jurors of assizes and inquests for six years or more, so that they dared not come to court or tell the truth out of fear of beating or loss of goods; and in particular he had terrorised the jurors who indicted him before Edmund Deincourt and his fellows, deriding them as 'rustics' [44, 45]. Ironically, Ranulf found himself in 1305 on a special commission of oyer and terminer concerning trespasses alleged to have been committed by Deincourt and other malefactors against Robert Godsfield of Sutton, a commission Deincourt was said to have tried to hinder by getting Robert falsely indicted before the justices of trailbaston (of whom he was one).[42] The conspiracy cases include accusations against bailiffs who abused their office by unjustly arresting ships [48, 49]; and allegations of false indictments (in one instance of a fictitious person) to shield the real felons or extort money [50]. Two persons were prosecuted by Ellis Preston, king's attorney, for a confederacy sealed by oath 'ad procurandum, abettandum et sustinendum falsa placita et querelas per ipsos moveri, et quosdam falso et maliciose indictari in comitatu isto' [52]; and another for taking 40s. 'per conspiracionem' from the dean and chapter of Lincoln to maintain their plea against the abbot of St Mary's and 40s. from the abbot to aid him against the dean and chapter, 'velud ambidexter' [52].

The prominence of conspiracy in its proceedings shows the necessity of putting trailbaston in a longer perspective. The plague of local conspiracies to pervert the course of justice is to be explained, not primarily by the war, but by longer-term changes in the organisation and processes of justice which trailbaston itself exemplifies. There are two closely-linked changes to be considered: the increasing use of lay justices on local or regional commissions to deal with trespasses, and the growing importance of plaints and bills in legal procedure. Knights from the counties had been used for much of the thirteenth century to help in taking assizes and delivering gaols.[43] The emergence of the 'custos pacis' on a county basis during the Barons' War, and the statute of Winchester of 1285 which was given him to enforce, marked new stages in bringing the mass of local disturbances labelled 'trespasses' within the scope of royal justice.[44] The justice of the peace appears for the first time with the three knights assigned to each county in 1300 to enforce the peace according to the statute of Winchester and also to hear and determine the 'querelas omnium et singulorum de eodem Comitatu tam infra libertates quam extra conquerencium seu conqueri volencium' of infringements of the charters.[45] The lay members of the inquests of 1304–5 and of the commission of trailbaston itself have already been noticed.

Oral complaints were first invoked in numbers against royal officials, but in the last quarter of the thirteenth century bills (which were simply plaints written down) were being presented to the justices in eyre against all sorts of defendants and entered on membranes headed 'Querele de transgressionibus' or 'Placita de querelis et bilettis'. From 1278 onwards the eyre was instructed to hear and determine plaints against the king's ministers, baronial officials, 'and anyone else'. Commissions of oyer and terminer were defined by their concern with plaints and bills, and in his last years Edward I used them increasingly in an attempt to divert from the eyre's path the clogging mass of bills which eventually halted it. The general commissions of 1298 and 1300 to hear complaints of the abuses of royal officials and of infringements of the charters were commissions of oyer and terminer. There were also innumerable special commissions of oyer and terminer to deal with offences of particular kinds in single counties, or committed by particular persons, or against particular complainants.[46]

Trailbaston was the most concerted attempt to make up the backlog of eyre business by a general commission of oyer and terminer to deal with complaints of particular types of injury committed in a limited period of time; afterwards eyres 'ad omnia placita' were intended to resume.[47] Like eyre rolls, the rolls of trailbaston have conventional-looking crown pleas (presentments of felonies and trespasses), and also, like the eyre rolls, cases of trespass heard on the complaint of private individuals ('De petitionibus et querelis'[48]). The puzzlement of Pike and

[42] *CCR 1302–7*, 284.

[43] See R. B. Pugh, *Imprisonment in Medieval England* (Cambridge, 1968), cc.XII, XIII.

[44] A. Harding, 'The Origins and Early History of the Keeper of the Peace', *TRHS*, 5th ser., X (1960), 85–109.

[45] *Parl. Writs*, I, 398–400; [45].

[46] A. Harding, 'Plaints and Bills in the Growth of English Law' in *Legal History Studies 1972*, ed. D. Jenkins (Cardiff, 1975), 65–86.

[47] *RP*, I, 178; Sayles in *King's Bench*, II, cl.

[48] The heading of m.30 of the Lincoln roll.

Holdsworth that 'apparently these justices entertained suits between party and party' is dissolved if it is understood that trailbaston was intended to relieve the eyre of its burden of 'querele de transgressionibus'. The hearing of bills was precisely what made it an oyer and terminer.[49]

The peculiar circumstances of the trailbaston proceedings of 1305 – that they involved presentments made to an earlier inquest – reveal just how much the bill had been reacting with jury presentment to transform criminal procedure. It was assumed that behind all the presentments made to the inquests which the trailbaston oyer and terminer superseded there lay private complaints from individuals, and, as the 'ordinance of trailbastons' instructed, the private complainants were given a chance to prosecute trespasses before the justices, either for the king as well as themselves in the case of 'enormous trespasses', or for themselves alone in the case of 'light and personal' ones.[50] Many a victim of a trespass which 'presentatum fuit alias coram Edmundo de Eyncurt' now appears to complain (*nunc sequitur et queritur*), and may be awarded damages by the 'inquisitio' on which 'defendens' and 'querens' agree or on which the 'defendens' alone relies, perhaps after being asked by the justices how he wishes to acquit himself.[51] If 'nullus sequitur', then the person indicted is tried 'ad sectam regis' or 'pro pace regis observanda inquiratur rei veritas' (the old formula of the appeal after the nonsuiting of the appellor) [22, 23, 43, 44]. Sometimes a case [e.g. 25] is brought 'ad presentationem xij etc. et ad sectam N. querentis'. Indictment as we know it from the late fourteenth-century proceedings before the justices of the peace, 'the Verdite of the Jurours, grounded upon the accusation of a third person: so that a Presentment, is but a declaration of the Jurours (or Officers) without any bill offered before: and an Enditement is their finding of a bill of accusation to be true', was clearly established in the 'Placita de indictamentis' of the trailbaston rolls.[52]

Also of great importance for the future is the prosecution of the king's suit by the bill of an individual prosecutor. A defendant may be summoned 'ad respondendum tam domino regi quam Willelmo filio Walteri et pluribus aliis' [29, 53], or an 'inquisitio' be held 'tam ad sectam Fulconis Juliain quam ad sectam regis' [37]. A complainant may 'tam sequitur pro domino rege quam pro seipso' [53], or in a plea of conspiracy of false indictments be 'paratus . . . verificare tam pro domino rege quam pro seipso'.[53] A private complainant may even seek to prosecute a mere trespass 'de bonis asportatis' (albeit by a crowd of people) on the king's suit only (*hoc petit verificare pro domino rege*) [53]; and so, on the basis of private complaints of trespass, was established the prosecution of crimes by the king's attorney. At Lincoln, bills alleging conspiracy seem normally to have been prosecuted by Ellis Preston 'qui sequitur pro domino rege' or 'paratus est verificare pro domino rege' [50, 52].[54]

The future of these developments in criminal prosecution lay in king's bench, because in 1305 the justices coram rege were used as justices of trailbaston and assize in the home counties and in 1323 were given a permanent trailbaston commission throughout England, so that in 1336 the court needed a separate division to cope with bills.[55] An attempt to revive the general eyre, promised in 1305 as the real medicine which would follow the 'beverage' of trailbaston, failed conclusively in 1330, and the government fell back once more on a combination of inquests by the 'custodes pacis' and sessions of oyer and terminer held by the 'plus Grantz' of the counties.[56] The determining as well as the receiving of the great mass of bills of trespass eventually passed to the 'custodes pacis', rarely disturbed by commissions of trailbaston from Westminster.

To this victory of the bill and lay justices in combination can be attributed a good deal of the disorder of later medieval England. Together they turned legal processes into potent new weapons in local struggles

49 Holdsworth, I, 273.

50 *RP*, I, 178.

51 [7, 12, 16, 17, 18, 19, 20, 21, 27, 28, 38, 42.]

52 The definition of indictment is Lambard's in *Eirenarcha,* quoted by B. H. Putnam in *Procs before JPs,* c. W. C. Bolland, *Select Bills in Eyre* (SS, XXX, 1914), 79, prints a bill in eyre of 1286 endorsed *Ista billa est vera* . . . See E 36/88, no. 29 for a bill presented to the justices of trailbaston in Gloucestershire in 1321 alleging assault and the extortion of money 'par leur manasses', including a threat of false indictments, to the grave damage of the king; the bill is endorsed *Affidavit quia pauper . . . nulla transgressio ad patriam; postea non prosecutus; misericordia xl d.; Finit'.* The headings 'Placita de Indictamentis', 'Placita Indictamentorum' and 'Indictamenta' appear in the Surrey, Herefordshire and Cornwall rolls for 1305–6.

53 M.18, first case (not printed).

54 cf. [15], in which William Thornton 'sequitur pro rege'.

55 Sayles in *King's Bench,* IV, lxviii.

56 ibid., II, cl; H. M. Cam, *Liberties and Communities in Medieval England* (London, 1963 edn), 157.

for power. It was too easy for gentry, who might themselves be justices, to get false bills endorsed by fearful jurors. In the trailbaston rolls there is a new concern with the conspiring of false plaints, indictments and informations, as much as false appeals [44, 47, 50–52].[57] The trouble was that an increase in the opportunities for such manipulation was an inevitable concomitant of any attempt to bring 'enormous trespasses' within the scope of royal justice. The concern with conspiracy was part of a desperate attempt to protect the jury of inquest. At Burstwick just across the Humber from Lincolnshire, on 24 November 1304, the day after the reissue of the commission of inquiry to Deincourt and his colleagues with a new clause about assaults on jurymen for telling the truth, King Edward ordered that civil writs of conspiracy were not to be granted without his express approval for use against indicting jurors, for 'if this were suffered many people would fear to be put on inquests and indict no man however guilty'.[58] At the spring parliament of 1305, the king received a petition that the delivery of gaols was being held up by charges that the jurymen were 'not good'. But other petitions alleging false indictment before Deincourt's inquest could not be ignored, nor the petition of 'poor men of England' that the king should ordain a remedy concerning jurymen who were 'so commonly corrupted by the gifts of the rich that no truth could be known by them'.[59] By the time of the parliament in the summer of 1306, petitions were arriving from 'those who served the king before the justices of Trailbaston', complaining that men convicted of conspiracy and other trespasses subsequently bought themselves on to inquests to confound those who had faithfully indicted them.[60] The warning that men would no longer serve on inquests if this continued may have been justified, for in June 1306 the king found it necessary to suspend the law that no one should be taken and imprisoned unless indicted by the oath of twelve jurymen.[61]

In the parliament which met in January 1315, the 'community of England' complained of conspirators in every borough and hundred of the land who corrupted jurors to give the verdicts they wanted and threatened 'les Aturnez de la Court le Roi' acting for their opponents.[62] Edward II's answer was that remedy should be sought from his chancery, but all the chancellor could do in answer to a bill of complaint was to issue a commission of oyer and terminer to take indictments. As the community of the realm complained in that same parliament, when a 'grant Seignur, ou homme de poer' wished to ruin a man, he simply alleged a trespass by him or maintained someone else to do so and bought commissions of oyer and terminer to justices favourable to himself.[63] The seeking of a commission was too often a declaration of war by one magnate upon another, and the justices were often enough men of war rather than of law.[64] In this, too, trailbaston was a landmark on a road which began much further back. By appointing as justices men such as Deincourt, or Mauley, 'the king's yeoman', who had returned with him from the siege of Stirling to Burstwick in the winter of 1304, Edward I fostered the conditions of civil war which he had set himself to quell.[65]

57 cf. Sayles in *King's Bench,* III, liv, lxxvi.

58 *CCW,* I, 241–2.

59 *Memoranda de Parliamento,* 11, 38, 122, 305.

60 *RP,* I, 201 (no. 63).

61 *CCR 1302–7,* 397.

62 *RP,* I, 289 (no. 3).

63 ibid., 290 (no. 8).

64 Sayles in *King's Bench,* VII, xxxvi–xxxvii.

65 *CCW,* I, 207, 224, 243; Sayles in *King's Bench,* IV, lvi.

TEXT

JUST 1/509, m.l.

PLACITA CORAM PETRO DE MALO LACU, EDMUNDO DE EYNCURT, WILLELMO LE VAVASUR, JOHANNE DE INSULA ET THOMA DE FISCHEBURN' JUSTICIARIIS DOMINI REGIS AD DIVERSAS FELONIAS ET TRANSGRESSIONES IN COMITATU LINCOLN' FACTAS AUDIENDUM ET TERMINANDUM ASSIGNATIS[66] DIE LUNE PROXIMA POST OCTABAS NATIVITATIS SANCTI JOHANNIS BAPTISTE APUD LINCOLN' ANNO REGNI DOMINI REGIS EDWARDI FILII DOMINI REGIS HENRICI TRICESIMO TERTIO

Wapentagium de Hawordeshowe venit per xij^{cim}

[1] Compertum est per juratores in quos Adam de Fulestowe cappellanus se posuit quod ipse simul cum Johanne de Rothewell' et Thoma fratre eius ex precepto Alani de Rothewell' persone ratione cuiusdam leporarii eiusdem Alani elongati et ex inimicia[67] perhabita verberavit, wlneravit, lapidavit et male tractavit Johannem filium Johannis de la Launde. Et similiter ratione quod idem Johannes conventionem factam in secretis cum predicto Johanne de Rothewell' et Thoma in pleno tridingio apud Castre revelavit. Et similiter dicunt quod idem Adam est communis verberator[68] et pacis domini regis purturbator. Ideo committitur gayole. Postea fecit finem per quadraginta solidos per plegium Radulfi de Fulestowe et Johannis de Trehampton' de Thoresby. Et similiter iidem Radulfus et Johannes manuceperunt eum quod bene se geret et honeste versus omnes de regno nemini injuriando nec injuriari procurando secundum formam per consilium regis provisam etc.

Et de predictis Johanne, Thoma et Alano preceptum fuit vicecomiti quod attachiaret eos per corpora etc. Et vicecomes testatur quod Thomas obiit et Johannes abjuravit regnum et predictus Alanus est in prisona. Ideo custodiatur quousque etc. Et Johannes exigatur et utlagetur si non comparuerit. Et si comparuerit tunc eum capiat etc. et salvo etc. quousque etc.

[*Marginated*] Gayole, xl s. [*deleted*]; Gayole, exigatur et utlagetur.

Jordeburg'

[2] Compertum est per inquisitionem in quam Thomas de Stutevill' se posuit quod predictus Thomas verberavit et maletractavit quendam hominem ignotum in villa de Barwe contra pacem domini regis etc. Et quod Johannes Comyn dedit garcionem Roberti de Scures unum ictum contra pacem etc. Et quod Simon le Porter verberavit, vulneravit et male tractavit Ricardum Scotte cum quodam baculo usque ad effusionem sanguinis etc. Et quod idem Simon simul cum Willelmo de la Haye cepit de bonis et catallis Stephani super Montem ad valenciam duorum solidorum. Et quod Johannes filius Johannis filii Radulfi de Gresseby verberavit et male tractavit Thomam Fabrum de Seuerby contra pacem etc. Ideo committantur gaole. Et postea Thomas de Stutevill' fecit finem per unam marcam per plegium Roberti Crispin et Herberti de Saltfletby. Et Johannes Comin fecit finem per duas marcas per plegium Roberti Crispyn et Herberti de Saltfletby. Et Simon le Porter fecit finem per viginti solidos per plegium Johannis Comyn et Herberti de Saltfletby. Et Johannes filius Johannis filii Radulfi de Gresseby fecit finem per viginti solidos per plegium Walteri le Girdeler de Linc' [et] [69] Johannis le Irnemonger de eadem.
[*Marginated*] Gaole; finis j marca, finis ij marce, finis xx s., finis xx s. [*deleted*].

Thomas de Stutvill' et Simon le Porter fecerunt finem cum domino rege per quadraginta solidos per plegium Jacobi de Tankerlegh de comitatu Linc'[70] persone de Wallesby, Willelmi de Stutvill' et Jacobi de Wandeslegh de comitatu Ebor'.
[*Marginated*] xl s.

Membrane 1d

[*Continuation heading*] Wappentagium de Yortheburgh' venit per xij

[3] Item compertum est per inquisitionem in quam Walterus Beveryge se posuit quod ipse verberavit et maletractavit Thomam le Blound de Ulseby in foro de Barton' ita quod mahemiatus est[71] et est communis verberator in feriis et mercatis. Ideo predictus Walterus committatur gayole. Postea venit predictus

[66] *AUDIENDUM . . . ASSIGNATIS* interlined.

[67] Here and elsewhere for *inimicitia*?

[68] MS *verbator*.

[69] Omitted.

[70] *de comitatu Linc'* interlined.

[71] *ita . . . est* interlined.

Walterus et fecit finem per sexaginta solidos per plegium Herberti de Saltefleteby et Willelmi de Thorp' de Goushill'. Et similiter iidem plegii manuceperunt eum quod decetero bene et pacifice se geret secundum formam etc.
[*Marginated*] Gayole [*deleted*].

[4] Presentatum fuit quod Adam Haucepe de Barton' qui dicitur Tayllur die lune proxima post festum Purificationis Beate Marie anno regni regis nunc xxxiij venit ad domum Willelmi de Houeden in villa de Stretton' et bona et catalla eiusdem Willelmi ibidem inventa videlicet pannos et vasa ad valenciam quadraginta solidorum vi et armis cepit et asportavit contra pacem etc. Et predictus Adam attachiatus venit. Et Willelmus non venit. Et ideo predictus Adam ad sectam regis quesitus qualiter se velit inde aquietare dicit quod non est inde culpabilis. Et de hoc ponit se super patriam. Et juratores ipsius wappintagii simul cum juratoribus wappintagiorum de Coringham et Manle ad hoc electis dicunt super sacramentum suum quod predictus Adam in nullo est culpabilis de transgressione predicta. Ideo ipse inde quietus.
[*Marginated*] Quietus.

[5] Item compertum est per inquisitionem in quam Henricus Langus de Barowe se posuit quod ipse verberavit et vulneravit Stephanum de Waddeword' in campis de Killyngholm' ex inimicitia perhabita. Et similiter quod predictus Henricus simul cum aliis verberavit, vulneravit et male tractavit Willelmum[72] de Outhenby et Ricardum Kenet servientes abbatis de Thorneton' in Barowe per preceptum Johannis de Eyvill' eo quod predicti Willelmus et Ricardus averia sua capta et imparcata per predictum Johannem de Eyvill' petierunt replegiari, et quod idem Henricus est communis malefactor in feriis et mercatis. Et similiter compertum [est][73] quod predictus[74] Henricus simul cum Galfrido de Hodersfeld verberavit et maletractavit Walterum Dolfyn de Gousill' janitorem abbatis de Thornton' et brachium suum fregit et quamdam rochetam de canebo ab eo extorsit de qua adhuc seisitus est. Et similiter compertum est quod idem Henricus verberavit et maletractavit Hugonem Horsehirde in contemptu abbatis de Thornton', et similiter verberavit Willelmum Archer ex inimicitia perhabita. Ideo idem Henricus committatur gaole. Postea venit Henricus et fecit finem per viginti solidos per plegium Henrici de Rideford' et Walteri de Rideford'. Et iidem manuceperunt eum quod bene etc. secundum provisionem etc.
[*Marginated*] Gaole, xx s. [*deleted*].

[6] Item compertum est per inquisitionem in quam Stephanus de Waddeword' de Kyllyngholm' se posuit quod ipse ex inimicitia perhabita Alexandrum Attegrene extra domum suam propriam in Killyngham violenter extraxit et ipsum verberavit et maletractavit ita quod de vita sua disperabatur. Et similiter idem Stephanus verberavit ex inimicitia perhabita Henricum Langus et Gilbertum de Pikeryng'. Et similiter vulneravit Gilbertum de Aylsby ita quod pulmo et vicera apparuerunt. Et est communis verberator in feriis et mercatis. Ideo predictus Stephanus committatur gayole. Postea venit predictus Stephanus et fecit finem per xxx s. per plegium Thome Rudde de Ormesby et Willelmi le Forester de Utterby. Et similiter iidem plegii manuceperunt pro eodem Stephano quod de cetero bene se geret etc.
[*Marginated*] Gaiole, finis xxx s. [*deleted*].

[7] Item presentatum fuit alias etc. quod Robertus de la Sale de Walde Neuton' simul cum aliis die sabbati in media septimana Quadragesime anno regni regis nunc xxxj apud Stalingburgh' vi et armis et contra pacem verberavit, vulneravit et male tractavit Rogerum de la Launde de Stalingburgh' ita quod tria ossa a capite eiusdem Rogeri fuerunt extracta. Et predictus Robertus attachiatus venit. Et similiter predictus Rogerus qui nunc queritur de predicta transgressione. Et dicit quod deterioratus est et dampnum habet ad valenciam lx li. Et predictus Robertus dicit quod in nullo est culpabilis. Et de hoc ponit se super patriam. Juratores dicunt super sacramentum suum quod predictus Robertus equo scansus et armatus simul cum aliis quadam die venit in campo de Stalingburgh' et jugum aratri bobus junctum amputavit. Et boves eiusdem Rogeri postea ad manerium Radulfi de Stalingburgh' fugavit. Et postea fuit presens et in auxilium ubi predictus Rogerus verberatus fuit et vulneratus. Et similiter dicunt quod predictus Robertus fuit conductor predictorum malefactorum. Ideo consideratum est quod predictus Rogerus recuperat dampna sua que taxantur per juratores ad C solidos. Et predictus Robertus comittatur gaole. Postea Robertus fecit finem per viginti solidos, per plegium Ricardi de Cateby de Neuton' et Ricardi de la Mare de eadem etc. Et quod bene etc.
[*Marginated*] Gaole, xx s. [*deleted*].
Dampna C s. unde clericis xx s.

[72] Interlined. [73] Omitted.

[74] *Et . . . predictus* on erasure.

[8] Item compertum est per inquisitionem in quam Willelmus Broun se posuit quod ipse odio antiquo verberavit et male tractavit Alanum de Ruda. Ideo predictus Willelmus comittatur gayole. Postea fecit finem per unam marcam per plegium Johannis de Cotes de Gousehill' et Alani Broun de eadem. [*Marginated*] Gayole, j m. [*deleted*].

[9] Item compertum est per inquisitionem in quam Willelmus filius Henrici Fabri de Kirnington' se posuit quod ipse est communis pugnator et pacis perturbator in feriis et mercatis. Ideo predictus Willelmus committatur gaole. Postea venit predictus Willelmus et finem fecit per viginti solidos per plegium Walteri de Kirketon', Herberti de Saltfletby et Henrici de Ridford'. Et iidem plegii manuceperunt eum quod bene etc. secundum provisionem etc. [*Marginated*] Gaole, xx s. [*deleted*].

Membrane 2

Presentationes de Laur'

[10] Item presentatum fuit alias etc. quod Viotus frater persone de Ingham, Willelmus Clavering' de Saxeby, Willelmus de Topclive de eadem, Willelmus Forestarius de Le et Willelmus de Kyme de Ingham venerunt vi et armis ad grangiam de Scampton' et obstupaverunt portas grangie grangiario dicentes se ibi venire ad verberandum garciones dicti grangiarii. Qui cum hoc vidit verbis blandissimis ac pacificis iram eorum tunc sedavit. Et contra pacem ceperunt ab eo decem solidos.

[11] Item presentatum fuit alias quod Philippus de[75] Hille fecit assultum Rogero de Thurelby et fregit portas manerii sui apud Upton' et amputavit arbores suas contra pacem. Et ipsum Rogerum occidisse voluisset si ipsum attingisse potuisset.

[12] Item compertum est per eosdem in quos Willelmus Steffan se posuit quod ipse ex inimicia perhabita verberavit et male tractavit Johannem Fayryng'[76] qui nunc sequitur et queritur et digitum eiusdem Johannis violenter fregit in villa de Midilrasene. Ideo consideratum est quod predictus Johannes recuperat dampna sua que taxantur per justiciarios ad viginti solidos. Et predictus Willelmus comittatur gaole. Fecit finem supra in proxima loquela. [*Marginated*] Gaole [*deleted*]. Dampna xx s.

Aslachow

[13] Compertum est per inquisitionem in quam Robertus Coddelyng' de Wyllyeton' se posuit quod ipse[77] est communis verberator hominum pro lucro recipiendo et pacis regis perturbator. Et quod cepit de quodam Rogero Catte de Helmeswelle ne ipsum verberaret xij d. Et quod idem Robertus verberavit quemdam Thomam Fabrum de Helmeswell' et ipsum male wlneravit contra pacem. Ideo predictus Robertus Coddelyng' committatur gaole. Postea fecit finem per unam marcam per plegium Johannis de Thornhaghe et Ricardi de Hatheleseye. Et manuceperunt eum quod bene se geret etc. [*Marginated*] Gaole, finis j m. [*deleted*].

[14] Item compertum est per inquisitionem in quam Robertus Spykynge de Helmeswelle se posuit quod ipse est[78] contumeliosus et pluries verberat homines contra pacem in feriis etc. contra pacem. Ideo committatur gaole. Postea venit et fecit finem per unam marcam per plegium Willelmi de Stokkyng' et Johannis filii Simonis de Helmeswell'. Et similiter manuceperunt eum quod de cetero bene se geret etc. [*Marginated*] Gaole, finis j m. [*deleted*].

Membrane 4

Wappentachium de Mannelay venit per xij juratores

[15] Johannes de Eyvle de Eggemanton', Johannes Deyvile de Anstan, Willelmus de Houedene [et][79] Robertus Crispin attachiati fuerunt ad respondendum domino regi de placito quare cum dominus nuper rex tenuisset parliamentum suum apud Linc' ac vicecomes Linc' tunc temporis tenuisset comitatum suum in eadem civitate in quo comitatu Hugo de Bussey et Johanna Dysni[80] in placitaverunt Johannem de Eyvile de Anstan et Johannam uxorem eius per breve patens domini regis de recto de quibusdam tenementis in Barewe[81] predicti Johannes, Johannes, Robertus et Willelmus vi et armis intraverunt in domum ubi comitatus tenebatur proferendo verba contumeliosa sub vicecomite et aliis ministris domini regis in eodem comitatu existentibus minando ac predictus Johannes

[75] Over *del* erased.

[76] The *y* in the first syllable of *Fayryng'* is interlined.

[77] *se . . . ipse* interlined.

[78] Interlined.

[79] Omitted.

[80] On erasure.

[81] The *rewe* of *Barewe* is interlined, after *Ba* on erasure.

de Eyvile miles manum ad misericordiam suam ponendo per quod fere omnes in dicto domo existentes pretimore teriti exierunt et fugerunt per quod placita dicti comitatus ad illum diem debito modo tenere non potuerunt nisi tantummodo placita corone contra pacem domini regis et in contemptum ipsius domini regis M lib. etc. Et predicti et alii venerunt et defendunt vim [et][82] quicquid est contra pacem domini regis etc. Et predictus Johannes de Eyvile miles dicit quod ipse fuit in civitate Linc' die quo dictus comitatus tenebatur in civitate predicta. Ad quem quidem comitatum ad instanciam dicti Johannis de Eyvile de Anstan consangueney[83] sui qui[84] inplacitatus fuit de terra uxoris sue in Barewe[85] accessit ipse[86] ad ipsum auxiliandum et consulendum secundum legem terre consilio regni etc. nulli minando obbrobria seu verba contumeliosa proferendo nec manum suam ad misericordiam suam ponendo nec ibidem aliquid contra pacem domini regis fecit et [de][87] hoc ponit se super patriam. Et Johannes de Eyvile de Anstan defendit etc. Et bene defendit quod nichil ad dictum comitatum ad predictum diem fecit contra pacem immo ad dictum comitatum accessit pro terra uxoris sue defendenda unde ipse et uxor eius in placitati fuerunt prout ei bene licuit et de hoc ponit se etc. Et predicti Willelmus et Robertus dicunt quod ipsi sunt narratores in comitatu Linc' et quod ad robas dicti Johannis de Anstan tunc temporis fuerunt [et][87] venerunt ad comitatum eodem die cum predicto Johanne domino suo ad ipsum consulendum et auxiliandum secundum legem terre. Et quod nichil ibidem contra pacem fecerunt ponunt se super patriam et petunt quod inquiratur. Et predictus Willelmus de Thornton' qui sequitur pro rege similiter petit quod inquiratur. Et dies datus est eis apud Snaynton' die sabbati in septimana Pascha.

Ad quem diem prefati Johannes et alii veniunt. Et similiter juratores de consensu predictorum Johannis et aliorum electi. Qui dicunt super sacramentum suum quod quidam Hugo de Buscy et quedam Johanna de Yseni tulerunt quoddam breve regis de recto in curia ipsius domini regis apud Barwe quod est de feodo Albe Marle versus Johannem de Eyvill' de Anstan et Johannam uxorem[88] eius de quibusdam tenementis in Barwe. Et quod loquela illa postea inter eos mota fuit usque ad comitatum Linc'. Et quod predicti Johannes et Johanna summoniti fuerunt essendi ad comitatum tentum apud Linc' tempore quo dominus rex ultimo ibidem parliamentum suum tenuit. Ad quem comitatum quoddam essonium intratum fuit pro predicto Johanne de Eyvill' de Anstan et adjornatum. Et statim postea venerunt Johannes de Eyvill' miles et Johannes de Eyvill' de Anstan, Willelmus de Houeden' et Robertus Crispin et alii plures tam milites quam armigeri. Et prefatus Johannes de Eyvill' de Anstan et Johanna uxor eius optulerunt se versus predictos Hugonem et Johannam in placito predicto. Et quidem Henricus de Fenton' subvicecomes et tenens locum vicecomitis dixit quod tam predictus Johannes de Eyvill' quam predicti Hugo et Johanna adjornati fuerunt usque ad proximum comitatum super essonio pro predicto Johanne de Anstan intrato et adjornato. Et quod servarent diem suum ad proximum comitatum. Et prefati Johannes de Eyvill' miles, Johannes de Eyvill' de Anstan et Willelmus de Houeden' hoc audientes statim predicto Henrico dixerunt quod ipse falso et infideliter se habuit et fecit in hac parte asserentes ipsum et quemdam Johannem de Cresseby tunc indicto comitatu existentem dictum essonium falso et maliciose intrasse et adjornasse in deceptionem predictorum Johannis de Anstan et Johanne uxoris eius. Et idem Johannes de Eyvill' miles super hoc precepit eidem Henrico subvicecomiti quod ipse adnullaret dictum essonium et quod faceret dicto Johanni de Anstan justiciam minando ei quod si non faceret hoc lueret. Et quod de eo domino regi conquereretur. Et super hoc venit Willelmus de Ros dominus de Hamelak'. Et predictus Henricus dixit ei verba et minas quas predictus Johannes de Eyvill' ei fecerat et petiit quod esse posset in protectionem ipsius Willelmi de Ros. Et predictus Willelmus statim abiit et prefatus Henricus similiter cum rotulis suis placitorum dicti comitatus in conductu predicti Willelmi a domo ubi comitatus tentus fuit cum eodem Willelmo recessit. Et post recessum predicti Johannis de Eyvill' et aliorum secum venientium idem Henricus rediit ad comitatum et placita eiusdem comitatus tenuit et cetera fecit que ad diem illum in dicto comitatu fieri debebant. Et bene dicunt quod Johannes de Eyvill' miles nec alii secum venientes non extraxit aliquam misericordiam sicut ei inponitur. Et quo ad Robertum Crispin dicunt quod ipse nichil fecit inprejudicium domini regis nec aliqua verba minatoria seu contumeliosa eidem Henrico intulit. Ideo consideratum est

[82] Omitted. [83] Recte *consanguinei.*
[84] Interlined. [85] On erasure.
[86] Interlined. [87] Omitted.
[88] *quod est . . . uxorem* on erasure.

quod predictus Robertus Crispin eat inde sine die. Et quia per istam inquisitionem compertum est quod predicti Johannes de Eyvill' miles, Johannes de Eyvill' de Anstan et Willelmus de Houeden' prefatum Henricum ministrum domini regis et locum vicecomitis tenentem in comitatu et in plena curia dicti domini regis verbis enormibus et contumeliosis insultaverunt maliciam et falsitatem imponendo et minas per predictum Johannem de Eyvill' militem inferendo per quod idem Henricus tanquam perteritus de dicta curia recessit. Consideratum est quod predicti Johannes et alii comittantur gayole. Postea manucapti sunt etc. Et datus est eis dies in parliamento regis apud Westm' in vigilia Penticoste proxima futuri. Postea Willelmus de Houedeyn'[89] fecit finem per sexaginta solidos per plegium Ade de Kydale[90] de Barton' et Thome de Amecotes. Et Johannes de Eyvill' milit'[91] fecit finem per quadraginta libras per plegium Petri Fenne de comitatu Nttingh' et Thome de Anecote de comitatu Linc'. Et Johannes de Eyvill' de Anestan fecit finem per quadraginta marcas per plegium Johannis de Harecourt de comitatu Leyc' et[92] Petri Fenne de comitatu Notingh'.
[*Marginated*] Gayole, lx s., xl li., xl m.

Membrane 4d

[16] [*Marginated*] Geyrtree
Compertum est per inquisitionem in quam Willelmus de Horneby querens et Johannes filius Roberti de Tynton' senior defendens se posuerunt quod idem Johannes die dominica proxima post festum Sancti Johannis Baptiste anno regni regis nunc xxix in villa de Stykeswolde ex odio antiquo vi et armis prefato Willelmo insultum fecit, verberavit, vulneravit et maletractavit contra pacem etc. ad dampnum ipsius Willelmi quadraginta solidorum. Et similiter quod idem Johannes filius Roberti de Tynton' alias die veneris proxima post festum Michaelis anno predicto prefato Willelmo insultum fecit et duas alapas ei dedit contra pacem etc. ad dampnum ipsius Willelmi qui sequitur ij s. etc. Ideo consideratum est quod predictus Willelmus recuperet dampna sua que taxantur per juratores [ad] xlij s. Et predictus Johannes committatur gaiole. Postea Johannes filius Roberti de Tyntton' senior fecit finem per viginti solidos per plegium Willelmi Gregor' de Querington' et Ricardi de Hanlay. Et iidem plegii manuceperunt eum quod bene se etc.

[*Marginated*] Gaiole, xx s. [*deleted*].
Dampna xlij s. unde clericis dimidia marca.

Membrane 5

[17] [*Marginated*] Mannele
Presentatum fuit alias etc. coram Edmundo de Eyncurt etc. per xij juratores de Mannelay quod Radulfus Takel de Haxay die Sancti Laurencii anno regni regis nunc xxxj hostia et fenestras Rogeri Drink' Halpeny apud Westwode in Insula vi et armis et contra pacem fregit et ipsum Rogerum verberavit, vulneravit et male tractavit et postea ipsum Rogerum ad quamdam tabernam cervisie in eadem villa vi secum duxit et sanguinem a vulnere capitis predicti Rogeri defluentem et in quodam cypho effusum et receptum cum cervisia mixtum bibere coegit minando ipsum quod aliter interficeret ut asseruit.

Et tunc a predicto Rogero per minas suas et pro pace habenda sex solidos violenter extorsit.

Et predictus Radulfus attachiatus venit et similiter predictus Rogerus qui nunc queritur. Et dictus Radulfus quesitus per justiciarios qualiter de predictis trangressionibus se velit inde acquietare dicit quod clericus est et quod non debet hic inde respondere. Et quia predictus Radulfus sepius requisitus aliud non respondit nisi quod clericus est et quod precise aliud non dicit predictus Radulfus per considerationem curie habeatur pro indefenso. Et super hoc inquiratur de dampnis. Et xij juratores de wappentagio de Mannelay ubi hoc fieri debuit de dampnis predicti Rogeri jurati et onerati dicunt super sacramentum suum quod predictus Rogerus dampna habuit ad valenciam x librarum. Ideo consideratum est quod predictus Rogerus recuperet dampna sua que taxantur per juratores ad decem libras. Et predictus Radulfus committatur gayole.
[*Marginated*] Gayole.
Dampna x libre unde clericis xx s. et marescallo x s.

[18] Item presentatum fuit per eosdem etc. quod Radulfus Takel die jovis proxima ante festum Epiphanie Domini anno regni regis nunc xxxij verberavit, vulneravit et mahemiavit Gilbertum le Mouner de Westewode noctanter in domo sua propria ita quod languidus fuit per sexdecim septimanas et unum digitum amisit et equum predicti Gilberti precii decem solidorum nequiter et contra pacem interfecit. Et postea a predicto Gilberto per minas suas tres solidos

89 Penultimate letter ill written.

90 *de Kydale* interlined.

91 Interlined; recte *miles.*

92 Repeated.

violenter extorsit et novem lagenas cervisie secum finiri coegit de quibus tribus solidis predictus Radulfus seisitus est. Et predictus Radulfus attachiatus venit. Et similiter predictus Gilbertus qui nunc queritur. Et predictus Radulfus quesitus per justiciarios qualiter de predictis transgressionibus se velit inde acquietare dicit quod clericus est et quod non debet hic inde respondere. Et quia predictus Radulfus sepius requisitus et aliud non respondit nisi quod clericus est et quod precise aliud non dicit predictus Rogerus[93] habeatur pro indefenso. Et super hoc inquiratur de dampnis. Et xij de wappentagio de Mannelay ubi hoc fieri debuit de dampnis predicti Gilberti jurati et onerati dicunt super sacramentum suum quod predictus Gilbertus dampnum habuit ad valenciam viginti librarum. Ideo consideratum est quod predictus Gilbertus recuperet dampna sua que taxantur per juratores ad viginti libras. Et predictus Radulfus committatur gaiole.
[*Marginated*] Gayole.
Dampna xx libre unde clericis x m. et marescallo xl s.

Membrane 5d

Manlee

[19] Item compertum est per inquisitionem in quam Radulfus Takel se posuit quod ipse simul cum aliis die jovis proxima ante festum Sancti Petri ad vincula anno regni regis nunc xxix domum Ade Swayneson' maliciose intravit et Hugonem filium Ade Swayneson' verberavit, vulneravit etc. et brachium suum sinistrum fregit ita quod de vita eius desperabatur. Et predictus Hugo nunc sequitur et queritur. Et similiter dicunt quod idem Radulfus die Sancti Michaelis anno supradicto eundem Hugonem in marisco de Westbutterwyk' inventum odio antiquo vulneravit, et ambo brachia sua in quatuor locis et tria ossa coste sue fregit et plantas pedis gladio suo abscidit ad dampnum dicti Hugonis xv li. Ideo consideratum est quod dictus Hugo recuperet dampna sua que taxantur ad xv li. Et predictus Radulfus committatur gaole.
[*Marginated*] Gaole.
Dampna quindecim libre.

[20] Item compertum est per inquisitionem in quam Radulfus Takel et Rogerus frater eius se posuerunt quod ipsi die Sancti Martini anno regni regis nunc xxxj apud Kynardfery vi et armis et contra pacem Johanni Chaunterel qui nunc queritur[94] insultum fecerunt. Et dixerunt quod nisi idem Johannes eisdem Radulfo et Rogero de denariis suis daret quod eum interficerent unde idem Johannes minis suis et timore fugit in ecclesiam eiusdem ville usque ad magnum altare et ibi eum interfecisse voluerunt nisi idem Johannes[95] finem fecisset cum eis de xxx s. quos eis statim solvit. Ideo consideratum [est][96] quod predictus Johannes recuperet dampna sua que taxantur per juratores ad x li. Et dicti Radulfus et Rogerus committantur gaole.
[*Marginated*] Gaole.
Dampna x libre unde clericis C s.

Membrane 7

Belteslawe

[21] Item presentatum fuit alias etc. coram E. de Eynecourt etc. per xij etc. quod Johannes Darcy miles vulneravit et male tractavit ex inimicia[97] perhabita homines abbatis de Valle Dei in villa de Scotilsthorp' contra pacem etc. Et predictus Johannes[98] attachiatus venit. Et quesitus qualiter velit inde[98] acquietare dicit quod in nullo est culpabilis. Et de hoc ponit se super patriam.[99] Juratores de consensu ipsius Johannis electi[100] dicunt super sacramentum suum quod predictus Johannes venit ad manerium Philippi de Arcy militis in Scotilsthorp'. Et quendam Johannem Wysse hominem predicti abbatis ad tabernam in eadem villa simul cum aliis inventum odio antiquo insultavit, verberavit, vulneravit et maletractavit contra pacem etc. Et dicunt quod homines predicti Johannis tunc secum venientes[101] verberaverunt, vulneraverunt et male tractaverunt ceteros homines predicti abbati[102] ad predictam tabernam inventos, predicto Johanne precipiente et sciente. Ideo predictus Johannes de Arcy comittatur gaole. Postea venit coram thesaurario et barones de scaccario et fecit finem per decem libras.
[*Marginated*] Gaole, x li. [*deleted*].

[22] Item presentatum fuit alias etc. per eosdem etc. quod Philippus de Arcy miles cepit de abbate[103]

[93] Recte *Radulfus.* [94] *qui . . . queritur* interlined.
[95] Interlined. [96] Omitted.
[97] Recte *inimicitia.* [98] Interlined.
[99] *super patriam* interlined.
[100] *de consensu . . . electi* interlined.
[101] *tunc . . . venientes* interlined.
[102] Recte *abbatis.*
[103] Interlined.

[de] [104] Valle Dei per minas suas centum solidos. Et similiter presentatum fuit quod idem Philippus cepit per minas suas de Johanne Wysse homine predicti abbatis xxx s. quem Johannes Darcy prius[105] verberaverat. Et predictus Philippus attachiatus venit. Et nullus sequitur. Ideo pro pace regis observanda inquiratur rei veritas. Juratores de consensu ipsius electi[106] dicunt super sacramentum suum quod predictus abbas quadam die[107] cum amicis suis ad villam de Scotilsthorp' accessit ratione cuiusdam verberationis hominibus predicte abbatis prius[108] facte in villa de Scotilsthorp' per quendam Johannem de Arcy et alios.[109] Et per graves minas predicti Philippi et metu aliorum transgressionum que eidem abbati et suis inposterum evenire potuerunt, in capella eiusdem Philippi in predicta villa de amore cum predicto Philippo tractavit. Et dicunt quod idem abbas timore[110] C solidos. Et dicunt quod nisi hoc fecisset timuit quod sine dampno[111] aliter evadere non potuit,[112] quos quidem C solidos predictus abbas statim ei[113] solvit. Et quo ad Johannem Wysse dicunt quod predictus Philippus cepit de eodem Johanne per graves minas suas xxx s. Ideo predictus Philippus comittatur gaole.
[*Marginated*] Gaole.

[23] Item presentatum est per eosdem quod Philippus de Arcy per minas suas coegit Agnetem quondam uxorem Ricardi de Arcy manerium suum relinquere ita quod amisit proficuum eiusdem manerii per unum annum unde medio tempore[114] predicta Agnes perhendinavit apud Linc' et ibi moram traxit quousque timore et cohercione predicti Philippi finem fecit cum predicto Philippo per xx marcas quas eidem Philippo statim[115] solvit. Et predictus Philippus attachiatus venit set nullus sequitur. Ideo pro pace regis inquiratur rei veritas. Juratores dicunt[116] super sacramentum suum quod predicta Agnes tenuit tertiam partem manerii de Flixburgh' nomine dotis quo tempore eadem Agnes perquisivit feodum et jus predicte tertie partis de Willelmo de Arcy filio Ricardi de Arcy quondam[117] viri predicte Agnetis tenendum eidem Agneti et heredibus suis[118] in feodo simplici. Et dicunt quod predictus Philippus hoc intelligens predictam Agnetem a predicto manerio violenter ejecit. Et eam extra seisinam per sex septimanas tenuit quousque predicta Agnes timore amissionis predicti manerii et[119] per graves[119] minas et cohercíones predicti Philippi finem fecit cum eo per[120] viginti marcas quas ei solvit. Ideo predictus Philippus committatur gaiole.
[*Marginated*] Gaiole.

[24] Item presentatum fuit per eosdem quod idem Philippus injuste impedivit priorem de Nocton' cariare blada sua per quod amisit blada sua ad valenciam centum solidorum. Et preterea deadjunxit rotas carettarum suarum ita quod amisit opera carettarum illarum per octo dies et amplius quousque finem fecit eidem Philippo per viginti marcas. Et preterea presentatum [est] [121] quod predictus Philippus amputavit caudam unius equi super quem quidem canonicus equitavit. Et[122] in posteriora parte eiusdem equi fecit quemdam garcionem equum illum osculari. Et Philippus attachiatus venit et dicit quod si aliqua transgressio inde facta fuit predicto priori, hoc fuit ante tempus justiciariis hic limitatum. Et juratores quesiti si predicta transgressio facta fuit ante tempus vel post, dicunt quod transgressio facta fuit ante tempus. Ideo Philippus inde sine die.

[25] Item ad presentationem xij etc. et ad sectam Willelmi Darcy querentis compertum est per inquisitionem in quam predictus Philippus se posuit quod idem Philippus die Sancti Egidii abbatis anno regis nunc xxxij⁰ injuste et contra pacem etc. cepit in villa de Flixburgh' sexdecim boves, quatuor equos, quinque vaccas et centum bidentes predicti Willelmi Darcy et eos detinuit absque aliqua causa rationabili et pro eo quod idem Philippus desiderabat quod predictus Willelmus dimitteret ei manerium suum de Flixburgh' et similiter eidem Willelmo de corpore suo graviter minabatur et dicta averia sic imparcata detinuit quousque predictus Willelmus finem fecit cum eo per

104 Omitted. 105 Interlined.
106 *de consensu . . . electi* interlined.
107 *quadam die* interlined.
108 Interlined. 109 *et alios* interlined.
110 There is a gap in the MS, several words having been erased.
111 *timuit . . . dampno* interlined.
112 Interlined above *potuisset,* struck through.
113 Interlined.
114 *per idem tempus* interlined above *medio tempore,* not deleted.
115 *postea* interlined and erased.
116 Repeated. 117 Interlined.
118 Repeated. 119 Interlined.
120 *cum eo per* interlined.
121 Interlined.
122 *super quem . . . equitavit. Et* interlined.

quatuor marcas quas ei postea solvit ad dampnum ipsius Willelmi centum solidorum. Ideo consideratum est quod predictus Willelmus recuperet dampna sua et predictus Philippus committatur prisone.
[*Marginated*] Gaole.

Membrane 7d

Wappintachium de Langhou et Flaxwelle

[26] Item compertum est per inquisitionem in quam Willelmus filius Walteri Fabri de Bloxham se posuit quod ipse ex malicia preconcepta verberavit, vulneravit et male tractavit per vices Johannem Pandolf de Bloxolm, Adam le Spenser de Bloxam et Robertum de Rouston' contra pacem. Ideo comittatur gayole. Postea predictus Willelmus filius Walteri fecit finem per decem solidos per plegium Ricardi Bellard de Bloxam, Johannis le Warde de Dounesby, Willelmi Aubray de Bloxham et Ricardi filii Willelmi de eadem. Et iidem manuceperunt eum quod bene etc. secundum provisionem etc.
[*Marginated*] Gayole, x s. [*deleted*].

Manlee

[27] Item presentatum fuit per eosdem quod predictus Philippus Darcy dicto Willelmo Darcy tam graviter minabatur quod moram trahere non audebat ad manerium suum de Flixburgh' nec terram suam colere nec seminare a festo Purificationis Beate Marie anno regni regis xxxij° usque Pentecoste proximo sequens, et firmam de villanis ipsius Willelmi de termino Pasche levavit. Et villano[123] illos talliavit vi et armis et contra pacem. Et predictus Willelmus modo venit et sequitur versus predictum Philippum de predicta transgressione. Et dicit quod deterioratus est et dampnum habet ad valenciam xx librarum. Et predictus Philippus defendit vim et injuriam quando etc. Et dicit quod nullam ei fecit injuriam. Et de hoc ponit se super patriam. Juratores ex consensu partium electi dicunt super sacramentum suum quod predictus Philippus simul cum aliis venit ad predictam villam de Flixburgh' et domum cuiusdam[124] villani ipsius Willelmi contra voluntatem suam intravit et ibidem morabatur per tres dies per quod predictus Willelmus Darcy ad manerium suum de Flixeburgh' venire ut moraretur non audebat, et villanos dicti Willelmi minabatur et eos graviter distrinxit ita quod ipsi in septimana proxima ante Pascha solverunt ei de firmis suis de eodem termino Pasche x libras et nichilominus eos talliavit et de eisdem C solidos levavit. Et bene dicunt quod predictus Willelmus ausus non fuit ibidem venire nec comodum suum facere ad dampnum ipsius Willelmi xx librarum. Ideo consideratum est quod predictus Willelmus recuperet dampna sua que taxantur per juratores ad xx libras. Et predictus Philippus committatur gaole.
[*Marginated*] Gaole.
Dampna xx li. unde clericis C s.

Membrane 10

Staunford'

[28] Presentatum fuit alias etc. quod Ricardus de Baldeswelle, Johannes de Walmesford' et Thomas de Morton' per preceptum Roberti de Stokton' Robertum filium Philippi de Tynewelle vi et armis in libertate abbatis de Burgo Sancti Petri de Estaunford' ceperunt et ipsum extra libertatem illam usque castrum de Staunford' duxerunt et ibi ipsum detinuerunt per unum mensem et in profundo gaole ipsum posuerunt ita quod per tres dies non permiserunt aliquem ei victum exhibere sic quod fere fame periit contra pacem etc. Et predicti Ricardus et alii veniunt et similiter predictus Robertus qui queritur quod predicti Ricardus, Johannes et Thomas ipsum Robertum in libertate abbatis de Burgo Sancti Petri in Estaunford' vi et armis ceperunt et ipsum usque castrum de Staunford' duxerunt et ipsum in profundo gaole detinuerunt fere per unum mensem nec per tres dies aliquem victum sibi exhibere permiserunt ita quod ibi fere fame periit. Et unde dicit quod deterioratus est et dampnum habet ad valenciam centum librarum et inde producit sectam etc. Et Ricardus, Johannes et Thomas defendunt vim et injuriam quando etc. et bene defendunt quod nuncquam predictis die et anno predicto Roberto predictam transgressionem fecerunt et de hoc ponunt se super patriam.

Juratores dicunt super sacramentum suum quod quidam Robertus de Stoketon' senescallus Comitis Warenn' in partibus de Staunford' preceperat Ricardo de Baldeswelle capitali ballivo ville de Staunford' et ceteris ballivis eiusdem ville quod ipsi caperent predictum Robertum de Tynewelle ubicumque ipsum inveniri contigerit et ipsum ad prisonam castri ducerent et ipsum ibidem inprisonarent. Qui quidem Ricardus pretextu illius precepti quodam die cum predictus Robertus ad villam de Staunford' accessisset

[123] Recte *villanos.*

[124] There is a blank in the MS where the villein's name should be.

precepit predictis Thome et Johanni quod venirent secum ad capiendum predictum Robertum sicut predictus senescallus eis preceperat qui quidem Thomas et Johannes simul cum predicto Ricardo ad capiendum predictum Robertum iverunt usque ad pontem de Staunford'. Set predicti Thomas et Johannes, nolentes metas predicti comitis domini sui excedere ibidem morabantur. Et predictus Ricardus pontem illum cum aliis ignotis usque infra libertatem abbatis de Burgo Sancti Petri de Staunford' intravit et predictum Robertum ibidem inventum vi et armis cepit et eum ultra pontem predictum versus prisonam duxit. Et cum ad predictos Thomam et Johannem venisset ipsi Thomas et Johannes qui priori precepto ipsius Ricardi resistere non audebant tancquam ballivi ville predicte insimul usque ad portam castri predicti ipsum Robertum conduxerunt. Et dicunt quod quidam Bartholomeus de Wodenewton' janitor porte eiusdem castri noluit permittere predictos Thomam et Johannem castrum predictum ingredi per quod ipsi statim exinde recedentes ipsum Robertum cum predictis Ricardo et Bartholomeo dimiserunt nec aliquid aliud malum ei fecerunt. Et dicunt quod predictus Ricardus simul cum predictis Bartholomeo et Waltero Bere qui modo non veniunt ad quamdam prisonam infra dictum castrum existentem [eum] [125] duxerunt et eum per quamdam gaolam usque in profundiorem locum illius gaole descendere per quamdam scalam coegerunt. Et cum per dictam scalam descendere incepisset, prefati Ricardus et alii qui modo non veniunt dictam scalam revolventes ipsum Robertum de Tynewell' usque in profundum projecerunt et postea per tres dies et noctes non permiserunt aliquem victum sibi portari nec exhiberi ita quod fere fame periit. Et dicunt quod cum propincqui amici dicti Roberti accessissent ad dictum castrum secum loquituri et victualia sibi exhibituri responsum fuit per janitorem et per predictum Ricardum quod predictus Robertus missus fuit ad castrum de Reygate ibidem incarcerandus ut per huiusmodi cautelam ipsum Robertum in predicto carcere voluerit periisse, quousque amici ipsius Roberti et alii horribilem tumultum et clamorem ipsius Roberti cognoscentes propter magnam famem quam patiebatur audiverunt, et quod[126] ipsum in prisona illa fere per unum mensem detinuerunt quousque deliberatus fuit per preceptum domini regis. Et quia compertum est per juratam istam quod predictus Ricardus[127] cepit predictum Robertum sine waranto et sine aliqua causa rationabili incarceravit et in carcere detinuit nec permisit aliquem victum sibi afferri nec exhiberi sicut predictum est. Consideratum est quod predictus Robertus de Tynewell' recuperet dampna sua que taxantur per juratores ad quadraginta libras et predictus Ricardus committatur gaole. Et quia predicti Johannes et Thomas[128] fuerunt in auxilium predicto Ricardo ad conducendum ipsum Robertum de ponte predicto usque ad portam castri de Staunford', ideo ipsi Thomas et Johannes committantur gaole. Postea predictus Thomas fecit finem per j marcam per plegium Willelmi de Spanneby et Johannis de Walmesford. Et Johannes de Walmesford' fecit finem per j marcam per plegium Willelmi de Spanneby et Thome de Morton'. Et iidem plegii manuceperunt eos quod de cetero bene se gerent etc. Et Ricardus de Baldeswelle fecit finem per quadraginta solidos per plegium Thome le Mercer de Staunfford' et Thome de Morton'. Et iidem plegii etc.[129]

[*Marginated*] Gaole j m., j m. [*deleted*] ; xl s. Dampna xl li. unde clericis x m. et marescallo xl s.

Wappentagium de Nesse

[29] Preceptum fuit vicecomiti quod attachiaret Willelmum Wyldegos de Est Deping' communem verberatorem quod esset hic ad respondendum tam domino regi quam Willelmo filio Walteri et pluribus aliis de diversis[130] transgressionibus contra pacem domini regis factis. Et quod attachiaret Henricum le Bercher de Manthorp' ad respondendum domino regi quare fecit rescussum ballivis domini regis pro debitis regis levandis contra pacem etc. Et vicecomes testatur quod non sunt inventi nec aliquid habent per quod possunt attachiari. Ideo preceptum fuit vicecomiti quod caperet eos si etc. Et salvo custodiret etc. ita quod haberet hic corpora eorum etc. Et vicecomes itero testetatur[131] quod non sunt inventi nec aliquid habent etc. Ideo exigantur et utlagentur si non comparuerint etc. Et si comparuerint tunc eos capiat et salvo etc. quousque etc.

[*Marginated*] Exigatur et utlagetur, exigatur et utlagetur.

125 Omitted.

126 Interlined.

127 *quod predictus Ricardus* interlined.

128 *et Thomas* interlined.

129 An attempt seems to have been made to erase the last two sentences from *Et Ricardus* . . . onward.

130 *de diversis* interlined.

131 Recte *testatur.*

Staunfford'

[30] Compertum est per inquisitionem in quam Thomas Smerman de Staunfford' se posuit quod non est communis malefactor nisi de modicis alapis. Ideo Henricus de Empingham et Willelmus de Apethorp' manuceperunt eum quod bene et honeste de cetero se geret etc.

Membrane 10d

Ellou

[31] Presentatum fuit quod Willelmus de Spalding' tempore quo fuit ballivus domini regis in Hoyland' cepit de Jordano le Fevre quendam latronem captum per villatam de Sutton' et corpus predicti Jordani deliberatum fuit predicto Willelmo ad salvo et secure[132] ducendum ad prisonam domini regis Linc' etc. Et predictus Willelmus cepit de predicto Jordano quatuor marcas ut ipsum dimitteret per manucaptionem etc. Ideo committitur gaole. Postea fecit finem pro omnimodis transgressionibus contra pacem domini regis factis in comitatu Linc' exceptis articulis coronam tangentibus si que sint per viginti solidos per plegium Rogeri de Morwode de comitatu Notingh' et Roberti Wyly de Wakefeld de comitatu Ebor'.
[*Marginated*] Gaole, xx s. [*deleted*].

Membrane 11

Villata de Staunford' venit per xij

[32] Compertum est[133] per inquisitionem in quam Ricardus de Hameldon' de Staunford', Ricardus Sampson[134] et Elena Bere de eadem se posuerunt quod predictus Ricardus verberavit Willelmum Frankhom de Weston' de comitatu Roteland in pleno foro de Staunford' ita quod brachia et tibias suas et totum corpus enormiter quassaverunt ita quod de vita desperabatur pro eo quod idem Willelmus fuit in servicio domini regis coram Roberto de Harwden tenente locum H. le Despenser justiciario domini regis ad inquirendum de malefactoribus venationis domini regis. Et hoc per procuramentum et assensum Elene Bere de eadem. Ad dampnum ipsius Willelmi viginti marcarum contra pacem etc. Et ideo consideratum [est][135] quod predictus Robertus[136] recuperet dampna sua predicta. Et predictus Ricardus et Elena et Ricardus[137] comittatur gaole.
[*Marginated*] Gayole.

Membrane 11d

Ellowe

[33] Compertum est per inquisitionem in quam Fulco Julian se posuit quod ipse ex impetu et non ex malicia preconcepta[138] percussit Johannem Juett'[139] cum quodam baculo contra pacem etc. Et quod ipse fecit resistenciam cuidam Johanni de Wyrham qui venit ex parte vicecomitis cum waranto ad levandum de ipso Fulcone decem libras adjudicatas in curia domini regis Roberto Hakebek' pro eo quod idem Johannes de Wirkham non fuit ballivus domini regis juratus in[140] patria cognitus. Ideo predictus Fulco comittatur gayole. Postea finem fecit infra.
[*Marginated*] Gayole [*deleted*].

[34] Compertum est per inquisitionem in quam Johannes de Berford se posuit quod ipse procuravit Johannem de Driffeld' et dedit ei duos solidos ut verberaret Fulconem Julian ad quam procurationem idem Johannes de Driffeld' ipsum Fulconem verberavit, vulneravit et male tractavit. Ideo predictus Johannes de Berford' comittatur gayole. Postea finem fecit per viginti solidos per plegium Willelmi de Bereford' et Willelmi de Havercroft de Holebeche.
[*Marginated*] Gayole, xx s. [*deleted*].

[35] Item compertum est quod Alexander Herre procuravit quamdam Adam de Hachebek' et alios ignotos ad verberandum Fulconem filium Thome de Quappelade qui ipsum per procurationem verberaverunt ad dampnum ipsius Fulconis viginti solidorum. Ideo predictus Fulco recuperet dampna sua predicta. Et predicti[141] Alexander comittatur gayole. Postea fecit finem per xx s. per plegium Thome de Burnham et Willelmi de Welleby. Et iidem manuceperunt quod de cetero bene se geret etc.
[*Marginated*] xx s. [*deleted*].

[36] Item compertum est per inquisitionem in quam Simon Digel se posuit quod ipse conduxit homines ignotos ad verberandum Robertum le Salter qui verbe-

[132] *et secure* interlined. [133] Interlined.

[134] *Ricardus Sampson* interlined.

[135] Omitted.

[136] Recte *Willelmus.*

[137] *et Elena et Ricardus* interlined but verb remains unchanged.

[138] *et non . . . preconcepta* interlined.

[139] Or *Ivett.* [140] Interlined. [141] Recte *predictus.*

ratus fuit. Et dedit eis ad jentaculandum contra pacem etc. Ideo comittatur gayole. Postea fecit finem per dimidiam marcam per plegium Willelmi de Bakwell' et Everardi de Flete. Et ipsi manuceperunt eum quod bene etc. secundum provisionem etc.
[*Marginated*] Gayole, dim. m. [*deleted*].

[37] Item compertum est per inquisitionem in quam Johannes Athelard' et Alexander de Wappelade ad sectam regis, et Simon Randolf tam ad sectam Fulconis Juliain quam ad sectam regis, se posuerunt quod ipsi verberaverunt et vulneraverunt et male tractaverunt predictum Fulconem Julian contra pacem etc. Et unde predictus Fulco se queritur quod predictus Simon ad Pascham Florum anno regni regis nunc xxxj ipsum verberavit et male tractavit ad dampnum ipsius Fulconis viginti solidorum et contra pacem etc. Ideo consideratum [est][142] quod predictus Fulco recuperet dampna sua predicta. Et predicti Johannes, Alexander et Simon comittatur[143] gayole. Postea Johannes Athelard' fecit finem pro se per xl d. Alexander filius Johannis fecit finem per dimidiam marcam per plegium Hugonis de Quappelade et Fulconis Julian et Alexandri Herre. Et Simon Randolf fecit finem pro se per unam marcam per plegium Willelmi de Berford' et Johannis de Berford'. Et iidem pleggii manuceperunt eos quod bene etc. secundum provisionem etc.
[*Marginated*] Gayole, xl d., dim. m., j m. [*deleted*].

Membrane 12

Villata de Graham venit per xij

[38] Presentatum fuit alias coram Edmundo de Eyncurt et sociis suis etc. per juratores de Wymersbrigge et Graham quod Thomas de Sancto Laudo et Thomas de Skyrlound simul cum Waltero de Shyryngton' et Nigello de Horssington' et aliis ignotis venerunt vi et armis tam equos et pedites ad manerium Willelmi de Horton' de Woleby in Wywolle et ipsum Willelmum ibidem verberaverunt, vulneraverunt et male tractaverunt per procurationem et abettum Willelmi de Woleby. Et predicti Thomas, Thomas et Willelmus attachiati veniunt. Set Willelmus de Horton' non sequitur. Ideo ad sectam regis predicti Thomas, [Thomas] et Willelmus quesiti qualiter se velint inde acquietare, predicti Thomas et Thomas dicunt quod ipsi nuncquam transgressiones fecerunt. Et Willelmus dicit quod si aliqua transgressio per predictos Thomam et Thomam facta fuisset, ipse nuncquam ad hoc faciendum procuravit nec aliquem assensum eis inde prebuit. Et de hoc ponunt se super patriam. Juratores dicunt super sacramentum suum quod quidam ignotus de familia dicti Thome de Sancto Laudo quodam die intraverunt[144] manerium predicti Willelmi de Horton' in Wywelle et predictum Willelmum in aula sua invenerunt et Willelmus eos percipiens et eorum maliciam timens fugit in cameram suam. Et ipsi ignoti in cameram suam insequebantur ipsum capientes et extra portas manerii sui trahentes ipsum verberaverunt et male tractaverunt. Et postea predicti Thomas et Thomas equos venerunt et ipsum sic verberatum invenientes extransverso ipsum equitaverunt et pedibus suis equinis eum conculcaverunt contra pacem etc. Et dicunt quod predictus Willelmus de Welleby ipsos Thomam et Thomam et alios ignotos procuravit et ad hoc faciendum eis assensum prebuit. Ideo predicti Thomas, Thomas et Willelmus committantur gayole. Postea dictus Thomas de Sancto Laudo fecit finem pro se et pro Thoma de Sherlound'[145] per decem libras per plegium Thome de Burnham et Ade de Welles. Et iidem plegii manuceperunt eum quod decetero bene se geret etc. secundum formam etc. Et Willelmus de Welleby fecit finem per xx s. per plegium Rogeri de Goldestan et Thome de Swyneford'. Et de pace de cetero.
[*Marginated*] Gaiole, x li., xx s. [*deleted*].

Lovedon'

[39] Compertum est per inquisitionem in quam Johannes Crane de Cathorp', Willelmus Sharp' de eadem et Hugo Morsyn de eadem se posuerunt quod predicti Johannes, Willelmus et Hugo simul cum aliis ignotis venerunt ad domum Willelmi de Burlee apud Anecastre et ibidem insultum fecerunt et predictum Willelmum in pede cum quadam sagitta sagittaverunt. Et ignem ter ad hostium dicti Willelmi posuerunt ad domum predictam comburendam. Et postea insultum domui illi viriliter fecerunt sagittando ad hostium et fenestras, et agnos in falda dicti Willelmi inparcatos vi et armis ceperunt et abduxerunt contra pacem domini regis. Ideo predicti Johannes Crane, Willelmus et Hugo committantur gayole. Et postea predicti Johannes, Willelmus et Hugo fecerunt finem per j marcam per plegium Rogeri Mot' de Stubton' et Rogeri Almot de eadem.
[*Marginated*] Gaiole, j marca [*deleted*].

142 Omitted.

143 Recte *comittantur.*

144 Recte *intravit.*

145 *et pro . . . Sherlound'* interlined.

Membrane 12d

Wappentachium de Calsewath' venit per xij juratores

[40] Compertum est per inquisitionem in quam Johannes de Mikelbergh de Moubray se posuit quod predictus Johannes est communis perturbator pacis et vacabundus de nocte contra pacem domini regis etc. Ideo predictus Johannes committitur gaole etc. Et postea predictus Johannes fecit finem per dimidiam marcam per plegium Walteri de Gymesland de Wynthorp' et Simonis filii Rose de Mumby. Et iidem plegii manuceperunt eum quod de cetero bene se geret etc.
[*Marginated*] Gaole, finis dim. m. [*deleted*].

[41] Compertum est per inquisitionem in quam Patricius persona ecclesie de Southerston' se posuit quod ipse Johanni Belle de Southerston' insultum fecit et cum pugno suo ipsum percussit ex inpetu animi contra pacem etc. ad dampnum ipsius Johannis ij s. Ideo consideratum est quod predictus Johannes recuperet dampna sua predicta. Et predictus Patricius committatur gayole. Postea fecit finem per quinque solidos per plegium Roberti le Charpentier de Gayton' et Willelmi Oby de Hoton'. Et similiter quod bene se geret etc.
[*Marginated*] Gaiole, v s. [*deleted*].

Membrane 15

Villata de Sancto Botulfo

[42] Item presentatum fuit alias quod dominus Ranulphus de Frixenay simul cum aliis in festo Sancti Thome apostoli anno regni regis nunc xxix° apud Sanctum Botulfum odio antiquo verberavit et maletractavit Willelmum de Wormelay servientem domini regis ad providencias domini regis faciendas. Et predictus Ranulphus attachiatus venit et similiter predictus Willelmus qui nunc queritur de predicta transgressione. Et dicit quod deterioratus est et dampnum habet ad valenciam sexaginta librarum etc. Et predictus Ranulphus dicit quod in nullo est culpabilis et de hoc ponit se super patriam. Juratores dicunt super sacramentum suum quod predictus Willelmus de Wormelay tanquam minister domini regis ad blada in partibus comitatus Linc' capienda et per vicecomitem assignatus venit quadam die apud Sanctum Botulfum et in domo cuiusdam Johannis de Thumby blada venditioni exposita invenit. Qui quidem Willelmus illis in domo tunc existentibus dixit quod denarios domini regis habuit ad sufficienciam et pro predictis bladis solvendos. Predictus Johannes hoc audiens statim domus ostium ubi predicta blada posita fuerunt clausit sub serura. Et dicunt quod predictus Willelmus tunc auctoritate sibi commissa predicta blada ad opus domini regis attachiavit et ostium domus sigillo suo signavit. Et dicunt quod idem[146] Johannes statim predicto Ranulpho de Frik' accessit et omnia premissa sibi intimavit, qui quidem Ranulphus hoc audiens predictum Willelmum quesivit et eidem Willelmo tandem obviavit et verbis contumeliosis rationavit et cum pugno suo predictum Willelmum in capite percussit et ad terram[147] prostravit. Et dicunt quod Nicholaus Belle et Rogerus Gernoun valetti eiusdem Ranulphi faciem predicti Willelmi cum capicio suo velaverunt et ipsum verberaverunt et maletractaverunt et in quodam lacu ipsum[148] postea projecerunt et warantum suum in eodem loco conculcaverunt. Et postea sigillum predicti Willelmi predicto ostio appositum predictus Ranulphus in contemptum domini regis violenter eradicavit.[149] Ideo consideratum est quod predictus Willelmus recuperet dampna sua que taxantur per juratores ad xl s. Et predictus Ranulphus committatur gaole.
Dampna xl s. unde clericis j marca et marescallo dimidia marca quos xl s.[150] postea solvit in curia hic.

[43] Item presentatum fuit alias etc. quod Ranulfus de Friskenay miles simul cum Alano de Seldik' et Nicholao Belle et aliis ignotis injuste et contra pacem etc. domum Johannis de le Fendik' intravit et uxorem eiusdem Johannis in eadem domo verberavit et cum pedibus suis conculcavit et male tractavit et postea per minas suas violenter extorsit et[151] predicto Johanne xv solidos. Et predictus Ranulphus attachiatus venit. Et predictus Johannes non sequitur. Ideo pro pace regis observanda inquiratur rei veritas. Juratores dicunt super sacramentum suum quod homines predicti Ranulphi quadam die cum caretta sua de meremio cariata per mediam villam de Skyrebek' transerunt et linosium Johannis de Fendik' positum ad siccandum regiam viam dimittendo cum caretta[152] conculcaverunt. Et idem Johannes emendas de predictis hominibus ratione predicte transgressionis

146 Interlined. 147 *ad terram* interlined.

148 Interlined.

149 Interlined. A cross is drawn against this line.

150 *xl s.* interlined.

151 Recte *de*.

152 *regiam . . . caretta* interlined.

petiit. Et dicunt quod homines predicti Ranulphi hoc statim eidem Ranulpho scire fecerunt et dicti homines[153] predictum Johannem de regia strata usque in domum suam consecuti fuerunt. Et in eadem domo uxorem predicti Johannis verberaverunt et maletractaverunt et eidem Johanni minabantur. Set dicunt quod predictus Ranulphus non interfuit nec aliquod malum contra pacem fecit,[154] set dicunt quod timore illius verberationis et alterius transgressionis que inposterum predicto Johanni evenire potuerunt per predictum Ranulphum et homines suos[155] predictus Johannes per quemdam Radulfum Cokewald intereuntem et exorantem pro pace predicti Ranulphi habenda finem fecit cum predicto Ranulpho per[156] xv s. quos eidem Ranulpho statim solvit. Et super hoc predictus Ranulphus dixit quod predicta transgressio facta fuit iam per sex annos elapsos de qua quidem transgressione et aliis transgressionibus per ipsum prius factis dominus rex sectam pacis sue que ad ipsum pertinet perdonavit per quandam cartam quam profert que testatur etc. quod dominus rex perdonavit eidem Ranulpho de Friskeneye pro bono servicio suo quod sibi in partibus Scotie inpendebat sectam pacis sue que ad ipsum pertinet de[156] homicidiis, robboriis, incendiis, latrociniis, recettamentis et omnibus aliis transgressionibus in regno suo contra pacem suam factis unde idem Ranulphus rettatus est. Data eiusdem carte apud Oggerstan xiij die januarii anno regni regis sui xxvij°. Unde petit quod predicta carta pro predictis transgressionibus sibi allocetur. Et quia predictus Ranulphus predictam cartam antequam se posuit in inquisitionem predictam non allegavit nec illam ante veredictum predictum in curia porrexit de perdonatione predicta, dies datus est ei de audiendo judicio suo inde in proximo[156] parleamento etc.
[*Marginated*] Gaole.

[44] Presentatum fuit alias etc. quod Ranulphus de Friskeney consuetus est minari juratoribus in assisis et inquisitionibus que ad curiam domini regis seu alibi ausi[156] sunt venire. Et similiter minatus fuit juratoribus illius inquisitionis qui se coram Edmundo de Eyncurt et sociis suis indictarunt quod alicubi non sunt ausi venire. Et predictus Ranulphus attachiatus venit et nullus sequitur. Ideo inquiratur rei veritas. Juratores [dicunt] [157] super sacramentum suum quod predictus Ranulphus de Friskenay est communis sustentator et manutentor placitorum et querelarum. Et sepissime juratoribus in assisis et inquisitionibus dicentibus contra partem suam quam fovet per sex annos et amplius iam elapsos minabatur ita quod ad loca ubi fuerunt summoniti timore verberationis et amissionis bonorum suorum accedere seu veritatem dicere non fuerunt ausi. Et similiter dicunt quod idem Ranulphus post quam indictatus fuit coram predicto Edmundo et sociis suis, juratoribus illius indictamenti sepissime eis[158] de vita et membris minatus fuit ipsos rusticos et falsos vocando. Ideo predictus Ranulphus comittatur gayole.
[*Marginated*] Gayole.

[45] Item presentatum fuit alias etc. quod Ranulphus de Friskeney miles tempore quo fuit justiciarius domini regis apud Sanctum Botulphum ad pacem domini regis observandam quod eos qui coram ipso indictati fuerunt semper hucusque ad robas suas sustinuit et manutenuit videlicet Nicholaum Belle et Joceum Aurifabrum et plures alios. Et predictus Ranulphus attachiatus venit. Et dicit quod non est culpabilis. Et de hoc ponit se super patriam. Juratores dicunt super sacramentum suum quod predictus Ranulphus custos pacis per breve domini regis quodam die apud Sanctum Botulphum de malefactoribus et pacis regis perturbatoribus inquirere fecit ubi compertum fuit per inquisitionem ibi captam quod quidam Nicholaus Belle et Joceus le Orfevere fuerunt communes malefactores in feriis et mercatis. Et dicunt quod predictus Ranulphus semper postea[158] hucusque et ante predictos Nicholaum[158] et Joceum ad robas suas tamquam familiares sustinuit. Et similiter dicunt quod predicti Nicholaus et Joceus post predictam inquisitionem per predictum Ranulphum captam quamplures sepissime in feriis et mercatis hucusque verberaverunt et male tractaverunt contra pacem etc. predicto Ranulpho eos fovente et manutenente. Ideo predictus Ranulphus comittatur gayole.
[*Marginated*] Gayole.

Membrane 18

Nortr' et Sutr' de conspiratoribus

Wappentagium de Bradele

[46] Compertum est per inquisitionem in quam Nicholaus Prophet' de Gerlethorp' se posuit quod ipse cepit de quodam Roberto Turny de Gerlethorp'

[153] *et dicti homines* interlined.

[154] *et eidem Johanni . . . contra pacem fecit* interlined; *malum* is interlined above this interlineation.

[155] *per predictum . . . homines suos* interlined.

[156] Interlined.

[157] Omitted.

[158] Interlined.

qui dudum implacitavit Willelmum Torneye avunculum suum de quadam terra in Gerlethorp' que fuit jus ipsius Roberti viginti quarteria cuiuslibet generis bladi quolibet anno tota vita ipsius Nicholai ad cambipartem pro medietate predicte terre quam habuisse debuit pro predicto placito movendo et sustentando et hoc fecit iam sex annis elapsis etc.

[47] Et compertum est per eandem inquisitionem in quam Johannes le Aumoner de Stowe, Walterus de Freston' et Johannes Costantyn se posuerunt quod predictus Johannes le Aumoner et alii sunt procuratores, abbettatores et conspiratores ad diversas assisas et[158] inquisitiones maliciose procurendas et sustinendas. Ideo committantur gaole. Et similiter quod Ricardus de Lyndewode abbettavit Robertum de Burton' qui neptem dicti Ricardi duxit in uxorem ad placitandum Simonem de Nevill' maliciose etc. Et Johannes de Ryseby attachiatus fuit ad respondendum domino regi de placito quare falso et[159] maliciose procuravit Cristianam Seward' appellare Thomam le Bocheler et Thomam filium Willelmi de morte Willelmi viri sui etc. Et predictus Johannes venit et defendit vim etc. Et dicit quod placitum inter ipsum et[160] Thomam le Bocher et Thomam filium Willelmi pendet coram rege de eodem conspiratione et petit judicium si de hoc debet respondere. Postea Johannes le Aumener fecit finem per unam marcam per plegium Nicholai de Grouce et Reginaldi de Kedelsthorp'. Et Johannes Costantyn fecit finem per unam marcam per plegium Johannis de Nevill' de Snarford' et Gilberti filii Roberti de eadem.
[*Marginated*] Gaole,[161] j marca, j marca.

[48] Compertum est per inquisitionem in quam Willelmus le Clerk' de Kyme se posuit quod ipse ratione officii sui et ballivie sue injuste arrestavit et attachiavit navem Ricardi le Couper in communi aqua que se extendit versus Kyme et ibi eam detinuit quousque finem fecit cum eo per quadraginta solidos. Ideo comittitur gaole. Postea predictus Willelmus fecit finem per dimidiam marcam per plegium Willelmi de Welleby et Johannis de Pateshulle.
[*Marginated*] Gaole, finis dimidia marca [*deleted*].

[49] Compertum est per inquisitionem in quam Robertus filius Willelmi de Keleseye se posuit quod predictus Robertus[162] fecit seipsum ballivum domini regis sine waranto et attachiavit quendam navem de Mysen' et eam detinuit quousque magister navis finem fecit cum eo pro quatuordecim denariis.

[50] Willelmus Randolf' de Rouceby et Walterus Clericus de Thorp' et frater Willelmus de Grafton' preceptor de Bruera attachiati fuerunt ad respondendum domino regi de placito conspirationis. Et unde Elyas de Preston' qui sequitur pro domino rege dicit quod cum quidam Willelmus Thomay occisus fuit in Cranewelle, predicti Willelmus Randolf' et Walterus falso coram coronatoribus[163] procuraverunt indictare quendam ignotum Ricardum le Messager de Hibernia nomine[164] qui nuncquam fuit in rerum natura ut creditur. Et si quis talis fuerat in nullo fuit culpabilis de morte predicta. Et quendam Egideum de Templo qui predictum Willelmum[165] Thomay occidit ut creditur per procurationem predicti fratris Willelmi preceptoris predictus Willelmus Randolf' qui erat unus de duodecim et de robis ipsius preceptoris simul cum predicto Waltero de morte predicta totaliter aquietaverunt coram justiciariis hic. Et quendam Robertum le Graunt qui in nullo fuit culpabilis de morta[166] predicta maliciose ipsum coram justiciariis hic indictaverunt.

Et Willelmus, Walterus et frater Willelmus preceptor veniunt et Walterus dicit quod tempore inquisitionis coram coronatoribus capte de morte predicti Willelmi Thomay erat Lond' diu ante et diu post. Et similiter quando capta fuit inquisitio coram justiciariis hic tam de aquietatione predicti Egidii quam de indictamento Roberti le Graunt ipse tunc temporis erat apud Sanctum Botulphum, unde dicit quod est incius utriusque inquisitionis predicte[167] tam coram coronatoribus quam coram justiciariis hic capte. Et quod[167] in nullo eos falso procuravit ponit se super patriam. Et Willelmus Randolf' quod tempore captionis predicte inquisitionis coram justiciariis hic ipse calumpniavit se ipsum et ostendit curie quod fuit de robis et de consilio Templariorum et quod ipse invitus positus fuit in inquisitione coram justiciariis hic capta, unde idem Willelmus Randolf' dicit quod nuncquam procuravit predictas inquisitiones falso nec maliciose. Et [de] hoc ponit se super patriam. Et predictus frater Willelmus preceptor dicit quod tempore felonie facte et predicte inquisitionis coram coronatoribus capte stetit in partibus Ciprie ita quod fuit ignorans quis fuit inde[167] culpabilis vel quietus

[159] *falso et* interlined. [160] Interlined.

[161] Deleted and reinstated. [162] Interlined.

[163] *coram coronatoribus* interlined.

[164] Interlined above *de Hibernia.*

[165] Interlined.

[166] Recte *morte.* [167] Interlined.

et dicit quod ipse nuncquam falso vel maliciose aliquam inquisitionem ad culpabilem de morte predicta aquietandum vel innocentem inde condempnandum procuravit. Et [de] [168] hoc ponit se super patriam.

Juratores dicunt super sacramentum suum quod predicti Willelmus Randolf'[169] et Walterus falso et maliciose coram coronatoribus in prima inquisione[170] inde facta indictare procuraverunt predictum[171] Ricardum le Messager de morte predicta[172] qui in nullo inde fuit culpabilis. Et postea Egidium de Templo qui predictum Willelmum Thomay occidit ut intelligunt inde coram justiciariis hic falso acquietare procuraverunt. Et quendam Robertum le Graunt qui in nullo de morte predicta fuit culpabilis de novo coram justiciariis hic indictare procuraverunt. Et dicunt quod predictus frater Willelmus preceptor nuncquam aliquos indictare coram coronatoribus predictis vel justiciariis hic de morte predicta falso vel maliciose indictare, condempnare seu acquietare procuravit. Ideo consideratum est quod predictus frater Willelmus de Grafton' preceptor eat inde quietus. Et predicti Willelmus Randolf' et Walterus committantur gaole. Postea predictus Radulfus[173] Randolf fecit finem per viginti libras per plegium Willelmi Gregori et Roberti de Gonewardby. Et Walterus fecit finem per iiij li. per plegium Roberti de la Grene de Gunwardby et Gilberti de Crosholm.
[*Marginated*] Gaole,[174] xx li., iij li.

[51] Compertum est per inquisitionem in quam Willelmus Gregor' se posuit quod ipse maliciose indictare fecit Nicholaum de Anecastr' ad turnum vicecomitis pro quo indictamento idem Nicholaus fecit finem cum predicto Willelmo per unam marcam. Et pro qua marca feoffavit predictum Willelmum Gregor' de dimidia[175] acra terre cum pertinenciis in Querington'. Ideo committitur gaole. Et quod Robertus Turry cepit per conspiracionem de Willelmo filio Alani quatuor solidos in quodam placito versus personam de Ketelsthorp'. Et postea cepit de eundem[176] persona in eodem placito duos solidos. Ita quod est ambidexter. Ideo committitur gaole. Et postea predictus Willelmus Gregor' fecit finem per[177] per plegium Willelmi Thebaud de Lafford', Galfridi de Swarreby, Simonis de Wymbilthorp' et Willelmi Randolf' de Rouceby etc.
[*Marginated*] Gaole.

Membrane 18d

Kesteven'

[52] Robertus Nicholas de Hermesthorp' et Alanus Grigori de Hermesthorp', Willelmus de Ingelton', Hugo de Sowe de Lunderthorp', Willelmus de Notyngham', Galfridus de Burton', Thomas de Poynton' in[178] Canewyk', Galfridus Clack' de Hadyngton' attachiati fuerunt ad respondendum domino regi de placito conspiracionis unde Elyas de Preston' qui sequitur pro domino rege dicit quod predicti Robertus et Alanus confederati sunt adinvicem sacramento ad procurandum, abettandum et sustinendum falsa placita et querelas per ipsos moveri, et quosdam falso et maliciose indictari in comitatu isto et maxime predicti Robertus et Alanus maliciose et falso procuraverunt quemdam probatorem appellare quemdam Willelmum Letherwane de Hermesthorp' de diversis latrociniis et unde postea per patriam fuit inde acquietatus.

Et quod[179] predictus Willelmus de Ingelton' est procurator et abettator falsorum placitorum et querelarum et maxime pro quodam David de Fletwyk' versus quemdam Ricardum de Appelgarth' de placito detentionis averiorum cuius partem maliciose movebat et fovebat et aliorum etc. Et quod predictus Hugo de Sowe falso et maliciose procuravit indictare Thomam Sytel de morte cuiusdam Radulfi de Crophil coram coronatoribus etc. qui in nullo fuit inde culpabilis. Et Nicholaum filium eiusdem Hugonis qui inde fuit culpabilis inde acquietare. Et quod predictus Willelmus de Notingham per conspiracionem cepit de decano et capitulo Linc' ad manutenendum placitum eorum versus abbatem Beate Marie[180] quadraginta solidos. Et postea de eodem abbate alios quadraginta solidos ad ipsos juvandum in eodem placito contra predictos etc. velud ambidexter. Et quod predictus Thomas de Poynton' et Galfridus Clack'[181] ceperunt denarios de preceptore de Bruera ad manutenendum placitum suum versus Johannem filium Hugonis de Brauncewell'. Et postea sicut ambidextri partem

[168] Omitted. [169] Interlined.

[170] Recte *inquisitione.* [171] Interlined.

[172] *de morte predicta* interlined.

[173] Recte *Willelmus.* [174] Deleted and reinstated.

[175] Interlined above *una,* underscored.

[176] Recte *eodem.*

[177] There is a blank where the sum should be.

[178] ?Recte *de.* [179] Interlined.

[180] *Beate Marie* interlined.

[181] *et Galfridus Clack'* interlined.

eiusdem Johannis contra eundem preceptorem in eodem placito pro suo dando fovebant etc. Et quod predictus Galfridus de Burton' est conspirator et maxime in hoc quod stetit cum Willelmo de Shaddeworthe contra Johannem de Stircheslee. Et postea partem dicti Johannis contra predictum[182] Willelmum dominum suum[182] fovebat. Et hoc paratus est verificare pro domino rege.

Et predicti Robertus et alii veniunt. Et Thomas de Poynton' et Galfridus Clack' non possunt dedicere conspiracionem nec transgressionem predictam. Ideo ipsi committantur gaole. Et predicti Robertus et alii defendunt omnem conspiracionem, falsam procurationem et abettum et maliciosam sustentationem predictam. Et quod in nullo inde sunt culpabiles ponunt se super patriam. Juratores dicunt super sacramentum suum quod predictus Robertus et omnes alii preter Galfridum de Burton' sunt culpabiles de conspiracionibus et transgressionibus ipsis in forma predicta inpositis. Ideo predictus Galfridus ad conspiracionem et transgressionem sibi inpositam eat inde quietus. Et predictus Robertus et omnes alii committantur gaole. Postea Alanus Gregori fecit finem per quinquaginta solidos per plegium Roberti Baroun de Wylesthorp' et Thome de Morton' de Staunford'. Et Willelmus de Ingelton' fecit finem per quadraginta solidos per plegium Roberti de Broucton' de Linc' et Roberti de Wywell' de Thurleby. Et Hugo de Stouwe fecit finem per quatuor marcas per plegium Willelmi de Welleby et Willelmi de Notyngh'. Et Willelmus de Notingh' fecit finem per triginta solidos per plegium Willelmi de Welleby.

[*Marginated*] Gaole, gaole, l s., xl s., iiij marce, xxx s.

Membrane 22

Ad huc de Wappentagio de Aswordehirne

[53] Brianus de Herdeby, Nigellus de Horsyngton', Robertus Denys de Carleton',[183] Henricus Yungman de Basingham, Adam de Ringesthorp', Thomas filius Hugonis de Veteri Lafford', Willelmus filius Willelmi de Fletewyk', Godefridus de Carleton', Reginaldus frater eius, Ricardus Tupplayn, Johannes de Aswordebi prepositus, Simon filius Radulfi Bariona prepositus, Johannes le Warner, Thomas le Westerne, Thomas filius Stephani, Walterus Scot', Simon filius eius,[184] Willelmus Ryvell', Robertus de Heyeby, Simon Fole, Simon de Haynton', Johannes Broun, Hugo Crok', Willelmus Fole, Elyas de Merston', Johannes filius Thome de Kirkeby, Thomas de Chadele et Robertus de Asgerby, Willelmus Benette [et][185] Walterus frater eius attachiati fuerunt ad respondendum tam domino regi quam Willelmo filio Johannis Gregor' de placito quare ipsi simul cum Rogero filio Radulfi de Veteri Lafford', Johanne de Helpiston', Thoma de Wraggeby, Ricardo le Blount', Waltero le White, Simone fratre eius, Willelmo Meynard', Johanne Bozon, Johanne Beneyt' et Simone filio Rogeri prepositi bona et catalla predicti Willelmi apud Querington' inventa ad valenciam trescentarum librarum depredaverunt et asportaverunt contra pacem etc. Et unde predictus Willelmus qui tam sequitur pro domino rege quam pro seipso dicit quod predicti Brianus et omnes alii qui nunc veniunt simul cum Rogero filio Radulfi et omnibus aliis qui modo non veniunt venerunt vi et armis ad predictum manerium de Querington' in vigilia Natalis Domini anno regni regis nunc xxxvij°. Et manerium illud intraverunt et cistam ipsius Willelmi in camera sua existentem fregerunt et quadraginta libras in pecunia numerata, monilia aurea et anulos aureos, zonas de serico, ciphos et pecia argentea et alia jocalia et unum aketonem pro se precii viginti marcarum et alia diversa bona ad valenciam trescentarum librarum ceperunt, depredaverunt et asportaverunt contra pacem etc. Et hoc petit verificare pro domino rege etc.

Et Brianus de Herdebi et alii veniunt. Et Brianus, Robertus Denys, Henricus Yungman, Adam de Rynggesthorp', Thomas filius Hugonis, Willelmus filius Willelmi, Godefridus de Carleton', Ricardus Tupplayn et Hugo Crok' dicunt quod clerici sunt. Et salva sibi libertate clericali predicti Brianus, Robertus, Henricus, Thomas filius Hugonis, Willelmus filius Willelmi de Fletewyk' dicunt quod quidem Johannes Gregor' pater ipsius Willelmi alias coram Willelmo Ingge et Ada de Crokedayk' justiciariis domini regis ad assisas in comitatu Linc' capiendas assignatis arramiavit assisam nove disseisine versus eos de predicto manerio per cuius assise recognitionem ipse recuperavit predictum manerium de Querington' etc. Et dampna sua versus eos trescentarum librarum. Et dicunt quod omnia bona de predicto manerio asportata tempore predicte disseisine facte continebantur in predictis dampnis sic recuperatis. Et petunt judicium si pro uno et[186] eodem delicto de quo alias in curia domini regis fuerunt puniti debeant hic iterato respondere et duplicem penam inde portare. Et Godefridus de Carleton' salva sibi libertate

182 Interlined. 183 *f* is written above this name.

184 *Simon filius eius* interlined.

185 Omitted.

186 Interlined.

clericali, et Reginaldus frater Godefridi, Ricardus Tupplayn, Nigellus de Horsyngton', Johannes prepositus de Aswordebi, Johannes le Warner, Thomas le Westerne, Simon filius Radulfi de Bariona dicunt quod ipsi alias in curia regis coram prefatis justiciariis assignatis puniti fuerunt per prisonam et redemptionem pro eodem delicto. Et de[186] hoc ponunt se super patriam. Et petunt judicium si iterato hic nunc debeant respondere. Et Thomas le Harpur, Willelmus Beneyt', Walterus frater eius, Elyas de Merston',[187] Robertus de Heytheby, Simon Fole, Willelmus Fole, Simon de Haynton' et Thomas de Chadeleye dicunt quod ipsi nuncquam predictam transgrescionem predicto Willelmo nuncquam fecerunt nec aliqua[188] bona vel catalla[189] sua depredaverunt nec asportaverunt. Et [de] [190] hoc ponunt se super patriam. Et Thomas filius Stephani de Veteri Lafford', Walterus Scot', Willelmus Rivell', Johannes Broun, Robertus de Asgerbi, Johannes filius Thome de Kirkebi dicunt quod ipsi nuncquam predictis die et anno predictum manerium vi et armis intraverunt nec aliqua bona seu catalla predicti Willhelmi depredaverunt seu asportaverunt nec aliquam transgressionem ei fecerunt. Et [de] [190] hoc ponunt se super patriam. Juratores dicunt super sacramentum suum quo ad predictos Thomam le Harpur, Simonem filium Walteri Scot', Willelmum Beneyt, Walterum fratrem eius, Robertum de Haytheby, Simonem Fole, Willelmum Fole, Simonem de Haynton', Hugonem Crok', Elyam de Merston' et Thomam de Schadele, nuncquam fecerunt predicto Willelmo[191] predictam transgressionem. Ideo eant ipsi inde quieti. Et quo ad predictos Nigellum, Robertum Denys, Thomam filium Stephani, Adam de Ringgesthorp', quod ipsi alias in curia domini regis coram prefatis justiciariis pro eadem transgressione nomine disseisine facte fuerunt inde puniti juxta quod hoc[192] inde deliquerunt. Ideo ipsi inde ad presens eant quieti. Et quo ad Walterum Scot', Willelmum Ryvell', Johannem filium Thome de Kirkeby, Robertum de Asgerby, Johannem Broun, Godefridum de Carleton', Reginaldum fratrem eius, Ricardum Tupplein, Johannem filium Thome de Aswordebi, Simonem filium Radulfi Barioney prepositum, Johannem le Warner, dicunt quod ipsi venerunt ad predictum manerium vi et armis cum aliis prenominatis ad predictam disseisinam faciendam set nulla bona aut catalla predicti Willelmi Gregor' ceperunt, depredaverunt seu asportaverunt. Ideo ipsi Walterus Scot' et alii pro transgressione contra pacem regis facta committantur gaole. Et quo ad predictos Brianum, Henricum Yungman, Thomam filium Hugonis de Veteri Lafford' et Willelmum filium Willelmi de Fletewyk' qui dicunt quod clerici sunt, venit decanus christianitatis Linc' et petit eos quasi clericos, set ut sciatur quales ei debent liberari inquiratur de eis rei veritas. Juratores dicunt super sacramentum suum quod predicti Brianus, Henricus, Thomas et Willelmus venerunt predictis die et anno vi et armis ad predictum manerium de Querington'. Et cameram predicti Willelmi Gregorii intraverunt. Et cistam suam in eadem nequiter fregerunt et bona et catalla ipsius Willelmi tam in eadem cista quam in predicto manerio inventa ad valenciam triginta librarum depredaverunt et asportaverunt. Ideo predicti Brianus, Henricus, Thomas et Willelmus predicto decano pro talibus etc. ei liberentur custodiendi sub pena inde provisa. Et postea Johannes Broun de Aswardeby, Robertus de Asgerby et Johannes filius Thome de Kirkeby fecerunt finem per triginta solidos per plegium Ricardi de Asgerby et Johannis de Mora de eadem. Et Robertus Denys de Carleton' fecit finem per unam marcam per plegium Thome filii Alicie Oky de Carleton' et Alani filii Rogeri de eadem. Et Walterus Scot' fecit finem per quadraginta denarios per plegium Johannis de Reynevill'.

[187] *Elyas de Merston'* interlined. [188] Interlined.

[189] *vel catalla* interlined. [190] Omitted.

[191] *predicto Willelmo* interlined.

[192] Interlined.

Three courts of the hundred of Penwith, 1333

edited by

G. D. G. HALL

INTRODUCTION*

The tortuous history of the Cornish lands of the earldom, later duchy, of Cornwall needs no rehearsal here. The relevant period has recently been summarised thus: 'John of Eltham, the brother of Edward III, had been created Earl of Cornwall in 1328, but the title remained an empty one until 10 October 1331 when he was finally granted the Cornish lands associated with the Earldom . . . he died at Perth in the autumn of 1336 . . . [and] the estates of the Earldom once more returned to the Crown'.[1] There is, for the present purpose, an important addition to be made to this account. Not until 3 October 1333 did John of Eltham receive, inter alia, those profits of the courts in Cornwall which had, until then, gone to the crown.[2] The change made with effect from that date may in part explain the remarkable coincidence that there exist in the Public Record Office three virtually contemporaneous rolls of legal proceedings covering the period 5 July to 3 October 1333: Lostwithiel borough court – three monthly courts;[3] Cornish stannary courts – three courts for each of the four stannaries;[4] Cornish county and hundred courts – four sessions at monthly intervals of the county courts (all at Lostwithiel), three courts at three-weekly intervals for each of the nine hundreds, and the sheriff's account for these county and hundred courts.[5] The third of these rolls is probably unique in containing county and hundred court proceedings covering the same area and period of time, and it is from this roll that the text of the three courts of the hundred of Penwith has been printed here.

The roll consists of membranes of various length, stitched together at the top. Each hundred begins at the top of the face of a new membrane, its three courts following consecutively: thus the three Penwith courts occupy mm.12, 12d, 13 and 13d and are followed by those for Kirrier hundred which begin at the top of m.14, though only about one-third of m.13d has been used up by Penwith. To judge from the nature of some of the errors contained in the main text of the roll as we now have it (even in cases making their first appearance), it is a copy of some other document or documents. Most of the entries have, written above the main text, special interlineations which indicate what happened at the next court and which would enable an experienced clerk, not necessarily present at the hearing, to write up the entry of a case in one court from the main text and interlineations in the previous court: but this is not always so (there are instances where information not in either the main text or interlineations in one court appears in the main text of the next court), and it could not be so when a case was a new case making its first appearance. Much of the main text for all the nine hundreds seems to be in the same hand, but the hand sometimes changes in the middle of a court. The special interlineations mentioned above seem to be in a different hand from the main text. A point which is probably relevant, and certainly additionally confusing, is that a map plot, based on the dates and places where the hundred courts met, suggests a clockwise judicial circuit of the county,[6] each circuit beginning in Powder hundred and ending in West hundred, and the circuits lasting from 15 to 27 July, 5 to 13 August, and 7 to 22 September; but, to take the extreme case, it is not easy to believe in a judicial circuit of the nine hundreds which took only nine days to complete, and it is contrary to the general belief that the hundred bailiff of each hundred would hold the court of that hundred.[7]

Some very tentative conclusions from this evidence now follow. The sittings of the hundred courts were centrally organised by the sheriff, but held by the hundred bailiff in each hundred; the timetable giving the impression of a circuit was for the convenience of litigants who had business in more than one

* The whole of this contribution was completed before Mr Hall's death.

[1] J. Hatcher, *Rural Economy and Society in the Duchy of Cornwall 1300–1500* (Cambridge, 1970), 5.

[2] *CChR*, IV, 302. [3] SC 2/161/5.

[4] E 101/260/1.

[5] SC 2/161/74: county courts at mm.1–11; hundred courts at mm.12–23d; account at m.24, stitched to the foot of m.23d. There is, unfortunately, no tourn among the hundred courts.

[6] Apart from two exceptions in the case of adjoining hundreds (9 Aug. – Pyder and Trigg; 11 Aug. – Lesnewth and Stratton), all the hundred courts are held on a different day: the sequence of hundreds is the same in all three sessions.

[7] e.g. H. M. Cam, *The Hundred and the Hundred Rolls* (London, 1963), 157, 185. Eight of the nine hundreds were certainly 'royal' in the period 5 July to 3 October 1333: the special problem of Penwith is discussed below, 171–2.

hundred court and proposed to act personally and not by attorney; it may also have allowed for an officer of the sheriff to itinerate the county, distributing to each hundred bailiff the official membrane or membranes containing at least the proceedings of the previous court. When the hundred court sat, the bailiff (or one of his officials) interlineated the official text of the previous court as 'old' cases came on, and made notes elsewhere of new cases making their first appearance.[8] Later, using these materials supplemented by his memory, he wrote out (*not* on the official membranes which we now have and which had been delivered to him) the proceedings of the whole court – this would explain the additional or different matter sometimes found in the main text of a case and not attributable to the main text and special interlineation of that case in the previous court. In this version were marginalia arising from the court and already known to him: these included obvious words like 'Inquisitio', 'Districtio' and 'Attachiamentum'. Also included were fines and their amount: in all such cases [10, 16, 17, 46, 57] the amount of the fine was available when he wrote his version. The version also contained, in appropriate places, a marginal 'c' ('clericis') indicating dues to the crown known as 'damages cleer': these were a part or all of the damages recovered by a successful plaintiff and given to the clerks of the court – hence 'dampna clericorum' or 'damages cleer'.[9] In the case of amercements, however, his version had a marginal 'misericordia' or 'misericordie' without the amount: the affeerors, suitors selected to assess the actual amount of amercements, made up, probably at the end of the court session, a separate list of amercement figures. The official membrane or membranes delivered before the sitting of the court and now interlineated, together with the hundred official's version of the proceedings and the affeerors' list of amercements, were then sent to or collected by the sheriff's office. Here, a fair and uncritical[10] copy of the court was added to the official membrane or membranes which had travelled out to the hundred and back. It was made up in the following order, which is consistent with the conjectures so far advanced and with the evidence of the physical condition of the manuscript: first, a copy of the hundred official's version; secondly, amounts of amercement; thirdly, the 'summa' at the end of each court; lastly, the word 'probatur' which follows the 'summa'. All was then ready for the next 'circuit', when the process would be repeated.

The choice of Penwith is odd, but not without interest. Chance has much to do with it. Work on the county court led to this Cornish roll and to the printed text of part of the Penwith section of the county court part of the roll.[11] This in turn led to an interest in the Penwith hundred courts and the hope, after a summary inspection of the other eight hundred rolls, that it might be possible to write a general article on Cornish hundred courts.[12] As a preliminary the Penwith hundred court rolls have been transcribed and are offered here, very much as 'work in progress', as an inadequate tribute to Mr Meekings for the generosity of many years. The difficulties inherent in writing even a brief introduction to the rolls will be indicated below, but they are greatly eased by a long and invaluable article by Mr P. A. S. Pool, which courageously attempts to delineate, with a map and supporting notes, the tithings of Penwith in relation to its parishes. The same article also deals with the special position of Penwith as a private hundred from whose courts two-thirds of the profits went at this time to the Arundells of Lanherne.[13] This is evidenced for the courts here printed by the note at the foot of

[8] M.17 may be a fragment of such informal notes.

[9] There are three relevant cases in the text printed here [10, 21, 26]. 'c' appears in the margin of each case at the stage where it is decided, and recorded for the first time in the basic text, as distinct from interlineation or repetition in the basic text, that part or all of the damages should go to the clerks; i.e. [10] at p.190, [21] at p.195 and [26] at p.188. It seems impossible to say, in these cases, whether the clerks in question were officials of the hundred or of the county. 'Damages cleer' are considered briefly by Holdsworth (I, 255–6).

[10] There are so many errors in the surviving version (e.g. in the number of defaults, and in cases disappearing for no evident reason) that it is impossible to believe that any check, or any serious check, was made when the fair copy was made in the sheriff's office. One result of this, which deserves closer investigation, would be loss of revenue from amercements and fines in cases which disappeared: some of the other hundreds are much worse than Penwith in this respect.

[11] W. A. Morris, *The Early English County Court* (Berkeley, Calif, 1926), 181–97: the Penwith transcript is at pp.181–91. Morris seems to have made no use at all of this material in writing the book; perhaps this is just as well, since his transcript is seriously defective.

[12] A very long-term, and probably over-ambitious, hope is that a study of county, hundred, stannary and other (e.g. manorial and central) court rolls might throw light on where and how people litigated in practice as distinct from theory.

[13] P.A.S. Pool, 'The Penheleg Manuscript', *Jnl R. Instn Corn*, New ser., III, pt 3 (1959), 163–228. The section on tithings and parishes is at pp.212–28; the map is at p.215 (corrections ibid., pt 4 (1960), 284); the crucial documents granting the manor of Connerton with the hundred of Penwith, except

m.13d in the Latin text, and also by a note in the sheriff's account at m.24 which reads: 'reddit compotum de xij s. vj d. de tertia parte placitorum et perquisitorum hundredi de Penwith per predictum tempus et non plus quia Johannes Arundel percipit duas partes profituorum eiusdem hundredi'.[14] To what extent does this mean that Penwith is 'odd' as a choice and likely to be atypical?

The distinction customarily drawn between royal and private hundreds seems generally to turn on three points not always distinguished: the right to take the profits; the right to hold the court; the jurisdiction of the court, i.e. whether it has additional jurisdiction conferred on it over and above the normal. Judged by the first criterion, Penwith was a mixture. The right to hold the court is less easy to determine. The vital charter of 1227–43[15] certainly favours the view that the Arundells could appoint a hundred bailiff, and the statement in the Caption of Seisin of 1337 that John Arundell was bailiff in fee of Penwith[16] may be a mis-statement of the true position – that the Arundells were lords of the hundred with power to appoint a bailiff.[17] It is probably of no great significance, for the Caption gives the prior of Bodmin as bailiff in fee of Pyder hundred and it seems improbable that he would do other than appoint someone to act for him as bailiff, and this in a hundred undoubtedly royal and not private.[18] More significant for our present purpose is that all nine hundreds (and this includes Penwith) fitted in with the 'circuit' scheme and exhibit (Penwith again included) the general characteristics which led to the tentative conclusions about the modus operandi in making up the surviving rolls: moreover, there is nothing in the headings to the Penwith courts which would suggest that they are in some way different from the other hundred courts.[19] There remains the question of jurisdiction – is there anything in the content of the Penwith rolls to mark them off from the others? Generally speaking there is not.[20] Some special points deserve consideration, since they seem prima facie to suggest otherwise. There are three cases of trespass [10,70, 71] in which, though not at every stage of the case, 'contra pacem domini regis' is alleged; this is rare, but occurs also in Trigg.[21] In no case where the interlineation 'curia' indicates a claim of court is it said whose court is claimed; elsewhere this is sometimes stated but more often, as in Penwith, it is not.[22] Wager of law does not occur in the Penwith rolls: in other hundreds it can generally, but not always, be found.[23] Lastly, careless mention of 'raptus' in the narratio of Penwith [27] produces an objection based on lack of jurisdiction to which the court has no ready answer: if it is relevant at all, this is an argument against any special jurisdiction in Penwith.[24]

Whether or not we classify Penwith as a private hundred, there does not seem to be much evidence that the procedure or jurisdiction of the court was atypical for Cornwall at that date. Yet it is fair to say that only a full analysis of the other eight hundreds

for one-third of the hundred court income, to the predecessors of the Arundells, and so creating 'a private hundred', are discussed at pp.165–7.

14 As the note at the foot of m.13d (end of printed text) indicates, the actual receipts for the three courts were 37s. 6d., exactly three times the amount accounted for by the sheriff.

15 Pool, *Jnl R. Instn Corn,* New ser., III, pt 3, 166–7.

16 *The Caption of Seisin of the Duchy of Cornwall (1337),* ed. P. L. Hull (Devon & Corn Rec. Soc., New ser., XVII, 1971), 134.

17 The suggestion about a 'mis-statement' comes from Mr Pool. In the Penwith rolls the two candidates for the post of hundred bailiff are William Hobba [47, 59] and, more probable, John Rosculian [103, 104].

18 *Caption of Seisin,* 134. The prior had been in trouble in the Cornish eyre of 1302 for having an excessive staff: JUST 1/118, m.56; this reference was kindly provided by Mr J. M. Kaye.

19 It might even be argued that the form of words used at the foot of m.13d suggests a court held by a royal official, from which two-thirds of the proceeds were handed over to John Arundell, rather than the reverse. The equivalent annotations for other courts (mm.5d, 6d, 7d, 8d, 10d, 11d, 15d, 18d, 19d, 20d, 21d, 22d, 23d) all include *probatur,* and are in a hand closely similar to that of the account at m.24.

20 The general question of jurisdiction, some of which is anticipated here, is considered more fully below, 175–7.

21 SC 2/161/74, m.19, about three-quarters down, beginning *Inquiratur si Mariota.*

22 For more about claim of court, see below, 176.

23 For more about wager of law, see below, 176.

24 A more complex problem arises from two examples given by Mr Pool, which illustrate the possibility of confusion between manor and hundred: *Jnl R. Instn Corn,* New ser., III, pt 3, 167 (in 1302 the lord of Connerton and Penwith appeared before the eyre justices to justify the hanging of a thief 'apprehended within the liberty of Penwith'); and 169 n.42 ('The Assize Rolls of 1284 and 1302 often refer to wreck being taken within various Penwith tithings, but always by the Crown or the Earldom, not the lords of the hundred. The case of 1753 says that records were preserved of wreck taken by the Arundells from about 1400'). Wreck here was firmly reserved to the crown in 1330: C 260/188, no. 10.

(not yet undertaken) can prove this. Moreover, Cornwall itself is 'suspect' in a number of ways. It is a long way from the central courts,[25] and this may have led to an unusually high number of cases held locally: but this would only affect the issue in cases where a theoretical choice of jurisdictions existed, and it is the county rather than the hundred court where this is likely to be so. It is Mr J. M. Kaye's view, based in particular on the Cornish eyre rolls of 1284 and 1302, that Cornwall was not then 'a standard county': there were peculiarities in enrolment and in content, and some local customs not found elsewhere.[26] Among the special customs claimed for Cornwall were the right to sue without writ in cases of mesne and dower,[27] the non-presentment of Englishry,[28] and a special rule about the effect of marriage out of the manor by female villeins:[29] but none of these customs is relevant to the work of the hundred court. As to enrolment, what is said by Mr Kaye of eyre rolls may well be true also of our hundred rolls of 1333: they are certainly more orderly (perhaps 'professional' is the word) than, to take three well-known cases, those of Whorwellsdown (1269),[30] Clackclose (1284)[31] and Highworth (1275–87).[32] The disparity in dates between 1262/1287 and 1333, the fact that the earlier rolls are from courts in private hands whereas the Cornish hundreds were royal (and Penwith is, as we have seen, no exception so far as final enrolment is concerned) makes it the more regrettable that no comparison has been made with court rolls of a royal hundred from another county in the 1330s.[33]

Granted all these difficulties, it was tempting to leave the rolls to 'speak for themselves' without any further attempt at introduction: but it has, on balance, seemed right to add something by way of analysis. There are 107 distinct cases in the three courts. Turnover was reasonably brisk. There are 68 cases in the first court, [69–83] come as new cases into the second court, [84–107] as new cases into the third court; by the end of the third court some result has been achieved in 46 of the 107 cases. In inter partes cases, 29 out of 61 cases were ended; in those which involved presentment by a tithing or tithingman, 17 out of 46 had a 'result', that is, came to a partial or total end.[34] An analysis of the types of case and result produces the following conclusions.[35] Inter partes cases total 61, of which 26 are trespass (14 ended),[36] 30 debt-detinue (14 ended),[37] 4 covenant (1 ended)[38] and 1 rescue.[39] Cases involving the

[25] The court of common pleas normally sat at Westminster, but from Michaelmas octave 1333 sat for some years at York: T. F. Tout, *Chapters in the Administrative History of Mediaeval England* (Manchester, 1920–33), III, 58–9 and references. In Michaelmas 1333 king's bench sat at York and Lincoln: Putnam in *Procs before JPs,* 30.

[26] I am grateful to Mr Kaye for this comment, which is based on wide reading of the eyre rolls of the period.

[27] *Reg. Brev.: Orig.,* ff.160v 1st *Nota,* 240v *Nota.*

[28] *YB 30–31 Edw. I,* ed. A. J. Horwood (RS, 1863), 240.

[29] ibid., 164.

[30] *Select Pleas in Manorial Courts,* ed. F. W. Maitland (SS, II, 1889), 176–82. It is a single 'arrear hundred': ibid., 178 n.1.

[31] *Court Rolls of Ramsey Abbey and the Honor of Clare,* ed. W. O. Ault (New Haven, Conn, 1928), xli-xlv, 146–69. The hundred courts are not easy to study because of the editorial method, described at pp.x-xi.

[32] *The Rolls of Highworth Hundred 1275–1287,* ed. B. Farr (Wilts Rec. Soc., XXI, XXII, 1966, 1968).

[33] This may be attributable to lack of editorial diligence rather than to an absence of rolls.

[34] It is necessary to distinguish between cases where, in the course of the three courts, there is (i) a partial end, that is (a) a case in which the inter partes aspect of the case is settled, but the tithing still has an interest which is not settled (seven such cases [9, 25, 32, 33, 71, 88, 104] and – provisionally – two others [11, 26]) and (ii) a total end, which may arise either in (b) a case in which the inter partes aspect has already been settled in a previous court, but the tithing still has an interest which is settled by fine (two such cases [42, 46]) or (c) a case in which are settled both the inter partes aspect and, by fine or because there is no need for further action, the tithing's interest (five such cases [10, 16, 17, 50, 57] and – provisionally – one other [52]). This gives the total of 17 'results' mentioned in the text. Clearly it is arguable that only (c), or perhaps (b) and (c), should count: this would give 6 or 8 'results'. The discussion of procedure by presentment (below, 174–5) should make this easier to follow.

[35] Based solely on the three courts and not attempting to predict, from interlineations in the third court, the outcome of cases in the following court.

[36] Failure to prosecute, 5; plaintiff wins, 3; defendant wins, 4; removal by claim of court, 2.

[37] Licence to concord, 1; failure to prosecute, 4; plaintiff wins, 5; removal by claim of court, 4.

[38] Removal by claim of court, 1.

[39] Unfinished.

tithing total 46, of which 34 are trespass (13 'results'),[40] 6 rescue (3 'results'),[41] 1 'vexavit in curia christianitatis', 1 concealment of hue, and 4 cases not disclosing the cause of action (1 'result').[42]

It will readily be seen that, with the exception of rescue where only 1 case [87] in 7 is inter partes,[43] the only area of overlap is trespass, where there are 26 inter partes cases and 34 presentment cases. Can any clear distinction be drawn between them, using those cases which reveal something, however little, of the facts? Most of the inter partes cases are about trespass to land and/or chattels and not to the person, but battery [63], the beating of a servant [56], and a puzzling case arising from a plea of covenant [93] also occur. Most of the presentment cases concern personal injuries, with or without other ingredients, but the taking of animals [10], house-breaking [50], corn-reaping [72], and gorse-burning [74, 75] also occur. Another distinguishing feature of tithing cases is that certain formal words like *vi armata, vi et armis, contra pacem* or *contra pacem domini regis* are found in some cases,[44] whereas no such formulae ever appear in inter partes cases; but many presentment cases lack any formal words of this sort.[45] The very sparse evidence on damages alleged and recovered suggests that the range was higher in presentment cases.[46] A summary of these differences would be little more than a repetition of them: what it would be really interesting to know is why, especially in the seemingly exceptional cases, the plaintiff raised the hue and cry. It is just possible that he balanced the hope of fairly quick proceedings inter partes against the more complex but (for the defendant in particular) potentially more damaging consequences of procedure by presentment. An examination of that procedure may help to illuminate this proposition.[47]

A simple case would begin with the raising of the hue. The tithing or tithingman then has a duty to present the case, and there will be trouble if the hue is concealed [73] or if the tithing or tithingman fails to turn up in court.[48] At some point before the court sits the tithing decides whether the hue has been justly or unjustly raised,[49] and this is almost always indicated at some stage in the enrolment of a case. The normal situation is 'justly raised', and this will be considered first. The presentment will be made and the plaintiff may, in 'prosecuting his hue', recite the alleged wrong in some detail [e.g. 13, 16, 27]. The defendant will normally plead not guilty, ask for, and get, a jury. If the jury finds for the plaintiff, the defendant will be amerced and will pay damages to the plaintiff; there will also be an order to arrest and imprison the defendant, which may or may not be successfully executed, the tithing generally being amerced if it is not.[50] The defendant can finally extricate himself by paying a fine [42, 46]. There

[40] In analysing the presentment cases the highest 'results' figure (17: see above, n.34) has been used throughout. The analyses in this and the next two footnotes of the reasons for these 'results' sometimes produce totals in excess of the number given in the text, because, for example, a case where both the inter partes aspect and the tithing's interest are disposed of in the course of the three courts may produce not only a licence to concord between the parties but also a subsequent fine to dispose of the tithing's interest. So trespass is licence to concord, 3; failure to prosecute, 4; plaintiff wins, 2; defendant wins, 1; death of party, 1; fine, 6; no need for further action by the tithing, 1; so there are 18 reasons for 13 'results', because 5 of the 'results' are in class (c), where there are always 2 reasons; 6 are in class (a) and 2 in class (b): see above, n.34.

[41] Licence to concord, 2; plaintiff wins, 1: all class (a).

[42] Failure to prosecute, 1; no need for further action by tithing, 1: class (c).

[43] The presentment cases are [32, 51, 88, 103, 104, 106]. There is no obvious explanation for the different procedure in [87].

[44] *vi armata* [10, 27]; *vi et armis* [16]; *contra pacem* [27, 72, 83, 102]; *contra pacem domini regis* [10, 70, 71].

[45] e.g. [25, 41], cases chosen because they also illustrate a variety of enrolment which makes it unsafe to depend heavily on the presence or absence of a particular formula in any one entry. [25] has, in three successive courts, *vulneravit, bateria* and *percussit*; [41] has *percussit, bateria* and *transgressio.*

[46] In inter partes cases damages alleged range from 2s. to 100s.; damages recovered from 2d. to 1s. In presentment cases damages alleged were either 100s. or £100; damages recovered range from 1s. to 1 mark.

[47] The examination is no more than a speculative outline based on the three Penwith courts and clearly subject to modification in the light of evidence from the other hundreds.

[48] [88, 102], chosen because they are 'new' cases in Court 3 and therefore have no missing previous history, and because both contain the seeming paradox that the 'Dec" presents and yet is amerced 'quia . . . recusavit venire ad presentandum'. This suggests that the presentments may have been put in before the sitting of the court.

[49] If the suggestion in the previous note is correct, the decision would be taken before the presentment was put in.

[50] [42, 44, 45, 65, 71], and [104], a case in which too much seems to have happened in one court.

are other possibilities. In nine cases the plaintiff fails to prosecute[51] – this costs him an amercement; but that is not the end of the matter, because the defendant still has to face the presentment. If he is not already in court he has to be got there (not always easy) [9, 25, 58]; once there he may ask for a jury which will, if he continues to turn up and the jury makes any progress [e.g. 43, 51, 61], lead, in the case of an adverse decision, to arrest.[52] From that point, process is the same as that described above in cases of conviction. Oddly, there are two cases [16, 57] in which the defendants, after amercement of the plaintiff for non-prosecution, immediately pay a fine; the explanation may be that they could predict only too well the likely outcome of going to a jury. In five cases the defendant gets licence to concord, either before or after a jury has been summoned [10, 17, 32, 33, 88];[53] in all cases he is amerced for the licence, gives security ranging from 'nil' to half a mark, and is ordered to be arrested. Subsequent proceedings involve the payment of a fine in two cases [10, 17], and repeated orders to the tithing to imprison the defendant in two cases [32, 33]. It is not clear whether, as with non-prosecution, the intent, in the absence of a fine, was to settle by jury the question of guilt (i.e. the truth of the presentment) or whether the licence to concord was regarded as making that question irrelevant – strictly speaking the question was still relevant from a presentment point of view.

In five cases [12, 26, 50, 52, 102] the presentment is that the hue has been 'unjustly raised', and the standard response is for the plaintiff to deny this and to set out his version of the facts.[54] The defendant then pleads not guilty and seeks a jury [12, 26, 50, 102]. Where the jury finds for the plaintiff [26], he gets damages; the defendant is amerced and ordered to be arrested and imprisoned; it is not clear whether the tithing, which is amerced for failure to imprison, also gets into trouble for wrongly saying 'unjustly', but on principle it should. Where the jury finds for the defendant [50], the plaintiff is amerced for a false hue; there is no suggestion of further action involving the tithing, and that seems correct in principle, given their initial statement that the hue was unjustly raised. Where the plaintiff fails to prosecute [52], he is amerced, and there, in contrast to cases where the presentment says 'justly raised', the matter ends: this is somewhat surprising because it leaves open the question whether the presentment was correct. The remaining two cases yield no useful evidence.

Finally, what do the Penwith rolls reveal about jurisdiction? The ordinary business of the hundred court was summarised in 1234 as consisting of 'pleas of battery and brawls that do not mention felony, of the wounding and maiming of beasts and of debts and other similar complaints without a royal writ'.[55] Miss Cam found this summary 'confirmed by the surviving records of thirteenth-century hundred courts'[56] and she goes on to give some account of the main heads of jurisdiction.[57] There is a considerable similarity between Miss Cam's survey and what took place inter partes in Penwith.[58] 'Trespass is the plea that recurs most frequently; it was . . . freely used in complaints not only of battery but of all kinds of violence'.[59] And not only direct violence or even violence in any ordinary sense of the word: Miss Cam's cases of passing off an inferior fish or failing to shut up a valuable bitch in the breeding season[60] have their pale parallels in the Penwith case of beating the plaintiff's servant [56], two cases of taking a girl from the custody or arrest of the plaintiff [27, 38], and a difficult case springing from a plea of covenant [93]. 'After trespass the commonest pleas are those of debt . . . Detention of chattels is another heading under which cases are recorded, very often cases of breach of contract'.[61] In Penwith too, debt-detinue comes second in total:[62] the 30 debt-detinue cases

[51] [9, 16, 25, 37, 43, 51, 57, 58, 61.]

[52] [37], assuming that failure to prosecute, jury decision, and order to arrest have all taken place in previous courts.

[53] [74, 75], presentment cases, are excluded here: note A, below, 179.

[54] 'Dec' male presentat' as in [12, 50, 102]; or 'tamen querens dicit quod juste' as in [26; cf. 52].

[55] *BNB,* III, no. 1110.

[56] Cam, *Hundred and Hundred Rolls,* 181.

[57] ibid., 181–4.

[58] Miss Cam had come across hundred courts, other than tourns, 'in which presentments were made by the tithing-man of the village' (ibid., 184); it is not clear whether she included such presentments in her account of the main heads of jurisdiction, but her examples seem all to be inter partes cases. For this reason the comparison here is limited to the inter partes Penwith cases.

[59] ibid., 181; in Penwith it comes an easy first if inter partes and presentment cases are aggregated, and is just behind debt-detinue if presentment cases are excluded.

[60] ibid., 181–2.

[61] ibid., 182.

[62] First, if only inter partes cases are counted.

are, alas, wholly uninformative as to the details or reason for the debt, apart from the three cases of detention of chattels [3, 20, 53], an action where the money was given to acquit the plaintiff against a third party [1], and three cases where the allegation is 'solvisse debuit ad terminum qui preteriit' [39, 60, 90]. It is perhaps worth mentioning at this point that in the two 'solvisse debuit' cases which make any progress, it is by way of jury [60, 90]; elsewhere in Cornwall it is not uncommon to find wager of law in such cases,[63] but in Penwith wager of law makes no appearance at all. 'Pleas of convention' are next to be mentioned by Miss Cam and were next in order of popularity in Penwith:[64] unfortunately only one [96] of the four cases [28, 40, 81, 96] reveals the facts, which were, and were to remain, very common in covenant – breach of an agreement to serve for a fixed term. Miss Cam's list ends with slander, not found in Penwith.

To look at the question of jurisdiction in a negative way, what have the rolls to say about limitations on jurisdiction? The only point positively taken in any of the cases concerns 'raptus'. In [27] there is a jurisdictional objection to what was probably a narrator's error in using this ambiguous technical term after an initial, and quite possibly acceptable, allegation 'ceperunt et abduxerunt Johannam . . . in custodia sua existentem': it caused difficulty which was not resolved in the course of three courts.[65] There are also seven cases, all inter partes, where it seems clear that 'claim of court' has removed a case from the hundred court to some other jurisdiction.[66] The indication that this is so is an interlineated 'cur'' (extended as 'curia') in one court, followed in the next court either by no entry at all or by a tidying-up entry amercing the defendant for any defaults he may have accumulated:[67] indeed, the tidying-up entries are of such standard and unique form that they entitle one to deduce an interlineated 'curia' in the previous court.[68] None of the Penwith examples (which, incidentally, produce no pattern when examined as a block) gives any indication where the case has gone to. The most probable answer, on principle, is to a feudal or seignorial court or other hundred court.[69] This probability is strengthened by claims in other Cornish courts where the claimant's name is sometimes given – examples are John prior of Bodmin and William de Botreaux – but where it also becomes apparent that the Penwith examples are to some extent misleading, for matters did not always proceed as smoothly as the Penwith cases suggest.[70]

The 'claim of court' cases are, as has been said, all inter partes. In presentment cases there are no objections to jurisdiction. It is, however, probable that presentments were limited to cases where the hue was raised in the presenting tithing, and that this meant cases where the wrong complained of was done in the presenting tithing. Few of the cases printed here enable this to be said as more than a guess, and many of them (if one can assume jurisdiction to be properly founded on the basis just described) point clearly to the danger of identifying common place-names as belonging to one parish rather than an alternative possibility merely because the former parish is in the tithing which presents. The whole area of Penwith is not great,[71] and there is no improbability in parties (even both parties) living outside a tithing being involved in, for example,

[63] e.g. Powder hundred, two cases near the top of m.18, beginning *Marcus Pavun est ad legem* and *Bernardus Cawel est ad legem*; Pyder, near the top of m.15d, beginning *Michael de Tresitheny est ad legem*; East, near the top of m.22, beginning *Hugo de Hille est ad legem.*

[64] Cam, *Hundred and Hundred Rolls,* 183: for Penwith this excludes rescue, where only one out of seven cases was inter partes.

[65] It is hoped to investigate this case in detail in the general article on Cornish hundred courts.

[66] [5, 6, 7, 28, 78, 80, 82.] [92] and [97], which appear for the first time in Court 3, have 'curia' interlineated but, in accordance with the general rules adopted here, have not been counted.

[67] A case of interlineated 'curia' followed by no entry in the next court, because there are no defaults to tidy up, is [5]; cases of interlineated 'curia' followed by a tidying-up entry in the next court are [6, 7, 78, 80, 82].

[68] [28] (Court 1): a puzzling feature of this case is that a case [81] with the same plaintiff, defendant and cause of action turns up in Court 2 in a sequence of new cases [76–83] and is continued in Court 3 with no suggestion of claim of court.

[69] Alternative answers are considered in note B, below 179.

[70] Note C, below, 179.

[71] Roughly twenty miles from east to west and ten miles from north to south: in many places bays and indentations much reduce the north-south figure.

a trespass or rescue in that tithing. To add to the difficulty, it is not necessarily the case that X de Y lives at Y, though in the case of 'lesser men' it is probably necessary to assume it.[72] This gloomy recital of difficulties can be lightened in one respect. There are five cases [10, 50, 70, 72, 102] where the presentment alleges the actual place where the alleged deed was done, and in all of them the place is, so far as can be ascertained on present knowledge, in the tithing which presents.[73] This is some small confirmation of the assumptions about the jurisdictional basis of presentment made above.

There is, finally, the question of a financial limit on claims made in the hundred court. It is generally said that, as a result of a curious interpretation of the statute of Gloucester (1278), c.8, the civil jurisdiction of local (including hundred) courts in personal pleas was limited to claims for less than 40s.[74] Recently, and convincingly, Dr Beckerman has substituted two different rules.[75] The first is that claims in debt-detinue for amounts under 40s. would lie without writ, and claims for 40s. or more would lie only if a viscontiel writ were employed. The limited evidence of the inter partes Penwith cases,[76] to which viscontiel writs, triable in the county court, are irrelevant, supports this solely in the negative sense that the maximum claim for debt-detinue was for 16s. [39].[77] The second rule is that in pleas of trespass, with or without writ (and this *is* relevant to the Penwith cases), there was no financial limit on the amount claimed. Again, the Penwith rolls support this: there are several trespass pleas inter partes in which damages of 100s. are claimed [23, ?63, 77, 79].[78]

Editorial note

The cases have been numbered consecutively in order of enrolment on first appearance, and thereafter retain the same number in subsequent courts if they reappear there. A table of cases, with page references, comes at the end of this introduction.

Most of the entries have one or more marginal notes in an abbreviated form: e.g. *mia iij d.* The marginal notes for each entry have been extended; in some cases there is no marginal note in the roll, but merely a line depending from the previous marginal note and indicating that the same marginal note is implied: in such cases the implied marginal note is printed within square brackets.

Interlineations are of two kinds: (a) words intended to be part of the basic text, but in fact interlined: this is indicated by a footnote; (b) 'special' interlineations

[72] All this makes identification of place names difficult. Invaluable help has been given by Mr P. A. S. Pool in correspondence and in his recent *The Place-Names of West Penwith* (Fedn Old Corn Socs, 1973), and Mr O. J. Padel has kindly provided a number of identifications.

[73] Subject to exceptions noted below, the location of tithings is based on the map by Mr Pool referred to above, n.13. [10]: animals taken at Roscroggan in Illogan parish in Tehidy tithing; Tehidy presents. [50]: house entered etc. at Trevaskis in Gwinear parish in the main, eastern, section of Connerton tithing; Connerton presents. [70]: breaking into house at Mousehole in Paul parish in Alverton tithing; Alverton presents (this involves redrawing the tithing map to bring Mousehole into Alverton and not Kemyell, and Mr Pool accepts the case as 'very strong evidence' for doing so – there are supporting reasons). [72]: taking crops at Boswarva in Madron parish in the detached, western, part of Binnerton tithing; Binnerton presents. [102]: expulsion from house at Porthenys by Mousehole; Alverton presents (see [70] in this note). It is clear from Mr Pool's map (above, n.13) and illustrated by [50] and [72] in this note, that in many cases tithings embraced more than one parish: the index identifications by parish are merely for general guidance.

[74] e.g. T. F. T. Plucknett, *A Concise History of the Common Law,* 5th edn (London, 1956), 93; J. H. Baker, *An Introduction to English Legal History* (London, 1971), 18, 21.

[75] J. S. Beckerman, 'The forty-shilling jurisdictional limit in medieval English personal actions', in *Legal History Studies 1972,* ed. D. Jenkins (Cardiff, 1975), 110–17.

[76] It is improbable that the traditional 40s. rule had presentment cases in mind and the new rules do not; but some parallel presentment evidence has been added in the following two footnotes.

[77] There are several claims for 10s. [24, 30, 31, 60]. There is, alas, no sign of the claims for 39s. 11½d. which 'recur with monotonous regularity' in the many hundred court rolls inspected by Miss Cam: *Hundred and Hundred Rolls,* 182. There are, of course, no presentment claims in debt-detinue.

[78] It is interesting to note that in the only case [21] in which the allegation of damage can be matched with the damages actually awarded, there is a marked disparity: damages of 3s. were alleged and 6d. was awarded, all of which went to the clerks. In presentment cases the only amounts alleged are £100 [17, 27, 71, 72, 102] and 100s. [10, 12, 13, 16, 70, 83], and in the only case [71] where damages alleged and awarded can be matched the figures are £100 and 1s.; in fact, the highest damages awarded in presentment cases were 1 mark [26, 44].

made at the following court and in a different hand (see above, 170): these are enclosed in diamond brackets. Words or passages from other sources are in square brackets and have a footnote explanation.

In a few instances the extension of contractions has presented problems. The form *huttesium* has been used throughout, although its contracted form would sometimes allow the reading *hutesium*; similarly, *plevinam* has been used, although its contracted form would sometimes allow forms of *plegium* to be read. The manuscript forms offer no guidance in distinguishing between *decenna* and *decennarius*; in view of the complete ambiguity of most instances, *dec'* is here used without any attempt at editorial discrimination, even where this is clearly possible.

I have had much assistance in preparing this contribution and hope that it has been acknowledged in the appropriate places. My greatest debt is to Dr J. B. Post, without whose encouragement and very considerable assistance the contribution would never have appeared.

Supplementary Notes to Introduction

A. [74, 75], presentment cases, are excluded here because no result was reached in the three courts, but they are prima facie surprising because in both cases the first entry of the presentment (Court 2) has *dia* (*dies amoris*?) interlineated, and the second entry (Court 3) begins *Dies datus est* and has *da* (*dies amoris*?) in the margin and *licencia concordandi, nil vadiat, arrestetur* interlineated: this makes it very probable that in Court 4 the defendants were amerced for licence to concord and ordered to be arrested. If the meaning given to *dia* and *da* is correct (I owe it to Dr Paul Brand, but responsibility for its use here and elsewhere in the text is mine), then it illustrates very clearly the separation in presentment cases between the inter partes aspect, which is dealt with first and where a licence to concord is entirely appropriate, and the subsequent proceedings, if any are needed, between tithing and plaintiff or defendant. There are, it should be said, several inter partes cases involving a 'dies amoris', but they are no cause for surprise. 'Dies amoris' (loveday) deserves further investigation, though there is much helpful material in J. W. Bennett, 'The Mediaeval Loveday', *Speculum*, XXXIII (1958), 351–70.

B. Had the cases been bound for the king's bench or common pleas, one would expect a writ at the instigation of one of the parties and some mention of the writ on the hundred court roll. It is not surprising that none of these cases is found in either bench in the term immediately following (CP 40/296; KB 27/294), although individual litigants and even pairs (*Taverner* v. *Coswiniva*: CP 40/296, m.304) occur; rolls for later terms have not been searched. It may be that the statute of Westminster (1275), c.35, is relevant here (it raises, inter alia, the question whether hundred courts had jurisdiction over trespasses and agreements done or made outside the hundred by those living in the hundred), but the trespass writ given by the statute is not easy to reconcile with the quiet disappearance of the 'curia' cases, which suggests a quick decision by the hundred itself that the claim is valid. The courts of the stannaries are a possibility, for there were constant conflicts and petitions over jurisdiction at this time: for a brief, recent and rather over-simplified survey, see R. P. Pennington, *Stannary Law* (Newton Abbot, 1973), 11–18. The most likely answer is transfer to some other local court of roughly the same level of importance which had the right to try the case either because of a special grant of jurisdiction or because the offence happened or the agreement was made outside the jurisdiction of the Penwith hundred court: for an illustration, involving claims by the prior of Ely, see H. M. Cam, *Liberties and Communities in Medieval England* (Cambridge, 1944), 201.

C. John prior of Bodmin: Pyder hundred, about half-way down m.15d (Court 3), beginning *Johannes de Penros*: the case 'remanet sub calumpnia curie Johannis prioris Bodminie' with marginal *remanet*, in this, its first and only appearance, and there are no interlineations.

William de Botreaux: Pyder, about one-quarter of the way down m.15 (Court 1), beginning *Loquela inter David de Reswaltes* with marginal *remanet*; near the top of m.15d (Court 2), beginning *Michael de Tresitheny* with marginal *lex*; about three-quarters of the way down m.15d (Court 3), beginning *David de Reswaltes* with marginal *lex*. Here, in spite of complexities in Court 1, which ends with the words 'Et super hoc Willelmus de Botreaux calumpniat curiam suam', the case continues in Courts 2 (with William as one of the sureties) and 3 with no mention of any claim of court.

There are other cases in which *sub calumpnia curie* appears in the text of an entry in which defaults are tidied up, and yet the case continues in the next court: e.g. Powder hundred, about one-third of the way down m.16 (Court 1), beginning *Loquela inter Robertum Hobba* with marginal *remanet* and *misericordia ij d.*; about half-way down m.16d (Court 2), beginning *Robertus Hobba in misericordia quia non prosequitur* with marginal *misericordia ij d.*: there is no mention of claim of court in Court 2. There is a short discussion of claim of court by Farr in *Rolls of Highworth Hundred,* I, 13–15, where it is said (14) that 'the line [between allowing and disallowing claim of court] was usually drawn at hue raised and blood shed'; certainly no claim was even made in any Penwith presentment case.

Table of Cases

The first column gives the *number* of the case: the other columns give the *page(s)* at which the entry or entries for that case (including essoins, marked *e*) can be found.

Case No.	*Court 1*	*Court 2*	*Court 3*
1	181	190	193
2	181		
3	181	190	
4	181		
5	181 and 181*e*	190 and 186*e*	
6	181 and 181*e* (bis)	190	
7	181	190	
8	181	190	193
9	181	190	193
10	181	190	
11	182	190	193
12	182	190	194
13	182	191	194
14	182		
15	182		
16	182	191	194
17	182	188	195
18	182	188	195
19	182	188	
20	182	188	
21	182	188	195
22	182	188	
23	183 and 181*e*	188	195
24	183		
25	183	188	196
26	183	188	196
27	183	188	196
28	183		
29	183 and 181*e*	188	196
30	183		
31	183		
32	183	189	196
33	183	189	196
34	184	189	
35	184	189	
36	184	189	196
37	184	189	196
38	184	189	196
39	184	189	196
40	184	189	196
41	184	189	196
42	184	189	196
43	184	189	196
44	184	189	196
45	184	189	196
46	184		
47	184	187 and 189	195
48	185		
49	185	191	194
50	185	191	194
51	185	191	194
52	185		
53	185	191 and 186*e*	194
54	185	191	194
55	185	187	195
56	185	187 and 186*e*	
57	185		
58	185	187	194
59	185		
60	185	187	195
61	185	187	195
62	185	187	195
63	186	187	
64	186	188	195
65	186	188	195
66	186	188	195
67	186	188	195
68	186		
68A	181*e*		
69		186	194
70		186	194
71		186	194
72		186	194 and 191*e*
73		187	195
74		187	195
75		187	195
76		190	193 and 191*e*
77		190	193 (bis)
78		190	193
79		190	193 (bis)
80		190	193
81		190	193
82		190	193
83		190	193
84			191
85			191
86			191
87			191
88			192
89			192
90			192
91			192
92			192
93			192
94			192
95			192
96			192
97			192
98			192
99			192
100			192
101			192
102			192
103			193
104			193
105			193
106			193
107			194

TEXT

Court 1

SC 2/161/74, m.12

PENWITH: TRETHEWY VICECOMES

HUNDREDUM TENTUM APUD MARCASION DIE LUNE PROXIMA ANTE FESTUM SANCTE MARGARETE VIRGINIS ANNO REGNI REGIS SEPTIMO [9 July 1333]

[23] [79] Teobaldus de Eskels versus Vivianum de Maen de placito transgressionis unde inquisitio per Rogerum Pencros.

[29] Johannes Gentil versus Thomas [80] de Trembaighwartha de placito transgressionis per Johannem Castellek.

[68A] [81] Henricus Mareis versus Anabillam que fuit uxor Johannis Fraunces de placito debiti per David Coly.

[5] Ricardus Baker de Moshole versus Herveum Josian de placito transgressionis per Ogerum de Caran.

[6] Ricardus Baker versus Henricum Mares de placito debiti per Willelmum Magur.

[6] Henricus Mares versus Ricardum Baker de placito debiti per Odonem Bosfrancan.

[1] [*Marginated*] Inquiratur
Inquiratur si Laurencius subballivus injuste detinet ij s. Alano Trethiles quos tradidit ei ad acquietandum eum versus Willelmum de Treloscan ad dampnum suum v s. nec ne.

[2] [*Marginated*] Misericordia iij d. Misericordia iij d.
Bonia Lulyn in misericordia quia non prosequitur versus David de Basily in placito transgressionis. Idem David in misericordia pro una defalta versus eandem Boneam in eodem placito.

[3] [*Marginated*] Districtio
Odo de Bosfrancan queritur de Nicholao Wychard ⟨misericordia: detinet iij hakas⟩ qui unam fecit defaltam in placito debiti.

[4] [*Marginated*] Misericordia iij d. Misericordia iij d.
Gilbertus de Douron[82] in misericordia quia non prosequitur versus Willelmum Prestour et Johannam uxorem eius in placito debiti. Iidem Willelmus et Johanna in misericordia pro una defalta versus eundem Gilbertum in eodem placito.

[5] [*Marginated*] Districtio
Ricardus Baker de Mousehole essoniatus ⟨attornatus⟩ queritur de Herveo Josyan apparente ⟨essonium⟩ in placito transgressionis.

[6] [*Marginated*] [Districtio]
Idem Ricardus queritur de Henrico Mares ⟨misericordia defalta: curia⟩ qui unam fecit defaltam in placito debiti.

[7] [*Marginated*] [Districtio]
Laurencius Basset queritur per attornatum de Stephano Mertherderwa ⟨misericordia defalta: curia⟩ qui unam fecit defaltam in placito debiti.

[8] [*Marginated*] [Districtio]
Walterus Goythel[83] per attornatum queritur de Johanne Barat ⟨defalta: plegii ballivus, Robertus Orylly⟩ qui unam fecit defaltam in placito transgressionis.

[9] [*Marginated*] Misericordia vj d. Attachiamentum
Juliana uxor Johannis de Trefula in misericordia quia non prosequitur huttesium versus Robertum de Caran ⟨defalta⟩ quod Dec' de Tiehidy presentavit juste pro eo quod ipsam percussit: qui quidem Robertus modo non venit nec stetit paci, ideo attachietur.

[10] [*Marginated*] Inquiratur
Inquiratur si Rogerus de Roscrogen ⟨ licencia concordandi, vadiat xij d., clericis vj d.: arrestetur: finis xviij d., pleg' Dec'⟩ cepit et abduxit animalia Johannis Ran Dec' de Tehidy apud Roscrogen vi armata contra

[79] This and the following five entries are essoins.

[80] Undeclined.

[81] There is no further sign of this case: hence its numbering.

[82] *Gilbertus de Douron* written over an erasure.

[83] Above *Gossel,* deleted.

pacem domini regis ad dampnum suum C s. prout Dec' de Tehidy presentavit juste.

[11] [*Marginated*] Attachiamentum Misericordie vj d.
Dec' de Alwerton presentat quod David Bolyer levavit huttesium juste super Henricum Spyk ⟨defalta⟩ pro eo quod fregit attachiamentum suum de piscibus attachiatis, qui modo non venit. Et attachiatus est per plevinam Henrici Auny et Nicholai Auny qui in misericordia quia ipsum non habuerunt. Et nihilominus attachietur.

[12] [*Marginated*] Inquiratur
Dec' de Alwerton presentat quod Robertus Yedden levavit huttesium injuste super Rogerum de Tregughion. Et Robertus dicit quod Dec' male presentat quia dicit quod ipsum verberavit ad dampnum suum C s. Et predictus Rogerus dicit quod non est culpabilis et petit quod inquiratur.

[13] [*Marginated*] [Inquiratur] Attachiamentum
Dec' de Alwerton presentat quod Rogerus de Tregughion levavit huttesium juste super Robertum Yedden Ricardum filium[84] eius ⟨ apparens: Inquiratur si fuit huttesium⟩ et Johannem Randal ⟨apparens: apparens: si fuit huttesium⟩ pro eo quod insultum fecerunt ei. Et in[85] quidem Ricardus et Johannes modo non venerunt, ideo attachientur. Et in prosequendo dictum huttesium dicit quod[86] predictus Robertus apparens et alii qui non venerunt insultum ei fecerunt et asportaverunt blada sua precii C s. contra eius voluntatem ad dampnum suum C s. Et predictus Robertus dicit quod nullum fecit huttesium et petit quod inquiratur. Et ceteri attachientur.

[14] [*Marginated*] Misericordia iij d.
Willelmus filius Willelmi de Magur in misericordia quia non prosequitur versus Ricardum de Trefrynk et Andream de eadem in placito transgressionis.

[15] [*Marginated*] Misericordia iij d.
Willelmus filius Willelmi de Magur in misericordia quia non prosequitur versus Thomam de Nans et Laurencium subballivum in placito transgressionis.

[16] [*Marginated*] Inquiratur
Dec' de Bray presentat quod Henricus Bras levavit huttesium juste super Philippum de Rosconnen pro eo quod invenit eum concubentem uxorem suam. Et predictus Henricus dicit quod predictus Philippus vi et armis fregit ostium domus sue et domum suam contra eius voluntatem et uxorem suam[87] ad dampnum suum C s. Et predictus Philippus dicit quod Dec' male presentavit et quod non est culpabilis et petit quod inquiratur.

[17] [*Marginated*] [Inquiratur]
Dec' de Ludevon presentat quod Philippus Meneg' levavit huttesium juste super Rogerum Lywer ⟨licencia concordandi, nil vadiat: arrestetur⟩ pro eo quod ipsum percussit. Et in prosequendo dictum huttesium ponit dampna sua ad C libri. Et predictus Rogerus dicit quod Dec' male presentavit et quod non est culpabilis de transgressione predicta et petit quod inquiratur.

[18] [*Marginated*] [Districtio]
⟨dies amoris⟩ Reginaldus de Trembethou ⟨attornatus⟩ queritur de Odone Bosou ⟨misericordia defalta⟩ qui unam fecit defaltam in placito transgressionis.

[19] [*Marginated*] [Districtio]
David Dolen ⟨non prosequitur⟩ queritur de Thome Burwyk et Exon uxore eius ⟨misericordia defalta⟩ qui unam fecerunt defaltam in placito debiti.

[20] [*Marginated*] Summonitio
Johannes Gorvothou ⟨non prosequitur⟩ queritur de Reginaldo de Bosuelok et Edmundo[88] fratre[89] eius non summonito[90] in placito detentionis unius tripedis.

[21] [*Marginated*] Inquiratur
⟨pro defectu juratorum in billa⟩ Inquiratur si Rogerus de Coyswynyve intravit domum Nicholai le Taver[91] de Lananta apud Trevalscoys et asportavit clavem aule sue precii vj d. ad dampnum suum iij s.

[22] [*Marginated*] [Inquiratur] Misericordia iij d.
Inquiratur si Ricardus Goddag' asportavit turbas Nicholai de Haie ⟨misericordia pro falsa querela⟩ precii vj d. in . . .[92] ad dampnum suum ij s. Idem Ricardus

[84] Above *fratrem*, not deleted; *filium* is correct.

[85] For *unde*? [86] Written twice.

[87] Followed by missing word or words.

[88] Could read *Edwardo*.

[89] But see Court 2, which has *filium*.

[90] Recte *summonitis*.

[91] For *Taverner:* see Courts 2 and 3.

[92] Illegible.

in misericordia pro una defalta versus eundem Nicholaum in eodem placito.

[23] [*Marginated*] Inquisitio
Inquisitio inter Vivianum de Maen[93] querentem et Teobaldum de Eskels[94] et Ricardum Scrougy ⟨defalta⟩ in placito transgressionis de eo quod asportaverunt pisces suos et sagenam suam precii xl s. fregerunt ad dampnum suum C s. remanet.

[24] [*Marginated*] Misericordia iij d.
Johannes Chaillard in misericordia pro injusta detentione x s. versus Nicholaum Taverner de Mosehole ad dampnum suum vj d. q' P.[95]

[25] [*Marginated*] Attachiamentum Inquisitio Misericordia vj d.
Dec' de Ludevon presentavit alias quod Hugo de Lananta levavit huttesium juste super Willelmum filium Michaelis de Enys ⟨defalta⟩ pro eo quod ipsum vulneravit, qui non venit nec stetit paci. Et secutus fuit ad Dec' de Ridwey et inde ad Dec' de Killeryon qui illud dedixit. Et quia idem Dec' de Killerion non venit hic hodie ideo in misericordia.

[26] [*Marginated*] Inquisitio
Inquisitio inter Nicholam de Porkellom querentem et Johannem de Trevranek ⟨defalta: misericordia transgressio dampna j marca unde clericis ij s.: attachiamentum[96]⟩ in placito transgressionis huttesii quod Dec' de Werwill presentavit injuste, tamen querens dicit juste pro eo quod ipsam verberavit, remanet.

[27] [*Marginated*] Judicium Attachiamentum
Dec' de Ludevon presentavit alias quod Johanna serviens Viviani Poer ⟨attornatus⟩ levavit huttesium juste super Martinum Petyt ⟨defalta⟩ apparentem Johannem ⟨apparens: defalta: defalta⟩ et Walterum ⟨defalta: defalta⟩ fratres ipsius Martini et Laurencium de Treveilar ⟨defalta: apparens⟩ pro eo quod ceperunt et abduxerunt Johannam filiam Thome de Trevreythiel in custodia sua existentem. Et in prosequendo dictum huttesium predictus Vivianus se junxit servienti[97] sue et dicit quod predictus Martinus apparens et alii qui modo non venerunt vi armata dictam Johannam de custodia sua rapuerunt contra pacem ad dampnum suum C libri. Et predictus Martinus defendit vim et injuriam etc. et petit judicium si curia cognoscere velut istud placitum[98] eo quod predictus Vivianus narrat versus eum de raptu ubi curia non est de potestate donandi penam etc. Et nihilominus predicti Johannes Walterus et Laurencius qui non venerunt attachientur.

[28] [*Marginated*] Misericordia iij d.
Petrus de Trevanwyn in misericordia pro una defalta versus Edmundum[99] de Carhurta in placito conventionis.

[29] [*Marginated*] Districtio
Thomas de Trembaigh Bartha[100] queritur de Johanne Gentil de Nancotthan ⟨misericordia defalta: Inquiratur si intravit domum suam apud Trembaigh et abduxit unam vaccam in custodia existentem[101]⟩ qui duas fecit defaltas in placito transgressionis.

[30] [*Marginated*] Misericordia iij d.
Johannes Robert in misericordia pro una defalta et injusta detentione x s. versus Alanum de Treverthion.

[31] [*Marginated*] Misericordia iij d.
Johannes Simon de Trevugluth in misericordia pro una defalta et injusta detentione x s. versus predictum Alanum.

[32] [*Marginated*] Misericordia vj d. Arrestetur
Johannes Stouorn in misericordia pro licencia concordandi cum Galfrido serviente Johannis Michel in placito transgressionis huttesii quod Dec' de Conerton ⟨misericordia quia nihil fecit⟩ presentavit juste pro eo quod fecit ei rescussum de averiis. Et vadiat ei dimidium marce. Et arrestetur.

[33] [*Marginated*] Misericordia iij d. Arrestetur
Johannes Stouorn in misericordia pro licencia con-

93 Above *Bodilen,* not deleted; *Maen* is correct: see Courts 2 and 3.

94 *Maen,* deleted and incorrect (see Courts 2 and 3), written above.

95 Reminiscent of 'damages cleer' (*q.c.:* see above, 171), but who or what is *P*?

96 *unde clericis ij s.* written later after *attachiamentum:* see above, 171.

97 Above *uxori,* deleted. See above, 176, for this and for the strange interlineations earlier in the entry.

98 The sense of *si curia . . . placitum* is clear, but a word is probably missing.

99 Possibly *Edwardum;* the MS would support either.

100 Recte *Wartha.*

101 *misericordia defalta* interlineated first, between *Trembaigh* and *et.*

cordandi cum predicto Galfrido in placito transgressionis huttesii quod Dec' de Conerton presentavit juste pro eo quod ipsum percussit. Et nil vadiat. Et arrestetur.

[34] [*Marginated*] Inquisitio Misericordia ix d.
Inquisitio inter Gervasium de Bossvyen querentem et Willelmum Jocelyn ⟨misericordia transgressio dampna ij d.⟩ in placito transgressionis in blado remanet pro defectu Johannis Eskels ⟨iij d.⟩ Thome de eadem ⟨iij d.⟩ et Nicholai de Caseweladra ⟨iij d.⟩ qui in misericordia quia non venerunt inquisitioni.

[35] [*Marginated*] Inquisitio
Inquisitio inter Willelmum Jocelyn ⟨misericordia pro falsa querela⟩ querentem et Gervasium de Bosvyen in placito transgressionis in blado remanet.

[36] [*Marginated*] Districtio
⟨dies amoris⟩ Johannes Castalletz de Trevor queritur de Johanne Fabro de Treworian ⟨misericordia defalta⟩ qui unam fecit defaltam in placito debiti.

[37] [*Marginated*] Misericordia vj d. Arrestetur
Dec' de Werwill ⟨non venit⟩ in misericordia quia non duxit prisone David de Boskenal arrestatum pro huttesio super ipsum juste levato per Andream de Treloghdeves qui est non prosecutus. Et nihilominus preceptum est ei etc.

[38] [*Marginated*] Attachiamentum
Preceptum est attachiare Johannem Wynnon ⟨defalta⟩ ad respondendum tam presentamento Dec' de Ludevon quam Ranulpho Ammalwyn Dec' de Ludevon in placito transgressionis huttesii juste levati pro eo quod abstulit[102] ab eo Gildam uxorem David Parys arrestatam et ei liberatam.[103]

[39] [*Marginated*] Judicium
⟨remanet⟩ Ranulphus de Albo Monasterio per attornatum queritur de Rogero Chauntecler apparente per attornatum in placito debiti et unde queritur quod injuste detinet ei xvj s. quos solvisse debuit ad terminum qui preteriit ad dampnum suum x s. et inde ostendit factum ipsius Rogeri curie quod hoc testatur. Et predictus Rogerus dicit quod istud factum quod ostendit non est factum suum. Et sic remanet.

[40] [*Marginated*] Districtio
Petrus Kemyel per attornatum queritur de Petro Westva ⟨defalta⟩ qui viij fecit defaltas in placito conventionis.

[41] [*Marginated*] Attachiamentum
Attachiare Ricardum de Tregos ⟨defalta plegius ballivus de Kerrier⟩ ad respondendum tam presentamento Dec' de Ludevon quam Thome Leig' in placito transgressionis huttesii levati juste pro eo quod ipsum percussit.

[42] [*Marginated*] Misericordia vj d. Arrestetur
Decen' de Ludevon ⟨misericordia quia nil fecit⟩ in misericordia quia non duxit prisone Johannem Geffrey arrestatum pro transgressione facta Thome Penntyn unde dampna taxantur ad xij d. Et nihilominus preceptum est ei etc.

[43] [*Marginated*] Inquisitio
Inquisitio inter Dec' de Marchal et Robertum de Bosvaynon ⟨defalta⟩ Willelmum Poer ⟨defalta⟩ Hugonem de Trewoef ⟨defalta⟩ et Johannem de Penros ⟨defalta⟩ de huttesio super ipsos juste levato per Aliciam que fuit uxor Johannis Chauntecler que est non prosecuta.

[44] [*Marginated*] Misericordia vj d. Arrestetur
Dec' de Marchal ⟨misericordia quia nil fecit⟩ in misericordia quia non duxit prisone Vivianum Poer arrestatum pro transgressione facta Willelmo Basset unde dampna taxantur ad j marcam. Et nihilominus preceptum est ei etc.

[45] [*Marginated*] Misericordia vj d. Arrestetur
Dec' de Alwerton ⟨misericordia quia nil fecit⟩ in misericordia quia non duxit prisone Ricardum de Trethewy arrestatum pro transgressione facta Reimundo de Argensawth unde dampna taxantur ad xij d. Et nihilominus preceptum est ei.

[46] [*Marginated*] Finis xij d.
Johannes Geffrey fecit finem pro xij d. de transgressione facta Johanni Uda ad dampnum suum iiij s. per plevinam Dec' de Conerton.

[47] [*Marginated*] Attachiamentum
Preceptum est attachiare Andream Pauly de Bossankut ⟨defalta⟩ et Johannem Maiour de Sancta Beriana ⟨defalta⟩ ad respondendum tam presentamento Dec' de Kemyel quam Willelmo Hobbe ballivo com' de Pen' in placito transgressionis huttesii juste [levati] [104] pro eo quod ipsum percusserunt.

102 Making sense of a difficult reading.

103 Arguably the MS reads *libtata* or *libertata*.

104 Omitted.

[48] [*Marginated*] Misericordia iij d.
Thomas filius Bugel de Treyouran in misericordia pro transgressione facta Benedicto de Boswolvel ad dampnum suum xij d. sicut compertum est.

[49] [*Marginated*] Districtio
Thomas Cauntilbers queritur de Hugone de Boskeures ⟨defalta plegius ballivus⟩ qui iiij fecit defaltas in placito debiti.

[50] [*Marginated*] Inquisitio
Inquisitio inter Rogerum Yve querentem et Nicholaum Taverner in placito transgressionis huttesii quod Dec' de Conerton presentavit injuste. Et predictus Rogerus dicit quod Dec' male presentavit quia dicit quod fregit seruram super ostia domus sue positam apud Trevalscoys fregit[105] et domum suam ibidem intravit contra eius voluntatem.

[51] [*Marginated*] [Inquisitio]
Inquisitio inter Decen' de Rosmeren et Dianam uxorem Johannis Molendinarii ⟨defalta⟩ de huttesio super ipsam juste levato per Thomam servientem Martini de Talvargh qui est non prosecutus pro rescussu.

[52] [*Marginated*] Misericordia vj d.
Alicia de Trencrom in misericordia quia non prosequitur huttesium versus Willelmum Molendinarium de Draynek quod Dec' de Draynek presentavit injuste.

[53] [*Marginated*] Inquisitio
Inquisitio inter Johannem Sandon de Bosvargus querentem et Johannam que fuit uxor Nicholai Sterling in placito detentionis averiorum de iiij ovibus matricibus [et] ij hogastribus precii v s. remanet.

[54] [*Marginated*] Districtio
Robertus Ourilly per attornatum queritur de Thoma fratre vicarii Sancti Maderni ⟨defalta plegius ballivus⟩ qui unam fecit defaltam in placito debiti.

Respice intergo.[106]

Membrane 12d

[55] [*Marginated*] Attachiamentum
Preceptum est attachiare Thomam Clericum de Nampian ⟨defalta⟩ ad faciendum finem de eo quod vexavit Johannem Kynysiek juniorem et Robertum de Boswen in curia christianitatis etc. prout presentatum per xij juratores.

[56] [*Marginated*] Inquisitio
Inquisitio inter Benedictum de Moelvre juniorem ⟨non prosequitur⟩ querentem et Johannem de Maen in placito transgressionis de eo quod verberavit Johannam servientem ipsius Benedicti ad dampnum suum xl s.

[57] [*Marginated*] Misericordia vj d. Finis xij d.
Willelmus Lywere in misericordia quia non prosequitur huttesium versus Johannem Chaillard quod Dec' de Alwerton presentavit juste pro eo quod ipsum percussit. Johannes Chaillard fecit finem pro xij d. pro pace sibi habenda de dicto presentamento per plevinam Johannis Treguvan.

[58] [*Marginated*] Attachiamentum
Attachiare Willelmum Fauntiston ⟨defalta⟩ ad respondendum presentamento Dec' de Tehidy pro transgressione facta Johanni Freimount qui est non prosecutus.

[59] [*Marginated*] [Attachiamentum]
Attachiare Andream Pauly de Bossankut ⟨defalta⟩ ad faciendum finem pro transgressione facta Willelmo Hobbe prout presentatum per xij juratores.

[60] [*Marginated*] Districtio Misericordie iiij d.
Ricardus de Penpons per attornatum queritur de Rogero de Porkellom apparente Willelmo Waryn ⟨defalta⟩ et Johanna uxore eius ⟨defalta pleg' prius⟩ qui ix fecerunt defaltas in placito debiti. Et modo attachiati sunt per plevinam ballivi qui in misericordia quia ipsos non habuit.

[61] [*Marginated*] Inquisitio
Inquisitio inter Decen' de Conerton et Radulphum Bevile et Johannem Herefort de huttesio super ipsos juste levato per Ricardum Coyswyn qui est non prosecutus remanet, unde iidem Radulphus et Johannes dixerunt quod nullum fuit huttesium.

[62] [*Marginated*] [Inquisitio]
Inquisitio inter Thomam Bast querentem et Gregorium Curryer ⟨defalta: defalta⟩ qui fecit defaltam in placito transgressionis huttesii quod Dec' de Alwertun presentavit juste de attachiamento fracto de coreo.

105 This, or the previous *fregit*, is otiose.

106 Recte *in tergo*.

[63] [*Marginated*] [Inquisitio]
Inquisitio inter Ricardum Lanry de Tregemran ⟨misericordia pro falsa querela⟩[107] querentem et Johannem Gorogan in placito transgressionis de bateria remanet. Dampna C s.[108]

[64] [*Marginated*] Districtio Misericordie iiij d.
Martinus Capellanus de Laneskele per attornatum queritur de Nicholao[109] Webber de Chymedir ⟨defalta⟩ qui v fecit defaltas in placito debiti. Et attachiatus est per plevinam ballivi qui in misericordia quia ipsum non habuit.

[65] [*Marginated*] Remanet
Preceptum est Dec' de Marchal ⟨misericordia quia nil fecit⟩ ducere prisone Vivianum Poer et Radulphum filium eius arrestatos pro transgressione facta Willelmo Bassett unde dampna taxantur ad ij s.

[66] [*Marginated*] Attachiamentum
Attachiare Johannem Noble ⟨defalta⟩ ad respondendum tam presentamento Dec' de Draynek quam Reginaldo Bevile in placito transgressionis huttesii juste levati.

[67] [*Marginated*] Districtio
Oliverus de Carmynou queritur de Johanne Fegam ⟨defalta⟩ qui xxj fecit defaltas in placito debiti.

[68] [*Marginated*] Misericordia iij d.
Thomas de Trewoef in misericordia pro licencia concordandi cum Joc' de Tirebuer in placito debiti: nil vadiat.

Summa xj s. xj d. probatur.[110]

Court 2

HUNDREDUM TENTUM APUD RIDRUTH DIE SABATI PROXIMA POST FESTUM SANCTI PETRI AD VINCULA ANNO REGNI REGIS SUPRA [7 Aug. 1333]

[5][111] Hervicus Josian versus Ricardum Baker de Mousehole de placito debiti per Henricum Mares.

[56] Benedictus de Moelvre junior versus Johannem de Maen de placito transgressionis unde inquisitio per Stephanum de Dref.

[53] Johannes Sandon de Bosvargus versus Johannam que fuit uxor Nicholai Sterling de placito detentionis averiorum unde inquisitio per Ogerum de Caran.

[69] [*Marginated*] Attachiamentum Districtio
Dec' de Treiewal presentat quod Robertus Burwyk levavit huttesium juste super Martinum Mark ⟨defalta⟩ et Michaelem de Sandwich ⟨defalta⟩ pro eo quod insultum ei fecerunt cum cultellis extractis qui modo non venerun⁺ et non steterunt paci: et secuti fuerunt ad Dec' Sancti Michaelis ⟨Inquiratur si fecit huttesium⟩ qui non venit, ideo distringatur.

[70] [*Marginated*] Attachiamentum Misericordie vj d.
⟨Inquiratur si verberavit [ad][112] dampnum C s.: pleg'⟩ Dec' de Alwarton presentat quod Amabilla serviens Johannis Vivian levavit huttesium juste super Johannem Chaillard pro eo quod noctanter fregit ostium domus sue apud Mosehole qui modo non venit. Et attachiatus est per plevinam Thi[113] Hugon' de Trewoef et Roberti de Bosvaynon qui in misericordia quia ipsum non habuerunt. Et nihilominus attachietur.

[71] [*Marginated*] Inquiratur
Inquiratur si Joceus Chalouner ⟨misericordia transgressio dampna xij d.: arrestetur⟩ verberavit vulneravit Johannam Certys contra pacem domini regis ad dampnum suum C libri in placito transgressionis huttesii quod Dec' de Alwerton presentavit juste.

[72] [*Marginated*] Inquisitio Misericordie xij d.
Attachiamentum
⟨pro defectu juratorum⟩ Dec' de Bynnerton presentat quod Stephanus de Dref et Robertus de Bosvaynon ⟨attornatus⟩ levaverunt huttesium juste super David de Lynyen Johannem filium eius David Tyek Johannem Crom Johannem Bellor Nicholaum Dug Gregorium Mur Rogerum de Resik apparentes,[114] Johannem Julian Rogerum Bellor Benedictum Payun Madocum

[107] *falsa querela* (see Court 2) is obscured by *Lanry*, written over *Lanyn* deleted: *Tregemran* should read *Tregeuvran*, but there are only three minims.

[108] *Dampna C s.* added later.

[109] Preceded by *Willelmo*, deleted.

[110] *probatur* added later.

[111] This and the two following entries are essoins.

[112] Omitted.

[113] Probably a faulty genitive of *Thomas;* the scribe had a lot of trouble with this name.

[114] It looks as if the scribe first wrote *J* (for the beginning of *Johannem Julian*?) and then wrote *app'* over it, correctly.

de Bossuoloubian et Martinum de eadem pro eo quod ceperunt et asportaverunt vesturam trium acrarum siliginis apud Bosuorvet Wartha. Et in prosequendo dictum huttesium dicunt quod predictus David et[115] alii apparentes et alii qui non venerunt messuerunt et asportaverunt vesturam trium acrarum siliginis contra pacem ad dampnum eorundem C libri. Et predicti David Johannes filius eius David Johannes Johannes Nicholaus Gregorius et Rogerus dicunt quod Dec' male presentavit et quod de transgressione predicta non sunt culpabiles et petunt quod inquiratur. Et predicti Johannes Julian Rogerus Bellour Benedictus Payun Madocus et Martinus qui modo non venerunt attachiati sunt per plevinam David Tyek Lynyen[116] et Martini de Bossiwolou qui in misericordia quia ipsos non habuerunt. Et nihilominus attachientur.

[73] [*Marginated*] Inquiratur
Inquiratur si Dec' de Bynnerton concellavit huttesium quod Johannes serviens David de Lynyen levavit super Robertum de Bosvaynon et Edwardum fratrem eius.

[55] [*Marginated*] Attachiamentum
Attachiare Thomam Clericum de Nampian ⟨defalta⟩ ad faciendum finem.

[56] [*Marginated*] Misericordia iij d.
Benedictus de Moelvre junior in misericordia quia non prosequitur versus Johannem de Maen in placito transgressionis eo quod essoniator non expectavit[117] diem.

[58] [*Marginated*] Attachiamentum
Attachiare Willelmum Fauntiston ⟨defalta⟩ ad respondendum presentamento Dec' de Tehidy.

[47][118] [*Marginated*] [Attachiamentum]
Attachiare Andream Pauly ⟨defalta⟩ et Johannem Maiour ⟨defalta⟩ ad respondendum tam presentamento Dec' de Kemyel quam Willelmo Hobbe[119] ballivo in placito transgressionis huttesii juste levati.

[74] [*Marginated*] [Attachiamentum] Misericordie xij d.
⟨dies amoris⟩ Dec' de Bynnerton presentat quod Nicholaus de Caseweladrabian levavit huttesium juste super David filium Edwardi de Botalek et Goganum fratrem suum ⟨plegii essendi ad proximam [curiam][120] Jacobus Tregemynon et Dec'⟩ pro eo quod combusserunt jaones suos apud . . .[121] qui non venerunt. Et attachiati sunt per plevinam Willelmi Ils et Johannis Rous qui in misericordia quia ipsos non habuerunt.

[75] [*Marginated*] Attachiamentum Misericordie vj d.
⟨dies amoris: plegii supra⟩ Dec' de Bynnerton presentat quod Nicholaus de Casweladramur levavit huttesium juste super predictos David et Goganum pro eo quod combusserunt jaones suos qui modo non venerunt. Et attachiati sunt per plevinam Willelmi Ils et Johannis Rous qui in misericordia quia ipsos non habuerunt. Et nihilominus attachientur.

[60] [*Marginated*] Districtio Misericordie iiij d.
⟨Inquiratur si debet x s.⟩ Ricardus de Penpons queritur de Rogero de Porthkellom apparente et Willelmo Waryn ⟨misericordia defalta⟩ et Johanna uxore eius ⟨misericordia defalta⟩ qui xj fecerunt defaltas in placito debiti. Et predicti Willelmus et Johanna attachiati sunt per plevinam ballivi qui in misericordia quia ipsos non habuit.

[61] [*Marginated*] Inquisitio
Inquisitio inter Decen' de Conerton et Radulphum Beville et Johannem Herfort de huttesio super ipsos juste levato per Ricardum Coyswyn qui est non prosecutus.

[62] [*Marginated*] [Inquisitio]
Inquisitio inter Thomam Bast querentem et Gregorium Cyryer ⟨defalta⟩ qui fecit defaltam in placito transgressionis huttesii quod Dec' de Alwarton presentavit juste de attachiamento fracto remanet.

[63] [*Marginated*] Misericordia iij d.
Ricardus Lanry de Tregeuvran in misericordia pro falsa querela versus Johannem Gorogan in placito transgressionis sicut compertum est.

[115] Interlineated.

[116] For *de Lynyen* or *David de Lynyen*?

[117] A conjectural reading which makes sense: the essoin is the second entry in this court.

[118] This entry has been renumbered from '[59]' in accordance with Mr Hall's later notes, where he suggested clerical or procedural muddle as an explanation for the entry of [47] twice in Court 2, and the disappearance of case [59] after Court 1. The introduction is not affected by this revision. J.B.P.

[119] Preceded by *Basset*, deleted.

[120] Omitted.

[121] Gap in MS.

[64] [*Marginated*] Districtio
Martinus Capellanus de Lannskely[122] per attornatum queritur de Nicholao[123] Webber de Chymedir ⟨defalta⟩ qui vj fecit defaltas in placito debiti.

[65] [*Marginated*] Misericordia vj d. Arrestentur
Dec' de Marchal in misericordia quia non duxit prisone Vivianum Poer [et][124] Radulphum filium eius arrestatos pro transgressione facta Willelmo Basset unde dampna taxantur ad ij s. Et nihilominus preceptum est ei.

[66] [*Marginated*] Attachiamentum
Attachiare Johannem Noble ⟨defalta⟩ ad respondendum tam presentamento Dec' de Draynek quam Reginaldo Beville in placito transgressionis huttesii juste levati.

[67] [*Marginated*] Districtio
Oliverus de Carmynou queritur de Johanne Fecam ⟨defalta⟩ qui xxiij fecit defaltas in placito debiti.

[17] [*Marginated*] Misericordia vj d. Arrestetur
Rogerus Liwere in misericordia pro licencia concordandi cum Philippo Meneg' in placito transgressionis huttesii quod Dec' de Ludefon presentavit juste pro eo quod ipsum percussit. Nil vadiat ⟨finis vj d.⟩. Et arrestetur.

[18] [*Marginated*] Dies amoris Misericordia iij d.
Dies datus est Reginaldo de Trembethou querenti per attornatum et Odoni Bosou in placito transgressionis. Idem Odo in misericordia pro una defalta versus eundem Reginaldum in eodem placito.

[19] [*Marginated*] Misericordia iij d. Misericordia iij d.
David Dolen in misericordia quia non prosequitur versus Thomam Burwyk et Exon uxorem eius in placito debiti. Iidem Thomas et Exon in misericordia pro una defalta versus eundem David.

[20] [*Marginated*] Misericordia iij d.
Johannes Gorvothou in misericordia quia non prosequitur versus Reginaldum de Bosuolek et Edmundum filium[125] eius in placito detentionis unius tripedis.

[21] [*Marginated*] Inquisitio
Inquisitio inter Nicholaum le Taverner de Lananta querentem et Rogerum de Coyswynyve ⟨misericordia transgressio vj d. que clericis⟩ in placito transgressionis remanet pro defectu.

[22] [*Marginated*] Misericordia iij d.
Nicholaus de Haye in misericordia pro falsa querela versus Ricardum Goddag' in placito transgressionis sicut compertum est.

[23] [*Marginated*] Inquisitio
Inquisitio inter Vivianum de Maen ⟨non prosequitur⟩ querentem et Teobaldum Eskels et Ricardum Scrougy in placito transgressionis remanet ut supra.

[25] [*Marginated*] Attachiamentum
Attachiare Willelmum filium Michaelis de Enys ⟨defalta⟩ ad respondendum tam presentamento Dec' de Ludevon quam Hugoni de Lananta ⟨non prosequitur⟩ in placito transgressionis huttesii juste levati pro bateria.

[26] [*Marginated*] Misericordia vj d. Clericis Attachiamentum
Johannes de Trevranek in misericordia pro transgressione facta Nicholae de Porkellom ad dampnum suum j marca unde clericis ij s. in placito transgressionis huttesii quod Dec' de Werwill ⟨misericordia quia non venit⟩ presentavit sicut compertum est per inquisitionem captam per eius defaltam. Et nihilominus attachietur.

[27] [*Marginated*] Judicium Attachiamentum
Judicium inter Johannem servientem Viviani Poer cui idem Vivianus se junxit querentem per attornatum et Martinum Petyt qui fecit defaltam in placito transgressionis huttesii quod Dec' de Ludevon presentavit juste. Et nihilominus preceptum est attachiare Johannem[126] ⟨apparens⟩ et Walterum ⟨defalta⟩ fratres predicti Martini et Laurencium de Treveilar ⟨apparens⟩ ad respondendum presentamento Dec' de huttesio predicto.

[29] [*Marginated*] Inquiratur Misericordia iij d.
Inquiratur si Johannes Gentil de Nancoithan intravit domum Thomas[127] de Trembaigh Wartha apud

[122] Above *Chymedir*, deleted. *Lannskely* is correct: see Courts 1 and 3.

[123] Preceded by *Willelmo*, deleted.

[124] Omitted.

[125] But see Court 1, which has *fratre*.

[126] Above *Laurencium*, which is correctly deleted.

[127] Undeclined.

Trembaigh et unam vaccam in custodia ipsius Thomas[127] existentem cepit et abduxit ad dampnum suum xl s. Idem Thomas in misericordia pro una defalta versus eundem Thomas.[127]

[32 and 33] [*Marginated*] Misericordia vj d. Arrestetur
Dec' de Conerton in misericordia quia non duxit prisone Johannem Stouorn arrestatum pro licencia concordandi cum Galfrido serviente Johannis Michel unde vadiat ei dimidium marce. Et nihilominus preceptum est ei. Et preceptum est eidem Dec' ducere predictum Johannem arrestatum pro licencia concordandi cum predicto Galfrido.

[34] [*Marginated*] Misericordia ij d.
Willelmus Jocelyn in misericordia pro transgressione facta Gervasio de Bosvyen ad dampnum suum ij d.

[35][128] [*Marginated*] Misericordia ij d.
Willelmus Jocelyn in misericordia pro falsa querela versus predictum Gervasium in placito transgressionis sicut compertum est.

[36] [*Marginated*] Dies amoris Misericordia iij d.
Dies datus est Johanni Castellec de Trevor querenti et Johanni Fabro de Treworian in placito debiti. Idem Johannes Faber in misericordia pro una defalta versus eundem Johannem.

[37] [*Marginated*] Misericordia vj d. Arrestetur
Decen' de Werwill in misericordia quia non venit nec duxit prisone David de Boskenal arrestatum pro huttesio super ipsum juste levato per Andream de Treloghdyves qui est non prosecutus. Et nihilominus preceptum est ei etc.

[38] [*Marginated*] Attachiamentum
Attachiare Johannem Wynnon ⟨defalta⟩ ad respondendum tam presentamento Dec' de Ludevon quam Ranulpho de Ammalwyn Dec' de Ludvon in placito transgressionis huttesii juste levati pro eo quod abstulit ab eo Gildam uxorem David Parys arrestatam et ei liberatam.

[39] [*Marginated*] Judicium
Adhuc judicium inter Ranulphum de Albo Monasterio querentem per attornatum et Rogerum Chaunteclir apparentem per attornatum in placito debiti.

[40] [*Marginated*] Districtio
Petrus de Kemyel per attornatum queritur de Petro Westva ⟨essonium⟩[129] qui ix fecit defaltas in placito conventionis.

[41] [*Marginated*] Misericordia iij d. Attachiamentum
Ballivus de Kerrier in misericordia quia non habuit Ricardum de Tregos ⟨defalta⟩ ad respondendum tam presentamento Dec' de Ludevon quam Thome Leig' in placito transgressionis huttesii juste levati pro bateria. Et nihilominus attachietur.

[42] [*Marginated*] Remanet
Preceptum est Dec' de Ludefon ducere prisone Johannem Geffrey arrestatum pro transgressione facta Thome Penntyn.

[43] [*Marginated*] Inquisitio
Inquisitio inter Dec' de Marchal et Robertum Bosvaynon ⟨defalta⟩ Hugonem de Treweef Willelmum Poer ⟨defalta⟩ et Johannem de Penros[130] ⟨defalta⟩ de huttesio super ipsos [juste levato].[131]

[44] [*Marginated*] Misericordia iij d. Arrestetur
Dec' de Marchal in misericordia quia non duxit prisone Vivianum Poer arrestatum pro transgressione facta Willelmo Basset unde dampna taxantur ad j marcam. Et nihilominus preceptum est ei etc. sub pena etc.

[45] [*Marginated*] Misericordia vj d.
Dec' de Alwerton in misericordia quia non duxit prisone Ricardum de Trethewy ⟨defalta⟩ arrestatum pro transgressione facta Reimundo Argensawith unde dampna taxantur ad xij d.

[47] [*Marginated*] Attachiamentum
Attachiare Andream Pauly de Bossankut ⟨defalta⟩ et Johannem Meyour de Sancta Beriana ad responden-

[128] From here to the foot of the membrane [47] the marginalia present a small problem. The editorial work was done initially from photographs made before the MS underwent a thorough overhaul. Some minor loss shortly before or during overhaul means that the photographs preserve fuller readings than can now be seen. There is, because of the context, never any doubt what should be there, whether it is/was or not; square brackets and notes have therefore been discarded.

[129] MS clearly *e*, but in fact he defaulted and did not essoin himself in Court 3.

[130] Over a blunder at the beginning of the word.

[131] Omitted.

dum tam presentamento Dec' de Kemyel quam Willelmo Hobbe ballivo com' in placito transgressionis huttesii juste levati. Et nihilominus attachientur.

Respice in alio rotulo.

Membrane 13

[76] [*Marginated*] Districtio
Johanna de Bollegh ⟨attornatus⟩ queritur de Rogero le Rous de Treguvan ⟨essonium⟩ et Marina uxore eius ⟨essonium⟩ qui unam fecerunt defaltam in placito debiti.

[77] [*Marginated*] Districtio
⟨Inquiratur si asportavit meremium⟩ Nicholaus de Talgullou queritur de Marco de Sancto Maudutto ⟨misericordia defalta⟩ qui unam fecit defaltam in placito transgressionis.

[78] [*Marginated*] [Districtio]
Nicholaus de Talgollou queritur de Marco de Sancto Maudutto ⟨misericordia defalta: curia⟩ qui unam fecit defaltam in placito debiti.

[79] [*Marginated*] [Districtio]
⟨Inquiratur si disscoperuit domum⟩ Nicholaus de Talgollou queritur de Marco de Sancto Maudutto ⟨misericordia defalta⟩ qui unam fecit defaltam in placito transgressionis.

[80] [*Marginated*] [Districtio]
Laurencius Basset queritur de Roberto Cecely de Mousehole ⟨misericordia defalta: curia⟩ qui unam fecit defaltam in placito debiti.

[81] [*Marginated*] [Districtio]
Edmundus[132] de Carhurta queritur de Petro de Trevanwyn ⟨defalta plegius ballivus⟩ qui unam fecit defaltam in placito conventionis.

[82] [*Marginated*] [Districtio]
Robertus Faber de Mousehole queritur de Willelmo Tidy ⟨misericordia defalta: curia⟩ qui unam fecit defaltam in placito transgressionis.

[83] [*Marginated*] Inquiratur
Inquiratur si Johanna Whegen vulneravit et verberavit Johannam Martyn contra pacem ad dampnum suum C s. in placito transgressionis huttesii quod Dec' de Tehidy presentavit juste.

[1] [*Marginated*] Inquisitio
Inquisitio inter Alanum de Trethiles querentem et Laurencium subballivum in placito debiti ij s.

[3] [*Marginated*] Misericordia iij d.
Nicholaus Wychard in misericordia pro una defalta et injusta detentione iij hakis[133] versus Odonem de Bosfrancan.

[5] [*Marginated*] Remanet
Ricardus Bakere de Mousehole per attornatum queritur de Herveo Josian ⟨curia⟩ essoniato in placito transgressionis.

[6] [*Marginated*] Misericordia ij d.
Henricus Mares in misericordia pro una defalta versus Ricardum Bakere in placito debiti.

[7] [*Marginated*] Misericordia iij d.
Stephanus de Mertherderwa in misericordia pro una defalta versus Laurencium Basset in placito debiti.

[8] [*Marginated*] Districtio Misericordia iiij d.
Walterus Goichel per attornatum queritur de Johanne Barat ⟨defalta⟩ qui duas fecit defaltas in placito transgressionis. Et attachiatus est per plevinam ballivi et Roberti Ourily qui in misericordia quia ipsum non habuerunt.

[9] [*Marginated*] Attachiamentum
Attachiare Robertum de Caran ⟨defalta⟩ ad respondendum presentamento Dec' de Tehidy.

[10] [*Marginated*] Misericordia vj d. Clericis Finis xviij d.
Rogerus de Roscrogen in misericordia pro licencia concordandi cum Johanne Ran Dec' de Tehidy, vadiat ei xij d. unde clericis vj d., in placito transgressionis huttesii juste levati. Et arrestetur. Et postea fecit finem pro xviij d. per plevinam Dec'.

[11] [*Marginated*] Attachiamentum
Attachiare Henricum Spyk ⟨defalta⟩ ad respondendum tam presentamento Dec' de Alwerton quam David Bolier est[134] placito transgressionis huttesii juste levati.

[12] [*Marginated*] Inquisitio
Inquisitio inter Robertum Yedden querentem et Rogerum de Tregughion in placito transgressionis

[132] Possibly *Edwardus;* the MS would support either.

[133] Recte *hakarum*?

[134] Recte *in.*

huttesii quod Dec' de Alwerton presentavit injuste esse levatum.

[13] [*Marginated*] [Inquisitio]
Inquisitio inter Rogerum de Tregughion querentem et Robertum Yedden Ricardum filium[135] eius et Johannem Randal in placito transgressionis huttesii quod Dec' de Alwerton presentavit juste.

[16] [*Marginated*] [Inquisitio]
Inquisitio inter Henricum Bras ⟨non prosequitur⟩ querentem et Philippum de Rosconnen ⟨finis xij d.⟩ in placito transgressionis huttesii quod Dec' de Bray presentavit juste.

[49] [*Marginated*] Districtio Misericordie iiij d.
Thomas de Cauntilbers queritur de Hugone de Boskeurys ⟨defalta: pleg' prius⟩ qui v fecit defaltas in placito debiti. Et modo attachiatus est per plevinam ballivi qui in misericordia quia ipsum non habuit.

[50] [*Marginated*] Inquisitio Misericordie xxj d.
Inquisitio inter Rogerum Ive ⟨misericordia pro falso huttesio⟩ et Nicholaum Taverner de Lananta in placito transgressionis huttesii quod Dec' de Conerton presentavit injuste esse levatum remanet pro defectu Rogeri Chauntecler ⟨iij d.⟩ David de Boskenal ⟨iij d.⟩ Willelmi de Trefrancon ⟨iij d.⟩ Johannis de Risiou ⟨iij d.⟩ Henrici de Treglistyn ⟨iij d.⟩ Willelmi Roscasewal junioris ⟨iij d.⟩ et Golwani Chyengworth ⟨iij d.⟩ qui in misericordia quia non venerunt inquisitioni.

[51] [*Marginated*] Inquisitio
Inquisitio inter Dec' de Rosmoren et Dianam uxorem Johannis Molendinarii ⟨apparens⟩[136] de huttesio super ipsam juste levato remanet.

[53] [*Marginated*] [Inquisitio]
Inquisitio inter Johannem Sandon de Bosvargus essoniatum querentem et Johannam que fuit uxor Nicholai Sterling in placito detentionis averiorum.

[54] [*Marginated*] Districtio Misericordie iij d.
Robertus Orilly per attornatum queritur de Thoma fratre[137] vicarii Sancti Maderni ⟨defalta⟩ qui ij fecit defaltas in placito debiti. Et attachiatus est per plevinam ballivi qui in misericordia quia ipsum non habuit. Et nihilominus distringatur.

Summa xiiij s. ix d. probatur.[138]

Court 3

HUNDREDUM TENTUM APUD MOUSEHOLE DIE VENERIS PROXIMA POST FESTUM NATIVITATIS BEATE MARIE ANNO REGNI REGIS SUPRADICTO [10 Sept. 1333]

[*Marginated*] Essonia

[76] Rogerus Rous de Treguvan versus Johannam de Trethyn[139] de placito debiti per Rogerum Tregughion. Marina uxor eiusdem Rogeri Rous de eodem per Ogerum Caran.

[72] Robertus de Bosvannon versus David de Lynyen Johannem filium eius David[140] Tyek Johannem Crom Johannem Bellor Nicholaum Duk Gregorium Mur Rogerum de Resik de placito transgressionis huttesii unde inquisitio per Nicholaum Taverner.

[84] [*Marginated*] Districtio
Robertus Faber de Mousehole queritur de Willelmo Tony de Deverel ⟨misericordia defalta: licencia concordandi vadiat iij d.⟩ qui unam fecit defaltam in placito transgressionis.

[85] [*Marginated*] Summonitio Misericordia ij d.
Martinus Molendinarius de Treiewal queritur de Johanne Whyteby de Pensans ⟨curia⟩ non summonito in placito debiti. Et quia ballivus ipsum non summonuit ideo in misericordia.

[86] [*Marginated*] Attachiamentum
Martinus Molendinarius de Treiewal queritur de Johanne Whyteby de Pensans ⟨licencia concordandi⟩ et Mabilla uxore eius ⟨licencia concordandi vad'[141] xij d.⟩ non attachiatis in placito transgressionis.

[87] [*Marginated*] Inquiratur
Inquiratur si Ricardus de Trefrenk et Andreas de

135 Correct; written above *fratrem*, deleted.

136 Preceded by *defalta*, deleted.

137 Correct; preceded by *filio*, deleted.

138 *probatur* added later.

139 *Bollegh/Bolleygh* in Courts 2 and 3.

140 Correct; written above *Johannem*, deleted.

141 Could be *vadiat* or *vadiant*.

Trefrenk fecerunt rescussum Henrico filio Willelmi de Magour ⟨per custodem⟩ de vj milonibus bladii attachiatis per ipsum Henricum ad dampnum suum xl s.

[88] [*Marginated*] Misericordia vj d. Arrestetur Misericordia vj d.
Nicholaus Farwill in misericordia pro licencia concordandi cum Johanne Luce in placito transgressionis huttesii quod Dec' de Treiewal presentat juste pro rescussu facto: vadiat ei xviij d. Et arrestetur. Et quia Decen' recusavit venire ad presentandum ideo in misericordia.

[89] [*Marginated*] Inquiratur
Inquiratur si Johannes le Gof de Brueny ⟨licencia[142] concordandi nil vadiat⟩ verberavit Johannam Paucok de Lulyn querentem per attornatum et dilaceravit pannos suos ad dampnum suum lx s.

[90] [*Marginated*] [Inquiratur]
Inquiratur si Johannes Faber de Brueny ⟨licencia concordandi⟩ injuste detinet vj s. viij d. Johanni de Trefruthken querenti per attornatum quos solvisse debuit ad terminum qui preteriit ad dampnum suum v s.

[91] [*Marginated*] [Inquiratur]
Inquiratur si Johannes Pydr' ⟨licencia concordandi vadiat iij d.⟩ deterioravit blada Roberti Fabri de Mousehole noctanter ad dampnum suum xl s.

[92] [*Marginated*] Summonitio
Laurencius Basset per attornatum queritur de Paulo de Mertherderwa ⟨curia⟩ non summonito in placito debiti.

[93] [*Marginated*] Inquiratur
David de Penwolva ⟨non prosequitur⟩ queritur de Johanne Nobelot de placito transgressionis. Et unde queritur quod ubi dedisset ei unam querelam versus Henricum Yedden de placito conventionis idem Johannes preposuit Johannam uxorem eius in dicta querela ad dampnum suum xl d. Et predictus Johannes dicit quod non est culpabilis et petit quod inquiratur.

[94] [*Marginated*] Districtio
Johannes de Lyme per attornatum queritur de Ranulpho de Bosvaynon ⟨misericordia detinet iiij s. iiij d.⟩ qui unam fecit defaltam in placito debiti.

[95] [*Marginated*] Inquiratur
Inquiratur si Salmista[143] que fuit uxor Thome Aude deterioravit blada Rogeri Luky ⟨non prosequitur⟩ apud Mosehole ad dampnum suum x s.

[96] [*Marginated*] [Inquiratur]
Inquiratur si Gervasius filius Sandon de Skewyek[144] fregit conventionem Henrici Capellani de Treverian de hoc quod serviet ei per certum tempus contra quam conventionem adivit ad dampnum suum xl s.

[97] [*Marginated*] Districtio
Laurencius Basset per attornatum queritur de Nicholao Taillour de Lananta ⟨misericordia defalta: curia⟩ qui unam fecit defaltam in placito debiti.

[98] [*Marginated*] [Districtio]
Benedictus de Botissava et Johannes Brice per attornatum queruntur de David de Boskenal ⟨defalta plegius ballivus⟩ qui unam fecit defaltam in placito debiti.

[99] [*Marginated*] [Districtio]
⟨dies amoris⟩ Benedictus de Moelvre junior queritur de Johanne de Maon ⟨misericordia defalta⟩ qui unam fecit defaltam in placito transgressionis.[145]

[100] [*Marginated*] Misericordia iij d.
Henricus Yedden in misericordia pro fatua querela versus Gregorium de Bossankuth in placito transgressionis.

[101] [*Marginated*] Misericordia iij d.
Drogo de Rosplethe in misericordia pro injusta detentione v s. vj d. versus Vivianum de Bodilen in placito debiti.

[102] [*Marginated*] Inquiratur Misericordia vj d.
⟨remanet⟩ Dec' de Alwerton presentat quod Ricardus Venour levavit huttesium injuste super Benedictum Nogth ⟨essonium⟩ Johannam uxorem eius Nicholaum le Taverner de Mosehole et Margeriam uxorem eius. Et predictus Ricardus dicit quod Dec' male presentavit quia dicit quod ipsum verberaverunt et ipsum de domo sua apud Porthenys traxerunt contra pacem ad dampnum suum C li. Et predicti Benedictus Johanna

[142] Preceded by *defalta*, very faint and probably erased.

[143] A guess: *Sal* is followed by four minims, of which the last is *i*.

[144] Above *Steynek*, deleted.

[145] Preceded by *debiti*, deleted.

Nicholaus et Margeria dicunt quod non sunt culpabiles et petunt quod inquiratur. Et quia Decen' recusavit venire ad presentandum ideo in misericordia.

[103] [*Marginated*] Attachiamentum Misericordie vj d.
⟨Inquiratur si Dec' bene presentavit: plegii de expectare inquisitionem Ogerus Carran W. Magur⟩ Dec' de Conerton presentat quod Johannes de Rosculian ballivus levavit huttesium juste super Alanum de Tredygembr'[146] pro eo quod fecit ei rescussum, qui modo non venit. Et attachiatus est per plevinam Michaelis Roget et Johannis de Tredygembr' qui in misericordia quia ipsum non habuerunt.

[104] [*Marginated*] Misericordia vj d. Arrestetur Willelmus de Magur [in misericordia][147] quia falso dedixit presentamentum Dec' de Tyhidy et[148] rescussu facto Johanni de Rosculian ballivo hundredi de uno jumento capto ⟨remanet⟩ per ipsum ballivum sicut compertum est per inquisitionem. Et arrestetur.

[105] [*Marginated*] Attachiamentum
Dec' de Tresuif presentat quod Johannes de Risiou levavit huttesium juste super Aliciam de Tremythek ⟨defalta plegius ballivus: dic' quod attach' blada⟩ pro eo quod fregit attachiamentum bladorum attachiatorum in feodo suo attach',[149] que modo non venit ideo attachietur.

[106] [*Marginated*] [Attachiamentum]
Dec' de Marchal presentat quod Vivianus Poer et ballivus com' de Pen' levaverunt huttesium juste super David de Boskenal ⟨defalta⟩ pro eo quod fecerunt[150] eis rescussum de duabus vaccis qui modo non venit nec stetit paci ideo attachietur.

[76] [*Marginated*] Districtio
⟨dies amoris⟩ Johanna de Bolleygh per attornatum queritur de Rogero le Rous de Treguvan ⟨misericordia defalta⟩ et Marina uxore eius ⟨ misericordia defalta⟩ essoniatis post unam defaltam in placito debiti.

[77] [*Marginated*] Inquiratur
Inquiratur si Marcus de Sancto Maudutto cepit et asportavit meremium Nicholai de Talgullou de domo sua apud Marcasion ad dampnum suum C s.

[79] [*Marginated*] [Inquiratur]
Inquiratur si Marcus de Sancto Maudutto discooperuit domum Nicholai de Talgullou et asportavit meremium ad dampnum suum C s.

[77, 78 and 79] [*Marginated*] Misericordia vj d.
Idem Marcus in misericordia pro iij defaltis versus eundem Nicholaum in eisdem querelis.

[80] [*Marginated*] Misericordia ij d.
Robertus Cecily de Mousehole in misericordia pro una defalta versus Laurencium Basset in placito debiti.

[81] [*Marginated*] Districtio Misericordie iij d.
Edmundus[151] de Carhurta queritur de Petro de Trevenwyn ⟨defalta plegius ballivus⟩ qui duas fecit defaltas in placito conventionis. Et modo attachiatus est per plevinam ballivi qui in misericordia quia ipsum non habuit.

[82] [*Marginated*] Misericordia iij d.
Willelmus Tidy in misericordia pro una defalta versus Robertum Smith de Mousehole in placito transgressionis.

[83] [*Marginated*] Inquisitio
Inquisitio inter Johannam Martyn querentem et Johannam Whegen in placito transgressionis huttesii quod Dec' de Tehidy presentavit juste remanet.

[1] [*Marginated*] [Inquisitio]
Inquisitio inter Alanum de Trethiles querentem ⟨essonium: tamen pars defendens petit judicium de essonio etc.⟩ et Laurencium subballivum in placito debiti ij s.

[8] [*Marginated*] Districtio
Walterus Gotthel ⟨non prosequitur⟩ per attornatum queritur de Johanne Barat ⟨misericordia defalta⟩ qui iij fecit defaltas in placito transgressionis.

[9] [*Marginated*] Attachiamentum
Attachiare Robertum de Caran ⟨defalta⟩ ad respondendum presentamento Decen' de Tihidy.

[11] [*Marginated*] [Attachiamentum]
Attachiare Henricum Spik ⟨defalta: mortuus⟩ ad

[146] *defalta* interlined and deleted.

[147] Omitted.

[148] Recte *de*.

[149] Surely otiose?

[150] Recte *fecit*. No other verb is extended to indicate singular or plural: but only *fecit eis* and the other extensions as printed here will make sense.

[151] Possibly *Edwardus;* the MS would support either.

respondendum tam presentamento Dec' de Alwerton quam David Boliere in placito transgressionis huttesii juste levati.

[58] [*Marginated*] [Attachiamentum]
Attachiare Willelmum Fauntiston ⟨defalta⟩ ad respondendum presentamento Dec' de Tehidy.

[12] [*Marginated*] Inquisitio
Inquisitio inter Robertum Yedden ⟨non prosequitur⟩ querentem et Rogerum de Tregughion in placito transgressionis huttesii quod Dec' de Alwertun presentavit injuste.

[13] [*Marginated*] [Inquisitio]
Inquisitio inter Rogerum de Tregughion ⟨non prosequitur⟩ querentem et Robertum Yedden Ricardum filium eius et Johannem Randal in placito transgressionis huttesii quod Dec' de Alwerton presentavit injuste.[152]

[16] [*Marginated*] Misericordia vj d. Finis xij d.
Henricus Bras in misericordia quia non prosequitur huttesium versus Philippum de Rosconnen quod Dec' de Bray presentavit juste. Philippus de Rosconnen fecit finem de predicto attachiamento super ipsum continuato pro xij d.

[49] [*Marginated*] Districtio Misericordie iij d.
Thomas de Cauntilbers ⟨non prosequitur⟩ queritur de Hugone de Boskeures ⟨misericordia defalta⟩ qui vj fecit defaltas in placito debiti. Et modo attachiatus est per plevinam ballivi qui in misericordia quia ipsum non habuit.

[50] [*Marginated*] Misericordia vj d.
Rogerus Yve in misericordia pro falso huttesio versus Nicholaum Taverner de Lananta quod Dec' de Conerton[153] presentavit injuste sicut compertum est.

[51] [*Marginated*] Inquisitio
Inquisitio inter Decen' de Rosmoren et Dianam uxorem Johannis Molendinarii de huttesio super ipsam juste levato.

[53] [*Marginated*] [Inquisitio]
Inquisitio inter Johannem[154] Sandon de Bosvargus querentem et Johannam que fuit uxor Nicholai Sterling ⟨misericordia detentio iiij ovium matricum et ij hogastriorum precii ij s. dampna vj d.⟩ apparentem per attornatum in placito detentionis averiorum.

[54] [*Marginated*] Districtio Misericordie iij d.
⟨Inquiratur si debet iij s. dampna iij s.⟩ Robertus Ourelly per attornatum queritur de Thoma fratre vicarii Sancti Maderni ⟨misericordia defalta⟩ qui iij fecit defaltas in placito debiti. Et modo attachiatus est per plevinam ballivi qui in misericordia quia ipsum non habuit.

[69] [*Marginated*] Attachiamentum Inquiratur
Attachiare Martinum Mark ⟨defalta⟩ et Michaelem de Sandwich ⟨defalta⟩ ad respondendum tam presentamento Dec' de Treiewal quam Roberto Burwyk in placito transgressionis huttesii juste levati, et non steterunt paci et secuti fuerunt ad Decen' Sancti[155] Michaelis qui illud dedicit ideo inquiratur.

[70] [*Marginated*] [Inquiratur]
Inquiratur si Johannes Chaillard verberavit Amabillam servientem Johannis Vivien contra pacem domini regis ad dampnum suum C s. prout Dec' de Alwerton presentavit juste. Dec' on' de corpore defend'.[156]

[71] [*Marginated*] Misericordia vj d. Arrestetur
Joceus Chalouner in misericordia pro transgressione facta Johanne Certis ad dampnum suum xij d. prout Dec' de Alwerton presentavit sicut compertum est per inquisitionem. Et arrestetur.

[72] [*Marginated*] Inquisitio
Inquisitio inter Stephanum de Dreef et Robertum de Bosvaynon querentes per attornatum et David de Lynyen Johannem filium eius David Tyek Johannem Crom Johannem Bellour Nicholaum Duk Gregorium Mur Rogerum de Resik Johannem Julian Rogerum Bellor Benedictum Payun Madocum de Bosiwoloubian et Martinum de eadem in placito transgressionis huttesii quod Dec' de Bynnerton presentavit juste remanet.

[107] [*Marginated*] Districtio
Benedictus de Botissavo et Johannes Brice per attornatum ⟨essonium⟩ queruntur de Johanne Sandon de Treviscan ⟨misericordia defalta⟩ qui unam fecit defaltam in placito debiti.

[152] Surely recte *juste*, as in Courts 1 and 2.

[153] Preceded by *Lana*, deleted.

[154] Preceded by *Decen'*, deleted.

[155] Preceded by *de*, deleted.

[156] *oneratur de corpore defendendo*?

[73] [*Marginated*] Inquiratur
Inquiratur si Dec' de Bynnerton concellavit huttesium quod Johannes serviens David de Lynyen levavit super Robertum de Bossvaynon et Edwardum fratrem eius.

[55] [*Marginated*] Attachiamentum
Attachiare Thomam Clericum de Nanpian ad faciendum finem.

[47][157] [*Marginated*] [Attachiamentum]
Attachiare Andream Pauly ⟨defalta⟩ et Johannem Maiorir ⟨defalta⟩ ad respondendum tam presentamento Dec' de Kemyel quam Willelmo Hobbe ballivo in placito transgressionis huttesii juste levati.

[74] [*Marginated*] Dies Amoris
Dies datus est Nicholao Casweladrabian querenti et David filio Edwardi de Botalek ⟨licencia concordandi⟩ et Gogano fratri suo ⟨licencia concordandi nil vad' arr'[158]⟩ in placito transgressionis huttesii quod Dec' de Bynnerton presentavit juste pro eo quod combusserunt jamnes[159] suos.

[75] [*Marginated*] [Dies Amoris]
Dies datus est Nicholao de Caseweladramur querenti et predictis David ⟨licencia concordandi⟩ et Gogano ⟨licencia concordandi nil vad' arr'[160]⟩ in placito transgressionis huttesii quod Dec' de Bynnerton presentavit juste pro eo quod combusserunt jamnes[161] suos.

Respice in tergo.

Membrane 13d

[60] [*Marginated*] Inquiratur
Inquiratur si Rogerus de Porthkellom ⟨essonium⟩ Willelmus Waryn et Johanna uxor eius que per attornatum est injuste detinent x s. Ricardo de Penpons querenti per attornatum quos solvisse debuissent ad terminum diu preteritum ad dampnum suum v s.

[61] [*Marginated*] [Inquisitio][162]
⟨Willelmus Magur Vivianus Bodilen Johannes Risiou⟩ Inquisitio inter Dec' de Conerton et Radulphum Beville et Johannem Herefort de huttesio super ipsos juste levato remanet.

[62] [*Marginated*] [Inquisitio]
Inquisitio inter Thomam Bast querentem et Gregorium Curyer qui fecit defaltam in placito transgressionis huttesii quod Dec' de Alwerton presentavit juste.

[64] [*Marginated*] Districtio
Martinus Capellanus de Lannskely per attornatum queritur de Nicholao Webber ⟨defalta⟩ de Chymeder qui vj fecit defaltas in placito debiti.

[65] [*Marginated*] Misericordia iij d. Arrestentur
Decen' de Marchal in misericordia quia non duxit prisone Vivianum Poer et Radulphum filium eius arrestatos pro transgressione facta Willelmo Basset unde dampna taxantur ad j marcam. Et nihilominus preceptum est ei etc.

[66] [*Marginated*] Attachiamentum
Attachiare Johannem Noble ⟨defalta⟩ ad respondendum tam presentamento Decen' de Draynek quam Reginaldo Bevile de Draynek in placito transgressionis huttesii juste levati.

[67] [*Marginated*] Districtio
Oliverus de Carmynou queritur de Johanne Fegam ⟨defalta⟩ qui xxiiij fecit defaltas in placito debiti.

[17] [*Marginated*] Finis vj d.
Rogerus Liwere fecit finem de attachiamento super ipsum diu continuato pro vj d.

[18] [*Marginated*] Dies Amoris
Adhuc dies datus est Reginaldo de Trembethou querenti per attornatum et Odoni Bosou ⟨licencia concordandi vadiat xij d.⟩ in placito transgressionis.

[21] [*Marginated*] Misericordia iij d. Clericis
Rogerus de Coyswynyve in misericordia pro transgressione facta Nicholao le Taverner ad dampnum suum vj d. que clericis sicut compertum est per inquisitionem.

[23] [*Marginated*] Misericordia iij d.
Vivianus de Maen in misericordia quia non prosequi-

[157] Renumbered: see above, n.118.

[158] *vad' arr'* could be *vadiat arrestetur,* but is more probably *vadiant arrestentur,* covering David and Gogan.

[159] Here, and in the next case, this form – not found in the *Revised Medieval Latin Word-List,* ed. R. E. Latham (London, 1965) – is used for 'jampnum': cf. Court 2, where *jaones* is the form used.

[160] See above, n.158.

[161] See above, n.159.

[162] The marginal *Inquiratur* of [60] has a straight line depending from it and covering [61, 62], which should, however, have marginal *Inquisitio:* hence [*Inquisitio*] at the beginning of [61, 62].

tur versus Teobaldum de Eskels et Ricardum Scrougy in placito transgressionis.

[25] [*Marginated*] Misericordia vj d. Attachiamentum
Hugo de Lananta in misericordia quia non prosequitur huttesium versus Willelmum filium Michaelis de Enys quod Dec' de Ludefon presentavit juste pro eo quod ipsum percussit. Preceptum est attachiare Willelmum filium Michaelis de Enys ⟨defalta⟩ ad respondendum presentamento dicti Dec' de huttesio predicto.

[26] [*Marginated*] Misericordia vj d. Arrestetur
Decen' de Werwill in misericordia quia non duxit prisone Johannem de Trevanrek arrestatum pro transgressione facta contra pacem Nicholae de Porkellom ad dampnum suum j marca unde clericis ij s.

[27] [*Marginated*] Judicium Attachiamentum
Adhuc judicium inter Johannam servientem Viviani Poer cui idem Vivianus se junxit querentem per attornatum et Martinum le Petit qui alias fecit defaltam Johannem fratrem eiusdem Martini et Laurencium de Treveilar apparentes ad hunc diem, unde judicium in placito transgressionis huttesii quod Dec' de Ludefon presentavit juste. Et nihilominus preceptum est attachiare Walterum fratrem predicti Martini ad respondendum de eodem.

[29] [*Marginated*] Inquisitio
Inquisitio inter Thomas[163] de Trembaighwartha querentem et Johannem Gentil de Nancoithan ⟨defalta⟩ in placito transgressionis remanet.

[32 and 33] [*Marginated*] Arrestetur
Preceptum est Dec' de Conerton ducere prisone Johannem Stouorn arrestatum pro licencia concordandi cum Galfrido serviente Johannis Michel unde vadiavit dimidium marce.

[36] [*Marginated*] Misericordia iij d.
Johannes Castellek de Trevor in misericordia quia non prosequitur versus Johannem Fabrum de Treworian in placito debiti.

[37] [*Marginated*] Arrestetur
Preceptum est Dec' de Werwill ducere prisone David de Boskenal ⟨defalta⟩ arrestatum pro huttesio super ipsum juste levato per Andream Treloghdyves qui est non prosecutus.

[38] [*Marginated*] Attachiamentum
Attachiare Johannem Wynnon ⟨defalta⟩ ad respondendum tam presentamento Dec' de Ludevon quam Ranulpho de Ammalwyn Dec' de Ludefon in placito transgressionis huttesii juste levati.

[39] [*Marginated*] Judicium
Adhuc judicium inter Ranulphum de Albo Monasterio querentem per attornatum et Rogerum Chauntecler apparentem per attornatum in placito debiti remanet.

[40] [*Marginated*] Districtio
Petrus de Kemyel per attornatum queritur de Petro Westva ⟨defalta⟩ qui x fecit defaltas in placito conventionis.

[41] [*Marginated*] Attachiamentum
Attachiare Ricardum de Tregos ⟨defalta⟩ ad respondendum tam presentamento Dec' de Ludefon quam Thome Leig' in placito transgressionis huttesii juste levati.

[42] [*Marginated*] Finis vj d.
Johannes Geffrey fecit finem de attachiamento super ipsum continuato pro vj d.

[44] [*Marginated*] Remanet
Preceptum est Dec' de Marchal ducere prisone Vivianum Poer arrestatum pro transgressione facta Willelmo Basset unde dampna taxantur ad ij s.

[43] [*Marginated*] Inquisitio
Inquisitio inter Dec' de Marchal et Robertum de Bosvaynon Hugonem de Trewoef Willelmum Poer et Johannem de Penros de huttesio super ipsos juste levato.

[45] [*Marginated*] Misericordia vj d. Arrestetur
Dec' de Alwerton in misericordia quia non duxit prisone Ricardum de Trethewy arrestatum pro transgressione facta Reymundo Argensawith unde dampna taxantur ad xij d.

Summa x s. x d. probatur.[164]

[*At foot of membrane*] [165] Summa istorum ij rotulorum xxxvij s. vj d. unde Johannes Arundel percipit duas partes. Et rem' domino regi xij s. vj d.

[163] Undeclined.

[164] *probatur* added later.

[165] Much faded but clear under the lamp.

A medieval robber baron Sir John Molyns of Stoke Poges, Buckinghamshire

edited by

NATALIE FRYDE

INTRODUCTION

The name of Sir John Molyns has not passed into the history books except the works of a few antiquarians and genealogists of the county where he resided, Buckinghamshire. To them he has a double importance. Firstly, he was the holder, for a time, of the beautiful and wealthy manor of Stoke Poges, whose churchyard provided the setting for the poet Thomas Gray's *Elegy*. Secondly, he was of considerable genealogical importance as the ancestor of one branch of the Hungerford family into which the last Molyns heiress, Eleanor, married in 1441. It was through her that this branch of the Hungerfords bore the title of Lord Moleyns. Eleanor's husband earned fame as the disseisor of Margaret Paston, whose troubles with Lord Moleyns are woefully reported in the Paston Letters. It is because of this later intermarriage with the Hungerfords that a splendid source for John Molyns' landed wealth, and that of his descendants, exists in the large and magnificent cartulary of the Hungerford family preserved in the Somerset County Record Office. Through the Hungerford connection Molyns was also an ancestor of one branch of the Hastings family, who ultimately succeeded to the manor of Stoke Poges where they erected a fine new house.

No Molyns ancestor of this illustrious line can be securely traced further back than John Molyns' father, who bore the unusual christian name of Vincent. Vincent Molyns was member of parliament for Hampshire in 1301, but otherwise remains obscure.[1] I have been unable to discover the patronymic of Molyns' mother, Isabella. Dugdale believed that the family stemmed from one Robert Molyns who had been disinherited and banished from England by Henry I, and that it hailed ultimately from a town in Bourbonnais.[2] John was apparently the younger son of Vincent Molyns. Not surprisingly, because of this, his earliest property holdings seem to have come through his marriage. His wife, Egidia, or to modernise her name, Gill, was better connected and enjoyed better prospects of inheritance than her husband. She was the only daughter, by his first marriage, of John Mauduit of Little Somerford.[3] Mauduit had been a follower of Thomas, earl of Lancaster, in the troubled times of Edward II's reign, and the family must have known difficult times when the Despenser régime fined John Mauduit 1000 marks for his adherence to Lancaster in the earl's rebellion in 1322. However, he made his peace with the régime and was employed by the Despensers later in the reign. He lived to see his son-in-law's spectacular rise to influence and wealth and his disgrace in 1340, for he survived until 1347. Gill's mother was Margaret, daughter of Robert Poges of Stoke Poges and a descendant of a Frenchman, Imbert Poges, steward of the household to King Henry III between 1257 and 1262. This well-connected wife was indubitably of inestimable value to Molyns' early career, but the obvious factor which turned him into one of the wealthiest men in Buckinghamshire and one of the most important men in England later on was his own forceful personality and great ability.

His early career belongs to the reign of Edward II. The few glimpses which we have of him suggest an ambivalent line of political conduct, a necessary prerequisite for survival in the terrible days of the civil war followed by the Despenser régime. One of our problems is that confusion can arise between him and two other men named John Molyns, both also quite prominent. One of these is more easily distinguishable as he seems always to be called 'John Molyns of Fareham'. He died in 1346.[4] The other, slightly more problematic since he sometimes appears without an additional territorial name, was the John Molyns who acted as custodian of Odiham castle for the Despensers. The year before, the keeper was named as John of 'Aulton'. This suggests that the custodian was the John Molyns of 'Aulton' who executed a recognisance in 1322. As our John Molyns, among his many and ever-changing landholdings, never held the manor of Alton in Hampshire, he was probably not the custodian of Odiham castle.[5] However problematic their origins, by the fourteenth century the Molynses were clearly a far-flung clan and may have been quite closely related. A James Molyns appears as an attorney for our John.[6] A Ralph Molyns

[1] *DNB*, XXXVIII, 127–8.

[2] W. Dugdale, *The Baronage of England* (London, 1675), II, 145.

[3] G.E.C., VIII, 551–3.

[4] *CIPM*, VIII, no. 667 (pp.492–3).

[5] *CMR 1326–7*, no. 2240 (John Molyns, keeper of Odiham, 1326); *CCR 1323–7*, 289 (John of 'Aulton', keeper of Odiham, 1325); ibid. *1318–23*, 677 (John Molyns of 'Aulton', 1322).

[6] *CPR 1324–7*, 171.

appears as a squire of the household in the 1330s at the time when Molyns was most prominent at court.[7]

On 10 September 1325 it was apparently the John Molyns who concerns us who was given protection to go abroad with the young prince, Edward, on the fateful journey to France which was to enable his mother, Queen Isabella, to use him as a pawn, to turn her leadership of a peace mission into exile and lead an invasion of her husband's realm.[8] Molyns seems, however, either never to have actually gone or to have returned very quickly because, in the following month, he acted as royal messenger on an important mission. He took a letter from the chancellor to the bishop of Winchester and the earl of Richmond empowering them to prorogue a treaty with the duke of Brittany.[9] Molyns does not appear again under the Despenser régime, but the queen's invasion and the revolution of 1326 gave him the chance to become an important landowner through acquiring Stoke Poges manor. This he accomplished under terrible circumstances which will be discussed later. Sometime during the régime of Mortimer and Isabella he found an important patron and protector in the person of William Montague the younger, the future earl of Salisbury. He repeatedly appears at Montague's side in the dangerous days of the régime. In March 1329 he was summarily and mysteriously summoned to the king 'in person immediately on sight' of the royal letter.[10] In June he was one of the mainpernors to produce in court a London merchant called Benedict Forsham.[11] Molyns was keeping dangerous company because Forsham fell foul of the régime for his association with Eleanor Zouche. She was one of its least favoured subjects. Formerly married to the younger Despenser, after his execution she eloped and married William Zouche without either permission or royal licence. She was also charged with stealing some jewels from the Tower. However, Forsham was later released and no proceedings were taken against Molyns. In September Molyns went abroad with his patron, Montague, probably on the mission which Montague used to transmit a highly confidential message from the young King Edward to the pope. He made an arrangement which would enable the young king to communicate with the Holy See without his letters and wishes being confused with those of his mother and Roger Mortimer who were effectively ruling the country. All letters reflecting the king's personal will would have written on them, in the king's own hand, the words 'pater sancte'.[12] The king was beginning to break away from his mother's control and Montague was his chief aide in this. Molyns' next appearance in history is as a leading follower of Montague at the coup d'état at Nottingham castle on 19 October 1330.

Participation in this risky venture began the most successful period of Molyns' life. Its success hung in the balance until the last moment. The young king and Montague, together with a number of their friends, were questioned one by one by Mortimer and his associates, who suspected a plot. It was Montague's aplomb and capacity to lie which saved the day and allayed suspicion. When the party made their way into the castle secretly by an underground passage, Molyns was with the king.[13] His part in this dangerous adventure earned him a place at the king's side and, in 1337, an earldom for his master.

An account of his subsequent career from 1330 to 1340, as it can be pieced together, yields a portrait of a respected and loyal royal servant. Concurrently, from other sources, one can see that Molyns was pursuing a life of banditry, murder and disinheritance, often between missions on the king's behalf. His career as a royal servant began with his appointment as a household squire which, for the son of a lesser landowner, was a considerable honour.[14] He also received a pardon for his support for the Despensers and of all his debts to the crown.[15] In January 1331 he established the first of a number of religious chantries for the souls of his family.[16] Also included amongst those spiritually provided for was his patron, Montague, and Montague's wife. He also gave his lord help of a more practical sort. It was he who collected for Montague his fees as a banneret of the household and acted as his attorney when his master was abroad.

[7] Wardrobe Book of John Ferriby, 8 Edw. III: BL, MS Cotton Nero C. VIII, f. 225v.

[8] *CPR 1324–7*, 171.

[9] ibid., 183 (20 Oct. 1325).

[10] *CCR 1327–30*, 531 (8 Mar. 1329).

[11] ibid., 553 (29 June 1329). Another of them was John Pulteney, the famous London merchant, who appears on other occasions associated with Molyns.

[12] *CPR 1327–30*, 442 (24 Sept. 1329). One of these letters, annotated with the words 'pater sancte', is printed in C. Johnson and H. Jenkinson, *English Court Hand, A.D. 1066–1500* (Oxford, 1915), II, plate XXIIb.

[13] *CPR 1330–4*, 110 (28 Mar. 1331).

[14] *CMR 1326–7*, no. 2271 (p.379).

[15] *CPR 1330–4*, 518–19 (1 Mar. 1334).

[16] *VCH Bucks*, III, 183, 312.

He also extended loans to Montague.[17] There is no doubt that he was the right-hand man of a member of the highest circle of trust which revolved around the king.

It is very difficult to get an idea of the personalities of important, let alone relatively unknown, medieval people. One can observe certain things about Molyns. He was clearly a considerable military figure. By 1334 he had become Montague's knight. By 1337 he had himself become a royal banneret.[18] In 1338 he served on the Dunbar campaign in Scotland under Montague's high command and he lost a number of horses, suggesting an active part in the fighting.[19] That he was a prominent soldier, although it was an important factor in his success at Edward III's court, was only one of his useful spheres of activity. He was also employed as a strong-arm man off the field of war. In 1337 he was given two extremely difficult tasks. The first was to round up all the foreign merchants in London, saving the king's own Tuscan bankers.[20] One can imagine the problems of arresting what must have been a very motley and tough group of men. In the same year he was put in charge of requisitioning a number of Spanish ships from their reluctant owners so that they could be used for the war.[21] That such arrests did not always proceed smoothly is attested by the result of his commission to capture another foreigner, Hermann la Nuyte, in 1340. Molyns killed him in the course of making the arrest.[22] Molyns was also active throughout the 1330s on ordinary commissions of the peace in Buckinghamshire and on numerous commissions of oyer and terminer.

As if this were not enough, he received tasks of other sorts. The scope of his activities gives us a good idea of the burdensome nature of the responsibilities thrust on a trusted royal servant in the fourteenth century. The least troublesome was his position as marshal of the goshawks, which went with the royal grant of the manor of Ilmer in Buckinghamshire.[23] Even this was probably no sinecure. He obviously impressed the king as an efficient manager of his ever-growing properties, because he gave him custody of one of the greatest royal chamber estates, the lordship of Burstwick. Molyns kept this until it was sold to William Pole.[24] He also became steward of the chamber lands and keeper of the royal stud.[25] These offices would have kept Molyns constantly on the move. In London, he and his friend John Pulteney, the London merchant, received a commission to survey the Tower which was in a state of neglect at this time.[26] An outstanding knowledge of military fortifications is implicit in this commission. Since he was, during this same period towards the end of the 1330s, also spasmodically campaigning abroad, acting as one of the chief royal envoys between England and the Low Countries, arranging foreign loans, it is clear that he must have been an enormously active and enterprising man.

Such strenuous activities on the king's behalf went well rewarded. His successive rise to squire, knight and banneret of the royal household has already been mentioned. He also acquired a huge number of manors by lawful, and partly unlawful, means. Royal grants of these came particularly thick and fast during the period when Molyns was most active on the king's behalf in ways described in the previous paragraph. His turnover of property, either through direct sale or leasing out, was rapid, and a conservative estimate of his income would be £800 a year at the time of his fall in 1340.[27] This excludes income from lands which he might be renting and which do not therefore appear in royal grants or the list of Molyns' charters. The appendix to this introduction shows the build-up of these estates in more detail. No year passed when Molyns did not obtain some royal licence or concession to improve his properties by crenellating them, imparking huge areas, assarting from royal forests or establishing fairs. He also assured himself the maximum control over his tenants by obtaining return of writs and of summonses to the exchequer, view of frankpledge, his own assize of bread and ale, and so forth. He also obtained immunity from dreary and unimportant local

[17] BL, MS Cotton Nero C. VIII, f. 223: payment of 10 marks half-yearly to William Montague through John Molyns, his knight. He acted as Montague's attorney from 22 Apr. 1337: *CPR 1334–8*, 421. On 27 Oct. 1331 John Mauduit and William Montague acknowledged a debt of 330 marks to Molyns: *CCR 1330–3*, 395.

[18] E 101/388/5.

[19] Dugdale, *Baronage*, II, 146

[20] *CPR 1334–8*, 506 (1 Sept. 1337); C 81/238, no. 10236 (by privy seal).

[21] C 81/239, no. 10385 (26 Oct. 1337).

[22] *CPR 1340–3*, 56 (8 Oct. 1341).

[23] *CCR 1337–9*, 322 (5 Mar. 1338).

[24] *CPR 1338–40*, 286 (13 June 1339).

[25] ibid. *1334–8*, 429 (1 Apr. 1337).

[26] ibid., 214 (15 Oct. 1335).

[27] See appendix to this introduction.

responsibilities like sitting on juries and burdensome ones like being required to act as sheriff or royal bailiff. In view of his character it was admittedly fortunate for the county of Buckingham that he chose to abstain from these activities. The heart of wealth and power lay for him at court in London. He also had other useful connections in the capital among important London merchants, and it may have been through them that he was able to be so forthcoming with ready cash, both to the king and Montague.[28] He was better able than almost any other magnate to get repayment of royal debts between 1338 and 1340. He also registered all his royal grants and licences most carefully, having obtained these expensive guarantees free of charge.[29]

Molyns' fall from grace was extremely sudden. He had played a very active part in what were to be the first stages of the Hundred Years War. He was back from the continent early in January 1339, returned abroad to the king and then came back to England with a royal message in February. He returned yet again from the Low Countries with another royal message to the council in April. Finally he travelled with money and other supplies for Edward III in May 1339 and was on the king's council at Antwerp later in that year.[30] In 1340, however, he did not return abroad and this may have been his undoing. It was now that the king's resentment against the home government built up. This came to a head when he was campaigning in Flanders in the summer of 1340 and reached its culmination in the autumn, after the siege of Tournai had had to be abandoned through failure of supplies and lack of funds. At the same time news was coming from England of incipient rebellion at home. Greatly disturbed, Edward and a small group of followers left the field of operations and sailed for home. They arrived in the middle of the night of 30 November and the king wasted no time in summoning those whom he suspected of causing the disaffection. The leading members of the home administration were hauled before him. Molyns was among those summoned and his close associate and future brother-in-law, Nicholas Beech, keeper of the Tower, was another victim of royal fury. Molyns' offence was simply stated to be 'rebellion'.[31] When he was eventually pardoned, 'giving wrongful counsel' was also specified.[32] It is possible that Molyns' offence consisted only in those charges presented against him in Buckinghamshire when the king inaugurated a special inquiry into abuses and infringements of law and order committed since the beginning of the reign. These offences were quite sufficient to hang a lesser man. The alternative is that 'rebellion' means precisely what it says and that Molyns was in some way mixed up with the party of the erstwhile chancellor, Stratford, who had also been summoned to the Tower. The king accused him of causing disaffection in the country and of endangering his throne. Stratford, during his debate with the king over his dismissal, also made scantily veiled threats of deposition against Edward. Molyns, unlike the rest of those summoned, decided not to risk appearing before the king raging in the Tower. Edward sent the knight's old patron, William Montague, now earl of Salisbury, to capture him. This Montague succeeded in doing.[33] He also ordered the seizure of all Molyns' lands and properties and, as early as 3 December, Gill was trying to provide herself with a good supply of ready money in the face of the catastrophe, by pawning a large quantity of the family silver to William Dalling, a London mercer. The mercer did not do well out of the deal because, when the king learned about the transaction, he confiscated the silver. The unfortunate mercer petitioned for it back in vain.[34] The day after this transaction by Molyns' wife, Edward personally led a treasure hunt to St Albans abbey to seize the wealth which Molyns was reputed to have left there. According to the single source

[28] That the king owed him £608 3s. 5d. at the time of Molyns' fall in 1340 can be estimated from the debts to him noted on the wardrobe accounts of Norwell (E 101/398/11, m.6), Cusance (E 101/22/35), Beech (E 101/388/9, f. 28v), and Ferriby (BL, MS Cotton Nero C. VIII, f. 196v).

[29] E 101/212/1.

[30] E. B. Fryde, 'Dismissal of Robert de Wodehouse from the Office of Treasurer, December 1338', *EHR*, LXVII (1952), 74–8. I am grateful to my husband both for first introducing me to Sir John and for much help with this contribution, especially the appendix. For Molyns' missions to England in 1339 see C 49/7, no. 9 (Feb.–Mar.); ibid., no. 7, and SC 1/38, no. 158 (Apr.–May).

[31] N. Fryde, 'Edward III's Removal of his Ministers and Judges, 1340–1', *BIHR*, XLVIII (1975), 149–61; *CCR 1343–5*, 192 (4 Nov. 1343); SC 6/1293/3 ('par cause de sa rebelte').

[32] *CPR 1345–8*, 29 (10 Jan. 1346, by privy seal).

[33] ibid. *1340–3*, 104 (5 Dec. 1340). He wasted no time in seizing Molyns' estates, sending swiftly a member of the household, William Trussell, and a party, long before the writ had reached the sheriff: *CIM*, II, no. 1760.

[34] E 143/11/12. It was worth £87 12s. 1d.

which relates this story, the treasure included royal money appropriated by Molyns. The king found Molyns' hoard in one of the abbey rooms and removed it.[35] He did not, however, succeed in visiting justice upon Molyns because, the next day, Salisbury reported that Molyns had escaped from his custody. For the next five years he remained an outlaw and fugitive whose whereabouts were unknown to the king. They were, however, known to Salisbury.[36]

The day after his return the king sent a long explanatory letter to his sheriffs describing the serious reasons for his return and setting out the organisation of the inquiry which he intended to inaugurate into corrupt officials whose misdeeds had caused his premature return and the abandonment of his campaign.[37] One of the most notable features of the precautions he took when setting up the inquiry was to try to prevent intimidation of those who wished to complain against powerful men.[38] Molyns emerged as the most notable of these in the proceedings of the inquiry.

The charges against Molyns consisted of criminal offences against his own family, including murder, and subverting a justice of king's bench to escape detection; straightforward terrorism in Buckinghamshire, of which the most notable case was his kidnapping of some of the tenants of the prior of Christchurch, Canterbury, at Monks Risborough; thirdly the usual legal chicanery and illegal appropriations of lands, often of relations or quite small people; and finally his offences against the king, including seizure of a quantity of royal wool and depredations in royal forests.

The evidence of the king's letter of 1 December shows that Edward had fully formulated the idea of an inquiry virtually on his arrival. Robert Parving, who had replaced John Willoughby as chief justice of king's bench at Michaelmas, was undoubtedly the mind behind it.[39] He was ready to start acting in Bedfordshire and Northamptonshire on 10 December.[40] There is some evidence that he acted in the most seriously disaffected counties, as a second commission had to be issued for Bedfordshire and Northamptonshire in November 1341.[41] He was also one of the justices in Buckinghamshire, where most of the cases against Molyns were brought, though in that county the head of the commission was the even more prestigious figure of the king's close friend, William Bohun, earl of Northampton. The first commission was against the abuses by royal officials. Six days later the justices in the midland counties received additional powers to seek out malefactors and disturbers of the peace.[42] On 13 January 1341 the commission was extended to examine and try other serious crimes as well.[43] This created in aggregate a general oyer and terminer inquiry with a wide jurisdiction, and the variety of charges against him made Molyns the most serious quarry in Buckinghamshire.

There is evidence, either through the survival of a roll of proceedings or the record of payments to the justices, that the inquiry actually operated in the counties of Bedford, Buckingham, Cambridge, Derby, Dorset, Essex, Gloucester, Hertford, Warwick, Leicester, Lincoln, Middlesex, Norfolk, Northumberland, Nottingham, Oxford, Suffolk, Surrey, Somerset, Worcester and York. The terms of reference of the articles allowed the justices to investigate misdeeds committed since the king had begun to reign. In its timing, its character and its resulting proceedings it closely resembles the commission which Edward I had inaugurated after he had concluded a truce with Philip the Fair of France and returned home in 1298 after a four-year period of warfare.[44] Such inquiries had been put on a legal basis by the statute of Northampton in 1328.

The best source of how the inquiry actually worked is to be found in the roll of the Bedfordshire proceedings,[45] which still has the lists of jurors and some of the accompanying writs attached to it and

[35] *Croniques de Londres*, ed. G. J. Aungier (Camden Soc. [Old ser.], XXVIII, 1844), 84.

[36] It was while he was in hiding that Montague obtained his rights to the manor of Stoke Trister: C 81/271, no. 13532 (by privy seal).

[37] Cambridge Univ. Lib., MS Dd ix 38, ff. 107–8.

[38] *CPR 1340–3*, 104 (10 Dec. 1340). A good list of the articles of the inquiry is in unsorted Exchequer Miscellanea B.

[39] For his career, see Sayles in *King's Bench*, VI, xxiv.

[40] *CPR 1340–3*, 111; JUST 1/31, m.1 (Beds special commission); 638, m.1 (Northants commission). For payments to the justices see E 372/186, Beds & Bucks; 188, Item Norht, Res. Norht; E 159/118, m.72d (Beds); E 368/155, m.155d (Northants).

[41] *CPR 1340–3*, 366 (27 Nov. 1341); E 159/119, m.63; E 368/114, m.147d; E 372/187, Norht.

[42] *CPR 1340–3*, 105, 107.

[43] ibid., 108.

[44] For proceedings in one county held under this commission see *A Lincolnshire Assize Roll for 1298*, ed. W. S. Thomson (Linc. Rec. Soc., XXXVI, 1944).

[45] JUST 1/31. The lists of jurors are pricked and annotated.

for which Mr Meekings found a particularly large number of connected documents. The reason for their particular survival is probably that Parving, as chief justice, brought the various ancillary materials back with him to Westminster. As always, it was the sheriff's job to prepare the court before the justices' arrival, and the justices sat in various parts of the county to spread the weight of royal authority and to make it easier for those who wanted to bring actions. The sheriff summoned the parties and the jurymen. In the case of our inquiry all the local officials who had acted since 1327 were supposed to appear too, bringing their records. It must have been a crowded and tumultuous scene in the court! Lists of potential jurors of presentment had already been drawn up by the hundred bailiffs. They listed them under the two headings of 'milites' and 'liberi et legales homines'. These lists survive for Bedfordshire and one of them is headed 'returned by Richard Oakley, bailiff of the liberty of Wallingford'. In this period the minimum requirement for a juror of presentment was that he had to be a forty-shilling freeholder. Normally these lists contained a few more names than were necessary and the justices' clerk checked on the spot, as soon as he arrived in the county, who could and could not serve. The sheriff then chose jurors from these and could be amerced for choosing people who were ineligible. In addition to the hundred and town juries, a jury 'diversorum hundredorum', or a grand inquisition of more substantial jurors, was made up. Its purpose was to bring indictments in more important cases and indictments which spread beyond the borders of one hundred, as was true of the charges against Molyns.

Unfortunately we have no similar lists drawn up for the trial juries, the 'patria' who actually tried those defendants who had been presented. Described as 'electi et triati', they were probably chosen on the spot from among those who attended the court proceedings and who were eligible, that is, unrelated to the defendant but from his locality. We know that the sheriff was responsible for them because one of the charges against John Inge was of procuring juries in oyer and terminer cases on Molyns' behalf who were not chosen by the sheriff. Those defendants who did not appear to answer the charges were summoned by a writ of venire facias directed by the sheriff to the hundred bailiffs. Those who still did not appear might be summoned up to five times and then outlawed.[46] Such was the case with Molyns who heads the list of those outlawed in Buckinghamshire. In most serious cases, like the conspiracies between Molyns and Inge, the proceedings could be transferred to the court of king's bench. This was probably done by royal orders under the privy seal and we do not have records of it as such documents rarely survive and their registers have disappeared.[47]

The Buckinghamshire proceedings started on 21 January 1341 and did not end until 9 July of that year, leaving behind two important rolls. Charges against Molyns appear on both. The most serious of them belonged to the very beginning of Edward III's rule. On 16 November 1326 Edward II had been captured at Neath. The anarchy which had accompanied his wife's invasion continued over parts of the country for the rest of 1326. After the invasion there had occurred an orgy of looting both by the noble leaders of the invasionary forces and by the foreign mercenaries whom they brought with them. All over England men took advantage of the situation to dispose of their private enemies. On 19 November Molyns' agents, led by his servant Henry Inde, went to the manor of Stoke Poges which belonged to his wife's uncle, Peter Poges. They murdered Peter, his son John and the family cook [8, 9]. At the time, the grandfather of Gill, Peter's father Robert, was still alive. By not murdering him, Molyns avoided a writ of novel disseisin. However, by the time that the old man died in 1330, a jury testified that he had surrendered his lands to Molyns.[48] The Poges inheritance henceforth constituted the core of Molyns' growing landed fortune. The Poges estates contributed the bulk of his income and formed the centres for further expansion of his properties in the adjoining districts. Having avoided the danger of detection through a writ of novel disseisin, Molyns secured immunity from further prosecution by securing an acquittal at the hands of a justice of oyer and terminer whose commission he himself had secured through influence in chancery. The connection which he used was John Inge, justice of king's bench. Inge came to Buckinghamshire and apparently saw to it that the jury, summoned to try the case at Aylesbury, was one which could be relied upon to acquit Molyns [9]. In the 1341 inquiry a joint jury of the Chiltern hundreds

46 W. A. Morris, *The Early English County Court* (Berkeley, Calif, 1926), 116.

47 P. Chaplais, *English Royal Documents, King John – Henry VI, 1199–1461* (Oxford, 1971), 34.

48 *CIPM*, VII, no. 274.

raised the case again. Because of the basic principle of English law that a man cannot be tried a second time for an offence of which he has been acquitted, it was impossible to present Molyns himself for the murder. However, in 1341 Henry Inde, who had actually committed the deed, was hanged, and Justice Inge's part in covering up the true culprit was uncovered. Molyns had consolidated his control over the Poges inheritance by terrorising the other coheiresses, his wife's two sisters.[49]

The Stoke Poges murder is only the first example of coöperation between Molyns and Inge to thwart the course of justice. With Inge's aid Molyns seems to have been able to manipulate any legal decision that he wanted, however slight his case. The Sinclair wardship is a clear example. The true facts only came to light through one of the indictments in 1341. Molyns coveted the wardship and marriage of young Robert Sinclair whose father, of the same name, had been an important Buckinghamshire landowner. He sent out a party of men to obtain the boy's custody in the most assured way, by kidnapping him. A ferocious fight broke out between Molyns' men and the boy's friends in which the kidnappers got the worse of the mêlée. Molyns then contrived that his injured men should bring a case against the boy's friends and once again arranged in chancery for Inge to be sent to try it, this time with Philip Aylesbury, a local knight. Ominously, the justices sat at Stoke Poges, Molyns' chief manor. Inge brought a verdict favourable to Molyns, Aylesbury being unaware that a fraud was involved. The unfortunate defendants earned a massive fine of 200 marks, more than some of Edward II's opponents had had to pay to redeem themselves from high treason. Terrified of Molyns, they paid up. In 1341 the Buckinghamshire jury also levelled a more general charge against Molyns of bringing unreasonable writs against his local opponents and of employing Inge to arrange for the court to be held at Stoke Poges. Because of this his opponents had been too frightened to appear and lawyers had been discouraged from acting for them. This allowed Molyns to obtain damages as the result of uncontested proceedings. In this way Molyns was said to have obtained 122 marks [7].

Molyns obviously wielded tremendous power in Buckinghamshire and terrorised the country at will before his prosecution. Two cases of strong-arm tactics apparently unconnected with seizures of land or wards clearly reveal this. The most amazing is an attack on the home of Gerard Braybrooke, the sheriff [2]. Braybrooke was a member of a very important Bedfordshire family whose prominence went back to a noted official of King John.[50] We do not know the origin of the hostility between him and Molyns, but it came to a head in July 1340. Molyns sent a band of followers, headed by the man who was perhaps his most trusted agent, John Hay, vicar of Weston Turville, one of Molyns' manors, to Braybrooke's house at Horsenden. There this band of men attacked the sheriff, his wife and family and ran amok in Horsenden village. Afterwards, at Molyns' command, the gang rode night and day through the county, attacked Braybrooke's tenants and so terrorised the countryside that no work could be done on Braybrooke's lands. Only the intercession of neighbours of the two men stopped the attacks and restored the peace, but not before great damage had been done to Braybrooke's property.

This was not the only occasion on which Molyns brought violence to the unfortunate population of Bedfordshire and Buckinghamshire. One of the most serious outrages committed by him was his intervention in the dispute between the prior of Christchurch, Canterbury, and his tenants of Monks Risborough. The struggle arose because the prior claimed that the tenants of Monks Risborough, a manor which the priory already held before the Conquest,[51] were villeins [6]. In June 1333 the prior asked the steward of Monks Risborough, James Frisel, to come to him because the tenants were claiming that they were freer than was the case and because they were establishing a fund to promote the claim that they were freemen.[52] By 1335 the prior was desperate. A visit by the Christchurch steward in February had only made things worse,[53] and in March the prior was proposing to find a powerful patron, perhaps the earl of Hereford or William Montague, to intercede and 'uphold the rights of our church against our rebels and opponents in those parts'.[54] Our next surviving letter from the prior is to John Stratford, by then archbishop of Canterbury, in which the prior ner-

[49] *VCH Bucks*, III, 305; BL, Egerton Roll 8762.

[50] They first came into prominence as favourites of King John in whose time they already possessed Horsenden: *VCH Bucks*, II, 253. An account of the later Braybrookes is in Margaret Bassett, *Knights of the Shire for Bedfordshire* (Beds Hist. Rec. Soc., XXIX, 1949), 20–4.

[51] *VCH Bucks*, I, 280–1.

[52] *Literae Cantuarienses*, ed. J. B. Sheppard, II (RS, 1888), nos 501, 548.

[53] ibid., no. 560.

[54] ibid., no. 566.

vously admitted that he had seized the recalcitrant tenants. He begged the archbishop's protection as the priory was going to be legally prosecuted.[55] What he did not mention was that Molyns had been responsible for seizing them and that they were kept in conditions so rigorous that two of them died [6]. The prior wrote this letter in October 1336. The attack had taken place at dawn on 20 May. Molyns and his men had ridden into Monks Risborough, broken into the houses of the ringleaders of the opposition and carried them off in a couple of carts to the priory. It may have been to forestall the charges of kidnapping and murder that the prior and Molyns obtained the services of John Inge to sit on a commission of oyer and terminer into the murder of the bailiff of Monks Risborough, Henry Plumber. The ringleaders were summoned before the commission. Since they were imprisoned in the priory gaol they could not put in an appearance. Consequently they were outlawed which made it impossible for them to bring an action against the prior! A smug letter written by the prior in February 1339 records 'dear friend, know that our bondmen belonging to Risborough who live at Risborough are from day to day entreating us that they may be allowed to make a solemn recognition of their servile condition'.[56]

In spite of the seriousness of these charges, it was not these last two offences which had brought Molyns to justice. It was not his offences against the king's peace so much as his offences against Edward personally. Edward not only suspected him of stealing royal treasure. He had also seized a large quantity of royal wool. Molyns' old enemy, Gerard Braybrooke, with another collector, Geoffrey Lucy, was collecting wool in Buckinghamshire as part of the royal wool levy of 1340 when Molyns attacked them with his armed men and seized the twenty-four sacks of wool which they were carrying [1, 3]. Edward III probably viewed this offence with particular seriousness, as the failure of the wool tax was one of the reasons for the collapse of his finances while he was abroad and the consequent abandonment of his campaign. It was particularly ironic that he had also given Molyns permission to export free of customs a large quantity of wool.[57]

Molyns' forest offences fall into a complicated class of their own. Molyns was charged with felling and then selling or giving away a total of 8,128 trees, mainly oaks, quite apart from shrubbery and undergrowth. Part of it was admitted to have gone to the king's service, but the rest was supposed to have been converted to Molyns' own use. Two foresters declared that they had seen the waste but had not dared to make a fuss about it for terror of Molyns [4].

Molyns never presented himself to answer these charges and was outlawed in his absence. His disappearance must have been viewed with delight, not only by rivals like Braybrooke but by a large number of ordinary people in Buckinghamshire as well. After his fall a number of petitions were presented against him. According to Ela, wife of William Butler of Wem, Molyns had illegally obtained presentation rights to the church of Weston Turville against her.[58] He had then made his right-hand man, John Hay, vicar. A chaplain, William Winchendon, complained that Molyns disseised him of a parcel of land at Brill.[59] In the other centre of Molyns' operations, London, he was also responsible for a number of misdeeds, if petitions are to be believed. Thomas Hart complained that Molyns had disseised him of three tenements, including one which Molyns made his town house.[60] He then put this property to ill use by imprisoning there a prominent London citizen and cornmerchant, Hamo Barber. Molyns threatened him with death until he abandoned a recognisance of £30 owed to him by one of Molyns' Buckinghamshire friends, Richard Millward of Great Marlow.[61] Another incident of about this time which illustrates both how well Molyns was able to tap his sources of influence at court to get his ends and then how brutal he could be in implementing his desires is the Peterborough case. Having obtained an assignment of £200 in repayment of royal debts, he enquired of the treasurer, Robert Woodhouse, how best he might implement it.[62] Most immediate sources of revenue had already been promised to merchants. However, Woodhouse suggested the £200 fine owed by the abbot and convent of Peterborough which they were required to make to retain custody of their abbey during a vacancy. Molyns followed this counsel and

[55] ibid., no. 602. [56] ibid., no. 672.

[57] *CCR 1337–9*, 439 (5 July 1338).

[58] C 81/279, no. 14339 (29 Sept. 1341); C 81/276, no. 14044 (16 May 1341).

[59] C 81/272, no. 13685 (1 Feb. 1341).

[60] C 81/281, nos 14596, 14597 (4 Mar. 1342).

[61] *YB 15 Edw. III*, ed. L. O. Pike (RS, 1891), 482–5.

[62] E. B. Fryde, *EHR*, LXVII, 78.

without further ado held up the abbey's representative on Westminster bridge and demanded his due. The abbey had to get a loan from Italian money-lenders to pay him off.[63]

Millward was kept in prison until 1344 and then pardoned. In the same year Molyns' much more prominent associate, Inge, was pardoned though he was never employed on the bench again.[64] Then in 1345 Molyns himself received a royal pardon and, in the course of August, the king gave him back his lands.[65] Edward apparently thought that this enterprising royal servant had learnt his lesson. Molyns recovered much of his former position. The next year he once again received the concession that he should not be put on any local jury or in any office without his consent and his swans were given protection from the royal bailiffs.[66] He managed to get back his old manor of Stoke Trister, even against the claims of the executors of his now dead patron, the earl of Salisbury.[67] In 1346–7 he served with the king in France on the Crécy campaign.[68] In 1347 Edward III squared old debts, pardoning him a debt of £1750 14s. 4d. in return for Molyns abandoning claims of £1807 2s. 5d.[69] He was summoned as a magnate to the great council of 1347, and therefore his descendants had the right to be summoned as peers.[70] In 1350 he headed the commission of the peace for Buckinghamshire.[71] Finally, in 1352 Queen Philippa, who had long ago favoured Molyns with a land grant in return for the romantic and unburdensome customary rent of a rose at Midsummer, made him steward of her household.[72]

However, rumblings of trouble reappeared in the 1350s. In 1353, in a royal council, there were complaints against Molyns' oppressiveness as the queen's steward.[73] The complaints could probably be pursued because the queen herself was dissatisfied with Molyns' conduct of his office. In 1354 the queen complained because her cofferer had given Molyns a fee of £83 whereas only 40 marks were due and she stated that it was against her commands. Molyns had overreached himself in his desire to profit from his office.[74] In 1355 Molyns, summoned to the court of king's bench to answer a suit of Thomas Parslow, 'did not trouble to answer the royal writ'.[75] On this occasion he still escaped disaster, but it was lurking around the next corner. The next year the king ominously prevented Molyns from proceeding with a legal action against one of his fellow officers in the queen's household.[76] In February 1357 he and Gill were charged with 'treasons, felonies, robberies, conspiracies and confederations'.[77]

On this second occasion Molyns did not escape arrest, though his final attempts to escape conviction have a comic touch. William Shareshill was put in charge of the special commission against Molyns and, as was often the case with important oyer and terminer proceedings, the trial and judgment of Molyns appear on the rolls of the court of king's bench [10]. The Buckinghamshire jurors presented a formidable dossier against him, about half of which was not confirmed by trial jurors. As it is, the charges for which he was eventually imprisoned provide an extraordinary conclusion to the career of an important councillor and steward of the queen's household. They included conviction for stealing the vicar of Stoke Poges' horse, theft of another two horses and a huge quantity of firewood, theft of half a dozen swans and an attempt to cover this up by cutting off their legs and necks! This last nasty deed brought an outcry in Buckinghamshire. What convicted him, however, was receiving on two separate occasions the murderers of two unnamed persons, one of them the murderer of a foreign merchant. One of these murderers, John Gamage, found refuge with Molyns for a year after he committed the offence.

Not surprisingly, Molyns challenged the jurors. The extent of his 'lordship' in Buckinghamshire must indeed have made it difficult to find men of substance who were not in some way acquainted with his activities in a manner which he would not have found acceptable.

63 J. Sparke, *Historiae Anglicanae Scriptores Varii* (London, 1723), 236–7.

64 B. H. Putnam, *The Place in Legal History of Sir William Shareshull* (Cambridge, 1950), 138–9.

65 *CPR 1345–8*, 76.

66 ibid., 154 (24 July 1346).

67 ibid., 63 (20 Apr. 1346).

68 G. Wrottesley, *Crécy and Calais* (London, 1898), 5–6.

69 *CPR 1345–8*, 417 (16 Oct. 1347).

70 G.E.C., IX, 38.

71 *CPR 1348–50*, 526 (20 Feb. 1350).

72 ibid. *1350–4*, 228 (13 Feb. 1352).

73 The great council, 23 Sept.–3 Oct. 1353: *RP*, II, 253.

74 E 101/392/6.

75 *CPR 1354–8*, 259 (2 June 1355).

76 ibid., 345 (18 Feb. 1356).

77 ibid., 548 (12 Feb. 1357).

When his objections were eventually laid aside, Molyns pulled a last trick out of his hat which may have astounded the court as much as it did the present writer. After a life-time of royal military service, surveying manors, keeping the peace and, above all, breaking the peace, Molyns pleaded benefit of clergy. Not surprisingly the bishop would not claim him. The sceptical justices requested proof of his literacy and Molyns read out loud to the court. To judge from the list of goods taken from him at his committal, Molyns attempted to give credence to his story by appearing with a prayer roll and a paternoster. The reaction of Gill, also standing before the court and apparently abandoned by her husband who was making his own ingenious defence, is unfortunately not on record. It did not save Molyns from being convicted of felony and sent for imprisonment to the place which had been the scene of the action which had brought his rise to power, Nottingham castle.[78] He was later transferred to prison at Cambridge in the custody of his own son, William Molyns. He died in 1361, aged about 62 years.[79] Gill, who was quickly pardoned, died five years after him.

The obvious question which one poses at the end of a study of his career is, how far such violent and dangerous activities were a way of life of members of Edward III's court or important royal officials in the countryside. Amidst all the charges of official corruption which the royal inquiry of 1340 revealed, Molyns' case is unique. No other magnate appears who has terrorised his part of the world for such a length of time. On the other hand, the king's renewed favour towards him after 1346 does not give a very reassuring view of the attitude of King Edward and his wife to disorderly and over-mighty subjects.

[78] ibid. *1358–61*, 286 (24 Sept. 1359); *CIM*, III, no. 443.

[79] On 10 Mar.: *CCR 1361–4*, 192 (4 June 1361).

Appendix to Introduction

ESTATES OF JOHN MOLYNS BY DECEMBER 1340

This list is arranged in roughly chronological order of acquisition by Molyns. It does not include some additional small properties, unconnected with his main estates, nor rights of patronage over religious houses, advowsons and knight fees. Also excluded are reversionary rights to estates that Molyns had not yet entered by December 1340.

The list is based chiefly on SC 6/1120/10 (Jan.–June 1341) and 12 (June 1341–Jan. 1346) containing the accounts of the chamber custodians; E 163/4/32, a chamber inventory of the goods of Molyns on 18 June 1341; and C 81/1337, no. 26 (31 Aug. 1345, under the griffin seal) listing the former estates of Molyns that should be restored to him.

The dates of acquisition by Molyns have been reconstructed chiefly from the information in BL, Egerton Roll 8762, containing an inventory of Molyns' muniments compiled by royal officials after the sequestration of his properties in December 1340.

It is impossible to assess precisely Molyns' revenue. Between about Michaelmas 1342 and the spring of 1345 the custodians of his estates charged themselves with £2760 and spent or disbursed more than that sum. The net revenue paid into the king's chamber during that period totalled £1934.

1. Stoke Poges manor, Bucks

The chief manor and main residence of Molyns, held in fee. Inheritance of his wife Gill, made possible through the murder by Molyns on 19 Nov. 1326 of Gill's cousin, Peter Poges. Acquired by Molyns finally in Mar. 1331 but possibly in his possession as early as Feb. 1328. Various additional lands in Stoke Poges acquired 1332–40.
Inventory of June 1341: 138 acres of cultivated demesne arable, 22 oxen, 150 sheep.
Revenue Oct. 1342–Mar. 1345: £138 19s.

2. Ditton manor, Bucks

Acquired of Poges inheritance (as under 1) by Mar. 1331; held in fee. A park existed there by 1338 and was augmented through the grant to Molyns by Queen Philippa before May 1338 of further 8 acres (C 81/245, no. 10928, privy seal).

3. Riding Court manor, Bucks

Acquired lands in it in 1331 as damages in an action of novel disseisin won against Alice widow of Thomas Poges (uncle of Gill Molyns) and her husband, Richard Walden.
For value and goods see under 6.

4. Fulmer manor, Bucks

Acquired on 20 Sept. 1332 by gift of William Montague for the life of John Molyns.
Inventory of June 1341: 68½ acres of cultivated demesne arable, 6 oxen, 96 sheep, 12 lambs. Farmed in 1343–5 for £8 p.a.

5. Weston Turville manor, Bucks

Acquired by Jan. 1333 (*CChR 1327–41*, 303); held in fee. In 1338 Walter Turplington, son and heir of Hugh Turplington killed in 1330 by William Montague and his associates (including Molyns) in Nottingham castle, renounced to Molyns all his rights in this manor.
Inventory of June 1341: 125½ acres of cultivated demesne arable, 153 sheep, 8 lambs.

6. Datchet manor, Bucks

Possession of some property in Datchet acquired in May 1331 from Richard Walden (see under 3) who, later in 1331, granted to Molyns in fee all his lands in Datchet. The manor of Datchet granted to Molyns in fee on 5 May 1335 by William Montague.
Inventory of June 1341 (for Datchet, Riding Court and Ditton jointly): 247½ acres of cultivated demesne arable, 28 oxen, 140 sheep, 108 lambs.
Revenue 29 Sept. 1342–May 1345 (from these 3 estates jointly): £208 14s. 0½d.

7. Addington manor, Bucks

Acquired on 29 May 1335 in fee by grant of John son of John Blackett (*CPR 1345–8*, 76). Entailed in 1338 on William son of John Molyns.
Inventory of June 1341: 126 acres of cultivated demesne arable, 12 oxen, 154 sheep, 33 lambs.
Farmed in 1343–5 for £20 p.a.

8. Aston Mollins and Ilmer manors, Bucks

Acquired in Nov. 1335 in fee by grant of John

Blackett, knight. Owed the service of being marshal of the king's goshawks.
Inventory of June 1341:

(a) Aston Mollins: 124½ acres of cultivated demesne arable, 12 oxen, 130 sheep, 38 lambs.

(b) Ilmer: 121 acres of cultivated demesne arable, 14 oxen, 151 sheep, 35 lambs.

The two manors farmed jointly in 1343–5 for £48 p.a.

9. Brill manor, Bucks

Acquired (with Silverstone, Northants) by a royal grant of 23 June 1337 (*CPR 1334–8*, 464, 476, 528); held in fee.

(a) Inventory of June 1341 (for Brill only): 80 acres of cultivated demesne arable, 8 oxen, 340 sheep, 63 lambs.
Revenue Aug. 1342–Jan. 1346: £183 16s. 0¼d.

(b) Inventory of 1341 (for Silverstone only): 68½ acres of cultivated demesne arable, 6 oxen.

10. Henley manor in Ash, Surrey

Acquired by a grant of William Clinton, earl of Huntingdon, of 24 Aug. 1337; held in fee.
Inventory of June 1341: 164½ acres of cultivated demesne arable, 17 oxen, 173 sheep, 31 lambs.

11. Henley on Thames manor, Oxon (including Phyllis Court)

Held for life by Margaret Clare (apparently as dower from her former marriage to Peter Gaveston) and her husband, Hugh Audley, earl of Gloucester. Reversion of it granted to Molyns by the king on 23 Mar. 1337. On 26 Nov. 1337 Gloucester and his wife conceded immediate possession to Molyns reserving a rent of £22 p.a. during the life of Margaret.
Inventory of June 1341: 88½ acres of cultivated demesne arable, 4 oxen, 182 sheep, 54 lambs.
Revenue of manor and town Jan.–June 1341: net revenue (after payment to the countess of Gloucester of ½ year's rent) £22 5s. 0½d.
Farmed 1343–5 for £11 6s. 8d. p.a.
Phyllis Court farmed 1342–5 for £13 6s. 8d. p.a.

12. Denham, Bucks

15 acres of meadow acquired in two different transactions in the first half of 1339; held by Molyns in Dec. 1340.

13. Cippenham manor, Bucks

Granted in Jan. 1339 by John Thoresby and John Eton to Reginald Cobham with reversion to Molyns. Molyns acquired possession from Cobham at some later date and held it in Dec. 1340.
Inventory of June 1341: 247 acres of cultivated demesne arable, 21 oxen, 173 sheep, 23 lambs.
Revenue Sept. 1342–June 1345: £274 0¼d.

14. Littlecote manor, Bucks

Acquired before 29 Sept. 1339 (C 81/256, no. 12022, privy seal).
Inventory of June 1341: 113 acres of cultivated demesne lands, 6 oxen, 159 sheep, 23 lambs.
Revenue: farmed 1342–5 for £9 6s. 8d. p.a.

15. Swanbourne manor, Bucks

Acquired before 29 Sept. 1339 (source as under 14); held by Molyns for life.
Revenue: farmed for £4 p.a. in 1342–5.

16. Beachendon manor, Bucks

Acquired in or before Sept. 1339 from Walter Mauny (source as under 14).
Inventory of June 1341: 135½ acres of cultivated demesne arable, 12 oxen.
Revenue: July 1342–Jan. 1345: £145 10s. 6¼d.

17. Wendover manor, Bucks

Acquired by royal grant of 15 Dec. 1339 (C 81/260, no. 12482, privy seal), repeated on 5 Mar. 1340, in part implementation of the king's promise to grant him £100 p.a. to maintain his status of banneret (Egerton Roll 8762; C 81/266, no. 13029, privy seal).
Inventory of June 1341: 217 acres of cultivated demesne arable, 23 oxen, 89 sheep, 8 lambs.
Revenue: farmed 1342–5 for £93 6s. 8d. p.a.

18. Aylesbury, Bucks

£60 of annual rent from Eleanor, countess of Ormond, which she received by a previous royal grant from the farm of Aylesbury, acquired by Molyns on 5 Mar. 1340 by a royal grant together with Wendover (see 17). Sources the same as for 17 together with *CPR 1338–40*, 524, and C 49/46/1.

19. Gore manor, Wilts

Acquired from Agnes Avon as part of properties formerly of Ralph Coombe before 7 Mar. 1340 (*CCR 1339–41*, 457–8).
Inventory of June 1341: 80 acres of cultivated

demesne arable, 4 oxen.
Revenue: farmed 1342–5 for £6 13s. 4d. p.a.

20. Lea manor, Wilts

Acquired before 7 Mar. 1340 (as 19).
Inventory of June 1341: 49 acres of cultivated demesne arable, 6 oxen.

21. Brinkworth and Long Newnton manors, Wilts

Acquired before 7 Mar. 1340 (as 19).
Inventory of June 1341:
(a) Brinkworth: 51 acres of cultivated demesne arable, 9 oxen.
(b) Long Newnton: 43½ acres of cultivated demesne arable, 6 oxen.

22. Box manor, Wilts

Acquired, probably with other Wiltshire properties, before 7 Mar. 1340 (as 19).
Inventory of June 1341: 69 acres of cultivated demesne arable, 8 oxen.
Revenue: farmed 1342–5 for £13 6s. 8d. p.a.

23. Durnford manor, Wilts

Acquired, probably with other Wiltshire properties, before 7 Mar. 1340 (as 19).
Revenue: farmed 1341–5 for £18 p.a.

24. Stoke Trister manor, Somerset

Acquired in fee by Midsummer 1340 from Elizabeth widow of John Lorty, together with the manors of Cucklington and Bayford (*CPR 1345–8*, 136–9). In Dec. 1340 Molyns is only known for certain to have held Stoke Trister, but the other two were ordered to be restored to him in 1346.

25. Moreton Pinkney manor, Northants

Acquired before 25 Nov. 1340 from William son of Robert Pinkney without royal licence, which was given subsequently (*CPR 1340–3*, 62).
Inventory of June 1341: 195½ acres of cultivated demesne arable, 8 oxen.

26. Chesham Bois manor, Bucks

Acquired finally in Nov. 1340 from Thomas Abingdon. See also [2].
Inventory of June 1341: 92 acres of cultivated demesne land.
Revenue: farmed 1342–5 for £8 p.a.

27. Wardship of Simon de Senlis with the manors of Little Kimble and 'Sublecote', Bucks

Acquired at an unknown date and held by Molyns in Dec. 1340.

28. Plumpton manor, Northants

Acquired at an unknown date before Dec. 1340.
Inventory of June 1341: 100 acres of cultivated demesne arable, 10 oxen, 85 sheep, 21 lambs.
Revenue: farmed 1342–5 for £20 p.a.

29. Easton Neston manor, Northants

Acquired at an unknown date before Dec. 1340.
Inventory of June 1341: $^1/_8$ rood of demesne arable (sown with flax), a mill.
Revenue: farmed 1343–5 for £6 p.a.

30. Three tenements in London

Acquired at an unknown date.
(a) Messuage of Thomas Hart from which Molyns wrongfully removed him (*CIM*, II, no. 1875, inquiry of 21 May 1343).
(b) Two messuages with gardens in the parish of St Andrew by the Wardrobe, Castle Baynard ward, formerly of Rose Bowyer.

31. Littleton, Middlesex

Advowson of the church with glebe lands.
Revenue: farmed 1342–5 at 2s. p.a.

TEXT

JUST 1/74, m.4

PLACITA CORAM PREFATIS WILLELMO DE BOHUN COMITE NORHT', ROBERTO DE FERARIIS, ROBERTO PARVYNG', RICARDO DE MONTE CANYSO, JOHANNE MORYCE, RICARDO DE KELLESHULL' ET ROBERTO DE TEYE JUSTICIARIIS ETC. APUD WYCOMBE DIE LUNE PROXIMO POST OCTABAS SANCTI HILLARII ANNO REGNI REGIS EDWARDI TERTII POST CONQUESTUM ANGLIE QUINTODECIMO REGNI VERO SUI FRANCIE SECUNDO

Membrane 7d

[1] [*Marginated*] Aylesbury
Juratores de Aylesbury presentant quod ubi commissio domini regis directa fuit Roberto le Spicer de Aylesbury et aliis ad capiendum medietatem lanarum etc. in comitatu Buk'[80] anno regni domini regis nunc undecimo virtute cuius commissionis predictus Robertus cepit de diversis hominibus in comitatu Buk' viginti et duos sarplerios lane qui ponderarunt viginti et quatuor saccos et plus ad opus domini regis qui quidem Robertus postea obiit per quod alia commissio directa fuit dominis Galfrido de Lucy et Gerardo de Braybrok' ad capiendum huiusmodi lanas in eodem comitatu, qui quidem Galfridus et Gerardus predictos viginti et quatuor saccos lane invenerunt apud Aylesbury in domo cuiusdam Willelmi atte Crouche et virtute illius commissionis eis directe lanas illas ibidem ceperunt et signo domini regis consignaverunt et deinde lanas illas usque aquam de Merlawe apud Merlawe cariare fecerunt. Et super hoc venit Thomas Bever cum aliis et signum domini regis predictum super lanas predictas modo predicto consignatum omnino deposuit et signum domini Johannis de Molyns super easdem lanas apposuit per quod lane ille ad opus domini regis minime devenerunt. Ideo preceptum fuit vicecomiti quod venire faceret predictum Thomas Bever ad respondendum domino regi super premissis etc. Qui quidem Thomas postea venit et allocutus per justiciarios qualiter se velit de premissis sibi impositis acquietare. Qui dicit quod ipse in nullo est inde culpabilis. Et de hoc ponit se super patriam etc. Juratores de Aylesbury venerunt qui dicunt super sacramentum suum quod quedam commissio domini regis directa fuit prefato Roberto le Spicer ad huiusmodi lanas ubicumque fuerunt inventa[81] in comitatu predicto ad opus domini regis capiendas qui quidem Robertus virtute illius commissionis cepit de diversis hominibus predicti comitatus viginti et quatuor saccos lane tantum in viginti et duobus sarpleriis et easdem lanas apud Aylesbury cariavit et in domo predicti Willelmi atte Crouche posuit salvo custodiendas. Et postea predictus Robertus obiit per quod alia commissio domini regis directa fuit prefatis Galfrido de Lucy et Gerardo de Braybrok ad huiusmodi lanas in comitatu predicto capiendas qui quidem Galfridus et Gerardus pretextu illius commissionis predictos viginti et quatuor saccos lane in predictis viginti et duobus sarpleriis apud Aylesbury inventos ad opus domini regis arestarunt et eos signo domini regis consignarunt et deinde usque aquam de Merlawe apud Merlawe cariare fecerunt ut predictum est. Et quod postea quidem malefactores per preceptum domini Johannis de Molyns signum domini regis super predictas lanas domini regis modo predicto consignatum deposuerunt et signum predicti domini[82] Johannis de Molyns super lanas illas consignarunt et eas ad opus predicti domini Johannis abinde cariarunt vi et armis et asportarunt per quod lane ille ad opus domini regis nuncquam devenerunt. Et dicunt quod predictus Thomas Bever in nullo est culpabilis de premissis sibi impositis. Ideo consideratum est quod predictus Thomas eat inde sine die etc.

Membrane 11

[2] [*Marginated*] Esshedon'
Et etiam juratores de Esshedon' presentant quod cum quoddam judicium redditum fuit in curia domini regis nunc[82] anno regni sui quartodecimo pro abbate de Woubourn' versus Gerardum de Braybrok' virtute cuius judicii preceptum fuit vicecomiti ad[83] distringeret predictum Gerardum ad acquietandum dictum abbatem de serviciis que Johannes de Molyns de eo exegit. Idem Johannes misit apud Horsendon' predictum Thomam Frembaud et quosdam alios qui morabantur apud Kynebell' quasi obsedendo dictum manerium de Horsendon' per quod idem Gerardus nec aliquis pro se ausus fuit blada sua ibidem metere nec de eis disponere unde magna pars bladorum suorum periit.

80 *in comitatu Buk'* interlined.

81 Recte *invente.*

82 Interlined.

83 Interlined; recte *quod.*

[*Marginated*] Inquisitio Buk'
Et similiter juratores magne inquisitionis comitatus Buk' presentant quod predictus Thomas Frembaud intravit manerium de Chesham Boys anno regni regis nunc secundo clamando statum in eodem post mortem cuiusdam Nicholai fratris sui qui quidem Nicholaus nunquam statum habuit in eodem manerio nisi ad terminum duodecim annorum ex dimissione Johannis de Breaunsoun chivaler. Ita quod post decessum ipsius Johannis, Johannes de Tryple satisfecit capitali domino pro custodia et maritagio Johannis filii et heredis ipsius Johannis Breaunsoun habendis. Et de ipso fuit seisitus per quod ipse Johannes de Tryple clamavit predictum manerium de Chesham Boys de predicto Thoma Frembaud' ut de jure ipsius Johannis filii et heredis qui quidem Thomas de ingressu et clamio suo injuste se ammovere noluit quousque dictus Johannes de Tryple quinquaginta marcas injuste prefato Thome Frembaud dederat. Et postea idem Thomas appropinquavit dominum Johannem de Molyns et per confederationem et certam conventionem inter eos et quendam Thomam de Abyndon' factas videlicet quod idem Thomas de Abyndon'[84] sequeretur quandam assisam nove disseisine versus prefatos Thomam Frembaud, Henricum et Margeriam[85] de manerio predicto quam sectam idem Thomas Frembaud' et prefatus Johannes de Molyns nomine predicti Thome de Abyndon' in omnibus manutenerent et sequerentur quousque idem Thomas de Abyndon' manerium illud versus prefatos Thomam Frembaud' et alios per assisam illam recuperasset et executionem inde habuisset et cum idem Thomas de Abyndon' seisinam de predicto manerio in forma predicta habuisset inde feoffaret predictum Johannem de Molyns habendum sibi et heredibus suis imperpetuum et ad ea facienda idem Thomas de Abyndon' ligavit se prefato Johanni de Molyns in trescentis marcis per statutum mercatorum ad certum diem in dicto statuto contentum solvendis. Ubi idem Thomas de Abyndon' nullum jus ad idem manerium exigendum seu habendum habuit[86] aut aliquod factum illud testificans nisi tantum unam cartam et unam relaxationem nomine predicti Johannis de Breaunsoun chivaler fictas[87] supponentes ipsum Johannem Breaunsoun predictos Nicholaum et Thomam de Abyndon' de dicto manerio feoffasse optinuit ubi iidem Nicholaus et Thomas de Abyndon' cartam seu relaxationem aliquas a prefato Johanne Breaunsoun chivaler de predicto manerio nunquam habuerunt et sic per conventionem et confederationem inter ipsos Johannem de Molyns, Thomam et Thomam et per falsam manutenenciam ipsius Johannis predictas predicti Henricus et Margeria manerium predictum amiserunt et eorum heredes omnino exheredantur.[88] Ideo preceptum est vicecomiti quod venire faceret prefatum Thomam Frembaud' ad respondendum domino regi super premissis etc. Qui quidem Thomas Frembaud postea venit et allocutus est per justiciarios qualiter se velit de premissis sibi impositis acquietare etc. Qui dicit quod ad premissa super ipsum presentata per juratores hundredorum de Newport et Esshedon' in nullo est inde culpabilis. Et de hoc ponit se super patriam etc. Et juratores de hundredis predictis ad hoc electi et triati dicunt super sacramentum suum quod predictus Thomas Frembaud' quo ad hoc quod superius presentatur quod fuit consentiens et consulens ad ducendum predictum Johannem Evote[89] apud London' coram maiore London' et clerico statuti mercatorum ad recognitionem de predictis ducentis libris in forma predicta faciendam non est inde culpabilis. Set dicunt quod post predictam recognitionem modo predicto factam prefatis civibus, et post diem solutionis predictorum denariorum assignatum predictus Thomas Frembaud' cepit per conventionem viginti marcas de predictis Hugone, Benedicto et Willelmo[90] essendi de eorum consilio et ad prosequendum executionem predicti statuti ipso Thoma sciente de falsitate et deceptione predictis, et quod perquisivit predicta terras et tenementa in Denham cum denariis suis de prefato Simone[91] set causa manutenencionis et auxilii predictorum meliorem mercatum habuit de eisdem. Ideo committitur prisone in custodia vicecomitis etc. Et quo ad hoc quod presentatur superius per hundredum de Esshedon' iidem juratores[92] dicunt quod predictus Thomas Frembaud' in nullo est culpabilis etc. Ideo ipse inde quietus etc. ⟨Finis pro isto articulo unde quietus est, set remanet pro aliis prisone; quietus.⟩[93]

84 Repeated in margin. 85 sc. *de Valoynes.*

86 Interlined. 87 Recte *factas.*

88 Interlined.

89 sc. *Johannem Evote de Wenge.*

90 sc. *Hugone le Bever, Benedicto de Suffolk' et Willelmo atte Halle civibus London'.*

91 sc. *de Salford'.*

92 *iidem juratores* interlined.

93 *pro isto . . . aliis* written later between *Finis* and *prisone; quietus.*

Et quo ad hoc quod super predictum Thomam Frembaud' superius presentatur per juratores comitatus Buk' dicit idem Thomas Frembaud[94] quod predictus Thomas de Abyndon' tulit quamdam assisam nove disseisine versus ipsum Thomam Frembaud' et Henricun de Valoynes et Margeriam uxorem eius et alios in eodem breve nominatos de predicto manerio de Chesham Boys coram domino rege apud Aylesbury anno regni domini regis nunc quartodecimo. Per quam assisam tunc[95] compertum fuit quod predictus Thomas de Abyndon' seisitus fuit et disseisitus de predicto manerio per predictum Thomam Frembaud' et alios etc. Per quod tunc ibidem consideratum fuit quod prefatus Thomas de Abyndon' recuperaret inde seisinam suam versus predictos Henricum et Margeriam et alios in predicto breve nominatos per visum recognitionis assise predicte. Et dampna sua taxabantur per eandem assisam ad trescentas marcas. Et quia predicti Henricus et Margeria ut tenentes etc.[95] in breve predicto nominati non fuerunt sufficientes ad predicta dampna predicto Thome de Abyndon' persolvenda, dampna illa per statutum etc. fuerunt proportionata, et quilibet eorum in predicto breve nominatus statum aliquem habens in eodem manerio post disseisinam predictam prefato Thome de Abyndon' factam pro tempore suo[95] de portione sua onerabatur. Ita quod predictus Thomas Frembaud' qui pro tempore quo statum inde habuit de centum marcis onerabatur, de quibus centum marcis executio versus ipsum Thomam nondum est assecuta.[96] Unde petit judicium ex quo probatur per veredictum assise predicte quod actio predicti Thome de Abyndon' vera fuit et fidelis et quod adhuc predictum judicium inde redditum permanet in suo robore non adnichilatum per processum vel alio modo per legem etc. si de premissis super ipsum Thomam Frembaud' superius presentatis supponentibus contrarium predicti judicii dominus rex aliquam injuriam in personam ipsius Thome Frambaud' assignare possit etc.

Et Thomas Gervays qui sequitur pro domino rege dicit quo ex quo predictus Thomas Frambaud' non dedicit quin ipse intravit manerium predictum de injuria sua propria prout supradictum est eo quod nullum jus in eodem tunc temporis habuit. Et non dedicit quin injuste percepit de Johanne de Triple quinquaginta marcas antequam de dicto manerio se vellet ammovere et postea per confederationem et conventionem[97] inter ipsum Thomam Frembaud' et predictos[98] Johannem de Molyns et Thomam de Abyndon' prehabitas conspiraverunt quod prefatus Thomas de Abyndon' sequeretur versus prefatos Thomam Frembaud', Henricum et Margeriam assisam predictam ubi idem Thomas Frembaud' aliquem statum in eodem manerio tunc temporis non habuit, set ex mera voluntate sua et per conventionem inter ipsum Thomam Fremba[ud] et prefatos Johannem de Molyns et Thomam de Abyndon' in predicto breve se fecit nominari et non dedicit quin . . .[99] fuit consentiens et auxilians virtute predictarum cartarum et relaxationis factarum ad predictam falsam . . .[99] prosequendam et manutenendam. Et quod idem Thomas de Abyndon' cum manerium predictum per predictam assisam recuperasset inde feoffaret predictum Johannem de Molyns occasione manutenencie sue predicte . . .[99] pro domino rege etc. Et super hoc datus est ei et Thome Gervays qui sequitur pro domino rege[100] dies de audiendo judicio suo apud Crendon die martis in secunda septimana Quadragesime salvis sibi rationibus suis hinc inde . . .[101] quem diem venerunt ibi tam predictus Thomas Gervays quam predictus Thomas Frembaud'.[102] Et datus est [eis][103] inde dies in forma predicta apud Wycombe die jovis proxima post diem dominicam in medio Quadragesime salvis etc. Ad quem diem ibi tunc venerunt predicti Thomas [Gervays][104] et Thomas Frembaud'. Et datus est eis dies hic die jovis proxima post festum . . .[104] martiris in forma predicta salvis etc.

Membrane 13

[3] [*Marginated*] Buk'
Juratores ville de Ayllesbury presentant quod ubi commissio domini regis directa fuit Roberto le Spicer de Aylesbury ad capiendum ad opus domini regis medietatem lanarum predicti comitatus anno regni domini regis nunc undecimo,[105] idem Robertus virtute commissionis predicte de diversis hominibus

[94] *idem Thomas Frembaud* interlined.

[95] Interlined.

[96] *Nondum est assecuta* interlined.

[97] *et conventionem* interlined.

[98] Interlined.

[99] End of line illegible.

[100] *et Thome . . . rege* interlined.

[101] End of line illegible.

[102] Interlined.

[103] End of line illegible.

[104] Beginning of line missing.

[105] [1] concerns the same offence.

predicti comitatus cepit viginti et duos sarplarios lane qui ponderarunt viginti et quatuor saccos lane et plus qui quidem Robertus postea obiit per quod dominus rex nunc mandavit breve suum patens quibusdam dominis[106] Galfrido de Lucy et Gerardo de Braybrok' sub forma quam prius mandavit predicto Roberto ad huiusmodi lanas in predicto comitatu capiendas et quod iidem dominus[107] Galfridus et Gerardus percipientes et invenientes predictas lanas in domo Willelmi atte Crouche apud Aylesbury per predictum Robertum ad opus predicti domini regis in forma predicta captas virtute mandati predicti domini regis prefatis Galfrido et Gerardo directi predictas lanas ad opus eiusdem domini regis ibidem[108] arestarunt et signum domini regis super predictos sarplarios consignarunt et eos deinde apud aquam de Merlawe duci et cariari fecerunt et predictis lanis ibidem sic existentibus quidam dominus Johannes de Molyns mandavit dominum Johannem del Hay, dominum Robertum del Hay, Willelmum de Berkhampstede et Thomam Bever apud Merlawe ad predictas lanas ad opus predicti domini Johannis de Molyns capiendas qui quidem domini Johannes del Hay, Robertus del Hay, Willelmus et Thomas ex causa predicta ibidem venerunt et predictas lanas de signo domini regis signatas arestarunt nomine predicti domini Johannis de Molyns et signum illud de eisdem lanis deposuerunt et signum predicti domini Johannis de Molyns super easdem lanas apposuerunt et easdem lanas asportarunt per quod predicte lane ad opus domini regis nuncquam devenerunt etc. Ideo preceptum est vicecomiti quod venire faceret hic predictos Galfridum et Gerardum ad respondendum domino regi si de eisdem lanis in compoto suo domino regi ad scaccarium suum responderunt et se inde onerarunt nec ne etc. Et postea predicti Galfridus et Gerardus venerunt et allocuti sunt singillatim si ipsi de omnibus lanis virtute predicte commissionis domini regis eis directe per ipsos arestatis et captis in comitatu predicto compotum suum reddiderunt et erga dominum regem exonerarunt. Qui dicunt quod ipsi de omnibus lanis per ipsos virtute commissionis predicte captis et receptis preterquam de predictis viginti et duobus sarpleriis lane in compoto suo[109] se onerarunt et quod de predictis viginti et duobus sarplariis se non oneraverunt eo quod predicti[109] malefactores per preceptum predicti domini Johannis de Molyns prout superius presentatur venerunt apud Merlawe et lanas illas ibidem modo predicto inventas vi et armis asportaverunt unde dicunt et intelligunt quod dominus rex de lanis illis in forma predicta de possessione sua asportatis ipsos velit onerare etc. unde petunt judicium etc. Et quia predicti Galfridus et Gerardus cognoverunt hic in curia quod ipsi receperunt viginti et duos sarplarios lane virtute commissionis predicte et quod compotum suum de omnibus lanis predictis per ipsos Galfridum et Gerardum in comitatu predicto captis et receptis per warantum supradictum reddiderunt preterquam de predictis lanis unde nichil ostendunt curie hic quod erga dominum regem ipsos exonerare possit. Ideo consideratum est quod predicti Galfridus et Gerardus de predictis viginti et quatuor saccis lane in predictis viginti et duobus sarplariis contentis erga dominum regem onerentur. Et committuntur prisone pro concelamento predictarum lanarum in compoto suo facto ⟨ prisona prisona⟩.[110] Et postea venerunt et quilibet eorum fecit finem cum domino rege pro predicto concelamento videlicet predictus Galfridus pro dimidia marca per plegium predicti Gerardi et predictus Gerardus pro dimidia marca per plegium predicti Galfridi etc. ⟨ dimidia marca dimidia marca⟩.[110] Et postea habita inquisitione de predictis viginti et duobus sarplariis lane appreciandis. Qui dicunt super sacramentum suum quod quilibet saccus continens viginti et sex petras predictarum lanarum modo predicto per predictos Galfridum et Gerardum arestatarum valebat centum solidos unde summa centum et viginti libras unde iidem Galfridus et Gerardus onerantur etc. ⟨ vj^{xx} li.⟩.[110] Et pro eisdem committuntur prisone etc. Et postea tenor recordi predicti mittitur in cancellariam domini regis per breve suum cuius transcriptum huic rotulo est consutum etc.

[*Marginated*] Intratur inter rotulos finium set non invenit plegios etc.

Membrane 14

[4] Placita de ministris foreste domini regis de Bernewode

[*Marginated*] Buk'

Juratores onerati super diversis articulis forestam de Bernwod' ad veredicendum tangentibus presentant quod dominus Johannes de Molyns quondam venit apud Brehull' et vendidit Ricardo le Warde de bosco domini regis pertinente ad manerium suum de Brehull' quatercentum et octo quercus quas predictus

[106] Interlined. [107] Interlined; recte *domini.*

[108] Interlined.

[109] Followed by line over erasure.

[110] Marginated and struck through.

Ricardus succidit et diversis hominibus predicti comitatus vendidit annis regni domini regis nunc Anglie tertiodecimo et quartodecimo.

Item presentant quod Ricardus de Byfeld' et Johannes de Clere prepositus manerii de Brehull' per preceptum domini Johannis de Molyns succiderunt in foresta predicta mille et sexcentum et sex quercus et illos diversis hominibus predicti comitatus vendiderunt annis regni predicti domini regis Anglie predictis.

Item presentant quod dominus Johannes de Molyns donavit cuidam Johanni de Clere preposito de Brehull' subboscum grossum et minimum in predicta foresta ad quantitatem viginti acrarum quem predictus Johannes de Clere succidit et vendidit diversis hominibus predicti comitatus et denarios inde pervenientes ad usum suum proprium recepit et retinuit. Et quod predictus Johannes de Clere succidit et vendidit ibidem[111] decem et octo quercus et denarios de eisdem querquibus pervenientes ad usum suum percepit et retinuit. Et quod custodes foreste predicte quando viderunt wastum in eadem foresta esse factum sicut supra dictum est non ausi fuerunt inde facere perturbationem pro timore predicti domini Johannis de Molyns.[112]

Item presentant quod in bosco de Ixhull' qui est separale predicti domini regis succisi fuerunt sexaginta et duo grossi quercus de bono maheremio.

Item presentant quod in bosco de Paynsehale et le Fryth' succisi fuerunt post coronationem domini regis nunc usque nunc quinque milia novem centum et quaterviginti querci et rowours unde pars in obsequio domini regis et suo hospicio expendebatur. Per quod preceptum est vicecomiti quod venire faceret dominum Johannem de Haudlo custodem predicte foreste in feodo. Et similiter Johannem le Venour locum tenentem predicti domini Johannis et similiter omnes viridarios, forestarios et regardatores predicte foreste ad respondendum domino regi de premissis. Et postea venit predictus Johannes le Venour et allocutus est de premissis, qualiter officium suum[113] super eisdem[113] in foresta et boscis predictis exercuit et perpetravit, et quod hec que de premissis in officio suo facto curie hic in presencia predictorum viridariorum, forestariorum et regardatorum hic existentium ostenderet si etc. Qui dicit quo ad premissa per dominum Johannem de Molyns, Ricardum le Warde, Ricardum de Byfeld', Johannem de Clere facta et superius presentata quod dominus rex nunc mandavit breve suum Johanni de Haudlo custodi foreste sue de Bernewode vel eius locum tenenti ibidem[113] clausum in hec verba. Edwardus Dei gracia rex Anglie, dominus Hibernie et dux Aquitannie dilecto et fideli suo Johanni de Haudlo custodi foreste nostre de Bernewode vel eius locum tenenti ibidem salutem. Cum nuper de gracia nostra speciali concesserimus pro nobis et heredibus nostris dilecto et fideli nostro Johanni de Molyns quod ipse de boscis manerii sui de Brehull' qui sunt infra metas foreste predicte ut dicitur in locis ubi expedire videbitur usque ad numerum trescentarum acrarum succidere et arbores et boscum sic succisos quo voluerit abducere cariare et voluntatem suam inde facere nec non dictas trescentas acras assartare et in culturam redigere et eas sic assartatas et in culturam redactas parvo fossato et bassa haia secundum assisam foreste includere et tenere possit sibi et heredibus suis imperpetuum sine occasione vel impedimento nostri vel heredum nostrorum justiciariorum, escatorum, vicecomitum aut aliorum ballivorum seu ministrorum nostrorum foreste seu aliorum quorumcumque eo non obstante quod manerium et bosci illi infra metas foreste nostre predicte sic existunt prout in litteris nostris patentibus inde confectis plenius continetur, vobis mandamus quod ipsum Johannem de boscis suis predictis usque ad numerum predictum succidere et arbores et boscum sic succisos quo voluerit abducere cariare et voluntatem suam inde facere necnon terram predictam assartare et in culturam redigere et eam sic assartatam et in culturam redactam parvo fossato et bassa haia ut predicitur includere et tenere absque impedimento permittatis juxta tenorem litterarum nostrarum predictarum ipsum contra tenorem earundem non molestantes in aliquo seu gravantes. Teste meipso apud Westmonasterium vicesimo secundo die aprilis anno regni nostri duodecimo. Pretextu cuius mandati in presencia omnium et singulorum viridariorum et rewardatorum ac[113] predicti Johannis le Venour locum tenentis predicti Johannis de Haudlo capitalis forestarii foreste predicte visis litteris dicti[113] domini regis patentibus inde confectis admensuratum fuit per certas divisas infra forestam predictam usque ad numerum trescentarum acrarum bosci et predicto Johanni de Molyns liberatum qui quidem Johannes de Molyns habita inde liberatione in forma predicta vendidit predicto Ricardo le Warde

[111] Interlined.

[112] Followed by line over erasure.

[113] Interlined.

predictos[113] quatercentum et octo quercus de bosco infra precinctum predictarum trescentarum acrarum bosci[113] existentes ad faciendum de eis prout superius presentatur. Et quo ad predictos mille et sexcentum et sex quercus per predictos Ricardum et Johannem de Clere in foresta predicta succisos et venditos et etiam quo ad[114] subboscum grossum et minimum predictum per predictum Johannem de Clere succisum et venditum et ad decem et octo quercus per predictum Johannem de Clere succisos et venditos succisi fuerunt infra precinctum predictarum trescentarum acrarum postquam predictus Johannes de Molyns inde habuit liberationem in forma predicta[115] et quod idem Johannes de Molyns de predictis quercubus et boscis disposuit et voluntatem suam de eisdem fecit prout superius presentatur. Et hoc petit quod inquiratur etc.

Datus est ei dies apud Ailesbury die lune[116] proxima ante festum Sancti Laurencii etc. in statu quo nunc. Item die sabati proxima post festum Omnium Sanctorum apud Wycombe. Item deinde datus est dies prefato Johanni le Venour apud Wycombe die mercurii proxima post festum Sancte Trinitatis in statu quo nunc. Et vicecomes tunc venire faciat xxiiij etc. Et deinde dies datus est apud Edelesburgh' die lune proxima post festum Sancti Andree apostoli in statu quo nunc. Et adtunc veniat inde jurata etc.

Membrane 15

[5] [*Marginated*] Buk'
Juratores trium hundredorum de Aylesbury presentant quod die lune proxima ante festum Sancte Margarete anno regni regis nunc quartodecimo per preceptum et manutenenciam domini Johannis de Molyns venerunt quidam malefactores vi et armis in effrenatione pacis apud Horsenden videlicet Johannes de la Haye persona ecclesie de Weston' Torvile et alii de covina sua insidiantes dominum Gerardum de Braybrok' et effrenantes uxorem eiusdem domini Gerardi ac eius familiam et communitatem eiusdem ville de Horsenden'. Et postea idem Johannes de Molyns assignavit predictum Johannem de la Haye et quendam Ricardum de Byfeld' et plures alios ad arma ad eundum vagantes et equitantes per diemque noctem per totam patriam eiusdem comitatus qui quidem Johannes de la Haye, Ricardus et alii homines eiusdem patrie effrenarunt et predictum dominum Gerardum insidiarunt ipsumque tenentes suos perturbantes quod ipse Gerardus et tenentes sui terram suam waynare non potuerunt nec fena sua cariare vel sesonare blada sua nec metere quousque quedam concordia inter predictum dominum Johannem de Molyns et predictum Gerardum per vicinos amicabiles esset facta et contracta ad magnum dampnum predicti domini Gerardi ac tenentium suorum. Ideo preceptum est vicecomiti quod venire faceret etc. ad respondendum domino regi de premissis etc. Et postea predictus Ricardus venit et allocutus est qualiter de transgressione predicta se velit acquietare qui dicit quod premissa non potest dedicere. Ideo comittitur prisone in custodia vicecomitis etc. Et postea venit idem Ricardus et fecit finem cum domino rege pro transgressione predicta de quadraginta solidis quos eidem vicecomiti in presencia eorundem justiciariorum plene persolvit etc.
[*Marginated*] xl s.[117]

Membrane 15d

[6] [*Marginated*] Buk'. iij hundredi de Ciltr'
Juratores trium hundredorum de Ciltr' presentant quod cum contentio mota fuit inter priorem Cantuariensem et tenentes suos de Riseburgh' in comitatu Buk' eo quod prefatus prior predictos tenentes suos terram suam de eo tenere facere voluisset alio modo quam facere solebant et super hoc idem prior tantum locutus fuit cum domino Johanne de Molyns et eum de consilio suo retinuit pro suo donante quod idem Johannes querelam predictam manucepit et postea venit ibidem[118] vi et armis contra pacem etc. cum suis adherentibus scilicet predicto Roberto tunc custode manerii predicti qui quidem Robertus modo est prior Cantuariensis et aliis malefactoribus etc. die lune in festo Pentecoste anno regni domini regis nunc decimo et hostia domorum Willelmi de la Halle, Hugonis de la Grene, Ricardi le Hopper et septem aliorum tenentium predicti manerii fregerunt et corpora eorundem Willelmi, Hugonis, Ricardi et aliorum predictorum tenentium ceperunt et de cordis ligaverunt et deinde in duabus carettis usque ad prioratum Cantuariensem duxerunt et ibidem detinuerunt quousque duo eorum ibidem moriebantur scilicet Hugo de la Grene et Willelmus le Hopper et aliquos predictorum tenentium

[114] *quo ad* interlined.
[115] *in forma predicta* interlined.
[116] Written over an erased word ending *is*.

[117] Struck through.
[118] Interlined.

adhuc ibidem detinent et aliquos eorumdem tenentium per conventionem inter ipsos tenentes et predictos Robertum et dominum Johannem et alios malefactores factam ita quod predicti tenentes tenerent terram suam in eodem manerio ad voluntatem prefati prioris domui transire permiserunt. Et ad propositum suum plene absque periculo inde habendo performandum iidem Robertus nunc prior et dominus Johannes de Molyns inter se et quemdam Jacobum Frisel patrem etc. conspiraverunt et ordinaverunt apud Stok' Pogeis die lune proxima post festum Sancti Johannis ante portam latinam anno regni domini regis nunc decimo ad imppetrandum unam commissionem regis[118] domino Johanni de Inge et predicto domino Johanni de Molyns ad audiendum et terminandum quicquid mortem cuiusdam Henrici le Plomer ballivi predicti manerii tangens virtute cuius commissionis prefati Johannes et Johannes ad premissa facienda apud Wycombe in comitatu isto die lune proxima post festum Sancti Bonifacii anno predicti domini regis nunc decimo sederunt et coram eis unam inquisitionem de tenentibus et adherentibus prefati Johannis de Molyns venire fecerunt et qui voluntatem eiusdem Johannis de Molyns in aliquo contradicere non ausi fuerunt per quod ad sessionem illam coram prefatis justiciariis quidam Willelmus de la Halle, Ricardus le Hopper, tenentes predicti manerii, Hugo de la Halle et Willelmus le Hopper de morte predicti Henrici indictati extiterunt ac etiam quidam Alexander de Saunderdon' de receptamento eorundem Willelmi, Ricardi, Hugonis, et Willelmi le Hopper sciens de predicta felonia indictatus fuit ubi predictus Alexander nuncquam eosdem Willelmum, Ricardum, Hugonem, et Willelmum le Hopper receptavit et quod iidem justiciarii processum super huiusmodi indictamento tam versus illos qui in forma predicta apud Cantuariam detenti fuerunt quam versus alios non in prisona existentes velociter continuaverunt quousque predicti indictati in exigendo positi fuerunt. Et quod postea predictus Alexander apud Aylesbury in comitatu isto ex causa predicta se prisone ibidem reddidit et manucaptionem vicecomiti invenit essendi coram prefatis justiciariis apud Agmoundesham ad diem in eodem brevi de exigendo prefixum ad quem diem iidem justiciarii ibidem non venerunt per quod processus super predicto indictamento in forma predicta factus discontinuatus fuit. Ideo preceptum est vicecomiti quod venire faceret predictum Jacobum simul etc. ad respondendum domino regi de conspiracione et falsitate predictis etc. Postea predictus Jacobus venit. Et allocutus est qualiter se velit de premissis acquietare. Qui dicit quod predicta presentatio nullam injuriam per ipsum esse factam supponit set quod quoddam breve domini regis de audiendo et terminando ad predictam feloniam puniendam imppetratum fuit quod quidem indictamentum virtute commissionis predicte factum nondum probatum est falsum aut expresse terminatum secundum legem Anglie per quod predictum indictamentum adhuc permanet in suo robore non adnichelatum unde intelligit quod dominus rex aliquam injuriam in personam ipsius Jacoby assignare possit aut ad[118] aliquod in predicta presentatione contentum velit responderi etc. Et petit judicium etc. Et Thomas Gervays qui sequitur pro domino rege dicit quod ex quo predictus Jacobus non dedicit predicta facinora per predictum priorem et dominum Johannem de Molyns et alios etc. in forma prout superius presentantur esse perpetrata et non dedicit quod predicta commissio domini regis per conspiracionem inter ipsum Jacobum[118] et predictos dominum Johannem de Molyns et priorem ad predicta facinora in forma predicta male et non debito modo secundum legem Anglie audienda et terminanda per ipsum Jacobum[119] imppetrata fuit per quod predicti Willelmus de la Halle, Ricardus le Hopper, Hugo, et Willelmus le Hopper de morte predicti Henrici maliciose indictati fuerunt et in exigendo positi prout superius presentatur. Unde petit judicium pro domino rege etc. Et super hoc datus est dies tam prefato Thome Gervays qui sequitur pro domino rege quam prefato Jacobo hic die jovis proxima post diem dominicam in medio Quadragesime de audiendo inde judicio suo etc. Ad quem diem predictus Jacobus venit. Et datus est ei dies hic et Thome Gervays qui sequitur pro domino rege[120] die lune proxima post festum translationis Sancti Thome martiris salvis sibi et domino regi rationibus suis hic inde dicendis etc. Ad quem diem venit predictus Jacobus. Et datus est ei dies ulterius coram prefatis justiciariis apud Aylesbury die lune proxima ante festum Sancti Laurencii salvis etc. Ad quem diem venit predictus Jacobus et datus est ei dies in statu quo nunc apud Wycombe die sabati proxima post festum Omnium Sanctorum. Ad quem diem non venit. Et super hoc testatum est quod predictus Jacobus mortuus est. Ideo etc.

Membrane 16d

[7] [*Marginated*] Buk'
Juratores trium hundredorum de Ciltr' presentant

[119] *per ipsum Jacobum* interlined.

[120] *et Thome . . . rege* interlined.

quod dominus Johannes de Molyns post mortem Roberti le Sencler petiit custodiam et maritagium cuiusdam Roberti filii et heredis eiusdem Roberti Sencler imponens ei quod tenuit de eo per homagium et escuagium et mandavit Johannem de Bracy, Thomam Golye et alios apud villam de Stoue ad corpus predicti heredis noctanter capiendum qui quidem puer de eorum adventu maxime timore ductus ab inde velociter diffugit. Et quod ibi contumelia inter amicos predicti heredis et predictos Johannem de Bracy et Thomam in tanto oriebatur quod pigatium caputii dicti Johannis de Bracy de uno gladio fuit abcisum set per quem ignorant per quod postea predictus dominus Johannes Molyns secutus fuit in cancellaria domini regis pro una commissione habenda Johanni de Inge et Philippo de Aylesbury militibus ad audiendum et terminandum contumeliam predictam que quidem commissio predictis Johanni et Philippo directa existit et in qua commissione predictus Johannes de Bracy et alii[121] ut querentes nominabantur. Et quidam Willelmus de Grenevill', Thomas Golie, Johannes Golie et alii defendentes nominabantur. Virtute cuius commissionis predicti justiciarii apud villam de Stok' Pugeis ad premissa facienda postea sederunt. Et quod per conspiracionem inter predictum Johannem de Molyns, Johannem de la Haye personam ecclesie de Weston' Turvill' et Johannem Inge chivaler prehabitam et locutam apud Stoke Pugeis existit ordinatum in octabis Circumcisionis Domini anno regni regis nunc decimo quod Thomas Golie unus predictorum defendentum ductibilis ad voluntatem predicti Johannis de la Haye veniret coram prefatis justiciariis apud Stoke Pugeis ad diem in mandato eorundem justiciariorum contentum responsurus prefatis conquerentibus et congnosceret transgressionem predictam in forma prout supponebatur per comissionem et narrationem predictorum conquerentium qui quidem Thomas premissa in omnibus per preceptum predicti Johannis de la Haye perpetravit per quod tunc consideratum fuit quod predicti querentes recuperarent dampna sua occasione predicta ducentarum marcarum. Et postea iidem justiciarii continuando predictum processum virtute comissionis predicte versus predictos Willelmum de Grenevill' et alios ubi idem Willelmus et alii defendentes pro timore quem a prefato Johanne de Molyns habuerunt per amicos intromittentes fecerunt satisfactionem cum predicto Johanne de Molyns pro predicta secta extinguenda versus eos de centum marcis quas eidem Johanni de Molyns plene solverunt. De quibus conspiracione et falsitate predictus Philippus de Aylesbury miles nichil scivit seu in aliquo erat consentiens. Ideo preceptum est vicecomiti quod venire faceret Johannem de la Haye simul cum aliis etc. ad respondendum domino regi de premissis. Qui postea per vicecomitem venit ductus et allocutus est qualiter de premissis se velit acquietare qui dicit quod predicta presentatio supponit primo unam transgressionem esse perpetratam per alias personas et non per ipsum.

[*Marginated*] Datus dies apud Ailesb' die lune ante festum Sancti Laurencii. Item die sabati proximo post festum Omnium Sanctorum.

Membrane 17

DELIBERATIO PRISONUM FACTA APUD WYCOMBE CORAM WILLELMO DE BOHUN COMITE NORHAMPTON', ROBERTO PARVYNG', JOHANNE MORICE, RICARDO DE MONTE CANYSO, RICARDO DE KELLESHULL' ET ROBERTO DE TEYE JUSTICIARIIS DOMINI REGIS AD DIVERSAS FELONIAS IN COMITATU BUK' FACTAS AUDIENDAS ET TERMINANDAS ASSIGNATIS DIE LUNE PROXIMO ANTE FESTUM PURIFICATIONIS BEATE MARIE ANNO REGNI REGIS EDWARDI TERTII POST CONQUESTUM ANGLIE QUARTODECIMO REGNI VERO SUI FRANCIE PRIMO FINIENTE

[8] [*Marginated*] Buk'

Juratores trium hundredorum de Chilterne presentant quod Henricus Inde ⟨suspendatur⟩ et alii die mercurii in festo Sancti Edwardi [anno regni][122] regis Edwardi patris domini regis nunc vicesimo noctanter felonice interfecerunt Petrum Pugeys dominum manerii de Stokepogeys et Johannem filium et heredem ipsius Petri et Johannem Pikerel cocum eiusdem Petri apud Stokepugeys in comitatu Buk'. Ideo preceptum fuit vicecomiti quod caperet prefatum Henricum si etc. et salvo etc. Ita quod haberet corpus eius coram prefatis[123] justiciariis domini regis hic ad[124] respondendum domino regi de feloniis predictis. Qui quidem Henricus coram prefatis justiciariis ad diem illum per vicecomitem captus venit et allocutus est per justiciarios qualiter se velit de feloniis predictis acquietare. Qui dicit quod ipse in nullo est culpabilis. Et inde de bono et malo se ponit super patriam etc. Juratores adhoc electi et triati dicunt super sacra-

121 *et alii* interlined.

122 Omitted.

123 Interlined.

124 Followed by line over erasure.

mentum suum quod predictus Henricus Inde culpabilis est de feloniis predictis. Ideo ipse suspendatur.[125] Catalla eius xxxiiij s. viij d. ⟨catalla forisfacta xxxiiij s. viij d.⟩.[126] Et terra ij acre terre que modo seisiantur precii acre xv d. et inde habuit statum per duos annos proximo post festum Sancti Michaelis ultimo preterito sequentem.

JUST 1/75, m.8

[9] [*Marginated*] iij hundredi de Chilterne
Juratores trium hundredorum de Chilterne presentant quod ubi Johannes de Molyns felonice interfecerat Petrum Pogeys, Johannem filium eius et Johannem Pikerel cocum dicti Petri apud Stokepogeys die mercurii in festo Sancti Edwardi anno regni regis Edwardi patris domini regis nunc vicesimo postmodum pro isto malefacto cooperiendo per conspiracionem inter predictum Johannem de Molyns et Johannem Inge chivaler apud Stokepogeys die lune proxima post festum Sancte Trinitatis anno regni regis nunc primo prehabitam pro predicto Johanne de Molyns de predicta felonia falso acquietando inter eos ordivanerunt et impetraverunt quandam commissionem de cancellaria domini regis dirigi prefato Johanni Inge et quibusdam aliis de covina predicti Johannis de Molyns ad predictam feloniam audiendam et terminandam assignatis quo pretextu predicti Johannes Inge et socii sui accesserunt apud Ayllesbury ad certum diem coram quibus predictus Johannes de Molyns ductus fuit tanquam priso ad barram et de feloniis predictis ubi idem Johannes de Molyns de bono et malo se posuit super patriam quod non fuit inde culpabilis et per juratores minus sufficientes et procuratos per predictos Johannem de Molyns et Johannem Inge et qui nuncquam per vicecomitem retornati fuerunt predictus Johannes de Molyns inde extitit falso acquietatus et hoc per ordinationem et machinationem predicti Johannis Inge. Et dicunt ulterius quod predicti Johannes et Johannes sunt communes conspiratores. Per quod preceptum fuit vicecomiti quod venire faceret predictum Johannem Inge etc. Et modo venit predictus Johannes Inge et allocutus super premissis etc.
[*Marginated*] Judicium.

KB 27/388, Rex m.22

[10] [*Marginated*] Buk'
Juratores diversorum hundredorum comitatus Buk' alias coram Willelmo de Shareshull' et sociis suis justiciariis domini regis ad diversas proditiones, felonias, roberias, transgressiones, conspiraciones, confederaciones et manutenencias per Johannem de Molyns chivaler et Egidiam uxorem eius et alios de comitiva sua de eorum precepto in comitatu predicto factas audiendas et terminandas assignatis presentaverunt quod ubi Johannes Gamage ⟨utlagatus⟩ et alii felones interfecerunt quendam extraneum mercatorem in Stokewode videlicet secundo die augusti anno regni regis nunc vicesimo sexto, predictus Johannes de Molyns ipsum Johannem Gamage sciens ipsum fecisse feloniam predictam et quod fuit communis latro receptavit et manutenuit apud Stoke Pugeys continue per unum annum post feloniam illam factam scienter ⟨culpabilis per primam inquisitionem⟩.[127] Item presentaverunt quod ubi Robertus Hiestre ⟨utlagatus⟩ felonice interfecit Johannem Lambard' apud Stoke Pugeys decimo die februarii anno regni regis nunc vicesimo quarto dictus Johannes de Molyns ipsum Robertum receptavit apud Stoke et alibi in comitatu Buk' et ipsum manutenuit post feloniam predictam factam usque in hunc diem sciens ipsum fecisse feloniam predictam ⟨culpabilis per primam inquisitionem⟩.[127] Item presentaverunt quod Johannes de Molyns et Egidia uxor eius primo die marcii anno regni regis nunc tricesimo felonice ceperunt et asportaverunt in aqua de Thamise duodecim cignos de diversis hominibus et eosdem cignos noctanter cariarunt usque maneria ipsius Johannis de Molyns videlicet Wendovere, Aston', Bychyndon' et eos in cameris incluserunt usque diem Parasceves anno supradicto quo die idem Johannes precepit Roberto de Boscham amputare colla et pedes cignorum predictorum et corpora eorum comburere eo quod tota patria percepta fuit de felonia predicta et idem Robertus sic fecit ⟨culpabilis de vj cignis et de aliis vj non culpabilis⟩.[127] Item presentaverunt quod idem Johannes de Molyns quarto die marcii anno regni regis nunc vicesimo octavo apud Wendovere felonice depredavit Johannem Bray de Wendovere de una vacca precii decem solidorum, triginta bidentibus precii sexaginta solidorum, sex quarteriis bracii et aliis bonis et catallis ad valenciam centum solidorum ⟨quietus per primam inquisitionem⟩.[127] Item presentaverunt quod dictus Johannes de Molyns primo die augusti anno regni regis nunc vicesimo octavo apud Stoke Pugeys felonice depredavit Cristinam la Daye de decem quarteriis brasii et aliis bonis et catallis ad valenciam

[125] Repeated in margin.

[126] Marginated; *xxxiiij s. viij d.* struck through.

[127] Marginated.

decem librarum ⟨quietus⟩.[127] Item presentaverunt quod dictus Johannes de Molyns primo die septembris anno regni regis nunc vicesimo quinto domum vicarii ecclesie de Stoke Pugeys apud Stoke Pugeys felonice fregit et unum equum ipsius vicarii precii sexdecim solidorum felonice cepit et abduxit ⟨culpabilis de equo et non de fractione⟩.[127] Item presentaverunt quod Johannes de Molyns chivaler die mercurii proxima post festum Sancte Trinitatis anno regni regis nunc Anglie vicesimo tertio apud Donyngton' felonice fregit domum Willelmi de Berkynge piscenarii London' et ibidem quinque equos ipsius Willelmi precii centum solidorum duos boves precii triginta solidorum unam vaccam precii octo solidorum et alia bona et catalla ipsius Willelmi ad valenciam centum librarum ibidem inventa cepit et asportavit ⟨quietus⟩.[127] Item presentaverunt quod predictus Johannes de Molyns chivaler et Egidia uxor eius venerunt in campo de Stoke vocato Appelton' circa festum Sancte Margarete virginis anno vicesimo sexto regis nunc et ibidem unum equum Johannis de Alderugge precii viginti solidorum felonice furati fuerunt et abduxerunt etc. ⟨quietus⟩.[127] Item presentaverunt quod predictus Johannes de Molyns chivaler receptavit Willelmum Forde ⟨utlagatus⟩, Robertum Boseham ⟨utlagatus⟩, et Robertum Hyestre ⟨utlagatus⟩ apud Dytton' et alibi ad alias domos suas in comitatu Buk' a die dominica in medio Quadragesime anno regni regis nunc tricesimo usque festum Pasche extunc proximo sequens[128] sciens ipsos felonice furatos fuisse duodecim cignos Oliveri de Burdeaux, Johannis de Remenham, et alios[129] apud Dorneiemore et in aqua Thamisie circa predictam diem dominicam in medio xlme anno regis nunc supradicto ⟨culpabilis de receptione omnium trium⟩.[130] Item presentaverunt quod quidam bos Andree Crups de Huggelee precii xvj solidorum pervenisset infra libertatem predicti Johannis de Molyns apud Stoke tanquam extrahura statim predictus Johannes predictum bovem cepit et ad carucam suam posuit ita quod predictus Andreas nullam deliberationem habere potuit nec inde probationem facere prout lex communis exposcit. Et sic dicunt quod predictus Johannes de Molyns circa festum Sancti Michaelis anno vicesimo septimo regis nunc predictum Andream de predicto bove felonice depredavit et ad lardarium suum ipsum interfecit ⟨quietus⟩.[130] Item presentaverunt quod predictus Johannes de Molyns circa festum Sancti Mathei apostoli anno vicesimo septimo regis nunc apud Cippenham Johannem Durewyne de octo bobus et xix porcis precii decem marcarum felonice depredavit ⟨quietus⟩.[130] Item presentaverunt quod predictus Johannes de Molyns et Egidia uxor eius simul cum aliis ignotis venerunt in campum de Upton' circa festum inventionis Sancte Crucis anno vicesimo quinto regis nunc et ibidem duo grossa jumenta precii decem librarum domini prioris de Merton' felonice ceperunt et abduxerunt usque la Ruydyngge ad domum predicti Johannis etc. ⟨culpabilis⟩.[130] Item presentaverunt quod predictus Johannes de Molyns venit cum aliis ignotis apud Adynton' circa festum Pentecoste anno vicesimo tertio regis nunc et ibidem in campo juxta manerium abbatis de Sancto Albano vocatum la Byggynge CC multones precii viginti librarum que fuerunt domini Rogeri Jargevill' et in custodia Johannis Boueton' existentes felonice furatus fuit et eosdem ad domus predicti Johannis de Molyns apud Aston' et Wendovere felonice fugavit etc. ⟨quietus⟩.[130] Item presentaverunt quod predictus Johannes de Molyns chivaler circa festum Natalis Domini anno vicesimo sexto regis nunc apud Dachet tria millia busce in fagotos facte precii septem librarum Johannis Bonet civis London' felonice cepit et abduxit ⟨culpabilis⟩.[130] Que quidem indictamenta inter alia dominus rex venire fecit coram eo terminanda etc. que remanent in custodia Thome Chirchehull' custodis rotulorum etc. in baga de secretis apud Wycombe in xv^{a} Sancti Johannis Baptiste de isto eodem termino etc. Et modo scilicet die jovis in festo Sancte Mildrede virginis isto eodem termino coram domino rege apud Wycombe venerunt predicti Johannes de Molyns et Egidia uxor eius per vicecomitem ducti per breve de exigendo redditi etc. Et pro eo quod predicti Johannes Gamage, Robertus Hiestre, Willelmus Forde et Robertus Boseham superius de principalibus etc. indictati utlagati sunt ideo idem Johannes de Molyns de receptamento et manutenencia eorundem ac etiam iidem Johannes et Egidia uxor eius de omnibus aliis feloniis superius super ipsos presentatis allocuti sunt qualiter de feloniis illis se velint acquietare dicunt separatim quod ipsi in nullo sunt inde culpabiles. Et inde de bono et malo ponunt se super patriam etc. Et juratores per predictum vicecomitem retornati videlicet Thomas de[131] Reynes chivaler, Johannes atte Penne, Alanus Carbonel, Johannes Loveday, Johannes Baudewyne, Henricus Baudewyne, Johannes Holt de Mersh', Nicholaus Barn', Thomas Poynaunt, Adam Bolestrode, Thomas Brayles et Johannes de Aylesbury venerunt quos quidem juratores predicti Johannes de Molyns et Egidia uxor eius omnino calumpniarunt. Ideo

128 Recte *sequentem*.

129 Recte *aliorum*.

130 Marginated.

131 Interlined.

iidem Johannes et Egidia pro defectu patrie remittuntur prisone in custodia Johannis de Essex' mariscalli etc. ⟨mariscallus⟩.[132] Et amotis predictis calumpniatis etc. preceptum est vicecomiti quod venire faceret coram domino rege in octabis Sancti Michaelis ubicumque etc. tot et tales etc. de balliva sua per quos etc. Et qui nec etc. ad recognoscendum etc. Et super hoc predicti Johannes et Egidia de mandato domini regis mittuntur per Johannem de Hampden' vicecomitem ad castrum ipsius regis de Wyndesore ibidem in prisona moraturi quousque idem rex alius de eis duxerit ordinandum etc. Et continuato inde processu usque in crastinum Sancti Martini tunc proximo sequentem etc. ad quem diem coram domino rege apud Dunstaple venerunt predicti Johannes et Egidia per dominum regem missi et per predictum vicecomitem ducti. Et similiter juratores virtute brevis domini regis retornati venerunt de quibus dictus Johannes de Molyns calumpniavit Rogerum Louthe chivaler, Walterum Rabbe, Simonem Rous, Willelmum Denton' et Ricardum Cave de Dorneye, Henricum Wydemere, Johannem de Couele, Walterum Portreve, Petrum de Ayete, Johannem Remenham, Adam Poynant, Ricardum Bataille, Radulfum Symely, Johannem Salford' seniorem, Johannem Tosty et Willelmum Saleman. Et Petrus de Salford', Johannes Cheyne, Radulfus Eccleshale, Johannes de Broghton', Ricardus Duraunt, Philippus Brayles, Johannes le Brok', Ricardus Pycot', Willelmus Broun, Johannes atte Forde, Johannes Asshwelle et Johannes Aldrugge jurati et onerati super ipsum Johannem de Molyns de receptamento predicti Johannis Gamage apud Stokbugeys et Roberti de Heghestr' apud Stoke dicunt super sacramentum suum quod idem Johannes de Molyns est inde culpabilis in forma qua superius presentatum est. Et super hoc idem Johannes de Molyns dicit quod ipse clericus est et non potest ulterius sine ordinario suo respondere. Et super hoc ob defectu ordinarii tradito sibi libro per curiam legit ut clericus etc. Et ut sciatur pro quali tam inde quam pro aliis articulis unde nondum convictus est debeat ordinario liberari inquiratur inde rei veritas per patriam etc. Et super hoc juratores videlicet Thomas de Reynes chivaler, Rogerus de Louthe chivaler, Walterus Rabbe, Johannes de Remenham, Willelmus Salman, Ricardus Cave de Dorneye, Ricardus Cave de Shirynton', Johannes Loveday, Adam Bolstrode, Johannes atte Penne, Johannes Cave et Johannes Couele ex officio jurati et onerati dicunt super sacramentum suum quo ad sex singnos in aqua Thamisie captos de predictis duodecim cingnis de diversis hominibus etc. Et quo ad depredationem de Johanne de Bray de predicta vacca et quo ad depredationem Cristiane le Daye de brasio etc. Et quo ad fractionem domus vicarii ecclesie de Stoke et quo ad fractionem domus Willelmi de Berkyng' piscenarii London' et captionem equorum, bovum, vacce ac aliorum bonorum et catallorum eiusdem Willelmi etc. Et quo ad depredationem equi predicti Johannis de Aldrugge et quo ad depredationem bovis predicti Andree Crups et quo ad depredationem dictorum octo bovum decem et novem porcorum predicti Johannis Durein etc. Et quo ad depredationem predictorum ducentorum multonum que fuerunt predicti domini Rogeri de Jargevile etc. predictus Johannes de Molyns in nullo est inde culpabilis. Ideo idem Johannes eat inde quietus etc. Et quo ad sex cingnos de predictis duodecim cingnis etc. et quo ad depredationem equi vicarii ecclesie de Stoke Pugeys et quo ad receptationem predictorum Willelmi Forde, Roberti Boseham et Roberti Heighestr' apud Dytton' et quo ad depredationem predictorum duorum jumentorum de priore de Merton' et quo ad predicta tria milia busce in fagottos etc. Iidem juratores dicunt quod predictus Johannes Molyns est inde culpabilis prout superius [*membrane 22d*] super ipsum presentatum est. Ideo pro defectu ordinarii committitur prisone in custodia predicti vicecomitis etc. salvo custodiendo [sub][133] periculo quod incumbit quousque etc. Catalla super ipsum Johannem inventa decem solidi et decem solidi[134] in denariis numeratis et due zone de argento ornate, unum par de pater noster de aunbre, unum tabularium de yvoir, et unum rotulum[135] de orationibus super ipsum inventa fuerunt que appressiantur per eosdem juratores ad decem solidos unde dictus vicecomes respondebit. Et quia curia non advisatur ad presens de procedendo ad deliberationem predicte Egidie. Ideo ipsa remittitur prisone in custodia eiusdem vicecomitis salvo custodienda quousque etc. Et quod omnia bona et catalla terre et tenementa ipsius Johannis de Molyns occasione predicta in manum regis seisiantur etc.[136]

[132] Marginated.

[133] Omitted.

[134] Recte *denarii*?

[135] Recte *unus rotulus*.

[136] *Et quod omnia . . . etc.* interlined. There follow charters of pardon to Gill dated 22 May 34 Edward III and consequent procedure.

The tenants of the bishops of Coventry and Lichfield and of Worcester after the plague of 1348-9

edited by

EDMUND FRYDE

INTRODUCTION

In the conclusion to her study of *The Black Death on the Estates of the Bishopric of Winchester*[1] the late Professor A. E. Levett expressed a hope that other comparable surveys might be published and that they should include some precise statistics. It appears that she herself 'was planning a survey of the effects of the Black Death over the country as a whole' and her surviving study of what happened on the estates of St Albans would have formed one fragment of this projected work.[2] More recently the inadequacy of the results obtained hitherto has been brought sharply to the notice of historians by the publication of Professor J. F. D. Shrewsbury's *History of Bubonic Plague in the British Isles.*[3] He argues that scholars have considerably exaggerated the number of deaths in the epidemic of 1348–9. I am not concerned here with discussing his attempt to evaluate from a medical point of view the contemporary descriptions of the plague, though even that is highly controversial.[4] But Professor Shrewsbury's methods of handling the evidence derived from various official records are certainly unsatisfactory. It is regrettable that he should rely mainly on printed records and that he was unable to explore the unpublished sources that lie behind them. Thus, he refers[5] to a short passage in the Victoria County History of Worcestershire mentioning the inquiry into the tenants of the bishopric of Worcester when that see was in the hands of the royal custodians in 1349.[6] Professor Shrewsbury treats it as merely another instance of what he regards as questionable allegations about the high rate of mortality from the plague, but he made no effort to look at the original evidence on the L.T.R. exchequer memoranda roll. He missed thereby a valuable reference to an important type of fresh evidence which forms the core of my own study. This Worcester evidence does not bear out Dr Shrewsbury's main contention that the death rate in 1348–9 was much lower than scholars usually suggest.

I have chosen to concentrate mainly on the two neighbouring bishoprics of Worcester and of Coventry and Lichfield because exceptionally valuable evidence happens to be readily available in these two cases. There are contrasts as well as similarities and the differences between the estates of the two bishops are very instructive. The choice of this region of England is particularly appropriate as the city of Worcester and the beautiful countryside around it were very familiar to Mr Meekings. In the course of his researches on the hearth tax at Worcester he investigated all the urban tenements that had once formed part of seventeenth-century Worcester.

I

Between 1349 and 1364 there were as many as four episcopal vacancies at Worcester in quick succession, a welcome source of information to a historian. Two of these occurred because of the transfer of bishops to other, richer dioceses. The first vacancy was due to the death of the aged Bishop Wolstan on 6 August 1349. The temporalities of the see were taken into the king's hands by the escheator, Leo Perton, who was joined soon afterwards by a second custodian, Robert Warcop (de Warthecop). Together they held the vacant bishopric unti 28 November 1349. Their two accounts[7] thus cover the crucial period during the last stages of the plague when the population had reached its lowest level.[8] The vacancy yielded to the king a mere £137 6s. 7d.,[9] much less than could normally be expected. The exchequer officials had certainly every reason for alarm as they scrutinised the records of previous vacancies at

[1] In Oxford Studies in Soc. & Leg. Hist., ed. P. Vinogradoff, V (Oxford, 1916), 154.

[2] A. E. Levett, *Studies in Manorial History* (Oxford, 1938), 248–86, especially 248 n.l.

[3] Cambridge, 1970.

[4] See, e.g., the review by R. M. S. McConaghey, *Medical History*, XV (1971), 309–11, and C. Morris, 'The Plague in Britain', *Hist. Jnl*, XIV (1971), 205–15.

[5] *Bubonic Plague*, 67–9.

[6] *VCH Worcs*, IV, 448–9. This evidence is also noted in another recent work on the plague of 1348–9: P. Ziegler, *The Black Death* (Pelican edn, Harmondsworth, 1970), 194–5.

[7] E 357/3, m.53; E 372/196, m.47; E 368/124, mm. 256–9: below, [1–61].

[8] The duration of the epidemic in the diocese of Worcester can be approximately reconstructed from the records of the ordination of new parish clergy. Cf. Shrewsbury, *Bubonic Plague*, 66–7 and fig. 7.

[9] E 372/196, m.47.

Worcester and listened to the long list of allowances claimed by Perton by reason of the plague. As far as the total revenue was concerned, comparisons with the past were very disturbing. Thus in 1317 a slightly longer period of royal custody in the summer and autumn of that year had produced £250 9s. 4¼d.[10] In 1349 there was a particularly catastrophic decline in renders depending on the numbers of tenants and on the size of the tenements occupied by them. The 'recognition' paid to the royal custodians by the servile tenants at the beginning of each vacancy slumped appallingly. In a more normal year, like 1337, this had yielded £24 15s.,[11] but in 1349 Perton and his colleagues could apparently collect no more than £1 8s. 8d.[12] The exchequer naturally set on foot a more detailed inquiry. The resultant inquisitions [28–33] provide invaluable information including precise statements about the number and condition of unfree tenants and smallholders who had survived the plague. The inquiry vindicated Perton and Warcop and they were excused £84 4s. ½d. of revenue lost by reason of the plague.[13]

The same thing happened after a vacancy of around seven weeks in February–March 1353. Perton had the custody of the episcopal estates in Worcestershire,[14] while the sheriff of Gloucestershire answered for properties in that county.[15] On this occasion Perton asked to be excused £57 15s. 5¼d. of revenues lost through the plague. After another detailed inquiry the exchequer gave him allowance for this amount. The returns of 1353 confirm the overall picture revealed by the previous inquiry, but some of the figures are slightly different. The two sets of returns appear, therefore, to be independent of each other. If they do reflect two different situations at an interval of four years, as they seem to do, this would suggest that the tenant population on the episcopal estates was recovering only very slowly from the disaster of 1348–9.

The next vacancy of the bishopric lasted two months, from 10 December 1361 to 9 February 1362. The records compiled on this occasion by the indispensable Leo Perton and his associates reveal a fresh decline in the revenue from the episcopal properties.[16] Some of the details suggest that this fresh setback may have been due to another fall in the tenant population, presumably as the result of the second plague epidemic which started in 1361 and continued in some places during the following winter. Three years later there occurred yet another vacancy at Worcester, lasting from 6 April to 28 June 1364. We owe to it an elaborate extent of the episcopal estates again drawn up, of course, by Leo Perton.[17] This document suggests that after the crisis of 1361 the new bishop, John Barnet, had modified somewhat the fiscal policies of his predecessors.

The information about the situation at the end of 1349 and in 1353 can be compared with the bishops' own surveys, dating mainly from c.1299, preserved in the Red Book of Worcester.[18] This alone makes it feasible to hazard a guess about the extent of the fall in the tenant population during the plague of 1348–9. It can be no more than a very tentative estimate because we know almost nothing about the changes in population between c.1299 and 1348. For comparisons of revenue good use can also be made of the records compiled during the long vacancy of the see of Worcester between 3 January 1302 and 4 February 1303.[19] This is what the exchequer officials themselves did in 1349 and 1353 and we still possess some of the sources of information that they utilised on these occasions.[20]

It is also possible to study in great detail the estates of the bishops of Worcester in the later decades of the fourteenth century because from the 1360s onwards the bishops' own manorial accounts and court rolls survive for some of their properties and this series of records becomes fuller in the reign

[10] SC 6/1143/19; E 372/165, m.30 (account of Henry Cobham, 20 June–20 Nov. 1317).

[11] SC 6/1143/20.

[12] E 372/196, m.47; E 136/12/10.

[13] E 372/196, m.47.

[14] E 368/126, stat. et vis. comp., Mich., mm.19–23; E 136/13/25A (particulars of escheator's account for the vacancy of 1353).

[15] E 357/3, m.55; E 136/13/9.

[16] E 136/13/28 (account) and 28A (extent), both for Worcs properties; E 136/14/13 (Glos properties). For further details see below, 000.

[17] SC 11/roll 724. Other evidence in E 136/13/30 (Worcs properties) and E 136/14/16 (Glos properties). Also see below, 235.

[18] *The Red Book of Worcester,* ed. M. Hollings (Worcs Hist. Soc., 4 pts, 1934–50), hereafter cited as *RBW.*

[19] The account of Humphrey Walden for the vacancy: SC 6/1143/18. It is published by Hollings: *RBW,* pt 4, 498–547. I have preferred to use the original account.

[20] e.g. Walden's account cited in the preceding note. The exchequer also used the extent compiled by Walden which seems to be no longer extant, but information derived from it is scattered in E 136/13/25A (particulars of the escheator's account, 1353).

of Richard II.[21] These manorial records confirm that the startling decline in the number of tenants revealed by Perton's inquiries remained an enduring feature to which the bishops had to adjust.

The records arising out of the long vacancy of the see of Coventry and Lichfield from 23 November 1358 to 19 September 1360 form the principal source of evidence for the position of the tenants on the estates of the bishops in Derbyshire, Staffordshire, Shropshire and Warwickshire,[22] but they do not cover properties in Cheshire. As at Worcester in 1349 and 1353, the exchequer officials became alarmed at the decline in the revenue from the bishopric. The inquiries ordered by the exchequer resulted in this case in lists of tenants who died during the epidemic. We can name 91 unfree tenants who were victims of the plague and we can find out what happened to their vacant holdings. Unfortunately only in the case of the Warwickshire estates is it possible to compare this very complete and precise evidence with earlier information contained in the hundred rolls of 1279[23] and the vacancy records of 1321–2.[24]

II

The detailed study of these two groups of episcopal estates must be prefaced by a wider inquiry into the reactions of government officials and of landlords to disastrous changes of this magnitude. In commenting upon the exaction of a 'recognition' from the much depleted body of the tenants of St Albans on the election of a new abbot in 1350, Professor Levett sadly remarked that 'evidently consideration for the Abbey's tenants had not been increased by the visitation of the pestilence'.[25] The fresh evidence that I have tried to collect from various parts of England points in the same direction. The heavy mortality from the plague did not on the whole produce on the part of either government authorities or landlords a more tolerant or more charitable attitude to their underlings, though there were some admirable exceptions.

Faced with the disaster of the plague, the exchequer officials continued in most cases to enforce the normal exchequer rules, just as they tried to do later on, after the revolts of 1381.[26] Aymer Fitz Warren, the sheriff of Devon, for failing to appear at the exchequer to account on 16 June 1348, was fined £20. It was subsequently proved that he was so ill of the plague that he was not expected to survive. All his subordinate staff, including the undersheriff, two clerks and two laymen, died of the pestilence at that time so that nobody could deputise for him. Only after much delay was an inquiry set in motion in 1351 and the fine was not cancelled until 1357.[27] Similarly, as we have already seen, the exchequer subjected to an elaborate scrutiny the claims of the custodians of the vacant bishoprics that they had been unable to collect some of the normal revenues. To this we owe our best evidence about the estates of our two bishoprics. Only in the case of the archbishopric of York was the exchequer willing in 1353 to accept the claim of the custodians for allowances on their personal oaths, without insisting on a more detailed inquiry.[28]

The exchequer always compared the accounts of the custodians of a vacant bishopric with earlier records arising out of previous vacancies. In 1359 the exchequer auditors at first declined to deal with the account of Philip Lutley, keeper of the Coventry estates, because they could not find any relevant earlier records, which was not surprising as there had been no vacancy since 1322. They were looking both for surveys of the bishopric and the accounts of cus-

21 These manorial accounts and court rolls as well as some other miscellaneous estate records are preserved in the Hereford and Worcester Record Office, St Helen's, Worcester.

22 E 368/132, stat. et vis. comp., Mich., mm.8–9, and Pas., mm.12, 15–21; E 368/133, stat. et vis. comp., Mich., mm.10–14; SC 6/1132/7. The original inquisitions can no longer be traced but modern transcripts of them are preserved in BL, Add. MSS 6165, 6167.

23 E 164/15, ff.28–30, 66–8. Some of the evidence is briefly quoted in *VCH Staffs,* V, 88, and VI, 122, using Dugdale's transcripts. The statement in ibid., VI, 122 n.24, that the entry for Bishops Itchington is now illegible is untrue.

24 SC 6/1132/5 (account of John Walwyn). The extent on which Walwyn's account is based is now lost, but some evidence derived from it is mentioned in E 136/12/17 (Warw).

25 Levett, *Manorial History,* 255.

26 E. B. Fryde, 'English Parliament and the Peasants' Revolt of 1381', in *Liber Memorialis Georges de Lagarde* (Studies presented to the International Comm. for the Hist. of Representative and Parliamentary Instns, XXXVIII, Louvain, 1970), 85–7.

27 E 368/121, communia, Trin.; E 372/194, Devon; E 13/77, m.40.

28 E 368/126, stat. et vis. comp., Mich., mm.10–11. William Kelsey, one of the two custodians, was a veteran financial official of the crown.

todians on these earlier occasions.[29] Ultimately their search covered more than a century and one of the items with which Lutley was confronted came from an account enrolled on an exchequer pipe roll as far back as 1251.[30] The officials of the exchequer seem to have assumed that economic values did not alter much over long periods. They deemed it quite practicable to charge accountants after the disaster of 1348–9 'according to the ancient accounts before the pestilence', to quote the harassed complaint of the custodian of the bishopric of Norwich in 1355.[31] During the vacancy of the bishopric of Coventry in 1358–9 the exchequer auditors used mainly the yardstick of the extents and accounts of 1321–2. For the two vacancies at Worcester in 1349 and 1353 they went back to the last prolonged vacancy in 1302–3.

In dealing with the manorial officials and the tenants of the vacant bishoprics the exchequer varied its demands according to what was required by the individual custodians. The officials of the exchequer provided the framework within which unjustly oppressive demands might be enforced, but the initiative for doing this came from the custodians. After the vacancy at York lasting from July 1352 to February 1353 fourteen different manorial officials from eleven estates were menaced with imprisonment by the keeper of the bishopric, William Kelsey, a veteran royal official. He was demanding from them debts totalling £48 6s. 4d. which they could not pay for the time being.[32] They were rescued by the new archbishop, John Thoresby, who became a surety on their behalf. This sufficed to satisy the exchequer. Thoresby was acting charitably 'in order to save the said tenants from imprisonment',[33] though it was in his interest to do so.

The same contrast between inexorable enforcement of claims by the custodian and a more humane attitude of the archbishop is to be found on the Canterbury estates in 1349. The new archbishop, Simon Islip, secured from Edward III the remission of the royal claim to a payment of £219 14s. 1½d. due from the tenants as 'recognition' on the death from the plague in May 1349 of Archbishop John Offord.[34] The Canterbury tenants had already paid one 'recognition' on the death of Archbishop John Stratford in August 1348,[35] and it was obviously in Islip's interest to protect the men on his properties from further impoverishment. He may have also been influenced by the spectacle of the harassment of the Canterbury tenants by the outgoing custodian, William Epworth.[36] This man, who had been removed from the office of custodian a month after Islip's election, appears to have been both unscrupulous and inefficient. Some of Epworth's legal proceedings against the various manorial officials on Canterbury estates were clearly unjustified and he had to admit the groundlessness of several of his accusations. He also later alleged that his receiver, Alan Botoweyn, had fled to Ireland carrying off £152 belonging to Epworth, which suggests that the latter was grossly incompetent in his choice of subordinates. Epworth had acted as custodian from 20 May to 19 October 1349. The exchequer simply enforced Epworth's claims and, in the pursuit of the charges made by him, detained a number of manorial officials. The groups of tenants responsible for the debts of these men were harassed for several years.

Epworth's total claims against various officials amounted initially to £264. Some of them were imprisoned for lengthy periods in 1353–5. The most detailed example of Epworth's indifference to the havoc wrought by the plague is provided by his proceedings against the bailiff of Otford in Kent. This official, Robert Malmesbury, had been elected by the tenants on 25 July 1349, on the death of his predecessor, and he claimed that, according to the local custom, he was not responsible for any sums collected by the previous bailiff. He refused to answer for £1 6s. 8d. of amercements imposed on six men responsible for making presentments who had been absent from the lord's court. He also denied liability for £4 4s. 7¾d. due for rents from holdings

29 ibid. 132, stat. et vis. comp., Mich.

30 E 372/204, m.43, mentioning that the custodian of the bishop's palace was allowed 1½d. per day during the vacancy of the see in 1251–2, as recorded on the pipe roll for 35 Henry III.

31 SC 6/1297/26.

32 E 368/126, stat. et vis. comp., Mich., mm.10–11.

33 ibid. Thoresby acted thus 'volens cum tenentibus suis predictis agere graciose ne iidem tenentes pro huiusmodi debitis carcerali custodie mancipentur, cum ad solutionem eorundem non sufficiant in presenti'.

34 ibid. 125, m.265.

35 SC 6/1128/11, 12.

36 E 368/122, m.260; 125, mm.265–6; E 13/76–78, passim.

which were, in fact, in the lord's hands, and from deserted mills that could not be leased. On all these points the jurors upheld Malmesbury.[37]

On the manors of Charing and Maidstone, Epworth clashed with the whole body of the tenants. At Charing two reeves had died in quick succession and Epworth claimed that the community of the tenants (the 'homage'), who had elected their successor, should be responsible for his debts. Epworth asserted that this was a customary rule applying to all elections of reeves made during a vacancy of the archbishopric. The men of Charing did ultimately pay £8 6s. 8d. exacted of them.[38] But at Maidstone the custodian encountered bitter resistance. The 'homage' of Maidstone had elected as reeve on 1 August 1349 Walter Tilden, a member of a prominent local family.[39] Epworth had made matters worse by trying to make Tilden responsible for the liabilities of his dead predecessor. Tilden's total debts were put at £51 3s. 6¼d. The 'homage' of Maidstone refused to bear responsibility for this huge debt. In denying their collective liability they maintained that the manorial custom of Charing did not apply to Maidstone while Epworth claimed that it was identical on all the estates of the archbishop. The 'homage' of Maidstone did not consist merely of humble peasants. It comprised the prior of Leeds, the master of the school at Maidstone and at least one knight, Ralph Farningham. In the summer of 1353 the sheriff of Kent seized the goods of tenants of Maidstone worth £30 but could find no buyers for them. The sheriff remained responsible for the whole debt.[40] It is pleasing to discover after all this that Epworth ended up by being himself imprisoned in the Fleet for £43 10s. due to the king at the end of his account.[41]

There is a clear contrast between the harsh treatment meted out to the tenants of Canterbury and the conditions on the estates of the bishops of Worcester and Coventry. Epworth was foolish in charging himself with sums that could not be collected. The custodians of Worcester and Coventry estates prudently from the start claimed allowance for revenues that were likely to be lost through the plague and the local juries in every case upheld their statements.

These two bishoprics had therefore one thing in common. The episcopal tenants do not appear to have been unduly harassed after the plague either by the royal custodians or by their own bishops. In other important respects there were significant differences between the two bishoprics. On the estates of Worcester there was a heavy mortality among the servile tenants. A considerable number of full holdings, virgates and half-virgates lapsed into the lord's hands and for many of them no new tenants could be found. The surviving unfree tenants did not, however, gain any immediate concessions of importance. On the estates of Coventry far fewer tenants died. The bishop was able to fill many of the resultant vacancies, but only at the cost of a permanent remission of servile burdens to all the new tenants, even if the newcomers were the heirs or close relatives of the previous holders.[42]

III

The diocese of Worcester suffered severely from the plague. 'Between 1 April and 6 August 1349 one hundred and thirty nine holders of rectories, vicarages and chantries are known to have died . . . This cannot represent much less than a third of the total.'[43] Bishop Wolstan's death on 6 August 1349, while the plague was still raging, was followed by extensive depredations on the episcopal estates and large quantities of animals and other goods belonging to the deceased bishop were carried off. Some losses had occurred during earlier vacancies. In the winter of 1338–9 the steward of Thomas Hempnall, the previous bishop, who had died on 21 December 1338,

37 ibid. 76, mm.20–2. Some private landlords were likewise very unwilling to drop demands for rents from vacant holdings. For example, Thomas Braose procured the arrest of the official who in 1348 had been in charge of his estate at Bosham, Sussex, for arrears of account, including £2 6s. 2d. of rents from vacant holdings of ten tenants (ibid., mm.27–9). Rents due from vacant holdings were included in £242 exacted in 1352–6 from the bailiff of Queen Philippa at Havering atte Bower, Essex: ibid. 79, mm.22d–26d.

38 E 368/125, m.265d; E 13/78, m.110d.

39 'The Kent Lay Subsidy Roll of 1334/5', ed. H. A. Hanley and C. W. Chalklin, in *Documents Illustrative of Medieval Kentish Society* (Kent Recs, XVIII, 1964), 117.

40 E 368/125, m.265d; E 13/78, m.111.

41 E 368/125, m.266d.

42 For a detailed discussion of the evidence and of possible reasons for these contrasts see below, 232–5.

43 R. M. Haines, 'Wolstan de Bransford, prior and bishop of Worcester, c.1280–1349', *Univ. Birmingham Hist. Jnl*, VIII (1962), 111. See also *A Calendar of the Register of Wolstan de Bransford, Bishop of Worcester, 1339–49*, ed. R. M. Haines (Worcs Hist. Soc., New ser., IV, 1966), li–lii and *The Register of the Diocese of Worcester . . . sede vacante, 1301–1435*, ed. J. W. Willis-Bund (Worcs Hist. Soc., VIII, 1893–7), 241–2.

apparently disposed of at least 146 oxen of his deceased master valued at £124. He was accused of selling them to the abbot of Evesham and of pretending that they were his own animals.[44] But in August 1349 unusually huge quantities of goods were carried off. Wolstan's executors described the looting as occurring during 'the time of the late pestilence', and this reveals something of the demoralisation spread by the plague. 'Certain sons of perdition whose names we do not know' were to be solemnly denounced for this after mass in all the parish churches of the diocese.[45] The new bishop, John Thoresby, prosecuted Wolstan's executors for the losses he had suffered and was awarded £766 13s. 4d. in compensation.[46]

Before studying the details of Leo Perton's inquiries we should glance at some tax records for Worcestershire. In 1360 the assessment of a royal tax of a tenth and fifteenth on Worcestershire was temporarily diminished by £55 7s. 10d., and this amount was distributed among all the towns and villages according to the degree of impoverishment that they were supposed to have suffered in recent years.[47] The highest abatement of taxation (£5 10s.) was given to the city of Worcester. Eleven other localities secured abatements of between £1 and £4. None of the estates of the bishops of Worcester was in this highest category. Presumably they were not considered to be among the worst-afflicted places in the county. Judging by this evidence, there was a group of particularly impoverished or depopulated localities in the north-eastern corner of Worcestershire and on its eastern border, close to the valley of the river Avon. Three of the most depopulated or distressed estates of the bishops lay within these two regions. Hanbury by Droitwich was a flourishing village in 1299. The bishop had 61 tenants there, including 38 holders of half-virgates. Only 4 tenants remained in 1349, holding between them 4 virgates [51].[48] In 1349 the custodians of the bishopric could collect there only 2s. 7½d. out of a total of £4 3s. 6¼d. due for rents and commuted services. In nearby Alvechurch they received £1 16s. 5¼d. out of a total of £9 5s. 10¾d. [15]. In 1360 Hanbury's share of royal taxation was reduced by 13s. 4d. and that of Alvechurch by 14s.[49] The third especially afflicted group of properties lay in the valley of the Avon, between Pershore and Evesham. They were known collectively as the manor of Fladbury, which included the neighbouring vill of Throckmorton. Comparison between 1299 and 1349 does not suggest any disastrous changes. The bishop's tenants were almost as numerous in 1349 as they had been in 1299.[50] But in 1360 the two villages secured important remissions of taxation. It is probable that there had been here a considerable expansion of population in the first half of the fourteenth century, after the survey of 1299, and that the plague wiped out this recent surplus. Whatever the explanation, the two villages seem to have suffered severely from the plague. In 1349 the royal custodians collected only £1 15s. 6d. out of a total of £8 4s. 1d. due to them [16]. In 1360 as much as 16s. 8d. was remitted to the two vills in taxation.

In the middle of the fourteenth century the bishops of Worcester possessed properties in 24 localities, consisting of 16 manors in Worcestershire, 5 in Gloucestershire and 3 in Warwickshire.[51] There exists adequate detailed evidence about the number of the bishop's tenants at the end of 1349 on fourteen estates.[52] For nine of these there is also comparable information in the inquisitions of 1353.[53]

In 1299 the majority of the bishop's estates were well populated manors. The income of the bishop and of his more substantial tenants was derived from prosperous arable farming combined with the keeping of cattle and sheep. Out of our previously mentioned sample of fourteen properties in Worcestershire and

44 E 202/35.

45 Register of Bishop John Thoresby (HWRO, 716:093 (B.A. 2648)/3(ii)), p.51.

46 ibid., pp.11, 49. Thoresby's final agreement with the executors of Bishop Wolstan was dated 4 Feb. 1350 and he gave his acquittance to the executors for the entire sum on 3 Dec. 1350.

47 E 13/82B, mm.32d, 73.

48 See also Table D.

49 E 13/82B, m.73.

50 See Table C.

51 R. H. Hilton, *A Medieval Society: the West Midlands at the end of the Thirteenth Century* (London, 1966), 34. Professor Hilton's figure refers to the end of the thirteenth century but there was probably little change in the bishop's possessions during the first half of the fourteenth century.

52 Bibury, Bishops Cleeve, Blockley, Henbury, Withington, all in Gloucestershire (see Tables A and B); Alvechurch, Bredon, Fladbury, Hanbury, Hartlebury, Kempsey, Northwick, Ripple, Wick Episcopi, all in Worcestershire (see Tables A, C and D).

53 Bishops Cleeve, Blockley, Bredon, Fladbury, Hartlebury, Henbury, Kempsey, Ripple, Wick Episcopi.

Gloucestershire, four could be regarded in 1299 as large estates on which the bishop controlled more than 100 servile tenants and smallholders. On nine other properties these two groups numbered together between 50 and 85. A considerable proportion of his dependent peasants were apparently very poor men, smallholders or cottars. On at least two estates these very humble groups formed more than half of the bishop's dependents, 40 out of 58 at Bishops Cleeve and 34 out of 62 at Alvechurch.

In counting the episcopal tenants on these estates I shall say nothing of the more substantial freeholders as they formed a very miscellaneous group and included men who were squires rather than peasants. But two other groups are sufficiently homogenous to merit study. While we have no evidence about the wholly landless men and women, immediately above them came the group of smallholders. They included people of diverse legal status, some free, others servile, but they were mostly very poor and could only earn a living by working for others as servants or labourers. The counting of the members of this group must be a very laborious and tricky task. The baffling variety of types of tenure makes it difficult to secure uniform results. But, as I have mentioned before, it is a relatively large group and some possible errors of classification would not seriously invalidate the usefulness of the overall statistics. I have tried to be consistent in including or omitting particular categories of people, but some estates required special treatment. Thus tenants of 'forlands' have normally been omitted as they were not necessarily residents at the manors to which they were attached. But I have consistently included them at Henbury (formerly Henbury Saltmarsh). This was an unusual estate very near Bristol and the holders of 'forlands' figure here prominently both in the episcopal survey of 1299 and in the inquisitions after the vacancy of 1349. The other main category of tenants that could be counted were the unfree tenants occupying substantial holdings. This was the category that underwent the most striking change as the result of the plague.

If a comparison is made between the very complete episcopal surveys of c.1299 and the figures at the end of 1349, this reveals on fourteen estates a fall in the tenant and smallholder population of about 36%. Around 1299 these two groups taken together totalled about 1160, but their successors at the end of 1349 numbered only 681.[54] Probably not all of this decline can everywhere be attributed to the disaster of 1348–9, but statements of juries imply that much of it was certainly due to the plague. The figures for 1353 seem to confirm for nine estates the reliability of the shockingly low figures of 1349.

The overall fall in population as the result of the plague was in fact probably greater than a comparison with 1299 can reveal on a cursory inspection. Some of the episcopal estates may have experienced a period of considerable economic growth between 1299 and 1348. I have suggested this already in the case of Fladbury.[55] At Northwick, just outside the city of Worcester, even at the end of 1349 population was appreciably larger than it had been in 1299.[56]

It is also instructive to compare the number of full holdings (virgates and large fractions of virgates) held by the unfree tenants in 1299 with the situation in the first few years after the plague. On our sample of fourteen estates in 1299 the servile tenants held between them 432¾ virgates as against 276¾ virgates held by their successors on the same properties at the end of 1349.[57] The decline in the number of tenants was matched fairly exactly by the decline in the number of virgates they were able to cultivate. In 1299 the number of virgates in cultivation represented 41% of the total number of unfree tenants and smallholders.[58] For 1349 the corresponding percentage was 40%: the ratio of servile tenants and smallholders to the number of virgates effectively exploited was almost the same in both 1299 and 1349.

There was very little change between 1349 and 1353. In those first years after the plague, recovery was very slow. In that period the smallholders and landless men were presumably either unwilling or unable to take up many of the vacated larger holdings. These lesser men were likely to be discouraged by the scarcity and the heavy cost of essential equipment and animals as well as by lack of reserves and experience. Only on the exceptionally valuable and populous estates of Stoke Bishop and Henbury, which lay just outside Bristol, are there signs of quick recuperation, so that in 1353 the actual number of servile virgates in

[54] The evidence for 1349 is printed below [47–60].

[55] Above, 229. [56] See Table C.

[57] The evidence for 1349 is printed below [47–60].

[58] This percentage is based on a slightly larger sample to make it as representative as possible. In addition to the fourteen estates in Gloucestershire and Worcestershire listed above I have included two Warwickshire estates of the bishop, Hampton Lucy and Tredington, for which there is adequate information in the survey of 1299.

cultivation was nearly the same as it had been in 1299. Later on this will happen on some, but not all, of the other estates, as will appear more fully when I deal with particular properties in the last section of this paper.

Until the manorial accounts of the bishops of Worcester begin to survive from the late 1360s onwards it is difficult to speak with any assurance of what was happening on the episcopal estates. The records connected with the vacancies of 1361–2 and 1364 suggest that the bishops attempted no general reorganisation of their methods before 1361, though they were forced into some piecemeal adjustments by the distressed condition of the tenants on some of their properties. Another outbreak of plague in 1361 produced a new crisis. Its possible consequences will be studied in more detail later on.

At the beginning of the fourteenth century the bishops of Worcester held large areas of demesne arable on most of their estates.[59] These demesne lands were chiefly cultivated by the bishop's servants and by hired labour. Only a relatively small amount of ploughing, harrowing and other work was required of the unfree tenants.[60] Perhaps only at the time of the harvest did the bishop tap effectively the large amount of tenant labour available to him, and not always then. On some of the biggest estates, such as Henbury or Hartlebury,[61] the amount of the servile labour at the bishop's disposal was so large that one wonders whether there ever had been a time when all these services had really been needed for the cultivation of the lord's land. In practice much of this labour was commuted every year for money.

Just as the catastrophe of 1348–50 did not produce a 'dislocation of the manorial system' on the Winchester estates studied by Professor Levett and Father E. Robo,[62] so likewise the disappearance of perhaps a third of the tenants of the bishop of Worcester did not destroy his domanial organisation. The Worcester extents of 1361 and 1364 show that on most estates the bishop still retained considerable areas of demesne arable.[63] Manorial accounts dating from the next three decades confirm that the bishops of Worcester continued to exploit directly their demesne lands, though they were now doing this on a smaller scale than had been practicable around 1300.[64]

Two episcopal vacancies occurred in quick succession at Worcester, in 1349–50 and in 1353. This makes it possible to pinpoint some of the concessions made to the tenants in the first few years after the plague, during the short episcopate of John Thoresby. Unfortunately the vacancy of 1353 only lasted some seven weeks, during the months of February and March, when comparatively few services would normally be exacted. Apart from one exception ('the recognition') that will be discussed in due course, neither this evidence nor the subsequent records suggest that Bishop Thoresby and his immediate successor were pursuing any uniform policy. At the manor of Northwick, Thoresby gave up the customary render of 'fishfee', due from the servile tenants on the first day of Lent.[65] It was a very slight payment, but it continued to be levied on other episcopal manors.[66] As has been already noted, the inhabitants of Fladbury had been particularly impoverished by the plague. After 1349 the bishop's surviving tenants at Fladbury were freed from the duty of ploughing and harrowing their lord's demesne in Lent 'because their tenure has been changed into a different service', which implies a permanent concession.[67] At Ripple similarly the tenants were exempted from having to plough and harrow 18 acres of demesne during Lent, while at Kempsey all the servile tenants were excused these particular labour services during Lent. It is interesting to note that all these three estates continued to decline during the 1350s.[68] But in other places, as for

59 cf. the table in T. H. Lloyd, 'Ploughing services on the demesnes of the bishop of Worcester in the late thirteenth century', *Univ. Birmingham Hist. Jnl,* VIII (1962), 196.

60 ibid., 189–96. See also below for a discussion of some of these estates in the later fourteenth century.

61 For Henbury see Table B and for Hartlebury see Table D.

62 E. Robo, 'The Black Death in the Hundred of Farnham', *EHR,* XLIV (1929), 570.

63 Extents of 1361: E 136/13/28A (Worcs); ibid. 14/13 (Glos). Extents of 1364: SC 11/724 (Worcs) and E 136/14/16 (Glos).

64 Long-term changes on these estates, mainly after 1364, are discussed in more detail in the final section of this introduction.

65 This and all the following examples in this paragraph are based on E 368/126, mm.19–22 and E 136/13/25A (inquiries of 1353).

66 e.g. in 1384–5 it was being collected at Bredon at the rate of 1d. per virgate (HWRO, 009:1 (B.A. 2636)/158, no. 92015).

67 'Eo quod tenura residui dictorum tenentium mutatur in aliud servicium et nulla huiusmodi opera facere tenebantur post pestilenciam videlicet post annum xxiij^{um}'.

68 See Table C.

example at Blockley and Hartlebury, ploughing and harrowing services still continued to be exacted, though they had declined greatly in value through the disappearance of about half the tenants.[69]

During the vacancy of 1302–3 the royal keepers collected £40 7s. 4d. from the 'recognition' due from the servile tenants.[70] In 1433, at the start of another prolonged vacancy, the royal custodians still regarded this as a target to aim at. Their ill-considered demand led on this occasion to the refusal of the tenants to pay anything at all.[71] These fifteenth-century tenants knew that 'recognition' had become much lighter in the second half of the preceding century.[72] In 1349 the royal keepers collected a mere £1 8s. 8d. in Worcestershire and Warwickshire. Bishop Thoresby may have carried out a revision of the quotas due from each village. At any rate in 1353, after Thoresby's promotion to York, the royal custodians put into operation a reduced scale of payments and collected no more than £3. In 1361 the 'recognition' yielded slightly less, £2 6s. 6d. This decline may have reflected deaths of tenants in the plague epidemic of 1361. In 1364 there was instead a rise to £5 8d., partly because the quota of the wealthy manors of Stoke Bishop and Henbury had been increased by £1 6s. 8d.

Apart from a few examples already noted, there is no evidence of any general policy of reducing servile renders in the decade after the plague of 1348–9, though the deaths of many tenants were bound to diminish this part of the bishop's revenue. The bishop's tallage certainly suffered in this way, though there is nowhere any mention of a deliberate scaling down of this annual tax. In 1349 the men of Henbury paid, for example, £3 in tallage, which represented less than a third of what they should have normally contributed. The extent of the Worcestershire manors compiled during the vacancy of 1364 mentions tallage on eleven estates. £15 9s. were then due, as compared with £25 12s. collected from the same estates in 1302. One gets a similar picture of piecemeal reductions and adjustments from a glance at the assized (fixed) rents paid by the unfree peasants. Later on, from at least 1364 onwards, the bishops began to revise upwards the assized rents, but this came as a part of a general revision of their methods of estate management which will be discussed in the final section of this article.

IV

In contrast with the bishopric of Worcester, the estates of the see of Coventry and Lichfield were in 1349 the scene of far-reaching immediate concessions to the bishop's tenants. Here there was no episcopal vacancy to add to the disruption caused by the plague. Roger Northborough (Northburgh), who held the bishopric of Coventry from 1322 to 1348, was a veteran household official of Edward II. He had held a succession of high household offices during the exceptionally turbulent years 1312–22. He served twice as treasurer of the exchequer, in 1328 and 1340. In 1349, faced with a loss of nearly a hundred servile tenants, he freed a number of villein holdings from their servile burdens, but he most probably agreed to do this only because he had no other choice.

The main group of the bishop's estates lay in Staffordshire. In addition to Lichfield itself the bishop had seven main manors: Haywood, Baswich, Longdon, Brewood, Rugeley, Cannock and Eccleshall, with tenants in a whole number of lesser hamlets.[73] The bulk of these properties lay in the south-eastern part of the county. Several of them adjoined Cannock forest. The presence of ample woodland pastures, the scattering of some of the tenants through small hamlets, the abundant possibilities of reclaiming new land within the forest area:[74] all these were factors encouraging the bishop's unfree men to assert a measure of independence in the years after 1348.

For purposes of administration the Staffordshire properties were combined with the manors of Sawley in Derbyshire and of Prees in Shropshire.[75] These estates were much more valuable early in the

69 See Tables A and D.

70 See Table E.

71 This incident has been described by C. Dyer, 'A redistribution of incomes in fifteenth-century England', *Past & Present*, XXXIX (1968), 19–22. This is the first attempt to use the manorial records of the bishops at the Hereford and Worcester Record Office in a really adequate way.

72 For all the evidence that follows in this and the next paragraph see Table E.

73 R. H. Hilton, *The English Peasantry in the Later Middle Ages* (Oxford, 1975), 221.

74 ibid., 230.

75 The main sources for this group of estates during the vacancy of 1358–60 are: E 368/132, stat. et vis. comp., Pas., mm.15–21; 133, stat. et vis. comp., Mich., mm.10–14; SC 6/1132/7. The original inquisitions returned to the exchequer cannot now be traced but modern transcripts of them exist in BL, Add. MS 6165, pp.189–206.

fourteenth century than in the years after the plague of 1349. When this group of properties was in the king's hands for a year from Michaelmas 1307 to Michaelmas 1308 by reason of the disgrace and imprisonment of Bishop Walter Langton, the gross income amounted to £775 16s. 3¼d.,[76] and, after deduction of expenses, the custodians were held liable for £628 11s. 5½d.[77] The amounts received during the vacancy after the death of Bishop Roger Northborough on 22 November 1358 were a good deal lower. Between that date and Michaelmas 1359 Philip Lutley, the royal escheator, received with another colleague a gross income of £410 2s. 3¼d. and remained liable for £395 18s. 1¼d.[78] Lutley continued to be in charge of these properties for almost another year, from Michaelmas 1359 to 19 September 1360. For this second year his net liability amounted to £308 4½d.[79]

Ninety-one unfree tenants died of plague in 1349 on the Staffordshire, Shropshire and Derbyshire estates of the bishops.[80] The evidence about them is exceptionally detailed. We have their names as well as the names of their successors so that the fate of their holdings can be studied. There is also a lot of information about the concessions that the bishop was forced to make.

I have no information about the possessions of the bishop in the county of Chester. He also held four properties in Warwickshire.[81] In this case there is no evidence about the tenants themselves but only about the tenements vacated by them. 12¾ virgates fell into the bishop's hands on his Warwickshire properties, representing the holdings of perhaps 13 or 14 tenants. None of these tenements was ever reoccupied in Bishop Northborough's lifetime because nobody else wanted 'to perform the services which the previous tenants had been accustomed to render before the pestilence'.[82]

Fortunately it is possible to compare the evidence of 1358–60 with earlier information in the hundred rolls of 1279 and the records connected with the vacancy before the appointment of Northborough, in 1321–2. The figures for 1279 and 1321–2 are broadly similar, so that the extent of the decline in 1349 can be readily compared with the earlier information. Only at Bishops Tachbrook can severe economic decline be alleged as a possible reason for the bishop's inability to find new tenants. He still retained 170 acres of demesne arable. But he could not find fresh occupants for five virgates. In place of the 25 tenants of the 1279 survey and of the 18 of 1321, only 9 tenants remained in 1358. While the villeins of 1279 held between them 16½ virgates, their successors in 1358 held only 4. The remaining three estates continued to be fairly well populated. At Chadshunt and Gaydon 4 virgates had remained vacant since 1349. The bishop still retained, however, 38 tenants, only 4 fewer than in 1279, and they held between them 28½ virgates. At Bishops Itchington 3¾ virgates could not be reoccupied after 1349, but the bishop still retained 36 tenants.

The bishop does not appear to have possessed any servile tenants at his valuable Staffordshire manor of Eccleshall. Two of his other Staffordshire properties, Baswich and Rugeley, contained only small groups of episcopal bondmen. Of Baswich we only know that four unfree tenants had died and that one third of the servile tallage had to be permanently remitted. At Rugeley, Brewood, Haywood and Longdon in Staffordshire and at Prees in Shropshire the bishop was able to find new tenants for 26½ vacant virgates and for two other holdings of an uncertain size. At Sawley he managed to replace the deceased tenants of either 27 or 29 bovates. But in every case this had to be done at a heavy price. All the new holders had to be released from all the servile burdens. In every case the money rent remained unchanged, but the customary servile tallage called 'stuth' had to be abandoned,[83] together with all the labour services due from these holdings.

Prees and Sawley form a group apart because on these two estates the bishop was at least able to replace in this way all the lost tenants. At Sawley 11 deceased villeins were replaced by the same number of

[76] My total from E 358/13. [77] ibid., m.3.

[78] E 372/204, m.35. [79] ibid., m.43.

[80] The evidence about the three most important Staffordshire estates (Brewood, Haywood, Longdon) is set out in Table G.

[81] See Table F on which is based the remainder of this and of the next paragraph.

[82] E 368/132, stat. et vis. comp., Pas., m.12: 'pro dictis operibus faciendis, prout custumarii, qui terram illam ante pestilenciam tenuerunt, prius facere consueverunt'.

[83] ibid., m.15 (under Longdon). The tenements of these 'nativi' are now 'in manibus liberorum tenentium pro certo redditu inde reddendo, absque eo quod quicquam ultra redditum illud nomine dicte consuetudinis aliqualiter solverunt per dictum tempus nec in vita ultimi episcopi post dictam pestilenciam'.

new holders, who were only obliged to pay fixed rents.[84] One of the newcomers was the son of the previous tenant and three others bore the same surnames as their predecessors. At Prees seven men holding one virgate each had died and five others whose individual holdings apparently added up to three-quarters of a virgate. They were all replaced by the same number of people, each taking up one vacant holding.

On the Staffordshire estates even generous offers of better terms of tenure failed to attract enough new tenants. At Rugeley the bishop failed to replace any of the five smallholders who had died. Fifty-nine of the bishop's unfree tenants disappeared on the three important estates of Brewood, Haywood and Longdon.[85] At Haywood a shortage of inhabitants may have been the reason why 13 of the holdings that fell vacant in 1349 were still without tenants in 1358.[86] The 5 men who took up the remaining vacant holdings (6 half-virgates) were described as newcomers (*adventiti*) and were, presumably, immigrants from other localities. But Brewood and Longdon were rich and, apparently, well populated estates and it is most unlikely that the bishop's inability to find new tenants for some of the vacated holdings could have been due to lack of inhabitants after the plague.

Brewood was one of the most important episcopal manors. In 1307 the bishop was entitled to receive here £25 16s. a year from the assized rents of free and unfree tenants.[87] In 1358 he owned here four carucates of demesne arable, an unusually large amount of land. Some twenty years later there were, according to the poll tax returns of 1377, as many as 280 'adults' at Brewood,[88] so that it is reasonable to conjecture that quite a considerable population existed there in 1358. Yet in the place of 20 holders of servile half-virgates who died in 1349, only 10 new tenants could be found. The new holders were all rent-paying tenants, 9 as half-virgaters and the tenth as a holder of an entire virgate. At least one of these men was related to the previous tenant: a clerk named William Stuche took up the holding of William Stuche the elder. The bishop sadly missed the labour of the new tenants as well as the services of the 9 half-virgates that could not be filled. He had to exact instead more labour from his remaining 29 unfree tenants. Their status had remained unaltered. Among other services they had to provide 3 days of ploughing in the autumn, before the sowing of the winter crops. These 'works', which used to be commuted in the past, were again being exacted in the last decade of Bishop Northborough's life.

Longdon resembled Brewood. In 1307 the free and unfree tenants owed to the bishop the huge sum of £49 8s. in assized rents.[89] 165 persons were liable to the poll tax in 1377.[90] Here too 20 tenants died of plague, 11 of whom held one virgate each. Three new tenants took up four of the vacated virgates and the remaining seven holdings remained permanently in the bishop's hands for lack of takers. In place of the 9 deceased tenants of half-virgate holdings 3 new tenants were found, of whom one leased 2 whole virgates and another was a descendant of the previous holder. Three remaining half-virgates remained unoccupied.

The bishop's financial losses from these changes can only be computed in part, but there is, at least, a complete record on all the estates discussed here of his loss of revenue from the servile tallage ('stuth'). In 1358 it yielded £11 6s. 8d., representing 44½% of the total amount due to the bishop from this tax before the plague. £14 4s. 2d. had been lost. Stuth was assessed on holdings according to their size and the rate of charges varied from manor to manor. It is, therefore, impossible to deduce from these figures what proportion of the bishop's servile dependents had ceased to be liable to villein services. In spite of losing a significant part of his unfree labour, Bishop Northborough still retained on most estates large arable demesnes. But there is a hint of trouble in the statement that at Prees only 3 out of the 6 demesne carcucates were being cultivated in 1358–9.

Another type of loss on the bishop's demesne is recorded under Longdon. In 1321 the revenue from pasture in his park of Beaudesert had amounted to £4 5s. In 1359–60 this was reduced to a mere 8s. 6d.

[84] BL, Add. MS 6165, p.205: 'Et predictus episcopus in vita sua terra et tenementa, que ipsi qui sic moriebantur in pestilencia tenuerunt, dimisit liberis tenentibus pro quoddam certo redditu inde reddendo ad incrementum redditus assisi liberorum tenentium per annum'.

[85] See Table G.

[86] BL, Add. MS 6165, p.197: e.g. 'tres dimid' virgate terre, quos Will. Norman, J. le Kyng et Ran. Morcok quondam tenuerunt, remanserunt in manibus domini a tempore dicte pestilencie hucusque'.

[87] E 358/13, m.16d (accounts for the estates of Bishop Walter Langton during his imprisonment by Edward II).

[88] E 179/177/20.

[89] E 358/13, m.2.

[90] E 179/177/19.

and there had been a similar decline in all the previous years since the time of the plague. The majority of the peasant holdings around the park were now abandoned and uncultivated and the remaining landholders had therefore abundant pasturage elsewhere. 'They had little need of the pasturage in the aforesaid park.'[91]

V

The vacancy account for the bishopric of Coventry dealt with the period just before the second onset of plague in 1361–2. The effects of this new disaster can, however, be studied on the estates of the bishop of Worcester,[92] because Bishop Reginald Brian died on 10 December 1361. The extent of the bishopric drawn by Leo Perton during the vacancy in the winter of 1361–2 is susceptible of more than one interpretation.[93] On some estates it tells us how many unfree tenants have remained liable to servile renders and labour services. More often it merely shows how many standard holdings continued to bear those liabilities. As the numbers are usually smaller than in 1353 it would be possible to interpret this evidence as a sign simply of extensive commutations of servile renders and labour services in or before 1361. This may be the true explanation in a few cases. But rents increased very little on Worcester estates between 1353 and 1361.[94] Besides, at Blockley and Bredon, for which manorial accounts happen to survive, it is quite clear that the number of undertenants and servile holdings increased again in subsequent years.[95] On these two estates, at any rate, the depressed figures of 1361 seem to arise out of a real temporary loss of some of the tenants and I am assuming that this is also true of the other estates of the bishops of Worcester.

The largest losses are recorded at Kempsey where all categories of tenants declined in number. If the figures of 1353 are compared with those of the 1361–2 vacancy, it seems that as many as 20 tenants may have disappeared.[96] On five estates, Alvechurch, Blockley, Fladbury, Kempsey and Ripple, as many as 29½ virgates were vacated by tenants.[97] The recognition paid by the servile tenants on all the estates, after declining to a mere £3 in 1353, slumped to £2 6s. 6d. during the vacancy of 1361–2. Other financial renders were affected much less. Only at Alvechurch did the assized rents slump from £1 2s. to 6s. 6d. per term. On the other hand some properties seem to have been affected very slightly or not at all.[98]

The extent drawn up during the next vacancy, in 1364,[99] reveals one important change in the sources of the bishop's income. While between 1353 and 1361 the assized rents changed very little, rising slightly on some estates and falling on a few properties, between 1361 and 1364 the income from this item of revenue jumped from £23 7s. 6d. to £32 16s. 5d. a term.[100] A change of this order points to a deliberate reform by Bishop John Barnet in 1362–3. It is to be assumed that after the setback of 1361 Barnet decided to commute some of the labour services and servile renders of unfree tenants into fixed rent charges or that he was filling some of the vacant holdings by offering purely financial charges to new tenants. Such a partial commutation of servile renders is revealed by the manorial accounts when they begin to survive from the late 1360s onwards.[101] Lastly, on some of the more prosperous estates, the bishop probably raised the amount of existing financial charges. This appears to have happened on the thriving and heavily populated estate of Henbury near Bristol.[102]

On the properties of the bishops of Worcester the initial decline in population caused by the disaster of 1348–9 was not reversed for the rest of the fourteenth century, though there were considerable differences between estates.[103] A few small places, Hatton in Warwickshire, Wontley by Bishops Cleeve in Gloucestershire, had to be abandoned altogether by their inhabitants. Hanbury by Droitwich, north of Worcester, was temporarily crippled by the plague.[104] The great majority of the bishops' estates remained as going concerns. In contrast with the properties of the

[91] E 368/132, stat. et vis. comp., Pas., m.15: 'homines patrie illius minus indiguerunt pastura dicti parci'.

[92] An archiepiscopal mandate of July 1362 dealing with the administrative problems arising 'a tempore succedentis posterioris epidemie' is enrolled in the register of Bishop John Barnet (HWRO, 716:093 (B.A. 2648)/4(i)), ff.24v–25v.

[93] E 136/13/28A. [94] See Table E.

[95] See Table A. [96] See Table C.

[97] See Tables A, C and D.

[98] Rents and other monetary renders are set out in Table E.

[99] E 136/13/30. [100] See Table E.

[101] See the detailed survey of particular estates in the last section of this introduction.

[102] Below, 239, and Table E.

[103] See Tables A–D. Many of the details are discussed below.

[104] See below for more details about these exceptionally afflicted localities.

bishops of Coventry, there is no evidence here of deliberate immediate conversions of villein tenements into rent-paying holdings, though all manner of concessions had to be made to face up to the brute fact that a part of the tenantry had vanished and could never be replaced.

As has been mentioned earlier, the decline in tenant labour did not, in most cases, compel the bishops to give up the direct exploitation of their own demesnes. While on a few particularly decayed estates direct farming was abandoned by the bishops fairly quickly, there is no evidence of any widespread leasing of their manorial demesnes before the first decade of the fifteenth century.[105] The other main components of the revenue of the bishops were the assized rents of the free and unfree tenants. This part of the episcopal income, after suffering a serious eclipse immediately after the plague, began to rise appreciably only after 1361. Where manorial accounts survive they show that by the 1370s the damage done by the plague to this item of the bishop's revenue had been largely repaired. Income from rents was back roughly to the level of c.1300 and in some cases had surpassed it.[106]

This process of adjustment can be studied particularly well at Bredon in eastern Worcestershire.[107] Its tenantry was badly hit by the plague. If comparison is made between 1299 and 1350, only one third of the holders of half-virgates were left after the plague (8 out of 24), and only 6 holders of full virgates out of 21. While there were altogether 58 customary tenants and smallholders in 1299, only 15 are recorded in 1350. It is not surprising that, while in 1302 the bishop's yearly revenue from free and servile assized rents amounted to £21 2s. 6½d., it was down to £9 7s. 10¾d. in 1353. If the extent of 1364 can be trusted, by that time the income from rents had returned to the level of 1302. The first surviving manorial account for Bredon dates from 1375–6.[108] It does not give the number of customary tenants, but it reveals that they occupied almost as many holdings as had been held by their predecessors in 1299. According to the survey of 1299, unfree tenants then held 33 virgates. There had been a decline to 12½ or 13 virgates in 1349, but in 1375–6 at least 30½ virgates were again held by villein tenants. At some earlier date, presumably soon after the epidemic of 1348–9, the tenants had secured a considerable reduction of tallage and of another servile render called 'spenyngfee'. In 1299 tallage had yielded £3 at Bredon, but in 1375–6 the reeve claimed that he could only collect 17s. 6d. He alleged that while in the past tallage and 'spenyngfee' had been paid at the rate of 2s. a virgate, he could now receive only 6d. a virgate. The auditors refused to give him allowance for the missing 42s. and added a laconic note, 'because it has not been ascertained'.[109]

In 1375–6 the reeve received £24 4s. 5½d. from rents. This included the proceeds of a new arrentation of four half-virgates and of two virgates, which had been recently freed from tallage and other servile burdens in return for an increase of rent. This was, apparently, a permanent change. An account of 1384–5 mentions, in addition, nine other virgates either in the lord's hands or newly arrented.[110] A court roll of 1389 records that 21 tenants, holding between them 17½ virgates, were willing to offer £11 13s. 4d. (at 13s. 4d. per virgate) beyond their ordinary rents for a remission of their services and [servile] customs for one year.[111] We learn from a later record that the lord still reserved to himself certain carriage services.[112] This arrangement had to be confirmed annually at the lord's will, as we are told in the account for 1393–4, where the reeve again answered for these £11 13s. 4d. from 'terra nativorum arrentata'.[113] The bishop's demesne had been leased by 1409, but the complaints made by the local jurors in October 1409 about the alleged malpractices of

105 A rental compiled in 1408 on the order of Bishop Thomas Peverel includes a list of revenues received from the leasing of demesnes (HWRO, 009:1 (B.A. 2636)/9(iv), pp.33–38).

106 The changes in the servile rents are set out in Table E. The information about the rents paid by freeholders comes from the following sources. The figures for 1299 are derived from *RBW*, passim. For 1302 see SC 6/1143/18; E 368/126, stat. et vis. comp., Mich., mm.19–23; E 136/13/25A. The latter two sources also give the figures for 1353. For the extent of 1364 see ibid. 30; SC 11/roll 724. Detailed references are given below to the episcopal manorial accounts.

107 See Table A for the figures of tenants and unfree holdings that follow.

108 HWRO, 009:1 (B.A. 2636)/158, no. 92014.

109 ibid.: 'quia non constat'. The same reeve claimed similar allowances in his account for 1384–5 (HWRO, 009:1 (B.A. 2636)/158, no. 92015).

110 ibid.

111 HWRO, 009:1 (B.A. 2636)/158, no. 92016: 'pro operibus et consuetudinibus suis relaxatis'.

112 ibid., 157, no. 92012$\frac{1}{8}$.

113 ibid.

the farmers of the demesne suggest that this change was then quite recent.[114]

A few miles south of Bredon, just across the Gloucestershire border, lies the manor of Bishops Cleeve.[115] In 1299 the bishop had here 58 unfree tenants, the same number as at Bredon. In 1349 many more of the bishop's tenants survived at Bishops Cleeve than at Bredon. Forty-four were still left at Bishops Cleeve, including 5 virgaters and 8 out of 11 holders of half-virgates. By 1372–3 the total number of tenants rose again to 55. But at Wontley, an outlying hamlet to the east of Bishops Cleeve, disastrous changes had occurred. In 1299 the bishop had possessed there 8 tenants holding half-virgates, as well as some other dependants.[116] In 1372–3 there were, apparently, no inhabitants at Wontley,[117] and in the account of 1393–4 it was said to be in the lord's hands.[118] The disappearance of Wontley is one of the reasons for the permanent decline in the bishop's income from Bishops Cleeve. In 1299 the revenue from rents of tenants had amounted to £18 14s. 6¾d. It came to only £8 19s. 5d. in 1353.[119] According to the first surviving manorial account, dating from 1372–3, the reeve in that year received £14 14s. He claimed deficiencies amounting to £3 19s. 11d., including £2 lost at Wontley. The reeve mentioned also a loss of 7s. 5d. in tallage and other dues, ascribing it all to the death of tenants.[120]

The manor of Bibury lies in the south-eastern corner of Gloucestershire. It was neither a valuable nor a well populated property.[121] In 1299 the bishop had here 24 tenants holding between them 12 virgates. In 1349 the number of tenants was reduced to 5 persons holding between them 5 virgates, of whom one actually occupied 2½ virgates. By 1372–3 there were again 24 tenants of the bishop at Bibury and in 1381 the poll tax was assessed on 47 people.[122] In 1372–3 the reeve claimed that the rent due from the unfree tenants had declined and asked for allowance of 39s. 2¼d. (at the rate of 2s. 4½d. on 16½ virgates).[123] Even after this reduction, he received slightly more (£6 3s. 9¾d.), than did the bishop's officials in 1299 (£5 9s. 3d.).

The great manor of Blockley, comprising several settlements, lies in eastern Gloucestershire, about fourteen miles north-east of Bishops Cleeve. Its history in the fourteenth century is difficult to reconstruct.[124] The account of the escheator for the vacancy of 1353 does include statements about conditions in 1302, but they are so much at variance with the figures in the survey of 1299 that it is impossible to use them. Most probably the information about tenants and holdings in 1302 refers to only some parts of the manor. The plague clearly caused some decline in the numbers of unfree tenants in the various localities which made up this manor. Upton, one of these hamlets, had disappeared altogether by 1381.[125] In 1299 the bishop had here 16 tenants holding between them 13 virgates, but there is no reference to Upton in the earliest surviving manorial account of Blockley, dating from 1383–4.[126] Unfortunately it is damaged and some essential evidence is missing. No satisfactory comparison is possible with any other record, as the next surviving account dates from 1458–9.[127] A few impressions can be gleaned from the account of 1383–4. Blockley was again at that date a very wealthy manor. The bishop had at least 64 unfree tenants. It was the bishop's main centre for marketing wool. A list of sheep kept on various episcopal manors in 1381 shows that nearly a thousand were concentrated at Blockley, representing about a quarter of his entire flock.[128] As far as can be judged from the account of 1383–4, the bishop's income from rents was much higher at that date than it had been at the beginning of the fourteenth century. We get glimpses of the transformations that were under way in the early years of Richard II's reign. By 1383–4 ten half-virgates were already

114 ibid., 159, no. 92030: court roll of Bredon, 11 Hen. IV.

115 See Table B. There is a good account of the history of Bishops Cleeve in *VCH Glos*, VIII, 14–15.

116 ibid., 2, 14. Its site is occupied today by Wontley Farm.

117 HWRO, 009:1 (B.A. 2636)/161, no. 92113$\frac{5}{6}$.

118 ibid., 193, no. 92627$\frac{11}{12}$.

119 The changes in servile rents are set out in Table E. For the free rents in 1353 see E 136/13/9.

120 HWRO, 009:1 (B.A. 2636)/161, no. 92113$\frac{5}{6}$: 'quia mortui'.

121 See Tables B and E.

122 E 179/113/35A.

123 HWRO, 009:1 (B.A. 2636)/159, no. 92049$\frac{3}{7}$.

124 For some of the evidence see Tables A and E.

125 See R. H. Hilton and P. A. Rahtz, 'Upton, Gloucestershire, 1959–1964', *Trans. Bristol & Glos Arch. Soc.*, LXXXV (1966), 70–146.

126 HWRO, 009:1 (B.A. 2636)/157, no. 92007.

127 ibid., no. 92008.

128 HWRO, 009:1 (B.A. 2636)/154, no. 52586$\frac{1}{8}$.

freed from labour services and paid only rent.[129] There had been some recent increases in rents. Eight virgaters at Ditchford who used to render between them £3 a year were now paying another £1, and a holder of a virgate at Paxford was contributing 2s. beyond his former rent of 8s. Various smaller charges were being imposed on divers lesser tenants.

The two neighbouring estates of Stoke Bishop and Henbury lay in the extreme south-western corner of Gloucestershire, just outside Bristol.[130] Throughout the fourteenth century this pair of manors continued to form one of the most valuable possessions of the bishops. In 1299 there were here at least 128 tenants and 99 of their successors still survived after the plague was over. A generation later, in 1375, there were 67 servile tenants at Henbury, besides 3 freeholders of standard peasant tenements.[131] Unfortunately there is no corresponding information for Stoke Bishop. Manorial records of the 1370s suggest that at least 50 virgates were then occupied by tenants on these two estates, which corresponds very closely to the number of virgates exploited in 1299. Direct exploitation of the demesnes was maintained by the bishops at Henbury and Stoke Bishop until at least the second decade of the fifteenth century. This meant that the liability of the servile tenants to labour services was likewise being preserved, though in practice most of these services were being commuted each year for money payments. The revenue from rents gradually crept upwards through attempts to demand slightly more from all the tenants as well as through the transformation of some villein holdings into purely rent-paying tenements. One virgate was thus arrented in 1375–6, two and a half virgates in 1377–8 and three and a half in 1379–80. By 1395 there appears in the manorial account a separate fresh item of £5 1s.10¾d. of supplementary rents from newly arrented servile tenements.[132]

I have already had occasion to mention the sad decline of Hanbury by Droitwich, north of Worcester.[133] In 1299 there had been 61 unfree episcopal tenants holding between them 19 virgates, but by 1349 there remained only 4 holders of 4 virgates. While in 1302 the combined tenants of Hanbury paid £1 as 'recognition', this sank to 2s. in 1353. By 1375 the 'recognition' on the accession of Bishop Wakefield amounted again to 10s., but the bishop had partly lost control over his tenants. At a session of the manorial court held in January 1376,[134] five men were accused of having withdrawn their services for several years past. In the case of three of them defaults were said to have extended over fourteen years. A jury of tenants declined to pronounce on the truth of these charges. By the beginning of the reign of Richard II the bishop had given up the direct exploitation of the manor. In 1377–8 his demesne was being farmed for £34 a year and, in addition, small bits of arable and meadow had been leased to two villeins.[135] Direct farming was never resumed here by the bishop. By 1408 the episcopal surveyors recorded, however, the existence of at least 21 tenants holding between them 13 virgates.[136]

At Kempsey, lying in the valley of the Severn some three miles south-east of Worcester, the second half of the fourteenth century was a time of gradual decline.[137] The 108 tenants of 1299 had been reduced to 57 by 1349. The survey made during the episcopal vacancy in the winter of 1361–2 showed that a further loss of perhaps as many as 20 tenants had occurred by that time, while the number of holdings occupied by servile tenants had shrunk by another third. In 1408 the bishop had only 28 tenants at Kempsey.[138]

One of the fullest series of episcopal manorial accounts survives for Hampton Lucy in Warwickshire. This has enabled Mr C. Dyer to reconstruct in great detail the history of this manor in the later fourteenth century.[139] It consisted of two localities, Hampton Lucy itself and Hatton. Between 1371 and 1385 the latter was gradually abandoned by its tenants. In 1385 the bishop merged together the demesne and the vacated holdings and transformed the whole of Hatton into one vast pasture.

129 This entry is partly damaged in the account (ibid., 157, no. 92007), but can be reconstructed from identical charges in ibid., no. 92008.

130 The details that follow are based on Tables B and E and on a series of manorial accounts for Henbury in HWRO, 009:1 (B.A. 2636)/165, 166.

131 ibid., 165, no. 92226$\frac{4}{7}$ (a record of 'recognition' by tenants, most probably dating from 1375).

132 ibid., 166, no. 92261.

133 See Tables D and E.

134 HWRO, 009:1 (B.A. 2636)/165, no. 92229.

135 HWRO, 705:7 (B.A. 57).

136 HWRO, 009:1 (B.A. 2636)/9(iv), pp.29–30.

137 See Tables C and E.

138 HWRO, 009:1 (B.A. 2636)/9(iv), p.27.

139 'Population and agriculture on a Warwickshire manor in the late Middle Ages', *Univ. Birmingham Hist. Jnl*, XI (1968), 114–27.

The shortage of inhabitants in the region of Hampton may perhaps help to account for the exorbitant wages paid by its reeves to hired labourers. This is the one aspect of Hampton Lucy's history not discussed by Mr Dyer. It gives us illuminating glimpses of the non-observance of the Statute of Labourers by the bishop's officials. For comparison we have a Warwickshire roll of proceedings before the justices of labourers.[140] Some of these took place at Stratford on Avon, very near Hampton Lucy. In 1357 a number of people were prosecuted for receiving excessive wages for reaping corn. On this occasion 3d. was described as the lawful daily wage of a reaper and several labourers were indicted for having received 6d. a day for such work. But in August 1372 the reeve of Hampton Lucy was paying labourers employed in gathering the harvest as much as 6½d. a day. Thirty men were employed in this fashion for 3½ days in the second week of August and 34 more during most of the following week. That autumn the harvesting of corn on the 172 acres of the bishop's demesne worked out at 12½d. an acre.[141] An even worse situation developed in 1377. The reeve, Walter Shayl, had fled from the manor on 1 June and could never be recaptured.[142] A lord's bailiff took over. His attempts to get in the harvest involved an expenditure of almost 13d. an acre on the demesne arable. Just over 13d. an acre was actually paid to gather the crops from the 35 acres of Shayl's holding now in the lord's hands.[143] In the autumn of 1378 the bishop's bailiff had again to spend 12½d. an acre over the harvest.[144] If we want to find parallel rates of wages on properties of other landlords, we would discover them on a Winchester estate only at the height of the disaster of 1349.[145]

Temporary shortages of labour in times of exceptional emergency could occur on most medieval estates. Henbury was one of the largest properties of the bishops of Worcester. The boon works due from its numerous tenants could normally suffice to clear the bishop's harvest, without there being any need to hire additional labour. The special expenses in the autumn averaged about 10s. and the reeve's annual expense bill might not exceed £5.[146] But something went badly wrong in 1375–6.[147] The reeve's annual expenses rose to £26.

Bibury and Blockley were the two other episcopal estates for which we have detailed evidence about the cost of hiring labour during harvest. The inflated rates paid at Hampton do not recur anywhere else. At Bibury the reeve did pay 10¼d. an acre in the autumn of 1381, but this was changed to 10d. by the auditors.[148] Eightpence an acre appears to have been the most usual rate. It occurs at Hampton in the autumn of 1376 and at Blockley in 1384.[149] At Bibury the bishop's auditors seem to have regarded the hiring of labourers as inevitable. The charge for it appears in every account save one.[150] They seem to have accepted 8d. an acre as the normal rate. In the account for 1382–3 they disallowed the reeve's original charge of 9d. and changed it to 8d.[151] In 1379–80 they did condone the higher rate of 9d. only because some of the corn might have been lost if exceptionally high wages had not been paid.[152] Similarly, bad weather necessitated special expenditure in 1382. This included the hiring of 10 additional men with five carts to move corn quickly 'for fear of rain'.[153] In the autumn of 1372 the reeve had to take the drastic step of hiring for one day as many as 127 men, at 5d. each, to gather and bind the lord's corn.[154] He also used 47 tenants of the bishop. The latter probably represented the entire labour force available locally at Bibury, as ten years later the royal poll tax was collected here from 47 persons.[155] The crowd of 127 hired labourers must have been specially brought from outside and this single day did cost the reeve 53s.

It has been the main aim of this article to add to

140 B. H. Putnam, *The Enforcement of the Statutes of Labourers during the First Decade after the Black Death, 1349–59* (New York, 1908), 226–7.

141 HWRO, 009:1 (B.A. 2636)/163, no. 92160.

142 ibid., no. 92161; Dyer, *Univ. Birmingham Hist. Jnl,* XI, 117–8.

143 HWRO, 009:1 (B.A. 2636)/163, no. 92161.

144 ibid., no. 92162.

145 Robo, *EHR*, XLIV, 568–9. The figures for other Winchester estates quoted by Levett, *Black Death,* 98–9, are lower. See also ibid., 101–2.

146 These general impressions are based on HWRO, 009:1 (B.A. 2636)/165, nos. 92227 (1363), 92228 (1369), 92226$\frac{2}{7}$ (1377–8), 92225$\frac{6}{8}$ (1378–9).

147 ibid., 166, no. 92230.

148 ibid., 159, no. 92049$\frac{7}{7}$.

149 ibid., 163, no. 92158$\frac{1}{7}$ (Hampton); 157, no. 92007 (Blockley).

150 The exception was in 1375–6: ibid., 160, no. 92052.

151 ibid., no. 92055.

152 ibid., no. 92054.

153 HWRO, 009:1 (B.A. 2636)/159, no. 92049$\frac{6}{7}$.

154 ibid., 160, no. 92051.

155 E 179/113/35A.

the available body of evidence about the effects of the disaster of 1348–9 on the rural communities and to do so by drawing more attention to the information that can be found in the records of the exchequer. By studying manorial accounts a historian may be able to reconstruct some of the changes that were occurring on the great estates after 1348, but it is valuable to have in the exchequer memoranda rolls and plea rolls explicit statements of well informed contemporaries about these changes. The questionings to which the keepers of the vacant bishoprics were subjected by the exchequer officials did produce some statements of this sort, most notably with reference to conditions on the properties of the bishops of Coventry. These exchequer records can also throw useful light on the reactions in the minds of contemporaries faced with such terrible and unprecedented problems.

TABLES

The estates of the bishops of Worcester have been split into four groups, partly for geographical reasons and partly because of differences in the types of evidence available for each group. These four tables present the evidence about the numbers of tenants and about their holdings. A fifth table, dealing with rents and other money renders, combines together all the estates.

There are two tables for the estates of the bishops of Coventry and Lichfield, one for their Warwickshire properties and the other for the principal Staffordshire properties.

Table A
TENANTS OF THE BISHOPS OF WORCESTER AT BLOCKLEY (GLOS) AND BREDON (WORCS)

Estate	*Virgaters*	*Half-virgaters*	*Quarter-virgaters*	*Inch-landers*	*Monday-men*	*Cottars*	*Others*	*Remarks and Sources*	*Total of Tenants*	*Total of Virgates*
BLOCKLEY (including Paxford) 1299	68				5			*RBW*, 295–311, 317–21	112	88½
		18		14				14 inchlanders held ½ virgate each		
						21		Including 10 holding 12 acres each (⅓ virgate) and 4 holding 5 acres each		
1302–3	44					9		E 136/13/25A (a partial list)	53	45
1349	32	7	2			4		E 368/124, m.258	45	36
1353	32	7	2			4		E 368/126, stat. et vis. comp., Mich., mm.21–2; E 136/13/25A	45	36
1361–2	24	5	12					E 136/13/28A	41	29½
1383–4								HWRO, 009:1 (B.A. 2636)/157, no. 92007 54 customary tenants rendered boonwork and in addition 10 holders of ½ virgates held only for rent	64	
BREDON 1299		24			1	5	7	*RBW*, 94–104	58	33
	21			4				4 inchlanders held 1 virgate each		
1302–3					1			E 136/13/25A (a partial list)	43	28½
1349	6	8						E 368/124, m.258	15	
								Add the holding of 1 reeve		12+
								No other tenants remained		
1353								E 368/126, stat. et vis. comp., Mich., m.20d; E 136/13/25A Add the holding of 1 reeve		14½ +
1361–2	13	8						E 136/13/28A (only tenants of virgates and ½ virgates given)		
1375–6	19?	17?		2		2		HWRO, 009:1 (B.A. 2636)/158, no. 92014 Labour services rendered by 25 virgates, 4 virgates arrented, 1½ virgates held by officials Add the holdings of 2 inchlanders		30½

Table B
TENANTS ON THE GLOUCESTERSHIRE ESTATES OF THE BISHOPS OF WORCESTER

Estate	*Virgaters*	*Half-virgaters*	*Inch-landers*	*Monday-men*	*Cottars*	*Others*	*Remarks and Sources*	*Total of Tenants*	*Total of Virgates*
BIBURY 1299		12			5		*RBW*, 368–75	24	12
	5						One held 2 virgates		
			3				One held ½ virgate, the others 16 acres each		
1349	3	1			1		E 368/124, m.258 1 virgater held 2½ virgates	5	5
1372–3 and 1380–81							HWRO, 009:1 (B.A. 2636)/159, no. 92049 $^{3}/_{7}$, $^{4}/_{7}$, $^{7}/_{7}$		
							12 at Bibury and 12 at Ablington	24	16½?
BISHOPS CLEEVE 1299	5	11		13	27		*RBW*, 327–48	58	10½ + ?
						2	One held a lease of 17 demesne acres		
1349	5	8			7		E 368/124, m.258	44	9
						24	20 six-acre tenants and 4 holders of pennylands		+5
1353	5	9		11			E 136/13/9	49	9½ +
						24	24 fardel tenants		6
1372–3	5	10		12			HWRO, 009:1 (B.A. 2636)/161, no. 92113 $^{5}/_{6}$	55	10 +
						28	Six-acre tenants		7
1393–4	5	10		12			HWRO, 009:1 (B.A. 2636)/193, no. 92627 $^{11}/_{12}$	55	10 +
						28	Six-acre tenants		7

Table B *continued*
TENANTS ON THE GLOUCESTERSHIRE ESTATES OF THE BISHOPS OF WORCESTER

Estate	*Virgaters*	*Half-virgaters*	*Inch-landers*	*Monday-men*	*Cottars*	*Other*	*Remarks and Sources*	*Total of Tenants*	*Total of Virgates*
HENBURY (including Stoke Bishop) 1299	23	48					*RBW*, 377–402	128	48 + ?
						48	Include 3 tenants of ⅓ virgate		
1349	16	39			5		E 368/124, m.258d To add the holdings of 2 reeves	99	35½+
						37	16 five-acre tenants and 21 forelands		
1353				16		5 or 6	E 136/13/9 (incomplete) Labour services of holders of 50 virgates performed		50 + ?
HENBURY 1363				1			HWRO, 009:1 (B.A. 2636)/165, no. 92227 24½ virgates charged Labour services of holders of 23 virgates performed and ½ virgate held by a beadle and 8 five-acre holdings		23½
Recognitio tenentium November 1375 ?	7	31		1			HWRO, 009:1 (B.A. 2636)/165, no. 92226 4/7		
						3	Ten-acre tenants		
						2	Five-acre tenants		
						23	Tenants of forelands	67	22½
							In addition 1 tenant held two free virgates and 2 tenants held half a free virgate each		
STOKE BISHOP 1372–3			1		4		HWRO, 009:1 (B.A. 2636)/192, no. 92626 10/12		
						14	Five-acre tenants		
							Labour services of holders of 27 virgates exacted and ½ virgate held by reeve		27½
1381–2					4		HWRO, 009:1 (B.A. 2636)/171, no. 92417		
						14	Five-acre tenants		
							Labour services of holders of 27 virgates exacted and 1 virgate held by reeve		28

Table B *continued*
TENANTS ON THE GLOUCESTERSHIRE ESTATES OF THE BISHOPS OF WORCESTER

Estate	*Virgaters*	*Half-virgaters*	*Inch-landers*	*Monday-men*	*Cottars*	*Others*	*Remarks and Sources*	*Total of Tenants*	*Total of Virgates*
WITHINGTON 1299	9				7		*RBW*, 354–65	51	17½
		17					One virgate tenant also held two ½ virgates		
				15			Including two men who also held ½ virgates and one who held two holdings		
						4	Three assarts and one smallholding		
			5				One was also a holder of ½ virgate		
1349	8		3		5		E 368/124, m.258	16	8
1353	8			9			E 136/13/9	21	

Table C
TENANTS OF THE BISHOPS OF WORCESTER IN CENTRAL AND WESTERN WORCESTERSHIRE AND AT TREDINGTON (WARWICKSHIRE)

Estate	*Virgaters*	*Half-virgaters*	*Inch-landers*	*Cottars*	*Others*	*Remarks and Sources*	*Total of Tenants*	*Total of Virgates*
FLADBURY (including Throckmorton) 1299	23	26				*RBW*, 129–40		35½
			4			3 inchlanders held one virgate each		
					33		83	
1349	31	37		6		E 368/124, m.258		
						Add the holding of 1 reeve	75	49½ +
1353	31	37		6		E 368/126, stat. et vis. comp., Mich., mm.20d., 21		
						Add the holding of 1 reeve	75	49½ +
1361–2				4		E 136/13/28A		40½

Table C *continued*

TENANTS OF THE BISHOPS OF WORCESTER IN CENTRAL AND WESTERN WORCESTERSHIRE AND AT TREDINGTON (WARWICKSHIRE)

Estate	*Virgaters*	*Half-virgaters*	*Inch-landers*	*Cottars*	*Others*	*Remarks and Sources*	*Total of Tenants*	*Total of Virgates*
KEMPSEY 1299	2	76				*RBW*, 64–79		30
					30	Not including the holders of forelands	108	
1302						E 136/13/25A (only holders of ½ virgates mentioned)	77	
1349		31		11		E 368/124, m.258		
					14	Holders of nooklands		
						Add the holding of 1 reeve	57	15½ +
1353		31		11		E 368/126, stat. et vis. comp., Mich., m.20d		
					14	Holders of nooklands		
						Add the holding of 1 reeve	57	15½ +
1361–2		21?		6		E 136/13/28A		10½ +
					10	Holders of nooklands	37?	
NORTHWICK 1299		25		12		*RBW*, 16–25		6+
					43	Consisting of 2 holders of ¼ virgates, 16 avermen, 25 millers (not including the holders of forelands)	80	
1349	15			43		E 368/124, m.258		
					50	Consisting of 13 holders of nooklands, 16 avermen, 23 molmen Add the holding of 1 reeve	108	15+
1361–2						E 136/13/28A (only holders of virgates mentioned)		15

Table C *continued*

TENANTS OF THE BISHOPS OF WORCESTER IN CENTRAL AND WESTERN WORCESTERSHIRE AND AT TREDINGTON (WARWICKSHIRE)

Estate	*Virgaters*	*Half-virgaters*	*Inch-landers*	*Cottars*	*Others*	*Remarks and Sources*	*Total of Tenants*	*Total of Virgates*
RIPPLE 1299	1	73		2		*RBW*, 154–64		36
			5			Including two holding ½ virgate each		
					6	Including two holding 6 acres each and three holding 10 acres each	85	
1302	3	65			3	E 136/13/25A (an incomplete list)	71	32½
1349	30	2		4		E 368/124, m.258		
					6	Holders of pennylands	42	31
1353	30	2		4		E 368/126, stat. et vis. comp., Mich., m.20		
					6	Holders of pennylands Add the holding of 1 reeve	43	31+
1361–2	25	2				E 136/13/28A (only holders of virgates and half-virgates mentioned)		26
TREDINGTON 1299	12	18	3			*RBW*, 281–8		21½
				11		Including 8 holding full cotlands and 3 holding half-cotlands		
					12	Smallholdings of various sizes	56	
1302						E 136/13/25A 33 tenants		22½
					14	Holding between them 146 acres	47	
1353	13	10		5		E 368/126, stat. et vis. comp., Mich., m.22 Add the holding of 1 reeve	29	18+

Table D
TENANTS OF THE BISHOPS OF WORCESTER IN NORTH-EASTERN WORCESTERSHIRE

Estate	*Virgaters*	*Half-virgaters*	*Quarter-virgaters*	*Cottars*	*Others*	*Remarks and Sources*	*Total of Tenants*	*Total of Virgates*
ALVECHURCH 1299		21	7	34		*RBW*, 208–16 These totals include four ½ virgates and four ¼ virgates held for rent only	62	12¼
1302–3						E 136/13/25A (a partial list)	51	9⅜
1349		13		32		E 368/124, m.258	45	6½
1361–2		11				E 136/13/28A (only the tenants of half-virgates given)		5½
HANBURY (by Droitwich) 1299		38			23	*RBW*, 176–84 Consisting of smallholders	61	19
1302–3		39				E 136/13/25A (a partial list)		19½
1349	4					E 368/124, m.258 No other tenants remained	4	4
1353	?	3				E 368/126, stat. et vis. comp., Mich., mm.21d, 22 Entry partly torn off. The number of virgate-holders is missing Add the holding of 1 reeve		

Table D *continued*
TENANTS OF THE BISHOPS OF WORCESTER IN NORTH-EASTERN WORCESTERSHIRE

Estate	*Virgaters*	*Half-virgaters*	*Quarter-virgaters*	*Cottars*	*Others*	*Remarks and Sources*	*Total of Tenants*	*Total of Virgates*
HARTLEBURY 1299	76					*RBW*, 191–202 Holding 66 virgates		
		7				Including 2 tenants who also held virgates		
			13	4				
					13	Including 7 tenants of 1 acre holdings	111	72¾
1349	38			4		E 368/124, m.258		
			13			13 holders of nooklands, each probably holding ¼ virgate		
					21	Consisting of avermen		
						Add the holding of 1 reeve	77	41¼ +
1353	38		13	2		E 368/126, stat. et vis. comp., Mich., m.21d		
					21	Consisting of avermen		
						Add the holding of 1 reeve	75	41¼ +

Table D *continued*
TENANTS OF THE BISHOPS OF WORCESTER IN NORTH-EASTERN WORCESTERSHIRE

Estate	*Virgaters*	*Half-virgaters*	*Quarter-virgaters*	*Cottars*	*Others*	*Remarks and Sources*	*Total of Tenants*	*Total of Virgates*
WICK EPISCOPI 1299	6					*RBW*, 45–55 2 tenants holding 1 virgate; 4 tenants holding 1 virgate of the bishop's demesne for rent		
		23				Holding between them 16 half-virgates		
			7			Holding between them 1¼ virgates (include one tenant holding also a further ½ virgate)		11¼
				11		Including 9 tenants of 3 acre holdings		
					33	Consisting of 10 tenants of 12 acre holdings and 23 with a variety of smallholdings	79	
1349		7		12		E 368/124, m.258	49	
					29	Consisting of 25 holders of nooklands and of 4 avermen		
						Add the holding of 1 reeve		3½ +
1353		7		11		E 368/126, stat. et vis. comp., Mich., m.21; E 136/13/25A		
					29	Consisting of 25 holders of nooklands and of 4 avermen		
						Add the holding of 1 reeve	48	3½ +
1361–2					16	E 136/13/28 A Consisting of holders of nooklands and of avermen		6½

Table E
RENDERS PAID BY THE CUSTOMARY TENANTS ON THE ESTATES OF THE BISHOP OF WORCESTER

Estate	*Recognition*	*Tallage*	*Fine*	*Rents (1 term of payment)*	*Fishfee and 'Spenyngfee*	*Sources and Remarks*
ALVECHURCH (Worcs) 1302–3	£1 0 0	£1 0 0	£1 0 0	£1 19 1¼		*RBW*, 531–3; SC 6/1143/18; E 364/71, m.3; E 136/13/25A
1353	2 0			£1 2 0		E 368/126, stat. et vis. comp., Mich., m.22; E 136/13/25A
1361–2	3 0			6 6		E 136/13/28A
1364	3 4	16 0		£2 13 0		E 136/13/30; SC 11/724
ASTON (Worcs) 1302–3	4 0					*RBW*, 517–8; SC 6/1143/18; E 136/13/25A
1353	none			none		E 368/126, stat. et vis. comp., Mich., m.20d. No customary tenants
1361–2	6					E 136/13/28A
BIBURY (Glos) 1302–3	10 0	£1 0 0	14 0	18 8½	4 10½	*RBW*, 504–5; SC 6/1143/18; E 364/71, m.3 (rents in 1299)
1353	3 4			1 3		E 136/13/9; E 357/3, m.55d
1364	2 0					E 136/14/16
1372–3			14 0			HWRO, 009:1 (B.A. 2636)/159, r.o. 92049 $^{3}/_{7}$, $^{4}/_{7}$
BLOCKLEY (Glos) 1302–3	£3 0 0	£3 0 0	10 0	£3 1 10	16 6	Includes PAXFORD *RBW*, 538–42; SC 6/1143/18; E 136/13/25A
1353	3 4			£2 2 3½	3 0	E 368/126, stat. et vis. comp., Mich.; E 136/13/25A
1361–2	3 0			£2 2 3½		E 136/13/28A
1364	3 4	£1 10 0		£2 17 6	2 6	E 136/13/30; SC 11/724
1383–4			15 6			HWRO, 009:1 (B.A. 2636)/157, r.o. 92007

Table E *continued*

RENDERS PAID BY THE CUSTOMARY TENANTS ON THE ESTATES OF THE BISHOP OF WORCESTER

Estate	*Recognition*	*Tallage*	*Fine*	*Rents (1 term of payments)*	*Fishfee and 'Spenyngfee'*	*Sources and Remarks*
BREDON (Worcs)						Tallage (including 'Spenyngfee') charged at 1s. per virgate (c.1300)
1302–3	£2 10 0	£3 0 4	£1 0 4	£2 13 10½	2 4	*RBW*, 510–12; SC 6/1143/18; E 364/71, m.3; E 136/13/25A
1353	3 4			£1 10 2	2 4½	E 368/126, stat. et vis. comp., Mich., m.20; E 136/13/25A
1361–2	5 0			£1 10 2		E 136/13/28A
1364	3 4	10 0		£3 10 9	2 0	E 136/13/30; SC 11/724
1375–6		17 6	£1 0 4		2 6	HWRO, 009:1 (B.A. 2636)/158, no. 92014 Tallage (including 'Spenyngfee') levied by reeve at 6d. per virgate
BISHOPS CLEEVE (Glos)						
1302–3	£2 0 0	£2 0 0	£1 4 0	£3 11 1	4 0	*RBW*, 327–48, 508–9; SC 6/1143/18; E 364/71, m.3 (rents in 1299)
1353	6 8			£1 3 2¼		E 136/13/9; E 357/3, m.55d
1364	13 4					E 136/14/16
1372–3		£2 0 0	£1 4 0			HWRO, 009:1 (B.A. 2636)/161, no. 92113 5/6
FLADBURY (Worcs)						Includes THROCKMORTON
1302–3	£3 0 0	£2 0 0	10 0	£3 3 3	13 2½	*RBW*, 518–20; SC 6/1143/18; E 364/71, m.3; E 136/13/25A
1353	3 4			£2 7 0	6 2	E 136/13/25A
1361–2	3 0			£2 7 0		E 136/13/28A
1364	3 4	£1 0 0		£3 4 0	1 6	E 136/13/30; SC 11/724
HAMPTON LUCY (Warw)						Includes HATTON
1302–3	£1 0 0	£1 6 8	12 0	£1 11 3		*RBW*, 263–74, 533–4; SC 6/1143/18; E 364/71, m.3 (rents in 1299)
1349–50	2 0					E 136/12/10
1353	2 0					E 136/12/13B
1361–2	6 8			£3 15 0		E 136/12/20

Table E *continued*
RENDERS PAID BY THE CUSTOMARY TENANTS ON THE ESTATES OF THE BISHOP OF WORCESTER

Estate	*Recognition*	*Tallage*	*Fine*	*Rents (1 term of payments)*	*Fishfee and 'Spenyngfee'*	*Sources and Remarks*
HANBURY (Worcs)						
1302–3	£1 0 0	£1 0 0	13 4	£1 17 9		*RBW*, 530–1; SC 6/1143/18; E 364/71, m.3; E 136/13/25A
1353	2 0			£1 1 1½		E 368/126, stat. et vis. comp., Mich., mm.21d, 22; E 136/13/25A
1361–2	3 4			£1 0 0¾		E 136/13/28A
1364	3 4	17 0		£2 15 6		E 136/13/30; SC 11/724
1375–7	10 0		10 0			HWRO, 009:1 (B.A. 2636)/165, no. 92229
HARTLEBURY (Worcs)						
1302–3	13 4	£3 8 0	£1 0 0	£3 15 8¼		*RBW*, 527–9; E 136/13/25A
1353	3 4			£1 4 9½		E 368/126, stat. et vis. comp., Mich., m.21d; E 136/13/25A
1361–2	2 0			£1 12 9½		E 136/13/28A
1364	3 4	£2 8 0		£3 15 2		E 136/13/30; SC 11/724
HENBURY (Glos)						Includes STOKE
1302–3	£10 0 0	£10 6 11¼	£3 19 4	£4 7 7	10 7½	*RBW*, 377–402, 498–503; SC 6/1143/18; E 364/71 m.3 (rents in 1299)
1349		£3 0 0				E 368/124, m.258
1353	13 4			2 1		E 136/13/9; E 357/3, m.55d
1364	£2 0 0					E 136/14/16
1372–3 & 1378–9		£9 11 4	£4 2 4		10 7½	HWRO, 009:1 (B.A. 2636)/165, no. 92225 6/8; 192, no. 92626 10/12
KEMPSEY (Worcs)						
1302–3	£3 0 0	£1 1 11	£1 0 0	£4 8 9	4 3½	*RBW*, 514–6; SC 6/1143/18; E 364/71, m.3; E 136/13/25A
1353	3 4			£2 14 0	4 4	E 368/126, stat. et vis. comp., Mich., m.19d; E 136/13/25A
1361–2	4 0			£2 13 0		E 136/13/28A
1364	4 0	£1 0 0		£3 4 0		E 136/13/30; SC 11/724

Table E *continued*
RENDERS PAID BY THE CUSTOMARY TENANTS ON THE ESTATES OF THE BISHOP OF WORCESTER

Estate	*Recognition*	*Tallage*	*Fine*	*Rents (1 term of payments)*	*Fishfee and 'Spenyngfee'*	*Sources and Remarks*
NORTHWICK (Worcs) 1302–3	£3 0 0	£2 18 4	£1 4 0	£5 3 7	4 1½	Includes KNIGHTWICK *RBW*, 2–26, 523–5; E 364/71, m.3 (rents in 1299)
1353	3 4			£2 12 9	No fishfee since 1349	E 368/126, stat. et vis. comp., Mich., mm.21, 21d; E 136/13/25A
1361–2	6 0			£2 10 9		E 136/13/28A
1364	3 4	£2 10 0		£2 19 6		E 136/13/30; SC 11/724
RIPPLE (Worcs) 1302–3	£3 0 0	£4 0 0	15 0	£4 0 3	10 0	*RBW*, 512–14; SC 6/1143/18; E 364/71, m.3; E 136/13/25A
1353	2 0			£1 15 9¼		E 368/126, stat. et vis. comp., Mich., mm.20, 20d; E 136/13/25A
1361–2	3 0			£1 15 9¼		E 136/13/28A
1364	4 0	£2 0 0		£3 4 6	6 0	E 136/13/30; SC 11/724
TREDINGTON (Warw) 1302–3	£2 10 0	£1 2 8½	10 0	£2 0 0½		*RBW*, 536–8; SC 6/1143/18; E 364/71, m.3; E 136/13/25A
1353	2 0			£1 16 0½		E 368/126, stat. et vis. comp., Mich., m.22; E 136/13/25A
1361–2	3 0			£2 3 6		E 136/13/28A
1364	4 0	16 0		£2 7 6		E 136/13/30; SC 11/724
WICK EPISCOPI (Worcs) 1302–3	£2 0 0	£3 0 11	£1 0 0	£3 5 10½		*RBW*, 521–3; SC 6/1143/18; E 364/71, m.3; E 136/13/25A
1353	3 4			£2 0 7		E 368/126, stat. et vis. comp., Mich., m.21
1361–2	4 0			£2 0 7		E 136/13/28A
1364	3 4	£2 2 0		£3 15 0		E 136/13/30; SC 11/724

Table E *continued*
RENDERS PAID BY THE CUSTOMARY TENANTS ON THE ESTATES OF THE BISHOP OF WORCESTER

Estate	*Recognition*	*Tallage*	*Fine*	*Rents (1 term of payments)*	*Fishfee and 'Spenyngfee'*	*Sources and Remarks*
WITHINGTON (Glos) 1302–3	£1 0 0	£1 6 8	19 8	£2 1 0		*RBW*, 354–65, 506–7; SC 6/1143/18; E 364/71 m.3 (rents in 1299)
1353	3 4			11 7½		E 136/13/9; E 357/3, m.55d
1364	6 8					E 136/14/16
TOTALS						
1302–3	£40 7 4	£41 12 5¾	£17 1 8	£47 19 7½		Include £1 of 'recognition' and 10s. of fine at Stratford not listed in the table above (*RBW*, 534–6).
1317		£35 16 9¼				SC 6/1143/19
					£1 7 0¼	Minute certe consuetudines
1334	£11 13 4					E 372/178, m.19 (vacancy 3–15 March 1334)
1337	£24 15 0					SC 6/1143/20 (vacancy 21 May–25 July 1337)
1349	£1 8 8					E 357/3, m.53, received by Leo Perton, escheator, between 7 August 1349 (death of Bishop Wolstan Bransford) and 28 August 1349. Nothing more received from 'recognitions' during 1349–50 vacancy (E 372/196, m.147)
1353	£3 0 0			£22 4 8		
1361	£2 6 6			£23 7 5		
1364	£5 0 8	£15 9 0		£32 16 5		

Table F
TENANTS ON THE WARWICKSHIRE ESTATES OF THE BISHOPS OF COVENTRY AND LICHFIELD

	CHADSHUNT (with Gaydon)					BISHOPS ITCHINGTON					BISHOPS TACHBROOK					
Date	*Virgaters*	*Half-virgaters*	*Others*	*Total of Tenants*	*Total of Virgates*	*Virgaters*	*Half-virgaters*	*Others*	*Total of Tenants*	*Total of Virgates*	*Virgaters*	*Half-virgaters*	*Others*	*Total of Tenants*	*Total of Virgates*	
c.1279	22 at Gaydon	17 at Chads-hunt	2 cottars	42	30½											1
						15	34	16 cottars	65	34¼						2
											14	5	6 cottars	25	16½	3
1321–2	24 at Gaydon	17 at Chads-hunt	?	41 + ?	32½	20	1	10 acremen	31 + ?			18	?	18 + ?	9	4
Immediately after 1348–9 plague	20	?	?			16	None	?				8	?			5
1358–60	20 + reeve	17		38	28½	25	1	10 acremen	36	30½		8 + reeve		9	4	6

Sources and Remarks

[1] E 164/15, f.66.

[2] E 164/15, ff. 28–30. 2 virgaters held 3¼ virgates between them.

[3] E 164/15, ff. 67–8.

[4] SC 6/1132/5; E 136/12/17. Evidence probably incomplete.

[5] E 368/132, stat. et vis. comp., Pas., m.12; E 136/12/17.

[6] ibid.; *VCH Staffs*, V1, 122; BL, Add. MS 6167, pp.173–4.

Table G
TENANTS ON SOME OF THE STAFFORDSHIRE ESTATES OF THE BISHOPS OF COVENTRY AND LICHFIELD

	BREWOOD					HAYWOOD					LONGDON					
Date	*Half-virgaters*		*Others*		*Holdings vacant*	*Half-virgaters*		*Quarter-virgaters*		*Holdings vacant*	*Virgaters*		*Half-virgaters*		*Holdings vacant*	Source
	Alive	*Dead*	*Alive*	*Dead*		*Alive*	*Dead*	*Alive*	*Dead*		*Alive*	*Dead*	*Alive*	*Dead*		
Before 1348	29															1
During the plague of 1348–9	9	20			20 half-virgates		13		6	13 half-virgates + 6 quarter-virgates		11		9	11 virgates + 9 half-virgates	2
1358–60	19 (one holding 2 half-virgates)				9 half-virgates					7 half-virgates + 6 quarter-virgates					7 virgates + 3 half-virgates	3

Sources [1] E 368/132, stat. et vis. comp., Pas., m.16. [2] ibid., mm. 16–20; BL, Add. MS 6165, p.197. [3] ibid.

TEXT

E 368/124, m.256

ADHUC STATUS ET VISUS COMPOTORUM DE TERMINO SANCTE TRINITATIS ANNO XXVJ°

[*Marginated*] Wygorn'

[1] Audito compoto Roberti de Warthecop' et Leonis de Perton' de exitibus temporalium episcopatus Wygorn' vacantis in manu regis existentis per mortem Wolstani nuper episcopi ibidem a xxviij° die augusti anno xxiij° usque xxviij diem novembris proximo sequentem, antequam liberarunt omnia temporalia predicta magistro Willelmo de Fenton et Willelmo de Evesham custodienda quamdiu dicta vacatio duraret, ita quod de exitibus de episcopatu predicto et temporalibus eiusdem provenientibus responderet[156] Johanni episcopo Menev' cui rex dictos exitus una cum aliis profituis inde a predicto xxviij° die novembris provenientes, que ad ipsum regem pertinere deberent, concessit de dono ipsius regis per breve de magno sigillo datum predicto xxviij° die novembris per quod rex mandavit prefato Roberto custodi quod eisdem Willelmo et Willelmo temporalia predicta cum pertinenciis liberarent custodienda in forma predicta, debent CCxxxviij li. v s. ob.

[2] De quibus solverunt lxvj li. xiij s. iiij d. per unam talliam levatam xix° die octobris anno xxiiij^{to}. Et petunt sibi allocari xxx li. viij s. viij d. ob. quos solverunt Willelmo de Cusaunce nuper thesaurario garderobe regis super expensis hospicii regis unde ostendunt duas acquietancias sub nomine ipsius Willelmi. Et debent Cxlj li. iij s. De quibus calumpniantur xv li. v s. vij d. ob. qu. de quibus onerantur infra summam suam predictam de firmis et aliis exitibus manerii de Stretford' super Aven', quos quidem firmas et exitus dicunt se non recepisse nec recipere potuisse, eo quod diu ante mortem prefati Wulstani ultimi episcopi, per cuius mortem dictus episcopatus vacabat, manerium illud per ipsum Wulstanum dimissum fuit Johanni de Peyto ad terminum vite sue qui toto tempore vacationis predicte tenuit et adhuc tenet dictum manerium ex assensu totius capituli Wygorn' et de licencia regis pro certa firma certis terminis inde reddenda et nullus terminus redditus accidebat infra tempus dicti compoti, ut dicunt per sacramentum suum, unde dictum est eis quod sequantur versus prefatum Johannem de Peyto citra quindenam Sancti Michaelis proximo futuram de respondendo et satisfaciendo regi de exitibus dicti manerii in exonerationem ipsorum custodum si etc. Et interim habeant respectum etc.

[3] Et xxiiij li. vj s. v d. de quibus onerantur infra summam suam predictam videlicet de decima garbarum et feni ecclesie de Hilendon' et vj s. v d. de redditu debito ad eandem ecclesiam de Hilendon' ad terminum Sancti Michaelis, de quibus quidem decima sive redditu dicunt se nichil percepisse seu percipere potuisse eo quod decanus et capitulum London' clamant habere fructus dicte ecclesie de Hilendon' tempore cuiuslibet vacationis dicti episcopatus Wygorn' et fructus ecclesie illius una cum redditu predicto habuerunt tempore vacationis predicte, unde dictum est eisdem custodibus quod sequantur versus dictos decanum et capitulum de respondendo regi de decima et redditu predictis citra dictam quindenam Sancti Michaelis si etc.

[4] Et xxxiij s. iiij d. de quibus onerantur infra summam predictam de pensione ecclesie de Berkeleye debita manerio de Hambury quod est de temporalibus dicti episcopatus videlicet ad terminum Sancti Michaelis de qua pensione dicunt se nichil percepisse eo quod prior Wygorn' clamavit habere pensionem illam et eam habuit unde dictum est eis quod sequantur versus dictum priorem citra dictam quindenam Sancti Michaelis de respondendo regi de predicta pensione in exonerationem ipsorum custodum si etc.

[5] Et calumpniantur iiij^{xx} iiij li. iiij s. ob. de quibus dicunt se[157] superoneratos esse infra summam predictam de redditibus tam assise quam custumariorum ac aliis minutis redditibus et consuetudinibus necnon de operibus autumpnalibus, precariis, operibus trituracionis arrure et herciature, cariaturis et tassationibus bladorum et aliis minutis redditibus in diversis maneriis dicti episcopatus ultra id quod inde perceperunt vel percipere potuerunt pro defectu tenentium qui dictos redditus reddere et pro defectu custumariorum et operariorum qui dicta opera facere solebant et qui moriebantur in pestilencia mortali que vigebat in terris dicti episcopatus infra tempus dicti compoti et ante, quorum quidem redditruum et operum particule per eosdem custodes in hac parte

156 Recte *responderent*.

157 Interlined.

levate[158] et nomina liberorum tenentium de quibus eosdem redditus levaverunt et numerus virgatariorum, noklandes, arkemen et cotagiariorum de quibus precaria huiusmodi operum perceperunt continentur in ij rotulis quos iidem custodes liberarunt hic et que sunt inter billas de hoc termino.[159] Et petunt exonerari de predictis iiij^{xx}iiij li. iiij s. ob. prout etc. asserentes se eosdem iiij^{xx}v li. xij s. j d. ob. qu. seu quicquam inde levasse nec levare potuisse per tempus predictum ex causis supradictis. Et hoc pretendunt verificare prout curie etc.[160] Ideo dictum est eis quod sequantur versus regem de brevi habendo thesaurario et baronibus hic super exoneratione sua in hac parte citra quindenam Sancti Michaelis proximo futuram si sibi viderint expedire. Et interim habeant respectum etc. Et debent xv li. xiij s. vj d. ob. qu. qui respitiantur eis usque dictam quindenam pro majori summa quam petunt sibi allocari pro custodia temporalium predictorum per tempus predictum. Et datus est eis dies hic ad dictam quindenam ad faciendum et recipiendum super premissis quod etc., dicto videlicet Leoni per manucaptionem Willelmi de Barton' et Johannis de Peolesdon' de comitatu Salop' qui alias presentes hic manuceperunt habere corpus dicti Leonis hic de die in diem et termino in terminum quousque computaverit et satisfecerit etc. necnon fecerit finem cum rege pro contemptu quem idem Leo fecit non veniendo hic in crastino Sancti Michaelis anno xxiiij^{to} ad computandum de escaetria in comitatu Wygorn' prout assumpserat et sicut continetur alibi in hiis memorandis inter recorda de termino Sancti Hillarii.

Et ad dictam quindenam Sancti Michaelis predicti Robertus de Warthecop' et Leo venerunt. Idemque Leo fecit finem cum rege pro[161] contemptu predicto sicut continetur in memorandis de anno xxvij^{o} regis nunc inter fines de termino Sancti Michaelis.

[6] Et quia predicti Robertus et Leo sunt in prosequendo versus prefatum Johannem de Peyto pro predictis xv li. v s. vij d. ob. qu. de exitibus manerii de Stratford' et versus predictos decanum et capitulum London' pro predictis xxiiij li. vj s. v d. de fructubus ecclesie de Hylendon' et versus priorem Wygorn' pro xxxiij s. iiij d. de pensione ecclesie de Berkeleye de respondendo et satisfaciendo regi de summis illis separatim in exonerationem ipsorum custodum per brevia retornabilia coram baronibus ad placita in octabis Sancti Hillarii proximo futuris concessum est eisdem custodibus per thesaurarium quod interim habeant respectum de summis predictis. Et quoad predictos iiij^{xx}iiij li. iiij s. ob. de quibus dicunt se superoneratos esse de redditibus tam liberorum quam custumariorum et operariorum ultra id quod dicunt se inde levasse vel levare potuisse exibuerunt curie breve regis de magno sigillo quod est inter communia de termino Sancti Michaelis anno xxvij^{o} in hec verba:

[7] Edwardus dei gracia rex Anglie et Francie et dominus Hibernie thesaurario et baronibus suis de scaccario salutem. Cum vicesimo octavo die augusti anno regni nostri Anglie vicesimo tertio per litteras nostras patentes commiserimus dilecto clerico nostro Roberto de[162] [*membrane 256d*] Warthecop' et Leoni de Perton' custodiam episcopatus Wygorn' tunc vacantis et in manu nostra existentis habendam cum omnibus ad custodiam illam spectantibus, ita quod de exitibus inde provenientibus nobis ad scaccarium nostrum responderent, prout in litteris nostris predictis plenius continetur, et licet iidem Robertus et Leo omnia servicia exitus et profitua que de omnibus liberis tenentibus et villanis ac de omnibus terris et tenementis ad dictum episcopatum tunc pertinentibus, considerata pestilencia que tunc in partibus, ubi temporalia ad dictum episcopatum pertinentia extiterant, invaluit, levaverint et nobis inde satisfecerint, auditores tamen compoti eorundem Roberti et Leonis per vos ad hoc deputati, detrimentis et distractionibus reddituum et serviciorum tenentium ac diminutione valoris terrarum et tenementorum minime ponderatis seu consideratis, ipsum[163] Robertum et Leonem de tanta pecunie summa quanta de temporalibus episcopatus predicti anno regni domini Edwardi quondam regis Anglie avi nostri tricesimo primo pro rata temporis vacationis predicte levata extitit, indebite onerarunt, sicut ex querela sua accepimus. Super quo nobis supplicarunt sibi per nos de remedio provideri. Nos nolentes ipsos Robertum et Leonem indebite onerari in hac parte vobis mandamus quod, viso et recitato compoto predicto auditisque rationibus eorundem Roberti et Leonis, si per inquisitionem vel alio modo legitimo vobis constare potuerit ipsos Robertum et Leonem omnes pecunie summas, que de serviciis omnium liberorum ac nativorum tenentium ac

158 From this point until the interlineation the text is written in a smaller hand.

159 For what seems to be a copy of these two rolls delivered into the exchequer on 28 Nov. 1352, see [36–61].

160 *per tempus . . . etc.* interlined.

161 *rege pro* interlined.

162 Written at the bottom of the membrane: *plus in tergo.*

163 Recte *ipsos.*

terrarum et tenementorum ad episcopatum predictum pertinentium tempore quo custodiam eiusdem episcopatus habuerunt, considerata pestilencia predicta, levasse et levare potuisse et nobis inde fideliter ad scaccarium predictum respondisse, tunc ipsos de majori summa, quam inde levaverunt seu levare potuerunt, super ipsos per predictos auditores onerata ad idem scaccarium exonerari et quietos esse faciatis. Teste me ipso apud Westm' xxvij die octobris anno regni nostri Anglie vicesimo sexto, regni vero nostri Francie tertiodecimo.

[8] Et petunt dicti custodes ut prius exonerari et quietos fieri de supradictis iiij^{xx}iiij li. iiij s. ob. juxta formam dicti brevis, asserentes se oneratos esse de eadem summa particulariter de redditibus liberorum tenentium et custumariorum ac operibus nativorum in diversis maneriis dicti episcopatus per tempus predictum ultra id quod inde perceperunt vel recipere potuerunt per tempus predictum ob causas superius allegatas, videlicet.

[9] De Cij s. viij d. ob. ultra Cix s. iij d. qu. inde receptos in manerio de Hertilbury.

[10] De iiij li. v s. iiij d. ob. ultra xxiij s. x d. inde receptos in manerio de Northwyke.

[11] De liij s. iiij d. ob. ultra vij li. xij s. v d. ob. inde receptos in manerio de Wyke juxta Wygorn'.

[12] De iiij li. xj s. vj d. ob. ultra iiij s. iiij d. ob. inde receptos in manerio de Kemeseye.

[13] De xv s. xj d. ob. ultra v s. ob. inde receptos in manerio de Aston'.

[14] De iiij li. x d. ob. qu. ultra ij s. vij d. ob. inde receptos in manerio de Hanbury juxta Wyche.

[15] De vij li. ix s. v d. ob. ultra xxxvj s. v d. qu. inde receptos in manerio de Alvechurch'.

[16] De vj li. viij s. vij d. ultra xxxv s. vj d. inde receptos in manerio de Fladebury.

[17] De vij li. v s. vj d. ultra lxiv s. ix d. qu. inde levatos in manerio de Blokley.

[18] De viij li. viij s. j d. qu. ultra Cvj s. xj d. qu. inde receptos in manerio de Riple.

[19] De Cj s. iv d. ultra iiij li. v s. ix d. ob. qu. inde levatos in manerio de Bredon'.

[20] De iiij li. xv s. iiij d. ob. ultra xlv s. vij d. qu. inde levatos in manerio de Clyve.

[21] De iiij li. xvij s. ix d. ob. qu. ultra lxxiv s. ix d. ob. qu. inde levatos in manerio de Withyndon'.

[22] De iiij li. ij s. vj d. ob. ultra xxv s. v d. inde levatos in manerio de Bibury.

[23] De xlviij s. v d. ob. qu. ultra iiij li. viij s. vij d. inde levatos in manerio de Bisshopeshampton.

[24] De xij li. iij s. vij d. ultra vij li. xix s. iij d. qu. inde levatos in manerio de Hambury Saltmerssh'.

[25] Asserentes dicti custodes se predictos iiij^{xx}iiij li. iv s. ob. seu quicquam inde non levasse nec levare potuisse per tempus predictum ob causas superius allegatas. Et hoc pretendunt verificare qualitercumque curia etc.

[26] Et viso rotulo de particulis compoti predicti compertum est in eodem quod dicti custodes onerantur de redditibus liberorum et custumariorum ac operibus nativorum in maneriis predictis usque ad summam Cxxiij li. xvj s. ij d. particulariter juxta videlicet ratam summarum dictorum superoneris et recepte conjunctaram et superius annotatarum per evidenciam videlicet compoti Humfridi de Waleden' qui fuit custos dicti episcopatus vacantis anno xxx^{o} regni regis avi regis nunc. Quibus compertis concordatum est quod inquiratur super premissis antequam ulterius etc. Et quod Johannes de Wyndesovere persona ecclesie de Clyve, Johannes de Sudyngton', Stephanus de Dudlegh' persone[164] ecclesie de Strengesham et Johannes Worthyn tres et duo eorum assignentur per commissionem huius scaccarii ad inquirendum etc. Et fit eis huiusmodi commissio.[165] Mandatumque est eis quod inquirant, ita quod inquisitionem inde habeant hic a die Pasche in xv dies. Et transcriptum predictorum duorum rotulorum simul cum transcriptum istius processus mittitur prefatis Johanni, Johanni, Stephano et Johanni sub pede sigilli huius scaccarii pro informatione et idem dies datus est predictis custodibus ad audiendum judicium et ad faciendum et recipiendum quod etc. prefato videlicet Leoni per manucaptionem predictam sicut continetur in memorandis de anno xxvij^{o} inter dies datos de termino Sancti Michaelis. Postea videlicet xxxj^{o} die maii anno xxvij^{o} huius regis prefatus Johannes de Peyto soluit regi pro predictis Roberto de Warthecop' et Leone de Perton' supradictos xv li. v s. viij d. per unam talliam levatam predicto xxxj^{o} die maii quam idem Johannes de Peyto ostendit.

[27] Postea, videlicet in quindena Sancti Michaelis dicto anno xxvij^{o} finiente predicti Robertus de Warthecop' et Leo de Perton' venerunt et prefati Johannes de Sodyngton' et Stephanus de Dudlegh' retornaverunt hic dictam commissionem cum transcripto predicto et vj inquisitionibus coram eis

164 Recte *persona.*

165 Marginated: *Transcriptum commissionis inter billas de termino Sancti Michaelis anno xxvij^{o}.*

captis super premissis, que insimul consuta sunt inter brevia executa pro rege de termino Sancti Michaelis anno xxviij°.[166]

[28] Primam videlicet captam apud Alvechirche xxviij° die marcii dicto anno xxvij° per sacramentum Johannis de Bechynton', Johannis Wade et aliorum juratorum quorum nomina annotantur in eadem inquisitione. Qui juratores dicunt per sacramentum suum quod non fuerunt[167] [*membrane 259*][168] in maneriis de Alvechirche et Blokkeleye plures libere tenentes nec major numerus custumariorum aut aliorum native tenentium ultra illos in rotulis per Robertum de Wardecop' et Leonem de Perton ad scaccarium liberatis[169] specificatos, causa pestilencie, a xxviij° die augusti anno xxiij° usque xxviij diem novembris proximo sequentem, per quod tempus predicta maneria fuerunt in manu domini regis, de quibus Robertus de Warthecop' et Leo de Perton', tunc custodes temporalium episcopatus Wygorn' vacantis tempore predicto, aliquos alios redditus liberorum tenentium seu custumariorum ac opera nativorum nec aliquod aliud profituum non levaverunt nec levasse potuerunt ultra summam xxix li. xij s. j d. ob., prout patet per duos rotulos sub pede sigilli de scaccario domini regis transmissos, et dicunt quod predicti libere tenentes et custumarii ac alii native tenentes in dictis rotulis specificati nec aliquis eorum predictis custodibus nec eorum alteri non plus solverunt vel solvit nec solvere tenebantur vel tenebatur ultra summam predictam.

[29] [*Marginated*] ij

Et secundam inquisitionem captam coram prefatis Johanne de Sodyngton' et Stephano de Dudlegh' apud Northwyck' quarto die januarii anno xxvj^to^ per sacramentum Thome de Abyndon', Walteri de Folkenham et aliorum juratorum quorum nomina annotantur in eadem inquisitione. Qui juratores dicunt per sacramentum suum quod non fuerunt in maneriis de Kemseye, Northwyk' et Wyk' juxta Wygorn' plures libere tenentes nec major numerus custumariorum aut aliorum native tenentium ultra illos in dictis rotulis specificatos, causa pestilencie, a xxviij° die augusti anno xxiij° usque xxviij diem novembris proximo sequentem, per quod tempus maneria predicta fuerunt in manu domini regis, de quibus Robertus de Warthecop' et Leo de Perton', tunc custodes temporalium episcopatus Wygorn' vacantis tempore predicto, aliquos alios redditus liberorum tenentium et custumariorum ac opera nativorum nec aliquod aliud profituum non levaverunt nec levasse potuerunt ultra summam xxxix li. xij s. j d. ob., prout patet per duos rotulos sub pede sigilli de scaccario domini regis transmissos.

[30] [*Marginated*] iij

Et tertiam inquisitionem captam coram predictis Johanne de Sodynton' et Stephano de Dudlegh' apud Hertelbury vj die decembris anno xxvj^to^ per sacramentum Roberti de Hyndelep', Johannis de Gatebrugg' et aliorum juratorum quorum nomina annotantur in eadem inquisitione. Qui dicunt per sacramentum suum quod non fuerunt in maneriis de Hertilbury et Hambury juxta Wich' plures redditus liberorum tenentium et custumariorum nec opera nativorum ultra illos in dictis[170] rotulis specificatos, causa pestilencie, a xxviij° die augusti anno xxiiij° usque xxviij diem novembris proximo sequentem, per quod tempus maneria predicta fuerunt in manu domini regis, de quibus Robertus de Warthecop' et Leo de Perton', tunc custodes temporalium episcopatus Wygorn' vacantis[170] tempore predicto, aliquos redditus liberorum tenentium et custumariorum ac opera nativorum nec aliquod aliud profituum non levaverunt nec levasse potuerunt ultra summam xxxix li. xij s. j d. ob., prout patet per duos rotulos sub pede sigilli de scaccario domini regis transmissos.

[31] [*Marginated*] iiij

Et quartam inquisitionem captam coram prefatis Johanne de Sodynton' et Stephano de Duddelegh' apud Bredon' vj die februarii anno xxvij° per sacramentum Walteri le Bakere, Ricardi Large et aliorum juratorum quorum nomina annotantur in eadem inquisitione. Qui dicunt per sacramentum suum quod non fuerunt in maneriis de Bredon', Rippull' et Fladbury plures libere tenentes nec major numerus custumariorum aut aliorum native tenentium ultra illos in dictis[170] rotulis specificatos, causa pestilencie, a xxviij° die augusti anno xxiij° usque xxviij diem novembris proximo sequentem, per quod tempus maneria predicta fuerunt in manu domini regis, de quibus Robertus de Warthecop' et Leo de Perton', tunc custodes temporalium episcopatus Wygorn' vacantis tempore predicto, aliquos alios redditus

166 *que insimul . . . xxviij°* interlined.

167 Written at the foot of the membrane: *plus in rotulo sequenti.*

168 Written at the top of the membrane: *Adhuc Warthecop' et Perton'.*

169 *de Wardecop' . . . liberatis* interlined.

170 Interlined.

liberorum tenentium seu custumariorum ac opera nativorum nec aliquod aliud profituum non levaverunt nec levasse potuerunt ultra summam xxxix li. xij s. j d. ob., prout patet per duos rotulos sub pede sigilli de scaccario domini regis transmissos, et dicunt quod predicti liberi tenentes et custumarii ac alii native tenentes in predictis rotulis specificati nec aliquis eorum predictis custodibus nec eorum alteri plus solverunt vel solvit nec solvere tenebantur vel tenebatur.

[32] [*Marginated*] v
Et quintam inquisitionem captam coram predictis Johanne de Sodynton' et Stephano de Duddelegh' apud Clyve in comitatu Glouc' xij° die junii anno xxvij° per sacramentum Johannis le Cook', Johannis de Clyve et aliorum juratorum quorum nomina annotantur in eadem inquisitione. Qui dicunt per sacramentum suum quod non fuerunt in maneriis de Clyve, Withyngdon' et Bibury plures libere tenentes nec major numerus custumariorum aut aliorum native tenentium ultra illos in dictis[170] rotulis specificatos, causa pestilencie, a xxviij° die augusti anno xxiij° usque xxviij diem novembris proximo sequentem, per quod tempus maneria predicta fuerunt in manu domini regis, de quibus Robertus de Warthecop' et Leo de Perton', tunc custodes temporalium episcopatus Wygorn' tempore predicto, aliquos alios redditus liberorum tenentium seu custumariorum ac opera nativorum nec aliquod aliud profituum non levaverunt nec levasse potuerunt ultra summam xxxix li. xij s. j d. ob., prout patet per duos rotulos sub pede sigilli[171] [*membrane 259d*][172] de scaccario domini regis transmissos, et dicunt quod predicti liberi tenentes et custumarii ac alii native tenentes in predictis rotulis specificati nec aliquis eorum predictis custodibus nec eorum alteri non plus solverunt vel solvit vel solvere tenebantur vel tenebatur ultra summam predictam.

[33] [*Marginated*] vj
Et sextam inquisitionem captam apud Hambury Saltmerssh' in comitatu Glouc' coram prefatis Johanne de Sodynton' et Stephano de Duddelegh' xxvij° die septembris anno xxvij° per sacramentum Thome de Daudeswell', Johannis le Hunte et aliorum juratorum quorum nomina annotantur in eadem inquisitione. Qui dicunt super sacramentum suum quod non fuerunt in manerio predicto de Hambury plures liberi tenentes nec major numerus custumariorum aut aliorum native tenentium ultra illos in rotulis specificatos, causa pestilencie, a xxviij° die augusti anno xxiij° usque xxviij diem novembris proximo sequentem, per quod tempus maneria predicta fuerunt in manu domini regis, de quibus Robertus de Warthecop' et Leo de Perton', tunc custodes temporalium episcopatus Wygorn' tempore predicto, aliquos alios redditus liberorum tenentium seu custumariorum ac opera nativorum nec aliquod aliud profituum non levaverunt vel levasse potuerunt ultra summam xxxix li. xij s. j d. ob., prout patet per duos rotulos sub pede sigilli de scaccario domini regis transmissos, et dicunt quod predicti liberi tenentes et custumarii ac alii native tenentes in predictis rotulis specificati nec aliquis eorum predictis custodibus nec eorum alteri non plus solverunt vel solvit vel solvere tenebantur vel tenebatur ultra summam predictam.

Ideo consideratum est quod predicti Robertus de Warthecop' et Leo de supradictis iiij^{xx}iiij li. iiij s. ob. exonerentur et quieti existant pretextu premissorum.

[*Marginated*] In compoto predictorum Roberti et Leonis.

[34] Et quo ad predictos xxiv li. vj s. v d. de quibus dicti custodes onerantur pro ecclesia de Hilendon' et xxxiij s. iiij d. de quibus similiter onerantur de pensione ecclesie de Berkle, de quibus duabus summis habuerunt respectum usque ad dictam quindenam Sancti Michaelis, quia iidem custodes sunt in prosequendo coram baronibus ad placita versus decanum et capitulum London' et priorem Wygorn' ad respondendum regi de summis illis separatim in exonerationem ipsorum custodum de summisque illis fit executio per summonitionem, non fiat inde executio ulterius hic.

[35] Postea, videlicet xxix° die novembris dicto anno xxvij°, pretextu cuiusdam brevis de magno sigillo quod predicti decanus et capitulum London' detulerunt hic, et quod est inter communia de termino Sancti Michaelis eodem anno xxvij°, concordatum est quod predicti custodes exonerantur de predictis xxiv li. de quibus onerantur pro decima garbarum et feni ecclesie de Hilendon' et quod predicti decanus et capitulum inde onerentur.

[*Marginated*] In compoto predictorum Roberti et Leonis.

Membrane 257

Nomina liberorum tenentium episcopi Wygorn' in

[171] Written at the foot of the membrane: *plus in tergo.*

[172] Written at the top of the membrane: *Adhuc Warthecop' et Perton'.*

maneriis ipsius episcopatus subscriptis tempore quo Robertus de Wardecop' et Leo de Perton' fuerunt custodes eiusdem episcopatus videlicet

[36] [*Marginated*] Hertelbury
Johannes de Gatebruge reddit ad festum Sancti Michaelis vj d.
Prior de Dodeford' reddit ad idem festum xx d.
Terra que fuit Juliane atte[173] Mille jacet inculta pro defectu heredum. Ideo nichil.
Magister Hugo de Penbrugge reddit ad dictum festum v d.
Her' Willelmi le Walkere redd' ad idem festum iij d.
Summa ij s. x d. probatur.

[37] [*Marginated*] Wyk' juxta Wygorniam. Liberi tenentes.
Dominus Baldewynus de Fryvill' reddit ad idem festum[173] iiij s. vj d.
Rogerus Power reddit ad idem festum j d.
Willelmus de Abyndon' reddit ad idem terminum iiij s. iij d.
Johannes atte Hyde reddit ad idem terminum v s.
Editha Prechet reddit ad idem terminum ix d.
Prior Sancti Oswaldi reddit ad idem terminum iij s. iij d.
Willelmus Clement reddit ad idem terminum vj d.
Nicholaus le Copsmyth reddit ad idem terminum vj d.
Willelmus Rokulf' reddit ad idem terminum iiij s. iij d.
Henricus atte Grene ad idem terminum ix d.
Sacrista Wygorn' reddit ad idem terminum xvj d. qu.
Pitanciarius Wygorn' reddit ad idem terminum ix d. ob. qu.
Johannes de Stone reddit ad idem terminum iij s. iiij d.
Johannes de Wyche reddit ad idem terminum xv d.
De terra Johannis atte Feld' quia obiit tempore ultimi episcopi et nullus heres et terra jacet inculta nichil.
Hugo de Cokeseye reddit ad idem terminum xv d.
Bernardus Skynnere reddit ad idem terminum iiij d.
Hugo Priche reddit ad idem terminum viij d.
Alicia atte Brigge reddit ad idem terminum viij d.
Walterus Longeley reddit ad idem terminum xv d.
Petrus de Grete reddit ad idem terminum xj d.
Et idem reddit ad idem terminum pro prato xviij d.
Willelmus atte Walle reddit ad idem terminum xxj d.
Galfridus Ouewyn reddit ad idem terminum xiij d. ob.
Johannes atte Pyrye reddit ad idem terminum xij d.
Ricardus Wethel reddit ad idem terminum x d. ob.
Ricardus Brette reddit ad idem terminum x d. ob.
Isabella Devenysh' reddit ad idem terminum x d. ob.
Summa xliij s. viij d.

[173] Interlined.

[38] [*Marginated*] Alvecherche
Petrus de la Chambre reddit ad terminum Michaelis vj d.
Et idem reddit pro quodam tenemento in Hopwod' ad eundem terminum vij d.
Margeria Brid reddit ad eundem terminum v d.
Petrus le Muleward reddit ad eundem terminum iiij d. ob. qu.
Johannes Barel reddit ad eundem terminum ij d.
Ricardus Cade reddit ad eundem terminum ij s.
Ricardus de Seggele reddit ad eundem terminum j d.
Johannes Balle reddit ad eundem terminum viij d. ob.
Johannes de Ardern' custos terre et heredis Petri atte Rouney reddit ad eundem terminum xix d. ob. qu.
Ricardus Blyke reddit ad eundem terminum vj d.
Thomas de Belne reddit ad eundem terminum vj d.
Thomas de Henle reddit ad eundem terminum iij s. ix d.
Dominus Willelmus de Salwarp' reddit ad eundem terminum x d.
Summa totalis xij s. probatur.

[39] [*Marginated*] Liberi tenentes de Fladebury.
Johannes de Sudyngton' reddit ad terminum Michaelis ij s. vj d.
Ricardus Peris reddit ad eundem terminum v s.
Thomas de Stoure reddit ad eundem terminum xij d.
Ricardus Irish reddit ad eundem terminum vj d.
Alicia Toky reddit ad eundem terminum xv d.
Henricus Rote reddit ad eundem terminum xij d.
Et idem Henricus reddit ad eundem terminum pro alia tenura xj d. qu.
Johannes Basly reddit pro pastura ad eundem terminum iij d.
Dominus Ricardus vicarius reddit ad eundem terminum ix d.
Matilldis la Sclatere reddit ad eundem terminum ix d.
Summa reddituum[173] liberorum xiij s. xj d. qu. probatur.

[40] [*Marginated*] Rippil
Thomas le Botiler reddit ad terminum Michaelis xxv s.
Ricardus de Ryhale reddit ad eundem terminum ij s. x d.
Idem reddit ad eundem terminum x d.
Thomas de la Rye reddit ad eundem terminum xix d. ob.
Willelmus Benet' reddit ad eundem terminum ix d.
Summa xxxj s. ob. probatur.

[41] [*Marginated*] Bredon'
Alienora Despenser reddit ad festum Sancti Martini xij s.
Prior de Parva Malverne reddit ad festum Sancti Michaelis v s.
Johannes de Westmancote reddit ad eundem terminum ij s.
Johannes Large reddit ad eundem terminum xij d.
Robertus Mundy reddit ad eundem terminum ij s. v d.
Johannes Neghebore reddit ad eundem terminum xij d. ob. qu.
Ricardus Large reddit ad eundem terminum iiij d. ob.
Dominus Henricus Capellanus reddit ad eundem terminum ix d.
Dominus Johannes Baueyn reddit ad eundem terminum ij s. iij d. ob. qu.
Johannes Wade reddit ad eundem terminum ij s. viij d.
Johannes le Wyte reddit ad eundem terminum ij s. viij d.
Ricardus de Hardewyk' reddit ad eundem terminum ij s. viij d.
Johanna Scryveyn reddit ad eundem terminum ij s.
Agatha Ive de Hardewyk' reddit ad eundem terminum v s. vj d.
Robertus Waupol reddit ad eundem terminum iij s. viij d. ob.
Her' Margerie Rolf redd' ad eundem terminum xv d.
Adam Moyses reddit ad eundem terminum vij s. vij d.
Willelmus Pagen reddit ad eundem terminum viij d.
Ricardus de Barnet reddit ad eundem terminum v d. ob. qu.
Ricardus Ode reddit ad eundem terminum viij d.
Dominus Nicholaus Bacon' reddit ad eundem terminum xvij d. ob.
Johannes Rolf reddit ad eundem terminum iij d.
Ricardus Grundil reddit ad eundem terminum ij s. ix d.[174]
Membrane 257d
Ricardus Branelard' reddit ad eundem terminum xix d.
Johannes le Hayward' reddit ad eundem terminum ix d. ob. qu.
Thomas Gilleson' reddit ad eundem terminum iij s. vij d. qu.
Summa reddituum[175] liberorum tenentium lxvij s. ij d. ob. qu.

[42] [*Marginated*] Clyve
Abbas de Teukesbury reddit ad terminum Michaelis ij d. ob.
Johannes le Cok' reddit ad eundem terminum vij d. ob.
Johannes de Clyve reddit ad eundem terminum iiij s. ob.
Johannes Sampson reddit ad eundem terminum x d.
Willelmus de Pendok' reddit ad eundem terminum iij s. iiij d.
Willelmus le Chamoun reddit ad eundem terminum ob.
Emma Marreny pro herede Johannis Marreny infra etatem reddit ad eundem terminum ij s. vj d. ob.
Margeria Durrel reddit ad eundem terminum viij d.
Emma Marshall' reddit ad eundem terminum v s. iiij d.
Juliana Peres reddit ad eundem terminum ij d. ob. qu.
Johannes de Fladbury reddit ad eundem terminum ij d. ob. qu.
Johannes atte Hall' reddit ad eundem terminum vij s.
Willelmus Preez reddit ad eundem terminum j d.
Matildis la Smythis reddit ad eundem terminum xiij d.
Johanna Hobkynes reddit ad eundem terminum xij d.
Willelmus Pigate reddit ad eundem terminum ob. qu.
Robertus de Luttelton reddit ad eundem terminum iij d. ob.
Johannes Botiler reddit ad eundem terminum xij d.
Summa xxviij s. vj d. qu. probatur.

[43] [*Marginated*] Wythyndon'
Johannes Russel reddit ad terminum Sancti Michaelis iij s. iiij d.
Thomas dele Mare reddit ad eundem terminum xv d.
Abbas de Brewern' reddit ad eundem terminum ij s. vj d.
Ricardus atte Stable reddit ad eundem terminum ij s. ix d.
Ricardus de Reynham reddit ad eundem terminum v d.
Margeria de Stretford' reddit ad eundem terminum v d.
Johannes le Marshal reddit ad eundem terminum v d.
Summa reddituum[175] liberorum xj s. j d. probatur.

[44] [*Marginated*] Bibury
Robertus Dun reddit pro herede Johannis Dun ad terminum Sancti Michaelis ij s.
Agneta Chestre reddit ad eundem terminum xv d.
Johannes de Wellyngton' reddit ad eundem terminum xvj s. viij d.
Summa xix s. xj d. probatur.

[45] [*Marginated*] Hambury Saltmersh'
Johannes de Wythyngton' reddit ad festum Sancti Michaelis xvj s. viij d.

[174] Written at the foot of the membrane: *plus in tergo.*

[175] Interlined.

Thomas de Douduswelle reddit ad eundem terminum xx s.
Johannes le Hunte reddit ad eundem terminum iiij s.
Walterus Condriche reddit ad eundem terminum v s.
Henricus atte More reddit ad eundem terminum iij s. x d. ob.
Johannes de Trye reddit ad eundem terminum vij d. ob.
Nicholaus le Sawyare reddit ad eundem terminum iiij d. ob.
Johannes de Stonore reddit ad eundem terminum vj d.
Willelmus le Blak' reddit ad eundem terminum vj d.
Alicia Tillyng' reddit ad eundem terminum vj d.
Summa lij s. ob. probatur.

[46] Summa totalis reddituum liberorum tenentium levata in dictis maneriis de Hertilbury, Wyke juxta Wygorn', Alvechurch', Fladebury, Ripple, Bredon', Clyve, Withyndon', Bybury et Hambury Saltmersh' xiiij li. ij s. iij d.

Membrane 258

Numerus custumariorum et aliorum native tenentium in maneriis episcopatus Wygornie subscriptis tempore ultime vacationis eiusdem episcopatus, videlicet a xxviij° die augusti anno xxiij° regis Edwardi tertii usque xxviij diem novembris proximo sequentem per quod tempus Robertus de Wardecop' et Leo de Perton' fuerunt custodes eiusdem episcopatus videlicet

[47] [*Marginated*] Hertilbury
In manerio de Hertilbury fuit Simon Botte prepositus et fuerunt ibidem xxxviij tenentes vocati virgatarii quorum quilibet tenuit j virgatam terre. Et xiij tenentes vocati nokelondes. Et xxj tenentes vocati arkmen. Et iiij cotagiarii qui reddiderunt per tempus predictum Cvj s. xj d. qu. de redditu custumariorum et communi tallagio custumariorum ac quadam custuma vocata yerdselver necnon operibus post autumpnum particulariter et non fuerunt plures custumarii seu native tenentes in manerio predicto per tempus predictum unde quicquam ultra illos Cvj s. xj d. qu. levasse potuerunt eo quod moriebantur in pestilencia mortali antequam dicti custodes admiserunt custodiam temporalium episcopatus.

[48] [*Marginated*] Northwyk'
In manerio hic fuerunt Willelmus Mewe prepositus. Et fuerunt ibidem xv tenentes vocati virgatarii. Et xiij tenentes vocati noklondes. Et xvj tenentes vocati arkmen. Et xxiij vocati melemen. Et xliij cotagiarii et non remanserunt plures superstiti per causam ut supra. Et isti simul reddiderunt xxiij s. x d. de operibus post autumpnum et seminibus consuetis ad semen iemale et non plus ob causam predictam.

[49] [*Marginated*] Wyk' juxta Wygorn'
In manerio hic fuerunt Ricardus atte Hethe prepositus. Et vij alii dimid'[175] virgatarii. Et xxv tenantes vocati noklondes. Et iiij vocati arkmen. Et xij cotagiarii et non remanserunt plures causa pestilencie. Qui simul reddiderunt vij s. ix d. de operibus post autumpnum et non plus ob causam predictam.

[50] [*Marginated*] Kemsey
In manerio hic fuerunt Andreas Herdeman prepositus. Et xxxj dimid' virgatarii. Et xiiij noklondes. Et xj cotagiarii et non remanserunt plures per causam ut supra. Et isti simul reddiderunt iiij s. iiij d. ob. de operibus arrure et herciature et non plus ob causam predictam.

[51] [*Marginated*] Hambury juxta Wych'
In manerio hic fuit Walterus Kyng' ballivus et loco prepositi et ipse et alii juratores dixerunt quod fuerunt hic iiij virgatarii et non plures superstiti per tempus compoti nec alii tenentes per causam ut supra. Et isti simul reddiderunt ij s. vij d. ob. de operibus post autumpnum et non plus ob causam predictam.

[52] [*Marginated*] Alvechirche
In manerio hic fuerunt Ricardus de la More prepositus et alii xij dimid' virgatarii. Et xxxij cotagiarii et non remanserunt plures per causam ut supra. Et isti simul reddiderunt v s. ij d. ob. de operibus post autumpnum et non plus ob causam predictam.

[53] [*Marginated*] Fladebury
In manerio hic fuerunt Thomas Balle prepositus. Et alii xxxj virgatarii et xxxvij dimid' virgatarii. Et vj cotagiarii et non plures per causam ut supra. Qui simul reddiderunt vj s. iiij d. ob. de operibus post autumpnum et non plus ob causam predictam.

[54] [*Marginated*] Blokley
In manerio hic fuerunt Henricus Warner ballivus et loco prepositi et alii xxxij virgatarii. Et vij dimid' virgatarii. Et ij tenentes noklondes. Et iiij cotagiarii et non plures per causam ut supra. Et isti simul reddiderunt lxiiij s. ix d. qu.[176] pro semine iemali, arruris

[176] *ix d. qu.* interlined.

et herciaturis et non plus ob causam predictam.

[55] [*Marginated*] Rippull'
In manerio hic fuerunt Ricardus de Gatebrugge ballivus et loco prepositi. Et xxx virgatarii. Et ij dimid' virgatarii. Et vj tenentes penilondes. Et iiij cotagiarii et non plures per causam ut supra. Et isti simul reddiderunt tam de redditu custumariorum quam de aliis operibus in compoto contentis lxxv s. x d. ob. de redditu custumariorum et operibus post autumpnum cum semine ad festum Sancti Martini et non plus ob causam predictam.

[56] [*Marginated*] Bredon'
In manerio hic Ricardus de Morton' ballivus et Ricardus Balle prepositus et alii juratores dixerunt quod fuerunt hic vj virgatarii. Et viij dimid' virgatarii. Et nulli cotagiarii neque alii superstiti per causam ut supra. Qui simul reddiderunt xviij s. vij d. de redditu gallinarum ad terminum Sancti Martini et de auxilio nativorum[177] et non plus ob causam predictam.

[57] [*Marginated*] Clyve
In manerio hic fuerunt Willelmus Sherston ballivus et Thomas le Reve prepositus et alii juratores dixerunt quod fuerunt hic iiij virgatarii. Et viij dimid' virgatarii. Et iiij tenentes penilondes. Et xx tenentes vocati sexacrelinges. Et vij cotagiarii et non plures per causam ut supra. Qui simul reddiderunt xvij s. j d. de arruris et herciaturis et non plus ob causam predictam.

[58] [*Marginated*] Wythyndon'
In manerio hic fuerunt viij virgatarii quorum Galfridus de Chuton' prepositus est unus et iij tenentes vocati inchemen et v cotagiarii et non plures per causam ut supra. Qui similiter reddiderunt lxiij s. viij d. ob. qu. de redditu custumariorum et redditu tenentium terrarum vocatarum penilond et redditu tenentium vocatorum inchemen et redditu gallinarum, auxilio nativorum, ac redditu de cherset ad festum Sancti Martini et non plus ob causam predictam.

[59] [*Marginated*] Bibery
In manerio hic fuit Galfridus Sare prepositus, dimid' virgatarius et j virgatarius. Et ij et dimid' virgatarii et unus cotagiarius et non plures per causam ut supra. Qui simul reddiderunt v s. vj d. de redditu custumariorum ad festum Sancti Michaelis et redditu bladi ad festum Sancti Martini et non plus ob causam predictam.[178]

Membrane 258d

[60] [*Marginated*] Hambury Saltmersh'
In manerio hic fuerunt ij prepositi Willelmus atte Wode et Johannes Whyte qui cum aliis juratoribus dixerunt quod fuerunt xvj virgatarii. Et xxxix dimid' virgatarii. Et xvj tenentes vocati fyveacrelynges. Et xxj tenentes vocati forlondes. Et v cotagiarii et non plures per causam ut supra. Qui simul reddiderunt Cvij s. ij d. ob. qu. particulariter videlicet xxx s. de custuma vocata auxilium sive lardarium de custumariis et tenentibus ad festum Sancti Michaelis, vj d. ob. qu. de custumariis pro vinis custodiendis in Severna ad idem festum et xxx s. de custumariis de Stoke et xxxiiij s. vj d. de xxxiiij arruris, xj s. iij d. de arrura xlv acrarum terre ad semen yemale et xj d. de xxij herciaturis.

[61] Summa totalis omnium denariorum ex utraque parte rotuli xxv li. ix s. x d. ob.[179]

[177] *et de auxilio nativorum* interlined.

[178] Written at the foot of the membrane: *plus in tergo.*

[179] *ob.* interlined. Lower down on the membrane is written: *Hos duos rotulos liberarunt hic Robertus de Warthecop' et Leo de Perton' nuper custodes temporalium episcopatus Wygorn' vacantis xxviij^{o} die novembris anno xxvj^{to} regis Edwardi tertii post conquestum.*

Reports, writs and records in the common bench in the reign of Richard II

edited by

L. C. HECTOR

INTRODUCTION

Ever since the days of L. O. Pike, who pioneered the practice,[1] year book editors have done their best to identify on the plea rolls the cases reported in their year book texts. The thorough examination of the rolls needed to accomplish their purpose has been accepted, despite the difficulties that daunted Pike,[2] as an important part of their editorial task; and the success they have achieved has served to confirm the view that the record, when found, is the complement of the report, and the report of the record.

But even the most painstaking search is likely to leave a certain number of year book cases unidentified; and if the conscientious editor is not to find himself hunting through the rolls with no very clear idea of what he is seeking and with more hope than confidence that he will recognise his quarry when he sees it, he must know the limits to the potential usefulness of the rolls.

By about the middle of Richard II's reign it was usual for the terminal de banco roll to contain distinct groups of membranes (often beginning at mm. 101, 201, 301, etc.) devoted to the enrolment of the plaintiff's count and the ensuing formal exchanges in actions which began to be pleaded in the term concerned.[3] This at least makes easier the search for the records corresponding to the reports of pleading which form most of the entries in any year book. But the roll for a given term is very far from constituting the minutes of the court's proceedings during that term. There are two reasons for this.

First, the date borne by a roll is a terminus a quo, in that many of the entries, even of mesne process, remain capable of receiving later additions. Actions pleaded to an issue or demurrer might be respited term after term, even year after year, 'because the sheriff did not send the writ', or 'for want of jurors', or because 'the justices were not yet advised as to their decision'; and all such continuations were entered by way of addition to the original record of the pleadings. If, therefore, the year book reports the discussion of a situation arising in such a case between issue and verdict, the record of that discussion may well be in the roll for a term long before that of the report. But how far back is it reasonable to carry the search for it?

In the second place, the rolls entirely ignore everything in the proceedings they record that can be regarded as abortive or irrelevant. Thus the plea abandoned by its proponent or declared inadmissible by the court, the disallowed claim to jurisdiction by the bailiffs of a franchise, the waived or the overruled objection, and the unsuccessful aid-prayer are all passed over in a silence as complete as if they had never been advanced. The defendant whose right to appear by attorney is not recognised by the court, or whose letters of protection are revoked by a patent produced by his opponent, is recorded, in an entry indistinguishable in form from hundreds of others on the roll, simply as having defaulted. If, after considering the precedents, the court decides that the widow of a peer is not exempt from arrest, the roll records the award of a capias against her without the slightest hint that the possibility of her being privileged was ever entertained. There is even good reason to think that a writ could be quashed, abandoned or replaced by another, without provoking any mention of the fact in the roll.[4] Yet abortiveness and irrelevance might have been determined only after lengthy debate, faithfully reported in the year book, whose compiler was as interested in failure (or at least the reasons for it) as in success.

[1] *YB 12–13 Edw. III* (RS, 1885), xvii: 'The present volume differs . . . from its predecessors in the frequent references, never before attempted, to the records of the cases which have been identified on the rolls, especially those of *Placita de Banco'*.

[2] 'the absence [from the report] of all names of persons and places' [and, he might have added, the presence of wholly distorted forms when names *are* given], 'the enormous bulk of the unindexed rolls', 'the physical labour . . . of turning over, each by itself, the successive membranes': ibid.

[3] cf. M. Hastings, *The Court of Common Pleas in Fifteenth-Century England* (New York, 1947), 124.

[4] At the octave of Hilary 8 Richard II the sheriffs of London returned the original writ of debt brought by Thomas Rose against the dowager countess of Ormond: CP 52/4/30/2. The countess had remarried before the issue of the writ, which must therefore have abated, but no reference to the case has been found on the plea rolls.

The roll for Michaelmas 8 Richard II records the default of the defendants, and the award of a capias against them, in *Ormesby and wife* v. *Bereford and wife,* a plea of £40 debt, laid in London: CP 40/495, m.623. The case then disappears from the rolls, but in Hilary term (CP 40/496, m.420d) a new action, *Ormesby* v. *Bereford,* for £40 debt, laid in London, has begun between the husbands. Cf. YB 8 Ric. II, Hil. 13: A. Fitzherbert, *La Graunde Abridgement* (London, 1577), Briefe 930.

Sometimes the deficiencies of the rolls can be offset, and the labour of searching them reduced, by recourse to the surviving common bench writs. At least the return date on the cover of a file is valid for every writ in it; and the errors, anomalies, inconsistencies and irregularities in its contents have not been edited out. The systematic arrangement of original files strongly suggests, moreover, that they were always intended to be capable of being consulted without difficulty.

It was the duty of every sheriff to return the writs for his county on or before the third of the four calendar days constituting the return day specified in them; and the plea rolls contain recurrent references to the amercement of sheriffs who failed to return their writs 'ante quartum diem placiti'.[5] Each writ was endorsed with a statement of the action taken by the sheriff to execute it or of the circumstances precluding execution. Within the file for each county the writs were arranged, without regard to whether they were original[6] or judicial,[7] simply in order of size, the smallest at the top and the largest at the bottom. Since the horizontal dimension of all the writs was about ten inches, and they were filed with their top and side edges flush, the position of any one writ in the file was determined by its depth (i.e. the number of lines of manuscript composing its text) or the depth of any annexure to it, such as an inquisition, a supersedeas enjoining non-execution of the writ, or a jury panel. This arrangement makes examination of the file easier in that smaller documents are not masked by larger ones. In the office of the *custos brevium* all the writs returned at the same day were assembled, without alteration or disturbance of their existing internal arrangement, in the following order of counties:

Westmorland, Cumberland, Northumberland, Yorkshire, Lincolnshire, Derbyshire, Nottinghamshire, Leicestershire, Warwickshire, Staffordshire, Shropshire, Rutland, Northamptonshire, Bedfordshire, Buckinghamshire, Berkshire, Oxfordshire, Gloucestershire, Worcestershire, Herefordshire, Cornwall, Devon, Bristol, Dorset, Somerset, Wiltshire, Hampshire, Sussex, Surrey, Kent, London, Middlesex, Huntingdonshire, Cambridgeshire, Hertfordshire, Essex, Suffolk, Norfolk.

If the number of writs returned at a given day was not too large, they could all now be restrung on one general file for the whole of England, beginning, at the bottom, with the Norfolk writs and ending, at the top, with those for Westmorland.[8] But by Richard II's time it was usual for the writs for the first and second return days of each term[9] to form two files, superscribed respectively, from the counties with which filing began at their bases, *Norf'* (writs from Norfolk to Gloucestershire inclusive) and *Oxon'* (Oxfordshire to Westmorland). The *Norf'* file for the first return day of each term began, below the Norfolk writs, with writs of an administrative nature addressed to the justices, the *Oxon'* file, below the Oxfordshire writs, with writs of exigi facias for the whole of England.

A contemporary, knowing who were the parties to an action and where it was laid, and consulting the files before they had suffered any loss or damage, was thus able to lay his hand very quickly on any writ he sought. Indeed, it would have been quite possible for him, with no other resource than the writ files, to construct a list of references to the plea roll entries recording every stage in almost[10] any action, from the return of the original writ throughout mesne process to pleading and issue.

The modern year book editor is much less well placed. The reports seldom afford any trustworthy clue as to the names of parties or counties, and the search must usually be for a writ (or the return to a writ) having about it something distinctive enough to have been reported. The files have moreover suffered badly since they were first made up. Probably less than half of them now survive in their original form: the rest are wholly or partly missing, mutilated, coagulated, or reduced to thousands of loose writs and fragments. Their condition must be largely due to the low opinion of their usefulness

5 e.g. CP 40/496, mm.19 (Northants), 36 (Bristol); 499, m.71 (Heref).

6 Writs by which proceedings were instituted, issued from the chancery and returnable in the common bench, to which they gave jurisdiction.

7 Writs issued in pursuance of a 'judicium' or decision in the common bench, to the enrolment of which they carried a precise reference.

8 In 11 Richard II, when a Lancashire case was proceeding in the common bench, the writs relating to it were filed above (i.e. after) those for Westmorland.

9 See *Hdbk of Dates,* 67.

10 The chief exceptions would be cases in which the defendant appeared and conceded the plaintiff's claim at the return of the original writ, and those in which no judicial writ issued after pleading had begun, as when the parties pleaded to a demurrer in law and no jury was summoned to determine an issue of fact.

which has been generally held ever since they ceased to serve their contemporary purpose. When the task of sorting, labelling and listing them was undertaken in the Public Record Office of the 1920s it was partly as an act of conscious virtue in archivists to whom any class of unsorted documents was a theoretical reproach, partly as a means of training junior staff. So knowledgeable a scholar as the late Sir Cyril Flower was persuaded that the writs contained nothing that was not to be found on the rolls.

Yet even in their present state the writs remain capable of occasional service to the year book editor; and the half dozen cases printed below are intended to exemplify some of the ways in which they can clarify and complement not only the reports but the enrolled records themselves. In each case the material printed consists of a year book report, followed by a brief statement of the considerations guiding the search for a potentially useful writ; the text of the writ found; and finally the text of the enrolled record. Three of the cases [2, 4, 5] owe their interest primarily to the fact that the relevant writs or returns are themselves the subjects of the discussion reported in the year book and contain (as the corresponding records do not) convincing evidence of the correctness of the identification. All the cases illustrate the use of the writs to shorten or make unnecessary the examination of the rolls as a means of tracing the record.

I am indebted to the Trustees of the Ames Foundation of America for permission to make use of some material prepared for publication in a forthcoming edition of the year books for 8–10 Richard II. Reports falling within this period are cited by the references allotted to them in that edition and not, for example, by the numbers or pages of Bellewe.

Throughout the text the palatalised 'c' has been retained, and not rendered as 't'.

TEXT

[1]

Prior of Hertford v. *Newehawe*

[a] *Report*: BL, Add. MS 32087, f.165v (YB 8 Ric. II, Trin. 2)

Autrefoitz un bref dannuite[11] fuist porte devers un persone; et pria eide de patron et de ordenarie; et leide graunte; quex viendrent et joindrent en eide. Et fuerent a issue, et venire facias issist.

Et ore, le venire facias retourne, vient la partie defendaunt et dit que le patron fuist mort, et pria eide dun J. come fitz et heire de patron.

Belk' [CJ]. Eit leide.

Et nota qen prochein terme devaunt, quaunt Belk' fuist en parlement de Sar',[12] tiel matere fuist graundement debatuz: et tota curia in oppinione pluis qil navera mye leide qe qil avereit, pur ceo qil ne poet mye chaunger lissue devaunt pris et si cest patron en sa vie nust mye venuz a le primer jour apres ceo qil fuist prie, si le bref ust este servie, la persone ust respondu soule. Mes la cause, per Belk', fuist pur la charge quel cherreit sur lesglise en perpetuete, quel nest mye resoun qe soit fait saunz assent du patron et saunz qil soit partie etc. Et fuist bien graunte par toutz qun persone poet charger pur terme de sa vie demesne sa esglise saunz assent de son patron etc.

Mes quere quaunt le patron vient ore sil variera[13] al issue pris devaunt etc.

Bealknap's decision authorised the issue of a writ in the form exemplified at *Reg. Brev.: Jud.*, f.41v, where it is called *scire facias petito in auxilium.* It was reasonable to suppose that this writ would have been returnable in the succeeding (Michaelmas) term,[14] and to hope that the new patron would appear in it as somebody's son and heir. Search in the files for Michaelmas 8 Richard II disclosed the writ printed below. Slight physical damage has impaired its text in a few places; and the readings in square brackets are taken from the record or supplied by conjecture.

[b] *Writ of scire facias petito in auxilium*: CP 52/4/29/1 (octave of Mich. 8 Ric. II)

[Ricardus Dei] gracia rex Anglie et Francie et dominus Hibernie vicecomiti Warr' salutem. Cum quidam nuper prior de Hertford' in curia domini Edwardi nuper regis Anglie avi nostri apud Ebor', scilicet a die [Pasche] in xv dies anno regni sui tercio, coram Willelmo de Herle et sociis suis tunc justiciariis eiusdem avi nostri de banco per consideracionem eiusdem curie ipsius avi nostri recuperasset versus [quendam] Robertum de Beverle tunc personam ecclesie de Sulihull' quendam annuum redditum duarum marcarum singulis annis eidem nuper priori et successoribus suis ad duos anni terminos, videlicet in octabis Sancti Michaelis unam marcam et in octabis Pasche unam marcam, imperpetuum solvendum (prout per recordum et processu[m] loquele predicte coram justiciariis apud Westmonasterium ad prosecucionem Johannis nunc prioris de Hertford' successoris predicti nuper prioris loci predicti de mandato nostro missa liquet manifeste), duodecim marce de arreragiis annui redditus predicti post predictum judicium redditum, videlicet de sex annis tunc proximo preteritis, prefato Johanni nunc priori de Hertford' aretro fuerunt ([prout] ex insinuacione ipsius nunc prioris accepimus); per quod tibi preceperimus quod per probos et legales homines de comitatu tuo scire faceres Willelmo Newenhawe clerico [nunc] persone ecclesie predicte successori prefati Roberti nuper persone eiusdem ecclesie quod esset coram justiciariis nostris apud Westmonasterium a die Sancte Trinitatis in xv dies anno regnorum nostrorum secundo incipiente ostensurus si quid pro se haberet vel dicere sciret quare predicte duodecim marce de arreragiis annui redditus predicti de terris et catallis suis in balliva [tua] fieri et prefato nunc priori reddi non deberent, si sibi vidisset expedire; idem Willelmus postea venit in eadem curia nostra et dixit quod ipse invenit ecclesiam suam [predictam] de annuo redditu predicto exoneratam, et non potuit ecclesiam illam sine Roberto Coventrensi et Lich' episcopo loci predicti diocesano et Hugone le Despenser chivaler filio et herede [Alicie] que fuit

[11] It was in fact scire facias to execute the judgment in a plea of annuity between the parties' predecessors: below, n.36.

[12] This parliament met on 29 April 1384 and lasted about 30 days.

[13] MS *varier'*. Perhaps *poet* has been omitted before it.

[14] For the system of continuances from day to day see the 'statute' Dies Communes in Banco: *SR*, I, 208. Of 72 judicial writs returned by the sheriff of Northamptonshire at the octave of Michaelmas 8 Richard II, 65 bear dates of issue in the preceding term.

uxor Johannis Trussell' ecclesie predicte patrono de eodem annuo redditu onerare; et peciit auxilium de ipsis episcopo et patrono. Et ideo tibi precipimus quod per probos et [legales homines] de comitatu tuo scire facias predictis episcopo et Hugoni quod sint coram justiciariis nostris apud Westmonasterium in octabis[15] Sancti Michaelis ad respondendum predicto priori simul cum [predicto] Willelmo de predicto placito, si sibi viderint expedire; et habeas ibi nomina eorum per quos eis scire feceris et hoc breve. Teste R. Bealknapp' apud Westmonasterium xv die julii anno regni nostri octavo.
Wakefeld'
Trin' secundo ro. Cxj.[16]
[*Endorsed*] Willelmus Bagot vicecomes. Scire feci Roberto episcopo Coventrensi et Lich' et Hugoni le Despenser chivaler filio et heredi Alicie que fuit uxor Johannis Trussell' per Willelmum Hawes et Thomam Blith' quod sint ad diem et locum in brevi isto contentos ad respondendum recipiendum et faciendum quod breve istud requirit.

[c] *Record*: CP 40/471, m.111 (Trin. 2 Ric. II)

[*Marginated*] Warr'
Preceptum fuit vicecomiti, cum quidam nuper prior de Hertford' in curia domini Edwardi nuper regis Anglie avi domini regis nunc apud Ebor', scilicet a die Pasche in xv dies anno regni sui tercio, coram Willelmo de Herle et sociis suis tunc justiciariis eiusdem avi domini regis nunc de banco per consideracionem eiusdem curie ipsius avi domini regis nunc recuperasset versus quendam Robertum de Beverele tunc personam ecclesie de Sulihull' quendam annuum redditum duarum marcarum singulis annis eidem nuper priori et successoribus suis ad duos anni terminos, videlicet in octabis Sancti Michaelis unam marcam et in octabis Pasche unam marcam, imperpetuum solvendum (prout per recordum et processum loquele predicte coram justiciariis domini Ricardi regis nunc hic ad prosecucionem Johannis nunc prioris de Hertford' successoris predicti nuper prioris loci predicti de mandato domini regis nunc missa liquet manifeste), duodecim marce de arreragiis annui redditus predicti post predictum judicium redditum, videlicet de sex annis proximo preteritis, prefato Johanni nunc priori de Hertford' aretro existunt (prout ex insinuacione ipsius nunc prioris acceperat rex); et quia etc.; quod per probos etc. scire faceret Willelmo Newehawe clerico nunc persone ecclesie predicte successori prefati Roberti nuper persone eiusdem ecclesie quod esset hic ad hunc diem, scilicet a die Sancte Trinitatis in xv dies [1378] ostensurus si quid pro se haberet vel dicere sciret quare predicte duodecim marce de arreragiis annui redditus predicti de terris et catallis suis in balliva sua fieri et prefato nunc priori reddi non debeant, si sibi vidisset expedire.[17]

Et modo veniunt tam predictus prior per Johannem de Bretton' attornatum suum quam predictus Willelmus per Henricum Broun attornatum suum. Et vicecomes modo mandat quod scire fecit eidem Willelmo per Johannem Bukkemore et Willelmum de Otteley essendi hic ostensuro etc. in forma predicta. Et super hoc predictus prior petit versus eum execucionem etc.

Et predictus Willelmus dicit quod tam prefatus nuper prior etc. quam predictus Robertus de Beverle nuper persona etc. et similiter tam Johannes nuper episcopus Eliensis ecclesie illius tempore recuperacionis predicte patronus etc. quam quidam Rogerus nuper Coventrensis et Lich' episcopus loci predicti ordinarius mortui sunt et quod ipse nunc est persona ecclesie predicte et invenit ecclesiam suam predictam de predicto annuo redditu exoneratam, et non potest eandem ecclesiam sine Johanne Trussell' et Alicia uxore eius nunc patronis ecclesie predicte et Roberto Coventrensi et Lich' episcopo loci illius diocesano onerare sive exonerare; et petit auxilium de ipsis Johanne Trussell' et Alicia patronis etc. et prefato Roberto nunc Coventrensi et Lich' episcopo loci illius ordinario etc. Habeat etc. Ideo tam predicti Johannes et Alicia quam prefatus Robertus nunc episcopus etc. premuniantur quod sint hic a die Sancti Michaelis in xv dies ad respondendum simul etc. si etc.[18] Ideo[19] dies datus [est][20] partibus predictis hic etc.

Ad quem diem veniunt partes etc. Et vicecomes non misit breve etc. Ideo sicut prius predicti episcopus Johannes et Alicia premuniantur quod sint

[15] Contrast the return day named in the record: below, 277.

[16] The reference to the entry, on a plea roll for twenty-four terms before, warranting the issue of the writ. See above, 271.

[17] *cum quidam . . . expedire* is founded on the actual writ from which the scire facias de annuo redditu at *Reg.Brev.: Jud.*, f.41, is taken.

[18] This is the actual writ from which the scire facias petito in auxilium at *Reg.Brev.:Jud.*, f.41v, is taken.

[19] Recte *Idem*. [20] Omitted.

hic in octabis Sancti Martini ad respondendum simul etc. si etc. Idem dies datus est partibus predictis hic etc.

Ad quem diem veniunt tam predictus prior quam prefatus Willelmus per attornatos suos predictos; et similiter predicti Robertus nunc episcopus Coventrensis et Lych' Johannes Trussell' et Alicia per premunicionem eis factam per Willelmum Otleye et Johannem de Bretford' per Willelmum Strethay attornatum suum veniunt et se jungunt eidem Willelmo in respondendo etc. Et super hoc dies datus est tam predicto priori quam prefato Willelmo et similiter predictis Roberto nunc episcopo Johanni Trussell' et Alicie qui se jungunt etc. hic in octabis Sancti Hillarii [1379] etc.

Ad quem diem veniunt tam predictus prior per attornatum suum predictum quam predicti episcopus Johannes et Alicia per attornatos suos predictos. Et super hoc iidem episcopus Johannes et Alicia petunt auditum recordi unde breve predictum warantizatur; et eis legitur in hec verba:

PLACITA CORAM WILLELMO DE HERLE ET SOCIIS SUIS JUSTICIARIIS DOMINI REGIS APUD WESTMONASTERIUM VIDELICET DE TERMINO PASCHE ANNO REGNI REGIS EDWARDI TERCII A CONQUESTU TERCIO [1329] Rotulo Clxvij[21]

[*Marginated*] Warr'

Robertus de Beverle persona ecclesie de Sulihull' summonitus fuit ad respondendum priori de Hertford' de placito quod reddat ei duodecim libras que ei aretro sunt de annuo redditu duarum marcarum quem ei debet etc.; et unde idem prior per Galfridum de Sheryngg' attornatum suum dicit quod cum quidam Rogerus quondam prior de Hertford' predecessor suus dudum fuisset seisitus de duabus partibus decimarum proveniencium de omnibus terris et dominicis quondam Johannis de Lymesy in Hulverle in parochia de Sulihull', ac contencio mota fuisset inter ipsum Rogerum tunc priorem et quendam Radulfum de Lacok' tunc personam ecclesie predicte super decimis predictis; qui quidem prior predecessor etc. et Radulfus se submiserunt ordinacioni Rogeri tunc Coventrensis et Lich' episcopi loci ordinarii, qui quidem episcopus ordinavit quod decime memorate imperpetuum remanerent prefato Radulfo et successoribus suis personis eiusdem ecclesie et quod idem Radulfus et successores sui solverent prefato priori et successoribus suis singulis annis imperpetuum duas marcas sterlingorum apud Sulihull' ad duos anni terminos, videlicet unam marcam in octabis Sancti Michaelis et unam marcam in octabis Pasche; et predictus prior predecessor etc. et similiter predictus Radulfus quondam persona [etc.] predicte ordinacioni ipsius episcopi sigilla sua alternatim apposuerunt: pretextu cuius ordinacionis predictus Radulfus tunc persona etc. seisitus fuit de predictis decimis et similiter omnes persone eiusdem ecclesie hucusque de eisdem tenementis seisiti extiterunt et predictus Robertus nunc persona [etc.] adhuc seisitus existit, et similiter predictus Rogerus quondam prior etc. a tempore ordinacionis predicte seisitus fuit de predicto annuo redditu duarum marcarum per manus predicti Radulfi et eciam omnes priores successores etc. hucusque seisiti fuerunt de predicto annuo redditu per manus personarum eiusdem ecclesie usque per novem annos ante diem impetracionis brevis, scilicet sextumdecimum die[m] maii anno regni domini regis nunc secundo [1328], quod predictus Robertus predictum annuum redditum reddere contradixit et adhuc contradicit; unde dicit quod deterioratus est et dampnum habet ad valenciam quinquaginta librarum; et inde producit sectam etc. Et profert quoddam scriptum indentatum quod predictas submissionem et ordinacionem testatur in hec verba:

Universis sancte matris ecclesie filiis ad quos presens scriptum pervenerit Rogerus miseracione divina Coventrensis et Licheff' ecclesie minister humilis eternam in Domino salutem.

Noverit universitas vestra quod cum questio mota fuisset inter abbatem de Sancto Albano et priorem et monachos de Hertford' ex parte una et magistrum Radulfum de Lacok' rectorem ecclesie de Sulihull' nostre diocesis ex altera super duabus partibus decimarum proveniencium de omnibus terris et dominicis quondam Johannis de Lymesy in Hurverle[22] de parochia ecclesie de Sulihull' predicte, quas proponebant prenominati monachi ad se pertinere ex spesiali collacione prefati Johannis et predecessorum suorum et confirmacione bone memorie Willelmi Coventrensis episcopi predecessoris nostri et sui capituli seque eciam in pacifica possessione earundem diu extitisse, memorato magistro Radulfo in contrarium proponente quod decime ipse ad ecclesiam suam predictam jure parochiali spectabant et sic eidem ecclesie de jure debebant adjudicari, tandem partes post diversas com[m]issiones hinc inde ad

[21] CP 40/277, m.167d, from which the readings in square brackets are taken.

[22] *Hulverle* in CP 40/277.

diversos judices a sede apostolica super premissis optentas omnibus impetratis super eisdem et eciam impetrandis renunciantes nostre se super decimis prefatis ordinacioni absolute subjecerunt, nos autem visis instrumentis predictorum monacorum super premissis optentis et jure utriusque partis ponderato sufficienter et intellecto de juris peritorum consilio in nomine Patris et Filii et Spiritus Sancti taliter ordinavimus, quod decimas prefatas totaliter percipiat ecclesia de Sulihull' prefata imperpetuum et quod prenominatus magister Radulfus rector ipsius ecclesie et successores sui imperpetuum solvant apud Sulihull' annuatim monachis de Hertford' predictis pro bono [pacis][23] et pro decimis ipsis duas marcas sterlingorum, unam marcam scilicet in octabis festivitatis Beati Michaelis et unam marcam in octabis Pasche, ita scilicet quod quocienscumque aliquo terminorum predictorum pecuniam ipsam non solverit rector quilibet illius ecclesie qui pro tempore fuerit dabit dictis monachis de Hertford' nomine pene dimidiam marcam sterlingorum infra octo dies proximo sequentes una cum debito principali, rata et firma nichilhominus manente ordinacione. Hanc autem ordinacionem partes adinvicem gratanter acceptarunt et huic instrumento super ea in [modum][24] cyrographi confecto una cum sigillo nostro et capituli nostri sigilla sua apposuerunt et bona fide servare eandem promiserunt. Actum apud Coventre anno Domini millesimo CC^{mo} quadragesimo sexto die lune Rogacionum [14 May 1246] etc.

Et Robertus per Thomam de Milford' attornatum suum venit et defendit vim et injuriam quando etc., et dicit quod ipse tempore quo fuit admissus et institutus in ecclesia predicta invenit ipse[25] ecclesiam illam exoneratam de predicto redditu, unde dicit quod ipse non potest inde sine Johanne episcopo Eliensi eiusdem ecclesie patrono et Rogero Couventrensi et Lich' episcopo eiusdem loci diocesano respondere; et petit auxilium de eis. Ideo ipsi summoneantur quod sint hic a die Sancti Michaelis in xv dies ad respondendum simul etc.

Ad quem diem veniunt partes predicte per attornatos suos predictos; et vicecomes non misit breve [etc.] Ideo sicut prius preceptum est vicecomiti quod summoneat eos quod sint hic a die Sancti Hillarii in xv dies [1330] ad respondendum simul etc.

Ad quem diem venerunt tam predictus Robertus quam predictus prior per predictos attornatos suos; et predictus episcopus Eliensis fecit se tunc inde essoniari versus predictum priorem, et [habuit][26] inde diem per essoniatorem suum hic ad hunc diem, scilicet a die Sancte Trinitatis in xv dies proximo sequen' etc. Idem dies datus fuit predicto Roberto per Nicholaum de Rysyng' attornatum suum hic in banco. Et predictus Coventrensis et Lich' episcopus ad diem illum summonitus non venit; per quod tunc consideratum fuit quod predictus Robertus responderet sine etc., ut patet rotulo essoniorum de eodem die nono.

Et modo venit predictus prior per predictum attornatum suum et similiter predictus Robertus per predictum Nicholaum attornatum suum; et predictus episcopus Eliensis non venit. Ideo consideratum est quod predictus Robertus respondeat sine etc.

Et predictus Robertus dicit quod ipse non potest dedicere quin ipse tenetur[27] eidem priori in predicto annuo redditu virtute composicionis predicte in forma predicta et[28] quin predicta arreragia eidem priori aretro sunt.[29] Ideo consideratum est quod predictus prior recuperet versus eum predictum annuum redditum et arreragia predicta ante diem impetracionis brevis etc.; et idem Robertus in misericordia. Nichil de arreragiis post diem impetracionis brevis usque ad hanc quindenam Sancte Trinitatis nec de dampnis, quia predictus attornatus ipsius prioris gratis remittit ei arreragia illa et dampna etc.; et eciam [idem] attornatus ipsius prioris remittit ei predicta arreragia ante predictum diem impetracionis brevis etc. usque ad centum solidos etc.

Et super hoc audito recordo predicto, protestando quod decime predicte modo non valent decem solidos, iidem Willelmus episcopus Johannes et Alicia dicunt quod predictus locus in predicto recordo vocatus Hulverle, de quo predictus prior supponitur habere duas partes decimarum, est et a tempore quo non extat memoria fuit infra bundas et parochiam de Solihull', et quod tam predictus Robertus de Beverlee qui fuit pars recordo predicto quam predictus Radulfus Lacok' in eodem recordo similiter contentus et omnes predecessores ipsius Willelmi habuerunt et integre perceperunt a tempore cuius contrarii memoria non existit omnes decimas de Hulverlee ut de jure

[23] *pace* in CP 40/471.

[24] *modicum* in CP 40/471.

[25] So also in CP 40/277.

[26] *habent* in CP 40/471.

[27] So also in CP 40/277; recte *teneatur*.

[28] So also in CP 40/277; recte *nec*.

[29] So also in CP 40/277; recte *sint*.

ecclesie sue de Solihull' tam tempore confeccionis composicionis predicte quam antea absque hoc quod predictus Rogerus nuper prior qui fuit pars composicioni predicte seu aliquis predecessorum suorum uncquam habuerunt possessionem duarum parcium decimarum predictarum prout in composicione et recordo predictis fit mencio; et cum hoc dicunt quod composicio predicta et similiter recuperare predictum facta fuerunt per covinam inter predecessorem ipsius Willelmi et predecessorem predicti nunc prioris; et ulterius dicunt quod prefatus Johannes de Hothom nuper episcopus Eliensis non fuit patronus ecclesie predicte tempore recuperacionis predicte, immo quidam Johannes filius Johannis de Hothom tunc temporis fuit patronus eiusdem ecclesie; et hoc parati sunt verificare si exitum placiti facere possit; unde petunt judicium si predictus nunc prior execucionem in hac parte de aliquibus arreragiis annui redditus predicti versus eundem Willelmum habere debeat etc.

Et predictus prior dicit quod tempore recuperacionis predicte prefatus nuper episcopus Eliensis fuit patronus ecclesie predicte; et hoc paratus est verificare si etc. Et ulterius dicit quod quidam Radulfus de Lymesy diu ante tempus memorie fundavit predictum prioratum de Hertford' et inter alia tenementa que eidem prioratui contulit decimas suas in Hulverle in bosco et in plano unde in recordo predicto fit mencio dedit et concessit; et profert hic in curia quandam codicillam que premissa testatur in forma predicta. Et postea quidam Johannes de Lymesy consanguineus et heres eiusdem Radulfi decimas illas inter alia que predictus Radulfus prioratui predicto prius contulit per quandam cartam suam quam hic in curia profert concessit et confirmavit Deo et ecclesie Sancti Albani et monachis eiusdem monasterii apud Hertford' manentibus, virtute quarum donacionis concessionis et confirmacionis omnes predecessores predicti nunc prioris seisiti fuerunt de decimis predictis, videlicet de duabus partibus decimarum predictarum in recordo predicto contentarum quousque quidam Willelmus le Bele nuper persona ecclesie de Solihull' predecessor predicti Willelmi Newehawe nunc persone etc. injuste impedivit quendam tunc priorem de Hertford' ad capiendum decimas predictas; super quo ad prosecucionem predicti tunc prioris per bullas apostolicas Honorii pape tunc prioribus de Waltham et de Ware ac tunc decano de Braghyng' Londoniensis diocesis delegatis ad querimoniam eiusdem tunc prioris de Hertford' super materia predicta determinandam visis examinatis et intellectis cum diligencia altercacione et querela predictis ac diversis instrumentis tam patronorum ecclesie predicte quam episcoporum loci illius diocesanorum per delegatos predictos, prefato Willelmo le Bele prius coram eis comparente, idem Willelmus le Bele habita consideracione ad jus predicti tunc prioris de Hertford' recognovit omnes decimas predictas tam jure proprietatis quam possessionis esse jus predicti tunc prioris de Hertford'; et profert hic in curia quasdam litteras sigillis predictorum priorum de Waltham et de Ware ac predicti tunc decani de Braghyng' et prefati Willelmi le Bele signatas premissa testificantes; quiquidem tunc prior de Hertford' statim post discussionem predictam per delegatos predictos virtute bullarum a sede apostolica factam amicis intervenientibus per quoddam scriptum indentatum tempore Henrici regis filii regis Johannis concessit et dimisit eidem Willelmo decimas predictas tenendas ad terminum vite eiusdem Willelmi le Bele, reddendo inde eidem tunc priori de Hertford' et successoribus suis duas marcas; quam quidem dimissionem Gregorius tunc papa per bullas apostolicas confirmavit et ratificavit; et profert hic in curia tam predictas bullas apostolicas quam alteram partem predicti scripti indentati, que dimissionem admissionem et confirmacionem predictas testatur[30] in forma supradicta; et sic dicit quod prefatus nuper prior qui fuit pars composicioni et recordo predictis et omnes predecessores sui a tempore quo [non][31] extat memoria seisiti fuerunt de decimis predictis aut de predicta firma duarum marcarum pro eisdem, [et] eciam quod omnes persone ecclesie predicte a tempore confeccionis composicionis predicte unde in recordo predicto fit mencio et virtute eiusdem composicionis de decimis predictis seisiti fuerunt et idem Willelmus Newehawe nunc persona de eisdem decimis virtute eiusdem composicionis adhuc seisitus existit, et similiter prefatus nunc prior et predecessores sui post composicionem et judicium predicta de annuo redditu predicto per manus personarum ecclesie predicte pro tempore existencium seisiti [fuerunt] quousque predictus nunc persona annuum redditum predictum eidem nunc priori subtraxit; et hoc [paratus] est verificare; unde petit judicium et execucionem etc.

Et predicti Willelmus episcopus Johannes et Alicia dicunt quod tempore predicti judicii in curia predicti avi domini [regis] nunc redditi prefatus Johannes filius Johannis fuit patronus ecclesie predicte et non predictus nuper episcopus [de] Ely; et hoc parati sunt

30 Recte *testantur*?

31 The edge of the membrane is missing. From this point readings in square brackets are conjectural.

verificare si exitum placiti facere possit etc. Et ulterius dicunt quod [tam predictus] Robertus de Beverle quam prefatus Rogerus[32] Lacok' predecessores ipsius Willelmi nunc persone etc. et o[mnes alii] predecessores sui persone ecclesie predicte fuerunt seisiti de decimis predictis de Hulverle et illas habuerunt et [integre] perceperunt ut de jure ecclesie predicte de Solihull' a tempore quo non extat memoria [tam] tempore confeccionis composicionis predicte quam antea, absque hoc quod predictus nuper prior [de] Hertford' qui fuit pars composicioni illi seu aliquis predecessorum suorum uncquam habuerunt possessionem duarum parcium decimarum predictarum; et hoc parati sunt verificare; unde petunt judicium etc.

Et predictus nunc prior dicit quod prefatus nuper prior qui fuit pars composicioni predicte et [omnes alii] predecessores sui fuerunt seisiti de predictis duabus partibus decimarum predictarum aut de predicta firma [duarum] marcarum pro eisdem decimis a tempore quo non extat memoria; et hoc petit quod [inquiratur] per patriam. Et predicti Willelmus episcopus Johannes et Alicia similiter. Ideo preceptum est vicecomiti quod venire [faciat] hic a die Pasche in tres septimanas xij etc. per quos etc. et qui nec etc. ad recognoscendum [etc., quia] tam etc.

Ad quem diem veniunt partes etc.; et vicecomes non misit breve etc. Ideo sicut prius [preceptum est] vicecomiti quod venire faciat hic in octabis Sancti Johannis Baptiste xij etc. ad recognoscendum in forma predicta [etc.]

Ad quem diem vic'[33] veniunt partes etc.; et vicecomes non misit breve. Ideo sicut pluries preceptum est vicecomiti [quod] venire faciat hic a die Sancti Michaelis in xv dies xij etc. per quos etc. et qui nec etc. [ad] recognoscendum etc., quia tam etc. Idem dies datus est omnibus partibus predictis hic etc.

Ad quem diem veniunt partes etc.; et jurata inde inter eos ponitur in [respectum] hic usque a die Sancti Hillarii in xv dies [1380] pro defectu juratorum quia nullus venit. Ideo vicecomes habeat [corpora] etc. Idem dies datus est omnibus partibus predictis hic etc.

Ad quem diem veniunt partes etc.; et jurata [inde] inter eos ponitur in respectum hic usque a die Pasche in tres septimanas pro defectu juratorum quia nullus [venit]. Ideo vicecomes habeat corpora etc. Idem dies datus est omnibus partibus predictis hic etc.

Ad quem diem veniunt [partes] etc.; et jurata predicta ponitur in respectum hic usque a die Sancte Trinitatis in xv dies pro defectu juratorum quia nullus venit. [Ideo] vicecomes habeat corpora etc. Idem dies datus est omnibus partibus predictis hic etc.

Ad quem diem veniunt partes etc.; et jurata predicta ponitur in respectum hic usque a die Sancti Michaelis in xv dies pro defectu juratorum quia nullus venit. Ideo vicecomes habeat corpora [etc.] Idem dies datus est partibus predictis hic etc.

Ad quem diem veniunt partes etc.; et jurata predicta ponitur in respectum hic usque a die Sancti Hillarii in xv dies [1381] pro defectu juratorum quia nullus venit. Ideo vicecomes habeat corpora etc. Idem dies datus est omnibus partibus predictis hic etc.

Ad quem diem veniunt partes etc.; et jurata predicta ponitur in respectum hic usque a die Sancte Trinitatis in xv dies pro defectu juratorum quia nullus venit. Ideo vicecomes habeat corpora etc. Idem dies datus est partibus predictis hic etc.

Ad quem diem veniunt partes etc.; et jurata predicta ponitur in respectum hic usque in crastino Sancti Martini pro defectu juratorum quia nullus etc. Ideo vicecomes habeat corpora etc. Idem dies datus est partibus predictis hic etc.

Ad quem diem veniunt partes etc.; et vicecomes non misit breve. Ideo predicta jurata ponitur in respectum hic [usque] a die Pasche in tres septimanas [1382] pro defectu juratorum etc. Ideo vicecomes habeat corpora etc.

Ad quem diem [veniunt] partes; et vicecomes non misit breve. Ideo predicta jurata ponitur in respectum hic usque a die Sancti Michaelis [in xv] dies pro defectu juratorum etc. Ideo vicecomes habeat corpora etc.

Ad quem diem veniunt partes; et vicecomes non misit [breve]. Ideo predicta jurata ponitur in respectum hic usque a die Sancti Hillarii in xv dies [1383] in forma [predicta] etc.

Ad quem diem veniunt partes; et vicecomes non misit breve. Ideo predicta jurata ponitur in respectum hic usque in [octabis] Sancte Trinitatis in forma supradicta etc.

Ad quem diem veniunt partes; et vicecomes non misit breve. Ideo predicta [jurata ponitur] in respectum hic usque in crastino Animarum in forma predicta pro defectu etc.

Ad quem diem vicecomes non misit breve. [Ideo] jurata predicta ponitur in respectum hic usque a die Pasche in xv dies [1384] in forma predicta pro defectu etc. [Ideo vicecomes] habeat corpora etc.

32 Recte *Radulfus.*

33 The scribe began to anticipate the second part of his sentence.

Ad quem diem veniunt tam predictus prior quam predicti Willelmus et episcopus per attornatos suos predictos; et predicti Johannes [et Alicia] quarto die placiti solempniter exacti non venerunt. Et super hoc idem prior petit quod jurata predicta inter ipsum et predictos Willelmum et episcopum [ponatur] sine die. Et super hoc idem Willelmus dicit quod predicta Alicia mortua est,[34] et petit auxilium de Hugone le Despe[nser] chivaler filio et herede eiusdem Alicie patrono ecclesie predicte et predicto episcopo. Et quia justiciarii hic nondum avisantur si predictus Willelmus [tale] auxilium de predicto Hugone in hac parte habere debeat, ideo dies datus est partibus predictis hic in octabis Sancte [Trini]tatis in statu quo nunc etc.; et jurata predicta ponitur in respectum hic usque ad predictum terminum pro defectu juratorum quia [nullus] venit. Ideo vicecomes habeat corpora.

Ad quem diem veniunt tam predictus prior quam predictus Willelmus per attornatos suos predictos. Et [quia] consideratum est quod idem Willelmus habeat auxilium tam de predicto episcopo quam de predicto Hugone patrono etc., ideo ipsi premuniantur [quod sint] hic a die Sancti Michaelis in xv dies[35] ad respondendum simul etc. si etc. Idem dies datus est partibus predictis hic etc.[36]

[2]

Brokhull v. *Cantays*

[a] *Report*: Lincoln's Inn, Hale MS 77, f.215[37] (YB 8 Ric. II, Mich. 5)

En bref de dette lez partiez furent a issue; et al venire facias retourne le vicount retourna quod mandavit ballivo libertatis Cantuar', qi avoit fait larray; et puis habeas corpora fuist retourne par la maner; et al distringas le vicount retourna quod mandavit ballivo libertatis Cantuar' et libertatis regine. Issint en le distringas un fraunchise fuist nomme pluis qe en ascun autre bref devaunt; et pur celle cause larray fuist chalenge par Hill' et Wadd' etc.

Belk' [CJ]. Le venire facias voille de visneto etc., issint qe ceo bref referre al lieu et nemye al persone; mez le habeas corpora et distringas referrent al persones: qar poet estre qe[38] ceux de lenquest furent al temps del venire facias agarde deinz le franchise de Cant' et en le mesne temps ount vendu lour terrez et sount demuranz en lautre franchise; et sil fuist issint, larray serra bon; et uncore il covient qe cel cause soit certifie a nous par le vicount; et ceo nest pas fait, par qi etc.

Et hoc non obstante larraye fuist agarde bon et lenquest jurre; qi passa[39] pur le pleintiff.

Mention of the 'franchise of Canterbury' and of 'the queen's franchise' (which could be presumed to be that of her hundred of Milton, about twelve miles from Canterbury along Watling Street) suggested that the Kent writs returned this term should be searched for a distringas juratores (*Reg. Brev.: Jud.*, f.22) bearing an endorsement of execution in some such words as those given in the report; and the document printed below was found.

[b] *Writ of distringas juratores*: CP 52/4/29/2 (octave of Mich. 8 Ric. II)

Ricardus Dei gracia rex Anglie et Francie et dominus Hibernie custodibus placitorum corone sue[40] in comitatu Kanc' salutem. Precipimus vobis quod distringatis Adam Broscombe Ricardum Royton' Willelmum Mayhew de Westwell' Leonardum de Grenestede Johannem Surryndenn' Johannem Gelot de Smerdenn' Johannem atte Melle de Smerdenn' Johannem Frend Johannem Elys de Hedecrone Ricardum Pemel Robertum Barlynge Johannem Eytherst Thomam Walssh' de Egerton' Willelmum Richard Johannem Foghelesle Thomam Richard Rogerum Bakere de Hothfelde Ricardum Sydenore Ricardum Seyntcler Ricardum Hamond Henricum Hemmyng' Laurencium de Dene Johannem Warde Willelmum de Dew Willelmum Beaugraunt et

[34] She had in fact died over four years before, on 5 or 6 Oct. 1379: *CIPM*, XV, nos.220–3.

[35] Contrast the return day named in the writ [1b].

[36] A new scire facias to execute the judgment of 3 Edward III was returned in Hilary term 8 Richard II: CP 40/496, m.351d. The defendant pleaded as here and prayed, and was granted, aid of Robert bishop of Coventry and Hugh Despenser. A writ warning the prayees for the quindene of Easter was not returned and was renewed, with recurrent entries of non misit, for the octave of Michaelmas 1385; the octave of Hilary and the octave of Trinity 1386; the octave of Hilary, the quindene of Easter and the octave of Michaelmas 1387. Here the record ends.

[37] Where the case is attributed to Trinity term.

[38] *qar poet estre qe* interlined.

[39] Corrected in MS from *passassa.*

[40] The sheriff was the plaintiff in this action.

Johannem de Mere,[41] juratores summonitos in curia nostra coram justiciariis nostris apud Westmonasterium inter Thomam Brokhull' querentem et Johannem Cantays de Brabourne de placito debiti, per omnes terras et catalla sua in balliva vestra[42] ita quod nec ipsi nec aliquis per ipsos ad ea manum apponat donec aliud a nobis inde habueris[43] preceptum, et quod de exitibus eorundem nobis respondeatis[44] et quod habeas[45] corpora eorum coram justiciariis nostris apud Westmonasterium in octabis Sancti Michaelis ad faciendum juratam illam et ad audiendum judicium suum de pluribus defaltis; et habeatis ibi hoc breve. Teste R. de Bealknapp' apud Westmonasterium xiij die julii anno regni nostri octavo.

Wakefeld'

ro. CCClvj.[46]

[*Endorsed*] Fecimus retornum huius brevis Willelmo Topeclyve senescallo libertatis archiepiscopi Cantuariensis et Ricardo Pope ballivo liberatatis domine Anne regine Anglie hundredi sui de Middelton', quibus execucio inde tantummodo pertinent[47] facienda; quorum responsiones patent in panello huic brevi consuto.

Per Thomam Holbeam Willelmum de Medmenham Rogerum Delham Ricardum Stokke et Johannem Proude custodes placitorum corone domini regis in comitatu Kanc'.

Ar' habet.[48]

[*Endorsed on the panel annexed*][49] Juratores dicunt quod persona optulit in ecclesia de Murston'; et recusavit. Ad dampnum xx librarum, unde clericis v marce.[50]

Finit' } – est
Finit' }

W. Topclyve deppon'[51]

Hill' ultimo ro. Dxx[52]

W. Topclyve[53]

[c] *Record*: CP 40/492, m.520 (Hil. 7 Ric. II)

[*Marginated*] Kanc'

Johannes Cantays de Brabourne summonitus fuit ad respondendum Thome Brokhull' de placito quod reddat ei ducentas libras quas ei debet et injuste detinet etc.; et unde idem Thomas per Willelmum Emery attornatum suum dicit quod cum predictus Johannes tercio die januarii anno regnorum domini regis nunc quarto [1381] per quoddam scriptum obligatorium concessisset se teneri prefato Thome in predictis ducentis libris solvendis ei apud Cherryng' ad festum Purificacionis Beate Marie tunc proximo sequens, pre-

41 The following geographical associations of these jurors derive from E 179/123/27, 29, 38 and 40. Broscombe, Royton', Surryndenn' and Sydenore with the hundred of Calehill (which had its meeting-place in Little Chart); Grenestede and Foghelesle with the hundred of Chart; Frend with Pluckley, near Little Chart; Pemel with Egerton; Eytherst with Smarden; Warde, Beaugraunt and Mere with the hundred of Milton; the Richard family with the hundreds of Calehill and Chart; and the Hamond and Dene families with the hundred of Chart.

The parishes of Westwell, Smarden, Headcorn, Egerton and Hothfield were wholly or partly in the franchise of the archbishop of Canterbury: R. Kilburne, *Topographie or Survey of . . . Kent* (London, 1659).

42 Obliterating *tua*.

43 Recte *habueritis*.

44 MS *respond* .

45 Recte *habeatis*.

46 The reference to the entry in the Trinity roll (CP 40/494, m.356) warranting the issue of this writ and respiting the jury until the octave of Michaelmas 'unless the assize justices should first come to Rochester on Monday before St Margaret the virgin [18 July]'.

47 Recte *pertinet*.

48 This may be for *archiepiscopus habet returnum brevium* or it may be meant to convey that the steward of the archbishop's franchise has received a precept; cf. *mandavit* in the report, and *fecimus retornum* above. Brief notes, such as this, that a writ falls to be executed in a franchise or in a hundred not in the king's hand take slightly different forms in the offices of different sheriffs. In Essex, for example, the abbreviated name of the (owner of the) franchise or hundred is preceded by *tra* (for *traditum, transmissum*?); in Somerset by a process mark (cf. [4b]). Written very unobtrusively near the bottom edge of the back of the writ, these jottings were made for the purposes of the sheriff's staff and form no part of the endorsed return, which, of course, they precede in time. It is possibly significant that the note here mentions only the archbishop's franchise.

49 The panel itself, which is not here transcribed, contains the array in the order of the distringas, each juror's name being docketed *Exitus ij s.* and followed by the bracketed names of four (presumably fictitious) sureties. Broscombe, Royton, Grenstede, Pemel, Barlynge, Walssh, Foghelesle, Bakere, Sydenore, Seyntcler, Dene and Warde are pricked and sworn; Surryndenn, Frend and Thomas Richard are pricked and struck through; Eytherst is pricked and marked with a cross; and Dew is pricked. The triers are Foghelesle and Sydenore.

50 The verdict at nisi prius, which it is interesting to compare with the issue and verdict as recorded in the roll [2c] .

51 Reading uncertain. Whatever this phrase means, it seems to show the steward of the archbishop's franchise to be alone concerned in the action taken.

52 The reference to the record of the pleadings and the issue taken.

53 This name is written the other way up.

dictus Johannes licet sepius requisitus predictas ducentas libras prefato Thome nondum reddidit set illas ei hucusque reddere contradixit et adhuc contradicit; unde dicit quod deterioratus est et dampnum habet ad valenciam centum librarum; et inde producit sectam etc.; et profert hic in curia predictum scriptum obligatorium quod predictum debitum testatur die et anno supradictis etc.; et dicit quod scriptum predictum factum fuit apud Cherryng' die et anno supradictis etc.

Et predictus Johannes Cantays in propria persona sua venit; et defendit vim et injuriam quando etc. Et dicit quod prefatus Thomas accionem de debito predicto versus eum habere non debet, quia dicit quod predicto tercio die januarii anno regnorum domini regis nunc supradicto apud Cherryng' convenit inter eosdem Thomam et Johannem, videlicet quod idem Johannes et Lucia uxor eius et Magister Ricardus[54] persona ecclesie de Morston' ante festum Pasche tunc proximo futurum concederent eidem Thome heredibus et assignatis suis per factum vel per finem in curia regis levandum ad custagia ipsius Thome reversionem tercie partis manerii de Morston' et de omnibus aliis terris et tenementis redditibus et reversionibus cum pertinenciis que Bartholomeus de Morston' habuit die mortis sue in comitatu Kanc' pro ducentis marcis argenti, unde idem Johannes recepit die confeccionis scripti predicti sexaginta et decem marcas, et idem Thomas per scriptum illud ulterius concessit quod si iidem Johannes et Lucia ex parte sua tenerent et teneri facerent in quantum in eis fuit convenciones supradictas absque fraude seu malo ingenio quod extunc predictum scriptum obligatorium vacuum foret et pro nullo haberetur. Et dicit quod ipse et predicta Lucia per totum tempus predictum parati fuerunt ad faciendum quicquid ad ipsos pertinuit in premissis et quod prefatus Thomas infra tempus illud nullum breve de convencione de tercia parte predicta perquisivit nec aliqua custagia eisdem Johanni et Lucie optulit. Et hec omnia paratus est verificare; unde petit judicium si idem Thomas accionem de predictis ducentis libris in hac parte versus eum habere debeat. Et profert hic in curia alteram partem cuiusdam scripti indentati sigillo predicti Thome signati convenciones predictas testificantis, cuius data est apud Cherryng' die et anno supradictis etc.

Et predictus Thomas dicit quod ipse per aliqua preallegata ab accione sua predicta precludi non debet; quia dicit quod diu ante confeccionem predicti scripti indentati predicta Lucia dum sola fuit, cui reversio tercie partis predicte pertinuit, concessit post mortem Johanne Morston' matris eiusdem Lucie reversionem illam prefato Ricardo et heredibus suis sub condicione de habendo eandem reversionem ad voluntatem eiusdem Lucie. Et dicit quod ipse die lune proxima post festum Purificacionis Beate Marie anno supradicto [4 Feb. 1381] apud Parvam[55] Chart juxta Lenham[56] requisivit prefatum Ricardum ad concedendum eidem Thome predicta terciam partem et tenementa, et racionabilia custagia ipsi Ricardo ibidem optulit; et idem Ricardus adtunc dixit quod terciam partem et tenementa predicta eidem Thome concedere noluit set quod eadem terciam partem et tenementa prefatis Johanni et Lucie libenter concedere vellet; et postea, scilicet die veneris proxima post octabas Purificacionis Beate Marie anno supradicto [15 Feb. 1381], idem Ricardus apud Parvam[57] Chart juxta Lenham[58] optulit eisdem Johanni et Lucie predicta terciam partem et tenementa et ad illa eis concedenda ibidem paratus fuit; et sic terciam partem et tenementa illa habuisse potuerunt si voluissent; et iidem Johannes et Lucia eadem terciam partem et tenementa sive aliquam concessionem inde admittere recusarunt; et sic in ipsis Johanne et Lucia defectus in ea parte in premissis extitit. Et hoc paratus est verificare; unde petit judicium et debitum predictum una cum dampnis sibi adjudicari etc.

Et predictus Johannes dicit quod prefatus Ricardus non optulit eidem Johanni et prefate Lucie predicta terciam partem et tenementa nec ad eadem terciam partem et tenementa eis concedenda paratus fuit prout predictus Thomas superius allegavit. Et hoc paratus est verificare; unde petit judicium etc.

Et predictus Thomas dicit quod prefatus Ricardus optulit prefatis Johanni et Lucie predicta terciam partem et tenementa et ad illa eis concedenda paratus fuit prout ipse preallegavit. Et hoc petit quod inquiratur per patriam: et predictus Johannes similiter.[59] Et quia predictus Thomas modo est vicecomes comitatus predicti, ideo preceptum est custodibus placitorum corone regis in comitatu pre-

[54] Richard Hornington: see R. Griffin, 'The Lepers' Hospital at Swainestrey', *Arch. Cantiana,* XXXIV (1920), 64, and *Registrum Simonis Langham,* ed. A. C. Wood (Cant. & York Soc., LIII, 1956), 399, where the reference is to Murston.

[55] Interlined. [56] *juxta Lenham* interlined.

[57] Interlined. [58] *juxta Lenham* interlined.

[59] The enrolled pleadings disclose no reason why the issue should not have been decided by a jury drawn exclusively from the Little Chart area; and only one of those sworn seems to have been in fact domiciled elsewhere. Was the array drawn up in the knowledge that the disputed offer was made at Murston and not at Little Chart?

dicto quod venire faciant hic a die Pasche in xv dies xij etc. per quos etc. et qui nec etc. ad recognoscendum etc.; quia tam etc.

Ad quem diem veniunt partes; et custodes placitorum corone regis non miserunt breve. Ideo sicut prius preceptum est custodibus placitorum corone regis in comitatu predicto quod venire faciant hic a die Sancte Trinitatis in xv dies[60] xij etc. ad recognoscendum in forma predicta etc.

Postea continuato inde processu inter partes predictas per juratas positas inde inter eas in respectum hic usque ad hunc diem, scilicet in octabis [Sancti Michaelis][61] anno regnorum domini regis nunc octavo: et modo hic ad hunc diem veniunt partes predicte in propriis personis suis; et similiter juratores veniunt, qui de consensu parcium predictarum ad hoc electi triati et jurati dicunt super sacramentum suum quod predictus Ricardus optulit prefatis Johanni et Lucie predicta terciam partem et tenementa et ad illa eis concedenda paratus fuit prout predictus Thomas superius allegavit,[62] et assident dampna predicti Thome occasione detencionis debiti predicti ad viginti libras. Ideo consideratum est quod predictus Thomas recuperet versus predictum Johannem debitum suum predictum et dampna sua predicta superius ad viginti libras assessa; et idem Johannes in misericordia etc.

Dampna viginti libre, unde clericis v marce.

[3]

Prior of Plympton v. *Bolham*

[a] *Report*: Lincoln's Inn, Hale MS 77, f.221 (YB 8 Ric. II, Mich. 33)

Annuite fuist porte vers un persoun, qi pria eide dordinarie et de patroun, et leide fuist graunte; quex furent somouns et viendrent prest de joindre par attourne. Et la persoun fist defaute; par qi bref issist al evesque[63] a distreindre la persone en lieu de petit cape, qi fuist retourne ore et servye; et lez autres avoient jour par idem dies et viendrent par attourne; et la persone autrefoitz fist defaute.

Par qi Fulthorp' [J] agarda qe le pleintiff recoverast lannuite et lez arreragez et lez damagez etc.

[b] *Report*: BL, Add. MS 32087, f.166 (YB 8 Ric. II, Mich. 33)

En bref dannuite vers un persone le persone pria aide del evesqe comme del ordenarie et del evesqe ensy comme de patron; et leide graunte et somounce ad auxiliendum[64] issist[65] devers levesqe et le somounce tesmoigne par le vicount. Et levesqe vient par attourne et le persoun fait defaute; sur qi distringas issist devers le persone ad audiendum jugement.

Et ore le jugement est rendu devers luy par sa defaut; et unqore, apres le somounce en eide tesmoigne devers levesqe et le persone fist defaut, nulle proces en rolle ne aillours ne fuist fait avaunt devers levesqe: et bene, ut dicitur, etc.

Postea Hill' viij levesqe retourne sur un bref qi issist, levari fac[iatis] et[66] xij libras de bonis et catallis etc. un T. rectoris talis ecclesie, ita quod habeas[67] coram etc. ad deliberandum etc. de arreragiis cuiusdam annui redditis[68] etc., quod non potest levare etc., set sequestrari facias[69] de fructibus eiusdem ecclesie ad valenciam tanti etc. Et sur ceo bref issist a evesqe pur vendre lez ditz fruitz etc., ita quod habeat denarios hic etc. ad deliberandum etc.

The 'distringas against the parson', returned this (Michaelmas) term, should have been fairly easily recognisable even if it was not (as the scribe of [a] was at pains to say that it was) addressed to the bishop; but the surviving files for Michaelmas contain no writ describable in the terms of either report. Better success, however, attended a search for the writ of execution to which [b] refers as a *levari fac'* (*Reg. Brev.: Jud.*, f.22) returned by the bishop at the octave of Hilary. It turned out to be the fieri facias (*Reg. Brev.: Jud.*, f.26v) transcribed below.

[c] *Writ of fieri facias*: CP 52/4/30/2 (octave of Hil. 8 Ric. II)

Ricardus Dei gracia rex Anglie et Francie et dominus Hibernie venerabili in Christo patri T. eadem gracia episcopo Exoniensi salutem. Mandamus vobis quod de bonis ecclesiasticis Ricardi Bolham persone ecclesie de Bratton' juxta Okhampton' clerici vestri in diocesi vestra fieri faciatis viginti et tres marcas et illas

60 Neither the venire facias nor the habeas corpora juratorum in this case is known to survive. Their endorsements would, of course, have been conclusive for or against the identification of the year book case with *Brokhull* v. *Cantays*.

61 Edge of membrane worn.

62 Contrast the verdict given at nisi prius: above, 278.

63 Preceded by *vic'*, expunged.

64 Recte *auxiliandum*.

65 Written above *issint*, deleted.

66 Repeated.

67 Recte *habeat*.

68 Recte *redditus*.

69 Recte *fecit*.

habeatis coram justiciariis nostris apud Westmonasterium in octabis Sancti Hillarii ad reddendum priori de Plympton' de arreragiis cuiusdam annui redditus octo marcarum quem idem prior in curia nostra coram justiciariis nostris apud Westmonasterium recuperavit versus eum singulis annis ad festa Sancti Michaelis Natalis Domini Pasche et nativitatis Sancti Johannis Baptiste per equales porciones solvendum. Mandamus eciam vobis quod de bonis ecclesiasticis predicti Ricardi clerici vestri in diocesi vestra fieri faciatis quinque marcas et illas habeatis coram prefatis justiciariis nostris apud Westmonasterium ad prefatum terminum ad reddendum predicto priori que eidem priori in eadem curia nostra adjudicate fuerunt pro dampnis suis que habuit occasione detencionis annui redditus predicti; et unde vicecomes noster Devon' alias mandavit justiciariis nostris apud Westmonasterium quod predictus Ricardus clericus est et non habet laicum feodum in balliva sua. Et habeatis ibi hoc breve. Teste R. Bealknapp' apud Westmonasterium quarto die novembris anno regni nostri octavo.
Wakefeld'
Hill' ultimo ro. CCxxiiij.[70]
[*Endorsed*] Viginti tres marcas ac eciam quinque marcas de quibus in infrascripto brevi plenior fit mencio de bonis ecclesiasticis infranominati Ricardi ad reddendum infrascripto priori loco et termino in hoc brevi limitatis fieri facere non possumus. Ideo fructus redditus et proventus quoscumque ad ecclesiam dicti Ricardi pertinentes sequestrari et sub arto et salvo sequestro fecimus custodiri quousque eidem priori de eisdem pecuniarum summis fuerit satisfactum.

Honorabilibus et circumspectis viris justiciariis domini nostri regis in banco suo communi.
Per Thomam Exoniensem episcopum.

[d] *Record*: CP 40/492, m.224 (Hil. 7 Ric. II)

[*Marginated*] Devon'
Ricardus Bolham persona ecclesie de Bratton' juxta Okhampton' summonitus fuit ad respondendum priori de Plympton' de placito quod reddat ei novem marcas que ei a retro sunt de annuo redditu octo marcarum quem ei debet etc.; et unde idem prior per Willelmum Burleston' attornatum suum dicit quod ipsemet fuit seisitus de annuo redditu predicto per manus predicti Ricardi nunc persone etc. ut de jure ecclesie sue Apostolorum Petri et Pauli de Plympton' singulis annis apud Plympton' ad festa Sancti Michaelis Natalis Domini Pasche et nativitatis Sancti Johannis Baptiste per equales porciones solvendo tempore pacis tempore domini regis nunc, de quo quidem annuo redditu idem prior et omnes predecessores sui priores loci predicti de Plympton' seisiti fuerunt de annuo redditu predicto per manus predicti Ricardi et predecessorum suorum personarum predicte ecclesie de Bratton' qui pro tempore fuerint[71] a tempore quo non extat memoria usque iam per unum annum et unum quarterium anni proxima ante diem impetracionis brevis etc., scilicet duodecimum diem januarii anno regni domini regis nunc Anglie sexto [1383], quod predictus Ricardus annuum redditum predictum subtraxit et redditum illum hucusque reddere contradixit et adhuc contradicit; unde dicit quod deterioratus est et dampnum habet ad valenciam viginti librarum; et inde producit sectam etc.

Et predictus Ricardus per Thomam Polsagh' attornatum suum venit et defendit vim et injuriam quando etc. Et super hoc dies datus est partibus predictis per attornatos suos predictos hic a die Pasche in tres septimanas in statu quo nunc salvis partibus racionibus etc.

Ad quem diem veniunt partes predicte per attornatos suos predictos. Et predictus Ricardus dicit quod ipse est persona ecclesie predicte de Bratton' et quod ipse invenit ecclesiam illam de predicto annuo redditu exoneratam et quod ipse non potest sine Thoma episcopo Exoniensi loci illius ordinario et prefato episcopo predicte ecclesie de Bratton' patrono ecclesiam predictam de aliquo redditu onerare sive exonerare; et petit auxilium de ipsis ordinario et patrono. Habeat etc. Ideo preceptum est vicecomiti quod summoneat etc. predictos ordinarium et patronum quod sint hic a die Sancte Trinitatis in xv dies ad respondendum predicto priori simul cum predicto Ricardo si etc. Idem dies datus est partibus hic etc.

Ad quem diem venit predictus prior per attornatum suum predictum: et predictus Ricardus Bolham quarto die placiti solempniter exactus non venit. Super quo predictus prior petit breve vicecomiti comitatus predicti directum ad distringendum Thomam episcopum Exoniensem ad habendum hic predictum Ricardum clericum suum, eo quod idem episcopus alias districtus fuit ad habendum clericum suum predictum hic in forma predicta etc.: et ei conceditur etc. Ideo preceptum est vicecomiti quod distringat predictum episcopum per omnes terras etc. et quod de exitibus

70 The reference to the plea roll entry warranting the issue of the writ.

71 Recte *fuerunt*.

etc. ita quod idem episcopus habeat hic a die Sancti Michaelis in xv dies per justiciarios[72] predictum Ricardum clericum suum ad respondendum predicto priori de predicto placito et ad audiendum inde judicium suum etc.

Ad quem diem venit predictus prior per attornatum suum predictum et optulit se quarto die versus predictum Ricardum Bolham de predicto placito: et ipse non venit: et vicecomes modo mandat quod predictus episcopus districtus est per catalla ad valenciam viginti et sex solidorum et octo denariorum et manucapitur per Willelmum Tille et Henricum Joye. Ideo ipsi in misericordia; et consideratum est quod predictus prior recuperet versus predictum Ricardum annuum redditum predictum et arreragia eiusdem tam ante diem impetracionis brevis sui quam post, que se extendunt ad viginti et tres marcas, et dampna sua, que taxantur per justiciarios ad quinque marcas; et predictus Ricardus in misericordia.

Dampna et arreragia [*blank*].[73]

[4]

Wallegh v. *Shyryg*

[a] *Report*: Lincoln's Inn, Hale MS 77, f.221v[74] (YB 8 Ric. II, Mich. 45)

En precipe quod reddat porte vers iij al petit cape retourne le demaundaunt soy tint al defaute.

Wadd' alleggea qe le bref original fuist porte vers iij et le petit cape suy vers ij, et le tierce entrelesse: issint le proses discontinue; par qi etc.

Et pur ceo qe le proses fuist bien continue en le roulle, il avoit petit cape sicut alias etc.

The inference from Wadham's argument and from the reported decision of the court was that the writs for this term should be searched for a parvum cape (*Reg. Brev.: Jud.*, f.2) naming two defendants but issued in pursuance of a plea roll entry naming three. The writ, when found, was not immediately recognisable for what it was, because it was one of three writs of parvum cape combined in one document, which is transcribed below.

[b] *Writ of parvum cape*: CP 52/4/29/4 (morrow of All Souls 8 Ric. II)

Ricardus Dei gracia rex Anglie et Francie et dominus Hibernie vicecomiti Somers' salutem. Cape in manum nostram unum mesuagium quadraginta acras terre et tres acras prati cum pertinenciis in Bicheuestoke que Johannes filius Johannis Wallegh' in curia nostra coram justiciariis nostris apud Westmonasterium clamat ut jus suum versus Henricum Shyryg' et Johannam uxorem eius pro defectu ipsorum Henrici et Johanne; cape eciam in manum nostram unum mesuagium et duodecim acras terre cum pertinenciis in eadem villa que predictus Johannes in eadem curia nostra coram prefatis justiciariis nostris apud Westmonasterium clamat ut jus suum versus Hawisiam Smyth' pro defectu ipsius Hawisie; cape eciam in manum nostram triginta acras terre [et][75] septem acras prati cum pertinenciis in eadem villa quas idem Johannes in eadem curia nostra coram prefatis justiciariis nostris apud Westmonasterium clamat ut jus suum versus Walterum Hayward et Aliciam uxorem eius et Johannem filium eiusdem Walteri Hayward pro defectu ipsorum Walteri Alicie et Johannis filii Walteri. Et summone per bonos summonitores predictos Henricum Johannam Margeriam[76] Hawisiam Walterum et Aliciam et Johannem filium Walteri quod sint coram justiciariis nostris apud Westmonasterium in crastino Animarum audituri inde judicium suum; et habeas ibi summonitores et hoc breve. Teste R. Bealknapp' apud Westmonasterium xxvj die junii anno regni nostri septimo.[77]
Wakefeld'
ro. CCCxvij.[78]
[*Endorsed*] Cepi in manum domini regis omnia terras

[72] *per justiciarios* interlined. This is the writ described in both reports as distress against the parson and in [3a] as having been addressed to the bishop. No Devon writs are known to survive for the quindene of Michaelmas this year.

[73] The tenor of the writ of fieri facias and of the bishop's return [3c] is recorded in the roll for Hilary 8 Richard II (CP 40/496, m.463d), where it is followed by: Ideo preceptum est eidem episcopo quod fructus redditus et proventus predictos . . . vendicioni disponat et denarios inde provenientes habeat hic a die Pasche in tres septimanas . . . ad reddendum predicto priori . . . This writ was not returned, and was issued sicut alias for return at the octave of St John the Baptist.

[74] Where the case is attributed to Hilary term.

[75] Omitted.

[76] Not previously mentioned.

[77] Recte *octavo*. The eighth year had begun only four days before, when Trinity term was already ten days old.

[78] The reference to the entry in the plea roll for the current term warranting the issue of the writ.

et tenementa in isto brevi petita secundum formam huius brevis.[79]

Summonitores: Johannes atte Hele Willelmus Barry

Johannes Strecche vicecomes

÷[80]

E[piscopus] B[athoniensis] [81]

[c] *Record*: CP 40/494, m.317d (Trin. 8 Ric. II)

[*Marginated*] Somers'

Johannes filius Johannis Wallegh' in propria persona sua optulit se quarto die versus Henricum Shyryg' et Johannam uxorem eius et Margeriam filiam eiusdem Henrici de placito unius mesuagii quadraginta acrarum terre et trium acrarum prati cum pertinenciis in Bicheuestoke, et versus Hawisiam Smyth' de placito unius mesuagii et duodecim acrarum terre cum pertinenciis in eadem villa, et versus Walterum Hayward' et Aliciam uxorem eius et Johannem filium eiusdem Walteri de placito triginta acrarum terre et septem acrarum prati cum pertinenciis in eadem villa, que clamat ut jus suum separatim versus eos; et ipsi non veniunt, et habuerunt inde diem hic ad hunc diem postquam alias comparuerunt hic in curia etc. Judicium. Predicta tenementa cum pertinenciis capiantur in manum domini regis etc.; et ipsi summoneantur quod sint hic in crastino Animarum[82] audituri inde judicium suum etc.

Ad quem diem quoad capiendum in manum domini regis predicta tenementa versus predictos Henricum et Johannam et Margeriam [petita] [83] vicecomes non misit breve.[84] Ideo sicut prius fiat inde breve in forma predicta retornabile hic a die Pasche in xv dies etc.

[5]

Basage v. *Bolle*

[a] *Report*: Lincoln's Inn, Hale MS 77, f.221v[85] (YB 8 Ric. II, Mich. 46)

En bref de dower proses suy tanqe al petit cape vers le baron et sa femme; a quel jour ils furent demaundez, et le baron fist defaute et la femme par attourne pria destre resceu etc. par bref de chauncellerie.

Wadd'. Ele ne serra pas resceu si ele ne fuist en propre persoun; par qi par lour defaute nous prioms seisin de terre.

Belk' [CJ]. Le roy ad nous comaunde qil ne poet mye venir pur ceo qil est si prest[86] son temps denfaunt; et autres ount este resceuz en tiel cas et autres semblables, come le cas Daudeley,[87] ou le roy recorda qil fuist maledie; par qi il semble qe ele est resceivable.

Et fuist touche qe tout ceo qe le roy avoit recorde ne fuit forsqe par suggestion a luy fait; et poet estre qe la suggestioun est faux: et non allocatur. Par qi Wadd' granta le resceit.

Pynch' dit qun J. fuist seisi de ceux tenementz et dautres tenementz etc. et murust saunz heire de son corps, par qi mesmez lez tenementz descendirent apres sa mort a un Alice et Elizabeth' come a ij soers etc., et Alice prist a baron mesme cestui W. vers qi le bref est ore porte, et Elizabeth' prist a baron un T., et firent purpartie entre eux, issint qe ceux tenementz dount la tierce partie est ore en demaunde fuist[88] allote al purpartie cestui W. et A. sa femme en allowaunce dautres tenementz qi furent allotez al purpartie Elizabeth'. Et T. baron Elizabeth' murust, et ele prist autre baron, un W. Wilby: et prioms eide [de] [89] mesmez ceux W. et E. nostre parcener, nient conisant qe mesmez lez tenementz sount si grant quantite dacres ne de meses come il ad suppose.

Wadd'. Lestatut done qe ele defendra sa tenance, qi ne poet estre forsqe par plee al accion, come voucher etc., et prier en eide nest qun dilatorie etc.

Fulth' [J]. Si leide soit grante lez ij averont la gard';[90] par qi respoignez.

Wadd'. Lou il ad dit qun J. fuit seisi ut supra, nous dioms par protestacion qe mesme cestui J. dount il parle fuist fitz nostre baron et murust en la vie soun piere. Et nous vous dioms en fait qil ne murust pas

[79] cf. the language of the record [4c].

[80] See above, n.48.

[81] cf. *Rotuli Hundredorum* (RC, 1812–18), II, 126 (4 Edw. I): Episcopus Batoniensis . . . habet returnum brevium in hundredo [de Chyu].

[82] *in crastino Animarum* inserted later in a space (a little too large) left blank.

[83] Omitted.

[84] Contrast the report [4a] and the return endorsed on the parvum cape [4b]. Admirers of the Gilbert and Sullivan operas will perhaps be reminded of Ko-Ko's suggestion to the Mikado: 'When your Majesty says, "Let a thing be done," it's as good as done – practically, it *is* done . . . and . . . why not say so?'

[85] Where the case is attributed to Hilary term.

[86] Recte *pres.*

[87] This case has not been identified. Fitzherbert (*Graunde Abridgement,* Resceit 87) shows that in 1367 (41 Edw. III, Hil. 8) the precedent invoked was that of 'Arundel' (found by Dr J. B. Post).

[88] Recte *furent.*

[89] Omitted.

[90] Recte *garrauntie*?

seisi de cest terre come il ad suppose; prest; jugement si eide doit ele aver.

Mez primerement il chalengea lour plee de ceo qils ne moustrerent pas en certein le quel le purpartie soy fist devaunt le murant soun baroun ou apres; 'qar si il fuist fait devaunt, ceo ne fuist nullement rienz a purpos, a ceo qi nous semble'.

Et puys per oppinionem curie ils serrount oustes del eide etc.

The court's refusal to grant aid removed the possibility that a writ warning the prayees (cf. [1]) was to be found in the files; but there remained the hope that the chancery writ of attorney produced by the woman defendant, and quoted by Bealknap in the discussion about receipt, might be discoverable among the writs addressed to the justices. Such writs were filed before (i.e. below) the Norfolk writs for the first return day of term. The writ transcribed below, found in the 'Norfolk' file for the octave of Michaelmas this year, contains identifying particulars which do not appear in the enrolled record; and though it does not, of course, provide any direct reference to that record, by giving the names of the parties and of the county concerned it greatly shortens and simplifies the search of the plea roll.

[b] *Writ of attorney*: CP 52/4/29/2 (octave of Mich. 8 Ric. II)
Ricardus Dei gracia rex Anglie et Francie et dominus Hibernie justiciariis suis de banco salutem. Sciatis quod cum Beatrix que fuit uxor Roberti Besage de Welyngore petat in curia nostra coram vobis per breve nostrum versus Willelmum Bolle de Swynesheved' et Isabellam uxorem eius terciam partem decem et septem mesuagiorum trium carucatarum terre unius molendini ventritici et octo libratarum quinque solidatarum et octo denariatarum redditus cum pertinenciis in Market Staynton' Marum Welyngore Wylkesby et Wodenderby ac in placito predicto taliter sit processum quod predicti Willelmus et Isabella postquam in curia nostra predicta coram vobis comparuerunt defaltam fecerunt, per quod vicecomiti nostro Lincoln' per breve nostrum de judicio preceperimus quod caperet in manum nostram terciam partem predictam et prefatos Willelmum et Isabellam summoneret quod sint coram vobis a die Sancti Michaelis in unum mensem proximo futur' ad audiendum inde judicium suum; ac eadem Isabella adeo gravida et partui vicina existens quod absque inevitabili mortis sue periculo usque Westmonasterium ad diem predictum laborare non possit metuensque quod prefatus Willelmus vir suus per collusionem inter ipsum et prefatam Beatricem factam ad diem illum iterato defaltam facere intendat (quod si fieret in ipsius Isabelle grave dampnum et exheredacionis periculum cederet manifeste) attornaverit coram nobis Humfridum de Haneworth' et Johannem Symond ad petendum se admitti ad defensionem juris ipsius Isabelle de tercia parte predicta si ipsum Willelmum ad diem predictum defaltam facere contingat et ad lucrandum vel perdendum in loquela predicta necnon ad omnia et singula facienda que eadem Isabella faceret si presens esset; vobis mandamus quod ipsos Humfridum et Johannem vel alterum ipsorum si ambo interesse non possint loco ipsius Isabelle ad hoc recipiatis. Teste me ipso apud Westmonasterium primo die octobris anno regni nostri octavo.
Roderh'
[*Endorsed*] Thomas de Pynchebek' recepit attorn[atos] per breve.[91]

[c] *Record*: CP 40/495, m.506 (Mich. 8 Ric. II)
[*Marginated*] Lincoln'
Beatrix que fuit uxor Roberti Basage de Welyngore in propria persona sua optulit se quarto die versus Willelmum Bolle de Swynesheved' de placito tercie partis decem et septem mesuagiorum trium carucatarum terre unius molendini ventritici octo libratarum quinque solidatarum et octo denariatarum redditus cum pertinenciis in Marketstaynton' Marum Welyngore Wilkesby et Wodenderby quam clamat in dotem ex dotacione prefati Roberti quondam viri etc. versus eum et Isabellam uxorem eius; et ipse non venit, et tam ipse quam prefata Isabella alias fecerunt defaltam hic, scilicet in octabis Sancti Johannis Baptiste proximo preteritis, postquam alias comparuerunt hic in curia etc., ita quod tunc preceptum fuit vicecomiti quod non omitteret propter libertatem Johannis ducis Lancastr' in partibus de Kesteven' et libertatem ville de Horncastre quin caperet predictam terciam partem cum pertinenciis in manum domini regis etc. et quod summoneret eos quod essent hic ad hunc diem, scilicet a die Sancti Michaelis in unum mensem tunc proximo sequen', audituri inde judicium suum; et vicecomes modo mandat quod cepit etc. et quod summonuit etc. Et super hoc predicta Beatrix petit seisinam de predicta tercia parte cum pertinenciis per defaltam etc. sibi adjudicari. Et super hoc venit predicta Isabella per Humfridum de Haneworth' attornatum suum per breve domini regis constitutum et dicit quod predicta

[91] i.e. a writ of dedimus potestatem recipiendi attornatos.

tenementa unde etc. sunt jus suum, unde exquo ipsa venit ante judicium etc. petit quod ipsa non amittat jus suum set quod ad defensionem juris sui inde admittatur. Et super hoc viso predicto brevi de attornacione eadem Isabella admittitur. Super quo prefata Beatrix petit versus ipsam Isabellam predictam terciam partem tenementorum predictorum ut dotem suam in forma predicta etc.

Et predicta Isabella, protestando quod predicta tenementa unde etc. non sunt nisi decem mesuagia unum molendinum ventriticum due carucate terre et quadraginta solidate redditus, dicit quod prefatus Robertus quondam vir predicte Beatricis diu ante desponsalia inter ipsum et predictam Beatricem celebrata dedit eadem tenementa cum pertinenciis unde etc. cuidam Johanni Besage avunculus[92] ipsius Isabelle, cuius una heredum ipsa est, habenda et tenenda eidem Johanni et heredibus ac assignatis suis imperpetuum, virtute quarum donacionis et concessionis idem Johannes inde seisitus fuit et statum suum de tenementis illis continuavit tota vita ipsius Johannis et inde seisitus obiit in dominico suo ut de feodo, absque hoc quod prefatus Robertus quondam vir predicte Beatricis die quo ipsam Beatricem desponsavit vel uncquam postea de tenementis illis unde etc. seisitus fuit in dominico suo ut de feodo ita quod ipsam Beatricem inde dotare potuit; et hoc paratus[93] est verificare; unde petit judicium etc.

Et predicta Beatrix dicit quod post desponsalia inter ipsam et predictum Robertum celebrata idem Robertus fuit seisitus de predictis tenementis cum pertinenciis unde etc. in dominico suo ut de feodo[94] ita quod ipsam Beatricem inde dotare potuit; et hoc petit quod inquiratur per patriam: et predicta Isabella similiter. Ideo preceptum est vicecomiti quod venire faciat hic in octabis Sancti Hillarii[95] xij etc. per quos etc. et qui nec etc. ad recognoscendum etc. quia tam etc.

Ad quem diem veniunt partes etc.; et vicecomes mandat quod breve adeo tarde etc. Ideo sicut prius preceptum est vicecomiti quod venire faciat hic a die Pasche in xv dies xij etc. per quos etc. et qui nec etc. ad recognoscendum in forma predicta etc. Idem dies datus est partibus etc.

Ad quem diem veniunt partes etc.; et vicecomes non misit breve. Ideo sicut pluries preceptum est vicecomiti quod venire faciat hic in octabis Sancte Trinitatis xij etc. ad recognoscendum etc. in forma predicta etc.

Postea continuato inde processu per juratas inter partes predictas positas in respectum hic usque in octabis Sancti Michaelis anno regni domini regis nunc undecimo [1387] nisi justiciarii domini regis ad assisas in comitatu predicto capiendas assignati per formam statuti etc. die veneris proxima ante festum Sancti Petri advincula [26 July 1387] apud Lincoln' prius venissent etc.; et modo ad hunc diem venit tam predicta Beatrix in propria persona sua quam predicta Isabella[96] per attornatum suum predictum; et justiciarii ad assisas etc. coram quibus etc. miserunt hic recordum suum in hec verba:

> Postea die et loco[97] infra contentis coram Rogero de Fulthorp' et Johanne de Lokton' justiciariis domini regis ad assisas etc. veniunt tam predicta Beatrix in propria persona sua quam predicta Isabella per attornatum suum predictum; et juratores similiter veniunt; qui ex consensu parcium super premissis infra contentis electi triati et jurati dicunt super sacramentum suum quod predictus Robertus Basage quondam vir predicte Beatricis diu ante sponsalia inter ipsum et predictam Beatricem celebrata dedit tenementa infra contenta cum pertinenciis prefato Johanni Besage in forma qua predicta Isabella inferius implacitando allegavit, absque hoc quod predictus Robertus Basage quondam vir predicte Beatricis die quo ipsam Beatricem desponsavit ven[98] uncquam postea de tenementis predictis seisitus fuit in dominico suo ut de feodo ita quod ipsam Beatricem inde dotare potuit.

Ideo consideratum est quod predicta Beatrix nichil capiat per breve suum predictum set sit in misericordia pro falso clamio suo etc.

[6]

Taillour v. *Brounyng*

[a] *Report*: Lincoln's Inn, Hale MS 77, f.272 (YB 10 Ric. II, Hil. 11)

Un homme porta bref de transgression devers un autre; proses suy tanqe il fuist utlage, par qi leschetour par cause de celle utlagarie seisist lez bienz et chateux dun autre homme qi porta mesme le noun, qi ne fuist pas mesme la persone vers qi le pleintiff suyst etc.

[92] Recte *avunculo;* interlined above a much shorter word (*patri*? *fratri*?) which has been erased.

[93] Recte *parata.*

[94] *in dominico . . . feodo* interlined.

[95] *in octabis Sancti Hillarii* was inserted later in a space left blank.

[96] Over an erasure.

[97] Followed by *die.*

[98] Recte *vel.*

Par qi il vint en comine bank et moustra tout ceo a la court et pria remedie. Et le pleintiff qi suyst le bref vint ovesqe luy et recorda qil ne fuist pas mesme la persone vers qi il avoit pursuy.

Et sur ceo Belk' justice [CJ] luy fist jurer sur un livere sil fuist mesme la persone ou noun; le qel jure qil ne fuist pas mesme la persone. Et nientmeyns la court ne dona pleyn credence a ceo, mez agarda un bref de idemptitate nominis a le vicount denquerrer sil fuist mesme la persone ou noun.

Et ore cest terme le vicount retourna qil ne fuist pas mesme la persone vers qi le pleintiff pursuya etc. Par qi il pria pur aver bref al eschetour a deliverer et faire restitucion de sez bienz etc.

Belk'. Vous naverez tiel bref, qar nous [ne][99] sumes pas appris leqel leschetour ad seisi voz chateux ou nient; mez vous averez un bref, si vous voillez, direct al eschetour qe vous ne serrez endamage par ly par cause de celle utlagarie; par qi suez etc.

Et nota qe tiel bref il suist etc.

This report pointed to the possibility that the files for this (Hilary) term might contain the writ de idemptitate nominis (*Reg. Brev.: Jud.*, f.81v). A writ to the required general effect (having only its last clause in the same words as the specimen in *Reg.Brev.: Jud.*) was found and is transcribed below; but the plea in which it was issued was of debt, not trespass. For all their carelessness and caprice in the rendering of such particulars as the names of people and places, the dates of fines, and even the sex of litigants, year book reporters seldom err over the form of action. Yet reference to the record suggests that *Taillour* v. *Brounyng* has in common with the reported case enough other circumstances (including the court's reluctance to accept the plaintiff's sworn statement without corroboration) to make the identification at least reasonably probable.

[b] *Writ de idemptitate nominis*: CP 52/4/38/2 (octave of Candlemas 10 Ric. II)

Ricardus Dei gracia rex Anglie et Francie et dominus Hibernie vicecomitibus London' salutem. Precipimus vobis quod per sacramentum proborum et legalium hominum de parochia Sancti Laurencii in la Jewerie in warda de Chepe in presencia Henrici Taillour capellani si ad hoc interesse voluerit diligenter inquiratis si quidam Johannes Brounyng' de Colde Aston' sit illa eadem persona que ad sectam ipsius Henrici in quodam placito debiti quadraginta solidorum in hustengo nostro London' utlagatus[100] fuit an Johannes Brounyng' de Heriettesham de comitatu Kanc' qui per nomen Johannis Brounyng' tantum ad sectam predicti Henrici in hustengo predicto utlagatus fuit necne; et inquisicionem quam inde feceritis scire faciatis justiciariis nostris apud Westmonasterium in octabis Purificacionis Beate Marie sub sigillo vestro et sigillis eorum per quorum sacramentum inquisicionem illam feceritis. Et habeatis ibi nomina eorum per quorum sacramentum illam feceritis et hoc breve. Teste R. Bealknapp' apud Westmonasterium xxviij die novembris anno regni nostri decimo.
Broun'
ro. CCCxxiiij.[101]

[*Endorsed*] Execucio istius brevis patet in inquisicione huic brevi consuta.
Responsio Willelmi More et Willelmi Staundon' vicecomitum.

[*Annexed*] Inquisicio capta coram nobis Willelmo More et Willelmo Staundon' vicecomitibus London' vicesimo die januarii anno regni regis Ricardi secundi decimo virtute cuiusdam brevis domini regis nobis directi et presentibus consuti, in presencia Henrici Taillour in dicto brevi nominati, ad inquirendum si Johannes Brounyng' [*and so forth, as in the writ, with insignificant verbal variants, down to* necne], per sacramentum Ricardi atte Pytte Roberti Pedyngton' Johannis Stere Johannis Botmade Willelmi Fungery Thome Dunche Bartholomei Dekene Rogeri Lounde Walteri atte Wode Thome Eketon' Jacobi Cotiller et Thome de Isle, proborum et legalium hominum de parochia Sancti Laurencii in la Jewerye in warda de Chepe London' juxta formam brevis predicti et prout idem breve requirit; qui dicunt super sacramentum suum quod predictus Johannes Brounyng' de Coldeaston' de comitatu Glouc' non est eadem persona que ad sectam predicti Henrici in hustengo predicto utlagatus fuit, set dicunt quod predictus Johannes Brounyng' de Heriettesham de comitatu Kanc' est eadem persona qui per nomen Johannis Brounyng' tantum in eodem hustengo ad sectam predicti Henrici fuit utlagatus. In cuius rei testimonium juratores predicti huic inquisicioni sigilla sua apposuerunt. Data London' vicesimo die januarii anno decimo supradictis.
[*Endorsed*] Est.

99 Omitted.

100 Throughout both the writ and the record masculine forms are frequently found in this context.

101 The reference to the Michaelmas plea roll entry warranting the issue of this writ.

[c] *Record*: CP 40/503, m.324 (Mich. 10 Ric. II)

Dominus rex mandavit justiciariis suis hic breve suum in hec verba:

Ricardus Dei gracia rex Anglie et Francie et dominus Hibernie justiciariis suis de banco salutem. Monstravit nobis Johannes Brounyng' de Colde Aston' de comitatu Glouc'[102] ut cum Henricus Taillour capellanus nuper per breve nostrum implacitaverit Johannem Brounyng' coram vobis in banco predicto de eo quod idem Johannes Brounyng' reddat prefato Henrico quadraginta solidos quos ei debet et injuste detinet, ut dicitur, ac idem Johannes pro eo quod non venit coram vobis in banco predicto prefato Henrico inde responsurus positus fuerit in exigendis in hustengo nostro London' ad utlagandum et ea occasione postmodum utlagatus, sicut per tenorem recordi et processus loquele predicte, quem coram nobis in cancellaria nostra venire fecimus, plene liquet; iamque predictus Johannes Brounyng' de Colde Aston' pro idemptitate nominis et cognominis prefati Johannis Brounyng' sic utlagati, timens sibi posse periculum evenire in futuro, nobis supplicaverit sibi per nos in hac parte de remedio provideri, nos supplicacioni predicte annuentes vobis mandamus quod inspectis recordo et processu predictis et vocatis coram vobis, si necesse fuerit, partibus predictis auditisque racionibus earundem, si per assercionem partis vel alio modo legitimo vobis constare poterit ipsum Johannem Brounyng' et non predictum Johannem Brounyng' de Colde Aston' sic fuisse implacitatum et utlagatum, tunc, ne pretextu idemptitatis nominis et cognominis prefati Johannis Brounyng' sic utlagati eidem Johanni Brounyng' de Coldeaston' prejudicetur, ulterius pro securitate prefati Johannis Brounyng' de Colde Aston' fieri faciatis quod de jure et secundum legem et consuetudinem regni nostri Anglie fuerit faciendum. Teste me ipso apud Westmonasterium xvj die octobris anno regni nostri decimo.

Et super hoc venit predictus Johannes Brounyng' de Coldeaston' hic in curia in propria persona sua et petit breve vicecomitibus London' de venire faciendo predictum Henricum super premissis responsurum ulteriusque facturum et [recepturum] [103] quod curia regis hic consideraverit in hac parte. Et ei conceditur, returnabile hic in octabis Sancti Martini etc. Et super hoc Walterus Griffin Robertus Burdun Willelmus Staverton' et Thomas Kevele de comitatu Glouc' manuceperunt predictum Johannem Brounyng' habendi corpus eius hic ad prefatum terminum et sic de die in diem ad quemlibet diem placiti quousque placitum inde terminetur etc.

Ad quem diem veniunt tam predictus Johannes Brounyng' de Coldeaston' quam predictus Henricus Taillour in propriis personis suis. Et idem Henricus examinatus super sacramentum suum si predictus Johannes Brounyng' de Coldaston' est illa eadem persona que ad sectam ipsius Henrici in placito predicto utlagatus fuit necne, qui dicit quod non; set dicit quod ipse qui ad sectam ipsius Henrici sic utlagatus existit nominatur Johannes Brounyng' de Heriettesham de comitatu Kanc' et non Johannes Brounyng' de Colde Aston', nec aliquam noticiam de eodem Johanne Brounyng' de Colde Aston' habet. Et super examinacione illa predictus Johannes Brounyng' de Colde Aston' petit quod ipse a curia predicta recedere posset[104] etc.

Et Willelmus de Hornby, qui sequitur pro domino rege, dicit quod ipse paratus est verificare et manutenere pro domino rege quod predictus Johannes Brounyng' de Colde Aston' est illa eadem persona que ad sectam ipsius Henrici sic utlagatus fuit, et quod idem Johannes Brounyng' de Coldeaston' per collusionem inter ipsum et prefatum Henricum prosecutus fuit breve predictum de idemptitate nominis et cognominis prefati Johannis Brounyng' sic utlagati ad ipsum dominum regem in hac parte defraudendum,[105] et petit breve prefatis vicecomitibus ubi utlagaria predicta promulgata fuit, videlicet de parochia Sancti Laurencii in Juerie[106] in warda de Chepe.[107] Et ei conceditur. Ideo preceptum est vicecomitibus quod per sacramentum proborum etc. de parochia predicta in presencia predicti Henrici, per se premuniendi si ad hoc interesse voluerit, diligenter inquirant si predictus Johannes Brounyng' de Colde Aston' sit eadem persona que ad sectam predicti Henrici per nomen Johannis Brounyng' tantum sic utlagatus existit necne, et de premissis omnibus et singulis plenius veritatem,[108] et inquisicionem quam etc. scire faciant hic in octabis Purificacionis Beate Marie[109] sub sigillo etc. et sigillis etc.

Ad quem diem vicecomites miserunt hic quandam

[102] *de comitatu Glouc'* interlined.

[103] Omitted.

[104] Usually *possit.*

[105] Recte *defraudandum.*

[106] *in Juerie* interlined.

[107] *de Chepe* was apparently inserted later in a space (slightly too large) left blank.

[108] *et de premissis . . . veritatem* does not appear in the writ.

[109] *in octabis . . . Marie* was inserted later in a space left blank.

inquisicionem coram eis captam in presencia predicti Henrici per sacramentum xij etc., qui dicunt super sacramentum suum quod predictus Johannes Brounyng' de Coldeaston' de comitatu Glouc' non est eadem persona que ad sectam predicti Henrici in hustengo predicto utlagatus fuit, set dicunt quod predictus Johannes Brounyng' de Heriettesham de comitatu Kanc' est eadem persona que per nomen Johannis Brounyng' tantum in eodem hustengo ad sectam predicti Henrici fuit utlagatus. Ideo preceptum est escaetori domini regis in comitatu Glouc' quod eidem Johanni Brounyng' de Coldeaston' terras tenementa bona et catalla per ipsum escaetorem pretendentem prefatum Johannem Brounyng' de Coldeaston' esse eundem Johannem Brounyng' de Heriettesham racione idempnitatis[110] nominis et cognominis predictorum, pretextu cuiusdam brevis domini regis de banco ad inquirendum de tenementis terris bonis et catallis predicti Johannis Brounyng' de Heriettesham de comitatu Kanc', [qui] [111] sub nomine Johannis Brounyng' absque adjeccione aliqua nomini illi ad sectam predicti Henrici in placito predicto utlagatus fuit, et ad eadem terras tenementa bona et catalla extendenda et apprecianda et in manum domini regis capienda eidem escaetori directi, si in manu ipsius domini regis occasione predicta et non alia capta existant, deliberari faciat indilate, proviso semper quod escaetor domini regis in predicto comitatu Kanc' de terris tenementis bonis et catallis predicti Johannis Brounyng' de Heriettesham, qui sic utlagatus fuit, inquirat et ea in manum domini regis seisiri faciat etc.

110 Recte *idemptitatis.*

111 Omitted.

Courts, councils, and arbitrators in the Ladbroke manor dispute, 1382–1400

edited by

J. B. POST

INTRODUCTION

For the last twenty years of the fourteenth century, William Catesby and his son John conducted a complicated and successful defence of property in Warwickshire – principally the manor of Ladbroke – against the repeated attempts of their litigious relatives to oust them. The legal issues were those commonplaces of later medieval property disputes, the allegedly broken entail and the allegedly forged deed, but the doggedness of the plaintiffs and the caution of the defence gave rise to documentation which is of more than commonplace interest. In one form or another the dispute was heard in the courts of common pleas and king's bench, at assizes, in chancery, by the king's council, before the seignorial councils of four several magnates, and by a distinguished body of consultant lawyers; over the years, therefore, John Catesby compiled a remarkable roll of evidences. It includes transcripts of deeds, of proceedings in courts of record, and (apparently) of an official report to the earl of Warwick from a hearing before his council; these are interspersed, however, with an extensive piecemeal narrative, in which Catesby provided, by way of memoranda, an informal account of the official and private dealings, the negotiations and hearings which the dispute engendered, concluding with a summary – unique in some significant detail – of the Lancastrian usurpation, in which both his arbitrators died. After the final hearing, moreover, Catesby retained not only a sealed copy of the legal opinion but also two earlier drafts of it,[1] a pair of draft narratives, and other notes, evidently working papers prepared for or by the legal advisers and their staff. These materials, though incomplete, provide detailed and closely involved accounts of some typical contemporary problems, sued on a classic scale.[2]

The Ladbroke family were long-standing tenants of the manors of Ladbroke and Harbury,[3] and of an extensive tenement in Tanworth which became known as Ladbroke's Manor.[4] The Catesby family, though also of ancient lineage,[5] held nothing in these places until the fourteenth century, when a cadet branch, tardily adopting the family toponym, began collecting parcels of land in Ladbroke,[6] prompted perhaps by a marriage alliance.[7] The elder John Ladbroke probably died in 1323/4,[8] and his son Henry inherited his estates. Thus far the later litigants agreed, and for half a century the actual devolution of the lands followed right, as the Catesbys saw it. Henry Ladbroke promptly entailed Harbury upon his son John and John's wife Hawise, with remainder to his own right heirs [65, 133], and subsequently granted Ladbroke and Tanworth to John for life, with reversion to himself [4, 13, 134].[9] At some time in the next nine years Henry died; John inherited, and proceeded to dispose of his lands to feoffees – initially to two clerks and Nicholas Woodward [45, 47, 46], but subsequently replacing

[1] An inaccurate transcript of one of these drafts, accompanied by a seriously misleading preface (apparently based on a misinterpretation of the text), has appeared recently as Appendix VI to *King's Bench,* VII; below, n.116.

[2] A slightly later dispute at a similar social level, also involving an alleged breach of entail, is described and discussed by P. S. Lewis, 'Sir John Fastolf's Lawsuit over Titchwell 1448–55', *Hist. Jnl,* I (1958), 1–20.

[3] *CIPM,* I, no. 679; V, no. 615 (pp.405, 408).

[4] See, in general, S. H. A. H[arvey], *Ladbroke and its Owners* (Bury St Edmunds, 1914), c. VI, using deductions there with caution. When the Catesbys acquired Ladbroke, their manor in that vill was also known as Ladbroke's Manor.

[5] The most nearly accurate Catesby pedigree is in G. Baker, *The History and Antiquities of the County of Northampton* (London, 1822–30), I, 244–5; for the context of the present dispute, see below, 301. For a brief survey of the Catesby family in the fourteenth and fifteenth centuries, see J. S. Roskell, 'William Catesby, Counsellor to Richard III', *Bull. Jn Rylands Lib.,* XLII (1959–60), 148–9.

[6] Transactions before c.1335, in the name of John Hull of Flecknoe, otherwise John Flecknoe of Catesby, and his family, clearly relate to the father of William Catesby: *CAD,* IV, A 7050 (and see also A 8808); V, A 11519–11522 (and see also [3]). For other piecemeal acquisitions in Ladbroke, see *CAD,* IV, A 7924, A 9857, A 10242; E 42/147. The family name must have been fairly well established by 1336, when Catesby Lane in Coventry is so called: J. E. B. Gover and others, *The Place-Names of Warwickshire* (EPNS, XIII, 1936), 162.

[7] At visitation, John Catesby of Flecknoe was said by Camden to have married Isabel Ladbroke: *The Visitation of the County of Warwick . . . 1619,* ed. J. Fetherston (Harl. Soc., XII, 1887), 125. See below, 301.

[8] Between *CAD,* IV, A 7050 (5 Oct. 1323) and 1327: *The 1327 Lay Subsidy Roll for Warwickshire* (Midland Rec. Soc. Supp., 1899), 16 (Ladbroke), 26 (Tanworth); probably before [133] (14 July 1324).

[9] For grants presupposing these, see *CAD,* IV, A 9040 and A 8051.

one of the clerks with William Catesby [31–2].[10] He followed this feoffment with a release of Ladbroke to Catesby, for life, with successive remainders in tail male to his own sons Thomas, Hugh, and John, with contingent remainder to Catesby's heirs.[11] A similar entail of Tanworth included an initial life interest to Hawise [13], and was part of a bargain whereby no dower was to be claimed in Ladbroke [41; see also 5, 13]. John Ladbroke died in the summer of 1349, his son and heir, Thomas, being still under age [35; 13], and his disposition of these lands was apparently completed by fine in the following year, when Hawise and William Woodward confirmed the entail of Tanworth – young Thomas now being married to Catesby's daughter Alice – and made similar arrangements for Harbury, save that the contingent remainder was to the right heirs of Thomas [121].

Over the following twenty-five years the properties were subject to numerous grants and regrants, tending (broadly speaking) to consolidate the Catesby position; during the early negotiations after John Ladbroke's death Catesby was certainly raising money,[12] as well as acquiring additional land in Ladbroke.[13] Almost immediately, Nicholas Woodward enfeoffed Catesby, Catesby's brother Simon, John Vintner, and his own son William, of Harbury manor and the Tanworth estate [39; 49]. Soon afterwards Catesby and Nicholas Woodward granted Ladbroke (with exceptions) to Simon Catesby, John Cook, John Warkton, chaplain, and William Woodward [36; see also 26]; Thomas Ladbroke released his rights there to the same, omitting William Woodward and subsequently omitting Simon Catesby (probably on their respective deaths) [40; 62], and Warkton released his rights there to Cook [37]. In 1369 Hawise died [98; see also 13], and thereafter Catesby separated his interests. John Cook granted him Ladbroke, on the terms of John Ladbroke's earlier grant [38; see also 13], and afterwards[14] Thomas Ladbroke confirmed his rights there [44] upon John, Catesby's son, who was acting as lord of the manor two years later.[15] In contrast Tanworth and Harbury were leased, sometimes piecemeal, for short terms [42; 63; 64] or for William Catesby's life [43; 60; 61]. Thereafter, as the Catesbys insisted, all was straightforward. William died in 1383, and John's succession to Ladbroke and Tanworth was accomplished in fact and recognised by the chief lords of the fees [78–82, 84; see also 13]; Harbury returned to the Ladbroke family under the fine of 1350, although the Catesbys may have attempted to assert an interest later [137]. From the entailing of Hopsford manor on his son, posthumously via feoffees, it is clear that John Catesby made careful disposition of his lands,[16] and Ladbroke remained in the possession of the family until its sale in 1597.[17]

A different view of the legal position was the basis for the protracted litigation which began in 1383. This view argued, initially [126; 95; 131], that the inheritance should have descended, after the death of Hawise Ladbroke, to Thomas, and then to his son John; when John died,[18] after his uncle John and shortly before his uncle Hugh, all without heirs of the body, the right passed to his aunt Alice,[19] married to

[10] William Catesby was assessed at 8s., as was John Ladbroke, in the subsidy of 1332; nearly fifty years later he was assessed as an armiger, under Ladbroke manor. His career, in the interim, had included numerous royal commissions on a variety of business, particularly involving criminal matters, legal matters, and matters affecting the royal households. See *The Lay Subsidy Roll for Warwickshire of 6 Edward III (1332)*, ed. W. F. Carter (Dugdale Soc., VI, 1926), 28; E 179/192/23, m.17; for examples of commissions, see *CPR 1340–3*, 88; *1345–8*, 99, 178, 179, 183, 184, 307, 312, 314, 376, 465.

[11] This release, described below [13], must be that described by Dugdale, in which case he omitted the clause giving Catesby a life interest: W. Dugdale, *The Antiquities of Warwickshire* (Coventry, 1765), 232.

[12] *CCR 1349–54*, 239.

[13] *CPR 1348–50*, 567; see also *CIM*, III, no. 37.

[14] This is clearly so [44; see also 54], regardless of their respective express dates.

[15] View of frankpledge was held there in his name, 10 October 1374: SC 2/207/50, m.3. John Catesby was described as an assizes pleader when assessed at 20s. (compared with his father's 6s. 8d.) in the subsidies of 1377 and 1379. Shortly after his death, the net landed income of his son and heir was substantial at £30 a year, but his widow admitted to thrice this amount: E 179/155/30, m.3; 35, m.3; 52, m.4 (all under Ashby St Ledgers, Northants).

[16] *CAD*, III, A 4327, A 4363. See below, n.26.

[17] Harvey, *Ladbroke*, 99.

[18] On another roll, of miscellaneous evidences, John Catesby noted carefully the date of his nephew's death at Coventry priory, 11 Sept. 1381: E 41/394, m.4.

[19] According to litigants in the third quarter of the fifteenth century, Alice was ineffectually disinherited by her father for marrying Cardian (otherwise 'Cardigan'), who was Sir John's servant and cook: Baker, *History of Northants*, I, 352. Many ramifications of this branch of the family are explored, ibid., I, 351–5. Alice omitted her own daughter from her will, leaving bedding to her grandson and the residue of her estate to her executor, although Katherine inherited her moiety of Coombe Keynes: Guildhall Lib., MS 9171/3 [Commissary Court of London, Register 3],

Lewis Cook, otherwise Cardian.[20] Subsequently [152] the claim included the alleged authenticity of a deed [157] whereby, in 1326, Henry Ladbroke had entailed Ladbroke and Tanworth upon John and Hawise, with contingent remainder to John's right heirs male. As supporting evidence, two grants were adduced whereby Thomas Ladbroke had leased portions of the Tanworth estate in 1370 [146, 147].

The litigation began in 1383, when William Catesby brought a successful trespass suit against the Cardians and others for felling and removing trees at Ladbroke. When the defendants defaulted at nisi prius, verdict and judgment, with damages, were given in Catesby's favour, but the defence case, ominously, had rested on the claim that Ladbroke belonged to the Cardians [72–4].[21] In the meantime the Catesbys, who had already disputed the wardship of the Ladbroke heirs [51], had argued their case before the council of the earl of Warwick, as chief lord [52–9, 65–70], Thomas Archer being their chief opponent,[22] although, since he did not present much of a case, his current interest is unspecified [59, 71]. He may have been acting for the earl himself; subsequent pleadings showed Warwick in opposition to the Catesbys [131, 133], perhaps arising from the disputed tenurial status of Tanworth [136], and it was suggested that he was behind the direct action whereby the Cardians, with two of William Catesby's lessees, took over the Tanworth estate, and had to be ousted by action of novel disseisin [13; 83; 75–8; see also 59, 60].[23] In a countersuit for Harbury and Ladbroke, at the same assizes, the Cardians were nonsuited [71], and when the trespass suit finally went against them they sued a formedon for Tanworth against John Catesby [126], anticipating in dating of the writ, if not in fact, the death of William on the following day [79]. They were again nonsuited.

In the following year concerted action was planned against John Catesby: the Cardians brought a novel disseisin action for Ladbroke, while Archer, William Gammell, clerk, and Nicholas Odingsells, presumably as Cardian grantees [92], brought another for Tanworth [89, 127; 85–6, 128]. Archer's suit was evidently the more serious, and it was probably at this time that a list of Archer's alleged feudal defaults [140–2] was presented to the earl of Warwick, since the case was brought before Warwick's council concurrently with the novel disseisin. Initially Archer's case failed for lack of evidence [90], and the assize was nonsuited, despite a Yuletide agreement to expedite proceedings [92; 87, 91]. Suit was renewed, however, before both private and royal courts. The joint suit over Tanworth was continued for two years despite procedural hitches, but failed for want of proofs; Archer and Gammell each alleged that the other held a vital document [97]. Warwick's council, meanwhile, heard further representations [143; 94–6; 130–142], apparently without reaching any but a highly tentative and conditional decision; Catesby obtained a favourable inquisition post mortem to support his case [144; see also 13], but his opponents produced witnesses who attributed the dispute to suppressions and forgeries by William Catesby when acting as John Ladbroke's executor [13, 139]. The Cardians had fared less well in their efforts. Nothing came of their novel disseisin suit, and Catesby recovered a messuage in Ladbroke from them by cessavit, on their default [119–120]. Lewis Cardian persuaded successive employers, the bishop of Durham (then treasurer) and the duke of Gloucester, to hear the case before their councils, but on each occasion Catesby's defence survived, if only by default [13; 100].

At some stage Catesby seems to have made disposition of the lands in dispute. Robert Burgilon, a colleague of Catesby [97], purchased Tanworth from him [13; 164], and, indeed, initiated proceedings in his own right against Archer, Gammell, Odingsells, the Cardians, Hawkshaw, and others.[24] When, in 1390, the Cardians made a further effort to acquire

f.145Av (will dated 11 Sept. and proved 18 Sept. 1425); C 139/21, no. 11 (giving date of death as 8 Sept. 1425). See also J. Hutchins, *The History and Antiquities of the County of Dorset,* 3rd edn (London, 1861), I, 321, 347.

[20] Cardian remains an obscure figure. Despite this animosity towards the Catesby family, he held a dovecote and lands, at 5s. rent, from their Ladbroke estate: SC 6/1041/10, m.3. His tendency to change masters [13] resulted in litigation later, and in another land dispute he was excommunicated for defamation: *CCR 1399–1402,* 461, 512; *1409–13,* 389–90; *1413–19,* 36–7; *Select Cases in the Exchequer Chamber . . . 1377–1461,* ed. M. Hemmant (SS, LI, 1933), case 6; see also *VCH Warw,* V, 124–5.

[21] The record returned into chancery upon certiorari bears an endorsement of exemplification for John Catesby in November 1384: C 260/96, no. 33, mm.5–6.

[22] A few years earlier, Thomas and Juliana Walker, also disgruntled Tanworth landowners, complained that Archer was 'such a great maintainer, extortioner, and conducer of inquests in the area that none dare gainsay him': C 1/3/76–7.

[23] C 260/96, no. 33, mm.1–4: chancery record upon certiorari, without endorsement of exemplification.

[24] JUST 1/1501, m.34.

Ladbroke, they named in the writ both Catesby and William Brook, who was Catesby's receiver and feoffee, and sometime rector of Ladbroke.[25] The suit was unsuccessful; the Cardians were nonsuited after challenging the array [13; 148–51]. Brook and Burgilon, among several others, were also cited in the two writs sued by the Cardians in 1397 [166–170], and it seems likely that Ladbroke had passed, or was being passed, to feoffees.[26]

With the failure of their suit in 1390, the Cardians turned once more to private arbitration. They petitioned the earl of Warwick for reconsideration [152], and he arranged for a fresh hearing before two justices; Catesby, however, distrusted the adapted terms of reference suggested by the earl's chairman, and withdrew [99]. The Cardians again petitioned Warwick, without perceptible success [153–4]; at the same time they petitioned John of Gaunt, with like effect [155–6]. A petition to the king [158–9] was more successful, and the whole matter was rehearsed in chancery, where the chancellor, Arundel, found rather testily for Catesby [100], and offered the usual recourse to the common law. For a while this ruling had the desired effect, and the Cardians' case was not helped when Henry Ladbroke's supposed deed of entail was found in the possession of a clerk being investigated – perhaps at Catesby's suggestion – for forgery, and handed to Catesby [165]. Nevertheless the Cardians persisted. In another petition to Warwick they pointed out that Burgilon had sold his interest in Tanworth to the earl, and that their next step should be a formedon against the latter. Nothing came of it [164].

Two years later political events apparently played to the Cardians' advantage. On 12 July 1397 Warwick, as a former Appellant, was committed to the Tower and subsequently disgraced,[27] and on 18 August confiscations were ordered from Warwick and four of his major associates including Catesby [180]. On the first event the Cardians brought another novel disseisin against Catesby, perhaps at Gammell's instigation [177]; on the second they again petitioned the king [162]. Consequently a letter under the privy seal [160–1], elicited and conveyed by the Cardians' son-in-law, William Hathewick [13, 101], summoned Catesby before the council, where the plaintiffs were again referred to the common law [163]. Within a few days the confiscation order was revoked in Catesby's case [179; 125]. The Cardians followed the council's advice nonetheless, the more accessibly since king's bench was sitting in Warwickshire for the Michaelmas term. Twice they sued writs of novel disseisin against Catesby, his wife, Brook, Burgilon, and others, for Ladbroke, and twice they were nonsuited; on the latter occasion the court amerced them for persistent abuse of procedure [122–4; 166–71].[28] At the same sessions Bromley, the suspected forger, was presented by jury on various counts, including forgery of the Ladbroke entail and of the great seal [172–4, 178].[29] He pleaded guilty and made fine; he subsequently told differing tales about the origin of the disputed document [8–9; 12; 14; 116; 165; 175],[30] but no one defended the document itself, and suspicion remained and remains against Gammell and Cardian.[31]

Having failed to derive any advantage from the discomfiture of Warwick and Catesby, the Cardians resorted to direct action once more. The king's half-brother, the duke of Surrey, was now chief lord,[32] and Catesby was soon under instructions to produce his evidence yet again. Before anything could be done, the Cardians and others had occupied Ladbroke

25 As receiver general, he accounted to Catesby's wife Emma: E 101/511/15. He was one of the feoffees of 1384: *CAD*, III, A 4327.

26 E 41/376, mm.2, 3 are drafts (in hand IV, the second item being annotated by Catesby: below, 298) of enfeoffments of Ladbroke and several other holdings, to Catesby's use. In the first, dated Jan. 1388, the feoffees were William Trueman, parson of Ladbroke, William Brook, chaplain, and William Offchurch; in the second, undated but probably from the same period, they were Brook, rector of Barford, Offchurch, Purefoy, Metley, and John Astwell, chaplain – a list similar to that of co-defendants at [166].

27 *CCR 1396–9*, 140; *RP*, III, 379–80.

28 No record of these suits survives among the roll and writ files of king's bench for this term, save the stays of execution upon Gammell: below, n.446.

29 The jury in [172] includes numerous representatives of the Warwick interest.

30 The indictment returned into chancery upon certiorari bears an endorsement of exemplification for Catesby in July 1398: C 260/109, no. 30, mm.3–4d.

31 The deed of entail was still treated as significant by Catesby's opponents, despite this discredit [6–8, 13, 14, 107, 108, 115]; yet if it was genuine, or a reconstruction of a genuine entail destroyed by William Catesby when he had the opportunity [139], it was in John Catesby's interest to destroy it as soon as he obtained it – which clearly he did not do.

32 Ladbroke is not specified, but his other acquisitions from Warwick's estates are listed in *CPR 1396–9*, 429.

in force [103]. Catesby started novel disseisin proceedings with a writ dated the same day [103; 183], and the case was heard at assizes within a couple of months. The defence claimed judgment of the writ, because at the date when the writ was purchased the manor was occupied jointly by Hathewick, the duke of Surrey, and the duke of Exeter, who had been enfeoffed by the Cardians two days before the writ, which nevertheless failed to mention them. The jurors, unimpressed by this grand association, found for Catesby [104],[33] who was reseised accordingly [113]. Unfortunately for Catesby, Surrey, whose rôle in the affair was already suspect, was correspondingly unimpressed by the judgment, and appointed his own bailiff in Ladbroke [103, 105]. After fruitless conversations with Nicholas Gascoigne, Surrey's steward, Catesby therefore appealed directly to Surrey, by petition, that he might enjoy Ladbroke in peace or have a final arbitration by Surrey's council [105, 176]. Surrey complied, instructing Gascoigne to arrange the matter, and after some delays the duke's council, like its many predecessors, found for Catesby [13; 106–7]. Although apparently suspicious of Catesby's jealous guarding of the forged deed, Surrey seems to have accepted this decision, but early in the following year, perhaps at Hathewick's instigation, he enfeoffed his brother Exeter and his counsellor Shard, prior to departing for Ireland [108]. Shard, with the assistance of Spinney the escheator, took seisin shortly afterwards, and had to threaten the tenants when they spoke up for the Catesby claim [108, 181].

At this point someone – probably Hathewick[34] – petitioned the duke of Exeter, and arrangements were made for a definitive arbitrement by the dukes of Exeter and Surrey, to which the parties bound themselves by a hundred pounds apiece [109].[35] On 8 June 1399 a most distinguished legal gathering, explicitly supported by (among others) all but one of the justices of either bench, found for Catesby [109], and reinforced this with a written and sealed opinion a fortnight later [1–2]. Technically this should have been followed by an award of the arbitrators, Exeter and Surrey, but political activities supervened. Catesby followed the events of the Lancastrian revolution with a cautious eye [110–112], limiting his own involvement to a rather unsatisfactory conversation with Exeter, who had domestic worries at the time [110]. It was therefore with relief that he noted that, after the abortive conspiracy of Christmas 1399, the deaths of Surrey and Exeter as traitors released him from their potentially self-interested award [111], and left him with a testified opinion which effectively guaranteed his title against all comers.

The principal interest of this case lies in the wealth of judicial resorts invoked by the Cardians, and in the richness of the reporting. The common-law procedures, to which the matter was so often referred, were hardly selective in their operation; the Cardians defaulted again and again, without once offering justification for doing so. In their petitions they complained that John Catesby, as a 'man of law' and a 'man of the court', was obstructing them 'by mastery and maintenance', and by 'subtleties and cautels' arising from his professional expertise [158, 155], but they were not without their own subtleties. Their persistent defaults precluded issue and judgment, and the various authorities to which they appealed were thus unable to point to any definitive judgment, save perhaps the assize of novel disseisin (of its nature merely relative) against them in 1383. Technically if not in the fact of the matter, therefore, the Cardians' right to reopen the dispute survived at every stage. This was an elementary point of common law; but the position of decisions made elsewhere than in the common-law courts is more obscure.

One form of equitable decision was clearly defined, and was acknowledged by the courts: this was arbitrement, whereby parties to a dispute formally bound themselves, in writing and on pain of an agreed sum, to abide by the award of specified persons to whom the matter should be submitted for arbitration; a pending or completed arbitrement was a bar to action

33 C 260/109, no. 30, mm.1–2: chancery record upon certiorari, without endorsement of exemplification.

34 Catesby certainly prepared a petition to Exeter [184], but his account here [109] does not make sense if his own petition was involved; the Cardians and Hathewick, however, also stood to lose by the action of which Catesby complained.

35 Catesby retained the bond (now E 40/6408), dated 28 April 22 Richard II, whereby 'William Athewyk, and Lewis Cardian alias Lewis Cardigan' simply undertook to pay Catesby £100 at Trinity next. It is said to be sealed with 'our seals'; the second seal on the tongue is apparently from a signet ring crudely incised with three Ys, and is not readily attributable, but Miss Wendy Goldsmith points out that the first, being elliptical and bearing the Ladbroke blazon undifferentiated within a delicate foliate border, probably belonged to a female of the whole blood, and suggests that one of the parties used Alice Cardian's seal.

at common law.[36] Such procedures were well established by this date;[37] indeed, in a lesser dispute over Bubbenhall mill, in 1384, William Bagot suggested to Catesby the arbitrement of Lancaster and Warwick, or of four justices, or of twelve knights, but Catesby refused on the grounds of undue delay, and the matter was compromised at lovedays.[38] The final submission of the Ladbroke dispute to the dukes of Surrey and Exeter seems to have been the most nearly successful attempt at arbitrement made in this case [see also 87]; the award was never made, as Catesby noted [111], but there is no trace of further attempts at litigation, and the legal opinion itself may have been treated as a bar to action.[39]

It is, however, difficult to define the status of decisions made by councils. The evolution of private councils, and the sort of jurisdiction they exercised, are in general traced by the sparsest of data. Any magnate might be expected to organise meetings of his senior advisers and executives, and allusions to such councils survive from the twelfth century onwards.[40] Under feudal forms of allegiance this council would be closely similar to the honorial court, where disputes between major tenants were decided according to custom; but from the middle of the thirteenth century at the very latest, the professional administrator and the consultant specialist were often feed if not annuitant retainers,[41] and by the late fourteenth century a great lord would have as his council a diverse collection of wealthy and distinguished men.[42] In executing the lord's business, such a council of non-tenurial retainers would necessarily assume some sort of practical jurisdiction over lesser men related to the same lord by a similar nexus; it served, very approximately, as the honorial court of the bastard feudal structure.[43] This development did not take place without modification, extrapolation, and definition. The immediate relevance of a lord's conciliar jurisdiction was to disputes between his retainers, but it could clearly be invoked by a person of impermanent or tenuous connection, and as effectively as the lord's power could make it; we have John Catesby's word that he presented himself, and argued his case, before the council of the bishop of Durham and that of the duke of Gloucester, apparently summoned thither because Lewis Cardian was temporarily in employment successively with those lords [13; 100]. There is, indeed, reference to coercion in the statutes of 1391–3, which provide that defendants should not be 'bound, compelled, or constrained' to appear before seignorial councils.[44]

Although these statutes appear designed partly to prohibit this coercion, their main purpose evidently concerned definition of the jurisdiction which councils were coming to exercise. The enactment was

> That none of the king's lieges should henceforward be bound, compelled, or constrained in any way to come or appear before the council of any lord or

[36] e.g. *YB Ric. II: 12 Ric. II, 1388–9,* ed. G. F. Deiser (Ames Fdn, 1914), 164–6 (Pas.11), 37–8 (Mich.2); *YB Ric. II: 13 Ric. II, 1389–90,* ed. T. F. T. Plucknett (Ames Fdn, 1929), 20–22 (Trin.7), 104–5 (Hil.3). Chancery could, however, provide a forum for disputes about the terms of submission to arbitrement: C 44/33, no. 13 [1403].

[37] For an early reference, see *RP,* I, 58 (no. 148) [1290]. See also R. Brooke, *La Graunde Abridgement* (London, 1573), Arbitrement 6–9, 30, 53, for notes of reports from the middle of Edward III's reign onwards. For a better-known case from the 1420s, see *Paston Letters and Papers of the Fifteenth Century,* ed. N. Davis, I (Oxford, 1971), no. 5. Arbitration procedures, though lacking consistent evidence of the bonds which characterised arbitrement, were recognised by the common-law courts as early as the third quarter of the thirteenth century: e.g. KB 26/167, m.26 [I owe this reference to Dr P. A. Brand].

[38] E 41/394, m.3, schedules 4d, 6d.

[39] If the exclusion of real property from the scope of arbitrement (A. Fitzherbert, *La Graunde Abridgement* (London, 1577), Arbitrement 16 [1469]) was already current, the opinion would have been as effective as any award.

[40] T. F. T. Plucknett, *A Concise History of the Common Law,* 5th edn (London, 1956), 186 n.2; H. Johnstone in *Eng. Govt at Work,* I, 292; see also 'Baronial Councils and their Relation to Manorial Courts', in A. E. Levett, *Studies in Manorial History* (Oxford, 1938), 21–40.

[41] N. Denholm-Young, *Seignorial Administration in England* (London, 1937), 27–9.

[42] The working councils of the duke of Surrey [106] or the earl of Warwick [52] may be compared with the analysis of the roughly contemporary livery roll of the earl of Devon, in K. B. McFarlane, *The Nobility of Later Medieval England* (Oxford, 1973), 111.

[43] The history and work of one such council are explored in detail in C. Rawcliffe, 'The Staffords, Earls of Stafford and Dukes of Buckingham 1394–1521' (unpub. Ph.D. thesis, Univ. of Sheffield, 1974), pt 2, c. IV; I am grateful to Dr Rawcliffe for allowing me to use this work. See also R. Somerville, 'The Duchy of Lancaster Council and Court of Duchy Chamber', *TRHS,* 4th ser., XXIII (1941), 159–77; G. A. Holmes, *The Estates of the Higher Nobility in Fourteenth-Century England* (Cambridge, 1957), 76–8.

[44] 15 Ric. II, c.12; 16 Ric. II, c.2.

lady to answer for his freehold, or for any thing touching his freehold, or for any other real or personal thing pertaining to the law of the land, in any manner.

The commons' complaint, embodied in the first statute, objected specifically to 'the defeasance of the common law'. Plucknett apparently saw this complaint as a rearguard action against the adoption of equitable jurisdiction by seignorial councils,[45] but it seems possible to read it as a complaint against the abuses of those councils which invaded the territory of the common law (as, indeed, chancery was alleged to have done)[46] in attempting to extend what was becoming recognised as a proper equitable rôle;[47] in this context it is interesting that Catesby refused to submit to arbitration which might ignore his legal rights [99], although in general he was content to argue his case before seignorial councils, and even – at the last – to suspend his procedural rights, against the advice of the justices [cf. 1 with 2]. The close view of seignorial councils in action afforded by the Ladbroke documents reveals an elaborate and well-defined (though flexible) institution, and invites very close comparison with the royal equivalent, chancery and the king's council.[48] Procedure was or could be initiated by petitions of similar form and standard phraseology [152, 153, 164, to Warwick; 158, 162, to the king; 176, to Surrey]; hearings were formal, for the most part, the parties being represented by counsel in strength [52, 143, 130, before Warwick's council; 106, before Surrey's council; 100, in chancery]; matters thought to be accessible to common-law actions were referred accordingly [59, by Warwick's council; 100 and 163, by chancery and by the king's council].[49] The only conspicuous differences – apart from the greater volume of business and the more extensive sanctions which chancery had – are the delegation of business [96, 99] to a subcommittee of the seignorial council (which surely corresponds to the delegation of royal council business to chancery), and the likelihood that the earl of Warwick kept better records than chancery did [130n.].[50] The calling of witnesses is here only apparent at a session of Warwick's council [52–8], but it was a common practice.[51] The general homogeneity of these equity proceedings argues that seignorial councils exercised an accepted and possibly long-standing equitable jurisdiction;[52] it also reinforces the identification

[45] Plucknett, *Common Law*, 675: '. . . the feeling among contemporaries that the old institutions were no longer entirely adequate – even the seignorial courts felt the same difficulty, and met it in the same way by erecting councils . . . which became courts of equity. A long struggle in Parliament failed to check this development either at Westminster or in many seignorial jurisdictions, and in the end the situation was accepted.'

[46] *RP*, III, 267 (no. 33) [1389].

[47] It may be significant that the statute directed victims of such coercion to the chancellor, rather than to the courts. On conciliar rôles in litigation, see Rawcliffe, 'Staffords', especially 237–42.

[48] Since closely similar petitions, addressed to the king and seeking hearings before his council [158, 100], were treated respectively in chancery [100] and before the council [163], and since the council apparently referred the plaintiffs to the common law because that had been the judgment in chancery [163], there seems little point in attempting either to identify their practical functions or to distinguish qualitatively between their jurisdictions at this date, although it is possible that the council normally dealt with matters affecting lands in the king's hand [162–3]. See also G. O. Sayles, *The King's Parliament of England* (London, 1975), 110, and in *King's Bench*, V, xciii; cf. J. F. Baldwin, *The King's Council in England during the Middle Ages* (Oxford, 1913), 244–55.

[49] Settlement by seignorial council (if parties accepted it) was regarded as preferable to the problems of prolonged litigation: Rawcliffe, 'Staffords', 258–9.

[50] The 'probable loss of material from the earliest period' (i.e. before 1417) covered by Early Chancery Proceedings (C 1), suspected by M. E. Avery, 'The History of the Equitable Jurisdiction of Chancery before 1460', *BIHR*, XLII (1969), 130 – which would detract from her mainly quantitative account of developments before, and possibly after, 1417 – seems far more than probable; *Cardian* v. *Catesby* is one such item lost. Some materials relating to the earliest period of C 1 are to be found among the medievalia in Answers, etc. (C 4), currently under arrangement, and perhaps among the Common Law Pleadings (C 44), especially pieces 36–37B. At best the chancery records seems to have consisted of bills, answers, replications, and rejoinders, together with memoranda and examinations; there is no evidence of attempts to maintain a record of verbal proceedings or of decisions taken (perhaps because such decisions were insufficiently binding to be 'of record'), beyond the miscellaneous annotations sometimes jotted on the pleadings.

[51] For a record of the examination of witnesses in chancery in this period, see the proceedings in *Domingo* v. *Prophet* (1378): C 44/37B, unnumbered memorandum and examinations.

[52] At a humbler level, urban guilds and fraternities made provision for arbitration between their members, with recourse to formal legal procedures allowed – grudgingly, and sometimes under penalty – as a subsequent expedient: *A Book of London English 1384–1425*, ed. R. W. Chambers and M. Daunt (Oxford, 1931), 43–4, 55; *English Gilds*, ed. T. Smith, L. T. Smith, and L. Brentano (Early Eng. Text Soc.,

of chancery's equitable jurisdiction as, ultimately, a function of the king's council.[53] Yet in no case, excepting the internal crossreference from council to chancery, does an equitable judgment seem to have been binding;[54] indeed, two litigants in 1387 formally put themselves on the chancellor's arbitrement, thereby implying that his judgment did not of itself constitute a bar to further litigation.[55] The chancellor's threat to imprison Alice Cardian if she continued to pester Warwick [100] seems like a prerogative expedient rather than the declaration of a bar to equitable suit, and nothing but the arbitrement of 1399 (and, perhaps, the subsequent desire of maintainers for a quieter life)[56] inhibited appeals to noble or royal councils.

A further point of interest, as much for social as for legal history, is the tenacity of the litigation. The Cardians themselves give little evidence of ample means, and they were pressing an extremely doubtful claim to a manor worth – prestige apart – at best around twenty pounds a year,[57] against a seasoned administrator and his lawyer son, both of whom ranked with the upper gentry. The lawsuits were not merely frequent and protracted; employing, as did both sides, the finest lawyers of the day, they must have been heavily expensive.[58] This suggests that the Cardians' understandable desire to claim Ladbroke was being exploited for secondary purposes by wealthy patrons, and other evidence, together with John Catesby's occasional asides, supports this. Ladbroke was held of the honor of Warwick, and the Catesbys' involvement with the earl was complex. Nevertheless, William Catesby managed to annoy Warwick by disputing the wardship of the Ladbroke heir [51], and this may well explain why Warwick is twice mentioned as having supported the Cardians during the lifetime of William Catesby [6, 13]. With William's death, and John Catesby's rise in the earl's favour and administration,[59] almost to the point of sharing his political disgrace,[60] it is hardly surprising to find that the enthusiasm for the case was now sustained by Thomas Archer [71], whose representation of the earl's interests [130–8] was clearly self-interested. But at some stage – it is impossible to say precisely when – weightier influence was brought to bear. Sir William Bagot, that brazen but always successful turncoat, was of gentle birth,[61] but he probably owed much of his political rise to Warwick's patronage.[62] Hedging his political bets – he attached himself to the Lancastrian interest as well[63] – he entered parliament for

[Orig. ser.], XL, reissued 1924), 21, 76, 96, 101, 115, 158–9, 279–80. A late record shows formal arbitrement by the Exeter Tailors in 1481: ibid., 322–3. In the fifteenth century the mayor and sheriff of Bristol held informal arbitration sessions at regular intervals, to obviate litigation, thus providing (according to Ricart in 1479) 'the greatest preservation of peace and good rule . . . that can be imagined': ibid., 426. Dr Caroline Barron tells me that such procedures were frequently recorded in the fifteenth-century City of London Journals, in the Corporation of London Records Office.

53 Avery, *BIHR,* XLII, 141–3. For the 'administrative function' arguments see B. Wilkinson in *Eng. Govt at Work,* I, 190–5; cf. Sayles in *King's Bench,* V, lxvii–xcvii.

54 Much earlier, however, there were objections when a case settled before a seignorial council was reopened in king's bench: *Letters of Edward Prince of Wales 1304–1305,* ed. H. Johnstone (Roxburghe Club, 1931), xxiv–xxv.

55 *Domingo* v. *Prophet* (1378), cited above. This may, however, represent recognition of the distinction between the common-law and equity functions. Chancery had long had the power to enforce the conduct and observance of arbitrements undertaken: *RP,* I, 58 (no. 148) [1290]; see also III, 287–8 (nos. 17–18) [1391], 573 (no. 35) [1406].

56 See next paragraph.

57 SC 6/1041/10, mm.1–3; 12, m.2.

58 In 1386, for example, before Warwick's council [143], Catesby's counsel were Burgilon and Frisby (JPs), Cassy (later chief baron of the exchequer), and Clopton and Lockton (serjeants, destined for the bench). The Cardians' lesser array nonetheless comprised Wadham (serjeant, destined for the bench) and two apprentices, Woodrow and Kirkby.

59 Dugdale, *Warwickshire,* 553; the Warwick attorney in the exchequer must have been this John Catesby's son, and perhaps identifies the latter with the John Catesby who was a clerk in the exchequer in 1401: *CFR 1399–1405,* 147.

60 Catesby's connection with Warwick was very probably exaggerated in order to inculpate the former with the latter.

61 For an outline of his life, see G. Wrottesley, 'A History of the Bagot Family', Wm Salt Arch. Soc., *Hist. Colls,* New ser., XI (1908), 45–54.

62 ibid., 46; A. Goodman, *The Loyal Conspiracy: The Lords Appellant under Richard II* (London, 1971), 148. The famous doggerel on Richard II's ministers stressed Warwick's contribution: 'A bearward found a rag; of the rag he made a bag; he did in good intent': *Political Songs and Poems,* ed. T. Wright, I (RS, 1859), 364.

63 This allegiance is apparent from 1379 to 1393 at least, and revived miraculously after 1399: Wrottesley, Wm Salt Arch. Soc., New ser., XI, 47; T. F. Tout, *Chapters in the Administrative History of Mediaeval England* (Manchester, 1920–33), IV, 13. He also used the aegis of the earl of Nottingham: ibid., 12.

Warwickshire, in the period of Warwick's ascendancy as a Lord Appellant, while managing to maintain and foster his favour with Richard himself;[64] this enabled him to take Richard's side against Warwick when the time came [180]. It also enabled him to attack the Catesby interest. Some years earlier John Catesby had served with Nicholas Lilling on a commission which accused Bagot of waste on land in his charge,[65] and later, when Catesby was sitting as justice of the peace, Bagot was indicted for felony.[66] These incidents were part of a long feud. Catesby recorded the shady means by which Bagot acquired Baginton manor in 1383 and Draycote two years later, and his own acrimonious dispute with Bagot over the operation of Bubbenhall mill;[67] by 1397 he was sure that Bagot was behind the Cardians' latest attempts on Ladbroke.[68] The feud may have determined political sympathies: not only was Catesby attached to the disgraced Warwick, but his opposition to the court party is also evident from a draft petition for parliament, proposing revocation of the arbitrary proceedings at the 1397–8 session.[69] He was, however, unafraid of his adversary [102], who soon became too busy saving his own skin to maintain local feuds, and by the time litigation lapsed Catesby did not even trouble to note Bagot's escape from the general slaughter of Richard's favourites [110].[70] Catesby's right to Ladbroke manor, therefore, was not enought to protect him from the harassment of rival interests, and the elaboration of the legal defence shows how much cost in time and money such harassment could exact.

The surviving documentation, as mentioned earlier, falls into two categories: Catesby's roll of evidences, and the working papers preparatory to the legal opinion of 1399. Apart from the various loose transcripts attached to the roll of evidences, which were clearly commissioned from the originating courts of record, only four hands are found. Hand I – that of the preliminary repertory of deeds [31–50, 60–64] – may be associated with William Catesby's activities, before his son took over the estates and the litigation. Hand II, which was responsible for the abstract of title [15–30] and for most of the narrative, later transcripts, and annotations on the roll of evidences, is either that of John Catesby himself or (less plausibly) of his amanuensis. The fluent French of the man of law occasionally breaks into the first person, clearly referring to Catesby [103–8, 156], and the draft of Catesby's petition to Surrey [176], in the same hand, suggests that the author rather than his secretary was writing.[71] Sundry lapses such as *dy* for *ditz* [71] could be phonetic rather than calligraphic, but they are too few to weigh against such factors as the inconsistent use of first and third persons, or the rapid correction of minor blunders, for example in names, which would be unlikely to feature in dictated longhand. There is in the same hand a letter from the earl of Warwick to Robert Brown, his steward at Tanworth, notifying him of Catesby's fealty and authorising the taking of security for his relief.[72] There are minor inconsistencies in the hand between document and document, but comparison with a scrappier and more desultory compilation of evidences and memoranda proves the identity of hands beyond doubt.[73] This leaves two hands, both associated with the opinion of 1399. Hand III provided the shorter version of the

64 ibid., 11–15, 25, 48, 52, 55–6.

65 *CIM,* IV, no. 299 [1385].

66 ibid., VII, no. 36 [1396]. Catesby's friends on the Warwickshire bench also heard indictments relating to Bagot: *Rolls of the Warwickshire and Coventry Sessions of the Peace 1377–1397,* ed. E. G. Kimball (Dugdale Soc., XVI, 1939), 75–7 (nos. 15–18) [1396].

67 E 41/394, m.3, schedules 4–4d, 6d.

68 Bagot, as sheriff, had collaborated with Archer as early as 1384 [87], and in 1397, in maintenance of the suit, he had a jury empanelled at Baginton, his own manor [101], both the sheriff and the undersheriff being his henchmen [102]; he was still interfering when the Cardians took direct action [103–4], and Catesby noted that he was paying the expenses of the plaintiffs [167]. The losses were apparently borne by Gammell [177], who may have been Bagot's agent – one Henry Gammell was working for Bagot in 1383: E 41/394, m.3, schedule 4.

69 E 41/376, m.23: J. B. Post, 'A privately drafted common petition of 1398–9', *Jnl Soc. Archivists,* VI (1978).

70 Bagot survived to gain an exchequer annuity of £100 (17 Nov. 1400), a comprehensive pardon at the petition of the commons (26 Feb. 1401), and a peaceful death (10 Sept. 1407): *CPR 1399–1401,* 386, 502; *RP,* III, 458; Wrottesley, Wm Salt Arch. Soc., New ser., XI, 53. His career would repay detailed study.

71 A fragment of draft letter in the same hand is in a Catesby file: E 41/376, m.9.

72 Derby Central Lib., Palmer-Morewood Colln, unsorted Palmer-Morewood miscellanea. Despite the hand, and the fact that it is on paper, this is clearly the original, since the folds correspond to traces of an applied seal. Dated at London, 14 Nov. [1383].

73 E 41/394.

narrative [13], and perhaps – although comparison of a cursive memorandum with an engrossing hand is unreliable – the surviving original of the opinion [2]. Hand IV provided both drafts of the opinion, the note arguing that Ladbroke and Tanworth were not entailed, the transcript of the testimony of the men of Coventry, and the fuller exposition of the Catesby case [1, 3–14]. The writer was a Catesby employee, as is shown by (for example) an expense account for a trip to London,[74] and an account roll for the Catesby household.[75] Although no direct evidence to identify the writer is forthcoming, William Offchurch, clerk (otherwise William Clerk of Offchurch) is a strong candidate for association with this hand, on grounds of long connection with the family [e.g. 42, 60], his particular connection with the draft enfeoffments in a Catesby file,[76] and his employment by Catesby,[77] notably as steward.[78] If, however, John Offchurch, clerk [106], was the son of William, and was also the unnamed clerk paid with him in 1392, an entry on the household account roll, recording the purchase of wine 'for my father',[79] might support the identification of John rather than William as the writer of Hand IV. The association of this hand with the drafting of the opinion perhaps casts some doubt on the independence of the latter, but the provision of clerical staff was one way for Catesby to share the considerable expenses, and some of the subsidiary documents, especially the abstract of title in Catesby's hand [15–30], were ex parte submissions, or perhaps notes for counsel.

Since 1400 the documents have suffered various fates. All those presented here, and their related materials, were in the possession of John Catesby at that date, and descended with the family muniments. Robert Catesby sold Ladbroke to the Dudley family in 1597, and the absence from the attested opinion and the Warwick letter of the archival annotations found on their scattered cousins suggests that these two items accompanied the manor. The property passed to the Palmer family, and the opinion was in Sir William Palmer's possession when Dugdale wrote.[80] It was one of the 'fishes' which Harvey 'had not time to pull out' when searching the Palmer-Morewood muniments, then at Alfreton, in 1914,[81] since it is now in the Palmer-Morewood Collection, among documents which Harvey certainly used.[82] The residue remained in the Catesby family until the attainder of the late Robert Catesby in 1605 for his part in the Gunpowder Plot;[83] they then passed into the custody of Arthur Agarde, deputy chamberlain of the exchequer, who kept a bag of Catesby evidences 'selected by me out of two great hanapers delivered in to me'.[84] The selection thus described in 1610 had probably been made before March 1607, when the class was available to searchers,[85] and it was presumably then that Agarde gave the main roll its archival marking.[86] It is not certain how long the bulk of the Catesby evidences remained intact. In 1633, when Scipio Le Squire was deputy chamberlain, some of the evidences were released to Sir Simon Archer,[87] who – quite apart from his descent from the devious Thomas[88] – had the dual claim of

74 E 41/376, m.8. There are references to 'the master', William Brook, and Gadifer [Giles], and one of the expenses was the entertainment of John Reed.

75 E 101/510/21, headed with unintentional irony 'Rotulus expensarum domus Johannis de Catesby et yconomie facte per uxorem eiusdem . . . '

76 E 41/376, mm.2, 3.

77 E 101/511/15, m.1: fees to Offchurch and his clerk (1392).

78 SC 6/1041/12, r.1, m.2

79 E 101/510/21, m.2.

80 Dugdale, *Warwickshire,* 235, working from transcripts made by Dodsworth at Palmer's Clerkenwell house in 1650: N. Denholm-Young and H. H. E. Craster, 'Roger Dodsworth (1585–1654) and his Circle', *Yorks Arch. Jnl,* XXXII (1936), 32.

81 Harvey, *Ladbroke,* ix.

82 See the note of documents in use, signed S.H.A.H., 5 Apr. 1913, in Derby Central Lib., Palmer-Morewood Colln, unsorted Warwickshire miscellanea.

83 There is no indication that any muniments remained in crown custody after reversal of the forfeitures of 1397 and 1485, although in the latter case some lands had already been alienated: Roskell, *Bull. Jn Rylands Lib.,* XLII, 170–4.

84 Agarde's 'Compendium of the Records in the Treasury', in *The Antient Kalendars and Inventories of the Treasury of His Majesty's Exchequer,* ed. F. Palgrave (RC, 1836), II, 325.

85 St Loe Kniveton (for whom see Denholm-Young and Craster, *Yorks Arch. Jnl,* XXXII, 14–15) made extracts, apparently dated 31 Mar. 1607: Bodleian Lib., MS Dodsworth 82, f.16. I am grateful to Miss Sula Rayska for her efforts to document this elusive antiquary.

86 All the seventeenth-century archival markings consist of jottings of manors, counties, or occasionally subjects, in a convenient place on the outside of the document as stored.

87 *Ant. Kals,* III, 426 (now E 101/337/7).

88 J. Burman, *The Story of Tanworth-in-Arden, Warwickshire* (Birmingham, 1930), 57–8.

being the owner of several former Catesby holdings and of being a most zealous Warwickshire antiquary.[89] The main roll and one of the original deeds [48] remain in the Archer Collection, now with the Shakespeare Birthplace Trust. Those of the evidences which remained in crown custody suffered a countywise sortation, probably during Peter Le Neve's tenure of office between 1684 and 1713,[90] and the permanence of this scattering may be inferred from the variety of modern references which these documents now bear.

The documents fall into no natural sequence; here the drafts of the 1399 opinion [1] are followed by the final version [2] and then by the subsidiary notes [3–30], and lastly by the Catesby roll of evidences [31–183] and a related draft petition [184]. The roll offers no sequence of entries which is both physical and logical; the order adopted here (mm.1, 1d, 2 . . . , with schedules in sequence at the end) necessitates only trifling breaches of the sequence on the roll, and these are noted. All entries in Latin, and deeds in French, being overwhelmingly in common form or the language of common form, have been calendared fully; those in French, deeds excepted, have been transcribed. Variants and scribal blunders in orthography or calligraphy, together with contemporary or subsequent archival markings, have been omitted; semantic and material variants and alterations, together with doubtful readings unconfirmed by other sources, have been noted. Deletions, which in all cases were made by striking through, are noted, as are blanks and omissions; hiatus (. . .) indicate illegible or lost passages of text. Asterisks and daggers represent prickings and crosses as procedural annotations. As well as the normal extension of contractions, the proper names of persons and places have been supplied where the text lapses into initials, but only as sanctioned elsewhere in the text. Punctuation and capitals are editorial.

I am most grateful to the following for assistance in tracing documents and (where relevant) for obtaining or giving permission to print them: The Shakespeare Birthplace Trust (for the earl of Plymouth), Dr Levi Fox, and Mr Robert Bearman; Derby Central Library, Mrs Langworthy, and Miss Taylor; Mr Philip Styles; Mrs Ann Morton; the County Archivist for Warwickshire. The Shakespeare Birthplace Trust kindly released MS DR 37/82 on temporary deposit in the Public Record Office. I am also grateful to Mrs Christine Carpenter, Dr R. F. Hunnisett, Mrs Margaret Post, and, especially, Dr P. A. Brand, for their constructive criticisms during the preparation of these texts.

89 Dugdale, *Warwickshire,* dedication; P. Styles, *Sir Simon Archer, 1581–1662* (Dugdale Soc., Occ. Papers, VI, 1946).

90 The archival markings on most of the survivors bear a strong resemblance to Le Neve's annotations in Agarde's 'Compendium': *Ant. Kals,* II, 325; and see the original, now IND 17126, pt I, f.6. For Le Neve, see N. J. Williams, 'The Work of Peter Le Neve at Chapter House, Westminster', *Jnl Soc. Archivists,* I, 126–7.

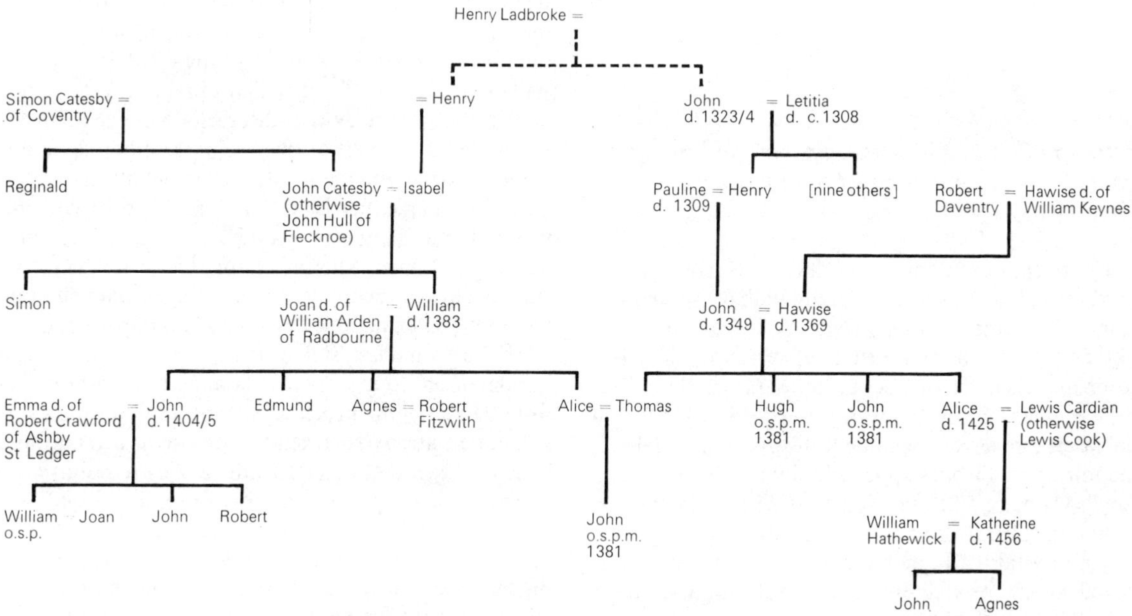

Principal sources (apart from documents printed here): the wills of Letitia and Pauline Ladbroke (E 40/4583 and 4580) printed in Harvey, *Ladbroke*, 64-5; Baker, *County of Northampton*, I, 244-5, 351-5; Dugdale, *Warwickshire*, 232, 551.

Broken lines indicate probable but uncertain relationships.

TEXT

E 163/6/46, ff.1, 2 [*Drafts, on paper; text from f.2 (here 'B') with variants noted from f.1 (here 'A'). Hand IV*]

[1] A trespuisantz princes les ducz de Surreie et Dexcestre, lour tresdotez seignurs William Gascoin,[91] Robert Tirewhit, [92] Johan Rede, et [93] William Skrene, [94] lours humblez suges et servauntz de la ley, totez maners de reverences et honours a si hautz princes duez. Et purtaunt, nos tresdotez seignurs, qe debat eit este entre Johan de Catesby, tenant del manoir de Lodbrokes appelle Lodbrokes maner, et Lowis Cardian, Alice sa femme, et William Hathewik, clamantz estat et droit en le dit manoir, de quele cleym et estat il ad este plesaunt[95] a vostre seignurie davoir nostre avys, discrecioun, et relacioun, desoutz nos seals, come apiert par vos hautz seneschalles et autres de vostre conseil dune part et dautre esteaunt presentz: sur qoi please a vostre treshaute seignurie entendre qe ore a la quynseine de la Trinite, en presence de parties susditz, nous avoms examine touz lours evidences del un part et del autre, les parties avantditz lun et lautre eyauntz ovesqe eaux serjauntez de la ley et autres sages de lour counseil; et[96] le dit Johan de Catesby ad moustre plusours grandes evidences de record et autrement,[97] qe lour entre ne poet ascunement estre meyntenuz par la ley.[98] Et nous sur ceo eiauntz lavys et discrecioun de monsire Walter de Clopton,[99] monsire William Tyrnyng,[100] monsire Johan Cassi,[101] monsire Johan Hull,[102] mounsire William Rychull,[103] Johan de Marcham,[104] William Hangford,[105] et William Brenchesle,[106] justices,[107] nostre avys et discrecioun est qe le dit Johan de Catesby eit et tigne sa possescioun en le dit maner, sanz ascunement estre ouste del dit manoir ou dascun parcel par les ditz Lowis, Alice, et William Hathwik, ou ascun altre clamaunt estat par eaux; et qe lez ditz Lowis, Alice sa femme,[108] et Wylliam Hathewich, ou ascun altre clamant estat par eaux ou par ascun de eaux, soient a lour accioun par voi de suyt a la[109] comune lay, si ils voient qe soit a fere; et qe si ils comensent lour suit entre la date dicestez et la feste de Pentecost prochein venant, et trovount a dit Johan de Catesby suffisaunt surtee qe ils attendrount issue et juggement de la dit suit sanz estre nounsuez[110] ou suffrer le dit proces estre discontinue,[111] qe adonqe le dit Johan de Catesby vendra,[112] par ly ou par son attorne, a primer jour del brief returnable, et pledera a lour accioun; et sils ne comencent lour suite avant le dit fest de Pentecost, ou[113] ne trovent le dit surtee come desuis, qe adonqe le dit Johan eit en chescun suite devers ly touz ses delays et avauntages par la ley luy durra.[114] Et ceo qe nous avoms ouste les delaies qe le dit Johan de Catesby avereit par la ley est soulement pur taunt qe les altres parties allegeount si grant povert qe ils ne sount mie del esee longement pursuer – les justices suisditz a ceo nient acordanz, pur taunt qe ceo est encountre la[115] ley et concience.[116] A qels avys, discrecioun, et relacioun a fere a vostre hautesse, nous vos ditz ser-

[91] KS 1396–1400; CJKB 1400–1413. Here and elsewhere, information on legal appointments is derived, unless otherwise stated, from Sayles in *King's Bench,* VI, App. II–XVII, and from Foss, *Judges of England,* IV.

[92] KS 1398–1408; JKB 1408–1428.

[93] Omitted B.

[94] KS 1408–1414. There is a brief Skrene pedigree at C 47/37/5, no. 46.

[95] Interlined above *pleynant,* deleted A.

[96] Omitted A.

[97] *et autrement* interlined above interlineation A.

[98] *le dit Johan . . . par la ley* interlined A.

[99] KS 1377–1388; CJKB 1388–1400.

[100] KS 1387; JCP 1388–1396; CJCP 1396–1413.

[101] Chief baron of the exchequer 1389–1400.

[102] JKB 1389–1407.

[103] KS 1383–8; JCP 1389–1407.

[104] KS 1388–95; JCP 1396–1408.

[105] KS 1389–98; JCP 1398–1413; CJKB 1413–22.

[106] KS 1389–98; JCP 1398–1406.

[107] Omitted A.

[108] *sa femme* omitted A.

[109] *a la* interlined above *de,* deleted A.

[110] *sanz estre nounsuy* interlined A.

[111] *ou suffret . . . discontinue* omitted A.

[112] After *qel,* deleted B.

[113] Above *et,* deleted B; *et* A.

[114] *et sils . . . durra* is inserted from the foot of the page by a double dagger A.

[115] Omitted A.

[116] *les justices . . . consience* interlined A. Dr Sayles, in *King's Bench,* VII, App. VI, takes the second part of this clause to be part of the plaintiffs' allegation, that 'to deny them justice because they were poor was "against law and conscience"'. It seems rather that the justices were dissociating themselves from Catesby's waiver of his procedural rights.

vantz William Gascoin, Robert Tyrewhit, Johan Rede, et William Skrene a ceste present briefe[117] patente[118] avoms mys nos seals. Escrit etc.[119]

Derby Central Lib., Palmer-Morewood Colln, unsorted Palmer-Morewood miscellanea [*Parchment, originally sealed close with four applied seals. Hand III?*][120]

[2] A lour tresdoutez seignurs les ducs de Surreie et Dexcestre, voz humblez servauntz William Gascoigne, Robert Tirewhit, Johan Rede, et William Skryne, totez maners de reverences et honours a si hautz seignurs duez. Et, tresdoutez seignurs, come Johan de Catesby dun part et William Athewyk et Lowis Cardyan dautre part soient entrechaungeablement obligez et chescun de eaux a autry en cent livers, come en les lettres obligatories appiert, sur condicioun qe siles parties avauntdites estoient a la garde de vous, tresdoutez seignurs, quant vous plerra a faire acordaunt a nostres discrecioun, avys, et relacioun, desouth noz sealx, sur due examinacioun par nous afaire sur les evidences des parties suisdites, a la quinszeyne de la Trinite darrain passee, a Loundres, de toutz debates et cleyms qe les ditz William et Lowis et Alice sa femme ount, ou ascun dels ad, ou ascun autre clamant estate par eux ou estate dependaunt de lour estate, devers le dit Johan de Catesby del manoir de Lodbrok appelle Lodbrokesmaner, et la dite agarde facent et perfournent en maner suisdite, qe adonqe les obligaciouns perdent lour force sicome par endentures eut faitz, et vers les dites parties demurantz, et par les dites[121] parties devant nous moustrez, appiert: please a voz treshautz seignuries entendre qe ore a la dite quinszeyne nous vos ditz servauntz avoms a noz scien, avys, et discrecioun, ove grand diligence, examinez toutz lour evidences des ambes parties; sur quelles examinementz nous voz ditz servauntz, a la reverence de vostre hautesse, eiauntz lavys et discrecioun de monsire Wauter de Clopton, monsire William Thirnyng, monsire Johan Cassy, monsire Johan Hulle, monsire William Rikhull, William Hankford, et William Brenchesle, justices nostre seignur le roi, de queux lour avys et discrecioun sount qe le dit Johan de Catesby tigne et occupie le dit manoir ove lez apertinances en peisible possessioun, saunz ascunement estre oustez ou destourbez sinoun par suite par brief a la comune ley, si les ditz clamantz veient qe soit afaire; sauvez a dit Johan de Catesby toutz avauntages qe la ley luy donne en cele partie. Certifions a voz hautessez qe noz discrecioun, avys, et relacioun sount solonqe lavys et discrecioun de lez justices avauntditz, et sicome desuis est declaree; et en outre please a voz hautessez entrendre qe le dit Johan de Catesby ad grauntee, al reverence de vos tresgraciousez seignuries, qe si les avantditz William Athewyk, Lowis, et Alice, ou ascun de eaux, ou ascun autre clamant estate par eaux, voillent user accioun a la comune ley devers le dit Johan de Catesby par brief del manoir avauntdit, ou de ascun parcell dycell, et purchecent eut lour brief entre cy et le fest de Penthecost proschein venant apres la date dicestez, et facent la sommons en mesme le brief estre fait duement par quinze jours devaunt la retourn dycell, et auxint facent sufficeant seurtee a dit Johan de Catesby qils pursueront ove effect sanz essoigne, et attendront le issue et le juggement de la dite pursuite sanz estre nounsuez ou suffrer la proces estre discontinuee, le dit Johan de Catesby pledera en chief a primer jour qils averount en court apres, sanz delay prendre par esson, voucher, eide prier, receyt, prorogacioun, ou proteccioun, sauvez a chescun des partiez lour chalanges et avantages a lez[122] array et les testez enpanelletz en la suite avantdite, la dite seurtee trove par quinsze jours avaunt le dit brief retournee; et si le dit Johan face dimise del dite manoir, ou de ascun parcell dicell, et les ditz clamantz demandent de dit Johan les nouns des enfeffez dicelles, il a els les delivera sanz delay noun resonable, parissint qe le dit Johan de Catesby soit garny duement a Asshby Legier par quinsze jours devant; et le dit Johan de Catesby, sur la dite seurtee a luy fait come desuis, ferra a ditz clamantz sufficeant seurtee qil ou sez enfeffez suisditz plederont en chief sanz delay, en la fourme avauntdite; purveu toute foitz qe si les avauntditz William Athewyk, Lowis, et Alice, ou ascun de eaux, ou ascun autre clamant estate par eaux, ne purchacent lour brief devant le dit fest de Penthecost come desuis est dit, ou sils purchacent lour brief et ne trovent seurtee come desuis est dit, adonqe le dit Johan de Catesby et sez enfeffez serrount a large a la comune ley en chescun suite qe serra pris envers eaux. Et cest nostre relacioun nous voz ditz servauntz certifioms a vostre hautesse desouth noz sealx par ycestez. Escript a Loundres le

[117] *bre'* B, perhaps in error for *l[ett]re*; *lettre* A.

[118] Interlined A.

[119] *Escrit a London* A.

[120] See [109] and note.

[121] Interlined.

[122] Altered from *le*.

vyntisme jour de juin, lan du regne le roi Richard le second vyntisme seconde [1399].[123]
[*Endorsed*] A lour tresdoutez seignurs les ducs de Surreie et Dexcestre.

E 40/6362 [*Paper. Hand IV*]

[3] A prover qe Lodbrok et Toneworth ne furent pas taillez: en primes, purtaunt qe monsire Henry de Lodbroke fuist mesmes seisi del manoir deus anz apres ceo qe lour faus fait purporte date, come est prove par soun fet de les fet a Adam Fleckenho et Roger soun fitz,[124] etc.
[4] Item, qe anno quarto le roi qe dirain moruist, le dit monsire Henry lessa les ditz manoirs a monsire Johan soun fitz a terme de sa vie, come est prove par soun fet endente. [*cf.* 135].
[5] Item, qe le dit mounsire Johan, en soun lit moriaunt, bargayna ove William de Catesby les ditz manoirs en maner, etc., qe Hawyse sa femme avereit le manoir de Toneworth a terme de sa vie, et pur ceo le lerroit tut soun dower en le manoir de Lodbrok, come est prove par fyn et par fet.
[6] Item, ils ne moustrerent unqe fet de tayll pendaunt le debat bien a qatre anx, Thomas de Beauchamp quorest, nadgairs count de Warr', esteaunt lour susteinour, ou ils graunteront le manoir de Lodbrok estre fee simple, et qe si Johan de Catesby purroit trover synk homes de Lodbrok, et un Johan Cook,[125] qi voudreyent jurer le fet de feffement, etc., estre boun et effectuel, qe le dit Johan tendroit le dit manoir sanz estre enpeche, en pees, etc., qele chose estoit fet, come est prove par mandamus et le serement Johan Cook [53], prove par le seignur de Fereres de Groby et altres, escrit de la meyn le clerc Frysby.
[7] Item, coment le faus fet fu trove en la garde Thomas Bromley, et par soun comaundement livere a Johan de Catesby, come le fet qe fuit faus et feynt, etc.
[8] Item, coment apres le fet fu trove faus en banc le roi, par chivalers et esqiers del comte de Warr', et par le conysance Bromley mesme, etc.
[9] Item, del instrument fet a Warr', et coment apres a Coventre le vicare de la Trinite conust certeins articles en le dit instrument estre faus, come est prove par les seals serteins bons gentz de Coventre, etc. [12]
dorse
[10] Item, atut ceo qe estoit fet en banc le roi a Coventre, Lowys et Alice et William Hathewyk estoient presentz, a quele temps Lowis et Alice porterent deus assises del dit manoir ver le dit Johan de Catesby, chescun de eaux apres autre, et estoient noun suez en lun et en lautre, et amerciez en cent soutz, etc.
[11] Item, a prover la continuace[126] le dit Johan est de lour porter de treis assises, etc.

E 40/14792 [*Transcript; paper. Hand IV*]

[12] A touz icels qe cestes lettres verrount ou orrount, Johan Northwode de Coventre, Johan Barewe, Johan Styward, et David Corby de mesme la vill,[127] saluz en Dieu. Come almoign et chose merytorie soit a tesmoigner verite, sachez nous tesmoignoms sur nostre foi par icestes, qen nostre presence, la samady prochein apres la feste de Seint Hill' derayn passe, en la esglise cathedral de Coventre, William Gamel, viker del esglise de la Trinyte de Coventre, jurra 'in verbo sacerdotii' qil soi repenti qil unqe soi avoit medle encountre Johan de Catesby tochant les manoirs de Lodbrok et Toneworth en le comte de Warr'; auxint qil unqe ne parla par ly mesme ne par altres ove Richard de Egebaston[128] tochant ascuns faitz tochant le manoir de Lodbrok en la counte de Warr', ne unqe luy paia ne dona, ne nul altre en soun noun[129] or ne argent ne ascunz altres rienz, pur ascuns faitz tochant le manoir de Lodbrok; mes il dit qil mesmes devoit a Lowys Cardian quatre livres, de quels quatre livres le dit Lowys envoia sa

123 The date clause, the single interlineation, and the rendering of *le array* into the plural are in the same hand as the main text, but in a different ink, presumably being added at the time of sealing.

124 Probably the Adam and Roger Somervile of *CAD*, V, A 11519–11520.

125 *et un Johan Cook* interlined.

126 Recte *continuance*.

127 All four are identifiable and probably prosperous Coventry citizens in this period: *The Register of the Guild of the Holy Trinity, St Mary, St John the Baptist, and St Katherine of Coventry*, ed M. D. Harris (Dugdale Soc., XIII, 1935), 6 and n.9, 17 and n.7, 20 and n.3.

128 Apart from his mysterious part in the matter of forged deeds [14], Edgbaston was a juror in Catesby's favour in 1383 [83].

129 *ne nul . . . noun* interlined.

lettre a dit William, viker, pur paier a Thomas Bromle qaraunt sold, les qelx il paia a dit Thomas pur deux faitz de taille del manoir de Lodbrok, al eops le dit Lowys; et auxint jurra illoq a donqe qil nies ne soi mellereit ne meinteindreit ascun partie encountre Johan de Catesby tochant le dit manoir, ne taille de icele, pur la pleine enformacioun de verite qil avoit de par le dit Johan de Catesby tochant le manoir suisdite. En tesmoignance de qele chose, a ceste nostre lettre patente nous avoms mis nos seals. Done a Coventre, le samady avaunt dit, lan de regne nostre seignur le roi Richard seconde puis le conqueste vintisme primer [19 Jan. 1398].

E 41/336 [*Here 'D', with variants noted from* E 163/6/46, f.4 (*here 'E'*).[130] *Both paper. D in Hand IV; E in Hand III*]

[13] Et le dit Johan dit qe la ou est allegge par[131] les ditz William Athewik, Lowis, et Alice qun Henri de Lodbrok le dit maner ove[132] autres terrez et tenementz, par un fait qe demurt en la garde Johan de Catesby, dona a Johan de Lodbrok soun fitz et a Hawis sa femme, a avoir et tener a eux et a lour heires de lour corps engendres, par force de quele don lez ditz Johan et Hawis fuerent seises, le quel fait del doun avantdit le dit William Athewik soi offrey de prover qil ad vewe es meyns et gard le dit Johan de Catesby: le dit Johan de Catesby dit qe le dit Henri unqe ne dona le[133] dit maner ove autres terres et tenementz en taille come desuis, ne le dit William unqe ne vit es meyns le dit Johan de Catesby autre[134] fait de taille, si noun un fet faux et contrefet a sa disheritesoun par un Thomas Bromle, qi contrefeta le grand seal de la[135] chauncellerie nostre seignur le roi, et utlahe, a cause de quele lez bailifs de la vill de Coventre pristerent le corps le dit Thomas, et en sa garde troverent le seal nostre seignur le roi contrefet, et la dite chartre de taill susdite[136] contrefet en desheritesoun le dit Johan, le quele chartre, purceo qe il fuist faux et nulle, le dit Thomas chargea lez ditz baillifs a bailer a dit Johan de Catesby,[137] la qele chartre apres[138] en banc le roi, lan de regne nostre seignur le roi qorest vint et primer, le term de Seint Michel, fut trove faux et contrefet en desheritesoun le dit Johan par les melz vaux[138] chevalers et esquiers . . . de la conte de Warr'[139] . . . par le . . . contrefait, come pura[138] estre moustre de record;[140] le quele chartre purporta date lan xix[141] le roi Edward fitz le roi Edward, le quele chartre est prove faux pur tant qe le dit Henry fuist seisi del dite maner en[142] fee simple long temps[143] apres la date de la dite chartre, et le dite maner ove le maner de Toneworth lessa a Johan soun fitz a terme de sa vie, la reverciounn de celle[144] estat save a lui et a sez herres; apres qi mort la revercion de fee simple descendy a dit Johan, le quel de celle[145] estat fuist seisi tanqe il soi demyst par sa chartre del dite maner de Lodbrok a William de Catesby, piere le dit Johan, et autres, et puis relessa par soun fait a dit William tut le droit qil avoit en le dit maner, et bargaina [146] ove le dit William de Catesby qe le dit William avera estat[147] en le dit maner a terme de sa vie, le remeindre a les heires madlz de corps[148] le dit Johan de Lodbrok engendrez;[149] et sil demast sanz heir male de soun corps, qe adonqz le dite maner remeyndreit a dit William de Catesby et a ses heires a touz jours, et qe le maner de Toneworth serroit taille par fin a la dite Hawis, le remeyndre apres soun decesse a dit William de Catesby a terme de sa vie, le remeyndre outre[150] come desuis; et pur ceo la dite Hawis relesseroit tut soun droit de dower en le maner Lodbrok suisdit; quelez choses estoient perfournez come apiert par fine et par relesse, pur un certein somme qe le dit Johan de Lodbrok devoit a dit William de Catesby;

130 The substantial interlineations in D which are not in E are apparently in the hand of John Catesby.

131 *depar* E.

132 After *duit*, deleted E.

133 After *pur*, deleted D.

134 *aucun* E.

135 *de la* interlined above *le*, deleted E.

136 Interlined D; omitted E.

137 Followed by *purceo qe ele fuist faux* DE, deleted D.

138 Reading uncertain.

139 *de la conte de Warr'*: reading conjectural.

140 *la qele chartre apres . . . de record* interlined D; *la qele chartre fut trove faux et contrefet en desheritesoun le dit Johan de Catesby en banc le roi a Coventre par chevalers et esquiers del counte de Warr' et par la conisaunce le dit Thomas come purra estre mostre de record* interlined E.

141 After *x et*, deleted E.

142 After *bien en*, deleted E.

143 *long temps* interlined above *bien entour a v ans*, deleted D.

144 *tiell* E.

145 *tiel* E.

146 *sur un* [above *et*, deleted] *bargaine* (*qil fit* interlined) altered to *bargaina* E.

147 Interlined E; omitted D.

148 *de corps* interlined E.

149 *engendres* interlined E.

150 *a dit William . . . outre* interlined D; omitted E.

et[151] apres la mort le dit Johan de Lodbrok,[152] Thomas nadgars count de Warr', pier Thomas de Beauchamp qore est, clayma la garde de Thomas fitz eigne le dit Johan, sur quoi a la suite le dit William de Catesby suyst[153] taunt a dit Thomas le pier nadgairs counte qe par testimoignance de bonz genz et plein enformacioun qe le feffement le[154] dit Johan de Lodbrok fist a dit William de Catesby et autres saunz[155] fraude ou collusioun de ly ou de sa seignurie, et accepta le dit William de Catesby soun verrai tenant de dit maner de Lodbrok, come est bien prove par ses lettres patentz ensealez desoutz le seal de ses armes; dez[156] ceo qe le[157] dit Thomas counte unqe nen prist de dit William de Catesby pur ceo fere;[158] quele estat le dit William de Catesby et autres de soun feoffament continueroun tauntqe[159] Thomas fitz le dit Johan de Lodbrok[160] graunta et suisrendre par[161] son fet[162] a Johan Cook, adonqe[163] tenant del dit maner et de lavowesoun, enseale de seal le dit Thomas fitz Johan de ses armes, fait a dit Johan Cook avant le dit feffement,[164] et voloit qe le doun soi a dit William a terme de sa vie et le remeyndre outre come desuis, et conust . . . dit fet qil unqe navoit altre estat en le dit manoir et lavowesoun si noun de la suffrance le dit Johan Cook,[165] par quele fet est prove qe le presentement fait par le dit Thomas ne doit ascunement desheriter le dit Johan de Catesby; le[166] quel Johan Cook, par son fet endentee, enfeoffa le dit William de Catesby a terme de sa vie, le remeyndre as heires madlz le dit Johan,[167] le remeindre as droitz heirs le dit William de Catesby,[168] come pleinement apiert par son fet endente;[169] les quex heirs madlz demerount sanz issue, le dit William einz[170] en le dit maner come en[171] fee simple, et en le maner de Toneworth apres la mort Hawis einz come de fee, apres la dit taill termynee,[172] la qele Hawyse vesqist bien entour a xx ou xix ans apres la mort son baron, et unqe rien dit demandant en le dit manoir de Lodbrok;[173] le quel William de Catesby cel estat continua en le dit manoir de Toneworth,[174] taunqe lez ditz Lowis et Alice, Johan Dolfyn, smyth,[175] et altres[176] ousterount le dit William de Catesby del dit manoir,[177] par sustinaunce de[178] Thomas Beauchamp[179] nadgairs counte de Warr', de quel ouster le dit William de Catesby porta lassise devers lez ditz Lowis et Alice[180] et le dit[181] Johan Dolfyn[182] et autres, et recovere, et les ditz Lowis, Alice, Johan, et autres atteintz disseisours ove force et armes, par quele puist bien estre prove qe le dit William de Catesby[183] ne voleit faire le dit Johan Dolfyne brokour[184] a la dite Alice a faire soun gree, come desuis est allegge;[185] et le dit manoir de Lodbrok les

151 After *le di* and *apres,* deleted E.

152 *de Lodbrok* interlined D; omitted E.

153 After *qi* interlined E.

154 After *qe* interlined E.

155 After *fut fait et* interlined above *et,* deleted E.

156 Reading uncertain.

157 After *unqe purra estre prove ?verita,* deleted D.

158 *dez ceo . . . ceo fere* interlined D; omitted E.

159 After *tanqe estat soi fist del dit manoir a dit William de Catesby a terme de sa vie, la remeyndre a les heirs madlez de corps le dit Johan de Lodbrok engendrez, et en defaut dissue, etc., le remeyndre as droitz heirs William de Catesby, come est prove par le graund,* deleted D.

160 *tauntqe . . . Johan de Lodbrok* interlined D.

161 After *le dit Thomas fet* DE, deleted D, and with *fiz Johan de Lodbrok* interlined above *Thomas* E.

162 *par son fet* interlined D; omitted E.

163 Interlined D; omitted E.

164 *fait . . . feffement* interlined E.

165 *et voloit . . . Johan Cook* interlined D; omitted E.

166 After *Hawyse,* deleted E.

167 *de Lodbrok* interlined E.

168 *le remeindre . . . Catesby* interlined E.

169 *son fet endente* interlined above *le dit fet* deleted D; *le dit fait* E.

170 After *e apo* [*apres*?], deleted E.

171 *de* E.

172 (*des heirs madlz* interlined) *terminee* E.

173 *la qele Hawyse . . . manoir de Lodbrok* interlined D; omitted E.

174 *en . . . Toneworth* interlined D; omitted E.

175 Assessed at 8d., under Tanworth, in 1379: E 179/192/23, m.14.

176 *Johan . . . altres* interlined D; omitted E.

177 Followed by *de Toneworth* DE, deleted D.

178 Interlined D.

179 *de Bewchamp* E.

180 *Lowys et Alice* interlined above *Hawyse Lowyse,* deleted E.

181 *et le dit* interlined after *s,* deleted E.

182 *Dolfyne de Tonworth par* (*par nom de Johan Dolfin de Tonworth, smyth,* interlined) E.

183 *William de Catesby* after *Johan Dolfyne,* deleted E.

184 After *mesme,* deleted D.

185 Presumably a reference to an earlier part of the text, now lost; very possibly a bill to which this was the answer.

ditz Lowis et Alice clamerent; sur[186] quoi le dit William[187] de Catesby porta brief de trespass[188] ou lissue fuit pris, le qel le francteneṁent fut as ditz Lowis et Alice ou as dit William Catesby,[189] et le franctenement trie en William de Catesby, et puis apres le dit William de Catesby mourut seisi de[190] fee; apres qi mort entra le dit Johan de Lodbrok[191] par descent de heritage, come par les lettres patentes de seignur de fee[192] est provez.[193] Et quant a ceo qe le dit William duist avoir pris le mayn le dit Johan hors de sa cist apres sa mort, et avoir enseale diversz blankes chartres dount le chartre par quele le dit Johan de Catesby cleyme le dit manoir de Lodbrok estoit une, le revers est prove si bien[194] par les lettres patentz le dit counte qi mort est, come par mandamus qissit hors de la chauncellerie apres la mort le dit Johan de Lodbrok,[195] par qel estoit trove qe le dit Johan de Lodbrok[196] ne mourut saisi de null terre ne tenement en le countee de Warr', a cause[197] qe le dit Johan de Lodbrok soi demit come desuis a William de Catesby et altres en fee,[198] quel Johan de Lodbrok unqe ne purchacea terres ne tenementz einz vendy terre et tenementz[199] et devoit grant dette a temps de son moriaunt. Et[200] outre Johan de Catesby dit qe long temps avant qe Robert Burgyloun purchacea le dit manoir de Toneworth ou purpose destre purchace a dit counte,[201] le dit counte oesta la meyn[202] par avis[203] de touz les sagez genz et autres de estat de soun counseil, quel Johan de Catesby cele estat continua; et les ditz Lowis et Alice porterount lassise del dit manoir de Lodbrok devant monsires William Thyrnyng et Richard de Sydenham,[204] et estoient nounsuez; et puis le dit Lowis servit sire Johan de Fordham, adonqe evesqe de Durem,[205] tresourer Dengleterre,[206] et devant soun counseil le dit Johan de Catesby[207] vient et declara sa matire tochant le maner suisdite, et le dit counseil osterent lour meyn; et puis le dit Lowys servist le duc de Glouc', et devant soun counseil le dit Johan de Catesby[208] vient en mesme la maner et declara sa matire tochant le dit maner de Lodbrok,[209] et le dit duc et soun counseil osterent lour meins; et puis[210] en la chauncellerie comaundez a suere a la comune lay sils verroient qil fusse a fere. Et puis le dit William Athewik fist le dit Johan de Catesby[211] venir devant le counseil nostre seignur le roi, a la xv de Seint Michel, lan xxj nostre seignur le roi qorest, ove sez fetz et munymentz tochant le dit maner de Lodbrok, ou fuist agardee par le dit counseil qe lez diz Lowis et[212] Alice suereient a la comune lay devers le dit Johan de Lodbrok;[213] et puis apres mesme le terme les diz Lowis et Alice, par meintenance de[214] dit William Athewik, suerent une assise de novel disseisin devers le dit Johan del dit manoir de Lodbrok en[215] bank le roi a Coventre, et furent[216] noumsuez; et puis porterount une altre[217] assise en[218]

186 After *et firent en le dit manoirs divers trespasses a dit William de Catesby,* interlined E.

187 After *Johan,* deleted D.

188 Interlined above *droit,* deleted D.

189 *ditz W. et C.* E.

190 After *del dit maner de Lodbrok en soun demesne come,* interlined E.

191 Recte *Catesby.*

192 *des* (*chiefs* interlined) *seignurs de fez* E.

193 *et le dit manoir . . . est provez* inserted here by double dagger from the dorse E.

194 *si bien* interlined E.

195 *apres la . . . de Lodbrok* interlined D; omitted E.

196 *qe le dit Johan de Lodbrok* interlined D; omitted E.

197 *ne mourut . . . a cause* interlined E.

198 *a William . . . fee* interlined above *par la dite chartre Johan de Lodbrok,* deleted D; *par . . . de Lodbrok* E.

199 *terre et tenement* interlined E.

200 After *come,* deleted E.

201 See also [164].

202 Here, since the chief lord of the fee is involved, some technical usage of *ouster le main* could apply, but subsequently in this entry the phrase is used loosely, to indicate non-interference by staying the hand, rather than judgment by withdrawing it. The usage in statutes of Edward I is not necessarily technical. Cf. *Prerogativa Regis: Tertia Lectura Roberti Constable de Lyncolnis Inne, Anno 11 H. 7,* ed. S. E. Thorne (New Haven, Conn, 1949), xxiv–xxvii; 28 Edw. I, c. 19, and 29 Edw. I (de Escaetoribus).

203 E dorse begins.

204 JCP 1389–1396; see Kimball in *Warwicks Sessions,* xli–xlii.

205 *evesqe de Durem* interlined DE.

206 Fordham was treasurer from 17 January to 24 October, 1386.

207 *Catesby* interlined above *Lodbrok,* deleted DE.

208 *Johan de Catesby* interlined E.

209 *de Lodbrok* interlined D; omitted E.

210 D dorse begins.

211 *Catesby* corrected from *Lodbrok* E.

212 *Lowis et* omitted E.

213 *devers . . . Johan de Lodbrok* [recte *Catesby*] interlined D; omitted E.

214 *le* E.

215 After *et furent,* deleted E.

216 *en banc . . . furent* interlined E.

217 Interlined E.

218 Omitted E.

mesme le terme en mesme le bank illeoq et nonsuez; sur quoi lez diz Lowis et Alice estoient amerciez a C s.; et les[219] diz Lowis et Alice et William Athewik[220] ousteront le dit Johan de Catesby del dit manoir de Lodbrok, de quel ouster il porta lassise, etc.,[221] devant mounsire William Thirning et Robert Tyrwhyt, ou le dit William Athewyk vint en propre persoun et pleda a lassise[222] et respondy par baillif pur les altres; et lassise prise des gens de grant estat, par qels fut trove qe le dit Johan fut seisi, et disseisi par les Lowys, Alice, et William Athewyk, sur quoy le dit Johan recovery, come de record . . .; et puis apres, le dit Johan de Catesby suist a soun tresdote seignur de Surrey . . . par bill le terme de Pasch adonqe prochein ensuaunt, par[223] qil peut estre my devant soun sage counseil, ou . . . dit seignur bailla la bill a Nicholas Gascoyn soun seneschal de assembler soun de ley et oier le dit suppliaunt, qel chose fut feat mesme le terme, a qel estoient sis serjaunz et Edward Scherd[224] illeoqs present; et puis le lundy en les simeign de Pentecost adonqe prochein ensuaunt, par relacioun qe le dit[225] Nicolas fit a dit tresdote seignur, comaunde fut qe le ministers soun dit seignur nies ne soi mellereient del[226] dit manoir depar soun dit seignur.

[14] [227] Apres cel terme, qaunt . . . les . . . Johan . . ., le dit William Hathewyk a Warr' fit le dit Thomas B. . . .[228] par instrument apiert qun William Gamel, viker de lesglise de la Trinite de Coventre, dut avoir done a Richard de Egebastoun xl s. pur deux chartres des manoirs de Lodbrok et Toneworth, les qels, come linstrument tesmoign, le dit Richard dut avoir livre a Thomas de Bromley; le qel viker puis apres a Coventre jura 'in verbo sacerdoti', en presence de serteins genz qi aceo ount avis,[229] quil unqe ne vit ne parla en . . . seals[230] le dit Richard de Egebastoun, par quel peut . . . la dite chartre estre faux. [*See also* 12]

E 163/6/46, f.3 [*Paper. Hand II*]

[15] [*Abstract of* 45.]

[16] [*Abstract of* 47, *describing the grant as being in fee simple.*]

[17] [*Abstract of* 46, *noting the omission of warranty.*]

[18] [*Abstract of* 31.]

[19] [*Abstract of* 34.]

[20] [*Abstract of* 33.]

[21] [*Abstract of* 48.]

[22] [*Abstract of* 32, *noting the omission of witnesses.*]

[23] [*Abstract of* 35, *paraphrasing the description of the feoffments as having been made* en bon foi et sanz collusion ou fraude dascun chief seignur de ly ou altre.]

[24] [*Abstract of* 39.]

[25] [*Abstract of* 49.]

[26] Abstract of a grant by William de Catesby and Nicholas le Wodeward of Long Itchington, to Simon brother of William de Catesby, John le Cook of Ladbroke, John de Werketon, chaplain, and William son of Nicholas le Wodeward, of all goods and chattels in the manor of Ladbroke. Dated Saturday the morrow of Hilary, 25 Edward III [14 Jan. 1352]. [*See* 36]

[27] [*Abstract of* 37, *noting the omissions of warranty and date.*]

[28] [*Abstract of* 40.]

Folio 3d

[29] [*Abstract of* 38, *correcting the expression of the contingent remainder and noting the limit of warranty.*]

[30] [*Abstract of* 42.]

219 After *puis en la ?vell,* deleted E.

220 *Lowis et . . . Athewik* deleted and then interlined D.

221 From this point E ends simply *et recovere,* followed by *et de tiel com* deleted.

222 Followed by *come de record,* deleted.

223 Possibly deleted; the rest of this clause was initially written after *Surrey,* and then deleted.

224 Interlined.

225 *le dit* interlined.

226 After *depar,* deleted.

227 The remainder of D is an inverted endorsement flagged by a paragraph mark, possibly for insertion in the text at a point not marked.

228 Perhaps *serement.*

229 *en . . . avis* interlined.

230 Marginated, apparently for this point.

Shakespeare Birthplace Trust, MS DR 37/82
[*Parchment roll of evidences, sewn chancery fashion, with schedules sewn to margins. Hands I and II, and others: see above, 298.*]

Membrane 1

[31] Grant by John de Lodbrok, knight, lord of Ladbroke, to Roger de Clifton,[231] parson of Ladbroke, William de Catesby, and Nicholas Wodeward, of the manor of Ladbroke, with appurtenances, excepting two virgates held in villeinage by William le Reve and Alice his mother, and forty shillings rent from tenements held for life by Roger de Clifton, parson of Ladbroke, Robert Hughwet, and William Dollyng, and the reversion of these tenements, previously granted by charter to William de Catesby; with warranty. Witnesses: Richard Hastank, William de Ardena, lord of Radbourn, William Saltleye, Henry de Flekeno, Nicholas Fraunceys. Dated at Ladbroke, Tuesday before St Barnabas, 21 Edward III [5 June 1347].

[32] Release by John de Lodbrok, knight, to William de Catesby, of two virgates and forty shillings rental in Ladbroke, with appurtenances, as previously granted; with warranty. Dated at Tanworth, Friday after St Philip and St James, 23 Edward III [8 May 1349].

[33] Grant by John de Lodbrok, knight, to William de Catesby and Nicholas le Wodeward of Long Itchington, of the advowson of Ladbroke, with appurtenances; with warranty. Witnesses: Gilbert de Chastilon, knight, John de Peyto the younger, Richard Hastang, William de Peyto, John Turvill, William de Arden. Dated at Tanworth, Friday after St Peter and St Paul, 23 Edward III [3 July 1349].

[34] Release by John de Lodbrok, knight, to William de Catesby and Nicholas le Wodeward of Long Itchington, of the manor of Ladbroke, with appurtenances; with warranty. Witnesses: Gilbert Chastilon, knight, John de Peyto the younger, Richard Hastang, William de Peyto, Guy Breton, John Turvill, William de Arden. Dated at Tanworth, Friday after St Peter and St Paul, 23 Edward III [3 July 1349].

[35] As touz ceux qi cestes lettres verront ou orront, Thomas de Beauchamp, counte de Warrewyk, salutz. Purceoqe nous avoms trove par bone examinement et tesmoignance de bone gent qi nostre trescher bacheler sire Johan de Lodbrok, qest a Dieu comande, enfeffa William de Catesby, ove altres qount relesse a dit William, en son manoir de Lodbrok, qest tenuz de nous en chief, saunz deceite ou collusioun de nous ou de nostre seignurie; vous fesoms a savoir qi nous avoms receu la fealte de dit William come de nostre verray tenant; en tesmoignance de quelle chose, as cestes nos lettres overtes avoms mys nostre seal. Escript a nostre chastel de Warrewyk, le disme jour daugst, lan du regne le roy Edward tiercz puis le conquest vintisme tiercz [1349].

[36] Grant by William de Catesby and Nicholas le Wodeward of Long Itchington, to Simon brother of William de Catesby, John le Cok of Ladbroke, John de Werketon, chaplain, and William son of Nicholas le Wodeward, of the manor and advowson of Ladbroke, which the grantors had of John de Lodbrok, knight, excepting two messuages, seven acres of meadow in 'le wete forowes', and fifteen shillings rent. Witnesses: Richard Hastang, William de Peyto, William de Ardena, lord of Radbourn, William Tomekyns, Nicholas Frаunceys, Henry Walding, John Colyns of Ladbroke. Dated at Ladbroke, Saturday the morrow of Hilary, 25 Edward III [14 Jan. 1352]. [*See* 26]

[37] Release by John de Werketon, rector of Sheepy Magna, to John Cok of Ladbroke, of the manor and advowson of Ladbroke, with appurtenances. Witnesses: William de Catesby, John son of William de Catesby, Thomas le Hore, Philip de Franketon, Richard de Teynton. [*No date.*]

[38] Grant by John le Cook of Ladbroke, to William de Catesby, of the manor and advowson of Ladbroke, with all other lands, tenements, and reversions there, with appurtenances, for life, with successive remainders in tail male to Thomas son of John de Lodbrok, knight, to Hugh brother of Thomas, and to John brother of Thomas and Hugh, with contingent remainder to William de Catesby and his heirs;[232] with warranty for the life of William de

[231] The distinction between *f* and long *s* is not clear here, and is seldom made in John Catesby's hand; *Cliston* is not an impossible name, but *Clifton,* as much more probable, is given throughout, regardless of the apparent palaeographical variants. Clifton was parson of Ladbroke 1340–9: Dugdale, *Warwickshire,* 233.

[232] Although probably an error, this might be intended to clarify (in the lord's favour) contemporary difficulties with contingent remainders, which were – perhaps surprisingly – not discussed: see S. F. C. Milsom, *Historical Foundations of the Common Law* (London, 1969), 161–5 and notes; Plucknett, *Common Law,* 562–5.

Catesby. Witnesses: John de Shukkeburgh,[233] John le Baillif of Southam,[234] Robert Emeley of Stockton,[235] Henry le Cook of Ladbroke, William Tomkyns of Ladbroke. Dated at Ladbroke, 3 June, 46 Edward III [1372].

Membrane 1d

[39] Grant by Nicholas le Wodeward of Long Itchington, to William de Catesby, Simon brother of William de Catesby, John le Vynter, and William son of Nicholas le Wodeward, of the manor of Harbury, with appurtenances; with warranty. Witnesses: Richard Harcourt, knight, William de Ardena, lord of Radbourn, Nicholas Fraunceys of Ladbroke, William de Ichinton, John Houdon, William Clerk (*clericus*). Dated at Harbury, Sunday after the Assumption, 23 Edward III [16 Aug. 1349]. [*Now* E 40/6771: *CAD,* IV, A 6771.]

[40] Release by Thomas de Lodbrok, to Simon brother of William de Catesby, John le Cook of Ladbroke, and John de Werketon, chaplain, of the manor, with appurtenances, and advowson of Ladbroke; with warranty. Witnesses: Robert le Fizwith, lord of Bubbenhall, dom Peter Barthelmeu, parson of the same,[236] William de Ardena, lord of Radbourn, John le Baillif of Southam, Henry le Cook of Ladbroke, William de Creek of Ladbroke. Dated at Ladbroke, Monday after St Peter's chains, 33 Edward III [5 Aug. 1359].

[41] Release by Hawise widow of John de Lodbrok, knight, to William de Catesby and Nicholas le Wodeward of Long Itchington, of her dower in the manor of Ladbroke. Witnesses: lord John de Oddingesele, Gilbert Chastilon, knight, Richard Hastang, William de Peyto, Thomas Larcher, Thomas Hamstede. Dated at Tanworth, Sunday after Michaelmas, 23 Edward III [4 Oct. 1349].

[42] Grant by William de Catesby, to William le Clerc of Offchurch,[237] of all rents and services in Harbury, late of John de Lodbrok, knight, for the term of two years. Witnesses: John de Catesby, Thomas de Meryngton, John Clifforde of Coventry, William de Allesleye, Hugh Bailly of Ladbroke. Dated at Harbury, 8 June, 47 Edward III [1373]. [*Now* E 40/7421: *CAD,* IV, A 7421.]

[43] Grant by William de Catesby, to William Clerc of Offchurch, of the manor of Harbury, with appurtenances, late of John de Lodbrok, knight, for the term of Catesby's life, for an annual rent of £6, payable in equal portions at the feasts of the Annunciation and St Peter's chains; the closes of the manor to be maintained without waste, by Clerc, and Catesby to have repossession should the rent be more than one month in arrears. Witnesses: John de Catesby, John de Shukkeburgh, Thomas Bawdewyne. Dated at Harbury, Friday of St Lawrence, 49 Edward III [10 Aug. 1375].

Membrane 2

[44] Confirmation by Thomas son of John de Lodbrok, to John de Catesby, that whereas the manor and advowson of Ladbroke, formerly held by John le Cook of Ladbroke, and subsequently granted to William de Catesby [38], has long been occupied by Thomas with Cook's permission, he has now granted all his right in the manor and advowson to John Catesby. Dated at Ladbroke, Wednesday the eve of Corpus Christi, 46 Edward III [26 May 1372].

[45] Grant by John de Lodbrok, to Roger Clifton, parson of Ladbroke, John de Lye, clerk, and Nicholas le Wodeward, of the manors of Harbury and Ladbroke, with all his lands and tenements in Tanworth, with appurtenances, excepting his house there; with warranty. Witnesses: Robert de Bereford, knight, William de Lucy, knight, Richard de Hastang, William de Catesby, John de Shuckeburgh. Dated at Ladbroke, Thursday after the Nativity of the Blessed Virgin, 17 Edward III [11 Sept. 1343].

[46] Release by John son of Henry de Lodbrok, knight, to Roger de Clifton, parson of Ladbroke, John de Leye, clerk, and Nicholas le Wodeward of Long Itchington, of the manors of Ladbroke, Harbury, and Tanworth, including his house in

233 Assessed at 40d., as farmer of Upper Shuckburgh, in 1379: E 179/192/23, m.17.

234 Assessed at 40d., as farmer of Southam, in 1379: ibid., m.17.

235 Assessed at 2s., as a franklin, in 1379: E 179/192/23, m.18.

236 Actually Ladbroke: *CPR 1358–61,* 147.

237 Assessed at 40d., as a franklin, in 1379: E 179/192/23, m.2. See also above, 299.

Tanworth, with appurtenances. Witnesses: John le Archer, Henry de Sydenhale,[238] Robert de Fulwode, Richard Aleyn, William Dolfyn of Tanworth. Dated at Tanworth, Thursday after St Barnabas, 20 Edward III [15 June 1346].

[47] Grant by John son of Henry de Lodbrok, knight, to Roger de Clifton, parson of Ladbroke, John de Leye, clerk, and Nicholas le Wodeward of Long Itchington, of his house in Tanworth; with warranty. Witnesses: John le Archer, Henry de Sidenhale, Robert de Fulwode, Richard Aleyn, William Dolfyn of Tanworth. Dated at Tanworth, Tuesday after St Barnabas, 20 Edward III [13 June 1346].

[48] Release by John de Lodbrok, knight, to Nicholas le Wodeward of Long Itchington, of the manor of Tanworth, with appurtenances; with warranty. Witnesses: Gilbert Chastilon, knight, John de Peyto the younger, Richard Hastang, William de Peyto, John Turvill, William de Arden. Dated at Tanworth, Friday after St Peter and St Paul, 23 Edward III [3 July 1349]. [*Now* Shakespeare Birthplace Trust, MS DR 37/652 (*temporary reference*).]

[49] Grant by Nicholas le Wodeward of Long Itchington, to William de Catesby, Simon brother of William de Catesby, John le Vynter of Solihull, and William son of Nicholas le Wodeward, of the manor of Tanworth, with appurtenances; with warranty. Witnesses: Thomas Larcher, Thomas de Hamstede, Robert de Crowenhale, Richard Aleyn. Dated at Tanworth, Sunday the morrow of the Assumption, 23 Edward III [16 Aug. 1349]. [*Now* E 40/10455: *CAD,* V, A 10455.]

[50] Grant by Hugh de Merinton of Coventry, to Henry de Lodbrok, knight, of the manor and advowson of Ladbroke, with appurtenances, as held by Hugh of Henry; with warranty. Witnesses: Robert de Stoke, Robert Sampson, William de Arden, William de London, Henry Sutham, Robert Balraven of the same, William Fraunceys of Ladbroke. [*No date.*]

Membrane 2d

[51] Chers et biens asmees: purceoqe nous est donnez a entendre comment vous pursuiez, par brief en le courte nostre seignur le roi, Thomas Haukeschawe, nostre neef,[239] et ceo par enemyte, a cause qe le dit Thomas et autres des tenantes nostre seignurie de Toncworth prcsentcront la garde et mariage des heirs de Thomas Lodebrok en nostre main; dont si ainsi soit, nous nous merveillons grandement, depuisqe nous nous affions en vous pluis qe en pluseurs autres; par quoi nous envoions pardevers vous apresent, endesirrant qe vous voillez cesser del pursuit vers nostre dit neif, tantqe nostre consaill eut vous purra enparler et savoir la certeinete dyceste matiere; et si soit trovez qe nostre dit neif ad meffait, par avys de nostre consaill il fera les amendes solonc droit et resone; et en mesme la manere nous desirrons de vous. A Dieu soietz. Escrit a nostre manoir de Sallewarp,[240] le xviij jour de feverer.

Le count de Warr', seignur de Gower, a nos chers et bien amez William Catesby et Johan Catesby son fiz.

[52] Et fait a remembrer, qe le mardi prochein apres la cluse Pasch, lan du regne le roi Richard seconde puis le conquest sisme [31 Mar. 1383], William de Catesby deinz nomez avoit jour, par assignement Thomas de Beauchamp, counte de Warr', seignur de Gower, devant le counseil le dit counte, a Warr', qel counseil estoit tenuz en la revestiarie de lesglise collegial de Nostre Dame illeqs, adonqs present de dit counseil monsire William de Beauchamp, frere a dit counte, frere Walter de Bykerston, confessour a dit counte, sire Richard de Pyriton, clerc, dean de Colcestre,[241] sire Johan de Hermesthorp,[242] un des chaumberleins de lescheqer et person de Hanslape, monsire Nicol Lyllyng,[243] Johan de Say,[244] sire Robert Mile, sire William de Morton, receivour del chastell, Robert Burgoillon,[245] Richard de Ryhale le pusnee, Robert Broun,[246] Johan Hambury del counte de Wyrc', Richard de Aston, clerc a Johan de Pole del counte de Staff', Edmund de Catesby, fiz pusne le dit William, William Broke, chapelein a Johan de Catesby, fiz eigne le [dit] [247] William de

[238] Assessed at 6s. 8d., as an armiger, under Tanworth, in 1379: E 179/192/23, m.14.

[239] Assessed at 4d., under Tanworth, in 1379: ibid., m.14.

[240] Salwarpe, Worcs.

[241] For Pirton, see Goodman, *Loyal Conspiracy,* 145.

[242] For Armthorpe, see ibid., 148.

[243] For Lilling, see ibid., 149–51.

[244] For Say, see ibid., 147–8.

[245] For Burgilon, see Kimball in *Warwicks Sessions,* xxxii.

[246] Probably Warwick's steward at Tanworth: above, 298 and note.

[247] Omitted.

Catesby, devant qels le dit Johan declara tute la matire tochaunt leritage Lodbrok, et tendy daverrer toz les faitz et fyns estre duement faitz[248] et executz par les genz southnomez:

[53] John Cook of Ladbroke, aged 100 years, father of William Lodbrok, now [under] sheriff of Warwickshire and Leicestershire, Roger Arleie of Ladbroke, aged 80 years, William Wryde, aged 80 years, Henry Waldyng, aged 60 years, Henry Paltok, aged 60 years, and William Colyns, aged 50 years, all witnessed the enfeoffment of William de Catesby by John de Lodbrok, knight, and offered to swear to it on halidom or housel before the same meeting of the council. Also, Roger de Clifton and others, by charter. And they and many others offered to verify the feoffment of John Cok by William de Catesby and Nicholas le Wodeward, as above.

[54] William Lyhtherne, chaplain, now living at Stratford on Avon with the brothers of the guild of Holy Trinity, John de Schuckebergh, lord of Upper Shuckburgh, John Baylly of Southam, William de Lodbrok, undersheriff, Robert de Stocton, Hugh de Luteryngton alias Bailly, John Cook, chaplain, Thomas Cook, Thomas Wylkyns, and Alan Salmon offered similarly to verify the feoffment of William de Catesby by John Cook, and the remainders as above [38], made in the presence of Thomas son of John de Lodbrok, knight, before the feoffment confirming the estate of John Cook, as above [44], and after the feoffment taking against him one part of the indenture, because of the remainder, after the death of William, as above. They were witnesses to this deed.

[55] Et William de Offechurch, clerc, illeqs present, tesmoigna qe en la vie le dit Thomas de Lodbrok il estoit a Lodbrok pur avoir tenu la court, et voleit avoir fait le title 'Curia Thome de Lodbrok', et le dit Thomas mesme le fit amender et ly fit escrire 'Curia Johannis Cook'. Item, qe a la reqeste le dit Thomas, le dit William de Catesby fit a dit Offechurch estat en le manoir de Herbury, pur une somme de monee qe le dit Thomas aprompta de ly, qel a profry a jurer en manere come desus.

[56] Item, Johan Cook, chapelein, et Johan fermer de la rectorie de Lodbrok tendira mesme la prove qen la vie le dit Thomas, le dit William de Catesby lessa al person de Lodbrok j mesuage et j verg' de terre en Lodbrok, en la vie le dit Thomas, qel le dit person tient unqore, etc.

[57] Et les genz de Busschopes Ichinton, ceste a savoir sire Hugh, viker illeqs, William Barbour de mesme la vill, Richard Balraven, Thomas Palmere, William Broke, Johan Barbour, tendirent daverrer qils unqe ne firent ne nul de lour veisins ne fit amendes pur trespas fait en le mulne hamme de Lodbrok qe gist sur els, si non a William de Catesby et a Johan Cook, checun pur son temps, et unqs a dit Thomas ne nul des seons, etc.

[58] Et les genz et tenantz de Herbury, cest a savoir Ralph, viker illeqs, Johan Bernard, Johan Ive, Johan Clerc, asoient qapres la mort Hawyse qe prist estat par la fyn, William de Catesby entra come en son remeindre, et unqes puis ne conissenent altre seignur, si non William Offechirch, qi tient le dit manoir de Herbury de son lees, modo quo supra, etc.

[59] Et apres tut ceo fait declarre et tenduz depar le dit William, Thomas Larcher[249] pur la partie adverse estoit apele, et rienz ne mostra, si non endentures par qels le dit Thomas dit avoir lesse certeins terres et venduz certeins boys en Toneworth, et pria outre qil pout avoir cours de la ley, qe ly fut grante, et dit ly fut outre qe mon dit seignur le counte ne soi mellereit ne dun part ne daltre; et sur ceo, a les assises tenuz a Warr', le joveday prochein apres le dit jour de mardy [2 Apr. 1383], devant monsire William de Skypwyth et William de Borgh,[250] Lowys Cardian et Alice sa feme furent essone, et pur doute del viscount le brief dassise et le panell remeinent es mains des justices avantdiz, etc.

Membrane 3

[60] Grant by William de Catesby, to Lawrence de Benteleye of Beoley,[251] at farm for Catesby's life, of all Catesby's lands and tenements in Tanworth, together with annual rents of 3s. there, excepting woods and fisheries, for an annual rent of 6m., in equal payments at the Annunciation and Michaelmas, to Catesby, and 31s. annually, payable similarly, to the earl of Warwick as chief lord of the fee; Benteleye, his heirs or assigns, undertaking to maintain the enclosure round 'Newenehewene' wood between 'Ladymede' and 'Birchenehurst' wood; Catesby to have repossession if the rent be in arrears, or the

248 *par les* written in error, and deleted, both after *fyns* and after *faitz*.

249 Assessed at 6s. 8d., as a 'squire', under Tanworth, in 1379: E 179/192/23, m.14.

250 cf. Kimball in *Warwicks Sessions*, xxxv: Skipwith was JCP 1376–88, and perhaps 1359–61; Burgh was JCP 1383–8.

251 Warwick's farmer there: *CIM*, VI, no. 302.

conditions unfulfilled, for one month. Witnesses: John de Catesby, Edmund de Catesby, William de Offechirche. Dated at Coventry, Sunday after Michaelmas, 49 Edward III [30 Sept. 1375]. [*Now* E 40/10225: *CAD,* IV, A 10225.]

[61] Lease by William de Catesby of Coventry, to John Dolphyn of Tanworth, smith, of the fisheries of Ladbroke, with all waters within the lands formerly belonging to John de Lodbrok in Tanworth, with appurtenances, to drain, fish, and otherwise use, with free access, for the term of Catesby's life, for an annual rent of 10s., payable at the Annunciation and Michaelmas in equal portions. Catesby will repair the head of the fishery within one year of the present date, Dolphyn maintaining it thereafter; the first rent is payable at Michaelmas now following. Dolphyn is at liberty to cut and to burn the underwood affecting the fishery and other waters. At the expiry of the lease Dolphyn is to leave in the fishery all pike of twelve inches and under, all bream of eight inches and under, and all perch and roach of four inches and under. Witnesses: Richard Mountford, Thomas Larcher, Henry Sidenhale, Thomas atte Berne,[252] Thomas Fulwode. Dated at Tanworth, St Matthias' day, 50 Edward III [25 Feb. 1376].

[62] Release by Thomas de Lodbrok, son and heir of John de Lodbrok, knight, to John de Werketon, chaplain, and John Cook of Ladbroke, of the manor of Ladbroke, and grant of the advowson. Dated at Ladbroke, Tuesday after St Denis, 36 Edward III [11 Oct. 1362].

[63] Grant by William de Catesby, to John Eyton of the same, of two cottages with curtilages and crofts adjacent, in Tanworth, lying between Park Field and the highway in one direction, and between Catesby's small granary and the road from Tanworth to Forshaw in the other, for nine years, at an annual rent of 2s., payable at the Annunciation and Michaelmas in equal portions; Eyton is to maintain all buildings and woodlands, and to make no alienations without permission, failing which conditions Catesby shall have repossession. Witnesses: John Crowleye,[253] John Dolfyn, Thomas Foluwode, John Foluwode,[254] Simon Tone. Dated at Tanworth, Monday after Michaelmas, 47 Edward III [3 Oct. 1373].

[64] Lease by William de Catesby, to Thomas Haukshawe, of three fields within Catesby's close at Tanworth, lying together, between 'Wynmelfeld' and the heath on one side, and the watercourse dividing Solihull and Tanworth parishes on the other, and from the highway to Tylers Grove, with free access to them between the watercourse and the 'Tylhous ovene', without damaging any woods, for the term of four years, at an annual rent of 3s. 4d., payable at Michaelmas and the Annunciation in equal portions. Catesby is to have repossession if alienation is made, and the conditions are broken, or the rent is three weeks in arrears. Witnesses: John de Crowleye, John Dolfyn, Thomas Foluwode, Simon Tone. Dated at Tanworth, Sunday of Easter quindene, 48[255] Edward III [16 Apr. 1374]. [*Now* E 40/6610: *CAD,* IV, A 6610.]

Membrane 3d

[65] Et fait a remembrer qe le jeovedy prochein devant la feste de la Trinite, mesme lan [12 May 1383], a Balsale, estoit pris un jour par frere Robert Normanton, comandour illeqs,[256] William Spernore,[257] et Gy Spynee, esquiers monseignur le count de Warr', entre les parties susditz, a tenir a Warr' le lundy en la veille de Seint Austyn prochein ensuaunt [25 May], et par certeins persones eslieuz depar les parties susditz, cest a savoir Thomas de Meryngton, Robert Burgoillon, et William Hopkyns de Warr' eslieuz depar le dit William, Rogger Harewelle de Waunes Wotton,[258] Johan Hambury del counte de Wyrc', et Estevene White del counte de Herford, a qel jour estoit mostre un fait de taille par qel le manoir de Herbury estoit done par Henry de Lodbrok a Johan son fiz et a Hawyse sa femme et a les heires de lour deux corps engendrez, et pur defaut dissue sauvant le revercioun a ly et a ses heirs;[259] et qe de ceo Hawyse continua et mourut seisi, et la fyn a qel Hawyse fut partie ele ne rienz ne conust; a [qi][260]

[252] Assessed at 2s., as a franklin, in 1379: E 179/192/23, m.14.

[253] Assessed at 2s., as a franklin, under Tanworth, in 1379: ibid.

[254] Assessed at 40d., as an armiger, under Tanworth, in 1379: ibid.

[255] MS '58'.

[256] i.e. the Templars' commandery at Temple Balsall, Warwickshire.

[257] For Spernore, see Goodman, *Loyal Conspiracy,* 146.

[258] Assessed at 6s. 8d., as an armiger, under Wootton Wawen, in 1379: E 179/192/23, m.5.

[259] Now E 40/8248: *CAD,* IV, A 8248.

[260] Omitted.

fut dit qe le dit Johan fit feffement, etc., issint, etc., Hawyse ne continua mie son estat, etc.

[66] Et del manoir de Lodbrok Johan fut seisi en son demeine come de fee simple, et mourut seisi; apres qi mort Thomas entra come fiz et heir, et mourut seisi; apres qi mort Johan entra come fiz et heir, et mourut seisi; apres qi mort entra cest Alice ove son baron, et issint, etc.; a qi furent dit qe Johan soi demist, come est prove par faitz de feffementz et de relesse, et les lettres patentes le count de Warr' qe darrein mourut, et par les confermentz le dit Thomas, et les feffementz et refeffementz, etc.

[67] Et qaunt a Toneworth, ils disoient qils entendirent qe le dit monsire Henry le dit [manoir][260] avoir done de pusne temps en taille, ut supra, etc., et qe Hawise mourut seisi, etc., ut supra; a qi fut alegge la demise, etc.; et auxint ils aleggent coment Thomas de Lodbrok dut avoir releve apres la mort son piere a count qi mort est, et avoir paie lxij s., issint double la rente pur taunt qe la tenure est sicage;[261] a qi est dit ceo est outreement faux, et la taille qils suppose outreement faux, etc.

[68] A qel jour les partie susditz ne purrount ascunement acorder, etc.

[69] Et pus le mardy en lendemain [26 May 1383], a Herbury, Johan Ive, Robert Colyns, et Richard Letice tesmoignent coment le dit monsire Henry soi avoit demis al person de Blaby[262] son frere del dit manoir de Herbury, et, come ils entendent, le dit person continua tute la vie le dit Henry, et apres sa mort mounsire Robert de Daventre ly voleit avoir oste,[263] etc. Inquiratur plus. Item qil[264] avoit bien a lx anz et plus puis qe le dit Henry mourut, etc.

[70] Item a Kyngeston mesme le jour, depar Katerine qe fuit la femme monsire Thomas de Bescles, estoient mostrez faitz faitz entre Johan de Lye, pere la dite Katerine, et Thomas son frere, des terres et tenementz nadgairs Johan Jecob en mesme la vill, par qels fut mostre qe le dit monsire Henry fut en vie le jeovedy prochein apres la feste de Seint Andreu, lan xv le roi Edward fiz le roi Edward fiz le roi Henry [3 Dec. 1321], et le meskerdy en la feste de Seint Michel, lan xvj de mesme roi [29 Sept. 1322], etc.

[71] Et sur cel departir apres a les assises, tenues le jour de Seinte Marie Magdelein prochein ensuaunt [22 July 1383], les diz Lowys et Alice estoient nonsuiz en lassise porte des manoirs de Lodbrok et Herbury, en quel assise les dy pleintifs avoient estee essone a darrein jour, come apiert devaunt [59]. Et Thomas Larcher de Toneworth lour meintenour ne apparut point a diz jour et lieu, etc.

[72] Et auxint le dit William de Catesby porta un brief de trespas del entre en le dit manoir de Lodbrok atort, etc., et de lemportement des biens, etc., et proces sur ceo continue taunt le nisi prius passa a mesme le jour devant mesme les justices dassises, devers Lowys Cook et Alice sa femme, Thomas Wattes, et William Wattes, par brief ensuaunt, etc.

[73] Writ to the sheriff of Warwickshire, ordering distraint of John de Schuckeborgh (sworn),[265] William Hikke (sworn), John Bray,[266] Walter Deyvill (sworn), Walter Farndon (sworn), John de Napton (sworn), John Pinke (sworn),[267] Robert Porter (sworn), John Budde, William Budde, Thomas Duston, John Grene of Grandborough (sworn), John de Grendon, John Bacon (sworn), John Colyns (sworn), Thomas Hert, Roger Hendeman, Thomas Bray, William Hemery (sworn), Robert de Stocton (sworn), John Ive of Harbury, Richard Truweman of Southam,[268] John Odams, William de Fylongleye, Philip of the Okes, John Raulyns, John Derset,[269] William Barbour, John Harryes of Wormleighton, John Harpour, and Adam Paynel, jurors summoned to Westminster in the plea of trespass by William de Catesby against Lewis Cook, Alice his wife, Thomas Wattes, and William Wattes, for their appearance at Westminster in Michaelmas octave [6 Oct.] unless the justices of assize for Warwickshire come there before the Wednesday of St Mary Magdalen [22 July]. Tested by Robert Belknap[270] at Westminster, 8

261 Recte *socage.*

262 Blaby in Leics was a Ladbroke manor of long standing: G. F. Farnham, *Leicestershire Medieval Pedigrees* (Leicester, 1925), 14–15.

263 cf. *CAD,* IV, A 9040 (demise by John Ladbroke, to Daventry, of rental in Harbury).

264 Followed by *et,* apparently in error.

265 Interlineations imitative of interlined annotations on the original.

266 Assessed at 40d., as a franklin, under Stretton on Dunsmore, in 1379: E 179/192/23, m.18. He was also a coroner at this time: Hunnisett, *Am.Jnl Leg.Hist.,* III, 345.

267 Assessed at 40d., as a franklin, under Thurlaston, in 1379: E 179/192/23, m.18d.

268 Assessed at 40d., as a hosteller, in 1379: ibid., m.17.

269 Assessed at 2s., as farmer of Thurlaston, in 1379: ibid., m.18d.

270 KS 1365–74; CJCP 1374–88.

July, 7 Richard II [1383]. 'Signed' Westwode. M.436.[271]

[74] Et[272] qel brief lissue fut pris, le qel le franctenement fut en le dit Lowys et Alice sa femme, come en dreit Alice, ou en le dit William de Catesby: qi disoient par lour serement qe le franctenement fut en le dit William de Catesby, etc., et assistreent les damages a quarant souch; et sur ceo jour fut done en banc ore a les oeptaves de Seint Michel prochein [6 Oct. 1383], etc.

Membrane 4

[75] Upon which recovery[273] William Catesby had a writ for reseisin of a messuage, 97a. of arable, 30a. of meadow, 100a. of pasture, 100a. of wood, 40a. of heath, and ten shillings rental in Tanworth, following his recovery of them against Lewis Cook and Alice his wife, Lawrence de Benteleye of Beoley, and John Dolphyn of Tanworth, before William de Skypwyth and William de Burgh, justices of assize in the county, at Warwick, on Wednesday of St Mary Magdalen [22 July]. Tested by William de Skypwyth at Warwick, 23 July, 7 Richard II [1383]. Authorised by Sadington.

[76] By virtue of this writ, on the Wednesday after,[274] at Tanworth, John Bray of Stretton on Dunsmore, by view of John Pinke of Thurlaston, William de Gersyndon, and other jurors, gave seisin in all these lands to John de Catesby, in the name of William de Catesby, in the presence of John Poleye, parker of Allesley,[275] William Tone, Thomas Cook, John Moton, John Jacob, and others.

[77] As for his damages, William de Catesby obtained a capias returnable on the Thursday following, but the sheriff returned that the defendants were not found, so Catesby obtained an exigent for as follows .[276]

[78] Et puis apres, a les freres menours de Coventre, le venderdy prochein devant la feste de Seint Bartholomeu mesme lan [21 Aug. 1383], estoit un jour tenuz entre le dit Johan de Catesby et les diz Laurence et Johan Dolphyn, etc., par mediacioun Johan de Croweleie, Johan Ray, Johan Barbour de Ichinton, et altres, ou ils covenaunterent issint qe le dit Laurence durreit iiij li., cest asavoir xl s. pur les arrerages de la rende et xl s. pur damages, et le dit Johan Dolphyn son estat del viver et des ewes, reservaunt a ly la moite del pesson qaunt ils serront debrusez, et v s. des arrerages, de qel paiement le dit Johan soi agreereit sil purreit estre servy des damages devers Lowyz et sa femme, et si non qils paiereient le remeindre en temps avenir; sur quoi le lundy en la dite feste de Seint Bertholomeu [24 Aug.], en le counte tenuz a Warr', le viscount fit sur le dit exigend un reddidit se pur les ditz Laurence et Johan Dolphyn, et lexigend avant devers les ditz Lowyz et sa femme.

[79] Et puis apres, le mardy[277] le septisme jour doctobre, le jour de Seint Marcz le pape, lan du regne [le] roi[278] Richard septisme [7 Oct. 1383], mourut le dit William de Catesby seisi des terres et tenementz avantditz et plusours altres, apres qi mort entra Johan son fiz et heir; et court tenuz en son noun a Lodbrok, le samady prochein devaunt la feste Seint Symond et Jude mesme lan [24 Oct.]; et le jeovedy prochein devant le dite feste [22 Oct.], il tient court a Schuckbergh;[279] et le lundy prochein devaunt[280] [26 Oct.] a Thorlaston. Et le venderdy prochein apres la feste de Seint Symond et Jude [30 Oct.], le dit Johan fit homage a Thomas de Beauchamp, counte de Warr', en presence de monsire William de Beauchamp, frere a dit counte, monsire Nicol Lylling, Robert Burgoillon, Henry Bruyn,[281] William Spernore, Johan Daniel,[282] Piers Holte,[283] William Cokeseie,[284] Edmund de Catesby, frere le dit Johan,[285] et plusours altres, si bien pur les terres et tenementz nadgaires monsire Johan de Lodbrok en Lodbrok come pur altres[286] terres et tenementz en mesme la vill, etc. Et pus apres, le xv jour de novembre, sire Johan de Belton,

[271] CP 40/490, m.436d. The membrane is authorised by *Stokkes.*

[272] For *A*? [273] i.e. [83]. [274] Blank in MS.

[275] Assessed at 12d., as farmer, in 1379: E 179/192/23, m.8.

[276] Blanks in MS. The capias, tested on 22 July and returnable on the following day (Thursday after St Mary Magdalen), and endorsed by Bagot as sheriff, survives, having strayed from Skipwith and Burgh's assize file to their gaol delivery file: JUST 3/67/5, m.3.

[277] Error for *meskerdy.*

[278] MS has *r' r',* as though for *regni regis.*

[279] Lower Shuckburgh, Warwickshire, at this time a separate manor from Upper Shuckburgh: *VCH Warw,* VI, 217.

[280] Interlined later.

[281] Probably Henry Bruin of Worcester, who was one of Warwick's creditors in 1397: *CIM,* VI, no. 303.

[282] For Daniel, see Goodman, *Loyal Conspiracy,* 146.

[283] For Holt, see ibid., 143.

[284] For Cooksey, see ibid., 146.

[285] Added later, in a space left.

[286] Interlined above *les,* deleted.

altrement apele Crisp,[287] person de lesglise de Swepston, qestoit de counseil monsire Henry de Ferers, seignur de Groby, bailla a dit Johan de Catesby une bill compernant la matire susdite en cels paroles:
[80] John de Lodbrok holds one messuage, two and a half virgates of land, a mill, and a holm, in Ladbroke, with the advowson of the church, of William de Ferariis, for a quarter of a knight fee.[288]
[81] Et puis apres, le xvj jour de novembre mesme lan,[289] Johan le fiz William de Catesby fit homage et fealte[290] pur les terres et tenementz susdiz a monsire Henry de Ferers, seignur de Groby, en la basse chapel de Seint Estevene a Westm', en presence de sire Johan Belton avantdite, Johan Farewell, Johan Schepeie, et plusours altres, de qi le dit Johan de Catesby ad les lettres le dit seignur, etc., patentes et closes, etc.
[82] Et auxint a mesme le temps le dit Johan de Catesby fit homage a Thomas de Mountbury, count de Notingham, pur le manoir de Hapsford en le counte de Warr', en presence dame Margaret countesse de Northfolk, aele le dit count, monsire Robert Belknap, monsire Rogger Fulthorp,[291] et monsire Robert de Plesington, chef baron de lescheqer,[292] et chief seneschal a dit count, ly chargeant de son homage, etc.

Membrane 4d

[83] Pleas of assize before William de Skypwyth and William de Burgh, justices of assize for Warwickshire, at Warwick, Wednesday of St Mary Magdalen, 7 Richard II [22 July 1383][293]

Assize to recognise whether Lewis Cook, Alice his wife, Lawrence de Benteleye of Beoley, and John Dolphyn of Tanworth, smith, unjustly disseised William de Catesby of his free tenement in Tanworth; Catesby complains of disseisin there of a messuage, 97a. of arable, 30a. of meadow, 100a. of pasture, 100a. of wood, 40a. of heath, and 10s. rental, with appurtenances. The defendants do not come; Lewis and Alice were attached by timber worth 12d., which is therefore forfeit, Dolphyn was attached by John Fox and Henry Hert, who are therefore in mercy, and Lawrence has no goods in the county and cannot be found. Let the assize be taken on default. Asked about the rental, Catesby says that William son of Nicholas le Wodeward was seised of the lands from which the rent derives, in demesne as of fee, and he granted them, by a fine [121], which is proffered in court. Thomas and Alice Ladbroke had one son, John; Hawise died, and thereupon William de Catesby entered by virtue of the fine;[294] then Thomas and Alice died, and John brother of Hugh died without heirs male; Catesby granted the lands whose rent is at issue to Dolphyn, for the life of Catesby, by indenture [61]; John son of Thomas and Alice died without heirs male of his body, and Hugh brother of Thomas likewise; after which Catesby was seised of the rental until the defendants disseised him. The recognitors say that the descent of the tenement and rental was as specified in the plaint,[295] until Catesby was unjustly disseised by the defendants, to his damage of £10. Judgment that Catesby have reseisin, and damages of £10;[296] capias on the defendants. [*See* 75–7] Names of the jurors: Richard de Eggebaston, Edmund de Compton, Thomas Corbet, William de Gersyndon, William de Fylongleye, Nicholas de Ayleston, John Napton, John Pynke, Thomas Baudewyn, John Bacon, William Laumprey, William Hemery.

Membrane 5

[84] Des qels homage et fealte, si ben de count de Warr' come del count de Not' et del seignur de Ferers de Groby, le dit Johan ad lour lettres patentes ceo tesmoignantes, etc.
[85] Et puis, le dit Johan continuant cel estat apres la mort William soun piere, un Thomas Larcher porta un assise de novel disseisin en son nom et en le non sir William Gamell, clerc, et Nicol de Oddingeseles,[297] issint, etc.

287 Interlined.

288 See the inquisition post mortem on William Ferrers of Groby: *CIPM,* XVI, no. 559.

289 *mesme lan* interlined.

290 Followed by *a,* in error.

291 JCP 1374–1388; see Kimball in *Warwicks Sessions,* xl.

292 Chief baron 1380–6.

293 This, and the chancery copy (C 260/96, no. 33, m.4), are transcripts of JUST 1/1488, m.59, omitting the postea noting Catesby's acknowledgement of receipt of damages – presumably made by John Catesby as executor – and the fines of the defendants.

294 Some of the text here is interlined and faint.

295 The detailing of this verdict was copied here rather inaccurately, with some interlineation and the omission of details of the lease, which were in the record itself: cf. the chancery copy, C 260/96, no. 33, m.4.

296 This passage is repeated, and the first time deleted, because sewing of the membranes obscured the reading. The entry runs over the top of m.5d.

297 Of Forshaw in Solihull: *VCH Warw,* IV, 221.

[86] [*Abstract of* 128.]

[87] Quele assise estoit araie encountre les assises qestoient tenuz a Warr' le meskerdy le jour de Seint Margaret, lan de mesme le roi viij [20 July 1384], devaunt monsire William Skypwyth et William de Burgh, tut a le devis le dit Thomas, par William Bagot,[298] viscount de dit counte, et puis jour soi pris par mediacioun monsire Nicol Lylling[299] et le dit viscount, ou il estoient esleuz depar le dit Thomas, monsire Johan de Peyto, et Richard de Ryhale, seneschal de la mar',[300] si le dit Thomas pout le dit Richard avoir, et si ne mye, le dit monsire Johan et Estevene Wyte del counte de Herford, et depar le dit Johan de Catesby, monsire Robert Destafford[301] et Robert de Burgoillon ou altre: qel arbitrement les dit monsire Johan et Ryhale ount refuse, et le dit jour dut avoir este tenuz a Warr' le mardy en lendemein de la feste de Lassumpcioun Nostre Dame [16 Aug.]. Et puis le dit Thomas, al prochein counte apres, tenuz a Warr', soi escusa del dit jour tenir, mes qil le tendreit volonters entour la Nativite Nostre Dame adonqe prochein [8 Sept.]; a qel jour de Seint Margaret toz les pleintifs furent esson', etc.

[88] La copie del panell de Toneworth est tiel de cest assise ore pendaunt:

Baldwin Montfort, knight, John Eynesford, knight, Thomas Raulee, Thomas Hubarrd, Thomas Busschopesdon, William Dede, John Boteler of Shustoke,[302] John Warde of Bromwich, Ralph Richardes,[303] William de Westyngton, John atte Lee of Tanworth, William Hawe, Ralph Hopwas, Leonard Worthin, Richard Hawe, Alexander Lyndon, Simon of the Hay, Richard Gowerne of Tanworth,[304] William Pycke, John Pynke, William Hemery, William Fylongleye, Thomas Broun, Robert atte Grene. [*cf.* 129]

[89] Axint clers de la chauncellerie conucent a dit Johan qil i ad un altre assise purchacea de Lodbrok issint: [*Abstract of* 127]. Quel assise nest mie unqore baille a viscount, etc.

[90] Et puis par le dit monsire Nicol Lylling, altre jour estoit assigne, entour le dit jour de la Nativite, cest a savoir le jeovedy en lendemain Seint Matheu, lan viij le dit roi [22 Sept. 1384], a temps qaunt les cessions de la pees estoient tenuz a Warr',[305] ou le dit Johan vient ove ses arbitours avantdiz et ove toz pl' des evidences et proves, et le dit Thomas vient et nulles proves ne amena, et issint sanz jour, etc.

[91] Et les diz justices dassises ajournerent les assises taunt entour la feste de Seint Piere en cathedre adonqe prochein ensuaunt [22 Feb. 1385], avant qel temps les diz justices estoient remuiz, et en lour lieu mis monsire Rogger Fulthorp et Johan de Lokton,[306] qi discontinuerent le dit jour et firent precept de novel[307] encountre le lundy en la symeigne de Pentecost adonqe prochein ensuaunt [22 May], a qel jour les diz William Gamell et Thomas Larcher furent nonsuiz; et le dit Nicol suit avant, et jour done tanqe jeovedy en lendemain Seint Nicolas, qestoit la veille de la Concepcioun Nostre Dame,[308] adonqe prochein ensuaunt, qest unqor avenir [7 Dec. 1385].

[92] Et fait a remembrer qentour la feste de Nowel, le dit an viij le roi qorest [1384], monsire Johan de Burmyngham,[309] monsire Nicol Lylling, monsire Johan de Eynesford, firent un acord entre le dit Johan de Catesby et Thomas Larcher, en la sale en le chastel de Warr', cest a savoir qe le dit Thomas suera et ferra le dit William Gamell suire avant lassise, issint qe lassise passereit a les procheins assises, et qe il livereit a dit Johan de Catesby les featz par qels il clame estat, qel abord il nad de rienz perfourmy, et puis sur ceo le dit Thomas envoia a dit Johan de Catesby, par Robert Broun de Warr', la copie dune chartre de feffement fait par Lowys Cardian et Alice sa femme as diz William, Thomas, et Nicol, en fez simple, et auxint un reles, etc.

[93] A qels jour des assises et de jeovedy les justices avantdiz ne vindrent pas, par qi les assises furent sanz jour. Et puis apres, le lundy prochein devant la feste

[298] For Bagot, see above, 297–8 and references.

[299] Followed by *mesme,* deleted.

[300] There is no evidence of his connection with the marshalsea either of the royal household or of king's bench; this might perhaps refer to an administrative function at the assizes session.

[301] For Stafford, see Kimball in *Warwicks Sessions,* xxxiii.

[302] Assessed at 2s., as a carpenter, in 1379: E 179/192/23, m.4d.

[303] Later coroner: Hunnisett, *Am. Jnl Leg. Hist.,* III, 345.

[304] Assessed at 2s., as a franklin, in 1379: E 179/192/23, m.14.

[305] See Kimball in *Warwicks Session,* xcii.

[306] JKB 1387–8; see also ibid., xl–xli.

[307] Followed by *tantqe,* deleted.

[308] *qestoit . . . Dame* interlined later, above *la feste de Seint Nicolas* deleted.

[309] For Birmingham, see Kimball in *Warwicks Sessions,* xxxiii.

Seint Thomas lapostre adonqe[310] prochein ensuaunt [18 Dec. 1385], apres manger en le gardyn del chastel a Warr', en presence le count mesmes, monsire Nicol Lylling, Margarete Wyltschire, William de Cokeseie, Janyn de la Butelerye, Nicolas Trymenell, et le dit Johan de Catesby, le count assigna jour as diz Margarete et Johan de Catesby en la dite matire a Loundres, devaunt son grant counseil a la xv de Seint Hillary adonqe prochein ensuaunt [27 Jan. 1386], etc.

[94] Qel jour continue tantqe le meskerdy prochein apres la Purificacioun Nostre Dame adonqe prochein ensuaunt [7 Feb.], a tenir en le meson de la chapitre de Seint Poul de Londres, a qel jour illeqs le dit count mesme,[311] monsire William son frere, monsire Johan Holte,[312] monsire David Hanmer,[313] monsire William de Burgh, sire Richard de Pyryton, clerc, dean de Colcestre, sire Johan de Ermesthorp, mestre de Seint Katerines, monsire Nicol Lilling, Robert de Cherleton,[314] William Thernyng, serjaunz de counseil le dit count, en presence des qels Thomas Archer pur Lewys et sa femme Alice, par Johan Wadham, serjaunt,[315] Johan Woderoue et Johan Kyrkeby del North, aprentiz, dit qe monsire Henry de Lodbrok dona les tenemenz en Toneworth a monsire Johan son fiz et a la dite Hawyse en fee taille, et evidence altre rienz ne mostre, si non la taille de Herbury, qe port date en temps le roi Edward secounde qe gist a Glouc'; en despreove de qi le dit Johan mostre un fait endente par qel le dit monsire Henry lessa a dit Johan soun fiz les manoirs de Lodbrok et Toneworth a terme de sa vie, remanent a ly pur terme de sa vie, par an xx li., qel fait desouz le seal de ses armes port date en temps[316] le roi Edward tierce puis le conqest, fiz le susdit roi Edward; issint fut lour dit fause supposer les tenemenz estre donez en fee taille en temps le dit roi Edward qe gist a Glouc'; et issint fut il tenuz pur faux, etc.

[95] Et qaunt a Lodbrok, ils coniseient bien qe ceo fut fee simple, mes ils disoient qe monsire Johan fut seisi et mourut seisi; apres qi mort entra Thomas come fiz et heyr, et mourut seisi; apres qi mort entra Johan son fiz et fut seisi, et mourut seisi; apres qi mort, pur ceo qil mourut sanz issue, le fee resorti ala dite Alice, seor Thomas, come a aunte et heir, etc.

[96] A qi fut dit qe le dit monsire Johan de Lodbrok soi demist par sa chartre desouz le seal de ses armes as certeins persones, et puis relessa en manere come les faitz et relesse purportent, le qel feffement apres la mort le dit monsire Johan fut tesmoigne desouth le seal des armes Thomas count de Warr', pier a count qorest, par ses lettres patentes, par qels il tesmoigne le feffement et accepta William de Catesby come son verroi tenant, et prist sa fealte, qele lettre patente le count mesme et monsire William son frere regarderent, et le seal, et disoient qe ceo fut verrement le seal count Thomas lour piere, et le dit count dit qe ceo fut trefort evidence si son piere fusse bien enfourme; a qi fut responduz qe sil fut ou bien ou mal, sire Richard de Pyriton, dean de Colcestre, qi seoit illeqs, les savoir bien enfourmer, pur ceo qil estoit demurant a tiel temps ove le dit count lour piere; le qel sire Richard lour dit qe lour dit piere fut bien et duement enfourme, et ceo prist il sur ly. Et puis apres le dit count comist la dite busoigne et les parties a dit sire Richard de Pyriton et a monsire David Hanmer et a monsire William de Burgh, les qels apres, le jeovedy en les oeptave de la dite Purificacioun [8 Feb. 1386], a Westm', en la chaumbre de counseil en lescheqer, firent fyn come piert par les cedules a cest roule consues, etc.

[97] Et puis a les prochein assises, jour fut pris entre Thomas Larcher et le dit Johan de Catesby, le dit an ix le roi Richard secounde, entour la feste Seint Pere in cathedra [22 Feb.],[317] par mediacioun monsire Nicol Lylling, destre tenuz a Wyrc' a les assises, esleux depar le dit Johan, Gy Spine et Robert Burgoillon[318] ou Thomas Purfrey,[319] et William Spernore estoit par le dit Nicol, et le dit Thomas soi mist en mesme les persones; a qel jour a Wyrc' le dit Thomas Purfrey ne vint point, et issint fut le dit jour sanz jour, etc. Et puis a les prochein assises apres, entour la feste de Seint Margaret prochein, lan disme mesme le roi [20 July 1386], qaunt lassise dut avoir passe, le dit Thomas Archer soi mist et ala a count de Warr', en son gardyn, qil envoiast pur un jour, qi envoia le dit monsire Nicol pur le dit jour, et le dit Thomas Archer dit qil ne ala pur null jour, et le dit monsire Nicol

[310] After *la*, deleted.

[311] This list is not identical with that given at [143].

[312] KS 1376–83; JCP 1383–8.

[313] KS 1377–83; JKB 1383–6.

[314] CJCP 1388–95.

[315] JCP 1389–98.

[316] The continuation (to [97] inclusive) from m.5d is inserted here by means of a crude Ladbroke blazon – azure, a chevron ermine – used as an asterisk (*plus in tergo ad hoc signum*); m.5 concludes with [98].

[317] *entour . . . cathedra* interlined.

[318] Followed by *William S*, deleted.

[319] For Purfrey, see Kimball in *Warwicks Sessions,* xli.

avowa sur ly qe il vint et requit le dit count del dit jour; issint, al instance del dit counte, le dit Johan granta la continuaunce, etc. Et apres, en le gardyn le dit count a Warr', le jour des assises, apres manger, en presence monsire Rogger Fulthorp et Johan de Locton, justices des assises, le count promist qil nies ne mellereit ne pur nul delai priereit; a[320] qel jour des assises le dit Johan de Catesby pria decem tales, et les avoit, et cour dona outre tantqe le mardy prochein devant la feste Seint Piere ad vincula, mesme lan disme [31 July 1386]; devant qel jour, cest a savoir en la Nowel, lan disme [25 Dec. 1385], le dit monsire Nicol, William Spernore, Gy Spynee, Piers Holte, Janyn of the Buterie,[321] Nicol Trymenell, esquiers, Henry Trimenell et laltre Trimenel, vadlez, firent un acord qe le dit Johan lerreit tut suites personels, sauve qe tochent enheritance, devers le dit Thomas et toz les seons, et le dit Thomas pursuereit lassise tantqe il fusse passe; et monsire Nicol et les esquiers ferreient lour pooir, et il le seon, qe William Gamel, clerc, vensist; a qel jour des assises, les parties demandez, Thomas vient et Nicholas Oddingeseles vint, et William Gamel ne vient point, et les justices agarderent la serveraince meintenant pur taunt qe toz aparurent a darrein jour par continuaunce prise, et puis qaunt Thomas et Nicol dussent avoir suy avant et fait lour pleinte des ij parties, le dit Thomas dit qil navoit mie patente, pur taunt (il dit) qe ceo fut a Coventre en la garde le dit William Gamel; et pur taunt qils navoient mie patente ne nul pleint ne fut fait adevant, fut agarde un nounsuit. Et puis lendamein le meskerdy en Cendres [21 Feb. 1387], a Coventre, le dit Johan de Catesby et Robert Burgoillon envoierent a William Gamel, viker, denqerrer sil ust la patente; qi dit qil delivra la patente et les faitz qils avoit, plus qun demy an passe, a ses compaignons, issint qe rienz ne revist en sa garde. Issint le dit Thomas fauxement debruse sa promes a son jour, etc. etc., et le dit Johan a large a pursuire ses vieles acciouns.

Membrane 5 (concluded)[322]

[98] Dame Hawyse mourut le meskerdy prochein devant la Toz Seintz [31 Oct. 1369], mesme lan qe le count Thomas de Warr' mourut; le venderdy prochein ensuaunt [2 Nov.],[323] Hugh Baillif de Lodbrok estoit envoie a Toneworth depar William de Catesby a prendre seisine illeqs, et il dit len lamener Thomas Larcher qorst enfaunt de tendre age, et Thomas Colles, etc.

Membrane 6

[99] Item par assignement le count de Warr' fait a Warr', le lundy prochein devant la feste des Palmes, lan du regne le roi Richard secounde qatorzisme [13 Mar. 1391], en presence sire Johan Hermesthorp, clerc, monsire Nicol Lylling, sire Thomas ,[324] receivour de Warr', et altres plusours, jour estoit assigne a Loundres destre tenuz devant monsire Walter de Clopton, chief justice de banc le roi, et Johan de Wadham, justice de comune banc, entre Lowys Cook et Alice sa femme dunpart, et le dit Johan de Catesby daltrepart, cest a savoir qe le dit Johan de Catesby declarreit tute la matire tochant les manoirs de Lodbrok et Toneworth, qe nadgairs furent a monsire Johan de Lodbrok, sauvant a dit Johan de Catesby tutes avauntages come la ley ly avoit done, et qe, la dite matire oiiz, les diz justices envoiereient lour avis a dit count; sur qel assignement, a dit jour, tenuz en lesglise de Seint Gregory desouz lesglise de Seint Poul, le samady en la veille de Seint Jeorge, le dit an [22 Apr. 1391], sire Johan Hermesthorp, un des chamberleyns de la receite, estoit, et monsire Nicol ne mie, qest a Wyndesore descuser le count de sa nonvenue illeqs; ou Hermesthorp rehercea qe tute la matire dut estre manye del foundement, sanz avoir regard a la ley, et ceo le dit Johan de Catesby traversa; et issint departirent sanz jour. Et puis le lundy prochein ensuaunt [24 Apr.], a Westm', le dit monsire Nicol[325] tesmoigne as diz justices ceo estre verrai qe Johan de Catesby avoit dit, etc. [*See also* 154]

[100] Et puis le samady prochein devant la feste de Seint Nicolas, lan du roi Richard seconde xvme [2 Dec. 1391], en la chauncellerie a West', devant lercevesqe Deverwyk, adonqe chaunceller, Thomas de Beuchamp, count de Warr', monsire William son frere, le seignur de Grey, William Thyrning, justice, et plusours altres, sur la bille baille a roi, la dite Alice illeqs present, Johan de Catesby reherceant tute la matire, et coment la matire avoit este manie devant le dit count et soun counseill, come plusours illeqs tesmoignent, et les ditz count et soun frere auxint, et

[320] After *issint si*, deleted.

[321] Perhaps one of the Buttery family of Berkswell: *VCH Warw*, IV, 30.

[322] See above [94 and n.]

[323] *le venderdy prochein ensuaunt* interlined above deletion.

[324] Blank in MS. Thomas Knight was receiver of Warwick in 1395: SC 6/1123/5.

[325] After *Johan de Catesby*, deleted.

justices et serjaunz; et auxint coment puis il estoit manie devant le counseil levesqz de Ely, Johan de Fordham, tantqe come il estoit evesqe de Duresme et tresorer Dengleterre, et illeqs dimis;[326] et puis devant le counseil le duc de Glouc', par temoignance monsire Robert de Plesington, monsire William Castelacre, et illeqs dimiss; et coment soun piere recovry par assise, dount la tenure estoit present en la chauncellerie, et soun dit pere mourut seisi: sur qoi fut dit a la dite Alice, par le chaunceller mesme, qele lessat a faire sa noise pur la dite matire, et nomeement sur le dit count, sur peine denprisonement; et si ele verroit qil fusse afaire en eese manere ele pursuereit la comune ley, et a ceo faire la court lasignereit volonters counseil, etc.

[101] Et puis apres, le lundy prochein apres la feste de Seint Mathe, lan du regne le roi Richard vint et primer [24 Sept. 1397], al hostel monsire Hugh Luterel en Southwerk, jouste Seint Jeorge, William Hathewyk aporta a Johan de Catesby lettre de prive seal nostre seignur le roi [160], qil serreit devant le counseil nostre dit seignur le roi a la xv de Seint Michel adonqe prochein venant [13 Oct.], ove ses fetz et evidences tochauntz le manoir de Lodbrok; a qel xv le dit Johan estoit, et declarra sa matere devant les presence de counseil en le Sterredchaumbre, especifiez sur lendocement de la copie de le lettre de prive seal escrit de la mein Frye, clerc de counseil; et sur la matire declarre pursuaunt fut agarde a suire la comune ley. Et puis apres le banc le roi vint a Coventre, a lendemein des Almes adonqe prochein ensuaunt [3 Nov.], a quel temps Lowys Cardian et Alice portent un assise retournable le lundy prochein apres la feste de Toz Seintz [5 Nov.] en le dit banc; a qel jour, en laube de jour, le panel estoit araie pur le pleintif a Bathekynton,[327] par Ilschawe le southviscount,[328] Robert de Gowshull[329] adonqe viscount, a la devis monsire William Bagot adonqe lour meintenour; et a demywey prime[330] le dit lundy, avaunt qe le dit Johan pout avoir la copie, et qaunt lassise apurut, le pleintif dit qe soun brief fut malement conceu, et pria conge de qerre meillour brief; et la court ne ly voleit recevire sanz dire en qey en especial, et puis ils furent nounsuiz.

[102] Et puis de diz Lowys et Alice purchacent un altre assise de novel, retournable en le dit banc le mardy prochein apres les uptaves de Seint Martin[331] adonqe prochein ensuaunt [18 Nov. 1397], de qel jour jour fut done tauntqe le jeovedy prochein ensuaunt [22 Nov.], a qel jour les pleintifs chalangent larray, et larray trie bon par William Hawe et Nicolas Sauser de Stretford,[332] et pur qaunt ix estoient jurrez, les pleintifs altre foith nounsuiz. Et pur taunt qe ceo fu la terce foith qe les pleintifs avoient este nonsuiz, cest a savoir un foith devant monsires William Thirning et Richard Sidenham, come piert amont,[333] et deux foith ore en le dit banc, les dez pleintifs estoient amerciez, et afurez par les diz jurours a cent soldz; duraunt qel temps des deux assises, monsire William Bagot tut meintenour, et les viscount et southviscount eueranz a dit monsire William, etc.; a qel temps, purtaunt qe le dit monsire William vit qe les assises letz a soun devis ne voleient point servir soun purpos, il envoia monsires Averay Trussel[334] et Gy Spyne a dit Johan de Catesby qil tendreit jour damour, et qil prendreit un chivaler et un esquier, et il mesme serreit ove les pleintifs et prendreit a ly un esquier; et Johan de Catesby respondit qe le chaunceller, par autorite de parlement,[335] avoit mis le pleintif a la comune ley, et puis le counseil, a la quinzeine de Seint Michel darrein, come desus, le pleintif conmis a la comune ley; et ore a la comune ley ils sont, la qele il est prest de atendre, et dit qil fut prest a tenir jours, par issint qe la comune ley ne fusse tarie. Et le dit William departy ove malencolie, etc.

326 One minim short.

327 Baginton, Warwickshire, the seat of Sir William Bagot.

328 William Illshaw: KB 37/2/21/1, unnumbered schedule of county officers, 1397.

329 Goxhill later married the widowed countess of Norfolk: G.E.C., IX, 604. His primary allegiance at this date was to the earl of Warwick.

330 See also G. Chaucer, *Complete Works,* ed. W. W. Skeat (Oxford, 1895), Canterbury Tales, T.3906: 'Lo, Depeford! and it is half-way pryme'.

331 Followed by *de qel,* deleted.

332 Saucer was coroner in this year: Hunnisett, *Am. Jnl Leg. Hist.,* III, 346.

333 i.e. on the attached schedules [148–151].

334 Alfred Trussell, lord of Milverton: *VCH Warw,* VI, 165.

335 This is probably a reference to the chancellor's regular function as a supplementary trier of petitions in parliament; this petition was heard in chancery after parliament had ended, and was not entered in the latter's proceedings: *RP,* III, 284–99; see [100].

Membrane 7[336]

[103] Et issint demura la matere en pees tauntqe en la Nowel adonqe prochein ensuaunt, le roi tenaunt son Nowel a Coventre, le jour de Nowel esteant sur un mardy, et le venderdy adonqe prochein ensuaunt [28 Dec. 1397], Thomas Purefey envoia a dit Johan de Catesby qe il serrait a Coventre la samady prochein, ove ses fetz et evidences, pur declarer soun droit devant le counseil le duc de Surreie; a qel samady le dit Johan de Catesby fut a Coventre par temps, et soi profry a dit counseil de avoir declarre ses evidences; et auxint, le dymenge en lendemein, par monsire William Daroundell et monsire Hugh Luterell en priaunt par els a dit duc, qe la dite matere purreit estre oie devant son counseil avaunt qe le duc plus soi mellereit. Et tut ceo nient countreesteaunt, le lundy en lendemein, cest a savoir la veille de la Circumcisioun Nostre Seignur [31 Dec.], Lowys Cardian et Alice, ove plusours de Herbury, entrerent en le dite manoir par covine et procurement le dit William Hathewyk, et puis entour x de la cloche vindrent monsire Robert de Clifton ove soun launcegay[337] soi xviij des persoun, archers et altres, et, come estoit dit, pristrent feffement a dit duc et monsire William Bagot, etc. Et puis le dit Johan de Catesby envoia par Johan Broke a la chauncellerie et purchacea deux assises et deux patentes de la date del xxxj jour de decembre, cest la veille de la Circumcision susdite, encontre les diz Lowis, Alice, et William Hathewyk; la qel assise estoit livre par Johan Broke a viscount le lundy en la veille de Seint Agaz mesme lan [4 Feb. 1398], en la receite a Warr'; et puis le mardy en lendemein, cest a savoir le jour de Seint Agaz, estoit lassise atache a Lodbrok par Chyrye, le southbaillif del hundred de Knytlowe;[338] et pus le lundy prochein devant la feste de Seint Juliane en Qaresme,[339] jeo parlai ove Nicolas Gascoyn pur Lodbrok, qi me dit qil ne voleit rienz fere sanz mandement ou comandement en especial; et le dymenge prochein, William Bakere envoia pur Wille Hogekyns[340] de venir a Warr', qe de illeqs vint a moi a Kenelworth et me counta qe le duc de Surreie ly avoit envoie ses lettres patentes pur estre soun baillif a Lodbrok; entour qel temps vient Johan le fiz Robert Broun a Lodbrok, et tient un court, et sen departy, etc.

[104] Et en le venderdy en la feste de Seint Piere en cathedra [22 Feb. 1398] passa lassise a Warr' pur moi encountre les diz Lowys et Alice et le dit William Hathewyk; a qel jour le dit William estoit, et respoundy par baillif pur les altres, et chalengea larrai, et estoient eslieu triours Aleyn Waldeyene de Elmedoun et William Hawe de Sulihull, qi trierent larrai bon, et puis lassise prise et passa pur moi, et en evidence il mostra soulement le fait de jointenaunce, par qel Lowys et Alice dussent avoir enfeffe le dit duc, Edmund soun frere, et le dit William Hathewyk, qel fait purporta date le xxix jour de decembre, la ou lentre les diz Lowys et Alice estoit fait deux jours apres, cest a savoir le xxxj jour de decembre, cest a savoir la veille de la Circumcision, a qel temps il ne oosa mostrer en evidence nul fait de taille pur la fauxine; et auxint la dite veille monsire William Bagot estoit enfeffe jount, etc., et pur taunt qil desclama, novel fait fut forge et le dite monsire William entrelesse. [*See* 114–115]

[105] Et puis le dymenge prochein [341] en Qaresme [10 *or* 17 Mar. 1398], vient Robert Walden a Stonleye en labbeye et mostra a moi les diz lettres patentes fetes a dit William Bakere, purportaunz date le iij jour de marcz; et issint demura tauntqe le meskerdy en la simeigne de Pasche adonqe prochein [10 Apr.], qe jeo parlai a Warr' ove Nicolas Gascoyn, a qel temps le dit William Hathewyk estoit, ou le dit Nicolas me respondy come devant, etc. Et puis le terme de Pasche adonqe prochein, jeo men alai a Londres, et le meskerdy prochein devaunt la feste de la Seint Crois en may [1 May 1398], jeo baillai un bille a dit duc, le matyn, en lostel de duc Dexcestre qe nadgairs estoit a dame Alice Perers; qi bailla la bille a Robert de Clifton soun chaumberlein, comaundaunt a ly qil baillast la bille a dit Nicolas Gascoyn son

336 M.6d contains only the continuation of m.7: below, [109n.]

337 Lancegays in particular, and armed force in general, had recently been subject to repeated complaint and legislation, when Bagot was MP for Warwickshire: *RP*, III, 164 (no. 56), 345 (no. 37); see 7 Ric. II, c.13 and 20 Ric. II, c.1.

338 Thomas Cherry, underbailiff of Knightlow hundred, Warwickshire: KB 37/2/21/1, unnumbered schedule of county officers, 1397.

339 Since both common feasts of St Juliana can occur in Lent, this should refer to 23 February, which alone fell within Lent in this year, giving 18 February as the date here; the alternative, however – St Juliana on 16 February and the previous Monday on 11 February – allows unbroken chronological sequence between this entry and the next.

340 Catesby's collector for Ladbroke: SC 6/1041/10, m.1; 12, m.2.

341 Blank in MS.

seneschal, et qil ferreit la dite matere estre manye par soun sage counseil, et qe relacioun fusse fait a ly solonc lour avis.

[106] Et puis jour moi fut assigne devant son counseil a les freres prechours a Londres, a la dymenge adonqe prochein ensuaunt [5 May 1398], aqel jour, en la meson de chapetre illeqs, esteanz presenz illeqs monsire Robert de Clyfton, chaumberlein, Nicolas Gascoyn, seneschal des terres, William Gascoyn, William Brencheslee, serjaunz le roi as plez, Robert Tyrwhyt, William Hornby,[342] serjaunz, et J. Scarclif,[343] chef auditour, et Edward[343] Scherd, de conseil le dit seignur, et auxint de counseil des parties,[344] et Johan Cokeyn[345] et Johan Rede, serjaunz, de mon counseil, Edward de Mettelee, William Danby, Stotesbury, Harewell, Throp, Osbern, Johan Offecherch, clerc, et altres, ou la matire estoit manie a leiser, et jour done a moi en la symeigne de Pentecost adonqe prochein, a Warr', a qel temps le dit Nicolas serreit illeqs, et le dit monsire Robert charge de fere relacioun.

[107] Et puis le lundy prochein devant la Pentecost, lan xxj le roi [20 May 1398], jeo aprochai a monseignur de Surreie, qi me fit bon chere; et pur taunt qe le dit Nicolas nestoit unqore, mon dit seignur mesmes me dona jour tantqe le lundy lendemein de la Pentecost adonqe prochein ensuaunt [27 May], davoir fyn finalment, a qel jour jestoie, et ove moi Asscheford, conestable de Kenelworth, Edward Metteleye, Thomas Purefey, William Pole, Johan Schuckeburgh, William Broke, persoun de Lodbrok, et sis altres des mielz vauiz de Lodbrok. Et sur la relacioun qe le dit Nicolas fit a mon dit seignur de soun grant counseil a Londres, agarde fut qe jeo tendreie en pees le manoir de Lodbrok, et William Baker comaunde par le dit monsire Robert, et par le dit Nicolas Gascoin, qil nies ne soi mellereit depar monseignur, devant plusours en la sale. Et qe si les diz Lowys et Alice voillent suire par brief de formedoun, a lour peril, qe monseignur ne envoiera nient plus pur Lowys et Alice qe pur moi ses lettres; et qe jeo baillereie un fait qe fit mencioun dun taille des manoirs de Lodbrok et Toneworth a Nicolas Gascoyn ou a Gy Spyne, seneschal, sur certeins condiciouns, le qel fait fut trove faux en le terme de Seint Michel, lan xxj le roi Richard, devant monsire Walter de Clopton et ses compaignons, justices de banc le roi, a Coventre.

[108] Et puis apres, le venderdy en lendemain de la translacioun Seint Benet [12 July 1398], monseignur de Surr' envoia Phelip son messager a Asscheby,[346] saunz lettre, qe jeo venisse a ly le dit jour, a North', esteauntz monsire Hugh Luterell et moi a manger, et apres manger jeo men departy et alai a North', et trovai monseignur a Oveston; et illeqs monseignur me dit qe jeo dusse avoir livere le fait avant la nativite Seint Johan [24 June], et jeo ly respondai qe ne mye a ma entente; et puis acorde fut qe jeo ferreie endenture entre le dit Nicolas et moi, et qe jeavoiereie le dit fait a Nicolas en la symeigne adonqe prochein ensuaunt a Londres; et puis le meskerdy en la dite symeigne [17 July], Gadifer Gyles bailla a Nicolas le dit fait a Loundres, en un hostel en la Garderobe, monseignur estoit ove la part dune note endente, dount jai laltre partie, ou monsire Gilbert Haydok et Nicolas, regardaunz le fait sembleit a els qele fut faux et defumee. Et puis moun dit seignur, sur soun alaunt en Irlaunde, le darrein jour de janvier adonqe prochein ensuaunt [1399], fit fere un chartre de feffement et un lettre datourne desouth son signet, a Lodelowe, par le procurement Edward Scherd et William Hathewyk, a le duc Dexcestre et a le dit Edward Scherd et a lours heirs del dit manoir, par vertue de qel feffement vindrent a Lodbrok Gy Spyne et Henry Trymenell, atournez, et Edward Scherd, et illeqs firent livre a dit Edward, en presence Thomas Lutterworth, messager,[347] etc., le meskerdy prochein apres la feste Seint Mathie en Qaresme adonqe prochein en lan de roi xxij [26 Feb. 1399].

Membrane 6d[348]

[109] Et puis apres, le primer dymenge de la Passion en la dite Qaresme [16 Mar. 1399], al enterement le duc de Lancastre,[349] bailla sa bille a Londres a dit

[342] King's attorney in common pleas 1382–96; KS 1398–1401.

[343] This word was entered later in a space left at the time of writing.

[344] *et auxint . . . parties* interlined later.

[345] JCP 1405–29.

[346] Ashby St Ledgers, Northants, the principal Catesby seat.

[347] Lutterworth acted as messenger for the earl of Warwick: SC 6/1123/5, m.2d.

[348] This continuation is flagged for insertion after m.7.

[349] This is somewhat late as Gaunt died 3 Feb. (G.E.C., VII, pt 2, 415–16), but it corresponds with the Kirkstall chronicler's 'modicum ante festum virginis gloriose' if this is taken as Lady Day (25 Mar.) and not, as various editors have supposed, the Purification (2 Feb.): *The Kirkstall Abbey*

duc Dexcestre en lostel nadgairs dame Alice Perers, par matyn; qele bille le duc me lut, et le bailla a monsire Thomas Schelley son senschal, presentz monsire William Cogeshale, soun chanberlein, monsire Johan Herle, seneschal del hostel, et plusours altres; et puis jour fut assigne as parties al mois de Pasch adonqe prochein; a qel jour de moys [28 Apr.][350] les parties, cest a savoir Johan de Catesby dunpart et Lowys Cardian et William Hathewyk daltre part, estoient entrechaungeablement lyez chescun a altre en cent li. dester a lagard des seignurs avauntdiz a faire acordaunt a lavis et discrecioun William Gascoin, Robert Tyrwyht, de counseil le duc de Surreie, Johan Rede et William Scryn de counseil le duc Dexcestre, serjaunz de la ley, enselez desouz lour seals, a la xv de la Trinite adonqe prochein ensuaunt [8 June], les qels serjaunz a la dite xv oiez a grant leiser de v simeignes les resons et evidences des ammbes partz, les parties eianz des ambes parz ove els serjaunz de la ley de counseil, cest a savoir, depar Hathewyk, Robert Hull, serjaunt, et altres aprentz, et depar Johan de Catesby, Johan Cokeyn, William Hornby, serjaunz, William Pole, les ij freres de Barton, et altres aprentiz; ou les diz qatre serjaunz certifierent, par deux lettres clos desouz lour seals as seignurs avauntdiz, et par un altre lettre overt dormaunt a demerer en la garde Johan de Catesby,[351] par avis des justices et altres sages, pur la droiturele posessioun le dit Johan de Catesby, et qe pur rien qestoit mostre nul ne avoit droit ne davoir possessioun si noun Johan de Catesby.

[110] Et puis apres,[352] entour la quinzeine de la nativite Seint Johan [8 July 1399],[353] arive Henry duc de Lancastre et de Herford a Ravenesporn en le counte Deverwyk, et comencea de chivaucher; et en sa compaignie le count de Northumbirlond, le count de Westmerlond, monsire Henry de Percy, fiz et her le dit count de Northumbirlond, le seignur de Wylugby, le fiz et heir a counte Daroundell,[354] Thomas Aroundell, ercevesqe Deverwyk, Phelip abbe de Leyc', et plusours chivalers et esquiers; et la soi passerent tant qe a Pountfreit, et de illeqs a Leyc',[355] et dileqes, la surveille de Seint Jame [23 July], a Coventre, et la veille de dit seint [24 July] a Warr'; a qel temps, la ou Thomas de Holand, count de Kent et puis duc de Surreie, fait par le roi Richard secounde, lan de soun regne xxj, avoit mis sur les portes del castel de Warr' un cerf de piere, corone, qestoit al hure la livre de dit roi Richard, et une blaunche bise,[356] qestoit al hure la livre del dit duc mesme, le dit duc de Lancastre comaunda de les abatre, et issint fut.[357] Et dileqs ils chivauchent tauntqe a Bristut, ou monsire William

Chronicles, ed. J. Taylor (Thoresby Soc., XLII, 1952), 76, 120–1; M. V. Clarke and N. Denholm-Young, 'The Kirkstall Chronicle, 1355–1400', *Bull. Jn Rylands Lib.*, XV (1931), 132. It also tallies exactly with the circumstantial evidence: J. B. Post, 'The Obsequies of John of Gaunt', *Guildhall Studies in London History* (1978).

350 A Monday, thus allowing Easter one month as a non-day: above, n.35.

351 The copy of the opinion now extant [2], and used by Dugdale (*Warwickshire,* 233), is not the patent here said to have been given to Catesby, but must, from its format, be one of the copies close sent to the arbitrators – if, indeed, two were sent, which the endorsement suggests was not the case.

352 There is no complete modern narrative of the Lancastrian usurpation and its immediate aftermath, although detailed and critical accounts can be found in E. F. Jacob, *The Fifteenth Century 1399–1485* (Oxford, 1961), c.I, and J. H. Wylie, *History of England under Henry the Fourth* (London, 1884–98), I, cc. I–III, V. For a summary both of events and of interpretations, see J. L. Kirby, *Henry IV of England* (London, 1970), cc.5–7. In this and the following entries, attention is drawn only to points of dispute and to material not found elsewhere.

353 Of various suggested dates, 4 July is offered most firmly: *Thomae Walsingham . . . Historia Anglicana* (*Chron. Mon. S. Albani,* ed. H. T. Riley, RS, 1863–76), II, 233; Clarke and Denholm-Young, *Bull. Jn Rylands Lib.*, XV, 132. The evidence is discussed in A. Tuck, *Richard II and the English Nobility* (London, 1973), 214, where a date late in June is preferred.

354 *le fiz . . . Daroundell* interlined.

355 The events between Pontefract and the west country are not mentioned by other authorities.

356 i.e. *biche,* hind, perhaps adopted by Holland from the crest of his (and Richard II's) mother: F. Sandford, *A Genealogical History of the Kings of England* . . . (London, 1677), 216.

357 If this anecdote is accurate in date and substance – and as careful local reporting this seems probable – the incident appears to be the earliest known overt indication that Lancaster was threatening the crown rather than claiming only his duchy, and thus supports a sceptical view of his supposed oath to limit his ambitions: see also J. M. W. Bean, 'Henry IV and the Percies', *History,* XLIV (1959), 215–21. Lancaster was certainly sensitive to the symbolism of liveries: *Chronicque de la Traison et Mort de Richart Deux Roy Dengleterre,* ed. B. Williams (London, 1846), 46, 194. Apart from this incident at Warwick castle, the earliest indication of usurpation remains the accroachment of the royal prerogative to appoint a warden of the west march towards Scotland, on 2 Aug.: privy seal warrant, translated in *English Historical Documents 1327–1485,* ed. A. R. Myers (Eng. Hist. Docs, IV, 1969), no. 79, and discussed by R. L. Storey, 'The Wardens of the Marches of England towards Scotland, 1377–1489', *EHR,* LXXII (1957), 603, and by Bean, *History,* XLIV, 219–20.

Lescrop, count de Wiltsch', tresorer Dengleterre, monsire Johan de Busscy, monsire Henry Grene estoient decolez, et monsire Johan Russell eschapa pur taunt qil estoit forsone;[358] et dileqs ils chivauchent tauntqe al chastel de Flynt, a qel temps le roi Richard, qestoit arive a Milford et soi passa al castel de Conewey, ou par mediacioun des diz arcevesqe, count de North', le dit roi Richard soi rendy a dit duc de Lanc',[359] a qel temps le dit duc de Surreie, et Johan count de Salesbyrs, estoient commiss' en le north en la garde le count de Westmerl', a qel temps le dit Johan de Catesby ne pout mie sure. Et entre les festes de Lassumpcioun et de la Nativite [15 Aug.–8 Sept.], gisaunt Elizabeth, seor a dit duc de Lanc', duchesse Dexcestre, sur sa deliverance denfant, Johan de Catesby aprocha a dit duc Dexcestre et mostre devant ly, present monsire T. Schelley, Johan Wylby, baillif de Daventre, et plusours altres, ces records, recovris, et altres evidences, qels mostrez le dit [duc][360] jura qil jammes pur ly ne perdreit le dit manoir de Lodbrok.

[111] Et puis apres, parlement estoit sommene en le noun le roi Richard, a tenir a Westm' le lundy lendemein de Seint Michel adonqe prochein; et lendemein del comencement de parlement [30 Sept.],[361] le roi Richard renuncia tut le droit qil avoit de regner, etc., et puis, le lundy prochein ensuaunt,[362] le dit duc Henry estoit corone roi par assent del dit roi Richard et de toz les spirituels et temperels et comunes del roialme, etc. Et puis en le dit temps, come le dit Johan de Catesby vient al corounement, dedeinz les iij jours apres, le duc[363] de Surreie et le count de Salesbyrs estoient arestuz come ils avoient sopee ove monsire Hugh le Despencer de Coly Weston,[364] et[365] comande a la Tour de Londres; a qel temps le dit Johan de Catesby sen ala del[366] hostel, et puis le parlement soit departy. Et puis apres le parlement soi departy, et le roi tient soun Noel adonqe prochein a Wyndesore, ou les ducs de Surreie et Dexcestre, le count de Salesbirs, levesqe de Cardoil, moigne[367] de Westm', avoient conspire de ly avoir trahy, le jour de lan reneof; et puis le dit duc de Surreie, a la ville de Circestre, en soun chivauche davoir rebelle, lendemein de Lepiphanie adonqe prochein [7 Jan. 1400],[368] ove le count de Salesbyrs, estoient par les comunes de paiis decolez. Et dedeins bref temps apres estoit le dit duc Dexcestre cole a Plasschis en Essex. Par ount le dit Johan de Catesby estoit descharge del agard des seignurs susdiz, et ad prist pur ly a mostre les avis et descrecioun des serjaunz susditz, etc.

[112] Et en bref temps apres, a la Tour de Loundres, estoient ajugge Thomas de Schelley, chivaler, monsire Bernard Brokaz le fiz, mestre Johan Fereby, Johan Magdeleyn, clerc, et levesqe, moisgne de Westm', et toz (forspris levesqe de Cardoil) estoient traine, penduz, et decole, etc.

Membrane 2 schedule 1

[113] Writ to the sheriff of Warwickshire, ordering reseisin following the recovery by John de Catesby of Ladbroke manor, as specified in the record. Tested by William Thirnyng, at Warwick, 23 February, 22[369] Richard II [1398]. 'Signed' Waldeby.
Endorsement of execution by Richard[370] Keman, undersheriff, and Richard his clerk, on the Thursday following, seisin being given to William Brok and

358 Capgrave, mentioning these four and William Bagot, and Walsingham and Harding, who omit Russell, are tacitly agreed that only Bagot escaped, but Russell's escape is confirmed by the Monk of Evesham: Walsingham, *Hist. Angl.*, II, 233; *The Chronicle of John Hardyng,* ed. H. Ellis (London, 1812), 350; J. Capgrave, *The Chronicle of England,* ed. F. C. Hingeston (RS, 1858), 270; *Historia Vitae et Regni Ricardi II Angliae Regis,* ed. T. Hearne (Oxford, 1729), 153.

359 This account of Richard's surrender, and that of his abdication, in the following entry, follow the official story subsequently maintained by the Lancastrians. The events described in the rest of this present entry are not mentioned by other authorities.

360 Omitted.

361 Parliament was summoned for Tuesday the morrow of Michaelmas, on which day, as the author correctly implies, Richard's abdication – which took place on the previous day – was announced: *RP,* III, 415–6.

362 This sentence accidentally conflates the last parliament summoned in Richard's name, for 30 Sept., with the first of his successor, summoned for 6 Oct.; the coronation was on the Monday *then* following, i.e. 13 Oct.: Kirby, *Henry IV,* 73; Wylie, *Henry IV,* I, 44; *RP,* III, 424 (no. 61).

363 MS *dit.*

364 The complicity of some members of the Despenser family is well established, but Hugh is not mentioned elsewhere: *Chronicon Adae de Usk A.D. 1377–1421,* ed. E. M. Thompson, 2nd edn (London, 1904), 43.

365 After *a qel,* deleted.

366 Reading uncertain.

367 After *le,* deleted.

368 This agrees with Usk, *Chronicon,* 42, but 6 January is also offered, less reliably: *Traison et Mort,* 88. Wylie, *Henry IV,* I, 99, accepts Evesham's suggestion of 8 January.

369 MS '21'.

370 Conceivably recte 'Robert'.

Godfrey Giles of Norton in Northamptonshire, in the name of the principal, in the presence of the tenants of the vill, the undersheriff having the white rod in one hand and the writ in the other.

Membrane 2 schedule 2

[114] Pleas before William Thirnyng and Robert Tyrwhit, justices of assize for Warwickshire, at Warwick, on Friday of St Peter's chair, 21 Richard II [22 Feb. 1398]

Assize of novel disseisin brought by John de Catesby against Lewis Cardian, Alice wife of Lewis, and William Hathewyk, concerning the manor of Ladbroke called 'Lodbrokesmanere'. Hathewyk appears on his own behalf and as bailiff for his co-defendants; he seeks judgment of the writ, because he holds the manor jointly with Thomas duke of Surrey and Edmund Holand the duke's brother, because he held thus on the day the writ was sued (31 December, 21 Richard II [1397]), and because Surrey and Holand, though yet surviving, were not named in the writ. He furthermore denies the disseisin. The parties put themselves on an assize; the recognitors – William de Peyto, Henry de Sutton, Edmund de Compton,[371] John Shukburgh, John Napton, Geoffrey Scarburgh, John Harryes, William Geydon,[372] Thomas Palmer, Roger Bulston, John Pynk, and John Derset of Thurlaston – say that the defendants were sole tenants of the manor on the day the writ was sued, Surrey and Holand having no interest in the manor at that time, and that the plaintiff was seised of the manor in demesne as a free tenement until disseised unjustly by the defendants, to his damage of 20s. Judgment of recovery and damages accordingly; the defendants in mercy.

[115] [*Endorsed*] Memorandum that at the time and place mentioned, the defendants challenged the array of the panel, and it was tried by Alan Waldeyene and William Hawe of Solihull that it was done well and reasonably, and by sufficient and worthy men; and afterwards they were sworn, as above, and the defendants did not dare to show any tail in evidence, but only the deed of joint tenancy, which was dated 29 December, on which day the named defendants disseised the plaintiff, and held the place for most of that day, and afterwards Lewis and Alice Cardian made the deed; upon which the assize found for the plaintiff, John Pynke giving the verdict on behalf of himself and his fellows. Counsel for the defence at that time were Guy Spyne and Robert Waldene, by letter of the earl of Surrey, Boteler the apprentice, cousin of the abbot of Evesham, and one Boteler of Warwick, who brought Catesby, at the same assizes, a writ under the privy seal, concerning the delivery to Lewis and Alice Cardian, or to Thomas earl of Surrey, of a certain deed of tail for the manor of Ladbroke, entailed to the same Lewis and Alice. [*Annotated*] Let it be exemplified.

Membrane 2 schedule 3

[116] Instrument dated 10 January 1398,[373] in the sixth indiction, and the ninth year of the papacy of Boniface IX, in the home of Robert Baxter of Warwick, diocese of Worcester, in the presence of the notary public and of the witnesses mentioned below, with William Hathewyk on the one part and Thomas Bromley on the other, concerning a charter of Ladbroke manor in Warwickshire. Bromley asserted openly that dom William Gamul, vicar of Holy Trinity, Coventry, once gave Richard Egebaston 40s. in silver for that charter and one other, which charter Egebaston delivered to Bromley, who retained it for a long time. At some time in Lent, 1392 – in March, but he cannot remember the day – Bromley was imprisoned at Coventry, in the custody of Walter Goldsmyth and Robert Cortenale, then town bailiffs, and he says that the bailiffs then took the charter from his house and carried it away, delivering it to John Catesby against Bromley's wishes. He also asserts that in 1397 – in November, but he cannot remember the day – John Catesby had him indicted at Coventry, claiming that he had falsely forged and sealed the charter; he, Bromley, appeared before Walter Clopton and his fellows, justices of king's bench, and, when examined, confessed to the forgery. Bromley claims that this confession in king's bench was made falsely, because he was in fear of his life, and he now swears as he will at the Last Judgment that of his own certain knowledge the charter should be regarded as true and valid, without fraud, and that it is essential to the rightful inheritance of Alice wife of Lewis Cardyan. He also says that when the charter was in his custody, it was intact and clean, without marks of smoke or fire. Taken in the presence of Henry Trymnell, 'domicellus', Nicholas Warrewyk, John Broun, John Lynton, Thomas Lutturworth,

[371] Compton was a coroner in this year: Hunnisett, *Am. Jnl Leg. Hist.*, III, 345.

[372] Gaydon was a former coroner: ibid.

[373] MS gives 1397 *secundum cursum et computationem ecclesie anglicane,* i.e. beginning the year at Lady Day: *Hdbk of Dates,* 5.

clerks, and William Baker and Robert Baxter, laymen, of the diocese of Worcester.
[*Endorsed*] Concorded with the original.
I.S. [*monogram*]

Membrane 2 schedule 4

[117] Grant by William son of Walter de Alspathe, to Ralph son of Henry Steel of Ladbroke, of a messuage in Ladbroke, with all the lands [there?] which Henry died holding of William, for the rent of ½m. and a pound of pepper at All Saints', for all services save foreign service of the king; with warranty; granted for 4m. Witnesses: John de Lodbrok, Henry de Sutham, William Frаunceys of Ladbroke, William Waldyng of Ladbroke, Giles de Esunhull, Roger Chaplain (*capellanus*), Henry son of Ralph de Wylmeleyghton, Simon son of Adam de Wylmeleyghton, John Clerk (*clericus*). Dated at Coventry, Friday after St Peter and St Paul, 23 Edward III [3 July 1349].

Membrane 3 schedule 1

[118] John Cook, Henry Waldyng, Roger Arlee, William Colyns, William Wryde, and Henry Paltok testify to the feoffment by John de Lodbrok, knight. John de Schuckeborgh, John Baylly of Southam, William Lodbrok, undersheriff, Robert de Stocton, Hugh[374] de Lothiryington, John Cook, chaplain, Thomas Cook, Thomas Wylkyns, and Alan Salmon testify to the feoffment by John Cok[375] to William de Catesby, and the remainders, as in the charter. William Offechirch testifies to the emendation of the court roll by Thomas de Lodbrok, and to the taking of rents and services for Harbury, on his behalf and at his request, by William de Catesby, in cash. John Cok, chaplain, and John farmer of the rectory, testify that the rector of Ladbroke had one message and one virgate of land by grant from William de Catesby for the debts of Thomas at his request. Hugh vicar of Bishops Itchington, William Barbour and Richard[376] Balraven of the same, Thomas Palmere, William Broke, and John Barbour testify that all trespassers at Ladbroke mill who were of the vill made their peace with William de Catesby or with John Cok of the same. [*See also* 53–57]

[374] After *Thomas,* deleted.

[375] 'John Cok' after 'William de Catesby', deleted.

[376] Interlined above 'William', deleted.

[377] CP 40/501, m.413.

Membrane 3 schedule 2

[119] Writ to the sheriff of Warwickshire ordering reseisin following the recovery by John de Catesby of one message and one and a half acres in Ladbroke, as specified in the record. Tested by Robert Bealknap at Westminster, 28 May, 9 Richard II [1386]. 'Signed' Stok.

Membrane 3 schedule 3

[120] Pleas before Robert Bealknapp and his fellows, justices of the common bench, at Westminster, Easter, 9 Richard II; m.413[377]

John de Catesby appears for the fourth day against Lewis Cook and Alice his wife, concerning a messuage and one and a half acres of land, with appurtenances, in Ladbroke, which he claims by writ of cessavit. The defendants do not come; since they also defaulted on Michaelmas[378] quindene last, the sheriff was to take the lands into the king's hand, and to summon the defendants for the fifth week after Easter. On further default recovery is awarded to the plaintiff, and the defendants are in mercy.

Membrane 3 schedule 4

[121] Fine,[379] dated the morrow of the Ascension, 24 Edward III [7 May 1350], before John de Stonore, William de Shareshull, Roger Hillary, Richard de Kelleshull, Richard de Wylughby, John de Stouford, and Thomas de Fencotes, justices, at Westminster, between Hawise widow of John de Lodbrok, knight, querent, and William son of Nicholas le Wodeward of Long Itchington, deforciant, for the manor of Harbury, with appurtenances, and one messuage, 100a. of arable, 30a. of meadow, 100a. of pasture, 100a. of wood, and 40a. of heath, with appurtenances, in Tanworth. Wodeward grants the lands to Hawise, and she regrants them to him to hold of her, for the term of her life, with remainder to William de Catesby, for life, and then with successive remainders of the manor to Thomas son of John de Lodbrok, knight, and Alice daughter of William de Catesby, to the heirs of their bodies, and to the right heirs of Thomas. Successive remainders in the tenement are to Thomas and Alice and their heirs, to the heirs of

[378] The record has 'Martinmas'.

[379] *Warwickshire Feet of Fines,* ed. L. Drucker, III (Dugdale Soc., XVIII, 1943), no. 2030.

Thomas, to Hugh brother of Thomas and his heirs, to John brother of Hugh and his heirs, all in tail male, and to the right heirs of William de Catysby. For 100m. paid by Hawise to William. 'Signed' Whiteman.

Membrane 4 schedule 1

[122] [*Writ of novel disseisin as* 166.]
[123] *Guy Breton, *Henry de Sutton, *Richard Botiller, *William Hore,[380] *John Bray, *Geoffrey Scarburgh, *William Geydon, *John Shukburgh, *John Napton, *John Fulwode, *Edmund de Compton, *William Hemery,[381] *John Derset of Thurlaston, *Thomas Palmer, *John Harrys, *Thomas Duston, †John Swyndon, *Roger Bulston, *Edmund Herdewyk, †Geoffrey Edmescote, *Eneas Badby, *Thomas Baron of Rugby, *John Scewer, †Peter Sloley, †Thomas atte Berne of Tanworth.[382]
[*cf.* 168]
[124] [*Endorsed*] At that day, in king's bench at Coventry, before Walter Clopton, John Hull, and Hugh Holes,[383] justices, the parties appeared, challenged the jury, and then withdrew the challenge; they then sought an adjournment to study the writ, which they said was defective. This was disallowed because they claimed no specific defect, and eventually, on Wednesday[384] following, at Coventry, it was not prosecuted.

Membrane 4 schedule 2

[125] Mandate from Robert Gowsill, king's commissioner, to the sheriff of Northamptonshire, requiring execution of the terms of letters close, dated 16 October, 21 Richard II [1397]. [*See also* 179, 180]

Membrane 5 schedule 1

[126] Writ of formedon to the sheriff of Warwickshire, concerning a messuage, one carucate of arable, 10a. of meadow, 40a. of wood, 10a. of heath, and 12d. rental, in Tanworth, given by Henry Lodbrok, knight, to John his son and Hawise wife of John, in tail, and then, after the deaths of John, Hawise, Thomas their son, and John son of Thomas, it ought to have descended to Alice as cousin and heir of John son of Thomas: if John Catesby does not surrender the land, and if Lewis Cardyan and Alice his wife find sufficient sureties for prosecution, Catesby is to be summoned to Westminster for Martinmas quindene [25 Nov.] to show cause. Tested at Westminster, 6 October, 7 Richard II [1383]. 'Signed' Pynyngton. [*Endorsed*] At that day Catesby essoined; on the next day given, Catesby being ready to plead, the plaintiffs were nonsuited.

Membrane 5 schedule 2

[127] Writ of novel disseisin to the sheriff of Warwickshire, on complaint by Lewis Cardian and Alice his wife that they have been unjustly disseised of a tenement in Ladbroke by John de Catesby; to be heard by William de Skipwyth and William Burgh. Tested at Westminster, 15 June, 7 Richard II [1384]. [*See also* 89]

[128] Similar writ concerning disseisin of William Gamel, clerk, Thomas Archer, and Nicholas Dodyngsels, by John de Catesby and John Bray of Dunsmore, from a tenement in Tanworth. Tested as above [127].

[129] Assize of Tanworth: Baldwin Mountfort, knight (not of the hundred), John Eynesford, knight (not of the hundred), †Thomas Raule,[385] Thomas Hubaud (not of the hundred), †Thomas Byssopesdon, *William Ode, John Boteler of Shustoke (not of the hundred), John Warde of Bromwich (not of the hundred), Ralph Richardes (not of the hundred), William Westyngton (not of the hundred), *John atte Lee of Tanworth, William Hawe (not of the hundred), Ralph Hopewas (not of the hundred), Leonard Worthyn (not of the hundred), Richard Hawe (not of the hundred), Alexander Lyndon (not of the hundred), Simon of the Hay[386] (unknown), *Richard Gowerne of Tanworth, William Pykke, John Pynke, William Hemery, William Fyllongleye, Thomas Broun (unknown), Robert atte Grene (unknown).[387]
[*cf.* 88]

Membrane 5 schedule 3

[130] xxix^{o} die octobris, anno regni regis Ricardi x^{mo} [1386]. Cest la copie des evidences et accordes

[380] Hore was a former coroner: Hunnisett, *Am. Jnl Leg. Hist.*, III, 346.

[381] Amery was a former coroner: ibid.

[382] Not all the prickings are in the same ink as the list; the crosses are in the same ink as 'William . . . ', struck through at the head of the list.

[383] JKB 1389–1414.

[384] After 'Tuesday', deleted.

[385] For Raleigh, see Kimball in *Warwicks Sessions,* xxxiv.

[386] *of the* interlined above *atte,* deleted.

[387] Richards, Worthen, and Fillongley had served or were to serve as coroners: Hunnisett, *Am. Jnl Leg. Hist.*, III, 345.

faites devant le conseill monseignur de Warr',[388] entre Johan de Catesby dun part et Thomas Archer et Lowys Cook dautre part, demuranz en le garde Richard de Piriton, clerk, escrit de la main W. Lyth . . . , clerc.

En primes, touchant le manoir de Lodebrok, Johan de Catesby ad moustre une chartre par quelle il suppose qe monsire Johan de Lodebrok se demyst par mesme le chartre de le dit manoir de Lodebrok a William de Catesby et as autres; et auxi ad moustre une relees par quelle il suppose qe le dit monsire Johan relessa toute son droit en le dit manoir au dit William et as autres, etc. [31; 13]

[131] A qi fuist responduz pur monseignur et le partie qe le dit monsire Johan murust seisi del dit manoir de Lodebrok, et outre fuit profree qe si Johan Cook et Johan Treweman, cosin du dit Johan Catesby, et autres quaters bones et loialx gentz de la dite ville de Lodebrok veullent jurere qe le dit monsire Johan delivera seiseyn du dit manoir par mesme la chartre au dit William et a les autres, et qe les tenantz du dit manoir attournerent, adonqs les ditz parties voillent bien suffrere le dit Johan Catesby tenir le dit manoir en pees, tanqe lour droit par fait ou par chose de record purra estre afferme en temps avenir, etc.

[132] Item, touchant le manoir de Herbury et les tenementz en Toneworth, le dit Johan Catesby ad moustre une chartre fait a Nicholas Wodeward et as autres del dit manoir de Herbury et de les ditz tenementz en Toneworth, et apres ad moustre coment William fitz le dit Nichol fuist seisi del dit manoir de Herbury et les tenementz en Toneworth, et les graunta a Hawise, femme le dit monsire Johan, a terme de sa vie, le remeindre, etc. [45, 121]

[133] A qi fuist responduz pur monseignur et le partie qe Henry de Lodebrok dona les ditz manoir de Herbury et les tenementz en Toneworth as ditz monsire Johan et Hawyse et a les heirs de lours dieux corps engendres;[389] et touchant le dit manoir de Herbury moustrerent une chartre endente prevant la dite taille, de quele chartre le dit Johan Catesby ad moustre lun parte. Et auxi fuist allegge qe le dit monsire Johan et Hawyse continuerunt toutes lours vies lours estate sanz ascune demise fait par le dit monsire Johan, et la dite Hawyse continua sa possessioun apres la mort le dit monsire Johan pur long temps, apres qi mort entra Thomas lours fitz par vertue de mesme le taille, et lessa les tenementz en Toneworth, et vendist bois illeoqs crescent, et illeoqes edifia, et touz autres choses fist come verraye tenant del manoir de Herbury et les tenementz en Toneworth, come par diverses endentures as diverses persones faitz par le dit Thomas, et par les parties moustres, pleinement appiert. Et auxi fuist allege qe semble chose deshonest et encountre bonne conscience qe le dit William Catesby assenta et ordeina de lever un fyne del manoir de Herbury pur son singuler profit et avauntage en countre le forme de la dite chartre endente, de qi le dit William avoit lun parte en sa garde demene; a qi plese, etc., prendre bonne garde, etc.

[134] Les parties susditz se sount en manere qensuit accordez ou pret, etc., qendroit des debaz des manoirs de Lodebrok et Toneworth en le contee de Warr' qe nadgaires furent a monsire Johan de Lodebrok, cestassavoir del manoir de Lodebrok, qe si Johan de Catesby purra faire Johan le Cook nadgairs de Lodebrok, qi ore demuret en le counte de Leyc', ove cynk hommes de mesme la ville de Lodebrok jurer qe la chartre de feffement qe le dit monsire Johan nadgairs fist a Roger de Clifton, nadgairs person de Lodebrok, William de Catesby, et Nichol Wodeward et a lour heirs del manoir de Lodebrok fuist duement execut en le livre de seisine faire ove atournement des tenanz, qadonqe les ditz Lowys Cook et Alice sa femme lerrount totes maneres des chalengz et clemys qils ount en le dit manoir. Et la quele matire le dit Johan est prest a moustre par plusours evidences qe le dit monsire Johan soy demist en manere susdite, etc.

[135] Et en droit des terres et tenemenz en Toneworth qels les ditz Lowys et Alice clement par force dun taille qe monsire Henry de Lodebrok duist avoir done a dit monsire Johan soun fitz et a Hawyse sa femme et a les [heirs] [390] de lour deux corps engendrez, en temps le roy Edward piere a roy Edward qi darrein murroit, de qel ele soy dit estre issue en la taille, Johan de Catesby dist qe le dit monsire Henry, en temps le roy qe darrein murrout,[391] lessa les ditz terres et tenemenz, par non de manoir ensemble ove le manoir de Lodebrok, a dit monsire Johan son fitz a terme de sa vie, rendant a dit monsire Henry xx li. pur celes, et par fait endente, enseale de seal de ses armes, qil ad moustre devant vostre conseill ove

[388] Lapses into the second person plural [e.g. in 136, 137] suggest that the original was the record kept for the use of the earl of Warwick. An earlier and rather more summary account, similarly 'official', describes decisions made by Lancaster's council in 1348: DL 42/11, f.67.

[389] Now E 40/8248: *CAD*, IV, A 8248.

[390] Omitted.

[391] In 4 Edw. III: above, [4].

autres plusours evidences, et tut temps est prest a moustre, sanz ceo qe le dit monsire Henry dona les ditz terres et tenemenz en le taille come desus est dit; et outre le dit Johan de Catesby, a la reverence de soun dit seignur, grante qe si les ditz Lowys et Alice vuillent suire a les comune ley accioun par force de la taille ou altre[392] qiconqe accioun qe lour plest, le dit Johan a primer jour de ple traversera lour accioun, et sur lissue elisent ils mesme un panell des chivalers et esquiers qe ne soient de affinite sanc ne aliance dune parte ou dautre, et qe chescun des diz enpanelles soit enherite de x livres de terre et tenement en le dit counte, et le dit Johan[393] atendra a lour verdit issint qe surtee soit fait qe les ditz Lowys et Alice atendrent le dit verdit sanz estre nonsuy en lour dite suite, etc.

[136] Et la ou est alegge pur monseignur qe les terres et tenemenz susditz sount tenuz en chivalerie, la dit Johan dit qe les terres et tenemenz susditz en Toneworth sount tenuz en sokage, come estoit presente en vostre court de Toneworth, et pur qels le dit Johan ad releve accordant a la tenure de sokage apres la mort William soun piere, et auxint herite[394] sanz ceo qils sount tenuz en chivalerie, etc.; et quaunt a ceo qe ils ount allegge qe Thomas de Lodebrok mourut seisi, il naveroit unqes rien si non a la volunte William de Catesby; et ceo serra le dit Johan prest daverrer par les mieux[395] vauiz de tut le counte, come la ley demande, et par plusours evidences, etc.

[137] Et qant a Herbury, a ceo qils diount qe Thomas mourut seisi, le dit Johan vous dist qe Thomas navoit unqe rienz si non a la volunte le dit William, come il est prest a moustre par plusours evidences, et auxint par totes les mieux vauiz de tote la paiis.

[138] Et prie outre le dit Johan de Catesby al noble conseil soun dit treshonure seignur qils vuillent certifier a soun dit seignur coment il lour semble des evidences moustres devant eux dun part et dautre tochant la matere susdite et les qels evidences il lour semble meillours, etc.

[139] [*Marginated*] Copie de bille baille a count de Warr' a Warr'[396]

Fait aremembrer qe Thomas de Horborn de Toneworth et Johan de Chestre de Boeleye sount serementz en la presence mon treshonure seignur conte de Warr', esteantz sire William Morton, Richard Brounk,[397] Robert Broun, Roger Hulbergh, Johan de la Botehye,[398] et autres, queux diount qe monsire Henry de Lodebrok dona et granta a Johan soun filz et a Hawys sa femme, fille a monsire Robert de Daventre, a eux et a lour heirs de lour corps engendrez, toutz ses terres et tenemenz en Toneworth, de qei ils ont grand notice de la seisine, etc., la quele possessioun les avantditz Johan et Hawys continuerount totes lours vies, et apres lour deces Thomas lour filz par vertue de la dite taille continua tote sa vie sanz enpechement de William de Catesby ou ascun autre, sanz demise ou alienacioun faites a ascun person en lours vies; et qe le dit William de Catesby vient a Toneworth apres la mort du dit Johan filz Henry, et illeoqs la cynkture la dite Hawyse ovesqz cliefs annexez a icelle, et les cofres le dit Johan filz Henry fist overer, et ovesqz lui chartres, escrites, et autres muniments tochant leheritage le dit Johan filz Henry ensemblement[399] ovesqz le seal mesme cestui Johan filz Henry prist et enporta, etc. Et auxint le dit Thomas Horburn dist qe y vient a Toneworth ovesqz un Thomas Hamsted a dit Johan filz Henry gisant en soun lit muriant, le quel Johan soy confessa as mesmes Thomas et Thomas qil avoit ordeignez le dit William de Catesby destre un de ses executours, et outre qil avoit grantez a dit William le mariage de Thomas soun filz et heir, disant qe null alienacioun ne demise avoit faite a dite William ne a null autre person de touz ses terres et tenemenz avantditz. Escrit a Warr' le v jour de marcz, lan ixme le roy Richard le secound [1386], etc.

[*Marginated*] Copie de la [bille][400] baille a count en contre Thomas Larcher

[140] A treshonure seignur le conte de Warr', plese entendre qe Thomas Larcher, piere au Thomas qore est, morust en vostre homage seisi de ceo qil tient de vous par service de chivaler en Tonneworth, le dit Thomas soun fitz esteant de deinz age, de qi voz ministres seiserunt la garde; et puis le dit Thomas, esteant de deinz age, soy maria, conge de vous de ceo nyent tue, pur quoi la forfature a vous atient, qamonta a centz livres, pur tant qe la sengle value

[392] Followed by *ou autre,* deleted.

[393] *et le dit Johan* interlined.

[394] MS *hiete,* ill written, with a general mark of contraction; perhaps, in the context, 'heriete'.

[395] The letter *a* at the beginning of this word, presumably erroneous, has not been struck through.

[396] This heading may have been intended for the succeeding entry.

[397] Possibly *Brounl'.*

[398] Error for *Botelrye*?

[399] Final letters doubtful.

[400] Omitted.

estoit a cynkqant livres, de quoy vous nesties unques servi.

[141] Item, par la ou voz estes seignur de tout la ville de Toneworth en demene et en services, et avez la cite de manoir, demenes terres, vewe, et suters a vostre court de troys symaignes en troys, le dit Thomas, qe nestoit si non vostre tenant en la dite ville, cleyme davoir les wastes de la dite ville en comune ovesqz vous, en desheretisoun de vous, et ad en les ditz wastes abatu keynes et altres maners des arbres, a grant nombre et de grant value, de quoi voz amendes nestoient unqs fait.

[142] Item, par la ou vous avez garreine en la dite ville la, le dit Thomas ad chace et pris divers bestes de garreine par plusours foithes, aforcement et voluntrement sanz conge de voz ministres illeoqs, mes expressement encontre lour gree, etc.

Membrane 5 schedule 3d

[143] Fait a remembrer qe le meskerdy prochein apres la feste de la Purificacioun Nostre Dame, lan du regne le roi Richard seconde puis le conquest ix (neofisme) [7 Feb. 1386], en presence Thomas counte de Warr', monsire William son frere, monsire Nicol Lylling, monsire Johan Holte, monsire David Hanmer, monsire William de Burgh, Richard de Pyryton, clerc, Johan Hermesthorp, clerc, Robert de Cherleton, et William Thirning, serjaunz, de counseil le dit count, Walter de Clopton, Johan de Lokton, serjaunz,[401] Robert Burgoillon, Johan de Cassy, Thomas Fryseby, de counseil le dit Johan de Catesby, Johan Wadham, serjaunt, Woderoue et Kyrkeby, de counseil Lewys Cook et Alice sa femme, etc., devant qels la matire deinz comprise estoit manie, etc. [*See* 94–96]

[144] Sur qel profre deinz comprise et acorde, le dit Johan de Catesby suist une commission hors de la chauncellerie nostre seignur le roi, direct a monsire Robert de Stafford, Robert Burgoillon, et altres, sur qel comission estoient jurez viij de Lodbrok et iiij bones gentz de paiis,[402] qi disoient pur le dit Johan de Catesby, come piert par lexemplification nostre seignur le roi eut fait, etc. [*See CIPM,* XVI, no.257 (*27 Mar. 1386*)]

[145] Et auxint le dit Johan Cook jura[403] en presence le seignur de Ferers, frere la countesse de Warr', monsire Rauf de Ferers, monsire Johan Fauconer, et plusours altres, come piert de south le seal de lour armes, etc.

Membrane 5 schedule 4

[*Endorsed*] Les copies des fauxes faitz mostrez par Thomas Larcher al entent davoir provee la seisine Thomas Lodbrok

[146] Grant by Thomas de Lodebrok of Tanworth, to Thomas de Haukesshawe of Tanworth, of a wood in Tanworth, lying between 'Brendeheth' and 'Somerheye', and between 'Longemedewe' and 'Wyndmellefeld', with free access by two routes, one via 'Newelond' and 'Brendeheth', the other via 'Somerheie', for life, to cut, and carry via 'Coderyng',[404] without waste, paying (in Tanworth church) for the first year £4 at the conversion of St Paul [25 Jan.] and £4 on St Mark's day [25 Apr.], and for the next year £4 13s. 4d. on St Luke's day [18 Oct.], and thereafter, annually on St Leo's day [28 June], £10; Lodebrok and his heirs are to have repossession if the rent be in arrears; Haukesshawe pledges his lands and chattels, and those of his heirs, to the payment of the initial £12 13s. 4d.; Lodebrok is to maintain the hedges and ditches, and Haukesshawe is to provide and maintain gates at the entrances. Witnesses: Thomas Archer, Henry Symondes, John Doufyn, smith. Dated at Tanworth, Sunday before the nativity of St John the Baptist, 44 Edward III [23 June 1370].

[147] Grant by Thomas son of John de Lodebrok, knight, to Thomas de Haukesshawe of Tanworth, of all the lands in Tanworth (except a messuage held by John de Eyton) which Sir John formerly held, together with all buildings, waters, and appurtenances, to hold of Thomas son of John, for life, for an annual rent of £4 2s. 4d., payable in equal portions at the Annunciation and Michaelmas, for the first five years, and subsequently for an annual rent of £20, payable similarly, together with all services and customs due; Lodebrok is to maintain the buildings and closes at

[401] *de counseil* deleted.

[402] Hugh Lotherton, Henry Walden, Thomas Wilkins, John Wryde the elder, John Spencer, Henry Paltock, Thomas Carter, and Roger Arley, all of Ladbroke, William Barber and William Brook, of Bishops Itchington, Robert Emley of Stockton (a 2s. franklin: E 179/192/23, m.9), and John Harris: C 136/39, no. 18, m.2.

[403] Followed by *come,* deleted.

[404] *excariando recte ad sepes dicte placee videlicet usque ad le coderyng.*

his own cost, and Haukesshawe is to cut wood only for fencing; Lodebrok is to have repossession if the rent be in arrears by one month in the first five years or one day subsequently. Witnesses: Thomas Archer, Thomas atte Berne, John de Creweleye, John de Yeveleshawe,[405] Thomas de Horbureie. Dated at Tanworth, Sunday after the Purification, 44 Edward III [3 Feb. 1370].

Membrane 6 schedule 1

[148] Writ of notification to the sheriff of Warwickshire, concerning assizes to be held by William Thirnyng and Richard Sydenham, at Warwick, on Monday of St Margaret the virgin [*no year given*].

Membrane 6 schedule 2

[149] Writ of novel disseisin to the sheriff of Warwickshire, on complaint by Lewis Cardian and Alice his wife that they have been unjustly disseised of a tenement in Ladbroke, by John de Catesby and William Broke, chaplain; to be heard by William Thirnyng and Richard Sidenham. Tested at Westminster, 12 May, 13 Richard II [1390]. [*Endorsed*] By John Bertun.

Membrane 6 schedule 3

[150] Panel returned by Ademar de Lychefeld alias Taverner, then sheriff of Warwickshire, on the above writ: John de Peyto, knight, John Mallory, knight, John de Napton, Richard Botiller, William Pykke, Edmund de Compton, John de Fulwode, John de Crowleye, William Emery, John Pynke, John Bacoun, John Colyns, Robert de Stokton, Eneas de Badby, William Barbour, Walter Deyvyll, John Harryes, John Raulyns, Thomas Hert of Lawford, John Derset of Thurlaston, Robert Porter of Ettington, John Hukyns of Warwick, John Ive of Harbury, William Budde of Napton on the Hill.

Membrane 6 schedule 3d

[151] La qele assise estoit araie en countre les assises tenues entour la feste Seint Margarete, lan xiiij le roi [20 July 1390], come pert par ceo panell; a qel jour les pleintifs chalengent le aray, et larrai trie bon par Aleyn Waldeyene de Ilmedon et Rauf Rich', apres qel trient ils estoient nounsuiz, etc., par la ou la pleint fut fait del manoir de Lodbrok; et Thomelyn West de soun counseil.

[405] Assessed at 12d., as a franklin, under Tanworth, in 1379: E 179/192/23, m.14.

Membrane 6 schedule 4

[152] A treshonurable et tresgracious seignur le conte de Warrewyk, moustrent Lowys Cardyan et Alice sa femme, file a monsire John de Lodbrok et Hawyse sa femme, qe come Henry de Lodbrok, chivaler, par ses chartres endentes, graunta as ditz Johan et Hawyse les manoirs de Lodbrok, Toneworth, et Herburbury, ove lour appurtenances, a tenir a eux et a lour heirs de lour corps engendres, come pleinement appiert par les ditz chartres, en quell estate les ditz Johan et Hawyse moroient seisez de mesmes les manoirs, et apres la mort les ditz Johan et Hawyse, Thomas Lodbrok, come fitz et heir as ditz Johan et Hawyse, entre en mesmes les manoirs, et sa possessioun continua toute sa vie, et de ceo morust seisez come heir en la taille, sanz issu de soun corps, par qei les ditz manoirs discenderunt a dite Alice come a soer et heire; nepurqant Johan de Catesby, come fitz et heir a William de Catesby, clayme davoir enheritance en mesmes les manoirs, et un des ditz manoirs a ore tient par vertue dun feffement qe le dit Johan de Lodbrok dussoit avoir fait al dit William et as autres de mesmes les manoirs, come le dit Johan de Catesby dit, la ou le dit Johan de Lodbrok morust seisez come desuis est dit, mais le dit William estoit executour, et avoit touz les biens et chateux le dit Johan de Lodbrok, et soun seal, par quy il purroit faire et ensealer touz manerez de feffementz qil voillent faire de mesmes les manoirs; et issint pur cause qe le dit Johan de Catesby est homme de ley, et si richez et de la conseil de les plus grantz du paiis, les ditz Lowys et Alice, come soere et heire al dit Thomas, ne purront avoir ascun recoverer par vertue del taille avantdite: qe vous please, pur Dieu et en oevre de charite, en vostre honurable presence, par gentz qont conissance de la ley, examiner et veier les evidences et chartres de ambedeux les parties, et faire ceo qe ley et droit demandent, issint qe la dite taille ne soit en toute defait et les heirs les ditz Johan de Lodbrok et Hawyse desheritez a touz jours, eiant regard, treshonurable seignur, qe les ditz Lowyse et Alice sont povres et riens nont de pursuir lour droit a la comune ley.
[*Endorsed*] La bille baille a count a Westm' en le parlement tenuz a Westm' le terme de Seint Michel, lan xiiij le roi Richard [1390].

Membrane 6 schedule 5

[153] A tresgracious et treshonurable seignur le counte de Warrewyk, moustrent Lowys Cardian et Alice sa femme, file a monsire Johan de Lodebrok et

Hawyse sa feme, qe come diverses temps passez, treshonurable seignur, la dite Alice pursua devers vostre tresgraciouse seignurie par diverses billes pur certeines terres et tenemenz queux furent donez en la taille as ditz Johan et Hawyse, come pleinement appiert par les ditz billes, en parcelle de queux terres et tenemenz certeines de vos gentz a vostre oeps sont feffez come lem dist par Johan de Catesby et ses feffees; et parcelle le dit Johan de Catesby fauxement et torceouousement occupe; et par vous, tresgracious seignur, estoit assentuz et accordez, et par assurance dun honurable homme, sire Johan Harmesthorp, clerk, qe le dit Johan de Catesby dussoit estre a Loundres et auxi les ditz Lowys et Alice ove touz ses chartres et evidences touchantes les ditz terres et tenemenz, a y demonstrere devant monsire Wauter de Clopton et Johan Wadham, justices nostre seignur le roy, a certein jour par eux assigner pur les ditz chartres et evidences triere qavoit droit en les ditz terres et tenemenz; a quel jour les ditz parties vendroient, et le dit Johan Harmesthorp dissoit pur vous, treshonurable seignur, graciousement qestoit vostre volentee de mettre toute ceo qe vous avoit en les ditz terres et tenemenz en juggement des ditz justices solonc ceo qils voillent respondre devant Dieu; et les ditz Lowys et Alice auxint se mistrent a mesme le juggement, moustrant la chartre endente de la taille avantdite et autres evidences; le quele juggement le dit Johan de Catesby nulle chartre ne evidences moustrantz refusa tout outrement, et dissoit qe vous, treshonurable seignur, poez bien grauntier, doner, et faire de voz terres ceo qe vous plest, mais il voudroit attender et prendre toute ceo qil poet prendre par la ley; et issint les ditz justice sen departirent sanz ascun autre chose faire: qe vous pleise, tresgracious seignur, de notifier cest matiere en paiis par voz tresgraciouses lettres a les pluis vauez genz, ou autrement come vous mieutz semble affaire, qest vostre volente qe les ditz Lowys et Alice eient droit en lour pursuyte quele ils sont en purpos affaire, et ne preignez a male, tresgracious seignur, pur la suyte qils sont affaire devers vostre treshonurable persone; pur Dieu et en oevre de charitee.

[154] [*Endorsed*] Cest la bille bailla a monseignur de Warr', en qele jour pris le dit Johan avoit reserve a ly tutes avantages qe la ley ly avoit done, come monsire Nicol Lylling tesmoigne, et monseignur le remenbrast; axint qele bille ly estoit baille en temps de parlement tenuz a Westm' lendemein des Almes, lan du roi Richard quinsime [3 Nov. 1391]. [*See also* 99]

Membrane 6 schedule 6

[155] Plese a treshaute et trespuissant seignur le duc de Guyen et de Lancastre graunter aide et socour a vostre povere oratrice Alice Lodbrok, feliz et heire a monsire Johan de Lodbrok, chivaler, en contre un Johan de Catesby, homme de ley, le quele ad detenue certeins terrez et tenement en Lodbrok et Tonworth en le counte de Warwic, al value de xl marc par an, de sa droit heritage, atorte et en contre resoun, et sanz title en droit, mes par forte mayne et mayntenaunce il ad occupia lez dit terrez et tenement par x ans et pluis, en queux le dit monsire Johan, pier audite Alice, murruste seisi en entaille, estoient de heir a heir come la taille est prist amoustrer; et la dite suppliant a fait graunte pursuyte pur les dit terrez et tenement envers le dit Johan par long temps, issint qe par dite pursuyte est tout entrement diffait et null recovere purra gayner pur lez subtiles et cautyles qe le dit Johan ad en la ley, et par sez mayntenours: ceo considerer, treshaute et tressocourable seignur, al honour de Dieu et en oevre de charite, et pur les almes de touz vous progenitours, queux Dieu assoille, et luy faire venir en la parlament devant vous et lez autres noble seignurs de ceste present parlement, et la dit suppliant auroi amoustrer lour evidence et sur ceo ordeigne fyne du dit pursuyte.

[156] [*Endorsed*] La bille dount ceste la copie estoit baille a monseignur de Lancastre[406] en le parlement tenuz a Westm' ledemein des Almes, lan xvme le roi Richard [3 Nov. 1391], ou monseignur me bailla mesme la bille, et jeo la copeay et puis reportai mesme la bille ariere et le baillai a mon dit seignur, et demanday de ly davoir un jour assigne, ou devant le roi et ly, ou devant le counseil de roi, ou devant son counseil demene; qi me respondit qil ne savoit ne ne voloit assigne a moi ne jour ne lieu par cele cause, qar cestoit chose a la comune ley, dount ils navoient rienz a faire par bill, et issint departy jeo de ly, etc.

Membrane 6 schedule 7

[157] Grant by Henry de Lodbrok, knight, to his son John de Lodbrok and Hawise his wife, and the heirs of John's body, of the manors of Ladbroke and Tanworth, with appurtenances, with remainder to the right heirs male of John; with warranty. Witnesses: Roger Grenvile, Nicholas Warrewyk, Eustace Burneby, Richard Gurmound, Walter Coyne, John de Shukburgh. Dated at Ladbroke, Monday the morrow of Trinity, 19 Edward II [19 May 1326].

[406] Followed by *et nie,* deleted.

Membrane 6 schedule 7d

[158] A nostre tresexcellent et tresredoute seignur le roy, moustrent treshumblement vous poverez lieges et simple oratours Lowys Cardian et Alice sa femme, qe coment Johan de Catesby, homme de ley, ad detenuz et detient certeyns terrez et tenementz en le countee de Warwyk hors dez mayns du dit Lowys et Alice, de queux la dite Alice est droit heir, come est bien conue as gentz du pais, et come appiert par diversez evydencez et par tayle de heire en heir; et par cause qil est homme de courte, lez ditz suppliantz ne purront gayner null homme de ley destre ove eaux ne de lour consaille envers le dit Johan en lour droit, et issint, par maistry et mayntenance et diversez cautilx qil sciet en la ley, il detient les ditz terres et tenementz torceuousement et sanz title ou bone reson, a grant damage et disaise de ditz suppliantz: qe plese a vostre tresexcellent et trespuissant seignurie faire venir le dit Johan ensemblement ove lez ditz suppliantz devant vostre tressage consaile, a moustrer toutz lour evidences sibien touchant les segniours[407] come le tenant, et sur ceo ordyne soie le[408] justice solonc droit et resoun demande, sanz pluis outre processe de ley, pur Dieu et en eovre de charite.
[159] . . . fauxement controve mestoit baille en la sale de Westm', le terme de Seint Michel, lan du roi Richard . . . ,[409] le temps de parlement qe comencea a lendemein des Almes, par Jankyn Charneles de Bedeworth,[410] avant ceo . . . estoit mis ou baille a roi.

Membrane 6 schedule 8

[160] Chier et bien ame: nostre ame lige Alice, file et heir a Johan Lodbrok, chivaler, nous ad moustrez en compleigniant coment par la ou ele, apres la mort de Thomas Lodbrok son frer, entra en les manoirs et terres queux furent a son dit pier en Lodbrok et Toneworth en counte Warrewyk, par vertue dun fait entaillez de mesme les manoirs et terres, vous aves torceuousment et contre nostre pees ouste la dite Alice, a ceo qele dit, hors de sa droit heritage suisdit, et laves ocupies tanque en cea, a graund damage et arrierissement de son estat; dont ele nous a suppliez de remedie. Et nous, ottroiantz a la supplicacioun de mesme celle Alice, volons et vous mandons et chargeons fermement, qe totes autres choses, lesses, et excusaciouns cessantz, soiez devant nostre conseil a Westmonster a la quinzime de Sceint Michel prochein venant, apportant oves vous totes vos munimentz et altres vos evidences tochantz les ditz manoirs et terres, au fin qe mesme nostre conseil purra avoir conusance de vostre droit en cele partie, et determiner par entre vous le droit des manoirs et terres avantditz. Et ceo en nulle manere nes lessez. Don souz nostre prive seal, a Westmester, le x jour de septembre [1397]. [*See also* 101]
[*Endorsed*] Sire Gy Mone esteaunt clerc de prive seal, et poi apres[411] cree en evesqe de Seint David.

Membrane 6 schedule 9

[161] [*Copy of* 160, *annotated* Lan xxj le roi Richard seconde, *and endorsed* La qele lettre enseale estoit susrenduz en loffice de prive seal en presence de tut le counseil.]

Membrane 6 schedule 10

[162] A nostre tresredoute et tresexcellent seignur nostre seignur le roi, supplie treshumblement vostre povre lige et oratrice Alice, fille et heire a monsire Johan Lodbrok, que come la dite Alice, apres la mort de Thomas Lodbrok son frere, entra ses manoirs et terres que feurent son dit piere en Lodbrok et Tonworth en le countee de Warr', par vertue dun fait entaillee de mesmes les manoirs et terres, vient un Johan Catesby, et, a tort et encontre vostre pees, horsmetta la dite Alice de soun droit heritage, et lad occupie tanqe encea; que mesmes les terres et manoirs sount sibien seisez en voz mains come seo propres terres,[412] a cause de certaine offense quil ad fait a vostre hautesse: quil plaise a vostre roial magestee comaunder a vostre tressage counsail de soubaeier[413] la veritee du droit de vostre dite povre suppliante, et la ordener liveree de sa dite heritage, selonc ce que la ley et reson requiert, pur Dieu et en oevre de charitez.
[163] [*Endorsed*] A la quinzeine de Seint Michel, lan vynt et primer [13 Oct. 1397], sibien la suppliante deinz escrite en propre persone et come Johan Catesby deinz comprise, par premunicion a lui faite par force

[407] Reading uncertain.
[408] *soie le*: reading uncertain.
[409] Probably 15 Ric. II, 1391.
[410] Margaret Charnels was lady of Bedworth, assessed at 6s. 8d.: E 179/192/24, m.1d.
[411] 11 Nov. 1397.
[412] There is no evidence that Catesby's lands were ever confiscate, although his chattels were, briefly [179–180]; this might simply be an exaggerative allusion to the effect of the forfeiture suffered by Warwick, chief lord of the fees.
[413] Reading uncertain.

des lettres du prive seal nostre seignur le roi a lui sur ce directes, viendrent devant le counsail, et la matire de ceste bille declaree,[414] par encheson qe la matire cy dedeinz fut nadgairs pendant en la chauncellerie et remys a la comun ley, selonc ce qe la nature dicelle requist, agardez est qe les parties soient remys a la comun ley, etc.

Presenz en counseil: lercevesqe Deverwyk, levesqe Dexcestre (chanceler Dengleterre), levesqe de Londres (Robert Braybrok), levesqe de Salesbury (Johan[415] de Metford), Rogger Walden, tresorer Dengleterre, Gy Mone, clerc de prive seal, Johan Stanle, clerc des roules, Johan Rome, clerc de parlement, Frye, clerc de counseil, monsire William Darondell, monsire William de Beauchamp, monsire Henry Grene, monsire Johan de Bussy, monsire Hugh Holes, justice de banc le roi.

Membrane 6 schedule 11

[164] A treshonurable et tresgracious seignur le count de Warrewyk, moustrent et suppliont voz poverez tenantz Lowys Cardian et Alice sa femme, fille a monsire Johan Lodebrok et Hawys sa femme, et lour heir en la taille des manoirs de Lodebrok et Toneworth ove les appurtenantz, par droit descent apres la mort Johan fitz Thomas Lodebrok soun frere, apres qi morte la dite Alice entra es ditz manoirs come droite heir en la dite taille, et continua sa possessioun tantqe ele fut atort desheritez par Johan de Catesby, apres vendi le dit manoir de Toneworth a Robert Burgylon et il puis la vendi a vous, monseignur,[416] vous fesant adonqe de certein entendre qil lavoit recoverez vers les ditz suppliantz par assise de novelle dissesine; quele chose nest par voir, qar lassise ne passa point, einz fut nounsuy, come piert par record de mesme lassise, dont les ditz suppliantz ont la copie prest a moustrer. Par qoi ne vous desplese, monseignur, qar si les ditz suppliantz dussent en ce cas pursuer par la comune ley, ils dussent pursuer par brief de forme de doun vers vous, monseignur, qestez en possessioun, quele chose ils ne voillent mie faire, einz par cause, monseignur, qe vous estez tenuz entre la gent droiturel seignur de seinte vie[417] et bone conscience, ils voillent et gracitont[418] qapres ce, monseignur, qe vous ensoiez duement enfourmez de lour droit, vewez auxi lour munimentz et evidences en celle partie, par bone avys et deliberacioun des sages et loiaulx gentz de la ley, ne mie suspectz en le cas desteer, et mestre outrement lour dit droit et claym en vostre agarde et juggement de mesme pur tout jours, quele chose ils sount prestez a faire et perfourmir a quel temps et lieu ou sitost come pleiser vous soit, monseignur, de lour assigner; et ce priont ils entierement en descharge de vostre conscience et salvacioun de vostre alme, et pur lamour Dieu et de seinte charite.

[*Endorsed*] Memorandum that this bill was handed to Thomas earl of Warwick by Alice Cardian, in London, in Hilary term, 18 Richard II [1395].

Membrane 6 schedule 12

[165] Memorandum that on Friday before Palm Sunday, 16 Richard II [28 Mar. 1393], in the presence of Edward de Metteley and William de Duncherche, gaolers of Coventry, and others, Walter Gooldsmyth and Robert de Cortynale, bailiffs of the town, delivered to John de Catesby a forged deed, whereby Henry de Lodbrok, knight, granted the manors of Ladbroke and Tanworth to John his son and Hawise wife of John, in tail. The deed had been found in a chest belonging to Thomas Bromley, clerk, who told Cortynale that he found it in a chest belonging to the vicar of Holy Trinity, Coventry, and told Duncherche that he acquired it in the house of Thomas Archer, among the deeds of Lewis Cook; now he says that he had it from the prior of Sandwell in Staffordshire. Bromley instructed the bailiffs to hand the deed to Catesby.[419]

[*Endorsed*] The deed in question corresponded exactly with the copy, given to John de Catesby by John Charnels of Bedworth, which is attached to this roll, above [157].

Membrane 7 schedule 1

[166] Writ of novel disseisin to the sheriff of Warwickshire, on complaint by Lewis Cardian and Alice his wife that John Catesby, William Catesby and Joan his wife, Thomas Purefey, Edward Metley, Robert Burgulon, John Ray, and William parson of Ladbroke have unjustly disseised them of a tenement in Ladbroke; to be heard in king's bench at Coventry

[414] Followed by two or three words erased.

[415] Recte *Richard*.

[416] On 22 Sept. 1388: BL, Add. MS 28024 [the Beauchamp cartulary], modern f.104–104v (Dugdale's f.99a–b).

[417] Repeated.

[418] Possibly *grantont*.

[419] At the foot of the membrane is written '£6 2s.', probably from an earlier use of the parchment.

on Monday after All Saints. Tested at Westminster, 18 October, 21 Richard II [1397].
[167] [*Endorsed*] Le qel jour de lundy [5 Nov. 1397], toz les jurours aparurent, et le pleintif dit qe son brief fut malement conceu, et pria conge de querre meillour brief, et la court ne ly voloit recevire sanz assigner en qey en especial, et puis il esteit nounsuy; et fait a remembrer qe monsire William Bagot avoit empris le meintenaunce le pleintif, etc.

Membrane 7 schedule 2

[168] Assize for Ladbroke: †Guy Breton, *Henry Sutton, *Richard Boteler, †William Hore, *John Bray, †Geoffrey Scarburgh, *William Geydon, *John Shukburgh, *John Napton, *John Fulwode, *Edmund de Compton, *William Hemery, *John Derset of Thurlaston, *Thomas Palmer, *John Harryes, *Thomas Duston, †John Swyndon, *Robert Bulston, *Edmund Herdewyk, †Geoffrey Edmescote, *Eneas Badby, *Thomas Baron of Rugby, *John Otewer,[420] †Peter Sloley, †Thomas atte Berne of Tanworth. [*Cf.* 123]

Membrane 7 schedule 3

[169] [*Writ of novel disseisin, as* 166 *above, but returnable on Tuesday after the octave of Martinmas (20 November), and tested 8 November, 21 Richard II (1397).*]
[170] [*Endorsed*] A qel jour, qaunt cels deinz nomez estoient jurez, les pleintifs estoient nonsuiz, et pur taunt qe ceo fut la tierce foith qils avoient este nounsuiz, Lowys et sa femme, pleintifs, estoient amerciez a C s. et afferez par les jurours.

Membrane 7 schedule 4

[171] *John Wolf, *William Peyto (sworn), *Thomas Seyvill, *Henry Sutton (sworn), *Robert de Aston (sworn), *Guy Breton (sworn), *Thomas Hubaud, *John Boteler of Shustoke (sworn), *William Hore (sworn), *John Shukburgh (sworn), *William Hawe (sworn), *Roger Bulston (sworn), *John Napton, *Thomas Blith, *John Harries, *Richard Boteler (sworn), *Geoffrey Scarburgh (sworn), *Leonard Worthyn, *Thomas Shukburgh, *Thomas Palmer, *William Geidon (sworn), *Thomas Duston, Peter Sloley, John Swyndon.

Membrane 7 schedule 5

[172] Alfred Trussell, knight, Thomas Asteley, knight, Baldwin Frevyll, knight, Thomas Erdyngton, William Peyto, Edward Metteley, Thomas Hubaud, Guy Spyne, Thomas Crewe, William Hore, Richard Boteler, Henry de Sutton, Guy Breton, Robert de Aston, John Boteler of Shustoke, John Fulwod, Thomas Wyncote, Peter Holt, John Lyle, Geoffrey Scarburgh, William Allesley, John Langoley, William Hawe, John Shukburgh, Thomas Blythe, William Geydon, Richard Waldene, John Harryes (all sworn).
[*Annotated*] Cels sount les nouns des jurours de divers hundreds qi present le fait[421] de taill del manoir de Lodbrok et Toneworth estre faux et contrefet en desheriteson de Johan de Catesby, en banc le roi, lan du roi Richard xxj. [*See* 173–4, 178, *and* KB 37/2/21/1, *unnumbered panel.*]

Membrane 7 schedule 6

[173] Thomas Bromlee appears in king's bench at Coventry, in the custody of the marshal, and pleads guilty, seeking the king's grace and asking to make fine; he is remanded in custody because he lacks sufficient pledges. Roll 27. [*See* KB 27/546, Rex m.27, *and* KB 37/2/21/1, *unnumbered writ and panel.*]
[*Endorsed*] Let it be exemplified.

Membrane 7 schedule 7

[174] Jurors of divers Warwickshire hundreds present in king's bench in the present term that Thomas Bromlee of Coventry, planning to disinherit John de Catesby of his manors of Ladbroke and Tanworth in Warwickshire, falsely, wickedly, and maliciously forged an indenture dated at Ladbroke, Monday the morrow of Trinity, 19 Edward II [19 May 1326], whereby Henry de Lodbrok, knight, granted to his son John de Lodbrook, and Hawise wife of John, and the heirs of the body of John, the said manors, writing the deed in his own hand and sealing it with green wax bearing the impression of a seal with Henry Lodbrok's arms; also, in order to conceal the forgery, and to make the document appear old enough for Edward II's reign, he held the document and its seal in smoke [*see also* 108]. They also say that he is a common counterfeiter of charters and seals. On appearance in custody of the marshal, in king's bench at Coventry, on Thursday after St Edmund the king [22 Nov. 1397], he pleads not guilty, and is remanded in custody until the Friday following, pending a jury. [*See* KB 27/546, Rex m.27.]
[*Endorsed*] To be exemplified.

[420] For *Scewer*?

[421] Followed by *estre*, deleted.

[175] Et fait a remembrer qe qaunt il conust la fauxine il bailla a la court une bille de papir, escrit de sa mayn demeine, enqel estoit compris qe Lowys Cardian avoit contrefait le seal monsire Henry deinz comprise, a Londres, et qe un Robert of the Dom, escrivein de Lychefeld, avoit escript le fait, et qe Alice la femme le dit Lowys aporta a Coventre le dit fait nient enseale, et qe le dit Thomas Bromlee et Alice enseleront le dit fait ove verte cyre, en desheritesoun del dit Johan de Catesby. Et fait a remembrer qe le primer jour qil conust, il estoit comande par monsire Wauter de Clopton a mareschal, de ly reprendre ariere, et le remener lendemein hors des fers, et qil soi aciusereit bien de sa conisaunce; a qel lendemein il conust de plein avis com desus. Et puis apres, le dymenge le jour de Seint Katerine [25 Nov. 1397], en lostel Johan Wychard, ou le mareschal estoit herbege, en la sale de stage, estoit Bromlee fait venir en presence William Broke, person de lesglise de Lodbrok, William le fiz de dit Johan de Catesby, le mareschal de banc, William Baudy, Gadifer Giles de Norton, le dit Johan de Catesby, et plusours altres, et soi confessa, et dit qe cely qi escrit le susdite fait escript le fait par quel ils pledent, de mein de rag,[422] qar il savoit escrire et lun et laltre, et qe le dit Bromlee mesme estoit al enseler del un et del altres, et qe tut estoit fait as custages William Gamel, viker, etc., et ceo prist il en peril de salvie, etc.

Membrane 7 schedule 8

[176] [*Variants noted from draft at* SC 1/51, 23 *(here 'F').*]

A soun tresexellent seignur le duc de Surreye, supplie le soun Johan de Catesby: come nadgairs William de Catesby soun pier, qe Dieux assoile, purchasa le manoir de Lodbrok en Lodbrok, appele Lodbrokes-maner, de monsire Johan de Lodbrok en fee, cinqant[423] anz passez,[424] et de ceo morust seisi, apres qi mort entra le dit suppliant come fitz et heir par descent, et releva as seignurs de fee;[425] et ore tard un William Hathewyk aporta a dit Johan un lettre de prive seal nostre seignur le roi, destre devant le conseil nostre dit seignur a la xv de Sceint Michel darrein, a respoundre a Alice, file a dit monsire Johan[426] a qel temps les parties estoient commis a la comune ley, par avis de tut le conseil.[427] Et puis un Lowys Cardian et la dite[428] Alice sa femme, par meyntenaunce le dit William Hathewyk, pursuerent devers le dit Johan de Catesby deux assises, chescun apres altre, del dit manoir, devant les justices de banc nostre seignur le roi a Coventre, mesme le terme, et furent nounsuiz;[429] et puis apres les diz Lowys et Alice, et le dit William Hathewyk,[430] la veille de la Circumsicioun Nostre Seignur darrein passe,[431] disseisirent le dit Johan de Catesby del dit manoir,[432] de qi le dit Johan porta lassise de la date de la dite

[422] The meaning of this phrase is not clear. The following suggestions, none of which is sanctioned by usage elsewhere, are offered: (i) a ragged hand, i.e. a slovenly hand disguising the writer's normal characteristics; (ii) a forger's hand, after Robert Rag, the Bruern abbey forger – see C. G. Crump, 'What became of Robert Rag, or some chancery blunders', in *Essays in Medieval History Presented to Thomas Frederick Tout,* ed. A. G. Little and F. M. Powicke (Manchester, 1925) [reference suggested by Mr L. C. Hector], and C 67/28B, m.13; (iii) a ragman hand, i.e. one typical of documents fifty or a hundred years old.

[423] After *bien a,* deleted F.

[424] Followed by *joint ove altres al eopes le dit William, et cel estat il et altres al eopes le dit William ount contenue tanteqe le dit William,* deleted F.

[425] Followed by *al counte de Warr' qadonqe mounsire de (le count Ferers de* interlined*) Groby qadonqe furent, des qe seignurs le dit manoir al temps estoit tenuz, et de tel estat est le dit Johan a present seisi,* deleted F.

[426] *a respondre . . . Johan* interlined F.

[427] This phrase interlined before *et puis le justices de banc nostre seignur le roi vindrent a Coventre al lendemain des almes darrein, devant qels Johan ne puis un,* deleted F.

[428] *la dite* interlined F.

[429] *deux assises . . . furent nounsuiz* interlined above *un assise de novel disseisin devers le dit Johan Catesby, et proces continua tauntqe ils furent nounsuis, et puis seaunt le dit banc en un altre assise altre foith,* deleted F.

[430] *et le . . . Hathewyk* interlined F.

[431] F deletes here a repetition of the subjects of the clause.

[432] *del dit manoir* interlined F.

veille,[433] par quel assise le dit Johan recovery et avoit execusioun,[434] qel estat le dit Johan ad contenue taunqe en ca; et ore il[435] eit entenduz qe William Bakere de Warr' ad vos lettres[436] patentez de pusne temps de ocupier;[437] et le dit Johan de grant age et de grant enfirmite, par assignement de vous et de vostre conseil, a grant disese et custage, ad travaille a Loundres a divers temps pur la matire avantdit;[438] par[439] qei[440] plese a vostre tresgraciouse seignurie comander vos[441] ministres en paiis qils nies ne soi medleint del dit manoir,[442] ou comander a vostre sage et discret conseil en ceste vill ore ceste terme de Pasch doier la matire suisdite ove les circumstances, et faire a dit suppliant[443] ceo qe ley et resoun demandount, pur Dieu et en eovre de charite.

Membrane 7 schedule 9

[177] John de Catesby complains that, despite statutory prohibition of maintenance, William, vicar of Holy Trinity, Coventry, by agreement made on the Monday before St , Richard II,[444] at Warwick, undertook to maintain Lewis and Alice Cardyan in their assize of novel disseisin, brought against the plaintiff before the justices of assize at Warwick, on Monday after St Margaret the virgin, 21 Richard II [23 July 1397], to Catesby's damage of £200. Pledges for prosecution: John Hale, Richard More.
[*Annotated*] Alcel bill des deux assises qil meinteint en banc le roi a Coventre le terme de Seint Michel, lan du roi Richard seconde xxj.
[*Endorsed*] Edmund de Compton, William Wylmecote, William Westyngdon, Ralph Saucer, William Elys, John Hopkyns of Wootton Wawen,[445] Richard Barell of Ullenhall, John Brasyer of Stratford, John Irmonger of Stratford, William Bronman, Thomas Merston, John James, Thomas Grene of Shottery, Robert Bereford, John Bronman, Henry Aldebury, George Bores, Thomas Aldebury, Robert Bailly and Robert Peyntour of Stratford on Avon, William Waleys, John Faukener, William Eyres, Otewell Power, Geoffrey Ive, John Hemery of Honiley, John Harpour of the same, Nicholas Ayleston, Simon Felton, John Godeshalve, William Pakwod. Summoner, Ralph . . . ler.
[*Annotated*] Les qels ij billes estoient suy tantqe le dit viker perdy en issues xlij marcz, sanz les cent s. qe Lowys et sa feme perdrent.[446]

Membrane 7 schedule 10

[178] [*Presentment in king's bench, as* 174.] Further presentment that, maliciously and falsely planning to disinherit divers of the king's lieges, and treasonably against the king's crown and allegiance, Thomas Bromlee counterfeited the chancery great seal from two pieces of lead, at Coventry, on Monday after the Purification, 16 Richard II [3 Feb. 1393], and sealed with white wax, in chancery fashion, divers forged letters close. Also, when Bromlee was steward of Great Wyrley, which is ancient demesne of the crown, he sent himself writs of right, close, assuming the royal power and without any warrant, forging them at Coventry on Monday the morrow of the close of Easter next [14 Apr.], addressing them to himself as steward of Wyrley, and by virtue of them he heard pleas, gave judgments, and required the execution of judgments in the court there, in disherison of the king and his laws. [*See* 172–4, *and* KB 27/546, Rex m.27–27d.]
In the name of Thomas in the Grene, concerning a messuage and 20a. of land, with appurtenances. [*?*]

Membrane 7 schedule 11

[179] Writ to William Bagot and Robert Goushill, requiring the restoration to John de Catesby of any chattels confiscated from him, notwithstanding a previous order to confiscate the chattels of Thomas earl of Warwick, Nicholas Lillyng, knight, John Catesby, William Spernole, and Robert Walden of

[433] *de Circumcision sur* deleted F.

[434] *execusion* interlined above *sa livre par le* (*south* interlined) *viscount ove sa blanche verge en sa mein,* deleted F.

[435] After *come come,* deleted F.

[436] After *honurez,* deleted F.

[437] *de pusne . . . ocupier,* interlined F.

[438] *pur . . . . avant dit* after *davoit declare sa matire devant vostre counseil,* interlined and deleted, followed by *come il serra prest a declarer,* deleted F.

[439] After *quels matires susdiz et plusours altres considerez* (*qil ad este . . . et travaille* interlined), deleted F.

[440] *par* omitted F.

[441] After *a vostre counseil destre comise,* deleted F.

[442] *de dit manoir* interlined F.

[443] Interlined after *Johan* F.

[444] Blanks in MS.

[445] Assessed at 4d. in 1379: E 179/192/23, m.5.

[446] This total – £33 – tallies with the sum forfeit in king's bench for which he obtained pardons: *CPR 1396–9,* 278, 291, and see also 283. The stays of execution on the offences and the debt survive in the Precepta Recordorum file: KB 145/3/21/2.

Warwick, in Warwickshire, Leicestershire, Northamptonshire, and Worcestershire. Tested at Westminster, 16 October, 21 Richard II [1397]. By the council. [*See* 125, *and CCR 1396–9,* 157.]

Membrane 7 schedule 12

[180] Writ mandamus to William Bagot and Robert Goushill, ordering confiscations [*as in previous entry*]. Tested at Woodstock, 18 August [1397]. By the king. [*CFR 1391–9,* 227.]

Membrane 7 schedule 13

[181] Fait a remembrer qe le meskerdy prochein apres la feste de Seint Mathie lapostre en Qaresme, lan du regne le roi Richard secounde vint et secounde [26 Feb. 1399], vindrent a Lodbrok Gy Spynee et Edward Scherd, Henry Trymenell et Thomas Lutterworth, messagers, et mostrerent le fait le duc de Surreie come ils as[er]oient de son signet, et Gy Spynee fesait livre a la porte del manoir depar le duc de Surreie[447] al duc Dexcestre, et le dit Edward Scherd, et des tenanz – William Hoggekyns, neif,[448] Thomas Wylkyns, et Johan Wryde leigne atournerent. Et Gy Spyne manacea Richard Stel qil serreit tret hors de sa mesoun sil les contredirreit; et manacea toz qe atornerent qils le comparreient sils ne voleient atourner, etc. Et cels qatournerent disoient qil ne voleient atorner al duc de Excestre, etc. Et le dit Thomas Wilkyns disoit qil ne conuit unqe altre seignur si non William de Catesby et Johan son fiz a present, et mesme ceo disoient toz les tenanz qi atournerent, etc. Et le dit fait porte date a Lodelowe le darrein jour de janvier, lan du roi Richard xxij [13 Jan. 1399].

[182] [*Endorsed*] Et puis apres, le lundy en la symeigne de Pasch adonqe prochein ensuaunt [31 Mar. 1399], Edward Scherd vint a Lodbrok et voleit avoir tenuz un court, et nul ne voleit venir a la court, nient countreesteaunt qil les demanda sur peine; et fit un Wille Fleckenho soun baillif, et amena ovesqe ly qatre gentz de Herbury, a pie, pur avoir pris destresse des tenanz; et Hugh Baillif, conestable, ly mostra un precept del viscount de deliveraunce de totiens quotiens, et qant Edward Scherd vit ceo il demanda sils voloient pleder, et ove ceo il sei departy sanz plus faire.

A quel jour les Trymenels de Herbury et altres debruserent les clos et hayes del dit manoir, etc.

Membrane 7 schedule 14

[183] Writ of novel disseisin to the sheriff of Warwickshire, on complaint by John de Catesby that Lewis Cardian, Alice his wife, and William Hathewyk have unjustly disseised him of a tenement in Ladbroke; to be heard by William Thirnyng and Robert Tirwyt, justices of assize. Tested at Westminster, 31 December, 21 Richard II [1397]. 'Signed' Stanle.

E 28/4, no. 82 [*?Draft, on parchment; interlineations in the hand of John Catesby.*[449]]

[184] A trespuissant prynce et son tresdoute seignour le duc Dexcestre, moustre et supplie le son Johan de Catesby. Come William de Catesby son pier nadgairs bien a sinqant et treis anz passes purchasa le manoir de Lodbrok appelle Lodbrokes Manoir de monsire Johan de Lodbrok, en fee, ove garrauntie,[450] William morust seisi del dit manoir, apres qi mort entra le dit suppliant come fitz et heir, et releva as seignours de fee;[451] et cele estat continua tanqe un Lowys Cardian et Alyce sa feme – qe soi dit estre fille et heir le dit monsire Johan – et un William Hathewyk ly disseiserunt, le lundy en la veille de la Circumcision Nostre Seignour, lan vintisme primer nostre seignour le roi quore est [31 Dec. 1397], de quele disseisyn[452] le dit suppliant porta lassise, et recoveri,[453] a Warrewyk, cest darrein an, et avoit execucion, et cele estat ad continue par verreie title, come il est prest a moustrer devaunt vous et vostre tresnoble et sage consail;[454] et oretard Henry

447 Above *Dexcestre,* deleted.

448 Interlined.

449 This is clearly a misplaced stray from the Catesby evidences; it bears the typical archival endorsement, probably by Le Neve. It shows, however, no signs of sewing-holes, and its folds suggest that it was stored with the notes rather than with the main roll. Although originally engrossed as a fair copy, the corrections indicate that this document was not itself sent, and it seems possible that another bill, perhaps from Hathewick, forestalled the need to send this one [109].

450 *ove garrauntie* interlined.

451 *de fee* interlined by the engrossing clerk.

452 Penultimate letter uncertain.

453 Last letter uncertain.

454 *et auxint et puis soun tresage seignur de Surreie par avis de son grand et sage counseil osta sa main de icele* interlined and deleted.

Trymunell et Edward Scherd, ove altres, viendront a Lodbrok, et clamerunt le dit manoir, et comaunderont as tenauntz qils ne paieront null rente si non a vous, tresdoute seignour, et a dit Edward, encountre ley et reson: qe please a vostre tresgraciouse seignorie comaunder a vostre noble et sage consail doier le dit suppliant en le matire suisdite ove les circumstancez, et sur ceo ordeigner pur le dit suppliant ceo qe ley et reson demandont: pur Dieu et en oepre[455] de charite.

[455] For *oevre*.

Clergy and common law in the reign of Henry IV

edited by

R. L. STOREY

INTRODUCTION

'More cruelty has been inflicted on prelates in England than in all Christendom.' Adam Usk wrote that he made this observation to Archbishop Arundel in a convocation when the archbishop had raised with his clergy the issue of violations of ecclesiastical liberties, particularly the trial of bishops as if they were laymen. Arundel quoted two instances of bishops thus treated;[1] his audience hardly needed to be reminded of his own impeachment in parliament and subsequent banishment in 1397. The convocation of Canterbury which discussed these grievances met on 6 October 1399. It had been called after the rebellion which was to make Henry IV king and restore Arundel as archbishop, but the mandates of summons had been issued before Richard II's formal deposition on 30 September and also well before Arundel was officially given restitution of the temporalities of his archbishopric on 21 October.[2] Arundel had resumed the title of archbishop since, after the capture of Richard, the rebellion's success was assured and he briefly held the office of chancellor[3] and in this capacity supervised the issue of writs calling a parliament to meet on 30 September. The convocation was thus called as the clerical counterpart of the assembly which gave constitutional form to Richard's deposition. Both bodies presented lists of grievances against the late king, the estates in the form of articles for his deposition, the clergy expressing theirs in the course of a lengthy series of proposed reforms.

Richard's violation of ecclesiastical liberties, despite his coronation oath, was instanced in the deposition articles by his demands that heads of religious houses should provide horses and carts for his expedition to Ireland, an issue also raised in convocation's articles.[4] The deposition articles alone refer to Richard's banishment of Arundel and to a matter of general clerical concern; this was that Richard had ordered church courts, by letters under his signet, to desist from hearing certain causes even though the chancellor had previously refused to issue writs of prohibition.[5] The convocation articles, other than those relating to matters which could be reformed by the prelates and clergy themselves (nos. 1–43), are concerned mainly with grievances suffered at the hands of the king's judges and officials (nos. 44–63). It was proposed that the new king be asked to confirm all clerical privileges, particularly those in Magna Carta, Circumspecte Agatis and Edward II's letters of 1316. Infringements of these concessions were illustrated in individual articles. Writs of prohibition had been improperly issued to prevent allegedly legitimate proceedings in church courts but the king's judges refused to grants writs of consultatio, the long-established practice whereby judges of church and common law courts resolved jurisdictional boundaries.[6] Altogether seven of the articles indicate that Richard's judges had taken a rigid stance after the issue of prohibitions. In some other articles the clergy might have added that the practices of royal officers, such as arresting priests during the performance of divine office, had been prohibited by parliamentary statute.[7] One article urged that the king should be asked to confirm benefit of clergy: even priests had been hanged after conviction on malicious indictments framed in particular terms.[8]

It is likely that Arundel and his clergy expected Henry IV to be more disposed to defend ecclesiastical liberties than Richard had been. That certain of the higher clergy at least welcomed Richard's replacement is indicated by Usk's notice of a committee of bishops and doctors which concluded that Richard's crimes justified his deposition in accordance with the verdict of the council of Lyons against the Emperor Frederick II.[9] Richard could also be accused of expelling some individual clergy from their benefices. After his deposition, he asked Henry to ease his conscience by restoring St Giles' hospital to the master of Burton Lazars.[10] In contrast, Henry's confirmation in parliament of a statute for the protection of

[1] *Chronicon Adae de Usk A.D. 1377–1421,* ed. E. M. Thompson, 2nd edn (London, 1904), 44, 204–5.

[2] *CPR 1399–1401,* 28–9.

[3] R. L. Storey, 'English Officers of State, 1399–1485', *BIHR,* XXXI (1958), 84.

[4] *RP,* III, 420 (no. 39); *Concilia Magnae Britanniae et Hiberniae,* ed. D. Wilkins (London, 1737), III, 245 (no. 61).

[5] *RP,* III, 421 (nos. 46–7, 50).

[6] Bracton, f.405b (IV, 252–3). See also stat. 50 Edw. III, c.4.

[7] ibid., c.5; 1 Ric. II, c.15.

[8] *Concilia,* III, 240–5; below, 343.

[9] Usk, *Chronicon,* 29–30, 181.

[10] *CPR 1401–5,* 120; below, 350.

incumbents and declaration of intent to moderate the statutes of provisors would have earned clerical satisfaction: both issues had been raised in the simultaneous convocation.[11] Four months after Henry's accession, however, Usk could chronicle with apparent disapproval that Thomas Marks, the ex-bishop of Carlisle, had been condemned before royal justices and a lay jury for his part in a rebellion.[12] At his trial on 27 January 1400, Marks had protested that as an anointed bishop he should not have been arraigned in king's bench, but the justices answered that no privilege could exempt persons indicted of treason from trial in a royal court.[13] This answer was amply supported by precedent and statute: treason was not clergyable.[14] Sentence was deferred, however, and Marks was subsequently pardoned because of the king's avowed respect for episcopal dignity and as an act of reverence.[15] Clerical opinion would also have been assuaged by the king's assent to anti-Lollard measures in the parliament of 1401, by his refusal to refrain from licensing provisions and to prohibit the appropriation of churches to religious houses, and by his referring to the prelates another commons' petition against pluralism.[16]

By the time Henry's third parliament met in September 1402, however, the clergy could no longer feel confident that they enjoyed royal protection. The execution for treason of nine Franciscans and three other priests in the previous June would have affronted clerical opinion, although king and council obviously endeavoured to prevent a public outcry by bringing to justice only the more deeply implicated suspects and by organising their trial so that their offence should be widely publicised as dangerous to all the king's subjects as well as to himself [1]. The clergy themselves conceded that they could not claim benefit if convicted of treason. What more greatly concerned them was that indictments for common felonies could be drawn up in terms alleging novel generalities which ensured that, after conviction, a clerk would be refused benefit. In this parliament a petition was submitted by Arundel, his suffragans and clergy, asking the king to confirm Edward III's statute of 1351 Pro Clero which reaffirmed benefit of clergy. Henry in fact confirmed this statute in its entirety, and all other liberties granted to the clergy, and he also met the petitioners' wishes by prohibiting the use in indictments of novel terms like 'depopulatores agrorum sive incidiatores viarum'. The convocation of October 1399 had complained about the inclusion of these particular words in malicious indictments.[17] As recently as the previous June (1402) a man had been hanged following conviction on an indictment with these words, and he may have been a priest because the point of the clergy's complaint in both 1399 and 1402 was that these terms would have prevented him from gaining benefit [2]. The petition of 1402 also referred to the use of the term *communes latrones* in indictments. It appears in the indictment of Adam Usk, also in Trinity 1402, and there is some reason to believe that this is an example of the false, malicious indictments with which, the clergy complained, their members were persecuted [3]. As Usk was a member of Arundel's household, this indictment doubtless helped to prompt the archbishop to present the petition three years after convocation had urged its necessity. Earlier in the same year, a number of the archbishop's *curiales* had been indicted for conspiracy and fraud, probably at the instigation of the ex-dean of Wells [4].

Usk thus had personal cause for bitterness about common law courts. His conversation with Arundel in 1399 and the articles of that year's convocation indicate that clergy regarded the king's judges as their most dangerous enemies. Henry IV may have been more benevolent than Richard II, but all the latter's judges were reappointed in 1399.[18] The availability of the year books of Henry's reign, unlike those of Richard's later years, provides a means of investigating whether these judges really were bitter opponents of the clergy and their judicial institutions. Few of the reports tend to confirm this opinion. While Henry's judges certainly opposed invasions of their own jurisdiction by church courts, they generally respected

11 13 Ric. II, stat.1, c.1; *RP*, III, 428, 438; *Concilia*, III, 241–2 (nos. 28, 30); W. E. Lunt, *Financial Relations of the Papacy with England, 1327–1534* (Cambridge, Mass, 1962), 400–1.

12 Usk, *Chronicon*, 43, 204. Usk misplaces this notice before he records his conversation in convocation, 1399, probably because he regarded Marks' trial as another example of the tribulations of English bishops: see also Thompson in ibid., xxxv–xxxvi.

13 *King's Bench*, VII, 102–5.

14 J. G. Bellamy, *The Law of Treason in England in the Later Middle Ages* (Cambridge, 1970), 60, 62–3, 88 n.3, 92; 25 Edw. III, stat.6, c.4.

15 *King's Bench*, VII, 105; *CPR 1399–1401*, 385.

16 *RP*, III, 459, 468, 470, 473–4.

17 ibid., 494–5; *SR*, II, 132–3; *Concilia*, III, 244 (no. 55).

18 *CPR 1399–1401*, 1, 14; Foss, *Judges of England*, IV, 17–18, 127, 136–7; Sayles in *King's Bench*, VII, lxii.

clerical privileges and the monopoly of church courts in their time-hallowed preserves. Occasionally, however, some judges were strangely ignorant of statutory concessions to the clergy.

Chief Justice William Gascoigne made a remarkable statement in 1406. He had it noted that a common law court could seize a bishop's temporalities if he refused to accept a felon who had been granted benefit of clergy. It had become normal practice, by the end of the fourteenth century, that a man indicted of felony made no claim to clerical privilege until he had been convicted. As is well known, felons who were not in clerical orders, who had been described in their indictments as having lay occupations, would be deemed clerks if they passed a simple test of literacy. Benefit of clergy was thus notoriously abused, sometimes by professional criminals.[19] Gascoigne's note shows that some bishops were not oblivious of this scandal and might refuse to receive convicted 'clerks' for detention in their prisons. The note reveals the judiciary in the surprising rôle of champion of benefit of clergy, even when it was being allowed to improbable clerks: there is no hint here that clergy need fear that their privilege might be denied in common law courts. Gascoigne, however, was not defending the principle of benefit but the right of common law courts to decide which felons were clergy; no bishop might presume to question their decision. A further point deserving emphasis is his dictum that this presumptuous bishop's temporalities could be seized, a sanction not only over severe but of dubious legality in such a case. Archbishop Islip had complained in parliament in 1351 about the tendency of the king's judges to seize temporalities whenever bishops might be deemed to be in contempt of court, and the remedy granted then was that in future judges were to impose a reasonable fine. Fortescue and his colleagues were more correct when they agreed in 1456 that the penalty for rejecting a convicted clerk was a fine.[20]

The statute which Gascoigne had overlooked was Pro Clero.[21] This statute was cited in defence of the bishop of Coventry and Lichfield against the king's suit by quare impedit in 1409. Horton, for the bishop, said that this statute barred the king from claiming the presentation in this case. Skrene, king's serjeant, replied that the statute had been repealed, but Hankford, JCP, agreed that it forbade the hearing of this plea. Thurning, CJCP, then asked that the statute should be read, after which he remarked 'it is different from what I had thought'. Tyldesley, king's serjeant, said that many similar actions had been tried in the courts and they had heard nothing of this statute. 'Et male', Horton rejoined. Thurning asked the serjeants if they wished to speak about the statute. Norton's answer was a negative, but he confirmed that the statute had not previously been cited, and Tyldesley observed that there had been a parliamentary ordinance about silva cedua which had never been used. Thurning ruled that Pro Clero did bar the king's title here and that it had not been repealed, while Hankford repeated that the statute was in force because it had been ordered in parliaments of Richard II and Henry IV that all statutes not repealed were to be observed.[22] What is most remarkable about this discussion is that the statute Pro Clero had been specifically confirmed as recently as 1402 in a parliament when some at least of these judges and serjeants were present.[23] It is hard to believe that their ignorance was genuine.

Some judicial discussions do suggest a critical attitude to clergy. In a suit for trespass brought by the friars minor of London in 1409, the defendant explained that he had entered the convent to retrieve his eleven-year-old son who had been enticed by the friars from his home at Winchester; the clothing he was accused of stealing was the habit his son was wearing, for otherwise he would have been naked. The court's sympathy was obviously with the father. Hankford made a harsh simile: if a husband recovered his wife from a lover, he might take her clad in her seducer's finery. The friars' writ was dismissed.[24] In the following term, two schoolmasters of Gloucester sued a third for trespass; they were licensed by the

19 L. C. Gabel, *Benefit of Clergy in the Later Middle Ages* (Northampton, Mass, 1928–9), 41–6, 76–9; *RP*, V, 151, 333. YB (1679) 10 Hen. IV, Mich.18, reports sentence on a married man claiming to be a clerk.

20 YB 7 Hen. IV (2nd ser.), Pas.6 (p.41); 34 Hen. VI, Trin.16. In 1409 Gascoigne refused a request by the king's serjeant to seize the temporalities of St Davids for failure to pay a pension to a king's clerk; seizure would be ordered only if the bishop (Chicheley) failed to execute the court's judgment: YB 10 Hen. IV, Hil.1. The case is in *King's Bench*, VII, 184–6.

21 25 Edw. III, stat.6, c.6.

22 YB 11 Hen. IV, Mich.20. For the case, see below, 351. Pro Clero was also cited in [20].

23 Reports from *The Lords Committees touching the Dignity of a Peer of the Realm* (London, 1826–9), IV, 783; *RP*, III, 486; above, 343.

24 YB 11 Hen. IV, Mich.27 (recte 57, p.31).

prior of Llanthony, but he was not, and since his arrival their fees from pupils had been halved. Hankford produced another simile: 'I might have a mill, a neighbour could erect another so that I lost business, but there is no remedy'. Thurning and Hill, JCP, were of the same opinion, the latter adding that teaching was a virtuous, charitable act and should not be punished. Skrene's suggestion that an action for nuisance was permissible was rejected by Hankford: the plaintiffs had no estate in 'le scholemastership', and it was against reason to prevent a master from holding a school wherever he pleased except in a town where there was a university or school of ancient foundation. The real point at issue, however, was whether the prior of Llanthony had the sole right to license schools in Gloucester, and as teaching was a spiritual matter, Thurning ruled, no remedy could be provided by the common bench. This writ was therefore also dismissed, but for the reason that the court would not interfere in a matter reserved to church courts.[25] In another case Gascoigne quoted subjects triable only by canon law [8]. In 1413, the judges refused to allow an action for trespass in what was really a dispute about tithes because a church court was the recognised forum for such an issue.[26]

There was opposition by the judges to the award of damages by church courts. Hankford pointed out that in practice the church courts did this by withholding absolution until compensation had been paid. He also cited an instance of a suit for enfeoffment in king's bench which failed; the plaintiff consequently sued in a church court, alleging the canonical offence of perjury, and so secured an order for fulfilment. Judges and king's serjeants agreed that violence to clergy was a spiritual offence and properly triable in a church court, but only if the object was to inform the court so that the offender should receive spiritual correction; if the injured clerk demanded damages, however, the suit pertained to common law. In at least one case of this kind a prohibition was allowed.[27] It is not known if the convocations of Henry's reign continued to complain about writs of prohibition, though an example is given below of one issued in very questionable circumstances [5]. A parliamentary petition in 1410 complained that church courts frequently cited people to answer for debt, contract, and the like, and that many defendants in such cases were too poor to sue for prohibitions. The king ignored the request for a statutory remedy, answering only that common law should be observed. The church courts were in fact to make increasing inroads into the common law's jurisdiction in debt on the pretext that the spiritual offence of perjury was thus committed.[28]

On the other hand, the judges continued to support the authority of church courts in their proper sphere. An excommunicate was not allowed to plead in common law courts and thus, in the instance shown, could not obtain remedy even for the abduction of his wife [6]. An excommunication certified by a bishop was respected because the court could order him to justify his sentence.[29] It was a different matter when an excommunication had been pronounced by papal authority. In the suit between the priors of Studley and Maxstoke [10], the latter claimed that he need not answer because of Studley's excommunication by the archbishop of Canterbury, whose certificate was produced. Hankford ruled that the excommunication was irrelevant: the archbishop had been acting as a papal judge-delegate and sentences by papal authority were not admissible in common law courts. Hankford's argument was that in contrast to English bishops, who could be compelled to justify their sentences by seizure of their temporalities, the pope was not similarly an officer of the common law courts: they could not compel his presence. Hankford later reported that he had consulted a 'doctor' (i.e. canonist) on this point and had his agreement, but in fact it had been the practice of common law judges to disregard excommunications by judges-delegate in Bracton's time.[30]

The common lawyers' opposition to papal authority was more widely expressed in the lengthy discussions of a quare impedit against Bishops Hallam of Salisbury and Chicheley of St Davids for the former's refusal to admit a royal nominee as chan-

[25] ibid., Hil.21; *VCH Glos,* II, 315.

[26] YB 14 Hen. IV, Hil.14.

[27] YB 7 Hen. IV (1st ser.), Mich.5 (p.1); 11 Hen. IV, Trin.40. *CPR 1408–13,* 266, refers to another prohibition in a similar case.

[28] *RP,* III, 645–6 (no. 72); B. L. Woodcock, *Medieval Ecclesiastical Courts in the Diocese of Canterbury* (Oxford, 1952), 84–90.

[29] See Littleton, in E. Coke, *The First Part of the Institutes of the Laws of England, or a Commentary upon Littleton* (London, 1628), 133b–134a.

[30] YB 14 Hen. IV, Hil.4; F. D. Logan, *Excommunication and the Secular Arm in Medieval England* (Pontifical Inst. Med. Studies, Toronto, Studies and Texts, XV, 1968), 30–1 (citing Bracton). For restatements of this doctrine by Littleton in 1478 and Hussey, CJ, in 1489, see YB 12 Edw. IV, Mich.18; 4 Hen. VII, Trin.12.

cellor of Salisbury. Chicheley was retaining this dignity by a papal grant in commendam made at the time of his provision to St Davids. It appears from these discussions that the judges and serjeants were completely unaware of the papal practice of so dispensing bishops to retain benefices. Grants in commendam may have been a novelty in England but as recently as 1402 the king had authorised the bishop of St Asaph to keep a rectory by virtue of papal letters.[31] This precedent was not quoted in the arguments about Chicheley's case. From the first report in Michaelmas 1409, all the judges denied the pope's right to license Chicheley's retention of the chancellorship: a papal grant could not change the law of England, said Thurning, and the law here was that a clerk's benefices became vacant if he was made a bishop. Although Hankford quoted 'Papa omnia potest', he would in similar circumstances have sued a clerk of his own by quare impedit. The statutes of provisors were brought into the debate: Horton, for Chicheley, said that they were not applicable as they referred only to provisions and reservations of benefices, whereas Chicheley was given a dispensation; but the king's serjeants said that on this line of argument Chicheley might have two bishoprics, which was against reason, and that the purpose of the statutes, to save the rights of patrons, must be respected. In later sessions Hankford showed that in practice the pope could moderate English law, by granting dispensations for benefices to be held in plurality or by monks, and by legitimising marriages and their issues. In Chicheley's case, he said, it was arguable that he had not vacated his benefices by his creation as bishop, for the papal grant was a dispensation. Thurning also changed his stance to saying that the law that a benefice was void was spiritual law, from which the pope could dispense; the judges had accepted papal dispensations in other actions. To the end, however, the general opinion was still opposed to Chicheley.[32] By this time (Trinity 1410) the judicial discussion was academic as the king had already agreed to a compromise made with the pope by Chicheley [9].

While the year books give some indications of how Henry IV's judges dealt with issues concerning church institutions and clergy, the extent to which they could be engaged with litigation about ecclesiastical affairs can be more amply illustrated from particular suits recorded in the plea rolls.[33] The common law courts' involvement with disputes of this nature had been increased as the result of parliamentary legislation designed to restrict papal influence in the English church, of which the statutes of provisors and praemunire are the best known. There were two statutes of praemunire seemingly designed to restrict litigation at the papal court on issues triable at common law; the statute of provisors of 1365 also had a clause about such suits.[34] The first of these measures was not in fact a statute made in parliament but an ordinance in great council, as the writs in which it is cited usually make clear [7, 9–11; but cf. 8]; it is never referred to as a statute, but as 'provisio et ordinacio' or 'ordinacio et concordia'. It is, however, enrolled on the statute roll, the courts obviously regarded it as having the force of a statute, and for centuries it has been called a statute.[35] It has been argued that this statute of 1353 did not make any new restraint on suits at the curia: common law courts were already able to forbid such litigation, and all the statute did was to provide a more stringent process for causing defendants to appear in common law courts; instead of citation by mesne process, they could now be summoned by the writs of praemunire facias which gave the statute its name, and failure to appear within two months would incur the penalties of loss of the king's protection and forfeiture.[36] This interpretation will be qualified later. As for the 'great statute' of praemunire of 1393, no evidence has been found in Henry IV's reign to challenge the conclusion of W. T. Waugh that it was a measure of temporary significance only, designed to meet the circumstances of Anglo-papal relations in the year of its enactment.[37]

[31] *CPR 1401–5*, 55–6; *Foedera*, VIII, 246.

[32] YB 11 Hen. IV, Mich.67, Pas.10, Trin.18.

[33] The selection from the coram rege rolls printed as [5–20] includes all the actions noticed by Arthur Agarde (d.1615) in his selective abridgment of pleas in king's bench in Henry IV's reign, which are said, sometimes mistakenly [e.g. 5], to be pleas under the statutes of praemunire and provisors (IND 17089). An examination of the rolls themselves would certainly provide more examples of such actions (see Appendix) but I was unfortunately unable to make a thorough inspection. As Agarde made notes about coram rege rolls only, there are no cases here extracted from the de banco rolls.

[34] Below, n.258.

[35] 'This statute of 27 E.3.': E. Coke, *The Third Part of the Institutes of the Laws of England* (London, 1644), 120.

[36] E. B. Graves, 'The Legal Significance of the Statute of Praemunire of 1353', in *Anniversary Essays in Medieval History by students of Charles Homer Haskins*, ed. C. H. Taylor (Boston, Mass, and New York, 1929), 57–80.

[37] W. T. Waugh, 'The Great Statute of Praemunire', *EHR*, XXXVII (1922), 173–205.

No actions under this statute have been traced: the statute of 1353 was preferred. As a remedy against litigation at Rome in contempt of the king's jurisdiction, the earlier statute was as adequate as that of 1393 and there was doubtless already a series of precedents for its invocation.[38] In this context, the only difference between the two statutes was that the first was directed against common law issues being taken to courts outside the realm, the 1393 statute named the courts to which such suits should not be taken as 'la courte de Rome ou aillours'.[39]

It was apparently Henry IV's policy to put restrictions on litigation by his subjects at the papal court. From time to time orders were given to keepers of ports to refuse passage abroad without a royal licence.[40] A small number of clergy were given passports to go to Rome.[41] Others suspected of intending to go there to make suits prejudicial to the crown were arrested, and released on security that they would desist.[42] Sometimes clergy at the curia were ordered to return to England under threats of dire penalties; six clerks were told in 1407 that if they dared to remain in Rome the king would make them an example to the terror of all others.[43] A further difficulty for the intending litigant was the need for a licence to send money to Rome, though these were granted more frequently than passports.[44] There is no question of resort to the curia being drastically reduced, but these administrative restrictions do indicate some measure of official disapproval which may have encouraged resort to process by praemunire facias in appropriate cases. Moreover, the scores of notices of orders for arrest and mainprises make it clear that the potential number of praemunire proceedings was reduced by the prevention of prejudicial litigation at the curia.

The five cases printed here allege citation to Rome on suits triable at common law.[45] One was said to be in contempt of a judgment already given in king's bench [7] and two others are known to have been the subjects of actions already pending on writs of quare impedit [9] and trespass [10]; all related to disputes for possession of benefices between clergy. In the other two cases the defendants cited by praemunire facias were alleged to have initiated suits triable as trespass in the curia [8, 11]. With the apparent exception of the suit in contempt of king's bench's judgment, the writs issued at the instance of plaintiffs who had to give security to prosecute their suits. Why did they choose process by praemunire instead of obtaining writs of prohibition? In the action against Bishop Chicheley, the reason must be that he was outside England, attending the papal court and council of Pisa [9].[46] Damages could be claimed in actions for contempt of prohibitions [5], but presumably if prohibitions had issued and been obeyed damages incurred up to that point could not easily be recovered. Damages were claimed in the three cases with narrations by plaintiffs: twice these are very large – £1000 [7] and £800 [8] – and in the only case recorded to its conclusion, the damages awarded were little short of the £100 claimed [11]. In one instance the circumstances strongly suggest that the suitor by praemunire wanted to inflict the maximum discomfiture on his adversary; this case, between two religious houses of the same order, is the only one shown to have led to the non-appearing defendants being put outside the king's protection [10].

There was also a strong element of malice in the action against the vicar of Sidlesham, who was said to have sued for trespass at Rome when the issue was really a claim for mortuary [8]. Fortunately for the vicar, the judges recognised that this was not a common law matter. Their discussion reveals how the statute of praemunire could enable novel challenges

[38] Graves, in *Haskins Anniversary Essays,* 74–8; cf. below, n.258.

[39] 27 Edw. III, stat.1, c.1; 16 Ric. II, c.4.

[40] *CCR 1399–1402,* 344, 540; *1402–5,* 421; *1405–9,* 99–100; *1409–13,* 275, 307.

[41] ibid. *1399–1402,* 529, 530; *1402–5,* 22; *1405–9,* 160, 460.

[42] e.g. ibid. *1399–1402,* 112, 123–4, 209, 310, 360, 488, 496, 516, 564, 578, 585.

[43] ibid., 430; *1402–5,* 352; *1405–9,* 195.

[44] ibid. *1402–5,* 203, 220, 441–3; *1409–13,* 195.

[45] Although this may not be the total number of such actions in the reign (see above, n.33), it may be noted that no references have been found to praemunire proceedings in the calendars of chancery rolls (cf. provisions: Appendix).

[46] The writ in this case differs from the other, earlier writs under the praemunire and other statutes. All declared the king's resolve that the laws, statutes, etc., should be observed, sometimes adding 'prout vinculo juramenti astringimur'. In the writ against Chicheley the words here are 'prout vinculo juramenti in coronacione nostra prestiti astringimur'. It may be significant that this original writ is dated at Canterbury, the chancellor (Archbishop Arundel) being absent from London in the summer vacation. These words also appear in a praemunire facias of 1412 [10], when Arundel was again chancellor.

to be made against the activity of church courts. In this case, it was said, a prohibition would not have been allowed by Circumspecte Agatis.[47] A defendant in a church court could thus avoid the restraints of Circumspecte Agatis by suing by praemunire. Writs of prohibition could be countered by writs of consultatio,[48] but writs of praemunire facias had to be obeyed by personal appearance in the king's court. In this case the judges had refused to allow an abuse of the statute. In another its application was extended. The latest of the actions terminated in 1415 with an award of damages not only for a citation to Rome but also for the calling of the plaintiff to a Canterbury court and being required there to give security to keep the peace. Thus although the statute was directed only against the trial of common law matters outside the realm, here it was also applied to proceedings in an English church court with a jury's approval [11]. It may be suggested, however, that this extension of the 1353 statute did not become a precedent.[49] From about twenty years later, when defendants in English church courts sought to impede their prosecution, they invoked the praemunire statute of 1393; in 1465 the judges could rule that the word *alibi* in its prohibition of common law actions 'in curia Romana vel alibi' applied to the courts of English bishops.[50]

Two statutes of Henry's reign provided for citation by praemunire facias. The first resulted from a complaint that Cistercian houses were obtaining papal letters exempting their lands leased to farmers from payment of tithes. It was enacted in 1401 that exemptions of this nature granted since Richard II's accession were not to be executed. A second statute was made in 1406 extending this prohibition to all other orders of religious and secular clergy, even though the first statute seemingly applied to them as well as to the Cistercians. These statutes gave parochial clergy the option of suing for non-payment of tithes in common law courts: a church court, the accepted forum for such litigation, would be obliged to respect papal letters. Actions by incumbents under both statutes appear below. The pattern of the writs is identical to that in writs in the statutory praemunire proceedings and, as there, the plaintiffs plead 'tam pro domino rege quam pro se ipso' and claim enormous damages. One record ends with the non-appearance of a jury [12]; the second suit was abandoned [13]. Another category of papal grant to certain religious, namely of independent status to heads of monastic cells, was challenged by proceedings under the statutes of provisors [15].

Of all the legislation of an anti-papal character, the most bitterly resented by the popes themselves were the statutes of provisors. Had these statutes been rigidly applied, the papacy would have been deprived of its major source of income in England, the annates and service charges it received from clergy obtaining their benefices by provision. In practice all bishops continued to be appointed by provision as the king was thus able to secure the promotion of his own candidates. Ever since parliaments had made enactments against provisions, however, Kings Edward III, Richard II and now Henry IV were also reluctant, in varying degrees, to observe the spirit of these statutes with regard to benefices of non-episcopal status. They seemingly regarded the statutes as negotiable according to the exigencies of Anglo-papal diplomacy. In periods when the king was anxious to have harmonious relations with Rome, he was ready to allow provisions to lesser benefices despite the statutes.[51] Henry IV's parliaments would not have repealed the statutes but he licensed individual clergy to sue the pope for grants of benefices by provision and in expectation of vacancies, and he granted pardons for any contempts of the statutes incurred by those who obtained benefices by these means. Significantly, the largest annual total of these licences in his reign, 54, was in 1406, when the king was anxious to repair his standing at Rome after the execution of Archbishop Scrope. Parliaments protested against the issue of these licences but Henry would not renounce his liberty to grant them.[52] Licences, like almost all other royal grants, were obtained by petitioning the king. These petitions were apparently considered with some care. John Catterick, for instance, asked the king to license his provision to prebends in Salisbury, York and Lincoln cathedrals; he was allowed the first two prebends. Thomas Field sought leave to sue for a prebend in Lincoln or Salisbury but was granted a licence in respect of prebends in York and Beverley minsters.

[47] YB 10 Hen. IV, Mich.2. [48] Above, 342.

[49] Coke cites actions under 27 Edw. III for suing in English church courts and chancery in Elizabeth I's reign: *Third Institute,* 122, 124–5.

[50] YB 5 Edw. IV, Mich.7; R. L. Storey, *Diocesan Administration in Fifteenth-Century England* (Borthwick Papers, XVI, 2nd edn, 1972), 27, 31.

[51] C. Davies, 'The Statute of Provisors of 1351', *History,* New ser., XXXVIII (1953), 116–33.

[52] Lunt, *Financial Relations,* 400–6.

In 1405, the bishop of Lincoln was authorised to license 24 clerks of his own choice to apply for provisions.[53]

As Henry IV so clearly approved of papal provisions in principle, subject to this measure of control, it might be supposed that litigation under the statutes of provisors was a rare occurrence in his reign. Professor Lunt traced references to three prosecutions in the calendars of chancery rolls; while admitting the possibility that other cases are omitted from these sources, he considered it 'more probable' that this tiny number was the result of 'better executive enforcement' of the statutes.[54] Closer investigation does not support this conclusion. Firstly, it is apparent that the number of statutory actions against provisors in the first ten years of the reign was well into double figures and was probably higher (see Appendix). Moreover, it cannot be maintained that these prosecutions supply evidence of official control over provisions. Most of the cases resulted from incumbents suing writs against provisors disturbing their possession. As with praemunire proceedings, those under the statutes of provisors were mostly initiated by subjects who had to give security to prosecute, as the statutes required; a plaintiff likewise pleaded 'as much for the lord king as for himself', the defendant was required to answer and perhaps pay for his contempt towards the king, but the plaintiffs demanded damages and engaged their own attorneys.

Defendants in these suits could quote royal licences, but these gave them no benefit. A licence hardly ever specified a particular benefice, and the hopeful provisor's subsequent bull was generally an expectative grant, again most frequently to one of a number of benefices. If he had such a provision to a prebend in a certain cathedral, for instance, he would have to engage a proctor to wait there until a canon died or resigned and then claim his vacant stall. The proctor needed extraordinary prescience to anticipate rival claimants by provision, but he was still likely to be foiled by another who, learning of the vacancy, straightway secured his own collation by the ordinary or obtained royal letters of presentation. In the latter case, even if the provisor or his proctor was instituted first, the royal candidate might prevail because he could prove the king's title to present at that particular vacancy [16–20]. If Henry IV did grant licences for provisions in good faith, he frequently frustrated their effect by his readiness to present clerks to vacant benefices. Despite all his licences to sue for provisions to benefices in York minster, for instance, only one recruit to the chapter in the whole reign entered by virtue of a provision: this was John Prophet, provided to the deanery in 1406, but as he was keeper of the privy seal he obviously enjoyed strong royal favour.[55]

Some provisors were not prepared to wait for vacancies. Thomas Stanley's usurpation of the deanery of Wells was a case of this kind, defeated by a statutory action but eventually achieved through good fortune [16]. John Warren was otherwise the only known provisor to have been sued and still held his benefice, but it was vacant when he entered and the prior of Launceston who prosecuted him was manifestly attempting to use the statute to further an unpopular purpose [14]. Provisors who attempted to enter occupied benefices could eventually be defeated by statutory actions. Two instances are known of clerks complaining to the pope that they dared not sue execution of their provisions for fear of death, outlawry and forfeiture, as threatened by the statutes.[56] These were, in fact, penalties only incurred by those who failed to appear on citation by writs of praemunire facias [17]. The first statute of provisors of 1351, being earlier than the first of praemunire, naturally did not prescribe its penalties for default, and no case under it has been traced. The statutes invoked were those of 1365 and 1390 (see Appendix). In cases when the rights of religious were threatened, there was cause to prefer the earlier statute [14, 15]. Why it should have been chosen by incumbents disturbed by provisors is less obvious. The statute of 1390, forbidding provisions to benefices otherwise occupied on 29 January of that year, must have been equally applicable, and in fact it does seem on balance that the later measure was preferred.

Provisors was thus generally defeated, sometimes at heavy cost. There is however one remarkable case of a provisor attempting to defend his title by litigation at common law. He claimed earlier possession than his rival and rested his action on a section of the statute Pro Clero and its confirmation in 1390. Both measures were made in response to complaints that the king presented clerks to benefices on their false allegations that the benefices were in his gift; patrons who thus lost their rights were allowed process. The

[53] C 81/1404, nos. 11, 18; *CPR 1405–8,* 3, 4, 44.

[54] Lunt, *Financial Relations,* 407, where it is supposed that only the statute of 1390 was enforced.

[55] J. Le Neve, *Fasti Ecclesiae Anglicanae, 1300–1541* (new edn, 1962–7), VI, 7; and preface to [17].

[56] *CPL,* V, 309–10; VI, 89.

1390 statute noted that the earlier remedy had not been applied because bishops failed to inspect the king's title to present and had instituted his nominees, thus expelling existing incumbents. A safeguard was provided, and if it was not observed the expelled incumbent might then sue for remedy provided that he began his suit one year after the induction of the king's nominee. In the case below, the frustrated provisor's plea was somewhat spurious: the defendant undoubtedly had received a royal presentation only three months before the original writ issued, but he could claim earlier institution [20].

The statutes unsucessfully invoked in this action in Michaelmas 1402 were confirmed on petition to the king in the parliament sitting at the same time; by what appears to be an example of retrospective legislation, Henry further agreed that no term should be set on the date when an expelled incumbent might begin his suit.[57] There is no doubt that beneficed clergy had good cause to feel insecure. After Richard II's deposition, a number alleged that he had deprived them in favour of his own nominees.[58] It was convenient to blame the ex-king, but his personal responsibility need not be presumed because the menace of spoliation persisted under Henry IV. The real perpetrators of this scandal were other clergy, particularly those in the king's service. The king was inundated by petitions for grants,[59] among them requests by clerks to be presented to certain livings. Sometimes these petitions were obviously granted without much consideration. Henry granted a hospital at Bridgnorth to John Shackle on 5 July 1403 and on 9 September following to John Rothbury, whose petition had alleged that the hospital was vacant.[60] No doubt some petitioners genuinely believed benefices to be vacant, but those ready to proceed by litigation were less innocent. Thomas Shelford, a king's clerk, petitioned for presentation to the prebend of Easton in Gordano, Wells, which 'a vostre dounison appertient au fin quil purra poursuyer pour la declaracion de vostre droit en celle partie'. This was in 1404: the prebend had been occupied, by a provisor, since 1400. Although the king acceded to the request and ordered a warrant to chancery, letters patent were seemingly not issued.[61] Robert Gow, the king's almoner, was presented to a prebend at Wherwell in 1405 on alleging that it was vacant and in the king's gift. It had been held by John Felbridge since 1371, and in 1406 he was sued by quare impedit.[62]

Quare impedit was the established process, described by Bracton, for a plaintiff to sue his right to present to a benefice; from 1285, by Westminster II, he was allowed six months after the occupation of the benefice by another's, allegedly wrongful, presentation to begin his suit for recovery.[63] This limitation was apparently not applied in Henry IV's reign, at least not in actions sued by the crown. It is improbable, however, that writs of quare impedit with the king as plaintiff issued on the king's personal direction. As Thomas Shelford's petition indicated, suitors for royal presentations were prepared to make them effective by litigation. Their favourite device was to claim that the king had the right to a presentation because he, or his predecessors, had held the estates of which the advowsons were a parcel. Most often this claim of royal right was made in respect of benefices in cathedrals, normally in the gift of their bishops, because in a recent episcopal vacancy the temporalities had been in crown custody. Henry made presentations on this pretext to dignities and prebends actually occupied at the time. The sequel was often an action by quare impedit against the bishop and incumbent to show why the king's nominee should not be instituted, and in the action the king's title from a past custody of the temporalities would be cited. In 1411, for instance, the king 'recovered' his presentation to the prebend of

57 *RP*, III, 507; stat. 4 Hen. IV, c.22.

58 *RP*, III, 430, 444; *CPR 1399–1401*, 32, 129, 311.

59 A. L. Brown, 'The Authorization of Letters under the Great Seal', *BIHR*, XXXVII (1964), 148–9, 154.

60 *CPR 1401–5*, 240, 259; *CCR 1405–9*, 2–3, 13. Gascoigne ruled in the same term that the later of two royal presentations should be preferred because the king could change his mind. This was not necessarily the same suit. Shackle sued in chancery by scire facias, while Gascoigne was referring to two actions by quare impedit, one in king's bench, the other in common pleas: YB 7 Hen. IV (2nd ser.), Mich.18 (p.32).

61 E 28/12 (18 Jan.); *Fasti*, VIII, 47.

62 E 28/15 (9 Nov.); *CPR 1401–5*, 464; A. B. Emden, *A Biographical Register of the University of Cambridge to 1500* (Cambridge, 1963), 223. Skrene, for Felbridge, claimed voidance of the writ as the patron was not shown as co-defendant. Thurning and Gascoigne rejected this plea, the latter saying that as a serjeant he had sued in similar cases. The year book rehearses Felbridge's title with several errors: the benefice is called a church, it became vacant by William of Wykeham's creation as bishop of Salisbury, and the defendant is called 'R. Feldbridge': YB 7 Hen. IV (2nd ser.), Mich.3 (pp.25–6), Hil.7 (pp.37, 39).

63 Pollock & Maitland, II, 139–40.

Handsacre in Lichfield cathedral; the defendants did not contest his claim that the last vacancy of the prebend occurred when Edward III held the temporalities.[64]

In the action previously noticed, when the judges were enlightened about the relevance and vitality of the statute Pro Clero, the co-defendant with the bishop of Coventry and Lichfield was Roger Westwood. He had been instituted to the Lichfield prebend of Sandiacre on the bishop's collation on 5 November 1408. The king presented William Wolf on 11 November; his letters patent alleged neither vacancy of the prebend nor the nature of the king's title. In the plea by quare impedit, the crown's case was that Edward I had appointed to the prebend in a vacancy of the see. That Henry IV was directly responsible for this preposterous suit is barely conceivable. Wolf may have been a king's clerk, but he was a very minor official in contrast to the incumbent Westwood, who was second baron of the exchequer.[65] Not all incumbents, however, had the necessary resources to defend themselves in quare impedit proceedings. Robert Watton had himself presented to the church of Melsonby on 2 July 1400. Quare impedit then issued against the rector of Melsonby, but on 14 October the two clerks came to terms: Watton renounced his claim in return for his institution to the defendant's prebend in Lanchester collegiate church. The king is unlikely to have been involved in this sordid affair. The patent roll shows no warrant for Watton's presentation; as he was a clerk of chancery, it may be suspected that he made his own letters patent. A similar presentation was made for his colleague Ganstead in 1399 [14]. The end of Watton's ecclesiastical record shows what manner of clerk he was. He obtained his prebend at Lanchester, but in 1410 it was vacant because of his marriage.[66] He was primarily a civil servant, never in major clerical orders, and for him church preferments were solely a source of additional income. As the king's clerks were so prone to abuse their position to seek preferments, some clergy took the precaution of obtaining royal presentations to benefices they already occupied [e.g. 17, 20]. It should be noted, therefore, that royal presentations recorded in the patent rolls are often not genuine: a number were really confirmations of existing incumbents, while others were speculative, only a proportion of which were effected as the result of subsequent litigation.[67]

In conclusion, it must be observed that there was no official machinery for the enforcement of legislation; like other forms of legal process, statutes had to be invoked by litigants. Legislation prohibiting certain acts usually provided procedures against those who committed them, but these could only be set in motion by private initiatives. The crown did not, indeed could not, act as a general overseer to detect breaches of statute and officially prosecute all their perpetrators. This was as true of the statutes in restraint of papal powers as of any other enactment. In most of the cases noticed, the parties who initiated proceedings under anti-papal statutes were themselves clergy, as were the defendants in these actions. These clerical plaintiffs turned to common law courts in self-defence and retaliation. Defendants in the Roman curia on issues triable at common law could have sued writs of prohibition: they resorted to process by praemunire facias by deliberate personal choice. It was not always necessary to invoke statutory procedure. For instance, the vicar of Saltash, disturbed by a provision to his benefice in 1405, submitted his cause to arbitration.

In this case, it is of particular significance that the arbitrators accepted by the provisor as well as by the threatened vicar were common law judges. Their award as well as their selection shows that they did not disapprove of papal provision in principle, because although they confirmed the vicar in his possession they also awarded compensation to the provisor.[68] The judges concerned were the two chief justices,

64 'Extracts from the Cheshire Plea Rolls . . . De Banco and Coram Rege Rolls . . .', ed. G. Wrottesley (Wm Salt Arch. Soc. *Hist. Colls,* Old ser., XVI, 1895), 78. This retrospective assertion of sede vacante royal patronage seems to have begun under Edward II: M. Howell, *Regalian Right in Medieval England* (1962), 183–4.

65 *Fasti,* X, 54; *CPR 1405–8,* 202; *1408–13,* 39; YB 11 Hen. IV, Mich.20; above, 344.

66 *CPR 1399–1401,* 332, 367; *1405–8,* 125; *1408–13,* 20; *CCR 1399–1402,* 274; *Register of Thomas Langley,* ed. R. L. Storey (Surtees Soc., 1956–70), I, 133. Watton's case in the quare impedit was presumably that the presentation to Melsonby belonged to the king because Deincourt lands were then in his wardship: A. H. Thompson, 'The Registers of the Archdeaconry of Richmond 1361–1442', *Yorks Arch. Jnl,* XXV (1920), 12 n.; G.E.C., IV, 124–5.

67 In York minster, for instance, two royal nominees were able to dispossess archdeacons of Cleveland (1411) and Richmond (1401), while crown presentations to the prebends of Bole (1404) and Fridaythorpe (1406) were not effected: *Fasti,* VI, 20, 26, 35–6, 51. See also preface to [17].

68 *CPL,* VI, 4; *CCR 1405–9,* 265, 327, 387–8. The vicar had been instituted in 1398: *Register of Edmund Stafford,* ed. F. C. Hingeston-Randolph (London, 1886), 206.

Gascoigne and Thurning, whose scrupulous regard for the jurisdictional areas of church courts has already been noticed. The third arbitrator was Hankford, undoubtedly the most learned member of the judiciary in this period, particularly well informed on ecclesiastical practice, and apparently having good personal relations with influential members of the church establishment;[69] all these factors doubtless weighed with Henry V when he appointed Hankford chief justice in 1413. In their wills, these three judges made considerable bequests to ecclesiastical institutions.[70] If these most eminent members of the legal profession were representative of their colleagues, Adam Usk's fears of the judiciary do not appear justified. Beneficed clergy at least had more cause to fear the king's clerks and other members of their own order who were ready to exploit political crises and royal as well as papal patronage in their pursuit of ecclesiastical preferment. For some clergy, common law offered a means of protection against deprivation, while to others it posed a threat through its abuse to further the insatiable ambitions of their fellow clerks.

Editorial note

Because of the importance of distinguishing between the letters 'c' and 't' in the transcription of [5], for the sake of consistency they have been rendered throughout these transcripts exactly as they are written in the manuscripts.

69 Above, 345. Reginald Kentwood [5] was one of Hankford's executors. His grandson and heir was a commoner at Winchester free of charge 'in regard' for the justice (A. B. Emden, *A Biographical Register of the University of Oxford to A.D. 1500* (Oxford, 1957–9), II, 866; III, xxvi).

70 *Register of Bishop Philip Repingdon,* ed. M. Archer (Linc. Rec. Soc., LVII–LVIII, 1963), II, 308–9 (Thurning); *Register of Henry Chichele,* ed. E. F. Jacob (Cant. & York Soc., 1937–47), II, 290–3, 656 (Hankford); *Testamenta Eboracensia,* pt 1, ed. J. Raine (Surtees Soc., IV, 1836), 390–5 (Gascoigne).

TEXT

[1]

Three of the records of trials for treason in 1402 have already been printed, two as early examples of treason by words.[71] There are actually five cases of treason on the roll for Trinity 1402. Four concern clergy and are given below. The first three are actually records of confessions to the coroner of king's bench and subsequent sentences, while the last is of a trial by jury following indictment before king's bench in Middlesex.[72]

All these trials resulted from the crown's determination to crush the spread of seditious rumours. The first victim of this policy, John Sparrowhawk of Cardiff, sentenced on 20 April, was obviously not an associate of those condemned in the following term. The burden of his purported speech at a place near Baldock on 19 March was adverse comment on the king's rule and parentage; he asserted that the earl of March was the rightful king. In contrast, the accused in Trinity term were all said to have maintained that Richard II was still alive and to have spread claims that his return to the throne was imminent; the majority were further charged with conspiring to assist Richard's restoration.

The actual order in which the accused were rounded up is not clear. The first recorded order for an arrest is that of Sir Roger Clarendon, Richard's illegitimate brother, and his clerk John Calf on 19 May. They were committed to the Tower four days later and by 1 June were joined there by thirteen friars minor and a Leicester quarrier.[73] There is apparently no record, however, of the arrest or committal to the Tower of the ex-prior Baldock, the chaplain Louth, and John Lawthe, who were subsequently executed. Clearly some persons were already in the Tower by 11 May, when commissions were appointed in every shire to publicise the king's resolve to preserve the laws and customs of the realm. The commissions make it clear that the principal means of impugning the king's good faith had been preaching, and the commissions were ordered to arrest all such preachers. Certain clergy, in fact, were regarded as the main purveyors of this seditious propaganda, and it was doubtless for this reason that bishops headed all these commissions.[74] The clergy in question were members of the order of friars minor; this episode in their history confirms that they were still performing their mission as itinerant preachers although hardly in a cause envisaged by St Francis.

It is fortunate that a contemporary chronicler, the continuator of the *Eulogium* who may himself have been a minorite,[75] gives a detailed account of the arrest and examination of some of the accused friars. The accuracy of this account is confirmed by the following records and it gives details which they lack about how some of the information was obtained. Although the records of the two friars and priest condemned on 9 June are their statements to the coroner [A, B, C below], the continuator shows that the king himself had questioned at least one of the friars. The continuator also shows that the accused friars had been betrayed to the king by some of their brethren. This account, correlated with the judicial records and orders for arrest and committal, suggests that the sequence of events was as follows.

According to the continuator, a lay brother of the minorite house at Aylesbury came to the king to tell him that a friar in priest's orders was rejoicing in the knowledge that Richard II was alive. Henry had the friar brought to him. The friar was obviously Henry Forster: the king asked what weapon he would use if he fought for Richard, and both question and reply – 'with a staff' – appear in Forster's formal confession [A]. The continuator records that the

[71] I. D. Thornley, 'Treason by Words in the Fifteenth Century', *EHR,* XXXII (1917), 556–61. These are the records of John Sparrowhawk (Easter) and Walter Walton (Trinity). Sparrowhawk's case is also printed in *King's Bench,* VII, 123–5, as is a second case in Trinity 1402, the appeal of John Bernard against William Balshalf (pp.126–8). Walton's case is printed again here for ease of reference [C].

[72] The original indictment is KB 9/190, m.36.

[73] *CPR 1402–5,* 126; *CCR 1399–1402,* 527–9. The Dominican prior of Winchelsea and rector of Horsmonden were also sent to the Tower on 27 May but probably in another connection: they were not indicted of treason and their south-eastern origin makes it unlikely that they were involved in what was essentially a conspiracy among friars *minor* of the east midlands.

[74] Except in Lancashire: *CPR 1402–5,* 126–30; *Foedera,* VIII, 255.

[75] *Eulogium Historiarum,* ed. F. S. Haydon (RS, 1858–63), III, 389–92. A slightly shorter version based on this account is in *An English Chronicle of the Reigns of Richard II, Henry IV, Henry V and Henry VI,* ed. J. S. Davies (Camden Soc., Old ser., LXIV, 1856), 23–5. For authorship, see C. L. Kingsford, *English Historical Literature in the Fifteenth Century* (Oxford, 1913), 28–30.

friar was then sent for trial at Westminster with a secular priest who had been caught carrying treasonable correspondence. Equally clearly this priest was Nicholas Louth, in whose statement a letter is quoted [B]. His implication of Walter Baldock was credible, for this deposed prior of Launde had won his election by ingratiating himself with Richard II.[76]

The continuator next records the friar (Forster)'s trial. After this, he wrote, a friar of Leicester came to the king and revealed that 500 men were ready to assemble on the Plain at Oxford on 23 June and thence proceed to find King Richard; he and ten of his fellows were ready to go. He accused an old friar of his house, a master in theology (i.e. Roger Frisby[77]), of quoting a prophecy that Richard would return, and also members of other mendicant houses. This informant may have been Walter Walton, whose statement does implicate Frisby [C]. Walton, however, is unlikely to have come forward voluntarily, moved by spite as the continuator claims, for he was accused by Forster of coming to Aylesbury about 9 April and then telling him that Richard was alive. Forster said that Robert Lowdham was with Walton then [A], and Walton's own account makes a first reference to 'le dit' Lowdham which suggests that the latter had been his companion until their return to Leicester in May. Forster, doubtless on his visitor's testimony, had also named Roger Frisby as a leading figure in the conspiracy.

Forster and Walton had been arrested before 27 May, when they were sent to the Tower with two other friars, Eyworth, also of Aylesbury, and Houghton, a limiter (alms-collector).[78] They may well have been in detention for some time before this, though Walton's account shows that he had been at liberty to visit Leicester after 8 May. He did, however, implicate Clarendon, whose arrest was ordered on 19 May. He also alleged that when at Leicester Frisby required him to recount his tale to a leech of Leicester named John, who must have been the same as the John Leech, former monk of St Albans, whose arrest with four others was ordered on 3 June.[79] Walton's confession to the coroner on 9 June, presumably, was a compilation of a series of statements made under prolonged examination; and the use of the term 'le dit' on the first occasions mention is made of Richard and Lowdham suggests that his confession was not delivered without prompting. Comparison with Forster's account reveals discrepancies. Walton alleged that he learned of Richard being alive when he visited Ralph Selby in Westminster abbey on 7 May and had confirmation from Clarendon in the following week; but Forster said that Walton told him about Richard a fortnight after Easter (i.e. about 9 April). The king's council may well have wondered why Walton should have gone to Westminster to see Selby, a former councillor of Richard's.[80] Walton, quoting Selby, accused Lord Fitz Walter. The council is not known to have taken any proceedings against this peer, whose record hardly suggests devotion to the late king.[81]

While Walton's credibility may have been suspect, his allegations could not all be ignored. A number of friars were brought before the council, when the king questioned Frisby. Frisby admitted to quoting John Bridlington's prophecy but denied saying that Richard was alive; he stoutly maintained that Richard would rightfully be king if he were alive. As in the exchange with Forster, Henry's final words were 'By my head, you shall lose your head'. In the subsequent discussion with his council, the continuator states, an unnamed knight notorious for his hatred of the church said 'We shall never cease this clamour of King Richard till these friars be destroyed'. The king rejected a request for grace by the friars' minister general, asserting that it was his duty, not the minister's, to punish them.[82]

The subsequent proceedings show, however, that the king was aware of the political hazards involved in punishing the friars as traitors. He had least cause for hesitation with the three who made confessions. The chaplain Louth had little choice, having been arrested with incriminating evidence. Of the two friars, Walton had clearly been over busy as an agent for the Ricardian cause. In contrast, Forster's rôle had been minor, as his judges evidently felt.[83] His fate had presumably been sealed by his bold words to the king rather than for the offences declared in his statement. As for the remaining suspects, it is evident that the council decided to limit the number to be sent for trial. It decided that the trial should be in king's bench; had it appointed a commission of oyer

76 He was prior 1388–95/8: *VCH Leics*, II, 11.

77 Frisby is first noticed in 1354 and was a doctor in theology: Emden, *Biog. Reg. Cambridge*, 244–5.

78 *CCR 1399–1402*, 527.

79 *CPR 1401–5*, 125–6.

80 Below, 404.

81 G.E.C., V, 480–1.

82 *Eng. Chron.*, 25; *Eulogium*, III, 392.

83 cf. sentences in A and B, C.

While for the sake of stilling dangerous rumour the king decided it was essential to make an example of some of his prisoners, a further complication was the nature of their offence. Richard II's statute making conspiracy against the king a treasonable offence had been repealed in October 1399, when the statute of 1352 was declared to define the only acts triable as treason. The 1352 statute did not include seditious speech in its catalogue, and no more than speech and sedition had been admitted by three of the accused. There was, however, the recent precedent of John Sparrowhawk. After the judges of king's bench had seen the record of his admission of treasonable speech, they asked why he should not be condemned as a traitor to the king and kingdom. Although his answer was that he knew no reason, the judges consulted the king's council before proceeding to sentence. The joint opinion of judges and councillors was that Sparrowhawk, although the king's liegeman, had knowingly made statements in public with the intention of seducing the king's subjects from their good will to their liege lord, and that this was high treason. On 20 April 1402, therefore, Sparrowhawk was sentenced as a traitor, to be drawn from the Tower to Tyburn and there hanged and beheaded.[92] Consequently, when the three confessed traitors appeared in king's bench on 9 June, the judges did not hesitate in passing sentence. Like Sparrowhawk, the three were asked – in identical terms – if they could give any reason why they should not be condemned as traitors to the king and kingdom. All answered 'non' and asked for the king's grace, but sentence followed immediately. The terms now differ: all were traitors for spreading falsehoods about the king, but in the cases of Walton and Louth it was then added that the intent of their words was to incite the king's people against their liege lord – the phrase which appeared in the opinion quoted before Sparrowhawk was sentenced – and lastly it was

89 *CPR 1401–5*, 125.

90 *CCR 1399–1402*, 529; *Eulogium*, III, 389. The 'old friar' had been accused of treasonable speech by a woman who withdrew the charge when required to prove her appeal by trial by battle.

91 Below, 357 and D.

92 Bellamy, *Law of Treason*, 116–18; above, n.71. Professor Bellamy has confused the issue by identifying Sparrowhawk with the friar of Aylesbury (actually Forster; above, 353–4); he consequently concludes that the king had a personal part in the creation of this precedent and, less explicably, places Sparrowhawk's trial in the context of the trials of the friars and others in Trinity term.

declared that the likely outcome (of their treason) was the final destruction of the realm of England. All three received the same sentence: it differed from Sparrowhawk's in that their beheaded corpses were to be quartered, but there was no directive about the exhibition of their remains nor any confiscation of their lands and goods. As the records do not quote second dates, presumably these sentences were passed, and possibly executed, on the same day, 9 June. They had certainly been executed by 18 June, when proclamations were ordered referring to the lies spread by members of religious orders planning rebellion, some of whom had been convicted on their own confessions and put to death.[93]

Two days later (20 June) a total of twenty others were arraigned in king's bench [D]. The date of their indictment before a Middlesex jury is not given. The prosecution's case would have been assisted had the indictment been presented after the conviction of Forster, Walton and Louth. Particulars from all three confessions appear in the indictment. The beginning of the preaching campaign is said to have been 9 April, the day Walton visited Forster [A]. The implication of ex-prior Baldock and the alleged identification of Richard II at Westminster appear in Louth's statement [B]. Despite Frisby's denial to Henry IV, as reported by the continuator,[94] he and Clarendon were alleged to have declared that Richard was in Wales, as Walton had stated. His claim that Frisby made him report his news in a council at Leicester [C] was presumably also the cause of the indictment of Leech, Neville and Ashby.[95] As these three were acquitted, the evidence against them cannot have been thought substantial.

By making a single, collective charge against all twenty, the prosecution made it appear that all had conspired together and in addition to spreading rumour had planned a treasonable rising. The continuator, in his account of the trial, quotes a judge (probably William Gascoigne) summarising the indictment against the friars: he spoke of their hypocrisy in preaching false sermons, as the record states, but he is also said to have accused them of urging their audiences to seek Richard in Scotland; while those who had made confessions before the friars were enjoined, as a penance, to look for him in Wales.[96] The reference to Scotland appears in none of the other records of this group of trials except the indictment. The king's council knew of the existence of a pretended Richard in Scotland. On 2 June two men apparently not connected with the friars were brought from the Tower to king's bench when one appealed the other of telling him that Richard was in Scotland and intended to enter England about 24 June.[97] This date is quoted in the indictment of the twenty as the time appointed for the culmination of their conspiracy. The indictment does not state that the twenty had any link with this precursor of Perkin Warbeck, but it does allege that their operations had encouraged the Scots to set up their pretender and invade under his banner. A Scottish invasion actually was expected at this time.[98] The judge is also said to have accused the friars of collecting money for despatch to Owain Glyn Dŵr. The Welsh rising was then at its peak and there were suspicions that he had financial support from English subjects hostile to their king.[99] The accused were thus being associated with real dangers to England.

The indictment was manifestly designed as official propaganda. The conspirators' purpose was said to be the slaughter not only of the king and magnates but of subjects of all ranks, the destruction of common law, and even the replacement of English by an alien tongue. Conspiracy and spreading rumour against the king had not previously been grounds for trial by jury and they lacked statutory definition as treason. By heightening the enormity of the accuseds' activities, the prosecution was portraying them as enemies of the English nation. The indictment, in fact, reaches a more modern concept of treason than did the statute of 1352, which reflects the essentially personal character of medieval government. The indictment was so designed that a jury would be faced with the responsibility of defending the national interest; it could also stand as a public justification of the crown for putting the accused on trial for their

93 *CCR 1399–1402,* 577.

94 Above, 354.

95 Leech is named in [C], but the arrest of all three was ordered on 3 June. When Ashby and Leech (but not Neville) were committed to the Tower on 12 June, they were accompanied by three Leicestershire priests (above, n.86) who may also have been present in Frisby's 'grant conseille': *CPR 1401–5,* 125; *CCR 1399–1402,* 532–3.

96 *Eulogium,* III, 392–3.

97 A proclamation ordering that no heed by given to rumours that Richard was in Scotland was issued on 5 June: *CCR 1399–1401,* 570; *Foedera,* VIII, 261. See also J. H. Wylie, *History of England under Henry the Fourth* (1884; reprinted 1969), I, 267–70; *King's Bench,* VII, 126–8.

98 Wylie, *Henry IV,* I, 289–90.

99 R. A. Griffiths, 'Some Secret Supporters of Owain Glyn Dŵr?', *BIHR,* XXXVII (1964), 77–89.

lives, and additionally it showed that the king was a conscientious defender of his people. Further points were made for general notice, the fact that Richard had been seen dead by numerous witnesses to still the rumour that he lived, and the constitutional argument that he had voluntarily abdicated and had also been rightfully deposed by the estates of the realm on account of his misgovernment, so answering those like Roger Frisby who maintained that Richard would lawfully be king were he still alive.[100]

Despite the crown's careful preparations, it seemingly met difficulty in empanelling a jury for the trial. The continuator alleges that men from London and Holborn refused to serve, and the twelve eventually found in Highgate and Islington subsequently sought forgiveness from other friars, saying that if they had not convicted they would themselves have been killed.[101] This statement cannot be entirely true, for the jurors were not afraid to acquit three of the fourteen who stood trial on 20 June. If the jurors did later feel remorse for their verdict, it was not because they doubted the guilt of those condemned but because they were friars. Clarendon and Lawthe were the only laymen convicted; the ex-prior, Clarendon's clerk and all seven friars were found guilty. Three of the other accused appeared at later dates and were acquitted,[102] and no verdict was recorded against the three monks of Westminster.[103]

The total of executions in June 1402 was thus fourteen: two laymen, an ex-prior of the Augustinian order, two secular priests, and nine minorites from houses at Leicester (3), Aylesbury (2), Northampton (2) and Nottingham, and one unattached (the limiter); two more Leicester friars were said to have been taken later and executed at Lichfield.[104] Never before had such a large number of clergy been executed in England. As has been argued, however, the number could have been higher, perhaps particularly among the minorites. The crown obviously acted with limited severity. It tried to allay further unease by announcing, on 18 June, that the king had no intention of prosecuting people who had listened to the friars.[105] He also apparently refrained from fully carrying out the sentence that the traitors' corpses should be quartered.[106] Heads only of the friars were put on the town walls of Leicester, Aylesbury, Northampton, Nottingham, Stamford, Coventry and Oxford; Frisby's head was appropriately delivered to the last on 23 June.[107] They remained on display until a parliament was meeting in Coventry in November 1404.[108]

[A]

KB 27/565, Rex m.3

[*Marginated*] Anglia

Frater Henricus Forster de ordine fratrum minorum pro diversis prodicionibus unde impetitus est in Turri London' nuper detentus et per consilium domini regis coram ipso rege apud Westmonasterium per Thomam de Rempston constabularium Turris predicti die veneris proximo post octabas Sancte Trinitatis isto eodem termino [9 June 1402] venit ductus, qui committitur marescallo. Et super hoc idem frater Henricus coram Thoma Couele coronatore domini regis coram ipso rege per consilium domini regis ad eundem fratrem Henricum pro prodicionibus predictis examinandis misso cognovit de recordo in hec verba:

Frere Henry Forster del ordour de frere menours conust que frere Walter Walton et frere Robert Loudam entour le xv^e du Pasche darrein passe [9 Apr. 1402] a Aillesbury countarent a luy que Richard qui fuist ore tard roy Dengleterre fuist en pleyn vie, pour le quels novels il soy rejoisa hautement de tout soun coer, et disoit outre que si ceo serroit verroi ou sil purroit voir le dit nadgairs roy Richard, que ove tout soun corps luy voilleit aider et ove luy steer encountre le roy qore est. Et outre conust qil nama poynt nostre seignur le roy qore est, mes qil de tout soun coer et soun poer luy haia et avoit haie puis le fest de Pasche darrein passe. Et dit que frere Roger Frysby meistre en divine del ordre de frere menours de Leycestre de tout cest traitrouse purpos et paroles ad este principal excitour, disaunt outrement a plusors hommes que

100 Above, 354. The point about Richard's abdication and deposition appeared in the indictment of Bishop Marks, as does the charge that his conspiracy was a national danger: *King's Bench,* VII, 102–3.

101 *Eulogium,* III, 393–4.

102 The delay with Ashby and Leech is sinister because they were in the Tower: above, n.95. Lynn, returned to the Marshalsea after his acquittal, was released on 3 March 1404 after petitioning the king: *CCR 1402–5,* 258.

103 Selby died in Westminster abbey in 1420: Emden, *Biog. Reg. Cambridge,* 517.

104 *Eulogium,* III, 394.

105 *CCR 1399–1401,* 577.

106 *Eulogium,* III, 393. For an example of similar clemency see *CCR 1402–5,* 357.

107 *Eulogium,* III, 394.

108 *CCR 1402–5,* 388–9.

le dit nadgairs roy par cronicle et profecie rejoiseroyt en graunt prosperite soun realme arere. Et le dit frere Henry conust que sil verroit le dit nadgairs roy Richard, que il luy aidera de tout soun poer, et demande fuist de luy ove quele wepene, et il disoit ove un bastoun.

Quamquidem cognicionem predictus coronator hic in curia recordatur et eciam[109] coram ipso rege[110] liberavit. Super quo predictus frater Henricus venit per marescallum ductus, et viso recordo coronatoris predicti in hac parte, idem frater Henricus instanter allocutus est si quid pro se habeat vel dicere sciat quare ex cognicione sua propria predicta ut proditor domini regis et regni sui Anglie pro premissis morti adjudicari non debeat, qui dicit quod non set se ponit inde in graciam domini regis. Per quod consideratum est quod idem frater Henricus ut proditor domini regis et regni sui Anglie tanta falsa et verba inhonesta de domino suo ligeo dicendo et advocando distrahatur a Turri London' per medium civitatis London' usque Tyburne et ibidem suspendatur et decapitetur et quod corpus suum postmodum in quatuor partes dividatur etc.

[*Marginated*] Distrahatur et suspendatur.

[B]

KB 27/565, Rex m.4d

[*Marginated*] Anglia

Nicholaus Louthe capellanus pro diversis prodicionibus [*as in* A, *mutatis mutandis* – verba]:

Nicholas Louthe chapeleyn conust qil venoit a Walkerne en le counte de Hertf' le mardy proschein apres le fest de Lascencion de Nostre Seignur darrein passe [9 May 1402] al meisoun dun barbour a luy disconuz, et la le dit barbour demanda a luy quels novels, et il luy disoit que Richard qui fuist ore tard roy Dengleterre est en pleyn vie et qil fuist ore tard a Seint James just Westm' et la fuist vew et conuz par femmes par un signe dune werte en sa fauce et qil sur celle werte avoit une blank drap de livere. Et disoit outre qe le duc de Lancastr' qui soi nomma roy Dengleterre ne fuist forsque profost et baillif al dit roy Richard et en brief temps renderoit a luy accomptez et[111] son realme, et que le dit nadgairs roy avoit xl cerves factz toutz prestez et ils a Wodesere joyousement et ameliiement pasturerent. Et conust outre il escria une lettre a sire Wauter Baldok priour de Launde, la quele lettre cy ensuit:

Gretyng to my dere frend Sir Walter. That I haf had mykyl dyssesse in this contre because I haf speryd after yow, and that I wold wyte fayn of yowr wele fare, for why it was told me that I scholde fynde yow here in this towne or elles here sholde I wyte ware that ye ware. For why I haf gone many contrees bothe in Kent and in Southsex' and in Sutheray and al Norffolk and Suthffolk and al Essex and al Middilsex', and now I am bone to London' to spyr and to wyte the ende of the conseyl, and than I shal go fro thennes northward. Bot now at this tyme I myght not speke wyt yow, bot be the grace of God I schal speke wyt yow in a nyghe tyme nought longe to. And the most frend that we lovede and we shul come so stronge that the erl of Darby that now is the kyng scholle not wyte whare he schol hold hym or abyd, and thare-fore I pray yow that ye pray for yowre leeth lord kyng Rychard and for al his men. And thare fore I haf no more to speke to yow at this tyme but that Yhesu kepe wel yowre tonge and be stylle, bot God yow kepe and save. A nother day I schal telle yow my name for wy [I] was dredand to tel tham what I was.

Et conust outre que la cause qil disoit en sa lettre qil fuist en Norff' Suff' et en les countes susditz fuist al entente davoir argent del dit priour de Launde pur soun grant labour enblant en lez countes suisditz.

Quamquidem cognicionem [*as in* A, *mutatis mutandis* – advocando] et quequidem verba per eundem Nicholaum ut evidenter apparet dicta fuerunt ad intensionem et finem excitandi populum domini regis contra dominum suum ligeum de eorum bono zelo ei naturaliter debito et econtra, et quod verisimile est finalis destruccio regni Anglie in hac parte consequeretur, quod ipse distrahatur [*as before*].

[*Marginated*] Distrahatur et suspendatur.

[C]

KB 27/565, Rex m.5d

[*Marginated*] Anglia

Frater Walterus Walton de Leycestre pro diversis prodicionibus [*as in* A, *mutatis mutandis* – verba]:

Frere Wauter Walton de Leycestre conust qil venoit a Westm' a meistre Rauf Selby commoigne de Westm' le dymeynge prochein devaunt le fest de Pentecoste darrein passe [7 May 1402] et demaunda

109 Recte *eam*, as in [B, C]. 110 Repeated. 111 Perhaps *a* (recte *de*?).

de luy en sa studie et puis en sa chambre qels novels, et ovesque celle mesme frere Wauter disoit qil oia en diversez parties Dengleterre et auxint dun homme de Gales qe le dit nadgairs roy fuist en plein vie, et le dit meistre Rauf disoit qe par profecie le dit roy Richard serroit en plein vie, et le dit frere Wauter disoit a luy qe meistre Roger Frysby frere de Leycestre disoit a dicte frere Wauter mesme le counte. Et le dit meistre Rauf disoit a luy qe fuist un seignur del mounde, et nomma le seignur FitzWauter, qe maunera qe M[l] liveres qe ceo fuist voir qil purroit oier bonez novels de luy. Et outre le dit meistre Rauff disoit 'Ales a moun seignur Roger Claryngdon qest frere du dit nadgairs roy en Suthwerk, et il vous sciet countera tout plein la verite en celle partie'; par quoy le dit frere Wauter le meskerdy adonques prochein ensuant [10 May 1402] venoit al mesoun du dit moun seignur Roger en Suthwerk et demaunda de luy en un bashalle la quels novels, et le dit moun seignur Roger disoit pur certayn a dit frere Wauter qe le dit nadgairs roy fuist en plein vie et qil fuist ove Oweyn Gleyndour en Gales et qe le dit Oweyn ferroit le dit frere Wauter parler ove le dit nadgairs roy. Et tant tost le dit Wauter ala a Leycestre et la tout celle matier counta a dit frere Roger Frysby et a un frere Richard Frysby soun frere, et la par lour assent pur acomplyer lour maveis et traiterous volunte et purpos ils ordinerent et assignerent un frere Roberd Colman pur aler ove le dit frere Wauter Walton en Gales al compler lour purpos suisdit, a cause qe sembla a dit frere Roger Frysby qe le dit frere Roberd Loudam feust trop june et de tendre age a ascun resistence faire. Et auxint le dit frere Wauter conust qe il est faux a nostre seigneur le roy. Et le dit frere Wauter Walton conust outre qe le dit frere Richard Frysby maunda pur le dit frere Wauter en sa chambre a Leycestre et pur un seignur John qest un leche en Leyc' et pur le dit frere Roger Frysby, et la furent ensemble en graunt conseille et la firent le dicte frere Wauter adonques countier a eux toutez les materez suisditez, et qant ils avoient oiez ils soi rejoisoient de oier pur celles novelles. Et conust outre qe soun purpos et volunte feust qil voilloit avoier eide le dicte roy Richard de tut soun poer encontre nostre seignur le roy qorest.

Quamquidem cognicionem [*as in* B, *mutatis mutandis*[112] – suspendatur].

[D]

KB 27/565, Rex m.11

[*Marginated*] Midd'

Juratores diversorum hundredorum comitatus predicti isto eodem termino coram domino rege apud Westmonasterium presentaverunt quod dominus Johannes Medicus de Leyc' nuper monachus de Sancto Albano[113] Walterus Baldok nuper prior de Launde Rogerus Claryngdon chivaler Johannes Calf serviens eiusdem Rogeri Johannes de York canonicus Beate Marie de Suthwerk magister[114] Radulphus Selby dompnus Johannes Barton et dompnus Johannes Bottesham monachi monasterii Westmonasterii Johannes Lawthe Thomas Assheby de Queneby Thomas Nevyll de Reresby frater Rogerus Frysby de Leycestre magister in divinis Willelmus Lake de Leyc' quarreour frater Johannes Eyworth de Ayllesbury frater Robertus Etone de Norht' frater Johannes Mody de Leyc' frater Rogerus Newegent de Norht' frater Rogerus Leyc' de Not' frater Johannes Howton lymytour magister Johannes Lynne[115] et alii, adunata sibi grandi potencia diversorum proditorum et rebellium de eorum falso assensu et covina tam de spiritualibus quam de temporalibus in diversis comitatibus Anglie, falso nequiter et proditorie premachinantes viis et modis falsisque et fictis sanctitate et coloribus quibus excogitare poterant, a quindena Pasche ultimo preterita [9 Apr. 1402] et diu antea et postea diversis vicibus apud Westmonasterium et alibi proposuerunt conspiraverunt et ymaginaverunt novam insurreccionem murmur et excitacionem infra regnum Anglie facere ad intencionem dominum nostrum ligium Henricum magnates et omnes fideles ligeos regni sui depredandi et interficiendi necnon omnes status

112 With (*quod idem*) *Nicholaus* for *frater Walterus.*

113 *dominus . . . Albano* interlined. In the indictment (KB 9/190, m.36) this name comes at the end of the list of those accused. The order there is otherwise the same as here, but has additional names. The full list in the indictment is as follows: Baldock, Clarendon, Calf, York (whose name is interlined), Selby, Barton, Bottisham, *frater Robertus Colman,* Lawthe, Ashby, Neville, *frater Johannes Lakinhithe, Thomas Wirhale,* Roger Frisby, *frater Ricardus Frysby de Leycestre,* Lake, Eyworth, Eton, Moody, Nugent, Roger Leicester, Howton, *frater Johannes Leycestre de ordine fratrum minorum de Stamford, frater Rogerus Gounfrey gardianus de ordine fratrum minorum de Notyngham,* Lynn and Leech. The abbreviations for *ponit se* and either *culpabilis* or *non culpabilis* are interlined over the names of those arraigned in king's bench, but not in the cases of the three monks of Westminster or the six others whose names appear only in the indictment.

114 Interlined.

115 *magister Johannes Lynne* interlined.

eiusdem regni legemque communem Anglie subvertendi adnullandi et destruendi et, quod verisimile fuit, terram istam lingua aliena de novo inhabitandi in finalem destruccionem tocius regni Anglie, et sic ad eorum falsum et proditorium propositum in hac parte perimplendum et colorandum in diversis comitatibus regni Anglie, ut in civitate London' comitatibus Midd' Essex Surr' Sussex' Kanc' Sutht' Norht' Warr' Leyc' Not' Derb' Bed' Buk' Norff' Suff' Cant' et Hunt' ac fere per totam boream, quidam ac quamplures eorum pro majori parte perambulaverunt dicendo per eosdem et pro vero nonnullis affirmando tam publice quam private ac predictus nuper prior publice predicando dominum Ricardum nuper regem Anglie, qui per mille milium infra civitatem London' et alibi nuper mortuus visus fuit et veraciter mortuus est, per antiquas propheciam et croniculas iam de novo debere revivere ac in diversis partibus regni Anglie ut apud hospitale Sancti Jacobi juxta Westmonasterium vivum nuper visum fore. Et predicti Rogerus Claryngdon frater Rogerus Frysby et alii publice et pro vero affirmaverunt et dixerunt ipsum nuper regem Ricardum vivere et cum Oweyno Gleyndurdo infra Walliam existere et ibidem visum fore, ut qui de eiusdem nuper regis retinencia et amicia perantea forent cum eis insurgerent ad dictum Oweynum inimicum mortalem domini nostri regis contra dominum nostrum regem Henricum et regnum Anglie de eorum toto velle et viribus adjuvandum et sustentandum. Preterea predicti nuper prior et fratres ex assensu omnium proditorum prenominatorum sub colore false et ficte sanctitatis et pietatis publice in quampluribus comitatuum predictorum predicaverunt ac quamplures eo modo excitaverunt et procuraverunt, dicendo meritorium fore et Deo placitum predictum nuper regem Ricardum, qui antea coronam Anglie sponte voluntarie et absolute resignavit imperpetuum idemque rex pro mala et iniqua gubernacione regni Anglie per omnes status eiusdem regni a regimine suo regni predicti non immerito depositus fuit, ad pristinam dignitatem suam reponendi et restituendi,[116] dicendo et false menciendo ipsum nuper regem Ricardum per propheciam et croniculas coronam Anglie prospere rehabere et regaudere. Et non tantum ad illum finem hec dicta fuerunt et imaginata, verum eciam ad finalem intencionem et conclusionem depredandi et interficiendi dominum nostrum regem ac omnes fideles ligeos regni istius qui eis ad eorum propositum predictum consentire nollent, si de eis prevaluissent in finalem destruccionem regni Anglie. Et sic quamplures complices suos ad numerum quatuor millium hominum in comitatibus predictis ad eorum falsum propositum predictum adunaverunt ipsosque insimul cum eis inter festum Pentecostes ultimo preteritum et festum nativitatis Sancti Johannis Baptiste proximo futurum [14 May to 24 June 1402] manuforti et potencia armata unanimiter insurgere consuluerunt procuraverunt et excitaverunt, causa quorum falsitatis ymaginacionis et mendacii sic subtiliter adinventi et de novo iam publicati adversarius noster Scocie et inimici nostri terre illius, attendentes divisionem istam et destruccionem Anglie in hac parte quod absit verisimiliter evenire, in decepcionem domini regis et populi sui quendam hominem similem dicto nuper rege Ricardo inter eos ibidem ut Ricardum regem Anglie iam tarde erexerunt et honoraverunt, ac vexillum de armis Anglie et standardum necnon alia signa de cervo de liberata sua quibus in vita sua uti solebat depingi fecerunt, et sic eo colore dictus adversarius Scocie et inimici ibidem manuforti et exercitu magno infra breve in terram Anglie cum armis et signis predictis ante predictam falsam fictam personam deportandis intrare nituntur et proponunt viribus suis de grandi fiducia adjutorii omnium proditorum et complicium suorum predictorum contra dominum nostrum regem Henricum et regnum suum Anglie, ut sic finalis divisio discensio murmur ac depredaciones infra regnum Anglie consequerentur imperpetuum in perpetuam adnullacionem tocius lingue regni et legis Anglicane etc.

Et modo, scilicet die mercurii proximo post festum Sancti Barnabe apostoli isto eodem termino [14 June 1402], coram domino rege apud Westmonasterium venerunt predicti Walterus Baldok Rogerus Claryngdon Johannes Calf Johannes de Yorke Johannes Lawthe Thomas Nevyll frater Rogerus Frysby Willelmus Lake frater Johannes Eyworth frater Robertus Eton frater Johannes Mody frater Rogerus Newegent frater Rogerus Leycester et frater Johannes Howton in custodia marescalli, in qua alias ex causis predictis commissi fuerunt. Et statim per marescallum ducti venerunt. Et allocuti sunt separatim qualiter de feloniis et prodicionibus predictis se velint acquietare, dicunt separatim quod ipsi in nullo sunt inde culpabiles. Et inde de bono et malo ponunt se super patriam. Ideo fiat inde juramenta etc. Et super hoc juratores per vicecomitem Midd' retornati venerunt, qui ad veritatem de premissis dicendam electi [triati][117] et jurati dicunt super sacramentum suum

116 Recte *reponendum et restituendum.*

117 Omitted.

quod predicti Johannes de Yorke canonicus Thomas Nevyll et Willelmus Lake de feloniis et prodicionibus predictis in nullo sunt culpabiles nec umquam hiis occasionibus se retraxerunt. Ideo consideratum est quod predicti Johannes de York canonicus Thomas Nevyll et Willelmus Lake eant inde quieti etc. ⟨Quietus. Quietus [nec] retraxit. Quietus⟩[118] Et ulterius dicunt quod predicti Walterus Baldok Rogerus Claryngdon Johannes Calf Johannes Lawthe frater Rogerus Frysby frater Johannes Eyworth frater Robertus Eton frater Johannes Mody frater Rogerus Newegent frater Rogerus Leycester et frater Johannes Howton de feloniis et prodicionibus predictis culpabiles sunt, per quod consideratum est quod iidem Walterus Baldok Rogerus Claryngdon Johannes Calf Johannes Lawthe frater Rogerus Frysby frater Johannes Eyworth frater Robertus Eton frater Johannes Mody frater Rogerus Newegent frater Rogerus Leycester et frater Johannes Howton ut proditores domini regis et regni sui Anglie distrahantur a Turri London' per medium civitatis London' usque Tyburne et ibidem suspendantur et decapitentur et quod corpora eorum postmodum in quatuor partes dividantur etc., et quod eorum capita et quarteria mittantur et ponantur ad quas partes regni Anglie domino regi placuerit ea mittere in conspectu omnium per partes illas transeuncium et ea intuencium ne in premissis seu hiis consimilibus exnunc delinquent exemplum, et quod ipsi forisfaciant omnia terras et tenementa, bona seu catalla sua etc. [*Marginated*] Distrahatur et suspendatur.[119]

[Subsequently Thomas Assheby of Quenby appeared on 16 June, John Medicus (brought by Thomas Rempston, constable of the Tower, by the king's order) on 19 December, and Master John Lynne on 10 February 1403. All were found not guilty, Assheby and Medicus were freed, but 'for certain other reasons' Lynne was meanwhile committed to the Marshalsea.]

[2]

There is no indication in this indictment in Trinity 1402 that the accused was a clerk. The terms 'depopulator agrorum et insidiator altarum viarum', and the allegations of notoriety and that his acts were treasonable, do however identically match the terms that the clergy complained about in convocation in 1399 and in their petition in the parliament which met in the September following this trial. Clergy indicted in these terms were said to be refused benefit of clergy, and this may be why no mention is made of benefit in this record. There were at least two other indictments of this nature in 1402.[120]

The literary style and exaggerated expression of this indictment suggest that it may have been drafted by the same counsel of the crown who were responsible for the indictment for treason in this term [1 D].

KB 27/565, Rex, m.5d

[*Marginated*] Midd'
Juratores diversorum hundredorum isto eodem termino coram domino rege apud Westmonasterium presentaverunt quod Johannes Leycestre de comitatu Kanc' die veneris proximo ante festum nativitatis Sancti Johannis Baptiste anno regni regis Henrici quarti post conquestum tercio [30 June 1402] apud Knottynghil in comitatu Midd' simul cum aliis felonibus ignotis, ut communes insidiatores altarum viarum et depopulatores agrorum, in alta via inter villam de Acton et London jacuit in insidiis ad communem populum regni regis Anglie et ligeos ipsius regis per viam predictam venientes depredandos et ex toto eius velle et opere felonice et proditorie murdrandos interficiendos et destruendos et principaliter homines legum Anglie, ita quod nulla lex in regno predicto uti poterit. Et sic per huiusmodi insidias felonice et proditorie, ut communis felo et proditor domini regis et regni sui ad destruendem et depredandum quoscumque ligeos domini regis per altas vias Anglie protereuntes, die anno loco et comitatu predictis quendam Laurencium Walter clericum de una zona harneisita cum argento precii decem solidorum et octo solidos argenti in pecunia numerata felonice et proditorie ibidem depredatus fuit. Et quod predictus Johannes sit[121] communis proditor et notarius[122] latro depopulator agrorum et insidiator altarum viarum ad communem populum domini regis per altas vias ad diversa mercata infra comitatum predictum transeuntem et cultores agrorum circa culturas laborantes felonice et proditorie depredandos interficiendos murdrandos et destruendos in maximam destruccionem populi domini regis et legum Anglie destruccionem.

Per quod preceptum est vicecomiti quod non omitteret etc. quin caperet eum si etc. Et modo

[118] Marginated. [119] Given eleven times.

[120] KB 27/563, Rex m.4d; Bellamy, *Law of Treason,* 116 n.6 where similar comment is made; and see above, 343. The original of the above indictment is KB 9/190, m.32.

[121] Recte *est.* [122] Recte *notorius.*

scilicet die martis proximo post festum nativitatis Sancti Johannis Baptiste isto eodem termino [27 June 1402] coram domino rege apud Westmonasterium venit predictus Johannes Leycestre in custodia marescalli, in qua alias commissus fuit, et allocutus[123] qualiter de prodicionibus et feloniis predictis se velit acquietare, dicit quod ipse in nullo est inde culpabilis et inde de bono et malo ponit se super patriam. Ideo fiat inde juramenta etc. Et super hoc juratores venerunt, qui ad hoc electi triati et jurati dicunt super sacramentum suum quod predictus Johannes Leycestre culpabilis est de prodicionibus et feloniis predictis. Nulla habet bona seu catalla, terras seu tenementa etc. Ideo consideratum est quod predictus Johannes Leycestre suspendatur etc.
[*Marginated*] Suspendatur.

[3]

The editor of Adam Usk's chronicle knew of the pardon granted on 16 June 1403 to Edward Usk on account of his being indicted as shown below; he accepted the pardon as proof that Adam had committed the felony and offers the fact of Adam being guilty as the reason why he abandoned his successful career in England and fled to Rome. In fact, Adam himself received a pardon from the same charge on 18 January 1403. It is suggested that these conclusions are mistaken. The pardon itself gives the date of the alleged felony as 3 November 1400.[124] Throughout the following year Adam was actively engaged in his practice as a canon and civil lawyer in London, and he was occasionally employed by the king in diplomatic negotiations there. It was not until February 1402, fifteen months after the alleged felony, that Adam found it necessary to leave the country.[125]

The indictment itself provides further cause to doubt its veracity. It was presented in Trinity 1402, eighteen months after the purported incident. Moreover, the charges against Sydenham and Ashton, naturally not mentioned in the Usks' pardons, add more cause for suspicion. Both were doctors of civil law, distinguished members of the London circle of ecclesiastical lawyers to which Adam belonged. At the time of the alleged robbery, and for three years later, Sydenham was lieutenant of the admiral of England, presiding in his court. It is no more credible that these two dignitaries should have been parties to highway robbery. Their careers were not interrupted by the accusation. Ashton became commissary general of Canterbury in 1405, while Sydenham was to conclude his career in royal diplomacy as bishop of Chichester.[126]

Usk was most probably the victim of a false indictment; the charge that he was a common thief was surely malicious. His chronicle refers, in another context, to personal enemies in high places, while its revelation of his officious, tactless and conceited personality suggests how easily he may have aroused antagonism.[127] The accusation was doubtless based on an actual incident, possibly a seizure ordered in the admiralty or a church court. A Westminster jury was not averse to endorsing a malicious bill against ecclesiastics [4]. Moreover, the current popular hostility against Welshmen, as well as Usk's flight abroad, would have eased his enemies' task of 'labouring' the jury. For the same reasons, it is unlikely that he would have been acquitted had he returned to stand his trial. It was preferable to obtain a royal pardon, no doubt by the mediation of his patron Archbishop Arundel, even though it could not clear Usk's reputation.

KB 9/190, m.26

[*Marginated*] Midd'
Inquiratur pro rege si Adam Usk clericus Edwardus Usk clericus Johannes Derby alias dictus Johannes Muleward de comitatu Derb' Nicholaus Broun de comitatu Stafford Nicholaus Edulffi de comitatu Glouc' et Ricardus Edven alias dictus Ricardus Walssheman die mercurii proximo post festum Omnium Sanctorum anno regni regis Henrici quarti post conquestum secundo [3 Nov. 1400] jacuerunt in insidiis apud villam Westmonasterii ad depredandum quoscumque ligeos domini regis et sic incidiandum ibidem Walterum Jakes de uno equo nigri coloris cum cella et freno precii centum solidorum et xiiij marcis in pecunia numerata ipsius Walteri[128] ibidem inventis felonice furati fuerunt et si sint communes latrones.

Item si Simon Sydenham clericus et Matheus Aston clericus fuerunt tunc ibidem presentes auxiliantes

[123] Followed by *est*.

[124] *CPR 1401–5*, 188, 234.

[125] Usk, *Chronicon*, xxi–xxii, 57–60, 63–4, 74, 220–5, 229–30, 242; Emden, *Biog. Reg. Oxford*, III, 1937–8.

[126] ibid., I, 64; III, 1838.

[127] Usk, *Chronicon*, xiv, xix, 86, 257.

[128] *ipsius Walteri* interlined.

abbettantes et confortantes predictis Ade et aliis felonibus ad feloniam predictam in forma predicta faciendam et si ipsos postea apud predictam villam Westmonasterii videlicet die jovis proximo sequenti receperunt,[129] scientes ipsos esse felones et feloniam predictam fecisse.
[*Endorsed*] Ista billa est vera.

[4]

This indictment is in the file for Hilary 1402 but there is no corresponding record on the Rex section of the coram rege roll for this term. It alleges that Nicholas Slack was deprived of the deanery of Wells by conspiracy and fraud. He could not have sued for remedy under statute as Rishton was to do in the following Trinity term, because the statutes invoked by the latter applied only against the king's presentations to benefices [20]. Since the presentation which deprived Slack was made by the archbishop of Canterbury, his reluctance to seek remedy by process at canon law in England is understandable, and the influence of his supplanter with the king may possibly have deterred Slack from resorting to the Roman curia. It may be noted that Thomas Tutbury, the new dean, is not accused in the indictment although those accused were said to have been acting for his benefit.

Slack had apparently become dean of Wells by election after the vacancy caused by Henry Beaufort's consecration as bishop of Lincoln in July 1398. The election had been confirmed by the former archbishop, Roger Walden.[130] As an intimate councillor of Richard II and dean of his chapel, Slack could feel his title to be secure. For this reason, however, he was arrested in the summer of 1399 and again in January 1400 at the time of the earls' plot to restore Richard.[131] On 25 January, the pope provided him to the deanery, stating that Slack's election was void because of a papal reservation; indeed, in February 1398 the pope had granted the deanery to a cardinal in expectation of Beaufort's consecration.[132] Possibly Slack's temporary detention in the Tower and his outlawry on a private plea of debt prevented him from being reinstalled as dean, but he was pardoned this outlawry on 10 December 1400, when he was described as the king's clerk.[133]

Archbishop Arundel collated the deanery to Tutbury on 24 February 1401. His letter states that the deanery was said to be vacant and the collation belonged to him in the vacancy of the bishopric of Bath and Wells. The second statement is remarkable because the temporalities were in crown custody and the king was accordingly making presentations to other benefices in the cathedral.[134] The king's assent to Tutbury's collation must therefore be presumed. The archbishop appointed the bishops of Hereford, Rochester and Bangor, and Master John Preen, to enquire into the vacancy of the deanery. They were to summon Slack, who was in possession, and if they determined it was vacant they were to institute Tutbury.[135] The proceedings described in the indictment, with its uncertain datings, doubtless followed this investigation. John Maidenhead is said to have acted in his capacity as official of Bath and Wells, an office he held in the vacancy of the diocese from 1400 to 1401. He was dean of Chichester and a canon lawyer.[136] Several of his alleged co-conspirators were also members of the establishment of ecclesiastical lawyers.[137] The archbishop affirmed that they had acted rightly in removing Slack from his unlawful occupation of the deanery in a mandate of 24 November 1401 requiring the new bishop of Bath and Wells to proceed against unknown persons still preventing Tutbury from enjoying possession.[138] The indictment shows that Slack's proctor was then occupying his decanal stall.

The indictment's allegations against Maidenhead and his colleagues do not command credit. At best, it is giving an adjusted version of proper canonical proceedings. It is hard to believe that Tutbury need

129 MS *recept'*, interlined.

130 *CPL*, V, 284; *CPR 1396–9*, 426; *1399–1401*, 288; *CCR 1402–5*, 276; *Fasti*, VIII, 4.

131 Usk, *Chronicon*, 28, 179; *CPR 1399–1401*, 214; A. L. Brown, 'The reign of Henry IV', in *Fifteenth-century England 1399–1509*, ed. S. B. Chrimes, C. D. Ross and R. A. Griffiths (Manchester, 1972), 5–6.

132 *CPL*, V, 112, 284.

133 *CPR 1399–1401*, 392.

134 ibid., 295, 442–3, 445, 447, 473.

135 Lambeth Palace Lib., Register of Archbishop Arundel, I, f.275.

136 Emden, *Biog. Reg. Oxford*, II, 1246–7.

137 Crass and Billesdon, a king's clerk, were also canonists: ibid., I, 508; *CPR 1399–1401*, 446. Ralph Canon and Terry were canons of Wells: *Fasti*, VIII, 45, 20. William Canon was a notary: C. R. Cheney, *Notaries Public in England* (Oxford, 1972), 182; so presumably were Hilton and Terry.

138 Lambeth Palace Lib., Reg. Arundel, I, f.280; *Registers of Walter Giffard and Henry Bowett*, ed. T. S. Holmes (Som Rec. Soc., XII, 1899), 21.

have resorted to the dubious expedients alleged by the indictment. His success in other suits at common law in defence of his titles to other benefices [16, 20] suggests that he would have emerged as victor in any judicial encounter with Slack. Undoubtedly Slack had been deprived of the deanery for reasons which remain unknown. His intimacy with Richard II may have weighed against him but he seems to have lived this down by 1401. It does appear that he was not entirely innocent of dubious practices. On 6 August 1401 the king granted him the deanery of the royal free chapel of Bridgnorth. Tutbury had been the previous dean,[139] and no doubt had resigned as his side to an arrangement with Slack. At the same time, however, Slack was negotiating an exchange of benefices with Thomas Stanley, whereby the latter was to become dean of Wells [16]. The indictment was obviously made on information provided by Slack. He had instigated the charge, perhaps to avenge himself on those who had thwarted his own double-dealing: an anti-clerical grand jury would have relished indicting so many members of the black establishment.

KB 9/187, m.43

Juratores presentant quod ubi quidam Nicholaus Slake in corporali possessione decanatus de Welles nuper existens et possessionem suam inde mero jure et justo titulo per tempus non modicum videlicet per tres annos proximo elapsos pacifice continuasset, quidam Johannes Maydenhithe clericus Thomas Redeman clericus Rogerus Royer Walterus Craas clericus Radulphus Canon clericus Willelmus Hethe clericus Nicholaus Barwe Willelmus[140] Byllesdon clericus Johannes Isaak clericus Johannes Hylton registrer Thomas[140] Terry re[gistrer][141] et Willelmus[140] Canon clericus adinvicem interligati et confederati, falso et maliciose machinantes et conspirantes qualiter et quomodo dictum Nicholaum Slake[142] a possessione sua decanatus predicti spoliare et expellere potuissent, die lune proximo post festum Sancti Bartholomei apostoli anno regni domini regis nunc tercio[143] apud villam Westmonasterii infra sanctuarium ibidem inter se ordinaverunt quod predictus Johannes Mayndenhith adtunc commissarius episcopatus Batoniensis et Welensis sede vacante quandam sitacionem faceret sub nomine suo predicto Willelmo Canon et aliis certis personis directam ad citandum dictum Nicholaum Slake[144] ad comparendum coram dicto commissario die lune proximo post festum Sancti Ambrosii anno supradicto[145] apud Aumesbury in ecclesia parochiali de Aumesbury ad respondendum Thome Tutbury super jure et titulo decanatus predicti, et quod idem com[m]issarius tunc sederet et curiam suam teneret in alio loco infra eandem villam ea intencione quod idem Nicholaus in ecclesia predicta locum suum limitatum servaret et ibidem expectaret donec quedam defalta in alio loco[146] propter eius contumaciam versus eum[147] adjudicaretur, virtute cuius false citacionis sic nequiter et maliciose machinate dictus Willelmus Canon apud predictam villam Westmonasterii eundem Nicholaum Slake die mercurii proximo post predictum festum Sancti Bartholomei[148] citavit ad comparendum coram dicto com[m]issario predicto die lune in ecclesia predicta ad respondendum prefato Thome Tutbury super jure et titulo decanatus predicti; quiquidem Nicholaus ignorans de falsitate predicta, in forma legis per Ricardum Lodelowe clericum et Johannem Danneby clericum procuratores suos in hac parte infra ecclesiam predictam dicto die lune proximo post festum Sancti Ambrosii[149] comparuit et ibidem expectabat donec quedam defalta versus eundem Nicholaum in quodam alio loco adjudicata fuit, videlicet in quodam orreo ad finem dicte ville de Ambresbury. Preteria[150] iidem Johannes Maydenhithe Thomas Redeman Rogerus Royer Walterus Craas Radulphus Canon Willelmus Hethe Nicholaus Barwe Willelmus Byllesdon Johannes Isaak Johannes Hulton et Willelmus Canon continuando eorum falsam conspiracionem et maliciam precogitatam, falso et maliciose proponentes per aliam decepcionem et falsitatem eundem Nicholaum Slake de decanatu predicto totaliter expellere, percipientes quendam Willelmum Fuller procuratorem dicti Nicholai Slake et stallum suum in choro apud Welles occupantem, die lune

139 *CPR 1399–1401*, 448, 485.

140 Dot over each of these three names.

141 *Thomas Terry re* [?] interlined.

142 Interlined.

143 Recte *secundo* and thus 29 Aug. 1401?

144 Interlined.

145 10 April 1402 (if in 3 Henry IV). This is too long after the citation to appear correct, and as is shown above sentence had then been given and Bath and Wells was no longer vacant. Perhaps another feast should have been cited, falling within a month of the citation.

146 *in alio loco* interlined.

147 *versus eum* interlined.

148 *Sancti Bartholomei* interlined.

149 *proximo . . . Ambrosii* interlined.

150 Recte *Preterea.*

proximo ante festum Sancti Andree apostoli anno supradicto [28 Nov. 1401] apud dictam villam Westmonasterii procuraverunt et excitaverunt dictum Rogerum Royer ad affirmandum quoddam falsum appellum per nomen Johannis Rede versus predictum Willelmum Fuller in curia militari ad intencionem quod idem Willelmus Fuller per corpus suum arestaretur et sic dictus Nicholaus Slake a possessione sua predicta spoliaretur, quiquidem Rogerus Royer juxta illorum falsum propositum sic precogitatum apud predictam villam Westmonasterii dicto die lune proximo ante dictum festum Sancti Andree quoddam falsum appellum supponendum ipsum de[151] diversis bonis et catallis suis per predictum Willelmum Fuller et alios in Wallia felonie depredari coram Thoma Pykworth militi marescallo per nomen Johannis Rede affirmavit, quiquidem Thomas Pykworth juxta officii sui debitum fieri fecit quoddam warantum Willelmo Frogenhale et aliis certis personis directum ad capiendum dictum Willelmum Fuller ubicumque inveniri potuit ad respondendum dicto Rogero per nomen Johannis Rede, quiquidem Willelmus Fuller adtunc occupans stallum predictum loco Nicholai Slake magistri sui per corpus suum arestatus fuit virtute waranti predicti, et statim postea iidem Johannes Mayndenhithe Thomas Redeman Rogerus Royer et alii etc. stallum predictum ut in jure dicti Thome Tuttebury intraverunt et sic per eorum falsam conspiracionem et confederacionem et occasione falsorum citacionis et appelli predictorum predictus Nicholaus Slake a possessione sua decanatus predicti spoliatus et expulsus fuit minus juste.
[*Endorsed*] Ista billa est vera.

[5]

Contempt of a writ of prohibition was alleged in this case in Hilary 1411. Both parties were clergy, the plaintiff rector of St Mary Somerset, London, and the defendant his archdeacon. The latter's well documented defence seems to make it clear that the rector had misrepresented the nature of their dispute. The record obviously quotes an award by Bishop Northborough (1354–61) which shows that the money-charge claimed by the archdeacon was not a rent, as the rector had alleged when suing his prohibiton. For good measure, by giving another reason for his citation, the archdeacon could draw attention to the rector's association with Rose of Grub Street and other prostitutes. The archdeacon did not mainprise in king's bench when the proceedings were adjourned, but on 2 April mainprise in £200 was given in chancery that he would not sue at Rome.[152]

Richard Comber alias Ludlow had been a notary public since 1391, five years before he became rector of St Mary Somerset.[153] His profession no doubt accounts for his ability to devise his prosecution of the archdeacon. He had already been excommunicated by the bishop of London in 1402 for non-appearance in a correction suit.[154] In July 1411 he was in trouble with the secular authorities for threatening violence against one John Blomtham.[155] It seems unlikely that the following suit would have been concluded to his satisfaction.

KB 27/599, m.92

[*Marginated*] London'
Reginaldus Kentwode archidiaconus London' in misericordia pro pluribus defaltis.

Idem Reginaldus attachiatus fuit ad respondendum Ricardo de Ludlowe persone ecclesie Beate Marie Somersete London' de placito quare cum placita de annuis redditibus in regno regis Anglie ad regem coronam et dignitatem suam specialiter pertineant, predictus archidiaconus secutus est placitum in curia[156] christianitatis de huiusmodi annuis redditibus in lesionem corone et dignitatis domini regis et grave dampnum ipsius Ricardi et contra prohibicionem domini regis. Et unde idem Ricardus in propria persona sua queritur quod cum placita de annuis redditibus in regno domini regis Anglie ad ipsum dominum regem coronam eiusdem regis et dignitatem suam specialiter pertineant, et idem Ricardus quoddam breve domini regis de prohibicione prefato Reginaldo ne ipse huiusmodi placitum in curia christianitatis prosequeretur apud London', videlicet in parochia Sancte Fidis virginis London' in warda de Farendon infra primo die februarii anno regni domini regis nunc undecimo [1410], in presencia Ricardi Haynard Johannis Cosyn capellani et Johannis Gerberd capellani et aliorum tunc ibidem presencium liberasset, predictus tamen Reginaldus Kentwode quoddam placitum de quodam annuo redditu[157] duorum solidorum versus ipsum Ricardum in curia christianitatis

[151] *ipsum de* interlined.

[152] *CCR 1409–13*, 209.

[153] *CPL*, IV, 360; Cheney, *Notaries Public*, 182; G. Hennessy, *Novum Repertorium Ecclesiasticum Parochiale Londinense* (London, 1898), 349.

[154] C 85/123, no.31; *CCR 1402–5*, 132.

[155] *CCR 1409–13*, 228.

[156] *in curia* interlined.

[157] Interlined.

secutus fuit, et ipsum Ricardum octavo die februarii anno undecimo supradicto apud London' in parochia Sancte Marie Somers' in warda de Quenhithe per quendam Willelmum Rowe citavit et citari fecit ad comparendum in curia christianitatis apud Sanctum Thomam de Acon' London' in warda de Chepe decimo die februarii tunc proximo sequenti coram ipso archidiacono[158] aut magistro Johanne Sproxton eiusdem officiale ad respondendum prefato Reginaldo de dicto annuo redditu duorum solidorum in domini regis contemptum ac contra prohibicionem predictam, unde dicit quod deterioratus est et dampnum habet ad valenciam centum librarum. Et inde producit sectam etc.

Et predictus Reginaldus per Johannem Corve attornatum suum venit. Et defendit vim et injuriam quando etc. et omnem contemptum et quicquid etc. Et protestando quod non cognovit de liberacione alicuius brevis domini regis de prohibicione eidem Reginaldo facti, prout predictus Ricardus superius versus eum declaravit, pro placito dicit quod cum nuper inter magistrum Johannem Barnet tunc archidiaconum London' predecessorem prefati Reginaldi ex parte una et quendam Nicholaum nuper personam ecclesie Beate Marie Somersete predecessorem predicti Ricardi et alios diversos priores rectores et vicarios ecclesiarum dicti archidiaconatus et jurisdiccioni eiusdem subjectarum super et de quadam prestacione et singulis singularum dictarum ecclesiarum rectoribus et vicariis dictarum suarum ecclesiarum nomine archidiacono pro tempore existenti solvi ut asserebatur solita annuatim, ac ipsius prestacionis causa et nomine lis fuisset suborta, tandem dictus nuper archidiaconus pro se et dicto suo archidiaconatu et suis successoribus ac dicti rectores et vicarii pro se et dictis suis ecclesiis et eorum successoribus super et de dictis prestacione[159] causa et nomine eiusdem et ea quoquomodo tangentibus se ordinacioni et diffinicioni Michaelis tunc Londoniensis episcopi concorditer et certa sciencia submiserunt, dictusque episcopus pro bono pacis et concordie necnon utilitate et perpetua tranquillitate tam dictorum rectorum et vicariorum omnium et singulorum et ecclesiarum predictarum quam dicti nuper archidiaconi et archidiaconatus predictorum,[160] mitigando et minuendo procuraciones canonicas in favorem rectorum et vicariorum etiam[161] laborem et onus archidiaconi predictorum racione ornamentorum plus in civitate London' quam alibi et etiam propinquitatis ordinarii ibidem, duxit ordinandum et diffiniendum pro omni tempore extunc futuro quod a qualibet ecclesia ecclesiarum predictarum per singulos earum rectores et vicarios singule summe pecuniarum, videlicet prefatus Nicholaus predecessor predicti Ricardi et successores sui dicto nuper archidiacono et successoribus suis duos solidos ad quatuor anni terminos, videlicet ad festa Pasche Omnium Sanctorum[162] Natalis Domini et Purificacionis Beate Marie Virginis, in singulis ecclesiis predictis equis porcionibus persolventur, quodque dicta prestacio cederet loco cuiuscumque prestacionis annue dicto[162] tunc archidiacono vel qui pro tempore foret sine racione honoris vel subjectionis et etiam loco procuracionis per dictos rectores et vicarios persolvende quamquam eundem nuper archidiaconum vel alium qui pro tempore foret qualitercumque aut ex quacumque causa prefatas ecclesias vel aliquam earum clerum et populum earumdem sive alicuius earum de facto contigeret visitare, prout in quadam composicione inter prefatum nuper archidiaconum et rectores et vicarios predictos de premissis habita et sub sigillis tam dicti nuper episcopi ad requisicionem et instanciam rectorum et vicariorum predictorum quam tunc decani et capituli ecclesie Sancti Pauli Londoniensis premissa confirmancium sigillata et per prefatum Reginaldum hic in curia monstrata plenius poterit apparere; quamquidem ordinacionem Urbanus papa sextus ex certa sciencia confirmavit, et Bonefacius papa ix[us] ordinacionem predictam ratificando mandavit tunc archiepiscopo Cantuariensi et tunc Londoniensi et Tudensi episcopis ad faciendum ordinacionem predictam auctoritate apostolica firmiter observari,[163] super quo Turibius episcopus Tudensis exequebatur huius[modi] mandatum et fecit processum in hac parte in forma consueta et demandata. Premissis tamen non obstantibus, quidam Radulphus Kestevene persona ecclesie Sancti Botolphi extra Aldrichgate et Johannes Malton persona ecclesie Sancte Mildrede in Bredstret London' cum aliis rectoribus eis in hac parte adherentibus post et contra ordinacionem huiusmodi sic confirmatam et per plures annos pacifice et fideliter hincinde observatam, primo ad curiam Cantuariensem, deinde ad sedem apostolicam racione peticionis dicte procuracionis sive prestacionis loco eiusdem appellarunt, deinde iidem rectores de dicto Bonefacio papa optinuerunt causam huiusmodi committi magistro Henrico

158 Repeated. 159 Recte *dicte prestacionis*?

160 Recte *predicti*.

161 Not *eciam*, indicating that this part of the archdeacon's case is an extract from the bishop's award, as the phraseology also suggests.

162 Interlined. 163 29 Aug. 1395 (as *CPL*, IV, 505–6).

Grunhard, quiquidem Henricus xx die decembris anno domini millesimo CCClxxxxv^to^ primam, Branda de Castellione secundam, Jacobus Floriani terciam sentencias diffinitivas conformes pro dicto[164] nuper archidiacono et contra eosdem rectores tulerunt, quasquidem tres sentencias dictus dominus Bonefacius papa confirmavit, demandando insuper dictis Cantuariensi archiepiscopo et Londoniensi et Tudensi episcopis conjunctim et divisim ad huiusmodi sentencias debite exequendas. Et dicit quod postea pretextu quarumdam litterarum nunc episcopi Londoniensis prefato Reginaldo archidiacono aut eius officiali directarum, idem Reginaldus citari fecit inter alios prefatum Ricardum Ludlowe et omnes alios rectores archidiaconatus sui predicti octavo die februarii anno undecimo supradicto ad comparendum coram prefato Reginaldo aut eius officiale in ecclesia Sancti Thome Acton' predicto decimo die februarii tunc proximo sequenti ad eligendum procuratores sufficientes ad comparendum coram reverendissimo in Christo patri Thoma archiepiscopo Cantuariensi aut eius in hac parte locumtenentibus vel commissariis in ecclesia Sancti Pauli London' xvij die februarii extunc proximo sequenti in generali convocacione cleri ibidem ad tractandum super arduis et urgentibus negociis statum defencionem et utilitatem ecclesie et regni Anglie concernentibus,[165] quoquidem Ricardo simul cum aliis rectoribus predictis pretextu citacionis huiusmodi ibidem tunc coram prefato Reginaldo archidiacono ad premissa facienda comparente, idem Reginaldus per quendam magistrum Willelmum Goodman requisitus fuit prefatum Ricardum ad solvendum eidem Reginaldo illud quod tunc aretro fuit de tempore suo de solucione predictorum duorum solidorum sibi in forma predicta solvendorum. Et similiter dicit quod pro eo quod predictus Ricardus per vicinos suos apprehensus fuit in adulterio cum diversis meretricibus, videlicet Emota Bray Alicia Spicer Rosa de Grubstret et Agnete Druer, et ea de causa in civitate London' palam et manifeste famatus, prefatus Reginaldus archidiaconus citari fecit prefatum Ricardum primo die julii anno regni[166] domini regis nunc xj^o^ in predicta parochia Beate Marie Somersete ad comparendum coram eodem archidiacono aut eius officiale in ecclesia Beate Marie Magdalene in Milkstrete London' viij die extunc proximo sequenti ad recipiendum tunc ibidem que ei pro correccione anime sue in premissis injungerentur; absque hoc quod prefatus Reginaldus archidiaconus citari fecit prefatum Ricardum ad comparendum coram eo aut eius officiale apud ecclesiam Sancti Thome Acton' ad respondendum eidem Reginaldo de annuo redditu predicto aut ipsum secutus fuit in curia christianitatis pro eodem annuo redditu modo et forma quibus predictus Ricardus superius declaravit. Et hoc paratus est verificare etc. Unde petit judicium si etc.

Et predictus Ricardus protestando quod non cognovit materiam predictam per predictum Reginaldum in forma predicta allegatam, dicit quod predictus Reginaldus dictum placitum de predicto annuo redditu duorum solidorum supradictorum in curia christianitatis versus ipsum Ricardum secutus fuit et eum citavit ad comparendum et respondendum de eodem annuo redditu in forma qua idem Ricardus supra per breve et narracionem sua supponit. Et de hoc ponit se super patriam etc. Et predictus Reginaldus similiter etc. Ideo veniat inde jurata coram domino rege a die Pasche in xv dies [26 Apr. 1411] ubicumque etc. Et qui nec etc. ad recognoscendum etc. Quia tam etc. Idem dies datus est partibus predictis etc.

[6]

This plea in Easter 1408 was dismissed sine die because the plaintiff Barrett was an excommunicate. The bishop's certificate shows that he had been excommunicated for contumacy in a matrimonial suit, suggesting that the woman abducted from his house was not his wife. It is apparent, however, that Barrett was subsequently absolved and proved his marriage was valid, because he resumed the prosecution, judgment was given in his favour and damages awarded in king's bench in Michaelmas 1409. In Hilary 1411 Brouneswolde was amerced in one mark and Thomas Porterd, an additional defendant in the second suit, produced letters of pardon dated 11 February.[167]

KB 27/588, m.36d

[*Marginated*] Essex'

Johannes Porterd de Colchestre Johannes Brouneswolde et Willelmus a Burton[168] de Colchestre attachi-

164 In 1395 the archdeacon of London was Thomas Bacton: *Fasti,* V, 8.

165 For the convocation of 17 Feb. 1410, see *Concilia,* III, 324.

166 Interlined.

167 KB 27/599, Fines, Rex m.13d; *CPR 1408–13,* 276.

168 MS *aburton* here and throughout the case.

ati fuerunt ad respondendum Willelmo Baret simul cum Johanne atte Hill de Hyntlisham de placito quare vi et armis Margaretam uxorem ipsius Willelmi Baret apud Colchestre rapuerunt et eam cum bonis et catallis eiusdem Willelmi Baret abduxerunt et ea ei adhuc detinent et alia enormia etc. ad grave dampnum etc. et contra pacem etc. ac contra formam statuti in huiusmodi casu provisi.[169]

Et unde idem Willelmus Baret per Johannem Wynchecombe attornatum suum queritur quod predicti Johannes Porterd Johannes Brouneswolde et Willelmus a Burton simul etc. die dominica proxima ante festum Omnium Sanctorum anno regni regis Henrici quarti post conquestum nono [30 Oct. 1407] vi et armis, videlicet gladiis baculis etc., Margaretam uxorem ipsius Willelmi Baret apud Colchestre rapuerunt et eam cum bonis et catallis eiusdem Willelmi Baret, videlicet pannum linei et lanei, vasa enea erea plumbea et lignea, anulos de auro et argento, cocliaria de argento, ciphos de macero, firmacula et alia jocalia, abduxerunt et ea ei adhuc detinent, et alia enormia ei intulerunt contra pacem domini regis nunc ac contra formam statuti in huiusmodi casu provisi, unde dicit quod deterioratus est et dampnum habet ad valenciam centum librarum. Et inde producit sectam etc.

Et predicti Johannes Porterd Johannes Brouneswolde et Willelmus a Burton in propria[170] personis suis venerunt. Et dicunt quod predictus [Willelmus] Baret responderi non debet quia dicunt quod idem Willelmus Baret excommunicatus existit, et proferunt hic in curia litteras episcopi Londoniensis sub sigillo suo sigillatas premissa testificantes que sequuntur in hec verba:

Universis sancte matris ecclesie filiis ad quos presentes littere pervenerint Ricardus permissione divina Londoniensis episcopus salutem in omnium salvatore. Quoniam expedit ut excommunicatorum nomina agnoscantur ne eorum dampnabilis communio Christi fideles inficiat ad similitudinem ovis morbide que inficit totum gregem, universitati vestre innotescimus per presentes quod, scrutato registro reverendi in Christo patris et domini domini Nicholai Bubbewith Dei gracia nuper Londoniensis episcopi predecessoris nostri, contineri invenimus in eodem quod Willelmus Baret de Colcestr' nostre diocesis propter ipsius contumacias rebelliones et offensas manifestas, in quadam causa matrimoniali nuper coram certo commissario eiusdem predecessoris nostri inter Johannem Kentissh partem actricem ex parte una ac prefatum Willelmum Baret et Margaretam Shapstere mulierem partem ream ex altera judicialiter contractas, ad instanciam prefati Johannis Kentissh fuit et est majoris excommunicacionis sentencia auctoritate ordinaria dicti predecessoris nostri legitime innodatus, et pro sic excommunicato publice et solempniter denunciatus, in quaquidem excommunicacionis sentencia idem Willelmus per quadraginta dies et amplius animo indurato perseveravit et adhuc perseverat, claves sancte matris ecclesie nequiter contempnendo. Vestram igitur universitatem obsecramus et in domino hortamur quatinus ipsius Willelmi sic excommunicati communionem ad ipsius maliciam convincendam tam in judicio quam extra arcius evitetis, ut sic demum rubore confusus cum ab aliis videat se contempni ad gremium sancte matris ecclesie cicius revertatur. In cuius rei testimonium sigillum nostrum fecimus hiis apponi. Datum in palacio nostro London' xviij die aprilis anno domini millesimo quadringentesimo octavo et nostre translacionis anno primo.

Pretextu quarum litterarum consideratum est quod loquela predicta remaneat sine die etc.
[*Marginated*] Sine die.

[7]

This is the earliest example printed here of an action under the statute of praemunire of 1353; the summons was for Hilary 1405 although the record dates from Easter. Unlike other writs under this statute [8–10], there is no indication that pledges to prosecute were required. The reason is clear enough: the writ issued because of alleged contempt of a judgment in king's bench.

This praemunire action reveals the real originator of the initial suit by quare impedit. Although this writ was sued for Robert, Lord Harington, on the reversal by king's bench of common pleas' sentence in his favour, the subsequent suit at Rome was begun by William Launde. He may be regarded as another example of clerks who obtained speculative presentations.[171]

The benefice to which the right of presentation was disputed was the rectory of Skirbeck. Thomas Carnyca was instituted on 22 January 1403 on presentation by Walter, Lord Fitz Walter, after the death of the previous rector. Fitz Walter held a third of the manor of Skirbeck and the right of patronage alternated: at the next vacancy it was Harington's

169 13 Edw. I (Westminster II), c.34.

170 Recte *propriis*.

171 Above, 350–1.

candidate who was admitted.[172] Presumably Launde, who was well connected locally,[173] persuaded Harington that it was his turn to present in 1403 and so obtained his own presentation. He was not the only other contender for Skirbeck: the king presented Robert Tunstall, one of his clerks, on 4 February. Çarnyca also was a king's clerk, apparently more highly placed as he was licensed to sue provisions to prebends.[174] He was thus in a good position to defend his title to Skirbeck.

The sentence in king's bench on the quare impedit action was made by 8 May 1404, the date of a writ ordering the bishop of Lincoln to institute Fitz Walter's nominee (i.e. Carnyca).[175] As the record shows, Launde must have already appealed to Rome because his proctor served Carnyca with a citation on 12 June following.

KB 27/576, m.51

[*Marginated*] Midd'
Preceptum fuit vicecomiti quod (cum per dominum Edwardum nuper regem avum domini regis nunc ac proceres magnates et communitatem regni sui Anglie in consilio suo apud Westmonasterium nuper tento[176] ordinatum et concordatum fuisset quod omnes et singuli de ligeancia sua cuiuscumque forent condicionis qui aliquem extra dictum regnum Anglie traherent in placitum de aliquo unde cognicio ad curias ipsius avi domini regis pertineret vel de aliquo unde judicia in curiis suis[177] redderentur, vel qui in aliena curia ad adnullandum vel impetendum judicia in curiis suis[177] reddita prosequerentur, haberent diem spacium duorum mensium continentem per premunicionem in loco ubi possessiones in debata existentes forent vel alibi ubi terras vel alias possessiones haberent per vicecomitem vel alium ministrum ipsius avi domini regis eis faciendam de essendo coram ipso avo domini regis vel consilio suo vel in cancellaria sua vel coram justiciariis suis de utroque banco vel aliis justiciariis suis per ipsum avum domini regis ad hoc assignandis ad respondendum[178] de contemptu facto in hac parte, et si ad diem predictum non venirent[179] ad standum legi, tunc ipsi procuratores executores notarii attornati et manutentores[180] sui ab illo die inantea ponerentur extra proteccionem ipsius avi domini regis et terre tenementa bona et catalla sua eidem avo domini regis essent forisfacta,[181] prout in ordinacione et concordia predictis plenius continetur; iamque intellexerit dominus rex quod Willelmus de la Launde clericus quamplures processus ad impetendum et adnullandum judicium nuper redditum in curia sua coram eo per breve suum de errore de loquela que fuit coram justiciariis suis de banco per breve suum quare impedit inter Robertum de Haryngton de Aleyngham militem et Walterum Fitz Wauter de Wodeham militem Thomam Carnyca clericum et Thomam Bekyngham clericum, de eo quod iidem Walterus Thomas et Thomas permitterent prefatum Robertum presentare idoneam personam ad ecclesiam de Skyrbek que tunc vacabat et ad donacionem predicti Roberti spectabat, cuiusquidem loquele recordum et processum cum omnibus ea tangentibus dominus rex coram eo causa erroris intervenientis venire fecit, contra ligeancie sue debitum in aliena curia extra regnum domini regis Anglie prosecutus fuit et indies prosequitur ac prefatum Thomam Carnyca ad respondendum inde in eadem curia extra regnum suum predictum apud villam de Westmonasterio citari fecit, et diversa processus provocaciones appellaciones et instrumenta ac notificaciones eorumdem in adnullacionem judicii predicti et quamplura alia domino regi et corone sue regie in hac parte prejudicialia fecit et fieri procuravit in domini regis contemptum et prejudicium suique et corone sue predicte exheredacionis periculum manifestum et ipsius Thome Carnyca dampnum non modicum et gravamen; dominus rex jura dicte corone sue ac judicia in curiis suis rite reddita prout vinculo juramenti astringitur illesa observari ac ordinacionem et concordiam predictas debite execucioni demandari

[172] Lincs Rec. Off., Bishops' Registers 13, f.152v; 14, f.66v; *CIPM*, XVI, 136.

[173] A John Launde was escheator of Lincs, 1401–2: *List of Escheators for England and Wales* (L & I Soc., LXXII, 1971), 79.

[174] *CPR 1401–5*, 83, 117, 193, 217, 309; *CCR 1409–13*, 76, shows Carnyca as the prince of Wales' receiver general.

[175] Lincs Rec. Off., Bishops' Regs 13, f.80. Miss J. A. Cripps kindly provided these references to the Lincoln registers.

[176] The ordinance known as the first statute of praemunire (27 Edw. III, stat. 1, c.1) is said to have been made in a 'grant conseil' at Westminster on 23 September 1353: *SR*, I, 329; see also *Hdbk Brit. Chron.*, 524.

[177] cf. 'la court nostre seignur le roi': *SR*, I, 329.

[178] cf. 'a respondre [en lour propre persones]'. The bracketed words are interlined in the statute roll.

[179] cf. 'sils ne veignent mie au dit jour [en propre persone]'.

[180] cf. 'procuratours attournez executours notairs et meintenours'.

[181] Omitting 'et soient lour corps, ou qils soient trovez, pris et emprisonez et reintz a la volunte le roi'.

volens) quod[182] per probos etc. premunire faceret predictum Willelmum ac Thomam de la Launde Johannem de la Launde Johannem Bailly de Quadryng Ricardum Pynchebek de Sancto Botolpho Johannem Judde clericum Henricum Davy clericum Thomam Cotyngwyth clericum Ricardum Dykson capellanum Nicholaum Granthame clericum Willelmum de Toft de Skyrbek et Johannem Haket clericum procuratores executores notorios[183] et manutentores ipsius Willelmi de la Launde in hac parte in locis ubi terras vel alias possessiones infra balliam suam haberent quod essent coram domino rege a die Sancti Hillarii in xv dies ultimo preterito [28 Jan. 1405] ubicumque etc. ad respondendum domino regi de contemptu et prejudicio predictis et prefato Thome Carnyca de dampnis et injuriis sibi illatis et in premissis perpetratis. Et ad faciendum ulterius etc.

Et modo scilicet a die Pasche in xv dies isto eodem termino [3 May 1405] coram domino rege apud Westmonasterium venerunt predictus Thomas Carnyca qui tam pro domino rege quam pro se ipso sequitur in propria persona sua, et predicti Thomas de la Launde Johannes de la Launde Johannes Bailly Ricardus Pynchebek Johannes Judde Thomas Cotyngwyth et Willelmus Tofte in propriis personis suis ac prefatus Nicholaus per Johannem Solas attornatum suum ex assensu predicti Thome Carnyca loco ipsius Nicholai in placito predicto positum.

Et super hoc predictus Thomas Carnyca tam pro domino rege quam pro se ipso queritur quod cum per dominum Edwardum [*as above*[184] – prosecutus fuit] ac prefatum Thomam Carnyca ad respondendum inde in eadem curia extra regnum domini regis predictum duodecimo die junii anno regni domini regis nunc quinto [1404] per Johannem Burbrigg capellanum apud villam Westmonasterii citari fecit ad comparendum in curia Romana octogesima die tunc proximo sequenti et diversa processus provocaciones appellaciones et instrumenta ac notificaciones eorumdem in adnullacionem judicii predicti et quamplura alia domino rege et corone sue regie in hac parte [prejudicialia] fecit et fieri procuravit. Et predicti Thomas de la Launde Johannes de la Launde et Ricardus Pynchebek fuerunt tunc ibidem procuratores et attornati et predicti Johannes Judde Johannes Bailly et Willelmus Tofte fuerunt tunc ibidem procuratores et manutentores et predictus Nicholaus Grantham ac prefatus Ricardus Dykson versus quem predictus Thomas Carnyca narraret, si presens esset, fuerunt notarii et executores predicti Willelmi de la Launde in hac parte in domini regis contemptum et prejudicium ipsiusque et corone sue predicte exheredacionis periculum manifestum, unde idem Thomas Carnyca dicit quod deterioratus est et dampnum habet ad valenciam mille librarum. Et inde tam pro domino rege quam pro se ipso producit sectam etc.

[Thomas and John de la Launde, Bailly, Pynchebek, Judde, Cotyngwyth, Grantham and Tofte denied contempt and pleaded not guilty, and a jury was called for 20 January 1406. Seven of the above (i.e. excluding Grantham), together with John de Flete, all of Lincolnshire, mainperned for each other, in groups of four, [*membrane 51d*] that they would not support William de la Launde in suits in any church court or attempt anything prejudicial to the king or his laws, all under pain of forfeiting £100. The seven made oaths to the same effect and renounced any prior suits.

Carnyca and all the defendants who had appeared earlier came on 20 January, but as the sheriff had not returned the writ, the parties and a jury were called for 6 October 1406.

A space 14 inches in depth follows, then the following]:

Idem Thomas Carnyca qui etc. in propria persona optulit se iiij^to^ die versus predictos Willelmum de la Launde Henricum Davy Ricardum Dykson Nicholaum Grantham et Johannem Haket de placito predicto etc. Et ipsi non venerunt. Et preceptum fuit vicecomiti comitatus Lincoln' ad premuniendum eos etc. eo quod testatum fuit quod ipsi possessiones in eodem comitatu habuerunt per quod etc. Et vicecomes retornavit quod predicti Henricus Davy et Johannes Haket mortui sunt etc. Ideo de eis nichil ulterius actum est. Et de predictis Willelmo de la Launde Ricardo Dykson et Nicholao idem vicecomes retornavit quod ipsi premuniti sunt in predicto loco in quo debata existit per Johannem Marche Henricum Abraham Johannem Murre et Johannem Jakson die sabbati ultimo die februarii ultimo preterito [28 Feb. 1405], quiquidem Willelmus Ricardus et Nicholaus licet sic premuniti et iiij^{to} die placiti solempniter exacti non venerunt. Et super hoc dies datus est prefato Thome

182 This is a repetition from before the first round bracket.

183 Recte *notarios.*

184 Differences are negligible, viz *iamque dominus rex intellexerit; in curia domini regis coram eo; inter predictum Robertum de Haryngton et prefatos Walterum; ad donacionem ipsius Roberti.*

Carnyca coram domino rege usque ad prefatas octabas Sancti Hillarii etc. in statu quo nunc etc. Ad quas octabas coram domino rege apud Westmonasterium venit predictus Thomas qui etc. Et super hoc dies datus ei coram domino rege usque ad predictas[185] octabas Sancti Michaelis ubicumque etc. in statu quo prius etc.

[8]

This prosecution under the 1353 statute of praemunire in Michaelmas 1408 alleged that the defendant Goodfather had cited the plaintiff to Rome to answer in a case of trespass. Goodfather, who was vicar of Sidlesham, replied that his suit was for a mortuary due to him by local custom (described at length) on the death of his parishioner John Segrome, junior, in 1404. He agreed that two years later he caused the plaintiff Lee to be cited to Rome because he had persuaded the young man's father to detain the beast he claimed. He had in fact begun his suit in the consistory court of Chichester and had subsequently had both Lee and John Segrome, senior, cited to Rome, where they had been excommunicated before 6 November 1406.[186] These proceedings in king's bench were extended until Michaelmas 1410 when the record ends.

In this term the suit was dismissed. Cheyne, for the vicar, pointed out that by Circumspecte Agatis a writ of prohibition would not be allowed in a suit for mortuary in a church court, and the judges agreed that the matter was outside their jurisdiction. Pole, counsel for Lee, argued that the vicar's claim was by custom, the local usage was that mortuary was not due on the death of a servant, and that John Segrome was his father's servant. Gascoigne told him that this point could be put in a church court and Hulse advised Pole to give up the suit. Pole claimed that the beast had never been in his client's possession and he sought damages. Hulse responded that offences concerning mortuary were not punishable in the king's court and it therefore could not award damages. The other judges made similar comments, Gascoigne observing that suits about bequests by testament and removal of tithes were also triable only in church courts, though with tithes a parson could sue for trespass if he chose.[187]

This ruling ended the praemunire suit. Goodfather was now able to proceed at Rome, and on 1 July 1411 papal letters ordered the bishop of Chichester to cite Lee and Segrome before him and terminate the dispute.[188]

Lee's quarrel with Goodfather had not been confined to preventing the payment of mortuary. In 1406 he had attempted to deprive him of the vicarage by arranging for the papal provision of another priest to Sidlesham. Goodfather defended himself by process under the 1390 statute of provisors; in May 1408 orders for the arrest of Lee, Segrome and two others in this connection were suspended.[189]

KB 27/590, m.6

[*Marginated*] Sussex'
Dominus rex mandavit vicecomiti Sussex' breve suum clausum in hec verba: Henricus [*etc.*] vicecomiti Sussex' salutem. Cum in parliamento domini Edwardi nuper regis Anglie avi nostri apud Westmonasterium nuper tento [*as in* 7[190] – continetur] ; ac iam intellexerimus quod licet placita de transgressionibus et aliis malefactis in regno nostro Anglie contra pacem nostram perpetratis ad nos et coronam nostram specialiter pertineant execucionesque eorumdem per nos et ministros nostros in curiis nostris regiis et non per alios fieri debeant, quidam tamen Willelmus Goodfader clericus machinans nos et coronam nostram regiam in hac parte exheredare et cognicionem quam nos et progenitores nostri quondam reges Anglie ut in jure corone nostre predicte ad huiusmodi placita infra regnum nostrum Anglie in curiis nostris regiis tenenda totis temporibus transactis habere consuevimus a nobis auferre, Nicholaum atte Lee ad respondendum in curia christianitatis extra regnum nostrum Anglie super quibusdam transgressionibus eidem Willelmo per prefatum Nicholaum apud Sydelesham infra regnum nostrum Anglie vi et armis et contra pacem nostram ut dicitur factis ac de aliis malefactis quorum cognicio ad nos et coronam nostram predictam in hac parte pertinet terminandi citari fecit, et quamplura alia nobis et corone nostre predicte prejudicialia et eidem Nicholao dampnosa in dicta curia christianitatis prosecutus fuit et indies prosequitur in nostri contemptum et prejudicium ac corone nostre predicte exheredacionem et ipsius Nicholai dampnum gravissimum ac contra formam

185 Interlined. 186 *CPL,* VI, 298.

187 YB 10 Hen. IV, Mich. 2. 188 *CPL,* VI, 298.

189 ibid., 86; *CCR 1405–8,* 360.

190 With only slight variations, e.g. *extra regnum nostrum Anglie* for *extra dictum regnum Anglie; avi nostri* for *avi domini regis;* and, more significant, *in curia sua* for *in curiis suis,* and *in eadem curia* for *in curiis suis.*

ordinacionis et concordie predictarum; nos huiusmodi contemptui prejudicio exheredacioni et dampno remedio congruo resistere ac ordinacionem et concordiam predictas debite execucioni demandari volentes ut tenemur, tibi preceperimus quod si predictus Nicholaus fecisset te securum de clamio suo prosequendo, tunc per probos et legales homines de balliva tua premuniri faceres prefatum Willelmum ac Adam Symond clericum Thomam Kytte clericum Willelmum Trot Johannem Amberle Johannem Gregge de Sydelesham seniorem Willelmum Chauntrell et Jacobum Dynmet procuratores attornatos notarios executores et manutentores ipsius Willelmi Goodfader in hac parte quod essent coram nobis in xv^{a} Pasche proximo preterita [29 Apr. 1408] ubicumque tunc fuissemus in Anglia ad respondendum nobis de contemptu prejudicio et exheredacione predictis et prefato Nicholao de dampnis et injuriis sibi illatis et in premissis perpetratis, tuque ad xv^{am} illam nobis retornavisti quod predictus Nicholaus non invenit tibi plegios de prosequendo, super quoquidem retorno idem Nicholaus invenit nobis plegios de clamio suo prosequendo in hac parte, scilicet Johannem Segrome et Willelmum Hydere; et ideo tibi precipimus sicut alias tibi precepimus quod per probos et legales homines de balliva tua premuniri facias prefatos Willelmum Goodfader ac predictos Adam Thomam Willelmum Trot Johannem Amberle Johannem Gregge Willelmum Chauntrell et Jacobum procuratores attornatos notarios executores et manutentores ipsius Willelmi Goodfader in hac parte quod sint coram nobis in octabis Sancti Michaelis [6 Oct. 1408] ubicumque tunc fuerimus in Anglia ad respondendum nobis de contemptu prejudicio et exheredacione predictis et prefato Nicholao de dampnis et injuriis sibi illatis et in premissis perpetratis et ad faciendum ulterius et recipiendum quod curia nostra consideraverit in hac parte, nobis vero de die et loco quo dictam premunicionem sibi feceris sub sigillo tuo distincte et aperte tunc certificans. Et habeas ibi nomina illorum per quos eos premuniri feceris et hoc breve. Teste Willelmo Gascoigne apud Westmonasterium quarto die maii anno regni nostri nono.

Indorsamentum brevis predicti sequitur in hec verba: Per Johannem Clipsham vicecomitem. Per Henricum Prat et Johannem Hyndon probos et legales homines de balliva mea quarto die augusti ultimo preterito apud Cicestr' premuniri feci Willelmum Goodfader ac Adam Symond Thomam Kytte Willelmum Trot Johannem Amberle Johannem Gregge Willelmum Chauntrell et Jacobum Dynmet infrascriptos procuratores attornatos notarios executores et manutentores ipsius Willelmi Goodfader quod sint coram domino rege ad diem in isto brevi contentum ubicumque tunc fuerit in Anglia ad respondendum et faciendum in omnibus secundum quod istud breve in se exigit et requirit.

Ad quasquidem octabas Sancti Michaelis coram domino rege apud Westmonasterium venerunt tam predictus Nicholaus in propria persona sua quam prefatus Willelmus Goodfader per Hugonem Cary attornatum suum per litteras domini regis patentes constitutum ac prefati[191] Adam Thomas Willelmus Trot Johannes Amberle Johannes Gregge Willelmus Chauntrell et Jacobus in propriis personis suis juxta premunicionem predictam eis in hac parte factam. Et unde predictus Nicholaus in propria persona sua queritur quod cum in parliamento domini Edwardi [*as above, mutatis mutandis*[192] – consueverunt] ab ipso domino rege auferre, prefatum Nicholaum citari fecit apud Sydelesham predictam vicesimo septimo die marcii anno regni domini regis nunc septimo [1406] ad comparendum in curia Romana sexagesimo die extunc proximo sequenti ad respondendum eidem Willelmo de eo quod ipse abscidisse debuisset apud predictam villam de Sydelesham unum folium de uno missali ecclesie de Sydelesham predicta et idem folium abinde asportare debuisset et quod debuit ymaginasse ibidem mortem ipsius Willelmi ac eciam quod ipse cepisse debuisset ibidem unam juvencam precii octo solidorum et eam abduxisse, quam predictus Willelmus exigebat pro mortuario per mortem Johannis Segrome filii Johannis Segrome de Sydelesham, et super isto processu dictus Willelmus prosequebatur prefatum Nicholaum in curia Romana quousque excommunicatus fuit et suspensus ab ingressu ecclesie, de quibus cognicio ad dominum regem et coronam domini regis predictam in hac parte pertinet terminandi, et quamplura alia domino regi et corone sue predicte prejudicialia et eidem Nicholao dampnosa in curia christianitatis prosecutus fuit et indies prosequitur in domini regis contemptum et prejudicium ac corone sue predicte exheredacionem ac contra formam ordinacionis et concordie predictarum. Et predicti Adam Thomas Willelmus Trot Johannes Amberle Johannes Gregge Willelmus Chauntrell et Jacobus diebus anno et locis[193] predictis fuerunt procuratores attornati notarii executores et manutentores ipsius Willelmi Goodfader in hac parte, unde dicit quod deterioratus est et dampnum habet

[191] Interlined. [192] i.e. with indirect reference to the king. [193] Recte *loco*.

ad valenciam quadringentarum librarum. Et inde tam pro domino rege quam pro seipso producit sectam etc.

Et predicti Willelmus Goodfader Adam Thomas Willelmus Trot Johannes Amberle Johannes Gregge Willelmus Chauntrell et Jacobus defendunt omnem contemptum. Et quiquid etc. Et iidem Adam Thomas Willelmus Trot Johannes Johannes Willelmus Chauntrell et Jacobus dicunt quod ipsi in nullo sunt culpabiles de aliquibus materiis supra in brevi et declaracione predicti Nicholai contentis. Et de hoc ponunt se super patriam. Et predictus Nicholaus atte Lee similiter etc. Et predictus [*membrane 6d*] Willelmus Goodfader quoad omnia in brevi et declaracione predictis contenta preter pro citacione juvence predicte dicit quod ipse in nullo est inde culpabilis. Et de hoc ponit se super patriam. Et predictus Nicholaus similiter etc.

Et quoad citacionem pro predicta juvenca, predictus Willelmus Goodfader dicit quod per totum dictum comitatum Sussex' consuetudo talis est, et fuit a tempore quo non extat memoria, quod quilibet rector ubi nullus sit vicarius, ac quilibet vicarius licet ibi aliquis rector fuerit, habere poterit mortuarium quocienscumque aliquis de eorum parochianis suis obierit. Et precipue dicit quod consuetudo talis est in dicta parochia de Sydelesham, et fuit a tempore quo non extat memoria, quod quocienscumque aliquis [de] parochianis in dicta parochia de Sydelesham non habens terras neque tenementa nec aliquod domicilium per se tenens, aceciam sive fuerit terras vel tenementa tenens sive domicilium per se habens et non habuerit uxorem nec filios aut filias de corpore suo procreatos, et aliqua animalia habuerit tempore mortis sue, vicarius ibidem qui pro tempore fuerit habere consuevit optimum animal nomine mortuarii quod idem parochianus habuit tempore mortis sue. Et si aliquis domicilium per se habens sive terras et tenementa tenens eiusdem parochie ibidem obierit habens aliquem bovem et plura alia animalia, licet aliquod animal eorumdem sit melius[194] quam aliquis bos eiusdem parochiani, et idem parochianus habuerit uxorem filios aut filias de corpore suo procreatos, vicarius ibidem qui pro tempore fuerit per consuetudinem in eadem parochia habere consuevit a toto tempore predicto post mortem eiusdem sic domicilium per se habentis sive terras et tenementa tenentis bovem et non aliud animal nomine mortuarii. Et dicit quod tempore quo idem Willelmus Goodfader fuit vicarius ecclesie de Sydelesham predicta, quidam Johannes Segrome junior nuper parochianus dicte parochie de Sydelesham in eadem parochia, videlicet xx^{mo} die septembris anno regni domini regis nunc quinto [1404], obiit habens plura animalia de quibus predicta juvenca fuit optimum animal suum quod habuit tempore mortis sue, quiquidem Johannes Segrome tempore mortis sue non fuit terras neque tenementa tenens nec domicilium per se tenens, ita quod juvenca predicta juxta consuetudinem in eadem parochia a tempore quo non extat memoria usitatam eidem Willelmo nomine mortuarii post mortem dicti Johannis Segrome accidebat. Et dicit quod juvenca predicta post mortem eiusdem Johannis Segrome remanebat in custodia Johannis Segrome senioris patris dicti Johannis Segrome junioris apud Sydelesham predicta. Et dicit quod predictus Nicholaus xxvj^{to} die septembris apud Sydelesham predictam consiluit predictum Johannem Segrome seniorem quod dictam juvencam nomine mortuarii non solveret, et ipsum Johannem Segrome seniorem ad solvendum dictum mortuarium ibidem eodem die impedivit, occasione quorum consilii et impeticionis predictus Johannes Segrome senior detinuit juvencam predictam apud Sydelesham predictam per unum annum extunc proximo sequentem et adhuc detineret per abbettamentum eiusdem Nicholai, causa quorum consilii et impedicionis diu post dictum xxvj^{um} diem septembris predictus Willelmus Goodfader prosequebatur nomine mortuarii et causa mortuarii versus prefatum Nicholaum, et ipsum citavit dicto vicesimo septimo die marcii anno septimo supradicto apud Sydelesham predictam ad comparendum in curia Romana centisimo die extunc proximo sequenti ad respondendum de mortuario predicto; absque hoc quod idem Willelmus Goodfader aliter seu alio modo citavit prefatum Nicholaum pro juvenca predicta seu aliquem processum fecit in curia Romana versus eundem Nicholaum pro eadem juvenca vel pro aliqua alia causa, nisi tantum prout per eundem Willelmum Goodfader superius declaratur, que omnia et singula idem Willelmus Goodfader paratus est verificare prout curia etc., unde peciit judicium si etc.

[Henry Pountfreyt, citizen and alderman of London, James Knottesford of Sussex, Henry Waryn of Cambridgeshire and Hugh Cary of Devonshire mainperned for Symond, Kytte, Trot, Amberle, Gregge, Chauntrell and Dymmet, viz that they would attempt nothing to the king's prejudice in a church court in England or abroad, each mainpernor in £40 and each defendant in £100, the latter also being sworn, etc. Further appearances (with Henry Chorley as attorney for Goodfader and the other defendants)

194 Recte *melior.*

were made on 27 January, 5 May and 27 October 1409, and 20 April 1410, when 27 October was the last day appointed.]

[9]

These writs against Henry Chicheley, then bishop of St Davids, issued under the 1353 statute of praemunire on behalf of William Farrington. When Chicheley was provided to St Davids on 4 October 1407, the pope dispensed him to hold his benefices,[195] which included the chancellorship of Salisbury. When the king granted Chicheley possession of the temporalities on 3 April 1408, however, he referred to him as former chancellor of Salisbury, and on 18 May following the king granted the chancellorship to Farrington. Farrington had been chancellor of Oxford university and must have been an old acquaintance of Chicheley himself.[196] As Chicheley retained the Salisbury dignity, Farrington attempted to remove him by process of quare impedit. The earliest of the lengthy discussions of this suit in the year books is dated Michaelmas 1409, but the first writ of praemunire facias shows that the quare impedit action had begun before 20 July 1409, a year after Farrington's presentation.

The judicial discussions relate only to the quare impedit and give no information on the progress of the praemunire action. The last of these reports belongs to Trinity 1410,[197] before the term appointed for the return of Chicheley's last recorded citation by praemunire facias. By this time, however, the grounds for Chicheley's further prosecution by Farrington had been removed. Chicheley, a delegate to the council of Pisa, made an arrangement with the pope which met the judges' objection that a bishop could not retain benefices while at the same time leaving unchallenged the pope's prerogative to make such grants in commendam. On 20 August 1409, Alexander V confirmed the previous dispensations to Chicheley and authorised the bishop of Winchester to receive Chicheley's resignation of his benefices and confer them on Chicheley's nominees. The king gave his approval to this plan on 28 April 1410 and pardoned Chicheley all contempts, forfeitures, etc.[198] The next chancellor of Salisbury was thus his nephew William Chicheley, a student at Oxford too young to be in major clerical orders.[199]

KB 27/594, m.13d

[*Marginated*] Wiltes'
Dominus rex mandavit breve suum clausum vicecomiti Wiltes'[200] in hec verba: Henricus [*etc.*] vicecomiti Wiltes' salutem. Cum per dominum Edwardum [*as in* 8, *mutatis mutandis* – continetur]; iamque intel[l]exerimus quod cum nuper vacante cancellaria ecclesie cathedralis Sarisbiriensis et ad nostram collacionem spectante, cancellariam illam Willelmo Faryngton clerico per litteras nostras patentes contulerimus, idemque Willelmus pro recuperacione cancellarie predicte in curia nostra per breve nostrum quare impedit versus Robertum episcopum Sarisbiriensem et Henricum episcopum Menevensem nomine nostro prosequatur, predictus episcopus Menevensis machinans prefatum Willelmum occasione predicta inquietari et cognicionem que ad curiam nostram pertinet in hac parte ad aliud examen extra regnum nostrum Anglie trahere, quamplures processus in curia Romana versus prefatum Willelmum prosecutus fuit et ipsum Willelmum ad respondendum inde[201] in eadem curia Romana extra regnum nostrum predictum citari fecit, et quamplura alia nobis et corone nostre in hac parte prejudicialia contra ligeancie sue debitum ibidem fecit et fieri procuravit in nostri contemptum et prejudicium et corone nostre exheredacionis periculum manifestum et ipsius Willelmi dampnum non modicum et gravamen ac contra leges et consuetudines regni nostri predicti necnon contra formam ordinacionis et concordie predictarum; nos jura corone nostre regie ac leges et consuetudines predictas illesa, prout vinculo juramenti in coronacione nostra prestiti astringimur, observari et ordinacionem et concordiam predictas debite execucioni demandari volentes, tibi precepimus quod, si predictus Willelmus fecerit te securum de clamio suo prosequendo, tunc per probos et legales homines de balliva tua premunire facias prefatum episcopum Menevensem ac Nicholaum Robertprest Cardewell et

[195] *CPL,* VI, 112.

[196] *Foedera,* VIII, 513; *CPR 1405–8,* 426, 470; Emden, *Biog. Reg. Oxford,* I, 410–12; II, 666.

[197] Above, 345–6.

[198] *CPL,* VI, 150, 156; *Foedera,* VIII, 632–3; *CPR 1408–13,* 187.

[199] *Fasti,* III, 17–18; *CPL,* VI, 228; Emden, *Biog. Reg. Oxford,* I, 413; *Reg. Chichele,* I, xxviii–xxix.

[200] *clausum . . . Wiltes'* interlined.

[201] Repeated in interlineation.

Johannem Smyth de Nova Sar' procuratores et manutentores ipsius episcopi Menevensis in hac parte apud Novam Sar' quod sint coram nobis a die Sancti Michaelis in xv dies [13 Oct. 1409] ubicumque tunc fuerimus in Anglia ad respondendum nobis de contemptu et prejudicio predictos[202] et prefato Willelmo de dampnis et injuriis sibi illatis in hac parte, et ad faciendum ulterius et recipiendum quod curia nostra consideraverit in premissis. Et habeas ibi nomina eorum per quos eos premunire feceris et hoc breve, nos de die quo dictam premunicionem sibi feceris sub sigillo tuo distincte et aperte tunc certificans. Teste me ipso apud Cantuar' xx die julii anno regni nostri decimo [1409].

Responcio eiusdem brevis sequitur in hec verba: Ego Robertus Corbet vicecomes vobis significo quod Willelmus Faryngton infrascriptus non fecit me securum de clamio suo prosequendo. Ideo de execucione istius brevis nichil actum est.

Et quia prefatus Willelmus Faryngton isto eodem termino coram domino rege apud Westmonasterium venit et invenit plegios de prosequendo, videlicet[203] David Holes et Henricum de Chorley, preceptum est vicecomiti quod per probos et legales homines de balliva sua premunire faceret prefatum episcopum Menevensem ac Nicholaum Robertprest Cardewell et Johannem Smyth de Nova Sar' procuratores et manutentores ipsius episcopi Menevensis in hac parte apud Novam Sar' quod sint coram domino rege in octabis Sancti Hillarii in xv dies [27 Jan. 1410] ubicumque etc. ad respondendum domino regi de contemptu et prejudicio predictis et prefato Willelmo de dampnis et injuriis sibi illatis in hac parte, et ad faciendum ulterius etc.

Ad quem diem coram domino rege apud Westmonasterium venit predictus Willelmus Faryngton per attornatum suum. Et vicecomes retornavit quod mandavit Willelmo Westbury ballivo libertatis episcopi Sarisbiriensis, qui plenum habet retornum omnium brevium domini regis etc., qui sibi inde nullum dedit responsum etc.,[203] per quod preceptum est vicecomiti quod non omitteret propter libertatem predictam quin per probos et legales homines de balliva sua premunire faceret prefatum episcopum Menevensem ac Nicholaum Robertprest Cardewell et Johannem Smyth de Nova Sar' quod sint coram domino rege in crastino Ascencionis Domini [2 May 1410] ubicumque etc. ad respondendum domino rege de contemptu et prejudicio predictis et prefato Willelmo de dampnis et injuriis sibi illatis in hac parte, et ad faciendum ulterius etc.

[KB 27/596 (11 Henry IV, Easter), m.77d, gives the text of the last-mentioned writ, attested by William Gascoigne and dated 28 January 1410. The sheriff, William Cheyne, returned that he had summoned the defendants at Salisbury by Nicholas Trenewoth and John Hull and was amerced in 20 shillings for an insufficient return in that he did not give the date of his summons; he was required to cite them again for 6 October 1410.]

[10]

For some twenty years two Warwickshire houses of Augustinian canons, Maxstoke and Studley, were in dispute at both Westminster and Rome for possession of the church of Aston Cantlow, and this action under the 1353 statute of praemunire was possibly Studley's final effort. The litigation apparently began in 1394–5 and Maxstoke's legal costs amounted to £930. Studley claimed the church by grant of William Cantilupe, who died in 1251, but although Edward III confirmed this grant in 1328 the advowsons remained with the lord of the manor until William Clinton, earl of Huntingdon, granted them to his new foundation of Maxstoke in 1345. The church was appropriated to Maxstoke for about fifty years, when Studley contrived to reëstablish its title.[204]

Studley appears to have been in possession by November 1399, when it obtained papal letters to authorise the church's appropriation.[205] This arrangement was frustrated. In 1401 the king twice presented his clerk Thomas Burdet to the church. Burdet's name suggests a Warwickshire origin and he was presumably exploiting local knowledge that Studley's title was insecure. In the event, he quickly had himself instituted after a suit by quare impedit in Michaelmas 1401 confirmed the king's title to present. Death soon ended Burdet's tenure as rector. Studley then presented another king's clerk to the church, perhaps hoping thus to gain tacit recognition of its title, but another quare impedit in Hilary 1404 reasserted the crown's patronage. Maxstoke may have had some hand in this litigation: these proceedings were presumably the occasion for the writs of prohibition which prevented execution of the papal

[202] Recte *predictis*. [203] Interlined.

[204] *VCH Warw*, III, 41. [205] *CPL*, VI, 359–60.

letters of November 1399 and Studley later alleged that Maxstoke was responsible for their issue.[206] At the same time, however, John Nassington, a canon of Maxstoke, was prevented from suing at Rome to the king's prejudice.[207]

After the second quare impedit, Maxstoke petitioned the king to grant it the advowsons. This he did on 14 May 1404, in return for an undertaking to celebrate divine service for the Lancastrian house and for £71 11s. paid into the hanaper. Two years later, Maxstoke's appropriation of Aston Cantlow church was confirmed by the king, and from 1407 it was appointing vicars there.[208]

Maxstoke had taken further common law proceedings against Studley: its prior and canons had been detained until they gave security not to sue outside the realm.[209] This ban was relaxed in November 1406, when the king licensed a canon of Studley to go to Rome.[210] Maxstoke also sued at Rome and won two sentences depriving Studley of the church; the archbishop of Canterbury was required to order Studley to surrender the church to Maxstoke. Studley made another appeal to Rome but failed to prosecute it and the archbishop's commissary declared the canons excommunicate and their house under interdict. At Studley's request, the pope referred the case to the bishop of Worcester in 1410, but if the bishop did give a sentence, it was not in Studley's favour. On 22 April 1412 the pope referred to Studley still being under sentence of excommunication and charged the archbishop and others to cite the canons as heretics if they refused to seek absolution within a year.[211]

By obtaining this papal letter, Maxstoke exposed itself to the following prosecution because Studley had already begun a common law action of trespass; the writ praemunire facias dated 12 July 1412 doubtless issued after the papal letter of 22 April had arrived in England. The plea that Maxstoke had seized the tithes of Aston Cantlow from Studley 'vi et armis' was thoroughly bogus as it entirely ignored the various sentences in Maxstoke's favour as well as the royal grant of 1404. That the action stood, however, enabled Studley to respond to the threat of prosecution for heresy by having the prior of Maxstoke and two of his canons appear in king's bench and another canon and Maxstoke's proctors put out of the king's protection.

Maxstoke's serjeant asked for the writ praemunire facias to be revoked: Maxstoke need not answer Studley because the latter was excommunicate by the archbishop's sentence for its failure to pay damages of 100 marks awarded to Maxstoke at Rome. It was in reply to this argument that Hankford maintained that papal sentences of excommunication were not recognised in common law courts.[212] Although Studley was thus permitted to proceed with its praemunire action, the suit presumably lapsed with the death of Henry IV soon after this discussion.[213] In fact, Maxstoke remained in possession of Aston Cantlow until the Dissolution, although Studley did not renounce its claim until 1493.[214]

KB 27/606, m.31

[*Marginated*] Warr'

Dominus rex mandavit vicecomiti Warr' breve suum clausum in hec verba: Henricus [*etc.*] vicecomiti Warr' salutem. Cum per dominum Edwardum [*as in* 8, *mutatis mutandis* – continetur] ; ac iam intellexerimus quod licet placita de transgressionibus vi et armis factis in regno nostro Anglie ad nos coronam et dignitatem nostram specialiter pertineant, quidam tamen Johannes prior de Maxstok machinans jus nostrum regium enervare et cognicionem que ad curiam nostram pertinet ad aliud examen extra regnum nostrum Anglie trahere, quamplures processus versus Willelmum priorem de Stodley prosecutus fuit et ipsum priorem de Stodley ad respondendum prefato priori de Maxstok in curiis christianitatis tam infra dictum regnum nostrum quam extra de quibusdam transgressionibus eidem priori de Maxstok per prefatum priorem de Stodley ut dicitur factis, quarum cognicio ad nos et coronam nostram pertinet, citari fecit, et quamplura alia nobis et corone nostre in hac parte prejudicialia contra ligeancie sue debitum ibidem fecit et fieri procuravit in nostri contemptum et prejudicium et corone nostre exheredacionis periculum manifestum et ipsius prioris de Stodley

[206] *CPR 1399–1401*, 513, 527; *1401–5*, 399–400; *CPL*, VI, 236.

[207] *CCR 1399–1402*, 496.

[208] E 28/12; *CPR 1401–5*, 399–400; *1405–8*, 260; *VCH Warw*, III, 41; W. Dugdale, *The Antiquities of Warwickshire* (Coventry, 1765), 585–6.

[209] *CPL*, VI, 236–7.

[210] *CCR 1405–9*, 160–1.

[211] *CPL*, VI, 236–7, 279.

[212] Above, 345. In the year book Studley is referred to as 'B' and Maxstoke as 'N': 14 Hen. IV, Hil. 4.

[213] cf. [11].

[214] *VCH Warw*, III, 41.

dampnum non modicum et gravamen et contra leges et consuetudines regni nostri Anglie necnon contra formam ordinacionis et concordie predictarum; nos jura corone nostre regie ac leges et consuetudines predictas illesa, prout vinculo juramenti in coronacione nostra prestiti astringimur, observari ac ordinacionem et concordiam predictas debite execucioni demandari volentes, tibi precepimus quod, si predictus prior de Stodley fecerit te securum de clamio suo prosequendo, tunc per probos et legales homines de balliva tua premunire facias prefatum priorem de Maxstok ac fratrem Johannem Nassyngton fratrem Johannem Atherston et fratrem Thomam Shystoke concanonicos predicti prioris de Maxstok et Robertum Heymere et Robertum Kirkeby juniorem procuratores attornatos executores notarios et manutentores ipsius prioris de Maxstok in hac parte apud Aston Cauntelou quod sint coram nobis a die Sancti Michaelis in xv dies [13 Oct. 1412] ubicumque tunc fuerimus in Anglia ad respondendum nobis de contemptu et prejudicio predictis et prefato priori de Stodley de dampnis et injuriis sibi illatis in hac parte et ad faciendum ulterius et recipiendum quod curia nostra consideraverit in premissis. Et habeas ibi nomina eorum per quos eos premunire feceris et hoc breve, nos de die quo dictam premunicionem sibi feceris sub sigillo tuo distincte et aperte tunc certificans. Teste me ipso apud Westmonasterium xij die julii anno regni nostri terciodecimo.

Ad quem diem coram domino rege apud Westmonasterium venit predictus prior de Stodley per Johannem Corve attornatum suum. Et Bartholomeus Brokesby vicecomes retornavit quod virtute dicti brevis domini regis die dominica proxima ante festum Assumpcionis Beate Marie Virginis ultimo preteritum [14 Aug. 1412] premunire fecit prefatos Johannem priorem de Maxstok ac fratrem Johannem Nassyngton fratrem Johannem Atherston et fratrem Thomam Shistoke concanonicos eiusdem prioris necnon Robertum Heymere et Robertum Kyrkeby juniorem per Willelmum Holt Simonem Felton Willelmum Pakwode et Thomam Pulton probos etc. apud Aston Cauntelou essendos coram domino rege ad prefatam xv^{am} Sancti Michaelis ubicumque etc. ad respondendum domino regi de contemptu et prejudicio supradictis et prefato priori de Stodley de dampnis et injuriis sibi illatis et perpetratis, et ad faciendum ulterius et recipiendum quod curia domini regis consideraverit in hac parte, prout dictum breve domini regis exigit et requirit etc. Quiquidem prior de Maxstok frater Johannes Nassyngton et frater Thomas Shistoke juxta premunicionem predictam sibi in forma predicta factam per Willelmum Waldeby attornatum suum venerunt. Et predicti frater[215] Johannem Atherston Robertus Heymere et Robertus Kirkeby, licet sic premuniti et iiij^{to} die placiti solenniter exacti, non venerunt. Ideo consideratum est quod ipsi ponantur extra proteccionem domini regis etc.,[215] et quod terre et tenementa, bona et catalla sua eidem domini regi sint forisfacta. Et preceptum est vicecomiti quod capiat eos si etc., et salvo etc., ita quod habeat corpora eorum coram domino rege in octabis Sancti Hillarii [20 Jan. 1413] ubicumque etc. ad respondendum tam domino regi quam prefato priori de Stodley de premissis etc. Idem dies datus est tam prefato priori de Stodley quam predicto priori de Maxstok ac[216] fratri Johanni Nassyngton et fratri Thome Shistoke coram domino rege usque ad prefatum terminum etc. in statu quo nunc etc.

[11]

This suit begun in Hilary 1413 is unusually recorded to a conclusion in Michaelmas 1415, being renewed after Henry IV's death and sustained despite failures to produce juries. The lengthy apportionment of damages is interesting in its own right but also because it shows an application of the 1353 statute of praemunire to proceedings in a church court in England even though the statute itself provided only for process in the event of litigation outside the country on issues triable at common law. The plaintiff Strange alleged that he was cited to Rome but also that he was brought before the Canterbury court of audience and there bound over to keep the peace. He was, of course, correct in stating that trespass was a common law issue, and the actual offence with which he was charged in the church courts, threatening violence, did have common law remedies. The defendant Richard was a clerk, however, and violence to clergy was a recognised subject of judicial proceedings in church courts.[217] As Strange also was a clerk, it hardly seems unreasonable of Richard to have had him cited to a church court.

The jury apportioned Strange's damages on the three points of citation to Rome, citation to the Canterbury court, and his binding over, at £20 each, with a further £20 for his costs. The proceedings in the Canterbury court were thus regarded as no less unlawful than the summons to Rome. Strange

215 Interlined.

216 *quam . . . ac* interlined.

217 Above, 345.

actually received only half of these damages. The principal defendant did not appear. His proctor, Master John Forster, presumably practised as a canon lawyer in London.[218] He would thus have been less elusive and doubtless also unwilling to jeopardise a profitable career by failing to answer. His payment of £40 satisfied the plaintiff, who then abandoned his pursuit of the other defendants.

KB 27/607, m.37

[*Marginated*] Midd'
Magister Johannes Forster premunitus fuit ad respondendum tam domino regi quam Johanni Straunge clerico simul cum Johanne Richard clerico et Johanne Neweport capellano de placito cum per dominum Edwardum [*as in* 7 – continetur]; ac iam intellexerit dominus rex nunc quod licet placita de transgressionibus vi et armis factis in regno ipsius regis Anglie ad ipsum regem coronam et dignitatem dicti domini regis specialiter pertineant, predictus tamen Johannes Richard clericus machinans dominum regem et coronam suam regiam exheredare et cognicionem que ad curiam ipsius domini regis pertinet ad aliud examen extra regnum regis Anglie trahere, quamplures processus in curiis christianitatis tam infra regnum ipsius domini regis Anglie quam extra versus predictum Johannem Straunge prosecutus fuit, et ipsum Johannem Straunge ad respondendum in eadem curia[219] christianitatis super huiusmodi transgressionibus citari procuravit et placitum inde ibidem prosecutus fuit et adhuc prosequitur, et sic cognicionem que ad dictam curiam dicti domini regis pertinet in hac parte in predicta curia[220] christianitatis deduci facere nititur viribus suis, et quamplura alia ad ipsum regem[221] et corone sue in hac parte prejudicialia contra ligeancie sue debitum ibidem fecit et fieri procuravit minus juste in domini regis nunc contemptum et prejudicium et corone sue exheredacionis periculum manifestum et ipsius Johannis Straunge dampnum non modicum et gravamen et contra leges et consuetudines regni ipsius domini regis Anglie necnon contra formam ordinacionis et concordie predictarum.

Et unde idem Johannes Straunge qui tam etc. per Johannem Solas attornatum suum queritur quod per dominum Edwardum nuper regem [*as above* – Johannes Richard clericus] versus quem predictus Johannes Straunge declararet, si[222] presens fuisset, machinans [*as above* – citari procuravit], videlicet[223] vicesimo die septembris anno regni regis Henrici quarti post conquestum terciodecimo [1412] apud villam Westmonasterii per quendam Johannem Somenour ad comparendum in curia audiencie domini Thome archiepiscopi Cantuariensis vicesimo septimo die septembris tunc proximo sequenti coram magistro Philippo Morgan auditore causarum in eadem curia apud ecclesiam Sancti Martini in Campis ville Westmonasterii ad respondendum predicto Johanni Richard de diversis transgressionibus sibi per prefatum Johannem Straunge contra pacem domini regis illatis, videlicet de eo quod idem Johannes Straunge sepius minatus fuisset predictum Johannem Richard ad ipsum verberandum vulnerandum et interficiendum, citari procuravit, et eciam idem Johannes Richard predicto vicesimo septimo die in predicta ecclesia Sancti Martini coram auditore predicto propter causas predictas exigebat securitatem pacis de predicto Johanne Straunge, et in eadem curia eodem vicesimo septimo die coram auditore predicto prosequebatur versus ipsum Johannem Straunge de securitate predicta eidem Johanni invenienda etc., et adtunc ibidem citari fecit ipsum Johannem Straunge per predictum Johannem Somenour ad comparendum in curia Romana centesimo die tunc proximo sequenti ad sibi respondendum de premissis. Et sic idem Johannes Richard placitum predictum in forma predicta versus ipsum Johannem Straunge prosecutus fuit et adhuc prosequitur, et sic cognicionem que ad dictam curiam dicti domini regis pertinet in hac parte in predictis curiis christianitatis deduci facere nititur viribus suis, et quamplura alia ad ipsum regem [*as above* – predictarum]. Et tam predictus magister Johannes Forster qui modo comparet quam predictus Johannes Neweport versus quem predictus Johannes Straunge similiter narraret, si presens fuisset, fuerunt tunc ibidem procuratores attornati executores notarii et manutentores ipsius Johannis Richard ad premissa omnia et singula in forma predicta facienda, unde dicit quod deterioratus est et dampnum habet ad valenciam centum librarum. Et inde tam pro domino rege quam pro se ipso producit sectam etc.

Et predictus magister Johannes Forster in propria persona sua venit et defendit omnem contemptum et quicquid etc. Et dicit quod ipse in nullo est culpabilis de aliquibus articulis superius in ipsum per predictum Johannem Straunge interpositis etc. Et de

[218] He may be the John Forster in Emden, *Biog. Reg. Oxford*, II, 708–9.

[219] MS *eadem cur'*; recte *eisdem curiis*?

[220] MS *predicta cur'*.

[221] Recte *alia domino regi*.

[222] Interlined.

[223] *citari . . . videlicet* interlined.

hoc ponit se super patriam etc. Et predictus Johannes Straunge similiter etc. Ideo veniat inde jurata coram domino rege a die Pasche in xv dies [7 May 1413] ubicumque etc. Et qui nec etc. ad recognoscendum etc. Quia tam etc. Idem dies datus est partibus predictis modo comparentibus etc.

Et super hoc venerunt Rogerus Welyley Urianus Seyntper Ricardus Bentley Willelmus Clud omnes de comitatu Salop', et manuceperunt pro predicto magistro Johanne Forster quod ipse non attemptabit nec attemptari procurabit per se nec per alios in curiis christianitatis citra mare neque extra quod in prejudicium domini regis et corone sue aut legum suarum regni Anglie cedere valeat quovismodo, quilibet eorumdem manucaptorum sub pena quadraginta librarum, quasquidem quadraginta libras iidem manucaptores cognoverunt et quilibet eorum pro se cognovit de terris et catallis suis fieri et ad opus domini regis levari si contingat ipsum magistrum Johannem Forster in premissis vel in aliquo premissorum delinquere et inde legitimo modo convinci etc.
[*Marginated*] Manucapcio. Pena xl libras.

Ante quem diem loquela predicta per mortem domini Henrici nuper regis Anglie quarti post conquestum[224] sine die remansit. Et postea, scilicet xij^{o} die maii anno regni regis Henrici quinti post conquestum primo, coram ipso rege apud Westmonasterium venit predictus Johannes Straunge in propria persona sua. Et petit breve ad venire faciendum xxiiij^{or} etc. et eciam breve ad premuniendum predictum magistrum Johannem Forster essendum coram domino rege audiendum juratam predictam si etc. Et ei conceditur etc.

[A jury was called for 8 July 1413, but only the parties came, with John Corve as Forster's attorney. The sheriff was to distrain the twenty-four named jurors to come on 2 November and again for 27 January 1414.]

Et postquam loquela predicta in forma predicta recontinuata fuit, continuato inde processu inter predictum Johannem Straunge et prefatum magistrum Johannem Forster coram domino rege per juratam ponitam inde inter eos in respectu usque in octabis Sancti Martini anno regni regis Henrici quinti post conquestum tercio [25 Nov. 1415] pro defectu juratorum etc.

Ad quem diem coram domino rege apud Westmonasterium venerunt tam predictus Johannes Straunge quam predictus Johannes Forster in propriis personis suis. Et juratores exacti similiter venerunt, qui ad veritatem super premissis dicendam ad hoc electi triati et jurati dicunt super sacramentum suum quod predictus Johannes Forster culpabilis est de omnibus et singulis articulis superius in brevi et declaracione predictis sibi impositis, prout predictus Johannes Straunge per breve et narracionem sua predicta supponit. Et assident dampna ipsius Johannis Straunge in hac parte ad quaterviginti libras. Et super hoc quesitum est per curiam hic a juratoribus predictis que dampna ex predictis dampnis quaterviginti librarum predictus Johannes Straunge sustinuit quoad hoc quod predictus magister Johannes Forster procuravit ipsum Johannem Straunge citari per predictum Johannem Somener ad comparendum in predicta curia audiencie predicti archiepiscopi coram prefato magistro Philippo Morgan auditore causarum in eadem curia ad respondendum prefato Johanni Richard de eo quod predictus Johannes Straunge sepius minatus fuisset predictum Johannem Richard ad ipsum verberandum vulnerandum et interficiendum, qui dicunt super sacramentum suum quod predictus Johannes Straunge ea occasione sustinuit dampna ad viginti libras de predicta summa quaterviginti librarum. Quesitum est eciam a prefatis juratoribus que dampna predictus Johannes Straunge sustinuit pro eo quod predictus Johannes Forster fuit procurator predicti Johannis Richard de eo quod idem Johannes coram auditore predicto exigebat securitatem pacis de prefato Johanne Straunge in forma predicta, et in eadem curia coram ipso auditore prosequebatur versus ipsum Johannem Straunge de securitate predicta eidem Johanni Richard invenienda, qui dicunt super sacramentum suum quod predictus Johannes Straunge ea occasione sustinuit dampna virginti librarum de predicta summa quaterviginti librarum. Et similiter [*membrane 37d*] quesitum est a prefatis juratoribus que dampna predictus Johannes Straunge sustinuit quoad hoc quod predictus magister Johannes Forster fuit procurator predicti Johannis Richard ad citari faciendum ipsum Johannem Straunge per predictum Johannem Somenour ad comparendum in curia Romana in forma predicta ad respondendum eidem Johanni Richard de premissis, quiquidem juratores assident dampna ipsius Johannis Straunge ea occasione ad viginti libras de predicta summa quaterviginti librarum. Quesitum est insuper a prefatis juratoribus que dampna predictus Johannes Straunge sustinuit pro misis et costagiis suis circa sectam suam in hac parte appositis, qui dicunt super sacramentum suum quod predictus Johannes Straunge de eadem summa quaterviginti librarum sustinuit

224 On 20 Mar. 1413.

dampna pro misis et costagiis suis circa sectam suam in hac parte habitis ad viginti libras. Adhuc quesitum est a prefatis juratoribus si contingat aliquod judicium reddi pro predicto Johanni Straunge versus predictum Johannem Forster pro eo quod ipse procuravit ipsum Johannem Straunge citari in forma predicta coram prefato magistro Philippo auditore etc. ad respondendum prefato Johanni Richard de eo quod idem Johannes Straunge sepius minatus fuisset ipsum Johannem Richard ad ipsum verberandum vulnerandum et interficiendum, que dampna ex causa illa eidem Johanni Straunge pro misis et costagiis suis in curia domini regis coram ipso rege habitis de predictis viginti libris generaliter pro costagiis assessis taxare velint, qui dicunt quod ipsi ea occasione pro misis et costagiis predicti Johannis Straunge in curia domini regis coram ipso rege habitis assident dampna eiusdem Johannis ad predictas viginti libras superius per ipsos juratores prius pro misis et costagiis dicti Johannis Straunge in toto assessas. Item quesitum est a prefatis juratoribus que dampna de predictis viginti libris pro costagiis generaliter taxatis taxari velint prefato Johanni Straunge pro misis et costagiis suis, si contingat judicium predictum reddi nisi solummodo pro illa causa quod predictus Johannes Forster fuit procurator in forma predicta quod predictus Johannes Richard exigebat coram prefato auditore securitatem pacis et coram ipso auditore prosequebatur versus predictum Johannem Straunge pro securitate predicta prefato Johanni Richard invenienda, qui dicunt super sacramentum suum quod licet judicium reddi debeat nisi solummodo pro illa causa, tamen ipsi assident dampna predicti Johannis Straunge pro misis et costagiis suis circa sectam suam in curia domini regis coram ipso rege habitis ad easdem viginti libras prius per ipsos juratores in toto et generaliter pro misis et costagiis predicti Johannis Straunge habitis. Item quesitum est a prefatis juratoribus que dampna de predictis dampnis generaliter pro misis et costagiis taxatis prefato Johanni Straunge taxari velint pro misis et costagiis suis coram domino rege habitis, si contingat judicium predictum reddi nisi solomodo pro illa causa quod predictus Johannes Forster fuit procurator predicti Johannis Richard ad citari faciendum predictum Johannem Straunge ad comparendum in forma predicta in curia Romana ad respondendum eidem Johanni Richard de premissis, qui dicunt super sacramentum suum quod licet judicium predictum reddi debeat nisi solomodo pro illa causa, tamen ipsi assident dampna predicti Johannis Straunge pro misis et costagiis suis circa sectam suam ea occasione in curia domini regis coram ipso rege factis et habitis ad predictas et easdem viginti libras prius et generaliter in omnibus causis et articulis predictis in eorum veredicto specificatis pro misis et costagiis ipsius Johannis Straunge taxatis.

Et super hoc predictus Johannes Straunge cognovit se nolle ulterius prosequi versus prefatos Johannem Richard et Johannem Neweport de premissis. Ideo consideratum est quod predictus Johannes Straunge recuperet versus predictum Johannem Forster viginti libras de dampnis predictis, pro eo quod ipse fuit procurator predicti Johannis Richard ad citari faciendum ipsum Johannem Straunge ad comparendum in curia Romana in forma predicta ad respondendum eidem Johanni de hoc unde cognicio pertinet ad curiam regis etc., et eciam viginti libras pro misis et custagiis suis circa sectam suam in hac parte appositis que in tot se attingunt ad quadraginta libras, et idem Johannes Forster capiatur etc. Et similiter prefatus Johannes Forster de predictis quadraginta libris residuis exoneretur etc.
[*Marginated*] Capiatur.
Dampna xl libras.

Idem Johannes Straunge qui tam etc. per attornatum suum predictum optulit se iiij^to^ die[225] versus predictum Johannem Richard clericum et Johannem Neweport capellanum de placito predicto. Et ipsi non venerunt. Et preceptum fuit vicecomiti quod premunire faceret eos. Et vicecomes retornavit quod nichil habent etc. nec sunt inventi etc. Ideo preceptum est vicecomiti sicut prius quod premuniri faceret eos quod sint coram domino rege ad prefatum terminum [7 May 1413] etc. Ante quemquidem terminum loquela predicta per mortem domini Henrici nuper regis Anglie quarti post conquestum sine die remansit. Postea, scilicet xij die maii anno regni regis Henrici quinti post conquestum primo, coram ipso rege apud Westmonasterium venit predictus Johannes Straunge in propria persona sua, et petit breve ad premuniendum predictos Johannem Richard et Johannem Neweport essendos coram ipso[226] domino rege ad respondendum etc. de placito predicto etc. Et ei conceditur etc. Ideo preceptum est vicecomiti quod premuniri faceret eos apud villam Westmonasterii[227] quod sint coram domino rege a die Sancti Johannis Baptiste in xv dies [8 July 1413] ubicumque etc., ita quod loquela etc.

[The sheriff returned that they had not been

225 In Michaelmas 1412. 226 Interlined. 227 *apud villam Westmonasterii* interlined.

found and further writs of praemunire issued for 2 November, and 27 January 1414.]

[12]

All houses of the Cistercian order were exempted by a bull of Alexander IV from payment of tithes on land cultivated by their own members. By the end of the fourteenth century the Cistercians were no longer personally working on their estates but had, like other landed proprietors, leased their lands to farmers. The privilege of exemption from tithes was not allowed in respect of land at farm and incumbents could sue for tithes on farmed land in church courts. In 1398, however, Boniface IX extended the privilege of exemption to Cistercians' estates farmed for periods not exceeding one year; he confirmed this concession in March 1400.[228] Three months later, Henry IV ordered a proclamation forbidding the execution of these bulls as contrary to English law and harmful to the clergy, reducing their means to give hospitality to the people and pay taxes to the king.[229] The statute of 1401 was obviously designed to provide incumbents with a legal process to enforce this prohibition.

In his narration, the vicar of Little Warley stated that the abbot of Coggeshall had granted a farm for two years. No reference has been found to a bull granted solely to Coggeshall at this time and the bulls mentioned by the vicar are presumably those to the Cistercian order. If so, and if the vicar's statement is correct, the abbot's lease exceeded the term allowed by the pope, and the vicar could doubtless have sued for his tithes in a church court. Since he said that he was refused the tithes on 27 June 1406, he must have immediately chosen to take proceedings under the statute, as his writ was returnable on 6 October following.

It may not be a coincidence that earlier that year it was discovered that Coggeshall had neglected to obtain a royal licence when it appropriated the church of Childerditch in 1380. On 5 April 1406 the abbot received a pardon which cost 100 shillings, with the proviso that he made provision for a vicarage and the dispensation of alms.[230] The statute for vicarages of 1391 was thus applied retrospectively.[231]

KB 27/582, m.9

[*Marginated*] Essex
Preceptum fuit vicecomiti (cum in statuto in parliamento domini regis apud Westmonasterium nuper tento edito[232] inter cetera contineatur quod viri religiosi ordinis Cisterciensis regni domini regis Anglie, qui certas bullas quod essent quieti et exonerati de decimis suis de terris tenementis et possessionibus suis ad firmam dimissis aut per alias personas quam per seipsos cultis et occupatis impetraverunt, starent in statu quo ante tempus impetracionis huiusmodi bullarum extiterunt, quodque processus per premunicionem duorum mensium per breve de premunire facias fieret tam versus ipsos ordinis predicti quam omnes alios religiosos et seculares cuiuscumque status vel condicionis fuerint et eorum quemlibet qui dictas bullas in execucionem ponerent vel extunc aliquas huiusmodi bullas de novo impetrarent aut colore earumdem bullarum impetratarum vel impetrandarum avantagium perciperent quovismodo, et si defaltam fecerint vel convicti fuerint incurrerent penas et forisfacturas in statuto de provisoribus anno regni domini Ricardi nuper regis Anglie secundi post conquestum terciodecimo edito contentas;[233] ac intellexerimus quod cum Rogerus Haldanby persona ecclesie de Estwarleye habere debeat ipseque et omnes predecessores sui persone ecclesie predicte ut de jure eiusdem ecclesie a tempore cuius contrarii memoria non existit successive habere consueverint omnimodas decimas de quibuscumque locis infra fines et limites parochie ecclesie sue predicte provenientes, quidam Johannes abbas de Coggeshale predicti ordinis Cisterciensis statuta predicta seu penas in eisdem contentas minime ponderans, quasdam bullas quod ipse et successores sui abbates abbatie predicte de huiusmodi decimis suis de terris tenementis et possessionibus suis ad firmam dimissis aut per alias personas quam per seipsos cultis et occupatis quieti essent et exonerati sibi a sede apostolica impetravit, et easdem bullas in execucionem poni fecit ac decimas de certis pratis ac aliis terris tenementis et possessionibus suis in predicta villa de Estwarleye per tempus non modicum provenientes et ad prefatum Rogerum ut de jure ecclesie sue predicte mere pertinentes colore bullarum predictarum detinuerit et adhuc detinet, easdem decimas predicto Rogero dare seu sibi inde satisfacere

228 *CPL*, IV, 40, 66; V, 161, 325, 516.
229 *CCR 1399–1402*, 146.
230 *CPR 1405–8*, 166; *VCH Essex*, II, 126.
231 See [14], below, 385.
232 2 Hen. IV, c.4.
233 See below, nn. 298, 302.

penitus recusando, sicque idem abbas avantagium bullarum predictarum percepit et percipere nititur viribus suis in domini regis contemptum et prejudicium et ipsius Rogeri grave dampnum ac contra vim formam et effectum dicti statuti in dicto parliamento domini regis editi; dominus rex statutum predictum inviolabiliter observari et illud impugnantes juxta eorum demerita castigari facere volens et puniri) quod per probos etc. premunire faceret prefatum abbatem ac fratrem Johannem Haverell commonachum eiusdem domus magistrum Johannem Fynchyngfeld et Radulphum Dyvys, qui bullas predictas in execucionem posuerunt ut dicitur, quod essent coram domino rege ad hunc diem, scilicet in octabis Sancti Michaelis [6 Oct. 1406], ubicumque etc. ad respondendum tam domino regi de contemptu et prejudicio predictis quam prefato Rogero de dampnis et injuriis sibi in premissis perpetratis et ad faciendum ulterius etc.

Ad quem diem coram domino rege apud Westmonasterium vicecomes retornavit quod virtute brevis predicti die lune proxima post festum Sancti Petri quod dicitur advincula [2 Aug. 1406] premunire fecit prefatos abbatem et fratrem Johannem Haverell magistrum Johannem Fynchyngfeld et Radulphum quod essent coram domino rege ad prefatum terminum etc. ad respondendum faciendum et recipiendum quod breve domini regis inde exigit et requirit per Johannem Cok et Johannem Nevard. Et modo ad eundem diem coram domino rege apud Westmonasterium venit predictus Rogerus Haldanby in propria persona sua. Et predicti abbas frater Johannes Haverell magister Johannes Fynchyngfeld et Radulphus in personis suis similiter venerunt.

Et super hoc predictus Rogerus tam pro domino rege quam pro seipso queritur quod cum in parliamento [*as above* – contentas]; ac cum prefatus Rogerus habere debeat ipseque et omnes predecessores sui persone ecclesie de Estwarley predicte [*as above*[234] – ponderans] die[235] in festo Sancti Michaelis archangeli anno regni regis Henrici quarti post conquestum sexto [29 Sept. 1405] dimisit sex[236] acras terre [et] triginta acras prati ad firmam cuidam Radulpho Dyvys ac alia terras et tenementa in Estwarleye de terris tenementis et possessionibus suis habenda a dicto festo Sancti Michaelis usque ad finem duorum annorum extunc proximo sequentium, quequidem decem acre terre et triginta acre prati sunt infra fines et limites parochie predicte ecclesie de Estwarleye, ac postea [quando] predictus Rogerus peciit decimas de predicto Radulpho Dyvys vicesimo septimo die junii anno regni dicti domini regis nunc septimo [1406] apud predictam villam de Estwarleye de feno eodem anno septimo crescenti in dictis triginta acris prati et avenis crescentibus eodem anno in dictis decem acris terre, predictus Radulphus per preceptum predictorum abbatis fratris Johannis Haverell et Johannis Fynchyngfeld dictas decimas eodem die in eadem villa solvere recusavit, quodquidem preceptum factum fuit virtute bullarum predictarum in predicto brevi contentarum, et sic predicti abbas frater Johannes Haverell Johannes Fynchyngfeld et Radulphus dictas bullas in execucionem posuerunt sicque idem abbas avantagium bullarum predictarum percepit et percipere nititur viribus suis in domini regis contemptum et prejudicium et contra vim formam et effectum dicti statuti in dicto parliamento domini regis editi, unde dicit quod deterioratus est et dampnum habet ad valenciam mille librarum. Et inde tam pro domino rege quam pro se ipso producit sectam etc.

[*Membrane 9d*] Et predicti abbas de Coggeshale et frater Johannes Haverell magister Johannes Fynchyngfeld et Radulphus veniunt et defendunt omnem injuriam et contemptum et quicquid etc. Et predictus frater Johannes Haverell dicit quod ipse est commonachus predicti abbatis et per breve predictum supponitur ipsum fratrem Johannem Haverell fore commonachum eiusdem domus et petit judicium de brevi etc. Et predictus Rogerus petit judicium si breve suum non sit satisbonum etc. Et predicti magister Johannes Fynchyngfeld et Radulphus Dyvys dicunt quod ipsi in nullo sunt inde culpabiles. Et de hoc ponunt se super patriam etc. Et predictus Rogerus similiter etc.

Et predictus abbas protestando quod non cognovit quod ipse unquam tales bullas prout predictus Rogerus superius per breve suum supponit sibi a sede apostolica impetravit, nec quod predictus Rogerus seu aliquis[237] predecessorum suorum unquam fuerunt seisiti de decimis predictarum decem acrarum terre et triginta acrarum prati, nec quod idem abbas seu aliqui predecessorum suorum unquam decimas de terris et prato predictis alicui persone ecclesie predicte solvit, pro placito dicit quod non precepit prefato Radulpho quod ipse decimas predictas solvere

234 With *predictus abbas* for *quidam Johannes abbas de Coggeshale*.

235 Followed by erasure of 0.5 inches.

236 Recte *decem*: see below.

237 Interlined.

non deberet neque idem Radulphus illas solvere recusavit virtute precepti predicti abbatis, nec posuit bullas aliquas in execucionem modo et forma quibus per predictum Rogerum supponitur. Et de hoc ponit se super patriam etc. Et predictus Rogerus similiter etc. Ideo veniat inde jurata coram domino rege in crastino Animarum [3 Nov. 1406] ubicumque etc. et qui nec etc. ad recognoscendum etc. Quia tam etc. Idem dies datus est partibus predictis etc.

Et sciendum quod predicti abbas frater Johannes et magister Johannes hic in curia Deo corporale prestiterunt sacramentum quod ipsi nec eorum aliquis attemptabunt seu attemptabit aliquid in curia christianitatis citra mare vel extra quod in lesionem statutorum domini regis in huiusmodi casu provisorum cedere valeat quovismodo etc. Et super hoc dies datus est tam prefato Rogero quam prefato fratri Johanni Haverell commonacho usque ad prefatum terminum de judicio suo inde audiendo de eo quod idem commonachus supra in cassacionem brevis predicti placitavit etc.

Ad quem diem coram domino rege apud Westmonasterium venerunt tam predictus Rogerus in propria persona sua quam predictus commonachus in propria persona sua. Et super hoc dies datus est eis coram domino rege usque in octabis Sancti Martini [18 Nov. 1406] de judicio suo audiendo de eo quod ipsi in judicium supra placitaverunt etc.

Ad quem diem coram domino rege apud Westmonasterium venerunt tam predictus Rogerus in propria persona sua quam predictus commonachus in propria persona sua. Et super hoc dies datus est eis coram domino rege in octabis Sancti Hillarii [20 Jan. 1407] de judicio suo audiendo in forma predicta etc.

[13]

This suit in Easter 1410 arose under the statute of 1406 extending to all religious houses the prohibition from refusal to pay tithes on land at farm by authority of papal letters not executed before 22 June 1377. In his narration the plaintiff refers to bulls granted by Pope Gregory, whose number is omitted. He is called 'late pope', a description which would have been applied to Gregory XII after his deposition by the council of Pisa in 1409. Gregory XII is not known to have granted a bull for the London Charterhouse. Its register mentions a bull of privileges from Gregory XI (1371–78), though no reference is made to tithes. The plaintiff also said, however, that the bull of exemption had been granted to the previous prior, i.e. John Luscote (1370–98).[238] It seems probable, therefore, that the exemption had been enjoyed before the limiting date set by the statute, and this was why the plaintiff abandoned his suit.

KB 27/596, m.71

[*Marginated*] Midd'
Preceptum fuit vicecomiti (cum in statuto in parliamento domini regis nunc apud Westmonasterium anno regni sui septimo tento inter cetera ordinatum sit et statutum[239] quod nulla persona religiosa seu secularis cuiuscumque status seu condicionis fuerit colore aliquarum bullarum privilegia de essendo quieta de decimis ad ecclesias parochiales prebendas hospitalia vel vicarias pertinentibus continencium ante annum regni domini Ricardi nuper regis Anglie secundi post conquestum primum vel postea impetratarum minime executarum huiusmodi bullas sic impetratas sive impetrandas exequatur, et quod si extunc aliqua persona religiosa seu secularis cuiuscumque status seu condicionis fuerit colore huiusmodi bullarum impediat aliquas personas ecclesiasticas prebendarios custodes hospitalium vel vicarios ita quod ipsi decimas sibi et beneficiis suis spectantes percipere et eis gaudere non possint, quod talis impeditorum tales processus et penam incurrat prout ordinatum est per statutum versus ipsos de ordine Cisterciensi anno regni domini regis nunc secundo editum,[240] prout in eodem statuto in parliamento domini regis predicto anno septimo edito plenius continetur; iamque intellexerit dominus rex quod licet Walterus Lynton ⟨non prosequitur⟩[241] magister ordinis de Burton Sancti Lazari in Anglia custos hospitalis Sancti Egidii extra London' racione custodie ipsius hospitalis habuerit, ipseque et omnes predecessores sui custodes eiusdem hospitalis a tempore quo non extat memoria ut de jure dicti hospitalis habere consueverint, omnimodas decimas tam majores quam minores de manerio de Blemondesbury ac de nutrimentis animalium et aliis rebus ibidem necnon de terris pratis et aliis possessionibus quibuscumque infra fines et limites parochie ecclesie parochialis infra idem hospitale situate existentibus pacifice et quiete; quidam tamen Johannes prior domus Salu-

[238] W. St J. Hope, *The History of the London Charterhouse* (London, 1925), 51, 147.

[239] 7 Hen. IV, c.6, here fully rehearsed.

[240] See [12].

[241] Marginated. There is a cross over *Walterus.*

tacionis Beate Marie prope London' Cartusiensis ordinis statutum predictum in parliamento domini regis anno septimo editum seu penam in eodem contentam minime ponderans, colore quarumdam bullarum nuper priori domus predicte predecessori predicti nunc prioris ac confratribus suis et eorum successoribus per tunc dominum summum pontificem confactarum privilegia ipsos de essendo quietos de decimis continencium et ante predictum annum regni regis Ricardi primum minime executarum, prefatum magistrum quominus ipse huiusmodi[242] decimas de manerio terris pratis et possessionibus predictis eidem magistro et hospitali suo predicto spectantes percipere et eis gaudere possit per tempus non modicum impedivit ac indies impedire non desistit, in domini regis nunc contemptum et ipsius magistri dampnum non modicum et gravamen ac contra formam et effectum ordinacionis et statuti in parliamento domini regis predicto anno septimo editorum; dominus rex eadem ordinacionem et statutum in parliamento domini regis predicto anno septimo edita inviolabiliter observari et ea impugnan[te]s juxta eorum demerita castigari facere volens et puniri) quod premunire faceret prefatum priorem apud parochiam Sancti Egidii extra barram Veteris Templi London' quod esset coram domino rege ad hunc diem, scilicet a die Pasche in unum mensem ultimo preteritum [20 Apr. 1410], ubicumque etc. ad respondendum tam domino regi de contemptu predicto quam prefato magistro de dampnis et injuriis sibi illatis in hac parte et ad faciendum ulterius et recipiendum quod curia domini regis consideraret in premissis.

Ad quem diem coram domino rege apud Westmonasterium venit predictus magister in propria persona sua. Et vicecomes retornavit quod virtute brevis predicti scire fecit prefato priori decimo octavo die februarii ultimo preterito apud parochiam Sancti Egidii extra barram Veteris Templi London' quod esset coram domino rege ad prefatum terminum etc. ad faciendum respondendum et recipiendum quod breve predictum in se exigebat et requirebat secundum vim et effectum eiusdem brevis per Johannem Frenssch Ricardum Mordon Willelmum Ryston et Johannem Lilleston probos et legales homines etc. Quiquidem prior juxta premunicionem ei in hac parte factam [venit] per Johannem Corve attornatum suum.

Et super hoc predictus magister dicit quod predictus prior statutum predictum in parliamento domini regis nunc anno septimo supradicto editum seu penam in eodem minime ponderans, colore quarumdam bullarum per dominum Gregorium[243] nuper dominum summum pontificem prefato[244] nuper priori domus predicte predecessori predicti nunc prioris ac confratribus suis et eorum successoribus per ipsum nuper summum pontificem confactarum privilegia ipsos de essendo quietos de decimis continencium et ante predictum annum regni nuper regis Ricardi primum minime executarum prefatum magistrum quominus ipse huiusmodi decimas,[245] videlicet decimas frumenti ordei avenarum fabarum pisarum messarum feni pasture et herbarum venditarum in herbis necnon de decimis de nutrimentis animalium ut de vitulis porcellis agnis lanis caseo butiro lacte ovis pullis gallinarum et ancarum pullis columbarum serecis pomis piris prunis avelanis nucibus melle oleribus porris allea capis canobo lino et omnibus aliis rebus decimalibus de manerio de Blemondesbury continente[246] sexviginti acras terre et sexdecim acras prati infra eundem manerium, et triginta acras terre et sex acras prati extra manerium predictum infra fines et limites parochie ecclesie parochialis Sancti Egidii infra idem hospitale situate existentes, per prefatum nunc priorem habere poterit a festo Natalis Domini anno regni domini regis nunc quinto [25 Dec. 1403] usque diem impetracionis brevis originalis inde, videlicet tercium diem februarii anno ipsius regis nunc undecimo [1410] impedivit ac indies impedire non desistit in domini regis contemptum, unde idem magister dicit quod deterioratus est et dampnum habet ad valenciam quadringintarum librarum. Et inde tam pro domino rege quam pro se ipso producit sectam etc.

Et predictus prior defendit omnem contemptum. Et quicquid etc. Et petit inde diem loquendi etc. Et ei conceditur. Et super hoc dies datus est partibus predictis usque in octabis Sancte Trinitatis [25 May 1410] ubicumque etc. in statu quo nunc etc.

Ad quem diem predictus Walterus Lynton, licet quarto die placiti solempniter exactus, non venit. Ideo ipse et plegii sui de prosequendo, videlicet Robertus Pyk et Johannes Morden, in misericordia etc.

[*Marginated*] Misericordia.

[14]

The statute of provisors of 1365 protected the ecclesiastical patronage of the king and other lay

242 Repeated.

243 Space of one inch: see preface to this case.

244 Interlined.

245 Recte *decimis*.

246 Recte *continenti*.

patrons, a description which could not be claimed in this suit by the prior of Launceston. The statute also allowed remedy against papal provisions to all benefices and other revenues appropriated to cathedrals and religious houses provided that these appropriations had not been annulled.[247] This clause of the statute, as well as its forerunner on lay patronage, was cited in the cause of summons; it likewise appears in the next case [15], also about a monastic benefice, but it is omitted when the action concerned a cathedral benefice [17]. The prior's argument was that the vicarage of Liskeard had been appropriated to his house by papal authority and with royal licence 'long before' John Warren entered by provision on 6 June 1400. In reality, the bull was dated 14 June 1398 and it allowed the appropriation to be made when the vicarage next became vacant, which occurred on 29 January following.[248]

Shortly before Warren's arrival, the prior had fended off a royal presentation to the church. Simon Ganstead had himself presented in October 1399; his letters patent were not warranted, a suspicious feature in the case of a chancery clerk. The prior opposed the presentation on the grounds that Launceston had appropriated the rectory before 1278, and as Ganstead remarkably failed to appear in chancery to answer the scire facias the presentation was revoked on 6 February 1400.[249] In the suit against Warren, the appropriation cited by the prior was of much more recent date than that claimed in Ganstead's case.

The record here, dating from Michaelmas 1400, opens with a notice of the attachment of the defendants, followed by the cause rehearsed from the writ of praemunire facias. There was thus no need to note that pledges for prosecution were required and given, as the statute enjoined. These were doubtless given before the attachment was ordered, probably in the previous term as the prior's citation to Rome was served on 6 June.

Warren's reply, made at an adjourned hearing on 17 April 1401, was that the pope had revoked the appropriation by a bull dated 17 January 1400. He anticipated the prior's rejoinder that the appropriation had been effected before this date by claiming that the prior had not met the condition of the royal licence, namely that alms should be assigned for the poor of the parish, a requirement made by a statute of 1391 in respect of all parish churches subsequently appropriated.[250] The prior rejoined that provision had been made for the poor, Warren denied this at a further hearing on 9 April 1402, and it was to determine this issue as well as the prior's plea that a jury was called.

Warren was a young canon lawyer, probably still at Oxford, and his conduct in this case proved the quality which was to win him a distinguished career as an ecclesiastical judge and administrator.[251] In the interval allowed by the court he secured another title to the vicarage despite his undertaking to do nothing to prejudice the case. He persuaded the archbishop of Canterbury that the right to present had lapsed to him as metropolitan, and on 19 January 1401 an enquiry in the diocese confirmed the archbishop's right and so Warren was collated to Liskeard.[252] The prior meanwhile petitioned the pope and obtained a revocation of the annulment of the appropriation.[253] Warren must have known this bull was on its way when the case in king's bench resumed on 17 April 1401, although the prior was unable or chose not to produce it then, and this was probably another reason why Warren raised the matter of alms for the poor. His knowledge of the bull by this stage is certain enough because on 9 May the pope cancelled the revocation and confirmed Warren's provision. The prior continued his suit at Rome and on 12 September Warren received the licence of his bishop, who was chancellor of England, to go there to defend his title to the vicarage.[254]

The record shows no conclusion to the suit. In fact the matter was settled in parliament in the autumn of 1402. A petition of the commons complained that the statute for vicarages was being ignored by religious houses which were appropriating

[247] The second statute of provisors: 38 Edw. III, stat. 2, cc.1, 2.

[248] *CPL*, V, 156; *Reg. Stafford*, 184.

[249] *CPR 1399–1401*, 11, 183; Foss, *Judges of England*, IV, 320. For another instance of non-warranty, see above, 350.

[250] 15 Ric. II, c.6. The licence, dated 7 Nov. 1398, is mistakenly shown in *CPR 1396–9*, 447, as allowing appropriation of the *churches* of Liskeard, Linkinhorne and Talland. The roll (C 66/351, m.35) and the warrant for these letters patent (C 81/577, no. 12456) describe the benefices as *vicarages*; in the roll, the margin has *De vicariis appropriandis*.

[251] Emden, *Biog. Reg. Oxford*, III, 1996.

[252] *Reg. Stafford*, 184.

[253] *CPL*, V, 357–8, undated but in 12 Boniface IX, so after 9 Nov. 1400.

[254] ibid., 391, 591–2; *Reg. Stafford*, 237; *Hdbk Brit. Chron.*, 85.

vicarages so that, instead of being served by secular priests instituted as vicars, parish churches were now having monks, canons or stipendiary priests exercising the cure of souls. The king's reply was to confirm the statute of 1391 and announce that all appropriations of vicarages made since 1377, even with royal licence, were to be annulled. The prior of Launceston had intended to appropriate the vicarages of Liskeard, Linkinhorne and Talland, three churches which had been appropriated since the thirteenth century and served by secular priests as vicars.[255] The people of these three parishes also petitioned in this parliament against the appropriation of their vicarages; the result would have deprived them of the resident ministry and hospitality of secular vicars, and they had no wish to be served by Augustinian canons. The archbishop of Canterbury and his suffragans, they said, had agreed in a recent convocation that the prior's purpose was illegal and they had so informed the pope, but the prior had illicitly sent great sums to Rome to support his cause. The king's answer was a reference to the adequate remedy provided in his reply to the more general petition.[256] Warren's tenure of the vicarage was thus secured.[257]

KB 27/558, m.55

[*Marginated*] Cornub'

Johannes Waryn clericus Walterus Dolbere clericus Johannes Cryk Johannes Fursdon et Willelmus Garrek attachiati fuerunt ad respondendum tam domino regi quam priori de Launceston de placito quare cum in statuto in parliamento domini Edwardi nuper regis Anglie avi domini regis nunc apud Westmonasterium nuper tento de communi consilio eiusdem avi domini regis inter alia provisum fuisset et ordinatum[258] quod omnes illi qui impetraverint in curia Romana decanatus archidiaconatus prepositu ras seu alias dignitates officia capellas vel alia beneficia ecclesiastica quecumque ad collacionem donacionem presentacionem vel disposicionem ipsius avi domini regis vel alterius laicalis patroni de regno suo spectancia, ac eciam omnes impetratores in curia predicta ecclesiarum capellarum officiorum beneficiorum ecclesiasticorum pensionum seu reddituum ecclesiis cathedralibus seu collegiatis abbatiis prioratibus cantariis hospitalibus aut aliis exiliis[259] domibus mortificatorum et appropriatorum priusquam appropriaciones et mortificaciones huiusmodi per debitum processum cassate et adnullate fuerint,[260] vel qui impetraverint extunc huiusmodi beneficia[261] per que prejudicium dampnum vel impeticio fuerit vel extunc fieri posset eidem avo domini regis vel subditis suis in personis hereditatibus possessionibus juribus aut bonis quibuscumque vel legibus usibus custumiis franchesiis et libertatibus eiusdem regni et corone sue, una cum omnibus manutentoribus conciliariis abettatoribus et aliis sibi auxiliantibus et fautoribus scienter, tam ad sectam ipsius avi domini regis quam partis seu alterius cuiuscumque de regno predicto invenientis plegium et securitatem de prosequendo contra eos in isto casu arestarentur et caperentur[262] per vicecomites locorum justiciarios in sessionibus suis deputatos ballivos et alios ministros ipsius avi domini regis, et per bonam et sufficientem manucapcionem replegiamentum ballium aut alios plegios[263] ad cicius quo fieri posset eidem avo domini regis et concilio suo presentarentur ad commorandum standum recto et recipiendum quod lex suaderet in hac parte, et si de aliquibus premissorum convicti forent haberent penam in statuto anno regni sui Anglie vicesimo quinto edito contentam,[264] et [265] si alique persone diffamate vel suspecte de huiusmodi impetracionibus prosecucionibus gravaminibus vel interprisis extra dictum regnum vel infra existentes non possent attachiari nec arestari in propriis personis suis et se

[255] *Taxatio Ecclesiastica . . . circa 1291*, ed. S. Ayscough and J. Caley (RC, 1802), 147.

[256] *RP*, III, 499–500, 505.

[257] *Reg. Stafford*, 364–5.

[258] Here is omitted citation of the first category of persons listed in the statute, viz those obtaining personal citations of the king and his subjects to the papal court on issues triable at common law: *SR*, I, 385–7. For a suit by the earl of Arundel against the bishop of Chichester under this clause in 1365, see *King's Bench*, VI, 143–5. Graves in *Haskins Anniversary Essays*, 76–7, mistakenly states that this action was under the statute of 1353.

[259] Interlined here and in repetition of statute below.

[260] Here omitting the statute's category of persons obtaining by provision dignities, offices, hospitals and benefices already occupied by natives having reasonable title.

[261] i.e. those named in the preceding note.

[262] cf. statute: 'en ceo caas soient toutes les dites persones diffames et suspectes violenment des tiels impetracions pursuites ou grevances arestuz et pris' (then continuing as above).

[263] Interlined; *traderentur et* omitted: cf. below, n.325.

[264] Omitting 'que commence Au parlement somons a Westm' etc.' (viz 25 Edw. III, stat. 5: *SR*, I, 319). The penalties were exclusion from the king's protection and consequent exposure to treatment as an enemy by any subject: c.22. This measure supplemented the first statute of provisors: 25 Edw. III, stat. 4.

[265] Here c.2 of statute begins.

non presentarent coram ipso avo domini regis et concilio suo infra duos menses proximo postquam super hoc forent premuniti in locis suis si aliqua loca haberent vel in locis inter eos in debata existentibus[266] vel aliquibus curiis ipsius avi domini regis vel comitatibus vel coram justiciariis suis in sessionibus suis vel alias sufficienter ad respondendum eidem avo domini regis et parti et ad commorandum et standum legi in isto casu coram ipso avo domini regis et concilio suo, punirentur per modum et formam in statuto anno regni sui Anglie vicesimo septimo edito contentam[267] et aliter sicut eidem avo domini regis et dicto concilio suo videretur faciendum absque gracia perdonacione seu remissione alicui eorum per dictum avum domini regis facienda sine voluntate et assensu partis que se probaret esse gravatam et nisi debitam ei facerent satisfaccionem in illo casu, prout in provisione et ordinacione predictis plenius continetur; iamque dominus rex intellexerit quod predictus Johannes Waryn provisionem et ordinacionem predictas minime ponderans quandam provisonem de vicaria de Leskyret prioratui de Lanceston debite appropriata, quamquidem vicariam dilecti domino regi in Christo prior et conventus prioratus predicti in proprios usus a diu est absque cassacione seu adnullacione appropriacionis eiusdem pacifice tenuerunt, sibi a sede apostolica fieri procuravit et quasdam litteras bullatas sibi inde factas infra regnum domini regis Anglie execucioni demandandas deferri fecit, ac quamplures processus versus prefatum priorem pretextu provisionis huiusmodi tam infra regnum domini regis Anglie quam extra prosecutus fuit et indies prosequitur, et quamplura alia domino regi et corone sue prejudicialia in hac parte fecit et fieri procuravit, in domini regis contemptum et prejudicium et ipsius prioris dampnum non modicum et gravamen ac contra formam et effectum provisionis et ordinacionis predictarum.

Et unde idem prior per Hugonem Holgot attornatum suum queritur quod cum in statuto [*as above* – continetur] ; iamque intellexerit dominus rex [quod] cum sanctissimum pater Bonifacius papa modernus ex proprio motu et libera voluntate suis per bullas suas apostolicas incorporaverit univerit et annexerit vicariam de Leskyret priori de Lanceston et eiusdem loci conventui habendam et tenendam eisdem priori et conventui[268] et successoribus suis imperpetuum, cuiusquidem vicarie ecclesiam iidem prior et conventus per nomen prioris et conventus prioratus Sancti Stephani de Lanceston et predecessorum suorum ordinis Sancti Augustini Exoniensis diocesis auctoritate apostolica a tempore quo memoria non existit habuerunt et tenuerunt et adhuc tenent in proprios usus pacifice et quiete, ad quamquidem vicariam quidam Henricus Frend capellanus per quendam Thomam Burdon tunc temporis priorem de Lanceston verum patronum eiusdem vicarie predecessorem predicti nunc prioris fuerat presentatus institutus et inductus in eadem ac ipsam vicariam per non modica tempora virtute dicte presentacionis pacifice et quiete possidebat, cuiusquidem vicarie dominus Ricardus nuper rex Anglie secundus post conquestum licenciam appropriacionis inde per litteras suas patentes dederit et concesserit prefato nunc priori et quod ipse vicariam predictam sibi et successoribus suis sic incorporatam unitam et annexam appropriare et eam sic appropriatam incorporatam unitam et annexam in proprios usus habere et tenere possit sibi et successoribus suis juxta vim formam et effectum bullarum apostolicarum predictarum imperpetuum, quocumque statuto in contrario edito non obstante, prout tam[269] in bullis apostolicis quam in litteris prefati nuper regis Ricardi patentibus curie hic ostensis plenius continetur, proviso semper quod quedam competens summa argenti juxta discrecionem loci illius ordinarii ordinaretur et assignaretur de fructibus et proficuis vicarie predicte per prefatos priorem et successores suos annuatim solvenda et destribuenda[270] inter pauperes parochianos eiusdem vicarie juxta formam statuti in consimili casu provisi, quiquidem prior quandam summam pecunie centum solidorum Edmundo Exoniensi episcopo loci illius ordinario et plus secundum eius discrecionem optulit inter pauperes parochianos vicarie predicte in forma predicta destribuendam[271] apud Leskyret annuatim, quam ipse adtunc fuit et adhuc paratus est solvere et distribuere secundum discrecionem ordinarii predicti. Et postea predictus Henricus Frend vicariam predictam [*membrane 55d*] ecclesie predicte apud Lanceston resignavit, virtute cuius resignacionis dicta

266 *vel in locis . . . existentibus* not in statute; presumably adopted from writ under statute of praemunire: see [7]. Nor are these words in writs in [15] and [17].

267 Recte *contentos.* Omitting 'que commence Nostre seignur le roi de lassent et a la priere etc.' (viz statute of praemunire of 1365: 27 Edw. III, stat. 1, c.1).

268 *et conventui* interlined.

269 Interlined.

270 Recte *distribuenda.*

271 Recte *distribuendam.*

vicaria vacavit. Et predictus prior qui nunc est possessionem vicarie predicte tam occasione bullarum apostolicarum predictarum et appropriacionis eiusdem quam pretextu litterarum prefati nuper regis Ricardi patencium inde sibi concessarum diu habuit et optinuit, quousque predictus Johannes Waryn provisionem et ordinacionem predictas minime ponderans quandam provisionem de vicaria predicta prioratui de Lanceston debite in forma predicta appropriata, quam predictus prior et conventus prioratus predicti in proprios usus a diu est absque cassacione seu adnullacione appropriacionis eiusdem pacifice tenuerunt, eidem Johanni a sede apostolica fieri procuravit et quasdam litteras bullatas sibi inde factas infra regnum Anglie execucioni demandandas deferri fecit et corporalem possessionem in eadem vicaria pretextu bullarum provisionis sue predicte die dominica in festo Pentecostes anno regni domini regis nunc primo [6 June 1400] cepit et optinuit ac quamplures processus versus ipsum priorem pretextu provisionis huiusmodi, videlicet citari fecit ipsum priorem apud Leskyret dicto die dominica anno regni regis nunc primo supradicto ibidem ad comparendum coram loci illius ordinario decimo die tunc proximo sequente ac eciam in curia Romana centesimo die tunc proximo sequente ad respondendum ad ea que ex parte dicti Johannis dicto priori ibidem obicerentur, tam infra regnum Anglie quam extra in forma predicta prosecutus fuit et indies prosequitur contra vim formam et effectum provisionis ac statuti et ordinacionis predictorum. Et predictus[272] Walterus Dolbere clericus Johannes Cryke Johannes Fursdon et Willelmus Garrek tunc ibidem fuerunt die et anno predictis manutentores conciliarii abettatores auxiliantes et fautores ipsius Johannis Waryn in hac parte, et quamplura alia tam domino regi et corone sue prejudicialia quam prefato priori in hac parte dampnosa, videlicet fructus decimas oblaciones et alia quecumque proficua dicte vicarie que eidem priori pertinent ceperunt et asportaverunt et ea fieri procuraverunt in domini regis contemptum et prejudicium, unde dicit quod deterioratus est et dampnum habet ad valenciam mille librarum. Et inde tam pro domino rege quam pro se ipso producit sectam etc.

Et predicti Johannes Waryn Walterus Johannes Cryke Johannes Fursdon et Willelmus Garrek in propriis personis suis venerunt et defenderunt omnem contemptum. Et quicquid etc. Et predicti Walterus Johannes Cryke Johannes Fursdon et Willelmus Garrek dicunt quod ipsi non fuerunt manutentores consiliarii abettatores auxiliantes et fautores predicti Johannis Waryn in forma predicta nec fructus decimas oblaciones seu alia quecumque proficua predicte vicarie ceperunt et asportaverunt seu ea fieri procuraverunt, prout predictus prior supra per breve et narracionem sua supponit. Et hoc parati sunt verificare per patriam etc.

Et predictus prior qui tam pro domino rege quam pro se ipso sequitur dicit quod predicti Walterus Johannes Cryke[273] Johannes Fursdon et Willelmus Garrek fuerunt manutentores consiliarii abbettatores auxiliantes et fautores predicti Johannis Waryn et fructus decimas oblaciones et alia quecumque proficua eiusdem vicarie ceperunt et asportaverunt et ea fieri procuraverunt, prout ipse supra per breve et narracionem sua supponit. Et hoc paratus est tam pro domino rege quam pro se ipso verificare per patriam etc. Et predicti Walterus Johannes Cryke Johannes Fursdon et Willelmus Garrek similiter etc. Ideo veniat inde jurata coram domino rege in octabis Sancti Hillarii [20 Jan. 1401] ubicumque etc. Et qui nec etc. ad recognoscendum etc. Quia tam etc.

Et predictus Johannes Waryn petit inde diem loquendi usque ad prefatum termimum etc. Et ei conceditur etc. Idem dies datus est tam prefato priori qui etc. quam predictis Waltero Johanni Cryk Johanni Fursdon et Willelmo etc. Et super hoc tam predictus Johannes Waryn quam quilibet predictorum Walteri Johannis Cryke Johannis Fursdon et Willelmi, tactis sacrosanctis evangeliis Dei, corporaliter prestiterunt sacramentum quod non temptarent nec temptari procurarent citra mare seu extra[274] aliquid in lesionem corone domini regis aut legum suarum prejudicium quoquomodo, et si quid in contrarium premissorum ante hec tempora fecerint seu presumpserint ea occasione renunciarent et recusarent imperpetuum etc.

Ad quem diem coram domino rege apud Westmonasterium venerunt tam predictus prior qui etc. per attornatum suum[275] quam predicti Walterus Johannes Cryke Johannes Fursdon et Willelmus Garrek per Johannem Lopynford attornatum suum. Et vicecomes non misit inde breve etc. Et predictus Johannes Waryn similiter in propria persona sua venit. Et preceptum est vicecomiti sicut prius quod veniat inde jurata coram domino rege a die Pasche in xv dies [17 Apr. 1401] ubicumque etc. Et qui nec etc. ad recognoscendum etc. Quia tam etc. Et predictus Johannes Waryn ut prius petit inde diem loquendi usque ad prefatum terminum etc. Et ei

272 Recte *predicti.*

273 Interlined.

274 *citra . . . extra* interlined.

275 *per . . . suum* interlined.

conceditur etc. Idem dies datus est tam prefato priori qui etc. quam predictis Waltero Johanni Cryke Johanni Fursdon et Willelmo etc.

Ad quem diem coram domino rege apud Westmonasterium venerunt tam predictus prior qui etc. per attornatum suum predictum quam predicti Walterus Johannes Cryke Johannes Fursdon et Willelmus Garrek per attornatum suum predictum. Et predictus Johannes Waryn in propria persona sua similiter venit.

Et predictus Johannes Waryn protestando quod non cognoscit quod predictus prior tenuit rectoriam in proprios usus nec quod vicaria predicta est de patronatu dicti prioris nec quod eadem vicaria dicto prioratui per licenciam dicti domini Ricardi nuper regis etc. appropriata fuit etc., dicit quod ubi predictus prior supponit quod ipse tenuit vicariam predictam in proprios usus pretextu appropriacionis predicte absque cassacione seu[276] adnullacione appropriacionis pacifice, dicit quod predictus[277] sanctissimus pater papa Bonifacius mero motu percipiens se fore deceptum in concessione de unione annexione et incorporacione predicte vicarie de Leskyret prioratui predicto factis, auctoritate sua propria et per bullas suas apostolicas unionem annexionem et incorporacionem predictas revocavit cassavit et irritas fore ac nullius esse roboris vel momenti pronunciavit, ipsamque vicariam in statum pristinum prout erat ante unionem annexionem et incorporacionem predictas reposuit et restituit etc., inhibens prefatis priori et conventui ac executoribus etc. in unione et annexione ac incorporacione predictis deputatis ne de vicaria predicta pretextu unionis annexionis et incorporacionis huiusmodi se intromittere quoquomodo presumerent, ac decernens extunc irritum et inane si secus super hiis a quoquam quavis auctoritate scienter vel ignoranter attemptatum forsan esset hactenus vel imposterum contigerit attemptari. Et profert hic in curia bullas predictas premissa testificantes quarum data est apud Sanctum Petrum xvj kalendas februarii pontificatus sui anno undecimo [17 Jan. 1400].[278] Et dicit quod predictus prior nunquam habuit corporalem possessionem vicarie predicte pretextu appropriacionis predicte ante datam dictarum bullarum de revocacione. Et absque hoc quod predictus ordinarius unquam ordinavit aliquam summam pecunie occasione appropriacionis predicte inter pauperes parochianos parochie predicte in forma predicta distribuendam apud Leskyret annuatim per formam statuti predicti etc. Et absque hoc quod predictus prior predictam summam pecunie centum solidorum prefato ordinario sive plus secundum eius discrecionem unquam optulit inter [pauperes] parochianos parochie predicte in forma predicta distribuendam apud Leskyret annuatim per formam statuti predicti etc. Et absque hoc quod ipse citari fecit predictum priorem ad comparendum in curia christianitatis citra mare vel extra, prout predictus prior supra allegavit, que omnia et singula ipse paratus est verificare prout curia etc. Et petit judicium si injuria in persona sua in hoc casu assignari possit etc.

Et predictus prior protestando quod non cognoscit bullas predictas de revocacione et adnullacione predicte appropriacionis quas predictus Johannes Waryn protulit hic in curia nec quod appropriacio predicta unquam revocata fuit, dicit quod ipse habuit corporalem possessionem vicarie predicte[279] per puram et liberam resignacionem predicti Henrici Frend nuper vicarii vicarie predicte pretextu appropriacionis unionis annexionis et incorporacionis predictarum et pretextu licencie dicti domini Ricardi nuper regis etc. diu antequam predictus Johannes Waryn supponit appropriacionem predictam revocari, et quod ipse fecit noticiam prefato ordinario apud Launceston quod ipse paratus fuit ad standum in eius discrecionem et arbitrium ad ordinandum certam summam pecunie majus vel minus secundum eius discrecionem inter pauperes parochianos parochie predicte distribuendam apud Leskyret annuatim per formam statuti predicti, et quod bulle papales provisionis dicti Johannis Waryn vicarie predicte facte fuerunt et gerunt datam diu ante datam predictarum bullarum revocacionis et adnullacionis predictarum, pretextu quarum bullarum provisionis dictus Johannes Waryn postea vicarie predicte corporalem possessionem cepit et optinuit et adhuc optinet, que omnia et singula ipse paratus est verificare, et exquo predictus Johannes Waryn non dedicit appropriacionem vicarie predicte predicto prioratui in forma predicta pretextu licencie dicti nuper regis Ricardi fore factam nec dedicit predictam provisionem a sede apostolica sibi factam contra formam provisionis et ordinacionis in contrarium editorum et ad aliqua alia superius per predictum Johannem Waryn allegata necesse non habet in lege ulterius respondere, petit judicium et dampna etc.

[*Following, unnumbered membrane*] Et super hoc dies datus est tam prefato priori quam dicto Johanni

[276] Interlined.

[277] Interlined. *dicit quod* seems unnecessary.

[278] Not in *CPL*, but their issue confirmed by ibid., V, 357–8.

[279] Omitting *vacantis*?

coram domino rege usque a die Sancte Trinitatis in xv dies [19 June 1401] ubicumque etc. in statu quo nunc etc. Et quoad venire faciendum xxiiij^{or} tam milites [etc.] inter prefatum priorem et predictos Walterum Johannem Cryke Johannem Fursdon et Willelmum Garrek ad prefatam quindenam Pasche etc., vicecomes non misit inde breve etc. Ideo sicut pluries veniat inde jurata coram domino rege ad prefatum terminum [*etc.*]

[The parties appeared as above, with the sheriff failing to return the writ, on 19 June and 13 October 1401. John Lopenford came as attorney for John Waryn on 13 October, when the parties and jury were ordered to come on 9 April 1402. The parties then appeared by their attorneys.]

Et predictus Johannes Waryn protestando quod non cognoscit materiam alias supra per predictum priorem allegatam etc., set quoad hoc quod predictus prior supra placitando allegavit quod ipse fecit noticiam prefato ordinario apud Launceston predictam quod ipse paratus fuit ad standum in eius discrecionem et arbitrium ad ordinandum certam summam pecunie magis vel minus secundum eius discrecionem inter pauperes parochianos parochie predicte distribuendam etc., predictus Johannes Waryn dicit quod predictus prior non fecit noticiam prefato ordinario nec se offerebat eidem ordinario ad standum in eius discrecionem et arbitrium ad ordinandum certam summam pecunie magis aut minus secundum [eius] discrecionem inter pauperes parochianos parochie predicte distribuendam, prout idem prior supra allegavit. Et hoc paratus est verificare per patriam etc. unde petit judicium si etc.

Et predictus prior dicit quod ipse fecit noticiam prefato ordinario apud Launceston predictam et se offerebat eidem ordinario ad standum in eius discrecionem et arbitrium ad ordinandum certam summam pecunie magis vel minus secundum eius discrecionem inter pauperes parochianos parochie predicte distribuendam etc., prout ipse supra allegavit. Et de hoc ponit se super patriam etc. Et predictus Johannes Waryn similiter etc. Ideo tam inde quam de exitu placiti inter predictum priorem et predictos Walterum Johannem Cryke Johannem Fursdon et Willelmum Garrek veniat jurata coram domino rege a die Sancte Trinitatis in xv dies [*etc.*]

[They accordingly appeared by attorney on 4 June, when Richard Repryna, John Jaybyn of Cornwall, Thomas Prens and John Laurence of Devon mainperned that John Waryn would make no suit prejudicial to the king in the Roman curia or any other church court, each (including Waryn) under pain of forfeiting £40, with Waryn again renouncing any prior suit. The sheriff made no return then nor when the parties reappeared as required on 13 October, 27 January and 17 June 1403. The record ends with another sicut pluries to the sheriff for 13 October 1403.]

[15]

In this record of Trinity 1401 the statute of provisors of 1365 was being invoked to prevent the prior of a monastic cell from achieving independence of his abbot by papal authority. The clause of the statute aimed to protect benefices and revenues of religious houses against provisors was regarded as applicable in such a case, for it is quoted (as in [14]). In the time of the Great Schism the papacy was facilitating the relaxation of monastic discipline by its readiness to grant privileges to individual religious.[280] Its occasional grants of independence to cells were naturally opposed by monastic superiors: they could sue the pope to revoke his bulls, but countermeasures could also be arranged in England. Henry IV was ready to support monastic discipline against its erosion by papal concessions.[281] In this instance, the countess of Suffolk, as patron of Snape, alleged that divine service was neglected because monks sent from Colchester were not required by their abbot to reside permanently. The pope consequently, on 10 January 1400, freed the prior of Snape from Colchester's authority.[282] The abbot must have complained to the king who, on 3 May following, ordered the prior of Snape to be arrested; the order was repeated on 15 July.[283]

This suit was extended until at least Easter 1402. The sheriff was amerced for a false return in Hilary 1402 and Mersea and his associates eventually appeared on 23 April 1402 when they mainperned not to sue to the prejudice of the king and his subjects.[284] The eventual outcome was that Snape remained a cell of Colchester.[285]

280 D. Knowles, *The Religious Orders in England* (Cambridge, 1948–59), II, 170–4.

281 e.g. *CPR 1399–1401*, 82, 315; *1401–5*, 64, 220.

282 *CPL*, V, 281–2; *Foedera*, VIII, 121–2.

283 *CPR 1399–1401*, 271, 347.

284 KB 27/563, Rex m.1.

285 *VCH Suff*, II, 79.

The prior was simultaneously suing the abbot in the common bench for trespass, alleging that the abbot had plundered Snape of its livestock and wasted its crops.[286] This was obviously an attempt by the prior to have his independence recognised at common law. The abbot refused to answer this plea, stating that the prior was under his obedience and removable at his will. The discussion of this point ended with a decision to require the local bishop to certify whether the prior was perpetual or not. There is no notice of the prior citing his papal letters in this context.[287]

KB 27/561, Rex m.29

[*Marginated*] Suff'

Dominus rex mandavit vicecomiti Suff' in hec verba: Henricus [*etc.*] vicecomiti Suff' salutem. Cum in statuto in parliamento domini Edwardi nuper regis Anglie avi nostri [*as in* 14, *mutatis mutandis* – continetur] ; iamque intellexerimus quod frater Johannes Merseye monachus provisionem et ordinacionem predictas minime ponderans, quandam provisionem de prioratu de Snapes qui est cella abbatis Sancti Johannis Colcestr', quequidem abbatia de nostro patronatu existit et quemquidem prioratum dilecti nobis in Christo abbas et conventus abbatie predicte et successores[288] sui in proprios usus a tempore cuius contrarii memoria non existit absque cassacione seu adnullacione appropriacionis seu mortificacionis eiusdem hucusque pacifice tenuerunt, sibi a sede apostolica fieri procuravit et quasdam litteras bullatas sibi inde factas infra regnum nostrum Anglie execucioni demandandas deferri fecit, ac quamplures processus versus prefatum abbatem pretextu provisionis huiusmodi tam infra regnum nostrum Anglie quam extra prosecutus fuit et indies prosequitur, et quamplura alia nobis et corone nostre regie in hac parte prejudicialia fecit et fieri procuravit in nostri contemptum et prejudicium ac contra formam et effectum provisionis et ordinacionis predictarum; nos provisionem et ordinacionem predictas ac leges et consuetudines regni nostri Anglie, prout vinculo juramenti astringimur, illesas observari ac contravenientes juxta vim firmam[289] et effectum earumdem et eorum demerita castigari facere volentes et puniri, tibi precepimus quod per probos et legales homines de balliva tua premunire facias prefatum Johannem ac Johannem Lene clericum et Johannem Menser manutentores consiliarios abettatores et fautores ipsius Johannis Merseye in hac parte apud Snapes quod sint coram nobis a die Sancti Johannis Baptiste in xv dies [8 July 1401] ubicumque tunc fuerimus in Anglia ad respondendum nobis de contemptu et prejudicio predictis et ad faciendum ulterius et recipiendum quod curia nostra consideraverit in premissis. Et habeas ibi nomina illorum per quos eos premuniri feceris et hoc breve, nos de die quo dictam premunicionem sibi feceris sub sigillo tuo distincte et aperte tunc certificans. Teste me ipso apud Westmonasterium vj die februarii anno regni nostri secundo.

[16]

Thomas Tutbury's collation to the deanery of Wells has already been noticed [4]. His possession was soon challenged by a papal provisor. He received the king's immediate support, an asset earned by his long service to John of Gaunt and more recently as treasurer of Henry IV's household.[290] On 14 September 1402 the chapter of Wells was ordered not to offend against the statutes of provisors by admitting 'one Thomas Stanley' who had been provided to the deanery[291] and on 20 September a writ issued under the statute of 1390 to arrest Stanley and his agents so that they appeared in king's bench exactly one month later. This was a crown prosecution. Stanley was required to answer only the king and the prosecution was conducted by Thomas Cowley, his attorney in king's bench.[292]

The 'certain Thomas Stanley' was keeper of the rolls of chancery, an office from which he was now dismissed.[293] In 1401 he had undertaken with Nicholas Slack to exchange certain of his benefices for the deanery of Wells. He had, however, already petitioned the pope for provision to a number of benefices. On 10 December he obtained a royal

[286] Wylie, *Henry IV*, I, 419–20.

[287] YB 2 Hen. IV, Trin. 14.

[288] Recte *predecessores.*

[289] Recte *formam.*

[290] R. Somerville, *History of the Duchy of Lancaster, 1265–1603*, I (London, 1953), 365; *Hdbk Brit. Chron.*, 79.

[291] *CPR 1401–5*, 136. See also *CCR 1399–1402*, 585, 595–6.

[292] *King's Bench*, VII, lxii.

[293] *CPR 1401–5*, 120; *CCR 1402–5*, 11; Foss, *Judges of England*, IV, 183.

licence thus to accept a prebend and major dignity in Salisbury cathedral; on the 27th he had this licence amended to read 'certain canonries and a major dignity in certain churches of the realm'. On 1 April 1402 further letters patent declared that the licence was to apply only to benefices becoming vacant after its date; he was thus prevented from obtaining his prebend at Salisbury, which the king had granted to another.[294] By this time he must have received his bull of provision to Wells but it required amendment and so could not be executed. The new version, dated at Rome on 29 April 1402, referred to the arrangements for an exchange with Slack. These had been concluded, Stanley told the pope, some twenty days before the issue of his original bull of provision to the deanery, and about the same time Slack had been deprived, a fact about which Stanley professed to be ignorant. The new bull was to allow him to receive the deanery despite his promise to exchange benefices with Slack, from which the pope absolved him.[295] The bull had doubtless arrived in England by 19 June when Tutbury further secured his title by obtaining the king's presentation to the deanery.[296] Stanley persisted in putting the bull into execution, relying on the king's licence to do so, with the result that proceedings were initiated against him.

The record states that the king's serjeants had not been instructed to proceed when Stanley appeared on 20 October and the case was therefore adjourned. In the interval Stanley, released on mainprise, seemingly tried to make his peace with Tutbury by resigning his deanery of St Martin le Grand so that Tutbury could have it. He was saved from further prosecution by Tutbury's death, and soon afterwards, on 4 March 1403, the king granted a pardon, authorising the provision and confirming his possession of the deanery.[297]

KB 27/566, Rex m.18

[*Marginated*] London'
Dominus rex mandavit vicecomitibus London' breve suum clausum in hec verba: Henricus [*etc.*] vicecomitibus London' salutem. Cum in statuto in parliamento domini Ricardi nuper regis Anglie secundi post conquestum apud Westmonasterium nuper tento edito inter cetera contineatur quod de quibuscumque beneficiis ecclesiasticis[298] que vicesimo nono die januarii anno regni eiusdem nuper regis terciodecimo seu postea de facto vacare inceperunt vel extunc infra idem regnum vacaverint, quoddam statutum in parliamento domini Edwardi nuper regis Anglie avi nostri anno regni sui Anglie[299] vicesimo quinto tento editum[300] in omnibus imperpetuum firmiter teneatur et debite execucioni demandetur de tempore in tempus, et siquis aliquam acceptacionem de aliquo beneficio ecclesiastico in contrarium dicti statuti in parliamento predicti nuper[301] regis Ricardi editi fecerit et hoc debite probato habeat penam in dicto statuto in parliamento eiusdem nuper regis Ricardi edito contentam,[302] et quod de aliqua dignitate vel beneficio ecclesiastico que vel quod dicto vicesimo nono die januarii plena vel plenum extitit aliquis occasione alicuius doni collacionis reservacionis vel provisionis aut alterius cuiuscumque gracie sibi per dominum summum pontificem de huiusmodi beneficio ecclesiastico facti et ante eundem vicesimum nonum diem januarii minime executi execucionem inde sub eadem pena nullatenus prosequatur, prout in eodem statuto in parliamento predicti nuper regis Ricardi edito plenius continetur; iamque intellexerimus quod cum nuper vacante decanatu ecclesie cathedralis Sancti Andree Wellensis et ad nostram donacionem spectante, decanatum illum dilecto clerico nostro Thome Tuttebury contulerimus, et licet idem Thomas decanatum illum virtute collacionis nostre predicte sit adeptus, quidam tamen Thomas Stanley clericus machinans jus nostrum regium in hac parte colore cuiusdam provisionis sibi a sede apostolica diu post dictum vicesimum nonum diem januarii facte impugnare et collacionem nostram eidem Thome[303] Tuttebury de decanatu predicto ut premittitur factam adnullare ac ipsum Thomam Tuttebury a possessione sua decanatus illius ammovere et possessionem eiusdem decanatus pretextu provisionis predicte sibi adquirere, quamplures processus moniciones

[294] On 4 Oct. 1401: *CPR 1401–5*, 2, 57; *Fasti*, III, 74.

[295] *CPR 1401–5*, 49, 53; *CPL*, V, 556.

[296] *CPR 1401–5*, 101.

[297] *CCR 1402–5*, 117; *CPR 1401–5*, 185, 205, 209. The notice in *Fasti*, VIII, 4–5, should therefore be corrected.

[298] cf.13 Ric. II, stat. 2, c.2 (*SR*, II, 73): 'de toutz erceveschees eveschees et autres dignites et benefices electives et autres benefices de seint esglise queconques'.

[299] *avi . . . Anglie* interlined.

[300] 25 Edw. III, stat. 4.

[301] Repeated.

[302] viz banishment and forfeiture. The bulk of the statute is now omitted from the writ and the following section gives the statute's last clause: *SR*, II, 73–4.

[303] Interlined.

citaciones inhibiciones appellaciones et notificaciones eorumdem necnon instrumenta publica ac quamplura alia nobis et corone nostre regie prejudicialia et eidem Thome Tuttebury dampnosa in hac parte apud London' prosecutus fuit et fieri procuravit, in nostri contemptum et prejudicium nostrique et corone nostre regie exheredacionis periculum manifestum necnon ipsius Thome Tuttebury in hac parte dampnum non modicum et gravamen et contra vim firmam[304] et effectum statutorum predictorum: nos statuta predicta ac leges et consuetudines regni nostri Anglie prout vinculo juramenti astringimur illesa observare[305] et ea contravenientes juxta vim formam et effectum statutorum predictorum ac eorum demerita debite castigari facere volentes et puniri, vobis precipimus quod prefatum Thomam Stanley ac Thomam Cotyngwyth Johannem Dautre capellanum Johannem Cressewelle capellanum et Johannem Russell de London' procuratores executores notarios et summonitores ipsius Thome Stanley in hac parte per corpora sua attachiatis, ita quod eos habeatis coram nobis a die Sancti Michaelis in tres septimanas ubicumque tunc fuerimus in Anglia ad respondendum nobis de contemptu et prejudicio predictis et ad faciendum ulterius et recipiendum quod curia nostra consideraverit in premissis. Et habeatis ibi hoc breve. Teste me ipso apud Westmonasterium xx die septembris anno regni nostri tercio.

Ad quem diem coram domino rege apud Westmonasterium venerunt predicti Thomas Stanley et Thomas Cotyngwyth in propriis personis suis, et predicti Johannes Dautre Johannes Cressewelle et Johannes Russell non venerunt. Ideo ipsi capiantur ita quod sunt[306] coram domino rege a die Pasche in xv dies [29 Apr. 1403] ubicumque etc. ad respondendum domino regi super premissis. Et quia servientes domini regis ad legem non informantur ad declarandum pro domino rege in hac parte, dies datus est tam Thome Couele qui sequitur etc. quam prefatis Thome Stanley et Thome Cotyngwyth.

Ad quamquidem quindenam coram domino rege apud Westmonasterium venerunt predicti Thomas Stanley et Thomas Cotyngwyth per Thomam Beeston attornatum suum. Et super hoc dictum est prefatis servientibus domini regis ad legem ac prefato ipsius regis attornato quod declarent jus et titulum domini regis, siquos dominus rex ad conferendum decanatum predictum habeat, et ad alia in eodem brevi contenta quoad acceptacionem et execucionem provisionis predicte pro ipso domino rege declaranda si voluerint, qui dicunt quod non sciunt nec aliquis est qui ipsos in hac parte informavit nec informare scit.

Et super hoc idem Thomas Stanley dicit quod dominus rex nunc de gracia sua speciali perdonavit eidem Thome ac executoribus et subexecutoribus bullarum procuratoribus et notariis suis omnimodos transgressiones mesprisiones contemptus et forisfacturas in quibus ipsi erga ipsum regem sunt incursi vel incurrere poterunt, aut aliquis eorum est incursus vel incurrere poterit, occasione acceptacionis et execucionis provisionis predicte et quantum ad ipsum regem pertinet aut pertinere poterit in hac parte; aceciam concessit quod prefatus Thomas decanatum predictum habeat et eo gaudeat virtute provisionis predicte, statuto de provisoribus anno regni domini Ricardi nuper regis Anglie secundi post conquestum terciodecimo seu aliis statutis aut ordinacionibus tam tempore suo quam tempore progenitorum suorum incontrarium factis aut aliqua collacione sive presentacione alicui de decanatu predicto per ipsum regem facta seu aliquo processu vel placito in curiis suis inde pendente non obstantibus. Et ulterius idem dominus rex statum et possessionem quos idem Thomas habet in decanatu predicto pro se et heredibus suis quantum in ipso est acceptavit approbavit ratificavit et confirmavit, nolens[307] quod ipse Thomas super possessione sua decanatus predicti racione alicuius juris vel tituli quod vel qui ipsi regi competit seu sibi aut heredibus suis infuturum competere poterit non impetatur inquietetur molestetur in aliquo seu gravetur. Et profert hic in curia litteras domini regis patentes premissa testificantes in hec verba:

Henricus [*etc.*] omnibus ad quos presentes littere pervenerint salutem. Sciatis quod cum sanctissimus in Christo pater papa modernus providisset dilecto clerico nostro Thome de Stanley de decanatu in ecclesia cathedrali Sancti Andree Wellensis dictusque Thomas pretextu provisionis predicte decanatum predictum acceptasset et inde plenam et corporalem possessionem habeat et adeptus existat, nos de gracia nostra speciali perdonavimus eidem Thome ac executoribus et subexecutoribus bullarum procuratoribus et notariis suis omnimodos transgressiones mesprisiones contemptus et forisfacturas in quibus ipsi erga nos sunt incursi vel incurrere poterunt, aut aliquis eorum est incursus vel incurrere poterit, occasione acceptacionis et execucionis provisionis predicte et quantum ad nos pertinet aut pertinere

304 Recte *formam*.

305 Recte *observari*.

306 Recte *sint*.

307 Recte *volens*: capital *N* in MS.

poterit in hac parte; aceciam concessimus quod prefatus Thomas decanatum predictum habeat et eo gaudeat virtute provisionis predicte, statuto de provisoribus anno regni domini Ricardi nuper regis Anglie secundi post conquestum terciodecimo seu aliis statutis aut ordinacionibus tam tempore nostro quam tempore progenitorum nostrorum incontrarium factis aut aliqua collacione sive presentacione alicui de decanatu predicto per nos facta seu aliquo processu vel placito in curiis nostris inde pendente non obstantibus. Et ulterius de uberiori gracia nostra acceptamus ratificamus et confirmamus statum et possessionem quos idem Thomas sic habet in decanatu supradicto, nolentes quod ipse super possessione sua decanatus illius racione alicuius juris vel tituli quod vel qui nobis competit seu nobis aut heredibus nostris infuturum competere poterit seu occasione statutorum aut ordinacionum predictorum per nos vel heredes nostros seu ministros nostros quoscumque futuris temporibus impetatur inquietetur molestetur in aliquo seu gravetur. In cuius rei testimonium has litteras nostras fieri fecimus patentes. Teste me ipso apud Eltham quarto die marcii anno regni nostri quarto.

Profert eciam hic in curia quoddam breve domini regis clausum justiciariis suis hic directum de non molestando ipsum Thomam Stanley contra tenorem litterarum domini regis predictarum, cuius data est apud Eltham quarto die marcii anno regni sui quarto. Super quo quesitum est a prefatis servientibus domini regis ad legem necnon a prefato attornato ipsius regis siquid in hac parte pro domino rege habeant vel dicere sciant quare littere patentes predicte super statu et possessione ipsius Thome Stanley de decanatu predicto ut premittitur factas eidem Thome allocari non debeant, qui dicunt quod non. Ideo consideratum est quod predicti Thomas Stanley et omnes alii eant inde sine die etc. salvo semper jure domini regis siquod etc.
[*Marginated*] Sine die.

[17]

Thomas Towton twice sued Master John Francis and his agents under the statute of provisors of 1365, first in Hilary 1406. This case is recorded to its conclusion in Michaelmas following [A]. In 1407 Francis repeated his offence and a second praemunire facias issued against him for Michaelmas, when Towton virtually duplicated his narration for the first suit and also his claim for damages of £1000 [B]. It appears that he was awarded damages only in respect of the first suit.

Francis was a bachelor of canon law who had been employed at the papal curia for some twenty years. In this time he had often been provided to canonries with expectations of prebends in a number of English cathedrals, with limited success. In 1402 the pope had provided him to the prebend of Masham in York, and soon afterwards also provided Thomas Stanley to the same stall.[308] A third provisor claimed the prebend by virtue of an expectation granted in 1399.[309] None of the three succeeded in obtaining Masham. The king granted the prebend to his treasurer of the household, Thomas More, and the royal presentation was confirmed by a suit at common law. After this rebuff, the pope and some cardinals wrote to the king on Francis' behalf, but all the king granted, on 5 January 1404, was a pardon for the attempt on Masham and licence to obtain prebends in York and Salisbury cathedrals by provision.[310] A year earlier Francis had obtained further papal letters granting him a canonry of York with expectation of a prebend.[311] He appointed Master John Willingham his proctor, presumably with instructions to claim the next prebend at York which became vacant. He was thus able to state in king's bench that Willingham had taken possession of the prebend of Stillington when it fell vacant by the death of Nicholas Ferriby, and he could produce the bull of 2 January 1403 and the king's licence of 5 January 1404 to justify this action.

Ferriby had died by 6 June 1404, when Thomas Walworth was admitted to Stillington on the archbishop's collation.[312] The plaintiff Towton knew this well enough because he then attempted to gain the prebend for himself. In a petition to the king, granted at Pontefract on 9 July, Towton asked for a royal presentation to Stillington; he did not say that the prebend was vacant but alleged that it was in the king's gift because the temporalities had recently

[308] *CPL*, IV, 269, 337, 412; V, 270–1, 296–7, 490–1.

[309] ibid., 183.

[310] *Hdbk Brit. Chron.*, 79; *Fasti*, VI, 67; *CPR 1401–5*, 332. The last reference makes it clear that More owed his institution to the king's grant. He was also provided to Masham, but his papal letters were dated 22 April 1402, the day before the king's grant, and may not have arrived in England before More was admitted on 10 June: *CPL*, V, 469; *CPR 1401–5*, 100.

[311] *CPL*, V, 523–4.

[312] *Fasti*, VI, 79.

been in the hands of the king's progenitors.[313] Towton, who was probably a fairly long-standing servant of the duchy of Lancaster,[314] doubtless hoped to oust Walworth by process of quare impedit, but a quicker way to achieve his end came to hand. In May 1405 Archbishop Scrope headed an abortive revolt against the king. Two days after Scrope's execution, Towton came to the king at Ripon and obtained another presentation to Stillington. This time the prebend was vacant: Walworth had resigned. He was a former vicar general of York and presumably a close adviser of the late archbishop[315] and thus likely to have been to some extent implicated in his master's treason. Towton may consequently have been able to put pressure on Walworth to resign Stillington. Walworth clearly was apprehensive about his security. He had also held the prebend of Bugthorpe since 1386, but on 10 June, the day of Towton's petition for Stillington, Walworth petitioned the king to present him to Bugthorpe[316] as if his title to it was no longer valid. Towton and Walworth were both admitted to their stalls on 17 June.[317]

This was not the only incident to suggest that Scrope's execution occasioned fears of insecurity in the York chapter. The three canons who received prebends from Scrope early in 1405 all took the safeguard of obtaining royal grants later that year.[318] In the case of one there certainly was a threat to his tenure. Richard Coniston, the archbishop's chancellor, was pardoned for his part in the revolt.[319] John Catterick, a clerk in royal service, attempted to take his prebend of Laughton by virtue of a provision. The crown then instituted proceedings under the statute of provisors against Catterick and his proctors; the latter would have been the more culpable, for Catterick himself was then on a royal mission to the pope.[320]

In their pleas in king's bench on 9 February 1406, Towton and Francis gave differing accounts of the descent of Stillington since it was vacated by Henry Wakefield. These are summarised as follows, with dates provided when known.[321]

According to Towton
Henry Wakefield (1370–75)
Nicholas Ferriby (1379–1404)
Thomas Walworth (1404–5)
Thomas Towton (1405–28)

According to Francis
Henry Wakefield (1370–75)
Cardinal Guy de Maillesec (1376)
John Sheepy (1376–78)
Cardinal Gerard de Puy (1378–79)
Nicholas Ferriby (1379–1404)
John Francis (no date)

Francis' research was obviously better than Towton's and the point he made was that the prebend had been filled by an unbroken series of papal provisors since 1375. Towton maintained that Francis had not followed Ferriby in the lifetime of Archbishop Scrope. This issue was eventually put to a jury at nisi prius on 20 June 1406; it found for Towton and awarded damages.

When the apportionment of damages between the principal and his accessories was considered, the king's attorney claimed that by statute forfeiture was due. Gascoigne corrected him: the statute prescribed forfeiture only in the event of failure to appear when praemunire facias was returnable.[322]

Despite this verdict, Francis made a second attempt in 1407 to cite Towton to the curia to answer for his opposition to Francis' provision to Stillington. Towton responded by suing a second writ under the same statute. Francis did not appear and was put out of the king's protection on 9 October 1407. A year later, he surrendered himself, paid the damages, resigned his claim to Stillington, and received a pardon.[323] His family connections had doubtless assisted his return to grace. Sir Robert Francis, who served the second citation, was one of the king's knights.[324]

313 E 28/12 (9 July); *CPR 1401–5,* 413.

314 His hospital of St Nicholas, Pontefract, was a duchy foundation: Somerville, *Duchy of Lancaster,* I, 149; *CPR 1408–13,* 198.

315 Emden, *Biog. Reg. Oxford,* III, 1977–8.

316 C 81/1404, no. 33; *CPR 1405–8,* 24.

317 *Fasti,* VI, 40, 79.

318 ibid., 31, 65, 89.

319 *CPR 1405–8,* 19; Emden, *Biog. Reg. Oxford,* III, 2164–5.

320 *CCR 1402–5,* 514; *Fasti,* VI, 65; Emden, *Biog. Reg. Oxford,* I, 372.

321 From *Fasti,* VI, 79.

322 YB 8 Hen. IV, Mich. 9B.

323 *CPR 1408–13,* 27.

324 *CPR 1399–1401,* 64; Somerville, *Duchy of Lancaster,* I, 573.

[A]

KB 27/579, m.69

[*Marginated*] Ebor'

Preceptum fuit vicecomiti (cum in parliamento domini Edwardi [*as in* 14[325] – continetur] ; iamque intellexerit dominus rex quod cum[326] nuper vacante prebenda de Styllyngton in ecclesia cathedrali Beati Petri Eboracensis et ad ipsius domini regis donacionem spectante racione temporalium archiepiscopatus Eboracensis in manu ipsius domini regis nunc existencium, prebendam illam dilecto domino regi Thome de Toueton clerico jure suo regio contulerit, qui ad eam pretextu collacionis sue[327] predicte concurrentibus hiis que de jure in hac parte requirebantur canonice admissus fuit ac institutus et inductus in eadem, sicut per litteras institucionis et induccionis eidem Thome in hac parte factas et in cancellaria ipsius domini regis ostensas plenius poterit apparere; quidam magister Johannes Fraunceys clericus machinans jus ipsius domini regis in hac parte adnullare et ipsum Thomam a justa possessione sua prebende predicte quam in eodem[328] jure suo regio optinet expellere, quandam provisionem de prebenda predicta a sede apostolica sibi fieri procuravit et colore eiusdem quamplures processus appellaciones citaciones et instrumenta publica ac notificaciones eorumdem in adnullacionem juris sui predicti et possessionis ipsius Thome in hac parte in curia christianitatis extra regnum domini regis Anglie prosecutus fuit et illos[329] infra idem regnum suum execucioni demandandos deferri fecit ac per eos possessionem eiusdem prebende sibi adquirere nititur viribus suis, et quamplura alia ipsi domino rege et corone sue regie prejudicialia in hac parte fecit et fieri procuravit in ipsius domini regis contemptum et prejudicium ipsiusque domini regis et corone sue predicte exheredacionis periculum et possessionis ipsius Thome in hac parte adnullacionem manifestam ac contra formam provisionis et ordinacionis predictarum; idem dominus rex provisionem et ordinacionem predictas ac leges et consuetudines regni sui Anglie prout vinculo juramenti astringitur illesas observari ac contravenientes juxta vim formam et effectum earumdem ac eorum demerita castigari volens et puniri) quod per probos etc. premunire faceret prefatum Johannem ac Johannem Savage de London capellanum magistrum Johannem Ragnell clericum Johannem Wylyngham clericum Johannem Bollesore de comitatu Derb' clericum et Willelmum Savage de London' manutentores consiliarios abbettatores auxiliatores et fautores ipsius Johannis Fraunceys in hac parte apud Styllyngton quod essent coram domino rege ad hunc diem, scilicet in octabis Purificacionis Beate Marie [9 Feb. 1406] ubicumque etc. ad respondendum domino regi de contemptu et prejudicio predictis et prefato Thome de dampnis et injuriis sibi illatis et in premissis perpetratis, et ad faciendum ulterius et recipiendum quod curia domini regis consideraret in hac parte.

Ad quem diem coram domino rege apud Westmonasterium venit predictus Thomas de Toueton per Henricum del Chambre attornatum suum. Et vicecomes retornavit breve quod premunire fecit apud Styllyngton die veneris proximo ante festum Sancti Nicholai episcopi ultimo preteritum [4 Dec. 1405] prefatos[330] magistrum Johannem Fraunceys clericum ac Johannem Savage de London capellanum magistrum Johannem Ragnell clericum Johannem Wylyngham clericum Johannem Bollesore de comitatu Derb' clericum et Willelmum Savage de London quod essent coram domino rege ad prefatas octabas Purificacionis Beate Marie ubicumque etc. ad faciendum et recipiendum quod breve domini regis predictum in se requirit secundum formam eiusdem brevis per Johannem Nikson de Styllyngton Robertum Baillyfman Willelmum Nicolson Robertum Perot Willelmum Blakmantill et Robertum de Crayke. Et predictus magister Johannes Fraunceys per Johannem Frank clericum attornatum suum per litteras domini regis nunc patentes constitutum curie hic ostensas, quarum data est apud Westmonasterium vicesimo tercio die junii anno regni domini regis nunc sexto [1405],[331] et predicti Johannes Savage Johannes Wylyngham Johannes Bollesore et Willelmus Savage in propriis personis suis similiter venerunt.

[325] The more substantial differences are: omission of *ac eciam omnes impetratores . . . adnullate fuerint;* omission of *seu alterius cuiuscumque de regno predicto; manucapcionem plegiagium vel ballium traderentur et ad cicius quo fieri posset sibi vel consilio suo presentarentur ad commorandum et standum recto;* omission of *vel in locis inter eos in debata existentibus; contentos vel aliter;* omission of *per dictum avum domini regis.*

[326] The record of the second suit summarised below [B] here has *licet.* There are some two dozen variants, none of substance, but showing that the second writ was not duplicated from the first. In contrast, differences between Towton's narration here and in the second suit are few and seem accidental.

[327] Interlined. [328] Recte *eadem.*

[329] [B] : *et processus illos.* [330] Interlined.

[331] Not traced in *CPR.*

Et predictus Thomas de Toueton qui tam pro domino rege quam pro seipso sequitur dicit quod quidam Johannes de Thoresby quondam archiepiscopus Eboracensis nuper fuit seisitus de patronatu prebende de Styllyngton predicte ut de jure ecclesie sue cathedralis Beati Petri Eboracensis et de eadem prebenda fecit collacionem cuidam Henrico de Wakefeld clerico, qui ad eandem prebendam per capitulum ecclesie predicte admissus fuit et installatus in eadem et corporalem possessionem suam inde pretextu collacionis predicte optinuit tempore pacis tempore domini Edwardi nuper regis Anglie avi etc. Et postea prebenda predicta vacavit pro eo quod idem Henricus consecratus fuit in episcopum Wygorniensem, per quod sanctissimus in Christo pater et dominus[332] Urbanus nuper papa per litteras suas apostolicas providit cuidam Nicholao de Fereby bacallario in legibus de prebenda predicta, qui virtute provisionis predicte per executores bullarum suarum et per capitulum ecclesie predicte admissus fuit et installatus in eadem tempore domini Ricardi[333] nuper regis etc. Et postea prebenda predicta vacavit per mortem predicti Nicholai, per quod Ricardus Lescrop adtunc archiepiscopus Eboracensis fuit seisitus de patronatu prebende predicte ut de jure etc. et de prebenda predicta fecit collacionem cuidam Thoma Walworth clerico suo, qui virtute collacionis predicte per capitulum ecclesie predicte admissus fuit et installatus in eadem tempore pacis tempore domini regis nunc. Et postea prebenda predicta vacavit per resignacionem predicti Thome Walworth, temporalibus archiepiscopatus predicti in manibus domini regis nunc per mortem dicti Ricardi nuper archiepiscopi existentibus, et sic collacio prebende predicte eidem domino regi pertinuit, per quod idem dominus rex per litteras [suas][334] patentes quas hic in curia profert, quarum data est apud Rypoun x die junii anno regni domini regis nunc sexto [1405],[335] predicto Thome de Toueton collacionem fecit, qui pretextu collacionis illius per capitulum ecclesie predicte admissus fuit et installatus in eadem et corporalem possessionem suam inde optinuit tempore pacis tempore eiusdem domini regis nunc etc. Et profert hic in curia litteras institucionis et inducccionis eidem Thome de Toueton in hac parte factas premissa[336] testificantes. Predictus tamen magister Johannes Fraunceys machinans jus domini regis in hac parte adnullare et ipsum Thomam de Toueton a justa possessione sua [prebende predicte][337] quam in eodem[338] jure suo regio optinet expellere, quandam provisionem de prebenda predicta a sede apostolica sibi fieri procuravit et colore eiusdem quamplures processus appellaciones citaciones et instrumenta publica ac notificaciones eorumdem in adnullacionem juris domini regis predicti et possessionis ipsius Thome in hac parte in curia christianitatis extra regnum domini regis Anglie prosecutus fuit et illos infra idem regnum domini regis execucioni demandandos deferri fecit, videlicet citari fecit predictum Thomam de Toueton apud Styllyngton predicta sexto die augusti anno regni regis Henrici post conquestum Anglie sexto [1405] per Johannem Hornyngsay et Willelmum Fraunceys notarios et procuratores ipsius Johannis Fraunceys ad comparendum in curia Romana extra regnum Anglie pro jure et possessione sua prebende predicte centesimo die tunc proximo sequenti, ac per eos possessionem eiusdem prebende sibi adquirere nititur viribus suis, et quamplura alia domino regi et corone sue regie prejudicialia [in hac parte][339] fecit et fieri procuravit in domini regis contemptum et prejudicium ipsiusque regis et corone sue exheredacionis periculum et possessionis ipsius Thome in hac parte adnullacionem manifestam ac contra formam provisionis et ordinacionis predictarum. Et dicit quod predicti Johannes Savage magister Johannes Ragnell Johannes Wylyngham Johannes Bollesore et Willelmus Savage fuerunt manutentores consiliarii abbettatores auxiliantes et fautores ipsius Johannis Fraunceys in hac parte, unde dicit quod deterioratus est et dampnum habet ad valenciam mille librarum. Et inde producit sectam etc.

Et ulterius idem Thomas de Toueton dicit quod predictus Willelmus Savage de London, qui modo comparet in propria persona sua, non est eadem persona versus quam ipse prosecutus est breve suum predictum, set dicit quod ipse versus quem ipse prosecutus est breve suum predictum est Willelmus Savage de London capellanus, et ipse qui modo comparet in propria persona sua est Willelmus Savage de parochia Sancte Brigide in Fletestrete London' in suburbiis eiusdem civitatis. Ideo predictus Willelmus Savage de parochia Sancte Brigide etc. eat inde sine die etc.

Et predicti magister Johannes Fraunceys Johannes

[332] Repeated.

[333] Recte *in eadem tempore pacis tempore Ricardi,* as in [B]?

[334] As in [B].

[335] *CPR 1405–8,* 24.

[336] Interlined.

[337] As in [B].

[338] Also in [B]; recte *eadem.*

[339] As in [B].

Savage Johannes Wylyngham et Johannes Bollesore defendunt omnem injuriam et contemptum et quicquid etc. Et predictus Johannes Savage dicit quod ubi predictus Thomas de Toueton per breve suum predictum supponit ipsum Johannem Savage esse Johannem Savage de London capellanum, ipse non est capellanus nec fuit die impetracionis brevis sui predicti, scilicet nono die novembris anno regni domini regis nunc septimo [1405], et petit judicium de brevi etc.

Et predictus Thomas de Toueton petit judicium si breve suum predictum non sit satis bonum etc. Et viso predicto Johanne Savage, consideratum est quod predictus Thomas de Toueton nichil capiat per breve suum predictum quoad predictum Johannem Savage set sit in misericordia pro falso clamio suo etc. Et predictus Johannes Savage eat inde sine die etc. Et predictus Johannes Bollesore dicit quod ipse in nullo est inde culpabilis. Et de hoc ponit se super patriam etc. Et predictus Thomas de Toueton similiter.

Et predictus magister Johannes Fraunceys dicit quod verum est quod predictus Johannes de Thoresby quondam archiepiscopus Eboracensis nuper fuit seisitus de patronatu prebende de Styllyngton predicte ut de jure ecclesie sue cathedralis Beati Petri Eboracensis, et de eadem prebenda fecit collacionem predicto Henrico Wakefeld clerico, qui ad eandem prebendam per capitulum ecclesie predicte admissus fuit et installatus in eadem et corporalem possessionem suam inde pretextu collacionis predicte optinuit tempore pacis tempore domini Edwardi nuper regis Anglie avi etc., et postea prebenda predicta vacavit pro eo quod idem Henricus consecratus fuit in episcopum Wygorniensem etc. Et ulterius dicit quod dominus papa tunc per bullas suas apostolicas de prebenda predicta fecit collacionem cuidam Guidoni tunc Sancte Crucis in Jerusalem' presbitero cardinali, qui pretextu provisionis et collacionis predictarum ad prebendam predictam per capitulum predictum admissus et installatus fuit et corporalem possessionem inde optinuit. Et dicit quod postea prebenda predicta vacavit per mortem predicti cardinalis, et tunc dominus papa per bullas suas apostolicas de prebenda predicta fecit collacionem et provisionem cuidam magistro Johanni Shepey, qui pretextu collacionis et provisionis predictarum ad prebendam predictam per capitulum predictum admissus et installatus fuit et corporalem possessionem inde optinuit tempore dicti domini Edwardi nuper regis Anglie etc., [*membrane 69d*] quiquidem Johannes[340] Shepey resignavit predictam prebendam in curia Romana, et tunc dominus papa per bullas suas apostolicas fecit collacionem et provisionem de prebenda predicta cuidam Geraldo tunc Sancti Clementis presbitero cardinali, qui pretextu collacionis et provisionis predictarum ad prebendam predictam per capitulum predictum admissus et installatus fuit et corporalem possessionem inde optinuit tempore domini Ricardi nuper regis Anglie secundi post conquestum. Et dicit quod postea prebenda predicta vacavit per mortem dicti Geraldi cardinalis, et tunc dominus papa per bullas suas apostolicas de prebenda predicta fecit collacionem et provisionem cuidam magistro Nicholao de Fereby clerico et subcollectori domini nostri pape in Anglia, qui pretextu collacionis et provisionis predictarum ad prebendam predictam per capitulum predictum admissus et installatus fuit et corporalem possessionem inde optinuit tempore[341] predicti domini Ricardi nuper regis Anglie tercio, et postea dominus Bonifacius nonus nuper papa per bullas suas apostolicas providebat prefato[342] magistro Johanni Fraunceys ad unam prebendam in ecclesia cathedrali Beati Petri Eboracensis tunc vacantem vel extunc vacaturam. Et profert hic in curia bullas apostolicas premissa testificantes, quarum data est Rome apud Sanctum Petrum iiij nonas januarii anno pontificatus sui xiiij [2 Jan. 1403].[343] Et dicit quod dominus papa predictus per alias bullas suas apostolicas executorias ordinavit et fecit dominum archiepiscopum nunc Cantuariensem dominum episcopum nunc Londoniensem et Thuribium Tudensem episcopum executores predictarum bullarum de provisione predicta predicto Johanni Fraunceys in forma predicta factarum. Et dicit quod postea dominus rex nunc per litteras suas patentes quas idem Johannes Fraunceys profert hic in curia, quarum data est apud Westmonasterium quinto die januarii anno regni sui quinto [1404],[344] perdonavit prefato magistro[345] Johanni Fraunceys transgressiones contemptus et mesprisiones per ipsum in ea parte factas,[346] et ulterius de uberiori gracia sua concessit quod executores et subexecutores bullarum predictarum et notarii quicumque processum et execucionem dictarum bullarum quantum videlicet ad unam prebendam et unam dignitatem extunc vacaturas de facto libere facere possent in dicta ecclesia Eboracensi, [et] quod prefatus Johannes per se ac procuratores notarios et servientes suos necnon alios quoscumque

340 Preceded by *predictus*, erased. 341 Recte *anno*.
342 Interlined. 343 *CPL*, V, 523–4.
344 *CPR 1401–5*, 332. 345 Interlined.
346 Recte *factos*.

de consilio suo canonicatum et prebendam necnon dignitatem in dicta ecclesia Eboracensi vacantem vel cum vacaverit de facto que cadent sub graciis et provisionibus supradictis acceptare possit. Et dicit quod predicta prebenda de Styllyngton vacavit per mortem predicti[347] Nicholai de Feriby ultimi prebendarii prebende predicte, et sub gracia predicti Johannis Fraunceys cadente[348] quidam magister Johannes Wylyngham procurator substitutus predicti[349] magistri Johannis Fraunceys predictam prebendam nomine magistri Johannis Fraunceys predicti acceptavit secundum consuetudinem et formam legis sancte ecclesie, et corporalem possessionem eiusdem prebende in vita predicti Ricardi Lescrop nuper archiepiscopi loci predicti optinuit et possessionem suam inde continuavit quousque ipse per predictum Thomam de Toueton amotus fuisset et expulsus; absque hoc quod ipse citari fecit predictum Thomam de Toueton ad comparendum in curia Romana predicta prout predictus Thomas de Toueton supra per breve et narracionem sua supponit. Et hoc paratus est verificare etc. Et petit judicium si predictus Thomas de Toueton accionem suam predictam versus eum manutenere debeat etc.

Et predictus Johannes Wylyngham dicit quod ipse fuit procurator predicti magistri Johannis Fraunceys in premissis et prebendam predictam nomine eiusdem magistri Johannis acceptavit et corporalem possessionem inde nomine eiusdem magistri Johannis in vita predicti Ricardi Lescrop nuper archiepiscopi loci predicti optinuit; absque hoc quod ipse citari fecit predictum Thomam de Toueton ad comparendum in curia Romana predicta prout predictus Thomas de Toueton supra per breve et narracionem sua supponit. Et hoc paratus est verificare etc. Et petit inde judicium etc.

Et predictus Thomas de Toueton protestando quod ipse non cognovit aliquam provisionem predicto Johanni Fraunceys in forma qua ipse supra allegavit factam, et protestando eciam quod predicti magister Johannes Fraunceys et Johannes Wylyngham citari fecerunt ipsum Thomam de Toueton ad comparendum in curia Romana prout ipse supra per breve et narracionem sua supponit, pro placito dicit quod predictus magister Johannes Fraunceys nunquam habuit corporalem possessionem prebende predicte in vita predicti Ricardi Lescrop nuper archiepiscopi loci predicti prout predicti magister Johannes Fraunceys et Johannes Wylyngham supra placitando allegarunt. Et de hoc ponit se super patriam. Et predicti magister Johannes Fraunceys et Johannes Wylyngham similiter. Ideo veniat inde jurata coram domino rege a die Pasche in xv dies [25 Apr. 1406] ubicumque etc. Et qui nec etc. ad recognoscendum etc. Quia tam etc. Idem dies datus est partibus predictis etc.

Et super hoc venerunt Henricus Bylyndon de comitatu Buk' Hugo Lyngeyn de eodem comitatu Robertus Othecote de comitatu Ebor' et Henricus Gedyngton de comitatu Norht' et manuceperunt pro predictis Johanne Bollesore et Johanne Wylyngham quod ipsi non attemptabunt nec aliquis eorum attemptabit nec attemptari facient in curia Romana nec in aliqua curia christianitatis citra mare vel extra aliquid quod in lesionem legum domini regis cedere valeat quovismodo, quilibet manucaptorum predictorum sub pena ducentarum marcarum et quilibet predictorum Johannis Bollesore et Johannis Wylyngham sub eadem pena, quasquidem summas quilibet manucaptorum predictorum ac predicti[350] Johannis Bollesore et Johannis Wylyngham separatim cognovit de terris et catallis suis ad opus domini regis levari si etc. Et quilibet predictorum Johannis Bollesore et Johannis Wylyngham, tactis sacrosanctis evangeliis, Deo corporale prestiterunt sacramentum quod nullus eorum in premissis attemptabit seu attemptari faciet, et siquid ante hec tempora in premissis attemptarunt illud omnino renunciabunt et quilibet eorum renunciabit etc.

Postea continuato inde processu inter partes predictas, pro jurata inde inter eas posita in respectum coram domino rege usque a die Sancte Trinitatis in xv dies anno regni domini regis nunc septimo [20 June 1406] ubicumque etc., nisi dilectus et fidelis domini regis Willelmus Gascoigne capitalis justiciarius ipsius regis prius die sabbati in vigilia Sancte Trinitatis [5 June 1406], apud Ebor' per formam statuti etc. venisset pro defectu juratorum etc.

Ad quem diem coram domino rege apud Westmonasterium venit predictus Thomas de[351] Toueton per attornatum suum predictum. Et prefatus Willelmus Gascoigne justiciarius coram quo etc. misit hic recordum coram eo inde habitum in hec verba:

Postea die et loco infracontentis coram Willelmo Gascoigne capitali justiciario etc. infranominato, associato sibi Willelmo de Waldeby, per formam statuti etc. venerunt tam Thomas de Toueton clericus infranominatus qui tam pro domino rege quam pro seipso sequitur in propria persona sua quam magister Johannes Fraunceys clericus Johannes Wylyngham clericus et Johannes Bollesore de comitatu Derb'

347 Interlined. 348 Recte *cadenti.* 349 Interlined. 350 Recte *predictorum.* 351 Interlined.

clericus infranominati per attornatum suum infranominatum. Et juratores exacti similiter venerunt, qui ad veritatem super infracontentis dicendam electi triati et jurati dicunt super sacramentum suum quod predictus magister Johannes Fraunceys nunquam habuit corporalem possessionem prebende de Stillyngton, unde infra fit mencio, in vita Ricardi Lescrop nuper archiepiscopi Eboracensis infranominati in forma qua idem Thomas infra placitando allegavit. Et dicunt ulterius super sacramentum suum quod predictus Johannes Bollesore culpabilis est de infracontentis in forma qua predictus Thomas per breve et narracionem sua infra supponit. Et assident dampna eiusdem Thome occasione unde infra fit mencio ad tricentas marcas.

Et super hoc dies datus est prefato Thome de[351] Toueton coram domino rege in octabis Sancti Michaelis [6 Oct. 1406] ubicumque etc. de judicio suo inde audiendo etc.

Ad quem diem coram domino rege apud Westmonasterium venit predictus Thomas de Toueton per attornatum suum predictum. Et super hoc quesitum est a prefato Thoma si ipse ulterius prosequi voluerit versus predictos magistrum Johannem Ragnell et Willelmum Savage de placito predicto, qui dicit quod non. Ideo consideratum est quod predictus Thomas de Toueton recuperet versus predictos Johannem Fraunceys Johannem Willyngham et Johannem Bollesore dampna sua predicta superius per juratores predictos ad trescentas marcas assessa. Et iidem Johannes Fraunceys Johannes Willyngham et Johannes Bollesore capiantur etc.

Postea, scilicet trecesimo[352] die[353] octobris anno regni regis Henrici quarti post conquestum decimo [1408],[354] coram ipso rege apud Westmonasterium venit predictus Thomas de Toueton in propria persona sua et cognovit se esse satisfactum de dampnis suis predictis etc.

[*Marginated*] Cognovit. Capiantur.

Dampna CCC marcas unde clericis xl s., custodi rotulorum xx s., Willelmo Waldby xx s., Hugoni Holgot j marca, Johanni Lambard dimidia marca.

[*At foot of membrane*] Idem Thomas de[355] Toueton in propria persona sua optulit se iiij^{to} die [12 Feb. 1406] versus predictos magistrum Johannem Ragnell et Willelmum Savage de London capellanum de placito predicto. Et ipsi non venerunt. Et preceptum fuit vicecomiti quod premunire faceret eos. Et vicecomes retornavit quod ipsi premuniti fuerunt prout patet supra etc. Ideo ipsi ponantur extra proteccionem domini regis. Et omnia terre et tenementa, bona et catalla sua foris[factura] fiant etc. Et preceptum est vicecomiti quod capiat eos si etc. ita quod habeat[356] corpora eorum coram domino rege ad prefatum terminum etc. Et unde in octabis Purificacionis[357] etc. Ad quem diem venit predictus Thomas in propria persona sua. Et vicecomes retornavit quod ipsi non sunt inventi. Ideo sicut prius capiantur quod sint coram domino rege a die Sancte Trinitatis in xv dies [20 June 1406] ubicumque etc. Ad quem diem vicecomes non misit inde breve. Ideo sicut prius capiantur quod sint coram domino rege in octabis Sancti Michaelis [6 Oct. 1407] ubicumque etc.

[B]

KB 27/586, m.38

[*Marginated*] Yorkshire

The sheriff was ordered (in terms nearly identical to [A]) to summon Master John Fraunceys and Robert Fraunceys, knight, Robert Scarclyf, clerk, John Savage, living at the hospital of St Anthony, London, John Macclesfeld, master of St Anthony's, John Hornyngsay of London, John Shilbotell, clerk, William Savage, clerk, Thomas, rector of St Mary 'atte Hill', London, William Lovell, clerk, William Fraunceys, clerk, and Robert Scargill, maintainors etc. of John Fraunceys, to be in king's bench on 6 October 1407 to answer the king and Thomas de Toueton. The latter then appeared by Henry de Chambre and the sheriff returned that he had summoned the defendants at Stillington on 29 July by John de Thornton of Farlington, Ellis de Tokwyth of Stillington, Robert Alwent, John Hikson, Robert de Stillyngton and John Bleuet [of Stillington]. Robert Fraunceys, Scarclyf, John Savage, Macclesfeld and Thomas the rector came in person.

Toueton's narration is identical to that in [A] save for the reference to his citation to the Roman curia here [*membrane 38d*] said to have been made at Methley, Yorkshire, on 11 March 1407 by Robert Fraunceys and John Savage as proctors and by Hornyngsay, Shilbotell and William Fraunceys as proctors and notaries of John Fraunceys. He concluded with accusing Scarclyf and Macclesfeld as

352 Recte *terciodecimo.*

353 Interlined.

354 The date of Francis' pardon: *CPR 1408–13,* 27.

355 Interlined.

356 Recte *haberet.*

357 Recte *in quindena Pasche*? (25 Apr. 1406, when the jury was to come for the main plea).

manutentores, William Savage and Thomas the rector as *fautores,* Lovell as *consiliarius* and Scargill as *abbettator et auxiliator.* He (again) claimed damages of £1000.

Following [only] denials of contempt and pleas of not guilty, a jury was called for 25 November 1407. John Hewet, Thomas Heuster of Staffordshire, Richard Lowe of Worcestershire and Thomas Wode of Shropshire mainperned for Robert Fraunceys, Robert Barry of Bedfordshire, Henry Gedyngton of Northamptonshire, Thomas Slautley of Warwickshire and Henry Chorley of Cheshire for Scarclyf, Hornyngsey and Thomas the rector, and John Lylleston of Middlesex, Barry, Slauteley and Gedyngton for John Savage and Macclesfeld, viz that they (the six defendants who did appear) would not harm the king or his laws by suing Toueton for the prebend in any church court without the king's licence, each mainpernor in £100 and each defendant in £200, the latter also being sworn to the same effect and renouncing previous attempts.

Before the appointed day the suit was adjourned *per commune adjornamentum* to 20 January 1408 when all appeared by attorneys. For want of jurors, 29 April was appointed, William Gascoigne, CJ, being named as justice of nisi prius at York on 19 April.

[*After space of 2½ inches*] Idem Thomas de Toueton per attornatum suum predictum optulit se iiij^to^ die [9 Oct. 1407] versus predictos Johannem Fraunceys Johannem Shilbotell Willelmum Savage Willelmum Lovell Willelmum Fraunceys et Robertum Scargill de placito predicto. Et ipsi non venerunt set super hoc venit predictus Robertus Scarclyf in propria persona sua. Et dicit quod ipse non cognoscitur tam per nomen Roberti Scarclyf quam per nomen Roberti Scargill, et petit quod predictus Thomas de Toueton narret versus eum de placito predicto. Et predictus Thomas de Toueton dicit quod predictus Robertus[358] Scarclyf qui modo comparet non est eadem persona versus quem ipse prosecutus est breve suum, set dicit quod ipse versus quem ipse prosecutus est breve etc. est Robertus Scargill de civitate Ebor'. Et preceptum fuit vicecomiti quod premunire faceret eos et vicecomes retornavit quod ipsi premuniti fuerunt prout patet supra etc. Ideo tam predicti Johannes Fraunceys Johannes Shilbotell Willelmus Savage Willelmus Lovell Willelmus Fraunceys quam predictus Robertus Scargill de civitate Ebor' ponantur extra proteccionem domini regis. Et terre tenementa bona et catalla sua domino regi forisfactura. Et preceptum est vicecomiti quod non omittat propter aliquam libertatem etc. quin capiat eos si etc. et salvo etc. ita quod habeat corpora eorum coram domino rege ad prefatum terminum etc.

[18]

As with the previously noticed prosecution under the 1390 statute of provisors [16], these proceedings in Michaelmas 1407 had been initiated on behalf of a king's clerk within days of his discomfiture by a papal provisor. John Root, fellow of Oriel college, had been granted papal letters of expectation for a benefice in the patronage of the abbot and convent of Westminster which the king authorised in 1405.[359] He attempted to execute these letters when the church of St Bride, Fleet Street, became vacant by the death of William Dennis in 1407. On 25 July, however, Henry Harborough, like Dennis a king's clerk, was instituted to the rectory.[360] A writ for the arrest of Root and his agents must have issued almost instantaneously, for on 5 August a supersedeas for their release was sealed; it states that the proceedings were under the statute of 1390.[361]

KB 27/586, m.39

[*Marginated*] London'

Preceptum fuit vicecomitibus quod Johannem Rote clericum Robertum Northlode Willelmum Byfflete de London' Gregorium Somenour de London' et Johannem Carter de London' cardewaner notarios procuratores manutentores et summonitores ipsius Johannis Rote etc. per corpora sua attachiarent ita quod haberent corpora eorum coram domino rege ad hunc diem, scilicet a die Sancti Michaelis in xv dies [13 Oct. 1407], ubicumque etc. ad respondendum domino regi de contemptu et prejudicio etc. et Henrico Harburgh clerico de dampnis et injuriis sibi per predictos Johannem Rote Robertum Willelmum Gregorium et Johannem Carter pro ecclesia Sancte Brigide London' factis ut dicitur.

Ad quem diem coram domino rege apud Westmonasterium venerunt tam predictus Henricus quam predicti Johannes Rote Robertus Willelmus Gregorius et Johannes Carter in propriis personis suis. Et super hoc dies datus est partibus predictis coram domino rege usque in octabis Sancti Hillarii [20 Jan. 1408] ubicumque etc. Et super hoc venerunt Willelmus

358 Interlined.

359 *CPR 1405–8,* 94; Emden, *Biog. Reg. Oxford,* III, 1592–3.

360 Hennessy, *Novum Repertorium,* 113; *CPR 1401–5,* 205.

361 *CCR 1405–9,* 291.

Rybode skynner de London' Laurencius Neuport de London' corsor' et Thomas Frome de comitatu Dors', et manuceperunt quod predicti Johannes Rote Robertus Willelmus Byfflete Gregorius et Johannes Carter non attemptabunt nec aliquis eorum attemptabit nec attemptari facient in curiis christianitatis citra mare vel extra aliquid quod in lesionem domini regis seu legum suarum quovismodo cedere valeat versus predictum Henricum pro ecclesia predicta sine speciali licencia domini regis, quilibet manucaptorum predictorum sub pena centum librarum et quilibet predictorum Johannis Rote Roberti Willelmi Byfflete Gregorii et Johannis Carter sub pena ducentarum librarum, quasquidem summas centum librarum quilibet manucaptorum predictorum et predictas summas ducentarum librarum quilibet predictorum Johannis Rote Roberti Willelmi Byfflete Gregorii et Johannis Carter separatim cognoverunt de terris et catallis suis[362] fieri et ad opus domini regis levari, si contingat predictos Johannem Rote Robertum Willelmum Byfflete Gregorium et Johannem Carter in premissis delinquere et inde legitimo modo convicti etc. Et predictus Johannes Rote, tactis sacrosanctis evangeliis, Deo corporale prestitit sacramentum quod in premissis non attemptabit seu attemptari faciet, et siquid ante hec tempora in premissis attemptaverit illud omnino recusabit etc.

Ad quem diem coram domino rege apud Westmonasterium venerunt tam predictus Henricus quam predicti Johannes Rote Robertus Willelmus Byfflete Gregorius et Johannes Carter in propriis personis suis. Et super hoc dies datus est eis coram domino rege usque a die Pasche in xv dies [29 Apr. 1408] ubicumque etc. in statu quo prius etc.

[19]

This record begun in Trinity 1409 and completed on 21 November 1410 concluded protracted litigation at Rome as well as in king's bench. Process under one of the statutes of provisors was not begun until some years after the parties opened their dispute for possession of the dignity of treasurer of Salisbury cathedral.

The contestants had both been king's clerks. George Lowthorpe was clerk to the treasurer of the exchequer when that office was held by John Waltham, bishop of Salisbury (1388–95), and he was one of the bishop's executors.[363] The bishop collated him to a prebend in Salisbury in 1393, he moved on to another in 1403, and he exchanged that prebend for the treasurership on 31 August 1404 and his estate as such was ratified by the king on 13 September following.[364]

William Glym was in Henry IV's service as clerk of the spicery.[365] He had already attempted to gain the Salisbury prebend of Chardstock, first by litigation at Rome which resulted in an adverse sentence and his excommunication for refusing to pay the damages.[366] He tried again in 1402 by the familiar ploy of obtaining a royal grant on the pretext that the presentation was the king's because the temporalities of the bishopric had recently been in royal custody (i.e. in 1395–96). If Glym did then raise an action by quare impedit it failed.

Glym then tried to enter the Salisbury chapter by provision. On 12 May 1404 the king granted his petition for a licence to sue for a papal grace of expectation for any benefice in the cathedral and for its execution, and on 27 July the grace was obtained, reserving Glym a prebend and dignity.[367] Lowthorpe was probably installed as treasurer before the papal letters reached England, but Glym was not deterred and obviously gave Lowthorpe cause for alarm because on 24 April 1405 the latter obtained a royal grant of the treasurership; this stated that the dignity was in the king's gift because of the recent voidance of the bishopric.[368] These letters patent, of course, were a safeguard against a suit at common law and, as the following record shows, allowed Lowthorpe to claim that as a provisor Glym was challenging the king's presentation.

Glym prosecuted his suit at Rome. Lowthorpe again betrayed fears about the validity of his title by obtaining, on 2 November 1405, papal letters which provided him to the treasurership.[369] The record indicates, however, that not long afterwards Glym won a sentence at Rome leading to the sequestration of the dignity by the bishop of Salisbury on 23 March 1406. Lowthorpe apparently fought back with some success because Glym was still in Rome in June 1407.[370] It was presumably at this point that

[362] Interlined.

[363] *CPR 1391–6*, 349; *1396–9*, 413; *CCR 1409–13*, 418.

[364] *Fasti*, III, 75, 51, 20; *CPR 1401–5*, 306.

[365] E 404/22, no. 268.

[366] *CPR 1401–5*, 88; *Fasti*, III, 39.

[367] E 28/12 (27 July); *CPR 1401–5*, 397; *CPL*, V, 618.

[368] *CPR 1405–8*, 8, 11.

[369] *CPL*, VI, 61.

[370] *CPR 1405–8*, 334.

Lowthorpe resorted to process under a statute of provisors: the case ended in Hilary 1408 with a jury awarding Lowthorpe damages of £800. After the sheriff, ordered by the court, had failed to arrest Glym and his proctor and had them outlawed, formidable commissions were appointed by chancery for their arrest in the following June, when it was understood that Glym was planning further proceedings at Rome to annul the verdict in king's bench.[371] Glym and Bilsthorpe remained at large until 19 November 1410, the date of their royal pardons and surrender into king's bench.[372] They were both fined twenty shillings 'pro quibusdam contemptibus et transgressionibus contra formam statuti de provisoribus'.[373]

KB 27/593, Rex m.21

[*Marginated*] Wiltes'

Alias scilicet termino Sancti Hillarii anno regni regis Henrici quarti post conquestum nono, preceptum fuit vicecomiti quod exigi faceret Willelmum Glym clericum et Thomam Billesthorp de London' de comitatu in comitatum quousque etc. utlagerentur si non etc., et si etc. tunc eos caperet, et salvo etc., ita quod haberet corpora eorum coram justiciarios domini regis apud Westmonasterium a die Sancti Johannis Baptiste tunc proximo sequenti in xv dies [8 July 1408] ad satisfaciendum domino regi de redempcionibus suis pro eo quod cum nuper vacante thesauraria in ecclesia cathedrali Beate Marie Sarisbiriensis et ad regis donacionem spectante racione episcopatus Sarisbiriensis nuper vacantis, thesaurariam illam Georgio Louthorp clerico contulerit rex, quiquidem Georgius pretextu collacionis domini regis predicte ad thesaurariam predictam, concurrentibus hiis que de jure in hac parte requirebantur, canonice admissus fuit ac institutus et inductus in eadem; predictus Willelmus machinans predictum Georgium maliciose inquietare et ipsum a possessione sua thesaurarie predicte quam ut premittitur optinet expellere, colore cuiusdam provisionis eidem Willelmo a sede apostolica ut dicitur facte ipsum Georgium ad respondendum super jure et titulo possessionis sue thesaurarie predicte in aliena curia extra regnum Anglie citari fecit, et quoddam mandatum ad sequestrandum super quadam sentencia in curia Romana versus eundem Georgium occasione premissa lata Ricardo episcopo Sarisbiriensi loci illius ordinario vicesimo secundo die marcii anno regni domini regis nunc septimo [1406] apud Novam Sar' per Thomam Billesthorp liberavit, et idem episcopus notificacionem eidem Georgio de sentencia et sequestracione predictis in adnullacionem et destruccionem presentacionis eidem Georgio per dominum regem facte vicesimo tercio die marcii anno regni domini regis nunc septimo apud Novam Sar' fecit, et predictus Thomas Billesthorp fuit manutentor consiliarius abbettator auxiliator et fautor predicti Willelmi ad premissa facienda; unde convicti sunt, prout per recordum et processum conviccionis predicte, que dominus rex certis de causis coram se venire fecit, plene liquet.

Ad quem diem coram prefatis justiciariis vicecomes retornavit quod ad comitatum tentum apud Wilton die martis proximo ante festum Nativitatis Sancti Johannis Baptiste anno regni domini regis nunc nono [19 June 1408], et sic ad quatuor comitatus proximo precedentibus, predicti Willelmus et Thomas exacti fuerunt et non comparuerunt; et quia ad nullum eorumdem comitatuum comparuerunt, utlagati fuerunt, per quod inquiratur de catallis suis.

Postea scilicet in quindena Sancti Martini extunc proximo sequenti [26 Nov. 1409][374] coram domino rege, venerunt predictus Georgius de Louthorp per Johannem Dalton attornatum suum per breve domini regis constitutum, quodquidem breve affilatur inter recorda anno undecimo etc., et cognovit sibi esse satisfactum de dampnis suis predictis etc.

Postea scilicet die mercurii proximo ante festum Sancti Clementis pape anno regni domini regis nunc duodecimo [19 Nov. 1410], venerunt predicti Willelmus Glym et Thomas Billesthorp in propriis personis suis et reddiderunt se prisone marescalcie domini regis coram ipso rege occasionibus predictis, qui committuntur marescallo. ⟨Mar'. Mar'.⟩[375]

Postea scilicet die veneris tunc proximo sequenti, venerunt predicti Willelmus Glym et Thomas Billesthorp in custodia marescalli et proferunt hic in curia litteras domini regis patentes de perdonacione eis separatim in hac parte facta, que secuntur in hec verba:

[Letters patent, both dated 19 November 1410, which virtually repeat the record above and pardon Glym and Billesthorp their outlawry.]

Et super hoc iidem Willelmus et Thomas petunt ipsos ad finem cum domino rege in hac parte faciendam admitti, et admittuntur prout patet per rotulos finium de termino Sancti Michaelis anno

371 ibid., 479–80. 372 *CPR 1408–13*, 263–4.
373 KB 27/598, Fines.

374 i.e. 11 Hen. IV.
375 Marginated.

regni domini regis nunc duodecimo. Ideo consideratum est quod predicti Willelmus Glym et Thomas Bilesthorp eant inde sine die etc. [*Marginated*] Sine die. Sine die.

[20]

This action was heard in Michaelmas 1402 when the king was defending Thomas Tutbury's possession of the deanery of Wells against a papal provisor [16]. Here the rôles are reversed, with Tutbury appearing as the defendant against a provisor calling in aid the statutes of 1352 and 1390 designed to protect incumbents against deprivation by royal presentations to their benefices. In such cases, as the judges noted in Hilary 1401, the deprived incumbent could only initiate proceedings for redress by petitioning the king,[376] and this action began with the plaintiff Rishton making a suit in chancery so that Tutbury was cited by scire facias. Rishton could quote letters patent of 10 March 1402 granting Tutbury the archdeaconry of Buckingham as if these were the cause of his expulsion from this benefice. In fact, Tutbury claimed earlier possession by episcopal collation: he had obtained the royal grant because, he claimed, the crown had a title to present to the archdeaconry as the temporalities of the see of Lincoln had been in royal custody in 1362–3. Tutbury had good cause to take this precaution in view of the experience of other incumbents.[377]

The record discloses another clerical casualty of the deposition of Richard II. Like Nicholas Slack [4], Ralph Selby was a councillor of Richard's arrested by the Londoners in the summer of 1399.[378] According to the record below, Selby had been professed as a monk by 19 August 1399 and his benefices thus became vacant. If he were indeed professed then, he must have received a special dispensation from the Benedictine rule. It is more probable that he embraced the cloister as a refuge.

In any event, Selby's retirement to Westminster abbey prompted a scramble for his benefices. Rishton was armed with papal letters of 1389 granting an expectation of a dignity in Lincoln cathedral and a licence of Richard II for their execution. He was not alone. Walter Cook had been granted, in 1398, expectations of prebends in York, Lincoln, Salisbury and Lichfield, and of a dignity in one of these cathedrals. With his London base, Cook was doubtless soon informed of Selby's arrest and tried to secure his benefices in the two cathedrals for which he had expectative provisions. Apparently he gained the Buckingham archdeaconry and a Salisbury prebend but after a fortnight was expelled by royal clerks supported by the ordinaries, and after being threatened with proceedings under the statutes of provisors desisted in his attempts.[379] Thus is confirmed Tutbury's claim to have obtained the archdeaconry by episcopal collation soon after Selby's entry to Westminster.

Rishton showed more resolution in pressing his claim. The grant to Tutbury by letters patent in 1402 gave him a pretext to invoke a statutory defence, and by this time he probably hoped for some influential support because he was employed by both the king and the archbishop of Canterbury. Although the record is not concluded, it is otherwise known that Tutbury remained archdeacon of Buckingham until his death in 1403 and Rishton continued to be excluded thereafter.[380]

KB 27/566, m.86

[*Marginated*] Lincoln'
Memorandum quod venerabilis pater Edmundus episcopus Exoniensis per manus suas proprias liberavit hic in curia isto eodem termino quoddam breve domini regis de scire facias indorsatum vicecomiti Lincoln' nuper directum et in cancellaria sua retornatum quod sequitur in hec verba:

Henricus [*etc.*] vicecomiti Lincoln' salutem. Cum per statutum anno regni domini Edwardi nuper regis Anglie avi nostri vicesimo quinto editum ordinatum fuisset quod quandocumque idem avus noster fecerit collacionem sive presentacionem ad aliquod beneficium in jure alterius, titulus super quo collacio sive presentacio illa fundaretur bene examinaretur quod esset verus, et quacumque hora ante judicium redditum titulus ille per bonam informacionem inveniretur non verus nec justus, collacio sive presentacio inde facta revocaretur;[381] ac in statuto in parliamento domini Ricardi nuper regis Anglie secundi post conquestum apud Westmonasterium anno regni sui ter-

[376] YB 2 Hen. IV, Hil. 26.

[377] Above, 350–1.

[378] Usk, *Chronicon*, 28, 179; below, 354.

[379] *CPL*, V, 102, 309; Emden, *Biog. Reg. Cambridge*, 157–8; *Fasti*, I, 15; III, 73.

[380] ibid., I, 15; *CPL*, VI, 59; Emden, *Biog. Reg. Oxford*, III, 1619–20.

[381] 25 Edw. III, stat. 6 (Pro Clero), c.3.

ciodecimo tento edito, pro eo quod quidam presentati regii dicto statuto predicto anno vicesimo quinto edito non obstante per favorem ordinariorum et aliquando per inquisiciones minus veraces favorabiliter captas in beneficiis ecclesiasticis absque debito processu partibus non premunitis nec vocatis fuerunt instituti et inducti et incumbentes eorumdem beneficiorum taliter amoti, ordinatum existat quod dictum statutum predicto anno vicesimo quinto editum firmiter teneatur et observetur quodque si idem nuper rex ad aliquod beneficium quod de aliquo incumbente[382] foret plenum presentaret, presentatus regius ad tale beneficium per ordinarium non admitteretur quousque idem nuper rex Ricardus in curia sua per processum legis presentacionem suam recuperasset, et quod si aliquis presentatus regius alio modo fuerit admissus et incumbens amotus absque debito processu ut predictum est, tunc idem incumbens prosecucionem suam infra unum annum post inductionem presentati regii ad ultimum inciperet;[383] iamque ex parte Nicholai de Rissheton clerici nobis sit ostensum quod licet archidiaconatum de Bukyngham qui est dignitas in ecclesia cathedrali Beate Marie Lincolniensis ex provisione apostolica mediante licencia regia canonice adeptus fuisset et possessionem suam in archidiaconatu illo per tempus non modicum continuasset ac verus incumbens in eodem[384] archidiaconatu extitisset, nos tamen decimo die marcii proximo preterito [1402] [385] ad minus veram suggestionem Thome Tuttebury clerici nobis suggerentis archidiaconatum predictum vacasse cum non vacaverit et ad nostram donacionem spectasse cum non spectaverit archidiaconatum illum per nomen archidiaconatus de Bukyngham eidem Thome per litteras nostras patentes contulerimus, colore cuius collacionis idem Thomas ad archidiaconatum predictum absque debito processu prefato Nicholao non premunito nec vocato admissus fuit ac institutus et inductus in eodem ut dicitur, sicque idem Nicholaus a possessione sua archidiaconatus illius expulsus existit minus juste in ipsius Nicholai dampnum non modicum et gravamen ac contra vim formam et effectum dicti statuti predicto anno terciodecimo editi, unde idem Nicholaus nobis supplicavit ut dictas litteras nostras eidem Thome sic factas et quicquid inde subsecutum fuerit revocari et adnullari ipsumque Nicholaum ad possessionem suam archidiaconatus predicti una cum fructibus et proficuis inde per prefatum Thomam medio tempore perceptis restitui jubere velimus: nos volentes predictum statutum dicto anno terciodecimo editum inviolabiliter observari et ulterius in hac parte fieri quod est justum, tibi precipimus quod scire facias prefato Thome quod sit coram nobis in cancellaria nostra in quindena Sancti Johannis Baptiste proximo futura [8 July 1402] ubicumque tunc fuerit ad ostendendum siquid pro nobis aut pro seipso habeat vel dicere sciat quare littere nostre predicte eidem Thome sic facte et quicquid inde subsecutum fuerit revocari et adnullari predictusque Nicholaus ad possessionem suam archidiaconatus predicti una cum fructibus et proficuis inde per prefatum Thomam medio tempore perceptis restitui non debeant, et ad faciendum ulterius et recipiendum quod curia nostra consideraverit in hac parte. Et habeas ibi nomina illorum per quos ei scire feceris et hoc breve. Teste me ipso apud Westmonasterium xiiij die junii anno regni nostri tercio.

Indorsamentum eiusdem brevis sequitur in hec verba: Responcio Thome Swynford vicecomes Lincoln'. Scire feci Thome Tuttebury clerico in brevi isto nominato ad stallum suum in ecclesia cathedrali Beate Marie Lincolniensi, ipso Thoma in balliva mea personaliter non invento, per Johannem Blake et Willelmum de Manfeld quod sit coram domino rege in cancellaria sua in quindena Sancti Johannis Baptiste proximo futura ubicumque tunc fuerit ad ostendendum siquid pro domino rege vel pro se ipso habeat vel dicere sciat quod istud breve in omnibus requirit secundum tenorem eiusdem brevis etc.

Ad quem diem coram domino rege apud Westmonasterium venerunt tam predictus Nicholaus Ryssheton quam predictus Thomas Tuttebury in propriis personis suis. Et predictus Nicholaus Rissheton dicit quod[386] ipse archidiaconatum de Bukyngham qui est dignitas in ecclesia cathedrali Beate Marie Lincolniensi ex provisione apostolica, videlicet per bullas sanctissimi patris Bonifacii undecimi[387] pape moderni quas idem Nicholaus profert hic in curia sigillo plumbeo sigillatas quorum[388] data est Rome apud Sanctum Petrum v idus novembris pontificatus sui anno primo [9 Nov. 1389][389] providebat[390] eidem Nicholao de dignitate personatu administracione vel officio eciam si dignitas ipsa

[382] Recte *incumbenti.* [383] 13 Ric. II, c.1.

[384] Interlined. [385] *CPR 1401–5,* 49.

[386] This clause has no verb (e.g. *optinuit*).

[387] Recte *noni.* [388] Recte *quarum.*

[389] Not traced in *CPL* but confirmed by *CPL,* V, 345–6.

[390] Recte *providentes*?

curata et in eadem ecclesia Lincolniensi post pontificalem major existeret etc., mediante licencia regia. Et profert hic in curia litteras domini Ricardi nuper regis Anglie secundi post conquestum quarum data est apud Westmonasterium xxiij° die marcii anno regni sui vicesimo secundo [1399],[391] inter alias provisiones recitans[392] provisionem ipsius Nicholai de archidiaconatu predicto etc. de gracia sua speciali perdonavit eidem Nicholao contemptus et transgressiones per ipsum factos pro impetracione et[393] acceptacione dictarum graciarum et provisionis in hac parte factarum; et ulterius concessit eidem Nicholao quod ipse per se procuratores executores subexecutores notarios et alios de consilio suo processum super[393] dictis gracia et provisione licite facere et execucionem eorumdem[394] juxta effectum et tenorem earumdem bullarum prosequi etc. et dignitatem que sub dictis gracia et provisione caderet acceptare et possessionem inde percipere et eos[395] habere et tenere ac eis juxta effectum bullarum predictarum gaudere et in curiis christianitatis, ubi sibi placeret, quicquid contigeret causas et materias predictas in hac parte prosequi valeret sine occasione vel impedimento ipsius nuper regis vel heredum suorum seu ministrorum suorum quorumcumque, et quod gracia et provisio predicte valerent et in suo robore et effectu permanerent a tempore date bullarum predictarum apostolicarum eidem Nicholao factarum, et quod idem Nicholaus quecumque beneficia vacancia seu de cetero vacatura tam in curia Romana quam alibi libere impetrare et acceptare posset, statuto de provisoribus anno regni dicti nuper regis terciodecimo edito aut aliquo alio statuto seu ordinacione per ipsum nuper regem vel progenitores suos in contrarium factis seu faciendis non obstantibus, et quod ipse graciis predictis etc. secundum tenorem et effectum dictarum bullarum uti posset etc. Et dicit quod archidiaconatus predictus est de patronatu episcopi Lincolniensis et fuit de patronatu eiusdem episcopi et predecessorum suorum a tempore cuius contrarii memoria non existit ut de jure ecclesie sue Beate Marie Lincolniensis. Et dicit quod quidam magister Radulphus Selby nuper archidiaconus loci predicti habitum religionis in abbatia Westmonasterii ante decimum nonum diem mensis augusti anno regni dicti nuper regis vicesimo tercio [1399] assumpsit et in eadem abbatia monachus professus fuit, per quod archidiaconatus predictus vacavit, quodque idem Nicholaus vigore dictarum bullarum seu litterarum apostolicarum necnon licencie predicti regis Ricardi eundem archidiaconatum Buk'[396] ut prefertur vacantem acceptavit, ac per subexecutorem in processibus dictarum litterarum apostolicarum deputatum [*membrane 86d*] de eodem archidiaconatu fecit sibi provideri ac stallum dicti archidiaconatus in choro dicte ecclesie Lincolniensis sibi assignari et in eiusdem stalli possessionem realem induci sub pretextu provisionis et licencie suarum predictarum. Idemque Nicholaus possessionem in dicto stallo ipsius archidiaconatus per tempus non modicum continuavit in predicta ecclesia cathedrali Lincolniensi tanquam verus incumbens in eodem archidiaconatu, quousque idem Thomas Tuttebury ipsum Nicholaum de[396] eodem archidiaconatu spoliavit. Dominus rex nunc tamen decimo die marcii [*as in the writ, mutatis mutandis* – anno terciodecimo editi]. Et petit quod predicte littere patentes prefato Thome de archidiaconatu predicto facte revocentur et penitus adnullentur, et quod ipse ad possessionem suam archidiaconatus predicti una cum fructibus et proficuis inde medio tempore perceptis restituatur etc.

Et predictus Thomas Tuttebury dicit quod verum est quod[397] archidiaconatus predictus est de patronatu episcopi Lincolniensis et fuit de patronatu predecessorum predicti nunc episcopi a tempore cuius contrarii memoria non existit ut de jure ecclesie sue Beate Marie Lincolniensis. Et dicit quod verum est[398] quod archidiaconatus predictus vacavit per professionem predicti Radulphi, prout predictus Nicholaus supra allegavit, et quod Henricus nunc episcopus Lincolniensis fecit collacionem prefato Thome Tuttebury de archidiaconatu predicto, pretextu cuius collacionis idem Thomas Tuttebury ad archidiaconatum predictum, concurrentibus hiis que de jure in hac parte requirebantur, admissus ac institutus et inductus fuit et corporalem possessionem inde habuit. Et dicit quod postmodum idem Thomas Tuttebury percipiens quod dominus rex nunc habuit jus collacionis ad archidiaconatum predictum, eo quod quidam Johannes Gynewell nuper episcopus Lincolniensis fuit seisitus de patronatu archidiaconatus predicti et fecit collacionem de archidiaconatu predicto cuidam Johanni Assheborn clerico tempore domini Edwardi nuper regis Anglie avi domini regis nunc, qui ad archidiaconatum predictum fuit admissus ac institutus

391 *CPR 1396–9*, 513. 392 Recte *recitantes.*

393 Interlined. 394 Recte *earumdem.*

395 This passage seems to be an extract from the licence which allowed entry to a number of benefices.

396 Interlined. 397 *verum est quod* interlined.

398 *quod verum est* interlined.

et inductus in eodem etc., et postmodum archidiaconatus predictus per mortem predicti Johannis Assheborn vacavit, temporalibus episcopatus predicti tunc in manibus predicti avi etc. existentibus per mortem dicti Johannis Gynewell nuper episcopi etc., per quod jus collacionis archidiaconatus predicti ad ipsum avum etc. pertinuit; et de ipso avo descendit jus collacionis archidiaconatus predicti Ricardo nuper regi Anglie secundo etc., videlicet filio Edwardi filii predicti avi etc., et de ipso Ricardo nuper rege etc., eo quod ipse de regimine regni sui se dimisit, descendit jus collacionis archidiaconatus predicti domino regi nunc. Et dicit quod dominus rex nunc per litteras suas patentes fecit eidem Thome Tuttebury collacionem de archidiaconatu predicto. Et dicit quod ipse post possessionem archidiaconatus predicti inde habitam pretextu collacionis predicti Henrici episcopi possessionem suam de archidiaconatu predicto continue post professionem predicti Radulphi continuavit et adhuc continuat, absque hoc quod predictus Nicholaus[399] aliquam possessionem de archidiaconatu predicto infra annum proximo ante datam brevis sui predicti, videlicet quartodecimo die junii anno regni eiusdem regis nunc tercio, habuit. Et hoc paratus est verificare. Et petit judicium de brevi suo predicto etc.

Et predictus Nicholaus[399] protestatur quod ipse non cognoscit aliquid per predictum Thomam Tuttebury supra allegatum, dicens quod placitum predicti Thome in forma predicta placitatum est ad accionem ipsius Nicholai. Et dicit quod archidiaconatus predictus nullam habet in dicto comitatu Buk' possessionem sive mansionem temporalem dicto archidiaconatui incorporatam nisi tantummodo visitacionem et jurisdiccionem spiritualem in dicto comitatu Buk' set stallum in ecclesia Lincolniensi antedicta in predicto comitatu Lincoln', et quod idem stallus a tempore cuius non extat memoria fuit et est in certo eidem archidiaconatui annexus assignatus ac pertinens.[400] Et dicit quod ipse post professionem predicti Radulphi, videlicet decimo nono die mensis augusti anno domini millesimo CCC° nonagesimo nono et anno regni dicti domini Ricardi nuper regis Anglie vicesimo tercio, per Hugonem Suthwell capellanum procuratorem suum in hac parte corporalem possessionem de archidiaconatu predicto apud Lincoln' in stallo in choro predicto optinuit et possessionem suam inde continuavit [et] antequam possessionem ipsius Nicholai predictus Thomas non fuit institutus nec inductus in archidiaconatu predicto, quousque predictus Thomas Tuttebury ipsum Nicholaum[401] archidiaconatu predicto spoliavit. Et postmodum idem Nicholaus[402] vicesimo septimo die aprilis anno domini millesimo CCCC° secundo et anno regni regis Henrici quarti tercio infra annum ante datam brevis sui predicti per Matheum Asshton advocatum curie Cantuariensis procuratorem ipsius magistri[403] Nicholai in hac parte corporalem possessionem archidiaconatus predicti in stallo predicto apud Lincoln' reassumpsit ac reintravit. Et sic idem Nicholaus fuit in possessione predicti archidiaconatus infra annum ante datam predicti brevis sui et hoc paratus est verificare etc. Et petit quod littere patentes prefato Thome inde facte revocentur etc.

Et predictus Thomas Tuttebury dicit quod predictus Nicholaus[404] non habuit aliquam possessionem archidiaconatus predicti infra annum proximo ante datam brevis sui predicti, prout ipse supra allegavit. Et hoc paratus est verificare etc. Et predictus Nicholaus[404] dicit quod ipse fuit in possessione predicti archidiaconatus, prout ipse superius allegavit. Et de hoc ponit se super patriam. Et predictus Thomas Tuttebury similiter etc. Et quia curia nondum avisatur utrum exitus placiti triari debet in dicto comitatu Buk' vel in predicto comitatu Lincoln', dies datus est partibus predictis coram domino rege usque in octabis Sancti Hillarii [20 Jan. 1403] ubicumque etc. in statu quo nunc etc.

Ad quem diem coram domino rege apud Westmonasterium venerunt tam predictus Nicholaus quam predictus Thomas Tuttebury per attornatos suos predictos. Et quia videtur curie quod exitus placiti predicti in predicto comitatu Lyncoln' triari debet, ideo preceptum est vicecomiti Lyncoln' quod venire faceret coram domino rege a die Pasche in xv dies [29 Apr. 1403][405] ubicumque etc. xxiiij^{or} tam milites etc. de visneto Lincoln'[406] per quos etc. Et qui nec etc. ad recognoscendum etc. Quia tam etc. Idem dies datus est partibus etc.

[399] *Nicholaus* is preceded by erasure and deletion mark of 0.8 inches at these two points and thrice later. The erased word was probably *magister* which occurs once below: n.403.

[400] *assignatus ac pertinens* interlined.

[401] *possessionem suam inde . . . Nicholaum,* comprising two lines of the MS, written over erasure adequate for one line of normal depth.

[402] See above, n.399.

[403] cf. above, n.399.

[404] See above, n.399.

[405] Tutbury was then dead: [16].

[406] Followed by *de Lincoln'.*

Appendix

LITIGATION UNDER THE STATUTES OF PROVISORS

Notices of pleas and issues of pardons and writs of supersedeas are clear evidence of common law proceedings. The other references, particularly to bonds, suggest that the disputes may have been settled 'out of court'.

This list cannot be complete. The chancery rolls obviously do not give a reference to every action in king's bench: there is none to the suits about Liskeard and St Teath. The chancery references make it clear that the coram rege rolls contain more cases than are printed here.[407] The St Teath case was discovered fortuitously: it shows John Stafford, the future archbishop, defending a prebend against the provisor Roger Sayer, who had a royal licence.[408]

Two of the notices listed show that provisions disputes were referred to chancery and others may have been settled at the king's council. The vicar of Burford initially petitioned parliament against his disturbance by a provisor.

Date	*Benefice*	*Nature of notice*	*Statute (if known)*	*References*
1399	Christchurch priory	Arrest		*CPR 1399–1401*, 82.
	Wigtoft vicarage	Supersedeas	1390	*CCR 1399–1402*, 103, 122; *CPL*, V, 303.
1400	Chesterton church	Petition		*Select Cases in Chancery 1364–1471*, ed. W. P. Baildon (SS, X, 1896), 95–7.
	St Goran vicarage	Supersedeas		*CCR 1399–1402*, 124.
	Liskeard vicarage	Plea	1365	Case [14].
	Salisbury: prebend	Supersedeas		*CCR 1399–1402*, 127.
1401	Snape priory	Plea	1365	Case [15].
1402	Burford vicarage	Proclamation (after sentence)	1390	*CCR 1399–1402*, 501–2; *RP*, III, 482.
	Ilkeston vicarage	Pardon	1365?	*CPR 1401–5*, 162.
	Roos church	Supersedeas	1390	*CCR 1399–1402*, 516; *CPL*, V, 594–5.
	Salisbury: prebend	Arrest		*CPR 1401–5*, 126.
	Sedgefield church	Bond		*CCR 1399–1402*, 495.
	Wells: deanery	Plea	1390	Case [16].
1403	Earls Colne priory	Pardon		*CPR 1401–5*, 220.
1405	Tawstock church	Bond		*CCR 1405–9*, 104.
	York: prebend	Attachment	1390	*CCR 1402–5*, 514.
1406	Salisbury: prebend	Bond		*CCR 1405–9*, 223.
	York: prebend	Plea	1365	Case [17].
1407	London, St Bride's	Plea	1390	Case [18].
	Salisbury: treasurer	Plea		Case [19].
	Saltash vicarage	Award in chancery		*CCR 1405–9*, 265, 327, 387–8.
1408	Sidlesham vicarage	Supersedeas	1390	ibid., 360.
1409	St Teath: prebend	Plea	1365	KB 27/599, m.34.

407 Above, n.33.

408 *CPR 1405–8*, 374; Emden, *Biog. Reg. Oxford*, III, 1751.

A Wiltshire sheriff's notebook, 1464-5

edited by

M. M. CONDON

The pore shreve quondam with his Quietus est
Singeth this anthem and taketh his rest
A turd for Tom Pyper now sorrowes are rype
My joyes are the greater By passyng the pype.

Francis Dyngley vic'
[sheriff of Worcestershire, 1597–8]
E 199/46/50, f.38v

INTRODUCTION[1]

Amongst the Darell papers,[2] which are mostly the estate papers, correspondence and legal papers of William Darell (d. 1589), and of his father (d. 1549) and great-grandfather (d. 1529), both called Edward, are several papers of earlier date, including a mutilated notebook of twelve folios concerned with the activities of George Darell (d. 1474) as sheriff of Wiltshire in 1464–5 and a bill of expenses in the passing of a shrieval account for Darell as sheriff of Somerset and Dorset two years later.[3] The bill of costs is not itself of any great interest, and there are other, similar, examples in the class of Sheriffs' Accounts (E 199) in the Public Record Office. It consists of notes of fees paid to the various officials of the exchequer and of expenditure on diet, and a few memoranda on Darell's debts at the end of his account. The first item, printed below, is, however, of much greater interest, for records remaining from the office of a medieval sheriff are by no means common, though a few examples are known to survive from the early fourteenth century.[4] The precise purpose of Darell's notebook remains, however, something of a mystery; it was almost certainly compiled after the events it records, and may not have been used during the term of his shrievalty.

This small book, of which eight and a half folios are written or partly written and the remainder are blank, contains the days of the sittings of the county court, presided over by the sheriff; the names of officials with whom he had to deal; royal and county officials such as the justices of the peace and the coroners; private officials such as the bailiffs of hundreds and liberties – though some hundred bailiffs were, of course, bailiffs of hundreds which had remained in the hands of the crown and who were thus themselves in the lower ranks of royal service;[5] and the names of the bailiffs itinerant who were there either by Darell's own appointment or by that of a predecessor. The greater part of the book is a record of writs received, with notes on the officials responsible for serving the process. It is by no means a complete record of such writs. Not only are all the writs judicial, concerned with securing the appearance of defendants in the course of litigation,[6] but even this record is not complete. For example, only twenty-two writs are listed as being returnable on the quindene of Easter 1465 [26–29],[7] whilst the de banco rolls for the two preceding terms (the unsorted writ files have not been examined) show that at least 124 writs were to be returned on this return day; and a further twelve are recorded on the coram rege rolls.[8] Notes amongst the now fragmentary exchequer bille

[1] I owe thanks to Dr M. A. Hicks for his helpful suggestions and for reading an earlier draft of this paper; and to Dr D. H. Gifford who gave me the opportunity to explore the respectably modern – or so it seemed – Darell papers.

[2] SP 46/44–46. C. E. Long, 'Wild Darell of Littlecote', *Wilts Arch. & Nat. Hist. Mag.*, VI (1860), 391, suggests that the documents have come to be amongst the state papers as a result of being produced and forgotten in the course of litigation between the attorney general, Sir John Popham, and the widow of Sir Francis Walsingham, both of whom had profited from William Darell's indiscretions, and both of whom might have expected to benefit from his will and estate. In addition to the Darell papers in the Public Record Office, there survives a cartulary, begun in the late fourteenth or, possibly, early fifteenth century, with substantial additions made by or for George Darell's father, William: BL, MS Harl. 1623. The matter which it contains is, however, of too early a date to be relevant to our text.

[3] SP 46/45, nos. 93, 94.

[4] *Rolls from the Office of the Sheriff of Beds and Bucks*, ed. G. H. Fowler (Beds Hist. Rec. Soc., Quarto ser., III, 1929); C. H. Jenkinson and M. H. Mills, 'Rolls from a Sheriff's Office of the Fourteenth Century', *EHR*, XLIII (1928), 21–32.

[5] There were, in 1274, thirteen royal and twenty-five private hundreds: H. M. Cam, *The Hundred and the Hundred Rolls* (London, 1930), 283–4. These had, by 1464, grouped themselves into a total of twenty-nine hundreds, of which twenty-one were in private and eight in royal hands. Two of these, Mere and Selkley, were farmed directly from the crown.

Darell himself farmed the hundred of Calne from Lord Zouche, and received a fee as his steward: E 357/120, m.52. The few surviving records show hundred bailiffs being paid sums ranging from 20s. to 26s. 8d. a year. William Stroud, bailiff of the honor of Trowbridge, the Wiltshire liberty of the duchy of Lancaster, received wages of 60s. 8d., but his duties included custody of the warren: SC 6/1056/5; 1050/2; 1054/8 (Thomas Mascall); DL 29/687/11145.

[6] cf. the variety of writs recorded in the roll edited by Fowler in *Sheriff's Rolls of Beds & Bucks.*

[7] In counting the number of writs, thoughout this essay the grouping suggested by the bracketing of the several defendants has been used, with only one exception. Thomas Wabcan is separated on the plea rolls from Thomas Edmunds and his fellows, and has therefore been separated in the count, as he is indeed in his first appearance in the memoranda.

[8] CP 40/813, 814; KB 27/814, 815.

which enumerate thirteen writs as returnable on the octave of Trinity 1464 seem fairly typical and, with the minimal figure of the three writs returnable on the quindene of Hilary 1465 found amongst chancery files, are a reminder of process outside the two common law courts.[9] Even where cases are represented in the notebook, they do not necessarily appear in each term nor are all the defendants always noted. In general, out-county defendants are omitted, although there are one or two writs of capias against men from adjacent counties [26, 33, 35].[10] In cases where men of substance are attached and writs of capias issued against those said to have no goods or chattels, only the latter appear.[11] The notes are not, however, consistent, and names of co-defendants were omitted for no apparent reason.[12] Nevertheless, to perform the tedious labour of relating book and plea roll, and to attempt to gain some insight into Darell's responsibilities as sheriff, is by no means unrewarding.

George Darell was no stranger to shrieval office or the king's service. He was sheriff of Wiltshire in 1454–5 and 1460–1. Within a month of Edward IV's accession he was appointed keeper of the great wardrobe. This office he held until 4 April 1465, midway through his shrievalty, when he was succeeded by Robert Cousin.[13] Although the keepership had declined from its earlier importance, and its duties could be performed largely by deputy, Darell must nevertheless have found its responsibilities onerous in conjunction with his duties as sheriff.[14] The tradition of service within the county ran in his family for more than a century, and between 1420 and 1519 members of the Darell family were fourteen times sheriffs of Wiltshire, this despite the long minority of Edward Darell.[15] George Darell was himself again sheriff in 1468–9, having been sheriff of Somerset and Dorset in 1466–7, and was a justice of the peace for Wiltshire from 1472 until his death on 21 March 1474.[16] Although he had served under both the Lancastrian and the Yorkist kings, his suing out of letters patent of pardon in March 1460, the dates of his two previous shrievalties and of his fourth tenure of office, which coincided with a major oyer and terminer commission designed to investigate a supposed Lancastrian plot, and the immediate preferment he received from Edward IV, suggest an early connection with the Yorkist cause.[17] This is confirmed by the survival of an indenture of 30 January 1453 signed by Richard, duke of York, retaining Darell for life with an annuity of £10 to be paid until he should have been provided with an office worth twenty marks.[18] Darell emerged from his third period of office as a knight rather than an esquire, but it was a dignity basically devoid of

[9] E 207/18/2; C 251/22. The second figure is, of course, much too low. Few of the files are complete, and many contain only one or two writs for the whole of England for these two years. Even so, one of these writs, for the attachment of William Sewey and others to appear in chancery to answer John Crook, a servant of the chancellor, on a plea of trespass, may be related to litigation in the common bench. Sewey, attached by the pledges of Robert Horwood and John Box, appeared in Hilary and Easter 1465 to answer to a plea of quare clausum fregit which ultimately involved a question of title: CP 40/814, mm.388, 400d; 815, m.146d.

[10] The second entry [37] of Thomas Tropenell's suit against Nicholas Bovey and others includes the name of John Keynsham, a glover of Frome Selwood, Som, although he is omitted from the first entry [28].

[11] e.g., *Fen* v. *Sprot and Hampton,* omitting John Bourne and William Beaushyn [26, 36]; *Francis* v. *Sussex,* omitting Robert Cove, who in this year was coroner of Salisbury, and omitting also the name of a Hampshire man [38]. This anticipates a similar dissociation occurring in the plea rolls, when writs of exigent were sued against these lesser men whilst the other defendants continued to be attached and distrained.

[12] e.g. *Ash* v. *Cromhall and other* omits two, and *Newbury* v. *Brown* omits four of the defendants grouped with them on the plea rolls [33, 34]. The explanation may be the grouping for convenience on the plea rolls of essentially unrelated suits for debt. Where there is more than one plaintiff, only the first is ever named in the memoranda.

[13] *CPR 1461–7,* 17, 436.

[14] Darell's account as keeper does not survive for this year, and very little financial evidence remains concerning his tenure of the office. For his receipts from the exchequer, and for a brief outline of his duties as laid down in the Black Book, see A. R. Myers, *The Household of Edward IV* (Manchester, 1959), 45–6, 114. The plea rolls of the exchequer do, however, show him both suing and being sued, sometimes appearing in person, for debts and non-payments concerning his office. It is interesting to note that not even his authority as sheriff could always secure the payment of fee farms within Wiltshire assigned to him as keeper, so that new assignments were made on the bad tallies one or two years later: E 13/150, 151; E 401/886A, 889.

[15] *List of Sheriffs to 1831* (PRO L & I, IX), 153.

[16] ibid., 153, 124; *CPR 1467–77,* 635; C 140/48, no. 14 (for date of death).

[17] *CPR 1452–61,* 576; J. H. Ramsay, *Lancaster and York* (Oxford, 1892), II, 185–9, 230–7. It is unfortunate that the pricked lists of sheriffs have not survived, for the rotation of names, and amendments to the lists, can be instructive.

[18] C 146/6400. This indenture is transcribed and discussed in F. M. Wright, 'The House of York' (Unpublished Ph.D. dissertation, Johns Hopkins Univ., 1959). I am indebted to Dr M. A. Hicks for this reference.

honour. On 12 April 1465 writs for distraint of knighthood were issued to all the counties of England, and Darell as sheriff had the execution of the writ in Wiltshire and returned himself at the head of those holding land worth more than £40 a year. Exchequer process pursuant to the writ ensued, and also a separate prosecution for an insufficient return to it, for Darell returned a distraint upon himself based on an obviously false assessment. But on 22 May 1465 Darell appeared before Edward IV at the Tower of London and was there knighted, so gaining his exoneration from further suit.[19] It was this change in Darell's status that materially assisted in the initial identification and dating of his notebook.

The first two folios of the notebook contain memoranda on dates and officials necessary to the sheriff. The list of days for the county court, held once every four weeks by the sheriff, confirms that it was held on Tuesdays throughout the middle ages.[20] It sat at Wilton, and here the process of exaction and eventual outlawry was enacted, for which an accurate record of county days might be required.[21] The process of exigent was utilised in at least 29% of the cases recorded in the notebook relating to suits in the common bench.[22] In general, at least a year and often two years or more elapsed before the writ of exigent was finally returned certifying the five statutory exactions which preceded the proclamation of outlawry. Only 12% of the exigents recorded as posteas to the Wiltshire entries on the de banco rolls of the five terms Michaelmas 1464 to Michaelmas 1465 have a further note recording the ultimate execution of the writ; 62% note only the non-return of the writ over periods of up to five years, although in two cases in king's bench the issue of the exigent proved sufficient to procure the appearance of the defendants.[23] For this reason it would be unwise to estimate the number of times on which Darell himself actually executed the writs, for return and reissue may well be noted only after the final entry of the suit which had led to the outlawry process. This process could itself be prolonged. William Coventry, William Pierce and William Herring [9] finally surrendered themselves to the Fleet in 1476, eleven years after the original exigent against them and eight years after the proclamation of their outlawry; seventeen years elapsed before John Dunstan, put in exigent at the suit of Thomas South, appeared to answer to the plea.[24] The frequency of outlawry was one result of the inefficacy of the writ of capias.[25] Within the period of the account, of only three cases in process in which the defendants had been imprisoned, one involved one of Darell's own bailiffs itinerant, Thomas Mascall, who was certified to be too sick to appear in court without danger to his life, which plea was invoked also on behalf of John Barry and his fellows.[26] The unreality of the capias process is underlined by at least two instances of the almost simultaneous return of a non est inventus

19 E 159/242, Recorda, Trin. 5 Edw. IV, mm.5d, 33. The original return also survives: E 202/171; his fine was paid in November 1465: E 401/888.

20 Thus *VCH Wilts,* V, 9.

21 KB 27/820, m.67: the voidance of an outlawry following a scribal error which had returned a Surrey county day as *xvij* rather than *xxvij* March underlines the need for accuracy in the returns if the process was to be upheld against an alert and well counselled defendant. This same plea includes an impressive catalogue of errors.

22 By comparison, 36% of the cases recorded in one of the earlier stages of mesne process by capias in Michaelmas term 1464 (CP 40/813) had, by Michaelmas 1465, proceeded to the issue of a writ of exigent. Cf. M. Hastings, *The Court of Common Pleas in the Fifteenth Century* (New York, 1947), 176, which appears to suggest a higher proportion; but the ratio of the membranes allotted to enrolment of exigent process to the size of the whole plea roll supports the lower figure. In only thirteen of the remaining cases represented on this Michaelmas 1464 de banco roll by mesne process, either capias or attachment, had the defendants appeared by Michaelmas 1465; the rest either disappear entirely or show a subsequent default by the sheriff in return of the writs.

23 KB 27/815, m.69d; 818, m.16d. KB 27/814, Rex m.28; 816, Rex m.31d.

24 C 88/170, nos. 21, 51, 52; CP 40/813, m.21d. See also J. G. Bellamy, *Crime and Public Order in Later Medieval England* (London, 1973), 105–6.

25 On mesne process, see Hastings, *Common Pleas,* 174–83. The Wiltshire entries conform to the process she describes, and also include several examples where more than one writ of sicut pluries capias was issued before the exigent. The Wiltshire escheators' accounts for 1464–7 return forfeitures of chattels on only four of the defendants mentioned in the notebook, a total of 20s. 8d: E 357/120, mm.26, 44d; E 136/198/1.

26 KB 27/817, m.88; CP 40/816, m.180. In the latter instance, however, the defendants appeared the following term, when they were given a day in Hilary 1466. This was the one case in which a final judgment was recorded: see below, 419.

and the presence on a jury of the county of the same defendant.[27]

The lists of officials are headed by the names of the coroners, who worked in close coöperation with, and might occasionally act instead of, the sheriff. One such instance, the issue of a writ to the county coroners rather than the sheriff, is enrolled on the de banco rolls of 1465, in a case involving Darell himself as plaintiff.[28] All the coroners are found suing in their own rights in the court of common pleas, and two of them, John Uffenham and Robert Fen, frequently acted as attorneys in cases originating in the county in both the common pleas and the exchequer. John Uffenham was, in addition, bailiff of the liberties of the bishop of Winchester and of the prior of St Swithun, though in the exchequer he accounted by John Cook as his attorney and within the county he seems to have delegated his responsibilities – in what was no doubt an admirable compromise, since the liberties had return of writs – to Thomas Mascall, a bailiff itinerant, and to William Holbeam, one of the more active of the hundred bailiffs.[29]

The names of the active justices of the peace follow: that is, of those men resident within the county, who sat at the sessions of the peace. Those members of the commission who, like George, duke of Clarence, gave it added prestige and who could if necessary be called upon to uphold the king's authority but who normally took no interest or part in the enforcement of law within the county, are omitted. The list does, however, include the name of John Baynton who, though a justice almost continuously in the last years of Henry VI's reign, from 1453, is not recorded in any of the commissions enrolled on the patent rolls of Edward IV, and who died in June 1465, before the close of the shrievalty.[30] The difference in personal status between the justices and the coroners is underlined by the fact that the justices listed include four past or future sheriffs, whereas none of the coroners was ever appointed to this office. One justice, Henry Long, was included amongst the returns for distraint of knighthood, though he fined for his default and never assumed the order.[31] In addition, all the justices and two of the coroners, John Uffenham and John Dauntsey, sat as MPs for various Wiltshire towns at least once between 1450 and 1480, though Darell himself is not known to have sat in parliament.[32] No payments to the justices are recorded on the pipe roll of this year, though the roll of the following year records that John Whittocksmead, Philip Morgan, Thomas Rogers and Henry Long had been paid for sitting for a combined total of fifteen days between 12 June 1465 and 26 March 1466, all save Long sitting for four days.[33] This confirms the evidence of the indictment files and subsidy commissions, that these four men were the most active of the county justices.[34] Again, all the justices are found as active litigants on their own behalfs in the common law courts, as was John Chaffin, the clerk of the peace, who acted as executor for several people within the county and is thus found suing in testamentary actions for recovery of debt, of which one example appears in the notebook itself [26].[35] Nor is it surprising to find one of the justices, John Whittocksmead, presiding over a jury which returned as a true bill an offence against himself, which charge then became translated into a qui tam action and so appears on the rex side of the coram rege rolls.[36] Roger Tocotes, who heads the list given in the notebook, was to end his long career of service to the crown as controller of the household and councillor of Henry VII, and his record of service within the county as three times sheriff almost matches Darell's own.[37] Of the others mentioned,

[27] John Omedeux: CP 40/816, m.178; KB 9/310, m.79; John Needler: CP 40/817, m.174; C 140/17/30. See also Fowler in *Sheriff's Rolls of Beds & Bucks,* 26 n.140.

The county prisons (at Old Sarum and Fisherton Anger) were not, of course, under-occupied, and there are extant several bills presented in chancery for the issue of a corpus cum causa for petitioners then in gaol: C 1/29/383; 46/51; 48/124; 64/1142. This suggests that arrests could have been as important before the opening of judicial proceedings as in the course of formal process. The county gaol at Fisherton Anger received a separate mention on the plea rolls when its keeper, John Cappes, was sued for debt: CP 40/813, m.41.

[28] CP 40/817, m.240d.

[29] E 368/237, 238, Adventus vicecomitum; [4].

[30] *CPR 1452–61,* 681. Biography in J. Wedgwood, *Parliamentary Biographies* (London, 1936), 53.

[31] E 159/242, Fines, Mich. 5 Edw. IV; E 401/890; E101/116/9 (the return of a distraint of half a mark on his lands).

[32] Wedgwood, *Parl. Biogs,* passim.

[33] E 372/311, Item Wilts. Whittocksmead and Morgan presided at the Marlborough sessions, 11 June 1465 [30]; KB 27/823, Rex m.6d; KB 9/310, m.25.

[34] KB 9/295–325; E 179/196/130; 239/194.

[35] As executor of William Cormaile, a former mayor of Salisbury: CP 40/814, m.235.

[36] KB 9/308, m.41; KB 27/818, Rex m.28.

[37] Wedgwood, *Parl. Biogs,* 858–9.

John Whittocksmead was also bailiff of the liberty of the bishop of Salisbury, and was frequently employed in royal commissions acting within the county,[38] whilst between them these justices accounted for no less than nine periods as sheriff between 1443 and 1485.[39]

With the bailiffs of the liberties, who were drawn from the same social classes as the justices and the coroners, the sheriff would have had little direct concern, for they accounted separately to the exchequer for the issues of their bailiwicks,[40] and within the liberties exercised the franchise of return of writs, thus excluding the sheriff. This franchise was invoked at least once by Darell as the reason for the non-execution of a writ.[41] One liberty is not mentioned, that of the prioress of Amesbury, whose bailiff was Richard Clevedon. Possibly it was omitted because the liberty was congruent with the hundred of Melksham, just as the hundreds of Damerham were omitted from the lists of hundreds because they formed the liberty of the abbot of Glastonbury.[42]

With the schedule of the bailiffs itinerant, we at once move to a group of men intimately associated with the sheriff in the business of the administration of the shire, and at the same time move a few points down the social scale. The coroners and the bailiffs of the liberties were gentry; the bailiffs itinerant, on the other hand, are variously described as yeoman or husbandman, or simply as bailiff. It is difficult to identify with any certainty their length of tenure of their offices, though endorsements of manucaptions on returnable writs of the exchequer, and suits for debts in the court of common pleas seem to suggest that John Box and Robert Horwood, at least, were still in office at the end of the decade, and it is not impossible that Box had been so acting some ten years earlier.[43] By Trinity term 1465, midway through his shrievalty, Darell was suing all four bailiffs, his undersheriff, Nicholas Reynold, and William Holbeam, bailiff of Dunworth,[44] in the court of common pleas on a plea that they should render him reasonable account for the period in which they were his receivers of monies. Not surprisingly – for it was the bailiffs itinerant who, as this notebook clearly shows, served many of the writs delivered originally to the sheriff[45] – they were continually returned non sunt inventi, and Darell was still suing them two terms later. Indeed, the process against them brought by Darell and by his predecessors went its full course to the issue of writs of exigent, at the same time as they were continuing to act as the sheriff's representatives in the serving of writs issued from the king's courts.[46] In their defence it might be suggested that their life cannot have been an easy one. It is surely no accident that we find them, particularly Thomas Mascall of Stockton and William Holbeam of Hindon, almost perpetual defendants in the common law courts on pleas of debt and unlawful caption or detinue of goods and chattels; some of the alleged debts and detentions must have been for goods lawfully taken in the course of their duties as bailiffs.[47] Thomas Mascall was even imprisoned for a brief period by Richard Bennet, a factious clerk who appears almost more than any other of the minor clergy in Wiltshire pleas of the period both as defendant and as plaintiff, and whose default

38 ibid., 944–5; *CPR 1461–7, 1467–77,* passim.

39 *List of Sheriffs,* 153.

40 E 368/237, 238, Adventus vicecomitum. Edward Basing, however, defaulted of appearance on at least two successive occasions: E 372/310, Item Wilts.

41 KB 27/815, m.42d.

42 *VCH Wilts,* V, 50–2.

43 E 202/169, 171. For Box as a summoner from 1453 see *The Tropenell Cartulary,* ed. J. S. Davies (Wilts Arch. & Nat. Hist. Soc., 1908) I, 80; II, 58.

44 For whom see below, 416.

45 cf. Fowler in *Sheriff's Rolls of Beds & Bucks,* 4, 54. Wiltshire seems closer to the practice in Berkshire rather than Bedfordshire in the use made of the bailiffs itinerant.

46 CP 40/816, m.273 (Darell's suit); 821, m.254 (*Darell* v. *Raunds, Cromhall and Holbeam* for debt, Mich. 1466); 825, m.21 (exigent at Darell's suit against Holbeam on a plea of debt); 819, m.172d (against Sotwell and Holbeam at the suit of Tocotes, 1466). By 1467 Box, Horwood, Reynold, Cromhall and Richman were being sued for debt by Darell's successor, Thomas Delamare: CP 40/822, m.272.

47 For example, it seems not impossible that John Payne's suit against Thomas Mascall for unlawfully seizing hens worth 60s. was connected with George Darell's suit against Payne on a plea of debt of 53s. 4d., which had begun the previous term: CP 40/817, m.240d; 818, m.243d. The Paston letters contain graphic pictures of both trespass and distraint; the Sandwich chamberlains' accounts of nearly two centuries later are equally revealing. Whilst 6s. 6d. was spent on dinner and a fire for two of the more senior officials, 'it being a well and boisterous day', 3s. was spent on Henry Bull and his companion, who took the distress, 'the weather being well and could': Kent Archives Office, Sa AC/7, ff. 290v-291v.

Darell's successor as sheriff, Thomas Delamare, brought an action in king's bench for an assault on his undersheriff, William Crouch: KB 27/825, m.67d.

of appearance was continually recorded in actions of both debt and trespass in one of which, at least, the alleged use of force may not have been wholly fictitious.[48]

The miscellaneous duties of the bailiff itinerant have been well described elsewhere.[49] Chancery proceedings of a few years later yield examples of action by the bailiffs itinerant when they, under warrant from the sheriff, attached Thomas Broomhall, parson of Stanton, and imprisoned his vicar, Thomas Monk, who had been appealed of felony; or, coming to Amesbury, questioned and imprisoned as a vagrant William Goldwich of Rochester, who complained to the chancellor that he had been on his way to Bristol about his lawful business;[50] the Tropenell cartulary shows the bailiffs serving writs of scire facias and venire facias.[51] Use of Darell's notebook does, however, raise some interesting questions concerning the process of manucaption (which Broomhall complained Monk had been debarred from entering, though he had offered sufficient sureties). In addition to their work in serving the writs, the bailiffs were frequently returned as pledges in process of attachment. All four bailiffs, with Nicholas Reynold and William Holbeam, and the hundred bailiffs, John Raunds, Robert Cromhall and Thomas Warren, all of whom are mentioned in the notebook, were returned, in varying combinations, in no less than thirty-one of the fifty manucaptions recorded on the de banco rolls in the three terms Hilary to Trinity 1465; Edmund Richman, who is once mentioned in the livery of writs, acted in ten further manucaptions, most of which involved Salisbury men.[52] The device was followed so often by default of appearance by the defendants and thus by fine upon the pledges[53] that a small surcharge on the anticipated fine may well have been one of the perquisites of office. How far the manucaptions were fictitious even when the names of the pledges were those of the bailiffs is impossible to determine. There certainly were fictitious returns, generally given as rhyming pairs of names;[54] at the same time the pledges were real enough when gentry and others of similar status were involved.[55] The use of the bailiffs in 1464–5, as they had been used in 1333–4,[56] suggests, as Godfrey Green, writing to Sir William Plumpton, implied,[57] that it may well have been the sufficiency of the return rather than the reality of the persons involved that vitiated the process, at least when applied to pledges for appearance.[58]

All these men – sheriff, justices, coroners and bailiffs – found employment not only in the king's service but also in the retinues and estates of magnates holding lands within the county. Darell himself held fees of William, Lord Zouche and Queen Elizabeth

[48] Mascall was sued by Bennet on a plea of trespass and surrendered himself to the county gaol once an exigent had been issued against him; Darell returned that he was too sick to appear in court, and it would indeed have been inconvenient to forgo his services: KB 27/817, m.88. Mascall himself brought an action in common pleas against Bennet, alleging that he had been unlawfully imprisoned by Bennet at Codford St Mary, and not released until he had given Bennet an obligation in £20: CP 40/815, m.243d. Bennet compounded for his assault on Thomas Tropenell's servant by a gift of wine, hoping thus to settle the dispute out of court; and a jury found him guilty of the taking of an ox but not of the assault nor of the taking of game: CP 40/816, m.343; 819, m.184. In 1465–6 Bennet forfeited chattels worth 10s.: E 136/198/1.

[49] H. M. Cam, 'Shire officials: coroners, constables and bailiffs', *Eng. Govt at Work,* III, 171–4.

[50] C 1/46/51; 67/159.

[51] *Tropenell Cartulary,* I, 80, 368, 393; II, 36, 58, 66, 69.

[52] None of the other returns is self-evidently fictitious, though several are uncertain; the roll of Michaelmas 1464 does, however, include Roo and Hoo and Rouce and Douce.

[53] Thus John Box, John Sotwell and Robert Horwood were, with John Hay, held responsible by the exchequer for fines totalling 5s. 3d. for twenty-four separate manucaptions in Trinity term 1466. John Box was included in addition in other manucaptions not here totalled: E 101/112/1.

[54] The same document gives John Weston and Richard Preston; John Broun and William Doun; John Payn and Richard Mayn. Rouce and Douce seem to have been more popular than Doo and Roo: E 101/112/1. Cf. the comments of C. A. F. Meekings on common essoiners in *List of Various Common-Law Records* (PRO L & I, Supp. ser., I), 76–8, 152–7, where some typical names are given.

[55] For example, John Mundy and Thomas Tropenell, two of Margaret Hungerford's feoffees, mainperned for her in 1476; and John Dauntsey, a coroner, for John Stradling. In 1458 Thomas Tropenell, who was negotiating for the purchase of certain lands, offered to act as a surety of the peace in perpetuity in king's bench and chancery, the prospective vendor being then in prison: *Tropenell Cartulary,* I, 351; E 202/171.

[56] Fowler in *Sheriff's Rolls of Beds & Bucks,* 54.

[57] *Plumpton Correspondence,* ed. T. Stapleton (Camden Soc., [Old ser.], IV, 1839), 29–30.

[58] cf. the comments of M. Hastings, *Common Pleas,* 166. Pledges for appearance by a surrendered outlaw are similar, but are men of slightly higher legal standing: John Hampton, Richard Nowers and Robert Fen, who frequently acted as attorneys in the common bench in Wiltshire cases, or the county coroner, John Dauntsey, for example, often acted as mainpernors in such circumstances. See also Fowler in *Sheriff's Rolls of Beds & Bucks,* 27.

Woodville; John Whittocksmead was retained of council with Walter, Lord Hungerford; Thomas Stone was of the council of the bishop of Salisbury whilst, at a more humble level, John Sotwell had been messor of East Harnham, part of the Hungerford estate.[59] This list is by no means exhaustive.

Of the hundred bailiffs, perhaps little need be said beyond generalities. Their duties are unlikely to have changed significantly from those described by Miss Cam for the early fourteenth century.[60] They executed writs delivered to the sheriff from the common law courts, exchequer and chancery, and those arising within the shire at the county and hundred courts which the bailiff was obliged to attend. They might assist in the assessment and collection of subsidies, fines and amercements; they were responsible for empanelling juries, and there is confirmation of this in the 1469 oyer and terminer file in which the bailiffs countersigned the returns.[61] Within the period under consideration one of the bailiffs, Nicholas Reynold, hundredor of Chalke, acted as Darell's undersheriff and accounted for him at the Easter proffer.[62] Thomas Mascall, a bailiff itinerant, was bailiff also of the hundreds of Warminster and Heytesbury. Four years later two others of the bailiffs itinerant, Robert Horwood and John Box, were bailiffs of the hundreds of Elstub and Chippenham respectively, and may well have so been during the period of the account.[63] Seven of the bailiffs mentioned by name in 1464 were still in office in 1469,[64] and John Raunds seems to have been bailiff of the hundreds of Amesbury and Alderbury for more than thirty years.[65] Apart from the bailiffs itinerant, only two of the hundred bailiffs are mentioned in the memoranda as serving writs: William Holbeam and John Raunds. Robert Oborne, an attorney in the exchequer, who delivered a writ pertaining to the hundred of Warminster, perhaps acted during the term of Mascall's incapacity, though he also held land in the area. William Holbeam seems almost to have been an honorary bailiff itinerant, for he is mentioned more than any other hundred bailiff, and is found delivering writs outside his own hundred of Dunworth and, unlike John Raunds, was sued with the other bailiffs itinerant by Darell in the court of common pleas for the render of a reasonable account. Holbeam had in fact been a bailiff itinerant in 1455, during the term of Darell's first period of office as sheriff, and it is thus possible either that he continued to act unofficially as a bailiff errant or that his name was omitted, in error, from the list given in the notebook.[66]

No rigid geographical pattern can be traced in the livery of writs, either in terms of a defined circuit for each bailiff, though most of the writs delivered to Horwood and Box were to be served in the north and east of the county, or in terms of office-holding within the hundred. Mascall was generally, but not always, entrusted with the execution of writs to be served on men resident within his own hundred of Warminster, and the same rather fluid pattern is true also of the other bailiffs itinerant and those of the hundred bailiffs mentioned. Although one of the more interesting features of the text is the division of labour between the bailiffs, no firm conclusions can be drawn because of the small size of the sample in relation to a complete file of writs. One would also hesitate to relate the book directly to Darell's actions in the common bench, for there is no exact correlation between the officials mentioned in the memoranda and those called as defendants to his suit.

These notes on officials and county days fill only the first two folios of the text, the rest of which consists of a record of writs delivered to the sheriff for execution. Apart from a few later annotations recording distraint, process of exigent or livery of writs to the undersheriff or sheriff rather than to one of the bailiffs, most marginal notes were written

59 E 357/120, m.52; SC 6/1094/1; 1119/12; CP 40/820, m.330. Stone had also been receiver general to Darell's father, William: unsorted exchequer miscellanea.

60 *Eng. Govt at Work,* III, 174–81.

61 KB 9/320. The Tropenell cartulary includes an illustration of the possibilities of abuse, for it was alleged that John Raunds, bailiff of the hundred of Amesbury, had laboured the jury and threatened amercements on them if they did not attend and return a predetermined verdict: *Tropenell Cartulary,* II, 324. See also C 1/35/197–201, another case alleging perversion of justice.

62 E 159/242, Adventus vicecomitum.

63 KB 9/320, m.33. 64 ibid.

65 Still bailiff not only in 1472 but also in 1492 when he was aged 70: *Tropenell Cartulary,* II, 291; DL 29/739/12118. Cf. the comments on tenure of office by Fowler in *Sheriff's Rolls of Beds & Bucks,* 5. Although the fact that so many of the hundreds cannot be directly compared in the two lists of 1464 and 1469 limits the value of the evidence, the discontinuity of office is more marked in royal than in private hundreds. Amesbury and Alderbury both belonged to the duke of Clarence.

66 *Tropenell Cartulary,* II, 36.

contemporaneously with the text and note the names of the persons responsible for the execution of the writs. It is clear that the entries in the text were made from the writs themselves, as occasional direct quotes, irrelevant in context, to *c t* (in comitatu tuo), prove [10, 32, 38]. The writs, which are listed under the terms in which they were to be returned,[67] are summarised in the briefest possible form. The entries record the process, which was almost invariably capias or sicut pluries capias; the name and domicile of the person against whom it was directed; the name of the party suing; and, on occasion, some idea of the charge. Only three kinds of offence are specified – debt, trespass and, for the sessions, felony. These entries correspond, with occasional clerical errors, to the entries on the plea rolls, though it has proved impossible to correlate all the entries in the memoranda to entries on the rolls of the common law courts. In addition, the non-survival of the peace rolls means that nothing is known of those cases heard at the sessions and it would be rash automatically to relate the appearance of a defendant mentioned amongst the sessions records with suits in which he might later be cited in the central courts at Westminster.[68] The book makes no distinction between writs emanating from each of the two common law courts;[69] but writs relating to cases in the common bench far outnumber the suits in king's bench. The latter account for only eleven[70] of the 128 entries[71] amongst the memoranda. This, of course, reflects the differing bulk of the proceedings passing through the two law courts. Wiltshire cases on the de banco rolls in the five terms from Michaelmas 1464 to Michaelmas 1465 total more than 795 entries in approximately 360 suits,[72] whilst king's bench enrolments total a mere 127 entries in 75 suits.

Of themselves, the cases recorded in Darell's notebook are not particularly interesting. Debt and trespass form the greater part of the pleas. Subdivided, fifty-three or 60% of the eighty-eight entries which relate to seventy separate suits in common pleas are suits for debt ranging from a minimal 40s. to the £20 demanded by Edith Golion from William Putain [36].[73] Amongst these debt cases mercantile suits predominate. The plea rolls record disputes between the leading merchants themselves, but the memoranda contain only some record of their actions against lesser tradesmen. William Swain, John Port and William Sturmy, of whom the first was mayor of Salisbury in 1444–5, 1454–5 and 1477–8 and the second in 1458–9 and 1466–9, all figure in the memoranda; William Hoar, Alan Collett and John Hall, the mayor of Salisbury during the shrievalty, who were equally, if not more, litigious do not.[74] The occupations of the defendants suggest that many were suits concerning debts incurred in the wool industry and cloth trade brought by the merchants against weavers, dyers and fullers, as well as for sale of the finished article. But there are also cases of, for

[67] This arrangement, suggested at some points within the book itself, was confirmed by drawing up a conspectus brevium for the entries in book and plea rolls.

[68] For example, John Oliver and John Scarlet both appear in the de banco rolls, and Thomas Swain and John Raunds in the coram rege rolls, but in view of the plurality of offences committed by some defendants, and the basic difficulty in identification of namesakes, it would be unwise to assume that these are the cases, or subsequent reappearance of cases, to which the book refers; unequivocal evidence in the form of suits on the rex side of the coram rege rolls or returns in the indictment files is lacking, whilst almost certainly the grouping of defendants in the book for the sessions is somewhat arbitrary. On translation of cases from sessions to king's bench, and on their eventual outcome, see Bellamy, *Crime and Public Order,* 100, 157–61; *Procs before JPs,* lvii–lxxvi, cx–cxi, and 237–74, 424–34, where none of the cases enrolled on the peace roll of the Worcestershire sessions of 1477–8 and few of those on the Southampton roll of 1474–5 have been traced to further proceedings in king's bench. This contrasts with the much greater incidence of further proceedings in the central courts found in, for instance, the Shropshire peace rolls edited by Elisabeth Kimball: *The Shropshire Peace Roll 1400–14* (Shrewsbury, 1959).

[69] cf. the Bedfordshire sheriff's roll: Fowler in *Sheriff's Rolls of Beds & Bucks,* 8.

[70] Possibly twelve, if John Nowers is a mistake for Richard, who sued John Leyot under the statute of maintenance of quarrels. Litigation in the common law courts involving the two families does suggest some connection between them, though Richard was also an attorney in the common bench.

[71] See above, n.7 for the method of counting entries and cases.

[72] Although no exhaustive count has been made, approximate figures may be derived by counting only suits in the first stages of process from Hilary 1465, and eliminating the first mention of suits given day within the same term for Michaelmas 1464.

[73] CP 40/817, m.240.

[74] Some idea of their financial standing may be gained from the subsidy assessments of 1450 and from ulnage accounts for the county: E 179/196/118; E 101/346/23; 345/9.

example, non-payment for wood received by a carpenter as part of his stock in trade, and others concerning arrears of rent; yet others are debts of whose origin we know nothing.[75] Twenty-nine or 33% of these entries concerning common bench suits are trespass cases, of which twenty-eight charge the breaking of a house or close. Six of these merely allege subsequent depasturing by animals; two the taking of wood or grain; nine concern the taking of hens or other farm animals such as horses and oxen, putting them to flight and setting on them with dogs (so ran the formula of the plea), or otherwise taking them away from their lawful owners, with or without a further charge of depasturing; five charge the taking of money or goods. In two instances, the charge is combined with an allegation of unlawful hunting and taking of game;[76] in one instance, fish were taken from a pond, whilst one plaintiff further pleaded assault on his servant to the great detriment of his master. None of these pleas cites the statutes De Ingressibus, though they are cited in support of eight pleas of trespass in Wiltshire in both king's bench and common pleas which are not mentioned in the memoranda,[77] and in the suit of Edmund Hungerford against Thomas Coventry and others [33], in which two of the defendants eventually appeared in king's bench after being put to outlawry, and for which damages seem finally to have been paid.[78] One charge of trespass, on an offence committed in 1457, was to the detriment of one of the coroners, Robert Fen. He pleaded that he had been fraudulently sold a horse, for although warranted by the vendor, John Ward, to be sound, it was in fact broken down and unfit for work, to his damage in £10. Even the authority of the county coroner was, however, insufficient to obtain the appearance of the defendant in court within two years, or the uninterrupted process of the law, for on two successive occasions the sheriff defaulted on the return of the writ of capias. It was returned in Michaelmas 1465 with a note of non est inventus, so that a further writ was issued for Ward's arrest. This, too, the sheriff failed to execute, and the writ was not returned the next term. Although Ward did eventually appear, in Easter term 1466, the story had by no means ended, for the case was adjourned by licence to imparl [9, 36].[79]

Not all the entries in the book are given a case description, and the remaining entries, which could nevertheless be fitted into the category of trespass, concerned the refusal to give seisin of land purchased, unlawful detention of goods, and assault. This catalogue of petty litigation roughly corresponds with the corpus of Wiltshire pleas enrolled on the plea rolls. Most are process entries. Indeed, only eight or 11% of the cases mentioned within the book and identified as relating to suits in the common bench came to the joinder of issue in the court within three years,[80] and this is a pattern true also of cases found on the plea rolls

[75] *Lavington* v. *Harris* [9]: CP 40/820, m.503d; *Sturmy* v. *Faunt* [11, 38]: CP 40/817, m.443; both these are suits in which issue was eventually joined, so that the origin of the debt was outlined in the course of the plea. For the frequent crises of credit in the wool and cloth industry, see *The Cely Papers,* ed. H. E. Malden (Camden, 3rd ser., I, 1900), from which examples are conveniently abstracted in E. E. Power, 'The Wool Trade in the Fifteenth Century', in *Studies in English Trade in the Fifteenth Century,* ed. E. E. Power and M. M. Postan (London, 1933), 62–70; and for the way in which the growth of the woollen industry in this area was associated with a rise in the number of trespass cases such as are described below, see *VCH Wilts,* IV, 132, 136–7.

[76] There are no forest proceedings amongst the public records sufficiently close in date to trace parallel or earlier actions against the same offenders, though one of the trespasses was committed within the king's chase of Aldbourne; proceedings of 17 Edward IV have been searched without success.

[77] All save John Whittocksmead cited, where the statute was named, that of 5 Ric. II, c.8; Whittocksmead, a JP and probably a lawyer, cited the enactment of 8 Hen. VI, c.9. The other statutes cited were one of the statutes of labourers, against a servant leaving his employment before the agreed time (23 Edw. III, c.2); and Edward IV's ordinance 'recently enacted' against maintenance of quarrels, 1461, for which see *RP,* V, 488a and Bellamy, *Crime and Public Order,* 114–5.

[78] KB 27/822, Rex m.33; 827, Rex mm.5, 24, Fines.

[79] CP 40/811, m.173; 812, m.220; 814, m.57d; 817, m.275d; 819, m.262.

[80] The de banco rolls have been searched to the end of Easter term 1468 (CP 40/827). William Swain, answering to a bill submitted in chancery by the vintner John Wise, pinpointed the problem when he complained that he had sued Wise for more than two years in the common bench, for lack of appearance of the defendants, alleging that, on this occasion the cause of delay was that they had been returned 'at small issues by special labour to the sheriffs . . .': C 1/48/302. The debt itself seems to have had its origin in an obligation given by Wise and others as security for a loan, possibly usurious, made by Swain to the mayor and corporation of Salisbury, though the two parties disputed the terms of its condition. M. Blatcher, 'Distress Infinite and the Contumacious Sheriff', *BIHR,* XIII (1936), 146–50, shows in detail the delay caused by the default or inactivity of one particular sheriff and its relation to litigation. See also Hastings, *Common Pleas,* 211–36.

which do not appear in the book. Where the entries in the memoranda relate to cases in the king's bench we are left with very little idea as to the nature of the suit. All those noted in the book are described as pleas of trespass, and only three can be traced to an appearance in the court. In the first of these, a qui tam action brought by Edmund Hungerford, the Goodcheaps went sine die because no one appeared to prosecute the plea [33].[81] The second, again at Hungerford's suit in a qui tam action, has already been mentioned. William and Edmund Coventry appeared on separate occasions, and obtained the king's pardon and exoneration from further suit [33].[82] The third involved the assault by Roger Perkins on Walter Hewster, servant of John Willoughby, a justice of the peace. Willoughby brought a parallel action, which is not mentioned in the notes, both for the assault and for the damage to himself for the loss of Hewster's services for nearly a year, an allegation given some credence by the delay between the date of the offence and the suing of the original writ.[83] Perkins, however, pleaded in answer to Hewster's suit that he had acted only in self-defence and so placed himself on the country, and the matter was still unresolved two years later [34].

Of those common bench cases which did result in an eventual appearance in court, one was adjourned on a wager of law; other defendants sought licence to imparl, many times renewed, and William Sturmy indeed eventually resumed his suit and process of capias five terms after the first appearance of the defendants [26, 33];[84] others again are lost to sight when the defendants placed themselves on the country and the case was continually deferred, either through failure to secure the appearance of a jury or by default by the sheriffs in returning the writ. In only one instance do we get a final judgment. This was on a plea of trespass in which the plaintiff, John Cranbourne, obtained judgment in his favour after the case had proceeded at nisi prius. He was awarded damages and costs which were finally paid in full in 1471, at the time of Henry VI's readeption, Cranbourne appearing in court to acknowledge that he had been satisfied of his claim [35].[85] Three cases which had proceeded to outlawry reëmerged when the defendants surrendered themselves to the Fleet. Pardoned in respect of the suit of the king and for their contempt, the whole dreary process resumed again on behalf of the unfortunate plaintiff.[86] In several instances discontinued cases were resumed one or two terms later, whilst others – no less than 55% of the cases in the notebook – disappear without trace before the completion of the capias process. Some of them may, of course, have been settled out of court. John Bookland's suit against Nicholas Rawlins for a debt of £10 may well be one such instance. The case in the notebook [36] came to no result, but two years later Rawlins appeared to answer a plea for recovery of a debt of £20, which proved to be the sum mentioned in an obligation given on 10 October 1465 to observe an arbitration to be had between them – at least, this was how Rawlins had understood the condition, for he was illiterate and the obligation had then been expounded to him.[87]

The full process of the law was not necessarily any disincentive to crime, or to the repetition of an offence. Robert Hooper is found repeating within two years his offence in breaking the close of Alexander Stanter, but this time in company with other malefactors [10].[88] Robert Sprot, who appears in the memoranda joined with Robert Hampton at the suit of Robert Fen, appears to have borne a charmed life. Outlawed in January 1463, he appeared in court in Michaelmas of the same year and pleaded exoneration from his outlawry on the technical ground that he should not have been outlawed because his domicile was given as *Ascheton Keynes* and that there was no such place within Wiltshire. This plea was upheld by a jury of the county, and his outlawry was accordingly made void.[89] The case underlines the need for correct orthography in writs if the process was to be upheld, for the error was almost certainly one of spelling;[90] though such errors would not necessarily be exploited unless the party

[81] KB 27/818, Rex m.18.

[82] KB 27/822, Rex m.33; 827, Rex mm.5, 24, Fines.

[83] Nearly eight months, from 22 May 1464 to 5 January 1465: KB 27/820, m.43.

[84] CP 40/816, m.424; 821, m.646.

[85] CP 40/818, m.363.

[86] On pleading and trial see Hastings, *Common Pleas*, 184–208.

[87] CP 40/826, m.344d.

[88] CP 40/813, m.389d; 819, m.363.

[89] CP 40/810, m.105d.

[90] Ashton Keynes. The spelling used at the time seems most usually to have been Assheton or Ayssheton.

defending was sufficiently alert and chose this method of reversal.[91] Sued for debt within the period of the account by the coroner, Robert Fen, Sprot was again outlawed, this time at the suit of John Lane, on 1 December 1466. He again obtained reversal of the sentence, this time on the excuse that he had been incorrectly described as a yeoman, whereas his true status was that of a gentleman [26, 36].[92] Yet it was easy enough to slip into error, and the notebook itself offers several such examples which, if they accurately record the precise wording of the original writs, could have given ground for the invalidation of the process. John Woodhouse, gentleman, is incorrectly described as husbandman in one entry, as was Sprot himself; whilst John Ranger is called Thomas in the first entry mentioning him [26, 36, 11].[93] In one case we can trace an error on the plea rolls. Robert Vincent, perhaps the lessor of Sutton Veny of 1448, is called William in the first entry of Margaret Hungerford's plea;[94] unfortunately his christian name in the memoranda is illegible owing to a fault in the manuscript at the point where the writ against him is entered. In the course of litigation between William Chandler and Thomas Maynard, whom William charged with breaking his close at Preshute and taking fish worth 100s. and goods worth 40s., the reversal of the rôles of plaintiff and defendant and of the details of the action, which occurred in the same term as the appearance in court of the original defendant, looks at first sight like a countersuit; but it seems more likely that this, too, was no more than a clerical error and a resumption of the original suit.[95] Such countersuits are, however, by no means unknown.

Using the plea roll evidence we can, in general, proceed only by inference. The fullest story comes when there is a shoring-up suit or related litigation in the English bill courts where pleadings, although partisan, were not yet hidebound by the constraints of accepted legal phraseology. There is no such instance amongst the memoranda, but included in the common bench suits of this year we find the beginnings of the litigation between the town of Salisbury, represented by its mayor, John Hall, and several of his fellow citizens, and the bishop of Salisbury, Richard Beauchamp, of which one facet was a dispute over the clearing of ground, to which both parties claimed title, for the building of a chantry chapel by William Swain, with whom John Hall had himself long been at odds,[96] though the fundamental dispute underlying the lengthy proceedings was one of conflicting jurisdictions and authority. In this case the interval between alleged offence and the suing of the original writ was brief,[97] though the full process of the law took fifteen years to pursue its course, necessitating some complicated manoeuvres within the administrative system, as Thomas Delamare, Darell's successor as sheriff, and one of the coroners, John Dauntsey, were related to the bishop, whilst a second coroner, Thomas Stone, was bound to the bishop by ties of livery and council. On the bishop's side, the prosecution of the trespass was initiated outside the city, in the 'sessions at large', since the mayor, who was also a justice of the liberty, was John Hall, one of the defendants to his suit.[98] There was in fact parallel litigation in four courts: in the chancery, where two of the bishop's servants alleged wrongful imprisonment and requested a corpus cum causa; in king's bench, on the trespass involving forcible entry, breach of the peace, and the removal of some of the building materials, and also the assault on the two servants; a similar action in the common bench; and, at another level, in the exchequer, where William Swain was charged with the breach of his obligation to keep the

[91] For reversals of outlawry see Hastings, *Common Pleas,* 179–82.

[92] CP 40/823, m.263; 817, m.21d is the enrolment of the exigent at the suit of Fen, and he is there termed franklin.

[93] At other points it is less easy to reconcile text and plea roll. The bailiff itinerant, John Sweetwell, invariably appears as John Sotwell in the plea rolls, though Tropenell's cartulary reflects the spelling of the memoranda; John Bowes [9] is John Dowes in the de banco rolls. Similarly, there are discrepancies in the forms of John James [9] and William Bore and Thomas Eastington [27].

[94] CP 40/816, m.272d.

[95] ibid., mm.454, 154d. It is the second action, Maynard's suit concerning the taking of fish worth 40s. and herbage worth 100s., that appears in the notebook.

[96] For this, and for the story of the dispute taken from the town archives, see F. Street, 'The Relations of the Bishops and Citizens of Salisbury between 1225 and 1612', *Wilts Arch. & Nat. Hist. Mag.*, XXXIX (1916), 233–57.

[97] The trespass, which was a deliberate act on the part of the city, was committed on 7 May 1465, and the first entry of the plea appears on the plea roll of Trinity term 1465: CP 40/816, m.271.

[98] CP 40/820, m.330; Street, *Wilts Arch. & Nat. Hist. Mag.*, XXXIX, 238.

peace, for he had been bound early in 1462 to appear before the king and council and to keep the peace against the king's subjects.[99] In addition, the council intervened in an attempt to achieve an aribitrated settlement.[100] If this case is exceptional in the status and tenacity of the parties, in the length of the proceedings and in the large body of evidence that remains concerning both its course and its motivation, it is also a reminder that the story of individual litigation may lie in the records of more than one court,[101] whilst many suits at common law would eventually have been settled out of court.

Many of the litigants or, at least, the plaintiffs,[102] are readily identifiable. The merchant community has already been mentioned, as have those holding office within the county. Most plaintiffs were drawn from the upper and middle ranks of county society: gentry such as Thomas Tropenell or Margaret Hungerford's receiver general, Gregory Westby; cathedral clergy such as John Cranbourne, prebendary of Hurstbourne and Burbage, or Henry Trevillian, prebendary of Warminster and also master of the hospital of St Katherine by the Tower, in virtue of which office he farmed crown lands within the county; heads of religious houses; or royal officials such as John Austin, formerly a receiver general of crown lands in several southern counties and who, within the period of the account, farmed of the crown the hundred of Selkley, or Richard Haynes, a merchant and clerk of the works at Clarendon. No less than thirteen of the plaintiffs mentioned in the memoranda (and another thirteen who are not) were of sufficient local importance to have acted, or to act within the next seven years, as MPs for boroughs within the shire.

Yet all this cannot explain the purpose of Darell's notes. The book itself is concerned principally with the bailiffs itinerant, rather than the hundred bailiffs, who would have shared with them the execution of process. One might expect the purpose of the notes to be financial, connected with debts owed to the crown either by Darell himself or by his subordinates. Yet it is unlikely that this was connected directly with default on the livery of writs. In only one term, Trinity 1465, did Darell return the writs after the due return day,[103] whilst only seven of those cases mentioned in the memoranda and traced through to a further process of capias, exigent or appearance, show an interruption of mesne process. We are left, then, with an interesting piece of evidence, but uncertain of its particular place in the history of the shrievalty. Yet it is clear that the use of such odd scraps of evidence to elucidate the formulae of the plea rolls and the process thereby ensuing not only underlines regional differences in the details of administration but may help to tell us something of medieval litigation and the way in which it operated at the local level.

99 C 1/27/474, 475 (the petition of Robert Boys and Thomas Cook); KB 9/310, m.25; KB 29/96, m.9; (the king's bench action seems not to have come to the joinder of issue, though it was more than ten years before the action in the court ceased); CP 40/817, m.538d; 820, m.330; 822, mm.135–135d; (judgment was given for the bishop on part of his plea, concerning the unlawful entry and the ill-treatment of his servants, though on the remainder he was amerced for false claim); E 159/242, Recorda, Mich. 5 Edw. IV, m.35 (the record of Swain's prosecution).

100 *HMC Various Collections,* IV, 206–7; Street, *Wilts Arch. & Nat. Hist. Mag.,* XXXIX, 240–7, 255–6.

101 See, for example, above, n.80.

102 It is very much more difficult to identify namesakes amongst the husbandmen and yeomen cited as defendants, though, for example, the court rolls of Castle Combe show that Thomas Hackborn, junior, had acted as reeve and collector of rent in the manor in 1461–2 and frequently acted as a juror, and would suggest that the William of the notebook is an error for Thomas Hackborn, senior, several times reeve of the manor, whose tenement fell into the lord's hands in 1464, 'for what legitimate cause the steward knew not': BL, Add. Ch. 18487. A cursory search has also been made in the court rolls in the Public Record Office. The defendants most readily identifiable tend to be of similar, or only slightly lower, status than the plaintiffs: merchants such as John Ranger, gentlemen such as John Woodhouse; Robert Sprot, several times employed in the assessment and collection of subsidies in Wiltshire; or Peter English, Margaret Hungerford's collector of rent at Heytesbury, who was indeed being sued by her in 1466 for arrears owed on his account.

103 KB 27/817, Fines.

TEXT

SP 46/45, no. 93, f.1

Memorandum Georgii Darell armig[eri vicecomiti]s Wiltes' anno r[egni regis] [104] Ed[war]di quarti post conquestum [quinto v]idelicet a crastino A[nimarum anno quarto regni regis] predicto usque idem festum [anno reg]ni eiusdem regis [quinto]

[1] Dies comitatus in eodem a[nno]
xviij° die decembris; xiiij° die januarii; xij° die februarii; xij° die marcii; ix° die aprilis; vij° die maii; iiij^to die junii; secundo die julii; xxx die julii; xxvij die augustii; xxiiij^to die septembris; xxij die octobris; xix die novembris.

[2] Nomina coronatorum comitatus predicti
Thomas Stone; Johannes Dauntesey; Johannes Uffonham; Robertus Fenne.

[3] Nomina justiciariorum pacis commorantium infra comitatum predictum
Rogerus Towkotes miles; Johannes Willughby miles; Johannes Boynton miles; Johannes Whittokesmede; Thomas Rogers;[105] [*folio* 1*v*] [Henricus L]onge;[106] [Philippus] [106] Morgan.

[4] [Nomina] ballivorum li[bertatum] comitatus predicti
Johannes Whittokes[mede] ballivus libertatis episcopi Sar'; Thomas Mascall ballivus libertatis episcopi Wynton'; Willelmus Holbem ballivus libertatis prioris Sancti Swithuni Wynton'; Edwardus Basy[ng] [107] ballivus libertatis abbatis Glaston'; ballivus libertatis ducatus Lancastr'; ballivus libertatis ducatus Ebor'.[108]

[5] Nomina ballivorum itinerantium comitatus predicti
Robertus Horewode; Johannes Box; Thomas Mascall; Johannes Swetwell.

[6] Nomina ballivorum hundredorum comitatus predicti
Willelmus White ballivus hundredi de Mere; Thomas Mascall ballivus hundredi de Wermester; Willelmus Holbem ballivus hundredi de Doneworth; Nicholaus Raynold ballivus hundredi de Chalke; Thomas Mascall ballivus hundredi de Heyghtesbury; [*folio 2*] Johannes Cappys ballivus hundredi de Brenchesburgh et [Dole]; Johannes Raundes ballivus hundredi de Cawdon et Cadewort; Henricus[109] ballivus hundredi de Frustesfeld; Johannes Raundes ballivus hundredi de Wanderdich; Johannes Raundes ballivus hundredi de Alwardbury; Johannes Raundes ballivus hundredi de Ambresbury; Willelmus Coke ballivus hundredi de Kynwardston; Robertus Cromale ballivus hundredi de Swanburgh; Thomas Wareyn ballivus hundredi de Whereweldoun; Willelmus Rydeler ballivus hundredi de Westbury; Thomas Wareyn ballivus hundredi de Bradeford; Willelmus Cary ballivus hundredi de Malmesbury; Johannes Halyday ballivus hundredi de Calne; Willelmus Wylkus ballivus hundredi de Kyngbrig; Hugo Fissher ballivus hundredi de Selkeley; Januarius Castelcombe ballivus hundredi de Hyworth, Criklade et Staple; ballivus hundredi[110]

[7] Hundreda libertatum
Hundredum de Dounton; hundredum de Wonderdich; hundredum de Melkesham; hundredum de Poterne et Canynges; hundredum de Remmesbury; hundredum de Selkeley; hundredum de Everley; hundredum de Elstubbe; hundredum de [111]

[*Folio 2v*]

[8] Ballivi burgi de Malmesbury; ballivi burgy de Devyses; ballivi burgi de Ludgarsale; ballivi burgi de Marleburgh; Johannes Bethe ballivi burgi de Wilton.[112]

[*Folio 3*]

[9] Waranta facta Johanni Box et Roberto Horewode termino . . .
Pluries capias Rogerum Taillour de Lytelhenton yoman, Ricardum Loveday de eadem yoman, Johannem Smyth de eadem yoman, Johannem Bowes

[104] This folio is badly rubbed and torn. The right-hand corner is missing from most folios.

[105] *verte* is written at the foot of the folio.

[106] *CPR 1461–7*, 575.

[107] E 368/237, Adventus vicecomitum.

[108] A space is left for the names of each of the last two bailiffs.

[109] A space is left for the surname.

[110] A space is left for a bailiff's name. The hundreds of Chippenham and of South and North Damerham, the latter two belonging to the abbot of Glastonbury, have been omitted from the list.

[111] Name of hundred omitted.

[112] Spaces have been left for the name of a second bailiff for Wilton and for two for each of the other boroughs.

de eadem yoman, Willelmum Coventre de Wanburgh husbondman, Willelmum Perys de eadem husbondman, Willelmum Heryng de eadem husbondman, octabis Hillarii ad sectam regis . . . fugac' in Aldeborn. Johannem Wodehous de Magna Cheverell gent' ad sectam Willelmi Flour . . .
Capias Johannem Blake de Monkenfarley yoman ad sectam Johannis Jones transgressionis. [*Marginated*] subvicecomiti.
Capias Johannem Spencer de Marleburgh bocher, Nicholaum[113] Broun de Clak bocher, respondendum Nicholao Bailly debiti.
Capias Johannem Kyng de Lacok husbondman, Johannem Swayn de Lacok husbondman milward, ad sectam abbatisse de Lacok transgressionis. Capias Johannem[114] Barley de Netelton husbondman ad sectam Nicholao[115] Richon' clerico[116] debiti. [*Marginated*] E[xitus] nichil.
Capias Willelmum Puddyng nuper de Lacok husbondman ad sectam abbatisse de Lacok debiti.
Pluries capias Johannem Warde nuper de Malmesbury yoman ad sectam Roberti Fenne in placito transgressionis.
Pluries capias Johannem Harryes de Chippenham husbondman ad sectam Ricardi Lavyngton debiti.
Capias Johannem Jamys [117] de Chilton Folyet yoman ad sectam Ricardi Darell transgressionis.
Capias Johannem Hayward nuper de Foxham husbondman ad sectam abbatis de Malmesbury.
Pluries capias Willelmum Gregory de Overwroughton husbondman ad sectam Johannis Austyn transgressionis.
Capias Robertum Scotte de Titcombe laborer, Willelmum Wheler nuper de Merton husbondman, ad sectam Ricardi Bocher transgressionis.
Capias Thomam Hakeborn de Castelcombe juniorem wever, Willelmum Taillour de eadem taillour, Willelmum Hakeborn de eadem seniorem wever, ad sectam Stephani Scrope.
Capias Johannem Dyer de Malmesbury mercer ad sectam Tilmanno[118] S . . . debiti.

[*Folio 3v*]

[10] Waranta facta Thome Mascall termino Sancti Hillarii . . . [Johanne]m[119] Craas nuper de Wermester chapman, Robertum Wattis nuper de Wermester husbondman, ad sectam Willelmi Sewester debiti.
Capias Johannem Clerk de Chitterne seniorem husbondman, Johannem Clerk de eadem juniorem husbondman, ad sectam prioris de Bradstoke; Thomam Mascall nuper de Stokton husbondman, Thomam Raulyns de Smalbroke husbondman, Aliciam uxorem eius, Johannem Rybus de Wermester in comitatu tuo husbondman, ad sectam Henrici Trivylyon clerici transgressionis.
Capias Willelmum Smyth de Deverell smyth ad sectam Roberti Burley transgressionis.
Capias Thomam[120] Warde de Chitterne husbondman, Thomam Warde de eadem husbondman, Robertum Warde de eadem shepherd, Bartholomeum Warde de eadem grome, ad sectam Philippi[121] Morgan transgressionis.
Capias Thomam Lecford de Busshopestrowe husbondman ad sectam abbatisse de Lacok transgressionis.
Capias Robertum Hoper de Hornyngesham husbondman ad sectam Alexandri Stanter transgressionis.

[11] Waranta facta Johanni Raundes
Capias Thomam[122] Renger nuper de Nova Sar' marchaunt ad sectam Johannis Palmer.
Capias Radulphum Joce de Nova Sar' bocher ad sectam Johannis Coteler debiti.
Capias Johannem Were de Stratford laborer, Johannem Hayward de Hele husbondman, Thomam Hykkys de Magna Wodeford laborer, Petrum Coffyn nuper de Wynterbornestoke husbondman, ad sectam Johannis Mundy; Johannem Spencer de Alwardbury husbondman, Willelmum Stephenes de Alwardbury husbondman, Willelmum Faunte de Nova Sar' carpenter, ad sectam Willelmi Swayne.

[*Folio 4*]

[12] Warenta facta Roberto Horewode et Nicholao Ray[nold]
Capias Thomam Gate de Berford clericum, Thomam Elyot de eadem husbondman, Johannem Notebem de eadem husbondman, Johannem Flewale de eadem husbondman, Walterum Vele de eadem husbondman, Ricardum Kyngman de eadem husbondman, Willelmum Clerkys de eadem yoman, Willelmum

[113] Preceded by *Johannem,* struck through.

[114] Recte *Georgium.* See [27, 33]; CP 40/813, m.79d.

[115] Recte *Nicholai.* Throughout the text the clerk confuses genitive and dative cases, particularly in second declension nouns where he tends to enter 'o' rather than 'i'.

[116] Recte *clerici.* [117] *Janyns* in CP 40/813, m.394d.

[118] Recte *Tilmanni.*

[119] CP 40/813, m.79d.

[120] Recte *Willelmum.* Cf. KB 27/815, m.13d.

[121] Followed by *P,* struck through.

[122] Recte *Johannem.* Cf. [35]; CP 40/813, m.79.

Carpenter de eadem husbondman, ad sectam Johannis Mompess[on]; Cristinam que fuit uxor Thome Dunster de Fissherton wydowe ad sectam Willelmi P[ope].[123]
[*Marginated*] xx d.

[13] Warenta facta Edmundo Rycheman
Attachias Johannem[124] Multon, Michaelem Morell, ad sectam Johannis Broun.

[*Folio 5*]

Registrum brevium de pace retornabilium ad sessionem ten[tam] . . .

[14] [*Marginated*] J. Swetwell
Capias Johannem Houchons de Alwardbury husbondman, Willelmum Ambrose de eadem husbondman, Johannem Yonge de eadem husbondman, Thomam Lavyngton de eadem husbondman, Johannem Yonge de eadem husbondman, ad sectam regis transgressionis.

[15] [*Marginated*] Subvicecomiti
Capias Johannem Bokeler de Polkrigge husbondman, Johannem Gernesey de Westbury taillour, Thomam Dekyn de eadem husbondman, Johannem Wyse de eadem husbondman, ad sectam regis transgressionis.

[16] [*Marginated*] R. Horewode
Capias Petrum Batte de Lokerigge husbondman, Aliciam uxorem eius, ad sectam regis transgressionis.[125]

[17] [*Marginated*] Johanni Swetwell
Johannem Howchons de Alwardbury husbondman ad sectam regis transgressionis.

[18] [*Marginated*] R. Horwode
Johannem Hulle de Cheverell yoman, Johannem Symond nuper de Shildon husbondman, ad sectam regis transgressionis.

[19] [*Marginated*] T. Mascall
Margaretam Lye nuper de Wermester wydowe ad sectam regis transgressionis.

[20] [*Marginated*] J. Swetwell
Willelmum Lanam nuper de Westmerton laborer, Thomam Curteys de Mere tanner, Johannem Clerk de Chitterne juniorem husbondman, Willelmum Busshop de Chitterne husbondman, Ricardum Bouyer alias Ballard de eadem servant, Johannem Olyver de Domerham clericum, ad sectam regis transgressionis.

[21] [*Marginated*] R. Horewode
Johannem Bokeler de Calston touker, Johannem Parham de Wilcote taillour, ad sectam regis transgressionis.

[22] [*Marginated*] Johanni Swetwell
Willelmum Blake nuper de Whiteparissh taillour ad sectam regis transgressionis.

[*Folio 5v*]

[23] Attachias Johannem Fabyan nuper de Bukkynton husbondman, Thomam Robardes nuper de Calne husbondman, Thomam Asshe nuper de Maydenbradley yoman, Thomam Chesterman nuper de Wilcote laborer, Willemum Dillyng nuper de Avbury clericum, Ricardum Grene de Semeley laborer, Johannem Bryan de Lanley Burell laborer, Johannem West nuper de Troubrigge servant, felonie.

[24] Capias Johannem Skarlet nuper de Nova Sar' taverner, Edwardum Kyng de Dauntesey husbondman.[126]

[25] [*Marginated*] [J.] Swetwell
Johannem Wodeford de Nova Sar' yoman, Hugonem Taillour de Knygton juxta Chalk taillour, Georgium Plowman de Quydhamton gent', Morganum Felip Vaughan de Merton clericum, Robertum Frank de Uphavyn clericum.

[*Folio 6*]

Brevia retornabilia xv Pasche

[26] Warenta facta R. Horewode
Johannem Poy de Cheselden clericum, Robertum

[123] CP 40/813, m.395. The plea roll entry gives Christina and John Leyot as co-defendants in a plea of debt brought against them by William, they being the executors of Thomas Dunster.

[124] The *J* is written over a *W*.

[125] *ad sectam regis transgressionis* is written only once in respect of [16–22] to which it is linked by a bracket. The initial *Capias* also relates to the same entries.

[126] These two names are bracketed with the first two of [25], but no offence is stated. *Capias* also relates to [25].

Pecok, Willelmum Pecok, ad sectam Willelmi West-[car].[127]
Thomam Wabcan de Draycote ⟨vicecomiti⟩,[128]
Rogerum Taillor de Lytelhenton, ad sectam Willelmi Sturmy.
Katerinam que fuit uxor Johannis Boteler de Marleburgh, Ricardum Baker nuper de Marleburgh tanner, ad sectam [Johannis] Chafyn.[129]
Thomam Edmondes nuper de Chissebury husbondman, Johannem Bocher nuper de eadem husbondman, Radulphum Burwode nuper [de][130] eadem husbondman, Willelmum Burwode nuper [de][130] eadem husbondman, Willelmum Abyngdon nuper de Rygge husbondman, ad sectam Willelmi Surmy.[131]
Thomas[132] Stephyn de Burbach repiar ad sectam Thome Tropnell.
Willelmum More de Okeburn Sancti Georgii husbondman, Robertum Morles de Upham yoman, ad sectam Thome Stylle.
Robertum Medford nuper de Shaldeborne, Willelmum Bailly nuper de eadem, ad sectam Willelmi Aston.
Johannem Eyleworth de Eyleworth ad sectam Thome Stone.
Johannem Spencer de Marleburgh bocher, Nicholaum Broun de Clakke bocher, ad sectam Nicholai Bailly.
Willelmum Coventre nuper de Wamburgh husbondman ad sectam episcopi Sar'.
Robertum Sprotte de Asshton, Robertum Hampton de Blontesdon, ad sectam Roberti Venne.

[*Folio 6v*]

[27] Johanni Box
[Johannem][133] Bailly de Bisshopeston husbondman ad sectam Johannis Aporte.
[Willelmum][134] Fryer de Benaker yoman Willelmi Lymborne.
[Jo]hannem Wodehous de Magna Cheverell husbondman[135] ad sectam Willelmi Flour.
Johannem Alway de Colerne husbondman, Johannem Islond de eadem, Thomam Swayn de Lye juxta Castelcombe, Thomam Huber de eadem husbondman, Johannem Cromale de eadem, Thomam Hunte de eadem, ad sectam Thome Norys.
Willelmum Bore nuper de Trowbrig tanner ad sectam Thome Estyng.[136]
Georgium Barly de Netelton ad [sectam][137] Nicholai Richon clerico.[138]

[28] Willelmo Holbem
Petrum Englyssh de Heigtesbury ad sectam Johannis Porte.
Hugonem John de Busshopestr husbondman ad sectam Henrici Grene.
Walterum Gibbys de Estcodford, Nicholaum Bovy de Maydenbradley ⟨xx d.⟩,[139] Thomam Hornar et Julianam uxorem eius, Willelmum Bury de Kyngeston Deverell, Thomam Launde de Wermester, ad sectam Thome Tropnell.
Johannem Clerk de Chitterne seniorem husbondman, Johannem Clerk de Chitterne juniorem husbondman, ad sectam prioris de Bradstok.

[29] Roberto Oborne
Ricardum Merywedyr de Middelton ad sectam Thome Benet.

[*Folio 7*]

Sessio pacis tenenda apud Marleburgh

[30] R. Horewode, J. Box
Thomam Swayne de Lygh juxta Castelcombe helyer ⟨e⟩, Johannem Swayne de eadem grome ⟨e⟩, Johannem Iselond de Colerne shepherd ⟨e⟩, Johannem Stronge de Lacok yoman, Adam Swayne de Shilden yoman ⟨e⟩,[140] Walterum Kember de Ludgarsale bailly, Johannem Stonham de Westchesyngbury husbondman, Thomam Symmes de Compton juxta Enford husbondman, Johannem Gardener de Colyngborn Suth husbondman, Thomam Niborne nuper de Brynkworth husbondman,

127 CP 40/813, m.219d. William Westcar was prior of Mottisfont.

128 Marginated.

129 CP 40/814, m.235.

130 Omitted. The following word has been changed from *de* to *eadem.*

131 Recte *Sturmy.*

132 Recte *Thomam.*

133 See [33, 36].

134 See [33].

135 *gent'* in [9] and CP 40/813, m.395.

136 CP 40/814, m.57d reads William Dore and Thomas Estynton.

137 Omitted.

138 Recte *clerici.*

139 Marginated.

140 These marginalia must indicate an outlawry process, either the initial summons to the county or, more probably, the final stages of outlawry. The cases mentioned in this record of the sessions of the peace cannot, however, be checked against independent sources. There was originally a marginal *e* against John Strong, but it was erased.

Johannem Boceler de Polkrich husbondman, nobis transgressionis.
Thomam Robardes nuper de Calne husbondman, Thomam Casterman nuper de Wilcote laborer, Willelmum Dillyng nuper de Avbury clericum, Willelmum Hawke rectorem parochie de Ludyngton, felonie.
Petrum Batte de Lokerigge husbondman, Willelmum Perys de Wamburgh husbondman, Johannem Harper de Cosham et Aliciam uxorem eius, Johannem Symond nuper de Shildon husbondman, Johannem Bokeler de Calston touker ⟨subvicecomiti⟩,[141] Johannem Parham de Wilcote taillour, transgressionis.

[31] Thome Mascall, W. Holbem
Thomam Asshe nuper de Maydenbradley laborer, Ricardum Grene nuper de Semeley laborer, felonie.
Thomam Curteys de Mere tanner, Johannem Clerk de Chitterne juniorem husbondman, Willelmum Busshop de eadem husbondman, Ricardum Bouyer de eadem laborer, transgressionis.

[*Folio 7v*]

[32] Johanni Swetwell et N. Raynold
Johannem Raundes de Brodchalk in comitatu seniorem husbondman, Thomam Felpus de Durneford clericum, Johannem Bartilmew de Whiteparisshe tiler juniorem, Johannem Bartilmewe de eadem seniorem tiler, Henricum Wakeman nuper de Whiteparisshe grome, Willelmum Lanam de Westmerton laborer, Willelmum Blake nuper de Whiteparisshe taillour.

Termino Trinitatis

[33] W.[142] Horewode et J. Box
Willelmum Fryer de Benacre yoman ad sectam Willelmi Lymborn.
Ricardum Hasard de Malmesbury yoman, Robertum Godechepe de Staunton husbondman, Edmundum Godechepe de eadem husbondman, Ricardum Godechepe de eadem laborer, Willelmum Godechepe de eadem laborer, regis.
Robertum Cromale de Worton husbondman, Thomam Touker de Poterne bocher, respondendum Willelmo Asshe.
Johannem Omedeux nuper de Chuyt husbondman respondendum Waltero Stake.
Thomam Edmondes nuper de Chisbury husbondman, Johannem Bocher nuper de Chissebury husbondman, Radulphum Burwode nuper de eadem husbondman, Willelmum Burwode de eadem miller, Willelmum Abyngdon nuper de Rigge husbondman, Thomam Wabbecan de Draycote husbondman, respondendum Willelmo Sturmy.
Georgium[143] Barly de Netelton juxta Castelcombe husbondman respondendum Nicholao Rych'.
[*Folio 8*]
Johannem Eyleworth de Elleworth[144] yoman respondendum Thome Stone.
Johannem Baylly de Busshopston husbondman respondendum Johanni a Porte.
Willelmum Whyte de Ludgarsale in comitatu tuo husbondman, Willelmum Towpe de eadem husbondman, ad sectam Humfrido Gower clerico.[145]
Nicholaum Rede de Froxfeld in comitatu tuo husbondman, Stephanum Rede de eadem husbondman, Thomam Rede de eadem husbondman, ad sectam Johannis Orpuddmann.[146]
Willelmum Wattys nuper de Colyngbourn husbondman, Johannem Cowper nuper de Ludgarsale husbondman, Johannem Bokelond nuper de eadem servant, ad respondendum Willelmo Colyngeborne.
Thomam Coventr' nuper de Wamburgh frankeleyn, Edmundum Coventr' de eadem yoman, Willelmum Coventr' de eadem yoman, utlagatos ad sectam Edmundi Hungerford.
Robertum Fryse de Marleburgh husbondman ad respondendum Agnetis Gilberd.

[34] Thome Mascall et Willelmo Holbem
Johannem Broun de Maydenbradley bocher ad sectam Johannis Newbury.
Henricum Prynce de Norton Bavent husbondman ad sectam Johannis Clyvedon.
Nicholaum Bovy de Maydenbradley in comitatu tuo bocher, Walterum Gibbes de Escodford laborer, Thomam Horner de Haydon et Julianam uxorem, Willelmum Bury de Kyngeston Deverell smyth, Thomam Launde de Wermester wever, ad sectam Thome Tropne[ll].
Rogerum Perkyns de Mere coteler ad sectam Walteri Heuster.

141 Marginated.

142 Recte *R*.

143 Written below *Thomam*, struck through.

144 The *ll* is written over another letter, probably *t*.

145 Recte *Humfridi Gower clerici*.

146 The first *d* is written over a *p*.

[*Folio 8v*]

[35] Johanni Swetwell, N. Reynold
[C]apias Robertum Bunker de Wyntreslowe clericum respondendum Henrico Rose.
[Jo]hannem Raynger nuper de Nova Sar' marchant respondendum Johanni Palmer.
Johannem Kent de Shafton' husbondman respondendum Johanni Haytour.
Johannem Kevell de Berford respondendum Anne Rous debiti.
Johannem Fraunceys nuper de Shafton' drover respondendum Margarete Hungerford.
Willelmum Stevenys de Alwardbury husbondman, Willelmum Faunte de Nova Sar' carpynter, ad sectam[147] Willelmi Swayn.
Johannem Dyer nuper de Magna Durneford husbondman ad sectam Ricardi Wodhill.
Johannem Farnhill nuper de Brifford yoman ad sectam prioris Ederose.
Willelmum Roper de Nova Sar' yoman, Johannem Parrok de Nova Sar' yoman, Ricardum Walker de eadem yoman, Thomam Beverley de Fissherton yoman, ad sectam Walteri Bergh.
Robertum Spray de Nova Sar' wever ad sectam Johannis Newburgh.
Johannem Lake de Suthtodeworth, Johannem Hurry de Thrukleston husbondman, ad sectam Thome Husey.
Johannem Colyns de Madyngton ad sectam Roberti Cromale. [*Marginated*] xx d.
Johannem Barry de Estgrymstede husbondman, Johannem Gyve de Netherwallop in comitatu S. husbondman, Johannem Hunte de Estgrymstede husbondman, Thomam Dodde de eadem husbondman, Johannem Bremmore de eadem husbondman, Ricardum Gybbys de eadem husbondman, ad sectam Johannis Crambourne.

[*Folio 9*]

Termino Michaelis

[36] R. Horewode et Johanni Box
Willelmum White de Ludgarsale husbondman, Willelmum Towpe de eadem husbondman, ad sectam Humfrido[148] Gow[er].
Willelmum Chaundeler de Marleburgh chaundeler ad sectam [Thome Maynard].[149]
Johannem Omedeux de Chuyt husbondman ad sectam Walteri Stake.
Willelmum Gryme de Catecombesmyll juxta Castelcombe [ad sectam Willelmi Upton].[150]
Willelmum Coventr' nuper de Wamburgh, Willelmum Palmer nuper de Calne yoman, ad sectam Willelmi . . .
Johannem Bailly de Bisshopeston husbondman ad sectam Johannis Aporte.
Robertum Sprot de Asshton Kaynes husbondman, Robertum Hampton de Brodbluntesdon gent', ad sectam Roberti Fenne.
Johannem Warde de Malmesbury yoman ad sectam Roberti Fenn[e].
Johannem Somerset personam ecclesie de Chilton respondendum nobis felonie.
Ricardum Denyse[151] de Crikkelade corveser, Robertum Godechepe de Staunton husbondman, Edmundum Godechepe de eadem husbondman, Ricardum Godechepe de eadem laborer, Willelmum Godechepe de eadem laborer, nobis.
Willelmum Bolde de Clakke husbondman ad sectam Johannis Gore.
Johannem Dyer de Malmesbure ad sectam[152] Rogeri Doget capell[ani].
Robertum Fryse nuper de Marleburgh husbondman ad sectam Agnetis Gilberd.
Ricardum Gilberd de Devyses smyth, Willelmum Perot de eadem clothmaker, ad sectam decani Sar'.
Nicholaum Rawelyns de Magna Somerford husbondman ad sectam Johannis Bokelond.
Johannem Hebdych de Devyses clothyer ad sectam Gregorio[153] Westby.
Willelmum Putteyn de Avbury husbondman ad sectam Edithe Golyon.
Willelmum Bolde nuper de Clakke husbondman ad sectam Johannis Gore.

[*Folio 9v*]

[37] Thome Mascall et W. Holbem
. . .[154] Vyncent de Fennysutton husbondman ad sectam Margarete Hungerford.
Johannem Kaynesham de Frome Selewode glover, Nicholaum Bury[155] de Maydenbradley bocher,

[147] *etc.* is written above this word.
[148] Recte *Humfridi.*
[149] CP 40/817, m.18.
[150] CP 40/816, m.217d.
[151] Possibly *Devyse.*
[152] The *s* is written over an *r,* for *respondendum.*
[153] Recte *Gregorii.*
[154] William in CP 40/816, m.272d; Robert in CP 40/817, m.171d.
[155] Recte *Bovy.*

Walterum Gibbys de Estcodford laborer, Willelmum Bury de Kyngeston Deverell smyth, Thomam Launde de Wermester wever, ad sectam Thome Tropnell.
Rogerum Strugge de Bekyngton clothmaker, Johannem Sherwyn de eadem husbondman, ad sectam Johannis Bartour.

[38] J. Swetwell et N. Raynold
Johannem Howchyns de Durneford husbondman ad sectam Ricardi Densill.
Henricum Fyseld[156] de Nova Sar' skynner, Johannem Mede nuper de Nova Sar' pewterer, Johannem Lemyngton de eadem capellanum, ad sectam Willelmi Grey.

[156] Recte *Fyfeld*.

Johannem Leyot de Nova Sar' yoman ad sectam Johannis Nowers.
Editham Crokker de Nova Sar' in comitatu tuo viduam ad sectam J. Heyton.
Willelmum Stephyns de Alwardbury husbondman, Willelmum Faunt de Nova Sar' carpenter, ad sectam Willelmi Swayn.
Thomam Norton de Wilton ad sectam Johannis Lyme.
Willelmum Wastell nuper de Devyse clothman regis.
Johannem Bysshop nuper de Fissyde husbondman ad sectam Johannis Martyn.
Johannem Nedeler de Nova Sar' yoman ad sectam Ricardi Hayne.
Robertum Sowsex de Nova Sar' baker ad sectam Johannis Fraunceys.

The Chancery corpus cum causa file, 10–11 Edward IV

edited by

PATRICIA M. BARNES

INTRODUCTION

In 1969,[1] as both compliment and complement to the work of Mr Meekings upon the king's bench writs, the present writer and colleagues past and present, permanent and temporary, embarked upon the formidable task of bringing order to the various and changing series of chancery files. Dr Hunnisett has recently described the methods used and the results achieved;[2] the purpose of this paper is to indicate some of the ways in which this hitherto almost inaccessible material can be used, and to look in some detail at one type of file in the middle years of the reign of Edward IV and at the use made of one particular type of document, the recognisance, in his reign and that of his brother, Richard III.

So much of the chronological framework of English medieval history from the thirteenth century onwards is derived from the incomparable series of chancery enrolments that we are tempted to forget that those very enrolments are not always particularly helpful in setting a date upon significant innovations in the chancery itself or in tracing the line from innovation to common practice. The recent sortation has made available a wealth of such chronological detail, detail which falls broadly into three categories. In the first category we can place those file series or writs which show the chancery exercising the functions laid upon it by statute and test the success of the statute itself. The clearest example of this is the series of Certificates of Statute Merchant and Statute Staple,[3] which owes its origin to the statutes of Acton Burnell, 1283, and of the Staple, 1353. By happy chance, the first file in this series is an original, and dates from the very year of Acton Burnell. The immediate and continuing popularity of the new procedure is marked by it and by the volume of certificates which flowed into the chancery thereafter.

Admittedly less precise than the first, the second category of chronological information relates to the date at which a new type of business not based upon a statute was entertained in the chancery, was then marked by the emergence of a set form of writ and, when business had become voluminous, the emergence of a new and separate file series to accommodate it. A few examples will sufficiently illustrate the process. The class Various Summonses[4] contains several examples of the chancery feeling its way to a set formula to meet a particular need; the earliest surviving writs of, for example, habeas corpus cum causa dated 27 Edward III[5] or sub pena dated 27 Edward III[6] mark the second stage, and the last stage, which can only confidently be dated from the first surviving original file, is seen in the sub pena file of 26 Henry VI.[7] This last stage is of especial interest, since we have so few precise indications from outside sources of the file series and the business they represent. A list from the reign of Richard II identifies six series: escheatries, inquisitions, privy seals, recorda, statutes merchant and brevia regis.[8] By the reign of Edward IV, fifteen series are identified – endorsed bills, privy seals, escheators, sub pena bills answered and unanswered, sub pena writs, corpus cum causa bills, corpus cum causa writs, protections, records upon outlawries, dedimus potestatem, excommunicates, the Horn bundle and non sunt inventi.[9] It is clear that neither list is complete: the dedimus potestatem series, for example, which begins in 14–15 Edward I, is missing from the first, and the Certificates of Statute Merchant series, whose survival into the reign of Edward IV and beyond is sufficiently marked by original files, is missing from the second. It is equally clear that, in the intervening period, a considerable process of subdivision had taken place, perhaps of the anomalous brevia regis files. Of these files which, by their title, appear to have had a particular association with the crown itself, no surviving example has been identified unless it be among the earlier files now classified as part of the corpus cum causa series. The first of these, from the seventh year of the reign of Henry VI, contains not only writs habeas corpus cum causa but also sub pena and attachias endorsed non sunt inventi;[10] nineteen years later these writs had been segregated into series of their own. Undoubtedly

[1] I am particularly indebted to my colleague Margaret Condon for her help in preparing this introduction and to Miss A. W. Goldsmith. Without the encouragement of the late H. C. Johnson, the long delayed sorting of the files would not have reached its present stage.

[2] R. F. Hunnisett, 'Early Chancery records: rolls and files', *Jnl Soc. Archivists,* V, no. 3 (1975), 158–68.

[3] C 241. [4] C 256. [5] C 250/1, no. 1.

[6] C 253/1, no. 1. [7] C 253/27.

[8] *List of Chancery Rolls preserved in the Public Record Office* (PRO L & I, XXVII), vii.

[9] *The Egerton Papers,* ed. J. P. Collier (Camden Soc., [Old ser.], XII, 1840), 2–3.

[10] C 244/1; for a detailed description of this file, see the introduction to the typescript list in the PRO search rooms.

this subdivision marked an increase of business, an increase which probably also dictated the change in form of the endorsements in the class Placita in Cancellaria noted as 'at once more frequent and more formal' by Professor Hargreaves from 1451 onwards[11] and the increasing employment of trained lawyers in the chancery attributed by Dr Pronay to the years after 1470.[12]

The last category of chronological information to be derived from the file series is the means to date other, undated chancery material and, in particular, the heterogenous mass known by the name of Early Chancery Proceedings. Some are dated by the file here calendared; Appendix I is the result of another exercise, using the sub pena file 11–12 Edward IV.[13] To the surviving writs whose return days fell between the octave of St John the Baptist in Edward's eleventh year and the quindene of Easter in his twelfth, some 127 proceedings can confidently be associated, notwithstanding the familiar difficulties of using the printed lists; some 47 cases have, so far, defied clear identification. These figures represent cases heard on fourteen out of the usual twenty return days,[14] suggesting that some 225 cases came before the English side of chancery in the full year. The results of so restricted a study are not necessarily valid, but they invite speculation whether something in the order of a quarter of the proceedings of this period have been lost or whether the same number were withdrawn at an early stage. A more prolonged study might resolve this issue as well as bring nearer to a conclusion the debate upon the volume of English-side business before the chancery at any given time.[15]

Aside from this chronological detail, a plenitude of other information could, with patience and fortitude, be extracted from the file series. Various fields of inquiry suggest themselves: the dedimus potestatem files[16] should illustrate the volume and type of legal business conducted by commissioners outside London, the inventories returned on writs elegit or capias et extendi facias[17] provide details of domestic, agricultural and trade implements, the certificates of statute merchant[18] enable the student to follow the commercial activities of named Englishmen and aliens and the sums of money they required to conduct them. Since the corpus cum causa series contains much evidence of the chancery's work, hitherto not well documented, as a court of common law, it seemed appropriate to calendar a file from this series;[19] the particular file was in part chosen because the contents of the series had become relatively stable by the middle of the reign of Edward IV and in part because, notwithstanding that stability, it contains some innovations.

The file has a good deal to tell us about the framework within which the Latin side of the chancery worked and, in particular, sheds light upon the dictum that 'Chancery is always open'.[20] To a certain extent this proves to be true, for the file contains writs issued on a Sunday [129, 43] and returnable on a feast day [154, 80]. It is arguable that these represent clerical errors, but the discrepancies between the endorsements on petitions and the return days written over erasures in the subsequent writs [152, 148, 125, 29, 22] suggest that considerable attention was paid to the accuracy of the dates; in the case of return days, such discipline must have been essential to marshal the daily list. The file also shows the chancery working out of term during the summer months; writs were issued and returned in late July and August 10 Edward IV [192–187] and in late July, August and September of the following year [e.g. 127, 125, 123, 119, 115, 99, 91]. If, however, we look at the date of the substantive action upon writs habeas corpus cum causa, which form the majority in the months under discussion as in the file it-

[11] A. D. Hargreaves, 'Equity and the Latin Side of Chancery', *Law Qtly Rev.*, LXVIII (1952), 498.

[12] N. Pronay, 'The Chancellor, the Chancery and the Council at the end of the fifteenth century', in *British Government and Administration*, ed. H. Hearder and H. R. Loyn (Cardiff, 1975), 91.

[13] The names of the plaintiffs are taken from the dorse of the writs.

[14] On return days see below, 440.

[15] See M. E. Avery, 'The History of the Equitable Jurisdiction of Chancery before 1460', *BIHR*, XLII (1969), 131; Pronay in *Brit. Govt and Admin.*, 89. Appendix I tends to confirm Dr Pronay's figures for the earlier part of the Yorkist period.

[16] C 254.

[17] C 131, C 239; for examples see *Wiltshire Extents for Debts, Edward I–Elizabeth I*, ed. A. Conyers (Wilts Rec. Soc., XXVIII, 1972).

[18] C 241.

[19] In the calendar, common forms and records sent up from inferior courts have been reduced to a minimum and the phrase *coram rege in cancellaria sua* has been rendered as 'in chancery'.

[20] A. Hopton, *Concordancy of Yeeres* (London, 1612), 245, cited by C. R. Cheney in *Hdbk of Dates*, 70.

self, it becomes clear that, outside the usual law terms, the service offered by the chancery was limited. A few examples will illustrate the point: John Hilbrond, William Smith, John King, Thomas Tailor, Richard Smith and John Cheyne were all released from prison in the summer months, but each had the full hearing of his case postponed until the following octave or quindene of Michaelmas [194, 192, 191, 123, 119, 115]; the same pattern is followed by recognisances drawn up during the summer [188, 130]. The chancery was thus offering a means of release from prison during the summer months, a service of not inconsiderable value, but the underlying framework of the Latin-side deliberations was that of the older courts. Two further documents underline this point, a writ attachias and a recognisance [16, 15]; the first was dated 20 November, to be returned on the quindene of St Martin (18 November), the second dated 30 January required attendance in chancery on the quindene of Hilary (27 January). Clearly, in chancery as in the other courts of common law, the return day encompassed the following days.[21]

Such a conclusion invites a comparison between the chancery and the other common law courts of the period, and the survival of a king's bench recorda file, which covers slightly more than the Michaelmas term 11 Edward IV,[22] makes this to some extent possible. While there is a marked difference in content between this and the calendared chancery file, both contain numerous writs habeas corpus cum causa. The number of these writs on the king's bench file, more than seventy, immediately corrects any impression that the majority of this type of business came into chancery, for our file, which covers more than a calendar year, contains 101. The speed with which a prisoner could obtain his release seems to have been, overall, about the same in either court in term time; for example, king's bench writs addressed to the sheriffs of London on 12 and 15 October were each returnable on 16 October, while those out of chancery dated 12 and 16 November were returnable on 14 and 19 November respectively [73, 72, 68, 67]. Out of term, there is a startling difference: a writ out of king's bench dated 11 July had, as its return day, 19 October, while one issued from chancery on 17 July, six days later, was returnable on 20 July, nearly three months earlier [192].

Of the chancery's relations with the other courts of common law there is scant direct evidence on the corpus cum causa file. While the calling up of a case of debt from a county court suggests an interference in business that would normally fall to the king's bench [17], the refusal of chancery to release from prison offenders held on writs out of king's bench [180, 18] argues a respect for, perhaps even a sense of subordination to, an older jurisdiction. The return of the sheriffs of Middlesex, officers well accustomed to dealing with all the central courts, that a chancery writ returnable on 3 February must give way to an exchequer writ returnable on 5 February [6] may merely represent the sheriffs' personal valuation of the two courts, yet it tends to confirm the impression that the Latin side of chancery at this date was considered to be of lesser importance than the more ancient courts of common law.

It is pertinent, therefore, to ask how the chancery court became so involved in the common law business recorded on the present file. We have seen that, out of term time, it had the advantage of speed in permitting preliminary actions upon writs habeas corpus cum causa;[23] if this was its prime attraction, a concentration of this type of business in the summer months might reasonably be expected, but this proves not to be the case. That, by reason of its jurisdiction in matters of statutes merchant and statutes staple, it was a familiar court in the great centres of commerce, and notably London, is certain[24] and the majority of the cases upon the file certainly came from London: so too did the majority of like business on the king's bench file. These factors undoubtedly have a bearing, direct or indirect, upon the origins of this aspect of the Latin side, but they are not decisive and we must look elsewhere for a further, and perhaps decisive, factor.

Of the hundred or so writs habeas corpus cum causa surviving on the calendared file, 58 can positively be identified with petitions or bills among the Early Chancery Proceedings; similarly 23 out of the 43 writs certiorari super causa captionis can be so linked.[25] It would not be unreasonable to conclude that the majority, if not all, of this side of the chancery's work was instituted by petition; indeed, the description of a file series as corpus cum causa bills confirms this.[26] A petition or bill addressed to

[21] *Hdbk of Dates*, 67.

[22] KB 145/7/11; the individual items are unnumbered.

[23] Above, 431–2.

[24] The point is forcibly made by Dr Pronay in *Brit. Govt and Admin.*, 94.

[25] See notes to individual items in the text.

[26] Above, 430.

the chancellor is generally regarded as more characteristic of the English rather than the Latin side of the period, but this is clearly not entirely so. Indeed, some petitions dating from about this period ask for both writs sub pena to bring the suit before the English side and writs habeas corpus cum causa to bring the same matter from an inferior court to the Latin side,[27] most strongly suggesting that litigants took advantage of both jurisdictions and regarded them as alternative means to a single end. The chancery held something of the same view: it filed its English- and Latin-side writs together well into the reign of Henry VI.[28] Moreover, while it had evolved the writ sub pena to open cases on the English side, the writ which came to be issued when the sub pena was ignored was an adaptation of the common law attachias [211A, 3]. This latter illustration is particularly interesting: it suggests a sequence of events, for no reïnforcing writ is designed before the writ it reïnforces. In this instance the Latin side was the handmaid of the English. It is at least arguable that this was the overall pattern of events, of one function being associated with another to increase the efficiency of the service offered, and it is, after all, not an unfamiliar one. In government, there is a ready parallel in the reprographic services of the Public Record Office, now governed by statute and statutory instrument,[29] which arise almost entirely from the duty laid upon successive Deputy Keepers and Keepers of the Public Records to make the records available to public inspection; outside government, one might instance those societies which enter into buying and selling at a lower than retail cost for the benefit of their members. That the chancery's association with both mercantile affairs and the council brought business to the English side, that some parts of the Latin side were required to supplement and reïnforce it[30] and that the common membership of both sides of the court combined with a certain flexibility in the days when the court sat, brought increasing business to the Latin side of chancery is not a wholly unlikely proposition.

The writs attachias discussed in the last paragraph are rare upon the calendared file; more common are those writs of attachment by which the court of chancery brought before itself the cases instituted by members of its staff and of their households. The suits, debt, trespass, detinue, were the daily portion of all common law courts of the period, but the writs themselves convey something of the family feeling of the chancery. John Davison, keeper of the hanaper, authorised[31] writs sued out by his servants Henry Brend and Simon Dynell [209, 16] and Richard Fryston another on behalf of his man, John Payne [116]. The file contains ten writs issued on behalf of such members of the clerks' households and five issued for the clerks themselves, together with one sued out by Thomas Bourchier, cardinal archbishop of Canterbury and former chancellor [14], and another by John Bate, a retired chancery clerk;[32] clearly, at this period, the privilege of suing in chancery was not necessarily surrendered upon leaving office. These writs attachias were for the most part[33] treated by their recipients as having the authority of a capias [e.g. 228, 60], while the chancery's precedence over the London courts is marked by the removal of a prisoner from the city prison to the Fleet [90]. Some of these writs met the fate, common to those of all courts that they could not, or would not, be executed, because it was said that the defendant was ill [209] or that he could not be found [193, 99, 21]. Such returns are found on other unexecuted writs upon the file; others are sufficiently unusual to merit comment. At York the mayor, who had been publicly insulted, kept to himself the habeas corpus cum causa, thus preventing the joint addressees, the city sheriffs, from executing it. Six of the city aldermen reported the circumstances to the chancellor, whose reply was to issue a second writ in favour of Thomas Helmsley, one of those named in the first, sub pena £500. This proved effective and Helmsley was produced in court and subsequently released [197], to reappear on the file as a surety [45]. In a second case, the court clearly suspected a fraudulent return and compelled the bailiffs' deputy to swear to its truth [117], and in a

27 For example C 1/40, no. 250; 43, nos. 102, 104; 44, no. 54.

28 Above, 430.

29 Public Records Act 1958 (6 & 7 Eliz. II, c.51) ss. 2(4)(d), 2(5), 2(6), 9(2).

30 26 files were required to accommodate writs sub pena earlier than 7 Henry VI and 17 for writs habeas corpus cum causa. With due allowance made for more than one defendant to be summoned sub pena, the figures seem to confirm the sequence of events proposed.

31 i.e. his name appears in the bottom right-hand corner of the writ.

32 Pronay in *Brit. Govt and Admin.*, 95.

33 The exceptions are [162, 99, 16].

third, the outgoing sheriffs delivered a writ duly endorsed with its return to the incoming sheriffs, but not the body of the prisoner concerned [91]. It is not clear whether two returns which deal with procedure, namely that a return required to a habeas corpus cum causa had already been made upon a certiorari super causa captionis and therefore cannot be repeated [95] and that the arrival of a de procedendo precludes the execution of a habeas corpus cum causa [64], represent established rules; the latter at least has the virtue of common sense. Neither writ gives any indication of the view taken by the chancery, nor is any reply recorded to the reasonable request for a judgment whether, if the subject of a recognisance to appear in court had died before the date of the hearing, one of his guarantors should forfeit the £100 in which he had stood surety [148].

The present file, indeed, is neither as forthcoming upon points of law and procedure as some of its predecessors and successors,[34] nor does it, as might reasonably have been expected, contain much overt trace of the political upheavals which interrupted its compilation. The preliminaries to that upheaval are recalled in the attempt of John Foster to obtain his release from the prison wherein the commissioners, Humphrey Bourchier, Lord Cromwell, and Sir John Scot, had placed him for sedition; his attempt to obtain his release failed, although he was moved to a London prison [186]. In another case, it is not until the initial petition is associated with the writ certiorari super causa captionis upon the file that it becomes clear that the plea of trespass brought by John Emyarn against Hugh Yarm arose from fighting in the streets when the Lancastrian party sought to take control of London from the Yorkists [93].

Although overt evidence of political problems is largely lacking from the calendared file, covert evidence is not. To discover it, we must turn to consider that system of imposing a threat of monetary penalties to secure the performance of a specified action which is a dominant characteristic of the chancery of this period. Mention has already been made of the £500 penalty threatened for failure to execute a writ habeas corpus cum causa.[35] Although in this instance the writ had the force of what elsewhere would have been a sicut alias,[36] it reïnforced an earlier writ which itself had been issued sub pena £200. Penalties of £40, £100 or £200 are found in other instances on the file, but no clear reason for their imposition emerges. While some doubts may have arisen whether the keeper of Ely gaol [120] or the bailiffs of the liberty of St Peter's, York [45] would necessarily have given the execution of a chancery order the priority demanded, the same ought not to have been true of the mayor and sheriffs of Bristol [213], the sheriff of Gloucestershire [17] or, least of all, the keeper of the Fleet prison, against whom penalties of £500 and £1000 are reported to have been threatened [151, 57]. While the majority of the penalties were associated with writs habeas corpus cum causa, which by their nature demanded immediate action, the certiorari super quibusdam loquelis [17] and the instructions to the keeper of the Fleet do not conform to this pattern. Neither does it appear that the sub pena process was used only when reïnforcing a previous writ; it is clear from the York case discussed above and from the endorsements upon the petitions associated with two other cases [45, 31] that no previous writ had issued. Thus, while we can safely conclude that the chancery had found that the threat of a substantial monetary penalty served wonderfully to concentrate the mind of the recipient upon the execution of a writ, there is insufficient evidence upon this file to show why such a threat was imposed in some instances and not in others.

Happily, the same problem does not arise from the financial penalties embodied in the considerable number of recognisances which are attached to writs habeas corpus cum causa and attachias upon the file. The purpose of such a recognisance was twofold: to secure the release of the defendant from the hazards of a medieval prison and to ensure his subsequent appearance in court coupled, from time to time, with a requirement to keep the peace. To all parties the making of such a recognisance was a serious matter. No evidence has been found that John Doe and Richard Roe had their equivalents in the chancery;

34 For example, injunctions (e.g. C 244/104, no. 34 (7 Edw. IV): upon Sir Thomas Etchingham not to obstruct coheiresses' claims to a manor) and memoranda of appearances (e.g. C 244/97, no. 144 (3 Edw. IV): a defendant appearing to answer an attachias before the writ was returned) are regularly if thinly scattered through the series. C 244/119, no. 3 (14 Edw. IV), a recognisance to appear in court, contains the singular provision that the man bound should observe any judgment made before the due appearance day and pay any moneys involved in that judgment.

35 Above, 433.

36 The formulae *sicut alias, sicut pluries* were regularly used in other chancery writ forms; numerous examples can be found in the Non Sunt Inventi files (C 251).

indeed, comparatively few sureties were involved in more than one case[37] and there is evidence, drawn from somewhat earlier in the reign of Edward IV, that they were carefully scrutinised.[38] Release from prison, then as now, was by no means certain; prisoners such as William Samson faced with many creditors [67] would, no doubt, have experienced some difficulty in finding friends willing to stand surety for them; others, such as the Dominican Robert Fulbrook and John Chambers, who had been imprisoned on the orders of a former chancellor, George Neville, archbishop of York, failed to persuade the court to reverse its earlier decision [151, 168]. The sum in which the sureties, most often four in number although eight are listed in one case [123], and the defendant stood bound could be as high as £700 [148] or as low as £10 [202], and was presumably fixed after consideration both of the sums of money involved, £250 and 99s. 9d. in these instances, and of the general financial standing of the sureties and of the defendant, upon whom the threatened penalty was normally higher. In addition, where a felony had been alleged, the sureties were required to swear *corpus pro corpore,* that is to surrender themselves to prison as well as forfeit the sum in which they stood bound if the defendant defaulted [192, 127, 119].[39] As the suit progressed, the sum fixed could remain the same [230], diminish, as in the case of Katherine Bachelor [214], or occasionally rise, as in the case of John Rouse [181]; the sureties could remain the same, change [230] or be discharged as their own request [215]. Katherine Bachelor, as feme coverte, could take no part in her own recognisance; defendants who were femes soles, such as the widow Joan Ormond [125], could and did, but there is no evidence on the file of any woman standing surety in this type of recognisance for other than herself. This apart, the rules and procedures involved in obtaining release from prison in the latter part of the fifteenth century seem familiar today. It is clear that the system was successful, for there is no evidence upon this file, and scant evidence elsewhere,[40] that any defendant defaulted at any stage of his suit in the chancery.

Thus far we have been considering routine recognisances attached to writs. The file does, however, contain a considerable number of others which, although markedly similar in form and content, even to the extent of including the phrase *corpus pro corpore* [135], are not attached to another document. Some twenty of these require the attendance of named persons in the chancery on a specified day on penalty of forfeiting sums on average rather higher than those discussed above, and rising to the considerable figure of £9000 [111].[41] In the majority of the recognisances no reason is given for the required attendance, but a preliminary investigation suggests that the persons named were involved in suits on either side of the chancery. William Reskymmer [15] had been involved in a suit at least since April 9 Edward IV and, in all, nine different persons are recorded as having stood surety for him on various occasions.[42] The clerk Walter Kingdon, for whom there are several recognisances upon the file, the last in a much reduced figure [103, 86, 62, 23], was with others being sued by Hugh Philip, a servant of John Davison, the keeper of the hanaper, on both the Latin and the English sides and it is noteworthy that the first recognisance for his appearance, dated 10 October 11 Edward IV [103], follows hard upon the heels of two writs attachias, dated 16 and 21 September 11 Edward IV, which had been returned non sunt inventi.[43] The five remaining recognisances of this kind are concerned with sureties to keep the peace, an area over which the chancery had some statutory authority.[44]

Apart from those which required attendance in the chancery, there are twenty-six recognisances on the file for parties to appear before the king and council,[45] and it is in these that the particular interest of the present file lies. Similar recognisances have been noted earlier in the reign: one in 3 Edward IV, another in 6 Edward IV, five in 9 Edward IV;[46] the present file contains twenty-five, those for 12–22

37 Thomas Ayloff [228, 22], Thomas Barford [184, 167] and John Friar [146, 125, 123] are examples from this file.

38 Memorandum quod predictus Johannes Kyngesfeld sufficiens est per certificationem Hugonis William sergeaunt: C 244/95, no. 19 (2 Edw. IV).

39 Holdsworth, II, 84, comments on the long survival of this provision.

40 Only one such example has been noted; the defendant forfeited £100 in which he stood bound: C 244/103, no. 6 (6 Edw. IV).

41 For a discussion on large sums of money see below, 438–9.

42 C 244/108, nos. 30, 163.

43 Appendix I, *Philip* v. *Kingdon*; C 1/45, no. 45; C 251/24, nos. 116, 119. This suit is a good example of the use of both sides of the court discussed above, 433.

44 Pronay in *Brit. Govt and Admin.*, 98–9 and the references there cited.

45 For a discussion of the phrase 'the king and council' see below, 440–1.

46 C 244/97, no. 93; 102, no. 231; 108, nos. 103, 104, 115, 173; 109, no. 34.

Edward IV sixteen, eight, one, seventeen, thirty-one, twenty, thirteen, twenty-one and eight respectively; sixteen survive from the brief two and a half months of the reign of Edward V and thirty-two for the rather more than two years of the reign of Richard III.[47] It is immediately clear that, throughout the reigns of Edward IV, his son and his brother, the chancery was in some respects acting as the secretariat of the council. The point is made abundantly clear by three items on the present file: in the first the clerk, accustomed to writing *cancellaria* had to amend the text to *consilio* [141], in the other two the recognisances had formally been entered into before the king and council but were duly filed among the chancery records [75, 74]. It is also clear that the method of dealing with the type of business which found its place upon the corpus cum causa file had in some way changed; the numbers of recognisances cited above show the general pattern of that change and the present file, which contains no such recognisance from Edward's tenth year and twenty-five from his eleventh, marks the turning point.

Like those for appearances in the chancery, not all of these recognisances give any reason for the required appearance. Seven [182, 178, 177, 141, 122, 56, 35] state no cause at all and two have the uninformative, if ominous, phrase 'to answer matters put to him' [171, 137]. The remaining seventeen are concerned with keeping the peace, a matter in which, as we have seen, the chancery had a jurisdiction. That the king and council should be involved in setting a curb upon wholesale breaches of the peace, the preoccupation of all medieval governments, is not remarkable, nor is it surprising that, after a period of political upheaval, their interest should be particularly keen. The evidence before us is susceptible of several interpretations: that the king and council were, for almost the first time in Edward IV's reign, using the chancery as a secretariat; or that in this year they found it necessary wholeheartedly to adopt the chancery system of recognisances to secure the attendance of parties to business that they already entertained; or, lastly, that they took business from chancery into their own hands, first at a time of particular difficulty and then as a matter of course. Further investigation will be required to establish the correct interpretation[48] but, for the moment, the balance of the evidence seems to favour the last view, particularly as the recognisances upon subsequent corpus cum causa files, taking one year with another, show that at least until the end of the reign of Richard III the king and council dealt with rather more cases concerning the maintenance of the peace than did the chancery.[49] Such a conclusion would accord happily with the view that Edward IV relied more upon council than upon departments for the government of the realm.[50] It would, however, be unwise in this context to place too great an emphasis upon the council as a separate institution. The chancellor and certain of the clerks were members of it[51] and the chancellor's leading role in its legal business is illustrated by the case of John Seaman, who was bound over to appear before the king and council but was dismissed quit sine die by the chancellor [141].[52] Indeed, the impression left by the scant evidence upon this file is of an interchange of business between two not wholly distinct bodies.[53] This interchange is admirably illustrated on the one hand by the council's authorisation of a writ habeas corpus cum causa returnable into the chancery [181] and on the other by the case of James Newnham which began in the chancery but moved to the king and council [163, 102].

While the recognisances upon this file, whether they relate to the chancery or to the king and council, offer points of considerable interest, they are concerned with a comparatively limited range of topics.

47 C 244/114–137.

48 It has not so far proved possible to link any case with documents preserved in Early Chancery Proceedings or Ancient Petitions.

49 On this file, the 'king and council' recognisances are concerned with 7 cases, *Sewster* v. *Lumner* [133], *Rex* v. *Osborne* [130], *Alway* v. *Newnham* [102] (from chancery), *Boughey* v. *Fitton* [83], *Paulet* v. *Hungerford et al.* [53–46], *Rex* v. *Shaw et al.* [39–36], *Ashen* v. *Stowell* [34], and chancery 4, *Alway* v. *Shute et al.* [164, 163] (to king and council), *Water* v. *Sturry* [42], *Rex* v. *Frostbury* [30] and *Vivian* v. *Reskymmer* [15] which began in 9 Edward IV: above 435. In comparison, the files for 9 Edward IV have one such suit before king and council and 10 heard in chancery (C 244/108, 109); the files 18–21 Edward IV and 1–2 Richard III contain – 'king and council' figures first – 16/6, 6/9, 12/9, 6/1, 3/5, 7/6: C 244/126–131, 135–137.

50 Pronay in *Brit. Govt and Admin.*, 101.

51 J. R. Lander, 'Council, Administration and Councillors, 1461 to 1485', *BIHR*, XXXII (1959), 138–80, lists councillors in the Appendix.

52 C 244/129, no. 150A (20 Edw. IV) is another example, which in confusion the clerk annotated *de mandato dicti cancellarii ista recognitio cancellatur et dampnatur.*

53 See also below, 440. There is some interesting evidence of written pleadings before the king and council when reference is made to goods etc. *que iidem . . . in quadam responsione sua coram prefato domino rege et consilio suo exhibita fatebantur et recognoscebant*: C 244/129, no. 30A (20 Edw. IV).

The other corpus cum causa files surviving from the reigns of the Yorkist kings contain recognisances, some of which in earlier years or in other circumstances would have found their place on the dorse of the close roll, dealing with a wide variety of matters. A proportion of them are concerned with the routine of the law. There are examples of a bond, having the force of a recognisance, entered into outside the chancery but registered in it, for parties to appear in the chancery.[54] Of greater interest, since they show something of the interrelation of the courts, are those which were intended to secure appearances before the justices of the peace at their next session[55] or in a town court.[56] The normal recognisance to secure attendance contains a clause, frequently so much abbreviated as to be unrecognisable, requiring attendance from day to day until given leave to depart. From time to time this was deemed insufficient and one party was prevented from going further from London than Westminster[57] and another restricted to a two-mile radius.[58] Once brought to court, sureties could be required that the expenses of a suit would be met,[59] title deeds produced,[60] the actions of an attorney supported[61] or a judgment given in court observed.[62] Beyond the confines of the court, similar undertakings were required from parties whose disputes were the subject of arbitration by senior officers of the crown, of whom the chancellor was often one, sitting alone[63] or with the chief baron,[64] the keeper of the rolls[65] or the chief justice of king's bench.[66] Two recognisances of this kind, which bound over Humphrey Stanley and Sir Walter Griffith, are of special interest since they provide for two levels of arbitration, the first by four lesser men, the second by Lord Hastings, the lord chamberlain, if the first was not successful within two months.[67] In two others, where rather longer terms were allowed, the case was to come before king and council if arbitration failed.[68]

In a sense, the crown was party to each recognisance entered into, both as the source of any process required to reïnforce it and as the recipient of any sums forfeited for failure to observe its terms.[69] There are, however, a number of recognisances in which the crown or, perhaps more correctly in these cases, the king himself had a more direct interest. On the one hand, recognisances were used to compel the performance of a particular action, whether it be the appearance of an officer in chancery to answer for neglect of duty[70] or the surrender before a specified date of a wool licence granted in the previous reign.[71] On the other hand, the same device was used to prevent a particular action. The area covered in this way was wide, ranging from fraudulent admixing in the grocery trade,[72] through travelling to Rome without licence,[73] writing letters abroad which ran contrary to the king's own letters,[74] behaving improperly in Furnival's Inn,[75] and breaching what was virtually house arrest,[76] to entering Southampton without licence.[77] Of these examples, the king's interest in the first three is obvious, and in the fourth a breach of the peace was involved. The king's interest in the last two is not obvious until one adds that they were

54 C 244/97, no. 116 (2 Edw. IV).

55 C 244/116, no. 118 (13 Edw. IV).

56 C 244/136, no. 25 (2 Ric. III).

57 C 244/126, no. 117 (18 Edw. IV).

58 C 244/134, no. 106 (1 Ric. III).

59 C 244/118, no. 39 (14 Edw. IV).

60 C 244/102, no. 295 (7 Edw. IV).

61 C 244/119, no. 48 (14 Edw. IV), on behalf of Gascon merchants.

62 C 244/130, no. 121 (21 Edw. IV); 136, no. 121 (2 Ric. III). Aliens were concerned in both cases.

63 C 244/136, no. 4 (2 Ric. III).

64 C 244/120, no. 171 (15 Edw. IV).

65 C 244/134, no. 4 (1 Ric. III).

66 C 244/136, nos. 2A, 2B (1 Ric. III).

67 C 244/129, nos. 52A, 52B (20 Edw. IV); the recognisances are dated 7 July and the term set for the first arbitration was the Nativity of the Virgin (8 Sept.). Curiously enough, neither man stood surety for himself.

68 C 244/116, nos. 90, 91 (13 Edw. IV), term allowed 7 Sept. – 2 Feb.; 126, nos. 65, 66 (18 Edw. IV), term allowed 27 July–2 Feb.

69 In one case a moiety, in two other cases the whole of the forfeited sum was to be paid to a third party: C 244/120, no. 121 (15 Edw. IV); 129, nos. 52A, 52B (20 Edw. IV); 130, no. 14 (21 Edw. IV).

70 An undersheriff of Warwickshire: C 244/97, no. 45 (3 Edw. IV).

71 C 244/135, no. 17 (1 Ric. III).

72 C 244/122, nos. 28, 99, 100 (16 Edw. IV).

73 The abbot of Wymondham (C 244/97, no. 53), for whom there are several subsequent recognisances in the same terms.

74 C 244/122, no. 104 (16 Edw. IV); the case concerned wool stolen in Spain.

75 C 244/119, nos. 25, 26 (14 Edw. IV).

76 In a house called the Bell in Carter Lane, London: C 244/120, no. 56 (15 Edw. IV).

77 C 244/100, no. 12 (4 Edw. IV).

coupled with the requirement in the first case to appear in chancery as often as and whenever reasonably summoned and in the second to appear before the king and council when summoned.

These two recognisances lead us into a field which has to some extent been explored but in which the full role of the chancery has yet to be appreciated. Professor Lander has traced the various forms and uses of monetary threats over the centuries, but his conclusion that under the Yorkist kings recognisances 'for almost all purposes except routine matters . . . were few in number'[78] requires, in the light of the evidence of the corpus cum causa files, some reconsideration. We have already looked at recognisances for appearances in court, keeping the peace, observing judgments and so on, which might fairly be described as routine, but any recognisance which imposes the condition of an appearance in chancery or before the king and council at an unspecified date or dates is not, prima facie, routine. In the majority of the seventeen such recognisances noted, the requirement to appear at an unspecified time seems to have been imposed as a matter of course. There are, however, two exceptions to this: in one case Richard Love, for whom three persons had originally stood surety, was subsequently bound over in his own surety to appear on reasonable summons,[79] and in another Thomas Hansard was doubly bound over, to appear on a fixed day before the king and council and at twenty days' notice before the council.[80] While in one example the threat of a summons to court held good only until the following Michaelmas,[81] and in two others the recognisances are noted as having been discharged,[82] the rest of them seem to have remained in force indefinitely. Only one can clearly be identified with a suit: two merchants of Almain were bound over to appear in chancery if their opponents pursued a suit against them, and it is noteworthy that this is one of the two known subsequently to have been discharged.[83] Undertakings to keep the peace were included in five instances,[84] and in these the threat of a subsequent summons to court clearly reïnforced the primary undertaking. In the remaining eleven,[85] no reason is given for the required appearance. It is probable that some, like the recognisances upon the calendared file, were concerned with routine matters, but there are two pieces of evidence to suggest that others were not. Only six of the seventeen recognisances required an appearance in the chancery and, with a single exception,[86] these were entered into in the early years of Edward IV's reign. The remainder were for appearances before the king and his council and follow the pattern of the transfer of business from chancery to king and council already discussed.[87] Moreover, in two cases substantial sums of money were involved, £1580 and £26,000.[88] The evidence requires further examination in the hope of establishing the cause of each recognisance; for the moment it would not be unreasonable to conclude that, at least in the instances where the larger sums of money were involved, the recognisances contain an element of coercion under threat of financial ruin.

The two sums quoted in the last paragraph are substantial, but they are not without parallel. Our file itself contains some fifteen recognisances for sums in excess of £1000 [177, 171, 137, 130, 123, 111, 94, 53–46]. Elsewhere in the series there is one in which eight parties, Genoese merchants, together stood bound in £64,000.[89] In another Sir William Stocker, kinsman of the Stonors, mayor of the Calais staple and subsequently of London, John Brampton, John Stocker and John Sturmyn each stood surety in the sum of 4000 marks that Thomas Spring would appear before the king and council, and Spring himself was bound over in 600,000 marks, apparently producing the staggering total of £410,667 at risk.[90] These high figures are some indication both of the importance attached to appearances before the court

[78] J. R. Lander, 'Bonds, Coercion and Fear', in *Essays presented to W.K. Ferguson* (Toronto, 1971), 338.

[79] C 244/124, no. 19 (17 Edw. IV).

[80] C 244/133, no. 15 (1 Edw. V).

[81] C 244/123, no. 49 (16 Edw. IV).

[82] C 244/97, nos. 54, 161 (3 Edw. IV).

[83] ibid., no. 54.

[84] C 244/97, nos. 14, 48 (3 Edw. IV); 102, no. 231 (6 Edw. IV); 120, no. 107 (15 Edw. IV); 133, no. 15 (1 Edw. V).

[85] C 244/95, no. 7 (2 Edw. IV); 97, no. 161 (3 Edw. IV); 116, no. 89 (13 Edw. IV); 120, no. 55 (15 Edw. IV); 122, nos. 20, 147 (16 Edw. IV); 123, no. 49 (16 Edw. IV); 126, nos. 28, 42 (18 Edw. IV).

[86] ibid., no. 28.

[87] Above, 436.

[88] C 244/120, no. 107 (15 Edw. IV); 97, no. 161 (3 Edw. IV).

[89] C 244/120, no. 140 (15 Edw. IV).

[90] C 244/114, no. 176, printed as Appendix II. The text is not without its difficulties; I am, however, inclined to place more reliance upon the first set of figures than the second, which occurs in the common form part of the recognisance.

and of the wealth of the merchants concerned. While it is true that the forfeiture of a small sum could, and indeed can, ruin a man of little substance, the forfeiture of these large sums would have had a profound effect not only upon the sureties themselves but also upon the world of commerce of which they were so significant a part. In a sense, therefore, coercion was being exercised upon the commercial community as a whole. Professor Lander has discussed whether sums of the magnitude of those set out above bore much relation to reality, or whether they represented simply a threat of unappreciable magnitude.[91] We have seen that, at least in the early years of the reign of Edward IV, the chancery took pains to establish the financial standing of sureties;[92] moreover, the sums in which sureties and parties alike stood bound vary so widely as to suggest that generally they were directly related to the resources of the individuals concerned. On balance, therefore, the evidence from the corpus cum causa files before us points towards the sums set out in the recognisances being a genuine guide to the available wealth of the period. The instances in which large sums were involved are, like great wealth, rare. If they, and those smaller but substantial sums which would ruin a poorer man, were not wholly related to realisable assets, then another factor contributed towards the threatened forfeiture, and we are forced to consider whether matters of state were involved.

It is doubtful whether, in medieval times, any valid distinction could be drawn between the maintenance of the peace and the proper functioning of the courts on the one hand, and the preservation of political stability on the other. Nevertheless, from the latter part of the reign of Edward IV and from that of his brother, there is some evidence, supplementary to that on the close roll, that the device of the recognisance was being used both to keep the peace and as a political tool, and that, thereby, the sums involved might be somewhat divorced from reality. For example, Robert Harrington was successively bound over on 25 November 13 Edward IV in £1000 to appear in chancery, on 28 November in the same year in 1000 marks not to leave London and to keep the peace, on 30 November in £3000 not to leave the king's presence and still, some eighteen months later, had to find sureties totalling £1400 to keep the peace.[93] His brother, Sir James Harrington, was certainly involved in a dispute with Sir Thomas Stanley and sureties of £5000 were required of them both.[94] Both the Harringtons and Stanley were substantial landowners in Lancashire and their disputes had the makings of an unacceptable local war. The series of recognisances taken from Edward Grey, Lord Lisle, and William Berkeley, Lord Berkeley, follow the same pattern.[95]

The texts printed in Appendix III are concerned with a third and apparently more serious case which involved disorder in South Wales and the dispute between the Herberts and the Vaughans. On 20 January 15 Edward IV, Thomas ap Roger Vaughan, esquire, Thomas ap Morgan, esquire, Sir John Morgan and William Herbert, earl of Pembroke, were bound over sub pena respectively 1200 marks, £400, £234 and £867, to appear before the king and council and to keep the peace towards each other.[96] On 4 February following, Vaughan was bound over to produce in the king's presence John ap Roger Vaughan, Roger Vaughan, Lewis Vaughan the bastard, senior, and Lewis Vaughan the bastard, junior, each sub pena 100 marks, while the earl entered into a recognisance in similar terms to produce Sir Walter Herbert, William Herbert of Pembroke the bastard, Richard Herbert the bastard, William bastard son of Sir Richard Herbert, Thomas Camoys, John Hughes, Matthew Craddock, John ap Howel and Walter Trehern, sub pena sums ranging from £100 to £40.[97] On 15 February Thomas ap Roger Vaughan, Thomas ap Morgan and the earl had their recognisances of 20 January renewed;[98] Morgan's recognisance was renewed once more on 15 March 16 Edward IV.[99] Vaughan's recognisance was twice more renewed, on that day[100] and on 24 April 17 Edward IV, then in the terms transcribed in Appendix III. By that time two other parties to the dispute, Roger ap Roger Vaughan and Sir Walter Herbert, had been bound over, on 28 May 16 Edward IV.[101] The final stage was reached in the recognisance dated 21 March 19

[91] Lander in *Essays presented to Ferguson,* 341 ff.

[92] Above, 434–5.

[93] C 244/116, nos. 53, 50, 48; 120, no. 188 (15 Edw. IV).

[94] C 244/116, nos. 54, 55 (13 Edw. IV). For the dispute see C. Ross, *Edward IV* (London, 1974), 408–10.

[95] C 244/125, nos. 81, 82 (17 Edw. IV); 126, no. 115 (18 Edw. IV); 127, no. 2 (19 Edw. IV); 129, no. 115A (20 Edw. IV).

[96] C 244/120, nos. 45–48.

[97] ibid., nos. 3, 4.

[98] ibid., nos. 6, 7, 10.

[99] C 244/123, no. 5.

[100] ibid., no. 6.

[101] ibid., nos. 22, 23.

Edward IV, printed in the Appendix, in which the earl and Sir Walter Herbert were forbidden to cross the river Severn, sub pena £5000. Within four months the earl had relinquished his title and a child not yet nine years old, the infant Edward V, had been created earl of Pembroke.

This part of the story of the Herbert–Vaughan feud has been told in some detail because it illustrates rather important points. In the first place, it is clear that while there was a sub pena tariff of sorts for the lesser protagonists, £100 for a knight, 100 marks and £40, the main protagonists were separately and variously assessed and the surety required of Vaughan was, on the first occasion, set higher than that required of the earl of Pembroke. Secondly, the solution arrived at in the case of the earl was a political one, tantamount to deprivation, which had the result of installing a royal administration in the Pembroke lands. These last two documents indeed have the flavour of those recognisances by which Henry VII enmeshed many of his subjects. Richard III followed his brother in setting a precedent for his conqueror. Sir William Hault[102] and Sir Richard Woodville had to find sureties of £1067 and 2000 marks respectively to guarantee their loyalty,[103] and Sir William Berkeley 2000 marks to guarantee both his loyalty and his undertaking to live in a place appointed by the king.[104] The complete, if infrequent, penetration of politics into the chancery system of taking sureties is marked by that recognisance wherein Christopher Colins, John Young and John Brampton, esquires, each stood surety in 500 marks for Robert Clifford, esquire, and Clifford himself stood bound in 1000 marks to be of good behaviour and to report at once to the king or the council anything prejudicial to the king that might come to his ears.[105]

In the calendared text the phrase *coram rege in cancellaria sua* has been rendered as 'in chancery', a free translation amply justified at this period. The phrase *coram rege et consilio suo* has, however, been more literally translated as 'before the king and council', a translation which may not, in the light of the available evidence, be wholly justified. It has already been suggested that there was no clear line of demarcation between the two courts described as 'the king in chancery' and 'the king and council';[106] we must now turn to consider whether 'the king and council' is, in relation to the business which is recorded on the corpus cum causa files, a single body composed of two parts or whether it is simply common form to describe the council alone in its judicial capacity. Common sense would dictate that this was so, for a king travelling at home and abroad with his immediate household would find difficulty in dealing with routine business generated in London; he would, however, expect to deal with the greater issues arising there and with matters brought before him at his stopping places by local petitioners. The weight of the evidence from the corpus cum causa files supports this view. In the first place, it is clear from the calendared file that 'the king and council' worked within a framework of return days borrowed from the older courts: the quindene of Michaelmas [130, 122], morrow of All Souls [141, 137, 39], octave of Hilary [34], morrow of the Purification [53], quindene of Easter [102], octave of Trinity [182, 83] and morrow of St John [171] all appear as days fixed for appearances before the king and council. This is not the framework of an itinerant court, as one entry on the present file [133] and another on a later file[107] make clear, by referring to the king and council at Westminster. If, then the court was static, we may next enquire whether it was ever, in dealing with this type of business, composed of the two elements, the king and the council. There is much evidence to support the view that it was not, and that the business was conducted by the council alone. The subjects of recognisances were certainly bound over to appear before 'the king and council', but the common form runs on 'wherever the council then may be'. This common form is supported by evidence of the council's power to bring a case to an end. There is an example of this upon the calendared file: Thomasin Catieyn was called before the king and council but dismissed quit sine die by the council alone [171]. The same pattern occurs in the document relating to Thomas Spring printed in Appendix II, and other files contain similar evidence of the council acting alone, for example releasing men from recognisances,[108]

102 Sheriff of Kent 1465–6, 1474–5, 1482–3.

103 C 244/134, no. 71 (1 Ric. III); 136, no. 130 (2 Ric. III).

104 C 244/134, no. 31.

105 C 244/136, no. 92: et si contingat aliquid quod in prejudicium predicti domini regis cedere valeat ad ipsius Roberti noticiam et intelligenciam pervenire tunc ipse eidem domino regi aut eius consilio quamcito poterit id declarabit et ostendet (2 Ric. III).

106 Above, 436.

107 C 244/125, no. 11 (17 Edw. IV).

108 C 244/114, nos. 13, 116 (12 Edw. IV); 120, no. 8 (15 Edw. IV).

assessing damages[109] and making judgments.[110] Perhaps the most telling pieces of evidence of the council's independent existence are the recognisance entered into on behalf of Robert Mason, archdeacon of Northumberland, who was bound over to appear before the king or the lords of the council whenever so instructed,[111] and the other, already discussed, which required Robert Clifford to report either to the king or to the council.

The council, then, could and did act on its own and was regarded as a body separate from the crown. There is, however, material to show both that the separation was not complete and that the king was to some extent involved in the deliberations of 'the king and council' and to some extent acted independently of it. On 18 February 18 Edward IV, William Enderby was bound over to appear before the king and council and go no further from London than Westminster; in place of the usual note of his subsequent dismissal by the council, the clerk has added the helpful postscript that on 24 March the king, by signet and sign manual, instructed Mr Robert Morton, keeper of the rolls, that the recognisance should be cancelled.[112] This is clear evidence of the king's personal participation in matters brought before 'the king and council'. There is equally clear evidence of the king acting alone. In the cases of Thomas ap Roger Vaughan, the earl of Pembroke and Sir Robert Harrington already discussed, the various parties were required to appear before the king himself, and similar provisions are found in the recognisances entered into by William Hatton and Edmund Finkle.[113] In sum, the evidence before us points to a flexible judicial administration in the latter part of the reign of Edward IV and in the reigns of Edward V and Richard III, in which some of the business with which the corpus cum causa files were concerned began and ended in the chancery, some was remitted to the chancery from the council and some from the chancery sent to the council, and that matters of greater moment were dealt with by the council acting alone or with the king, while others were dealt with by the king alone. To what extent this commonsense arrangement influenced the development of the conciliar courts is a field for others better versed in Tudor government than the present writer to investigate.

It has been the intention of this paper, however imperfectly fulfilled, to draw attention to records which have long been in existence but only recently open to public inspection, and to suggest ways in which they might be used. The pursuit of fragments of evidence through series of common form files, variations of formulae, addenda and endorsements is not to the taste of every historian, nor do the preoccupations of the modern academic world afford all those who have that taste to indulge it. If the present writer has indulged her own taste for this, one of the more obscure areas of historical enquiry, such a diversion is surely not improper in one brought up in the long traditions of the Public Record Office?

[109] C 244/127, no. 100 (19 Edw. IV).

[110] ibid., no. 10.

[111] C 244/122, no. 147 (16 Edw. IV).

[112] C 244/126, no. 117 (18 Edw. IV).

[113] ibid., nos. 3, 42.

Appendix I to Introduction

SUITS OPENED IN CHANCERY ON WRITS SUB PENA 11 EDWARD IV

The names of the plaintiffs and defendants are drawn from the sub pena file 11–12 Edward IV (C 253/44), an original file. The surviving writs on the file before the parchment stop, which normally indicates the end of a regnal year, were returnable between the octave of St John the Baptist 11 Edward IV and the quindene of Easter 12 Edward IV.

Plaintiffs	*Defendants*	*Early Chancery Proceedings (C 1)*
Aldrech, Isabella widow of William	Thomas Symson	–
Amesham, John, monk	John Stokton, kt	–
Asfordby, John	John Hardbien	–
Aunger, John, and Joan his wife	John Baldewyn	–
Baker, Margaret and Joan	Henry Baldewyne	40/71
Bath and Wells, bishop of	bishop of Hereford	–
Beauford, Agnes	Thomas Asshenden	43/171
Bemptbowe, John	prior of Tickford	43/169
Benet, Henry, and Alice his wife	Peter and William Glover	–
Bettenham, Stephen	Robert Kent and John Goldwell	41/48
Bisshop, Edward	John Bisshop	–
Blundell, Katherine	John Bechar	–
Botiller, Joan, widow of Lord Dunmow, and John Barkar	John Clerk	–
Boureman, Thomas, and Joan his wife	John Puryman	40/78
Bourgchier, Thomas, kt, and Isabella his wife, countess of Devon	William Browenyng	41/217
Brandon, William, kt	William Harlyston	–
The same	John Henyngham, kt	–
The same	John Heydon	–
The same	John Hopton, esq	–
Burgh, Joan, widow	William Neuport, esq, Thomas Mittone, esq, John Leghton, esq. John Lyngen, kt, and Lawrence Roche, clerk	44/243
The same	John Salter	–
Carewe, William, and Joan his wife	Elizabeth Drury	42/20
Carleton, John	Edmund Staley	40/84
Carowe, James, and Eleanor his wife	Thomas Hoo, esq	44/185
Cawode, James, and others	David John	–
Chacombe, Henry	Peter Emson and Richard Salforde	41/181
Chittock, John	John Jordan	43/194
Clerk, John	abbot of Chertsey	–
Clynton, John	John Hampton and John Dyve	40/21
Cobbe, William	William Elwyn and John Peers	–
Cobbe, William, and Katherine his wife	William Elwyn	42/48
Cole, Robert, and Margaret his wife	John Page	40/69
Colyngryge, John, and Isabella his wife, John FitzRobert and Agnes his wife	Henry Maknay	40/87
Comberworth, Richard, clerk	John Wynton, chaplain	–
Curteis, William	William Haryot, Richard Gardener and John Borell	–
Daventry, Thomas	William Hylles	–
Davy, Richard	Roger Tygo	–
Denney, abbess of	John Burgoyn	?40/30
?Dieneustn, John	William Seman	–
Dy. . ., John	Thomas Castell	–
Elmet, John, chaplain	Thomas Walron, Robert Morley and Thomas Ledenyll alias Wynter, chaplain	40/277
Englissh, John	John Jordan	–
Faireman, Richard	William Chaunterell	40/66
Felde, John, sen	Edward Gower, esq, and Agnes his wife	–
Frelbu. . ., John, and John Kyriel	William Covert	–
Gay, Thomas, jun	William Hampton	43/185
Glyn, John	Robert Knolle, clerk	?43/58
Goldewell, Emma, and others	John Samuel	44/1
Goman, John, and Marjorie his wife	William Heyne and Simon Halle	–
Gybbes, Thomas	Morgan ap Jenkyn	–
Haye, Matthew, and Ann his wife	John Owden	40/44
Hayward, Thomas, and Joan his wife	William Havelok, William Garston and Robert Baldewyn	–
Hilgerynden, John, and Alice his wife	John Holstrete	44/124
Hoper, Thomas	Matthew Glover	–

Plaintiffs	*Defendants*	*Early Chancery Proceedings (C 1)*
Hoton, Joan	Andrew Dungate and Robert Rayner	38/193
Hungerford, Walter, and Margaret his wife, widow of Lord Clynton	John Hampton and John Dyve	39/4
Huse, William	Richard Middelton	–
Ingoldesby, Thomas, and Robert Martin	John Midelton	–
Ishill, Joan widow of John	Thomas Urswyk	–
Ive, Thomas	Agnes widow of John Bagott	–
The same	Thomas and John Bourgchier, kts	–
The same	Joan Kyryell, widow	–
The same	Edmund Putvyne	–
The same	Thomas Seintleger	–
The same	William Charlewode and William Covert	40/73
Jakeman, Thomas	William Delamere	–
Kent, Joan, widow	John Seyve	38/221 or 45/320
Knesworth, Richard	John Mondy and John Beaufitz	44/54
Knoldene, George	Roger Brent	–
Lammonier, Rayner	Nicholas Aylewyn	43/129
Leuke[nor], Joan widow of John	John Goryng, Richard Pygot, Bartholomew Bolnay and Richard Forde	40/47
Lewes, Henry, kt	John Stokes	–
? Lewode, James, and others	Thomas Pounde	–
Lyghtfott, Thomas, his executors	Richard West	–
Lyteman, John, and Alice his wife	John Bone, Robert Weeld, Thomas Bernard and John Charvonell	41/99
Mascall, Thomas	William Taillour, kt	–
Maud, William, and John Toft	Robert Blower	–
Michell, George, and Alice his wife	Henry Santon	–
Middelton, John, and Ralph Wolseley	Alice Wyche and John Sulyard	–
Miller, Robert, and John Tyler	John Griffith	–
Molyneux, William	Thomas Littelton	–
Mydelton, Henry	Robert Rychard	–
Nanseglos, Nicholas	Richard Palmer	–
Olyver, William, and John Scoutop	John Bolles, Stephen Feltwell, John Welles, Thomas Tanner, Peter Smyth and William Tunbryge	39/226
Osbarne, Agnes	John and Thomas Longe	41/96
Otter, John	William Babyngton	10/218
Parrys, Robert, Robert Benet and William Straunge	Walter Yorke and Robert Dyer	43/189
Perepoynt, Henry	Henry Sotehill	39/35
Philip, Hugh, clerk	Walter Kyngdon, clerk	45/45
Philip, Matthew, kt, and Beatrice his wife	Thomas Hille, Robert Racheford and Thomas Gylmyn	–
The same	Bartholomew Bolney and John Goryng	40/47
Pulter, John, and Alice his wife	John and William Walkelyn	44/98
Ramys, James, clerk	Philip Berker	44/37
Raulyn, Alice widow of Richard	Richard Wode	?39/238
Renaker, Geoffrey, and Joan his wife	Robert Spayn	42/38
Riswik, Dietrich van	Katherine Ripplyngham	43/295
Rokke, William	John Ayrest	–
Rowethorne, John	Edmund Kervell and John Lambard	–
Russell, John, sen	Nicholas Molle and Nicholas Tillyer	44/131
Ry, John at	John Vyncent	–
Rygmere, John	John Oxenbrigge	–
Rylay, John, chaplain	William Bekbank and John Wraby, clerks	45/167
Sauston, Thomas	John Barre	44/203
Scotte, John	William Wodewarde	40/60 or 44/59
Sewester, John	Robert Richardes and Henry Middilton	–
Seymour, Roger, and Sibyl his wife	Nicholas Danyell	–
Smale, John	John Stopehill and John Coggare	40/36
Snowe, Henry	Thomas Leventhorp and Ralph Grey	39/216
Stevenson, John	William Tebald and Edmund Crosse, clerk	?39/201
Syff, Richard	Thomas Peytevin	–
Syscote, Thomas	William Hasylwode	–
Taillour, John	Joan widow of John Payn	40/33
Thorndon, Thomas	William Brandon, kt	45/381
Thornton, Thomas	The same	?45/381
Tryg, John	William Ricardis and Joan Jakelyn	40/40
Vavasour, William, and Joan his wife	Peter Bank	41/157
Wales, Matthew	Thomas Mason	38/184
Walwyn, Richard	Humphrey Gentile	45/36

Plaintiffs	*Defendants*	*Early Chancery Proceedings (C 1)*
Whitbarowe, William	Thomas Guyn, Walter Stokker and Thomas Bygge	40/82 or 42/49
The same	Richard Chircheman and Roger Reynold	–
White, Richard, and Alice his wife	Robert Grynell	–
Whynyngton, John, clerk	Thomas Fermour	45/346
Wilden, Thomasina widow of Robert	prior of Christchurch, London	41/249
Winchester, bishop of	William Paston, esq	?42/104
Wode, Henry, and Agnes his wife	Henry Lancastre	–
Wode, John	Hamon Clayton, Thomas Bokenham and William Pepri	–
Wyneslowe, Thomas	Thomas Hoo	40/20
'per cancellarium'	Thomas Faux	–
The same	Thomas Hadley, chaplain	–
The same	Thomas Norrey	–
The same	Richard Osbarn	–
The same	John Percyvall	–
The same	Richard Burton	–
The same	William Dawebes, vicar of Bassingbourne	–
The same	John Gray	–

Appendix II to Introduction

C 244/127, no. 16 (see above, 438)

Memorandum quod primo die maii anno regni regis Edwardi quarti duodecimo Willelmus Stokker de London miles Johannes Brampton de London marchaunt Johannes Stokker de London marchaunt et Johannes Sturmyn de London marchaunt coram eodem domino rege in cancellaria sua personaliter constituti manuceperunt videlicet quilibet eorum sub pena quatuor milium marcarum pro Thoma Spryng ac idem Thomas assumpsit pro se ipso sub pena sexcentarum milium marcarum quod ipse coram dicto domino rege et consilio suo in crastino Sancti Johannis Baptiste proximo futuro ubicumque idem consilium tunc fore contigerit personaliter comparebit, quam quidem summam quatuor milium librarum[114] quilibet manucaptorum predictorum per se ac predictus Thomas dictam summam sexcentarum librarum[114] concesserunt de terris et catallis suis ad opus dicti domini regis levari si prefatus Thomas coram prefato domino rege et consilio suo predicto in crastinum predictum in forma predicta minime comparuerit.

Ad quem quidem crastinum predictus Thomas Spryng coram prefato domino rege et consilio suo personaliter comparuit, et super hoc prefatus Thomas dimissus est de consilio quietus sine die per considerationem eiusdem consilii.

[114] Sic.

Appendix III to Introduction

C 244/127, no. 16

Memorandum quod vicesimo primo die marcii anno regni regis Edwardi quarti decimo nono Anna comitissa Pembroch, Walterus Devereux de Ferrers miles et Radulfus Hothom de Lekenfeld in comitatu Ebor' armiger coram nobis in cancellaria nostra personaliter constituti manuceperunt, videlicet quilibet eorum sub pena mille librarum, pro Willelmo comite Pembroch et Waltero Herbert milite fratre eiusdem comitis et eorum utroque, ac uterque predictorum comitis et Walteri assumpsit pro se ipso sub pena mille librarum quod ipsi nec ad neque in aliquas partes occidentales ultra aquam Sabrine nec ad neque in aliquas partes Wallie aliquo tempore infra unum annum integrum proxime futurum transibunt, nec se divertent, nec eorum alter transibit nec se divertet quovis modo, quam quidam summam mille librarum tam quilibet manucaptorum predictorum quam uterque predictorum comitis et Walteri per se concesserunt de terris et catallis suis ad opus dicti domini regis levari si predicti comes et Walterus ad et in aliquas partes occidentales ultra dictam aquam Sabrine aut ad et in aliquas partes Wallie aliquo tempore infra unum annum integrum proxime, ut predictum est, futurum transierint aut se diverterint vel eorum alter transierit aut se diverterit ullo modo.

C 244/125, no. 7

Memorandum quod vicesimo quarto die aprilis anno regni regis Edwardi quarti decimo septimo Thomas ap Roger Vaghan coram domino rege in cancellaria sua personaliter constitutus manucepit sub pena centum librarum pro Rogero ap Roger Vaghan quod ipse coram domino rege et consilio suo apud Westm' in quindena Pasche proxime futura personaliter comparebit ad faciendum et recipiendum quod sibi ex parte dicti domini regis tunc ibidem injungetur faciendum, et quod idem Rogerus dampnum vel malum aliquod Willelmo comiti Pembroch aut alicui de populo dicti domini regis de corpore suo interim non faciet nec fieri procurabit aliquo modo, nec aliquam gomortham contributionem sive impositionem alicui subditorum dicti domini regis in partibus Suthwall' pro fine eiusdem Rogeri coram dicto domino rege et consilio suo pro diversis transgressionibus riotis routis coadunationibus et conventiculis illatis per ipsum Rogerum ante primum diem maii ultimo preteritum in partis predictis factis illatis sive perpetratis assesso et adjudicato nullo modo fieri faciet aut levabit, quam quidam summam centum librarum prefatus Thomas concessit de terris et catallis suis ad opus dicti domini regis levari si idem Rogerus coram prefato domino rege et consilio suo predicto ad quindenam predictam in forma predicta minime comparuerit aut si dampnum vel malum aliquod prefato comiti aut alicui de populo dicti domini regis de corpore suo per prefatum Rogerum vel procurationem suam eveniat ullo modo, vel si aliquam gomortham contributionem sive impositionem alicui predictorum subditorum dicti domini regis pro fine predicto fieri fecit aut levavit.

TEXT

[In translating return days into calendar form, it has been assumed that all Sundays and the greater feasts are 'dies non juridici' *and that the quindene of Easter begins 17 days from Easter day. For a discussion on dating see above, 431–2. The entry numbers used are the subnumbers within the file; hence the reverse order.]*

C 244/112

[230] Habeas corpus cum causa captionis to the mayor and sheriffs of London: John Kyrkeman, chaplain, on the quindene of Easter [9 May]. Southampton, 29 April 10 Edward IV [1470].

[*Return*] Imprisoned in pleas of trespass brought by Thomas Hewetson, yeoman, of threats against the same, on suspicion of felony suggested by the same, and of debt for £20 brought by William Nele, rector of St Leonard's, Streatham, Surrey.

Recognisance: Thomas Bradeston of Winterbourne, Glos, gent., John Lylburn of Devizes, Wilts, gent., Ralph Shirley of Staunton Harold, Leics, gent., Richard Avard of Worcester, Worcs, gent., Thomas Alye of Westminster, Midd, tailor, Walter Hylle of Islington, Midd, gent., each sub pena 100 marks and corpus pro corpore, John Kyrkeman, chaplain, sub pena £100: Kyrkeman to appear in chancery on Tuesday next [15 May] and from day to day etc. and meanwhile not to do or cause to be done any physical harm to Thomas Hewetson. 14 May 10 Edward IV.

Recognisance: Lylburn, Shirley, Avard, Alye, Hylle [*as above*] and William Byrd of St Sepulchre's, London, chapman, each sub pena 100 marks and corpus pro corpore, John Kyrkeman sub pena £100: Kyrkeman to appear in chancery on the morrow of St John the Baptist [25 June], [*other terms as above*]. 4 June 10 Edward IV.

[229] Certiorari super causa captionis to the sheriffs of London: Thomas Malpas, yeoman, returnable on Saturday next [19 May]. Westminster, 16 May 10 Edward IV [1470].

[*Return*] Imprisoned in a plea of trespass brought by Agnes Apryen, widow.

[*The petition is* C 1/46/464, *endorsed*: Coram rege in cancellaria sua xix die maii.]

[228] Attachias to the sheriffs of London: Simon Smyth and William Heryet, former sheriffs of London and Middlesex, to answer Robert Spaldyng, serjeant at arms, servant of the bishop of Bath and Wells, chancellor, in a plea of debt on Tuesday next [22 May]. Westminster, 19 May 10 Edward IV [1470].

[*Return*] They have been imprisoned.

Recognisance: Thomas Aylofe of St George Botolph Lane, London, gent., Peter Sandes of St Nicholas Acons, London, draper, John Adam of Holy Trinity, London, draper, William Holgyll of St Martin Ludgate, London, tailor, each sub pena 40 marks, Simon Smyth and William Heryot each sub pena £40: Smyth and Heryot to appear in chancery on Wednesday next [23 May] and from day to day etc. 22 May 10 Edward IV.

[227] Habeas corpus cum causa captionis to the sheriffs of London: George Cok, on Wednesday next [23 May]. Westminster, 22 May 10 Edward IV [1470].

[*Return*] Imprisoned in a plea of debt for £8 14s. brought by Henry Bulstrode, citizen and mercer of London, and William Hekley of Southampton, Hants.

Cok was dismissed quit sine die by order of the keeper of the rolls.

[226] Habeas corpus cum causa captionis to the sheriffs of London: William Howeden, on Friday next [25 May]. Westminster, 23 May 10 Edward IV [1470].

[*Return*] Imprisoned in a plea of trespass brought by James Grey, carter.

Recognisance: Hugh Robynson of St Mary Matfelon, London, yeoman, John Johnson of the same, yeoman, John Willyam of the same, yeoman, Thomas Smyth of St Margaret Pattens, London, yeoman, William Howeden, each sub pena £20: Howeden to appear in chancery on Saturday next and from day to day etc. 25 May 10 Edward IV.

Howeden duly appeared.

[*The petition is* C 1/44/159, *endorsed*: R' xxv die maii proximo futuro.]

[225] Certiorari super causa captionis to the mayor

and sheriffs of London: John de Pounte and John Piers, returnable on Friday next [25 May]. Westminster, 23 May 10 Edward IV [1470].

[*Return*] Imprisoned in pleas of trespass, £100 damages, brought by Bonafanatus Berynger, merchant, and by John Fabian, draper.

[*The petition is* C 1/45/2, *endorsed*: Coram rege in cancellaria sua die veneris proximo futuro; C 1/45/7 *relates to the same suit.*]

[224] Habeas corpus cum causa captionis to the steward and marshal of the household: Thomas Lypney, on Wednesday next [23 May]. Westminster, 19 May 10 Edward IV [1470].

[*Return*] Attached in a plea of trespass within the verge brought by John Elgar; imprisoned to find surety of the peace towards Joan wife of John Elgar until Monday before Whit Sunday [4 June].

Recognisance: Henry Suttell of St Gregory by St Paul, London, draper, Robert Peke of St Botolph Aldgate, London, gent., each sub pena £40, Thomas Lypney sub pena 100 marks: Lypney to appear in chancery on Monday next [28 May] and from day to day etc. and meanwhile not to do or cause to be done any physical harm to Joan wife of John Elgar or other of the king's people. 23 May 10 Edward IV.

Lypney duly appeared and was dismissed quit sine die by the court and quit of the surety of the peace by supersedeas.

[223] Habeas corpus cum causa captionis to the mayor and sheriffs of London: Thomas Sharp, on this present Saturday [26 May]. Westminster, 26 May 10 Edward IV [1470].

[*Return*] Arrested on the king's mandate given both by the earl of Kent and by Robert Cosyns, keeper of the great wardrobe, for divers considerations.

Recognisance: Nicholas Sharp of Coggeshall, Essex, esq., John Kyng of the same, gent., Richard Manton of St Mary Woolnoth, London, vintner, Richard Preston of St Bartholomew's, London, brewer, Thomas Sharp, each sub pena 50 marks: Sharp to appear in chancery on Monday next [28 May] and from day to day etc. 26 May 10 Edward IV.

[222] Habeas corpus cum causa captionis to the mayor and sheriffs of London: John Drayton, chaplain, on this present Tuesday [29 May]. Westminster, 29 May 10 Edward IV [1470].

[*Return*] The writ was delivered too late to be executed.

[*See* 218]

[221–220] Certiorari super causa captionis to the mayor, aldermen and sheriffs of London: John Shukburgh, citizen and clothworker of London, returnable on the morrow of Ascension [1 June]. Salisbury, 9 May 10 Edward IV [1470].

[*Return*] Imprisoned in a plea of debt for £60 brought by Vesconte Cigala, merchant of Genoa.

[219] Habeas corpus cum causa captionis to the mayor and sheriffs of London: Henry Middelton, servant of William Sewester, mercer, on Saturday next [2 June]. Westminster, 1 June 10 Edward IV [1470].

[*Return*] Imprisoned in a plea of debt for £62 14s. 9d. brought by Rayner Lumner, lawnmaker (*lawen'man*).

[*See also* 133]

[218] Habeas corpus cum causa captionis to the mayor and sheriffs of London: John Drayton, chaplain, on Saturday next [2 June]. Westminster, 30 May 10 Edward IV [1470].

[*Return*] Imprisoned in pleas of trespass brought by William Bacheler, gardener, and of debt for 3s. and suspicion of felony in the parish of St Botolph Aldgate in Portsoken ward, at the suggestion of the same William Bacheler.

Recognisance: John Byrche of St Botolph Aldgate, London, yeoman, William Machon of Westminster, ostler, John Grene of the same, saddler, John Smyth of St Clement Danes, yeoman, each sub pena £20, John Drayton sub pena 40 marks: Drayton to appear in chancery on Monday next [4 June] and from day to day etc. 2 June 10 Edward IV.

Drayton duly appeared, and on the quindene of Michaelmas [30 Oct.], when he was dismissed quit sine die by the court in the plea of trespass and was given a day on the quindene of Easter [1 May] in the matter of the suspicion of felony and to appear from day to day etc. in the plea of debt.

[*See* 222, 214]

[217] Habeas corpus cum causa captionis to the mayor and bailiffs of Southampton: John Pynnok of Burford, Oxon, merchant, on the morrow of Ascen-

sion [1 June]. Southampton, 29 April 10 Edward IV [1470].

[*Return*] Imprisoned in a plea of detinue brought by Thomas Hongreford, esq.

[216] Habeas corpus cum causa captionis to the mayor and sheriffs of London: Rayner Lumner, lawnmaker (*lawndeman*) of Cambrai, on this present Friday [1 June]. Westminster, 1 June 10 Edward IV [1470].

[*Return*] Imprisoned on attachias out of king's bench on behalf of Walter Hille, to provide a surety of the peace, returnable on Saturday after Ascension [2 June].

Recognisance: William Pratte of St Mary Aldermanbury, London, mercer, Robert Yarum of St Michael Bassishaw, London, mercer, Rayner Lumner, each sub pena £100: Lumner to appear before the king and council on Saturday next [2 June]. 1 June 10 Edward IV.

Lumner duly appeared.

[215] Habeas corpus cum causa captionis to the mayor and sheriffs of London: Thomas Pynde, on Friday next [8 June]. Westminster, 3 June 10 Edward IV [1470].

[*Return*] Imprisoned in a plea of trespass brought by Thomas Graunger, citizen and tallowchandler of London.

Recognisance: John Beauchamp of St Michael Cornhill, London, draper, Thomas Kelet of St Martin Outwich, London, grocer, Thomas Pynde, each sub pena 100 marks: Pynde to appear in chancery on the octave of Trinity [25 June] and from day to day etc. 8 June 10 Edward IV.

Pynde duly appeared; on 6 December 14 Edward IV [1474], Kelet and Beauchamp asked to be released from the recognisance and on the same day found another surety, as appears in the chancery files of the 14th year, and the parties to the present recognisance were discharged.

[*The petition is* C 1/46/272, *endorsed*: Coram domino rege in cancellaria sua die veneris.]

[214] Habeas corpus cum causa captionis to the mayor and sheriffs of London: Katherine wife of William Bacheler, gardener, on Monday next [11 June]. Westminster, 7 June 10 Edward IV [1470].

[*Return*] Imprisoned in a plea of trespass brought against her and her husband by Robert Duk, tallow-chandler, and Joan his wife, and in a plea de minis brought against them and John Drayton, chaplain, by Margaret Walker.

Recognisance: William Kendall of London, serjeant, John Smyth of St Clement Danes, yeoman, Richard Smyth of St Nicholas Shambles, London, butcher, Reynold Baynam of St Mary Abchurch, London, shearman, each sub pena £40: Katherine to appear in chancery on the octave of Trinity [25 June] and meanwhile not to do or cause to be done any physical harm to Margaret Walker. 11 June 10 Edward IV.

Katherine duly appeared and was quit of the surety of the peace by supersedeas.

Recognisance: John and Richard Smyth [*as above*] each sub pena £20: Katherine to appear in chancery on Thursday next [28 June]. 27 June 10 Edward IV.

[*The petition is* C 1/46/397, *endorsed*: R' die lune proximo futuro. *See also* 218.]

[213] Habeas corpus cum causa captionis sub pena £100 to the mayor, sheriff and bailiffs of Bristol, the mayor and commonalty of the same: William Folkes, on 6 June. Westminster, 28 May 10 Edward IV [1470].

[*Return*] Imprisoned in two pleas of trespass brought by Moses Conteryn.

Recognisance: Robert Colyns of St Lawrence Jewry, London, cofferer, John Markaunt of St Nicholas Olave, London, fishmonger, Richard Tyffyn of St Clement Danes, brewer, John Pere of St Sepulchre's, London, grocer, each sub pena £100, William Folkes sub pena £200: Folkes to appear in chancery on the octave of St John the Baptist [2 July]. 7 June 10 Edward IV.

Folkes duly appeared.

Recognisance: Colyns, Markaunt [*as above*], Richard Snadnam of St Gregory by St Paul, London, barber, each sub pena £100, William Folkes sub pena £200: Folkes to appear in chancery on Thursday next [28 June] and from day to day etc. 27 June 10 Edward IV.

Folkes duly appeared; on 30 June Conteryn failed to appear and Folkes was dismissed quit sine die by the court.

[*The petition is* C 1/46/273, *endorsed*: Coram

domino rege in cancellaria sua vj die junii proximo futuro.]

[212] Habeas corpus cum causa captionis to the mayor and sheriffs of London: William Broun, chaplain, on the octave of Trinity [25 June]. Westminster, 19 June 10 Edward IV [1470].

[*Return*] Imprisoned in a plea of account brought by Richard Langston, brewer.

Recognisance: John Queldryk of St Leonard's, London, goldsmith, Hugh Longe of St John Zachary, London, yeoman, Nicholas Clerk of St Botolph Aldgate, London, skinner, William Tonge of the same, tailor, each sub pena £10, William Broun sub pena £20: Broun to appear in chancery on Thursday next [28 June] and from day to day etc. 27 June 10 Edward IV.

Broun duly appeared and was given a day on the quindene of Michaelmas [13 Oct.]

[*The petition is* C 1/46/316, *endorsed*: London: Coram rege in cancellaria sua in octabis Sancte Trinitatis.]

[211B] Certiorari super causa arestationis to the mayor and aldermen of London: £50 belonging to Idonea Hall of London, widow, taken into the hands of Richard Galyon, goldsmith, returnable on the octave of Trinity [25 June]. Westminster, 17 June 10 Edward IV [1470].

[*Return*] The money was attached in a plea of debt for £50 brought by John Aleyn of London, goldsmith.

[211A] Attachias to the sheriff of Warwickshire: Roger Grendon, who has failed to answer a sub pena delivered to him by John Staunton, to answer for contempt and other matters on the octave of Trinity [25 June]. Westminster, 10 May 10 Edward IV [1470].

[*Return*] Grendon has been taken.

Recognisance: William Byngham of London, gent., William Rokesby of the same, gent., each sub pena 20 marks, Roger Grendon sub pena 40 marks: Grendon to appear in chancery on Thursday next [28 June] and from day to day etc. 27 June 10 Edward IV.

[210] Habeas corpus cum causa captionis to the mayor and bailiffs of New Windsor: John Fremley, on the octave of Trinity [25 June]. Westminster, 5 June 10 Edward IV [1470].

[*Return*] Imprisoned in two pleas of trespass brought by Margaret Salveyn.

Recognisance: William Bullok of New Windsor, draper, Richard Grenewey of the same, mercer, each sub pena 100s., John Fremley sub pena £10: Fremley to appear in chancery on Friday next [29 June] and from day to day etc. 28 June 10 Edward IV.

Fremley duly appeared.

[*The petition is* C 1/46/312, *endorsed*: Coram rege in cancellaria sua in octabis Sancte Trinitatis.]

[209] Attachias to the sheriffs of Norwich: Thomas Faukoner of Norwich, skinner, to answer Henry Brende, servant of John Davyson, chancery clerk, in a plea of debt on the quindene of Trinity [2 July]. Westminster, 17 May 10 Edward IV [1470].

[*Return*] Faukoner has been imprisoned but is too ill to attend.

[*The writ was authorised by Davyson.*]

[208] Certiorari super causa captionis to the sheriffs of Norwich: Simon Peticlerk, returnable on the quindene of Trinity [2 July]. Westminster, 26 May 10 Edward IV [1470].

[*Return*] Imprisoned in a plea of account brought by Gregory Clerk.

[*The petition is* C 1/46/311, *endorsed*: Coram domino rege in cancellaria sua in quindena Sancte Trinitatis.]

[207] Habeas corpus cum causa captionis to the mayor and sheriffs of London: John Dokyng, on Monday next [30 June]. Westminster, 26 June 10 Edward IV [1470].

[*Return*] Imprisoned in a plea of debt for £20 brought by William Taillour, alderman, citizen and grocer of London.

Recognisance: Giles Dokkyng of St Giles Cripplegate, London, waxchandler, John Brode of the same, pattenmaker, each sub pena £20, John Dokyng sub pena £40: Dokyng to appear in chancery on Wednesday next [4 July] and from day to day etc. 2 July 10 Edward IV.

Dokyng duly appeared and was dismissed quit sine die with the agreement of the plaintiff.

[*The petitions* C 1/46/305, 308 *appear to relate to this suit.*]

[206] Certiorari super causa captionis to the sheriffs of London: John Tussy late of Ware, Herts, returnable on Tuesday next [3 July]. Westminster, 28 June 10 Edward IV [1470].

[*Return*] Imprisoned in a plea of debt for 57s.

A writ de procedendo was granted.

[*The petition is* C 1/46/438, *endorsed*: Coram domino rege in cancellaria sua tertio die junii proximo futuro etc.]

[205] Certiorari super causa captionis to the mayor of Canterbury: Adrian Martynson, returnable on the octave of St John the Baptist [2 July]. Westminster, 22 June 10 Edward IV [1470].

[*Return*] Imprisoned in pleas of debt brought by Henry van Melom for £22; by Maud widow of Henry Herryson; and by Maud widow of Gerard Gazazson alias Gerardson, hardwareman, alias Maud widow of Henry Herryson for £28.

A writ de procedendo was granted pro parte Henry van Melom.

[204] Habeas corpus cum causa captionis to the sheriffs of London: John Roberdson, alias John Roberdson, chaplain, on Thursday next [5 July]. Westminster, 3 July 10 Edward IV [1470].

[*Return*] Imprisoned in a plea of trespass brought by William Skyrmot, goldsmith.

Recognisance: John Toller of St Faith under St Paul, London, gent., William Birde of All Hallows Bread Street, London, fuller, John Roberdson, each sub pena £20: Roberdson to appear in chancery on Friday next [6 July] and from day to day etc. 5 July 10 Edward IV.

Roberdson duly appeared and was dismissed quit sine die by the court.

[*The petition is* C 1/46/162, *endorsed*: Coram rege in cancellaria sua die jovis.]

[203] Habeas corpus cum causa captionis to the sheriffs of London: William Howard, chaplain, on Tuesday next [3 July]. Westminster, 30 June 10 Edward IV [1470].

[*Return*] Imprisoned to find surety of the peace towards Richard Wolff, tailor.

Recognisance: Nicholas Andlaby of St Mary Barking, London, gent., Thomas Yonge of the same, mercer, John Parteriche of the same, dyer, William Ely of St Martin Vintry, London, tailor, each sub pena £20, William Howard sub pena £40: Howard to appear in chancery on Friday next [6 July] and meanwhile not to do or cause to be done any physical harm to Richard Wolf. 3 July 10 Edward IV.

Howard duly appeared and was dismissed quit sine die by the court since he had found sufficient surety of the peace.

[202] Habeas corpus cum causa captionis to the sheriffs of London: Agnes Payntour, on Saturday next [7 July]. Westminster, 6 July 10 Edward IV [1470].

[*Return*] Imprisoned in pleas of debt against herself and Robert Payntour, salter, her husband, brought by John Bever, husbandman, for 30s., Edward Vewter, citizen and fishmonger of London, for 30s. 8d., and by John Turke, maltman, for 39s.

Recognisance: Richard Shyngylton of St Peter Cornhill, London, upholsterer, Richard Forde of St Clement Danes, gent., each sub pena 100s.: Agnes to appear in chancery on Monday next [9 July] and from day to day etc. 7 July 10 Edward IV.

Agnes duly appeared.

[*The petition is* C 1/46/319, *endorsed*: Coram rege in cancellaria sua die sabbati proximo futuro.]

[201] Certiorari super causa arestationis to the bailiffs of Colchester: two horses belonging to Richard Maiston, returnable on the quindene of St John the Baptist [2 July]. Westminster, 22 June 10 Edward IV [1470].

[*Return*] The horses were attached in a plea of debt for 18s. brought by John Clerk, carter.

[200] Habeas corpus cum causa captionis to the mayor and sheriffs of London: Copyn Pylgryme, on Monday next [9 July]. Westminster, 5 July 10 Edward IV [1470].

[*Return*] Imprisoned in pleas of debt for 10s. 6d. brought by Thomas Balyngton, baker, and of trespass brought by John Dreyman, Robert Marston, shipman, and John Copyn, beerbrewer.

Recognisance: Thomas Edwardes of London, gent., William Harryson of Wapping, Midd, beerbrewer, each sub pena £20, Copyn Pylgryme sub pena £40:

Pylgryme to appear in chancery on Tuesday next [10 July] and from day to day etc. 9 July 10 Edward IV.

Pylgryme duly appeared and was given a day on the octave of Michaelmas [6 Oct.] for the pleas against Balyngton and Marston, and dismissed quit in the plea against Dreyman who, on 10 July, withdrew his actions against Pylgryme.

[*The petition is probably* C 1/45/124, *which is damaged.*]

[199] Certiorari super causa captionis to the mayor and bailiffs of New Windsor: Robert Ordewey, returnable on the quindene of St John the Baptist [9 July]. Westminster, 5 July 10 Edward IV [1470].

[*Return*] Imprisoned in a plea of debt for 4 marks brought by John Seynton.

[198] Habeas corpus cum causa captionis to the bailiff of the liberty of the Savoy: Thomas Molyneux, chaplain, returnable on Friday next [13 July]. Westminster, 12 July 10 Edward IV [1470].

[*Return*] Imprisoned in a plea of debt brought by Robert Grene. Molyneux was dismissed quit sine die by order of the chancellor.

[*The petition is* C 1/46/303, *endorsed*: Savoy: Coram rege in cancellaria sua die veneris videlicet xiij die julii proximo futuro.]

[197] Habeas corpus cum causa captionis sub pena £200 to the mayor and sheriffs of York: Thomas Hemelsey, merchant, and Henry Williamson, merchant, on 18 June. Westminster, 25 May 10 Edward IV [1470].

[*Return*] Hemelsey uttered offensive words against the mayor, tending towards public disorder, in speech with Thomas Fynche, serjeant of the key, and William Speght, constable of All Saints Pavement, and when he was arrested, under letters close dated at York, 26 March 10 Edward IV, and brought to the council chamber, Williamson attacked the mayor and was arrested.

Letter from John Thirsk, Thomas Stanceby, John Marshall, Richard York, Thomas Wrangwissh and John Tounge, aldermen of York, to the chancellor, witnessing that the mayor retained the writ of 25 May and therefore the sheriffs could not execute it.

Habeas corpus cum causa captionis sub pena £500 to the mayor and sheriffs of York: Thomas Hemelsey, merchant, on 9 July. Westminster, 22 June 10 Edward IV.

Hemelsey appeared on 9 July and on the quindene of Michaelmas [13 Oct.], when he was dismissed quit sine die by order of the chancellor.

[*The petition is* C 1/46/398, *endorsed*: Coram domino rege in cancellaria sua xviij die junii anno decimo.]

[196] Habeas corpus cum causa captionis to the sheriff of Oxfordshire: John Nowers, on Saturday next [7 July]. 6 July 10 Edward IV [1470].

[*Return*] Imprisoned on capias utlagatum out of the common bench dated 23 May 10 Edward IV and capias et extendi facias out of chancery dated 27 February 8 Edward IV [1469], in pleas of debt brought by John Verde, citizen and clothworker of London, and John Vyncent, citizen and skinner of London, respectively.

Nowers was committed to the Fleet prison.

[195] Certiorari super causa captionis to the mayor, aldermen and sheriffs of London: Robert Killyngham, citizen and tailor of London, returnable on Thursday next [12 July]. Westminster, 8 July 10 Edward IV [1470].

[*Return*] Imprisoned in a plea of debt for £16 brought by John Beauchamp, citizen and clothworker of London.

Killyngham was given a day on the octave of Michaelmas [6 Oct.].

[*The petition is* C 1/46/348, *endorsed*: R' coram domino rege in cancellaria sua xij die julii.]

[194] Habeas corpus cum causa captionis to the steward and marshal of the household: John Hilbrond, on Tuesday next [31 July]. Westminster, 25 July 10 Edward IV [1470].

[*Return*] Imprisoned in a plea of trespass within the verge brought by John Colyn of the king's household.

Recognisance: Robert Burnet of Westminster, skinner, William Wilkyns of the same, gent., John Forde of St Clement Danes, Midd, skinner, Thomas Marchall of Southwark, Surrey, yeoman, each sub pena £10, John Hilbrond sub pena £20: Hilbrond to appear in chancery on the quindene of Michaelmas [13 Oct.] and from day to day etc. 31 July 10 Edward IV.

[193] Attachias to the sheriffs of London: John Harrys, grocer, Robert Smythfeld, grocer, John Sander, draper, John Hoton, saddler, Roger Humphrey, currier, to appear to answer William Boweman, servant of John Davyson, chancery clerk, keeper of the hanaper, in pleas of trespass on the quindene of St John the Baptist [9 July]. Westminster, 4 June 10 Edward IV [1470].

[*Return*] Harrys, Sander, Hoton and Humfrey have been attached; Smythfeld has not been found.

Recognisance: John Robchaunt of London, girdler, Thomas Cotton of London, serjeant, each sub pena £20, John Harrys sub pena 40 marks: Harrys to appear in chancery on the quindene of Michaelmas [13 Oct.] and from day to day etc. 11 July 10 Edward IV.

Recognisance: Richard Tykerich of London, scrivener, John Porter of London, barber, each sub pena £20, John Sander sub pena 40 marks: similar terms for Sander. 11 July 10 Edward IV.

Sander duly appeared and was dismissed quit sine die by order of the keeper of the rolls.

Recognisance: John Broughton of London, saddler, Nicholas Assheby of London, saddler, each sub pena £20, John Houton sub pena 40 marks: similar terms for Houton. 11 July 10 Edward IV.

Recognisance: John Shukburgh of London, draper, Walter Smert of London, skinner, each sub pena £20, Roger Humfrey sub pena 40 marks: similar terms for Humfrey. 11 July 10 Edward IV.

Humfrey duly appeared and was dismissed quit sine die with the agreement of the plaintiff.

[192] Habeas corpus cum causa captionis to the sheriffs of London: William Smyth, on Friday next [20 July]. Westminster, 17 July 10 Edward IV [1470].

[*Return*] Detained in the parish of St Mary le Strand, Midd, and sent to the city Counter on suspicion of a homicide at Lambeth marsh and of the robbery of William Thornton and the archbishop of Canterbury at Lambeth, Surrey, on the information of William Thornton.

Recognisance: John Leigh of Flamston, Wilts, gent., John Wykes of St Clement Danes, gent., William Bowil of the same, gent., William Blake of Hilmarton, Wilts, gent., each sub pena £20 and corpus pro corpore, William Smyth sub pena £40: Smyth to appear in chancery on the quindene of Michalemas [13 Oct.] and from day to day etc. 20 July 10 Edward IV.

Smyth duly appeared and was dismissed quit sine die by the court since divers persons testified to his good behaviour and character.

[*The petition is* C 1/46/101, *endorsed*: Coram rege in cancellaria sua xix die julii.]

[191] Habeas corpus cum causa captionis to the sheriffs of London: John Kynge, bladesmith, on Monday next [30 July]. Westminster, 26 July 10 Edward IV [1470].

[*Return*] Imprisoned in pleas of debt for 60s. brought by William Walton, esq., and of detinue for 5 marks brought by Thomas Person, bladesmith.

Recognisance: Richard Baron of St Mary le Strand, Midd, yeoman, Richard Wardale of Hoddesdon, Herts, yeoman, Thomas Prese of All Hallows Bread Street, London, skinner, William Traynell of St Benet Fink, London, shearman, each sub pena 20 marks, John Kynge sub pena £20: Kynge to appear in chancery on the quindene of Michaelmas [13 Oct.] and from day to day etc. 30 July 10 Edward IV.

[*The petition is probably* C 1/46/321, *although it is endorsed*: Coram domino rege in cancellaria sua xxvij die julii.]

[190] Habeas corpus cum causa captionis to the mayor and sheriffs of London: Richard Garnett, on Saturday next [4 Aug.]. Westminster, 3 August 10 Edward IV [1470].

[*Return*] Imprisoned in a plea of debt for £4 brought by Richard Sokel, cutler, and Agnes his wife, widow and executrix of William Taillour, citizen and tailor of London, and Richard Bonavuntour, rector of Chelsfield, Kent, her coexecutor.

Recognisance: Peter Benett of London, gent., Thomas Mountgomery of St Mary Magdalen, London, yeoman, each sub pena 100s., Richard Garnett sub pena £10: Garnett to appear in chancery on the quindene of Michaelmas [13 Oct.] and from day to day etc. 4 August 10 Edward IV.

[*The petition is* C 1/46/352, *endorsed*: Coram rege die sabbati.]

[189, 187] Habeas corpus cum causa captionis to the sheriffs of London: Richard Burgham, on Saturday next [4 Aug.]. Westminster, 3 August 10 Edward IV [1470].

[*Return*] Imprisoned in two pleas of debt for 20 marks each and a plea de minis, all brought by William Sefowle, timbermonger alias carpenter, of London.

Recognisance: John Herynden of Staplehurst, Kent, gent., John Hamon of London, gent., John Osborn of London, . . . , William Borell of Staplehurst, yeoman, each sub pena £20, Richard Burgham sub pena £40: Burgham to appear in chancery on the quindene of Michaelmas [13 Oct.] and from day to day etc. 4 August 10 Edward IV.

Burgham duly appeared and on the morrow of St Martin [12 Nov.], when he was dismissed quit sine die by the court.

[188] Recognisance: John Kendall of St Andrew Holborn, London, gent., John Faukeswell of London, gent., Simon Wryxworth of London, gent., Richard White of London, gent., John Don of London, tailor, Nicholas Mille of London, tailor, each sub pena £40, William Saundres sub pena £100: Saundres to appear in chancery on the quindene of Michaelmas [13 Oct.] and from day to day etc. 22 September 10 Edward IV [1470].

[186] Habeas corpus cum causa captionis to the sheriff of Kent: John Foster, on 31 July. Westminster, 23 July 10 Edward IV [1470].

[*Return*] Imprisoned by Humphrey Bourgchier, Lord Cromwell, and John Scot, kt, councillors, for sedition.

Foster was committed to the Fleet prison.

[185] Mittatis recordum et processum to the mayor and constables of the Calais staple: pleas of debt brought by Thomas Keston against William Kilton, in which partiality has been alleged; no further action is to be taken in the suit, and they are to appear before him on the quindene of Trinity [2 July] to answer for contempt in failing to act upon instructions. Salisbury, 10 May 10 Edward IV [1470]. Breve de statuto. [The return is missing.]

[*There is a parchment stop in the file at this point, marking the division between the 10th and 11th regnal years.*]

[184] Habeas corpus cum causa captionis to the sheriffs of London: Thomas Plane, grocer, on Monday next [20 May]. Westminster, 18 May 11 Edward IV [1471].

[*Return*] Imprisoned in pleas of debt brought by Richard Arlyngton, fishmonger, for 8 marks, William Costantyne, grocer, for £7 9s. 6½d., by William Kenet, grocer, for 24s., and James Gelybrond, citizen and grocer of London, for £13 10s.

Recognisance: William Broke of St Andrew by the Wardrobe, London, tailor, Richard Wardall of Holy Trinity, London, gent., Thomas Prees of All Hallows the Great, London, skinner, Thomas Berford of St Michael Crooked Lane, London, fishmonger, each sub pena £40, Thomas Plane sub pena £50: Plane to appear in chancery on Friday next [24 May] and from day to day etc. 21 May 11 Edward IV.

Plane duly appeared and on the octave of Trinity [17 June], when he was given a day on the quindene [25 June].

[*The petition is* C 1/46/70, *endorsed*: London: Coram domino rege in cancellaria sua die lune videlicet xx die maii.]

[183] Habeas corpus cum causa captionis to the mayor and sheriffs of London: Roger Walkleyn, on Tuesday next [21 May]. Westminster, 18 May 11 Edward IV [1471].

[*Return*] Imprisoned in pleas of debt brought by John Bryan, maltman, for £3, and Edward Snoxhill, gent., for 40s.

Recognisance: Thomas Erly of All Hallows, London, shearman, Robert Taylour of St Sepulchre's, London, brewer, Robert Wyleston of the same, fuller, Thomas Semay of St Andrew Holborn, London, salter, each sub pena £10, Roger Walkleyn sub pena £20: Walkleyn to appear in chancery on Friday next [24 May] and from day to day etc. 20 May 11 Edward IV.

[*The petition is* C 1/46/420, *endorsed*: R' die lune coram rege in cancellaria videlicet vicesimo die maii.]

[182] Recognisance: Thomas Hiltofte of All Hallows Honey Lane, London, vintner, Stephen Hengeham of the same, girdler, Haunannus Voght, each sub pena £100: Voght to appear before the king and council on the octave of Trinity [17 June] and from day to day etc. 18 May 11 Edward IV [1471].

[181] Habeas corpus cum causa captionis to the steward and marshal of the household: John Rous,

on Thursday next [25 April]. Westminster, 23 April 11 Edward IV [1471].

[*Return*] Imprisoned on the king's order.

Recognisance: Roger Seymour of London, gent., Thomas Bisshoppestre of London, gent., each sub pena £40, John Rous sub pena £100: Rous to appear in chancery on Friday next [26 April]. 25 April 11 Edward IV.

Rous duly appeared.

Recognisance: William Dene of London, gent., John Benster of St Alphage's, London, gent., John Colshaie of St Nicholas Olave, London, butcher, John Fryston of St Nicholas Olave, London, yeoman, each sub pena £100, John Rous sub pena £200: Rous to appear in chancery on 6 May and from day to day etc. 27 April 11 Edward IV.

Rous duly appeared on 6 May, 12 May, the morrow of Ascension [27 May], the octave of Trinity [17 June] and 25 June, when he was dismissed quit sine die by the court.

[*The writ was authorised* per consilium.]

[180–179] Habeas corpus cum causa captionis to the sheriffs of London: Edmund Redknapp, on Friday next [10 May]. Westminster, 8 May 11 Edward IV [1471].

[*Return*] Imprisoned on a writ capias et extendi facias out of chancery, dated 22 February 49 Henry VI [1471], and in a plea of debt for £30 brought by William Lok, citizen and mercer of London.

Recognisance: William Skypwith of Norwich, Norf, gent., Robert Richardes of St Mary le Bow, London, mercer, each sub pena 200 marks, Edmund Redknap sub pena 400 marks: Redknap to appear in chancery on the octave of Trinity [17 June]. 10 May 11 Edward IV.

Redknap duly appeared and was committed to the Fleet prison, for reasons influencing the chancellor.

[*See also* 160, 57]

[178] Recognisance: John de Bardy of London, merchant, sub pena £4000: to appear before the king and council on Monday next [13 May] and from day to day etc. 6 May 11 Edward IV [1471].

Bardy duly appeared and on the morrow of Ascension [24 May], when he was given a day on the octave of Trinity [17 June].

[177] Recognisance: William Kerver, Philip Hardbene, Gerard Camzan, Philip Lomelyn, Michael de Chiperell, Hugh Pemberton, all of London, merchants, each sub pena £2000, John de Bardy sub pena £4000: Bardy to appear before the king and council on 6 May and from day to day etc. 27 April 11 Edward IV [1471].

[176] Recognisance: John Hanmer of London, mercer, William Fyncheham of London, mercer, each sub pena £20, John Bedell of London, gent., Thomas Bowes of London, gent., each sub pena £60, Roger Abyndon, mercer, sub pena 100 marks: Abyndon to appear in chancery on the octave of Trinity [17 June] and from day to day etc. 6 June 11 Edward IV.

Abyndon duly appeared.

[*This was probably once attached to at least one other document.*]

[175–173] Habeas corpus cum causa captionis to the sheriffs of London: Eleanor Cotton, on Thursday next [30 May]. Westminster, 28 May 11 Edward IV [1471].

[*Return*] Imprisoned in pleas of debt against herself and Thomas Cotton, esq., brought by Richard Comber, tailor, for £4, John Lokke, waxchandler, for 5s., William Hurste, cook, for 12s., John Comber, tailor, for 5s., Agnes Wythom, widow, for 10s., Thomas Elde, serjeant, for 5s., in a plea of trespass brought by William Dollyng, gent., and, by herself, to find sufficient surety of the peace against Christine Benet, singlewoman.

Recognisance: John Shute of Ipswich, gent., Ralph Mansert of St Swithun London Stone, London, gent., William Graystok of York, gent., John Gascoigne of York, gent., each sub pena £40, Eleanor Cotton sub pena £100: Eleanor to appear in chancery on the octave of Trinity [17 June] and meanwhile not to do or cause to be done any physical harm to Christine Benet or other of the king's people. 1 June 11 Edward IV.

Eleanor duly appeared.

Recognisance: John Rysley of the king's household, esq., John Glover of the same, gent., Robert Clavynger of London, gent., Walter Sonnyng of London, gent., each sub pena £20, Eleanor Cotton sub pena £40: Eleanor to appear in chancery on Thursday next [27 June] and from day to day etc. and meanwhile not to do or cause to be done any physical harm to Christine Benet or other of the king's people. 20 June 11 Edward IV.

Eleanor duly appeared.

[*The petition is* C 1/46/113, *endorsed*: Coram domino rege in cancellaria sua xxix die maii. *See also* 114.]

[172] Recognisance: William Heron of St Vedast Foster Lane, London, saddler, John Hoton of the same, saddler, John Harryes of the same, tailor, Thomas Ray of the same, saddler, each sub pena £20, Thomas Long sub pena £40: Long to appear in chancery on the octave of Trinity [17 June] and from day to day etc. 26 May 11 Edward IV [1471].

[171] Recognisance: Philip Lomelyn, Leonard Vivold, Ralph Vivold, Anthony Calvus, merchants of Genoa, each sub pena £2000, Thomasin Catieyn sub pena £3000: Catieyn to appear before the king and council on the morrow of St John the Baptist [25 June] to answer matters put to him. 13 June 11 Edward IV [1471].

Catieyn duly appeared and was dismissed quit sine die by the council.

[170] Habeas corpus cum causa captionis to the mayor and sheriffs of London: William Campion, on Friday next [14 June]. Westminster, 12 June 11 Edward IV [1471].

[*Return*] Imprisoned in pleas of debt for 40s brought by William Scarborgh, clerk, of account brought by Peter Boteler, esq., for £20, and of debt for 39s. 11d. brought by Henry Penhargar, cutler.

Recognisance: Thomas Prees of All Hallows, London, skinner, Thomas Barford of St Michael Crooked Lane, London, fishmonger, Richard Wardall of St Benet Paul's Wharf, London, gent., William Tranell of St Peter le Poer, London, shearman, each sub pena £20, William Campyon sub pena £40: Campyon to appear in chancery on the octave of Trinity [17 June] and from day to day etc. 14 June 11 Edward IV.

[*The petition is* C 1/45/139, *endorsed*: R' coram domino rege in cancellaria sua die veneris videlicet xiiij die junii.]

[169] Habeas corpus cum causa captionis to the mayor and sheriffs of London: John Martyn of London, mercer, on Saturday next [15 June]. Westminster, 12 June 11 Edward IV [1471].

[*Return*] Martyn has not been imprisoned.

[168] Habeas corpus cum causa captionis to the mayor and sheriffs of London: John Chambre, on Friday next [21 June]. Westminster, 20 June 11 Edward IV [1471].

[*Return*] Imprisoned on the order of the archbishop of York, former chancellor.

[*The petition is* C 1/45/137, *endorsed*: Coram domino rege in cancellaria sua die veneris videlicet xxj die junii.]

[167] Habeas corpus cum causa captionis to the mayor and sheriffs of London: Bartholomew Carecta, on Saturday next [22 June]. Westminster, 20 June 11 Edward IV [1471].

[*Return*] Imprisoned in pleas of debt for £150 and trespass brought by John Periz of La Réole, late patron of the carvel *St James* of Spain.

Recognisance: William a Thomas of St Benet Gracechurch Street, London, tailor, Richard Baron of St Martin in the Fields, gent., William Proves of St Dunstan in the East, London, tallowchandler, Thomas Berford of St Michael Crooked Lane, London, fishmonger, each sub pena £200, Bartholomew Carecta sub pena 300 marks: Carecta to appear in chancery on Tuesday next [25 June] and from day to day etc. 22 June 11 Edward IV.

Carecta duly appeared.

[*The petition is probably* C 1/46/334, *although it is endorsed*: R' in cancellaria die sabbati videlicet secundo die junii.]

[166] Certiorari super causa arestationis to the mayor and aldermen of London: 120 pounds of silver in plate belonging to Thomas Cooke, kt, now in the custody of Henry Chacombe, clothworker, at the suit of Ralph Josselyn, kt, executor of Philip Malpas, citizen and clothworker of London, returnable on Saturday next [22 June]. Westminster, 21 June 11 Edward IV [1471].

[*Return*] The silver was attached in a plea of debt for £196 13s. 4d. brought by Ralph Josselyn, kt.

[165] Habeas corpus cum causa captionis to the keeper of the Fleet prison: John Teddesley, on Saturday next [29 June]. Westminster, 23 June 11 Edward IV [1471].

[*Return*] Imprisoned on the order of the archbishop of York, former chancellor.

Teddesley was dismissed quit sine die by the court.

[164] Recognisance: John Midelton of Belsay, Northumb, kt, William Pomeray of Berry Pomeroy, Devon, esq., John Fortescu late of London, esq., John Wykes of London, gent., each sub pena £100, John Shute and Ralph Birte each sub pena £200: Shute and Birte to appear in chancery on the quindene of Michaelmas [14 Oct.] and meanwhile not to do or cause to be done any physical harm to John Alwey or other of the king's people. 22 June 11 Edward IV [1471].

Shute and Birte duly appeared; on 23 November 12 Edward IV [1472] Alway appeared and released the surety of the peace and Shute and Birte were dismissed quit sine die by the court.

[*See also* 102]

[163] Recognisance [*by the same persons and in the same terms*] for James Newnham. 22 June 11 Edward IV [1471]. Newenham duly appeared.

[*See also* 102]

[162] Attachias to the sheriff of Surrey: William Charlewode of Chipstead to answer Thomas Ive, chancery clerk, in a plea of trespass on the quindene of Trinity [25 June]. Westminster, 4 June 11 Edward IV [1471].

[*Return*] Charlewode has been attached.

Recognisance: Thomas Brodbrigge of Reigate, Surrey, gent., John Pope of the same, yeoman, John Colcok of Chipstead, yeoman, John Groffham of Leatherhead, yeoman, each sub pena £40, William Charlewode sub pena £100: Charlewode to appear in chancery on Thursday next [27 June] and from day to day etc. 26 June 11 Edward IV.

[*The writ was authorised by Ive.*]

[161] Habeas corpus cum causa captionis to the mayor and sheriffs of London: John Alwey, on Friday next [14 June]. Westminster, 12 June 11 Edward IV [1471].

[*Return*] Imprisoned in a plea of trespass brought by James Newham, esq.

[*See also* 163, 102]

[160] Habeas corpus cum causa captionis to the keeper of the Fleet prison: Edmund Redeknape, on Friday next [21 June]. Westminster, 19 June 11 Edward IV [1471].

[*Return*] Imprisoned on the king's order and by the justices of king's bench to find surety of the peace towards John Whitefot.

[*See also* 180, 57]

[159] Habeas corpus cum causa captionis to the sheriffs of London: Robert Boulde, kt, on Saturday next [22 June]. Westminster, 21 June 11 Edward IV [1471].

[*Return*] Imprisoned in pleas of trespass brought by Thomas Molyneux, esq., of debt for £6 18s. 8d. brought by Thomas Chaterley, citizen and mercer of London, of trespass brought by William Bulkley of Beaumaris, Anglesey, to find surety of the peace towards Robert Brygger, esq., to find better surety to keep the day of payment of £25 to the same, of debt, as constable of Denbigh castle, for £12 brought by Roger Chesshire, clerk, rector of Boston, Lincs, of debt for £10 brought by John Wykyng, husbandman, of debt for 25s. 8d. brought by Nicholas Baynard, hosier, and of debt for £40 brought by Thomas Smyth, yeoman.

On 27 June 11 Edward IV, Brygger came to court and released the surety of the peace.

[158] Habeas corpus cum causa captionis to the mayor and bailiffs of Cambridge: Thomas Gardyner, on the quindene of Trinity [25 June]. Westminster, 10 June 11 Edward IV [1471].

[*Return*] Imprisoned in pleas of debt brought by Thomas Bendissh sen. of Steeple Bumpstead, Essex, esq., and John Bendissh of London, gent., for £20 and Nicholas Burdon for 13s. 10d. The habeas corpus was delivered by Gardyner in court on 18 June.

Recognisance: Thomas Lacy of Westminster, gent., John Burgh of London, gent., each sub pena £30, Thomas Gardyner sub pena £40: Gardyner to appear in chancery on Saturday next [29 June] and from day to day etc. 28 June 11 Edward IV.

Gardyner duly appeared, and on the quindene of Michaelmas [14 Oct.]; on 21 October he was dismissed quit sine die by the court with the agreement of the other parties.

[157] Certiorari super causa arestationis to the

mayor and bailiffs of Southampton: 171 pokes of Spanish wool and 50 sacks of cork belonging to John de Castro and John Goveroves, returnable on the morrow of St John the Baptist [25 June]. Westminster, 24 May 11 Edward IV [1471].

[*Return*] The goods were attached in a plea of debt brought by David Colwell.

[C 1/45/153 *appears to relate to the same suit.*]

[156] Habeas corpus cum causa captionis to the sheriffs of London: Joan Style, on Monday next [1 July]. Westminster, 29 June 11 Edward IV [1471].

[*Return*] Imprisoned in a plea of trespass brought by Thomas Thuresby, waferer.

Recognisance: Robert Style of St Dunstan in the West, London, skinner, Richard Fawcet of St Mary [Aldermanbury, John] Hamond of the same, tailor, Thomas Wright of Islington, Midd, carpenter, each sub pena £40: Joan to appear in chancery on 2 July and from day to day etc. 1 July 11 Edward IV.

Joan duly appeared and was subsequently dismissed quit sine die by the court since the plaintiff did not appear.

[*The petition is* C 1/46/64, *endorsed*: Coram domino rege in cancellaria sua primo die julii.]

[155] Habeas corpus cum causa captionis to the sheriffs of London: Thomas Samon, on Tuesday next [2 July]. Westminster, 29 June 11 Edward IV [1471].

[*Return*] Imprisoned in a plea of trespass brought by Roger Shavelok, tailor, and to find sufficient surety of the peace towards the same.

Recognisance: John Dyve of London, gent., Matthew Cressy of London, gent., Thomas Gybbes of St Gregory by St Paul, London, vestmentmaker, Thomas Samon, each sub pena £40: Samon to appear in chancery on Wednesday next [3 July] and from day to day etc. and meanwhile not to do or cause to be done any physical harm to Roger Shavelok or other of the king's people. 2 July 11 Edward IV.

Samon duly appeared and was dismissed quit sine die with the agreement of the plaintiff.

[*The petition is* C 1/46/65, *endorsed*: R' coram domino rege in cancellaria sua die martis proximo futuro.]

[154] Certiorari super causa captionis to the mayor and sheriffs of London: Agnes Bate, widow, returnable on Monday next [24 June]. Westminster, 18 June 11 Edward IV [1471].

[*Return*] Imprisoned in a plea of debt for £100 brought by John Birlyng, goldsmith, and Alexander Brok, salter.

[*The petition* C 1/44/138, *for a certiorari super causa captionis upon which the substantive action took place on 23 November 11 Edward IV, appears to represent an earlier stage in the same suit*; C 1/46/335 *also appears to relate to the same suit.*]

[153] Habeas corpus cum causa captionis to the sheriff of Surrey: William Peryn, on Wednesday next [3 July]. Westminster, 2 July 11 Edward IV [1471].

[*Return*] Peryn is not in prison.

[152] Habeas corpus cum causa captionis to the mayor and sheriffs of London: Richard Lygett, on Wednesday next [3 July]. Westminster, 1 July 11 Edward IV [1471].

[*Return*] Imprisoned in a plea of trespass brought by Sarah Cornyssh, widow, and on suspicion of the homicide of John Cornyssh, yeoman, at Stanford Rivers, Essex, on the suggestion of John Cornyssh jun., saddler.

[*The petition is* C 1/45/135, *endorsed*: Coram domino rege in cancellaria sua secundo die julii. *In the writ the day of the week is written over an erasure. Lygett had been committed to prison by the council of Henry VI.*]

[151] Habeas corpus cum causa captionis to the keeper of the Fleet prison: Robert Fulbroke, friar preacher, on Wednesday next [3 July]. Westminster, 2 July 11 Edward IV [1471].

[*Return*] Imprisoned on 14 December last on the order of the archbishop of York, former chancellor, sub pena £500.

[*The petition is* C 1/46/394, *endorsed*: Coram rege in cancellaria die mercurii.]

[150–148] Habeas corpus cum causa captionis to the mayor and sheriffs of London: Thomas Conyngston, merchant, on Wednesday next [3 July]. Westminster, 28 June 11 Edward IV [1471].

[*Return*] Imprisoned in pleas of account for 30s. and

a pipe of Gascon wine, and of debt for £100, brought by John Neve, mercer.

Recognisance: Thomas Bourne of St Magnus the Martyr, London, yeoman, John Smyth of St Clement Danes, shearman, William Heryn of St Margaret's, Westminster, yeoman, Ambrose Smyth of St Mary le Strand, cordwainer, Thomas Burlace of St Martin in the Fields, tailor, each sub pena £100, Thomas Conyngston sub pena £200: Conyngston to appear in chancery on Friday next [5 July] and from day to day etc. 4 July 11 Edward IV.

Conyngston was committed to the Fleet prison. On the octave of Michaelmas [7 Oct.] William Heryn appeared and stated that Conyngston died on 13 September in St Botolph Billingsgate, and asked for judgment if he should be charged in the sum of £100 for the failure of Conyngston to appear.

[*The petition is* C 1/46/360, *endorsed*: Coram rege in cancellaria sua secundo die julii. *In the writ the day of the week is written over an erasure.*]

[147] Certiorari super causa captionis to the mayor and sheriffs of London: Hugh Adnette, returnable on the octave of St John the Baptist [1 July]. Westminster, 27 June 11 Edward IV [1471].

[*Return*] Imprisoned in pleas of debt brought by Humphrey Gentill, merchant of Lucca, for £39 5s., and William Cater, citizen and embroiderer of London, for £10.

[*The petition is* C 1/46/337, *endorsed*: Coram domino rege in cancellaria sua in octabis Sancti Johannis Baptiste proximis futuris.]

[146] Habeas corpus cum causa captionis to the mayor and sheriffs of London: William Hille, on Thursday next [4 July]. Westminster, 3 July 11 Edward IV [1471].

[*Return*] Imprisoned in pleas of trespass brought by Thomas Swan, esq., William Lexham, esq., and William Gray, bishop of Ely.

Recognisance: William Flamell of St Peter le Poer, London, brewer, Richard Milbery of Shoreditch, Midd, tailor, John Stykford of St Giles in the Fields, tailor, John Fakerell of All Hallows Lombard Street, London, saddler, John Frere of St Clement Danes, corviser, Richard Vygell of St Helen Bishopsgate, London, gent., each sub pena £60, William Hille sub pena £120: Hille to appear in chancery on 5 July and from day to day etc. 4 July 11 Edward IV.

Hille duly appeared and on 11 July was dismissed quit sine die by the court since the plaintiffs did not appear.

[145] Habeas corpus cum causa captionis to the sheriffs of London: Richard Treweman, on Friday next [5 July]. Westminster, 3 July 11 Edward IV [1471].

[*Return*] Imprisoned in a plea of trespass brought by Henry van Melom, jeweller.

Recognisance: Richard Westmyll of St John the Baptist upon Walbrook, London, tailor, Nicholas Swan of St Olave's, Southwark, Surrey, tailor, William Andreweson of St Margaret's, Southwark, whittawer, each sub pena £20, Richard Treweman sub pena £40: Treweman to appear in chancery on Saturday next [6 July] and from day to day etc. 5 July 11 Edward IV.

[*The petition is* C 1/46/409, *endorsed*: Coram domino rege in cancellaria sua quinto die julii.]

[144] Habeas corpus cum causa captionis to the mayor and sheriffs of London: Roger Austen, on Monday next [1 July]. Westminster, 27 June 11 Edward IV [1471].

[*Return*] Imprisoned in pleas of trespass brought by William Breton, grocer, and of debt for 25s. brought by Nicholas Grene, woodmonger.

Recognisance: Richard Hoo of Enfield, Midd, gent., Peter Benet of Eltham, Kent, gent., John Hoton of St Vedast Foster Lane, London, saddler, William Umfray of St Michael Wood Street, London, mercer, Thomas Bourn of St Magnus the Martyr, London, fishmonger, each sub pena £40, Roger Austen sub pena £80: Austen to appear in chancery on Saturday next [6 July] and from day to day etc. 5 July 11 Edward IV.

[*The petition* C 1/45/136 *may relate to the same suit.*]

[143] Habeas corpus cum causa captionis to the mayor and sheriffs of London: John Cokk jun., on Saturday next [6 July]. Westminster, 4 July 11 Edward IV [1471].

[*Return*] Imprisoned in a plea of trespass brought by Nicholas Barbur, gent.

Recognisance: John Lucas of St Dunstan in the West, London, tailor, Robert Pollard of the same, tailor,

Richard Fifeld of the same, tailor, John Hoby of the same, spurrier, each sub pena £40, John Cokk sub pena £100: Cokk to appear in chancery on Monday next [8 July] and from day to day etc. 6 July 11 Edward IV.

[*The petition is* C 1/46/472, *endorsed*: R' quinto die julii proximo futuro. *In the writ the day of the week is written over an erasure.*]

[142] Certiorari super causa captionis to the mayor and sheriffs of London: John Ingolsby of London, gent., and Robert Martyn of London, gent., returnable on Monday next [8 July]. Westminster, 3 July 11 Edward IV [147].

[*Return*] Imprisoned in a plea of debt for 100 marks brought by John Middelton sen., citizen and mercer of London.

[141] Recognisance: William Godyer of Oxford, LL.D., John Clerk of the same, fishmonger, each sub pena £100, John Seman of the same sub pena £200: Seman to appear before the king and council on the morrow of All Souls [2 Nov.]. 6 July 11 Edward IV [1471].

Seman duly appeared and was dismissed quit sine die by order of the chancellor.

[*In the text, the word* cancellaria *has been cancelled and* consilio *interlined above it.*]

[140] Habeas corpus cum causa captionis to the sheriffs of London: John Love, grocer, on Monday next [8 July]. Westminster, 3 July 11 Edward IV [1471].

[*Return*] Imprisoned in a plea of debt for £17 9s. 4d. brought by Thomas Kippyng, citizen and clothworker of London.

Recognisance: Thomas Lacy of Westminster, gent., Hugh Daryngton of London, grocer, each sub pena £20, John Love sub pena £40: Love to appear in chancery on Wednesday next [10 July] and from day to day etc. 8 July 11 Edward IV.

Love duly appeared and was dismissed quit sine die with the agreement of the plaintiffs.

[*The petition is* C 1/46/66, *endorsed*: Coram domino rege in cancellaria sua die lune videlicet viij die julii.]

[139] Habeas corpus cum causa captionis to the sheriffs of London: John Archar, on Monday next [8 July]. Westminster, 5 July 11 Edward IV [1471].

[*Return*] Imprisoned in a plea of trespass brought by David Panter, gent.

Recognisance: John Ellerton of London, gent., William Russell of London, gent., each sub pena 100 marks, John Archar sub pena 200 marks: Archar to appear in chancery on Tuesday next [9 July] and from day to day etc. 8 July 11 Edward IV.

Archar duly appeared and on the octave of Michaelmas [7 Oct.].

[*The petition is* C 1/46/73, *endorsed*: Coram rege in cancellaria die lune.]

[138] Habeas corpus cum causa captionis to the sheriffs of London: Richard Bailly, tailor, on Wednesday next [10 July]. Westminster, 4 July 11 Edward IV [1471].

[*Return*] Imprisoned on suspicion of a felony in St Nicholas Shambles, London, of which a jury has acquitted him.

[*The petition is* C 1/46/63, *endorsed*: Coram domino rege in cancellaria sua quarto die julii. *In the writ* quarto *in the dating clause is written over an erasure.*]

[137] Recognisance: Roger Denham of Nutwell, Devon, esq., William Pollet of London, gent., each sub pena £1000, John Neuburgh sen., sub pena 2000 marks: Neuburgh to appear before the king and council on the morrow of All Souls [2 Nov] to answer those matters put to him. 8 July 11 Edward IV [1471].

[136] Certiorari super causa captionis to the mayor and sheriffs of London: John Skirwith, leatherseller, returnable on Thursday next [11 July]. Westminster, 8 July 11 Edward IV [1471].

[*Return*] Imprisoned in a plea of debt for £5 10d. brought by John Marchall, mercer.

[*The petition is* C 1/46/333, *endorsed*: Coram domino rege in cancellaria sua die jovis videlicet undecimo die julii.]

[135] Recognisance: John Nores of St Sepulchre's, London, skinner, John Johnson of the same, smith, Richard Johnson of St Andrew Holborn, London, brewer, each sub pena £40 and corpus pro corpore, Robert Thorp sub pena £40: Thorp to appear in

chancery on the octave of Michaelmas [7 Oct.]. 11 July 11 Edward IV [1471].

[134] Recognisance: John Langford of Reading, Berks, esq., John Makeworth of Derby, esq., Robert Styrley, kt, each sub pena 200 marks: Styrley to appear in chancery on the quindene of Michaelmas [14 Oct.]. 19 July 11 Edward IV [1471].

[133] Recognisance: John Lamburn of London, gent., William Herte of London, gent., each sub pena £40, William Sewester, citizen and mercer of London, sub pena £100: Sewester to appear before the king and council on Monday next [15 July] and meanwhile not to do or cause to be done any physical harm to Rayner Lumner. 13 July 11 Edward IV [1471].

Sewester duly appeared, at Westminster.

[*See also* 219]

[132] Habeas corpus cum causa captionis to the mayor and sheriffs of London: Henry Whitrede, clerk, on Thursday next [25 July]. Westminster, 22 July 11 Edward IV [1471].

[*Return*] Imprisoned in a plea of trespass brought by John Stanard, parish clerk.

Recognisance: William Grene, clerk, Edward Stephens of St Andrew Holborn, London, gent., Walter Haltman of the same, carpenter, each sub pena £20, Henry Whitrede sub pena £40: Whitrede to appear in chancery on Monday next [29 July] and from day to day etc. 25 July 11 Edward IV.

Whitrede duly appeared.

[*The petition is* C 1/46/164, *endorsed*: R' xxv die julii.]

[131] Certiorari super causa captionis to the mayor and sheriffs of London: Thomas Wyssheton, returnable on Wednesday next [24 July]. Westminster, 22 July 11 Edward IV [1471].

[*Return*] Imprisoned in pleas of debt for 53s. 4d. brought by Thomas Lypney, citizen and barber of London, and of trespass brought by Thomas Hoton, ostler.

[*The petition is* C 1/45/125, *endorsed*: R' vicesimo quarto die julii.]

[130] Recognisance: Thomas Fraunces of London, chaplain, John Gloys of London, ironmonger, Richard Foote of London, draper, George Knevysworth of London, draper, Richard Smyth of St Mildred's, London, draper, each sub pena 500 marks, John Osbourne sub pena 1000 marks: Osbourne to appear before the king and council on the quindene of Michaelmas [4 Oct.] and meanwhile to be of good behaviour towards the king and his people. 5 August 11 Edward IV [1471].

[129] Certiorari super causa captionis to the mayor and sheriffs of London: William Pace, chaplain, returnable on Thursday next [11 July]. Westminster, 7 July 11 Edward IV [1471].

[*Return*] Imprisoned in a plea of trespass brought by James Belgrave, chaplain.

[*The petition is* C 1/46/52, *endorsed*: R' die lune videlicet octavo die julii. *In the writ the day of the week is written over an erasure.*]

[128] Recognisance: William Brandon of Southwark, Surrey, kt, Thomas Hoo of Horsham, Sussex, esq., John Martyn jun. of London, mercer, each sub pena 200 marks, John Martyn sub pena £100: Martyn to appear in chancery on Monday next [15 July] and from day to day etc. 12 July 11 Edward IV [1471].

[127] Habeas corpus cum causa captionis to the sheriff of Buckinghamshire: William Fryng, on 1 August. Westminster, 20 July 11 Edward IV [1471].

[*Return*] Imprisoned on an indictment of divers felonies and on a warrant issued by one of the keepers of the peace of the county.

Recognisance: William Carden of St Mary Abchurch, London, shearman, John Russell of the same, tailor, Edward Hide of the same, tailor, William Hacompleyn of the same, waxchandler, each sub pena £20 and corpus pro corpore, William Fryng sub pena £40: Fryng to appear in chancery on Friday next [2 Aug.] and from day to day etc., and meanwhile not to do or cause to be done any physical harm to William Proktour or other of the king's people. 30 July 11 Edward IV.

Fryng duly appeared and was given a day on the quindene of Michaelmas [14 Oct.].

[*The petition is* C 1/38/218, *endorsed*: R' coram domino rege in cancellaria sua primo die augusti proximo futuro. *The parties were involved in a suit concerning uses.*]

[126] Habeas corpus cum causa captionis to the mayor and sheriffs of London: Agnes Manfeld, on Wednesday next [24 July]. Westminster, 22 July 11 Edward IV [1471].

[*Return*] Imprisoned in a plea of trespass brought by Thomas Thuresby, waferer.

Recognisance: Thomas Hedeman of Westminster, gent., Maurice Aungell of St Sepulchre's, London, yeoman, John Shirryf of St Anne Aldersgate, London, goldsmith, John Hammond of St Mary Aldermanbury, London, tailor, each sub pena £20, Agnes Manfeld sub pena £40: Agnes to appear in chancery on Friday next [26 July] and from day to day etc. 24 July 11 Edward IV.

Agnes duly appeared and on the octave of Michaelmas [7 Oct.], when she was dismissed quit sine die by the court.

[*The petition is* C 1/46/84, *endorsed*: Coram domino rege in cancellaria sua xxiiij die julii.]

[125] Habeas corpus cum causa captionis to the sheriffs of London: Joan Ormond, widow, on Saturday next [3 Aug.]. Westminster, 31 July 11 Edward IV [1471].

[*Return*] Imprisoned in pleas of debt for 16s. brought by John Wode, chandler, of trespass brought by Richard Dygan, skinner, of debt for 39s. 11d. brought by John Watson, brewer, for £10 brought by Richard Dygan, for 3s. brought by Thomas Dowsyng, wheeler, and for 13s. 4d. brought by Margery Thurwet, widow.

Recognisance: Richard Vigill of St Helen Bishopsgate, London, gent., Henry Rodes of St Sepulchre's, London, yeoman, John Stykford of St Andrew Holborn, London, tailor, John Frere of St Clement Danes, cordwainer, each sub pena £20, Joan Ormond sub pena £40: Joan to appear in chancery on Monday next [5 Aug.]. 3 August 11 Edward IV.

Joan duly appeared and on the octave of Michaelmas [7 Oct.].

[*The petition is* C 1/46/83, *endorsed*: Coram rege in cancellaria die veneris videlicet secundo die augusti. *In the writ the day of the week is written over an erasure.*]

[124] Habeas corpus cum causa captionis to the sheriffs of London: Roger Blakwall, on Thursday next [11 July]. Westminster, 9 July 11 Edward IV [1471].

[*Return*] Imprisoned in pleas of trespass and to find surety of the peace brought by Roger Morys, clerk, of debt for 32s. brought by Thomas Hadley, prior of the new hospital of St Mary without Bishopsgate, and of trespass brought by the same and by William Haynes, gent.

Recognisance: John Bylawe of St Botolph Bishopsgate, London, waxchandler, Robert Staffe of the same, armourer, John Oldom of Southwark, Surrey, fuller, Thomas Grove of St Clement Danes, glover, each sub pena £20, Roger Blakwall sub pena £40: Blakwall to appear in chancery on the octave of Michaelmas [7 Oct.] and from day to day etc. and meanwhile not to do or cause to be done any physical harm to Roger Morys. 11 July 11 Edward IV.

Blakwall duly appeared and was dismissed quit sine die by the court with the agreement of the other parties; on 7 October Morys came to court and released the surety of the peace.

[*The petition is* C 1/46/85, *endorsed*: Coram rege in cancellaria sua die jovis (*over an erasure*) x die julii. *In the writ the day of the week is written over an erasure.*]

[123] Habeas corpus cum causa captionis to the mayor and sheriffs of London: Thomas Taylour, clerk, on Monday next [12 Aug.]. Westminster, 9 August 11 Edward IV [1471].

[*Return*] Imprisoned, as rector of Merthyr and canon of Llandaff, in a plea of debt for 200 marks brought by the archdeacon and chapter of Llandaff.

Recognisance: Philip Huske of London, clerk, Walter Enderby of London, gent., Philip Bitterley of Langley, Herts, gent., Thomas Lypney of London, barber, John Frere of St Clement Danes, cordwainer, Robert Swete of the same, surgeon, John Ratclyff of St Mary at Hill, London, ironmonger, Thomas Burlas of St Martin in the Fields, Midd, tailor, each sub pena 200 marks, Thomas Taillour sub pena 300 marks: Taillour to appear in chancery on the octave of Michaelmas [7 Oct.] and from day to day etc. 12 August 11 Edward IV.

Taillour duly appeared.

[*The petition is* C 1/46/76, *endorsed*: Coram rege in cancellaria sua die lune videlicet xij die augusti.]

[122] Recognisance: John Abbot of St Sepulchre's, London, barber, Simon Warde of the same, fuller, each sub pena £20, John Dalton sub pena £40: Dalton to appear before the king and council on the quindene of Michaelmas [14 Oct.]. 20 August 11 Edward IV [1471].

[121] Certiorari super causa captionis to the mayor and sheriffs of London: Thomas Hervy, esq., returnable on 10 August. Westminster, 2 August 11 Edward IV [1471].

[*Return*] Imprisoned in two pleas of trespass brought by John Mendham, vintner.

[*The petition appears to be* C 1/46/341.]

[120] Habeas corpus cum causa captionis sub pena £100 to Thomas Whitrigge, keeper of the prison of the prior of Ely: John Hardyng, chaplain, on 12 August. Westminster, 31 July 11 Edward IV [1471].

[*Return*] Imprisoned on suspicion of felony.

[119] Habeas corpus cum causa captionis to the sheriff of Buckinghamshire: Richard Smyth of Edlesborough, on Monday next [26 Aug.]. Westminster, 20 August 11 Edward IV [1471].

[*Return*] Imprisoned for the murder of John Annes of 'Norwhald' [?Northall in Edlesborough].

Recognisance: William Potyer of St Giles Cripplegate, London, gent., Thomas Fulcus of Leighton Buzzard, Beds, husbandman, William Salcok of Edlesborough, Bucks, yeoman, Thomas Crouche of Ivinghoe, Bucks, yeoman, each sub pena £40 and corpus pro corpore, Richard Smyth sub pena £100: Smyth to appear in chancery on the octave of Michaelmas [7 Oct.]. 26 August 11 Edward IV.

Smyth duly appeared and was dismissed quit sine die by the court.

[*The petition is* C 1/46/80, *endorsed*: Coram rege in cancellaria sua die lune proximo futuro.]

[118] Certiorari super causa captionis to the sheriffs of London: William Gilbard, leatherdresser, returnable on Tuesday next [3 Sept.]. Westminster, 30 August 11 Edward IV [1471].

[*Return*] Imprisoned in a plea of debt for £47 18s. 4d. brought by Robert Rychard, citizen and mercer of London.

[117] Habeas corpus cum causa captionis sub pena £200 to the bailiffs of Huntingdon: Thomas Kelde and Adrian Lapayn alias Lappyn, Dutchman, on 26 August. Westminster, 17 August 11 Edward IV [1471].

[*Return*] They are not imprisoned. The deputy of the bailiffs swore that the return was true.

[116] Attachias to the sheriffs of London: William Sayer, citizen and mercer of London, to answer John Payn, gent., servant of Richard Fryston, chancery clerk, in a plea of detinue on Thursday next [20 June]. Westminster, 19 June 11 Edward IV [1471].

[*Return*] Already imprisoned in a plea of trespass brought by John Broun, ostler.

Recognisance: Thomas Lacy of Westminster, gent., Thomas Coton of London, gent., John Vaus of Westminster, gent., William Sayer, each sub pena £10: Sayer to appear in chancery on the octave of Michaelmas [7 Oct.] and from day to day etc. 11 July 11 Edward IV.

[*The writ was authorised by Fryston.*]

[115] Habeas corpus cum causa captionis to the mayor and sheriffs of Norwich: John Cheny, on 4 September. Westminster, 26 August 11 Edward IV [1471].

[*Return*] Imprisoned in a plea of account brought by John Stevynson.

Recognisance: John Storowe of Morning Thorpe, Norf, gent., William Andrews of Norwich, yeoman, each sub pena £20, John Cheny sub pena £40: Cheny to appear in chancery on the quindene of Michaelmas [14 Oct.] and from day to day etc. 4 September 11 Edward IV.

Cheny duly appeared, and on the morrow of All Souls [2 Nov.] and the octave of Hilary [20 Jan.], when the plaintiff did not appear, and was then dismissed quit sine die by the court.

[*The petition is* C 1/46/393, *endorsed*: R' quarto die septembris.]

[114] Habeas corpus cum causa captionis to the mayor and sheriffs of London: Eleanor Cotton, on Monday next [2 Sept.]. Westminster, 30 August 11 Edward IV [1471].

[*Return*] Imprisoned in pleas of debt brought against

herself and Thomas Cotton, esq., her husband, by William Herst, cook, for 20s., and by Robert Henley and Richard Mason, drapers, for 39s.

Recognisance: Robert Clavynger of Hoo, Kent, yeoman, William Sherman of Westminster, tailor, John Swifte of Stamford, Lincs, baker, each sub pena £10, Eleanor Cotton sub pena £20: Eleanor to appear in chancery on the quindene of Michaelmas [14 Oct.] and from day to day etc. 2 September 11 Edward IV.

Eleanor duly appeared, and on the quindene of St Martin [25 Nov.], the quindene of Hilary [27 Jan.], the quindene of Easter [15 April], the following Friday [17 April], the octave of Trinity [1 June], the morrow of All Souls [2 Nov.], the quindene of Easter [5 May], the octave of St John the Baptist [1 July] and was then given a day on the quindene of Michaelmas [13 Oct.].

[*See also* 175–3]

[113] Recognisance: William Flamell of St Peter le Poer, London, brewer, John Chaundeler of St Andrew Holborn, London, tallowchandler, Robert Rawelyn of St Margaret's, Westminster, brewer, William Torkesey of St Andrew Holborn, London, brewer, each sub pena £20, Henry Sotell sub pena £40: Sotell to appear in chancery on Friday next [18 Oct.] and from day to day etc. 17 October 11 Edward IV [1471].

Sotell duly appeared.

[112] Habeas corpus cum causa captionis to the sheriffs of London: Alan Sheveler, William Pregent and John Morecok on Friday next [4 Oct.]. Westminster, 1 October 11 Edward IV [1471].

[*Return*] Sheveler and Pregent, Bretons, imprisoned in pleas of trespass brought by Richard Kesteyn, esq., and of debt for 10s. brought by William Rede; Morecok imprisoned in a plea of trespass and contempt brought by Kesteyn and the keeper of the Counter in Poultry.

Recognisance: Thomas Bryce of All Hallows Lombard Street, London, mercer, Roger Boge of the same, upholsterer, John Paye of the same, vintner, Valentine Doune of St Peter Cornhill, London, draper, each sub pena £40, Alan Sheveler, William Pregent, John Morecok each sub pena £100: Sheveler, Pregent and Morecok to appear in chancery on Wednesday next [9 Oct.] and from day to day etc. 4 October 11 Edward IV.

[*The petition is* C 1/45/142, *endorsed*: R' coram rege in cancellaria sua die veneris videlicet quarto die octobris.]

[111] Recognisance: John Holl of Holy Trinity, London, esq., Henry Westclyf of St Nicholas Olave, London, ironmonger, William Tenet of Mitcham, Surrey, gent., John Marshall of London, surgeon, William Sheffeld of St Nicholas Olave, London, fishmonger, each sub pena £1000, Richard Cheldesworth and John Westclyf each sub pena £2000: Cheldesworth and Westclyf to appear in chancery on the octave of Michaelmas [7 Oct.] and from day to day etc. 7 September 11 Edward IV [1471].

Both duly appeared; Cheldesworth was dismissed quit sine die on 19 October and Westclyf on 21 October by the court.

[110] Certiorari super causa captionis to the mayor and sheriffs of London: William Bretayn, returnable on the octave of Michaelmas [7 Oct.]. Westminster, 20 September 11 Edward IV [1471].

[*Return*] Imprisoned in a plea of debt for £60 brought by John Hungerforth, citizen and clothworker of London.

[109] Certiorari super causa captionis to the mayor and sheriffs of London: John Desford, returnable on the octave of Michaelmas [7 Oct.]. Westminster, 2 September 11 Edward IV [1471].

[*Return*] Imprisoned in pleas of debt for £3 brought by John Wode, citizen and grocer of London, and for £3 brought by John Fenkell, draper.

[108] Certiorari super causa captionis to the mayor and sheriffs of London: John Pykeryng, returnable on the octave of Michaelmas [7 Oct.]. Westminster, 30 July 11 Edward IV [1471].

[*Return*] Imprisoned in a plea of debt for £600 brought by Richard Cotes, and Alice his wife, widow and exectutrix of Thomas Plumer, scrivener (*scriptor littere curialis*) of London, Master Robert Barkby, clerk, John Geny, gent., John Forster, gent., and Robert Leget, scrivener, her coexecutors.

[*The petition is* C 1/46/373, *endorsed*: R' coram rege in cancellaria sua in octabis Sancti Michaelis; C 1/46/372 *appears to relate to the same suit. Plumer is described as a scrivener in Calendar of Letter Books of the City of London, Letter Book L, ed. R.R. Sharpe (London, 1912), 50.*]

[107] Certiorari super causa captionis to the bailiffs of Colchester: William Kynggushurst, chaplain, returnable on the octave of Michaelmas [7 Oct.]. Westminster, 4 October 11 Edward IV [1471].

[*Return*] Imprisoned in a plea of debt for £10 brought by Nicholas Rewys of Thaxted, Essex.

Kynggushurste was dismissed quit sine die by the court.

[*The petition is* C 1/46/381, *endorsed*: Coram domino rege in cancellaria octabis Michaelis.]

[106] Habeas corpus cum causa captionis to the sheriffs of London: Richard Broun, on the octave of Michaelmas [7 Oct.]. Westminster, 21 August 11 Edward IV [1471].

[*Return*] Imprisoned in pleas of trespass and to find surety of the peace brought by Thomas Frere, brewer.

Recognisance: John Porter of St Mary Bothaw, London, draper, William Jakson of London, serjeant, Henry Snow of London, gent., Philip Swyfte of London, skinner, each sub pena £20, Richard Broun sub pena £40: Broun to appear in chancery on Thursday next [10 Oct.] and from day to day etc. and meanwhile not to do or cause to be done any physical harm to Thomas Frere or other of the king's people. 9 October 11 Edward IV.

Broun duly appeared and was discharged from the surety of the peace by a writ de supersedendo.

[*The petition is* C 1/46/75.]

[105] Certiorari super causa captionis to the sheriffs of London: Joce Lamanva, Elizabeth his wife and Alice Ryder, returnable on the octave of Michaelmas [7 Oct.]. Westminster, 1 October 11 Edward IV [1471].

[*Return*] Joce has not been imprisoned; Elizabeth his wife is imprisoned in a plea of trespass brought by William Rotheley, armourer, against herself and her husband, and Alice Ryder in a similar plea brought by the same.

[*The petition is* C 1/46/47, *endorsed*: Coram domino rege in cancellaria sua in octabis Sancti Michaelis; C 1/46/115 *appears to relate to the same suit.*]

[104] Certiorari super causa captionis to the mayor and sheriffs of London: Henry Scarnyng, returnable on Friday next [11 Oct.]. Westminster, 5 October 11 Edward IV [1471].

[*Return*] Imprisoned in a plea of trespass brought by Gerard Morys, barber.

Scarnyng was dismissed quit sine die by the court.

[*The petition is* C 1/46/411, *endorsed*: Coram domino rege in cancellaria sua die veneris.]

[103] Recognisance: Michael Carvenan of London, gent., John Kewesale of London, gent., John Houghton of London, gent., John Wykes of London, gent., each sub pena 100 marks, Walter Kyngdon, clerk, sub pena £100: Kyngdon to appear in chancery on the morrow of All Souls [2 Nov.]. 10 October 11 Edward IV [1471].

Kyngdon duly appeared.

[*See also* 86, 62]

[102] Recognisance: John Middelton of Belsay, Northumb, kt, Alfred Corneburgh of London, esq., John Devyck of Okehampton, Devon, gent., John Wykes of the same, gent., each sub pena £100, James Neweham sub pena £200: Neweham to appear before the king and council on the quindene of Easter [15 April] and meanwhile not to do or cause to be done any physical harm to John Alwey or other of the king's people. 14 October 11 Edward IV [1471].

Neweham duly appeared.

[*See also* 163, 161]

[101] Recognisance: Thomas John of St Dunstan in the West, London, brewer, Richard Caley of St Clement Danes, brewer, Robert Mercer of the same, brewer, Thomas Hervy of the same, pattenmaker, each sub pena 100 marks, William Dawbys, clerk, sub pena 200 marks: Dawbys to appear in chancery on the morrow of All Souls [2 Nov.]. 15 October 11 Edward IV [1471].

Dawbys duly appeared.

[*See also* 84]

[100] Habeas corpus cum causa captionis to the sheriffs of London: Thomas Warmynton, chaplain, on Wednesday next [16 Oct.]. Westminster, 14 October 11 Edward IV [1471].

[*Return*] Imprisoned in a plea of trespass brought by Thomas Walcote, tailor.

Recognisance: Thomas Warmyngton of All Hallows Lombard Street, London, grocer, Roger Chadwyke of St Mary Magdalen, London, haberdasher, each sub pena 40 marks, Thomas Warmyngton sub pena £40: Warmyngton to appear in chancery on Thursday next [17 Oct.] and from day to day etc. 16 October 11 Edward IV.

Warmyngton duly appeared and was dismissed quit sine die with the agreement of the other party.

[*The petition is* C 1/46/401, *endorsed*: Coram domino rege in cancellaria sua xvj die octobris.]

[99] Attachias to the sheriff of Surrey: John Courtmyll sen. of Shere, yeoman, John Burton late of Carshalton, gent., John Courtmyll jun. late of Shere, and Henry Courtmyll of Caterham, yeoman, to answer Richard Ive, servant of Thomas Ive, chancery clerk, in a plea of trespass on the octave of Michaelmas [7 Oct.]. Westminster, 1 September 11 Edward IV [1471].

[*Return*] John Courtmyll sen. has been attached; the others have not been found.

Recognisance: John Sawyer of Shere, Surrey, husbandman, Thomas Rede of Southwark, Surrey, tailor, each sub pena £100, John Courtmyll sen. sub pena £200: Courtmyll to appear in chancery on Wednesday next [16 Oct.]. 15 October 11 Edward IV.

[*The writ was authorised by Ive.*]

[98] Certiorari super causa captionis to the mayor, aldermen and sheriffs of London: Joan Nele, widow, returnable on Wednesday next [16 Oct.]. Westminster, 14 October 11 Edward IV [1471].

[*Return*] Imprisoned in a plea of debt for £7 16s. brought by John Lethom of London, baker.

[97] Habeas corpus cum causa captionis to the mayor and sheriffs of London: James Ramys, on the quindene of Michaelmas [4 Oct.]. Westminster, 14 July 11 Edward IV [1471].

[*Return*] Imprisoned in a plea of debt for 5s. brought by John Forster, skinner, and in a plea of contempt and trespass brought by Thomas, bishop of London.

Recognisance: William Wade of London, scrivener, William Murton of London, barber, John Broun of London, mercer, Thomas Fyfeld of London, marbler, each sub pena £20, James Ramys sub pena £40: Ramys to appear in chancery on Thursday next [17 Oct.] and from day to day etc. 16 October 11 Edward IV.

Ramys duly appeared.

[96] Attachias to the sheriff of Middlesex: Robert Oldham, to answer John Davyson, chancery clerk, keeper of the hanaper, in a plea of trespass on the quindene of Michaelmas [14 Oct.]. Westminster, 8 October 11 Edward IV [1471].

[*Return*] Oldham has been taken.

Recognisance: James Annesley of Uxbridge, Midd, gent., Walter Stalworth of Westminster, tailor, each sub pena £20, Robert Oldham sub pena £40: Oldham to appear in chancery on Friday next [18 Oct.] and from day to day etc. 16 October 11 Edward IV.

[95] Habeas corpus cum causa captionis to the mayor, aldermen and sheriffs of London: Joan Nele, widow, on Thursday next [17 Oct.]. Westminster, 14 October 11 Edward IV [1471].

[*Return*] The cause of her imprisonment was returned to chancery on an earlier writ [98] and cannot again be returned.

Recognisance: Richard Holman of St Stephen Walbrook, London, grocer, John Frecok of St Botolph Billingsgate, London, tailor, Thomas Blake of St Dunstan in the East, London, salter, Thomas Cok of the same, weaver, each sub pena £20, Joan Nele, widow, sub pena £40: Joan to appear in chancery on Friday next [18 Oct.] and from day to day etc. 17 October 11 Edward IV.

Joan duly appeared and was dismissed quit sine die by the court.

[*The petition is* C 1/46/384, *endorsed*: Coram domino rege in cancellaria sua die martis proximo futuro. *In the writ the day of the week is written over an erasure.*]

[94] Habeas corpus cum causa captionis to the bailiffs of Kings Lynn and the keeper of the prison there: Richard Arnold, esq., on the quindene of Michaelmas [14 Oct.]. Westminster, 30 September 11 Edward IV [1471].

[*Return*] Imprisoned in pleas of account, debt and trespass brought by John Thorysby, merchant.

Recognisance: Thomas Jenney of London, gent., William Pryce of London, gent., each sub pena £500,

Richard Arnold sub pena 1000 marks: Arnold to appear in chancery on Friday next [18 Oct.] and from day to day etc. 17 October 11 Edward IV.

Arnold duly appeared; on 18 November he was dismissed quit sine die by the court with the agreement of the plaintiff.

[*The petition is* C 1/45/152, *endorsed*: Coram domino rege in cancellaria sua in quindena Michaelis.]

[93] Certiorari super causa captionis to the mayor and sheriffs of London: Hugh Yeram, bowyer, returnable on the quindene of Michaelmas [14 Oct.]. Westminster, 13 August 11 Edward IV [1471].

[*Return*] Imprisoned in a plea of trespass brought by John Emyarn, armourer.

[*The petition is* C 1/45/23, *concerning an affray 'on the Tuesday when the rebels and traitors of our sovereign lord intended to burn and destroy the city', endorsed*: R' coram rege in cancellaria quindena Michaelis.]

[92] Certiorari super causa captionis to the mayor and sheriffs of London: Henry Frank, returnable on Monday next [21 Oct.]. Westminster, 15 October 11 Edward IV [1471].

[*Return*] Imprisoned in a plea of debt for 33s. 4d. brought by Hugh Broke, draper.

[C 1/46/328 *appears to relate to the same suit.*]

[91] Habeas corpus cum causa captionis to the sheriffs of Norwich: John Emmys, on the quindene of Michaelmas [14 Oct.]. Westminster, 11 September 11 Edward IV [1471].

[*Return*] Imprisoned in a plea of debt for £6 brought by Roger Crabbe. The return was made by the former sheriffs, by whom the writ was delivered without the body of the prisoner to the present sheriffs.

[*The petition is* C 1/46/477, *endorsed*: R' in cancellaria in quindena Sancti Michaelis.]

[90] Attachias to the sheriffs of London: Richard Kelette of London, tailor, to answer Roger Elmley and Robert Denny, servants of the bishop of Bath and Wells, chancellor, in a plea of trespass 3 weeks from Michaelmas [21 Oct.]. Westminster, 12 September 11 Edward IV [1471].

[*Return*] He is already imprisoned in a plea of trespass brought by John Base, lattener.

Kelette was committed to the Fleet prison and thereafter dismissed quit sine die by the court.

[89] Habeas corpus causa captionis to the sheriffs of London: John Gladwyn, on Friday next [25 Oct.]. Westminster, 24 October 11 Edward IV [1471].

[*Return*] Imprisoned in a plea of debt for £40 brought by Thomas Ralf sen. of Totteridge, Herts, collier.

Recognisance: Thomas Gladwyn of Finchley, Midd, husbandman, Richard Gladwyn of Friern Barnet, Midd, husbandman, Thomas Hayne of Finchley, husbandman, John Hill of the same, husbandman, each sub pena £40, John Gladwyn sub pena £80: Gladwyn to appear in chancery on Saturday next [26 Oct.] and from day to day etc. 25 October 11 Edward IV.

Gladwyn duly appeared and was dismissed quit sine die by the court.

[*The petition is* C 1/46/329, *endorsed*: Coram domino rege in cancellaria sua die veneris proximo futuro videlicet xxv die octobris.]

[88] Certiorari super causa captionis to the sheriffs of London: Richard Deryvale, returnable on 28 October. Westminster, 22 October 11 Edward IV [1471].

[*Return*] Imprisoned in a plea of debt for £9 brought by William Kember and Robert Gylle.

[*The petition is* C 1/46/402, *endorsed*: Coram domino rege in cancellaria sua xxvij die octobris.]

[87] Certiorari super causa captionis to the mayor and sheriff of Kingston upon Hull: Agnes Saunderson, widow, returnable on the quindene of Michaelmas [14 Oct.]. Westminster, 24 July 11 Edward IV [1471].

[*Return*] Imprisoned in pleas of debt for £12 4s. brought by Alice Barkar, widow, of Kingston upon Hull, and Edmund Copendale, merchant, of the same.

[*The petition is* C 1/46/447, *endorsed*: Coram rege in cancellaria sua in quindena Michaelis.]

[86] Recognisance: Edward Kyngdon of Stanmore, Midd, gent., John Wykes of St Dunstan in the West, London, gent., each sub pena 100 marks, Walter Kyngdon, clerk, sub pena £100: Walter Kyngdon to

appear in chancery on the octave of St Martin [18 Nov.]. 6 November 11 Edward IV [1471].

Kyngdon duly appeared.

[*See also* 103, 62]

[85] Certiorari super causa captionis to the mayor and sheriffs of London: Owen Pole, returnable on Thursday next [7 Nov.]. Westminster, 3 November 11 Edward IV [1471].

[*Return*] Imprisoned in a plea of debt for 200 marks brought by John ap Richard, John Deverauxe, kt, and Thomas Brugge of 'Rosse', gent.

[84] Recognisance: Thomas John of St Dunstan in the West, London, brewer, Robert Mercer of St Clement Danes, brewer, William Atheley of the same, gent., each sub pena 100 marks, William Dawbys, clerk, sub pena 200 marks: Dawbys to appear in chancery on Friday next [8 Nov.] and from day to day etc. 7 November 11 Edward IV [1471].

Dawbys duly appeared.

[*See also* 101]

[83] Recognisance: William Brereton of Brereton, Ches, kt, Hugh Erdeswyke of Sandon, Staffs, esq., Roger Kelsall of the king's household, gent., Geoffrey Downe of London, gent., each sub pena £50, Thomas Fytton, kt, sub pena £100: Fytton to appear before the king and council on the octave of Trinity [1 June] and meanwhile not to do or cause to be done any physical harm to Robert Boughay or other of the king's people. 6 November 11 Edward IV [1471].

Fytton duly appeared.

[82] Certiorari super causa captionis to the mayor and bailiffs of Exeter: Robert Rawlyn of Exeland, Devon, dyer, returnable on the morrow of All Souls [2 Nov.]. Westminster, 27 September 11 Edward IV [1471].

[*Return*] Imprisoned in a plea of debt for £32 13s. 3½d. brought by William Mannyng of London, grocer, then released on bail and neither he nor his pledges subsequently appeared at the adjourned plea.

[*The petition is* C 1/44/265, *endorsed*: R' coram rege in cancellaria crastino Animarum; C 1/10/59 *and* C 1/46/209 *appear to relate to the same suit.*]

[81] Fieri facias executionem judicii to the bailiffs of the liberty of the bishop of Winchester in Southwark: in the plea of debt John Canon v. John Chapman. Westminster, 26 October 11 Edward IV [1471].

[*Return*] There neither is nor has been any such plea.

[80] Habeas corpus cum causa captionis to the keepers of the court of the fairs of the abbot of Westminster: Robert Palmer and Joan his wife, on Monday next [11 Nov.]. Westminster, 5 November 11 Edward IV [1471].

[*Return*] Imprisoned in a plea of trespass brought by William Cherden.

Recognisance: John Shorter of Salisbury, Wilts, yeoman, John Smyth of Westminster, yeoman, William Heron of the same, saddler, John a Chambre of the same, carpenter, each sub pena £20, Robert Palmer sub pena 40 marks: Palmer and Joan his wife to appear in chancery on Tuesday next [12 Nov.] and from day to day etc. 11 November 11 Edward IV.

[*The petition is* C 1/38/206, *endorsed*: Coram domino rege in cancellaria sua decimo die novembris.]

[79] Certiorari super causa captionis to the mayor and sheriffs of London: Edmund Bataill, chaplain, returnable on Monday next [11 Nov.]. Westminster, 8 November 11 Edward IV [1471].

[*Return*] The writ arrived too late to be executed.

[*See* 69]

[78] Habeas corpus cum causa captionis to the mayor and sheriffs of London: Henry Middelton, on Tuesday next [12 Nov.], before the king and council. Westminster, 11 November 11 Edward IV [1471].

[*Return*] The writ arrived too late to be executed.

[77] Habeas corpus cum causa captionis to the mayor and sheriffs of London: William Inglond, on Wednesday next [13 Nov.]. Westminster, 9 November 11 Edward IV [1471].

[*Return*] Imprisoned in a plea of debt for 46s. 8d. brought by John Calker, citizen and cutler of London.

Recognisance: Thomas Lytteney of St Bride Fleet Street, London, barber, Thomas Alisaundre of St Mary le Strand, sheather, Robert Yate of the same, sheather, John Wykes of St Bride Fleet Street, London, pinner, each sub pena 20 marks, William Inglond sub pena 40 marks: Inglond to appear in chancery on Friday next [15 Nov.] and from day to day etc. 13 November 11 Edward IV.

[76] Certiorari super causa captionis to the constable of New Windsor castle or his lieutenant: John Lese of Egham, Surrey, returnable on the morrow of St Martin [12 Nov.]. Westminster, 28 October 11 Edward IV [1471].

[*Return*] Imprisoned in a plea of trespass brought by the prioress of Ankerwyke.

[*The petition is* C 1/38/217, *endorsed*: Coram domino rege in cancellaria sua in crastino Sancti Martini proximo futuro.]

[75] Recognisance made before the king and council: Richard Norman of London, gent., John Tyryngham of London, esq., William Cressy of Nottingham, esq., William Garnon of Bucks, gent., each sub pena £100, Robert Olney of Weston Underwood, Bucks, gent., sub pena £200: Olney to appear before the king and council on Tuesday next, 19 November, and from day to day etc. 12 November 11 Edward IV [1471].

[74] Recognisance made before the king and council: John Turpyn of London, gent., Thomas Hampden of Kimble, Bucks, gent., John Bradshawe of London, gent., John Leveden of Long Crendon, Bucks, gent., each sub pena £100, Robert Ryseburgh, abbot of Missenden, sub pena £200: the abbot to appear before the king and council on Thursday next [14 Nov.] and from day to day etc. 12 November 11 Edward IV [1471].

[73] Habeas corpus cum causa captionis to the mayor and sheriffs of London: Mary Rykeward, widow, on Thursday next [14 Nov.]. Westminster, 12 November 11 Edward IV [1471].

[*Return*] Imprisoned in pleas of trespass brought by Richard Flemyng, gent., and by Robert Newerk.

Recognisance: Richard Gernes of Highgate, Midd, yeoman, William Flamell of St Peter le Poer, London, brewer, William Broke of St Andrew by the Wardrobe, London, woodmonger, Ambrose Smyth of St Mary le Strand, cordwainer, Mary Rikeward, widow, each sub pena 40 marks: Mary to appear in chancery on Friday next [15 Nov.] and from day to day etc. 14 November 11 Edward IV.

[72] Habeas corpus cum causa captionis to the sheriffs of London: Peter Warner, clerk, on Thursday next [14 Nov.]. Westminster, 12 November 11 Edward IV [1471].

[*Return*] Imprisoned in a plea of debt for £7 brought by Thomas Wake against Warner, Henry Crakhall, clerk, and William Warar, leatherdresser, executors of Richard Herman, clerk.

Recognisance: Richard Drax of St Mary Somerset, London, serjeant, William Warner of St Anne's, London, saddler, each sub pena £20, Peter Warner, clerk, sub pena £40: Warner to appear in chancery on Friday next [15 Nov.] and from day to day etc. 14 November 11 Edward IV.

Warner duly appeared.

[*The petition is* C 1/46/457, *endorsed*: Coram domino rege in cancellaria sua die jovis proximo futuro.]

[71] Habeas corpus cum causa captionis sub pena £1000 to the constable of Winchester castle or his lieutenant or deputy: John Kendale, Henry Hayne and John Blakett, on 15 November. Westminster, 28 October 11 Edward IV [1471].

[*Return*] The writ was delivered on 2 November; none of the above mentioned was then, or has since been, imprisoned.

[70] Habeas corpus cum causa captionis sub pena £200 to John Rogers, constable of Winchester castle, or his deputy: Henry Hayne and John Blakett, on the morrow of St Martin [12 Nov.]. Westminster, 27 October 11 Edward IV [1471].

[*Return*] When the writ was delivered neither of the above named was then, or has since been, imprisoned.

[69] Certiorari super causa captionis sub pena £100 to the mayor and sheriffs of London: Edmund Bataill, chaplain, returnable on Saturday next [16 Nov.]. Westminster, 13 November 11 Edward IV [1471].

[*Return*] Imprisoned in two pleas of debt, both for £6 6s. 8d. brought by Richard Walker, citizen and grocer of London.

[*See also* 79]

[68] Habeas corpus cum causa captionis to the mayor and sheriffs of London: Thomas Gare, on Tuesday

next [19 Nov.]. Westminster, 16 November 11 Edward IV [1471].

[*Return*] Imprisoned to find surety, with Margery his wife, to keep the peace toward John Johnson, blacksmith, in pleas of debt for £13 6s. 8d. brought by John Johnson and for £10 brought by John Fourmour, and of trespass brought by John Johnson against himself and his wife.

Gare was sent to the Fleet prison.

[67] Habeas corpus cum causa captionis to the mayor and sheriffs of London: William Sampson, on Tuesday next [19 Nov.]. Westminster, 16 November 11 Edward IV [1471].

[*Return*] Imprisoned in pleas of debt for 4 marks brought by Peter Caldecote and Edward Stone, masters of London Bridge, for 3s. 4d. brought by Ralph Cole, draper, for 33s. 4d. brought by Robert Brande, brewer, for 39s. brought by Godfrey Yonge, butcher, for 8s. 6d. brought by John Hertford, baker, for 4s. brought by Thomas Hunnesdon, maltman, for 17s. and 2s. 8d. for damages and costs brought by William Turnour, maltman, in a plea of trespass brought by Henry Langshote, cooper, and in pleas of debt for 36s. 8d. brought by Henry Langshote, for 2s. 2d. brought by William Touny, chaplain, for £3 4s. brought by John Taylefere, brewer, for 8s. 3d. and 2s. 8d. for damages and costs brought by William Aylward, tailor, for 2s. 6d. brought by John Dan, cordwainer, and for 36s. 6d. brought by Robert Leicrofte, fishmonger.

Sampson was committed to the Fleet prison.

[*See also* 33]

[66] Habeas corpus cum causa captionis to the sheriffs of London: James Strykland, on Wednesday next [20 Nov.]. Westminster, 19 November 11 Edward IV [1471].

[*Return*] Imprisoned at the suit of William Pounde, butcher.

Recognisance: William Parre of the king's household, kt, John Skelton of the chancellor's household, gent., James Strykland, each sub pena £10: Strykland to appear in chancery on Thursday next [21 Nov.] and from day to day etc. 20 November 11 Edward IV.

Strykland duly appeared but Pounde did not; Strykland was dismissed quit sine die by the court.

[*The petition is* C 1/10/129, *endorsed*: Coram rege in cancellaria sua die mercurii videlicet xx die novembris.]

[65] Habeas corpus cum causa captionis sub pena £100 to John Brumston, lieutenant of Canterbury, or his deputy: John Hawes and Thomas Barsham, on the octave of St Martin [18 Nov.]. Westminster, 5 November 11 Edward IV [1471].

[*Return*] Imprisoned in a plea of trespass brought by William Olyver. Hawes and Barsham were committed to the keeper of the Fleet prison; on 27 January 11 Edward IV [1472] they were dismissed quit sine die since Olyver failed to appear.

[64] Habeas corpus cum causa captionis to the mayor and bailiffs of Bedford: John Spelyng, on the octave of St Martin [18 Nov.]. Westminster, 10 October 11 Edward IV [1471].

[*Return*] Imprisoned in a plea of trespass brought by John, prior of Newnham; a writ de procedendo has now been delivered which precludes the execution of the habeas corpus.

[*The petition is* C 1/41/186, *endorsed*: R' coram rege in octabis Martini; *the petition* C 1/38/219 *for a certiorari appears to relate to the same suit.*]

[63] Habeas corpus cum causa captionis to the mayor and sheriffs of London: Adrian Lowes, on Thursday next [21 Nov.]. Westminster, 20 November 11 Edward IV [1471].

[*Return*] Imprisoned in pleas of trespass brought by John Parre, kt, and Maurice Arnold, esq., and by Robert Mores, shipman.

Recognisance: John Grene of Westminster, saddler, William Heron of the same, saddler, Richard Barbet of the same, carpenter, John Smyth of St Clement Danes, yeoman, each sub pena £10, Adrian Lowes sub pena £20: Lowes to appear in chancery on Friday next [29 Nov.] and from day to day etc. 22 November 11 Edward IV.

Lowes duly appeared.

[*See* 55]

[62] Recognisance: Edward Kyngdon of Stanmore, Midd, gent., sub pena 100 marks, Walter Kyngdon, clerk, sub pena £100: Walter to appear in chancery on Saturday next [23 Nov.]. 21 November 11 Edward IV [1471].

Walter duly appeared and was given a day on the octave of Hilary [20 Jan.] when he duly appeared and was dismissed quit sine die with the agreement of the other party.

[*See also* 103, 86]

[61] Certiorari super causa captionis to the sheriffs of London: John Salter of London, currier, returnable on the octave of St Martin [18 Nov.]. Westminster, 12 November 11 Edward IV [1471].

[*Return*] Imprisoned in a plea of trespass brought by Juliana Champeyn, widow.

[*The petition is* C 1/46/433, *endorsed*: Coram rege in cancellaria sua in octabis Martini.]

[60] Attachias to the sheriff of London: John Mortyn of London, tailor, to answer Richard Baxter, servant of the bishop of Bath and Wells, chancellor, in a plea of debt for 100s. on Friday next [25 Nov.]. Westminster, 20 October 11 Edward IV [1471].

[*Return*] Mortyn has been taken.

Recognisance: Thomas Norrey of London, gent., John Firth of St Nicholas', London, tailor, John Hepeston of St Bride Fleet Street, London, tailor, Nicholas Vicary of St Benet Fink, London, yeoman, each sub pena 100s., John Mortyn sub pena £10: Mortyn to appear in chancery on Saturday next [23 Nov.] and from day to day etc. 22 November 11 Edward IV.

[59] Certiorari super causa arestationis to the mayor and sheriffs of London: the goods of Alice Asshefeld, prioress of St Helen Bishopsgate, London, taken into the hands of Walter Mauntell, kt, and of 93 other named persons, at the suit of John Asshefeld, citizen and grocer of London, returnable on Monday next [25 Nov.]. Westminster, 20 November 11 Edward IV [1471].

[*Return*] Arrested in a plea of debt for £250 brought by John Asshefeld.

[58] Certiorari super causa arestationis to the mayor and sheriffs of London: £17 and £10 belonging to William Sauston, taken into the hands of John Barre at the suits of Simon Hogan and William Stokker, returnable on Friday next [22 Nov.]. Westminster, 20 November 11 Edward IV [1471].

[*Return*] Arrested in pleas of debt.

[*A later bill,* C 1/46/56, *is concerned with the same suit.*]

[57] Habeas corpus cum causa captionis to the keeper of the Fleet prison: Edmund Redknap, on Tuesday next [26 Nov.]. Westminster, 23 November 11 Edward IV [1471].

[*Return*] First committed to prison by the chancellor on 21 June last and on 20 November last recommitted by John Alcok, keeper of the rolls, sub pena £1000.

[*See also* 180, 160]

[56] Recognisance: Robert Danyell of London, gent., John Brewode of London, gent., Richard Spert of London, gent., Henry Langley of London, gent., each sub pena £20, Robert Dokkyng of Walpole, Lincs, sub pena £40: Dokkyng to appear before the king and council on Monday next [18 Nov.] and from day to day etc. 16 November 11 Edward IV [1471].

[55] Recognisance: Ambrose Smyth of St Mary le Strand, cordwainer, John Nottyngham of St Martin in the Fields, baker, each sub pena £100, Adrian Lowes sub pena £200: Lowes to appear in chancery on Thursday next [28 Nov.]. 27 November 11 Edward IV [1471].

[*See* 63]

[54] Certiorari super causa captionis to the mayor and bailiffs of Coventry: John Cliff, returnable on the morrow of All Souls [2 Nov.]. Westminster, 7 October 11 Edward IV [1471].

[*Return*] Imprisoned in a plea of debt for £18 brought by Thomas Hobbes of Coventry, girdler.

[*The petition is* C 1/46/357, *endorsed*: R' coram domino rege in crastino Animarum.]

[53] Recognisance: William Norreys, kt, Thomas Seintleger, John Walop, Walter Hungerford, each sub pena £200, Robert Playsay sub pena £400: Playsay to appear before the king and council on the morrow of the Purification [3 Feb.] and meanwhile not to do or cause to be done any harm to Eleanor wife of John Poulet, esq., or other of the king's people. 27 October 11 Edward IV [1471].

[*That part of the terms of the recognisance containing the surety of the peace is written in this and* 52–46 *over an erasure.*]

[52] Recognisance: William Noreys, kt, Thomas Seyntleger, esq., John Walop, Walter Hungerford, each sub pena £200, William Burley sub pena £400: [*terms,*

for Burley, as in 53]. 27 October 11 Edward IV [1471].

[51] Recognisance: William Norreys, kt, Thomas Seintleger, John Walop, Walter Hungerford, each sub pena £200, William Lee sub pena £400: [*terms, for Lee, as in* 53]. 27 October 11 Edward IV [1471].

[50] Recognisance: William Norreys, kt, Thomas Seintleger, John Walop, Walter Hungerford, each sub pena £200, William Austyn sub pena £400: [*terms, for Austyn, as in* 53]. 27 October 11 Edward IV [1471].

[49] Recognisance: William Noreys, kt, John Walop, Brian Talbotte, Walter Hungerford, each sub pena £200, Thomas Seyntleger, esq., sub pena £400: [*terms, for Seyntleger, as in* 53]. 27 October 11 Edward IV [1471].

Seyntleger duly appeared.

[48] Recognisance: William Noreys, kt, Thomas Seyntleger, esq., Brian Talbotte, Walter Hungerford, each sub pena £200, John Walop sub pena £400: [*terms, for Walop, as in* 53]. 27 October 11 Edward IV [1471].

[47] Recognisance: Thomas Seyntleger, John Walop, Brian Talbott, Walter Hungerford, each sub pena £200, William Norreys, kt, sub pena £400: [*terms, for Norreys, as in* 53]. 27 October 11 Edward IV [1471].

Norreys duly appeared.

[46] Recognisance: William Noreys, kt, Thomas Seintleger, esq., Brian Talbotte, Walter Hungerford, each sub pena £200, William Walop sub pena £400: [*terms, for Walop, as in* 53]. 27 October 11 Edward IV [1471].

[45] Habeas corpus cum causa captionis sub pena £100 to the bailiffs and keeper of the gaol of the liberty of St Peter's, York: Thomas Swanne, on the quindene of St Martin [25 Nov.]. Westminster, 12 November 11 Edward IV [1471].

[*Return*] Imprisoned in pleas of trespass brought by Richard Swan, cordwainer, and Robert Williamson of York.

Recognisance: Thomas Hemelsey of York, gent., John Todde of the same, merchant, each sub pena £10, Thomas Swanne sub pena £20: Swanne to appear in chancery on Monday next [2 Dec.] and from day to day etc. 28 November 11 Edward IV.

[*The petition is* C 1/46/248, *endorsed*: Coram domino rege in cancellaria sua quindena Sancti Martini; *for Hemelsey see* 197.]

[44] Certiorari super causa captionis to the bailiffs of Colchester: Robert Biby, returnable on the quindene of St Martin [25 Nov.]. Westminster, 4 November 11 Edward IV [1471].

[*Return*] Imprisoned in a plea brought by William Bourgchier, kt, to render account for the time he was Bourgchier's receiver in Colchester.

[43] Attachias to the sheriffs of London: Hugh Olyver to answer John Davyson, chancery clerk, keeper of the hanaper, in a plea of trespass on Friday next [29 Nov.]. Westminster, 24 November 11 Edward IV [1471].

[*Return*] Already imprisoned in a plea of trespass brought by Thomas Baily.

Recognisance: Richard Whityngton of London, shearman, Geoffrey Chirk of London, baker, Stephen John of London, shearman, James Holdernesse of London, shearman, each sub pena £10, Hugh Olyver sub pena £20: Olyver to appear in chancery on the octave of Hilary [20 Jan.] and from day to day etc. 29 November 11 Edward IV.

[42] Recognisance: Thomas Acton of London, gent., Thomas Hoorde of London, gent., John Leghton of Stretton, Salop, esq., Thomas Stuche of London, gent., each sub pena 100 marks, Alan Stury sub pena £100: Stury to appear in chancery on the morrow of the Purification [3 Feb.] and meanwhile not to do or cause to be done any physical harm to John Water or other of the king's people. 28 November 11 Edward IV [1471].

Stury duly appeared; Water appeared and released the surety of the peace and Stury was dismissed quit sine die by the court.

[41] Habeas corpus cum causa captionis to the sheriffs of London: Eleanor Martyn, widow, on Thursday next [5 Dec.]. Westminster, 3 December 11 Edward IV [1471].

[*Return*] Imprisoned in pleas of debt, as widow and executrix of Robert Martyn of Sutton, Suff, esq., for

10 marks and 10 marks brought by William Knyvet, esq.

Recognisance: Thomas Swan of Hatfield, Herts, gent., John Frethyll of Little Shelford, Cambs, gent., each sub pena 20 marks, Eleanor Martyn sub pena £20: Eleanor to appear in chancery on the quindene of Hilary [27 Jan.] and from day to day etc. 5 December 11 Edward IV.

Eleanor duly appeared.

[*The petition is* C 1/46/122, *endorsed*: Coram domino rege in cancellaria sua die jovis videlicet quinto die decembris.]

[40] Certiorari super causa arestationis to the mayor and aldermen of London: £339 9s., taken into the hand of John Neve, citizen and mercer of London, returnable on 16 December. Westminster, 11 December 11 Edward IV [1471].

[*Return*] The money was arrested in a plea of debt for £350 brought by William Cooke, gent., against John Isbury, gent.

[*The petition is* C 1/46/368, *endorsed*: Coram domino rege in cancellaria sua xvj die decembris.]

[39] Recognisance: Henry Grey of Codnor, kt, Roger Clyfford, kt, John Middelton, kt, Robert Ratcliff, esq., each sub pena £100, Thomas Shawe sub pena £200: Shawe to be of good behaviour towards the king and his people until All Saints [1 Nov.] 1472 and to appear before the king and council on the morrow of All Souls [2 Nov.] 1472. 26 October 11 Edward IV [1471].

[38] Recognisance: Henry Grey of Codnor, kt, Roger Clyfford, kt, John Middelton, kt, Robert Ratcliff, esq., each sub pena £100, Robert Hampson sub pena £200: [*terms, for Hampson, as in* 39]. 26 October 11 Edward IV [1471].

[37] Recognisance: Henry Grey of Codnor, kt, Roger Clifford, kt, John Middelton, kt, Robert Ratcliffe, esq., each sub pena £100, Thomas Hudson sub pena £200: [*terms, for Hudson, as in* 39]. 26 October 11 Edward IV [1471].

[36] Recognisance: Henry Grey of Codnor, kt, Roger Clyfford, kt, John Middelton, kt, Robert Ratclif, esq., each sub pena £100, Richard Alester sub pena £200: [*terms, for Alester, as in* 39]. 26 October 11 Edward IV [1471].

[35] Recognisance: John Wadham of White Lackington, Som, gent., William Wadham of the same, gent., Richard Waley of Ashbourne, Derb, gent., Richard Tyffan of St Clement Danes, gent., each sub pena £100, John Barentyn sub pena £200: Barentyn to appear before the king and council on the octave of Hilary [20 Jan.]. 26 October 11 Edward IV [1471].

[34] Recognisance: Reynold Stourton of Bower, Som, kt, Thomas Beauchamp late of London, esq., James Clyfford of Frampton, Glos, esq., Roger Seymour of London, gent., each sub pena £100, Robert Stowell, esq., sub pena £200: Stowell to appear before the king and council on the octave of Hilary [20 Jan.] and meanwhile not to do or cause to be done any physical harm to Joan wife of John Asshyn. 16 October 11 Edward IV [1471].

[33] Recognisance: John Dany of London, clerk, Hugh Payn of London, gent., each sub pena 100 marks: William Sampson to appear in chancery on the octave of Hilary [20 Jan.] and from day to day etc. 23 December 11 Edward IV [1471].

Sampson duly appeared.

[*See* 67]

[32] Certiorari super causa summonitionis to the mayor and bailiffs of Coventry: William Briscowe and William White, returnable on the octave of Hilary [20 Jan.]. Westminster, 8 November 11 Edward IV [1471].

[*Return*] Summoned in a plea of trespass brought by William Pere.

[31] Habeas corpus cum causa captionis sub pena £40 to the sheriff of Hertfordshire and the keeper of Hertford gaol: Richard Benet, on Tuesday next [7 Jan.]. Westminster, 2 January 11 Edward IV [1472].

[*Return*] Imprisoned on suspicion of felony.

Recognisance: William Debenham, esq., of the king's household, Richard Lovell of Westminster, gent., Robert Aylmer of the same, esq., William Dollyng of the same, gent., each sub pena £40, Richard Benet sub pena £80: Benet to appear in chancery on the octave of Hilary [20 Jan.] and from day to day etc. 7 January 11 Edward IV.

Benet duly appeared and was dismissed quit sine die by the court.

[*The petition is* C 1/46/201, *endorsed*: Coram rege in cancellaria sua die martis.]

[30] Recognisance: William Chirchey of London, gent., Robert Hillys of London, gent., John Bury of London, fishmonger, Thomas Ingram of London, butcher, each sub pena £40, John Frostbury sub pena £80: Frostbury to appear in chancery on the octave of Hilary [20 Jan.] and meanwhile to keep the peace. 24 September 11 Edward IV [1471].

[29] Habeas corpus cum causa captionis to the steward and marshal of the household: John West, on Saturday next [11 Jan.]. Westminster, 5 January 11 Edward IV [1472].

[*Return*] Imprisoned in a plea of trespass brought by Thomas Scoryet.

Recognisance: Richard Whyteher of Hackney, Midd, husbandman, John Grey of the same, husbandman, Lawrence Ben of the same, clerk, Robert Mors of London, shearman, each sub pena £10, John Weste of Hackney, labourer, sub pena £20: Weste to appear in chancery on the octave of Hilary [20 Jan.] and from day to day etc. 11 January 11 Edward IV [1472].

[*The petition is* C 1/46/453, *endorsed*: Coram domino rege in cancellaria sua octavo die januarii. *In the writ the day of the week is written over an erasure.*]

[28] Habeas corpus cum causa captionis to the sheriffs of Norwich: Lawrence Russhworth and John Hemmyng, on the octave of Hilary [20 Jan.]. Westminster, 8 January 11 Edward IV [1472].

[*Return*] Russhworth was imprisoned in pleas of debt for 40s. brought by William Barly, merchant, for 100s. brought by John Alforth and a plea of trespass brought by Richard Radley, and then released on the sureties of Richard Southwell, John Curson and John Hemmyng; John Hemmyng was imprisoned in a plea of trespass brought by Richard Radley and released on the sureties of Richard Courdon and Thomas Wygge; neither therefore can be produced.

[*The petition* C 1/46/12 *appears to relate to the same suit.*]

[27] Certiorari super causa captionis to the bailiffs of Colchester: Richard Boteler, returnable on the octave of Hilary [20 Jan.]. Westminster, 4 December 11 Edward IV [1471].

[*Return*] Imprisoned in a plea of trespass brought by Henry Haukewode, of debt for 26s. 8d. brought by Nicholas Seman and John Parker and of trespass brought by John Bermycham.

[26] Certiorari super causa captionis to the mayor and sheriffs of London: John Asshfeld, returnable on the octave of Hilary [20 Jan.]. Westminster, 7 January 11 Edward IV [1472].

[*Return*] Imprisoned in pleas of debt for £4 8s. 9d. brought by Simon Smyth and John Love, citizens and grocers of London, for 20s. brought by William Griffith, citizen of London, and for £11 10s. brought by Edmund Pygot, citizen and skinner of London.

[25] Certiorari super causa captionis to the sheriffs of London: Roger Radnore, returnable on the octave of Hilary [20 Jan.]. Westminster, 12 December 11 Edward IV [1471].

[*Return*] Imprisoned in a plea of trespass brought by William Whethall, chapman, and Alice his wife, and in pleas of debt for £5 brought by William Hynde, mercer, and for £5 brought by William and Alice Whethall.

[*The petition is* C 1/46/111, *endorsed*: Coram rege in cancellaria sua in octabis Hillarii.]

[24] Habeas corpus cum causa captionis to the steward and marshal of the household: John Hewet alias Huet, on the octave of Hilary [20 Jan.]. Westminster, 7 January 11 Edward IV [1472].

[*Return*] Imprisoned in a plea of trespass within the verge brought by Bartholomew Delves.

Recognisance: John Isbury of London, gent., Richard Nanseglos of London, gent., each sub pena 100 marks, John Hewet sub pena £100: Hewet to appear in chancery on Friday next [30 Jan.] and from day to day etc. 24 January 11 Edward IV [1472].

[23] Attachias to the sheriff of Middlesex: John Eltham, chaplain, to answer Hugh Philip, clerk of John Davyson, chancery clerk, keeper of the hanaper, in a plea of trespass on the octave of Hilary [20 Jan.]. Westminster, 5 November 11 Edward IV [1471].

[*Return*] He has been taken.

Recognisance: Walter Kyngdon, clerk, Edward Kyndon of Middlesex, yeoman, John Sandeacre, chaplain, John Pynson of Church Eaton, Staffs, yeoman, each sub pena 100 marks, John Eltham sub pena £100: Eltham to appear in chancery on 24 January next and from day to day etc. 23 January 11 Edward IV [1472].

Eltham duly appeared and was dismissed quit sine die.

[22] Habeas corpus cum causa captionis to the sheriffs of London: Thomas Bet[tys], on Friday next [24 Jan.]. Westminster, 22 January 11 Edward IV [1472].

[*Return*] Imprisoned in pleas of debt for 6 marks brought by Thomas Valans, yeoman, and Marion his wife, widow and executrix of Thomas Whatton of Greenwich, Kent, yeoman, and for 6 marks brought by the same parties and William Draper of Erith, Kent, yeoman, coexecutor.

Recognisance: Thomas Aylove of London, gent., Thomas Goodale of London, serjeant, William Hoppkyns of St Botolph Billingsgate, London, woodmonger, Robert Richars of St Magnus the Martyr, London, each sub pena 6 marks, Thomas Bettys sub pena 12 marks: Bettys to appear in chancery on 25 January and from day to day etc. 24 January 11 Edward IV [1472].

[*The petition is* C 1/46/301, *endorsed*: Coram rege in cancellaria die veneris videlicet xxj (*over an erasure*) die januarii. *In the writ the day of the week is written over an erasure.*]

[21] Attachias to the sheriffs of Coventry: William Bamburgh of Coventry, cooper, Thomas Michell of Coventry, shearman, William Broune of Coventry, barber, to answer John Bate, chancery clerk, in a plea of debt on the octave of Hilary [20 Jan.]. Westminster, 24 November 11 Edward IV [1471].

[*Return*] Michell and Broun cannot be found; Bamburgh has been attached.

Bamburgh was dismissed quit sine die by the court.

[20] Habeas corpus cum causa captionis to the sheriffs of London: John Rogerson, on Saturday next [25 Jan.]. Westminster, 24 January 11 Edward IV [1472].

[*Return*] Imprisoned in a plea of trespass brought by John Assheley, kt.

Recognisance: John Cole of St Mary Bothaw, London, brewer, Richard Streteley of St Michael Cornhill, London, draper, Thomas Frost of St Mary Magdalen, Southwark, Surrey, tiler, Nicholas Mille of St Botolph Billingsgate, London, cook, each sub pena £10, John Rogerson sub pena £20: Rogerson to appear in chancery on Monday next [27 Jan.] and from day to day etc. 25 January 11 Edward IV.

[19] Attachias to the sheriffs of Norwich: William Nobys of Norwich, Norf, bowyer, to answer Edward Cryche, servant of John Davyson, chancery clerk, keeper of the hanaper, in a plea of trespass on the octave of Hilary [20 Jan.]. Westminster, 16 December 11 Edward IV [1471].

[*Return*] He has been imprisoned.

Recognisance: Henry Clyderowe of Norwich, yeoman, William Neweton of the same, yeoman, each sub pena 100s., William Nobys sub pena £10: Nobys to appear in chancery on 25 January and from day to day etc. 24 January 11 Edward IV.

Nobys duly appeared and one month from Easter [27 April], when he was dismissed quit sine die.

[18] Habeas corpus cum causa captionis to the sheriffs of Middlesex: Ludovic Pynella, on Tuesday next [28 Jan.]. Westminster, 27 January 11 Edward IV [1472].

[*Return*] Imprisoned on a capias out of king's bench.

[17] Certiorari super quibusdam loquelis sub pena £100 to the sheriff of Gloucestershire: suits of debt, trespass and detinue in the county court between John Edwardys and Thomas, abbot of Keynsham, returnable on the octave of Hilary [20 Jan.]. Westminster, 16 November 11 Edward IV [1471].

[*Return*] A brief certificate.

[16] Attachias to the sheriffs of London: Richard Langton, gent., to answer Simon Dynell, servant of John Davyson, chancery clerk, keeper of the hanaper, in a plea of trespass on the quindene of St Martin [18 Nov.]. Westminster, 20 November 11 Edward IV [1471].

[*Return*] He has been attached.

Recognisance: William Meryng of Meering, Notts, esq., Thomas Knyght of Ingleby, Lincs, gent., each sub pena £40, Richard Langton sub pena £100: Langton to appear in chancery on the morrow of the Purification [3 Feb.]. 24 November 11 Edward IV.

Langton duly appeared and on the following Monday

[10 Feb.], when he was dismissed quit sine die by the court with the agreement of the other parties.

[*The writ was authorised by Davyson.*]

[15] Recognisance: John Tretherf of Trethurff, Corn, gent., Ralph Arundell of London, esq., John Leche of Chatsworth, Derb, gent., Richard Reynold of St Enoder, Corn, gent., each sub pena £20, William Reskymer sub pena £40: Reskymer to appear in chancery on the quindene of Hilary [27 Jan.] and meanwhile not to do or cause to be done any physical harm to John Vivyan or other of the king's people. 30 January 11 Edward IV [1472].

[14] Attachias to the sheriff of Sussex: William Hotheleye late of Rotherfield, yeoman, Nicholas Catell late of the same, husbandman, and John Slowman, late of the same, cooper, to answer Thomas, cardinal archbishop of Canterbury, former chancellor, in a plea of trespass on the quindene of Hilary [27 Jan.]. Westminster, 23 November 11 Edward IV [1471].

[*Return*] They have been imprisoned.

Recognisance: John Knyghte of Rotherfield, gent., William Gilderegge of Withyham, Sussex, gent., Hugh Snodle of Newington, Surrey, yeoman, Thomas Wylyng of Rotherfield, yeoman, each sub pena £40, William Hotheleye, Nicholas Catell, John Slowman, each sub pena £80: Hotheleye, Catell and Slowman to appear in chancery on Friday next [31 Jan.] and from day to day etc. 30 January 11 Edward IV.

They duly appeared and were given a day on the quindene of Easter [13 April].

[13] Certiorari super causa captionis to the sheriffs of Norwich: Alice Clerk alias Gunton, returnable on the quindene of Hilary [27 Jan.]. Westminster, 27 November 11 Edward IV [1471].

[*Return*] Imprisoned in a plea of debt for £18 brought by Thomas and Robert Houchons.

[12] Habeas corpus cum causa captionis to the sheriffs of Norwich: Thomas Grigges, gent., on the quindene of Hilary [27 Jan.]. Westminster, 27 November 11 Edward IV [1471].

[*Return*] Formerly imprisoned in a plea of trespass brought by Edward Sylk but subsequently released on bail and therefore cannot be produced.

[11] Habeas corpus cum causa captionis to the mayor and sheriffs of London: Edmund Broke, on Saturday next [1 Feb.]. Westminster, 29 January 11 Edward IV [1472].

[*Return*] Imprisoned in a plea of debt for 32s. 8d. brought by Michael Sax of London, surgeon.

Recognisance: John Randolf of All Hallows the Less, London, brewer, Robert Jonson of St Peter Cornhill, London, yeoman, John Wrighte of St Lawrence Pountney, London, weaver, Nicholas Tyler of All Hallows the Great, London, tiler, Edmund Broke, each sub pena 40s.: Broke to appear in chancery on Monday next [3 Feb.] and from day to day etc. 2 February 11 Edward IV.

Broke duly appeared and was dismissed quit sine die.

[*The petition is* C 1/42/108, *endorsed*: R' primo die februarii proximo futuro.]

[10] Certiorari super causa captionis to the mayor, sheriff and bailiffs, and commonalty of Bristol: Henry Colwell, merchant, returnable on the quindene of Hilary [27 Jan.]. Westminster, 2 January 11 Edward IV [1472].

[*Return*] Imprisoned in pleas of trespass and debt brought by Richard Bole of Bristol, merchant.

[*The petition is* C 1/46/290, *endorsed*: Coram domino rege in cancellaria sua quindena Hillarii.]

[9] Certiorari super causa captionis to the mayor and sheriffs of London: Robert Duplage and John Aylmer, returnable on Monday next [3 Feb.]. Westminster, 29 January 11 Edward IV [1472].

[*Return*] Duplage was imprisoned in a plea of debt for £4 brought by William Wetton, citizen and grocer of London; Aylmer in two pleas of debt, both for £140 12s. 6d., brought by Robert Drope, alderman, citizen and clothworker of London; Duplage and Aylmer jointly in two pleas of debt, both of £140 12s. 6d., brought by Drope.

[8] Habeas corpus cum causa captionis to the mayor and sheriffs of London: John Thrompton, on the octave of Hilary [27 Jan.]. Westminster, 3 December 11 Edward IV [1471].

[*Return*] Formerly imprisoned in a plea of trespass brought by John Shirwode, grocer, and subsequently released on bail; therefore he cannot be produced.

[*The petition is* C 1/46/107, *endorsed*: Coram rege in cancellaria sua in octabis Sancti Hillarii.]

[7] Certiorari super causa arestationis to the mayor and sheriffs of London: the goods of Thomas Pakeman, taken into the hands of William Wade and John Sheff at the suit of John Prolle, returnable on Monday next [3 Feb.]. Westminster, 30 January 11 Edward IV [1472].

[*Return*] Two wooden tables, two trestles, one cupboard, one ambry, one cist carved with divers instruments of the art or mystery of cutlery, another cist, two chairs (*cathedra*) of turner's work, 10 pairs of embroidered wall hangings, a cross coffin and two iron cupboards were arrested in a plea of debt for 30s. brought by John Prolle, brewer.

[6] Attachias to the sheriffs of Middlesex: Thomas Haldhous, late of Mendlesham, Suff, gent., to answer Robert Blakwall, chancery clerk, in a plea of trespass on the morrow of the Purification [3 Feb.]. Westminster, 28 November 11 Edward IV [1471].

[*Return*] Haldhous has been imprisoned but has been delivered to the exchequer on a subsequent habeas corpus cum causa captionis returnable on 5 February, and therefore cannot be produced in chancery.

[5] Certiorari super causa captionis to the sheriffs of London: Thomas Portyngton, clerk, returnable on the morrow of the Purification [3 Feb.]. Westminster, 12 December 11 Edward IV [1471].

[*Return*] Imprisoned in a plea of debt for £10 brought by Thomas Langton, brother and executor of William Langton, priest of Hazlewood, Yorks.

[*The petition is* C 1/46/345, *endorsed*: R' coram domino rege in cancellaria sua in crastino Purificationis Beate Marie.]

[4] Recognisance: Richard Messanger of St Edmund Lombard Street, London, goldsmith, Henry Norbury of the same, baker, John Haukyn of the same, draper, William Walter of the same, pouchmaker, each sub pena £100, John Polyngton sub pena £200: Polyngton to appear in chancery on Monday next [10 Feb.]. 5 February 11 Edward IV [1472].

Polyngton duly appeared and was dismissed quit sine die.

[3] Attachias to the sheriff of Essex: John Hunt, who has failed to answer a sub pena, returnable on the morrow of the Purification [3 Feb.]. Westminster, 24 January 11 Edward IV [1472].

[*Return*] The bailiff of the liberty of the abbess of Barking has executed the writ.

Recognisance: Stephen Shawe of West Ham, Essex, yeoman, John Danyell of the same, yeoman, each sub pena £20, John Hunt sub pena £40: Hunt to appear in chancery on Monday next [10 Feb.]. 5 February 11 Edward IV.

Hunt duly appeared.

[2] Attachias to the sheriffs of London: John Kydde of London, grocer, and Thomas Neweland of London, to answer John Davyson, chancery clerk, keeper of the hanaper, in a plea of trespass on the morrow of the Purification [3 Feb.]. Westminster, 18 December 11 Edward IV [1471].

[*Return*] They have been imprisoned.

Recognisance: John Murdon of St Dunstan in the West, London, barber, Thomas Horndon of London, grocer, each sub pena £20, Thomas Newelande sub pena £80: Newelande to appear in chancery on Friday next [7 Feb.] and from day to day etc. 5 February 11 Edward IV.

Newelande duly appeared, and on Easter three weeks [20 April], the quindene of Trinity [8 June] and the quindene of Michaelmas [13 Oct.], when he was dismissed quit sine die with the agreement of the plaintiff.

Recognisance: Thomas Herte of St Mary Colechurch, London, grocer, sub pena £40, John Kydde of London, grocer, sub pena £80: Kydde to appear in chancery on Saturday next [8 Feb.] and from day to day etc. 5 February 11 Edward IV.

Kydde duly appeared and on Easter three weeks and the quindene of Trinity, when he was dismissed quit sine die with the agreement of the plaintiff.

[1] Certiorari super causa captionis to the mayor and sheriffs of London: John Frounceis, returnable on Friday next [7 Feb.]. Westminster, 4 February 11 Edward IV [1472].

[*Return*] Imprisoned in a plea of debt for 33s. brought by John Togode, fishmonger.

INDEX OF PERSONS AND PLACES

INDEX OF SUBJECTS

Matters relating to the law are mostly grouped under the following main headings: Courts of law; Criminal and other offences; Inheritance and Conveyance; Jurisdiction; Procedure and Process; Punishment; Statutes and Ordinances; Writs. Other main groups are Agricultural buildings and equipment; Buildings; Ecclesiastical buildings and institutions; Ecclesiastics; Financial matters; Household articles; Land; Materials; Occupations and Trades; Officials; Records and Manuscripts; Rents and Services; Tenure.

Printed in England for Her Majesty's Stationery Office by Hobbs the Printers of Southampton
(96) Dd288850 K4 3/78